W9-CRB-234

Less managing. More teaching. Greater learning.

INSTRUCTORS...

Would you like your **students** to show up for class **more prepared**?
(Let's face it, class is much more fun if everyone is engaged and prepared...)

Want an **easy way to assign** homework online and track student **progress**?
(Less time grading means more time teaching...)

Want an **instant view** of student or class performance? *(No more wondering if students understand...)*

Need to **collect data and generate reports** required for administration or accreditation? *(Say goodbye to manually tracking student learning outcomes...)*

Want to **record and post your lectures** for students to view online?

With **McGraw-Hill's *Connect® Plus Finance*,**

INSTRUCTORS GET:

- Simple **assignment management**, allowing you to spend more time teaching.
- **Auto-graded** assignments, quizzes, and tests.
- **Detailed Visual Reporting** where student and section results can be viewed and analyzed.
- Sophisticated **online testing** capability.
- A **filtering and reporting** function that allows you to easily assign and report on materials that are correlated to accreditation standards, learning outcomes, and Bloom's taxonomy.
- An easy-to-use **lecture capture** tool.
- The option to **upload course documents** for student access.

www. accounting-degree.org/scandals/

Want an online, **searchable version** of your textbook?

Wish your textbook could be **available online** while you're doing your assignments?

Connect® Plus Finance eBook

If you choose to use *Connect® Plus Finance*, you have an affordable and searchable online version of your book integrated with your other online tools.

Connect® Plus Finance eBook offers features like:

- Topic search
- Direct links from assignments
- Adjustable text size
- Jump to page number
- Print by section

 Want to get more **value** from your textbook purchase?

Think learning finance should be a bit more **interesting**?

Check out the STUDENT RESOURCES section under the *Connect®* Library tab.

Here you'll find a wealth of resources designed to help you achieve your goals in the course. Every student has different needs, so explore the STUDENT RESOURCES to find the materials best suited to you.

Standard Edition

FUNDAMENTALS OF
CORPORATE FINANCE

The McGraw-Hill/Irwin Series in Finance, Insurance, and Real Estate

Stephen A. Ross
Franco Modigliani Professor of Finance and Economics
Sloan School of Management, Massachusetts Institute of Technology, Consulting Editor

Financial Management

Block, Hirt, and Danielsen
Foundations of Financial Management
Fourteenth Edition

Brealey, Myers, and Allen
Principles of Corporate Finance
Tenth Edition

Brealey, Myers, and Allen
Principles of Corporate Finance, Concise
Second Edition

Brealey, Myers, and Marcus
Fundamentals of Corporate Finance
Seventh Edition

Brooks
FinGame Online 5.0

Bruner
Case Studies in Finance: Managing for
Corporate Value Creation
Sixth Edition

Cornett, Adair, and Nofsinger
Finance: Applications and Theory
Second Edition

Cornett, Adair, and Nofsinger
M: Finance
First Edition

DeMello
Cases in Finance
Second Edition

Grinblatt (editor)
Stephen A. Ross, Mentor: Influence
through Generations

Grinblatt and Titman
Financial Markets and Corporate Strategy
Second Edition

Higgins
Analysis for Financial Management
Tenth Edition

Kellison
Theory of Interest
Third Edition

Ross, Westerfield, and Jaffe
Corporate Finance
Ninth Edition

Ross, Westerfield, Jaffe, and Jordan
Corporate Finance: Core Principles
and Applications
Third Edition

Ross, Westerfield, and Jordan
Essentials of Corporate Finance
Seventh Edition

Ross, Westerfield, and Jordan
Fundamentals of Corporate Finance
Tenth Edition

Shefrin
Behavioral Corporate Finance: Decisions
that Create Value
First Edition

White
Financial Analysis with an Electronic
Calculator
Sixth Edition

Investments

Bodie, Kane, and Marcus
Essentials of Investments
Eighth Edition

Bodie, Kane, and Marcus
Investments
Ninth Edition

Hirt and Block
Fundamentals of Investment Management
Tenth Edition

Hirschey and Nofsinger
Investments: Analysis and Behavior
Second Edition

Jordan, Miller, and Dolvin
Fundamentals of Investments: Valuation
and Management
Sixth Edition

Stewart, Piros, and Heisler
Running Money: Professional
Portfolio Management
First Edition

Sundaram and Das
Derivatives: Principles and Practice
First Edition

Financial Institutions and Markets

Rose and Hudgins
Bank Management and Financial Services
Ninth Edition

Rose and Marquis
Financial Institutions and Markets
Eleventh Edition

Saunders and Cornett
Financial Institutions Management: A Risk
Management Approach
Seventh Edition

Saunders and Cornett
Financial Markets and Institutions
Fifth Edition

International Finance

Eun and Resnick
International Financial Management
Sixth Edition

Robin
International Corporate Finance
First Edition

Real Estate

Brueggeman and Fisher
Real Estate Finance and Investments
Fourteenth Edition

Ling and Archer
Real Estate Principles: A Value Approach
Third Edition

Financial Planning and Insurance

Allen, Melone, Rosenbloom, and Mahoney
Retirement Plans: 401(k)s, IRAs, and Other
Deferred Compensation Approaches
Tenth Edition

Altfest
Personal Financial Planning
First Edition

Harrington and Niehaus
Risk Management and Insurance
Second Edition

Kapoor, Dlabay, and Hughes
Focus on Personal Finance: An Active Approach
to Help You Develop Successful Financial Skills
Third Edition

Kapoor, Dlabay, and Hughes
Personal Finance
Tenth Edition

Walker and Walker
Personal Finance: Building Your Future
First Edition

Standard Edition

Tenth Edition

FUNDAMENTALS OF CORPORATE FINANCE

Stephen A. Ross
Massachusetts Institute of Technology

Randolph W. Westerfield
University of Southern California

Bradford D. Jordan
University of Kentucky

McGraw-Hill Irwin

FUNDAMENTALS OF CORPORATE FINANCE

Published by McGraw-Hill/Irwin, a business unit of The McGraw-Hill Companies, Inc., 1221 Avenue of the Americas, New York, NY, 10020. Copyright © 2013, 2010, 2008, 2006, 2003, 2000, 1998, 1995, 1993, 1991 by The McGraw-Hill Companies, Inc. All rights reserved. Printed in the United States of America. No part of this publication may be reproduced or distributed in any form or by any means, or stored in a database or retrieval system, without the prior written consent of The McGraw-Hill Companies, Inc., including, but not limited to, in any network or other electronic storage or transmission, or broadcast for distance learning.

Some ancillaries, including electronic and print components, may not be available to customers outside the United States.

This book is printed on acid-free paper.

2 3 4 5 6 7 8 9 0 RJE/RJE 1 0 9 8 7 6 5 4 3 2

ISBN   978-0-07-803463-3 (standard edition)
MHID   0-07-803463-9 (standard edition)
ISBN   978-0-07-747945-9 (alternate edition)
MHID   0-07-747945-9 (alternate edition)

Vice president and editor-in-chief: *Brent Gordon*
Publisher: *Douglas Reiner*
Executive editor: *Michele Janicek*
Executive director of development: *Ann Torbert*
Development editor II: *Jennifer Lohn*
Vice president and director of marketing: *Robin J. Zwettler*
Marketing director: *Brad Parkins*
Senior marketing manager: *Melissa S. Caughlin*
Vice president of editing, design, and production: *Sesha Bolisetty*
Lead project manager: *Christine A. Vaughan*
Buyer II: *Debra R. Sylvester*
Cover/interior designer: *Pam Verros*
Lead media project manager: *Brian Nacik*
Media project manager: *Joyce J. Chappetto*
Cover image: *Getty Images*
Typeface: *10/12 Times Roman*
Compositor: *MPS Limited, a Macmillan Company*
Printer: *R. R. Donnelley*

Library of Congress Cataloging-in-Publication Data

Ross, Stephen A.
    Fundamentals of corporate finance / Stephen A. Ross, Randolph W. Westerfield, Bradford D. Jordan.—10th ed., Alternate ed.
        p. cm.—(The McGraw-Hill/Irwin series in finance, insurance and real estate)
    Includes index.
    ISBN-13: 978-0-07-803463-3 (standard ed. : alk. paper)
    ISBN-10: 0-07-803463-9 (standard ed. : alk. paper)
    ISBN-13: 978-0-07-747945-9 (alternate ed. : alk. paper)
    ISBN-10: 0-07-747945-9 (alternate ed. : alk. paper)
    1. Corporations—Finance. I. Westerfield, Randolph W. II. Jordan, Bradford D. III. Title.
HG4026.R677 2013
658.15—dc23
                                                            2011042532

www.mhhe.com

To our families and friends with love and gratitude.

S.A.R. R.W.W. B.D.J.

STEPHEN A. ROSS

Sloan School of Management, Franco Modigliani Professor of Finance and Economics, Massachusetts Institute of Technology

Stephen A. Ross is the Franco Modigliani Professor of Finance and Economics at the Sloan School of Management, Massachusetts Institute of Technology. One of the most widely published authors in finance and economics, Professor Ross is recognized for his work in developing the Arbitrage Pricing Theory and his substantial contributions to the discipline through his research in signaling, agency theory, option pricing, and the theory of the term structure of interest rates, among other topics. A past president of the American Finance Association, he currently serves as an associate editor of several academic and practitioner journals. He is a trustee of CalTech.

RANDOLPH W. WESTERFIELD

Marshall School of Business, University of Southern California

Randolph W. Westerfield is dean emeritus of the University of Southern California's Marshall School of Business and is the Charles B. Thornton Professor of Finance.

He came to USC from the Wharton School, University of Pennsylvania, where he was the chairman of the finance department and a member of the finance faculty for 20 years. He is a member of several public company boards of directors, including Health Management Associates, Inc. His areas of expertise include corporate financial policy, investment management, and stock market price behavior.

BRADFORD D. JORDAN

Gatton College of Business and Economics, University of Kentucky

Bradford D. Jordan is professor of finance and holder of the Richard W. and Janis H. Furst Endowed Chair in Finance at the University of Kentucky. He has a long-standing interest in both applied and theoretical issues in corporate finance and has extensive experience teaching all levels of corporate finance and financial management policy. Professor Jordan has published numerous articles on issues such as cost of capital, capital structure, and the behavior of security prices. He is a past president of the Southern Finance Association, and he is coauthor of *Fundamentals of Investments: Valuation and Management,* 6e, a leading investments text, also published by McGraw-Hill/Irwin.

Preface from the Authors

When the three of us decided to write a book, we were united by one strongly held principle: Corporate finance should be developed in terms of a few integrated, powerful ideas. We believed that the subject was all too often presented as a collection of loosely related topics, unified primarily by virtue of being bound together in one book, and we thought there must be a better way.

One thing we knew for certain was that we didn't want to write a "me-too" book. So, with a lot of help, we took a hard look at what was truly important and useful. In doing so, we were led to eliminate topics of dubious relevance, downplay purely theoretical issues, and minimize the use of extensive and elaborate calculations to illustrate points that are either intuitively obvious or of limited practical use.

As a result of this process, three basic themes became our central focus in writing *Fundamentals of Corporate Finance:*

AN EMPHASIS ON INTUITION

We always try to separate and explain the principles at work on a common sense, intuitive level before launching into any specifics. The underlying ideas are discussed first in very general terms and then by way of examples that illustrate in more concrete terms how a financial manager might proceed in a given situation.

A UNIFIED VALUATION APPROACH

We treat net present value (NPV) as the basic concept underlying corporate finance. Many texts stop well short of consistently integrating this important principle. The most basic and important notion, that NPV represents the excess of market value over cost, often is lost in an overly mechanical approach that emphasizes computation at the expense of comprehension. In contrast, every subject we cover is firmly rooted in valuation, and care is taken throughout to explain how particular decisions have valuation effects.

A MANAGERIAL FOCUS

Students shouldn't lose sight of the fact that financial management concerns management. We emphasize the role of the financial manager as decision maker, and we stress the need for managerial input and judgment. We consciously avoid "black box" approaches to finance, and, where appropriate, the approximate, pragmatic nature of financial analysis is made explicit, possible pitfalls are described, and limitations are discussed.

In retrospect, looking back to our 1991 first edition IPO, we had the same hopes and fears as any entrepreneurs. How would we be received in the market? At the time, we had no idea that 20 years later, we would be working on a tenth edition. We certainly never dreamed that in those years we would work with friends and colleagues from around the world to create country-specific Australian, Canadian, and South African editions, an International edition, Chinese, French, Polish, Portuguese, Thai, Russian, Korean, and Spanish language editions, and an entirely separate book, *Essentials of Corporate Finance,* now in its seventh edition.

Today, as we prepare to once more enter the market, our goal is to stick with the basic principles that have brought us this far. However, based on the enormous amount of feedback we have received from you and your colleagues, we have made this edition and its package even *more flexible* than previous editions. We offer flexibility in coverage, by continuing to offer two editions, and flexibility in pedagogy, by providing a wide variety of features in the book to help students to learn about corporate finance. We also provide flexibility in package options by offering the most extensive collection of teaching, learning, and technology aids of any corporate finance text. Whether you use only the textbook, or the book in conjunction with our other products, we believe you will find a combination with this edition that will meet your current as well as your changing course needs.

Stephen A. Ross
Randolph W. Westerfield
Bradford D. Jordan

Coverage

This book was designed and developed explicitly for a first course in business or corporate finance, for both finance majors and non-majors alike. In terms of background or prerequisites, the book is nearly self-contained, assuming some familiarity with basic algebra and accounting concepts, while still reviewing important accounting principles very early on. The organization of this text has been developed to give instructors the flexibility they need.

The following grid presents, for each chapter, some of the most significant features as well as a few selected chapter highlights of the 10th edition of *Fundamentals*. Of course, in every chapter, opening vignettes, boxed features, in-chapter illustrated examples using real companies, and end-of-chapter material have been thoroughly updated as well.

Chapters	Selected Topics of Interest	Benefits to You
PART 1 Overview of Corporate Finance		
Chapter 1 Introduction to Corporate Finance	Goal of the firm and agency problems.	Stresses value creation as the most fundamental aspect of management and describes agency issues that can arise.
	Ethics, financial management, and executive compensation.	Brings in real-world issues concerning conflicts of interest and current controversies surrounding ethical conduct and management pay.
	Sarbanes-Oxley.	Up-to-date discussion of Sarbanes-Oxley and its implications and impact.
	Minicase: The McGee Cake Company.	Examines the choice of organization form for a small business.
Chapter 2 Financial Statements, Taxes, and Cash Flow	Cash flow vs. earnings.	Clearly defines cash flow and spells out the differences between cash flow and earnings.
	Market values vs. book values.	Emphasizes the relevance of market values over book values.
	New! Brief discussion of average corporate tax rates.	Highlights the variation in corporate tax rates across industries in practice.
	Minicase: Cash Flows and Financial Statements at Sunset Boards, Inc.	Reinforces key cash flow concepts in a small business setting.
PART 2 Financial Statements and Long-Term Financial Planning		
Chapter 3 Working with Financial Statements	Expanded DuPont analysis.	Expands the basic DuPont equation to better explore the interrelationships between operating and financial performance.
	DuPont analysis for real companies using data from S&P *Market Insight.*	Analysis shows students how to get and use real-world data, thereby applying key chapter ideas.
	Ratio and financial statement analysis using smaller firm data.	Uses firm data from *RMA* to show students how to actually get and evaluate financial statement benchmarks.
	Understanding financial statements.	Thorough coverage of standardized financial statements and key ratios.
	New! The enterprise value–EBITDA ratio.	Defines enterprise value (EV) and discusses the widely used EV–EBITDA ratio.
	Minicase: Ratio Analysis at S&S Air, Inc.	Illustrates the use of ratios and some pitfalls in a small business context.

Chapters	Selected Topics of Interest	Benefits to You
Chapter 4 Long-Term Financial Planning and Growth	Expanded discussion of sustainable growth calculations.	Illustrates the importance of financial planning in a small firm.
	Explanation of alternative formulas for sustainable and internal growth rates.	Explanation of growth rate formulas clears up a common misunderstanding about these formulas and the circumstances under which alternative formulas are correct.
	Thorough coverage of sustainable growth as a planning tool.	Provides a vehicle for examining the interrelationships between operations, financing, and growth.
	Long-range financial planning.	Covers percentage of sales approach to creating pro forma statements.
	Minicase: Planning for Growth at S&S Air.	Discusses the importance of financial plan and capacity utilization for a small business.

PART 3   Valuation of Future Cash Flows

Chapters	Selected Topics of Interest	Benefits to You
Chapter 5 Introduction to Valuation: The Time Value of Money	First of two chapters on time value of money.	Relatively short chapter introduces just the basic ideas on time value of money to get students started on this traditionally difficult topic.
Chapter 6 Discounted Cash Flow Valuation	Growing annuities and perpetuities. Second of two chapters on time value of money.	Covers more advanced time value topics with numerous examples, calculator tips, and Excel spreadsheet exhibits. Contains many real-world examples.
	Minicase: The MBA Decision.	Explores the financial pros and cons of pursuing an MBA degree.
Chapter 7 Interest Rates and Bond Valuation	"Clean" vs. "dirty" bond prices and accrued interest.	Clears up the pricing of bonds between coupon payment dates and also bond market quoting conventions.
	NASD's new TRACE system and transparency in the corporate bond market.	Up-to-date discussion of new developments in fixed income with regard to price, volume, and transactions reporting.
	"Make-whole" call provisions.	Up-to-date discussion of a relatively new type of call provision that has become very common.
	Bond valuation.	Complete coverage of bond valuation and bond features.
	Interest rates.	Discusses real versus nominal rates and the determinants of the term structure.
	New! Islamic Finance.	New section briefly describes effect of shariah on Islamic finance.
	Minicase: Financing S&S Air's Expansion Plans with a Bond Issue.	Discusses the issues that come up in selling bonds to the public.
Chapter 8 Stock Valuation	Stock valuation.	Thorough coverage of constant and non-constant growth models.
	NYSE and NASDAQ Market Operations.	Up-to-date description of major stock market operations.
	New! Valuation using multiples.	New section illustrates using PE and price/sales ratios for equity valuation.
	Minicase: Stock Valuation at Ragan, Inc.	Illustrates the difficulties and issues surrounding small business valuation.

Coverage *(continued)*

Chapters	Selected Topics of Interest	Benefits to You
PART 4 Capital Budgeting		
Chapter 9 Net Present Value and Other Investment Criteria	First of three chapters on capital budgeting.	Relatively short chapter introduces key ideas on an intuitive level to help students with this traditionally difficult topic.
	NPV, IRR, payback, discounted payback, and accounting rate of return.	Consistent, balanced examination of advantages and disadvantages of various criteria.
	Minicase: Bullock Gold Mining.	Explores different capital budgeting techniques with nonstandard cash flows.
Chapter 10 Making Capital Investment Decisions	Project cash flow.	Thorough coverage of project cash flows and the relevant numbers for a project analysis.
	Alternative cash flow definitions.	Emphasizes the equivalence of various formulas, thereby removing common misunderstandings.
	Special cases of DCF analysis.	Considers important applications of chapter tools.
	Minicase: Conch Republic Electronics, Part 1.	Analyzes capital budgeting issues and complexities.
Chapter 11 Project Analysis and Evaluation	Sources of value.	Stresses the need to understand the economic basis for value creation in a project.
	Scenario and sensitivity "what-if" analyses.	Illustrates how to actually apply and interpret these tools in a project analysis.
	Break-even analysis.	Covers cash, accounting, and financial break-even levels.
	Minicase: Conch Republic Electronics, Part 2.	Illustrates the use of sensitivity analysis in capital budgeting.
PART 5 Risk and Return		
Chapter 12 Some Lessons from Capital Market History	Expanded discussion of geometric vs. arithmetic returns.	Discusses calculation and interpretation of geometric returns. Clarifies common misconceptions regarding appropriate use of arithmetic vs. geometric average returns.
	Capital market history.	Extensive coverage of historical returns, volatilities, and risk premiums.
	Market efficiency.	Efficient markets hypothesis discussed along with common misconceptions.
	The equity risk premium.	Section discusses the equity premium puzzle and latest international evidence.
	New! The 2008 experience.	New section on the stock market turmoil of 2008.
	Minicase: A Job at S&S Air.	Discusses selection of investments for a 401(k) plan.
Chapter 13 Return, Risk, and the Security Market Line	Diversification, systematic and unsystematic risk.	Illustrates basics of risk and return in a straightforward fashion.
	Beta and the security market line.	Develops the security market line with an intuitive approach that bypasses much of the usual portfolio theory and statistics.
	Minicase: The Beta for Colgate-Palmolive.	Detailed discussion of beta estimation.

Chapters	Selected Topics of Interest	Benefits to You
PART 6 Cost of Capital and Long-Term Financial Policy		
Chapter 14 Cost of Capital	Geometric vs. arithmetic growth rates.	Both approaches are used in practice. Clears up issues surrounding growth rate estimates.
	Cost of capital estimation.	Contains a complete, Web-based illustration of cost of capital for a real company.
	Minicase: Cost of Capital for Hubbard Computer, Inc.	Covers pure play approach to cost of capital estimation.
Chapter 15 Raising Capital	Dutch auction IPOs.	Explains uniform price auctions using recent Google IPO as an example.
	IPO "quiet periods."	Explains the SEC's quiet period rules.
	Rights vs. warrants.	Clarifies the optionlike nature of rights prior to their expiration dates.
	IPO valuation.	Extensive, up-to-date discussion of IPOs, including the 1999–2000 period.
	Minicase: S&S Air Goes Public.	Covers the key parts of the IPO process for a small firm.
Chapter 16 Financial Leverage and Capital Structure Policy	Basics of financial leverage.	Illustrates effect of leverage on risk and return.
	Optimal capital structure.	Describes the basic trade-offs leading to an optimal capital structure.
	Financial distress and bankruptcy.	Briefly surveys the bankruptcy process.
	Minicase: Stephenson Real Estate Recapitalization.	Discusses optimal capital structure for a medium-sized firm.
Chapter 17 Dividends and Payout Policy	Very recent survey evidence on dividend policy.	New survey results show the most important (and least important) factors considered by financial managers in setting dividend policy.
	Effect of new tax laws.	Discusses implications of new, lower dividend and capital gains rates.
	Dividends and dividend policy.	Describes dividend payments and the factors favoring higher and lower payout policies.
	Optimal payout policy.	Extensive discussion of the latest research and survey evidence on dividend policy, including life-cycle theory.
	Stock repurchases.	Thorough coverage of buybacks as an alternative to cash dividends.
	Minicase: Electronic Timing, Inc.	Describes the dividend/share repurchase issue for a small company.

Coverage *(continued)*

Chapters	Selected Topics of Interest	Benefits to You
PART 7 Short-Term Financial Planning and Management		
Chapter 18 Short-Term Finance and Planning	Operating and cash cycles.	Stresses the importance of cash flow timing.
	Short-term financial planning.	Illustrates creation of cash budgets and potential need for financing.
	New! Purchase Order Financing.	Brief discussion of PO financing, which is popular with small and medium-sized firms.
	Minicase: Piepkorn Manufacturing Working Capital Management.	Illustrates the construction of a cash budget and short-term financial plan for a small company.
Chapter 19 Cash and Liquidity Management	Float management.	Thorough coverage of float management and potential ethical issues.
	Cash collection and disbursement.	Examination of systems used by firms to handle cash inflows and outflows.
	Minicase: Cash Management at Webb Corporation.	Evaluates alternative cash concentration systems for a small firm.
Chapter 20 Credit and Inventory Management	Credit management	Analysis of credit policy and implementation.
	Inventory management	Brief overview of important inventory concepts.
	Minicase: Credit Policy at Howlett Industries.	Evaluates working capital issues for a small firm.
PART 8 Topics in Corporate Finance		
Chapter 21 International Corporate Finance	Foreign exchange.	Covers essentials of exchange rates and their determination.
	International capital budgeting.	Shows how to adapt basic DCF approach to handle exchange rates.
	Exchange rate and political risk.	Discusses hedging and issues surrounding sovereign risk.
	Minicase: S&S Air Goes International.	Discusses factors in an international expansion for a small firm.

In-Text Study Features

To meet the varied needs of its intended audience, *Fundamentals of Corporate Finance* is rich in valuable learning tools and support.

CHAPTER-OPENING VIGNETTES

Vignettes drawn from real-world events introduce students to the chapter concepts.

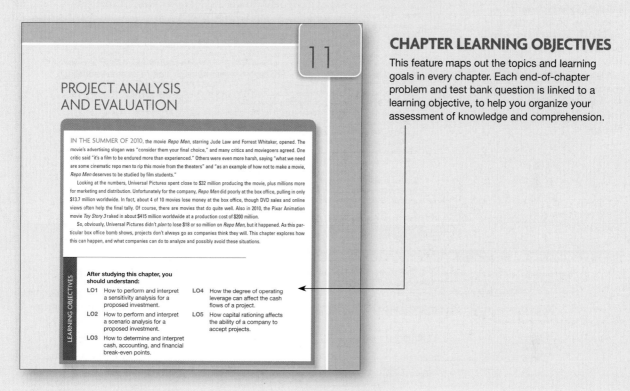

11

PROJECT ANALYSIS
AND EVALUATION

IN THE SUMMER OF 2010, the movie *Repo Men*, starring Jude Law and Forrest Whitaker, opened. The movie's advertising slogan was "consider them your final choice," and many critics and moviegoers agreed. One critic said "it's a film to be endured more than experienced." Others were even more harsh, saying "what we need are some cinematic repo men to rip this movie from the theaters" and "as an example of how not to make a movie, *Repo Men* deserves to be studied by film students."

Looking at the numbers, Universal Pictures spent close to $32 million producing the movie, plus millions more for marketing and distribution. Unfortunately for the company, *Repo Men* did poorly at the box office, pulling in only $13.7 million worldwide. In fact, about 4 of 10 movies lose money at the box office, though DVD sales and online views often help the final tally. Of course, there are movies that do quite well. Also in 2010, the Pixar Animation movie *Toy Story 3* raked in about $415 million worldwide at a production cost of $200 million.

So, obviously, Universal Pictures didn't *plan* to lose $18 or so million on *Repo Men*, but it happened. As this particular box office bomb shows, projects don't always go as companies think they will. This chapter explores how this can happen, and what companies can do to analyze and possibly avoid these situations.

After studying this chapter, you should understand:

LO1 How to perform and interpret a sensitivity analysis for a proposed investment.

LO2 How to perform and interpret a scenario analysis for a proposed investment.

LO3 How to determine and interpret cash, accounting, and financial break-even points.

LO4 How the degree of operating leverage can affect the cash flows of a project.

LO5 How capital rationing affects the ability of a company to accept projects.

LEARNING OBJECTIVES

CHAPTER LEARNING OBJECTIVES

This feature maps out the topics and learning goals in every chapter. Each end-of-chapter problem and test bank question is linked to a learning objective, to help you organize your assessment of knowledge and comprehension.

PEDAGOGICAL USE OF COLOR

This learning tool continues to be an important feature of *Fundamentals of Corporate Finance*. In almost every chapter, color plays an extensive, nonschematic, and largely self-evident role. A guide to the functional use of color is on the endsheets of the text.

FIGURE 9.3

Future Value of Project Cash Flows

	Future Value at 12.5%	
Year	$100 Annuity (Projected Cash Flow)	$300 Lump Sum (Projected Investment)
0	$ 0	$300
1	100	338
2	213	380
3	339	427
4	481	481
5	642	541

IN THEIR OWN WORDS BOXES

This series of boxes are the popular articles updated from previous editions written by a distinguished scholar or practitioner on key topics in the text. Boxes include essays by Merton Miller on capital structure, Fischer Black on dividends, and Roger Ibbotson on capital market history. A complete list of "In Their Own Words" boxes appears on page xli.

IN THEIR OWN WORDS ...

Robert C. Higgins on Sustainable Growth

Most financial officers know intuitively that it takes money to make money. Rapid sales growth requires increased assets in the form of accounts receivable, inventory, and fixed plant, which, in turn, require money to pay for assets. They also know that if their company does not have the money when needed, it can literally "grow broke." The sustainable growth equation states these intuitive truths explicitly.

Sustainable growth is often used by bankers and other external analysts to assess a company's creditworthiness. They are aided in this exercise by several sophisticated computer software packages that provide detailed analyses of the company's past financial performance, including its annual sustainable growth rate.

Bankers use this information in several ways. Quick comparison of a company's actual growth rate to its sustainable rate tells the banker what issues will be at the top of management's financial agenda. If actual growth consistently exceeds sustainable growth, management's problem will be where to get the cash to finance growth. The banker thus can anticipate interest in loan products. Conversely, if sustainable growth consistently exceeds actual, the banker had best be prepared to talk about investment products, because management's problem will be what to do with all the cash that keeps piling up in the till.

Bankers also find the sustainable growth equation useful for explaining to financially inexperienced small business owners and overly optimistic entrepreneurs that, for the long-run viability of their business, it is necessary to keep growth and profitability in proper balance.

Finally, comparison of actual to sustainable growth rates helps a banker understand why a loan applicant needs money and for how long the need might continue. In one instance, a loan applicant requested $100,000 to pay off several insistent suppliers and promised to repay in a few months when he collected some accounts receivable that were coming due. A sustainable growth analysis revealed that the firm had been growing at four to six times its sustainable growth rate and that this pattern was likely to continue in the foreseeable future. This alerted the banker to the fact that impatient suppliers were only a symptom of the much more fundamental disease of overly rapid growth, and that a $100,000 loan would likely prove to be only the down payment on a much larger, multiyear commitment.

Robert C. Higgins is the Marguerite Reimers Professor of Finance at the Foster School of Business at the University of Washington. He

WORK THE WEB BOXES

These boxes show students how to research financial issues using the Web and then how to use the information they find to make business decisions. Work the Web boxes also include interactive follow-up questions and exercises.

WORK THE WEB

Bond quotes have become more available with the rise of the Internet. One site where you can find current bond prices is cxa.marketwatch.com/finra/MarketData/Default.aspx. We went to the website and searched for bonds issued by Coca-Cola. Here is a look at part of what we found for one of the bonds:

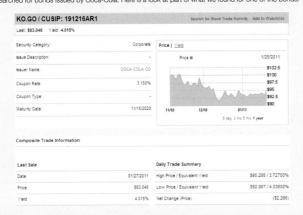

The bond has a coupon rate of 3.15 percent and matures on November 15, 2020. The last sale on this bond was at a price of 93.046 percent of par, which gives a yield to maturity of about 4.015 percent. Not only does the site provide the most recent price and yield information, but it also provides more important information about the bond, such as the credit rating, coupon date, call date, and call price. We'll leave it up to you to have a look at the page and the rest of the information available there.

Questions

1. Go to this website and find the bond shown above. When was this bond issued? What was the size of the bond issue? What were the yield to maturity and price when the bond was issued?
2. If you search for Chevron bonds (CVX), you will find bonds for several companies listed. Why do you think Chevron has bonds issued with different corporate names?

REAL-WORLD EXAMPLES

Actual events are integrated throughout the text, tying chapter concepts to real life through illustration and reinforcing the relevance of the material. Some examples tie into the chapter-opening vignette for added reinforcement.

SPREADSHEET STRATEGIES

This feature introduces students to Excel and shows them how to set up spreadsheets in order to analyze common financial problems—a vital part of every business student's education.

SPREADSHEET STRATEGIES

How to Calculate Present Values with Multiple Future Cash Flows Using a Spreadsheet

Just as we did in our previous chapter, we can set up a basic spreadsheet to calculate the present values of the individual cash flows as follows. Notice that we have simply calculated the present values one at a time and added them up:

	A	B	C	D	E
1					
2		Using a spreadsheet to value multiple future cash flows			
3					
4	What is the present value of $200 in one year, $400 the next year, $600 the next year, and				
5	$800 the last year if the discount rate is 12 percent?				
6					
7	Rate:	.12			
8					
9	Year	Cash flows	Present values	Formula used	
10	1	$200	$178.57	=PV($B$7,A10,0,−B10)	
11	2	$400	$318.88	=PV($B$7,A11,0,−B11)	
12	3	$600	$427.07	=PV($B$7,A12,0,−B12)	
13	4	$800	$508.41	=PV($B$7,A13,0,−B13)	
14					
15		Total PV:	$1,432.93	=SUM(C10:C13)	
16					
17	Notice the negative signs inserted in the PV formulas. These just make the present values have				
18	positive signs. Also, the discount rate in cell B7 is entered as $B$7 (an "absolute" reference)				
19	because it is used over and over. We could have just entered "=.12" instead, but our approach is				
20	more flexible.				
21					
22					

CALCULATOR HINTS

Brief calculator tutorials appear in selected chapters to help students learn or brush up on their financial calculator skills. These complement the Spreadsheet Strategies.

CALCULATOR HINTS

How to Calculate Present Values with Multiple Future Cash Flows Using a Financial Calculator

To calculate the present value of multiple cash flows with a financial calculator, we will simply discount the individual cash flows one at a time using the same technique we used in our previous chapter, so this is not really new. However, we can show you a shortcut. We will use the numbers in Example 6.3 to illustrate.

To begin, of course we first remember to clear out the calculator! Next, from Example 6.3, the first cash flow is $200 to be received in one year and the discount rate is 12 percent, so we do the following:

Enter	1	12			200
	N	I/Y	PMT	PV	FV
Solve for				−178.57	

Now, you can write down this answer to save it, but that's inefficient. All calculators have a memory where you can store numbers. Why not just save it there? Doing so cuts way down on mistakes because you don't have to write down and/or rekey numbers, and it's much faster.

CONCEPT BUILDING

Chapter sections are intentionally kept short to promote a step-by-step, building block approach to learning. Each section is then followed by a series of short concept questions that highlight the key ideas just presented. Students use these questions to make sure they can identify and understand the most important concepts as they read.

Concept Questions

3.3a What are the five groups of ratios? Give two or three examples of each kind.

3.3b Given the total debt ratio, what other two ratios can be computed? Explain how.

3.3c Turnover ratios all have one of two figures as the numerator. What are these two figures? What do these ratios measure? How do you interpret the results?

3.3d Profitability ratios all have the same figure in the numerator. What is it? What do these ratios measure? How do you interpret the results?

SUMMARY TABLES

These tables succinctly restate key principles, results, and equations. They appear whenever it is useful to emphasize and summarize a group of related concepts. For an example, see Chapter 3, page 67.

For example, an investment offers a perpetual cash flow of $500 every year. The return you require on such an investment is 8 percent. What is the value of this investment? The value of this perpetuity is:

Perpetuity $PV = C/r = \$500/.08 = \$6,250$

For future reference, Table 6.2 contains a summary of the annuity and perpetuity basic calculations we described. By now, you probably think that you'll just use online calculators to handle annuity problems. Before you do, see our nearby *Work the Web* box!

Preferred Stock	EXAMPLE 6.7

Preferred stock (or preference stock) is an important example of a perpetuity. When a corporation sells preferred stock, the buyer is promised a fixed cash dividend every period (usually every quarter) forever. This dividend must be paid before any dividend can be paid to regular stockholders—hence the term *preferred*.

Suppose the Fellini Co. wants to sell preferred stock at $100 per share. A similar issue of preferred stock already outstanding has a price of $40 per share and offers a dividend of $1 every quarter. What dividend will Fellini have to offer if the preferred stock is going to sell?

(continued)

LABELED EXAMPLES

Separate numbered and titled examples are extensively integrated into the chapters. These examples provide detailed applications and illustrations of the text material in a step-by-step format. Each example is completely self-contained so students don't have to search for additional information. Based on our classroom testing, these examples are among the most useful learning aids because they provide both detail and explanation.

KEY TERMS

Key Terms are printed in bold type and defined within the text the first time they appear. They also appear in the margins with definitions for easy location and identification by the student.

EXPLANATORY WEB LINKS

These Web links are provided in the margins of the text. They are specifically selected to accompany text material and provide students and instructors with a quick way to check for additional information using the Internet.

Bankruptcy Liquidation Chapter 7 of the Federal Bankruptcy Reform Act of 1978 deals with "straight" liquidation. The following sequence of events is typical:

1. A petition is filed in a federal court. Corporations may file a voluntary petition, or involuntary petitions may be filed against the corporation by several of its creditors.
2. A trustee-in-bankruptcy is elected by the creditors to take over the assets of the debtor corporation. The trustee will attempt to liquidate the assets.
3. When the assets are liquidated, after payment of the bankruptcy administration costs, the proceeds are distributed among the creditors.
4. If any proceeds remain, after expenses and payments to creditors, they are distributed to the shareholders.

The distribution of the proceeds of the liquidation occurs according to the following

The SEC has a good overview of the bankruptcy process in its "Online Publications" section at www.sec.gov.

KEY EQUATIONS

Called out in the text, key equations are identified by an equation number. The list in Appendix B shows the key equations by chapter, providing students with a convenient reference.

Based on our examples, we can now write the general expression for the value of a bond. If a bond has (1) a face value of F paid at maturity, (2) a coupon of C paid per period, (3) t periods to maturity, and (4) a yield of r per period, its value is:

$$\text{Bond value} = C \times [1 - 1/(1 + r)^t]/r \quad + \quad F/(1 + r)^t \qquad \text{[7.1]}$$

$$\text{Bond value} = \begin{array}{c} \text{Present value} \\ \text{of the coupons} \end{array} \quad + \quad \begin{array}{c} \text{Present value} \\ \text{of the face amount} \end{array}$$

HIGHLIGHTED CONCEPTS

Throughout the text, important ideas are pulled out and presented in a highlighted box—signaling to students that this material is particularly relevant and critical for their understanding. For examples, Chapter 10, page 306; Chapter 13, page 426.

EXCEL MASTER

New to this edition, icons in the sidebar identify concepts and skills covered in our unique, RWJ-created Excel Master program. For more training in Excel functions for finance, and for more practice, log on to the OLC at www.mhhe.com/rwj or to McGraw-Hill's Connect Finance for *Fundamentals of Corporate Finance* to access the Excel Master files. This pedagogically superior tool will help get your students the practice they need to succeed—and to exceed expectations.

QUESTIONS AND PROBLEMS

1. **Building a Balance Sheet [LO1]** Penguin Pucks, Inc., has current assets of $4,800, net fixed assets of $27,500, current liabilities of $4,200, and long-term debt of $10,500. What is the value of the shareholders' equity account for this firm? How much is net working capital?

2. **Building an Income Statement [LO1]** Billy's Exterminators, Inc., has sales of $734,000, costs of $315,000, depreciation expense of $48,000, interest expense of $35,000, and a tax rate of 35 percent. What is the net income for this firm?

3. **Dividends and Retained Earnings [LO1]** Suppose the firm in Problem 2 paid out $85,000 in cash dividends. What is the addition to retained earnings?

4. **Per-Share Earnings and Dividends [LO1]** Suppose the firm in Problem 3 had 110,000 shares of common stock outstanding. What is the earnings per share, or EPS, figure? What is the dividends per share figure?

5. **Market Values and Book Values [LO1]** Klingon Widgets, Inc., purchased new cloaking machinery three years ago for $6 million. The machinery can be sold to the Romulans today for $5.3 million. Klingon's current balance sheet shows net

SELF-QUIZ AND STUDY

New to this edition, this end-of-chapter feature gives students a quick overview of what resources are available in McGraw-Hill Connect's Self-Quiz and Study program. Students get a glimpse of our practice questions, the additional assets available to help students study and master the content, and the address to log on for more practice. This can be a great way to engage your Connect-using students in Corporate Finance!

CONNECT TO FINANCE

connect | FINANCE If you are using *Connect™ Finance* in your course, get online to take a Practice Test, check out study tools, and find out where you need additional practice.

▼ Chapter 8 Stock Valuation

8.1 Common Stock Valuation	eBook	Study	Practice
8.2 Some Features of Common and Preferred Stocks	eBook	Study	Practice
8.3 The Stock Markets	eBook	Study	Practice

NPPT 47–48

Can you answer the following questions?

Section 8.1 A stock is selling for $11.90 a share given a market return of 14 percent and a capital gains yield of 5 percent. What was the amount of the last annual dividend that was paid? (LO 8-1)

CHAPTER SUMMARY AND CONCLUSIONS

Every chapter ends with a concise, but thorough, summary of the important ideas—helping students review the key points and providing closure to the chapter.

CHAPTER REVIEW AND SELF-TEST PROBLEM

2.1 **Cash Flow for Mara Corporation** This problem will give you some practice working with financial statements and figuring cash flow. Based on the following information for Mara Corporation, prepare an income statement for 2012 and balance sheets for 2011 and 2012. Next, following our U.S. Corporation examples in the chapter, calculate cash flow from assets, cash flow to creditors, and cash flow to stockholders for Mara for 2012. Use a 35 percent tax rate throughout. You can check your answers against ours, found in the following section.

	2011	2012
Sales	$4,203	$4,507
Cost of goods sold	2,422	2,633
Depreciation	785	952
Interest	180	196
Dividends	225	250
Current assets	2,205	2,429
Net fixed assets	7,344	7,650
Current liabilities	1,003	1,255
Long-term debt	3,106	2,085

ANSWER TO CHAPTER REVIEW AND SELF-TEST PROBLEM

2.1 In preparing the balance sheets, remember that shareholders' equity is the residual. With this in mind, Mara's balance sheets are as follows:

Visit us at www.mhhe.com/rwj

CHAPTER REVIEW AND SELF-TEST PROBLEMS

Appearing after the Summary and Conclusions, each chapter includes a Chapter Review and Self-Test Problem section. These questions and answers allow students to test their abilities in solving key problems related to the chapter content and provide instant reinforcement.

CONCEPTS REVIEW AND CRITICAL THINKING QUESTIONS

This successful end-of-chapter section facilitates your students' knowledge of key principles, as well as intuitive understanding of the chapter concepts. A number of the questions relate to the chapter-opening vignette—reinforcing student critical thinking skills and the learning of chapter material.

CONCEPTS REVIEW AND CRITICAL THINKING QUESTIONS

1. **Liquidity [LO1]** What does liquidity measure? Explain the trade-off a firm faces between high liquidity and low liquidity levels.
2. **Accounting and Cash Flows [LO2]** Why might the revenue and cost figures shown on a standard income statement not be representative of the actual cash inflows and outflows that occurred during a period?
3. **Book Values versus Market Values [LO1]** In preparing a balance sheet, why do you think standard accounting practice focuses on historical cost rather than market value?
4. **Operating Cash Flow [LO4]** In comparing accounting net income and operating cash flow, name two items you typically find in net income that are not in operating cash flow. Explain what each is and why it is excluded in operating cash flow.

END-OF-CHAPTER QUESTIONS AND PROBLEMS

Students learn better when they have plenty of opportunity to practice; therefore, *FCF*, 10e, provides extensive end-of-chapter questions and problems. The end-of-chapter support greatly exceeds typical introductory textbooks. The questions and problems are segregated into three learning levels: Basic, Intermediate, and Challenge. Answers to selected end-of-chapter material appear in Appendix C. Also, all problems are available in McGraw-Hill's Connect—see page xxii for details.

QUESTIONS AND PROBLEMS

1. **Building a Balance Sheet [LO1]** Penguin Pucks, Inc., has current assets of $4,800, net fixed assets of $27,500, current liabilities of $4,200, and long-term debt of $10,500. What is the value of the shareholders' equity account for this firm? How much is net working capital?

2. **Building an Income Statement [LO1]** Billy's Exterminators, Inc., has sales of $734,000, costs of $315,000, depreciation expense of $48,000, interest expense of $35,000, and a tax rate of 35 percent. What is the net income for this firm?

3. **Dividends and Retained Earnings [LO1]** Suppose the firm in Problem 2 paid out $85,000 in cash dividends. What is the addition to retained earnings?

4. **Per-Share Earnings and Dividends [LO1]** Suppose the firm in Problem 3 had 110,000 shares of common stock outstanding. What is the earnings per share, or EPS, figure? What is the dividends per share figure?

5. **Market Values and Book Values [LO1]** Klingon Widgets, Inc., purchased new cloaking machinery three years ago for $6 million. The machinery can be sold to the Romulans today for $5.3 million. Klingon's current balance sheet shows net fixed assets of $3.2 million, current liabilities of $900,000, and net working capital of $215,000. If all the current assets were liquidated today, the company would

BASIC
(Questions 1–13)

Visit us at www.mhhe.com/rwj

END-OF-CHAPTER CASES

Located at the end of the book's chapters, these minicases focus on real-life company situations that embody important corporate finance topics. Each case presents a new scenario, data, and a dilemma. Several questions at the end of each case require students to analyze and focus on all of the material they learned from each chapter.

MINICASE

Bullock Gold Mining

Seth Bullock, the owner of Bullock Gold Mining, is evaluating a new gold mine in South Dakota. Dan Dority, the company's geologist, has just finished his analysis of the mine site. He has estimated that the mine would be productive for eight years, after which the gold would be completely mined. Dan has taken an estimate of the gold deposits to Alma Garrett, the company's financial officer. Alma has been asked by Seth to perform an analysis of the new mine and present her recommendation on whether the company should open the new mine.

Alma has used the estimates provided by Dan to determine the revenues that could be expected from the mine. She has also projected the expense of opening the mine and the annual operating expenses. If the company opens the mine, it will cost $450 million today, and it will have a cash outflow of $95 million nine years from today in costs associated with closing the mine and reclaiming the area surrounding it. The

Year	Cash Flow
0	−$450,000,000
1	63,000,000
2	85,000,000
3	120,000,000
4	145,000,000
5	175,000,000
6	120,000,000
7	95,000,000
8	75,000,000
9	−70,000,000

QUESTIONS

1. Construct a spreadsheet to calculate the payback period, internal rate of return, modified internal rate of return, and net present value of the proposed mine.

WEB EXERCISES (ONLINE ONLY)

For instructors interested in integrating even more online resources and problems into their course, these Web activities show students how to learn from the vast amount of financial resources available on the Internet. In the 10th edition of *Fundamentals,* these Web exercises are available to students and instructors on the Online Learning Center.

Comprehensive Teaching and Learning Package

This edition of *Fundamentals* has several options in terms of the textbook, instructor supplements, student supplements, and multimedia products. Mix and match to create a package that is perfect for your course!

TEXTBOOK

As with the previous editions, we are offering two versions of this text. Choose the length and topics suitable for your course.

- Standard Edition (21 Chapters)
- Alternate Edition (27 Chapters)

Instructor's CD-ROM

Keep all the supplements in one place! This CD contains all the necessary supplements—Instructor's Manual, Solutions, Test Bank, Computerized Test Bank, and PowerPoint—all in one useful product in an electronic format.

- **Instructor's Manual (IM)**

  A great place to find new lecture ideas! The annotated outline for each chapter includes lecture tips, real-world tips, ethics notes, suggested PowerPoint slides, and, when appropriate, a video synopsis.

- **Solutions Manual (SM)**

  Prepared by Joseph Smolira, Belmont University

  The *Fundamentals* Solutions Manual provides detailed solutions to the extensive end-of-chapter material, including concept review questions, quantitative problems, and cases.

- **Test Bank**

  Prepared by Terri Renner, Indiana University

  Over 100 questions and problems per chapter! Each chapter is divided into five parts. *Part I* contains questions that test the understanding of the key terms in the book. *Part II* includes questions patterned after the learning objectives, concept questions, chapter-opening vignettes, boxes, and highlighted phrases. *Part III* contains multiple-choice problems patterned after the end-of-chapter questions, in basic, intermediate, and challenge levels. *Part IV* provides essay questions to test problem-solving skills and more advanced understanding of concepts. *Part V* picks up questions directly from the end-of-chapter material and converts them into parallel test bank questions. For your reference, each TB question in this part is linked with its corresponding question in the EOC.

- **Computerized Test Bank (Windows)**

  Create your own tests in a snap! These additional questions are found in a computerized test bank utilizing McGraw-Hill's EZ Test testing software to quickly create customized exams. This user-friendly program allows instructors to sort questions by format; edit existing questions or add new ones; and scramble questions for multiple versions of the same test.

- **PowerPoint Presentations**

  Prepared by Eric McLaughlin, California State University–Pomona

  The PowerPoint slides for the 10th edition have been revised to include a wealth of instructor material, including lecture tips, real-world examples, and international notes. Each presentation now also includes slides dedicated entirely to ethics notes that relate to the chapter topics. In addition, the PPTs provide exhibits and examples both from the book and from outside sources. Applicable slides have

Web links that take you directly to specific Internet sites, or a spreadsheet link to show an example in Excel. Go to the Notes Page function for more tips and information while presenting the slides to your class.

Customize our content for your course! If you already have PowerPoint installed on your PC, you have the ability to add, delete, edit, print, or rearrange the complete presentation to focus on your course needs.

Videos (DVD Format)

Current set of videos on hot topics! McGraw-Hill/Irwin produced a series of finance videos that are 10-minute case studies on topics such as Financial Markets, Careers, Rightsizing, Capital Budgeting, EVA (Economic Value Added), Mergers and Acquisitions, and International Finance.

ONLINE SUPPORT

Online Learning Center at www.mhhe.com/rwj

The Online Learning Center (OLC) contains FREE access to additional Web-based study and teaching aids created for this text, such as:

Student Support

A great resource for those seeking additional practice, students can access self-grading quizzes, Excel template problems, and Excel Master, designed by Brad Jordan and Joe Smolira.

- **Premium Content Access**

    Narrated PowerPoint Slides—*Created by Lynn Kugele, University of Southern Mississippi.* The narrated PowerPoints provide real-world examples accompanied by step-by-step instructions and explanations for solving problems presented in the chapter. The Concept Checks from the text are also integrated into the slides to reinforce the key topics in the chapter. Designed specifically to appeal to the different learning methods of students, the slides provide a visual and audio explanation of topics and problems. Click on the slide and listen to the accompanying narration! You can view the slides via computer or download them onto your video iPod.

New! For this Edition—Study Finance Mobile App

The Study Finance mobile app was built with the student in mind. You are on the go and your study tools should be too!

McGraw-Hill is proud to offer a new mobile study app for students learning corporate finance from Ross/Westerfield/Jordan's *Fundamentals of Corporate Finance,* 10th edition. The Study Finance app that accompanies your textbook will allow you to study wherever you are and wherever you want to be.

Visit your mobile app store and download Study Finance today! Just search "Study Finance."

Teaching Support

Along with having access to all of the same material your students can view on the book's OLC, you also have password-protected access to the Instructor's Manual, solutions to end-of-chapter problems and cases, Instructor's PowerPoint, Excel Template Solutions, video clips, and video projects and questions.

WebCT and Blackboard course cartridges allow instructors to manage their course and administer examinations online. Increase ease, organization, and efficiency and ask your representative for more details about course cartridges today!

Wall Street Survivor

Students receive free access to this Web-based portfolio simulation with a hypothetical $100,000 brokerage account to buy and sell stocks and mutual funds. Students can use the real data found at this site in conjunction with the chapters on investments. They can also compete against students around the United States. This site is powered by Stock-Trak, the leading provider of investment simulation services to the academic community.

McGraw-Hill's Connect and Connect Plus

Are you looking for a way to spend less time grading and to have more flexibility with the problems you assign as homework and tests? McGraw-Hill's Connect is an exciting package option! Connect is a Web-based tool for instructors and students for delivering, answering, and grading end-of-chapter problems and tests and providing a limitless supply of self-graded practice for students.

All of the book's end-of-chapter Questions and Problems are loaded into Connect, and instructors can choose to assign the exact problems as stated in the book, or algorithmic versions of them so each student has a unique set of variables for the problems. You create the assignments and control parameters such as do you want your students to receive hints, is this a graded assignment or practice, etc. The test bank is also available in Connect, giving you the ability to use those questions for online tests. Both the problems and the tests are automatically graded and the results are stored in a private grade book, which is created when you set up your class. Detailed results let you see at a glance how each student does on an assignment or an individual problem—you can even see how many tries it took them to solve it. If you order this special package, students will receive a Connect User's Guide and an access code packaged with their text.

There is also an enhanced version of McGraw-Hill's Connect through the Connect Plus package option. If you order the text packaged with Connect Plus, your students will receive Connect as described above, but with an integrated online text included. When students are in Connect and need more help to solve a problem, there will be a link that takes them to the section of the text online that explains the concept they are struggling with. All of McGraw-Hill's media assets, such as videos, narrated lectures, and additional online quizzing, are also integrated at the appropriate places of the online text to provide students with a full learning experience. If you order this special package, students will receive the Connect Plus card packaged with their text, which gives them access to all of these products.

AVAILABLE FOR PURCHASE & PACKAGING

FinGame Online 5.0

By LeRoy Brooks, John Carroll University

(ISBN 10: 0077219880/ISBN 13: 9780077219888)

Just $15.00 when packaged with this text. In this comprehensive simulation game, students control a hypothetical company over numerous periods of operation. The game is now tied to the text by exercises found on the Online Learning Center. As students make major financial and operating decisions for their company, they will develop and enhance their skills in financial management and financial accounting statement analysis.

Assurance of Learning Ready

Assurance of Learning is an important element of many accreditation standards. *Fundamentals of Corporate Finance,* 10e, is designed specifically to support your assurance of learning initiatives. Each chapter in the book begins with a list of numbered learning objectives that appear throughout the chapter, as well as in the end-of-chapter problems and exercises. Every test bank question is also linked to one of these objectives, in addition to level of difficulty, topic area, Bloom's Taxonomy level, and AACSB skill area. Connect, McGraw-Hill's online homework solution, and EZ Test, McGraw-Hill's easy-to-use test bank software, can search the test bank using these and other categories, providing an engine for targeted Assurance of Learning analysis and assessment.

AACSB Statement

The McGraw-Hill Companies is a proud corporate member of AACSB International. Understanding the importance and value of AACSB Accreditation, *Fundamentals of Corporate Finance,* 10e, has sought to recognize the curricula guidelines detailed in the AACSB standards for business accreditation by connecting selected questions in the test bank to the general knowledge and skill guidelines found in the AACSB standards.

The statements contained in *Fundamentals of Corporate Finance,* 10e, are provided only as a guide for the users of this text. The AACSB leaves content coverage and assessment within the purview of individual schools, the mission of the school, and the faculty. While *Fundamentals of Corporate Finance,* 10e, and the teaching package make no claim of any specific AACSB qualification or evaluation, we have, within the test bank, labeled selected questions according to the six general knowledge and skills areas.

Acknowledgments

To borrow a phrase, writing an introductory finance textbook is easy—all you do is sit down at a word processor and open a vein. We never would have completed this book without the incredible amount of help and support we received from literally hundreds of our colleagues, students, editors, family members, and friends. We would like to thank, without implicating, all of you.

Clearly, our greatest debt is to our many colleagues (and their students) who, like us, wanted to try an alternative to what they were using and made the decision to change. Needless to say, without this support, we would not be publishing a 10th edition!

A great many of our colleagues read the drafts of our first and subsequent editions. The fact that this book has so little in common with our earliest drafts, along with the many changes and improvements we have made over the years, is a reflection of the value we placed on the many comments and suggestions that we received. To the following reviewers, then, we are grateful for their many contributions:

Ibrahim Affeneh
Mike Anderson
Sung C. Bae
Robert Benecke
Gary Benesh
Scott Besley
Sanjai Bhaghat
Vigdis Boasson
Elizabeth Booth
Denis Boudreaux
Jim Boyd
William Brent
Ray Brooks
Charles C. Brown
Lawrence Byerly
Steve Byers
Steve Caples
Asim Celik
Christina Cella
Mary Chaffin
Fan Chen
Raju Chenna
Barbara J. Childs
Charles M. Cox
Natalya Delcoure
Michael Dorigan
David A. Dumpe
Michael Dunn
Alan Eastman

Adrian C. Edwards
Uchenna Elike
Steve Engel
Angelo V. Esposito
Cheri Etling
Thomas H. Eyssell
Michael Ferguson
Deborah Ann Ford
Jim Forjan
Micah Frankel
Jennifer R. Frazier
Deborah M. Giarusso
Devra Golbe
A. Steven Graham
Darryl E. J. Gurley
Wendy D. Habegger
Karen Hallows
David Harraway
John M. Harris, Jr.
R. Stevenson Hawkey
Delvin D. Hawley
Robert C. Higgins
Karen Hogan
Steve Isberg
James Jackson
Pankaj Jain
James M. Johnson
Randy Jorgensen
Jarl G. Kallberg

Terry Keasler
David N. Ketcher
Jim Keys
Kee Kim
Robert Kleinman
David Kuipers
Morris A. Lamberson
Qin Lan
Dina Layish
Chun Lee
Adam Y. C. Lei
George Lentz
John Lightstone
Jason Lin
Scott Lowe
Robert Lutz
Pawan Madhogarhia
Timothy Manuel
David G. Martin
Dubos J. Masson
John McDougald
Bob McElreath
Bahlous Mejda
Gordon Melms
Richard R. Mendenhall
Wayne Mikkelson
Lalatendu Misra
Karlyn Mitchell
Sunil Mohanty

Scott Moore

Belinda Mucklow

Barry Mulholland

Frederick H. Mull

Michael J. Murray

Randy Nelson

Oris Odom

Keith Osher

Bulent Parker

Megan Partch

Samuel Penkar

Pamela P. Peterson

Robert Phillips

Greg Pierce

Robert Puelz

George A. Racette

Charu G. Raheja

Narendar V. Rao

Russ Ray

Ron Reiber

Thomas Rietz

Jay R. Ritter

Ricardo J. Rodriguez

Stu Rosenstein

Kenneth Roskelley

Ivan Roten

Gary Sanger

Travis Sapp

Martha A. Schary

Robert Schwebach

Roger Severns

Michael Sher

Dilip K. Shome

Neil W. Sicherman

Timothy Smaby

Ahmad Sohrabian

Michael F. Spivey

Vic Stanton

Charlene Sullivan

George S. Swales, Jr.

Lee Swartz

Philip Swensen

Philip Swicegood

Brian Tarrant

Rhonda Tenkku

John G. Thatcher

Harry Thiewes

A. Frank Thompson

Joseph Trefzger

George Turk

Michael R. Vetsuypens

Joe Walker

Jun Wang

James Washam

Alan Weatherford

Gwendolyn Webb

Marsha Weber

Jill Wetmore

Mark White

Annie Wong

Colbrin Wright

David J. Wright

Steve B. Wyatt

Tung-Hsiao Yang

Morris Yarmish

Michael Young

Mei Zhang

J. Kenton Zumwalt

Tom Zwirlein

Reviews from the following instructors helped us to shape our development plan for the tenth edition of *Fundamentals of Corporate Finance*.

Jan Ambrose
LaSalle University

James Estes
California State University–San Bernardino

Dave Fehr
Southern New Hampshire University

Mark Graham
James Madison University

Eric Haye
Ramapo College of New Jersey

Matthew Hood
University of Southern Mississippi

Daniel Jubinski
St. Joseph's University

Ashok Kapoor
Metropolitan State University

Howard Keen
Temple University

Deborah King
Springfield Technical Community College

Ladd Kochman
Kennesaw State University

Sophie Kong
Western Washington University

Qingzhong Ma
Cornell University

Mario Mastrandrea
Cleveland State University

Leslie Mathis
University of Memphis

Steve Pilloff
George Mason University

Kenneth Roskelley
Mississippi State University

Philip Russel
Philadelphia University

Alice Sun
California State Polytechnic University–Pomona

Susan White
University of Maryland–College Park

Several of our most respected colleagues contributed original essays for this edition, which are entitled "In Their Own Words," and appear in selected chapters. To these individuals we extend a special thanks:

Edward I. Altman
New York University

Robert C. Higgins
University of Washington

Roger Ibbotson
Yale University, Ibbotson Associates

Erik Lie
University of Iowa

Robert C. Merton
Harvard University

Jay R. Ritter
University of Florida

Richard Roll
University of California at Los Angeles

Fischer Black

Jeremy Siegel
University of Pennsylvania

Hersh Shefrin
Santa Clara University

Bennett Stewart
Stern Stewart & Co.

Samuel C. Weaver
Lehigh University

Merton H. Miller

We are lucky to have had skilled and experienced instructors developing the supplement material for this edition. Thank you to Eric McLaughlin for his work thoroughly revising and updating the PowerPoint presentations and for organizing and distributing the wealth of annotated instructor notes from the book into these teaching materials. We greatly appreciate the contributions of Joe Smolira, Belmont University, who worked closely with us to develop the Solutions Manual and to create Excel Templates for many of the end-of-chapter problems. Thank you also to Terri Renner, Indiana University, for her thorough updating, revising, and tagging of every problem in the test bank. Thanks to Lynn Kugele, Ole Miss, for expertly developing and extending the Student Narrated PowerPoint slides for the tenth edition.

The following University of Kentucky students did outstanding work on this edition of *Fundamentals:* Nathaniel Graham and Tim Riley. To them fell the unenviable task of technical proofreading, and in particular, careful checking of each calculation throughout the text and Instructor's Manual.

Finally, in every phase of this project, we have been privileged to have had the complete and unwavering support of a great organization, McGraw-Hill/Irwin. We especially thank the McGraw-Hill/Irwin sales group. The suggestions they provide, their professionalism in assisting potential adopters, and the service they provide to current users have been a major factor in our success.

We are deeply grateful to the select group of professionals who served as our development team on this edition: Michele Janicek, Executive Editor; Jennifer Lohn, Development Editor; Melissa Caughlin, Marketing Manager; Christine Vaughan, Lead Project Manager; Pam Verros, Designer; and Brian Nacik, Media Producer. Others at McGraw-Hill/Irwin, too numerous to list here, have improved the book in countless ways.

Throughout the development of this edition, we have taken great care to discover and eliminate errors. Our goal is to provide the best textbook available on the subject. To ensure that future editions are error-free, we gladly offer $10 per arithmetic error to the first individual reporting it as a modest token of our appreciation. More than this, we would like to hear from instructors and students alike. Please write and tell us how to make this a better text. Forward your comments to: Dr. Brad Jordan, c/o Editorial—Finance, McGraw-Hill/Irwin, 1333 Burr Ridge Parkway, Burr Ridge, IL 60527 or visit us online at www.mhhe.com/rwj.

Stephen A. Ross
Randolph W. Westerfield
Bradford D. Jordan

Brief Contents

Contents

PART 3   Valuation of Future Cash Flows

PART 5   Risk and Return

PART 8   Topics in Corporate Finance

In Their Own Words Boxes

CHAPTER 4

Robert C. Higgins *University of Washington*
On Sustainable Growth

CHAPTER 7

Edward I. Altman *New York University*
On Junk Bonds and Leveraged Loans

CHAPTER 10

Samuel C. Weaver *Lehigh University*
On Capital Budgeting at The Hershey Company

CHAPTER 12

Roger Ibbotson *Yale University*
On Capital Market History

Jeremy Siegel *University of Pennsylvania*
On Stocks for the Long Run

Richard Roll *University of California at Los Angeles*
On Market Efficiency

CHAPTER 14

Bennett Stewart *Stern Stewart & Co.*
On EVA
Samuel C. Weaver *Lehigh University*
On Cost of Capital and Hurdle Rates at The Hershey Company

CHAPTER 15

Jay R. Ritter *University of Florida*
On IPO Underpricing around the World

CHAPTER 16

Merton H. Miller
On Capital Structure: M&M 30 Years Later

CHAPTER 17

Fischer Black
On Why Firms Pay Dividends

INTRODUCTION TO CORPORATE FINANCE

COMPENSATION OF CORPORATE EXECUTIVES in the United States continues to be a hot button issue. It is widely viewed that CEO pay has grown to exorbitant levels (at least in some cases). In response, in July 2010, the Dodd–Frank Wall Street Reform and Consumer Protection Act became law. The "say-on-pay" portion of the bill requires that, beginning in January 2011, corporations with a market value over $75 million allow a nonbinding shareholder vote on executive pay. (Note that because the bill applies to corporations, it does not give voters a say on pay for U.S. representatives and senators.)

Specifically, the measure allows shareholders to approve or disapprove a company's executive compensation plans. Because the bill is nonbinding, it does not permit shareholders to veto a compensation package and does not place limits on executive pay. In February 2011, the shareholders of Beazer Homes USA and Jacobs Engineering Group became the first shareholders to vote against executive compensation under the new law. One analyst expected that these two companies would not be alone, as he expected at least 50 companies to receive negative votes during 2011.

Understanding how a corporation sets executive pay, and the role of shareholders in that process, takes us into issues involving the corporate form of organization, corporate goals, and corporate control, all of which we cover in this chapter.

LEARNING OBJECTIVES

After studying this chapter, you should understand:

LO1 The basic types of financial management decisions and the role of the financial manager.

LO2 The goal of financial management.

LO3 The financial implications of the different forms of business organization.

LO4 The conflicts of interest that can arise between managers and owners.

To begin our study of modern corporate finance and financial management, we need to address two central issues. First, what is corporate finance and what is the role of the financial manager in the corporation? Second, what is the goal of financial management? To describe the financial management environment, we consider the corporate form of organization and discuss some conflicts that can arise within the corporation. We also take a brief look at financial markets in the United States.

1.1 Corporate Finance and the Financial Manager

In this section, we discuss where the financial manager fits in the corporation. We start by defining *corporate finance* and the financial manager's job.

WHAT IS CORPORATE FINANCE?

Imagine that you were to start your own business. No matter what type you started, you would have to answer the following three questions in some form or another:

1. What long-term investments should you take on? That is, what lines of business will you be in and what sorts of buildings, machinery, and equipment will you need?
2. Where will you get the long-term financing to pay for your investment? Will you bring in other owners or will you borrow the money?
3. How will you manage your everyday financial activities such as collecting from customers and paying suppliers?

These are not the only questions by any means, but they are among the most important. Corporate finance, broadly speaking, is the study of ways to answer these three questions. Accordingly, we'll be looking at each of them in the chapters ahead.

THE FINANCIAL MANAGER

Check out the companion website for this text at www.mhhe.com/rwj.

For current issues facing CFOs, see www.cfo.com.

A striking feature of large corporations is that the owners (the stockholders) are usually not directly involved in making business decisions, particularly on a day-to-day basis. Instead, the corporation employs managers to represent the owners' interests and make decisions on their behalf. In a large corporation, the financial manager would be in charge of answering the three questions we raised in the preceding section.

The financial management function is usually associated with a top officer of the firm, such as a vice president of finance or some other chief financial officer (CFO). Figure 1.1 is a simplified organizational chart that highlights the finance activity in a large firm. As shown, the vice president of finance coordinates the activities of the treasurer and the controller. The controller's office handles cost and financial accounting, tax payments, and management information systems. The treasurer's office is responsible for managing the firm's cash and credit, its financial planning, and its capital expenditures. These treasury activities are all related to the three general questions raised earlier, and the chapters ahead deal primarily with these issues. Our study thus bears mostly on activities usually associated with the treasurer's office.

FINANCIAL MANAGEMENT DECISIONS

As the preceding discussion suggests, the financial manager must be concerned with three basic types of questions. We consider these in greater detail next.

capital budgeting
The process of planning and managing a firm's long-term investments.

Capital Budgeting   The first question concerns the firm's long-term investments. The process of planning and managing a firm's long-term investments is called **capital budgeting**. In capital budgeting, the financial manager tries to identify investment opportunities that are worth more to the firm than they cost to acquire. Loosely speaking, this means that the value of the cash flow generated by an asset exceeds the cost of that asset.

The types of investment opportunities that would typically be considered depend in part on the nature of the firm's business. For example, for a large retailer such as Walmart,

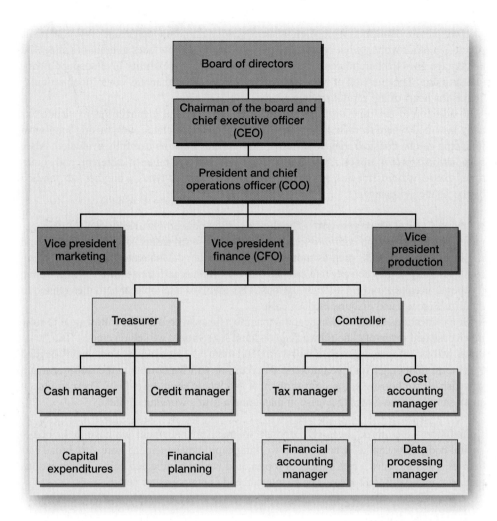

FIGURE 1.1

A Sample Simplified Organizational Chart

deciding whether to open another store would be an important capital budgeting decision. Similarly, for a software company such as Oracle or Microsoft, the decision to develop and market a new spreadsheet program would be a major capital budgeting decision. Some decisions, such as what type of computer system to purchase, might not depend so much on a particular line of business.

Regardless of the specific nature of an opportunity under consideration, financial managers must be concerned not only with how much cash they expect to receive, but also with when they expect to receive it and how likely they are to receive it. Evaluating the *size, timing,* and *risk* of future cash flows is the essence of capital budgeting. In fact, as we will see in the chapters ahead, whenever we evaluate a business decision, the size, timing, and risk of the cash flows will be by far the most important things we will consider.

Capital Structure   The second question for the financial manager concerns ways in which the firm obtains and manages the long-term financing it needs to support its long-term investments. A firm's **capital structure** (or financial structure) is the specific mixture of long-term debt and equity the firm uses to finance its operations. The financial manager has two concerns in this area. First, how much should the firm borrow? That is, what mixture of debt and equity is best? The mixture chosen will affect both the risk and the value of the firm. Second, what are the least expensive sources of funds for the firm?

capital structure
The mixture of debt and equity maintained by a firm.

If we picture the firm as a pie, then the firm's capital structure determines how that pie is sliced—in other words, what percentage of the firm's cash flow goes to creditors and what percentage goes to shareholders. Firms have a great deal of flexibility in choosing a financial structure. The question of whether one structure is better than any other for a particular firm is the heart of the capital structure issue.

In addition to deciding on the financing mix, the financial manager has to decide exactly how and where to raise the money. The expenses associated with raising long-term financing can be considerable, so different possibilities must be carefully evaluated. Also, corporations borrow money from a variety of lenders in a number of different, and sometimes exotic, ways. Choosing among lenders and among loan types is another job handled by the financial manager.

working capital
A firm's short-term assets and liabilities.

Working Capital Management   The third question concerns **working capital** management. The term *working capital* refers to a firm's short-term assets, such as inventory, and its short-term liabilities, such as money owed to suppliers. Managing the firm's working capital is a day-to-day activity that ensures that the firm has sufficient resources to continue its operations and avoid costly interruptions. This involves a number of activities related to the firm's receipt and disbursement of cash.

Some questions about working capital that must be answered are the following: (1) How much cash and inventory should we keep on hand? (2) Should we sell on credit? If so, what terms will we offer, and to whom will we extend them? (3) How will we obtain any needed short-term financing? Will we purchase on credit, or will we borrow in the short term and pay cash? If we borrow in the short term, how and where should we do it? These are just a small sample of the issues that arise in managing a firm's working capital.

Conclusion   The three areas of corporate financial management we have described—capital budgeting, capital structure, and working capital management—are very broad categories. Each includes a rich variety of topics, and we have indicated only a few questions that arise in the different areas. The chapters ahead contain greater detail.

Concept Questions

1.1a   What is the capital budgeting decision?

1.1b   What do you call the specific mixture of long-term debt and equity that a firm chooses to use?

1.1c   Into what category of financial management does cash management fall?

1.2 Forms of Business Organization

Large firms in the United States, such as Ford and Microsoft, are almost all organized as corporations. We examine the three different legal forms of business organization—sole proprietorship, partnership, and corporation—to see why this is so. Each form has distinct advantages and disadvantages for the life of the business, the ability of the business to raise cash, and taxes. A key observation is that as a firm grows, the advantages of the corporate form may come to outweigh the disadvantages.

SOLE PROPRIETORSHIP

sole proprietorship
A business owned by a single individual.

A **sole proprietorship** is a business owned by one person. This is the simplest type of business to start and is the least regulated form of organization. Depending on where you live, you might be able to start a proprietorship by doing little more than getting a business license and opening your doors. For this reason, there are more proprietorships than any other type of business, and many businesses that later become large corporations start out as small proprietorships.

The owner of a sole proprietorship keeps all the profits. That's the good news. The bad news is that the owner has *unlimited liability* for business debts. This means that creditors can look beyond business assets to the proprietor's personal assets for payment. Similarly, there is no distinction between personal and business income, so all business income is taxed as personal income.

The life of a sole proprietorship is limited to the owner's life span, and the amount of equity that can be raised is limited to the amount of the proprietor's personal wealth. This limitation often means that the business is unable to exploit new opportunities because of insufficient capital. Ownership of a sole proprietorship may be difficult to transfer because this transfer requires the sale of the entire business to a new owner.

For more information about forms of business organization, see www.incorporate.com.

PARTNERSHIP

A **partnership** is similar to a proprietorship except that there are two or more owners (partners). In a *general partnership,* all the partners share in gains or losses, and all have unlimited liability for *all* partnership debts, not just some particular share. The way partnership gains (and losses) are divided is described in the *partnership agreement.* This agreement can be an informal oral agreement, such as "let's start a lawn mowing business," or a lengthy, formal written document.

partnership
A business formed by two or more individuals or entities.

In a *limited partnership,* one or more *general partners* will run the business and have unlimited liability, but there will be one or more *limited partners* who will not actively participate in the business. A limited partner's liability for business debts is limited to the amount that partner contributes to the partnership. This form of organization is common in real estate ventures, for example.

The advantages and disadvantages of a partnership are basically the same as those of a proprietorship. Partnerships based on a relatively informal agreement are easy and inexpensive to form. General partners have unlimited liability for partnership debts, and the partnership terminates when a general partner wishes to sell out or dies. All income is taxed as personal income to the partners, and the amount of equity that can be raised is limited to the partners' combined wealth. Ownership of a general partnership is not easily transferred because a transfer requires that a new partnership be formed. A limited partner's interest can be sold without dissolving the partnership, but finding a buyer may be difficult.

Because a partner in a general partnership can be held responsible for all partnership debts, having a written agreement is very important. Failure to spell out the rights and duties of the partners frequently leads to misunderstandings later on. Also, if you are a limited partner, you must not become deeply involved in business decisions unless you are willing to assume the obligations of a general partner. The reason is that if things go badly, you may be deemed to be a general partner even though you say you are a limited partner.

Based on our discussion, the primary disadvantages of sole proprietorships and partnerships as forms of business organization are (1) unlimited liability for business debts on the part of the owners, (2) limited life of the business, and (3) difficulty of transferring ownership. These three disadvantages add up to a single, central problem: the ability of such businesses to grow can be seriously limited by an inability to raise cash for investment.

CORPORATION

The **corporation** is the most important form (in terms of size) of business organization in the United States. A corporation is a legal "person," separate and distinct from its owners,

corporation
A business created as a distinct legal entity composed of one or more individuals or entities.

and it has many of the rights, duties, and privileges of an actual person. Corporations can borrow money and own property, can sue and be sued, and can enter into contracts. A corporation can even be a general partner or a limited partner in a partnership, and a corporation can own stock in another corporation.

Not surprisingly, starting a corporation is somewhat more complicated than starting the other forms of business organization. Forming a corporation involves preparing *articles of incorporation* (or a charter) and a set of *bylaws*. The articles of incorporation must contain a number of things, including the corporation's name, its intended life (which can be forever), its business purpose, and the number of shares that can be issued. This information must normally be supplied to the state in which the firm will be incorporated. For most legal purposes, the corporation is a "resident" of that state.

The bylaws are rules describing how the corporation regulates its existence. For example, the bylaws describe how directors are elected. These bylaws may be a simple statement of a few rules and procedures, or they may be quite extensive for a large corporation. The bylaws may be amended or extended from time to time by the stockholders.

In a large corporation, the stockholders and the managers are usually separate groups. The stockholders elect the board of directors, who then select the managers. Managers are charged with running the corporation's affairs in the stockholders' interests. In principle, stockholders control the corporation because they elect the directors.

As a result of the separation of ownership and management, the corporate form has several advantages. Ownership (represented by shares of stock) can be readily transferred, and the life of the corporation is therefore not limited. The corporation borrows money in its own name. As a result, the stockholders in a corporation have limited liability for corporate debts. The most they can lose is what they have invested.

The relative ease of transferring ownership, the limited liability for business debts, and the unlimited life of the business are why the corporate form is superior for raising cash. If a corporation needs new equity, for example, it can sell new shares of stock and attract new investors. Apple is an example. The company was a pioneer in the personal computer business. As demand for its products exploded, it had to convert to the corporate form of organization to raise the capital needed to fund growth and new product development. The number of owners can be huge; larger corporations have many thousands or even millions of stockholders. For example, in 2011, General Electric Corporation (better known as GE) had about 4 million stockholders and about 10.7 billion shares outstanding. In such cases, ownership can change continuously without affecting the continuity of the business.

The corporate form has a significant disadvantage. Because a corporation is a legal person, it must pay taxes. Moreover, money paid out to stockholders in the form of dividends is taxed again as income to those stockholders. This is *double taxation,* meaning that corporate profits are taxed twice: at the corporate level when they are earned and again at the personal level when they are paid out.[1]

Today, all 50 states have enacted laws allowing for the creation of a relatively new form of business organization, the limited liability company (LLC). The goal of this entity is to operate and be taxed like a partnership but retain limited liability for owners, so an LLC is essentially a hybrid of partnership and corporation. Although states have differing definitions for LLCs, the more important scorekeeper is the Internal Revenue Service (IRS). The IRS will consider an LLC a corporation, thereby subjecting it to double taxation, unless it meets certain specific criteria. In essence, an LLC cannot be too corporation-like, or it will be treated as one by the IRS. LLCs have become common. For example, Goldman, Sachs and Co., one of Wall Street's last remaining partnerships, decided to convert from a private

How hard is it to form an LLC? Visit www.llc.com *to find out.*

---

[1]An S corporation is a special type of small corporation that is essentially taxed like a partnership and thus avoids double taxation. In 2012, the maximum number of shareholders in an S corporation was 100.

TABLE 1.1   International Corporations

Company	Country of Origin	Type of Company	
		In Original Language	**Translated**
Bayerische Motoren Werke (BMW) AG	Germany	Aktiengesellschaft	Corporation
Dornier GmBH	Germany	Gesellschaft mit Beschränkter Haftung	Limited liability company
Rolls-Royce PLC	United Kingdom	Public limited company	Public limited company
Shell UK Ltd.	United Kingdom	Limited	Corporation
Unilever NV	Netherlands	Naamloze Vennootschap	Joint stock company
Fiat SpA	Italy	Società per Azioni	Joint stock company
Volvo AB	Sweden	Aktiebolag	Joint stock company
Peugeot SA	France	Société Anonyme	Joint stock company

partnership to an LLC (it later "went public," becoming a publicly held corporation). Large accounting firms and law firms by the score have converted to LLCs.

As the discussion in this section illustrates, the need of large businesses for outside investors and creditors is such that the corporate form will generally be the best for such firms. We focus on corporations in the chapters ahead because of the importance of the corporate form in the U.S. and world economies. Also, a few important financial management issues, such as dividend policy, are unique to corporations. However, businesses of all types and sizes need financial management, so the majority of the subjects we discuss bear on any form of business.

A CORPORATION BY ANOTHER NAME . . .

The corporate form of organization has many variations around the world. The exact laws and regulations differ from country to country, of course, but the essential features of public ownership and limited liability remain. These firms are often called *joint stock companies, public limited companies,* or *limited liability companies,* depending on the specific nature of the firm and the country of origin.

Table 1.1 gives the names of a few well-known international corporations, their countries of origin, and a translation of the abbreviation that follows the company name.

Concept Questions

1.2a What are the three forms of business organization?

1.2b What are the primary advantages and disadvantages of sole proprietorships and partnerships?

1.2c What is the difference between a general and a limited partnership?

1.2d Why is the corporate form superior when it comes to raising cash?

The Goal of Financial Management   1.3

Assuming that we restrict ourselves to for-profit businesses, the goal of financial management is to make money or add value for the owners. This goal is a little vague, of course, so we examine some different ways of formulating it to come up with a more precise definition. Such a definition is important because it leads to an objective basis for making and evaluating financial decisions.

POSSIBLE GOALS

If we were to consider possible financial goals, we might come up with some ideas like the following:

> Survive.
>
> Avoid financial distress and bankruptcy.
>
> Beat the competition.
>
> Maximize sales or market share.
>
> Minimize costs.
>
> Maximize profits.
>
> Maintain steady earnings growth.

These are only a few of the goals we could list. Furthermore, each of these possibilities presents problems as a goal for the financial manager.

For example, it's easy to increase market share or unit sales: All we have to do is lower our prices or relax our credit terms. Similarly, we can always cut costs simply by doing away with things such as research and development. We can avoid bankruptcy by never borrowing any money or never taking any risks, and so on. It's not clear that any of these actions are in the stockholders' best interests.

Profit maximization would probably be the most commonly cited goal, but even this is not a precise objective. Do we mean profits this year? If so, we should note that actions such as deferring maintenance, letting inventories run down, and taking other short-run cost-cutting measures will tend to increase profits now, but these activities aren't necessarily desirable.

The goal of maximizing profits may refer to some sort of "long-run" or "average" profits, but it's still unclear exactly what this means. First, do we mean something like accounting net income or earnings per share? As we will see in more detail in the next chapter, these accounting numbers may have little to do with what is good or bad for the firm. Second, what do we mean by the long run? As a famous economist once remarked, in the long run, we're all dead! More to the point, this goal doesn't tell us what the appropriate trade-off is between current and future profits.

The goals we've listed here are all different, but they tend to fall into two classes. The first of these relates to profitability. The goals involving sales, market share, and cost control all relate, at least potentially, to different ways of earning or increasing profits. The goals in the second group, involving bankruptcy avoidance, stability, and safety, relate in some way to controlling risk. Unfortunately, these two types of goals are somewhat contradictory. The pursuit of profit normally involves some element of risk, so it isn't really possible to maximize both safety and profit. What we need, therefore, is a goal that encompasses both factors.

THE GOAL OF FINANCIAL MANAGEMENT

The financial manager in a corporation makes decisions for the stockholders of the firm. Given this, instead of listing possible goals for the financial manager, we really need to answer a more fundamental question: From the stockholders' point of view, what is a good financial management decision?

If we assume that stockholders buy stock because they seek to gain financially, then the answer is obvious: Good decisions increase the value of the stock, and poor decisions decrease the value of the stock.

Given our observations, it follows that the financial manager acts in the shareholders' best interests by making decisions that increase the value of the stock. The appropriate goal for the financial manager can thus be stated quite easily:

> **The goal of financial management is to maximize the current value per share of the existing stock.**

The goal of maximizing the value of the stock avoids the problems associated with the different goals we listed earlier. There is no ambiguity in the criterion, and there is no short-run versus long-run issue. We explicitly mean that our goal is to maximize the *current* stock value.

If this goal seems a little strong or one-dimensional to you, keep in mind that the stockholders in a firm are residual owners. By this we mean that they are entitled to only what is left after employees, suppliers, and creditors (and anyone else with a legitimate claim) are paid their due. If any of these groups go unpaid, the stockholders get nothing. So, if the stockholders are winning in the sense that the leftover, residual portion is growing, it must be true that everyone else is winning also.

Because the goal of financial management is to maximize the value of the stock, we need to learn how to identify investments and financing arrangements that favorably impact the value of the stock. This is precisely what we will be studying. In fact, we could have defined *corporate finance* as the study of the relationship between business decisions and the value of the stock in the business.

A MORE GENERAL GOAL

Given our goal as stated in the preceding section (maximize the value of the stock), an obvious question comes up: What is the appropriate goal when the firm has no traded stock? Corporations are certainly not the only type of business; and the stock in many corporations rarely changes hands, so it's difficult to say what the value per share is at any given time.

As long as we are dealing with for-profit businesses, only a slight modification is needed. The total value of the stock in a corporation is simply equal to the value of the owners' equity. Therefore, a more general way of stating our goal is as follows: Maximize the market value of the existing owners' equity.

With this in mind, it doesn't matter whether the business is a proprietorship, a partnership, or a corporation. For each of these, good financial decisions increase the market value of the owners' equity and poor financial decisions decrease it. In fact, although we focus on corporations in the chapters ahead, the principles we develop apply to all forms of business. Many of them even apply to the not-for-profit sector.

Finally, our goal does not imply that the financial manager should take illegal or unethical actions in the hope of increasing the value of the equity in the firm. What we mean is that the financial manager best serves the owners of the business by identifying goods and services that add value to the firm because they are desired and valued in the free marketplace.

SARBANES-OXLEY

In response to corporate scandals at companies such as Enron, WorldCom, Tyco, and Adelphia, Congress enacted the Sarbanes-Oxley Act in 2002. The act, better known as "Sarbox," is intended to protect investors from corporate abuses. For example, one section of Sarbox prohibits personal loans from a company to its officers, such as the ones that were received by WorldCom CEO Bernie Ebbers.

One of the key sections of Sarbox took effect on November 15, 2004. Section 404 requires, among other things, that each company's annual report must have an assessment of the company's internal control structure and financial reporting. An independent auditor must then evaluate and attest to management's assessment of these issues.

Sarbox contains other key requirements. For example, the officers of the corporation must review and sign the annual reports. They must explicitly declare that the annual report does not contain any false statements or material omissions; that the financial statements fairly represent the financial results; and that they are responsible for all internal controls. Finally, the annual report must list any deficiencies in internal controls. In essence, Sarbox makes company management responsible for the accuracy of the company's financial statements.

Because of its extensive reporting requirements, compliance with Sarbox can be very costly, which has led to some unintended results. Since its implementation, hundreds of public firms have chosen to "go dark," meaning that their shares are no longer traded on the major stock exchanges, in which case Sarbox does not apply. Most of these companies stated that their reason was to avoid the cost of compliance. Ironically, in such cases, the law had the effect of eliminating public disclosure instead of improving it.

For more about Sarbanes-Oxley, visit www.soxlaw.com.

Concept Questions

1.3a What is the goal of financial management?

1.3b What are some shortcomings of the goal of profit maximization?

1.3c Can you give a definition of *corporate finance?*

1.4 The Agency Problem and Control of the Corporation

We've seen that the financial manager acts in the best interests of the stockholders by taking actions that increase the value of the stock. However, we've also seen that in large corporations ownership can be spread over a huge number of stockholders. This dispersion of ownership arguably means that management effectively controls the firm. In this case, will management necessarily act in the best interests of the stockholders? Put another way, might not management pursue its own goals at the stockholders' expense? In the following pages, we briefly consider some of the arguments relating to this question.

AGENCY RELATIONSHIPS

The relationship between stockholders and management is called an *agency relationship.* Such a relationship exists whenever someone (the principal) hires another (the agent) to represent his or her interests. For example, you might hire someone (an agent) to sell a car you own while you are away at school. In all such relationships, there is a possibility of conflict of interest between the principal and the agent. Such a conflict is called an **agency problem.**

Suppose you hire someone to sell your car and agree to pay that person a flat fee when he or she sells the car. The agent's incentive in this case is to make the sale, not necessarily to get you the best price. If you offer a commission of, say, 10 percent of the sales price instead of a flat fee, then this problem might not exist. This example illustrates that the way in which an agent is compensated is one factor that affects agency problems.

agency problem
The possibility of conflict of interest between the stockholders and management of a firm.

MANAGEMENT GOALS

To see how management and stockholder interests might differ, imagine that the firm is considering a new investment. The new investment is expected to favorably impact the share value, but it is also a relatively risky venture. The owners of the firm will wish to take the investment (because the stock value will rise), but management may not because there is the possibility that things will turn out badly and management jobs will be lost. If management does not take the investment, then the stockholders may lose a valuable opportunity. This is one example of an agency cost.

More generally, the term *agency costs* refers to the costs of the conflict of interest between stockholders and management. These costs can be indirect or direct. An indirect agency cost is a lost opportunity, such as the one we have just described.

Direct agency costs come in two forms. The first type is a corporate expenditure that benefits management but costs the stockholders. Perhaps the purchase of a luxurious and unneeded corporate jet would fall under this heading. The second type of direct agency cost is an expense that arises from the need to monitor management actions. Paying outside auditors to assess the accuracy of financial statement information could be one example.

It is sometimes argued that, left to themselves, managers would tend to maximize the amount of resources over which they have control or, more generally, corporate power or wealth. This goal could lead to an overemphasis on corporate size or growth. For example, cases in which management is accused of overpaying to buy up another company just to increase the size of the business or to demonstrate corporate power are not uncommon. Obviously, if overpayment does take place, such a purchase does not benefit the stockholders of the purchasing company.

Our discussion indicates that management may tend to overemphasize organizational survival to protect job security. Also, management may dislike outside interference, so independence and corporate self-sufficiency may be important goals.

DO MANAGERS ACT IN THE STOCKHOLDERS' INTERESTS?

Whether managers will, in fact, act in the best interests of stockholders depends on two factors. First, how closely are management goals aligned with stockholder goals? This question relates, at least in part, to the way managers are compensated. Second, can managers be replaced if they do not pursue stockholder goals? This issue relates to control of the firm. As we will discuss, there are a number of reasons to think that even in the largest firms, management has a significant incentive to act in the interests of stockholders.

Managerial Compensation   Management will frequently have a significant economic incentive to increase share value for two reasons. First, managerial compensation, particularly at the top, is usually tied to financial performance in general and often to share value in particular. For example, managers are frequently given the option to buy stock at a bargain price. The more the stock is worth, the more valuable is this option. In fact, options are often used to motivate employees of all types, not just top managers. For example, in late 2010, Google's more than 20,000 employees owned enough options to buy 11.5 million shares in the company. Many other corporations, large and small, have adopted similar policies.

The second incentive managers have relates to job prospects. Better performers within the firm will tend to get promoted. More generally, managers who are successful in pursuing stockholder goals will be in greater demand in the labor market and thus command higher salaries.

In fact, managers who are successful in pursuing stockholder goals can reap enormous rewards. For example, the best-paid executive in 2010 was Stephen Hemsley, the CEO of United Health Group. According to *Forbes* magazine, he made about $120 million. By way of comparison, Hemsley made less than Oprah Winfrey ($290 million) and the band U2 ($195 million), but way more than Lady Gaga ($90 million). Over the period 2006–2010, Oracle CEO Lawrence Ellison was the highest-paid executive, earning about $961 million. Information about executive compensation, along with lots of other information, can be easily found on the Web for almost any public company. Our nearby *Work the Web* box shows you how to get started.

Business ethics are considered at www.business-ethics.com.

Control of the Firm   Control of the firm ultimately rests with stockholders. They elect the board of directors, who in turn hire and fire managers. The fact that stockholders control the corporation was made abundantly clear by Steven Jobs's experience at Apple. Even though he was a founder of the corporation and was largely responsible for its most successful products, there came a time when shareholders, through their elected directors, decided that Apple would be better off without him, so out he went. Of course, he was later rehired and helped turn Apple around with great new products such as the iPod, iPhone, and iPad.

An important mechanism by which unhappy stockholders can act to replace existing management is called a *proxy fight*. A proxy is the authority to vote someone else's stock. A proxy fight develops when a group solicits proxies in order to replace the existing board and thereby replace existing managers. For example, in early 2002, the proposed merger between Hewlett-Packard (HP) and Compaq triggered one of the most widely followed, bitterly contested, and expensive proxy fights in history, with an estimated price tag of well over $100 million. One group of shareholders, which included Walter B. Hewlett (a board member and heir to a cofounder of HP), opposed the merger and launched a proxy fight for control of HP. Another group, led by HP CEO Carly Fiorina, supported the merger. In a very close vote, Ms. Fiorina prevailed, the merger went through, and Mr. Hewlett resigned from the board.

Another way that managers can be replaced is by takeover. Firms that are poorly managed are more attractive as acquisitions than well-managed firms because a greater profit potential exists. Thus, avoiding a takeover by another firm gives management another incentive to act in the stockholders' interests. For example, in the summer of 2010, genetic drug maker Genzyme was battling an $18.5 billion unsolicited takeover bid from the French pharmaceutical firm Sanofi-Aventis. Genzyme's management argued that the bid significantly undervalued the company, even though it was 28 percent higher than the then current stock price. One sticking point was the potential sales of the multiple sclerosis drug Lemtrada. Genzyme estimated that the future sales would be about $3.5 billion per year, while Sanofi-Aventis estimated a more modest sales level of $700 million per year. Genzyme's board unanimously rejected the initial offer of $69 per share, arguing that a price of $80 per share was more reasonable. After an intense battle that lasted several months, Genzyme ultimately accepted an offer of $74 per share, with the possibility of an additional $14 per share if certain sales criteria for Lemtrada were met.

Conclusion   The available theory and evidence are consistent with the view that stockholders control the firm and that stockholder wealth maximization is the relevant goal of the corporation. Even so, there will undoubtedly be times when management goals are pursued at the expense of the stockholders, at least temporarily.

STAKEHOLDERS

Our discussion thus far implies that management and stockholders are the only parties with an interest in the firm's decisions. This is an oversimplification, of course. Employees, customers, suppliers, and even the government all have a financial interest in the firm.

Taken together, these various groups are called **stakeholders** in the firm. In general, a stakeholder is someone other than a stockholder or creditor who potentially has a claim on the cash flows of the firm. Such groups will also attempt to exert control over the firm, perhaps to the detriment of the owners.

stakeholder
Someone other than a stockholder or creditor who potentially has a claim on the cash flows of the firm.

Concept Questions

1.4a What is an agency relationship?

1.4b What are agency problems and how do they come about? What are agency costs?

1.4c What incentives do managers in large corporations have to maximize share value?

WORK THE WEB

The Web is a great place to learn more about individual companies, and there are a slew of sites available to help you. Try pointing your Web browser to finance.yahoo.com. Once you get there, you should see something like this on the page:

To look up a company, you must know its "ticker symbol" (or just ticker for short), which is a unique one- to four-letter identifier. You can click on the "Symbol Lookup" link and type in the company's name to find the ticker. For example, we typed in "PZZA," which is the ticker for pizza maker Papa John's. Here is a portion of what we got:

Papa John'S International, Inc. (NasdaqGS: PZZA)
REAL-TIME 28.35 ↓ 0.36 (1.25%) 1:53PM EST

Last Trade:	28.34	Day's Range:	28.26 - 28.69
Trade Time:	1:50PM EST	52wk Range:	21.51 - 28.84
Change:	↓ 0.37 (1.29%)	Volume:	45,295
Prev Close:	28.71	Avg Vol (3m):	115,866
Open:	28.63	Market Cap:	730.38M
Bid:	28.32 x 200	P/E (ttm):	14.83
Ask:	28.34 x 200	EPS (ttm):	1.91
1y Target Est:	31.20	Div & Yield:	N/A (N/A)

There's a lot of information here and many links for you to explore, so have at it. By the end of the term, we hope it all makes sense to you!

Questions
1. Go to finance.yahoo.com and find the current stock prices for Southwest Airlines (LUV), Harley-Davidson (HOG), and Starwood Hotels & Resorts (HOT).
2. Get a quote for American Express (AXP) and follow the "Key Statistics" link. What information is available on this link? What do mrq, ttm, yoy, and lfy mean?

Financial Markets and the Corporation   1.5

We've seen that the primary advantages of the corporate form of organization are that ownership can be transferred more quickly and easily than with other forms and that money can be raised more readily. Both of these advantages are significantly enhanced by the existence of financial markets, and financial markets play an extremely important role in corporate finance.

CASH FLOWS TO AND FROM THE FIRM

The interplay between the corporation and the financial markets is illustrated in Figure 1.2. The arrows in Figure 1.2 trace the passage of cash from the financial markets to the firm and from the firm back to the financial markets.

Suppose we start with the firm selling shares of stock and borrowing money to raise cash. Cash flows to the firm from the financial markets (A). The firm invests the cash in current and fixed assets (B). These assets generate cash (C), some of which goes to pay corporate taxes (D). After taxes are paid, some of this cash flow is reinvested in the firm (E). The rest goes back to the financial markets as cash paid to creditors and shareholders (F).

A financial market, like any market, is just a way of bringing buyers and sellers together. In financial markets, it is debt and equity securities that are bought and sold. Financial markets differ in detail, however. The most important differences concern the types of securities that are traded, how trading is conducted, and who the buyers and sellers are. Some of these differences are discussed next.

PRIMARY VERSUS SECONDARY MARKETS

Financial markets function as both primary and secondary markets for debt and equity securities. The term *primary market* refers to the original sale of securities by governments and corporations. The *secondary markets* are those in which these securities are bought and sold after the original sale. Equities are, of course, issued solely by corporations. Debt securities are issued by both governments and corporations. In the discussion that follows, we focus on corporate securities only.

Primary Markets In a primary market transaction, the corporation is the seller, and the transaction raises money for the corporation. Corporations engage in two types of primary

FIGURE 1.2

Cash Flows between the Firm and the Financial Markets

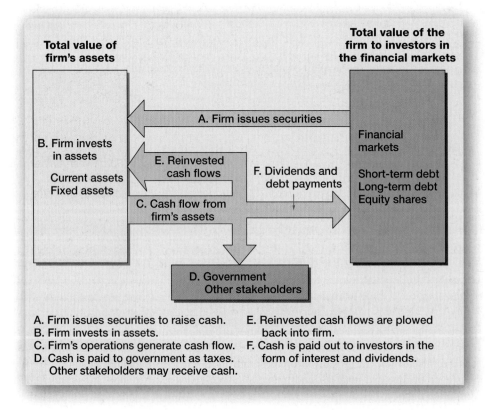

A. Firm issues securities to raise cash.
B. Firm invests in assets.
C. Firm's operations generate cash flow.
D. Cash is paid to government as taxes. Other stakeholders may receive cash.
E. Reinvested cash flows are plowed back into firm.
F. Cash is paid out to investors in the form of interest and dividends.

market transactions: public offerings and private placements. A public offering, as the name suggests, involves selling securities to the general public, whereas a private placement is a negotiated sale involving a specific buyer.

By law, public offerings of debt and equity must be registered with the Securities and Exchange Commission (SEC). Registration requires the firm to disclose a great deal of information before selling any securities. The accounting, legal, and selling costs of public offerings can be considerable.

To learn more about the SEC, visit www.sec.gov.

Partly to avoid the various regulatory requirements and the expense of public offerings, debt and equity are often sold privately to large financial institutions such as life insurance companies or mutual funds. Such private placements do not have to be registered with the SEC and do not require the involvement of underwriters (investment banks that specialize in selling securities to the public).

Secondary Markets   A secondary market transaction involves one owner or creditor selling to another. Therefore, the secondary markets provide the means for transferring ownership of corporate securities. Although a corporation is directly involved only in a primary market transaction (when it sells securities to raise cash), the secondary markets are still critical to large corporations. The reason is that investors are much more willing to purchase securities in a primary market transaction when they know that those securities can later be resold if desired.

Dealer versus Auction Markets   There are two kinds of secondary markets: *auction* markets and *dealer* markets. Generally speaking, dealers buy and sell for themselves, at their own risk. A car dealer, for example, buys and sells automobiles. In contrast, brokers and agents match buyers and sellers, but they do not actually own the commodity that is bought or sold. A real estate agent, for example, does not normally buy and sell houses.

Dealer markets in stocks and long-term debt are called *over-the-counter* (OTC) markets. Most trading in debt securities takes place over the counter. The expression *over the counter* refers to days of old when securities were literally bought and sold at counters in offices around the country. Today, a significant fraction of the market for stocks and almost all of the market for long-term debt have no central location; the many dealers are connected electronically.

Auction markets differ from dealer markets in two ways. First, an auction market or exchange has a physical location (like Wall Street). Second, in a dealer market, most of the buying and selling is done by the dealer. The primary purpose of an auction market, on the other hand, is to match those who wish to sell with those who wish to buy. Dealers play a limited role.

Trading in Corporate Securities   The equity shares of most of the large firms in the United States trade in organized auction markets. The largest such market is the New York Stock Exchange (NYSE). There is also a large OTC market for stocks. In 1971, the National Association of Securities Dealers (NASD) made available to dealers and brokers an electronic quotation system called NASDAQ (which originally stood for NASD Automated Quotation system and is pronounced "naz-dak"). NASDAQ-listed companies tend to be smaller and trade less actively. There are exceptions, of course. Both Microsoft and Intel trade OTC, for example. Nonetheless, the total value of NASDAQ stocks is much less than the total value of NYSE stocks.

To learn more about the exchanges, visit www.nyse.com *and* www.nasdaq.com.

There are many large and important financial markets outside the United States, of course, and U.S. corporations are increasingly looking to these markets to raise cash. The Tokyo Stock Exchange and the London Stock Exchange (TSE and LSE, respectively) are two well-known examples. The fact that OTC markets have no physical location means that

Visit us at www.mhhe.com/rwj

national borders do not present a great barrier, and there is now a huge international OTC debt market. Because of globalization, financial markets have reached the point where trading in many investments never stops; it just travels around the world.

Listing   Stocks that trade on an organized exchange are said to be *listed* on that exchange. To be listed, firms must meet certain minimum criteria concerning, for example, asset size and number of shareholders. These criteria differ from one exchange to another.

The NYSE has the most stringent requirements of the exchanges in the United States. For example, to be listed on the NYSE, a company is expected to have a market value for its publicly held shares of at least $100 million. There are additional minimums on earnings, assets, and number of shares outstanding.

Concept Questions

1.5a What is a dealer market? How do dealer and auction markets differ?
1.5b What does *OTC* stand for? What is the large OTC market for stocks called?
1.5c What is the largest auction market in the United States?

1.6 Summary and Conclusions

This chapter introduced you to some of the basic ideas in corporate finance:

1. Corporate finance has three main areas of concern:
   a. Capital budgeting: What long-term investments should the firm take?
   b. Capital structure: Where will the firm get the long-term financing to pay for its investments? In other words, what mixture of debt and equity should the firm use to fund operations?
   c. Working capital management: How should the firm manage its everyday financial activities?
2. The goal of financial management in a for-profit business is to make decisions that increase the value of the stock or, more generally, increase the market value of the equity.
3. The corporate form of organization is superior to other forms when it comes to raising money and transferring ownership interests, but it has the significant disadvantage of double taxation.
4. There is the possibility of conflicts between stockholders and management in a large corporation. We called these conflicts *agency problems* and discussed how they might be controlled and reduced.
5. The advantages of the corporate form are enhanced by the existence of financial markets. Financial markets function as both primary and secondary markets for corporate securities and can be organized as either dealer or auction markets.

Of the topics we've discussed thus far, the most important is the goal of financial management: maximizing the value of the stock. Throughout the text, we will be analyzing many different financial decisions, but we will always ask the same question: How does the decision under consideration affect the value of the stock?

CONNECT TO FINANCE

 If you are using *Connect™ Finance* in your course, get online to take a Practice Test, check out study tools, and find out where you need additional practice.

☐	▼ Chapter 1 Introduction to Corporate Finance			
☐	1.1 Corporate Finance and the Financial Manager	eBook	Study	Practice
☐	1.2 Forms of Business Organization	eBook	Study	Practice
☐	1.3 The Goal of Financial Management	eBook	Study	Practice
☐	1.4 The Agency Problem and Control of the Corporation	eBook	Study	Practice

Section Quiz

Can you answer the following questions?

Section 1.1   Deciding which fixed assets should be purchased is an example of what type of decision? (LO 1-1)

Section 1.2   What form of ownership is easiest to transfer? (LO 1-3)

Section 1.3   What best describes the goal of financial management? (LO 1-2)

Section 1.4   In a corporation, the primary agency conflict arises between which two parties? (LO 1-4)

Log on to find out!

CONCEPTS REVIEW AND CRITICAL THINKING QUESTIONS

1. **The Financial Management Decision Process [LO1]** What are the three types of financial management decisions? For each type of decision, give an example of a business transaction that would be relevant.

2. **Sole Proprietorships and Partnerships [LO3]** What are the four primary disadvantages of the sole proprietorship and partnership forms of business organization? What benefits are there to these types of business organization as opposed to the corporate form?

3. **Corporations [LO3]** What is the primary disadvantage of the corporate form of organization? Name at least two advantages of corporate organization.

4. **Sarbanes-Oxley [LO4]** In response to the Sarbanes-Oxley Act, many small firms in the United States have opted to "go dark" and delist their stock. Why might a company choose this route? What are the costs of "going dark"?

5. **Corporate Finance Organization [LO4]** In a large corporation, what are the two distinct groups that report to the chief financial officer? Which group is the focus of corporate finance?

6. **Goal of Financial Management [LO2]** What goal should always motivate the actions of a firm's financial manager?

7. **Agency Problems [LO4]** Who owns a corporation? Describe the process whereby the owners control the firm's management. What is the main reason that an agency relationship exists in the corporate form of organization? In this context, what kinds of problems can arise?

8. **Primary versus Secondary Markets [LO3]** You've probably noticed coverage in the financial press of an initial public offering (IPO) of a company's securities. Is an IPO a primary market transaction or a secondary market transaction?

9. **Auction versus Dealer Markets [LO3]** What does it mean when we say the New York Stock Exchange is an auction market? How are auction markets different from dealer markets? What kind of market is NASDAQ?

10. **Not-for-Profit Firm Goals [LO2]** Suppose you were the financial manager of a not-for-profit business (a not-for-profit hospital, perhaps). What kinds of goals do you think would be appropriate?

11. **Goal of the Firm [LO2]** Evaluate the following statement: Managers should not focus on the current stock value because doing so will lead to an overemphasis on short-term profits at the expense of long-term profits.

12. **Ethics and Firm Goals [LO2]** Can our goal of maximizing the value of the stock conflict with other goals, such as avoiding unethical or illegal behavior? In particular, do you think subjects like customer and employee safety, the environment, and the general good of society fit in this framework, or are they essentially ignored? Think of some specific scenarios to illustrate your answer.

13. **International Firm Goal [LO2]** Would our goal of maximizing the value of the stock be different if we were thinking about financial management in a foreign country? Why or why not?

14. **Agency Problems [LO4]** Suppose you own stock in a company. The current price per share is $25. Another company has just announced that it wants to buy your company and will pay $35 per share to acquire all the outstanding stock. Your company's management immediately begins fighting off this hostile bid. Is management acting in the shareholders' best interests? Why or why not?

15. **Agency Problems and Corporate Ownership [LO4]** Corporate ownership varies around the world. Historically individuals have owned the majority of shares in public corporations in the United States. In Germany and Japan, however, banks, other large financial institutions, and other companies own most of the stock in public corporations. Do you think agency problems are likely to be more or less severe in Germany and Japan than in the United States? Why? Over the last few decades, large financial institutions such as mutual funds and pension funds have been becoming the dominant owners of stock in the United States, and these institutions are becoming more active in corporate affairs. What are the implications of this trend for agency problems and corporate control?

16. **Executive Compensation [LO3]** Critics have charged that compensation to top managers in the United States is simply too high and should be cut back. For example, focusing on large corporations, David Novak of fast food operator Yum! Brands has been one of the best-compensated CEOs in the United States, earning about $29.67 million in 2010 alone and $199.88 million over the 2006–2010 period. Are such amounts excessive? In answering, it might be helpful to recognize that superstar athletes such as LeBron James, top entertainers such as Tom Hanks and Oprah Winfrey, and many others at the top of their respective fields earn at least as much, if not a great deal more.

MINICASE

The McGee Cake Company

In early 2005, Doc and Lyn McGee formed the McGee Cake Company. The company produced a full line of cakes, and its specialties included chess cake*, lemon pound cake, and double-iced, double-chocolate cake. The couple formed the company as an outside interest, and both continued to work at their current jobs. Doc did all the baking, and Lyn handled the marketing and distribution. With good product quality and a sound marketing plan, the company grew rapidly. In early 2010, the company was featured in a widely distributed entrepreneurial magazine. Later that year, the company was featured in *Gourmet Desserts,* a leading specialty food magazine. After the article appeared in *Gourmet Desserts,* sales exploded, and the company began receiving orders from all over the world.

Because of the increased sales, Doc left his other job, followed shortly by Lyn. The company hired additional workers to meet demand. Unfortunately, the fast growth experienced by the company led to cash flow and capacity problems. The company is currently producing as many cakes as possible with the assets it owns, but demand for its cakes is still growing.

* Chess cake is quite delicious and distinct from cheesecake. The origin of the name is obscure.

Further, the company has been approached by a national supermarket chain with a proposal to put four of its cakes in all of the chain's stores, and a national restaurant chain has contacted the company about selling McGee cakes in its restaurants. The restaurant would sell the cakes without a brand name.

Doc and Lyn have operated the company as a sole proprietorship. They have approached you to help manage and direct the company's growth. Specifically, they have asked you to answer the following questions.

QUESTIONS

1. What are the advantages and disadvantages of changing the company organization from a sole proprietorship to an LLC?

2. What are the advantages and disadvantages of changing the company organization from a sole proprietorship to a corporation?

3. Ultimately, what action would you recommend the company undertake? Why?

Visit us at www.mhhe.com/rwj

2

FINANCIAL STATEMENTS, TAXES, AND CASH FLOW

A WRITE-OFF BY A COMPANY frequently means that the value of the company's assets has declined. For example, in 2010, Bank of America announced a total of $34 billion in write-offs for bad loans. In addition, the company announced a $10.5 billion write-off because recent legislation reduced the value of its credit card business. The write-offs made by Bank of America during 2010 followed write-offs of $33.7 billion in 2009 and $16.2 billion in 2008. Of course, Bank of America was not alone. Moody's Investor Services estimated that banks had written off $476 billion during 2009 and 2010, and it expected bank write-offs of $286 billion during 2011.

Bank of America's write-off was a big one, but not a record. Possibly the largest write-offs in history were done by the media company Time Warner, which took a charge of $45.5 billion in the fourth quarter of 2002. This enormous write-off followed an earlier, even larger, charge of $54 billion.

So did stockholders in Bank of America lose $34 billion because of the write-offs? The answer is probably not. Understanding why ultimately leads us to the main subject of this chapter: that all-important substance known as *cash flow*.

LEARNING OBJECTIVES

After studying this chapter, you should understand:

LO1 The difference between accounting value (or "book" value) and market value.

LO2 The difference between accounting income and cash flow.

LO3 The difference between average and marginal tax rates.

LO4 How to determine a firm's cash flow from its financial statements.

In this chapter, we examine financial statements, taxes, and cash flow. Our emphasis is not on preparing financial statements. Instead, we recognize that financial statements are frequently a key source of information for financial decisions, so our goal is to briefly examine such statements and point out some of their more relevant features. We pay special attention to some of the practical details of cash flow.

As you read, pay particular attention to two important differences: (1) the difference between accounting value and market value and (2) the difference between accounting income and cash flow. These distinctions will be important throughout the book.

The Balance Sheet

The **balance sheet** is a snapshot of the firm. It is a convenient means of organizing and summarizing what a firm owns (its assets), what a firm owes (its liabilities), and the difference between the two (the firm's equity) at a given point in time. Figure 2.1 illustrates how the balance sheet is constructed. As shown, the left side lists the assets of the firm, and the right side lists the liabilities and equity.

ASSETS: THE LEFT SIDE

Assets are classified as either *current* or *fixed*. A fixed asset is one that has a relatively long life. Fixed assets can be either *tangible,* such as a truck or a computer, or *intangible,* such as a trademark or patent. A current asset has a life of less than one year. This means that the asset will convert to cash within 12 months. For example, inventory would normally be purchased and sold within a year and is thus classified as a current asset. Obviously, cash itself is a current asset. Accounts receivable (money owed to the firm by its customers) are also current assets.

LIABILITIES AND OWNERS' EQUITY: THE RIGHT SIDE

The firm's liabilities are the first thing listed on the right side of the balance sheet. These are classified as either *current* or *long-term*. Current liabilities, like current assets, have a life of less than one year (meaning they must be paid within the year) and are listed before long-term liabilities. Accounts payable (money the firm owes to its suppliers) are one example of a current liability.

A debt that is not due in the coming year is classified as a long-term liability. A loan that the firm will pay off in five years is one such long-term debt. Firms borrow in the long term from a variety of sources. We will tend to use the terms *bond* and *bondholders* generically to refer to long-term debt and long-term creditors, respectively.

Finally, by definition, the difference between the total value of the assets (current and fixed) and the total value of the liabilities (current and long-term) is the *shareholders' equity,* also called *common equity* or *owners' equity.* This feature of the balance sheet is intended to reflect the fact that, if the firm were to sell all its assets and use the money to pay off its debts, then whatever residual value remained would belong to the shareholders. So, the balance sheet "balances" because the value of the left side always equals the value

2.1

balance sheet
Financial statement showing a firm's accounting value on a particular date.

Three excellent sites for company financial information are finance.yahoo.com, finance.google.com, *and* money.cnn.com.

FIGURE 2.1

The Balance Sheet. Left Side: Total Value of Assets. Right Side: Total Value of Liabilities and Shareholders' Equity.

of the right side. That is, the value of the firm's assets is equal to the sum of its liabilities and shareholders' equity:[1]

$$\text{Assets} = \text{Liabilities} + \text{Shareholders' equity} \qquad [2.1]$$

This is the *balance sheet identity,* or equation, and it always holds because shareholders' equity is defined as the difference between assets and liabilities.

NET WORKING CAPITAL

net working capital
Current assets less current liabilities.

As shown in Figure 2.1, the difference between a firm's current assets and its current liabilities is called **net working capital**. Net working capital is positive when current assets exceed current liabilities. Based on the definitions of current assets and current liabilities, this means the cash that will become available over the next 12 months exceeds the cash that must be paid over the same period. For this reason, net working capital is usually positive in a healthy firm.

EXAMPLE 2.1	Building the Balance Sheet

A firm has current assets of $100, net fixed assets of $500, short-term debt of $70, and long-term debt of $200. What does the balance sheet look like? What is shareholders' equity? What is net working capital?

In this case, total assets are $100 + 500 = $600 and total liabilities are $70 + 200 = $270, so shareholders' equity is the difference: $600 − 270 = $330. The balance sheet would look like this:

Assets		Liabilities and Shareholders' Equity	
Current assets	$100	Current liabilities	$ 70
Net fixed assets	500	Long-term debt	200
		Shareholders' equity	330
Total assets	$600	Total liabilities and shareholders' equity	$600

Net working capital is the difference between current assets and current liabilities, or $100 − 70 = $30.

Table 2.1 shows simplified balance sheets for the fictitious U.S. Corporation. The assets on the balance sheet are listed in order of the length of time it takes for them to convert to cash in the normal course of business. Similarly, the liabilities are listed in the order in which they would normally be paid.

The structure of the assets for a particular firm reflects the line of business the firm is in and also managerial decisions about how much cash and inventory to have and about credit policy, fixed asset acquisition, and so on.

Disney has a good investor relations site at disney.go.com.

The liabilities side of the balance sheet primarily reflects managerial decisions about capital structure and the use of short-term debt. For example, in 2012, total long-term debt for U.S. was $454 and total equity was $640 + 1,629 = $2,269, so total long-term financing was $454 + 2,269 = $2,723. (Note that, throughout, all figures are in millions of dollars.) Of this amount, $454/2,723 = 16.67% was long-term debt. This percentage reflects capital structure decisions made in the past by the management of U.S.

---

[1]The terms *owners' equity, shareholders' equity,* and *stockholders' equity* are used interchangeably to refer to the equity in a corporation. The term *net worth* is also used. Variations exist in addition to these.

U.S. CORPORATION 2011 and 2012 Balance Sheets ($ in millions)					
Assets			**Liabilities and Owners' Equity**		
	2011	**2012**		**2011**	**2012**
Current assets			Current liabilities		
Cash	$ 104	$ 160	Accounts payable	$ 232	$ 266
Accounts receivable	455	688	Notes payable	196	123
Inventory	553	555	Total	$ 428	$ 389
Total	$1,112	$1,403			
Fixed assets					
Net plant and equipment	$1,644	$1,709	Long-term debt	$ 408	$ 454
			Owners' equity		
			Common stock and paid-in surplus	600	640
			Retained earnings	1,320	1,629
			Total	$1,920	$2,269
Total assets	$2,756	$3,112	Total liabilities and owners' equity	$2,756	$3,112

TABLE 2.1

Balance Sheets

There are three particularly important things to keep in mind when examining a balance sheet: liquidity, debt versus equity, and market value versus book value.

LIQUIDITY

Liquidity refers to the speed and ease with which an asset can be converted to cash. Gold is a relatively liquid asset; a custom manufacturing facility is not. Liquidity actually has two dimensions: ease of conversion versus loss of value. Any asset can be converted to cash quickly if we cut the price enough. A highly liquid asset is therefore one that can be quickly sold without significant loss of value. An illiquid asset is one that cannot be quickly converted to cash without a substantial price reduction.

Assets are normally listed on the balance sheet in order of decreasing liquidity, meaning that the most liquid assets are listed first. Current assets are relatively liquid and include cash and assets we expect to convert to cash over the next 12 months. Accounts receivable, for example, represent amounts not yet collected from customers on sales already made. Naturally, we hope these will convert to cash in the near future. Inventory is probably the least liquid of the current assets, at least for many businesses.

Fixed assets are, for the most part, relatively illiquid. These consist of tangible things such as buildings and equipment that don't convert to cash at all in normal business activity (they are, of course, used in the business to generate cash). Intangible assets, such as a trademark, have no physical existence but can be very valuable. Like tangible fixed assets, they won't ordinarily convert to cash and are generally considered illiquid.

Liquidity is valuable. The more liquid a business is, the less likely it is to experience financial distress (that is, difficulty in paying debts or buying needed assets). Unfortunately, liquid assets are generally less profitable to hold. For example, cash holdings are the most liquid of all investments, but they sometimes earn no return at all—they just sit there. There is therefore a trade-off between the advantages of liquidity and forgone potential profits.

Annual and quarterly financial statements (and lots more) for most public U.S. corporations can be found in the EDGAR database at www.sec.gov.

DEBT VERSUS EQUITY

To the extent that a firm borrows money, it usually gives first claim to the firm's cash flow to creditors. Equity holders are entitled to only the residual value, the portion left after creditors are paid. The value of this residual portion is the shareholders' equity in the firm, which is just the value of the firm's assets less the value of the firm's liabilities:

$$\text{Shareholders' equity} = \text{Assets} - \text{Liabilities}$$

This is true in an accounting sense because shareholders' equity is defined as this residual portion. More important, it is true in an economic sense: If the firm sells its assets and pays its debts, whatever cash is left belongs to the shareholders.

The use of debt in a firm's capital structure is called *financial leverage.* The more debt a firm has (as a percentage of assets), the greater is its degree of financial leverage. As we discuss in later chapters, debt acts like a lever in the sense that using it can greatly magnify both gains and losses. So, financial leverage increases the potential reward to shareholders, but it also increases the potential for financial distress and business failure.

MARKET VALUE VERSUS BOOK VALUE

Generally Accepted Accounting Principles (GAAP)
The common set of standards and procedures by which audited financial statements are prepared.

The home page for the Financial Accounting Standards Board (FASB) is www.fasb.org.

The values shown on the balance sheet for the firm's assets are *book values* and generally are not what the assets are actually worth. Under **Generally Accepted Accounting Principles (GAAP)**, audited financial statements in the United States generally show assets at *historical cost.* In other words, assets are "carried on the books" at what the firm paid for them, no matter how long ago they were purchased or how much they are worth today.

For current assets, market value and book value might be somewhat similar because current assets are bought and converted into cash over a relatively short span of time. In other circumstances, the two values might differ quite a bit. Moreover, for fixed assets, it would be purely a coincidence if the actual market value of an asset (what the asset could be sold for) were equal to its book value. For example, a railroad might own enormous tracts of land purchased a century or more ago. What the railroad paid for that land could be hundreds or thousands of times less than what the land is worth today. The balance sheet would nonetheless show the historical cost.

The difference between market value and book value is important for understanding the impact of reported gains and losses. For example, to open the chapter, we discussed the huge charges against earnings taken by Bank of America. What actually happened is that these charges were the result of accounting rule changes that led to reductions in the book value of certain types of assets. However, a change in accounting rules all by itself has no effect on what the assets in question are really worth. Instead, the market value of an asset depends on things like its riskiness and cash flows, neither of which have anything to do with accounting.

The balance sheet is potentially useful to many different parties. A supplier might look at the size of accounts payable to see how promptly the firm pays its bills. A potential creditor would examine the liquidity and degree of financial leverage. Managers within the firm can track things like the amount of cash and the amount of inventory the firm keeps on hand. Uses such as these are discussed in more detail in Chapter 3.

Managers and investors will frequently be interested in knowing the value of the firm. This information is not on the balance sheet. The fact that balance sheet assets are listed at cost means that there is no necessary connection between the total assets shown and the value of the firm. Indeed, many of the most valuable assets a firm might have—good management, a good reputation, talented employees—don't appear on the balance sheet at all.

Similarly, the shareholders' equity figure on the balance sheet and the true value of the stock need not be related. For example, in early 2011, the book value of IBM's equity was about $23 billion, while the market value was $193 billion. At the same time, Google's book value was $44 billion, while the market value was $202 billion.

For financial managers, then, the accounting value of the stock is not an especially important concern; it is the market value that matters. Henceforth, whenever we speak of the value of an asset or the value of the firm, we will normally mean its *market value*. So, for example, when we say the goal of the financial manager is to increase the value of the stock, we mean the market value of the stock.

| Market Value versus Book Value | EXAMPLE 2.2 |

The Klingon Corporation has net fixed assets with a book value of $700 and an appraised market value of about $1,000. Net working capital is $400 on the books, but approximately $600 would be realized if all the current accounts were liquidated. Klingon has $500 in long-term debt, both book value and market value. What is the book value of the equity? What is the market value?

We can construct two simplified balance sheets, one in accounting (book value) terms and one in economic (market value) terms:

	KLINGON CORPORATION **Balance Sheets** **Market Value versus Book Value**				
Assets			**Liabilities and Shareholders' Equity**		
	Book	**Market**		**Book**	**Market**
Net working capital	$ 400	$ 600	Long-term debt	$ 500	$ 500
Net fixed assets	700	1,000	Shareholders' equity	600	1,100
	$1,100	$1,600		$1,100	$1,600

In this example, shareholders' equity is actually worth almost twice as much as what is shown on the books. The distinction between book and market values is important precisely because book values can be so different from true economic value.

| Concept Questions |

2.1a What is the balance sheet identity?

2.1b What is liquidity? Why is it important?

2.1c What do we mean by *financial leverage?*

2.1d Explain the difference between accounting value and market value. Which is more important to the financial manager? Why?

The Income Statement

2.2

The **income statement** measures performance over some period of time, usually a quarter or a year. The income statement equation is:

$$\text{Revenues} - \text{Expenses} = \text{Income} \qquad\qquad [2.2]$$

If you think of the balance sheet as a snapshot, then you can think of the income statement as a video recording covering the period between before and after pictures. Table 2.2 gives a simplified income statement for U.S. Corporation.

income statement
Financial statement summarizing a firm's performance over a period of time.

TABLE 2.2

Income Statement

U.S. CORPORATION 2012 Income Statement ($ in millions)		
Net sales		$1,509
Cost of goods sold		750
Depreciation		65
Earnings before interest and taxes		$ 694
Interest paid		70
Taxable income		$ 624
Taxes (34%)		212
Net income		$ 412
Dividends	$103	
Addition to retained earnings	309	

The first thing reported on an income statement would usually be revenue and expenses from the firm's principal operations. Subsequent parts include, among other things, financing expenses such as interest paid. Taxes paid are reported separately. The last item is *net income* (the so-called bottom line). Net income is often expressed on a per-share basis and called *earnings per share (EPS)*.

As indicated, U.S. paid cash dividends of $103. The difference between net income and cash dividends, $309, is the addition to retained earnings for the year. This amount is added to the cumulative retained earnings account on the balance sheet. If you look back at the two balance sheets for U.S. Corporation, you'll see that retained earnings did go up by this amount: $1,320 + 309 = $1,629.

EXAMPLE 2.3	**Calculating Earnings and Dividends per Share**

Suppose U.S. had 200 million shares outstanding at the end of 2012. Based on the income statement in Table 2.2, what was EPS? What were dividends per share?

From the income statement, we see that U.S. had a net income of $412 million for the year. Total dividends were $103 million. Because 200 million shares were outstanding, we can calculate earnings per share, or EPS, and dividends per share as follows:

$$\text{Earnings per share} = \text{Net income/Total shares outstanding}$$
$$= \$412/200 = \$2.06 \text{ per share}$$
$$\text{Dividends per share} = \text{Total dividends/Total shares outstanding}$$
$$= \$103/200 = \$.515 \text{ per share}$$

When looking at an income statement, the financial manager needs to keep three things in mind: GAAP, cash versus noncash items, and time and costs.

GAAP AND THE INCOME STATEMENT

An income statement prepared using GAAP will show revenue when it accrues. This is not necessarily when the cash comes in. The general rule (the *recognition* or *realization principle*) is to recognize revenue when the earnings process is virtually complete and the value of an exchange of goods or services is known or can be reliably determined. In practice, this principle usually means that revenue is recognized at the time of sale, which need not be the same as the time of collection.

Expenses shown on the income statement are based on the *matching principle*. The basic idea here is to first determine revenues as described previously and then match those revenues with the costs associated with producing them. So, if we manufacture a product and then sell it on credit, the revenue is realized at the time of sale. The production and other costs associated with the sale of that product will likewise be recognized at that time. Once again, the actual cash outflows may have occurred at some different time.

As a result of the way revenues and expenses are realized, the figures shown on the income statement may not be at all representative of the actual cash inflows and outflows that occurred during a particular period.

NONCASH ITEMS

A primary reason that accounting income differs from cash flow is that an income statement contains **noncash items**. The most important of these is *depreciation*. Suppose a firm purchases an asset for $5,000 and pays in cash. Obviously, the firm has a $5,000 cash outflow at the time of purchase. However, instead of deducting the $5,000 as an expense, an accountant might depreciate the asset over a five-year period.

If the depreciation is straight-line and the asset is written down to zero over that period, then $5,000/5 = $1,000 will be deducted each year as an expense.[2] The important thing to recognize is that this $1,000 deduction isn't cash—it's an accounting number. The actual cash outflow occurred when the asset was purchased.

The depreciation deduction is simply another application of the matching principle in accounting. The revenues associated with an asset would generally occur over some length of time. So, the accountant seeks to match the expense of purchasing the asset with the benefits produced from owning it.

As we will see, for the financial manager, the actual timing of cash inflows and outflows is critical in coming up with a reasonable estimate of market value, so we need to learn how to separate the cash flows from the noncash accounting entries. In reality, the difference between cash flow and accounting income can be pretty dramatic. For example, consider the case of automaker Chrysler. For the third quarter of 2010, Chrysler reported a net loss of $84 million. Sounds bad, but Chrysler also reported *positive* cash flow of $419 million, a difference of about $503 million!

noncash items
Expenses charged against revenues that do not directly affect cash flow, such as depreciation.

TIME AND COSTS

It is often useful to think of the future as having two distinct parts: the short run and the long run. These are not precise time periods. The distinction has to do with whether costs are fixed or variable. In the long run, all business costs are variable. Given sufficient time, assets can be sold, debts can be paid, and so on.

If our time horizon is relatively short, however, some costs are effectively fixed—they must be paid no matter what (property taxes, for example). Other costs such as wages to laborers and payments to suppliers are still variable. As a result, even in the short run, the firm can vary its output level by varying expenditures in these areas.

The distinction between fixed and variable costs is important, at times, to the financial manager, but the way costs are reported on the income statement is not a good guide to which costs are which. The reason is that, in practice, accountants tend to classify costs as either product costs or period costs.

---

[2]By *straight-line,* we mean that the depreciation deduction is the same every year. By *written down to zero,* we mean that the asset is assumed to have no value at the end of five years. Depreciation is discussed in more detail in Chapter 10.

WORK THE WEB

The U.S. Securities and Exchange Commission (SEC) requires that most public companies file regular reports, including annual and quarterly financial statements. The SEC has a public site named EDGAR that makes these free reports available at www.sec.gov. We went to "Search for Company Filings" and looked up Hewlett-Packard:

The two reports we look at the most are the 10-K, which is the annual report filed with the SEC, and the 10-Q. The 10-K includes the list of officers and their salaries, financial statements for the previous fiscal year, and an explanation by the company of the financial results. The 10-Q is a smaller report that includes the financial statements for the quarter.

Questions

1. *As you can imagine, electronic filing of documents with the SEC has not been around for very long. Go to www.sec.gov and find the filings for General Electric. What is the date of the oldest 10-K available on the website for General Electric? Look up the 10-K forms for IBM and Apple to see if the year of the first electronic filing is the same for these companies.*

2. *Go to www.sec.gov and find out when the following forms are used: Form DEF 14A, Form 8-K, and Form 6-K.*

Product costs include such things as raw materials, direct labor expense, and manufacturing overhead. These are reported on the income statement as costs of goods sold, but they include both fixed and variable costs. Similarly, *period costs* are incurred during a particular time period and might be reported as selling, general, and administrative expenses. Once again, some of these period costs may be fixed and others may be variable. The company president's salary, for example, is a period cost and is probably fixed, at least in the short run.

The balance sheets and income statement we have been using thus far are hypothetical. Our nearby *Work the Web* box shows how to find actual balance sheets and income statements online for almost any company. Also, with the increasing globalization of business, there is a clear need for accounting standards to become more comparable across countries. Accordingly, in recent years, U.S. accounting standards have become more closely tied to International Financial Reporting Standards (IFRS). In particular, the Financial Accounting Standards Board (FASB), which is in charge of U.S. GAAP policies, and the International Accounting Standards Board, which is in charge of IFRS polices, have been working toward a convergence of policies by June 2011. A decision about full adoption of IFRS by U.S.-based companies is expected to follow afterward.

For more information about IFRS, check out the website www.ifrs.org.

Concept Questions

2.2a What is the income statement equation?

2.2b What are the three things to keep in mind when looking at an income statement?

2.2c Why is accounting income not the same as cash flow? Give two reasons.

Taxes ~~Skip this~~   **2.3** z

Taxes can be one of the largest cash outflows a firm experiences. For example, for the fiscal year 2010, ExxonMobil's earnings before taxes were about $52.96 billion. Its tax bill, including all taxes paid worldwide, was a whopping $21.56 billion, or about 41 percent of its pretax earnings. Also for fiscal year 2010, Walmart had a taxable income of $23.54 billion, and the company paid $7.58 billion in taxes, an average tax rate of 32 percent.

The size of a company's tax bill is determined by the tax code, an often amended set of rules. In this section, we examine corporate tax rates and how taxes are calculated. If the various rules of taxation seem a little bizarre or convoluted to you, keep in mind that the tax code is the result of political, not economic, forces. As a result, there is no reason why it has to make economic sense.

Taxable Income	Tax Rate
$ 0– 50,000	15%
50,001– 75,000	25
75,001– 100,000	34
100,001– 335,000	39
335,001–10,000,000	34
10,000,001–15,000,000	35
15,000,001–18,333,333	38
18,333,334+	35

CORPORATE TAX RATES

Corporate tax rates in effect for 2012 are shown in Table 2.3. A peculiar feature of taxation instituted by the Tax Reform Act of 1986 and expanded in the 1993 Omnibus Budget Reconciliation Act is that corporate tax rates are not strictly increasing. As shown, corporate tax rates rise from 15 percent to 39 percent, but they drop back to 34 percent on income over $335,000. They then rise to 38 percent and subsequently fall to 35 percent.

According to the originators of the current tax rules, there are only four corporate rates: 15 percent, 25 percent, 34 percent, and 35 percent. The 38 and 39 percent brackets arise because of "surcharges" applied on top of the 34 and 35 percent rates. A tax is a tax is a tax, however, so there are really six corporate tax brackets, as we have shown.

AVERAGE VERSUS MARGINAL TAX RATES

average tax rate
Total taxes paid divided by total taxable income.

marginal tax rate
Amount of tax payable on the next dollar earned.

In making financial decisions, it is frequently important to distinguish between average and marginal tax rates. Your **average tax rate** is your tax bill divided by your taxable income—in other words, the percentage of your income that goes to pay taxes. Your **marginal tax rate** is the rate of the extra tax you would pay if you earned one more dollar. The percentage tax rates shown in Table 2.3 are all marginal rates. Put another way, the tax rates in Table 2.3 apply to the part of income in the indicated range only, not all income.

The difference between average and marginal tax rates can best be illustrated with a simple example. Suppose our corporation has a taxable income of $200,000. What is the tax bill? Using Table 2.3, we can figure our tax bill:

```
.15($  50,000)           = $  7,500
.25($  75,000 − 50,000)  =    6,250
.34($100,000 − 75,000)   =    8,500
.39($200,000 − 100,000)  =   39,000
                            $61,250
```

The IRS has a great website! (www.irs.gov)

Our total tax is thus $61,250.

In our example, what is the average tax rate? We had a taxable income of $200,000 and a tax bill of $61,250, so the average tax rate is $61,250/200,000 = 30.625%. What is the marginal tax rate? If we made one more dollar, the tax on that dollar would be 39 cents, so our marginal rate is 39 percent.

| **Deep in the Heart of Taxes** | **EXAMPLE 2.4** |

Algernon, Inc., has a taxable income of $85,000. What is its tax bill? What is its average tax rate? Its marginal tax rate?

From Table 2.3, we see that the tax rate applied to the first $50,000 is 15 percent; the rate applied to the next $25,000 is 25 percent; and the rate applied after that up to $100,000 is 34 percent. So Algernon must pay .15 × $50,000 + .25 × 25,000 + .34 × (85,000 − 75,000) = $17,150. The average tax rate is thus $17,150/85,000 = 20.18%. The marginal rate is 34 percent because Algernon's taxes would rise by 34 cents if it had another dollar in taxable income.

Table 2.4 summarizes some different taxable incomes, marginal tax rates, and average tax rates for corporations. Notice how the average and marginal tax rates come together at 35 percent.

With a *flat-rate* tax, there is only one tax rate, so the rate is the same for all income levels. With such a tax, the marginal tax rate is always the same as the average tax rate. As it stands now, corporate taxation in the United States is based on a modified flat-rate tax, which becomes a true flat rate for the highest incomes.

In looking at Table 2.4, notice that the more a corporation makes, the greater is the percentage of taxable income paid in taxes. Put another way, under current tax law, the average tax rate never goes down, even though the marginal tax rate does. As illustrated, for corporations, average tax rates begin at 15 percent and rise to a maximum of 35 percent.

Normally the marginal tax rate is relevant for financial decision making. The reason is that any new cash flows will be taxed at that marginal rate. Because financial decisions usually involve new cash flows or changes in existing ones, this rate will tell us the marginal effect of a decision on our tax bill.

There is one last thing to notice about the tax code as it affects corporations. It's easy to verify that the corporate tax bill is just a flat 35 percent of taxable income if our taxable income is more than $18.33 million. Also, for the many midsize corporations with taxable incomes in the range of $335,000 to $10,000,000, the tax rate is a flat 34 percent. Because we will normally be talking about large corporations, you can assume that the average and marginal tax rates are 35 percent unless we explicitly say otherwise.

We should note that we have simplified the U.S. tax code in our discussions. In reality, the tax code is much more complex and is riddled with various tax deductions and loopholes allowed for certain industries. As a result, the average corporate tax rate can be far from 35 percent for many companies. Table 2.5 displays average tax rates for various industries.

As you can see, the average tax rate ranges from 33.8 percent for electric utilities to 4.5 percent for biotechnology firms.

(1) Taxable Income	(2) Marginal Tax Rate	(3) Total Tax	(3)/(1) Average Tax Rate
$ 45,000	15%	$ 6,750	15.00%
70,000	25	12,500	17.86
95,000	34	20,550	21.63
250,000	39	80,750	32.30
1,000,000	34	340,000	34.00
17,500,000	38	6,100,000	34.86
50,000,000	35	17,500,000	35.00
100,000,000	35	35,000,000	35.00

TABLE 2.4

Corporate Taxes and Tax Rates

TABLE 2.5

Average Tax Rates

Industry	Number of Companies	Average Tax Rate
Electric utilities (Eastern U.S.)	24	33.8%
Trucking	33	32.7
Railroad	15	27.4
Securities brokerage	30	20.5
Banking	481	17.5
Medical supplies	264	11.2
Internet	239	5.9
Pharmaceutical	337	5.6
Biotechnology	121	4.5

Before moving on, we should note that the tax rates we have discussed in this section relate to federal taxes only. Overall tax rates can be higher if state, local, and any other taxes are considered.

Concept Questions

2.3a What is the difference between a marginal and an average tax rate?

2.3b Do the wealthiest corporations receive a tax break in terms of a lower tax rate? Explain.

2.4 Cash Flow

At this point, we are ready to discuss perhaps one of the most important pieces of financial information that can be gleaned from financial statements: cash flow. By *cash flow,* we simply mean the difference between the number of dollars that came in and the number that went out. For example, if you were the owner of a business, you might be very interested in how much cash you actually took out of your business in a given year. How to determine this amount is one of the things we discuss next.

No standard financial statement presents this information in the way that we wish. We will therefore discuss how to calculate cash flow for U.S. Corporation and point out how the result differs from that of standard financial statement calculations. There is a standard financial accounting statement called the *statement of cash flows,* but it is concerned with a somewhat different issue that should not be confused with what is discussed in this section. The accounting statement of cash flows is discussed in Chapter 3.

From the balance sheet identity, we know that the value of a firm's assets is equal to the value of its liabilities plus the value of its equity. Similarly, the cash flow from the firm's assets must equal the sum of the cash flow to creditors and the cash flow to stockholders (or owners):

cash flow from assets
The total of cash flow to creditors and cash flow to stockholders, consisting of the following: operating cash flow, capital spending, and change in net working capital.

operating cash flow
Cash generated from a firm's normal business activities.

Cash flow from assets = Cash flow to creditors + Cash flow to stockholders   **[2.3]**

This is the *cash flow identity*. It says that the cash flow from the firm's assets is equal to the cash flow paid to suppliers of capital to the firm. What it reflects is the fact that a firm generates cash through its various activities, and that cash is either used to pay creditors or paid out to the owners of the firm. We discuss the various things that make up these cash flows next.

CASH FLOW FROM ASSETS

Cash flow from assets involves three components: operating cash flow, capital spending, and change in net working capital. **Operating cash flow** refers to the cash flow that results from the firm's day-to-day activities of producing and selling. Expenses associated with the firm's financing of its assets are not included because they are not operating expenses.

As we discussed in Chapter 1, some portion of the firm's cash flow is reinvested in the firm. *Capital spending* refers to the net spending on fixed assets (purchases of fixed assets less sales of fixed assets). Finally, *change in net working capital* is measured as the net change in current assets relative to current liabilities for the period being examined and represents the amount spent on net working capital. The three components of cash flow are examined in more detail next.

Operating Cash Flow   To calculate operating cash flow (OCF), we want to calculate revenues minus costs, but we don't want to include depreciation because it's not a cash outflow, and we don't want to include interest because it's a financing expense. We do want to include taxes because taxes are (unfortunately) paid in cash.

If we look at U.S. Corporation's income statement (Table 2.2), we see that earnings before interest and taxes (EBIT) are $694. This is almost what we want because it doesn't include interest paid. We need to make two adjustments. First, recall that depreciation is a noncash expense. To get cash flow, we first add back the $65 in depreciation because it wasn't a cash deduction. The other adjustment is to subtract the $212 in taxes because these were paid in cash. The result is operating cash flow:

U.S. CORPORATION 2012 Operating Cash Flow	
Earnings before interest and taxes	$694
+ Depreciation	65
− Taxes	212
Operating cash flow	$547

U.S. Corporation thus had a 2012 operating cash flow of $547.

Operating cash flow is an important number because it tells us, on a very basic level, whether a firm's cash inflows from its business operations are sufficient to cover its everyday cash outflows. For this reason, a negative operating cash flow is often a sign of trouble.

There is an unpleasant possibility of confusion when we speak of operating cash flow. In accounting practice, operating cash flow is often defined as net income plus depreciation. For U.S. Corporation, this would amount to $412 + 65 = $477.

The accounting definition of operating cash flow differs from ours in one important way: Interest is deducted when net income is computed. Notice that the difference between the $547 operating cash flow we calculated and this $477 is $70, the amount of interest paid for the year. This definition of cash flow thus considers interest paid to be an operating expense. Our definition treats it properly as a financing expense. If there were no interest expense, the two definitions would be the same.

To finish our calculation of cash flow from assets for U.S. Corporation, we need to consider how much of the $547 operating cash flow was reinvested in the firm. We consider spending on fixed assets first.

Capital Spending   Net capital spending is just money spent on fixed assets less money received from the sale of fixed assets. At the end of 2011, net fixed assets for U.S. Corporation (Table 2.1) were $1,644. During the year, U.S. wrote off (depreciated) $65 worth of fixed assets on the income statement. So, if the firm didn't purchase any new fixed assets, net fixed assets would have been $1,644 − 65 = $1,579 at year's end. The 2012 balance sheet shows $1,709 in net fixed assets, so U.S. must have spent a total of $1,709 − 1,579 = $130 on fixed assets during the year:

Ending net fixed assets	$1,709
− Beginning net fixed assets	1,644
+ Depreciation	65
Net capital spending	$ 130

This $130 is the net capital spending for 2012.

Could net capital spending be negative? The answer is yes. This would happen if the firm sold off more assets than it purchased. The *net* here refers to purchases of fixed assets net of any sales of fixed assets. You will often see capital spending called CAPEX, which is an acronym for capital expenditures. It usually means the same thing.

Change in Net Working Capital   In addition to investing in fixed assets, a firm will also invest in current assets. For example, going back to the balance sheets in Table 2.1, we see that, at the end of 2012, U.S. had current assets of $1,403. At the end of 2011, current assets were $1,112; so, during the year, U.S. invested $1,403 − 1,112 = $291 in current assets.

As the firm changes its investment in current assets, its current liabilities will usually change as well. To determine the change in net working capital, the easiest approach is just to take the difference between the beginning and ending net working capital (NWC) figures. Net working capital at the end of 2012 was $1,403 − 389 = $1,014. Similarly, at the end of 2011, net working capital was $1,112 − 428 = $684. Given these figures, we have the following:

Ending NWC	$1,014
− Beginning NWC	684
Change in NWC	$ 330

Net working capital thus increased by $330. Put another way, U.S. Corporation had a net investment of $330 in NWC for the year. This change in NWC is often referred to as the "addition to" NWC.

Conclusion   Given the figures we've come up with, we're ready to calculate cash flow from assets. The total cash flow from assets is given by operating cash flow less the amounts invested in fixed assets and net working capital. So, for U.S., we have:

U.S. CORPORATION 2012 Cash Flow from Assets	
Operating cash flow	$547
− Net capital spending	130
− Change in NWC	330
Cash flow from assets	$ 87

From the cash flow identity given earlier, we know that this $87 cash flow from assets equals the sum of the firm's cash flow to creditors and its cash flow to stockholders. We consider these next.

It wouldn't be at all unusual for a growing corporation to have a negative cash flow. As we see next, a negative cash flow means that the firm raised more money by borrowing and selling stock than it paid out to creditors and stockholders during the year.

A Note about "Free" Cash Flow   Cash flow from assets sometimes goes by a different name, **free cash flow**. Of course, there is no such thing as "free" cash (we wish!). Instead the name refers to cash that the firm is free to distribute to creditors and stockholders because it is not needed for working capital or fixed asset investments. We will stick with "cash flow from assets" as our label for this important concept because, in practice, there is some variation in exactly how free cash flow is computed; different users calculate it in different ways. Nonetheless, whenever you hear the phrase "free cash flow," you should understand that what is being discussed is cash flow from assets or something quite similar.

free cash flow
Another name for cash flow from assets.

CASH FLOW TO CREDITORS AND STOCKHOLDERS

The cash flows to creditors and stockholders represent the net payments to creditors and owners during the year. Their calculation is similar to that of cash flow from assets. **Cash flow to creditors** is interest paid less net new borrowing; **cash flow to stockholders** is dividends paid less net new equity raised.

cash flow to creditors
A firm's interest payments to creditors less net new borrowing.

cash flow to stockholders
Dividends paid out by a firm less net new equity raised.

Cash Flow to Creditors   Looking at the income statement in Table 2.2, we see that U.S. paid $70 in interest to creditors. From the balance sheets in Table 2.1, we see that long-term debt rose by $454 − 408 = $46. So U.S. Corporation paid out $70 in interest, but it borrowed an additional $46. Thus, net cash flow to creditors is:

U.S. CORPORATION 2012 Cash Flow to Creditors	
Interest paid	$70
− Net new borrowing	46
Cash flow to creditors	$24

Cash flow to creditors is sometimes called *cash flow to bondholders;* we will use these terms interchangeably.

Cash Flow to Stockholders   From the income statement, we see that dividends paid to stockholders amounted to $103. To get net new equity raised, we need to look at the common stock and paid-in surplus account. This account tells us how much stock the company has sold. During the year, this account rose by $40, so $40 in net new equity was raised. Given this, we have the following:

U.S. CORPORATION 2012 Cash Flow to Stockholders	
Dividends paid	$103
− Net new equity raised	40
Cash flow to stockholders	$ 63

The cash flow to stockholders for 2012 was thus $63.

The last thing we need to do is to verify that the cash flow identity holds to be sure we didn't make any mistakes. From the previous section, we know that cash flow from assets is $87. Cash flow to creditors and stockholders is $24 + 63 = $87, so everything checks out. Table 2.6 contains a summary of the various cash flow calculations for future reference.

TABLE 2.6

Cash Flow Summary

I. The cash flow identity
Cash flow from assets = Cash flow to creditors (bondholders) + Cash flow to stockholders (owners)

II. Cash flow from assets
Cash flow from assets = Operating cash flow − Net capital spending − Change in net working capital (NWC) where: Operating cash flow = Earnings before interest and taxes (EBIT) + Depreciation − Taxes Net capital spending = Ending net fixed assets − Beginning net fixed assets + Depreciation Change in NWC = Ending NWC − Beginning NWC

III. Cash flow to creditors (bondholders)
Cash flow to creditors = Interest paid − Net new borrowing

IV. Cash flow to stockholders (owners)
Cash flow to stockholders = Dividends paid − Net new equity raised

As our discussion indicates, it is essential that a firm keep an eye on its cash flow. The following serves as an excellent reminder of why doing so is a good idea, unless the firm's owners wish to end up in the "Po'" house:

QUOTH THE BANKER, "WATCH CASH FLOW"

Once upon a midnight dreary as I pondered weak and weary
Over many a quaint and curious volume of accounting lore,
Seeking gimmicks (without scruple) to squeeze through
   some new tax loophole,
Suddenly I heard a knock upon my door, Only this, and nothing more.

Then I felt a queasy tingling and I heard the cash a-jingling
As a fearsome banker entered whom I'd often seen before.
His face was money-green and in his eyes there could be seen
Dollar-signs that seemed to glitter as he reckoned up the score.
   "Cash flow," the banker said, and nothing more.

I had always thought it fine to show a jet black bottom line.
But the banker sounded a resounding, "No.
Your receivables are high, mounting upward toward the sky;
Write-offs loom. What matters is cash flow."
   He repeated, "Watch cash flow."

Then I tried to tell the story of our lovely inventory
Which, though large, is full of most delightful stuff.
But the banker saw its growth, and with a mighty oath
He waved his arms and shouted, "Stop! Enough!
   Pay the interest, and don't give me any guff!"

Next I looked for noncash items which could add ad infinitum
To replace the ever-outward flow of cash,
But to keep my statement black I'd held depreciation back,
And my banker said that I'd done something rash.
   He quivered, and his teeth began to gnash.

When I asked him for a loan, he responded, with a groan,
That the interest rate would be just prime plus eight,
And to guarantee my purity he'd insist on some security—

All my assets plus the scalp upon my pate.
  Only this, a standard rate.

Though my bottom line is black, I am flat upon my back,
My cash flows out and customers pay slow.
The growth of my receivables is almost unbelievable:
The result is certain—unremitting woe!
And I hear the banker utter an ominous low mutter,
  "Watch cash flow."

Herbert S. Bailey Jr.

Source: Reprinted from the January 13, 1975, issue of *Publishers Weekly,* published by R. R. Bowker, a Xerox company. Copyright © 1975 by the Xerox Corporation.

To which we can only add, "Amen."

AN EXAMPLE: CASH FLOWS FOR DOLE COLA

This extended example covers the various cash flow calculations discussed in the chapter. It also illustrates a few variations that may arise.

Operating Cash Flow   During the year, Dole Cola, Inc., had sales and cost of goods sold of $600 and $300, respectively. Depreciation was $150 and interest paid was $30. Taxes were calculated at a straight 34 percent. Dividends were $30. (All figures are in millions of dollars.) What was operating cash flow for Dole? Why is this different from net income?

The easiest thing to do here is to create an income statement. We can then pick up the numbers we need. Dole Cola's income statement is given here:

DOLE COLA 2012 Income Statement	
Net sales	$600
Cost of goods sold	300
Depreciation	150
Earnings before interest and taxes	$150
Interest paid	30
Taxable income	$120
Taxes	41
Net income	$ 79
Dividends	$30
Addition to retained earnings	49

Net income for Dole was thus $79. We now have all the numbers we need. Referring back to the U.S. Corporation example and Table 2.5, we have this:

DOLE COLA 2012 Operating Cash Flow	
Earnings before interest and taxes	$150
+ Depreciation	150
− Taxes	41
Operating cash flow	$259

As this example illustrates, operating cash flow is not the same as net income because depreciation and interest are subtracted out when net income is calculated. If you recall our earlier discussion, we don't subtract these out in computing operating cash flow because depreciation is not a cash expense and interest paid is a financing expense, not an operating expense.

Net Capital Spending   Suppose beginning net fixed assets were $500 and ending net fixed assets were $750. What was the net capital spending for the year?

From the income statement for Dole, we know that depreciation for the year was $150. Net fixed assets rose by $250. Dole thus spent $250 along with an additional $150, for a total of $400.

Change in NWC and Cash Flow from Assets   Suppose Dole Cola started the year with $2,130 in current assets and $1,620 in current liabilities, and the corresponding ending figures were $2,260 and $1,710. What was the change in NWC during the year? What was cash flow from assets? How does this compare to net income?

Net working capital started out as $2,130 − 1,620 = $510 and ended up at $2,260 − 1,710 = $550. The addition to NWC was thus $550 − 510 = $40. Putting together all the information for Dole, we have the following:

DOLE COLA	
2012 Cash Flow from Assets	
Operating cash flow	$259
− Net capital spending	400
− Change in NWC	40
Cash flow from assets	−$181

Dole had a cash flow from assets of −$181. Net income was positive at $79. Is the fact that cash flow from assets was negative a cause for alarm? Not necessarily. The cash flow here is negative primarily because of a large investment in fixed assets. If these are good investments, the resulting negative cash flow is not a worry.

Cash Flow to Stockholders and Creditors   We saw that Dole Cola had cash flow from assets of −$181. The fact that this is negative means that Dole raised more money in the form of new debt and equity than it paid out for the year. For example, suppose we know that Dole didn't sell any new equity for the year. What was cash flow to stockholders? To creditors?

Because it didn't raise any new equity, Dole's cash flow to stockholders is just equal to the cash dividend paid:

DOLE COLA	
2012 Cash Flow to Stockholders	
Dividends paid	$30
− Net new equity raised	0
Cash flow to stockholders	$30

Now, from the cash flow identity, we know that the total cash paid to creditors and stockholders was −$181. Cash flow to stockholders is $30, so cash flow to creditors must be equal to −$181 − 30 = −$211:

Cash flow to creditors + Cash flow to stockholders = −$181
Cash flow to creditors + $30   = −$181
Cash flow to creditors   = −$211

Because we know that cash flow to creditors is −$211 and interest paid is $30 (from the income statement), we can now determine net new borrowing. Dole must have borrowed $241 during the year to help finance the fixed asset expansion:

DOLE COLA	
2012 Cash Flow to Creditors	
Interest paid	$ 30
− Net new borrowing	− 241
Cash flow to creditors	−$211

Concept Questions

2.4a What is the cash flow identity? Explain what it says.

2.4b What are the components of operating cash flow?

2.4c Why is interest paid not a component of operating cash flow?

Summary and Conclusions   2.5

This chapter has introduced some of the basics of financial statements, taxes, and cash flow:

1. The book values on an accounting balance sheet can be very different from market values. The goal of financial management is to maximize the market value of the stock, not its book value.

2. Net income as it is computed on the income statement is not cash flow. A primary reason is that depreciation, a noncash expense, is deducted when net income is computed.

3. Marginal and average tax rates can be different, and it is the marginal tax rate that is relevant for most financial decisions.

4. The marginal tax rate paid by the corporations with the largest incomes is 35 percent.

5. There is a cash flow identity much like the balance sheet identity. It says that cash flow from assets equals cash flow to creditors and stockholders.

The calculation of cash flow from financial statements isn't difficult. Care must be taken in handling noncash expenses, such as depreciation, and not to confuse operating costs with financing costs. Most of all, it is important not to confuse book values with market values, or accounting income with cash flow.

Visit us at www.mhhe.com/rwj

CONNECT TO FINANCE

If you are using *Connect™ Finance* in your course, get online to take a Practice Test, check out study tools, and find out where you need additional practice.

☐	▼ Chapter 2 Financial Statements, Taxes, and Cash Flow			NPPT 4–12
☐	2.1 The Balance Sheet	eBook	Study	Practice
☐	2.2 The Income Statement	eBook	Study	Practice
☐	2.3 Taxes	eBook	Study	Practice
☐	2.4 Cash Flow	eBook	Study	Practice

Can you answer the following questions?

Section 2.1   What types of accounts are the most liquid? (LO 2-1)

Section 2.2   What is an example of a noncash expense? (LO 2-2)

Section 2.3   The marginal tax rate is the tax rate which _____. (LO 2-3)

Section 2.4   Interest expense is treated as what type of cash flow? (LO 2-4)

Log on to find out!

Visit us at www.mhhe.com/rwj

CHAPTER REVIEW AND SELF-TEST PROBLEM

2.1   **Cash Flow for Mara Corporation**   This problem will give you some practice
working with financial statements and figuring cash flow. Based on the following information for Mara Corporation, prepare an income statement for 2012 and
balance sheets for 2011 and 2012. Next, following our U.S. Corporation examples
in the chapter, calculate cash flow from assets, cash flow to creditors, and cash flow
to stockholders for Mara for 2012. Use a 35 percent tax rate throughout. You can
check your answers against ours, found in the following section.

	2011	2012
Sales	$4,203	$4,507
Cost of goods sold	2,422	2,633
Depreciation	785	952
Interest	180	196
Dividends	225	250
Current assets	2,205	2,429
Net fixed assets	7,344	7,650
Current liabilities	1,003	1,255
Long-term debt	3,106	2,085

ANSWER TO CHAPTER REVIEW AND SELF-TEST PROBLEM

2.1   In preparing the balance sheets, remember that shareholders' equity is the residual.
With this in mind, Mara's balance sheets are as follows:

MARA CORPORATION 2011 and 2012 Balance Sheets					
	2011	**2012**		**2011**	**2012**
Current assets	$2,205	$ 2,429	Current liabilities	$1,003	$ 1,255
Net fixed assets	7,344	7,650	Long-term debt	3,106	2,085
			Equity	5,440	6,739
Total assets	$9,549	$10,079	Total liabilities and shareholders' equity	$9,549	$10,079

The income statement is straightforward:

MARA CORPORATION 2012 Income Statement		
Sales		$4,507
Cost of goods sold		2,633
Depreciation		952
Earnings before interest and taxes		$ 922
Interest paid		196
Taxable income		$ 726
Taxes (35%)		254
Net income		$ 472
Dividends	$250	
Addition to retained earnings	222	

Notice that we've used an average 35 percent tax rate. Also notice that the addition to retained earnings is just net income less cash dividends.

We can now pick up the figures we need to get operating cash flow:

MARA CORPORATION 2012 Operating Cash Flow	
Earnings before interest and taxes	$ 922
+ Depreciation	952
− Taxes	254
Operating cash flow	$1,620

Next, we get the net capital spending for the year by looking at the change in fixed assets, remembering to account for depreciation:

Ending net fixed assets	$7,650
− Beginning net fixed assets	7,344
+ Depreciation	952
Net capital spending	$1,258

After calculating beginning and ending NWC, we take the difference to get the change in NWC:

Ending NWC	$1,174
− Beginning NWC	1,202
Change in NWC	−$ 28

We now combine operating cash flow, net capital spending, and the change in net working capital to get the total cash flow from assets:

MARA CORPORATION 2012 Cash Flow from Assets	
Operating cash flow	$1,620
− Net capital spending	1,258
− Change in NWC	−28
Cash flow from assets	$ 390

To get cash flow to creditors, notice that long-term borrowing decreased by $1,021 during the year and that interest paid was $196:

MARA CORPORATION 2012 Cash Flow to Creditors	
Interest paid	$ 196
− Net new borrowing	−1,021
Cash flow to creditors	$ 1,217

Finally, dividends paid were $250. To get net new equity raised, we have to do some extra calculating. Total equity was up by $6,739 − 5,440 = $1,299. Of this increase, $222 was from additions to retained earnings, so $1,077 in new equity was raised during the year. Cash flow to stockholders was thus:

MARA CORPORATION 2012 Cash Flow to Stockholders	
Dividends paid	$ 250
− Net new equity raised	1,077
Cash flow to stockholders	−$ 827

As a check, notice that cash flow from assets ($390) equals cash flow to creditors plus cash flow to stockholders ($1,217 − 827 = $390).

CONCEPTS REVIEW AND CRITICAL THINKING QUESTIONS

1. **Liquidity [LO1]** What does liquidity measure? Explain the trade-off a firm faces between high liquidity and low liquidity levels.

2. **Accounting and Cash Flows [LO2]** Why might the revenue and cost figures shown on a standard income statement not be representative of the actual cash inflows and outflows that occurred during a period?

3. **Book Values versus Market Values [LO1]** In preparing a balance sheet, why do you think standard accounting practice focuses on historical cost rather than market value?

4. **Operating Cash Flow [LO4]** In comparing accounting net income and operating cash flow, name two items you typically find in net income that are not in operating cash flow. Explain what each is and why it is excluded in operating cash flow.

5. **Book Values versus Market Values [LO1]** Under standard accounting rules, it is possible for a company's liabilities to exceed its assets. When this occurs, the owners' equity is negative. Can this happen with market values? Why or why not?

6. **Cash Flow from Assets [LO4]** Suppose a company's cash flow from assets is negative for a particular period. Is this necessarily a good sign or a bad sign?

7. **Operating Cash Flow [LO4]** Suppose a company's operating cash flow has been negative for several years running. Is this necessarily a good sign or a bad sign?

8. **Net Working Capital and Capital Spending [LO4]** Could a company's change in NWC be negative in a given year? (*Hint:* Yes.) Explain how this might come about. What about net capital spending?

9. **Cash Flow to Stockholders and Creditors [LO4]** Could a company's cash flow to stockholders be negative in a given year? (*Hint:* Yes.) Explain how this might come about. What about cash flow to creditors?

10. **Firm Values [LO1]** Referring back to the Bank of America example used at the beginning of the chapter, note that we suggested that Bank of America's stockholders probably didn't suffer as a result of the reported loss. What do you think was the basis for our conclusion?

11. **Enterprise Value [LO1]** A firm's *enterprise value* is equal to the market value of its debt and equity, less the firm's holdings of cash and cash equivalents. This figure is particularly relevant to potential purchasers of the firm. Why?

12. **Earnings Management [LO2]** Companies often try to keep accounting earnings growing at a relatively steady pace, thereby avoiding large swings in earnings from period to period. They also try to meet earnings targets. To do so, they use a variety of tactics. The simplest way is to control the timing of accounting revenues and costs, which all firms can do to at least some extent. For example, if earnings are looking too low this quarter, then some accounting costs can be deferred until next quarter. This practice is called *earnings management*. It is common, and it raises a lot of questions. Why do firms do it? Why are firms even allowed to do it under GAAP? Is it ethical? What are the implications for cash flow and shareholder wealth?

QUESTIONS AND PROBLEMS

1. **Building a Balance Sheet [LO1]** Penguin Pucks, Inc., has current assets of $4,800, net fixed assets of $27,500, current liabilities of $4,200, and long-term debt of $10,500. What is the value of the shareholders' equity account for this firm? How much is net working capital?

    BASIC
    (Questions 1–13)

2. **Building an Income Statement [LO1]** Billy's Exterminators, Inc., has sales of $734,000, costs of $315,000, depreciation expense of $48,000, interest expense of $35,000, and a tax rate of 35 percent. What is the net income for this firm?

3. **Dividends and Retained Earnings [LO1]** Suppose the firm in Problem 2 paid out $85,000 in cash dividends. What is the addition to retained earnings?

4. **Per-Share Earnings and Dividends [LO1]** Suppose the firm in Problem 3 had 110,000 shares of common stock outstanding. What is the earnings per share, or EPS, figure? What is the dividends per share figure?

5. **Market Values and Book Values [LO1]** Klingon Widgets, Inc., purchased new cloaking machinery three years ago for $6 million. The machinery can be sold to the Romulans today for $5.3 million. Klingon's current balance sheet shows net fixed assets of $3.2 million, current liabilities of $900,000, and net working capital of $215,000. If all the current assets were liquidated today, the company would receive $1.25 million cash. What is the book value of Klingon's total assets today? What is the market value?

6. **Calculating Taxes [LO3]** The Anberlin Co. had $255,000 in 2011 taxable income. Using the rates from Table 2.3 in the chapter, calculate the company's 2011 income taxes.

7. **Tax Rates [LO3]** In Problem 6, what is the average tax rate? What is the marginal tax rate?

8. **Calculating OCF [LO4]** Chevelle, Inc., has sales of $39,500, costs of $18,400, depreciation expense of $1,900, and interest expense of $1,400. If the tax rate is 35 percent, what is the operating cash flow, or OCF?

9. **Calculating Net Capital Spending [LO4]** Earnhardt Driving School's 2010 balance sheet showed net fixed assets of $2.8 million, and the 2011 balance sheet showed net

Visit us at www.mhhe.com/rwj

Visit us at www.mhhe.com/rwj

fixed assets of \$3.6 million. The company's 2011 income statement showed a depreciation expense of \$345,000. What was net capital spending for 2011?

10. **Calculating Additions to NWC [LO4]** The 2010 balance sheet of Greystone, Inc., showed current assets of \$3,120 and current liabilities of \$1,570. The 2011 balance sheet showed current assets of \$3,460 and current liabilities of \$1,980. What was the company's 2011 change in net working capital, or NWC?

11. **Cash Flow to Creditors [LO4]** The 2010 balance sheet of Maria's Tennis Shop, Inc., showed long-term debt of \$2.3 million, and the 2011 balance sheet showed long-term debt of \$2.55 million. The 2011 income statement showed an interest expense of \$190,000. What was the firm's cash flow to creditors during 2011?

12. **Cash Flow to Stockholders [LO4]** The 2010 balance sheet of Maria's Tennis Shop, Inc., showed \$680,000 in the common stock account and \$4.3 million in the additional paid-in surplus account. The 2011 balance sheet showed \$715,000 and \$4.7 million in the same two accounts, respectively. If the company paid out \$540,000 in cash dividends during 2011, what was the cash flow to stockholders for the year?

13. **Calculating Total Cash Flows [LO4]** Given the information for Maria's Tennis Shop, Inc., in Problems 11 and 12, suppose you also know that the firm's net capital spending for 2011 was \$1,300,000 and that the firm reduced its net working capital investment by \$55,000. What was the firm's 2011 operating cash flow, or OCF?

INTERMEDIATE   ✗ 14. **Calculating Total Cash Flows [LO4]** Jetson Spacecraft Corp. shows the following
(Questions 14–22)   information on its 2011 income statement: sales = \$235,000; costs = \$141,000; other expenses = \$7,900; depreciation expense = \$17,300; interest expense = \$12,900; taxes = \$19,565; dividends = \$12,300. In addition, you're told that the firm issued \$6,100 in new equity during 2011 and redeemed \$4,500 in outstanding long-term debt.

 a. What is the 2011 operating cash flow?

 b. What is the 2011 cash flow to creditors?

 c. What is the 2011 cash flow to stockholders?

 d. If net fixed assets increased by \$25,000 during the year, what was the addition to NWC?

✗ 15. **Using Income Statements [LO1]** Given the following information for Calvani Pizza Co., calculate the depreciation expense: sales = \$52,000; costs = \$27,300; addition to retained earnings = \$5,300; dividends paid = \$1,800; interest expense = \$4,900; tax rate = 35 percent.

16. **Preparing a Balance Sheet [LO1]** Prepare a 2011 balance sheet for Cornell Corp. based on the following information: cash = \$127,000; patents and copyrights = \$630,000; accounts payable = \$210,000; accounts receivable = \$105,000; tangible net fixed assets = \$1,620,000; inventory = \$293,000; notes payable = \$160,000; accumulated retained earnings = \$1,278,000; long-term debt = \$845,000.

17. **Residual Claims [LO1]** Dimeback, Inc., is obligated to pay its creditors \$5,800 during the year.

 a. What is the market value of the shareholders' equity if assets have a market value of \$7,100?

 b. What if assets equal \$5,200?

18. **Marginal versus Average Tax Rates [LO3]** (Refer to Table 2.3.) Corporation Growth has \$76,000 in taxable income, and Corporation Income has \$7,600,000 in taxable income.

 a. What is the tax bill for each firm?

b. Suppose both firms have identified a new project that will increase taxable income by $10,000. How much in additional taxes will each firm pay? Why is this amount the same?

19. **Net Income and OCF [LO2]** During 2010, Raines Umbrella Corp. had sales of $850,000. Cost of goods sold, administrative and selling expenses, and depreciation expenses were $610,000, $110,000, and $140,000, respectively. In addition, the company had an interest expense of $85,000 and a tax rate of 35 percent. (Ignore any tax loss carryback or carryforward provisions.)

    a. What is Raines's net income for 2010?

    b. What is its operating cash flow?

    c. Explain your results in (a) and (b).

20. **Accounting Values versus Cash Flows [LO4]** In Problem 19, suppose Raines Umbrella Corp. paid out $63,000 in cash dividends. Is this possible? If spending on net fixed assets and net working capital was zero, and if no new stock was issued during the year, what do you know about the firm's long-term debt account?

21. **Calculating Cash Flows [LO2]** Zigs Industries had the following operating results for 2011: sales = $27,360; cost of goods sold = $19,260; depreciation expense = $4,860; interest expense = $2,190; dividends paid = $1,560. At the beginning of the year, net fixed assets were $16,380, current assets were $5,760, and current liabilities were $3,240. At the end of the year, net fixed assets were $20,160, current assets were $7,116, and current liabilities were $3,780. The tax rate for 2011 was 34 percent.

    a. What is net income for 2011?

    b. What is the operating cash flow for 2011?

    c. What is the cash flow from assets for 2011? Is this possible? Explain.

    d. If no new debt was issued during the year, what is the cash flow to creditors? What is the cash flow to stockholders? Explain and interpret the positive and negative signs of your answers in (a) through (d).

22. **Calculating Cash Flows [LO4]** Consider the following abbreviated financial statements for Parrothead Enterprises:

PARROTHEAD ENTERPRISES 2010 and 2011 Partial Balance Sheets					
Assets			**Liabilities and Owners' Equity**		
	2010	**2011**		**2010**	**2011**
Current assets	$ 914	$ 990	Current liabilities	$ 365	$ 410
Net fixed assets	3,767	4,536	Long-term debt	1,991	2,117

PARROTHEAD ENTERPRISES 2011 Income Statement	
Sales	$11,592
Costs	5,405
Depreciation	1,033
Interest paid	294

    a. What is owners' equity for 2010 and 2011?

    b. What is the change in net working capital for 2011?

    c. In 2011, Parrothead Enterprises purchased $1,890 in new fixed assets. How much in fixed assets did Parrothead Enterprises sell? What is the cash flow from assets for the year? (The tax rate is 35 percent.)

    d. During 2011, Parrothead Enterprises raised $378 in new long-term debt. How much long-term debt must Parrothead Enterprises have paid off during the year? What is the cash flow to creditors?

CHALLENGE
(Questions 23–26)

23. Net Fixed Assets and Depreciation [LO4] On the balance sheet, the net fixed assets (NFA) account is equal to the gross fixed assets (FA) account (which records the acquisition cost of fixed assets) minus the accumulated depreciation (AD) account (which records the total depreciation taken by the firm against its fixed assets). Using the fact that NFA = FA − AD, show that the expression given in the chapter for net capital spending, $NFA_{end} − NFA_{beg} + D$ (where D is the depreciation expense during the year), is equivalent to $FA_{end} − FA_{beg}$.

24. Tax Rates [LO3] Refer to the corporate marginal tax rate information in Table 2.3.

a. Why do you think the marginal tax rate jumps up from 34 percent to 39 percent at a taxable income of $100,001, and then falls back to a 34 percent marginal rate at a taxable income of $335,001?

b. Compute the average tax rate for a corporation with exactly $335,001 in taxable income. Does this confirm your explanation in part (*a*)? What is the average tax rate for a corporation with exactly $18,333,334? Is the same thing happening here?

c. The 39 percent and 38 percent tax rates both represent what is called a tax "bubble." Suppose the government wanted to lower the upper threshold of the 39 percent marginal tax bracket from $335,000 to $200,000. What would the new 39 percent bubble rate have to be?

Use the following information for Taco Swell, Inc., for Problems 25 and 26 (assume the tax rate is 34 percent):

	2010	2011
Sales	$ 11,573	$ 12,936
Depreciation	1,661	1,736
Cost of goods sold	3,979	4,707
Other expenses	946	824
Interest	776	926
Cash	6,067	6,466
Accounts receivable	8,034	9,427
Short-term notes payable	1,171	1,147
Long-term debt	20,320	24,696
Net fixed assets	50,888	54,273
Accounts payable	4,384	4,644
Inventory	14,283	15,288
Dividends	1,411	1,618

25. Financial Statements [LO1] Draw up an income statement and balance sheet for this company for 2010 and 2011.

26. Calculating Cash Flow [LO4] For 2011, calculate the cash flow from assets, cash flow to creditors, and cash flow to stockholders.

MINICASE

Cash Flows and Financial Statements at Sunset Boards, Inc.

Sunset Boards is a small company that manufactures and sells surfboards in Malibu. Tad Marks, the founder of the company, is in charge of the design and sale of the surfboards, but his background is in surfing, not business. As a result, the company's financial records are not well maintained.

The initial investment in Sunset Boards was provided by Tad and his friends and family. Because the initial investment was relatively small, and the company has made surfboards only for its own store, the investors haven't required detailed financial statements from Tad. But thanks to word of mouth among professional surfers, sales have picked up recently, and Tad is considering a major expansion. His plans include opening another surfboard store in Hawaii, as well as supplying his "sticks" (surfer lingo for boards) to other sellers.

Tad's expansion plans require a significant investment, which he plans to finance with a combination of additional funds from outsiders plus some money borrowed from banks. Naturally, the new investors and creditors require more organized and detailed financial statements than Tad has previously prepared. At the urging of his investors, Tad has hired financial analyst Christina Wolfe to evaluate the performance of the company over the past year.

After rooting through old bank statements, sales receipts, tax returns, and other records, Christina has assembled the following information:

Sunset Boards currently pays out 50 percent of net income as dividends to Tad and the other original investors, and it has a 20 percent tax rate. You are Christina's assistant, and she has asked you to prepare the following:

1. An income statement for 2010 and 2011.
2. A balance sheet for 2010 and 2011.
3. Operating cash flow for each year.
4. Cash flow from assets for 2011.
5. Cash flow to creditors for 2011.
6. Cash flow to stockholders for 2011.

QUESTIONS

1. How would you describe Sunset Boards' cash flows for 2011? Write a brief discussion.
2. In light of your discussion in the previous question, what do you think about Tad's expansion plans?

	2010	2011
Cost of goods sold	$ 163,849	$ 206,886
Cash	23,643	35,721
Depreciation	46,255	52,282
Interest expense	10,056	11,526
Selling and administrative	32,223	42,058
Accounts payable	41,786	47,325
Net fixed assets	204,068	248,625
Sales	321,437	391,810
Accounts receivable	16,753	21,732
Notes payable	19,046	20,796
Long-term debt	103,006	116,334
Inventory	32,255	43,381
New equity	0	20,500

Visit us at www.mhhe.com/rwj

3

WORKING WITH
FINANCIAL STATEMENTS

THE PRICE OF A SHARE OF COMMON STOCK in green tractor manufacturer John Deere closed at
about $89 on January 21, 2011. At that price, John Deere had a price–earnings (PE) ratio of 21. That is, investors were
willing to pay $21 for every dollar in income earned by John Deere. At the same time, investors were willing to pay
$72, $23, and $9 for each dollar earned by Amazon.com, Google, and Ford, respectively. At the other extreme were
General Motors (GM) and United States Steel. Both had negative earnings for the previous year, yet GM was priced
at about $37 per share and United States Steel at about $54 per share. Because they had negative earnings, their
PE ratios would have been negative, so they were not reported. At the time, the typical stock in the S&P 500 index of
large company stocks was trading at a PE of about 15, or about 15 times earnings, as they say on Wall Street.

Price-to-earnings comparisons are examples of the use of financial ratios. As we will see in this chapter, there
are a wide variety of financial ratios, all designed to summarize specific aspects of a firm's financial position. In
addition to discussing how to analyze financial statements and compute financial ratios, we will have quite a bit to
say about who uses this information and why.

LEARNING OBJECTIVES

**After studying this chapter, you
should understand:**

LO1 How to standardize financial
statements for comparison
purposes.

LO2 How to compute and, more
importantly, interpret some
common ratios.

LO3 The determinants of a firm's
profitability.

LO4 Some of the problems and
pitfalls in financial statement
analysis.

In Chapter 2, we discussed some of the essential concepts of financial statements and cash flow.
Part 2, this chapter and the next, continues where our earlier discussion left off. Our goal here
is to expand your understanding of the uses (and abuses) of financial statement information.

Financial statement information will crop up in various places in the remainder of our
book. Part 2 is not essential for understanding this material, but it will help give you an
overall perspective on the role of financial statement information in corporate finance.

A good working knowledge of financial statements is desirable simply because such
statements, and numbers derived from those statements, are the primary means of communicating financial information both within the firm and outside the firm. In short, much of
the language of corporate finance is rooted in the ideas we discuss in this chapter.

Furthermore, as we will see, there are many different ways of using financial statement
information and many different types of users. This diversity reflects the fact that financial
statement information plays an important part in many types of decisions.

In the best of all worlds, the financial manager has full market value information about all of the firm's assets. This will rarely (if ever) happen. So, the reason we rely on accounting figures for much of our financial information is that we are almost always unable to obtain all (or even part) of the market information we want. The only meaningful yardstick for evaluating business decisions is whether they create economic value (see Chapter 1). However, in many important situations, it will not be possible to make this judgment directly because we can't see the market value effects of decisions.

We recognize that accounting numbers are often just pale reflections of economic reality, but they are frequently the best available information. For privately held corporations, not-for-profit businesses, and smaller firms, for example, very little direct market value information exists at all. The accountant's reporting function is crucial in these circumstances.

Clearly, one important goal of the accountant is to report financial information to the user in a form useful for decision making. Ironically, the information frequently does not come to the user in such a form. In other words, financial statements don't come with a user's guide. This chapter and the next are first steps in filling this gap.

Cash Flow and Financial Statements: A Closer Look

At the most fundamental level, firms do two different things: They generate cash and they spend it. Cash is generated by selling a product, an asset, or a security. Selling a security involves either borrowing or selling an equity interest (shares of stock) in the firm. Cash is spent in paying for materials and labor to produce a product and in purchasing assets. Payments to creditors and owners also require the spending of cash.

In Chapter 2, we saw that the cash activities of a firm could be summarized by a simple identity:

Cash flow from assets = Cash flow to creditors + Cash flow to owners

This cash flow identity summarizes the total cash result of all transactions a firm engages in during the year. In this section, we return to the subject of cash flow by taking a closer look at the cash events during the year that lead to these total figures.

SOURCES AND USES OF CASH

Activities that bring in cash are called **sources of cash**. Activities that involve spending cash are called **uses** (or applications) **of cash**. What we need to do is to trace the changes in the firm's balance sheet to see how the firm obtained and spent its cash during some period.

To get started, consider the balance sheets for the Prufrock Corporation in Table 3.1. Notice that we have calculated the change in each of the items on the balance sheets.

Looking over the balance sheets for Prufrock, we see that quite a few things changed during the year. For example, Prufrock increased its net fixed assets by $149 and its inventory by $29. (Note that, throughout, all figures are in millions of dollars.) Where did the money come from? To answer this and related questions, we need to first identify those changes that used up cash (uses) and those that brought cash in (sources).

A little common sense is useful here. A firm uses cash by either buying assets or making payments. So, loosely speaking, an increase in an asset account means the firm, on a net basis, bought some assets—a use of cash. If an asset account went down, then on a net basis, the firm sold some assets. This would be a net source. Similarly, if a liability account goes down, then the firm has made a net payment—a use of cash.

sources of cash
A firm's activities that generate cash.

uses of cash
A firm's activities in which cash is spent. Also called *applications of cash*.

TABLE 3.1

PRUFROCK CORPORATION 2011 and 2012 Balance Sheets ($ in millions)			
	2011	**2012**	**Change**
Assets			
Current assets			
Cash	$ 84	$ 98	+$ 14
Accounts receivable	165	188	+ 23
Inventory	393	422	+ 29
Total	$ 642	$ 708	+$ 66
Fixed assets			
Net plant and equipment	$2,731	$2,880	+$149
Total assets	$3,373	$3,588	+$215
Liabilities and Owners' Equity			
Current liabilities			
Accounts payable	$ 312	$ 344	+$ 32
Notes payable	231	196	− 35
Total	$ 543	$ 540	−$ 3
Long-term debt	$ 531	$ 457	−$ 74
Owners' equity			
Common stock and paid-in surplus	$ 500	$ 550	+$ 50
Retained earnings	1,799	2,041	+ 242
Total	$2,299	$2,591	+$292
Total liabilities and owners' equity	$3,373	$3,588	+$215

Company financial information can be found in many places on the Web, including www.financials .com, finance.yahoo.com, finance.google.com, *and* money.msn.com.

Given this reasoning, there is a simple, albeit mechanical, definition you may find useful. An increase in a left-side (asset) account or a decrease in a right-side (liability or equity) account is a use of cash. Likewise, a decrease in an asset account or an increase in a liability (or equity) account is a source of cash.

Looking again at Prufrock, we see that inventory rose by $29. This is a net use because Prufrock effectively paid out $29 to increase inventories. Accounts payable rose by $32. This is a source of cash because Prufrock effectively has borrowed an additional $32 payable by the end of the year. Notes payable, on the other hand, went down by $35, so Prufrock effectively paid off $35 worth of short-term debt—a use of cash.

Based on our discussion, we can summarize the sources and uses of cash from the balance sheet as follows:

Sources of cash:	
Increase in accounts payable	$ 32
Increase in common stock	50
Increase in retained earnings	242
Total sources	$324
Uses of cash:	
Increase in accounts receivable	$ 23
Increase in inventory	29
Decrease in notes payable	35
Decrease in long-term debt	74
Net fixed asset acquisitions	149
Total uses	$310
Net addition to cash	$ 14

TABLE 3.2

PRUFROCK CORPORATION 2012 Income Statement ($ in millions)	
Sales	$2,311
Cost of goods sold	1,344
Depreciation	276
Earnings before interest and taxes	$ 691
Interest paid	141
Taxable income	$ 550
Taxes (34%)	187
Net income	$ 363
Dividends	$121
Addition to retained earnings	242

The net addition to cash is just the difference between sources and uses, and our $14 result here agrees with the $14 change shown on the balance sheet.

This simple statement tells us much of what happened during the year, but it doesn't tell the whole story. For example, the increase in retained earnings is net income (a source of funds) less dividends (a use of funds). It would be more enlightening to have these reported separately so we could see the breakdown. Also, we have considered only net fixed asset acquisitions. Total or gross spending would be more interesting to know.

To further trace the flow of cash through the firm during the year, we need an income statement. For Prufrock, the results for the year are shown in Table 3.2.

Notice here that the $242 addition to retained earnings we calculated from the balance sheet is just the difference between the net income of $363 and the dividends of $121.

THE STATEMENT OF CASH FLOWS

There is some flexibility in summarizing the sources and uses of cash in the form of a financial statement. However it is presented, the result is called the **statement of cash flows**.

We present a particular format for this statement in Table 3.3. The basic idea is to group all the changes into three categories: operating activities, financing activities, and investment activities. The exact form differs in detail from one preparer to the next.

Don't be surprised if you come across different arrangements. The types of information presented will be similar; the exact order can differ. The key thing to remember in this case is that we started out with $84 in cash and ended up with $98, for a net increase of $14. We're just trying to see what events led to this change.

Going back to Chapter 2, we note that there is a slight conceptual problem here. Interest paid should really go under financing activities, but unfortunately that's not the way the accounting is handled. The reason, you may recall, is that interest is deducted as an expense when net income is computed. Also, notice that the net purchase of fixed assets was $149. Because Prufrock wrote off $276 worth of assets (the depreciation), it must have actually spent a total of $149 + 276 = $425 on fixed assets.

Once we have this statement, it might seem appropriate to express the change in cash on a per-share basis, much as we did for net income. Ironically, despite the interest we might have in some measure of cash flow per share, standard accounting practice expressly prohibits reporting this information. The reason is that accountants feel that cash flow (or some component of cash flow) is not an alternative to accounting income, so only earnings per share are to be reported.

As shown in Table 3.4, it is sometimes useful to present the same information a bit differently. We will call this the "sources and uses of cash" statement. There is no such

statement of cash flows
A firm's financial statement that summarizes its sources and uses of cash over a specified period.

TABLE 3.3

PRUFROCK CORPORATION 2012 Statement of Cash Flows ($ in millions)	
Cash, beginning of year	$ 84
Operating activity	
Net income	$363
Plus:	
Depreciation	276
Increase in accounts payable	32
Less:	
Increase in accounts receivable	− 23
Increase in inventory	− 29
Net cash from operating activity	$619
Investment activity	
Fixed asset acquisitions	−$425
Net cash from investment activity	−$425
Financing activity	
Decrease in notes payable	−$ 35
Decrease in long-term debt	− 74
Dividends paid	− 121
Increase in common stock	50
Net cash from financing activity	−$180
Net increase in cash	$ 14
Cash, end of year	$ 98

TABLE 3.4

PRUFROCK CORPORATION 2012 Sources and Uses of Cash ($ in millions)	
Cash, beginning of year	$ 84
Sources of cash	
Operations:	
Net income	$363
Depreciation	276
	$639
Working capital:	
Increase in accounts payable	$ 32
Long-term financing:	
Increase in common stock	50
Total sources of cash	$721
Uses of cash	
Working capital:	
Increase in accounts receivable	$ 23
Increase in inventory	29
Decrease in notes payable	35
Long-term financing:	
Decrease in long-term debt	74
Fixed asset acquisitions	425
Dividends paid	121
Total uses of cash	$707
Net addition to cash	$ 14
Cash, end of year	$ 98

statement in financial accounting, but this arrangement resembles one used many years ago. As we will discuss, this form can come in handy, but we emphasize again that it is not the way this information is normally presented.

Now that we have the various cash pieces in place, we can get a good idea of what happened during the year. Prufrock's major cash outlays were fixed asset acquisitions and cash dividends. It paid for these activities primarily with cash generated from operations.

Prufrock also retired some long-term debt and increased current assets. Finally, current liabilities were not greatly changed, and a relatively small amount of new equity was sold. Altogether, this short sketch captures Prufrock's major sources and uses of cash for the year.

Concept Questions

3.1a What is a source of cash? Give three examples.

3.1b What is a use, or application, of cash? Give three examples.

Standardized Financial Statements   3.2 ✗

The next thing we might want to do with Prufrock's financial statements is compare them to those of other similar companies. We would immediately have a problem, however. It's almost impossible to directly compare the financial statements for two companies because of differences in size.

For example, Ford and GM are serious rivals in the auto market, but GM is bigger (in terms of market share), so it is difficult to compare them directly. For that matter, it's difficult even to compare financial statements from different points in time for the same company if the company's size has changed. The size problem is compounded if we try to compare GM and, say, Toyota. If Toyota's financial statements are denominated in yen, then we have size *and* currency differences.

To start making comparisons, one obvious thing we might try to do is to somehow standardize the financial statements. One common and useful way of doing this is to work with percentages instead of total dollars. In this section, we describe two different ways of standardizing financial statements along these lines.

COMMON-SIZE STATEMENTS

To get started, a useful way of standardizing financial statements is to express each item on the balance sheet as a percentage of assets and to express each item on the income statement as a percentage of sales. The resulting financial statements are called **common-size statements**. We consider these next.

common-size statement
A standardized financial statement presenting all items in percentage terms. Balance sheet items are shown as a percentage of assets and income statement items as a percentage of sales.

Common-Size Balance Sheets   One way, though not the only way, to construct a common-size balance sheet is to express each item as a percentage of total assets. Prufrock's 2011 and 2012 common-size balance sheets are shown in Table 3.5.

Notice that some of the totals don't check exactly because of rounding. Also notice that the total change has to be zero because the beginning and ending numbers must add up to 100 percent.

In this form, financial statements are relatively easy to read and compare. For example, just looking at the two balance sheets for Prufrock, we see that current assets were 19.7 percent of total assets in 2012, up from 19.1 percent in 2011. Current liabilities

TABLE 3.5

PRUFROCK CORPORATION Common-Size Balance Sheets 2011 and 2012			
	2011	**2012**	**Change**
Assets			
Current assets			
Cash	2.5%	2.7%	+ .2%
Accounts receivable	4.9	5.2	+ .3
Inventory	11.7	11.8	+ .1
Total	19.1	19.7	+ .7
Fixed assets			
Net plant and equipment	80.9	80.3	− .7
Total assets	100.0%	100.0%	.0
Liabilities and Owners' Equity			
Current liabilities			
Accounts payable	9.2%	9.6%	+ .3%
Notes payable	6.8	5.5	−1.4
Total	16.0	15.1	−1.0
Long-term debt	15.7	12.7	−3.0
Owners' equity			
Common stock and paid-in surplus	14.8	15.3	+ .5
Retained earnings	53.3	56.9	+3.6
Total	68.1	72.2	+4.1
Total liabilities and owners' equity	100.0%	100.0%	.0

declined from 16.0 percent to 15.1 percent of total liabilities and equity over that same time. Similarly, total equity rose from 68.1 percent of total liabilities and equity to 72.2 percent.

Overall, Prufrock's liquidity, as measured by current assets compared to current liabilities, increased over the year. Simultaneously, Prufrock's indebtedness diminished as a percentage of total assets. We might be tempted to conclude that the balance sheet has grown "stronger." We will say more about this later.

Common-Size Income Statements   A useful way of standardizing the income statement is to express each item as a percentage of total sales, as illustrated for Prufrock in Table 3.6.

This income statement tells us what happens to each dollar in sales. For Prufrock, interest expense eats up $.061 out of every sales dollar and taxes take another $.081. When all is said and done, $.157 of each dollar flows through to the bottom line (net income), and that amount is split into $.105 retained in the business and $.052 paid out in dividends.

These percentages are useful in comparisons. For example, a relevant figure is the cost percentage. For Prufrock, $.582 of each $1 in sales goes to pay for goods sold. It would be interesting to compute the same percentage for Prufrock's main competitors to see how Prufrock stacks up in terms of cost control.

TABLE 3.6

PRUFROCK CORPORATION Common-Size Income Statement 2012	
Sales	100.0%
Cost of goods sold	58.2
Depreciation	11.9
Earnings before interest and taxes	29.9
Interest paid	6.1
Taxable income	23.8
Taxes (34%)	8.1
Net income	15.7%
Dividends	5.2%
Addition to retained earnings	10.5

Common-Size Statements of Cash Flows   Although we have not presented it here, it is also possible and useful to prepare a common-size statement of cash flows. Unfortunately, with the current statement of cash flows, there is no obvious denominator such as total assets or total sales. However, if the information is arranged in a way similar to that in Table 3.4, then each item can be expressed as a percentage of total sources (or total uses). The results can then be interpreted as the percentage of total sources of cash supplied or as the percentage of total uses of cash for a particular item.

COMMON–BASE YEAR FINANCIAL STATEMENTS: TREND ANALYSIS

Imagine we were given balance sheets for the last 10 years for some company and we were trying to investigate trends in the firm's pattern of operations. Does the firm use more or less debt? Has the firm grown more or less liquid? A useful way of standardizing financial statements in this case is to choose a base year and then express each item relative to the base amount. We will call the resulting statements common–base year statements.

For example, from 2011 to 2012, Prufrock's inventory rose from $393 to $422. If we pick 2011 as our base year, then we would set inventory equal to 1.00 for that year. For the next year, we would calculate inventory relative to the base year as $422/393 = 1.07. In this case, we could say inventory grew by about 7 percent during the year. If we had multiple years, we would just divide the inventory figure for each one by $393. The resulting series is easy to plot, and it is then easy to compare companies. Table 3.7 summarizes these calculations for the asset side of the balance sheet.

common–base year statement
A standardized financial statement presenting all items relative to a certain base year amount.

COMBINED COMMON-SIZE AND BASE YEAR ANALYSIS

The trend analysis we have been discussing can be combined with the common-size analysis discussed earlier. The reason for doing this is that as total assets grow, most of the other accounts must grow as well. By first forming the common-size statements, we eliminate the effect of this overall growth.

For example, looking at Table 3.7, we see that Prufrock's accounts receivable were $165, or 4.9 percent of total assets, in 2011. In 2012, they had risen to $188, which was 5.2 percent of total assets. If we do our analysis in terms of dollars, then the 2012 figure would be $188/165 = 1.14, representing a 14 percent increase in receivables. However, if we work with the common-size statements, then the 2012 figure would be 5.2%/4.9% = 1.06. This tells us accounts receivable, as a percentage of total assets, grew by 6 percent. Roughly speaking, what we see is that of the 14 percent total increase, about 8 percent (= 14% − 6%) is attributable simply to growth in total assets.

TABLE 3.7

PRUFROCK CORPORATION Summary of Standardized Balance Sheets (Asset Side Only)						
	Assets ($ in millions)		Common-Size Assets		Common–Base Year Assets	Combined Common-Size and Base Year Assets
	2011	**2012**	**2011**	**2012**	**2012**	**2012**
Current assets						
Cash	$ 84	$ 98	2.5%	2.7%	1.17	1.08
Accounts receivable	165	188	4.9	5.2	1.14	1.06
Inventory	393	422	11.7	11.8	1.07	1.01
Total current assets	$ 642	$ 708	19.1	19.7	1.10	1.03
Fixed assets						
Net plant and equipment	$2,731	$2,880	80.9	80.3	1.05	.99
Total assets	$3,373	$3,588	100.0%	100.0%	1.06	1.00

NOTE: The common-size numbers are calculated by dividing each item by total assets for that year. For example, the 2011 common-size cash amount is $84/3,373 = 2.5%. The common–base year numbers are calculated by dividing each 2012 item by the base year (2011) dollar amount. The common-base cash is thus $98/84 = 1.17, representing a 17 percent increase. The combined common-size and base year figures are calculated by dividing each common-size amount by the base year (2011) common-size amount. The cash figure is therefore 2.7%/2.5% = 1.08, representing an 8 percent increase in cash holdings as a percentage of total assets. Columns may not total precisely due to rounding.

Concept Questions

3.2a Why is it often necessary to standardize financial statements?

3.2b Name two types of standardized statements and describe how each is formed.

3.3 Ratio Analysis

financial ratios
Relationships determined from a firm's financial information and used for comparison purposes.

Another way of avoiding the problems involved in comparing companies of different sizes is to calculate and compare **financial ratios**. Such ratios are ways of comparing and investigating the relationships between different pieces of financial information. Using ratios eliminates the size problem because the size effectively divides out. We're then left with percentages, multiples, or time periods.

There is a problem in discussing financial ratios. Because a ratio is simply one number divided by another, and because there are so many accounting numbers out there, we could examine a huge number of possible ratios. Everybody has a favorite. We will restrict ourselves to a representative sampling.

In this section, we only want to introduce you to some commonly used financial ratios. These are not necessarily the ones we think are the best. In fact, some of them may strike you as illogical or not as useful as some alternatives. If they do, don't be concerned. As a financial analyst, you can always decide how to compute your own ratios.

What you do need to worry about is the fact that different people and different sources seldom compute these ratios in exactly the same way, and this leads to much confusion. The specific definitions we use here may or may not be the same as ones you have seen or will see elsewhere. If you are ever using ratios as a tool for analysis, you should be careful to document how you calculate each one. And if you are comparing your numbers to numbers from another source, be sure you know how those numbers are computed.

We will defer much of our discussion of how ratios are used and some problems that come up with using them until later in the chapter. For now, for each of the ratios we discuss, we consider several questions:

1. How is it computed?
2. What is it intended to measure, and why might we be interested?
3. What is the unit of measurement?
4. What might a high or low value tell us? How might such values be misleading?
5. How could this measure be improved?

Financial ratios are traditionally grouped into the following categories:

1. Short-term solvency, or liquidity, ratios.
2. Long-term solvency, or financial leverage, ratios.
3. Asset management, or turnover, ratios.
4. Profitability ratios.
5. Market value ratios.

We will consider each of these in turn. In calculating these numbers for Prufrock, we will use the ending balance sheet (2012) figures unless we say otherwise. Also notice that the various ratios are color keyed to indicate which numbers come from the income statement and which come from the balance sheet.

SHORT-TERM SOLVENCY, OR LIQUIDITY, MEASURES

As the name suggests, short-term solvency ratios as a group are intended to provide information about a firm's liquidity, and these ratios are sometimes called *liquidity measures*. The primary concern is the firm's ability to pay its bills over the short run without undue stress. Consequently, these ratios focus on current assets and current liabilities.

For obvious reasons, liquidity ratios are particularly interesting to short-term creditors. Because financial managers work constantly with banks and other short-term lenders, an understanding of these ratios is essential.

One advantage of looking at current assets and liabilities is that their book values and market values are likely to be similar. Often (though not always), these assets and liabilities just don't live long enough for the two to get seriously out of step. On the other hand, like any type of near-cash, current assets and liabilities can and do change fairly rapidly, so today's amounts may not be a reliable guide to the future.

Go to www.reuters.com *to examine comparative ratios for a huge number of companies.*

Current Ratio   One of the best known and most widely used ratios is the *current ratio*. As you might guess, the current ratio is defined as follows:

$$\text{Current ratio} = \frac{\text{Current assets}}{\text{Current liabilities}} \qquad \text{[3.1]}$$

Here is Prufrock's 2012 current ratio:

$$\text{Current ratio} = \frac{\$708}{\$540} = 1.31 \text{ times}$$

Because current assets and liabilities are, in principle, converted to cash over the following 12 months, the current ratio is a measure of short-term liquidity. The unit of measurement is either dollars or times. So, we could say Prufrock has $1.31 in current assets for every $1 in current liabilities, or we could say Prufrock has its current liabilities covered 1.31 times over.

To a creditor—particularly a short-term creditor such as a supplier—the higher the current ratio, the better. To the firm, a high current ratio indicates liquidity, but it also may indicate an inefficient use of cash and other short-term assets. Absent some extraordinary circumstances, we would expect to see a current ratio of at least 1 because a current ratio of less than 1 would mean that net working capital (current assets less current liabilities) is negative. This would be unusual in a healthy firm, at least for most types of businesses.

The current ratio, like any ratio, is affected by various types of transactions. For example, suppose the firm borrows over the long term to raise money. The short-run effect would be an increase in cash from the issue proceeds and an increase in long-term debt. Current liabilities would not be affected, so the current ratio would rise.

Finally, note that an apparently low current ratio may not be a bad sign for a company with a large reserve of untapped borrowing power.

EXAMPLE 3.1	**Current Events**

Suppose a firm pays off some of its suppliers and short-term creditors. What happens to the current ratio? Suppose a firm buys some inventory. What happens in this case? What happens if a firm sells some merchandise?

The first case is a trick question. What happens is that the current ratio moves away from 1. If it is greater than 1 (the usual case), it will get bigger. But if it is less than 1, it will get smaller. To see this, suppose the firm has $4 in current assets and $2 in current liabilities for a current ratio of 2. If we use $1 in cash to reduce current liabilities, then the new current ratio is ($4 − 1)/($2 − 1) = 3. If we reverse the original situation to $2 in current assets and $4 in current liabilities, then the change will cause the current ratio to fall to 1/3 from 1/2.

The second case is not quite as tricky. Nothing happens to the current ratio because cash goes down while inventory goes up—total current assets are unaffected.

In the third case, the current ratio will usually rise because inventory is normally shown at cost and the sale will normally be at something greater than cost (the difference is the markup). The increase in either cash or receivables is therefore greater than the decrease in inventory. This increases current assets, and the current ratio rises.

The Quick (or Acid-Test) Ratio   Inventory is often the least liquid current asset. It's also the one for which the book values are least reliable as measures of market value because the quality of the inventory isn't considered. Some of the inventory may later turn out to be damaged, obsolete, or lost.

More to the point, relatively large inventories are often a sign of short-term trouble. The firm may have overestimated sales and overbought or overproduced as a result. In this case, the firm may have a substantial portion of its liquidity tied up in slow-moving inventory.

To further evaluate liquidity, the *quick,* or *acid-test, ratio* is computed just like the current ratio, except inventory is omitted:

$$\text{Quick ratio} = \frac{\text{Current assets} - \text{Inventory}}{\text{Current liabilities}} \qquad [3.2]$$

Notice that using cash to buy inventory does not affect the current ratio, but it reduces the quick ratio. Again, the idea is that inventory is relatively illiquid compared to cash.

For Prufrock, this ratio for 2012 was:

$$\text{Quick ratio} = \frac{\$708 - 422}{\$540} = .53 \text{ times}$$

The quick ratio here tells a somewhat different story than the current ratio because inventory accounts for more than half of Prufrock's current assets. To exaggerate the point, if this inventory consisted of, say, unsold nuclear power plants, then this would be a cause for concern.

To give an example of current versus quick ratios, based on recent financial statements, Walmart and Manpower Inc. had current ratios of .9 and 1.5, respectively. However, Manpower carries no inventory to speak of, whereas Walmart's current assets are virtually all inventory. As a result, Walmart's quick ratio was only .2, whereas Manpower's was 1.4, about the same as its current ratio.

Other Liquidity Ratios We briefly mention three other measures of liquidity. A very short-term creditor might be interested in the *cash ratio:*

$$\text{Cash ratio} = \frac{\text{Cash}}{\text{Current liabilities}} \qquad \textbf{[3.3]}$$

You can verify that for 2012 this works out to be .18 times for Prufrock.

Because net working capital, or NWC, is frequently viewed as the amount of short-term liquidity a firm has, we can consider the ratio of *NWC to total assets:*

$$\text{Net working capital to total assets} = \frac{\text{Net working capital}}{\text{Total assets}} \qquad \textbf{[3.4]}$$

A relatively low value might indicate relatively low levels of liquidity. Here, this ratio works out to be ($708 − 540)/$3,588 = 4.7%.

Finally, imagine that Prufrock was facing a strike and cash inflows began to dry up. How long could the business keep running? One answer is given by the *interval measure:*

$$\text{Interval measure} = \frac{\text{Current assets}}{\text{Average daily operating costs}} \qquad \textbf{[3.5]}$$

Total costs for the year, excluding depreciation and interest, were $1,344. The average daily cost was $1,344/365 = $3.68 per day.[1] The interval measure is thus $708/$3.68 = 192 days. Based on this, Prufrock could hang on for six months or so.[2]

The interval measure (or something similar) is also useful for newly founded or start-up companies that often have little in the way of revenues. For such companies, the interval measure indicates how long the company can operate until it needs another round of financing. The average daily operating cost for start-up companies is often called the *burn rate,* meaning the rate at which cash is burned in the race to become profitable.

LONG-TERM SOLVENCY MEASURES

Long-term solvency ratios are intended to address the firm's long-term ability to meet its obligations, or, more generally, its financial leverage. These are sometimes called *financial leverage ratios* or just *leverage ratios.* We consider three commonly used measures and some variations.

Total Debt Ratio The *total debt ratio* takes into account all debts of all maturities to all creditors. It can be defined in several ways, the easiest of which is this:

$$\text{Total debt ratio} = \frac{\text{Total assets} - \text{Total equity}}{\text{Total assets}}$$

$$= \frac{\$3,588 - 2,591}{\$3,588} = .28 \text{ times} \qquad \textbf{[3.6]}$$

The online Women's Business Center has more information about financial statements, ratios, and small business topics (www.onlinewbc.gov).

---

[1]For many of these ratios that involve average daily amounts, a 360-day year is often used in practice. This so-called banker's year has exactly four quarters of 90 days each and was computationally convenient in the days before pocket calculators. We'll use 365 days.

[2]Sometimes depreciation and/or interest is included in calculating average daily costs. Depreciation isn't a cash expense, so its inclusion doesn't make a lot of sense. Interest is a financing cost, so we excluded it by definition (we looked at only operating costs). We could, of course, define a different ratio that included interest expense.

In this case, an analyst might say that Prufrock uses 28 percent debt.[3] Whether this is high or low or whether it even makes any difference depends on whether capital structure matters, a subject we discuss in Part 6.

Prufrock has $.28 in debt for every $1 in assets. Therefore, there is $.72 in equity (=$1 − .28) for every $.28 in debt. With this in mind, we can define two useful variations on the total debt ratio—the *debt–equity ratio* and the *equity multiplier:*

$$\text{Debt–equity ratio} = \text{Total debt/Total equity}$$
$$= \$.28/\$.72 = .38 \text{ times}$$

[3.7]

$$\text{Equity multiplier} = \text{Total assets/Total equity}$$
$$= \$1/\$.72 = 1.38 \text{ times}$$

[3.8]

The fact that the equity multiplier is 1 plus the debt–equity ratio is not a coincidence:

$$\text{Equity multiplier} = \text{Total assets/Total equity} = \$1/\$.72 = 1.38$$
$$= (\text{Total equity} + \text{Total debt})/\text{Total equity}$$
$$= 1 + \text{Debt–equity ratio} = 1.38 \text{ times}$$

The thing to notice here is that given any one of these three ratios, you can immediately calculate the other two; so, they all say exactly the same thing.

Ratios used to analyze technology firms can be found at www.chalfin.com under the "Publications" link.

A Brief Digression: Total Capitalization versus Total Assets   Frequently, financial analysts are more concerned with a firm's long-term debt than its short-term debt because the short-term debt will constantly be changing. Also, a firm's accounts payable may reflect trade practice more than debt management policy. For these reasons, the *long-term debt ratio* is often calculated as follows:

$$\text{Long-term debt ratio} = \frac{\text{Long-term debt}}{\text{Long-term debt} + \text{Total equity}}$$
$$= \frac{\$457}{\$457 + 2{,}591} = \frac{\$457}{\$3{,}048} = .15 \text{ times}$$

[3.9]

The $3,048 in total long-term debt and equity is sometimes called the firm's *total capitalization,* and the financial manager will frequently focus on this quantity rather than on total assets.

To complicate matters, different people (and different books) mean different things by the term *debt ratio.* Some mean a ratio of total debt, some mean a ratio of long-term debt only, and, unfortunately, a substantial number are simply vague about which one they mean.

This is a source of confusion, so we choose to give two separate names to the two measures. The same problem comes up in discussing the debt–equity ratio. Financial analysts frequently calculate this ratio using only long-term debt.

Times Interest Earned   Another common measure of long-term solvency is the *times interest earned* (TIE) *ratio.* Once again, there are several possible (and common) definitions, but we'll stick with the most traditional:

$$\text{Times interest earned ratio} = \frac{\text{EBIT}}{\text{Interest}}$$
$$= \frac{\$691}{\$141} = 4.9 \text{ times}$$

[3.10]

---

[3]Total equity here includes preferred stock (discussed in Chapter 8 and elsewhere), if there is any. An equivalent numerator in this ratio would be Current liabilities + Long-term debt.

As the name suggests, this ratio measures how well a company has its interest obligations covered, and it is often called the *interest coverage ratio*. For Prufrock, the interest bill is covered 4.9 times over.

Cash Coverage   A problem with the TIE ratio is that it is based on EBIT, which is not really a measure of cash available to pay interest. The reason is that depreciation, a noncash expense, has been deducted out. Because interest is definitely a cash outflow (to creditors), one way to define the *cash coverage ratio* is this:

$$\text{Cash coverage ratio} = \frac{\text{EBIT} + \text{Depreciation}}{\text{Interest}}$$

$$= \frac{\$691 + 276}{\$141} = \frac{\$967}{\$141} = 6.9 \text{ times}$$

[3.11]

The numerator here, EBIT plus depreciation, is often abbreviated EBITD (earnings before interest, taxes, and depreciation—say "ebbit-dee"). It is a basic measure of the firm's ability to generate cash from operations, and it is frequently used as a measure of cash flow available to meet financial obligations.

A common variation on EBITD is earnings before interest, taxes, depreciation, and amortization (EBITDA—say "ebbit-dah"). Here *amortization* refers to a noncash deduction similar conceptually to depreciation, except it applies to an intangible asset (such as a patent) rather than a tangible asset (such as a machine). Note that the word *amortization* here does not refer to the repayment of debt, a subject we discuss in a later chapter.

ASSET MANAGEMENT, OR TURNOVER, MEASURES

We next turn our attention to the efficiency with which Prufrock uses its assets. The measures in this section are sometimes called *asset utilization ratios*. The specific ratios we discuss can all be interpreted as measures of turnover. What they are intended to describe is how efficiently or intensively a firm uses its assets to generate sales. We first look at two important current assets: inventory and receivables.

Inventory Turnover and Days' Sales in Inventory   During the year, Prufrock had a cost of goods sold of $1,344. Inventory at the end of the year was $422. With these numbers, *inventory turnover* can be calculated as follows:

$$\text{Inventory turnover} = \frac{\text{Cost of goods sold}}{\text{Inventory}}$$

$$= \frac{\$1,344}{\$422} = 3.2 \text{ times}$$

[3.12]

In a sense, Prufrock sold off or turned over the entire inventory 3.2 times.[4] As long as we are not running out of stock and thereby forgoing sales, the higher this ratio is, the more efficiently we are managing inventory.

If we know we turned our inventory over 3.2 times during the year, we can immediately figure out how long it took us to turn it over on average. The result is the average *days' sales in inventory:*

$$\text{Days' sales in inventory} = \frac{365 \text{ days}}{\text{Inventory turnover}}$$

$$= \frac{365 \text{ days}}{3.2} = 115 \text{ days}$$

[3.13]

---

[4]Notice that we used cost of goods sold in the top of this ratio. For some purposes, it might be more useful to use sales instead of costs. For example, if we wanted to know the amount of sales generated per dollar of inventory, we could just replace the cost of goods sold with sales.

This tells us that, roughly speaking, inventory sits 115 days on average before it is sold. Alternatively, assuming we have used the most recent inventory and cost figures, it will take about 115 days to work off our current inventory.

To give an example, in March 2011, the U.S. automobile industry as a whole had a 57-day supply of cars, just under the 60-day supply considered normal. This figure means that at the then-current rate of sales, it would have taken 57 days to deplete the available supply. Of course, there is significant variation across models, with newer, hotter-selling models in shorter supply (and vice versa). So, also in March 2011, the Mini Countryman had only 14 days of sales compared to 139 days for the Toyota Camry Hybrid.

It might make more sense to use the average inventory in calculating turnover. Inventory turnover would then be $1,344/[($393 + 422)/2] = 3.3$ times.[5] It depends on the purpose of the calculation. If we are interested in how long it will take us to sell our current inventory, then using the ending figure (as we did initially) is probably better.

In many of the ratios we discuss in this chapter, average figures could just as well be used. Again, it depends on whether we are worried about the past, in which case averages are appropriate, or the future, in which case ending figures might be better. Also, using ending figures is common in reporting industry averages; so, for comparison purposes, ending figures should be used in such cases. In any event, using ending figures is definitely less work, so we'll continue to use them.

Receivables Turnover and Days' Sales in Receivables   Our inventory measures give some indication of how fast we can sell product. We now look at how fast we collect on those sales. The *receivables turnover* is defined much like inventory turnover:

$$\text{Receivables turnover} = \frac{\text{Sales}}{\text{Accounts receivable}}$$

$$= \frac{\$2,311}{\$188} = 12.3 \text{ times} \qquad \text{[3.14]}$$

Loosely speaking, Prufrock collected its outstanding credit accounts and reloaned the money 12.3 times during the year.[6]

This ratio makes more sense if we convert it to days, so here is the *days' sales in receivables:*

$$\text{Days' sales in receivables} = \frac{365 \text{ days}}{\text{Receivables turnover}}$$

$$= \frac{365}{12.3} = 30 \text{ days} \qquad \text{[3.15]}$$

Therefore, on average, Prufrock collects on its credit sales in 30 days. For obvious reasons, this ratio is frequently called the *average collection period* (ACP).

Note that if we are using the most recent figures, we could also say that we have 30 days' worth of sales currently uncollected. We will learn more about this subject when we study credit policy in a later chapter.

EXAMPLE 3.2	Payables Turnover

Here is a variation on the receivables collection period. How long, on average, does it take for Prufrock Corporation to pay its bills? To answer, we need to calculate the accounts payable turnover rate using cost of goods sold. We will assume that Prufrock purchases everything on credit.

---

[5]Notice that we calculated the average as (Beginning value + Ending value)/2.

[6]Here we have implicitly assumed that all sales are credit sales. If they were not, we would simply use total credit sales in these calculations, not total sales.

The cost of goods sold is $1,344, and accounts payable are $344. The turnover is therefore $1,344/$344 = 3.9 times. So, payables turned over about every 365/3.9 = 94 days. On average, then, Prufrock takes 94 days to pay. As a potential creditor, we might take note of this fact.

Asset Turnover Ratios   Moving away from specific accounts like inventory or receivables, we can consider several "big picture" ratios. For example, *NWC turnover* is:

$$\text{NWC turnover} = \frac{\text{Sales}}{\text{NWC}}$$

$$= \frac{\$2,311}{\$708 - 540} = 13.8 \text{ times} \qquad [3.16]$$

This ratio measures how much "work" we get out of our working capital. Once again, assuming we aren't missing out on sales, a high value is preferred. (Why?)

Similarly, *fixed asset turnover* is:

$$\text{Fixed asset turnover} = \frac{\text{Sales}}{\text{Net fixed assets}}$$

$$= \frac{\$2,311}{\$2,880} = .80 \text{ times} \qquad [3.17]$$

With this ratio, it probably makes more sense to say that for every dollar in fixed assets, Prufrock generated $.80 in sales.

Our final asset management ratio, the *total asset turnover,* comes up quite a bit. We will see it later in this chapter and in the next chapter. As the name suggests, the total asset turnover is:

$$\text{Total asset turnover} = \frac{\text{Sales}}{\text{Total assets}}$$

$$= \frac{\$2,311}{\$3,588} = .64 \text{ times} \qquad [3.18]$$

In other words, for every dollar in assets, Prufrock generated $.64 in sales.

To give an example of fixed and total asset turnover, based on recent financial statements, Southwest Airlines had a total asset turnover of .8, compared to .9 for IBM. However, the much higher investment in fixed assets in an airline is reflected in Southwest's fixed asset turnover of 1.2, compared to IBM's 7.1.

More Turnover	EXAMPLE 3.3

Suppose you find that a particular company generates $.40 in sales for every dollar in total assets. How often does this company turn over its total assets?

The total asset turnover here is .40 times per year. It takes 1/.40 = 2.5 years to turn total assets over completely.

PROFITABILITY MEASURES

The three measures we discuss in this section are probably the best known and most widely used of all financial ratios. In one form or another, they are intended to measure how efficiently a firm uses its assets and manages its operations. The focus in this group is on the bottom line, net income.

Profit Margin   Companies pay a great deal of attention to their *profit margins:*

$$\text{Profit margin} = \frac{\text{Net income}}{\text{Sales}}$$

$$= \frac{\$363}{\$2,311} = 15.7\%$$

[3.19]

This tells us that Prufrock, in an accounting sense, generates a little less than 16 cents in profit for every dollar in sales.

All other things being equal, a relatively high profit margin is obviously desirable. This situation corresponds to low expense ratios relative to sales. However, we hasten to add that other things are often not equal.

For example, lowering our sales price will usually increase unit volume but will normally cause profit margins to shrink. Total profit (or, more important, operating cash flow) may go up or down; so the fact that margins are smaller isn't necessarily bad. After all, isn't it possible that, as the saying goes, "Our prices are so low that we lose money on everything we sell, but we make it up in volume"?[7]

Return on Assets   *Return on assets* (ROA) is a measure of profit per dollar of assets. It can be defined several ways, but the most common is this:

$$\text{Return on assets} = \frac{\text{Net income}}{\text{Total assets}}$$

$$= \frac{\$363}{\$3,588} = 10.12\%$$

[3.20]

Return on Equity   *Return on equity* (ROE) is a measure of how the stockholders fared during the year. Because benefiting shareholders is our goal, ROE is, in an accounting sense, the true bottom-line measure of performance. ROE is usually measured as follows:

$$\text{Return on equity} = \frac{\text{Net income}}{\text{Total equity}}$$

$$= \frac{\$363}{\$2,591} = 14\%$$

[3.21]

For every dollar in equity, therefore, Prufrock generated 14 cents in profit; but again this is correct only in accounting terms.

Because ROA and ROE are such commonly cited numbers, we stress that it is important to remember they are accounting rates of return. For this reason, these measures should properly be called *return on book assets* and *return on book equity*. In fact, ROE is sometimes called *return on net worth*. Whatever it's called, it would be inappropriate to compare the result to, for example, an interest rate observed in the financial markets. We will have more to say about accounting rates of return in later chapters.

The fact that ROE exceeds ROA reflects Prufrock's use of financial leverage. We will examine the relationship between these two measures in more detail shortly.

EXAMPLE 3.4	ROE and ROA

Because ROE and ROA are usually intended to measure performance over a prior period, it makes a certain amount of sense to base them on average equity and average assets, respectively. For Prufrock, how would you calculate these?

---

[7]No, it's not.

We first need to calculate average assets and average equity:

Average assets = ($3,373 + 3,588)/2 = $3,481
Average equity = ($2,299 + 2,591)/2 = $2,445

With these averages, we can recalculate ROA and ROE as follows:

$$\text{ROA} = \frac{\$363}{\$3,481} = 10.43\%$$

$$\text{ROE} = \frac{\$363}{\$2,445} = 14.85\%$$

These are slightly higher than our previous calculations because assets and equity grew during the year, so the average values are below the ending values.

MARKET VALUE MEASURES

Our final group of measures is based, in part, on information not necessarily contained in financial statements—the market price per share of stock. Obviously, these measures can be calculated directly only for publicly traded companies.

We assume that Prufrock has 33 million shares outstanding and the stock sold for $88 per share at the end of the year. If we recall that Prufrock's net income was $363 million, we can calculate its earnings per share:

$$\text{EPS} = \frac{\text{Net income}}{\text{Shares outstanding}} = \frac{\$363}{33} = \$11$$

Price–Earnings Ratio   The first of our market value measures, the *price–earnings* (PE) *ratio* (or multiple), is defined here:

$$\begin{aligned} \text{PE ratio} &= \frac{\text{Price per share}}{\text{Earnings per share}} \\ &= \frac{\$88}{\$11} = 8 \text{ times} \end{aligned}$$

[3.22]

In the vernacular, we would say that Prufrock shares sell for eight times earnings, or we might say that Prufrock shares have or "carry" a PE multiple of 8.

PE ratios vary substantially across companies, but, in 2011, a typical large company in the United States had a PE in the 15–20 range. This is on the high side by historical standards, but not dramatically so. A low point for PEs was about 5 in 1974. PEs also vary across countries. For example, Japanese PEs have historically been much higher than those of their U.S. counterparts.

Because the PE ratio measures how much investors are willing to pay per dollar of current earnings, higher PEs are often taken to mean the firm has significant prospects for future growth. Of course, if a firm had no or almost no earnings, its PE would probably be quite large; so, as always, care is needed in interpreting this ratio.

Sometimes analysts divide PE ratios by expected future earnings growth rates (after multiplying the growth rate by 100). The result is the PEG ratio. Suppose Prufrock's anticipated growth rate in EPS was 6 percent. Its PEG ratio would then be 8/6 = 1.33. The idea behind the PEG ratio is that whether a PE ratio is high or low depends on expected future growth. High PEG ratios suggest that the PE is too high relative to growth, and vice versa.

Price–Sales Ratio   In some cases, companies will have negative earnings for extended periods, so their PE ratios are not very meaningful. A good example is a recent start-up. Such companies usually do have some revenues, so analysts will often look at the *price–sales ratio:*

Price–sales ratio = Price per share/Sales per share

In Prufrock's case, sales were $2,311, so here is the price–sales ratio:

Price–sales ratio = $88/($2,311/33) = $88/$70 = 1.26

As with PE ratios, whether a particular price–sales ratio is high or low depends on the industry involved.

Market-to-Book Ratio   A third commonly quoted market value measure is the *market-to-book ratio:*

$$\text{Market-to-book ratio} = \frac{\text{Market value per share}}{\text{Book value per share}}$$

$$= \frac{\$88}{(\$2,591/33)} = \frac{\$88}{\$78.5} = 1.12 \text{ times}$$

[3.23]

Notice that book value per share is total equity (not just common stock) divided by the number of shares outstanding.

Because book value per share is an accounting number, it reflects historical costs. In a loose sense, the market-to-book ratio therefore compares the market value of the firm's investments to their cost. A value less than 1 could mean that the firm has not been successful overall in creating value for its stockholders.

Market-to-book ratios in recent years appear high relative to past values. For example, for the 30 blue-chip companies that make up the widely followed Dow Jones Industrial Average, the historical norm is about 1.7; however, the market-to-book ratio for this group has recently been twice this size.

Another ratio, called *Tobin's Q ratio,* is much like the market-to-book ratio. Tobin's Q is the market value of the firm's assets divided by their replacement cost:

Tobin's Q = Market value of firm's assets/Replacement cost of firm's assets
        = Market value of firm's debt and equity/Replacement cost of firm's assets

Notice that we used two equivalent numerators here: the market value of the firm's assets and the market value of its debt and equity.

Conceptually, the Q ratio is superior to the market-to-book ratio because it focuses on what the firm is worth today relative to what it would cost to replace it today. Firms with high Q ratios tend to be those with attractive investment opportunities or significant competitive advantages (or both). In contrast, the market-to-book ratio focuses on historical costs, which are less relevant.

As a practical matter, however, Q ratios are difficult to calculate with accuracy because estimating the replacement cost of a firm's assets is not an easy task. Also, market values for a firm's debt are often unobservable. Book values can be used instead in such cases, but accuracy may suffer.

Enterprise Value–EBITDA Ratio   A company's enterprise value is an estimate of the market value of the company's operating assets. By operating assets, we mean all the assets of the firm except cash. Of course, it's not practical to work with the individual assets of a firm because market values would usually not be available. Instead, we can use the right-hand side of the balance sheet and calculate the enterprise value as:

Enterprise value = Total market value of the stock
        + Book value of all liabilities − Cash

[3.24]

We use the book value for liabilities because we typically can't get the market values, at least not for all of them. However, book value is usually a reasonable approximation for market value when it comes to liabilities, particularly short-term debts. Notice that the sum

TABLE 3.8 Common Financial Ratios

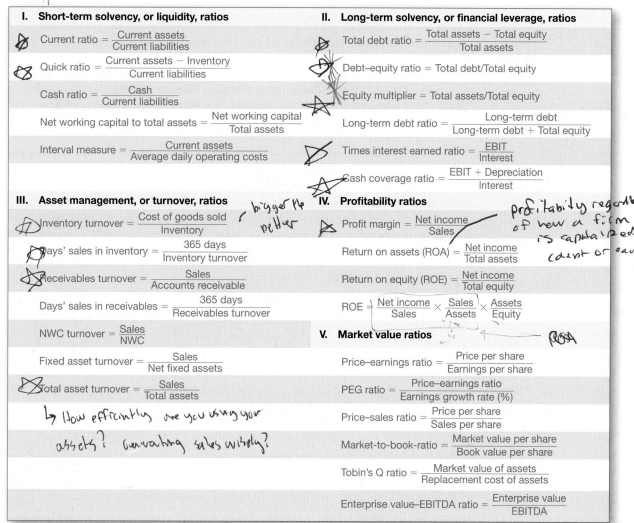

I. Short-term solvency, or liquidity, ratios

$$\text{Current ratio} = \frac{\text{Current assets}}{\text{Current liabilities}}$$

$$\text{Quick ratio} = \frac{\text{Current assets} - \text{Inventory}}{\text{Current liabilities}}$$

$$\text{Cash ratio} = \frac{\text{Cash}}{\text{Current liabilities}}$$

$$\text{Net working capital to total assets} = \frac{\text{Net working capital}}{\text{Total assets}}$$

$$\text{Interval measure} = \frac{\text{Current assets}}{\text{Average daily operating costs}}$$

II. Long-term solvency, or financial leverage, ratios

$$\text{Total debt ratio} = \frac{\text{Total assets} - \text{Total equity}}{\text{Total assets}}$$

$$\text{Debt–equity ratio} = \text{Total debt/Total equity}$$

$$\text{Equity multiplier} = \text{Total assets/Total equity}$$

$$\text{Long-term debt ratio} = \frac{\text{Long-term debt}}{\text{Long-term debt} + \text{Total equity}}$$

$$\text{Times interest earned ratio} = \frac{\text{EBIT}}{\text{Interest}}$$

$$\text{Cash coverage ratio} = \frac{\text{EBIT} + \text{Depreciation}}{\text{Interest}}$$

III. Asset management, or turnover, ratios

$$\text{Inventory turnover} = \frac{\text{Cost of goods sold}}{\text{Inventory}}$$

$$\text{Days' sales in inventory} = \frac{365 \text{ days}}{\text{Inventory turnover}}$$

$$\text{Receivables turnover} = \frac{\text{Sales}}{\text{Accounts receivable}}$$

$$\text{Days' sales in receivables} = \frac{365 \text{ days}}{\text{Receivables turnover}}$$

$$\text{NWC turnover} = \frac{\text{Sales}}{\text{NWC}}$$

$$\text{Fixed asset turnover} = \frac{\text{Sales}}{\text{Net fixed assets}}$$

$$\text{Total asset turnover} = \frac{\text{Sales}}{\text{Total assets}}$$

IV. Profitability ratios

$$\text{Profit margin} = \frac{\text{Net income}}{\text{Sales}}$$

$$\text{Return on assets (ROA)} = \frac{\text{Net income}}{\text{Total assets}}$$

$$\text{Return on equity (ROE)} = \frac{\text{Net income}}{\text{Total equity}}$$

$$\text{ROE} = \frac{\text{Net income}}{\text{Sales}} \times \frac{\text{Sales}}{\text{Assets}} \times \frac{\text{Assets}}{\text{Equity}}$$

V. Market value ratios

$$\text{Price–earnings ratio} = \frac{\text{Price per share}}{\text{Earnings per share}}$$

$$\text{PEG ratio} = \frac{\text{Price–earnings ratio}}{\text{Earnings growth rate (\%)}}$$

$$\text{Price–sales ratio} = \frac{\text{Price per share}}{\text{Sales per share}}$$

$$\text{Market-to-book-ratio} = \frac{\text{Market value per share}}{\text{Book value per share}}$$

$$\text{Tobin's Q ratio} = \frac{\text{Market value of assets}}{\text{Replacement cost of assets}}$$

$$\text{Enterprise value–EBITDA ratio} = \frac{\text{Enterprise value}}{\text{EBITDA}}$$

[handwritten annotations: "45 9 35 12", "286167", "bigger the better", "profitability regardless of how a firm is capitalized (debt or equity)", "ROA", "How efficiently are you using your assets? Generating sales wisely?"]

of the value of the market values of the stock and all liabilities equals the value of the firm's assets from the balance sheet identity. Once we have this number, we subtract the cash to get the enterprise value.

Enterprise value is frequently used to calculate the EBITDA ratio (or multiple):

$$\text{EBITDA ratio} = \text{Enterprise value/EBITDA} \qquad [3.25]$$

This ratio is similar in spirit to the PE ratio, but it relates the value of all the operating assets (the enterprise value) to a measure of the operating cash flow generated by those assets (EBITDA).

CONCLUSION

This completes our definitions of some common ratios. We could tell you about more of them, but these are enough for now. We'll go on to discuss some ways of using these ratios instead of just how to calculate them. Table 3.8 summarizes the ratios we've discussed.

Concept Questions

3.3a What are the five groups of ratios? Give two or three examples of each kind.

3.3b Given the total debt ratio, what other two ratios can be computed? Explain how.

3.3c Turnover ratios all have one of two figures as the numerator. What are these two figures? What do these ratios measure? How do you interpret the results?

3.3d Profitability ratios all have the same figure in the numerator. What is it? What do these ratios measure? How do you interpret the results?

3.4 The DuPont Identity

As we mentioned in discussing ROA and ROE, the difference between these two profitability measures is a reflection of the use of debt financing, or financial leverage. We illustrate the relationship between these measures in this section by investigating a famous way of decomposing ROE into its component parts.

A CLOSER LOOK AT ROE

To begin, let's recall the definition of ROE:

$$\text{Return on equity} = \frac{\text{Net income}}{\text{Total equity}}$$

If we were so inclined, we could multiply this ratio by Assets/Assets without changing anything:

$$\text{Return on equity} = \frac{\text{Net income}}{\text{Total equity}} = \frac{\text{Net income}}{\text{Total equity}} \times \frac{\text{Assets}}{\text{Assets}}$$

$$= \frac{\text{Net income}}{\text{Assets}} \times \frac{\text{Assets}}{\text{Total equity}}$$

Notice that we have expressed the ROE as the product of two other ratios—ROA and the equity multiplier:

$$\text{ROE} = \text{ROA} \times \text{Equity multiplier} = \text{ROA} \times (1 + \text{Debt–equity ratio})$$

Looking back at Prufrock, for example, we see that the debt–equity ratio was .39 and ROA was 10.12 percent. Our work here implies that Prufrock's ROE, as we previously calculated, is this:

$$\text{ROE} = 10.12\% \times 1.38 = 14\%$$

The difference between ROE and ROA can be substantial, particularly for certain businesses. For example, in 2010, American Express had an ROA of 2.78 percent, which is fairly typical for financial institutions. However, financial institutions tend to borrow a lot of money and, as a result, have relatively large equity multipliers. For American Express, ROE was about 24.81 percent, implying an equity multiplier of 8.92 times.

We can further decompose ROE by multiplying the top and bottom by total sales:

$$\text{ROE} = \frac{\text{Sales}}{\text{Sales}} \times \frac{\text{Net income}}{\text{Assets}} \times \frac{\text{Assets}}{\text{Total equity}}$$

If we rearrange things a bit, ROE looks like this:

$$\text{ROE} = \underbrace{\frac{\text{Net income}}{\text{Sales}} \times \frac{\text{Sales}}{\text{Assets}}}_{\text{Return on assets}} \times \frac{\text{Assets}}{\text{Total equity}}$$

[3.26]

$$= \text{Profit margin} \times \text{Total asset turnover} \times \text{Equity multiplier}$$

What we have now done is to partition ROA into its two component parts, profit margin and total asset turnover. The last expression of the preceding equation is called the **DuPont identity**, after the DuPont Corporation, which popularized its use.

We can check this relationship for Prufrock by noting that the profit margin was 15.7 percent and the total asset turnover was .64:

$$
\begin{aligned}
\text{ROE} &= \text{Profit margin} \times \text{Total asset turnover} \times \text{Equity multiplier} \\
&= 15.7\% \qquad\quad \times .64 \qquad\qquad\qquad \times 1.39 \\
&= 14\%
\end{aligned}
$$

This 14 percent ROE is exactly what we had before.

The DuPont identity tells us that ROE is affected by three things:

1. Operating efficiency (as measured by profit margin).
2. Asset use efficiency (as measured by total asset turnover).
3. Financial leverage (as measured by the equity multiplier).

Weakness in either operating or asset use efficiency (or both) will show up in a diminished return on assets, which will translate into a lower ROE.

Considering the DuPont identity, it appears that the ROE could be leveraged up by increasing the amount of debt in the firm. However, notice that increasing debt also increases interest expense, which reduces profit margins, which acts to reduce ROE. So, ROE could go up or down, depending. More important, the use of debt financing has a number of other effects, and as we discuss at some length in Part 6, the amount of leverage a firm uses is governed by its capital structure policy.

The decomposition of ROE we've discussed in this section is a convenient way of systematically approaching financial statement analysis. If ROE is unsatisfactory by some measure, then the DuPont identity tells you where to start looking for the reasons.

General Motors provides a good example of how DuPont analysis can be very useful and also illustrates why care must be taken in interpreting ROE values. In 1989, GM had an ROE of 12.1 percent. By 1993, its ROE had improved to 44.1 percent, a dramatic improvement. On closer inspection, however, we find that over the same period GM's profit margin had declined from 3.4 to 1.8 percent, and ROA had declined from 2.4 to 1.3 percent. The decline in ROA was moderated only slightly by an increase in total asset turnover from .71 to .73 over the period.

Given this information, how is it possible for GM's ROE to have climbed so sharply? From our understanding of the DuPont identity, it must be the case that GM's equity multiplier increased substantially. In fact, what happened was that GM's book equity value was almost wiped out overnight in 1992 by changes in the accounting treatment of pension liabilities. If a company's equity value declines sharply, its equity multiplier rises. In GM's case, the multiplier went from 4.95 in 1989 to 33.62 in 1993. In sum, the dramatic "improvement" in GM's ROE was almost entirely due to an accounting change that affected the equity multiplier and didn't really represent an improvement in financial performance at all.

AN EXPANDED DUPONT ANALYSIS

So far, we've seen how the DuPont equation lets us break down ROE into its basic three components: profit margin, total asset turnover, and financial leverage. We now extend this analysis to take a closer look at how key parts of a firm's operations feed into ROE. To get

DuPont identity
Popular expression breaking ROE into three parts: operating efficiency, asset use efficiency, and financial leverage.

TABLE 3.9

FINANCIAL STATEMENTS FOR DUPONT 12 months ending December 31, 2010 (All numbers are in millions)					
Income Statement		**Balance Sheet**			
Sales	$32,134	Current assets		Current liabilities	
CoGS	21,766	Cash	$ 6,801	Accounts payable	$ 4,440
Gross profit	$10,368	Accounts receivable	5,635	Notes payable	133
SG&A expense	4,828	Inventory	6,353	Other	4,816
Depreciation	1,380	Total	$18,789	Total	$ 9,389
EBIT	$ 4,160				
Interest	449	Fixed assets	$21,621	Total long-term debt	$21,281
EBT	$ 3,711				
Taxes	659			Total equity	$ 9,740
Net income	$ 3,052	Total assets	$40,410	Total liabilities and equity	$40,410

going, we went to the *S&P Market Insight* Web page (www.mhhe.com/edumarketinsight) and pulled abbreviated financial statements for science and technology giant DuPont. What we found is summarized in Table 3.9.

Using the information in Table 3.9, Figure 3.1 shows how we can construct an expanded DuPont analysis for DuPont and present that analysis in chart form. The advantage of the extended DuPont chart is that it lets us examine several ratios at once, thereby getting a better overall picture of a company's performance and also allowing us to determine possible items to improve.

Looking at the left side of our DuPont chart in Figure 3.1, we see items related to profitability. As always, profit margin is calculated as net income divided by sales. But as our chart emphasizes, net income depends on sales and a variety of costs, such as cost of goods sold (CoGS) and selling, general, and administrative expenses (SG&A expense). DuPont can increase its ROE by increasing sales and also by reducing one or more of these costs. In other words, if we want to improve profitability, our chart clearly shows us the areas on which we should focus.

Turning to the right side of Figure 3.1, we have an analysis of the key factors underlying total asset turnover. Thus, for example, we see that reducing inventory holdings through more efficient management reduces current assets, which reduces total assets, which then improves total asset turnover.

Concept Questions

3.4a Return on assets, or ROA, can be expressed as the product of two ratios. Which two?

3.4b Return on equity, or ROE, can be expressed as the product of three ratios. Which three?

FIGURE 3.1   Extended DuPont Chart for DuPont

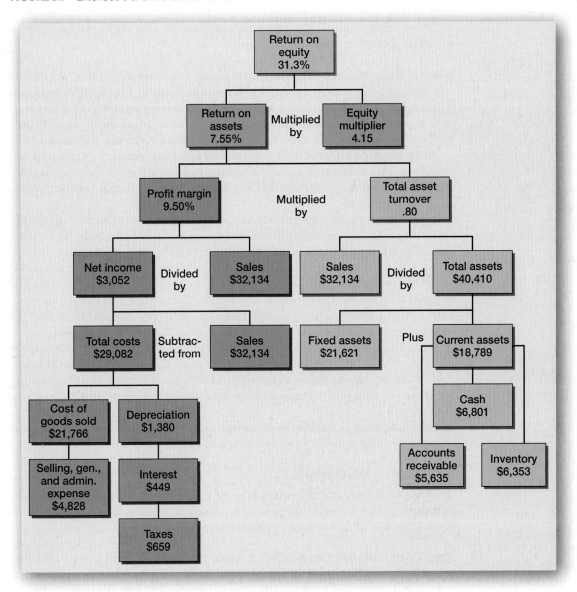

Using Financial Statement Information   3.5 ✗

Our last task in this chapter is to discuss in more detail some practical aspects of financial statement analysis. In particular, we will look at reasons for analyzing financial statements, how to get benchmark information, and some problems that come up in the process.

WHY EVALUATE FINANCIAL STATEMENTS?

As we have discussed, the primary reason for looking at accounting information is that we don't have, and can't reasonably expect to get, market value information. We stress that whenever we have market information, we will use it instead of accounting data. Also, if there is a conflict between accounting and market data, market data should be given precedence.

Financial statement analysis is essentially an application of "management by exception." In many cases, such analysis will boil down to comparing ratios for one business with average or representative ratios. Those ratios that seem to differ the most from the averages are tagged for further study.

Internal Uses   Financial statement information has a variety of uses within a firm. Among the most important of these is performance evaluation. For example, managers are frequently evaluated and compensated on the basis of accounting measures of performance such as profit margin and return on equity. Also, firms with multiple divisions frequently compare the performance of those divisions using financial statement information.

Another important internal use we will explore in the next chapter is planning for the future. As we will see, historical financial statement information is useful for generating projections about the future and for checking the realism of assumptions made in those projections.

External Uses   Financial statements are useful to parties outside the firm, including short-term and long-term creditors and potential investors. For example, we would find such information quite useful in deciding whether to grant credit to a new customer.

We would also use this information to evaluate suppliers, and suppliers would review our statements before deciding to extend credit to us. Large customers use this information to decide if we are likely to be around in the future. Credit-rating agencies rely on financial statements in assessing a firm's overall creditworthiness. The common theme here is that financial statements are a prime source of information about a firm's financial health.

We would also find such information useful in evaluating our main competitors. We might be thinking of launching a new product. A prime concern would be whether the competition would jump in shortly thereafter. In this case, we would be interested in learning about our competitors' financial strength to see if they could afford the necessary development.

Finally, we might be thinking of acquiring another firm. Financial statement information would be essential in identifying potential targets and deciding what to offer.

CHOOSING A BENCHMARK

Given that we want to evaluate a division or a firm based on its financial statements, a basic problem immediately comes up. How do we choose a benchmark, or a standard of comparison? We describe some ways of getting started in this section.

Time Trend Analysis   One standard we could use is history. Suppose we found that the current ratio for a particular firm is 2.4 based on the most recent financial statement information. Looking back over the last 10 years, we might find that this ratio had declined fairly steadily over that period.

Based on this, we might wonder if the liquidity position of the firm has deteriorated. It could be, of course, that the firm has made changes that allow it to more efficiently use its current assets, the nature of the firm's business has changed, or business practices have changed. If we investigate, we might find any of these possible explanations behind the decline. This is an example of what we mean by management by exception—a deteriorating time trend may not be bad, but it does merit investigation.

Peer Group Analysis   The second means of establishing a benchmark is to identify firms similar in the sense that they compete in the same markets, have similar assets, and operate in similar ways. In other words, we need to identify a *peer group*. There are obvious problems with doing this because no two companies are identical. Ultimately the choice of which companies to use as a basis for comparison is subjective.

Agriculture, Forestry, and Fishing	Transportation, Communication, Electric, Gas, and Sanitary Service
01 Agriculture production—crops	40 Railroad transportation
08 Forestry	45 Transportation by air
09 Fishing, hunting, and trapping	49 Electric, gas, and sanitary services
Mining	**Retail Trade**
10 Metal mining	54 Food stores
12 Bituminous coal and lignite mining	55 Automobile dealers and gas stations
13 Oil and gas extraction	58 Eating and drinking places
Construction	**Finance, Insurance, and Real Estate**
15 Building construction	60 Banking
16 Construction other than building	63 Insurance
17 Construction—special trade contractors	65 Real estate
Manufacturing	**Services**
28 Chemicals and allied products	78 Motion pictures
29 Petroleum refining and related industries	80 Health services
37 Transportation equipment	82 Educational services

TABLE 3.10

Selected Two-Digit SIC Codes

One common way of identifying potential peers is based on **Standard Industrial Classification (SIC) codes.** These are four-digit codes established by the U.S. government for statistical reporting. Firms with the same SIC code are frequently assumed to be similar.

The first digit in an SIC code establishes the general type of business. For example, firms engaged in finance, insurance, and real estate have SIC codes beginning with 6. Each additional digit narrows down the industry. So, companies with SIC codes beginning with 60 are mostly banks and banklike businesses; those with codes beginning with 602 are mostly commercial banks; and SIC code 6025 is assigned to national banks that are members of the Federal Reserve system. Table 3.10 lists selected two-digit codes (the first two digits of the four-digit SIC codes) and the industries they represent.

SIC codes are far from perfect. For example, suppose you were examining financial statements for Walmart, the largest retailer in the United States. The relevant two-digit SIC code is 53, General Merchandise Stores. In a quick scan of the nearest financial database, you would find about 20 large, publicly owned corporations with a similar SIC code, but you might not be comfortable with some of them. Target would seem to be a reasonable peer, but Neiman Marcus also carries the same industry code. Are Walmart and Neiman Marcus really comparable?

As this example illustrates, it is probably not appropriate to blindly use SIC code–based averages. Instead, analysts often identify a set of primary competitors and then compute a set of averages based on just this group. Also, we may be more concerned with a group of the top firms in an industry, not the average firm. Such a group is called an *aspirant group* because we aspire to be like its members. In this case, a financial statement analysis reveals how far we have to go.

Beginning in 1997, a new industry classification system was initiated. Specifically, the North American Industry Classification System (NAICS, pronounced "nakes") is intended to replace the older SIC codes, and it will eventually. Currently, however, SIC codes are still widely used.

With these caveats about industry codes in mind, we can now take a look at a specific industry. Suppose we are in the retail hardware business. Table 3.11 contains some condensed common-size financial statements for this industry from the Risk Management Association (RMA, formerly known as Robert Morris Associates), one of many sources of such information. Table 3.12 contains selected ratios from the same source.

Standard Industrial Classification (SIC) code
A U.S. government code used to classify a firm by its type of business operations.

Learn more about NAICS at www.naics.com.

TABLE 3.11   Selected Financial Statement Information

			Retail—Hardware Stores (NAICS 444130)						
COMPARATIVE HISTORICAL DATA				**CURRENT DATA SORTED BY SALES**					
			Type of Statement						
10	12	6	Unqualified					1	5
47	33	48	Reviewed	2	7	11	9	15	4
90	83	64	Compiled	5	27	10	18	4	
69	106	121	Tax Returns	29	55	18	15	4	
89	103	98	Other	10	39	15	13	9	12
4/1/07– 3/31/08 ALL 305	**4/1/08– 3/31/09 ALL 337**	**4/1/09– 3/31/10 ALL 337**	**NUMBER OF STATEMENTS**	**57 (4/1–9/30/09)**		**280 (10/1/09–3/31/10)**			
				0–1MM 46	**1–3MM 128**	**3–5MM 54**	**5–10MM 55**	**10–25MM 33**	**25MM & OVER 21**
%	%	%	**Assets**	%	%	%	%	%	%
6.4	6.4	7.2	Cash & Equivalents	10.1	6.7	8.6	6.5	6.7	3.5
12.8	10.3	10.0	Trade Receivables (net)	6.1	7.7	10.3	13.5	15.9	12.8
51.0	53.7	51.0	Inventory	53.9	53.4	47.2	47.7	51.1	47.8
2.2	2.6	1.7	All Other Current	2.0	1.5	1.5	1.6	2.0	3.1
72.4	73.0	69.9	Total Current	72.1	69.4	67.6	69.3	75.7	67.3
16.3	14.4	15.3	Fixed Assets (net)	13.0	13.6	16.0	18.2	14.4	22.3
1.8	2.3	3.9	Intangibles (net)	4.9	4.8	2.7	3.4	1.7	3.6
9.6	10.2	10.9	All Other Noncurrent	10.0	12.2	13.7	9.1	8.1	6.8
100.0	100.0	100.0	Total	100.0	100.0	100.0	100.0	100.0	100.0
			Liabilities						
10.3	12.1	8.9	Notes Payable-Short term	4.8	10.5	6.0	7.5	13.5	11.4
3.4	3.0	3.5	Cur. Mat.-L.T.D	4.4	3.8	3.3	3.0	2.1	3.2
13.8	13.2	12.0	Trade Payables	9.8	10.7	13.2	14.6	13.0	12.7
.2	.1	.2	Income Tax Payable	.5	.1	.1	.1	.3	.0
7.5	7.0	6.5	All Other Current	8.5	6.6	4.9	5.7	6.0	8.6
35.2	35.4	30.9	Total Current	28.0	31.7	27.5	30.8	34.9	35.9
21.0	19.8	22.7	Long-Term Debt	34.2	23.9	24.4	16.8	13.9	15.5
.1	.1	.1	Deferred Taxes	.0	.0	.1	.3	.3	.5
6.6	7.8	9.5	All Other Noncurrent	20.6	10.8	4.2	6.6	5.9	3.9
37.1	36.9	36.7	Net Worth	17.2	33.6	43.8	45.5	45.0	44.2
100.0	100.0	100.0	Total Liabilities & Net Worth	100.0	100.0	100.0	100.0	100.0	100.0
			Income Data						
100.0	100.0	100.0	Net Sales	100.0	100.0	100.0	100.0	100.0	100.0
36.7	36.4	38.9	Gross Profit	44.3	40.2	38.1	35.5	36.6	33.9
34.4	34.7	37.2	Operating Expenses	41.6	39.1	35.7	33.9	35.0	31.6
2.3	1.7	1.7	Operating Profit	2.7	1.1	2.4	1.6	1.6	2.3
.2	.0	.0	All Other Expenses (net)	.6	−.4	−.1	.1	.2	.1
2.0	1.7	1.8	Profit Before Taxes	2.1	1.5	2.5	1.5	1.3	2.2

M = $ thousand; MM = $ million.

Interpretation of Statement Studies Figures: RMA cautions that the studies be regarded only as a general guideline and not as an absolute industry norm. This is due to limited samples within categories, the categorization of companies by their primary Standard Industrial Classification (SIC) number only, and different methods of operations by companies within the same industry. For these reasons, RMA recommends that the figures be used only as general guidelines in addition to other methods of financial analysis.

© 2011 by RMA. All rights reserved. No part of this table may be reproduced or utilized in any form or by any means, electronic or mechanical, including photocopying, recording, or by any information storage and retrieval system, without permission in writing from RMA.

TABLE 3.12 Selected Ratios

Retail—Hardware Stores (NAICS 444130)									
COMPARATIVE HISTORICAL DATA				CURRENT DATA SORTED BY SALES					

			Type of Statement						
10	12	6	Unqualified					1	5
47	33	48	Reviewed	2	7	11	9	15	4
90	83	64	Compiled	5	27	10	18	4	
69	106	121	Tax Returns	29	55	18	15	4	
89	103	98	Other	10	39	15	13	9	12

4/1/07–3/31/08 ALL 305	4/1/08–3/31/09 ALL 337	4/1/09–3/31/10 ALL 337	NUMBER OF STATEMENTS	57 (4/1–9/30/09)		280 (10/1/09–3/31/10)			
				0–1MM 46	1–3MM 128	3–5MM 54	5–10MM 55	10–25MM 33	25MM & OVER 21
			Ratios						
4.1	4.2	4.9		6.0	5.1	5.4	4.0	4.3	2.6
2.4	2.6	2.8	Current	3.1	2.9	2.9	2.7	2.4	1.7
1.5	1.6	1.6		1.9	1.7	1.7	1.5	1.5	1.5
1.1	1.0	1.1		1.4	1.1	1.2	1.3	1.1	.9
(304) .5	.5	.5	Quick	.5	.5	.7	.5	.6	.5
.3	.2	.2		.2	.2	.3	.3	.2	.2
6 56.4	4 81.5	5 78.7		2 152.1	4 92.8	5 72.7	6 56.2	8 43.5	7 54.7
12 29.3	9 39.4	10 36.7	Sales/ Receivables	8 45.3	8 46.3	11 34.0	14 25.5	14 25.9	15 24.1
29 12.6	22 16.4	20 18.0		17 21.3	15 24.3	22 16.6	29 12.5	30 12.1	22 16.4
85 4.3	94 3.9	95 3.8		131 2.8	109 3.3	83 4.4	77 4.8	72 5.1	89 4.1
126 2.9	138 2.7	141 2.6	Cost of Sales/ Inventory	221 1.6	155 2.4	116 3.1	115 3.2	151 2.4	109 3.4
173 2.1	185 2.0	200 1.8		287 1.3	200 1.8	158 2.3	166 2.2	187 2.0	152 2.4
15 24.3	14 26.4	14 26.6		4 92.8	12 29.3	16 22.7	14 25.3	16 23.5	16 22.9
26 14.3	24 15.0	24 15.4	Cost of Sales/ Payables	20 18.1	22 16.5	28 12.8	26 14.1	24 15.4	24 15.2
42 8.6	38 9.5	37 9.8		43 8.6	34 10.9	39 9.3	38 9.6	35 10.4	34 10.8
4.2	3.8	3.7		2.6	3.7	3.8	4.5	4.1	5.9
5.9	5.6	5.5	Sales/Working Capital	3.9	5.3	6.2	5.6	5.1	8.1
11.7	10.5	9.2		6.3	9.0	10.4	9.7	11.5	11.7
5.2	6.5	6.7		3.2	6.6	5.9	7.4	6.0	11.8
(281) 2.4	(306) 2.4	(295) 2.6	EBIT/Interest	(34) 2.4	(111) 2.8	(50) 2.2	(49) 3.0	(30) 1.7	7.2
1.0	.9	.5		.6	.4	.3	1.0	−.2	1.3
4.3	4.1	4.2	Net Profit + Depr., Dep,. Amort/ Cur. Mat. L/T/D		3.4	3.2		4.9	
(61) 1.9	(54) 1.7	(50) 1.6			(10) 1.0	(11) 1.6		(10) 2.8	
.7	.4	.5			.5	.7		.1	
.1	.1	.1		.0	.1	.1	.1	.1	.2
.4	.3	.3	Fixed/Worth	.4	.4	.3	.3	.2	.5
1.0	1.1	1.6		−.9	−9.8	.9	1.0	.6	.9
.7	.6	.6		.7	.5	.4	.6	.6	.7
1.6	1.6	1.7	Debt/Worth	3.1	1.8	1.5	1.3	1.7	1.4
4.7	4.6	7.3		−11.4	−45.7	3.5	3.1	3.4	2.5
25.1	25.4	26.9	% Profit Before Taxes/Tangible Net Worth	47.6	30.6	23.0	20.0	20.5	24.0
(269) 9.7	(289) 12.2	(280) 11.0		(33) 19.5	(95) 11.4	(46) 7.9	(54) 8.4	(32) 6.1	(20) 14.1
1.6	1.5	1.9		3.5	2.9	1.1	.8	−3.0	.6
9.0	9.8	9.9	% Profit Before Taxes/Total Assets	11.4	11.6	7.7	9.0	9.8	9.4
3.5	4.2	4.1		4.2	4.3	3.6	4.1	2.5	6.2
.3	−.2	−.5		−2.2	−1.3	−2.2	.1	−1.0	1.0
53.3	73.0	56.5	Sales/Net Fixed Assets	146.1	53.4	54.2	59.3	34.3	47.6
23.1	26.0	24.4		36.8	27.2	19.7	25.5	24.1	14.1
10.2	10.2	9.7		9.1	11.4	9.1	6.3	16.0	6.4

(continued)

TABLE 3.12   (continued)

4/1/07–3/31/08 ALL 305		4/1/08–3/31/09 ALL 337		4/1/09–3/31/10 ALL 337		NUMBER OF STATEMENTS	57 (4/1–9/30/09)				280 (10/1/09–3/31/10)							
							0–1MM 46		1–3MM 128		3–5MM 54		5–10MM 55		10–25MM 33		25MM & OVER 21	
	2.9		3.0		2.9	Sales/Total Assets		2.3		2.9		3.1		3.1		3.0		3.1
	2.4		2.4		2.2			1.7		2.3		2.3		2.2		2.4		2.3
	1.8		1.8		1.7			1.4		1.7		1.8		1.7		1.9		1.7
	.5		.6		.6	% Depr., Dep., Amort/Sales	(29)	.6	(103)	.6	(47)	.7	(45)	.6	(29)	.6	(17)	.7
(256)	1.2	(269)	1.2	(270)	1.3			1.3		1.3		1.3		1.1		1.1		1.8
	1.8		2.0		2.2			3.4		2.6		2.0		2.1		1.5		2.0
	2.3		1.7		1.9	% Officers', Directors' Owners' Comp/ Sales	(26)	3.5	(75)	2.3	(40)	2.4	(39)	1.1	(16)	1.2		
(172)	4.0	(197)	3.1	(201)	3.5			5.7		3.9		3.8		2.0		2.8		
	6.4		5.4		5.6			9.2		5.3		5.4		5.6		3.8		
4482123M		5286386M		3234499M		Net Sales ($)	28058M		237156M		211693M		386738M		522395M		1848459M	
1909677M		2072674M		1496318M		Total Assets ($)	21422M		112110M		99184M		192442M		228535M		842625M	

M = $ thousand; MM = $ million.

© 2011 by RMA. All rights reserved. No part of this table may be reproduced or utilized in any form or by any means, electronic or mechanical, including photocopying, recording, or by any information storage and retrieval system, without permission in writing from RMA.

There is a large amount of information here, most of which is self-explanatory. On the right in Table 3.11, we have current information reported for different groups based on sales. Within each sales group, common-size information is reported. For example, firms with sales in the $10 million to $25 million range have cash and equivalents equal to 6.7 percent of total assets. There are 33 companies in this group, out of 337 in all.

On the left, we have three years' worth of summary historical information for the entire group. For example, operating profit fell from 2.3 percent of sales to 1.7 percent over that time.

Table 3.12 contains some selected ratios, again reported by sales groups on the right and time period on the left. To see how we might use this information, suppose our firm has a current ratio of 2. Based on these ratios, is this value unusual?

Looking at the current ratio for the overall group for the most recent year (third column from the left in Table 3.12), we see that three numbers are reported. The one in the middle, 2.8, is the median, meaning that half of the 337 firms had current ratios that were lower and half had bigger current ratios. The other two numbers are the upper and lower quartiles. So, 25 percent of the firms had a current ratio larger than 4.9 and 25 percent had a current ratio smaller than 1.6. Our value of 2 falls comfortably within these bounds, so it doesn't appear too unusual. This comparison illustrates how knowledge of the range of ratios is important in addition to knowledge of the average. Notice how stable the current ratio has been for the last three years.

EXAMPLE 3.5   **More Ratios**

Take a look at the most recent numbers reported for Sales/Receivables and EBIT/Interest in Table 3.12. What are the overall median values? What are these ratios?

If you look back at our discussion, you will see that these are the receivables turnover and the times interest earned, or TIE, ratios. The median value for receivables turnover for the entire group is 36.7 times. So, the days in receivables would be $365/36.7 = 10$, which is the boldfaced number reported. The median for the TIE is 2.6 times. The number in parentheses indicates that the calculation is meaningful for, and therefore based on, only 295 of the 337 companies. In this case, the reason is that only 295 companies paid any significant amount of interest.

There are many sources of ratio information in addition to the one we examine here. Our nearby *Work the Web* box shows how to get this information for just about any company, along with some useful benchmarking information. Be sure to look it over and then benchmark your favorite company.

PROBLEMS WITH FINANCIAL STATEMENT ANALYSIS

We close our chapter on financial statements by discussing some additional problems that can arise in using financial statements. In one way or another, the basic problem with financial statement analysis is that there is no underlying theory to help us identify which quantities to look at and to guide us in establishing benchmarks.

Other websites provide different information about a company's ratios. For example, www.reuters. com *provides some ratio analyses for five-year periods.*

As we discuss in other chapters, there are many cases in which financial theory and economic logic provide guidance in making judgments about value and risk. Little such help exists with financial statements. This is why we can't say which ratios matter the most and what a high or low value might be.

One particularly severe problem is that many firms are conglomerates, owning more or less unrelated lines of business. The consolidated financial statements for such firms don't

WORK THE WEB

As we discussed in this chapter, ratios are an important tool for examining a company's performance. Gathering the necessary financial statements to calculate ratios can be tedious and time-consuming. Fortunately many sites on the Web provide this information for free. One of the best is http://investing.businessweek. com. We went there, entered the ticker symbol "MCD" (for McDonald's), and then went to the ratio page. Here is an abbreviated look at the results:

MCDONALD'S CORP (MCD:New York)

LAST **$75.01** USD   CHANGE TODAY **-0.15 -0.20%**   VOLUME **9.8M**   MCD On Other Exchanges ▾

As of 8:04 PM 01/21/11 All times are local (Market data is delayed by at least 15 minutes).

Snapshot	News	Charts	Financials	Earnings	People	Ownership	Transactions	Options

Financial Statements   Ratios   Pensions & Options   SEC Filings

Ratio data TTM as of 09/30/2010   ▣ MCD

PROFITABILITY - MCDONALD'S CORP (MCD)

Return on Assets	14.68%	**Return on Equity**	36.68%
Industry Comparison		Industry Comparison	
Return on Capital	18.22%		
Industry Comparison			

This website is unique in that it shows the ratios compared to the industry quintile ratios. As you can see, McDonald's is in the top 20th percentile for all three profitability ratios calculated on this site.

Questions

1. Go to *investing.businessweek.com* and find the major ratio categories listed on this website. How do the categories differ from the categories listed in this textbook?
2. Go to *investing.businessweek.com* and find all the ratios for McDonald's. How is the company performing in each ratio category presented on this website?

fit any neat industry category. Well-known companies like General Electric (GE) and 3M fall into this category. More generally, the kind of peer group analysis we have been describing works best when the firms are strictly in the same line of business, the industry is competitive, and there is only one way of operating.

Another problem that is becoming increasingly common is that major competitors and natural peer group members in an industry may be scattered around the globe. The automobile industry is an obvious example. The problem here is that financial statements from outside the United States do not necessarily conform at all to GAAP. The existence of different standards and procedures makes it difficult to compare financial statements across national borders.

Even companies that are clearly in the same line of business may not be comparable. For example, electric utilities engaged primarily in power generation are all classified in the same group (SIC 4911). This group is often thought to be relatively homogeneous. However, most utilities operate as regulated monopolies, so they don't compete much with each other, at least not historically. Many have stockholders, and many are organized as cooperatives with no stockholders. There are several different ways of generating power, ranging from hydroelectric to nuclear, so the operating activities of these utilities can differ quite a bit. Finally, profitability is strongly affected by regulatory environment, so utilities in different locations can be similar but show different profits.

Several other general problems frequently crop up. First, different firms use different accounting procedures—for inventory, for example. This makes it difficult to compare statements. Second, different firms end their fiscal years at different times. For firms in seasonal businesses (such as a retailer with a large Christmas season), this can lead to difficulties in comparing balance sheets because of fluctuations in accounts during the year. Finally, for any particular firm, unusual or transient events, such as a one-time profit from an asset sale, may affect financial performance. In comparing firms, such events can give misleading signals.

Concept Questions

3.5a What are some uses for financial statement analysis?

3.5b Why do we say that financial statement analysis is management by exception?

3.5c What are SIC codes and how might they be useful?

3.5d What are some problems that can come up with financial statement analysis?

3.6 Summary and Conclusions

This chapter has discussed aspects of financial statement analysis:

1. *Sources and uses of cash:* We discussed how to identify the ways in which businesses obtain and use cash, and we described how to trace the flow of cash through a business over the course of the year. We briefly looked at the statement of cash flows.

2. *Standardized financial statements:* We explained that differences in size make it difficult to compare financial statements, and we discussed how to form common-size and
common–base period statements to make comparisons easier.

3. *Ratio analysis:* Evaluating ratios of accounting numbers is another way of comparing financial statement information. We therefore defined and discussed a number of
the most commonly reported and used financial ratios. We also discussed the famous
DuPont identity as a way of analyzing financial performance.

4. *Using financial statements:* We described how to establish benchmarks for comparison
and discussed some types of information that are available. We then examined potential problems that can arise.

After you have studied this chapter, we hope that you have some perspective on the uses
and abuses of financial statements. You should also find that your vocabulary of business
and financial terms has grown substantially.

CONNECT TO FINANCE

 If you are using *Connect™ Finance* in your course, get online to take a Practice
Test, check out study tools, and find out where you need additional practice.

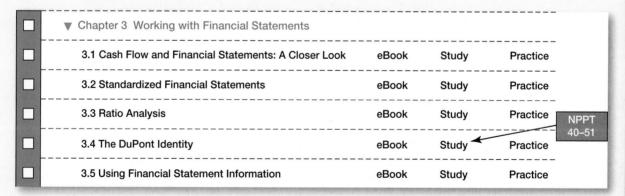

Can you answer the following questions?

Section 3.1   What is an example of a source of cash? (LO 3-1)

Section 3.2   Pioneer Aviation has total liabilities of $23,800 and total equity of $46,200.
Current assets are $8,600. What is the common-size percentage for the current assets?
(LO 3-1)

Section 3.3   What ratio measures the number of days that a firm can operate based on its
current assets? (LO 3-2)

Section 3.4   What is the correct formula for computing the return on equity? (LO 3-3)

Section 3.5   If you want to identify other firms that have similar assets and operations as
your firm, what should you refer to? (LO 3-4)

Log on to find out!

Visit us at www.mhhe.com/rwj

CHAPTER REVIEW AND SELF-TEST PROBLEMS

3.1 Sources and Uses of Cash Consider the following balance sheets for the Philippe Corporation. Calculate the changes in the various accounts and, where applicable, identify the change as a source or use of cash. What were the major sources and uses of cash? Did the company become more or less liquid during the year? What happened to cash during the year?

PHILIPPE CORPORATION
2011 and 2012 Balance Sheets
($ in millions)

	2011	2012
Assets		
Current assets		
Cash	$ 210	$ 215
Accounts receivable	355	310
Inventory	507	328
Total	$1,072	$ 853
Fixed assets		
Net plant and equipment	$6,085	$6,527
Total assets	$7,157	$7,380
Liabilities and Owners' Equity		
Current liabilities		
Accounts payable	$ 207	$ 298
Notes payable	1,715	1,427
Total	$1,922	$1,725
Long-term debt	$1,987	$2,308
Owners' equity		
Common stock and paid-in surplus	$1,000	$1,000
Retained earnings	2,248	2,347
Total	$3,248	$3,347
Total liabilities and owners' equity	$7,157	$7,380

3.2 Common-Size Statements Here is the most recent income statement for Philippe. Prepare a common-size income statement based on this information. How do you interpret the standardized net income? What percentage of sales goes to cost of goods sold?

PHILIPPE CORPORATION
2012 Income Statement
($ in millions)

Sales		$4,053
Cost of goods sold		2,780
Depreciation		550
Earnings before interest and taxes		$ 723
Interest paid		502
Taxable income		$ 221
Taxes (34%)		75
Net income		$ 146
Dividends	$47	
Addition to retained earnings	99	

3.3   Financial Ratios Based on the balance sheets and income statement in the previous two problems, calculate the following ratios for 2012:

Current ratio _____

Quick ratio _____

Cash ratio _____

Inventory turnover _____

Receivables turnover _____

Days' sales in inventory _____

Days' sales in receivables _____

Total debt ratio _____

Long-term debt ratio _____

Times interest earned ratio _____

Cash coverage ratio _____

3.4   ROE and the DuPont Identity Calculate the 2012 ROE for the Philippe Corporation and then break down your answer into its component parts using the DuPont identity.

ANSWERS TO CHAPTER REVIEW AND SELF-TEST PROBLEMS

3.1 We've filled in the answers in the following table. Remember, increases in assets and decreases in liabilities indicate that we spent some cash. Decreases in assets and increases in liabilities are ways of getting cash.

Philippe used its cash primarily to purchase fixed assets and to pay off short-term debt. The major sources of cash to do this were additional long-term borrowing, reductions in current assets, and additions to retained earnings.

PHILIPPE CORPORATION 2011 and 2012 Balance Sheets ($ in millions)				
	2011	**2012**	**Change**	**Source or Use of Cash**
Assets				
Current assets				
Cash	$ 210	$ 215	+$ 5	
Accounts receivable	355	310	− 45	Source
Inventory	507	328	− 179	Source
Total	$1,072	$ 853	−$219	
Fixed assets				
Net plant and equipment	$6,085	$6,527	+$442	Use
Total assets	$7,157	$7,380	+$223	
Liabilities and Owners' Equity				
Current liabilities				
Accounts payable	$ 207	$ 298	+$ 91	Source
Notes payable	1,715	1,427	− 288	Use
Total	$1,922	$1,725	−$197	
Long-term debt	$1,987	$2,308	+$321	Source
Owners' equity				
Common stock and paid-in surplus	$1,000	$1,000	+$ 0	—
Retained earnings	2,248	2,347	+ 99	Source
Total	$3,248	$3,347	+$ 99	
Total liabilities and owners' equity	$7,157	$7,380	+$223	

Visit us at www.mhhe.com/rwj

The current ratio went from $1,072/1,922 = .56$ to $853/1,725 = .49$, so the firm's liquidity appears to have declined somewhat. Overall, however, the amount of cash on hand increased by $5.

3.2   We've calculated the common-size income statement here. Remember that we simply divide each item by total sales.

PHILIPPE CORPORATION 2012 COMMON-SIZE INCOME STATEMENT		
Sales		100.0%
Cost of goods sold		68.6
Depreciation		13.6
Earnings before interest and taxes		17.8
Interest paid		12.3
Taxable income		5.5
Taxes (34%)		1.9
Net income		3.6%
Dividends	1.2%	
Addition to retained earnings	2.4%	

Net income is 3.6 percent of sales. Because this is the percentage of each sales dollar that makes its way to the bottom line, the standardized net income is the firm's profit margin. Cost of goods sold is 68.6 percent of sales.

3.3   We've calculated the following ratios based on the ending figures. If you don't remember a definition, refer back to Table 3.8.

Current ratio	$853/$1,725	= .49 times
Quick ratio	$525/$1,725	= .30 times
Cash ratio	$215/$1,725	= .12 times
Inventory turnover	$2,780/$328	= 8.48 times
Receivables turnover	$4,053/$310	= 13.07 times
Days' sales in inventory	365/8.48	= 43.06 days
Days' sales in receivables	365/13.07	= 27.92 days
Total debt ratio	$4,033/$7,380	= 54.6%
Long-term debt ratio	$2,308/$5,655	= 40.8%
Times interest earned ratio	$723/$502	= 1.44 times
Cash coverage ratio	$1,273/$502	= 2.54 times

3.4   The return on equity is the ratio of net income to total equity. For Philippe, this is $146/$3,347 = 4.4\%$, which is not outstanding.

Given the DuPont identity, ROE can be written as follows:

$$\text{ROE} = \text{Profit margin} \times \text{Total asset turnover} \times \text{Equity multiplier}$$
$$= \$146/\$4,053 \times \$4,053/\$7,380 \qquad \times \$7,380/\$3,347$$
$$= \quad 3.6\% \qquad \times \quad .549 \qquad \times \qquad 2.20$$
$$= \quad 4.4\%$$

Notice that return on assets, ROA, is $3.6\% \times .549 = 1.98\%$.

CONCEPTS REVIEW AND CRITICAL THINKING QUESTIONS

1. **Current Ratio [LO2]** What effect would the following actions have on a firm's current ratio? Assume that net working capital is positive.

    a. Inventory is purchased.
    b. A supplier is paid.
    c. A short-term bank loan is repaid.
    d. A long-term debt is paid off early.

    e. A customer pays off a credit account. — A/R
    f. Inventory is sold at cost.
    g. Inventory is sold for a profit.

2. **Current Ratio and Quick Ratio [LO2]** In recent years, Dixie Co. has greatly increased its current ratio. At the same time, the quick ratio has fallen. What has happened? Has the liquidity of the company improved?

3. **Current Ratio [LO2]** Explain what it means for a firm to have a current ratio equal to .50. Would the firm be better off if the current ratio were 1.50? What if it were 15.0? Explain your answers.

4. **Financial Ratios [LO2]** Fully explain the kind of information the following financial ratios provide about a firm:

    a. Quick ratio.
    b. Cash ratio.
    c. Total asset turnover.
    d. Equity multiplier.
    e. Long-term debt ratio.

    f. Times interest earned ratio.
    g. Profit margin.
    h. Return on assets.
    i. Return on equity.
    j. Price–earnings ratio.

5. **Standardized Financial Statements [LO1]** What types of information do common-size financial statements reveal about the firm? What is the best use for these common-size statements? What purpose do common–base year statements have? When would you use them?

6. **Peer Group Analysis [LO2]** Explain what peer group analysis is. As a financial manager, how could you use the results of peer group analysis to evaluate the performance of your firm? How is a peer group different from an aspirant group?

7. **DuPont Identity [LO3]** Why is the DuPont identity a valuable tool for analyzing the performance of a firm? Discuss the types of information it reveals compared to ROE considered by itself.

8. **Industry-Specific Ratios [L02]** Specialized ratios are sometimes used in specific industries. For example, the so-called book-to-bill ratio is closely watched for semiconductor manufacturers. A ratio of .93 indicates that for every $100 worth of chips shipped over some period, only $93 worth of new orders were received. In December 2010, the semiconductor equipment industry's book-to-bill ratio was .90, compared to .97 during the month of November 2010. The book-to-bill ratio reached a recent low of .47 during January 2009 and a recent high of 1.23 during July 2010. The three-month average of worldwide bookings in December 2010 was $1.7 billion, an increase of 8.7 percent from November 2010, while the three-month average of billings was $1.5 billion, a 1.4 percent decrease from November 2010. What is this ratio intended to measure? Why do you think it is so closely followed?

9. **Industry-Specific Ratios [LO2]** So-called same-store sales are a very important measure for companies as diverse as McDonald's and Sears. As the name suggests, examining same-store sales means comparing revenues from the same stores or restaurants at two different points in time. Why might companies focus on same-store sales rather than total sales?

Visit us at www.mhhe.com/rwj

10. **Industry-Specific Ratios [LO2]** There are many ways of using standardized financial information beyond those discussed in this chapter. The usual goal is to put firms on an equal footing for comparison purposes. For example, for auto manufacturers, it is common to express sales, costs, and profits on a per-car basis. For each of the following industries, give an example of an actual company and discuss one or more potentially useful means of standardizing financial information:

    a. Public utilities.   **d.** Online services.

    b. Large retailers.   **e.** Hospitals.

    c. Airlines.   **f.** College textbook publishers.

11. **Statement of Cash Flows [LO4]** In recent years, several manufacturing companies have reported the cash flow from the sale of Treasury securities in the cash from operations section of the statement of cash flows. What is the problem with this practice? Is there any situation in which this practice would be acceptable?

12. **Statement of Cash Flows [LO4]** Suppose a company lengthens the time it takes to pay suppliers. How would this affect the statement of cash flows? How sustainable is the change in cash flows from this practice?

QUESTIONS AND PROBLEMS

BASIC
(Questions 1–17)

1. **Calculating Liquidity Ratios [LO2]** SDJ, Inc., has net working capital of $2,710, current liabilities of $3,950, and inventory of $3,420. What is the current ratio? What is the quick ratio?

2. **Calculating Profitability Ratios [LO2]** Diamond Eyes, Inc., has sales of $18 million, total assets of $15.6 million, and total debt of $6.3 million. If the profit margin is 8 percent, what is net income? What is ROA? What is ROE?

3. **Calculating the Average Collection Period [LO2]** Boom Lay Corp. has a current accounts receivable balance of $327,815. Credit sales for the year just ended were $4,238,720. What is the receivables turnover? The days' sales in receivables? How long did it take on average for credit customers to pay off their accounts during the past year?

4. **Calculating Inventory Turnover [LO2]** The Cape Corporation has ending inventory of $483,167, and cost of goods sold for the year just ended was $4,285,131. What is the inventory turnover? The days' sales in inventory? How long on average did a unit of inventory sit on the shelf before it was sold?

5. **Calculating Leverage Ratios [LO2]** Perry, Inc., has a total debt ratio of .46. What is its debt–equity ratio? What is its equity multiplier?

6. **Calculating Market Value Ratios [LO2]** That Wich Corp. had additions to retained earnings for the year just ended of $375,000. The firm paid out $175,000 in cash dividends, and it has ending total equity of $4.8 million. If the company currently has 145,000 shares of common stock outstanding, what are earnings per share? Dividends per share? Book value per share? If the stock currently sells for $79 per share, what is the market-to-book ratio? The price–earnings ratio? If the company had sales of $4.7 million, what is the price–sales ratio?

7. **DuPont Identity [LO4]** If Roten Rooters, Inc., has an equity multiplier of 1.45, total asset turnover of 1.80, and a profit margin of 5.5 percent, what is its ROE?

8. **DuPont Identity [LO4]** Kindle Fire Prevention Corp. has a profit margin of 4.6 percent, total asset turnover of 2.3, and ROE of 19.14 percent. What is this firm's debt–equity ratio?

Visit us at www.mhhe.com/rwj

9. **Sources and Uses of Cash [LO4]** Based only on the following information for Shinoda Corp., did cash go up or down? By how much? Classify each event as a source or use of cash.

Decrease in inventory	$430
Decrease in accounts payable	165
Increase in notes payable	150
Increase in accounts receivable	180

10. **Calculating Average Payables Period [LO2]** Tortoise, Inc., had a cost of goods sold of $43,821. At the end of the year, the accounts payable balance was $7,843. How long on average did it take the company to pay off its suppliers during the year? What might a large value for this ratio imply?

11. **Enterprise Value–EBITDA Multiple [LO2]** The market value of the equity of Thompson, Inc., is $580,000. The balance sheet shows $35,000 in cash and $190,000 in debt, while the income statement has EBIT of $91,000 and a total of $135,000 in depreciation and amortization. What is the enterprise value–EBITDA multiple for this company?

12. **Equity Multiplier and Return on Equity [LO3]** Isolation Company has a debt–equity ratio of .80. Return on assets is 7.9 percent, and total equity is $480,000. What is the equity multiplier? Return on equity? Net income?

    Just Dew It Corporation reports the following balance sheet information for 2011 and 2012. Use this information to work Problems 13 through 17.

JUST DEW IT CORPORATION 2011 and 2012 Balance Sheets					
Assets			**Liabilities and Owners' Equity**		
	2011	**2012**		**2011**	**2012**
Current assets			Current liabilities		
Cash	$ 9,279	$ 11,173	Accounts payable	$ 41,060	$ 43,805
Accounts receivable	23,683	25,760	Notes payable	16,157	16,843
Inventory	42,636	46,915	Total	$ 57,217	$ 60,648
Total	$ 75,598	$ 83,848			
			Long-term debt	$ 40,000	$ 35,000
			Owners' equity		
			Common stock and paid-in surplus	$ 50,000	$ 50,000
			Retained earnings	200,428	236,167
Net plant and equipment	$272,047	$297,967	Total	$250,428	$286,167
			Total liabilities and		
Total assets	$347,645	$381,815	owners' equity	$347,645	$381,815

13. **Preparing Standardized Financial Statements [LO1]** Prepare the 2011 and 2012 common-size balance sheets for Just Dew It.

14. **Preparing Standardized Financial Statements [LO1]** Prepare the 2012 common–base year balance sheet for Just Dew It.

15. **Preparing Standardized Financial Statements [LO1]** Prepare the 2012 combined common-size, common–base year balance sheet for Just Dew It.

Visit us at www.mhhe.com/rwj

Visit us at www.mhhe.com/rwj

16. **Sources and Uses of Cash [LO4]** For each account on this company's balance sheet, show the change in the account during 2012 and note whether this change was a source or use of cash. Do your numbers add up and make sense? Explain your answer for total assets as compared to your answer for total liabilities and owners' equity.

17. **Calculating Financial Ratios [LO2]** Based on the balance sheets given for Just Dew It, calculate the following financial ratios for each year:

    a. Current ratio.
    b. Quick ratio.
    c. Cash ratio.
    d. NWC to total assets ratio.
    e. Debt–equity ratio and equity multiplier.
    f. Total debt ratio and long-term debt ratio.

INTERMEDIATE
(Questions 18–30)

18. **Using the DuPont Identity [LO3]** Y3K, Inc., has sales of $6,189, total assets of $2,805, and a debt–equity ratio of 1.40. If its return on equity is 13 percent, what is its net income?

19. **Days' Sales in Receivables [LO2]** A company has net income of $179,000, a profit margin of 8.3 percent, and an accounts receivable balance of $118,370. Assuming 70 percent of sales are on credit, what is the company's days' sales in receivables?

20. **Ratios and Fixed Assets [LO2]** The Caughlin Company has a long-term debt ratio of .35 and a current ratio of 1.30. Current liabilities are $910, sales are $6,430, profit margin is 9.5 percent, and ROE is 18.5 percent. What is the amount of the firm's net fixed assets?

21. **Profit Margin [LO4]** In response to complaints about high prices, a grocery chain runs the following advertising campaign: "If you pay your child $2 to go buy $50 worth of groceries, then your child makes twice as much on the trip as we do." You've collected the following information from the grocery chain's financial statements:

($ in millions)	
Sales	$680
Net income	13.6
Total assets	410
Total debt	280

Evaluate the grocery chain's claim. What is the basis for the statement? Is this claim misleading? Why or why not?

22. **Return on Equity [LO2]** Firm A and firm B have debt–total asset ratios of 45% and 35% and returns on total assets of 9% and 12%, respectively. Which firm has a greater return on equity?

23. **Calculating the Cash Coverage Ratio [LO2]** Hedgepeth Inc.'s net income for the most recent year was $15,185. The tax rate was 34 percent. The firm paid $3,806 in total interest expense and deducted $2,485 in depreciation expense. What was the cash coverage ratio for the year?

24. **Cost of Goods Sold [LO2]** Saunders Corp. has current liabilities of $435,000, a quick ratio of .95, inventory turnover of 6.2, and a current ratio of 1.6. What is the cost of goods sold for the company?

25. **Ratios and Foreign Companies [LO2]** Prince Albert Canning PLC had a net loss of £45,831 on sales of £198,352. What was the company's profit margin? Does the

fact that these figures are quoted in a foreign currency make any difference? Why? In dollars, sales were $314,883. What was the net loss in dollars?

Some recent financial statements for Smolira Golf Corp. follow. Use this information to work Problems 26 through 30.

SMOLIRA GOLF CORP.
2011 and 2012 Balance Sheets

Assets			Liabilities and Owners' Equity		
	2011	2012		2011	2012
Current assets			Current liabilities		
Cash	$24,046	$ 24,255	Accounts payable	$ 23,184	$ 27,420
Accounts receivable	12,448	15,235	Notes payable	12,000	10,800
Inventory	25,392	27,155	Other	11,571	15,553
Total	$61,886	$ 66,645	Total	$ 46,755	$ 53,773
			Long-term debt	$ 80,000	$ 95,000
			Owners' equity		
			Common stock and paid-in surplus	$ 40,000	$ 40,000
Fixed assets			Accumulated retained earnings	219,826	243,606
Net plant and equipment	324,695	365,734	Total	$259,826	$283,606
Total assets	$386,581	$432,379	Total liabilities and owners' equity	$386,581	$432,379

SMOLIRA GOLF CORP.
2012 Income Statement

Sales	$366,996
Cost of goods sold	253,122
Depreciation	32,220
Earnings before interest and taxes	$ 81,654
Interest paid	14,300
Taxable income	$ 67,354
Taxes (35%)	23,574
Net income	$ 43,780
Dividends	$20,000
Retained earnings	23,780

26. **Calculating Financial Ratios [LO2]** Find the following financial ratios for Smolira Golf Corp. (use year-end figures rather than average values where appropriate):

Short-term solvency ratios:

a. Current ratio

b. Quick ratio

c. Cash ratio

Asset utilization ratios:

d. Total asset turnover

e. Inventory turnover

f. Receivables turnover

Long-term solvency ratios:

g. Total debt ratio   .34

h. Debt–equity ratio   .52

i. Equity multiplier   1.52

j. Times interest earned ratio   5.71

k. Cash coverage ratio   xxx

Profitability ratios:

l. Profit margin   .12 (11.13) Net/sales

m. Return on assets   *RA*   10.13

n. Return on equity   *ROE*   13.44

27. **DuPont Identity [LO3]** Construct the DuPont identity for Smolira Golf Corp.
28. **Statement of Cash Flows [LO4]** Prepare the 2012 statement of cash flows for Smolira Golf Corp.
29. **Market Value Ratios [LO2]** Smolira Golf Corp. has 25,000 shares of common stock outstanding, and the market price for a share of stock at the end of 2012 was $43. What is the price–earnings ratio? What are the dividends per share? What is the market-to-book ratio at the end of 2012? If the company's growth rate is 9 percent, what is the PEG ratio?
30. **Tobin's Q [LO2]** What is Tobin's Q for Smolira Golf? What assumptions are you making about the book value of debt and the market value of debt? What about the book value of assets and the market value of assets? Are these assumptions realistic? Why or why not?

MINICASE

Ratio Analysis at S&S Air, Inc.

Chris Guthrie was recently hired by S&S Air, Inc., to assist the company with its financial planning and to evaluate the company's performance. Chris graduated from college five years ago with a finance degree. He has been employed in the finance department of a *Fortune* 500 company since then.

S&S Air was founded 10 years ago by friends Mark Sexton and Todd Story. The company has manufactured and sold light airplanes over this period, and the company's products have received high reviews for safety and reliability. The company has a niche market in that it sells primarily to individuals who own and fly their own airplanes. The company has two models; the Birdie, which sells for $53,000, and the Eagle, which sells for $78,000.

Although the company manufactures aircraft, its operations are different from commercial aircraft companies. S&S Air builds aircraft to order. By using prefabricated parts, the company can complete the manufacture of an airplane in only five weeks. The company also receives a deposit on each order, as well as another partial payment before the order is complete. In contrast, a commercial airplane may take one and one-half to two years to manufacture once the order is placed.

Mark and Todd have provided the following financial statements. Chris has gathered the industry ratios for the light airplane manufacturing industry.

S&S AIR, INC. 2012 Income Statement		
Sales		$36,599,300
Cost of goods sold		26,669,496
Other expenses		4,641,000
Depreciation		1,640,200
EBIT		$ 3,648,604
Interest		573,200
Taxable income		$ 3,075,404
Taxes (40%)		1,230,162
Net income		$ 1,845,242
Dividends	$560,000	
Add to retained earnings	1,285,242	

S&S AIR, INC. 2012 Balance Sheet			
Assets		**Liabilities and Equity**	
Current assets		Current liabilities	
Cash	$ 396,900	Accounts payable	$ 844,550
Accounts receivable	637,560	Notes payable	1,928,500
Inventory	933,400	Total current liabilities	$ 2,773,050
Total current assets	$ 1,967,860		
		Long-term debt	$ 5,050,000
Fixed assets			
		Shareholder equity	
Net plant and equipment	$15,411,620	Common stock	$ 322,500
		Retained earnings	9,233,930
		Total equity	$ 9,556,430
Total assets	$17,379,480	Total liabilities and equity	$17,379,480

Light Airplane Industry Ratios			
	Lower Quartile	Median	Upper Quartile
Current ratio	.50	1.43	1.89
Quick ratio	.21	.35	.62
Cash ratio	.08	.21	.39
Total asset turnover	.68	.85	1.38
Inventory turnover	4.89	6.15	10.89
Receivables turnover	6.27	9.82	14.11
Total debt ratio	.44	.52	.61
Debt–equity ratio	.79	1.08	1.56
Equity multiplier	1.79	2.08	2.56
Times interest earned	5.18	8.06	9.83
Cash coverage ratio	5.84	8.43	10.27
Profit margin	4.05%	6.98%	9.87%
Return on assets	6.05%	10.53%	13.21%
Return on equity	9.93%	16.54%	26.15%

QUESTIONS

1. Using the financial statements provided for S&S Air, calculate each of the ratios listed in the table for the light aircraft industry.

2. Mark and Todd agree that a ratio analysis can provide a measure of the company's performance. They have chosen Boeing as an aspirant company. Would you choose Boeing as an aspirant company? Why or why not? There are other aircraft manufacturers S&S Air could use as aspirant companies. Discuss whether it is appropriate to use any of the following companies: Bombardier, Embraer, Cirrus Design Corporation, and Cessna Aircraft Company.

3. Compare the performance of S&S Air to the industry. For each ratio, comment on why it might be viewed as positive or negative relative to the industry. Suppose you create an inventory ratio calculated as inventory divided by current liabilities. How do you think S&S Air's ratio would compare to the industry average?

Visit us at www.mhhe.com/rwj

4

LONG-TERM FINANCIAL PLANNING AND GROWTH

GROWTH RATES ARE IMPORTANT TOOLS for evaluating a company and, as we will see later, for valuing a company's stock. When thinking about (and calculating) growth rates, a little common sense goes a long way. For example, in 2010, retailing giant Walmart had about 603 million square feet of stores, distribution centers, and so forth. The company expected to increase its square footage by about 8 percent over the next year. This doesn't sound too outrageous, but can Walmart grow its square footage at 8 percent indefinitely?

We'll get into the calculation in our next chapter, but if you assume that Walmart grows at 8 percent per year over the next 156 years, the company will have about 100 trillion square feet of property, which is about the total land mass of the entire United States! In other words, if Walmart keeps growing at 8 percent, the entire country will eventually be one big Walmart. Scary.

Sirius XM Satellite Radio is another example. The company had total revenues of about $805,000 in 2002 and $2.82 billion in 2010. This represents an annual increase of about 177 percent! How likely do you think it is that the company can continue this growth rate? If this growth continued, the company would have revenues of about $27.07 trillion in just 9 years, which is about twice the gross domestic product (GDP) of the United States. Obviously, Sirius XM Radio's growth rate will slow substantially in the next several years. So, long-term growth rate estimates must be chosen very carefully. As a rule of thumb, for really long-term growth estimates, you should probably assume that a company will not grow much faster than the economy as a whole, which is about 1 to 3 percent (inflation-adjusted).

Proper management of growth is vital. Thus, this chapter emphasizes the importance of planning for the future and discusses some tools firms use to think about, and manage, growth.

LEARNING OBJECTIVES

After studying this chapter, you should understand:

LO1 How to apply the percentage of sales method.

LO2 How to compute the external financing needed to fund a firm's growth.

LO3 The determinants of a firm's growth.

LO4 Some of the problems in planning for growth.

A lack of effective long-range planning is a commonly cited reason for financial distress and failure. As we discuss in this chapter, long-range planning is a means of systematically thinking about the future and anticipating possible problems before they arrive. There are no magic mirrors, of course, so the best we can hope for is a logical and organized procedure for exploring the unknown. As one member of GM's board was heard to say, "Planning is a process that at best helps the firm avoid stumbling into the future backward."

Financial planning establishes guidelines for change and growth in a firm. It normally focuses on the big picture. This means it is concerned with the major elements of a firm's financial and investment policies without examining the individual components of those policies in detail.

Our primary goals in this chapter are to discuss financial planning and to illustrate the interrelatedness of the various investment and financing decisions a firm makes. In the chapters ahead, we will examine in much more detail how these decisions are made.

We first describe what is usually meant by *financial planning*. For the most part, we talk about long-term planning. Short-term financial planning is discussed in a later chapter. We examine what the firm can accomplish by developing a long-term financial plan. To do this, we develop a simple but useful long-range planning technique: the percentage of sales approach. We describe how to apply this approach in some simple cases, and we discuss some extensions.

To develop an explicit financial plan, managers must establish certain basic elements of the firm's financial policy:

1. *The firm's needed investment in new assets*: This will arise from the investment opportunities the firm chooses to undertake, and it is the result of the firm's capital budgeting decisions.
2. *The degree of financial leverage the firm chooses to employ*: This will determine the amount of borrowing the firm will use to finance its investments in real assets. This is the firm's capital structure policy.
3. *The amount of cash the firm thinks is necessary and appropriate to pay shareholders*: This is the firm's dividend policy.
4. *The amount of liquidity and working capital the firm needs on an ongoing basis*: This is the firm's net working capital decision.

As we will see, the decisions a firm makes in these four areas will directly affect its future profitability, need for external financing, and opportunities for growth.

A key lesson to be learned from this chapter is that a firm's investment and financing policies interact and thus cannot truly be considered in isolation from one another. The types and amounts of assets a firm plans on purchasing must be considered along with the firm's ability to raise the capital necessary to fund those investments. Many business students are aware of the classic three *P*s (or even four *P*s) of marketing. Not to be outdone, financial planners have no fewer than six *P*s: *P*roper *P*rior *P*lanning *P*revents *P*oor *P*erformance.

Financial planning forces the corporation to think about goals. A goal frequently espoused by corporations is growth, and almost all firms use an explicit, companywide growth rate as a major component of their long-term financial planning. For example, in September 2007, Toyota Motor announced that it planned to sell about 9.8 million vehicles in 2008 and 10.4 million vehicles in 2009, becoming the first auto manufacturer to sell more than 10 million vehicles in a year. Of course, Toyota's plans didn't come to fruition. In 2009, the company only sold 7.2 million cars, and it sold 8.6 million in 2010. General Motors currently holds the auto sales record with 9.55 million vehicles sold in 1978.

There are direct connections between the growth a company can achieve and its financial policy. In the following sections, we show how financial planning models can be used to better understand how growth is achieved. We also show how such models can be used to establish the limits on possible growth.

4.1 What Is Financial Planning?

Financial planning formulates the way in which financial goals are to be achieved. A financial plan is thus a statement of what is to be done in the future. Many decisions have long lead times, which means they take a long time to implement. In an uncertain world, this requires that decisions be made far in advance of their implementation. If a firm wants to build a factory in 2015, for example, it might have to begin lining up contractors and financing in 2013 or even earlier.

GROWTH AS A FINANCIAL MANAGEMENT GOAL

Because the subject of growth will be discussed in various places in this chapter, we need to start out with an important warning: Growth, by itself, is not an appropriate goal for the financial manager. Clothing retailer J. Peterman Co., whose quirky catalogs were made famous on the TV show *Seinfeld*, learned this lesson the hard way. Despite its strong brand name and years of explosive revenue growth, the company was ultimately forced to file for bankruptcy—the victim of an overly ambitious, growth-oriented expansion plan.

Amazon.com, the big online retailer, is another example. At one time, Amazon's motto seemed to be "growth at any cost." Unfortunately, what really grew rapidly for the company were losses. Amazon refocused its business, explicitly sacrificing growth in the hope of achieving profitability. The plan seems to be working as Amazon.com has become a profitable retailing giant.

As we discussed in Chapter 1, the appropriate goal is increasing the market value of the owners' equity. Of course, if a firm is successful in doing this, then growth will usually result. Growth may thus be a desirable consequence of good decision making, but it is not an end unto itself. We discuss growth simply because growth rates are so commonly used in the planning process. As we will see, growth is a convenient means of summarizing various aspects of a firm's financial and investment policies. Also, if we think of growth as growth in the market value of the equity in the firm, then goals of growth and increasing the market value of the equity in the firm are not all that different.

DIMENSIONS OF FINANCIAL PLANNING

It is often useful for planning purposes to think of the future as having a short run and a long run. The short run, in practice, is usually the coming 12 months. We focus our attention on financial planning over the long run, which is usually taken to be the coming two to five years. This time period is called the **planning horizon**, and it is the first dimension of the planning process that must be established.

In drawing up a financial plan, all of the individual projects and investments the firm will undertake are combined to determine the total needed investment. In effect, the smaller investment proposals of each operational unit are added up, and the sum is treated as one big project. This process is called **aggregation**. The level of aggregation is the second dimension of the planning process that needs to be determined.

Once the planning horizon and level of aggregation are established, a financial plan requires inputs in the form of alternative sets of assumptions about important variables. For example, suppose a company has two separate divisions: one for consumer products and one for gas turbine engines. The financial planning process might require each division to prepare three alternative business plans for the next three years:

1. *A worst case*: This plan would require making relatively pessimistic assumptions about the company's products and the state of the economy. This kind of disaster planning would emphasize a division's ability to withstand significant economic adversity, and

You can find growth rates at www.reuters.com and finance.yahoo.com.

planning horizon
The long-range time period on which the financial planning process focuses (usually the next two to five years).

aggregation
The process by which smaller investment proposals of each of a firm's operational units are added up and treated as one big project.

it would require details concerning cost cutting and even divestiture and liquidation. For example, on "Black Friday" in 2010, several retailers offered 40-inch to 42-inch high-definition television sets for $400 to $500. The previous year, similar TVs sold for more than $1,000. Excess inventories were blamed for the dramatic price drop. TV sales at the beginning of the year were much lower than expected due to relatively high prices, resulting in lower sales. Expecting increased demand later in the year that never materialized, TV production remained steady as the demand fell, resulting in the excess inventory.

2. *A normal case*: This plan would require making the most likely assumptions about the company and the economy.

3. *A best case*: Each division would be required to work out a case based on optimistic assumptions. It could involve new products and expansion and would then detail the financing needed to fund the expansion. Not planning for good outcomes can lead to lost profits. For example, in October 2010, Subaru's sales were up 47 percent over the same month the previous year. In fact, the company's sales for the year were up 22 percent over the previous year. While this sounds like a nice position to be in, the company could not produce enough vehicles and likely lost sales because of the unavailability of cars in some locations.

In this discussion, business activities are aggregated along divisional lines, and the planning horizon is three years. This type of planning, which considers all possible events, is particularly important for cyclical businesses (businesses with sales that are strongly affected by the overall state of the economy or business cycles).

WHAT CAN PLANNING ACCOMPLISH?

Because a company is likely to spend a lot of time examining the different scenarios that will become the basis for its financial plan, it seems reasonable to ask what the planning process will accomplish.

Examining Interactions   As we discuss in greater detail in the following pages, the financial plan must make explicit the linkages between investment proposals for the different operating activities of the firm and its available financing choices. In other words, if the firm is planning on expanding and undertaking new investments and projects, where will the financing be obtained to pay for this activity?

Exploring Options   The financial plan allows the firm to develop, analyze, and compare many different scenarios in a consistent way. Various investment and financing options can be explored, and their impact on the firm's shareholders can be evaluated. Questions concerning the firm's future lines of business and optimal financing arrangements are addressed. Options such as marketing new products or closing plants might be evaluated.

Avoiding Surprises   Financial planning should identify what may happen to the firm if different events take place. In particular, it should address what actions the firm will take if things go seriously wrong or, more generally, if assumptions made today about the future are seriously in error. As physicist Niels Bohr once observed, "Prediction is very difficult, particularly when it concerns the future." Thus, one purpose of financial planning is to avoid surprises and develop contingency plans.

For example, in August 2010, Boeing announced that the delivery of its new 787 Dreamliner would not occur until at least the first quarter of 2011, more than three years behind schedule. The reason for the delay was not lack of demand (Boeing had orders for more than 900 of the jets), but rather shortages of numerous parts and other bottlenecks.

The most recent delay arose because of problems with the supplier of the engines used to power the new jet. Several analysts noted that difficulties with other suppliers had already slowed test flights. Thus, a lack of proper planning can be a problem for even the biggest companies.

Ensuring Feasibility and Internal Consistency   Beyond a general goal of creating value, a firm will normally have many specific goals. Such goals might be couched in terms of market share, return on equity, financial leverage, and so on. At times, the linkages between different goals and different aspects of a firm's business are difficult to see. Not only does a financial plan make explicit these linkages, but it also imposes a unified structure for reconciling goals and objectives. In other words, financial planning is a way of verifying that the goals and plans made for specific areas of a firm's operations are feasible and internally consistent. Conflicting goals will often exist. To generate a coherent plan, goals and objectives will therefore have to be modified, and priorities will have to be established.

For example, one goal a firm might have is 12 percent growth in unit sales per year. Another goal might be to reduce the firm's total debt ratio from 40 to 20 percent. Are these two goals compatible? Can they be accomplished simultaneously? Maybe yes, maybe no. As we will discuss, financial planning is a way of finding out just what is possible—and, by implication, what is not possible.

Conclusion   Probably the most important result of the planning process is that it forces managers to think about goals and establish priorities. In fact, conventional business wisdom holds that financial plans don't work, but financial planning does. The future is inherently unknown. What we can do is establish the direction in which we want to travel and make some educated guesses about what we will find along the way. If we do a good job, we won't be caught off guard when the future rolls around.

Concept Questions

4.1a What are the two dimensions of the financial planning process?
4.2a Why should firms draw up financial plans?

⅀ 4.2   Financial Planning Models: A First Look

Just as companies differ in size and products, the financial planning process will differ from firm to firm. In this section, we discuss some common elements in financial plans and develop a basic model to illustrate these elements. What follows is just a quick overview; later sections will take up the various topics in more detail.

A FINANCIAL PLANNING MODEL: THE INGREDIENTS

Most financial planning models require the user to specify some assumptions about the future. Based on those assumptions, the model generates predicted values for many other variables. Models can vary quite a bit in complexity, but almost all have the elements we discuss next.

Sales Forecast   Almost all financial plans require an externally supplied sales forecast. In our models that follow, for example, the sales forecast will be the "driver," meaning that the user of the planning model will supply this value, and most other values will be calculated based on it. This arrangement is common for many types of business; planning will focus on projected future sales and the assets and financing needed to support those sales.

Frequently, the sales forecast will be given as the growth rate in sales rather than as an explicit sales figure. These two approaches are essentially the same because we can calculate projected sales once we know the growth rate. Perfect sales forecasts are not possible, of course, because sales depend on the uncertain future state of the economy. To help a firm come up with its projections, some businesses specialize in macroeconomic and industry projections.

As we discussed previously, we frequently will be interested in evaluating alternative scenarios, so it isn't necessarily crucial that the sales forecast be accurate. In such cases, our goal is to examine the interplay between investment and financing needs at different possible sales levels, not to pinpoint what we expect to happen.

Pro Forma Statements   A financial plan will have a forecast balance sheet, income statement, and statement of cash flows. These are called *pro forma statements*, or *pro formas* for short. The phrase *pro forma* literally means "as a matter of form." In our case, this means the financial statements are the form we use to summarize the different events projected for the future. At a minimum, a financial planning model will generate these statements based on projections of key items such as sales.

In the planning models we will describe, the pro formas are the output from the financial planning model. The user will supply a sales figure, and the model will generate the resulting income statement and balance sheet.

Spreadsheets to use for pro forma statements can be obtained at www.jaxworks.com.

Asset Requirements   The plan will describe projected capital spending. At a minimum, the projected balance sheet will contain changes in total fixed assets and net working capital. These changes are effectively the firm's total capital budget. Proposed capital spending in different areas must thus be reconciled with the overall increases contained in the long-range plan.

Financial Requirements   The plan will include a section about the necessary financing arrangements. This part of the plan should discuss dividend policy and debt policy. Sometimes firms will expect to raise cash by selling new shares of stock or by borrowing. In this case, the plan will have to consider what kinds of securities have to be sold and what methods of issuance are most appropriate. These are subjects we consider in Part 6 of our book, where we discuss long-term financing, capital structure, and dividend policy.

The Plug   After the firm has a sales forecast and an estimate of the required spending on assets, some amount of new financing will often be necessary because projected total assets will exceed projected total liabilities and equity. In other words, the balance sheet will no longer balance.

Because new financing may be necessary to cover all of the projected capital spending, a financial "plug" variable must be selected. The plug is the designated source or sources of external financing needed to deal with any shortfall (or surplus) in financing and thereby bring the balance sheet into balance.

For example, a firm with a great number of investment opportunities and limited cash flow may have to raise new equity. Other firms with few growth opportunities and ample cash flow will have a surplus and thus might pay an extra dividend. In the first case, external equity is the plug variable. In the second, the dividend is used.

Economic Assumptions   The plan will have to state explicitly the economic environment in which the firm expects to reside over the life of the plan. Among the more important economic assumptions that will have to be made are the level of interest rates and the firm's tax rate.

A SIMPLE FINANCIAL PLANNING MODEL

We can begin our discussion of long-term planning models with a relatively simple example. The Computerfield Corporation's financial statements from the most recent year are as follows:

COMPUTERFIELD CORPORATION Financial Statements					
Income Statement			**Balance Sheet**		
Sales	$1,000	Assets	$500	Debt	$250
Costs	800			Equity	250
Net income	$ 200	Total	$500	Total	$500

Unless otherwise stated, the financial planners at Computerfield assume that all variables are tied directly to sales and current relationships are optimal. This means that all items will grow at exactly the same rate as sales. This is obviously oversimplified; we use this assumption only to make a point.

Suppose sales increase by 20 percent, rising from $1,000 to $1,200. Planners would then also forecast a 20 percent increase in costs, from $800 to $800 × 1.2 = $960. The pro forma income statement would thus be:

Pro Forma Income Statement	
Sales	$1,200
Costs	960
Net income	$ 240

The assumption that all variables will grow by 20 percent lets us easily construct the pro forma balance sheet as well:

Pro Forma Balance Sheet			
Assets	$600 (+100)	Debt	$ 300 (+ 50)
		Equity	300 (+ 50)
Total	$600 (+100)	Total	$600 (+100)

Planware provides insight into cash flow forecasting (www.planware.org).

Notice that we have simply increased every item by 20 percent. The numbers in parentheses are the dollar changes for the different items.

Now we have to reconcile these two pro formas. How, for example, can net income be equal to $240 and equity increase by only $50? The answer is that Computerfield must have paid out the difference of $240 − 50 = $190, possibly as a cash dividend. In this case, dividends are the plug variable.

Suppose Computerfield does not pay out the $190. In this case, the addition to retained earnings is the full $240. Computerfield's equity will thus grow to $250 (the starting amount) plus $240 (net income), or $490, and debt must be retired to keep total assets equal to $600.

With $600 in total assets and $490 in equity, debt will have to be $600 − 490 = $110. Because we started with $250 in debt, Computerfield will have to retire $250 − 110 = $140 in debt. The resulting pro forma balance sheet would look like this:

Pro Forma Balance Sheet			
Assets	$600 (+100)	Debt	$110 (−140)
		Equity	490 (+240)
Total	$600 (+100)	Total	$600 (+100)

In this case, debt is the plug variable used to balance projected total assets and liabilities.

This example shows the interaction between sales growth and financial policy. As sales increase, so do total assets. This occurs because the firm must invest in net working capital and fixed assets to support higher sales levels. Because assets are growing, total liabilities and equity (the right side of the balance sheet) will grow as well.

The thing to notice from our simple example is that the way the liabilities and owners' equity change depends on the firm's financing policy and its dividend policy. The growth in assets requires that the firm decide on how to finance that growth. This is strictly a managerial decision. Note that in our example, the firm needed no outside funds. This won't usually be the case, so we explore a more detailed situation in the next section.

Concept Questions

4.2a What are the basic components of a financial plan?

4.2b Why is it necessary to designate a plug in a financial planning model?

The Percentage of Sales Approach

4.3

In the previous section, we described a simple planning model in which every item increased at the same rate as sales. This may be a reasonable assumption for some elements. For others, such as long-term borrowing, it probably is not: The amount of long-term borrowing is something set by management, and it does not necessarily relate directly to the level of sales.

In this section, we describe an extended version of our simple model. The basic idea is to separate the income statement and balance sheet accounts into two groups—those that vary directly with sales and those that do not. Given a sales forecast, we will then be able to calculate how much financing the firm will need to support the predicted sales level.

The financial planning model we describe next is based on the **percentage of sales approach**. Our goal here is to develop a quick and practical way of generating pro forma statements. We defer discussion of some "bells and whistles" to a later section.

percentage of sales approach
A financial planning method in which accounts are varied depending on a firm's predicted sales level.

THE INCOME STATEMENT

We start out with the most recent income statement for the Rosengarten Corporation, as shown in Table 4.1. Notice we have still simplified things by including costs, depreciation, and interest in a single cost figure.

Rosengarten has projected a 25 percent increase in sales for the coming year, so we are anticipating sales of $1,000 × 1.25 = $1,250. To generate a pro forma income statement, we assume that total costs will continue to run at $800/1,000 = 80% of sales. With this assumption, Rosengarten's pro forma income statement is shown in Table 4.2. The effect here

TABLE 4.1

Rosengarten Corporation
Income Statement

ROSENGARTEN CORPORATION Income Statement		
Sales		$1,000
Costs		800
Taxable income		$ 200
Taxes (34%)		68
Net income		$ 132
Dividends	$44	
Addition to retained earnings	88	

TABLE 4.2

Rosengarten Corporation
Pro Forma Income
Statement

ROSENGARTEN CORPORATION Pro Forma Income Statement	
Sales (projected)	$1,250
Costs (80% of sales)	1,000
Taxable income	$ 250
Taxes (34%)	85
Net income	$ 165

of assuming that costs are a constant percentage of sales is to assume that the profit margin is constant. To check this, notice that the profit margin was $132/1,000 = 13.2\%$. In our pro forma, the profit margin is $165/1,250 = 13.2\%$, so it is unchanged.

Next, we need to project the dividend payment. This amount is up to Rosengarten's management. We will assume Rosengarten has a policy of paying out a constant fraction of net income in the form of a cash dividend. For the most recent year, the **dividend payout ratio** was this:

dividend payout ratio
The amount of cash paid out to shareholders divided by net income.

$$\text{Dividend payout ratio} = \text{Cash dividends/Net income} \qquad [4.1]$$
$$= \$44/132 = 33\ 1/3\%$$

We can also calculate the ratio of the addition to retained earnings to net income:

$$\text{Addition to retained earnings/Net income} = \$88/132 = 66\ 2/3\%$$

retention ratio
The addition to retained earnings divided by net income. Also called the *plowback ratio*.

This ratio is called the **retention ratio** or **plowback ratio**, and it is equal to 1 minus the dividend payout ratio because everything not paid out is retained. Assuming that the payout ratio is constant, here are the projected dividends and addition to retained earnings:

Projected dividends paid to shareholders $= \$165 \times 1/3 = \$\ 55$
Projected addition to retained earnings $\ \ = \$165 \times 2/3 = \underline{\ \ 110}$
$\underline{\underline{\$165}}$

THE BALANCE SHEET

To generate a pro forma balance sheet, we start with the most recent statement, as shown in Table 4.3.

On our balance sheet, we assume that some items vary directly with sales and others do not. For items that vary with sales, we express each as a percentage of sales for the year just completed. When an item does not vary directly with sales, we write "n/a" for "not applicable."

TABLE 4.3   Rosengarten Corporation Balance Sheet

ROSENGARTEN CORPORATION Balance Sheet					
Assets			**Liabilities and Owners' Equity**		
	$	**Percentage of Sales**		**$**	**Percentage of Sales**
Current assets			Current liabilities		
Cash	$ 160	16%	Accounts payable	$ 300	30%
Accounts receivable	440	44	Notes payable	100	n/a
Inventory	600	60	Total	$ 400	n/a
Total	$1,200	120	Long-term debt	$ 800	n/a
Fixed assets			Owners' equity		
Net plant and equipment	$1,800	180	Common stock and paid-in		
			surplus	$ 800	n/a
			Retained earnings	1,000	n/a
			Total	$1,800	n/a
Total assets	$3,000	300%	Total liabilities and owners' equity	$3,000	n/a

For example, on the asset side, inventory is equal to 60 percent of sales (= $600/1,000) for the year just ended. We assume this percentage applies to the coming year, so for each $1 increase in sales, inventory will rise by $.60. More generally, the ratio of total assets to sales for the year just ended is $3,000/1,000 = 3, or 300%.

This ratio of total assets to sales is sometimes called the **capital intensity ratio**. It tells us the amount of assets needed to generate $1 in sales; so the higher the ratio is, the more capital-intensive is the firm. Notice also that this ratio is just the reciprocal of the total asset turnover ratio we defined in the last chapter.

capital intensity ratio
A firm's total assets divided by its sales, or the amount of assets needed to generate $1 in sales.

For Rosengarten, assuming that this ratio is constant, it takes $3 in total assets to generate $1 in sales (apparently Rosengarten is in a relatively capital-intensive business). Therefore, if sales are to increase by $100, Rosengarten will have to increase total assets by three times this amount, or $300.

On the liability side of the balance sheet, we show accounts payable varying with sales. The reason is that we expect to place more orders with our suppliers as sales volume increases, so payables will change "spontaneously" with sales. Notes payable, on the other hand, represent short-term debt such as bank borrowing. This item will not vary unless we take specific actions to change the amount, so we mark it as "n/a."

Similarly, we use "n/a" for long-term debt because it won't automatically change with sales. The same is true for common stock and paid-in surplus. The last item on the right side, retained earnings, will vary with sales, but it won't be a simple percentage of sales. Instead, we will explicitly calculate the change in retained earnings based on our projected net income and dividends.

We can now construct a partial pro forma balance sheet for Rosengarten. We do this by using the percentages we have just calculated wherever possible to calculate the projected amounts. For example, net fixed assets are 180 percent of sales; so, with a new sales level of $1,250, the net fixed asset amount will be 1.80 × $1,250 = $2,250, representing an increase of $2,250 − 1,800 = $450 in plant and equipment. It is important to note that for

TABLE 4.4

ROSENGARTEN CORPORATION **Partial Pro Forma Balance Sheet**					
Assets			**Liabilities and Owners' Equity**		
	Projected	**Change from Previous Year**		**Projected**	**Change from Previous Year**
Current assets			Current liabilities		
Cash	$ 200	$ 40	Accounts payable	$ 375	$ 75
Accounts receivable	550	110	Notes payable	100	0
Inventory	750	150	Total	$ 475	$ 75
Total	$1,500	$300	Long-term debt	$ 800	$ 0
Fixed assets					
Net plant and equipment	$2,250	$450	Owners' equity		
			Common stock and paid-in surplus	$ 800	$ 0
			Retained earnings	1,110	110
			Total	$1,910	$110
Total assets	$3,750	$750	Total liabilities and owners' equity	$3,185	$185
			External financing needed	$ 565	$565

items that don't vary directly with sales, we initially assume no change and simply write in the original amounts. The result is shown in Table 4.4. Notice that the change in retained earnings is equal to the $110 addition to retained earnings we calculated earlier.

Inspecting our pro forma balance sheet, we notice that assets are projected to increase by $750. However, without additional financing, liabilities and equity will increase by only $185, leaving a shortfall of $750 − 185 = $565. We label this amount *external financing needed* (EFN).

A PARTICULAR SCENARIO

Our financial planning model now reminds us of one of those good news–bad news jokes. The good news is we're projecting a 25 percent increase in sales. The bad news is that this isn't going to happen unless Rosengarten can somehow raise $565 in new financing.

This is a good example of how the planning process can point out problems and potential conflicts. If, for example, Rosengarten has a goal of not borrowing any additional funds and not selling any new equity, then a 25 percent increase in sales is probably not feasible.

If we take the need for $565 in new financing as given, we know that Rosengarten has three possible sources: short-term borrowing, long-term borrowing, and new equity. The choice of some combination among these three is up to management; we will illustrate only one of the many possibilities.

Suppose Rosengarten decides to borrow the needed funds. In this case, the firm might choose to borrow some over the short term and some over the long term. For example, current assets increased by $300, whereas current liabilities rose by only $75. Rosengarten could borrow $300 − 75 = $225 in short-term notes payable and leave total net working capital unchanged. With $565 needed, the remaining $565 − 225 = $340 would have to come from long-term debt. Table 4.5 shows the completed pro forma balance sheet for Rosengarten.

TABLE 4.5

ROSENGARTEN CORPORATION Pro Forma Balance Sheet					
Assets			**Liabilities and Owners' Equity**		
	Projected	**Change from Previous Year**		**Projected**	**Change from Previous Year**
Current assets			Current liabilities		
Cash	$ 200	$ 40	Accounts payable	$ 375	$ 75
Accounts receivable	550	110	Notes payable	325	225
Inventory	750	150	Total	$ 700	$300
Total	$1,500	$300	Long-term debt	$1,140	$340
Fixed assets					
Net plant and equipment	$2,250	$450	Owners' equity		
			Common stock and paid-in surplus	$ 800	$ 0
			Retained earnings	1,110	110
			Total	$1,910	$110
Total assets	$3,750	$750	Total liabilities and owners' equity	$3,750	$750

We have used a combination of short- and long-term debt as the plug here, but we emphasize that this is just one possible strategy; it is not necessarily the best one by any means. There are many other scenarios we could (and should) investigate. The various ratios we discussed in Chapter 3 come in handy here. For example, with the scenario we have just examined, we would surely want to examine the current ratio and the total debt ratio to see if we were comfortable with the new projected debt levels.

Now that we have finished our balance sheet, we have all of the projected sources and uses of cash. We could finish off our pro formas by drawing up the projected statement of cash flows along the lines discussed in Chapter 3. We will leave this as an exercise and instead investigate an important alternative scenario.

AN ALTERNATIVE SCENARIO

The assumption that assets are a fixed percentage of sales is convenient, but it may not be suitable in many cases. In particular, note that we effectively assumed that Rosengarten was using its fixed assets at 100 percent of capacity because any increase in sales led to an increase in fixed assets. For most businesses, there would be some slack or excess capacity, and production could be increased by perhaps running an extra shift. According to the Federal Reserve, the overall capacity utilization for U.S. manufacturing companies in May 2011 was 74.5 percent, up from a low of 64.4 percent in June 2009.

For example, in 2007, Toyota Motor announced that it would build its seventh manufacturing plant in North America in Mississippi. At about the same time, Ford announced it would close up to 12 plants over the next five years, and General Motors announced that it would close up to 13 plants over the same period. Evidently, both Ford and General Motors had excess capacity, whereas Toyota did not.

In another example, in early 2004, Simmons announced it was closing its mattress factory in Ohio. The company stated it would increase mattress production at other plants to compensate for the closing. Apparently, Simmons had significant excess capacity in its production facilities.

If we assume that Rosengarten is operating at only 70 percent of capacity, then the need for external funds will be quite different. When we say "70 percent of capacity," we mean that the current sales level is 70 percent of the full-capacity sales level:

Current sales = $1,000 = .70 × Full-capacity sales
Full-capacity sales = $1,000/.70 = $1,429

This tells us that sales could increase by almost 43 percent—from $1,000 to $1,429—before any new fixed assets would be needed.

In our previous scenario, we assumed it would be necessary to add $450 in net fixed assets. In the current scenario, no spending on net fixed assets is needed because sales are projected to rise only to $1,250, which is substantially less than the $1,429 full-capacity level.

As a result, our original estimate of $565 in external funds needed is too high. We estimated that $450 in net new fixed assets would be needed. Instead, no spending on new net fixed assets is necessary. Thus, if we are currently operating at 70 percent capacity, we need only $565 − 450 = $115 in external funds. The excess capacity thus makes a considerable difference in our projections.

EXAMPLE 4.1   EFN and Capacity Usage

Suppose Rosengarten is operating at 90 percent capacity. What would sales be at full capacity? What is the capital intensity ratio at full capacity? What is EFN in this case?

Full-capacity sales would be $1,000/.90 = $1,111. From Table 4.3, we know that fixed assets are $1,800. At full capacity, the ratio of fixed assets to sales is this:

Fixed assets/Full-capacity sales = $1,800/1,111 = 1.62

So, Rosengarten needs $1.62 in fixed assets for every $1 in sales once it reaches full capacity. At the projected sales level of $1,250, then, it needs $1,250 × 1.62 = $2,025 in fixed assets. Compared to the $2,250 we originally projected, this is $225 less, so EFN is $565 − 225 = $340.

Current assets would still be $1,500, so total assets would be $1,500 + 2,025 = $3,525. The capital intensity ratio would thus be $3,525/1,250 = 2.82, which is less than our original value of 3 because of the excess capacity.

These alternative scenarios illustrate that it is inappropriate to blindly manipulate financial statement information in the planning process. The results depend critically on the assumptions made about the relationships between sales and asset needs. We return to this point a little later.

One thing should be clear by now. Projected growth rates play an important role in the planning process. They are also important to outside analysts and potential investors. Our nearby *Work the Web* box shows you how to obtain growth rate estimates for real companies.

Concept Questions

4.3a What is the basic idea behind the percentage of sales approach?
4.3b Unless it is modified, what does the percentage of sales approach assume about fixed asset capacity usage?

WORK THE WEB

Calculating company growth rates can involve detailed research, and a major part of a stock analyst's job is to estimate them. One place to find earnings and sales growth rates on the Web is Yahoo! Finance at finance.yahoo.com. We pulled up a quote for 3M Corporation and followed the "Analyst Estimates" link. Here is an abbreviated look at the results:

Revenue Est	Current Qtr. Mar 11	Next Qtr. Jun 11	Current Year Dec 11	Next Year Dec 12
Avg. Estimate	6.95B	7.45B	29.35B	31.34B
No. of Analysts	5	5	13	12
Low Estimate	6.74B	7.32B	28.69B	30.44B
High Estimate	7.11B	7.56B	29.68B	32.97B
Year Ago Sales	6.35B	6.73B	26.66B	29.35B
Sales Growth (year/est)	9.50%	10.70%	10.10%	6.80%

As shown, analysts expect, on average, revenue (sales) of $29.35 billion in 2011, growing to $31.34 billion in 2012, an increase of 6.8 percent. We also have the following table comparing 3M to some benchmarks:

Growth Est	MMM	Industry	Sector	S&P 500
Current Qtr.	2.90%	7.20%	24.80%	67.30%
Next Qtr.	5.20%	20.80%	68.40%	43.00%
This Year	7.00%	17.60%	35.50%	35.00%
Next Year	11.40%	14.90%	14.70%	13.40%
Past 5 Years (per annum)	4.76%	N/A	N/A	N/A
Next 5 Years (per annum)	11.93%	14.17%	15.02%	10.51%
Price/Earnings (avg. for comparison categories)	14.39	15.94	15.29	13.70
PEG Ratio (avg. for comparison categories)	1.21	1.40	0.86	0.32

As you can see, the estimated earnings growth rate for 3M is lower than the industry growth rate over the next five years. What does this mean for 3M stock? We'll get to that in a later chapter.

Questions
1. One of the things shown here is the projected sales growth for 3M during 2011 at the time this was captured from finance.yahoo.com. How does the current sales projection or the actual sales number differ from this projection? Can you think of any reasons for the difference?
2. On the same Web page, you can find the earnings history for 3M. How close have analysts been to estimating 3M earnings? In other words, what has the "surprise" been in 3M earnings?

⚡ 4.4 External Financing and Growth

External financing needed and growth are obviously related. All other things staying the same, the higher the rate of growth in sales or assets, the greater will be the need for external financing. In the previous section, we took a growth rate as given, and then we determined the amount of external financing needed to support that growth. In this section, we turn things around a bit. We will take the firm's financial policy as given and then examine the relationship between that financial policy and the firm's ability to finance new investments and thereby grow.

Once again, we emphasize that we are focusing on growth not because growth is an appropriate goal; instead, for our purposes, growth is simply a convenient means of examining the interactions between investment and financing decisions. In effect, we assume that the use of growth as a basis for planning is just a reflection of the very high level of aggregation used in the planning process.

EFN AND GROWTH

The first thing we need to do is establish the relationship between EFN and growth. To do this, we introduce the simplified income statement and balance sheet for the Hoffman Company in Table 4.6. Notice that we have simplified the balance sheet by combining short-term and long-term debt into a single total debt figure. Effectively, we are assuming that none of the current liabilities varies spontaneously with sales. This assumption isn't as restrictive as it sounds. If any current liabilities (such as accounts payable) vary with sales, we can assume that any such accounts have been netted out in current assets. Also, we continue to combine depreciation, interest, and costs on the income statement.

Suppose the Hoffman Company is forecasting next year's sales level at $600, a $100 increase. Notice that the percentage increase in sales is $100/500 = 20%. Using the percentage of sales approach and the figures in Table 4.6, we can prepare a pro forma income statement and balance sheet as in Table 4.7. As Table 4.7 illustrates, at a 20 percent

TABLE 4.6

HOFFMAN COMPANY Income Statement and Balance Sheet					
Income Statement					
Sales		$500			
Costs		400			
Taxable income		$100			
Taxes (34%)		34			
Net income		$ 66			
Dividends	$22				
Addition to retained earnings	44				
Balance Sheet					
Assets			**Liabilities and Owners' Equity**		
	$	**Percentage of Sales**		**$**	**Percentage of Sales**
Current assets	$200	40%	Total debt	$250	n/a
Net fixed assets	300	60	Owners' equity	250	n/a
Total assets	$500	100%	Total liabilities and owners' equity	$500	n/a

TABLE 4.7

HOFFMAN COMPANY Pro Forma Income Statement and Balance Sheet					
Income Statement					
Sales (projected)			$600.0		
Costs (80% of sales)			480.0		
Taxable income			$120.0		
Taxes (34%)			40.8		
Net income			$ 79.2		
Dividends		$26.4			
Addition to retained earnings		52.8			
Balance Sheet					
Assets			**Liabilities and Owners' Equity**		
	$	Percentage of Sales		$	Percentage of Sales
Current assets	$240.0	40%	Total debt	$250.0	n/a
Net fixed assets	360.0	60	Owners' equity	302.8	n/a
Total assets	$600.0	100%	Total liabilities and owners' equity	$552.8	n/a
			External financing needed	$ 47.2	n/a

growth rate, Hoffman needs $100 in new assets (assuming full capacity). The projected addition to retained earnings is $52.8, so the external financing needed (EFN) is $100 − 52.8 = $47.2.

Notice that the debt–equity ratio for Hoffman was originally (from Table 4.6) equal to $250/250 = 1.0. We will assume that the Hoffman Company does not wish to sell new equity. In this case, the $47.2 in EFN will have to be borrowed. What will the new debt–equity ratio be? From Table 4.7, we know that total owners' equity is projected at $302.8. The new total debt will be the original $250 plus $47.2 in new borrowing, or $297.2 total. The debt–equity ratio thus falls slightly from 1.0 to $297.2/302.8 = .98.

Table 4.8 shows EFN for several different growth rates. The projected addition to retained earnings and the projected debt–equity ratio for each scenario are also given (you should probably calculate a few of these for practice). In determining the debt–equity ratios, we assumed that any needed funds were borrowed, and we also assumed any surplus funds were used to pay off debt. Thus, for the zero growth case, debt falls by $44, from $250 to $206. In Table 4.8, notice that the increase in assets required is simply equal to the original assets of $500 multiplied by the growth rate. Similarly, the addition to retained earnings is equal to the original $44 plus $44 times the growth rate.

Projected Sales Growth	Increase in Assets Required	Addition to Retained Earnings	External Financing Needed, EFN	Projected Debt–Equity Ratio
0%	$ 0	$44.0	−$44.0	.70
5	25	46.2	−21.2	.77
10	50	48.4	1.6	.84
15	75	50.6	24.4	.91
20	100	52.8	47.2	.98
25	125	55.0	70.0	1.05

TABLE 4.8

Growth and Projected EFN for the Hoffman Company

FIGURE 4.1

Growth and Related
Financing Needed for the
Hoffman Company

Table 4.8 shows that for relatively low growth rates, Hoffman will run a surplus, and its debt–equity ratio will decline. Once the growth rate increases to about 10 percent, however, the surplus becomes a deficit. Furthermore, as the growth rate exceeds approximately 20 percent, the debt–equity ratio passes its original value of 1.0.

Figure 4.1 illustrates the connection between growth in sales and external financing needed in more detail by plotting asset needs and additions to retained earnings from Table 4.8 against the growth rates. As shown, the need for new assets grows at a much faster rate than the addition to retained earnings, so the internal financing provided by the addition to retained earnings rapidly disappears.

As this discussion shows, whether a firm runs a cash surplus or deficit depends on growth. Microsoft is a good example. Its revenue growth in the 1990s was amazing, averaging well over 30 percent per year for the decade. Growth slowed down noticeably over the 2000–2010 period; nonetheless, Microsoft's combination of growth and substantial profit margins led to enormous cash surpluses. In part because Microsoft pays a relatively small dividend, the cash really piled up; in 2011, Microsoft's cash horde exceeded $44 billion.

FINANCIAL POLICY AND GROWTH

Based on our preceding discussion, we see that there is a direct link between growth and external financing. In this section, we discuss two growth rates that are particularly useful in long-range planning.

The Internal Growth Rate   The first growth rate of interest is the maximum growth rate that can be achieved with no external financing of any kind. We will call this the **internal growth rate** because this is the rate the firm can maintain with internal financing only. In Figure 4.1, this internal growth rate is represented by the point where the two lines cross. At this point, the required increase in assets is exactly equal to the addition to retained

internal growth rate
The maximum growth rate
a firm can achieve without
external financing of any
kind.

earnings, and EFN is therefore zero. We have seen that this happens when the growth rate is slightly less than 10 percent. With a little algebra (see Problem 31 at the end of the chapter), we can define this growth rate more precisely:

$$\text{Internal growth rate} = \frac{\text{ROA} \times b}{1 - \text{ROA} \times b} \qquad \text{[4.2]}$$

Here, ROA is the return on assets we discussed in Chapter 3, and b is the plowback, or retention, ratio defined earlier in this chapter.

For the Hoffman Company, net income was $66 and total assets were $500. ROA is thus $66/500 = 13.2\%$. Of the $66 net income, $44 was retained, so the plowback ratio, b, is $44/66 = 2/3$. With these numbers, we can calculate the internal growth rate:

$$\begin{aligned}
\text{Internal growth rate} &= \frac{\text{ROA} \times b}{1 - \text{ROA} \times b} \\
&= \frac{.132 \times (2/3)}{1 - .132 \times (2/3)} \\
&= 9.65\%
\end{aligned}$$

Thus, the Hoffman Company can expand at a maximum rate of 9.65 percent per year without external financing.

The Sustainable Growth Rate   We have seen that if the Hoffman Company wishes to grow more rapidly than at a rate of 9.65 percent per year, external financing must be arranged. The second growth rate of interest is the maximum growth rate a firm can achieve with no external *equity* financing while it maintains a constant debt–equity ratio. This rate is commonly called the **sustainable growth rate** because it is the maximum rate of growth a firm can maintain without increasing its financial leverage.

There are various reasons why a firm might wish to avoid equity sales. For example, as we discuss in Chapter 15, new equity sales can be expensive. Alternatively, the current owners may not wish to bring in new owners or contribute additional equity. Why a firm might view a particular debt–equity ratio as optimal is discussed in Chapters 14 and 16; for now, we will take it as given.

Based on Table 4.8, the sustainable growth rate for Hoffman is approximately 20 percent because the debt–equity ratio is near 1.0 at that growth rate. The precise value can be calculated (see Problem 31 at the end of the chapter):

$$\text{Sustainable growth rate} = \frac{\text{ROE} \times b}{1 - \text{ROE} \times b} \qquad \text{[4.3]}$$

This is identical to the internal growth rate except that ROE, return on equity, is used instead of ROA.

For the Hoffman Company, net income was $66 and total equity was $250; ROE is thus $66/250 = 26.4$ percent. The plowback ratio, b, is still 2/3, so we can calculate the sustainable growth rate as follows:

$$\begin{aligned}
\text{Sustainable growth rate} &= \frac{\text{ROE} \times b}{1 - \text{ROE} \times b} \\
&= \frac{.264 \times (2/3)}{1 - .264 \times (2/3)} \\
&= 21.36\%
\end{aligned}$$

Thus, the Hoffman Company can expand at a maximum rate of 21.36 percent per year without external equity financing.

sustainable growth rate
The maximum growth rate a firm can achieve without external equity financing while maintaining a constant debt–equity ratio.

EXAMPLE 4.2	Sustainable Growth

Suppose Hoffman grows at exactly the sustainable growth rate of 21.36 percent. What will the pro forma statements look like?

At a 21.36 percent growth rate, sales will rise from $500 to $606.8. The pro forma income statement will look like this:

HOFFMAN COMPANY Pro Forma Income Statement		
Sales (projected)		$606.8
Costs (80% of sales)		485.4
Taxable income		$121.4
Taxes (34%)		41.3
Net income		$ 80.1
Dividends	$26.7	
Addition to retained earnings	53.4	

We construct the balance sheet just as we did before. Notice, in this case, that owners' equity will rise from $250 to $303.4 because the addition to retained earnings is $53.4.

HOFFMAN COMPANY Pro Forma Balance Sheet					
Assets			**Liabilities and Owners' Equity**		
	$	Percentage of Sales		$	Percentage of Sales
Current assets	$242.7	40%	Total debt	$250.0	n/a
Net fixed assets	364.1	60	Owners' equity	303.4	n/a
Total assets	$606.8	100%	Total liabilities and owners' equity	$553.4	n/a
			External financing needed	$ 53.4	n/a

As illustrated, EFN is $53.4. If Hoffman borrows this amount, then total debt will rise to $303.4, and the debt–equity ratio will be exactly 1.0, which verifies our earlier calculation. At any other growth rate, something would have to change.

Determinants of Growth In the last chapter, we saw that the return on equity, ROE, could be decomposed into its various components using the DuPont identity. Because ROE appears so prominently in the determination of the sustainable growth rate, it is obvious that the factors important in determining ROE are also important determinants of growth.

From Chapter 3, we know that ROE can be written as the product of three factors:

$$\text{ROE} = \text{Profit margin} \times \text{Total asset turnover} \times \text{Equity multiplier}$$

If we examine our expression for the sustainable growth rate, we see that anything that increases ROE will increase the sustainable growth rate by making the top bigger and the bottom smaller. Increasing the plowback ratio will have the same effect.

Putting it all together, what we have is that a firm's ability to sustain growth depends explicitly on the following four factors:

1. *Profit margin*: An increase in profit margin will increase the firm's ability to generate funds internally and thereby increase its sustainable growth.

2. *Dividend policy*: A decrease in the percentage of net income paid out as dividends will increase the retention ratio. This increases internally generated equity and thus increases sustainable growth.

3. *Financial policy*: An increase in the debt–equity ratio increases the firm's financial leverage. Because this makes additional debt financing available, it increases the sustainable growth rate.

4. *Total asset turnover*: An increase in the firm's total asset turnover increases the sales generated for each dollar in assets. This decreases the firm's need for new assets as sales grow and thereby increases the sustainable growth rate. Notice that increasing total asset turnover is the same thing as decreasing capital intensity.

The sustainable growth rate is a very useful planning number. What it illustrates is the explicit relationship between the firm's four major areas of concern: its operating efficiency as measured by profit margin, its asset use efficiency as measured by total asset turnover, its dividend policy as measured by the retention ratio, and its financial policy as measured by the debt–equity ratio.

Given values for all four of these, there is only one growth rate that can be achieved. This is an important point, so it bears restating:

> **If a firm does not wish to sell new equity and its profit margin, dividend policy, financial policy, and total asset turnover (or capital intensity) are all fixed, then there is only one possible growth rate.**

As we described early in this chapter, one of the primary benefits of financial planning is that it ensures internal consistency among the firm's various goals. The concept of the sustainable growth rate captures this element nicely. Also, we now see how a financial planning model can be used to test the feasibility of a planned growth rate. If sales are to grow at a rate higher than the sustainable growth rate, the firm must increase profit margins, increase total asset turnover, increase financial leverage, increase earnings retention, or sell new shares.

The two growth rates, internal and sustainable, are summarized in Table 4.9.

TABLE 4.9

Summary of Internal and Sustainable Growth Rates

I.	**Internal Growth Rate**

$$\text{Internal growth rate} = \frac{\text{ROA} \times b}{1 - \text{ROA} \times b}$$

where

    ROA = Return on assets = Net income/Total assets

        b = Plowback (retention) ratio

          = Addition to retained earnings/Net income

The internal growth rate is the maximum growth rate that can be achieved with no external financing of any kind.

II.	**Sustainable Growth Rate**

$$\text{Sustainable growth rate} = \frac{\text{ROE} \times b}{1 - \text{ROE} \times b}$$

where

    ROE = Return on equity = Net income/Total equity

        b = Plowback (retention) ratio

          = Addition to retained earnings/Net income

The sustainable growth rate is the maximum growth rate that can be achieved with no external equity financing while maintaining a constant debt–equity ratio.

IN THEIR OWN WORDS ...

Robert C. Higgins on Sustainable Growth

Most financial officers know intuitively that it takes money to make money. Rapid sales growth requires increased assets in the form of accounts receivable, inventory, and fixed plant, which, in turn, require money to pay for assets. They also know that if their company does not have the money when needed, it can literally "grow broke." The sustainable growth equation states these intuitive truths explicitly.

Sustainable growth is often used by bankers and other external analysts to assess a company's creditworthiness. They are aided in this exercise by several sophisticated computer software packages that provide detailed analyses of the company's past financial performance, including its annual sustainable growth rate.

Bankers use this information in several ways. Quick comparison of a company's actual growth rate to its sustainable rate tells the banker what issues will be at the top of management's financial agenda. If actual growth consistently exceeds sustainable growth, management's problem will be where to get the cash to finance growth. The banker thus can anticipate interest in loan products. Conversely, if sustainable growth consistently exceeds actual, the banker had best be prepared to talk about investment products, because management's problem will be what to do with all the cash that keeps piling up in the till.

Bankers also find the sustainable growth equation useful for explaining to financially inexperienced small business owners and overly optimistic entrepreneurs that, for the long-run viability of their business, it is necessary to keep growth and profitability in proper balance.

Finally, comparison of actual to sustainable growth rates helps a banker understand why a loan applicant needs money and for how long the need might continue. In one instance, a loan applicant requested $100,000 to pay off several insistent suppliers and promised to repay in a few months when he collected some accounts receivable that were coming due. A sustainable growth analysis revealed that the firm had been growing at four to six times its sustainable growth rate and that this pattern was likely to continue in the foreseeable future. This alerted the banker to the fact that impatient suppliers were only a symptom of the much more fundamental disease of overly rapid growth, and that a $100,000 loan would likely prove to be only the down payment on a much larger, multiyear commitment.

Robert C. Higgins is the Marguerite Reimers Professor of Finance at the Foster School of Business at the University of Washington. He pioneered the use of sustainable growth as a tool for financial analysis.

A NOTE ABOUT SUSTAINABLE GROWTH RATE CALCULATIONS

Very commonly, the sustainable growth rate is calculated using just the numerator in our expression, ROE $\times$ b. This causes some confusion, which we can clear up here. The issue has to do with how ROE is computed. Recall that ROE is calculated as net income divided by total equity. If total equity is taken from an ending balance sheet (as we have done consistently, and is commonly done in practice), then our formula is the right one. However, if total equity is from the beginning of the period, then the simpler formula is the correct one.

In principle, you'll get exactly the same sustainable growth rate regardless of which way you calculate it (as long as you match up the ROE calculation with the right formula). In reality, you may see some differences because of accounting-related complications. By the way, if you use the average of beginning and ending equity (as some advocate), yet another formula is needed. Also, all of our comments here apply to the internal growth rate as well.

A simple example is useful to illustrate these points. Suppose a firm has a net income of $20 and a retention ratio of .60. Beginning assets are $100. The debt–equity ratio is .25, so beginning equity is $80.

If we use beginning numbers, we get the following:

ROE = $20/80 = .25 = 25%

Sustainable growth = .60 $\times$ .25 = .15 = 15%

For the same firm, ending equity is $80 + .60 $\times$ $20 = $92. So, we can calculate this:

ROE = $20/92 = .2174 = 21.74%

Sustainable growth = .60 $\times$ .2174/(1 − .60 $\times$ .2174) = .15 = 15%

These growth rates are exactly the same (after accounting for a small rounding error in the second calculation). See if you don't agree that the internal growth rate is 12%.

| **Profit Margins and Sustainable Growth** | **EXAMPLE 4.3** |

The Sandar Co. has a debt–equity ratio of .5, a profit margin of 3 percent, a dividend payout ratio of 40 percent, and a capital intensity ratio of 1. What is its sustainable growth rate? If Sandar desired a 10 percent sustainable growth rate and planned to achieve this goal by improving profit margins, what would you think?

ROE is .03 × 1 × 1.5 = 4.5 percent. The retention ratio is 1 − .40 = .60. Sustainable growth is thus .045(.60)/[1 − .045(.60)] = 2.77 percent.

For the company to achieve a 10 percent growth rate, the profit margin will have to rise. To see this, assume that sustainable growth is equal to 10 percent and then solve for profit margin, PM:

.10 = PM(1.5)(.6)/[1 − PM(1.5)(.6)]

PM = .1/.99 = 10.1%

For the plan to succeed, the necessary increase in profit margin is substantial, from 3 percent to about 10 percent. This may not be feasible.

Concept Questions

4.4a How is a firm's sustainable growth related to its accounting return on equity (ROE)?

4.4b What are the determinants of growth?

Some Caveats regarding Financial Planning Models

4.5

Financial planning models do not always ask the right questions. A primary reason is that they tend to rely on accounting relationships and not financial relationships. In particular, the three basic elements of firm value tend to get left out—namely cash flow size, risk, and timing.

Because of this, financial planning models sometimes do not produce meaningful clues about what strategies will lead to increases in value. Instead, they divert the user's attention to questions concerning the association of, say, the debt–equity ratio and firm growth.

The financial model we used for the Hoffman Company was simple—in fact, too simple. Our model, like many in use today, is really an accounting statement generator at heart. Such models are useful for pointing out inconsistencies and reminding us of financial needs, but they offer little guidance concerning what to do about these problems.

In closing our discussion, we should add that financial planning is an iterative process. Plans are created, examined, and modified over and over. The final plan will be a result negotiated between all the different parties to the process. In fact, long-term financial planning in most corporations relies on what might be called the Procrustes approach.[1] Upper-level managers have a goal in mind, and it is up to the planning staff to rework and ultimately deliver a feasible plan that meets that goal.

The final plan will therefore implicitly contain different goals in different areas and also satisfy many constraints. For this reason, such a plan need not be a dispassionate assessment of what we think the future will bring; it may instead be a means of reconciling the planned activities of different groups and a way of setting common goals for the future.

---

[1]In Greek mythology, Procrustes is a giant who seizes travelers and ties them to an iron bed. He stretches them or cuts off their legs as needed to make them fit the bed.

Visit us at www.mhhe.com/rwj

Concept Questions

4.5a What are some important elements that are often missing in financial planning models?

4.5b Why do we say planning is an iterative process?

4.6 Summary and Conclusions

Financial planning forces the firm to think about the future. We have examined a number of features of the planning process. We described what financial planning can accomplish and the components of a financial model. We went on to develop the relationship between growth and financing needs, and we discussed how a financial planning model is useful in exploring that relationship.

Corporate financial planning should not become a purely mechanical activity. If it does, it will probably focus on the wrong things. In particular, plans all too often are formulated in terms of a growth target with no explicit linkage to value creation, and they frequently are overly concerned with accounting statements. Nevertheless, the alternative to financial planning is stumbling into the future. Perhaps the immortal Yogi Berra (the baseball catcher, not the cartoon character) put it best when he said, "Ya gotta watch out if you don't know where you're goin'. You just might not get there."[2]

CONNECT TO FINANCE

 If you are using *Connect™ Finance* in your course, get online to take a Practice Test, check out study tools, and find out where you need additional practice.

▼ Chapter 4 Long-Term Financial Planning and Growth

			Section Quiz
4.1 What Is Financial Planning?	eBook	Study	Practice
4.2 Financial Planning Models: A First Look	eBook	Study	Practice
4.3 The Percentage of Sales Approach	eBook	Study	Practice
4.4 External Financing and Growth	eBook	Study	Practice
4.5 Some Caveats regarding Financial Planning Models	eBook	Study	Practice

Can you answer the following questions?

Section 4.1 Murphy's, Inc., is in the process of preparing a financial plan for the firm for the next five years. This five-year period is referred to as the. (LO 4-1)

Section 4.2 What is generally the first step in the financial planning process? (LO 4-1)

Section 4.3 A firm has current sales of $272,600 with total assets of $311,000. What is the full-capacity capital intensity ratio if the firm is currently operating at 68 percent capacity? (LO 4-1)

---

[2]We're not *exactly* sure what this means either, but we like the sound of it.

Section 4.4   What growth rate assumes that the debt–equity ratio is held constant? (LO 4-3)

Section 4.5   What is generally considered when compiling a financial plan? (LO 4-4)

Log on to find out!

CHAPTER REVIEW AND SELF-TEST PROBLEMS

4.1   **Calculating EFN**   Based on the following information for the Skandia Mining Company, what is EFN if sales are predicted to grow by 10 percent? Use the percentage of sales approach and assume the company is operating at full capacity. The payout ratio is constant.

<table>
<tr><td colspan="6" align="center">SKANDIA MINING COMPANY
Financial Statements</td></tr>
<tr><td colspan="2" align="center">Income Statement</td><td colspan="4" align="center">Balance Sheet</td></tr>
<tr><td></td><td></td><td colspan="2" align="center">Assets</td><td colspan="2" align="center">Liabilities and Owners' Equity</td></tr>
<tr><td>Sales</td><td>$4,250.0</td><td>Current assets</td><td>$ 900.0</td><td>Current liabilities</td><td>$ 500.0</td></tr>
<tr><td>Costs</td><td>3,875.0</td><td>Net fixed assets</td><td>2,200.0</td><td>Long-term debt</td><td>1,800.0</td></tr>
<tr><td>Taxable income</td><td>$ 375.0</td><td></td><td></td><td>Owners' equity</td><td>800.0</td></tr>
<tr><td>Taxes (34%)</td><td>127.5</td><td></td><td></td><td>Total liabilities and owners'</td><td></td></tr>
<tr><td>Net income</td><td>$ 247.5</td><td>Total assets</td><td>$3,100.0</td><td>equity</td><td>$3,100.0</td></tr>
<tr><td> Dividends</td><td>$ 82.6</td><td></td><td></td><td></td><td></td></tr>
<tr><td> Addition to retained earnings</td><td>164.9</td><td></td><td></td><td></td><td></td></tr>
</table>

4.2   **EFN and Capacity Use**   Based on the information in Problem 4.1, what is EFN, assuming 60 percent capacity usage for net fixed assets? Assuming 95 percent capacity?

4.3   **Sustainable Growth**   Based on the information in Problem 4.1, what growth rate can Skandia maintain if no external financing is used? What is the sustainable growth rate?

ANSWERS TO CHAPTER REVIEW AND SELF-TEST PROBLEMS

4.1   We can calculate EFN by preparing the pro forma statements using the percentage of sales approach. Note that sales are forecast to be $4,250 × 1.10 = $4,675.

<table>
<tr><td colspan="4" align="center">SKANDIA MINING COMPANY
Pro Forma Financial Statements</td></tr>
<tr><td colspan="4" align="center">Income Statement</td></tr>
<tr><td>Sales</td><td>$4,675.0</td><td colspan="2">Forecast</td></tr>
<tr><td>Costs</td><td>4,262.7</td><td colspan="2">91.18% of sales</td></tr>
<tr><td>Taxable income</td><td>$ 412.3</td><td colspan="2"></td></tr>
<tr><td>Taxes (34%)</td><td>140.2</td><td colspan="2"></td></tr>
<tr><td>Net income</td><td>$ 272.1</td><td colspan="2"></td></tr>
<tr><td> Dividends</td><td>$ 90.8</td><td colspan="2">33.37% of net income</td></tr>
<tr><td> Addition to retained earnings</td><td>181.3</td><td colspan="2"></td></tr>
<tr><td colspan="4" align="center">Balance Sheet</td></tr>
<tr><td colspan="2" align="center">Assets</td><td colspan="2" align="center">Liabilities and Owners' Equity</td></tr>
<tr><td>Current assets</td><td>$ 990.0</td><td>21.18%</td><td>Current liabilities</td></tr>
</table>

<table>
<tr><td colspan="2" align="center">Assets</td><td></td><td colspan="2" align="center">Liabilities and Owners' Equity</td><td></td></tr>
<tr><td>Current assets</td><td>$ 990.0</td><td>21.18%</td><td>Current liabilities</td><td>$ 550.0</td><td>11.76%</td></tr>
<tr><td>Net fixed assets</td><td>2,420.0</td><td>51.76%</td><td>Long-term debt</td><td>1,800.0</td><td>n/a</td></tr>
<tr><td></td><td></td><td></td><td>Owners' equity</td><td>981.3</td><td>n/a</td></tr>
<tr><td>Total assets</td><td>$3,410.0</td><td>72.94%</td><td>Total liabilities and
  owners' equity</td><td>$3,331.3</td><td>n/a</td></tr>
<tr><td></td><td></td><td></td><td>EFN</td><td>$ 78.7</td><td>n/a</td></tr>
</table>

Visit us at www.mhhe.com/rwj

4.2   Full-capacity sales are equal to current sales divided by the capacity utilization. At 60 percent of capacity:

$4,250 = .60 × Full-capacity sales

$7,083 = Full-capacity sales

With a sales level of $4,675, no net new fixed assets will be needed, so our earlier estimate is too high. We estimated an increase in fixed assets of $2,420 − 2,200 = $220. The new EFN will thus be $78.7 − 220 = −$141.3, a surplus. No external financing is needed in this case.

At 95 percent capacity, full-capacity sales are $4,474. The ratio of fixed assets to full-capacity sales is thus $2,200/4,474 = 49.17%. At a sales level of $4,675, we will thus need $4,675 × .4917 = $2,298.7 in net fixed assets, an increase of $98.7. This is $220 − 98.7 = $121.3 less than we originally predicted, so the EFN is now $78.7 − 121.3 = −$42.6, a surplus. No additional financing is needed.

4.3   Skandia retains $b = 1 − .3337 = 66.63\%$ of net income. Return on assets is $247.5/3,100 = 7.98%. The internal growth rate is thus:

$$\frac{ROA × b}{1 − ROA × b} = \frac{.0798 × .6663}{1 − .0798 × .6663}$$
$$= 5.62\%$$

Return on equity for Skandia is $247.5/800 = 30.94%, so we can calculate the sustainable growth rate as follows:

$$\frac{ROE × b}{1 − ROE × b} = \frac{.3094 × .6663}{1 − .3094 × .6663}$$
$$= 25.97\%$$

CONCEPTS REVIEW AND CRITICAL THINKING QUESTIONS

1. **Sales Forecast [LO1]** Why do you think most long-term financial planning begins with sales forecasts? Put differently, why are future sales the key input?

2. **Sustainable Growth [LO3]** In the chapter, we used Rosengarten Corporation to demonstrate how to calculate EFN. The ROE for Rosengarten is about 7.3 percent, and the plowback ratio is about 67 percent. If you calculate the sustainable growth rate for Rosengarten, you will find it is only 5.14 percent. In our calculation for EFN, we used a growth rate of 25 percent. Is this possible? (*Hint:* Yes. How?)

3. **External Financing Needed [LO2]** Testaburger, Inc., uses no external financing and maintains a positive retention ratio. When sales grow by 15 percent, the firm has a negative projected EFN. What does this tell you about the firm's internal growth rate? How about the sustainable growth rate? At this same level of sales growth, what will happen to the projected EFN if the retention ratio is increased? What if the retention ratio is decreased? What happens to the projected EFN if the firm pays out all of its earnings in the form of dividends?

4. **EFN and Growth Rates [LO2, 3]** Broslofski Co. maintains a positive retention ratio and keeps its debt–equity ratio constant every year. When sales grow by 20 percent, the firm has a negative projected EFN. What does this tell you about the firm's sustainable growth rate? Do you know, with certainty, if the internal growth rate is greater than or less than 20 percent? Why? What happens to the projected

EFN if the retention ratio is increased? What if the retention ratio is decreased? What if the retention ratio is zero?

Use the following information to answer the next six questions: A small business called The Grandmother Calendar Company began selling personalized photo calendar kits. The kits were a hit, and sales soon sharply exceeded forecasts. The rush of orders created a huge backlog, so the company leased more space and expanded capacity; but it still could not keep up with demand. Equipment failed from overuse and quality suffered. Working capital was drained to expand production, and, at the same time, payments from customers were often delayed until the product was shipped. Unable to deliver on orders, the company became so strapped for cash that employee paychecks began to bounce. Finally, out of cash, the company ceased operations entirely three years later.

5. **Product Sales [LO4]** Do you think the company would have suffered the same fate if its product had been less popular? Why or why not?

6. **Cash Flow [LO4]** The Grandmother Calendar Company clearly had a cash flow problem. In the context of the cash flow analysis we developed in Chapter 2, what was the impact of customers not paying until orders were shipped?

7. **Product Pricing [LO4]** The firm actually priced its product to be about 20 percent less than that of competitors, even though the Grandmother calendar was more detailed. In retrospect, was this a wise choice?

8. **Corporate Borrowing [LO4]** If the firm was so successful at selling, why wouldn't a bank or some other lender step in and provide it with the cash it needed to continue?

9. **Cash Flow [LO4]** Which was the biggest culprit here: too many orders, too little cash, or too little production capacity?

10. **Cash Flow [LO4]** What are some of the actions that a small company like The Grandmother Calendar Company can take if it finds itself in a situation in which growth in sales outstrips production capacity and available financial resources? What other options (besides expansion of capacity) are available to a company when orders exceed capacity?

Visit us at www.mhhe.com/rwj

QUESTIONS AND PROBLEMS

1. **Pro Forma Statements [LO1]** Consider the following simplified financial statements for the Fire Corporation (assuming no income taxes):

BASIC
(Questions 1–15)

Income Statement			Balance Sheet		
Sales	$32,000	Assets	$25,300	Debt	$ 5,800
Costs	24,400			Equity	19,500
Net income	$ 7,600	Total	$25,300	Total	$25,300

The company has predicted a sales increase of 15 percent. It has predicted that every item on the balance sheet will increase by 15 percent as well. Create the pro forma statements and reconcile them. What is the plug variable here?

2. **Pro Forma Statements and EFN [LO1, 2]** In the previous question, assume Fire pays out half of net income in the form of a cash dividend. Costs and assets vary with sales, but debt and equity do not. Prepare the pro forma statements and determine the external financing needed.

3. **Calculating EFN [LO2]** The most recent financial statements for Dockett, Inc., are shown here (assuming no income taxes):

Income Statement			Balance Sheet		
Sales	$7,100	Assets	$21,900	Debt	$ 9,400
Costs	4,370			Equity	12,500
Net income	$2,730	Total	$21,900	Total	$21,900

Assets and costs are proportional to sales. Debt and equity are not. No dividends are paid. Next year's sales are projected to be $8,449. What is the external financing needed?

4. **EFN [LO2]** The most recent financial statements for GPS, Inc., are shown here:

Income Statement			Balance Sheet		
Sales	$26,400	Assets	$65,000	Debt	$27,400
Costs	17,300			Equity	37,600
Taxable income	$ 9,100	Total	$65,000	Total	$65,000
Taxes (40%)	3,640				
Net income	$ 5,460				

Assets and costs are proportional to sales. Debt and equity are not. A dividend of $2,300 was paid, and the company wishes to maintain a constant payout ratio. Next year's sales are projected to be $30,360. What is the external financing needed?

5. **EFN [LO2]** The most recent financial statements for Xporter, Inc., are shown here:

Income Statement			Balance Sheet		
Sales	$5,700	Current assets	$ 3,900	Current liabilities	$ 2,200
Costs	4,200	Fixed assets	8,100	Long-term debt	3,750
Taxable income	$1,500			Equity	6,050
Taxes (34%)	510	Total	$12,000	Total	$12,000
Net income	$ 990				

Assets, costs, and current liabilities are proportional to sales. Long-term debt and equity are not. The company maintains a constant 40 percent dividend payout ratio. As with every other firm in its industry, next year's sales are projected to increase by exactly 15 percent. What is the external financing needed?

6. **Calculating Internal Growth [LO3]** The most recent financial statements for Live Co. are shown here:

Income Statement			Balance Sheet		
Sales	$17,500	Current assets	$10,400	Debt	$17,500
Costs	11,800	Fixed assets	28,750	Equity	21,650
Taxable income	$ 5,700	Total	$39,150	Total	$39,150
Taxes (40%)	2,280				
Net income	$ 3,420				

Assets and costs are proportional to sales. Debt and equity are not. The company maintains a constant 30 percent dividend payout ratio. No external equity financing is possible. What is the internal growth rate?

7. **Calculating Sustainable Growth [LO3]** For the company in the previous problem, what is the sustainable growth rate?

Visit us at www.mhhe.com/rwj

8. **Sales and Growth [LO2]** The most recent financial statements for McGovney Co. are shown here:

Income Statement		Balance Sheet			
Sales	$49,000	Current assets	$ 21,000	Long-term debt	$ 51,000
Costs	37,500	Fixed assets	86,000	Equity	56,000
Taxable income	$11,500	Total	$107,000	Total	$107,000
Taxes (34%)	3,910				
Net income	$ 7,590				

Assets and costs are proportional to sales. The company maintains a constant 30 percent dividend payout ratio and a constant debt–equity ratio. What is the maximum increase in sales that can be sustained assuming no new equity is issued?

9. **Calculating Retained Earnings from Pro Forma Income [LO1]** Consider the following income statement for the Heir Jordan Corporation:

HEIR JORDAN CORPORATION Income Statement	
Sales	$47,000
Costs	31,300
Taxable income	$15,700
Taxes (35%)	5,495
Net income	$10,205
Dividends	$2,500
Addition to retained earnings	7,705

A 20 percent growth rate in sales is projected. Prepare a pro forma income statement assuming costs vary with sales and the dividend payout ratio is constant. What is the projected addition to retained earnings?

10. **Applying Percentage of Sales [LO1]** The balance sheet for the Heir Jordan Corporation follows. Based on this information and the income statement in the previous problem, supply the missing information using the percentage of sales approach. Assume that accounts payable vary with sales, whereas notes payable do not. Put "n/a" where needed.

HEIR JORDAN CORPORATION Balance Sheet					
Assets			**Liabilities and Owners' Equity**		
	$	Percentage of Sales		$	Percentage of Sales
Current assets			Current liabilities		
Cash	$ 2,950	—	Accounts payable	$ 2,400	—
Accounts receivable	4,100	—	Notes payable	5,400	—
Inventory	6,400	—	Total	$ 7,800	—
Total	$13,450	—	Long-term debt	$28,000	—
Fixed assets					
Net plant and equipment	$41,300	—	Owners' equity		
			Common stock and paid-in surplus	$15,000	—
			Retained earnings	3,950	—
			Total	$18,950	—
Total assets	$54,750	—	Total liabilities and owners' equity	$54,750	—

Visit us at www.mhhe.com/rwj

11. **EFN and Sales [LO2]** From the previous two questions, prepare a pro forma balance sheet showing EFN, assuming a 15 percent increase in sales, no new external debt or equity financing, and a constant payout ratio.

12. **Internal Growth [LO3]** If the Boddy Shoppe has a 7 percent ROA and a 25 percent payout ratio, what is its internal growth rate?

13. **Sustainable Growth [LO3]** If Rondo Corp. has a 14 percent ROE and a 30 percent payout ratio, what is its sustainable growth rate?

14. **Sustainable Growth [LO3]** Based on the following information, calculate the sustainable growth rate for Kaleb's Kickboxing:

Profit margin	= 7.1%
Capital intensity ratio	= .75
Debt–equity ratio	= .60
Net income	= $48,000
Dividends	= $13,000

15. **Sustainable Growth [LO3]** Assuming the following ratios are constant, what is the sustainable growth rate?

Total asset turnover	= 2.70
Profit margin	= 6.5%
Equity multiplier	= 1.2
Payout ratio	= 35%

INTERMEDIATE
(Questions 16–26)

16. **Full-Capacity Sales [LO1]** Alter Bridge Mfg., Inc., is currently operating at only 92 percent of fixed asset capacity. Current sales are $640,000. How fast can sales grow before any new fixed assets are needed?

17. **Fixed Assets and Capacity Usage [LO1]** For the company in the previous problem, suppose fixed assets are $490,000 and sales are projected to grow to $730,000. How much in new fixed assets are required to support this growth in sales? Assume the company maintains its current operating capacity.

18. **Growth and Profit Margin [LO3]** Abacus Co. wishes to maintain a growth rate of 13 percent per year, a debt–equity ratio of 1.20, and a dividend payout ratio of 30 percent. The ratio of total assets to sales is constant at .95. What profit margin must the firm achieve?

19. **Growth and Assets [LO3]** A firm wishes to maintain an internal growth rate of 6.5 percent and a dividend payout ratio of 25 percent. The current profit margin is 6 percent, and the firm uses no external financing sources. What must total asset turnover be?

20. **Sustainable Growth [LO3]** Based on the following information, calculate the sustainable growth rate for Clapton Guitars, Inc.:

Profit margin	= 5.3%
Total asset turnover	= 1.60
Total debt ratio	= .45
Payout ratio	= 30%

21. **Sustainable Growth and Outside Financing [LO3]** You've collected the following information about Odyssey, Inc.:

Sales	= $165,000
Net income	= $14,800
Dividends	= $9,300
Total debt	= $68,000
Total equity	= $51,000

What is the sustainable growth rate for the company? If it does grow at this rate, how much new borrowing will take place in the coming year, assuming a constant debt–equity ratio? What growth rate could be supported with no outside financing at all?

22. **Sustainable Growth Rate [LO3]** Cambria, Inc., had equity of $145,000 at the beginning of the year. At the end of the year, the company had total assets of $275,000. During the year, the company sold no new equity. Net income for the year was $26,000 and dividends were $5,500. What is the sustainable growth rate for the company? What is the sustainable growth rate if you use the formula ROE × b and beginning of period equity? What is the sustainable growth rate if you use end of period equity in this formula? Is this number too high or too low? Why?

23. **Internal Growth Rates [LO3]** Calculate the internal growth rate for the company in the previous problem. Now calculate the internal growth rate using ROA × b for both beginning of period and end of period total assets. What do you observe?

24. **Calculating EFN [LO2]** The most recent financial statements for Fleury, Inc., follow. Sales for 2012 are projected to grow by 20 percent. Interest expense will remain constant; the tax rate and the dividend payout rate will also remain constant. Costs, other expenses, current assets, fixed assets, and accounts payable increase spontaneously with sales. If the firm is operating at full capacity and no new debt or equity is issued, what external financing is needed to support the 20 percent growth rate in sales?

FLEURY, INC. 2011 Income Statement		
Sales		$743,000
Costs		578,000
Other expenses		15,200
Earnings before interest and taxes		$149,800
Interest paid		11,200
Taxable income		$138,600
Taxes		48,510
Net income		$ 90,090
Dividends	$27,027	
Addition to retained earnings	63,063	

FLEURY, INC. Balance Sheet as of December 31, 2011			
Assets		**Liabilities and Owners' Equity**	
Current assets		Current liabilities	
Cash	$ 20,240	Accounts payable	$ 54,400
Accounts receivable	32,560	Notes payable	13,600
Inventory	69,520	Total	$ 68,000
Total	$122,320	Long-term debt	$126,000
Fixed assets		Owners' equity	
Net plant and equipment	$330,400	Common stock and paid-in surplus	$112,000
		Retained earnings	146,720
		Total	$258,720
Total assets	$452,720	Total liabilities and owners' equity	$452,720

25. **Capacity Usage and Growth [LO2]** In the previous problem, suppose the firm was operating at only 80 percent capacity in 2011. What is EFN now?

26. **Calculating EFN [LO2]** In Problem 24, suppose the firm wishes to keep its debt–equity ratio constant. What is EFN now?

CHALLENGE
(Questions 27–32)

27. **EFN and Internal Growth [LO2, 3]** Redo Problem 24 using sales growth rates of 15 and 25 percent in addition to 20 percent. Illustrate graphically the relationship between EFN and the growth rate, and use this graph to determine the relationship between them. At what growth rate is the EFN equal to zero? Why is this internal growth rate different from that found by using the equation in the text?

28. **EFN and Sustainable Growth [LO2, 3]** Redo Problem 26 using sales growth rates of 30 and 35 percent in addition to 20 percent. Illustrate graphically the relationship between EFN and the growth rate, and use this graph to determine the relationship between them. At what growth rate is the EFN equal to zero? Why is this sustainable growth rate different from that found by using the equation in the text?

29. **Constraints on Growth [LO3]** Seether, Inc., wishes to maintain a growth rate of 12 percent per year and a debt–equity ratio of .40. Profit margin is 5.8 percent, and the ratio of total assets to sales is constant at 1.55. Is this growth rate possible? To answer, determine what the dividend payout ratio must be. How do you interpret the result?

30. **EFN [LO2]** Define the following:

S = Previous year's sales

A = Total assets

E = Total equity

g = Projected growth in sales

PM = Profit margin

b = Retention (plowback) ratio

Assuming all debt is constant, show that EFN can be written as follows:

$$EFN = -PM(S)b + (A - PM(S)b) \times g$$

Hint: Asset needs will equal $A \times g$. The addition to retained earnings will equal $PM(S)b \times (1 + g)$.

31. **Growth Rates [LO3]** Based on the result in Problem 30, show that the internal and sustainable growth rates are as given in the chapter. *Hint:* For the internal growth rate, set EFN equal to zero and solve for g.

32. **Sustainable Growth Rate [LO3]** In the chapter, we discussed the two versions of the sustainable growth rate formula. Derive the formula $ROE \times b$ from the formula given in the chapter, where ROE is based on beginning of period equity. Also, derive the formula $ROA \times b$ from the internal growth rate formula.

MINICASE

Planning for Growth at S&S Air

After Chris completed the ratio analysis for S&S Air (see Chapter 3), Mark and Todd approached him about planning for next year's sales. The company had historically used little planning for investment needs. As a result, the company experienced some challenging times because of cash flow problems. The lack of planning resulted in missed sales, as well as periods when Mark and Todd were unable to draw salaries. To this end, they would like Chris to prepare a financial plan for the next year so the company can begin to address any outside investment requirements. The income statement and balance sheet are shown here:

S&S AIR, INC.	
2011 Income Statement	
Sales	$36,599,300
Cost of goods sold	26,669,496
Other expenses	4,641,000
Depreciation	1,640,200
EBIT	$ 3,648,604
Interest	573,200
Taxable income	$ 3,075,404
Taxes (40%)	1,230,162
Net income	$ 1,845,242
Dividends	$ 560,000
Add to retained earnings	1,285,242

S&S AIR, INC.
2011 Balance Sheet

Assets		Liabilities and Equity	
Current assets		**Current liabilities**	
Cash	$ 396,900	Accounts payable	$ 844,550
Accounts receivable	637,560	Notes payable	1,928,500
Inventory	933,400	Total current liabilities	$ 2,773,050
Total current assets	$ 1,967,860	Long-term debt	$ 5,050,000
Fixed assets			
Net plant and equipment	$15,411,620	Shareholder equity	
		Common stock	$ 322,500
		Retained earnings	9,233,930
		Total equity	$ 9,556,430
Total assets	$17,379,480	Total liabilities and equity	$17,379,480

QUESTIONS

1. Calculate the internal growth rate and sustainable growth rate for S&S Air. What do these numbers mean?

2. S&S Air is planning for a growth rate of 12 percent next year. Calculate the EFN for the company assuming the company is operating at full capacity. Can the company's sales increase at this growth rate?

3. Most assets can be increased as a percentage of sales. For instance, cash can be increased by any amount. However, fixed assets must be increased in specific amounts because it is impossible, as a practical matter, to buy part of a new plant or machine. In this case, a company has a "staircase" or "lumpy" fixed cost structure. Assume S&S Air is currently producing at 100 percent capacity. As a result, to increase production, the company must set up an entirely new line at a cost of $5,000,000. Calculate the new EFN with this assumption. What does this imply about capacity utilization for the company next year?

Visit us at www.mhhe.com/rwj

5

INTRODUCTION TO VALUATION: THE TIME VALUE OF MONEY

TOYOTA MOTOR CREDIT CORPORATION (TMCC), a subsidiary of Toyota Motor, offered some securities for sale to the public on March 28, 2008. Under the terms of the deal, TMCC promised to repay the owner of one of these securities $100,000 on March 28, 2038, but investors would receive nothing until then. Investors paid TMCC $24,099 for each of these securities; so, they gave up $24,099 on March 28, 2008, for the promise of a $100,000 payment 30 years later. Such a security, for which you pay some amount today in exchange for a promised lump sum to be received at a future date, is about the simplest possible type. Is giving up $24,099 in exchange for $100,000 in 30 years a good deal? On the plus side, you get back about $4 for every $1 you put up. That probably sounds good; but on the down side, you have to wait 30 years to get it. What you need to know is how to analyze this trade-off; this chapter gives you the tools you need.

LEARNING OBJECTIVES

After studying this chapter, you should understand:

LO1 How to determine the future value of an investment made today.

LO2 How to determine the present value of cash to be received at a future date.

LO3 How to find the return on an investment.

LO4 How long it takes for an investment to reach a desired value.

One of the basic problems faced by the financial manager is how to determine the value today of cash flows expected in the future. For example, the jackpot in a PowerBall™ lottery drawing was $110 million. Does this mean the winning ticket was worth $110 million? The answer is no because the jackpot was actually going to pay out over a 20-year period at a rate of $5.5 million per year. How much was the ticket worth then? The answer depends on the time value of money, the subject of this chapter.

In the most general sense, the phrase *time value of money* refers to the fact that a dollar in hand today is worth more than a dollar promised at some time in the future. On a practical level, one reason for this is that you could earn interest while you waited; so a dollar today would grow to more than a dollar later. The trade-off between money now and money later thus depends on, among other things, the rate you can earn by investing. Our goal in this chapter is to explicitly evaluate this trade-off between dollars today and dollars at some future time.

A thorough understanding of the material in this chapter is critical to understanding material in subsequent chapters, so you should study it with particular care. We will present a number of examples in this chapter. In many problems, your answer may differ from ours slightly. This can happen because of rounding and is not a cause for concern.

Future Value and Compounding

5.1

The first thing we will study is future value. **Future value (FV)** refers to the amount of money an investment will grow to over some period of time at some given interest rate. Put another way, future value is the cash value of an investment at some time in the future. We start out by considering the simplest case: a single-period investment.

future value (FV)
The amount an investment is worth after one or more periods.

INVESTING FOR A SINGLE PERIOD

Suppose you invest $100 in a savings account that pays 10 percent interest per year. How much will you have in one year? You will have $110. This $110 is equal to your original *principal* of $100 plus $10 in interest that you earn. We say that $110 is the future value of $100 invested for one year at 10 percent, and we simply mean that $100 today is worth $110 in one year, given that 10 percent is the interest rate.

In general, if you invest for one period at an interest rate of r, your investment will grow to $(1 + r)$ per dollar invested. In our example, r is 10 percent, so your investment grows to $1 + .10 = 1.1$ dollars per dollar invested. You invested $100 in this case, so you ended up with $100 \times 1.10 = \$110$.

INVESTING FOR MORE THAN ONE PERIOD

Going back to our $100 investment, what will you have after two years, assuming the interest rate doesn't change? If you leave the entire $110 in the bank, you will earn $110 \times .10 = \$11$ in interest during the second year, so you will have a total of $110 + 11 = \$121$. This $121 is the future value of $100 in two years at 10 percent. Another way of looking at it is that one year from now you are effectively investing $110 at 10 percent for a year. This is a single-period problem, so you'll end up with $1.10 for every dollar invested, or $110 \times 1.1 = \$121$ total.

This $121 has four parts. The first part is the $100 original principal. The second part is the $10 in interest you earned in the first year, and the third part is another $10 you earn in the second year, for a total of $120. The last $1 you end up with (the fourth part) is interest you earn in the second year on the interest paid in the first year: $10 \times .10 = \$1$.

This process of leaving your money and any accumulated interest in an investment for more than one period, thereby *reinvesting* the interest, is called **compounding**. Compounding the interest means earning **interest on interest**, so we call the result **compound interest**. With **simple interest**, the interest is not reinvested, so interest is earned each period only on the original principal.

compounding
The process of accumulating interest on an investment over time to earn more interest.

interest on interest
Interest earned on the reinvestment of previous interest payments.

compound interest
Interest earned on both the initial principal and the interest reinvested from prior periods.

simple interest
Interest earned only on the original principal amount invested.

Interest on Interest   **EXAMPLE 5.1**

Suppose you locate a two-year investment that pays 14 percent per year. If you invest $325, how much will you have at the end of the two years? How much of this is simple interest? How much is compound interest?

At the end of the first year, you will have $325 \times (1 + .14) = \$370.50$. If you reinvest this entire amount and thereby compound the interest, you will have $370.50 \times 1.14 = \$422.37$ at the end of the second year. The total interest you earn is thus $422.37 - 325 = \$97.37$. Your $325 original principal earns $325 \times .14 = \$45.50$ in interest each year, for a two-year total of $91 in simple interest. The remaining $97.37 - 91 = \$6.37$ results from compounding. You can check this by noting that the interest earned in the first year is $45.50. The interest on interest earned in the second year thus amounts to $45.50 \times .14 = \$6.37$, as we calculated.

We now take a closer look at how we calculated the $121 future value. We multiplied $110 by 1.1 to get $121. The $110, however, was $100 also multiplied by 1.1. In other words:

$$\begin{aligned}
\$121 &= \$110 \times 1.1 \\
&= (\$100 \times 1.1) \times 1.1 \\
&= \$100 \times (1.1 \times 1.1) \\
&= \$100 \times 1.1^2 \\
&= \$100 \times 1.21
\end{aligned}$$

At the risk of belaboring the obvious, let's ask: How much would our $100 grow to after three years? Once again, in two years, we'll be investing $121 for one period at 10 percent. We'll end up with $1.10 for every dollar we invest, or $121 \times 1.1 = \$133.10$ total. This $133.10 is thus:

$$\begin{aligned}
\$133.10 &= \$121 \times 1.1 \\
&= (\$110 \times 1.1) \times 1.1 \\
&= (\$100 \times 1.1) \times 1.1 \times 1.1 \\
&= \$100 \times (1.1 \times 1.1 \times 1.1) \\
&= \$100 \times 1.1^3 \\
&= \$100 \times 1.331
\end{aligned}$$

For a discussion of time value concepts (and lots more) see www.financeprofessor.com.

You're probably noticing a pattern to these calculations, so we can now go ahead and state the general result. As our examples suggest, the future value of $1 invested for t periods at a rate of r per period is this:

$$\text{Future value} = \$1 \times (1 + r)^t \qquad \textbf{[5.1]}$$

The expression $(1 + r)^t$ is sometimes called the *future value interest factor* (or just *future value factor*) for $1 invested at r percent for t periods and can be abbreviated as FVIF(r, t).

In our example, what would your $100 be worth after five years? We can first compute the relevant future value factor as follows:

$$(1 + r)^t = (1 + .10)^5 = 1.1^5 = 1.6105$$

Your $100 will thus grow to:

$$\$100 \times 1.6105 = \$161.05$$

The growth of your $100 each year is illustrated in Table 5.1. As shown, the interest earned in each year is equal to the beginning amount multiplied by the interest rate of 10 percent.

TABLE 5.1

Future Value of $100 at 10 percent

Year	Beginning Amount	Simple Interest	Compound Interest	Total Interest Earned	Ending Amount
1	$100.00	$10	$ .00	$10.00	$110.00
2	110.00	10	1.00	11.00	121.00
3	121.00	10	2.10	12.10	133.10
4	133.10	10	3.31	13.31	146.41
5	146.41	10	4.64	14.64	161.05
		Total $50 simple interest	Total $11.05 compound interest	Total $61.05 interest	

FIGURE 5.1

Future Value, Simple
Interest, and Compound
Interest

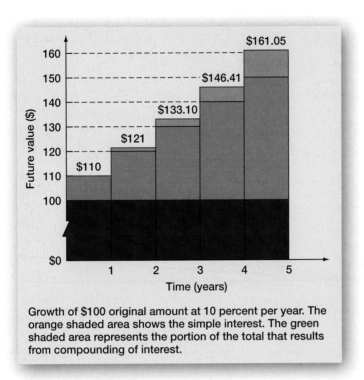

Growth of $100 original amount at 10 percent per year. The
orange shaded area shows the simple interest. The green
shaded area represents the portion of the total that results
from compounding of interest.

In Table 5.1, notice the total interest you earn is $61.05. Over the five-year span of this
investment, the simple interest is $100 × .10 = $10 per year, so you accumulate $50 this
way. The other $11.05 is from compounding.

Figure 5.1 illustrates the growth of the compound interest in Table 5.1. Notice how the
simple interest is constant each year, but the amount of compound interest you earn gets
bigger every year. The amount of the compound interest keeps increasing because more
and more interest builds up and there is thus more to compound.

*A brief introduction
to key financial
concepts is available at
www.teachmefinance.com.*

Future values depend critically on the assumed interest rate, particularly for long-lived
investments. Figure 5.2 illustrates this relationship by plotting the growth of $1 for differ-
ent rates and lengths of time. Notice the future value of $1 after 10 years is about $6.20 at
a 20 percent rate, but it is only about $2.60 at 10 percent. In this case, doubling the interest
rate more than doubles the future value.

To solve future value problems, we need to come up with the relevant future value factors. There are several different ways of doing this. In our example, we could have multiplied 1.1 by itself five times. This would work just fine, but it would get to be very tedious
for, say, a 30-year investment.

Fortunately, there are several easier ways to get future value factors. Most calculators
have a key labeled "y^x". You can usually just enter 1.1, press this key, enter 5, and press the
"=" key to get the answer. This is an easy way to calculate future value factors because it's
quick and accurate.

Alternatively, you can use a table that contains future value factors for some common
interest rates and time periods. Table 5.2 contains some of these factors. Table A.1 in the
appendix at the end of the book contains a much larger set. To use the table, find the column
that corresponds to 10 percent. Then look down the rows until you come to five periods.
You should find the factor that we calculated, 1.6105.

Tables such as 5.2 are not as common as they once were because they predate inexpensive calculators and are available only for a relatively small number of rates. Interest rates

FIGURE 5.2

Future Value of $1 for Different Periods and Rates

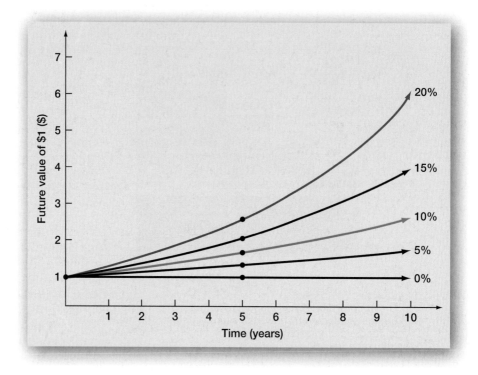

TABLE 5.2

Future Value Interest Factors

	Interest Rate			
Number of Periods	**5%**	**10%**	**15%**	**20%**
1	1.0500	1.1000	1.1500	1.2000
2	1.1025	1.2100	1.3225	1.4400
3	1.1576	1.3310	1.5209	1.7280
4	1.2155	1.4641	1.7490	2.0736
5	1.2763	1.6105	2.0114	2.4883

are often quoted to three or four decimal places, so the tables needed to deal with these accurately would be quite large. As a result, the real world has moved away from using them. We will emphasize the use of a calculator in this chapter.

These tables still serve a useful purpose. To make sure you are doing the calculations correctly, pick a factor from the table and then calculate it yourself to see that you get the same answer. There are plenty of numbers to choose from.

EXAMPLE 5.2	**Compound Interest**

You've located an investment that pays 12 percent per year. That rate sounds good to you, so you invest $400. How much will you have in three years? How much will you have in seven years? At the end of seven years, how much interest will you have earned? How much of that interest results from compounding?

Based on our discussion, we can calculate the future value factor for 12 percent and three years as follows:

$$(1 + r)^t = 1.12^3 = 1.4049$$

Your $400 thus grows to:

$$\$400 \times 1.4049 = \$561.97$$

After seven years, you will have:

$$\$400 \times 1.12^7 = \$400 \times 2.2107 = \$884.27$$

Thus, you will more than double your money over seven years.

Because you invested $400, the interest in the $884.27 future value is $884.27 − 400 = $484.27. At 12 percent, your $400 investment earns $400 × .12 = $48 in simple interest every year. Over seven years, the simple interest thus totals 7 × $48 = $336. The other $484.27 − 336 = $148.27 is from compounding.

The effect of compounding is not great over short time periods, but it really starts to add up as the horizon grows. To take an extreme case, suppose one of your more frugal ancestors had invested $5 for you at a 6 percent interest rate 200 years ago. How much would you have today? The future value factor is a substantial $1.06^{200} = 115{,}125.90$ (you won't find this one in a table), so you would have $5 × 115,125.90 = $575,629.52 today. Notice that the simple interest is just $5 × .06 = $.30 per year. After 200 years, this amounts to $60. The rest is from reinvesting. Such is the power of compound interest!

How Much for That Island?   EXAMPLE 5.3

To further illustrate the effect of compounding for long horizons, consider the case of Peter Minuit and the American Indians. In 1626, Minuit bought all of Manhattan Island for about $24 in goods and trinkets. This sounds cheap, but the Indians may have gotten the better end of the deal. To see why, suppose the Indians had sold the goods and invested the $24 at 10 percent. How much would it be worth today?

About 385 years have passed since the transaction. At 10 percent, $24 will grow by quite a bit over that time. How much? The future value factor is roughly:

$$(1 + r)^t = 1.1^{385} \approx 8{,}600{,}000{,}000{,}000{,}000$$

That is, 8.6 followed by 14 zeroes. The future value is thus on the order of $24 × 8.6 = $207 *quadrillion* (give or take a few hundreds of trillions).

Well, $207 quadrillion is a lot of money. How much? If you had it, you could buy the United States. All of it. Cash. With money left over to buy Canada, Mexico, and the rest of the world, for that matter.

This example is something of an exaggeration, of course. In 1626, it would not have been easy to locate an investment that would pay 10 percent every year without fail for the next 385 years.

CALCULATOR HINTS

Using a Financial Calculator

Although there are the various ways of calculating future values we have described so far, many of you will decide that a financial calculator is the way to go. If you are planning on using one, you should read this extended hint; otherwise, skip it.

A financial calculator is simply an ordinary calculator with a few extra features. In particular, it knows some of the most commonly used financial formulas, so it can directly compute things like future values.

Financial calculators have the advantage that they handle a lot of the computation, but that is really all. In other words, you still have to understand the problem; the calculator just does some of the arithmetic. In fact, there

(continued)

is an old joke (somewhat modified) that goes like this: Anyone can make a mistake on a time value of money problem, but to really screw one up takes a financial calculator! We therefore have two goals for this section. First, we'll discuss how to compute future values. After that, we'll show you how to avoid the most common mistakes people make when they start using financial calculators.

How to Calculate Future Values with a Financial Calculator

Examining a typical financial calculator, you will find five keys of particular interest. They usually look like this:

For now, we need to focus on four of these. The keys labeled **PV** and **FV** are just what you would guess: present value and future value. The key labeled **N** refers to the number of periods, which is what we have been calling t. Finally, **I/Y** stands for the interest rate, which we have called r.[1]

If we have the financial calculator set up right (see our next section), then calculating a future value is very simple. Take a look back at our question involving the future value of $100 at 10 percent for five years. We have seen that the answer is $161.05. The exact keystrokes will differ depending on what type of calculator you use, but here is basically all you do:

1. Enter −100. Press the **PV** key. (The negative sign is explained in the next section.)
2. Enter 10. Press the **I/Y** key. (Notice that we entered 10, not .10; see the next section.)
3. Enter 5. Press the **N** key.

Now we have entered all of the relevant information. To solve for the future value, we need to ask the calculator what the FV is. Depending on your calculator, either you press the button labeled "CPT" (for compute) and then press **FV** or you just press **FV**. Either way, you should get 161.05. If you don't (and you probably won't if this is the first time you have used a financial calculator!), we will offer some help in our next section.

Before we explain the kinds of problems you are likely to run into, we want to establish a standard format for showing you how to use a financial calculator. Using the example we just looked at, in the future, we will illustrate such problems like this:

Enter	5	10		−100	

Solve for					161.05

Here is an important tip: Appendix D contains more detailed instructions for the most common types of financial calculators. See if yours is included; if it is, follow the instructions there if you need help. Of course, if all else fails, you can read the manual that came with the calculator.

How to Get the Wrong Answer Using a Financial Calculator

There are a couple of common (and frustrating) problems that cause a lot of trouble with financial calculators. In this section, we provide some important *dos* and *don'ts*. If you just can't seem to get a problem to work out, you should refer back to this section.

There are two categories we examine: three things you need to do only once and three things you need to do every time you work a problem. The things you need to do just once deal with the following calculator settings:

1. *Make sure your calculator is set to display a large number of decimal places.* Most financial calculators display only two decimal places; this causes problems because we frequently work with numbers—like interest rates—that are very small.
2. *Make sure your calculator is set to assume only one payment per period or per year.* Most financial calculators assume monthly payments (12 per year) unless you say otherwise.
3. *Make sure your calculator is in "end" mode.* This is usually the default, but you can accidently change to "begin" mode.

---

[1]The reason financial calculators use N and I/Y is that the most common use for these calculators is determining loan payments. In this context, *N* is the number of payments and *I/Y* is the interest rate on the loan. But as we will see, there are many other uses of financial calculators that don't involve loan payments and interest rates.

If you don't know how to set these three things, see Appendix D or your calculator's operating manual. There are also three things you need to do *every time you work a problem*:

1. *Before you start, completely clear out the calculator*. This is very important. Failure to do this is the number one reason for wrong answers; you must get in the habit of clearing the calculator every time you start a problem. How you do this depends on the calculator (see Appendix D), but you must do more than just clear the display. For example, on a Texas Instruments BA II Plus you must press 2nd then CLR TVM for *clear time value of money*. There is a similar command on your calculator. Learn it!

   Note that turning the calculator off and back on won't do it. Most financial calculators remember everything you enter, even after you turn them off. In other words, they remember all your mistakes unless you explicitly clear them out. Also, if you are in the middle of a problem and make a mistake, *clear it out and start over*. Better to be safe than sorry.

2. *Put a negative sign on cash outflows*. Most financial calculators require you to put a negative sign on cash out-flows and a positive sign on cash inflows. As a practical matter, this usually just means that you should enter the present value amount with a negative sign (because normally the present value represents the amount you give up today in exchange for cash inflows later). By the same token, when you solve for a present value, you shouldn't be surprised to see a negative sign.

3. *Enter the rate correctly*. Financial calculators assume that rates are quoted in percent, so if the rate is .08 (or 8 percent), you should enter 8, not .08.

If you follow these guidelines (especially the one about clearing out the calculator), you should have no prob-lem using a financial calculator to work almost all of the problems in this and the next few chapters. We'll provide some additional examples and guidance where appropriate.

A NOTE ABOUT COMPOUND GROWTH

If you are considering depositing money in an interest-bearing account, then the interest rate on that account is just the rate at which your money grows, assuming you don't remove any of it. If that rate is 10 percent, then each year you simply have 10 percent more money than you had the year before. In this case, the interest rate is just an example of a compound growth rate.

The way we calculated future values is actually quite general and lets you answer some other types of questions related to growth. For example, your company currently has 10,000 employ-ees. You've estimated that the number of employees grows by 3 percent per year. How many employees will there be in five years? Here, we start with 10,000 people instead of dollars, and we don't think of the growth rate as an interest rate, but the calculation is exactly the same:

$$10,000 \times 1.03^5 = 10,000 \times 1.1593 = 11,593 \text{ employees}$$

There will be about 1,593 net new hires over the coming five years.

To give another example, according to Value Line (a leading supplier of business informa-tion for investors), Walmart's 2010 sales were about $423 billion. Suppose sales are projected to increase at a rate of 15 percent per year. What will Walmart's sales be in the year 2015 if this is correct? Verify for yourself that the answer is about $851 billion—just over twice as large.

Dividend Growth	EXAMPLE 5.4

The TICO Corporation currently pays a cash dividend of $5 per share. You believe the dividend will be increased by 4 percent each year indefinitely. How big will the dividend be in eight years?

Here we have a cash dividend growing because it is being increased by management; but once again the calculation is the same:

Future value = $5 $\times$ 1.04^8 = $5 $\times$ 1.3686 = $6.84

The dividend will grow by $1.84 over that period. Dividend growth is a subject we will return to in a later chapter.

Concept Questions

5.1a What do we mean by the future value of an investment?

5.1b What does it mean to compound interest? How does compound interest differ from simple interest?

5.1c In general, what is the future value of $1 invested at r per period for t periods?

5.2 Present Value and Discounting

When we discuss future value, we are thinking of questions like: What will my $2,000 investment grow to if it earns a 6.5 percent return every year for the next six years? The answer to this question is what we call the future value of $2,000 invested at 6.5 percent for six years (verify that the answer is about $2,918).

Another type of question that comes up even more often in financial management is obviously related to future value. Suppose you need to have $10,000 in 10 years, and you can earn 6.5 percent on your money. How much do you have to invest today to reach your goal? You can verify that the answer is $5,327.26. How do we know this? Read on.

THE SINGLE-PERIOD CASE

We've seen that the future value of $1 invested for one year at 10 percent is $1.10. We now ask a slightly different question: How much do we have to invest today at 10 percent to get $1 in one year? In other words, we know the future value here is $1, but what is the **present value (PV)**? The answer isn't too hard to figure out. Whatever we invest today will be 1.1 times bigger at the end of the year. Because we need $1 at the end of the year:

Present value × 1.1 = $1

Or solving for the present value:

Present value = $1/1.1 = $.909

In this case, the present value is the answer to the following question: What amount, invested today, will grow to $1 in one year if the interest rate is 10 percent? Present value is thus just the reverse of future value. Instead of compounding the money forward into the future, we **discount** it back to the present.

present value (PV)
The current value of future cash flows discounted at the appropriate discount rate.

discount
Calculate the present value of some future amount.

EXAMPLE 5.5	**Single-Period PV**

Suppose you need $400 to buy textbooks next year. You can earn 7 percent on your money. How much do you have to put up today?

We need to know the PV of $400 in one year at 7 percent. Proceeding as in the previous example:

Present value × 1.07 = $400

We can now solve for the present value:

Present value = $400 × (1/1.07) = $373.83

Thus, $373.83 is the present value. Again, this just means that investing this amount for one year at 7 percent will give you a future value of $400.

From our examples, the present value of $1 to be received in one period is generally given as follows:

$$PV = \$1 \times [1/(1 + r)] = \$1/(1 + r)$$

We next examine how to get the present value of an amount to be paid in two or more periods into the future.

PRESENT VALUES FOR MULTIPLE PERIODS

Suppose you need to have $1,000 in two years. If you can earn 7 percent, how much do you have to invest to make sure you have the $1,000 when you need it? In other words, what is the present value of $1,000 in two years if the relevant rate is 7 percent?

Based on your knowledge of future values, you know the amount invested must grow to $1,000 over the two years. In other words, it must be the case that:

$$\$1,000 = PV \times 1.07 \times 1.07$$
$$= PV \times 1.07^2$$
$$= PV \times 1.1449$$

Given this, we can solve for the present value:

Present value = $1,000/1.1449 = $873.44

Therefore, $873.44 is the amount you must invest to achieve your goal.

Saving Up   EXAMPLE 5.6

You would like to buy a new automobile. You have $50,000 or so, but the car costs $68,500. If you can earn 9 percent, how much do you have to invest today to buy the car in two years? Do you have enough? Assume the price will stay the same.

What we need to know is the present value of $68,500 to be paid in two years, assuming a 9 percent rate. Based on our discussion, this is:

$$PV = \$68,500/1.09^2 = \$68,500/1.1881 = \$57,655.08$$

You're still about $7,655 short, even if you're willing to wait two years.

As you have probably recognized by now, calculating present values is quite similar to calculating future values, and the general result looks much the same. The present value of $1 to be received t periods into the future at a discount rate of r is:

$$PV = \$1 \times [1/(1 + r)^t] = \$1/(1 + r)^t \qquad [5.2]$$

The quantity in brackets, $1/(1 + r)^t$, goes by several different names. Because it's used to discount a future cash flow, it is often called a *discount factor*. With this name, it is not surprising that the rate used in the calculation is often called the **discount rate**. We will tend to call it this in talking about present values. The quantity in brackets is also called the *present value interest factor* (or just *present value factor*) for $1 at r percent for t periods and is sometimes abbreviated as PVIF(r, t). Finally, calculating the present value of a future cash flow to determine its worth today is commonly called **discounted cash flow (DCF) valuation**.

To illustrate, suppose you need $1,000 in three years. You can earn 15 percent on your money. How much do you have to invest today? To find out, we have to determine the

discount rate
The rate used to calculate the present value of future cash flows.

discounted cash flow (DCF) valuation
Calculating the present value of a future cash flow to determine its value today.

TABLE 5.3

Present Value Interest Factors

Number of Periods	5%	10%	15%	20%
		Interest Rate		
1	.9524	.9091	.8696	.8333
2	.9070	.8264	.7561	.6944
3	.8638	.7513	.6575	.5787
4	.8227	.6830	.5718	.4823
5	.7835	.6209	.4972	.4019

present value of $1,000 in three years at 15 percent. We do this by discounting $1,000 back three periods at 15 percent. With these numbers, the discount factor is:

$$1/(1 + .15)^3 = 1/1.5209 = .6575$$

The amount you must invest is thus:

$$\$1,000 \times .6575 = \$657.50$$

We say that $657.50 is the present or discounted value of $1,000 to be received in three years at 15 percent.

There are tables for present value factors just as there are tables for future value factors, and you use them in the same way (if you use them at all). Table 5.3 contains a small set. A much larger set can be found in Table A.2 in the book's appendix.

In Table 5.3, the discount factor we just calculated (.6575) can be found by looking down the column labeled "15%" until you come to the third row.

CALCULATOR HINTS

You solve present value problems on a financial calculator just as you do future value problems. For the example we just examined (the present value of $1,000 to be received in three years at 15 percent), you would do the following:

Enter 3 15   1,000

| N | I/Y | PMT | PV | FV |

Solve for   −657.50

Notice that the answer has a negative sign; as we discussed earlier, that's because it represents an outflow today in exchange for the $1,000 inflow later.

EXAMPLE 5.7   Deceptive Advertising?

Businesses sometimes advertise that you should "Come try our product. If you do, we'll give you $100 just for coming by!" If you read the fine print, what you find out is that they will give you a savings certificate that will pay you $100 in 25 years or so. If the going interest rate on such certificates is 10 percent per year, how much are they really giving you today?

What you're actually getting is the present value of $100 to be paid in 25 years. If the discount rate is 10 percent per year, then the discount factor is:

$$1/1.1^{25} = 1/10.8347 = .0923$$

This tells you that a dollar in 25 years is worth a little more than nine cents today, assuming a 10 percent discount rate. Given this, the promotion is actually paying you about .0923 × $100 = $9.23. Maybe this is enough to draw customers, but it's not $100.

FIGURE 5.3

Present Value of $1 for Different Periods and Rates

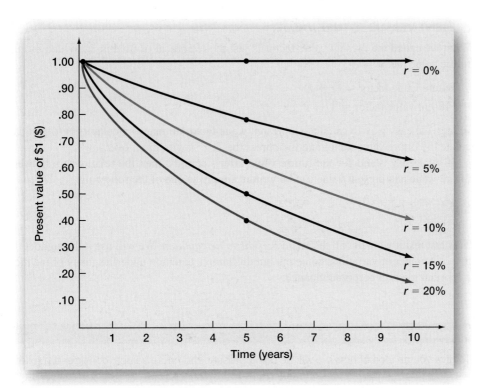

As the length of time until payment grows, present values decline. As Example 5.7 illustrates, present values tend to become small as the time horizon grows. If you look out far enough, they will always approach zero. Also, for a given length of time, the higher the discount rate is, the lower is the present value. Put another way, present values and discount rates are inversely related. Increasing the discount rate decreases the PV and vice versa.

The relationship between time, discount rates, and present values is illustrated in Figure 5.3. Notice that by the time we get to 10 years, the present values are all substantially smaller than the future amounts.

Concept Questions

5.2a What do we mean by the present value of an investment?
5.2b The process of discounting a future amount back to the present is the opposite of doing what?
5.2c What do we mean by discounted cash flow, or DCF, valuation?
5.2d In general, what is the present value of $1 to be received in t periods, assuming a discount rate of r per period?

More about Present and Future Values   **5.3** ℤ

If you look back at the expressions we came up with for present and future values, you will see a simple relationship between the two. We explore this relationship and some related issues in this section.

PRESENT VERSUS FUTURE VALUE

What we called the present value factor is just the reciprocal of (that is, 1 divided by) the future value factor:

Future value factor $= (1 + r)^t$

Present value factor $= 1/(1 + r)^t$

In fact, the easy way to calculate a present value factor on many calculators is to first calculate the future value factor and then press the "$1/x$" key to flip it over.

If we let FV_t stand for the future value after t periods, then the relationship between future value and present value can be written simply as one of the following:

$$PV \times (1 + r)^t = FV_t$$
$$PV = FV_t/(1 + r)^t = FV_t \times [1/(1 + r)^t]$$

[5.3]

This last result we will call the *basic present value equation*. We will use it throughout the text. A number of variations come up, but this simple equation underlies many of the most important ideas in corporate finance.

| EXAMPLE 5.8 | Evaluating Investments |

To give you an idea of how we will be using present and future values, consider the following simple investment. Your company proposes to buy an asset for $335. This investment is very safe. You would sell off the asset in three years for $400. You know you could invest the $335 elsewhere at 10 percent with very little risk. What do you think of the proposed investment?

This is not a good investment. Why not? Because you can invest the $335 elsewhere at 10 percent. If you do, after three years it will grow to:

$$\$335 \times (1 + r)^t = \$335 \times 1.1^3$$
$$= \$335 \times 1.331$$
$$= \$445.89$$

Because the proposed investment pays out only $400, it is not as good as other alternatives we have. Another way of seeing the same thing is to notice that the present value of $400 in three years at 10 percent is:

$$\$400 \times [1/(1 + r)^t] = \$400/1.1^3 = \$400/1.331 = \$300.53$$

This tells us that we have to invest only about $300 to get $400 in three years, not $335. We will return to this type of analysis later on.

DETERMINING THE DISCOUNT RATE

For a downloadable, Windows-based financial calculator, go to www.calculator.org.

We frequently need to determine what discount rate is implicit in an investment. We can do this by looking at the basic present value equation:

$$PV = FV_t/(1 + r)^t$$

There are only four parts to this equation: the present value (PV), the future value (FV_t), the discount rate (r), and the life of the investment (t). Given any three of these, we can always find the fourth.

Finding *r* for a Single-Period Investment	**EXAMPLE 5.9**

You are considering a one-year investment. If you put up $1,250, you will get back $1,350. What rate is this investment paying?

First, in this single-period case, the answer is fairly obvious. You are getting a total of $100 in addition to your $1,250. The implicit rate on this investment is thus $100/1,250 = 8 percent.

More formally, from the basic present value equation, the present value (the amount you must put up today) is $1,250. The future value (what the present value grows to) is $1,350. The time involved is one period, so we have:

$$\$1{,}250 = \$1{,}350/(1 + r)^1$$
$$1 + r = \$1{,}350/1{,}250 = 1.08$$
$$r = 8\%$$

In this simple case, of course, there was no need to go through this calculation. But as we describe next, it gets a little harder with more than one period.

To illustrate what happens with multiple periods, let's say we are offered an investment that costs us $100 and will double our money in eight years. To compare this to other investments, we would like to know what discount rate is implicit in these numbers. This discount rate is called the *rate of return,* or sometimes just the *return,* on the investment. In this case, we have a present value of $100, a future value of $200 (double our money), and an eight-year life. To calculate the return, we can write the basic present value equation as:

$$PV = FV_t /(1 + r)^t$$
$$\$100 = \$200/(1 + r)^8$$

It could also be written as:

$$(1 + r)^8 = \$200/100 = 2$$

We now need to solve for *r*. There are three ways we could do it:

1. Use a financial calculator.
2. Solve the equation for $1 + r$ by taking the eighth root of both sides. Because this is the same thing as raising both sides to the power of ⅛ or .125, this is actually easy to do with the "y^x" key on a calculator. Just enter 2, then press "y^x," enter .125, and press the "=" key. The eighth root should be about 1.09, which implies that *r* is 9 percent.
3. Use a future value table. The future value factor after eight years is equal to 2. If you look across the row corresponding to eight periods in Table A.1, you will see that a future value factor of 2 corresponds to the 9 percent column, again implying that the return here is 9 percent.

Actually, in this particular example, there is a useful "back of the envelope" means of solving for *r*—the Rule of 72. For reasonable rates of return, the time it takes to double your money is given approximately by $72/r\%$. In our example, this means that $72/r\% =$ eight years, implying that *r* is 9 percent, as we calculated. This rule is fairly accurate for discount rates in the 5 percent to 20 percent range.

EXAMPLE 5.10   ## Baseball Collectibles as Investments

In April 2008, the last baseball hit for a home run by Barry Bonds was auctioned off for about $376,000. The price of the ball was considered a bargain, in part because potential buyers were unsure if Bonds would play again. "Experts" on such collectibles often argue that collectibles such as this will double in value over a 10-year period.

So would the ball have been a good investment? By the Rule of 72, you already know the experts were predicting that the ball would double in value in 10 years; so the return predicted would be about 72/10 = 7.2 percent per year, which is only so-so.

Why does the Rule of 72 work? See www.moneychimp.com.

At one time at least, a rule of thumb in the rarefied world of fine art collecting was "your money back in 5 years, double your money in 10 years." Given this, let's see how an investment stacked up. In 1998, the Alberto Giacometti bronze statue *L'Homme Qui Marche III* sold for $2,972,500. Five years later, the statue was sold again, walking out the door at a price of $4,039,500. How did the seller do?

The rule of thumb has us doubling our money in 10 years; so, from the Rule of 72, we have that 7.2 percent per year was the norm. The statue was resold in almost exactly five years. The present value is $2,972,500, and the future value is $4,039,500. We need to solve for the unknown rate, *r*, as follows:

$$\$2,972,500 = \$4,039,500/(1 + r)^5$$
$$(1 + r)^5 = 1.3590$$

Solving for *r*, we find the seller earned about 6.33 percent per year—less than the 7.2 percent rule of thumb. At least the seller made his money back.

What about other collectibles? To a philatelist (a stamp collector to you and us), one of the most prized stamps is the 1918 24-cent inverted Jenny C3a. The stamp is a collectible because it has a picture of an upside-down biplane. One of these stamps sold at auction for $345,000 in 2010. At what rate did its value grow? Verify for yourself that the answer is about 16.66 percent, assuming a 92-year period.

Other famous collectibles exist because of mistakes. For example, there is the 1944D Lincoln penny, which was struck in zinc rather than copper. In 2010, one of these pennies sold for $60,375. Assuming that 66 years had passed, see if you don't agree that this collectible gained a whopping 26.69 percent per year.

Not all collectibles do as well. Also in 2010, a 1796 $10 gold coin was auctioned for $57,500. While this seems like a huge return to the untrained eye, check that, over the 214-year period, the gain was only about 4.13 percent per year.

Perhaps the most desired coin for numismatists (coin collectors) is the 1933 $20 gold double eagle. Outside of the U.S. Mint and the Smithsonian, only one of these coins is in circulation. In 2002, the coin sold at auction for $7,590,020. See if you agree that this collectible gained about 20.5 percent per year.

A slightly more extreme example involves money bequeathed by Benjamin Franklin, who died on April 17, 1790. In his will, he gave 1,000 pounds sterling to Massachusetts and the city of Boston. He gave a like amount to Pennsylvania and the city of Philadelphia. The money had been paid to Franklin when he held political office, but he believed that politicians should not be paid for their service (it appears that this view is not widely shared by modern politicians).

Franklin originally specified that the money should be paid out 100 years after his death and used to train young people. Later, however, after some legal wrangling, it was agreed that the money would be paid out in 1990, 200 years after Franklin's death. By that time, the Pennsylvania bequest had grown to about $2 million; the Massachusetts bequest had grown to $4.5 million. The money was used to fund the Franklin Institutes in Boston and Philadelphia. Assuming that 1,000 pounds sterling was equivalent to $1,000, what rate of return did the two states earn? (The dollar did not become the official U.S. currency until 1792.)

For Pennsylvania, the future value is $2 million and the present value is $1,000. There are 200 years involved, so we need to solve for r in the following:

$$\$1,000 = \$2 \text{ million}/(1 + r)^{200}$$
$$(1 + r)^{200} = 2,000$$

Solving for r, we see that the Pennsylvania money grew at about 3.87 percent per year. The Massachusetts money did better; verify that the rate of return in this case was 4.3 percent. Small differences in returns can add up!

CALCULATOR HINTS

We can illustrate how to calculate unknown rates using a financial calculator with these numbers. For Pennsylvania, you would do the following:

Enter	200			−1,000	2,000,000
	N	**I/Y**	**PMT**	**PV**	**FV**
Solve for		3.87			

As in our previous examples, notice the minus sign on the present value, representing Franklin's outlay made many years ago. What do you change to work the problem for Massachusetts?

Saving for College   EXAMPLE 5.11

You estimate that you will need about $80,000 to send your child to college in eight years. You have about $35,000 now. If you can earn 20 percent per year, will you make it? At what rate will you just reach your goal?

If you can earn 20 percent, the future value of your $35,000 in eight years will be:

$$FV = \$35,000 \times 1.20^8 = \$35,000 \times 4.2998 = \$150,493.59$$

So, you will make it easily. The minimum rate is the unknown r in the following:

$$FV = \$35,000 \times (1 + r)^8 = \$80,000$$
$$(1 + r)^8 = \$80,000/35,000 = 2.2857$$

Therefore, the future value factor is 2.2857. Looking at the row in Table A.1 that corresponds to eight periods, we see that our future value factor is roughly halfway between the ones shown for 10 percent (2.1436) and 12 percent (2.4760), so you will just reach your goal if you earn approximately 11 percent. To get the exact answer, we could use a financial calculator or we could solve for r:

$$(1 + r)^8 = \$80,000/35,000 = 2.2857$$
$$1 + r = 2.2857^{(1/8)} = 2.2857^{.125} = 1.1089$$
$$r = 10.89\%$$

EXAMPLE 5.12   **Only 18,262.5 Days to Retirement**

You would like to retire in 50 years as a millionaire. If you have $10,000 today, what rate of return do you need to earn to achieve your goal?

The future value is $1,000,000. The present value is $10,000, and there are 50 years until payment. We need to calculate the unknown discount rate in the following:

$$\$10,000 = \$1,000,000/(1 + r)^{50}$$
$$(1 + r)^{50} = 100$$

The future value factor is thus 100. You can verify that the implicit rate is about 9.65 percent.

How much do you need at retirement? Check out the "Money in Your 20s" link at www.about.com.

Not taking the time value of money into account when computing growth rates or rates of return often leads to some misleading numbers in the real world. For example, the most loved (and hated) team in baseball, the New York Yankees, had the highest payroll during the 1988 season, about $19 million. In 2010, the Yankees again had the highest payroll, a staggering $206 million: an increase of 984 percent! If history is any guide, we can get a rough idea of the future growth in baseball payrolls. See if you don't agree that this represents an annual increase of 11.4 percent, a substantial growth rate, but much less than the gaudy 984 percent.

How about classic maps? A few years ago, the first map of America, printed in Rome in 1507, was valued at about $135,000, 69 percent more than the $80,000 it was worth 10 years earlier. Your return on investment if you were the proud owner of the map over those 10 years? Verify that it's about 5.4 percent per year—far worse than the 69 percent reported increase in price.

Whether with maps or baseball payrolls, it's easy to be misled when returns are quoted without considering the time value of money. However, it's not just the uninitiated who are guilty of this slight form of deception. The title of a feature article in a leading business magazine predicted the Dow Jones Industrial Average would soar to a 70 percent gain over the coming five years. Do you think it meant a 70 percent return per year on your money? Think again!

FINDING THE NUMBER OF PERIODS

Suppose we are interested in purchasing an asset that costs $50,000. We currently have $25,000. If we can earn 12 percent on this $25,000, how long until we have the $50,000? Finding the answer involves solving for the last variable in the basic present value equation, the number of periods. You already know how to get an approximate answer to this particular problem. Notice that we need to double our money. From the Rule of 72, this will take about $72/12 = 6$ years at 12 percent.

To come up with the exact answer, we can again manipulate the basic present value equation. The present value is $25,000, and the future value is $50,000. With a 12 percent discount rate, the basic equation takes one of the following forms:

$$\$25,000 = \$50,000/1.12^t$$
$$\$50,000/25,000 = 1.12^t = 2$$

We thus have a future value factor of 2 for a 12 percent rate. We now need to solve for t. If you look down the column in Table A.1 that corresponds to 12 percent, you will see that a future value factor of 1.9738 occurs at six periods. It will thus take about six years, as we calculated. To get the exact answer, we have to explicitly solve for t (or use a financial calculator). If you do this, you will see that the answer is 6.1163 years, so our approximation was quite close in this case.

CALCULATOR HINTS

If you use a financial calculator, here are the relevant entries:

Enter	12			-25,000	50,000
	N	**I/Y**	**PMT**	**PV**	**FV**
Solve for	6.1163				

Waiting for Godot	**EXAMPLE 5.13**

You've been saving up to buy the Godot Company. The total cost will be $10 million. You currently have about $2.3 million. If you can earn 5 percent on your money, how long will you have to wait? At 16 percent, how long must you wait?

At 5 percent, you'll have to wait a long time. From the basic present value equation:

$$\$2.3 \text{ million} = \$10 \text{ million}/1.05^t$$
$$1.05^t = 4.35$$
$$t = 30 \text{ years}$$

At 16 percent, things are a little better. Verify for yourself that it will take about 10 years.

U.S. EE Savings Bonds are a familiar investment for many. You purchase them for half of their $100 face value. In other words, you pay $50 today and get $100 at some point in the future when the bond "matures." You receive no interest in between, and the interest rate is adjusted every six months, so the length of time until your $50 grows to $100 depends on future interest rates. However, at worst, the bonds are guaranteed to be worth $100 at the end of 17 years, so this is the longest you would ever have to wait. If you do have to wait the full 17 years, what rate do you earn?

Because this investment is doubling in value in 17 years, the Rule of 72 tells you the answer right away: $72/17 = 4.24\%$. Remember, this is the minimum guaranteed return, so you might do better. This example finishes our introduction to basic time value concepts. Table 5.4 summarizes present and future value calculations for future reference. As our

Learn more about using Excel for time value and other calculations at www.studyfinance.com.

TABLE 5.4

Summary of Time Value Calculations

I.	**Symbols:**
	PV = Present value, what future cash flows are worth today
	FV_t = Future value, what cash flows are worth in the future
	r = Interest rate, rate of return, or discount rate per period—typically, but not always, one year
	t = Number of periods—typically, but not always, the number of years
	C = Cash amount
II.	**Future Value of C Invested at r Percent for t Periods:**
	$FV_t = C \times (1 + r)^t$
	The term $(1 + r)^t$ is called the *future value factor*.
III.	**Present Value of C to Be Received in t Periods at r Percent per Period:**
	$PV = C/(1 + r)^t$
	The term $1/(1 + r)^t$ is called the *present value factor*.
IV.	**The Basic Present Value Equation Giving the Relationship between Present and Future Value:**
	$PV = FV_t/(1 + r)^t$

SPREADSHEET STRATEGIES

Using a Spreadsheet for Time Value of Money Calculations

More and more, businesspeople from many different areas (not just finance and accounting) rely on spreadsheets to do all the different types of calculations that come up in the real world. As a result, in this section, we will show you how to use a spreadsheet to handle the various time value of money problems we presented in this chapter. We will use Microsoft Excel™, but the commands are similar for other types of software. We assume you are already familiar with basic spreadsheet operations.

As we have seen, you can solve for any one of the following four potential unknowns: future value, present value, the discount rate, or the number of periods. With a spreadsheet, there is a separate formula for each. In Excel, these are shown in a nearby box.

In these formulas, pv and fv are present and future value, nper is the number of periods, and rate is the discount, or interest, rate.

Two things are a little tricky here. First, unlike a financial calculator, the spreadsheet requires that the rate be entered as a decimal. Second, as with most financial calculators, you have to put a negative sign on either the present value or the future value to solve for the rate or the number of periods. For the same reason, if you solve for a present value, the answer will have a negative sign unless you input a negative future value. The same is true when you compute a future value.

To Find	Enter This Formula
Future value	= FV (rate,nper,pmt,pv)
Present value	= PV (rate,nper,pmt,fv)
Discount rate	= RATE (nper,pmt,pv,fv)
Number of periods	= NPER (rate,pmt,pv,fv)

To illustrate how you might use these formulas, we will go back to an example in the chapter. If you invest $25,000 at 12 percent per year, how long until you have $50,000? You might set up a spreadsheet like this:

	A	B	C	D	E	F	G	H
1								
2	**Using a spreadsheet for time value of money calculations**							
3								
4	If we invest $25,000 at 12 percent, how long until we have $50,000? We need to solve							
5	for the unknown number of periods, so we use the formula NPER(rate,pmt,pv,fv).							
6								
7	Present value (pv):	$25,000						
8	Future value (fv):	$50,000						
9	Rate (rate):	.12						
10								
11	Periods:	6.1162554						
12								
13	The formula entered in cell B11 is =NPER(B9,0,-B7,B8); notice that pmt is zero and that pv							
14	has a negative sign on it. Also notice that rate is entered as a decimal, not a percentage.							

nearby *Work the Web* box shows, online calculators are widely available to handle these calculations; however, it is still important to know what is really going on.

Concept Questions

5.3a What is the basic present value equation?

5.3b What is the Rule of 72?

WORK THE WEB

How important is the time value of money? A recent search on one Web search engine returned over 26.5 million hits! Although you must understand the calculations behind the time value of money, the advent of financial calculators and spreadsheets has eliminated the need for tedious calculations. In fact, many websites offer time value of money calculators. The following is one example from www. investopedia.com. You have $10,000 today and will invest it at 10.5 percent for 35 years. How much will it be worth at that time? With the Investopedia calculator, you simply enter the values and hit "Calculate". The results look like this:

Interest Rate Per Time Period:	10.5	%
Number of Time Periods:	35	
Present Value:	10000	
	Calculate	
Future Value:	$329,366.73	

Who said time value of money calculations are hard?

Questions

1. Use the present value calculator on this website to answer the following: Suppose you want to have $140,000 in 25 years. If you can earn a 10 percent return, how much do you have to invest today?
2. Use the future value calculator on this website to answer the following question: Suppose you have $8,000 today that you plan to save for your retirement in 40 years. If you earn a return of 10.8 percent per year, how much will this account be worth when you are ready to retire?

Visit us at www.mhhe.com/rwj

Summary and Conclusions   5.4

This chapter has introduced you to the basic principles of present value and discounted cash flow valuation. In it, we explained a number of things about the time value of money, including these:

1. For a given rate of return, we can determine the value at some point in the future of an investment made today by calculating the future value of that investment.
2. We can determine the current worth of a future cash flow or series of cash flows for a given rate of return by calculating the present value of the cash flow(s) involved.

3. The relationship between present value (PV) and future value (FV) for a given rate r and time t is given by the basic present value equation:

$$PV = FV_t/(1 + r)^t$$

As we have shown, it is possible to find any one of the four components (PV, FV_t, r, or t) given the other three.

The principles developed in this chapter will figure prominently in the chapters to come. The reason for this is that most investments, whether they involve real assets or financial assets, can be analyzed using the discounted cash flow (DCF) approach. As a result, the DCF approach is broadly applicable and widely used in practice. Before going on, therefore, you might want to do some of the problems that follow.

CONNECT TO FINANCE

 If you are using $Connect^{TM}$ *Finance* in your course, get online to take a Practice Test, check out study tools, and find out where you need additonal practice.

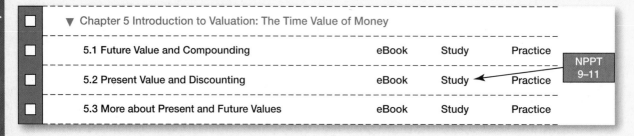

▼ Chapter 5 Introduction to Valuation: The Time Value of Money			
5.1 Future Value and Compounding	eBook	Study	Practice
5.2 Present Value and Discounting	eBook	Study	Practice
5.3 More about Present and Future Values	eBook	Study	Practice

NPPT 9–11

Can you answer the following questions?

Section 5.1   You deposited $2,000 in a bank account that pays 5 percent simple interest. How much will you have in this account after three years? (LO 5-1)

Section 5.2   What is the present value of $11,500 discounted at 9 percent for 11 years? (LO 5-2)

Section 5.3   Charlie invested $6,200 in a stock last year. Currently, this investment is worth $6,788.38. What is the rate of return on this investment? (LO 5-3)

Log on to find out!

CHAPTER REVIEW AND SELF-TEST PROBLEMS

5.1   **Calculating Future Values** Assume you deposit $10,000 today in an account that pays 6 percent interest. How much will you have in five years?

5.2   **Calculating Present Values** Suppose you have just celebrated your 19th birthday. A rich uncle has set up a trust fund for you that will pay you $150,000 when you turn 30. If the relevant discount rate is 9 percent, how much is this fund worth today?

5.3   **Calculating Rates of Return** You've been offered an investment that will double your money in 10 years. What rate of return are you being offered? Check your answer using the Rule of 72.

Visit us at www.mhhe.com/rwj

5.4   Calculating the Number of Periods You've been offered an investment that will pay you 9 percent per year. If you invest $15,000, how long until you have $30,000? How long until you have $45,000?

ANSWERS TO CHAPTER REVIEW AND SELF-TEST PROBLEMS

5.1   We need to calculate the future value of $10,000 at 6 percent for five years. The future value factor is:

$$1.06^5 = 1.3382$$

The future value is thus $10,000 \times 1.3382 = \$13,382.26$.

5.2   We need the present value of $150,000 to be paid in 11 years at 9 percent. The discount factor is:

$$1/1.09^{11} = 1/2.5804 = .3875$$

The present value is thus about $58,130.

5.3   Suppose you invest $1,000. You will have $2,000 in 10 years with this investment. So, $1,000 is the amount you have today, or the present value, and $2,000 is the amount you will have in 10 years, or the future value. From the basic present value equation, we have:

$$\$2,000 = \$1,000 \times (1 + r)^{10}$$
$$2 = (1 + r)^{10}$$

From here, we need to solve for r, the unknown rate. As shown in the chapter, there are several different ways to do this. We will take the 10th root of 2 (by raising 2 to the power of $1/10$):

$$2^{(1/10)} = 1 + r$$
$$1.0718 = 1 + r$$
$$r = 7.18\%$$

Using the Rule of 72, we have $72/t = r\%$, or $72/10 = 7.2\%$; so, our answer looks good (remember that the Rule of 72 is only an approximation).

5.4   The basic equation is this:

$$\$30,000 = \$15,000 \times (1 + .09)^t$$
$$2 = (1 + .09)^t$$

If we solve for t, we find that $t = 8.04$ years. Using the Rule of 72, we get $72/9 = 8$ years, so once again our answer looks good. To get $45,000, verify for yourself that you will have to wait 12.75 years.

CONCEPTS REVIEW AND CRITICAL THINKING QUESTIONS

1.   **Present Value [LO2]** The basic present value equation has four parts. What are they?

2.   **Compounding [LO1, 2]** What is compounding? What is discounting?

3.   **Compounding and Period [LO1]** As you increase the length of time involved, what happens to future values? What happens to present values?

Visit us at www.mhhe.com/rwj

4. **Compounding and Interest Rates [LO1]** What happens to a future value if you increase the rate *r*? What happens to a present value?

5. **Ethical Considerations [LO2]** Take a look back at Example 5.7. Is it deceptive advertising? Is it unethical to advertise a future value like this without a disclaimer?

   To answer the next five questions, refer to the TMCC security we discussed to open the chapter.

6. **Time Value of Money [LO2]** Why would TMCC be willing to accept such a small amount today ($24,099) in exchange for a promise to repay about four times that amount ($100,000) in the future?

7. **Call Provisions [LO2]** TMCC has the right to buy back the securities on the anniversary date at a price established when the securities were issued (this feature is a term of this particular deal). What impact does this feature have on the desirability of this security as an investment?

8. **Time Value of Money [LO2]** Would you be willing to pay $24,099 today in exchange for $100,000 in 30 years? What would be the key considerations in answering yes or no? Would your answer depend on who is making the promise to repay?

9. **Investment Comparison [LO2]** Suppose that when TMCC offered the security for $24,099, the U.S. Treasury had offered an essentially identical security. Do you think it would have had a higher or lower price? Why?

10. **Length of Investment [LO2]** The TMCC security is bought and sold on the New York Stock Exchange. If you looked at the price today, do you think the price would exceed the $24,099 original price? Why? If you looked in the year 2019, do you think the price would be higher or lower than today's price? Why?

QUESTIONS AND PROBLEMS

BASIC
(Questions 1–15)

1. **Simple Interest versus Compound Interest [LO1]** First City Bank pays 7 percent simple interest on its savings account balances, whereas Second City Bank pays 7 percent interest compounded annually. If you made a $6,000 deposit in each bank, how much more money would you earn from your Second City Bank account at the end of nine years?

2. **Calculating Future Values [LO1]** For each of the following, compute the future value:

Present Value	Years	Interest Rate	Future Value
$ 2,250	11	13%	
8,752	7	9	
76,355	14	12	
183,796	8	6	

3. **Calculating Present Values [LO2]** For each of the following, compute the present value:

Present Value	Years	Interest Rate	Future Value
	13	7%	$ 15,451
	4	13	51,557
	29	14	886,073
	40	9	550,164

Visit us at www.mhhe.com/rwj

4. **Calculating Interest Rates [LO3]** Solve for the unknown interest rate in each of   ✗
   the following:

Present Value	Years	Interest Rate	Future Value
$ 240	4		$ 297
360	18		1,080
39,000	19		185,382
38,261	25		531,618

5. **Calculating the Number of Periods [LO4]** Solve for the unknown number of   ✗
   years in each of the following:

Present Value	Years	Interest Rate	Future Value
$ 560		9%	$ 1,389
810		10	1,821
18,400		17	289,715
21,500		15	430,258

6. **Calculating Interest Rates [LO3]** Assume the total cost of a college education
   will be $300,000 when your child enters college in 18 years. You presently have
   $65,000 to invest. What annual rate of interest must you earn on your investment to
   cover the cost of your child's college education?

7. **Calculating the Number of Periods [LO4]** At 6.5 percent interest, how long does
   it take to double your money? To quadruple it?

8. **Calculating Interest Rates [LO3]** In January 2010, the average house price in
   the United States was $283,400. In January 2000, the average price was $200,300.
   What was the annual increase in selling price?

9. **Calculating the Number of Periods [LO4]** You're trying to save to buy a new
   $190,000 Ferrari. You have $40,000 today that can be invested at your bank. The
   bank pays 4.8 percent annual interest on its accounts. How long will it be before
   you have enough to buy the car?

10. **Calculating Present Values [LO2]** Imprudential, Inc., has an unfunded pension
    liability of $575 million that must be paid in 20 years. To assess the value of the
    firm's stock, financial analysts want to discount this liability back to the present. If
    the relevant discount rate is 6.8 percent, what is the present value of this liability?

11. **Calculating Present Values [LO2]** You have just received notification that you
    have won the $1 million first prize in the Centennial Lottery. However, the prize
    will be awarded on your 100th birthday (assuming you're around to collect),
    80 years from now. What is the present value of your windfall if the appropriate
    discount rate is 9 percent?

12. **Calculating Future Values [LO1]** Your coin collection contains fifty 1952 silver
    dollars. If your grandparents purchased them for their face value when they were
    new, how much will your collection be worth when you retire in 2060, assuming
    they appreciate at a 4.1 percent annual rate?

13. **Calculating Interest Rates and Future Values [LO1, 3]** In 1895, the first U.S.
    Open Golf Championship was held. The winner's prize money was $150. In 2010,
    the winner's check was $1,350,000. What was the percentage increase per year in
    the winner's check over this period? If the winner's prize increases at the same rate,
    what will it be in 2040?

Visit us at www.mhhe.com/rwj

14. **Calculating Interest Rates [LO3]** In 2010, a gold Morgan dollar minted in 1895 sold for $125,000. For this to have been true, what rate of return did this coin return for the lucky numismatist?

15. **Calculating Rates of Return [LO3]** Although appealing to more refined tastes, art as a collectible has not always performed so profitably. During 2003, Sotheby's sold the Edgar Degas bronze sculpture *Petite Danseuse de Quatorze Ans* at auction for a price of $10,311,500. Unfortunately for the previous owner, he had purchased it in 1999 at a price of $12,377,500. What was his annual rate of return on this sculpture?

INTERMEDIATE
(Questions 16–20)

16. **Calculating Rates of Return [LO3]** Referring to the TMCC security we discussed at the very beginning of the chapter:

    a. Based on the $24,099 price, what rate was TMCC paying to borrow money?

    b. Suppose that, on March 28, 2019, this security's price is $42,380. If an investor had purchased it for $24,099 at the offering and sold it on this day, what annual rate of return would she have earned?

    c. If an investor had purchased the security at market on March 28, 2019, and held it until it matured, what annual rate of return would she have earned?

17. **Calculating Present Values [LO2]** Suppose you are still committed to owning a $190,000 Ferrari (see Problem 9). If you believe your mutual fund can achieve a 12 percent annual rate of return and you want to buy the car in 9 years on the day you turn 30, how much must you invest today?

18. **Calculating Future Values [LO1]** You have just made your first $5,000 contribution to your retirement account. Assuming you earn an 11 percent rate of return and make no additional contributions, what will your account be worth when you retire in 45 years? What if you wait 10 years before contributing? (Does this suggest an investment strategy?)

19. **Calculating Future Values [LO1]** You are scheduled to receive $15,000 in two years. When you receive it, you will invest it for six more years at 7.1 percent per year. How much will you have in eight years?

20. **Calculating the Number of Periods [LO4]** You expect to receive $15,000 at graduation in two years. You plan on investing it at 11 percent until you have $85,000. How long will you wait from now?

DISCOUNTED CASH FLOW VALUATION

THE SIGNING OF BIG-NAME ATHLETES is often accompanied by great fanfare, but the numbers are often misleading. For example, in late 2010, catcher Victor Martinez reached a deal with the Detroit Tigers, signing a contract with a reported value of $50 million. Not bad, especially for someone who makes a living using the "tools of ignorance" (jock jargon for a catcher's equipment). Another example is the contract signed by Jayson Werth of the Washington Nationals, which had a stated value of $126 million.

It looks like Victor and Jayson did pretty well, but then there was Carl Crawford, who signed to play in front of Boston's Red Sox Nation. Carl's contract has a stated value of $142 million, but this amount was actually payable over several years. The contract consisted of a $6 million signing bonus, along with $14 million in the first year plus $122 million in future salary to be paid in the years 2011 through 2017. Victor's and Jayson's payments were similarly spread over time. Because all three contracts called for payments that are made at future dates, we must consider the time value of money, which means none of these players received the quoted amounts. How much did they really get? This chapter gives you the "tools of knowledge" to answer this question.

LEARNING OBJECTIVES

After studying this chapter, you should understand:

LO1 How to determine the future and present value of investments with multiple cash flows.

LO2 How loan payments are calculated and how to find the interest rate on a loan.

LO3 How loans are amortized or paid off.

LO4 How interest rates are quoted (and misquoted).

In our previous chapter, we covered the basics of discounted cash flow valuation. However, so far, we have dealt with only single cash flows. In reality, most investments have multiple cash flows. For example, if Target is thinking of opening a new department store, there will be a large cash outlay in the beginning and then cash inflows for many years. In this chapter, we begin to explore how to value such investments.

When you finish this chapter, you should have some very practical skills. For example, you will know how to calculate your own car payments or student loan payments. You will also be able to determine how long it will take to pay off a credit card if you make the minimum payment each month (a practice we do not recommend). We will show you how to compare interest rates to determine which are the highest and which are the lowest, and we will also show you how interest rates can be quoted in different—and at times deceptive—ways.

FIGURE 6.1

Drawing and Using a Time Line

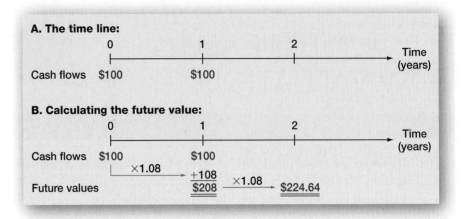

6.1 Future and Present Values of Multiple Cash Flows

Thus far, we have restricted our attention to either the future value of a lump sum present amount or the present value of some single future cash flow. In this section, we begin to study ways to value multiple cash flows. We start with future value.

FUTURE VALUE WITH MULTIPLE CASH FLOWS

Suppose you deposit $100 today in an account paying 8 percent. In one year, you will deposit another $100. How much will you have in two years? This particular problem is relatively easy. At the end of the first year, you will have $108 plus the second $100 you deposit, for a total of $208. You leave this $208 on deposit at 8 percent for another year. At the end of this second year, it is worth:

$$\$208 \times 1.08 = \$224.64$$

Figure 6.1 is a *time line* that illustrates the process of calculating the future value of these two $100 deposits. Figures such as this are useful for solving complicated problems. Almost anytime you are having trouble with a present or future value problem, drawing a time line will help you see what is happening.

In the first part of Figure 6.1, we show the cash flows on the time line. The most important thing is that we write them down where they actually occur. Here, the first cash flow occurs today, which we label as Time 0. We therefore put $100 at Time 0 on the time line. The second $100 cash flow occurs one year from today, so we write it down at the point labeled as Time 1. In the second part of Figure 6.1, we calculate the future values one period at a time to come up with the final $224.64.

| **EXAMPLE 6.1** | **Saving Up Revisited** |

You think you will be able to deposit $4,000 at the end of each of the next three years in a bank account paying 8 percent interest. You currently have $7,000 in the account. How much will you have in three years? In four years?

At the end of the first year, you will have:

$$\$7,000 \times 1.08 + 4,000 = \$11,560$$

At the end of the second year, you will have:

$11,560 × 1.08 + 4,000 = $16,484.80

Repeating this for the third year gives:

$16,484.80 × 1.08 + 4,000 = $21,803.58

Therefore, you will have $21,803.58 in three years. If you leave this on deposit for one more year (and don't add to it), at the end of the fourth year, you'll have:

$21,803.58 × 1.08 = $23,547.87

When we calculated the future value of the two $100 deposits, we simply calculated the balance as of the beginning of each year and then rolled that amount forward to the next year. We could have done it another, quicker way. The first $100 is on deposit for two years at 8 percent, so its future value is:

$100 × 1.08^2 = $100 × 1.1664 = $116.64

The second $100 is on deposit for one year at 8 percent, and its future value is thus:

$100 × 1.08 = $108

The total future value, as we previously calculated, is equal to the sum of these two future values:

$116.64 + 108 = $224.64

Based on this example, there are two ways to calculate future values for multiple cash flows: (1) Compound the accumulated balance forward one year at a time or (2) calculate the future value of each cash flow first and then add them up. Both give the same answer, so you can do it either way.

To illustrate the two different ways of calculating future values, consider the future value of $2,000 invested at the end of each of the next five years. The current balance is zero, and the rate is 10 percent. We first draw a time line, as shown in Figure 6.2.

On the time line, notice that nothing happens until the end of the first year, when we make the first $2,000 investment. This first $2,000 earns interest for the next four (not five) years. Also notice that the last $2,000 is invested at the end of the fifth year, so it earns no interest at all.

Figure 6.3 illustrates the calculations involved if we compound the investment one period at a time. As illustrated, the future value is $12,210.20.

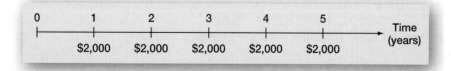

FIGURE 6.2

Time Line for $2,000 per Year for Five Years

FIGURE 6.3   Future Value Calculated by Compounding Forward One Period at a Time

FIGURE 6.4   Future Value Calculated by Compounding Each Cash Flow Separately

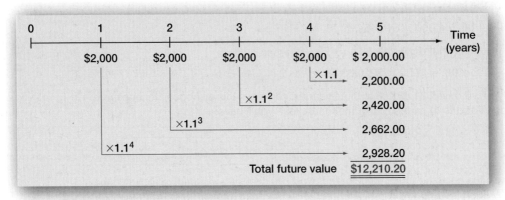

Figure 6.4 goes through the same calculations, but the second technique is used. Naturally, the answer is the same.

EXAMPLE 6.2   **Saving Up Once Again**

If you deposit $100 in one year, $200 in two years, and $300 in three years, how much will you have in three years? How much of this is interest? How much will you have in five years if you don't add additional amounts? Assume a 7 percent interest rate throughout.

We will calculate the future value of each amount in three years. Notice that the $100 earns interest for two years, and the $200 earns interest for one year. The final $300 earns no interest. The future values are thus:

$$\$100 \times 1.07^2 = \$114.49$$
$$\$200 \times 1.07 = 214.00$$
$$+\$300 = \underline{300.00}$$
$$\text{Total future value} = \$628.49$$

The total future value is thus $628.49. The total interest is:

$$\$628.49 - (100 + 200 + 300) = \$28.49$$

How much will you have in five years? We know that you will have $628.49 in three years. If you leave that in for two more years, it will grow to:

$$\$628.49 \times 1.07^2 = \$628.49 \times 1.1449 = \$719.56$$

Notice that we could have calculated the future value of each amount separately. Once again, be careful about the lengths of time. As we previously calculated, the first $100 earns interest for only four years, the second deposit earns three years' interest, and the last earns two years' interest:

$$\$100 \times 1.07^4 = \$100 \times 1.3108 = \$131.08$$
$$\$200 \times 1.07^3 = \$200 \times 1.2250 = 245.01$$
$$+\$300 \times 1.07^2 = \$300 \times 1.1449 = \underline{343.47}$$
$$\text{Total future value} = \$719.56$$

PRESENT VALUE WITH MULTIPLE CASH FLOWS

We often need to determine the present value of a series of future cash flows. As with future values, there are two ways we can do it. We can either discount back one period at a time, or we can just calculate the present values individually and add them up.

Suppose you need $1,000 in one year and $2,000 more in two years. If you can earn 9 percent on your money, how much do you have to put up today to exactly cover these amounts in the future? In other words, what is the present value of the two cash flows at 9 percent?

The present value of $2,000 in two years at 9 percent is:

$2,000/1.09^2 = $1,683.36

The present value of $1,000 in one year is:

$1,000/1.09 = $917.43

Therefore, the total present value is:

$1,683.36 + 917.43 = $2,600.79

To see why $2,600.79 is the right answer, we can check to see that after the $2,000 is paid out in two years, there is no money left. If we invest $2,600.79 for one year at 9 percent, we will have:

$2,600.79 × 1.09 = $2,834.86

We take out $1,000, leaving $1,834.86. This amount earns 9 percent for another year, leaving us with:

$1,834.86 × 1.09 = $2,000

This is just as we planned. As this example illustrates, the present value of a series of future cash flows is simply the amount you would need today to exactly duplicate those future cash flows (for a given discount rate).

An alternative way of calculating present values for multiple future cash flows is to discount back to the present, one period at a time. To illustrate, suppose we had an investment that was going to pay $1,000 at the end of every year for the next five years. To find the present value, we could discount each $1,000 back to the present separately and then add them up. Figure 6.5 illustrates this approach for a 6 percent discount rate; as shown, the answer is $4,212.37 (ignoring a small rounding error).

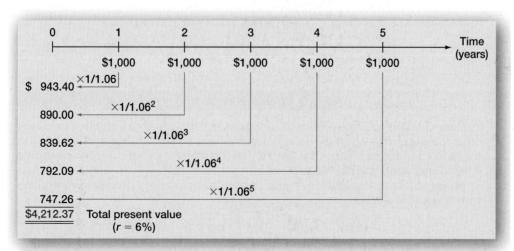

FIGURE 6.5

Present Value Calculated by Discounting Each Cash Flow Separately

FIGURE 6.6   Present Value Calculated by Discounting Back One Period at a Time

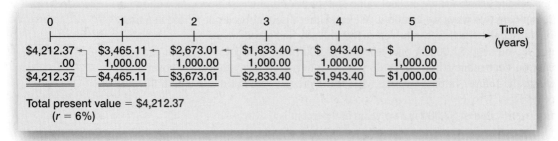

Alternatively, we could discount the last cash flow back one period and add it to the next-to-the-last cash flow:

$$(\$1,000/1.06) + 1,000 = \$943.40 + 1,000 = \$1,943.40$$

We could then discount this amount back one period and add it to the Year 3 cash flow:

$$(\$1,943.40/1.06) + 1,000 = \$1,833.40 + 1,000 = \$2,833.40$$

This process could be repeated as necessary. Figure 6.6 illustrates this approach and the remaining calculations.

EXAMPLE 6.3   **How Much Is It Worth?**

You are offered an investment that will pay you $200 in one year, $400 the next year, $600 the next year, and $800 at the end of the fourth year. You can earn 12 percent on very similar investments. What is the most you should pay for this one?

We need to calculate the present value of these cash flows at 12 percent. Taking them one at a time gives:

$$
\begin{aligned}
\$200 \times 1/1.12^1 &= \$200/1.1200 = \$\ \ 178.57 \\
\$400 \times 1/1.12^2 &= \$400/1.2544 = \ \ \ \ 318.88 \\
\$600 \times 1/1.12^3 &= \$600/1.4049 = \ \ \ \ 427.07 \\
+\$800 \times 1/1.12^4 &= \$800/1.5735 = \underline{\ \ \ \ 508.41} \\
\text{Total present value} &= \underline{\$1,432.93}
\end{aligned}
$$

If you can earn 12 percent on your money, then you can duplicate this investment's cash flows for $1,432.93, so this is the most you should be willing to pay.

EXAMPLE 6.4   **How Much Is It Worth? Part 2**

You are offered an investment that will make three $5,000 payments. The first payment will occur four years from today. The second will occur in five years, and the third will follow in six years. If you can earn 11 percent, what is the most this investment is worth today? What is the future value of the cash flows?

We will answer the questions in reverse order to illustrate a point. The future value of the cash flows in six years is:

$$(\$5,000 \times 1.11^2) + (5,000 \times 1.11) + 5,000 = \$6,160.50 + 5,550 + 5,000$$
$$= \$16,710.50$$

The present value must be:

$16,710.50/1.11^6 = $8,934.12$

Let's check this. Taking them one at a time, the PVs of the cash flows are:

$$\$5,000 \times 1/1.11^6 = \$5,000/1.8704 = \$2,673.20$$
$$\$5,000 \times 1/1.11^5 = \$5,000/1.6851 = 2,967.26$$
$$+\$5,000 \times 1/1.11^4 = \$5,000/1.5181 = \underline{3,293.65}$$
$$\text{Total present value} = \underline{\underline{\$8,934.12}}$$

This is as we previously calculated. The point we want to make is that we can calculate present and future values in any order and convert between them using whatever way seems most convenient. The answers will always be the same as long as we stick with the same discount rate and are careful to keep track of the right number of periods.

CALCULATOR HINTS

How to Calculate Present Values with Multiple Future Cash Flows Using a Financial Calculator

To calculate the present value of multiple cash flows with a financial calculator, we will simply discount the individual cash flows one at a time using the same technique we used in our previous chapter, so this is not really new. However, we can show you a shortcut. We will use the numbers in Example 6.3 to illustrate.

To begin, of course we first remember to clear out the calculator! Next, from Example 6.3, the first cash flow is $200 to be received in one year and the discount rate is 12 percent, so we do the following:

Enter   1   12   200

Solve for   −178.57

Now, you can write down this answer to save it, but that's inefficient. All calculators have a memory where you can store numbers. Why not just save it there? Doing so cuts way down on mistakes because you don't have to write down and/or rekey numbers, and it's much faster.

Next we value the second cash flow. We need to change N to 2 and FV to 400. As long as we haven't changed anything else, we don't have to reenter I/Y or clear out the calculator, so we have:

Enter   2   400

Solve for   −318.88

You save this number by adding it to the one you saved in your first calculation, and so on for the remaining two calculations.

As we will see in a later chapter, some financial calculators will let you enter all of the future cash flows at once, but we'll discuss that subject when we get to it.

SPREADSHEET STRATEGIES

How to Calculate Present Values with Multiple Future Cash Flows Using a Spreadsheet

Just as we did in our previous chapter, we can set up a basic spreadsheet to calculate the present values of the individual cash flows as follows. Notice that we have simply calculated the present values one at a time and added them up:

	A	B	C	D	E
1					
2		Using a spreadsheet to value multiple future cash flows			
3					
4	What is the present value of $200 in one year, $400 the next year, $600 the next year, and				
5	$800 the last year if the discount rate is 12 percent?				
6					
7	Rate:	.12			
8					
9	Year	Cash flows	Present values	Formula used	
10	1	$200	$178.57	=PV($B$7,A10,0,−B10)	
11	2	$400	$318.88	=PV($B$7,A11,0,−B11)	
12	3	$600	$427.07	=PV($B$7,A12,0,−B12)	
13	4	$800	$508.41	=PV($B$7,A13,0,−B13)	
14					
15		Total PV:	**$1,432.93**	=SUM(C10:C13)	
16					
17	Notice the negative signs inserted in the PV formulas. These just make the present values have				
18	positive signs. Also, the discount rate in cell B7 is entered as $B$7 (an "absolute" reference)				
19	because it is used over and over. We could have just entered "=.12" instead, but our approach is				
20	more flexible.				
21					
22					

A NOTE ABOUT CASH FLOW TIMING

In working present and future value problems, cash flow timing is critically important. In almost all such calculations, it is implicitly assumed that the cash flows occur at the *end* of each period. In fact, all the formulas we have discussed, all the numbers in a standard present value or future value table, and (very important) all the preset (or default) settings on a financial calculator assume that cash flows occur at the end of each period. Unless you are explicitly told otherwise, you should always assume that this is what is meant.

As a quick illustration of this point, suppose you are told that a three-year investment has a first-year cash flow of $100, a second-year cash flow of $200, and a third-year cash flow of $300. You are asked to draw a time line. Without further information, you should always assume that the time line looks like this:

On our time line, notice how the first cash flow occurs at the end of the first period, the second at the end of the second period, and the third at the end of the third period.

We will close this section by answering the question we posed at the beginning of the chapter concerning baseball player Carl Crawford's contract. Recall that the contract called for a $6 million signing bonus and $14 million in 2011. The remaining $122 million was to be paid as $19.5 million in 2012, $20 million in 2013, $20.25 million in 2014, $20.5 million in 2015, \$20.75 million in 2016, and \$21 million in 2017. If 12 percent is the appropriate discount rate, what kind of deal did the Red Sox outfielder snag?

To answer, we can calculate the present value by discounting each year's salary back to the present as follows (notice we assume that all the payments are made at year-end):

Year 0 (2010): \$ 6,000,000   = \$ 6,000,000.00
Year 1 (2011): \$14,000,000 $\times$ 1 / 1.12^1 = \$12,500,000.00
Year 2 (2012): \$19,500,000 $\times$ 1 / 1.12^2 = \$15,545,280.61
Year 3 (2013): \$20,000,000 $\times$ 1 / 1.12^3 = \$14,235,604.96
...
...
Year 7 (2017): \$21,000,000 $\times$ 1 / 1.12^7 = \$ 9,499,333.52

If you fill in the missing rows and then add (do it for practice), you will see that Carl's contract had a present value of about \$92.8 million, or about 65 percent of the stated \$142 million value.

Concept Questions

6.1a Describe how to calculate the future value of a series of cash flows.
6.2a Describe how to calculate the present value of a series of cash flows.
6.3a Unless we are explicitly told otherwise, what do we always assume about the timing of cash flows in present and future value problems?

Valuing Level Cash Flows: Annuities and Perpetuities

6.2

We will frequently encounter situations in which we have multiple cash flows that are all the same amount. For example, a common type of loan repayment plan calls for the borrower to repay the loan by making a series of equal payments over some length of time. Almost all consumer loans (such as car loans) and home mortgages feature equal payments, usually made each month.

More generally, a series of constant or level cash flows that occur at the end of each period for some fixed number of periods is called an ordinary **annuity**; more correctly, the cash flows are said to be in *ordinary annuity form*. Annuities appear frequently in financial arrangements, and there are some useful shortcuts for determining their values. We consider these next.

annuity
A level stream of cash flows for a fixed period of time.

PRESENT VALUE FOR ANNUITY CASH FLOWS

Suppose we were examining an asset that promised to pay \$500 at the end of each of the next three years. The cash flows from this asset are in the form of a three-year, \$500 annuity. If we wanted to earn 10 percent on our money, how much would we offer for this annuity?

From the previous section, we know that we can discount each of these \$500 payments back to the present at 10 percent to determine the total present value:

$$\text{Present value} = (\$500/1.1^1) + (500/1.1^2) + (500/1.1^3)$$
$$= (\$500/1.1) + (500/1.21) + (500/1.331)$$
$$= \$454.55 + 413.22 + 375.66$$
$$= \$1,243.43$$

This approach works just fine. However, we will often encounter situations in which the number of cash flows is quite large. For example, a typical home mortgage calls for monthly payments over 30 years, for a total of 360 payments. If we were trying to determine the present value of those payments, it would be useful to have a shortcut.

Because the cash flows of an annuity are all the same, we can come up with a handy variation on the basic present value equation. The present value of an annuity of C dollars per period for t periods when the rate of return or interest rate is r is given by:

$$\text{Annuity present value} = C \times \left(\frac{1 - \text{Present value factor}}{r} \right)$$
$$= C \times \left\{ \frac{1 - [1/(1 + r)^t]}{r} \right\}$$

[6.1]

The term in parentheses on the first line is sometimes called the *present value interest factor for annuities* and abbreviated PVIFA(r, t).

The expression for the annuity present value may look a little complicated, but it isn't difficult to use. Notice that the term in square brackets on the second line, $1/(1 + r)^t$, is the same present value factor we've been calculating. In our example from the beginning of this section, the interest rate is 10 percent and there are three years involved. The usual present value factor is thus:

$$\text{Present value factor} = 1/1.1^3 = 1/1.331 = .751315$$

To calculate the annuity present value factor, we just plug this in:

$$\text{Annuity present value factor} = (1 - \text{Present value factor})/r$$
$$= (1 - .751315)/.10$$
$$= .248685/.10 = 2.48685$$

Just as we calculated before, the present value of our $500 annuity is then:

$$\text{Annuity present value} = \$500 \times 2.48685 = \$1,243.43$$

EXAMPLE 6.5 **How Much Can You Afford?**

After carefully going over your budget, you have determined you can afford to pay $632 per month toward a new sports car. You call up your local bank and find out that the going rate is 1 percent per month for 48 months. How much can you borrow?

To determine how much you can borrow, we need to calculate the present value of $632 per month for 48 months at 1 percent per month. The loan payments are in ordinary annuity form, so the annuity present value factor is:

$$\text{Annuity PV factor} = (1 - \text{Present value factor})/r$$
$$= [1 - (1/1.01^{48})]/.01$$
$$= (1 - .6203)/.01 = 37.9740$$

With this factor, we can calculate the present value of the 48 payments of $632 each as:

$$\text{Present value} = \$632 \times 37.9740 = \$24,000$$

Therefore, $24,000 is what you can afford to borrow and repay.

Annuity Tables   Just as there are tables for ordinary present value factors, there are tables for annuity factors as well. Table 6.1 contains a few such factors; Table A.3 in the appendix to the book contains a larger set. To find the annuity present value factor we calculated just before Example 6.5, look for the row corresponding to three periods and then find the column for 10 percent. The number you see at that intersection should be 2.4869 (rounded to four decimal places), as we calculated. Once again, try calculating a few of these factors

Number of Periods	Interest Rate			
	5%	10%	15%	20%
1	.9524	.9091	.8696	.8333
2	1.8594	1.7355	1.6257	1.5278
3	2.7232	2.4869	2.2832	2.1065
4	3.5460	3.1699	2.8550	2.5887
5	4.3295	3.7908	3.3522	2.9906

TABLE 6.1

Annuity Present Value Interest Factors

yourself and compare your answers to the ones in the table to make sure you know how to do it. If you are using a financial calculator, just enter $1 as the payment and calculate the present value; the result should be the annuity present value factor.

CALCULATOR HINTS

Annuity Present Values

To find annuity present values with a financial calculator, we need to use the PMT key (you were probably wondering what it was for). Compared to finding the present value of a single amount, there are two important differences. First, we enter the annuity cash flow using the PMT key. Second, we don't enter anything for the future value, FV. So, for example, the problem we have been examining is a three-year, $500 annuity. If the discount rate is 10 percent, we need to do the following (after clearing out the calculator!):

Enter	3	10	500		
	N	**I/Y**	**PMT**	**PV**	**FV**
Solve for				−1,243.43	

As usual, we get a negative sign on the PV.

SPREADSHEET STRATEGIES

Annuity Present Values

Using a spreadsheet to find annuity present values goes like this:

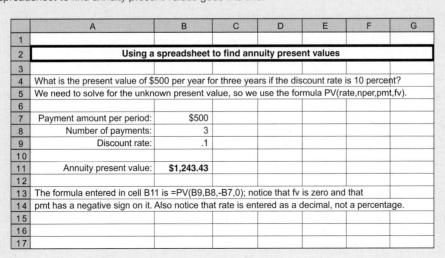

	A	B	C	D	E	F	G
1							
2	**Using a spreadsheet to find annuity present values**						
3							
4	What is the present value of $500 per year for three years if the discount rate is 10 percent?						
5	We need to solve for the unknown present value, so we use the formula PV(rate,nper,pmt,fv).						
6							
7	Payment amount per period:	$500					
8	Number of payments:	3					
9	Discount rate:	.1					
10							
11	Annuity present value:	$1,243.43					
12							
13	The formula entered in cell B11 is =PV(B9,B8,-B7,0); notice that fv is zero and that						
14	pmt has a negative sign on it. Also notice that rate is entered as a decimal, not a percentage.						
15							
16							
17							

Finding the Payment   Suppose you wish to start up a new business that specializes in the latest of health food trends, frozen yak milk. To produce and market your product, the Yakkee Doodle Dandy, you need to borrow $100,000. Because it strikes you as unlikely that this particular fad will be long-lived, you propose to pay off the loan quickly by making five equal annual payments. If the interest rate is 18 percent, what will the payment be?

In this case, we know the present value is $100,000. The interest rate is 18 percent, and there are five years. The payments are all equal, so we need to find the relevant annuity factor and solve for the unknown cash flow:

$$
\begin{aligned}
\text{Annuity present value} = \$100,000 &= C \times [(1 - \text{Present value factor})/r] \\
&= C \times \{[1 - (1/1.18^5)]/.18\} \\
&= C \times [(1 - .4371)/.18] \\
&= C \times 3.1272 \\
C &= \$100,000/3.1272 = \$31,977.78
\end{aligned}
$$

Therefore, you'll make five payments of just under $32,000 each.

CALCULATOR HINTS

Annuity Payments

Finding annuity payments is easy with a financial calculator. In our yak example, the PV is $100,000, the interest rate is 18 percent, and there are five years. We find the payment as follows:

Enter	5	18		100,000	
	N	**I/Y**	**PMT**	**PV**	**FV**
Solve for			−31,977.78		

Here, we get a negative sign on the payment because the payment is an outflow for us.

SPREADSHEET STRATEGIES

Annuity Payments

Using a spreadsheet to work the same problem goes like this:

	A	B	C	D	E	F	G
1							
2		**Using a spreadsheet to find annuity payments**					
3							
4	What is the annuity payment if the present value is $100,000, the interest rate is 18 percent, and						
5	there are five periods? We need to solve for the unknown payment in an annuity, so we use the						
6	formula PMT(rate,nper,pv,fv).						
7							
8	Annuity present value:	$100,000					
9	Number of payments:	5					
10	Discount rate:	.18					
11							
12	Annuity payment:	-$31,977.78					
13							
14	The formula entered in cell B12 is =PMT(B10,B9,B8,0); notice that fv is zero and that the payment						
15	has a negative sign because it is an outflow for us.						
16							

Finding the Number of Payments   **EXAMPLE 6.6**

You ran a little short on your spring break vacation, so you put $1,000 on your credit card. You can afford only the minimum payment of $20 per month. The interest rate on the credit card is 1.5 percent per month. How long will you need to pay off the $1,000?

What we have here is an annuity of $20 per month at 1.5 percent per month for some unknown length of time. The present value is $1,000 (the amount you owe today). We need to do a little algebra (or use a financial calculator):

$$\$1,000 = \$20 \times [(1 - \text{Present value factor})/.015]$$
$$(\$1,000/20) \times .015 = 1 - \text{Present value factor}$$
$$\text{Present value factor} = .25 = 1/(1 + r)^t$$
$$1.015^t = 1/.25 = 4$$

At this point, the problem boils down to asking, How long does it take for your money to quadruple at 1.5 percent per month? Based on our previous chapter, the answer is about 93 months:

$$1.015^{93} = 3.99 \approx 4$$

It will take you about 93/12 = 7.75 years to pay off the $1,000 at this rate. If you use a financial calculator for problems like this, you should be aware that some automatically round up to the next whole period.

CALCULATOR HINTS

Finding the Number of Payments

To solve this one on a financial calculator, do the following:

Enter		1.5	−20	1,000	
	N	I/Y	PMT	PV	FV
Solve for	93.11				

Notice that we put a negative sign on the payment you must make, and we have solved for the number of months. You still have to divide by 12 to get our answer. Also, some financial calculators won't report a fractional value for N; they automatically (without telling you) round up to the next whole period (not to the nearest value). With a spreadsheet, use the function =NPER(rate,pmt,pv,fv); be sure to put in a zero for fv and to enter −20 as the payment.

Finding the Rate   The last question we might want to ask concerns the interest rate implicit in an annuity. For example, an insurance company offers to pay you $1,000 per year for 10 years if you will pay $6,710 up front. What rate is implicit in this 10-year annuity?

In this case, we know the present value ($6,710), we know the cash flows ($1,000 per year), and we know the life of the investment (10 years). What we don't know is the discount rate:

$$\$6,710 = \$1,000 \times [(1 - \text{Present value factor})/r]$$
$$\$6,710/1,000 = 6.71 = \{1 - [1/(1 + r)^{10}]\}/r$$

So, the annuity factor for 10 periods is equal to 6.71, and we need to solve this equation for the unknown value of r. Unfortunately, this is mathematically impossible to do directly. The only way to do it is to use a table or trial and error to find a value for r.

If you look across the row corresponding to 10 periods in Table A.3, you will see a factor of 6.7101 for 8 percent, so we see right away that the insurance company is offering just about 8 percent. Alternatively, we could just start trying different values until we got very close to the answer. Using this trial-and-error approach can be a little tedious, but fortunately machines are good at that sort of thing.[1]

To illustrate how to find the answer by trial and error, suppose a relative of yours wants to borrow $3,000. She offers to repay you $1,000 every year for four years. What interest rate are you being offered?

The cash flows here have the form of a four-year, $1,000 annuity. The present value is $3,000. We need to find the discount rate, r. Our goal in doing so is primarily to give you a feel for the relationship between annuity values and discount rates.

We need to start somewhere, and 10 percent is probably as good a place as any to begin. At 10 percent, the annuity factor is:

Annuity present value factor $= [1 - (1/1.10^4)]/.10 = 3.1699$

The present value of the cash flows at 10 percent is thus:

Present value $= \$1,000 \times 3.1699 = \$3,169.90$

You can see that we're already in the right ballpark.

Is 10 percent too high or too low? Recall that present values and discount rates move in opposite directions: Increasing the discount rate lowers the PV and vice versa. Our present value here is too high, so the discount rate is too low. If we try 12 percent, we're almost there:

Present value $= \$1,000 \times \{[1 - (1/1.12^4)]/.12\} = \$3,037.35$

We are still a little low on the discount rate (because the PV is a little high), so we'll try 13 percent:

Present value $= \$1,000 \times \{[1 - (1/1.13^4)]/.13\} = \$2,974.47$

This is less than $3,000, so we now know that the answer is between 12 percent and 13 percent, and it looks to be about 12.5 percent. For practice, work at it for a while longer and see if you find that the answer is about 12.59 percent.

To illustrate a situation in which finding the unknown rate can be useful, let us consider that the Tri-State Megabucks lottery in Maine, Vermont, and New Hampshire offers you a choice of how to take your winnings (most lotteries do this). In a recent drawing, participants were offered the option of receiving a lump sum payment of $250,000 or an annuity of $500,000 to be received in equal installments over a 25-year period. (At the time, the lump sum payment was always half the annuity option.) Which option was better?

To answer, suppose you were to compare $250,000 today to an annuity of $500,000/ 25 = $20,000 per year for 25 years. At what rate do these have the same value? This is the same type of problem we've been looking at; we need to find the unknown rate, r, for a present value of $250,000, a $20,000 payment, and a 25-year period. If you grind through the calculations (or get a little machine assistance), you should find that the unknown rate is about 6.24 percent. You should take the annuity option if that rate is attractive relative to

---

[1]Financial calculators rely on trial and error to find the answer. That's why they sometimes appear to be "thinking" before coming up with the answer. Actually, it is possible to directly solve for r if there are fewer than five periods, but it's usually not worth the trouble.

other investments available to you. Notice that we have ignored taxes in this example, and taxes can significantly affect our conclusion. Be sure to consult your tax adviser anytime you win the lottery.

CALCULATOR HINTS

Finding the Rate

Alternatively, you could use a financial calculator to do the following:

Enter	4		1,000	−3,000	
	N	**I/Y**	**PMT**	**PV**	**FV**
Solve for		12.59			

Notice that we put a negative sign on the present value (why?). With a spreadsheet, use the function =RATE(nper,pmt,pv,fv); be sure to put in a zero for fv and to enter 1,000 as the payment and −3,000 as the pv.

FUTURE VALUE FOR ANNUITIES

On occasion, it's also handy to know a shortcut for calculating the future value of an annuity. As you might guess, there are future value factors for annuities as well as present value factors. In general, here is the future value factor for an annuity:

$$\text{Annuity FV factor} = (\text{Future value factor} - 1)/r$$
$$= [(1 + r)^t - 1]/r \qquad \textbf{[6.2]}$$

To see how we use annuity future value factors, suppose you plan to contribute $2,000 every year to a retirement account paying 8 percent. If you retire in 30 years, how much will you have?

The number of years here, t, is 30, and the interest rate, r, is 8 percent; so we can calculate the annuity future value factor as:

$$\begin{aligned}
\text{Annuity FV factor} &= (\text{Future value factor} - 1)/r \\
&= (1.08^{30} - 1)/.08 \\
&= (10.0627 - 1)/.08 \\
&= 113.2832
\end{aligned}$$

The future value of this 30-year, $2,000 annuity is thus:

$$\begin{aligned}
\text{Annuity future value} &= \$2,000 \times 113.28 \\
&= \$226,566.42
\end{aligned}$$

CALCULATOR HINTS

Future Values of Annuities

Of course, you could solve this problem using a financial calculator by doing the following:

Enter	30	8	−2,000		
	N	**I/Y**	**PMT**	**PV**	**FV**
Solve for					226,566.42

Notice that we put a negative sign on the payment (why?). With a spreadsheet, use the function =FV(rate,nper, pmt,pv); be sure to put in a zero for pv and to enter −2,000 as the payment.

Sometimes we need to find the unknown rate, r, in the context of an annuity future value. For example, if you had invested $100 per month in stocks over the 25-year period ended December 1978, your investment would have grown to $76,374. This period had the *worst* stretch of stock returns of any 25-year period between 1925 and 2005. How bad was it?

Here we have the cash flows ($100 per month), the *future* value ($76,374), and the time period (25 years, or 300 months). We need to find the implicit rate, r:

$$\$76,374 = \$100 \times [(\text{Future value factor} - 1)/r]$$
$$763.74 = [(1 + r)^{300} - 1]/r$$

Because this is the worst period, let's try 1 percent:

$$\text{Annuity future value factor} = (1.01^{300} - 1)/.01 = 1,878.85$$

We see that 1 percent is too high. From here, it's trial and error. See if you agree that r is about .55 percent per month. As you will see later in the chapter, this works out to be about 6.8 percent per year.

A NOTE ABOUT ANNUITIES DUE

annuity due
An annuity for which the cash flows occur at the beginning of the period.

So far we have only discussed ordinary annuities. These are the most important, but there is a fairly common variation. Remember that with an ordinary annuity, the cash flows occur at the end of each period. When you take out a loan with monthly payments, for example, the first loan payment normally occurs one month after you get the loan. However, when you lease an apartment, the first lease payment is usually due immediately. The second payment is due at the beginning of the second month, and so on. A lease is an example of an **annuity due**. An annuity due is an annuity for which the cash flows occur at the beginning of each period. Almost any type of arrangement in which we have to prepay the same amount each period is an annuity due.

There are several different ways to calculate the value of an annuity due. With a financial calculator, you simply switch it into "due" or "beginning" mode. Remember to switch it back when you are done! Another way to calculate the present value of an annuity due can be illustrated with a time line. Suppose an annuity due has five payments of $400 each, and the relevant discount rate is 10 percent. The time line looks like this:

0	1	2	3	4	5
$400	$400	$400	$400	$400	

Time value applications abound on the Web. See, for example, www.collegeboard.org, *and* personal.fidelity.com.

Notice how the cash flows here are the same as those for a *four*-year ordinary annuity, except that there is an extra $400 at Time 0. For practice, check to see that the value of a four-year ordinary annuity at 10 percent is $1,267.95. If we add on the extra $400, we get $1,667.95, which is the present value of this annuity due.

There is an even easier way to calculate the present or future value of an annuity due. If we assume cash flows occur at the end of each period when they really occur at the beginning, then we discount each one by one period too many. We could fix this by simply multiplying our answer by $(1 + r)$, where r is the discount rate. In fact, the relationship between the value of an annuity due and an ordinary annuity is just this:

$$\text{Annuity due value} = \text{Ordinary annuity value} \times (1 + r) \qquad \textbf{[6.3]}$$

This works for both present and future values, so calculating the value of an annuity due involves two steps: (1) Calculate the present or future value as though it were an ordinary annuity and (2) multiply your answer by $(1 + r)$.

I. Symbols:
PV = Present value, what future cash flows are worth today
FV_t = Future value, what cash flows are worth in the future
r = Interest rate, rate of return, or discount rate per period—typically, but not always, one year
t = Number of periods—typically, but not always, the number of years
C = Cash amount
II. Future Value of C per Period for t Periods at r Percent per Period:
$FV_t = C \times \{[(1 + r)^t - 1]/r\}$ A series of identical cash flows is called an *annuity*, and the term $[(1 + r)^t - 1]/r$ is called the *annuity future value factor*.
III. Present Value of C per Period for t Periods at r Percent per Period:
$PV = C \times \{1 - [1/(1 + r)^t]\}/r$ The term $\{1 - [1/(1 + r)^t]\}/r$ is called the *annuity present value factor*.
IV. Present Value of a Perpetuity of C per Period:
$PV = C/r$ A *perpetuity* has the same cash flow every year forever.

TABLE 6.2

Summary of Annuity and Perpetuity Calculations

PERPETUITIES

We've seen that a series of level cash flows can be valued by treating those cash flows as an annuity. An important special case of an annuity arises when the level stream of cash flows continues forever. Such an asset is called a **perpetuity** because the cash flows are perpetual. Perpetuities are also called **consols**, particularly in Canada and the United Kingdom. See Example 6.7 for an important example of a perpetuity.

Because a perpetuity has an infinite number of cash flows, we obviously can't compute its value by discounting each one. Fortunately, valuing a perpetuity turns out to be the easiest possible case. The present value of a perpetuity is simply:

$$\text{PV for a perpetuity} = C/r \qquad \qquad [6.4]$$

For example, an investment offers a perpetual cash flow of $500 every year. The return you require on such an investment is 8 percent. What is the value of this investment? The value of this perpetuity is:

$$\text{Perpetuity PV} = C/r = \$500/.08 = \$6,250$$

For future reference, Table 6.2 contains a summary of the annuity and perpetuity basic calculations we described. By now, you probably think that you'll just use online calculators to handle annuity problems. Before you do, see our nearby *Work the Web* box!

perpetuity
An annuity in which the cash flows continue forever.

consol
A type of perpetuity.

Preferred Stock	**EXAMPLE 6.7**

Preferred stock (or preference stock) is an important example of a perpetuity. When a corporation sells preferred stock, the buyer is promised a fixed cash dividend every period (usually every quarter) forever. This dividend must be paid before any dividend can be paid to regular stockholders—hence the term *preferred*.

Suppose the Fellini Co. wants to sell preferred stock at $100 per share. A similar issue of preferred stock already outstanding has a price of $40 per share and offers a dividend of $1 every quarter. What dividend will Fellini have to offer if the preferred stock is going to sell?

(continued)

The issue that is already out has a present value of $40 and a cash flow of $1 every quarter forever. Because this is a perpetuity:

Present value = $40 = $1 × (1/r)

r = 2.5%

To be competitive, the new Fellini issue will also have to offer 2.5 percent *per quarter;* so if the present value is to be $100, the dividend must be such that:

Present value = $100 = C × (1/.025)

C = $2.50 (per quarter)

WORK THE WEB

As we discussed in our previous chapter, many websites have financial calculators. One of these sites is Calculatoredge, which is located at www.calculatoredge.com. Suppose you retire with $2,000,000 and want to withdraw an equal amount each year for the next 30 years. If you can earn an 8 percent return, how much can you withdraw each year? Here is what Calculatoredge says:

Enter your values:

Currency:	US Dollars
Starting Principal:	2000000 US Dollars
Annual Interest Rate:	8 %
Repayment Period:	30 Years

[Calculate] [Clear]

Results:

Annuity Payment: 164495.25 US Dollars / Year

According to the Calculatoredge calculator, the answer is $164,495.25. How important is it to understand what you are doing? Calculate this one for yourself, and you should get $177,654.87. Who is right? You are, of course! What's going on is that Calculatoredge assumes (but does not tell you) that the annuity is in the form of an annuity due, not an ordinary annuity. Recall that with an annuity due, the payments occur at the beginning of the period rather than the end of the period. The moral of the story is clear: *Caveat calculator.*

Questions

1. *Go to the calculator at www.calculatoredge.com and find out how much the website says you could withdraw each year if you have $2,500,000, earn an 8 percent interest rate, and make annual withdrawals for 35 years. How much more are the withdrawals if they are in the form of an ordinary annuity?*

2. *Suppose you have $500,000 and want to make withdrawals each month for the next 10 years. The first withdrawal is today and the appropriate interest rate is 9 percent compounded monthly. Using this website, how much are your withdrawals?*

GROWING ANNUITIES AND PERPETUITIES

Annuities commonly have payments that grow over time. Suppose, for example, that we are looking at a lottery payout over a 20-year period. The first payment, made one year from now, will be $200,000. Every year thereafter, the payment will grow by 5 percent, so the payment in the second year will be $200,000 × 1.05 = $210,000. The payment in the third year will be $210,000 × 1.05 = $220,500, and so on. What's the present value if the appropriate discount rate is 11 percent?

If we use the symbol g to represent the growth rate, we can calculate the value of a growing annuity using a modified version of our regular annuity formula:

$$\text{Growing annuity present value} = C \times \left[\frac{1 - \left(\frac{1 + g}{1 + r} \right)^t}{r - g} \right] \qquad \text{[6.5]}$$

Plugging in the numbers from our lottery example (and letting $g = .05$), we get:

$$\text{PV} = \$200,000 \times \left[\frac{1 - \left(\frac{1 + .05}{1 + .11} \right)^{20}}{.11 - .05} \right] = \$200,000 \times 11.18169 = \$2,236,337.06$$

There is also a formula for the present value of a growing perpetuity:

$$\text{Growing perpetuity present value} = C \times \left[\frac{1}{r - g} \right] = \frac{C}{r - g} \qquad \text{[6.6]}$$

In our lottery example, now suppose the payments continue forever. In this case, the present value is:

$$\text{PV} = \$200,000 \times \frac{1}{.11 - .05} = \$200,000 \times 16.6667 = \$3,333,333.33$$

The notion of a growing perpetuity may seem a little odd because the payments get bigger every period forever; but, as we will see in a later chapter, growing perpetuities play a key role in our analysis of stock prices.

Before we go on, there is one important note about our formulas for growing annuities and perpetuities. In both cases, the cash flow in the formula, C, is the cash flow that is going to occur exactly one period from today.

Concept Questions

6.2a In general, what is the present value of an annuity of C dollars per period at a discount rate of r per period? The future value?

6.2b In general, what is the present value of a perpetuity?

Comparing Rates: The Effect of Compounding

6.3

The next issue we need to discuss has to do with the way interest rates are quoted. This subject causes a fair amount of confusion because rates are quoted in many different ways. Sometimes the way a rate is quoted is the result of tradition, and sometimes it's the result of legislation. Unfortunately, at times, rates are quoted in deliberately deceptive ways to mislead borrowers and investors. We will discuss these topics in this section.

EFFECTIVE ANNUAL RATES AND COMPOUNDING

If a rate is quoted as 10 percent compounded semiannually, this means the investment actually pays 5 percent every six months. A natural question then arises: Is 5 percent every six months the same thing as 10 percent per year? It's easy to see that it is not. If you invest $1 at 10 percent per year, you will have $1.10 at the end of the year. If you invest at 5 percent every six months, then you'll have the future value of $1 at 5 percent for two periods:

$$\$1 \times 1.05^2 = \$1.1025$$

This is $.0025 more. The reason is simple: Your account was credited with $1 × .05 = 5 cents in interest after six months. In the following six months, you earned 5 percent on that nickel, for an extra 5 × .05 = .25 cents.

As our example illustrates, 10 percent compounded semiannually is actually equivalent to 10.25 percent per year. Put another way, we would be indifferent between 10 percent compounded semiannually and 10.25 percent compounded annually. Anytime we have compounding during the year, we need to be concerned about what the rate really is.

In our example, the 10 percent is called a **stated**, or **quoted, interest rate**. Other names are used as well. The 10.25 percent, which is actually the rate you will earn, is called the **effective annual rate (EAR)**. To compare different investments or interest rates, we will always need to convert to effective rates. Some general procedures for doing this are discussed next.

stated interest rate
The interest rate expressed in terms of the interest payment made each period. Also known as the *quoted interest rate*.

effective annual rate (EAR)
The interest rate expressed as if it were compounded once per year.

CALCULATING AND COMPARING EFFECTIVE ANNUAL RATES

To see why it is important to work only with effective rates, suppose you've shopped around and come up with the following three rates:

Bank A: 15 percent compounded daily
Bank B: 15.5 percent compounded quarterly
Bank C: 16 percent compounded annually

Which of these is the best if you are thinking of opening a savings account? Which of these is best if they represent loan rates?

To begin, Bank C is offering 16 percent per year. Because there is no compounding during the year, this is the effective rate. Bank B is actually paying .155/4 = .03875 or 3.875 percent per quarter. At this rate, an investment of $1 for four quarters would grow to:

$$\$1 \times 1.03875^4 = \$1.1642$$

The EAR, therefore, is 16.42 percent. For a saver, this is much better than the 16 percent rate Bank C is offering; for a borrower, it's worse.

Bank A is compounding every day. This may seem a little extreme, but it is common to calculate interest daily. In this case, the daily interest rate is actually:

$$.15/365 = .000411$$

This is .0411 percent per day. At this rate, an investment of $1 for 365 periods would grow to:

$$\$1 \times 1.000411^{365} = \$1.1618$$

The EAR is 16.18 percent. This is not as good as Bank B's 16.42 percent for a saver, and not as good as Bank C's 16 percent for a borrower.

This example illustrates two things. First, the highest quoted rate is not necessarily the best. Second, compounding during the year can lead to a significant difference between the quoted rate and the effective rate. Remember that the effective rate is what you actually get or what you pay.

If you look at our examples, you see that we computed the EARs in three steps. We first divided the quoted rate by the number of times that the interest is compounded. We then added 1 to the result and raised it to the power of the number of times the interest is compounded. Finally, we subtracted the 1. If we let m be the number of times the interest is compounded during the year, these steps can be summarized simply as:

$$EAR = [1 + (\text{Quoted rate}/m)]^m - 1 \qquad\qquad\qquad \textbf{[6.7]}$$

For example, suppose you are offered 12 percent compounded monthly. In this case, the interest is compounded 12 times a year; so m is 12. You can calculate the effective rate as:

$$
\begin{aligned}
EAR &= [1 + (\text{Quoted rate}/m)]^m - 1 \\
&= [1 + (.12/12)]^{12} - 1 \\
&= 1.01^{12} - 1 \\
&= 1.126825 - 1 \\
&= 12.6825\%
\end{aligned}
$$

What's the EAR?	**EXAMPLE 6.8**

A bank is offering 12 percent compounded quarterly. If you put $100 in an account, how much will you have at the end of one year? What's the EAR? How much will you have at the end of two years?

The bank is effectively offering $12\%/4 = 3\%$ every quarter. If you invest $100 for four periods at 3 percent per period, the future value is:

$$
\begin{aligned}
\text{Future value} &= \$100 \times 1.03^4 \\
&= \$100 \times 1.1255 \\
&= \$112.55
\end{aligned}
$$

The EAR is 12.55 percent: $\$100 \times (1 + .1255) = \$112.55$.

We can determine what you would have at the end of two years in two different ways. One way is to recognize that two years is the same as eight quarters. At 3 percent per quarter, after eight quarters, you would have:

$$\$100 \times 1.03^8 = \$100 \times 1.2668 = \$126.68$$

Alternatively, we could determine the value after two years by using an EAR of 12.55 percent; so after two years you would have:

$$\$100 \times 1.1255^2 = \$100 \times 1.2668 = \$126.68$$

Thus, the two calculations produce the same answer. This illustrates an important point. Anytime we do a present or future value calculation, the rate we use must be an actual or effective rate. In this case, the actual rate is 3 percent per quarter. The effective annual rate is 12.55 percent. It doesn't matter which one we use once we know the EAR.

Quoting a Rate	**EXAMPLE 6.9**

Now that you know how to convert a quoted rate to an EAR, consider going the other way. As a lender, you know you want to actually earn 18 percent on a particular loan. You want to quote a rate that features monthly compounding. What rate do you quote?

(continued)

In this case, we know the EAR is 18 percent, and we know this is the result of monthly compounding. Let q stand for the quoted rate. We thus have:

$$EAR = [1 + (\text{Quoted rate}/m)]^m - 1$$
$$.18 = [1 + (q/12)]^{12} - 1$$
$$1.18 = [1 + (q/12)]^{12}$$

We need to solve this equation for the quoted rate. This calculation is the same as the ones we did to find an unknown interest rate in Chapter 5:

$$1.18^{(1/12)} = 1 + (q/12)$$
$$1.18^{.08333} = 1 + (q/12)$$
$$1.0139 = 1 + (q/12)$$
$$q = .0139 \times 12$$
$$= 16.68\%$$

Therefore, the rate you would quote is 16.68 percent, compounded monthly.

annual percentage rate (APR)
The interest rate charged per period multiplied by the number of periods per year.

EARs AND APRs

Sometimes it's not altogether clear whether a rate is an effective annual rate. A case in point concerns what is called the **annual percentage rate (APR)** on a loan. Truth-in-lending laws in the United States require that lenders disclose an APR on virtually all consumer loans. This rate must be displayed on a loan document in a prominent and unambiguous way.[2]

Given that an APR must be calculated and displayed, an obvious question arises: Is an APR an effective annual rate? Put another way, if a bank quotes a car loan at 12 percent APR, is the consumer actually paying 12 percent interest? Surprisingly, the answer is no. There is some confusion over this point, which we discuss next.

The confusion over APRs arises because lenders are required by law to compute the APR in a particular way. By law, the APR is simply equal to the interest rate per period multiplied by the number of periods in a year. For example, if a bank is charging 1.2 percent per month on car loans, then the APR that must be reported is $1.2\% \times 12 = 14.4\%$. So, an APR is in fact a quoted, or stated, rate in the sense we've been discussing. For example, an APR of 12 percent on a loan calling for monthly payments is really 1 percent per month. The EAR on such a loan is thus:

$$EAR = [1 + (APR/12)]^{12} - 1$$
$$= 1.01^{12} - 1 = 12.6825\%$$

EXAMPLE 6.10	**What Rate Are You Paying?**

Depending on the issuer, a typical credit card agreement quotes an interest rate of 18 percent APR. Monthly payments are required. What is the actual interest rate you pay on such a credit card?

---

[2]By law, lenders are required to report the APR on all consumer loans. In this text, we compute the APR as the interest rate per period multiplied by the number of periods in a year. According to federal law, the APR is a measure of the cost of consumer credit expressed as a yearly rate, and it includes interest and certain noninterest charges and fees. In practice, the APR can be much higher than the interest rate on the loan if the lender charges substantial fees that must be included in the federally mandated APR calculation.

Based on our discussion, an APR of 18 percent with monthly payments is really .18/12 = .015 or 1.5 percent per month. The EAR is thus:

$$EAR = [1 + (.18/12)]^{12} - 1$$
$$= 1.015^{12} - 1$$
$$= 1.1956 - 1$$
$$= 19.56\%$$

This is the rate you actually pay.

It is somewhat ironic that truth-in-lending laws sometimes require lenders to be *un*truthful about the actual rate on a loan. There are also truth-in-saving laws that require banks and other borrowers to quote an "annual percentage yield," or APY, on things like savings accounts. To make things a little confusing, an APY is an EAR. As a result, by law, the rates quoted to borrowers (APRs) and those quoted to savers (APYs) are not computed the same way.

There can be a huge difference between the APR and EAR when interest rates are large. For example, consider "payday loans." Payday loans are short-term loans made to consumers, often for less than two weeks, and are offered by companies such as AmeriCash Advance and National Payday. The loans work like this: You write a check today that is postdated (the date on the check is in the future) and give it to the company. They give you some cash. When the check date arrives, you either go to the store and pay the cash amount of the check, or the company cashes it (or else automatically renews the loan).

For example, in one particular state, Check Into Cash allows you to write a check for $115 dated 14 days in the future, for which you get $100 today. So what are the APR and EAR on this arrangement? First, we need to find the interest rate, which we can find by the FV equation as follows:

$$FV = PV \times (1 + r)^1$$
$$\$115 = \$100 \times (1 + r)^1$$
$$1.15 = (1 + r)$$
$$r = .15 \text{ or } 15\%$$

That doesn't seem too bad until you remember this is the interest rate for *14 days!* The APR of the loan is:

$$APR = .15 \times 365/14$$
$$APR = 3.9107 \text{ or } 391.07\%$$

And the EAR for this loan is:

$$EAR = (1 + \text{Quoted rate}/m)^m - 1$$
$$EAR = (1 + .15)^{365/14} - 1$$
$$EAR = 37.2366 \text{ or } 3,723.66\%$$

Now that's an interest rate! Just to see what a difference a small difference in fees can make, Advance America Cash Advance will let you write a check for $117.50 in exchange for the same $100 amount. Check for yourself that the APR of this arrangement is 456.25 percent and the EAR is 6,598.65 percent—not a loan we would like to take out!

Compounding Period	Number of Times Compounded	Effective Annual Rate
Year	1	10.00000%
Quarter	4	10.38129
Month	12	10.47131
Week	52	10.50648
Day	365	10.51558
Hour	8,760	10.51703
Minute	525,600	10.51709

TAKING IT TO THE LIMIT: A NOTE ABOUT CONTINUOUS COMPOUNDING

If you made a deposit in a savings account, how often could your money be compounded during the year? If you think about it, there isn't really any upper limit. We've seen that daily compounding, for example, isn't a problem. There is no reason to stop here, however. We could compound every hour or minute or second. How high would the EAR get in this case? Table 6.3 illustrates the EARs that result as 10 percent is compounded at shorter and shorter intervals. Notice that the EARs do keep getting larger, but the differences get very small.

As the numbers in Table 6.3 seem to suggest, there is an upper limit to the EAR. If we let q stand for the quoted rate, then, as the number of times the interest is compounded gets extremely large, the EAR approaches:

$$\text{EAR} = e^q - 1 \qquad\qquad [6.8]$$

where e is the number 2.71828 (look for a key labeled "e^x" on your calculator). For example, with our 10 percent rate, the highest possible EAR is:

$$
\begin{aligned}
\text{EAR} &= e^q - 1 \\
&= 2.71828^{.10} - 1 \\
&= 1.1051709 - 1 \\
&= 10.51709\%
\end{aligned}
$$

In this case, we say that the money is continuously, or instantaneously, compounded. Interest is being credited the instant it is earned, so the amount of interest grows continuously.

EXAMPLE 6.11   **What's the Law?**

At one time, commercial banks and savings and loan associations (S&Ls) were restricted in the interest rates they could offer on savings accounts. Under what was known as Regulation Q, S&Ls were allowed to pay at most 5.5 percent, and banks were not allowed to pay more than 5.25 percent (the idea was to give the S&Ls a competitive advantage; it didn't work). The law did not say how often these rates could be compounded, however. Under Regulation Q, then, what were the maximum allowed interest rates?

The maximum allowed rates occurred with continuous, or instantaneous, compounding. For the commercial banks, 5.25 percent compounded continuously would be:

$$
\begin{aligned}
\text{EAR} &= e^{.0525} - 1 \\
&= 2.71828^{.0525} - 1 \\
&= 1.0539026 - 1 \\
&= 5.39026\%
\end{aligned}
$$

This is what banks could actually pay. Check for yourself to see that S&Ls could effectively pay 5.65406 percent.

Concept Questions

6.3a If an interest rate is given as 12 percent compounded daily, what do we call this rate?

6.3b What is an APR? What is an EAR? Are they the same thing?

6.3c In general, what is the relationship between a stated interest rate and an effective interest rate? Which is more relevant for financial decisions?

6.3d What does continuous compounding mean?

Loan Types and Loan Amortization   6.4 ℀

Whenever a lender extends a loan, some provision will be made for repayment of the principal (the original loan amount). A loan might be repaid in equal installments, for example, or it might be repaid in a single lump sum. Because the way that the principal and interest are paid is up to the parties involved, there are actually an unlimited number of possibilities.

In this section, we describe a few forms of repayment that come up quite often, and more complicated forms can usually be built up from these. The three basic types of loans are pure discount loans, interest-only loans, and amortized loans. Working with these loans is a very straightforward application of the present value principles that we have already developed.

PURE DISCOUNT LOANS

The *pure discount loan* is the simplest form of loan. With such a loan, the borrower receives money today and repays a single lump sum at some time in the future. A one-year, 10 percent pure discount loan, for example, would require the borrower to repay $1.10 in one year for every dollar borrowed today.

Because a pure discount loan is so simple, we already know how to value one. Suppose a borrower was able to repay $25,000 in five years. If we, acting as the lender, wanted a 12 percent interest rate on the loan, how much would we be willing to lend? Put another way, what value would we assign today to that $25,000 to be repaid in five years? Based on our work in Chapter 5, we know the answer is just the present value of $25,000 at 12 percent for five years:

$$
\begin{aligned}
\text{Present value} &= \$25,000/1.12^5 \\
&= \$25,000/1.7623 \\
&= \$14,186
\end{aligned}
$$

Pure discount loans are common when the loan term is short—say a year or less. In recent years, they have become increasingly common for much longer periods.

Treasury Bills   **EXAMPLE 6.12**

When the U.S. government borrows money on a short-term basis (a year or less), it does so by selling what are called *Treasury bills,* or *T-bills* for short. A T-bill is a promise by the government to repay a fixed amount at some time in the future—for example, 3 months or 12 months.

Treasury bills are pure discount loans. If a T-bill promises to repay $10,000 in 12 months, and the market interest rate is 7 percent, how much will the bill sell for in the market?

Because the going rate is 7 percent, the T-bill will sell for the present value of $10,000 to be repaid in one year at 7 percent:

Present value = $10,000/1.07 = $9,345.79

INTEREST-ONLY LOANS

A second type of loan repayment plan calls for the borrower to pay interest each period and to repay the entire principal (the original loan amount) at some point in the future. Loans with such a repayment plan are called *interest-only loans*. Notice that if there is just one period, a pure discount loan and an interest-only loan are the same thing.

For example, with a three-year, 10 percent, interest-only loan of $1,000, the borrower would pay $1,000 × .10 = $100 in interest at the end of the first and second years. At the end of the third year, the borrower would return the $1,000 along with another $100 in interest for that year. Similarly, a 50-year interest-only loan would call for the borrower to pay interest every year for the next 50 years and then repay the principal. In the extreme, the borrower pays the interest every period forever and never repays any principal. As we discussed earlier in the chapter, the result is a perpetuity.

Most corporate bonds have the general form of an interest-only loan. Because we will be considering bonds in some detail in the next chapter, we will defer further discussion of them for now.

AMORTIZED LOANS

With a pure discount or interest-only loan, the principal is repaid all at once. An alternative is an *amortized loan,* with which the lender may require the borrower to repay parts of the loan amount over time. The process of providing for a loan to be paid off by making regular principal reductions is called *amortizing* the loan.

A simple way of amortizing a loan is to have the borrower pay the interest each period plus some fixed amount. This approach is common with medium-term business loans. For example, suppose a business takes out a $5,000, five-year loan at 9 percent. The loan agreement calls for the borrower to pay the interest on the loan balance each year and to reduce the loan balance each year by $1,000. Because the loan amount declines by $1,000 each year, it is fully paid in five years.

In the case we are considering, notice that the total payment will decline each year. The reason is that the loan balance goes down, resulting in a lower interest charge each year, whereas the $1,000 principal reduction is constant. For example, the interest in the first year will be $5,000 × .09 = $450. The total payment will be $1,000 + 450 = $1,450. In the second year, the loan balance is $4,000, so the interest is $4,000 × .09 = $360, and the total payment is $1,360. We can calculate the total payment in each of the remaining years by preparing a simple *amortization schedule* as follows:

Year	Beginning Balance	Total Payment	Interest Paid	Principal Paid	Ending Balance
1	$5,000	$1,450	$ 450	$1,000	$4,000
2	4,000	1,360	360	1,000	3,000
3	3,000	1,270	270	1,000	2,000
4	2,000	1,180	180	1,000	1,000
5	1,000	1,090	90	1,000	0
Totals		$6,350	$1,350	$5,000	

Notice that in each year, the interest paid is given by the beginning balance multiplied by the interest rate. Also notice that the beginning balance is given by the ending balance from the previous year.

Probably the most common way of amortizing a loan is to have the borrower make a single, fixed payment every period. Almost all consumer loans (such as car loans) and mortgages work this way. For example, suppose our five-year, 9 percent, $5,000 loan was amortized this way. How would the amortization schedule look?

We first need to determine the payment. From our discussion earlier in the chapter, we know that this loan's cash flows are in the form of an ordinary annuity. In this case, we can solve for the payment as follows:

$$\$5,000 = C \times \{[1 - (1/1.09^5)]/.09\}$$
$$= C \times [(1 - .6499)/.09]$$

This gives us:

$$C = \$5,000/3.8897$$
$$= \$1,285.46$$

The borrower will therefore make five equal payments of $1,285.46. Will this pay off the loan? We will check by filling in an amortization schedule.

In our previous example, we knew the principal reduction each year. We then calculated the interest owed to get the total payment. In this example, we know the total payment. We will thus calculate the interest and then subtract it from the total payment to calculate the principal portion in each payment.

In the first year, the interest is $450, as we calculated before. Because the total payment is $1,285.46, the principal paid in the first year must be:

Principal paid = $1,285.46 − 450 = $835.46

The ending loan balance is thus:

Ending balance = $5,000 − 835.46 = $4,164.54

The interest in the second year is $4,164.54 × .09 = $374.81, and the loan balance declines by $1,285.46 − 374.81 = $910.65. We can summarize all of the relevant calculations in the following schedule:

Year	Beginning Balance	Total Payment	Interest Paid	Principal Paid	Ending Balance
1	$5,000.00	$1,285.46	$ 450.00	$ 835.46	$4,164.54
2	4,164.54	1,285.46	374.81	910.65	3,253.88
3	3,253.88	1,285.46	292.85	992.61	2,261.27
4	2,261.27	1,285.46	203.51	1,081.95	1,179.32
5	1,179.32	1,285.46	106.14	1,179.32	0.00
Totals		$6,427.30	$1,427.31	$5,000.00	

Because the loan balance declines to zero, the five equal payments do pay off the loan. Notice that the interest paid declines each period. This isn't surprising because the loan balance is going down. Given that the total payment is fixed, the principal paid must be rising each period.

If you compare the two loan amortizations in this section, you will see that the total interest is greater for the equal total payment case: $1,427.31 versus $1,350. The reason for this is that the loan is repaid more slowly early on, so the interest is somewhat higher. This doesn't mean that one loan is better than the other; it simply means that one is effectively paid off faster than the other. For example, the principal reduction in the first year is $835.46 in the equal total payment case as compared to $1,000 in the first case. Many websites offer loan amortization schedules. See our nearby *Work the Web* box for an example.

WORK THE WEB

Preparing an amortization table is one of the more tedious time value of money applications. Using a spreadsheet makes it relatively easy, but there are also websites available that will prepare an amortization schedule very quickly and simply. One such site is www.bankrate.com. This site has a mortgage calculator for home loans, but the same calculations apply to most other types of loans such as car loans and student loans. Suppose you graduate with a student loan of $30,000 and will repay the loan over the next 10 years at 6.8 percent. What are your monthly payments? Using the calculator we get:

Try this example yourself and click the "Show/Recalculate Amortization Table" button. You will find that your first payment will consist of $175.24 in principal and $170.00 in interest. Over the life of the loan you will pay a total of $11,428.92 in interest.

Questions

1. Suppose you take out a 30-year mortgage for $250,000 at an interest rate of 6.8 percent. Use this website to construct an amortization table for the loan. What are the interest payment and principal amounts in the 110th payment? How much in total interest will you pay over the life of the loan?

2. You take out a 30-year mortgage for $275,000 at an interest rate of 7.3 percent. How much will you pay in interest over the life of this loan? Now assume you pay an extra $100 per month on this loan. How much is your total interest now? How much sooner will the mortgage be paid off?

We will close this chapter with an example that may be of particular relevance. Federal Stafford loans are an important source of financing for many college students, helping to cover the cost of tuition, books, new cars, condominiums, and many other things. Sometimes students do not seem to fully realize that Stafford loans have a serious drawback: They must be repaid in monthly installments, usually beginning six months after the student leaves school.

Some Stafford loans are subsidized, meaning that the interest does not begin to accrue until repayment begins (this is a good thing). If you are a dependent undergraduate student under this particular option, the total debt you can run up is, at most, $23,000. The maximum interest rate in 2010–2011 is 6.8 percent, or $6.8/12 = .5667$ percent per month. Under the "standard repayment plan," the loans are amortized over 10 years (subject to a minimum payment of $50).

Suppose you max out borrowing under this program and also get stuck paying the maximum interest rate. Beginning six months after you graduate (or otherwise depart the ivory tower), what will your monthly payment be? How much will you owe after making payments for four years?

Given our earlier discussions, see if you don't agree that your monthly payment assuming a $23,000 total loan is $264.68 per month. Also, as explained in Example 6.13, after making payments for four years, you still owe the present value of the remaining payments. There are 120 payments in all. After you make 48 of them (the first four years), you have 72 to go. By now, it should be easy for you to verify that the present value of $264.68 per month for 72 months at .50 percent per month is about $15,613, so you still have a long way to go.

Partial Amortization, or "Bite the Bullet"	**EXAMPLE 6.13**

A common arrangement in real estate lending might call for a 5-year loan with, say, a 15-year amortization. What this means is that the borrower makes a payment every month of a fixed amount based on a 15-year amortization. However, after 60 months, the borrower makes a single, much larger payment called a "balloon" or "bullet" to pay off the loan. Because the monthly payments don't fully pay off the loan, the loan is said to be partially amortized.

Suppose we have a $100,000 commercial mortgage with a 12 percent APR and a 20-year (240-month) amortization. Further suppose the mortgage has a five-year balloon. What will the monthly payment be? How big will the balloon payment be?

The monthly payment can be calculated based on an ordinary annuity with a present value of $100,000. There are 240 payments, and the interest rate is 1 percent per month. The payment is:

$$\$100,000 = C \times [(1 - 1/1.01^{240})/.01]$$
$$= C \times 90.8194$$
$$C = \$1,101.09$$

Now, there is an easy way and a hard way to determine the balloon payment. The hard way is to actually amortize the loan for 60 months to see what the balance is at that time. The easy way is to recognize that after 60 months, we have a $240 - 60 = 180$-month loan. The payment is still $1,101.09 per month, and the interest rate is still 1 percent per month. The loan balance is thus the present value of the remaining payments:

$$\text{Loan balance} = \$1,101.09 \times [(1 - 1/1.01^{180})/.01]$$
$$= \$1,101.09 \times 83.3217$$
$$= \$91,744.69$$

The balloon payment is a substantial $91,744. Why is it so large? To get an idea, consider the first payment on the mortgage. The interest in the first month is $100,000 \times .01 = $1,000. Your payment is $1,101.09, so the loan balance declines by only $101.09. Because the loan balance declines so slowly, the cumulative "pay down" over five years is not great.

Of course, it is possible to rack up much larger debts. According to the Association of American Medical Colleges, medical students who borrowed to attend medical school and graduated in 2009 had an average student loan balance of $160,000. Ouch! How long will it take the average student to pay off her medical school loans?

SPREADSHEET STRATEGIES

Loan Amortization Using a Spreadsheet

Loan amortization is a common spreadsheet application. To illustrate, we will set up the problem that we examined earlier: a five-year, $5,000, 9 percent loan with constant payments. Our spreadsheet looks like this:

	A	B	C	D	E	F	G	H
1								
2			**Using a spreadsheet to amortize a loan**					
3								
4			Loan amount:	$5,000				
5			Interest rate:	.09				
6			Loan term:	5				
7			Loan payment:	$1,285.46				
8				Note: Payment is calculated using PMT(rate,nper,-pv,fv).				
9		Amortization table:						
10								
11		Year	Beginning	Total	Interest	Principal	Ending	
12			Balance	Payment	Paid	Paid	Balance	
13		1	$5,000.00	$1,285.46	$450.00	$835.46	$4,164.54	
14		2	4,164.54	1,285.46	374.81	910.65	3,253.88	
15		3	3,253.88	1,285.46	292.85	992.61	2,261.27	
16		4	2,261.27	1,285.46	203.51	1,081.95	1,179.32	
17		5	1,179.32	1,285.46	106.14	1,179.32	.00	
18		Totals		6,427.31	1,427.31	5,000.00		
19								
20		Formulas in the amortization table:						
21								
22		Year	Beginning	Total	Interest	Principal	Ending	
23			Balance	Payment	Paid	Paid	Balance	
24		1	=+D4	=$D$7	=+$D$5*C13	=+D13-E13	=+C13-F13	
25		2	=+G13	=$D$7	=+$D$5*C14	=+D14-E14	=+C14-F14	
26		3	=+G14	=$D$7	=+$D$5*C15	=+D15-E15	=+C15-F15	
27		4	=+G15	=$D$7	=+$D$5*C16	=+D16-E16	=+C16-F16	
28		5	=+G16	=$D$7	=+$D$5*C17	=+D17-E17	=+C17-F17	
29								
30		Note: Totals in the amortization table are calculated using the SUM formula.						
31								

Let's say she makes a monthly payment of $1,000, and the loan has an interest rate of 7 percent per year, or .5833 percent per month. See if you agree that it will take about 466 months, or almost 39 years, to pay off the loan. Maybe MD really stands for "mucho debt"!

Concept Questions

6.4a What is a pure discount loan? An interest-only loan?

6.4b What does it mean to amortize a loan?

6.4c What is a balloon payment? How do you determine its value?

Summary and Conclusions   6.5

This chapter rounded out your understanding of fundamental concepts related to the time value of money and discounted cash flow valuation. Several important topics were covered:

1. There are two ways of calculating present and future values when there are multiple cash flows. Both approaches are straightforward extensions of our earlier analysis of single cash flows.

2. A series of constant cash flows that arrive or are paid at the end of each period is called an ordinary annuity, and we described some useful shortcuts for determining the present and future values of annuities.

3. Interest rates can be quoted in a variety of ways. For financial decisions, it is important that any rates being compared be first converted to effective rates. The relationship between a quoted rate, such as an annual percentage rate (APR), and an effective annual rate (EAR) is given by:

$$\text{EAR} = [1 + (\text{Quoted rate}/m)]^m - 1$$

where m is the number of times during the year the money is compounded or, equivalently, the number of payments during the year.

4. Many loans are annuities. The process of providing for a loan to be paid off gradually is called amortizing the loan, and we discussed how amortization schedules are prepared and interpreted.

The principles developed in this chapter will figure prominently in the chapters to come. The reason for this is that most investments, whether they involve real assets or financial assets, can be analyzed using the discounted cash flow (DCF) approach. As a result, the DCF approach is broadly applicable and widely used in practice. For example, the next two chapters show how to value bonds and stocks using an extension of the techniques presented in this chapter. Before going on, therefore, you might want to do some of the problems that follow.

Visit us at www.mhhe.com/rwj

CONNECT TO FINANCE

 |FINANCE

If you are using *Connect™ Finance* in your course, get online to take a Practice Test, check out study tools, and find out where you need additional practice.

▼ Chapter 6 Discounted Cash Flow Valuation			
6.1 Future and Present Values of Multiple Cash Flows	eBook	Study	Practice
6.2 Valuing Level Cash Flows: Annuities and Perpetuities	eBook	Study	Practice
6.3 Comparing Rates: The Effect of Compounding	eBook	Study	Practice
6.4 Loan Types and Loan Amortization	eBook	Study	Practice

Section 6.4
Practice Quiz

Can you answer the following questions?

Section 6.1   Two years ago, you opened an investment account and deposited $5,000. One year ago, you added another $2,000 to the account. Today, you are making a final deposit of $7,500. How much will you have in this account three years from today if you earn a 14 percent rate of return? (LO 6-1)

Section 6.2   A stream of equal payments that occur at the beginning of each month for one year is called a(n). (LO 6-1)

Section 6.3   Your credit card charges interest of 1.2 percent per month. What is the annual percentage rate? (LO 6-4)

Section 6.4   What type of loan is repaid in a single lump sum? (LO 6-3)

Log on to find out!

CHAPTER REVIEW AND SELF-TEST PROBLEMS

6.1   **Present Values with Multiple Cash Flows**   A first-round draft choice quarterback has been signed to a three-year, $25 million contract. The details provide for an immediate cash bonus of $2 million. The player is to receive $5 million in salary at the end of the first year, $8 million the next, and $10 million at the end of the last year. Assuming a 15 percent discount rate, is this package worth $25 million? If not, how much is it worth?

6.2   **Future Value with Multiple Cash Flows**   You plan to make a series of deposits in an individual retirement account. You will deposit $1,000 today, $2,000 in two years, and $2,000 in five years. If you withdraw $1,500 in three years and $1,000 in seven years, assuming no withdrawal penalties, how much will you have after eight years if the interest rate is 7 percent? What is the present value of these cash flows?

6.3   **Annuity Present Value**   You are looking into an investment that will pay you $12,000 per year for the next 10 years. If you require a 15 percent return, what is the most you would pay for this investment?

6.4   **APR versus EAR**   The going rate on student loans is quoted as 8 percent APR. The terms of the loans call for monthly payments. What is the effective annual rate (EAR) on such a student loan?

6.5   **It's the Principal That Matters**   Suppose you borrow $10,000. You are going to repay the loan by making equal annual payments for five years. The interest rate on the loan is 14 percent per year. Prepare an amortization schedule for the loan. How much interest will you pay over the life of the loan?

6.6   **Just a Little Bit Each Month**   You've recently finished your MBA at the Darnit School. Naturally, you must purchase a new BMW immediately. The car costs about $21,000. The bank quotes an interest rate of 15 percent APR for a 72-month loan with a 10 percent down payment. You plan on trading the car in for a new one in two years. What will your monthly payment be? What is the effective interest rate on the loan? What will the loan balance be when you trade the car in?

ANSWERS TO CHAPTER REVIEW AND SELF-TEST PROBLEMS

6.1   Obviously, the package is not worth $25 million because the payments are spread out over three years. The bonus is paid today, so it's worth $2 million. The present values for the three subsequent salary payments are:

$$(\$5/1.15) + (8/1.15^2) + (10/1.15^3) = (\$5/1.15) + (8/1.32) + (10/1.52)$$
$$= \$16.9721 \text{ million}$$

The package is worth a total of $18.9721 million.

6.2 We will calculate the future values for each of the cash flows separately and then add them up. Notice that we treat the withdrawals as negative cash flows:

$$
\begin{aligned}
\$1,000 \times 1.07^8 = \quad \$1,000 \times 1.7182 &= \$ 1,718.19 \\
\$2,000 \times 1.07^6 = \quad \$2,000 \times 1.5007 &= 3,001.46 \\
-\$1,500 \times 1.07^5 = -\$1,500 \times 1.4026 &= -2,103.83 \\
\$2,000 \times 1.07^3 = \quad \$2,000 \times 1.2250 &= 2,450.09 \\
-\$1,000 \times 1.07^1 = -\$1,000 \times 1.0700 &= -1,070.00 \\
\text{Total future value} \quad &= \$ 3,995.91
\end{aligned}
$$

This value includes a small rounding error.

To calculate the present value, we could discount each cash flow back to the present or we could discount back a single year at a time. However, because we already know that the future value in eight years is $3,995.91, the easy way to get the PV is just to discount this amount back eight years:

$$
\begin{aligned}
\text{Present value} &= \$3,995.91/1.07^8 \\
&= \$3,995.91/1.7182 \\
&= \$2,325.64
\end{aligned}
$$

We again ignore a small rounding error. For practice, you can verify that this is what you get if you discount each cash flow back separately.

6.3 The most you would be willing to pay is the present value of $12,000 per year for 10 years at a 15 percent discount rate. The cash flows here are in ordinary annuity form, so the relevant present value factor is:

$$
\begin{aligned}
\text{Annuity present value factor} &= (1 - \text{Present value factor})/r \\
&= [1 - (1/1.15^{10})]/.15 \\
&= (1 - .2472)/.15 \\
&= 5.0188
\end{aligned}
$$

The present value of the 10 cash flows is thus:

$$
\begin{aligned}
\text{Present value} &= \$12,000 \times 5.0188 \\
&= \$60,225
\end{aligned}
$$

This is the most you would pay.

6.4 A rate of 8 percent APR with monthly payments is actually $8\%/12 = .67\%$ per month. The EAR is thus:

$$\text{EAR} = [1 + (.08/12)]^{12} - 1 = 8.30\%$$

6.5 We first need to calculate the annual payment. With a present value of $10,000, an interest rate of 14 percent, and a term of five years, the payment can be determined from:

$$
\begin{aligned}
\$10,000 &= \text{Payment} \times \{[1 - (1/1.14^5)]/.14\} \\
&= \text{Payment} \times 3.4331
\end{aligned}
$$

Therefore, the payment is $10,000/3.4331 = $2,912.84 (actually, it's $2,912.8355; this will create some small rounding errors in the following schedule). We can now prepare the amortization schedule as follows:

Year	Beginning Balance	Total Payment	Interest Paid	Principal Paid	Ending Balance
1	$10,000.00	$ 2,912.84	$1,400.00	$ 1,512.84	$8,487.16
2	8,487.16	2,912.84	1,188.20	1,724.63	6,762.53
3	6,762.53	2,912.84	946.75	1,966.08	4,796.45
4	4,796.45	2,912.84	671.50	2,241.33	2,555.12
5	2,555.12	2,912.84	357.72	2,555.12	0.00
Totals		$14,564.17	$4,564.17	$10,000.00	

6.6 The cash flows on the car loan are in annuity form, so we need to find only the payment. The interest rate is 15%/12 = 1.25% per month, and there are 72 months. The first thing we need is the annuity factor for 72 periods at 1.25 percent per period:

$$\text{Annuity present value factor} = (1 - \text{Present value factor})/r$$
$$= [1 - (1/1.0125^{72})]/.0125$$
$$= [1 - (1/2.4459)]/.0125$$
$$= (1 - .4088)/.0125$$
$$= 47.2925$$

The present value is the amount we finance. With a 10 percent down payment, we will be borrowing 90 percent of $21,000, or $18,900. To find the payment, we need to solve for C:

$$\$18,900 = C \times \text{Annuity present value factor}$$
$$= C \times 47.2925$$

Rearranging things a bit, we have:

$$C = \$18,900 \times (1/47.2925)$$
$$= \$18,900 \times .02115$$
$$= \$399.64$$

Your payment is just under $400 per month.

The actual interest rate on this loan is 1.25 percent per month. Based on our work in the chapter, we can calculate the effective annual rate as:

$$\text{EAR} = (1.0125)^{12} - 1 = 16.08\%$$

The effective rate is about one point higher than the quoted rate.

To determine the loan balance in two years, we could amortize the loan to see what the balance is at that time. This would be fairly tedious to do by hand. Using the information already determined in this problem, we can instead simply calculate the present value of the remaining payments. After two years, we have made 24 payments, so there are 72 − 24 = 48 payments left. What is the present value of 48 monthly payments of $399.64 at 1.25 percent per month? The relevant annuity factor is:

$$\text{Annuity present value factor} = (1 - \text{Present value factor})/r$$
$$= [1 - (1/1.0125^{48})]/.0125$$
$$= [1 - (1/1.8154)]/.0125$$
$$= (1 - .5509)/.0125$$
$$= 35.9315$$

Visit us at www.mhhe.com/rwj

The present value is thus:

Present value = $399.64 × 35.9315 = $14,359.66

You will owe about $14,360 on the loan in two years.

CONCEPTS REVIEW AND CRITICAL THINKING QUESTIONS

1. **Annuity Factors [LO1]** There are four pieces to an annuity present value. What are they?

2. **Annuity Period [LO1]** As you increase the length of time involved, what happens to the present value of an annuity? What happens to the future value?

3. **Interest Rates [LO1]** What happens to the future value of an annuity if you increase the rate r? What happens to the present value?

4. **Present Value [LO1]** What do you think about the Tri-State Megabucks lottery discussed in the chapter advertising a $500,000 prize when the lump sum option is $250,000? Is it deceptive advertising?

5. **Present Value [LO1]** If you were an athlete negotiating a contract, would you want a big signing bonus payable immediately and smaller payments in the future, or vice versa? How about looking at it from the team's perspective?

6. **Present Value [LO1]** Suppose two athletes sign 10-year contracts for $80 million. In one case, we're told that the $80 million will be paid in 10 equal installments. In the other case, we're told that the $80 million will be paid in 10 installments, but the installments will increase by 5 percent per year. Who got the better deal?

7. **APR and EAR [LO4]** Should lending laws be changed to require lenders to report EARs instead of APRs? Why or why not?

8. **Time Value [LO1]** On subsidized Stafford loans, a common source of financial aid for college students, interest does not begin to accrue until repayment begins. Who receives a bigger subsidy, a freshman or a senior? Explain. In words, how would you go about valuing the subsidy on a subsidized Stafford loan?

9. **Time Value [LO1]** Eligibility for a subsidized Stafford loan is based on current financial need. However, both subsidized and unsubsidized Stafford loans are repaid out of future income. Given this, do you see a possible objection to having two types?

10. **Time Value [LO1]** A viatical settlement is a lump sum of money given to a terminally ill individual in exchange for his life insurance policy. When the insured person dies, the purchaser receives the payout from the life insurance policy. What factors determine the value of the viatical settlement? Do you think such settlements are ethical? Why or why not?

11. **Perpetuity Values [LO1]** What happens to the future value of a perpetuity if interest rates increase? What if interest rates decrease?

12. **Loans and Interest Rates [LO4]** In the chapter, we gave several examples of so-called payday loans. As you saw, the interest rates on these loans can be extremely high and are even called predatory by some. Do you think such high interest loans are ethical? Why or why not?

BASIC
(Questions 1–28)

Visit us at www.mhhe.com/rwj

1. **Present Value and Multiple Cash Flows [LO1]** Wainright Co. has identified an investment project with the following cash flows. If the discount rate is 10 percent, what is the present value of these cash flows? What is the present value at 18 percent? At 24 percent?

Year	Cash Flow
1	$ 720
2	930
3	1,190
4	1,275

2. **Present Value and Multiple Cash Flows [LO1]** Investment X offers to pay you $5,200 per year for eight years, whereas Investment Y offers to pay you $7,300 per year for five years. Which of these cash flow streams has the higher present value if the discount rate is 5 percent? If the discount rate is 15 percent?

3. **Future Value and Multiple Cash Flows [LO1]** Toadies, Inc., has identified an investment project with the following cash flows. If the discount rate is 8 percent, what is the future value of these cash flows in Year 4? What is the future value at a discount rate of 11 percent? At 24 percent?

Year	Cash Flow
1	$1,375
2	1,495
3	1,580
4	1,630

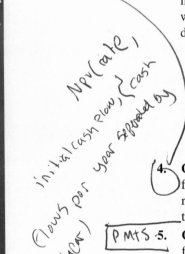

4. **Calculating Annuity Present Value [LO1]** An investment offers $6,100 per year for 15 years, with the first payment occurring one year from now. If the required return is 6 percent, what is the value of the investment? What would the value be if the payments occurred for 40 years? For 75 years? Forever?

5. **Calculating Annuity Cash Flows [LO1]** If you put up $45,000 today in exchange for a 6.25 percent, 15-year annuity, what will the annual cash flow be?

6. **Calculating Annuity Values [LO1]** Your company will generate $68,000 in annual revenue each year for the next seven years from a new information database. If the appropriate interest rate is 8.5 percent, what is the present value of the savings?

7. **Calculating Annuity Values [LO1]** If you deposit $5,000 at the end of each of the next 20 years into an account paying 10.8 percent interest, how much money will you have in the account in 20 years? How much will you have if you make deposits for 40 years?

8. **Calculating Annuity Values [LO1]** You want to have $75,000 in your savings account 12 years from now, and you're prepared to make equal annual deposits into the account at the end of each year. If the account pays 6.8 percent interest, what amount must you deposit each year?

9. **Calculating Annuity Values [LO2]** Dinero Bank offers you a $60,000, five-year term loan at 7.5 percent annual interest. What will your annual loan payment be?

10. **Calculating Perpetuity Values [LO1]** The Maybe Pay Life Insurance Co. is trying to sell you an investment policy that will pay you and your heirs $30,000 per year

forever. If the required return on this investment is 5.8 percent, how much will you pay for the policy?

11. **Calculating Perpetuity Values [LO1]** In the previous problem, suppose a sales associate told you the policy costs $475,000. At what interest rate would this be a fair deal?

12. **Calculating EAR [LO4]** Find the EAR in each of the following cases:

Stated Rate (APR)	Number of Times Compounded	Effective Rate (EAR)
9%	Quarterly	
18	Monthly	
14	Daily	
11	Infinite	

13. **Calculating APR [LO4]** Find the APR, or stated rate, in each of the following cases:

Stated Rate (APR)	Number of Times Compounded	Effective Rate (EAR)
	Semiannually	11.5%
	Monthly	12.4
	Weekly	10.1
	Infinite	13.8

14. **Calculating EAR [LO4]** First National Bank charges 13.2 percent compounded monthly on its business loans. First United Bank charges 13.5 percent compounded semiannually. As a potential borrower, which bank would you go to for a new loan?

15. **Calculating APR [LO4]** Barcain Credit Corp. wants to earn an effective annual return on its consumer loans of 15 percent per year. The bank uses daily compounding on its loans. What interest rate is the bank required by law to report to potential borrowers? Explain why this rate is misleading to an uninformed borrower.

16. **Calculating Future Values [LO1]** What is the future value of $2,600 in 19 years assuming an interest rate of 7.9 percent compounded semiannually?

17. **Calculating Future Values [LO1]** Gold Door Credit Bank is offering 6.7 percent compounded daily on its savings accounts. If you deposit $5,100 today, how much will you have in the account in 5 years? In 10 years? In 20 years?

18. **Calculating Present Values [LO1]** An investment will pay you $43,000 in 10 years. If the appropriate discount rate is 7 percent compounded daily, what is the present value?

19. **EAR versus APR [LO4]** Big Dom's Pawn Shop charges an interest rate of 27 percent per month on loans to its customers. Like all lenders, Big Dom must report an APR to consumers. What rate should the shop report? What is the effective annual rate?

20. **Calculating Loan Payments [LO2, 4]** You want to buy a new sports coupe for $83,500, and the finance office at the dealership has quoted you a 6.5 percent APR loan for 60 months to buy the car. What will your monthly payments be? What is the effective annual rate on this loan?

21. **Calculating Number of Periods [LO3]** One of your customers is delinquent on his accounts payable balance. You've mutually agreed to a repayment schedule of $500 per month. You will charge 1.7 percent per month interest on the overdue balance. If the current balance is $16,000, how long will it take for the account to be paid off?

22. Calculating EAR [LO4] Friendly's Quick Loans, Inc., offers you "three for four or 1 knock on your door." This means you get $3 today and repay $4 when you get your paycheck in one week (or else). What's the effective annual return Friendly's earns on this lending business? If you were brave enough to ask, what APR would Friendly's say you were paying?

23. Valuing Perpetuities [LO1] Live Forever Life Insurance Co. is selling a perpetuity contract that pays $1,500 monthly. The contract currently sells for $115,000. What is the monthly return on this investment vehicle? What is the APR? The effective annual return?

24. Calculating Annuity Future Values [LO1] You are planning to make monthly deposits of $400 into a retirement account that pays 10 percent interest compounded monthly. If your first deposit will be made one month from now, how large will your retirement account be in 30 years?

25. Calculating Annuity Future Values [LO1] In the previous problem, suppose you make $4,800 annual deposits into the same retirement account. How large will your account balance be in 30 years?

26. Calculating Annuity Present Values [LO1] Beginning three months from now, you want to be able to withdraw $2,500 each quarter from your bank account to cover college expenses over the next four years. If the account pays .47 percent interest per quarter, how much do you need to have in your bank account today to meet your expense needs over the next four years?

27. Discounted Cash Flow Analysis [LO1] If the appropriate discount rate for the following cash flows is 9 percent compounded quarterly, what is the present value of the cash flows?

Year	Cash Flow
1	$ 830
2	910
3	0
4	1,500

28. Discounted Cash Flow Analysis [LO1] If the appropriate discount rate for the following cash flows is 7.38 percent per year, what is the present value of the cash flows?

Year	Cash Flow
1	$2,480
2	0
3	3,920
4	2,170

INTERMEDIATE
(Questions 29–56)

29. Simple Interest versus Compound Interest [LO4] First Simple Bank pays 9 percent simple interest on its investment accounts. If First Complex Bank pays interest on its accounts compounded annually, what rate should the bank set if it wants to match First Simple Bank over an investment horizon of 10 years?

30. Calculating EAR [LO4] You are looking at an investment that has an effective annual rate of 14 percent. What is the effective semiannual return? The effective quarterly return? The effective monthly return?

31. Calculating Interest Expense [LO2] You receive a credit card application from Shady Banks Savings and Loan offering an introductory rate of .5 percent per year, compounded monthly for the first six months, increasing thereafter to 17 percent compounded monthly. Assuming you transfer the $6,000 balance from your existing credit card and make no subsequent payments, how much interest will you owe at the end of the first year?

32. **Calculating Annuities [LO1]** You are planning to save for retirement over the next 30 years. To do this, you will invest $800 a month in a stock account and $400 a month in a bond account. The return of the stock account is expected to be 10 percent, and the bond account will pay 6 percent. When you retire, you will combine your money into an account with a 7 percent return. How much can you withdraw each month from your account assuming a 25-year withdrawal period?

33. **Calculating Future Values [LO1]** You have an investment that will pay you .98 percent per month. How much will you have per dollar invested in one year? In two years?

34. **Calculating Annuity Payments [LO1]** You want to be a millionaire when you retire in 40 years. How much do you have to save each month if you can earn an 11 percent annual return? How much do you have to save each month if you wait 10 years before you begin your deposits? 20 years?

35. **Calculating Rates of Return [LO2]** Suppose an investment offers to quadruple your money in 12 months (don't believe it). What rate of return per quarter are you being offered?

36. **Comparing Cash Flow Streams [LO1]** You've just joined the investment banking firm of Dewey, Cheatum, and Howe. They've offered you two different salary arrangements. You can have $75,000 per year for the next two years, or you can have $64,000 per year for the next two years, along with a $20,000 signing bonus today. The bonus is paid immediately, and the salary is paid in equal amounts at the end of each month. If the interest rate is 10 percent compounded monthly, which do you prefer?

37. **Growing Annuity [LO1]** You have just won the lottery and will receive $1,000,000 in one year. You will receive payments for 30 years, which will increase 3 percent per year. If the appropriate discount rate is 7 percent, what is the present value of your winnings?

38. **Growing Annuity [LO1]** Your job pays you only once a year for all the work you did over the previous 12 months. Today, December 31, you just received your salary of $60,000 and you plan to spend all of it. However, you want to start saving for retirement beginning next year. You have decided that one year from today you will begin depositing 8 percent of your annual salary in an account that will earn 10 percent per year. Your salary will increase at 3 percent per year throughout your career. How much money will you have on the date of your retirement 40 years from today?

39. **Present Value and Interest Rates [LO1]** What is the relationship between the value of an annuity and the level of interest rates? Suppose you just bought a 20-year annuity of $7,500 per year at the current interest rate of 10 percent per year. What happens to the value of your investment if interest rates suddenly drop to 5 percent? What if interest rates suddenly rise to 15 percent?

40. **Calculating the Number of Payments [LO2]** You're prepared to make monthly payments of $290, beginning at the end of this month, into an account that pays 7 percent interest compounded monthly. How many payments will you have made when your account balance reaches $20,000?

41. **Calculating Annuity Present Values [LO2]** You want to borrow $95,000 from your local bank to buy a new sailboat. You can afford to make monthly payments of $1,950, but no more. Assuming monthly compounding, what is the highest rate you can afford on a 60-month APR loan?

Visit us at www.mhhe.com/rwj

✗ 42. **Calculating Loan Payments [LO2]** You need a 30-year, fixed-rate mortgage to buy a new home for $290,000. Your mortgage bank will lend you the money at a 5.85 percent APR for this 360-month loan. However, you can afford monthly payments of only $1,300, so you offer to pay off any remaining loan balance at the end of the loan in the form of a single balloon payment. How large will this balloon payment have to be for you to keep your monthly payments at $1,300?

43. **Present and Future Values [LO1]** The present value of the following cash flow stream is $8,400 when discounted at 9 percent annually. What is the value of the missing cash flow?

Year	Cash Flow
1	$2,000
2	?
3	2,600
4	3,200

44. **Calculating Present Values [LO1]** You just won the TVM Lottery. You will receive $1 million today plus another 10 annual payments that increase by $600,000 per year. Thus, in one year, you receive $1.6 million. In two years, you get $2.2 million, and so on. If the appropriate interest rate is 7 percent, what is the present value of your winnings?

✗ 45. **EAR versus APR [LO4]** You have just purchased a new warehouse. To finance the purchase, you've arranged for a 30-year mortgage loan for 80 percent of the $3,400,000 purchase price. The monthly payment on this loan will be $17,500. What is the APR on this loan? The EAR?

✗ 46. **Present Value and Break-Even Interest [LO1]** Consider a firm with a contract to sell an asset for $145,000 four years from now. The asset costs $81,000 to produce today. Given a relevant discount rate on this asset of 13 percent per year, will the firm make a profit on this asset? At what rate does the firm just break even?

47. **Present Value and Multiple Cash Flows [LO1]** What is the value today of $4,000 per year, at a discount rate of 10 percent, if the first payment is received 6 years from today and the last payment is received 20 years from today?

48. **Variable Interest Rates [LO1]** A 15-year annuity pays $1,750 per month, and payments are made at the end of each month. If the interest rate is 10 percent compounded monthly for the first seven years, and 6 percent compounded monthly thereafter, what is the present value of the annuity?

49. **Comparing Cash Flow Streams [LO1]** You have your choice of two investment accounts. Investment A is a 13-year annuity that features end-of-month $1,500 payments and has an interest rate of 7.5 percent compounded monthly. Investment B is a 7 percent continuously compounded lump sum investment, also good for 13 years. How much money would you need to invest in B today for it to be worth as much as investment A 13 years from now?

✗ 50. **Calculating Present Value of a Perpetuity [LO1]** Given an interest rate of 4.7 percent per year, what is the value at date $t = 7$ of a perpetual stream of $3,100 payments that begins at date $t = 15$?

51. **Calculating EAR [LO4]** A local finance company quotes a 17 percent interest rate on one-year loans. So, if you borrow $25,000, the interest for the year will be $4,250. Because you must repay a total of $29,250 in one year, the finance company requires you to pay $29,250/12, or $2,437.50, per month over the next 12 months. Is this a 17 percent loan? What rate would legally have to be quoted? What is the effective annual rate?

52. Calculating Present Values [LO1] A five-year annuity of ten $8,000 semiannual payments will begin 9 years from now, with the first payment coming 9.5 years from now. If the discount rate is 8 percent compounded monthly, what is the value of this annuity five years from now? What is the value three years from now? What is the current value of the annuity?

53. Calculating Annuities Due [LO1] Suppose you are going to receive $13,500 per year for five years. The appropriate interest rate is 8.4 percent.

   a. What is the present value of the payments if they are in the form of an ordinary annuity? What is the present value if the payments are an annuity due?

   b. Suppose you plan to invest the payments for five years. What is the future value if the payments are an ordinary annuity? What if the payments are an annuity due?

   c. Which has the highest present value, the ordinary annuity or annuity due? Which has the highest future value? Will this always be true?

54. Calculating Annuities Due [LO1] You want to buy a new sports car from Muscle Motors for $78,000. The contract is in the form of a 60-month annuity due at a 7.25 percent APR. What will your monthly payment be?

55. Amortization with Equal Payments [LO3] Prepare an amortization schedule for a five-year loan of $63,000. The interest rate is 8 percent per year, and the loan calls for equal annual payments. How much interest is paid in the third year? How much total interest is paid over the life of the loan?

56. Amortization with Equal Principal Payments [LO3] Rework Problem 55 assuming that the loan agreement calls for a principal reduction of $12,600 every year instead of equal annual payments.

57. Calculating Annuity Values [LO1] Bilbo Baggins wants to save money to meet three objectives. First, he would like to be able to retire 30 years from now with retirement income of $24,000 per month for 25 years, with the first payment received 30 years and 1 month from now. Second, he would like to purchase a cabin in Rivendell in 10 years at an estimated cost of $340,000. Third, after he passes on at the end of the 25 years of withdrawals, he would like to leave an inheritance of $1,500,000 to his nephew Frodo. He can afford to save $2,500 per month for the next 10 years. If he can earn a 10 percent EAR before he retires and a 7 percent EAR after he retires, how much will he have to save each month in Years 11 through 30?

CHALLENGE
(Questions 57–78)

58. Calculating Annuity Values [LO1] After deciding to buy a new car, you can either lease the car or purchase it on a three-year loan. The car you wish to buy costs $35,000. The dealer has a special leasing arrangement where you pay $99 today and $499 per month for the next three years. If you purchase the car, you will pay it off in monthly payments over the next three years at a 6 percent APR. You believe you will be able to sell the car for $23,000 in three years. Should you buy or lease the car? What break-even resale price in three years would make you indifferent between buying and leasing?

59. Calculating Annuity Values [LO1] An All-Pro defensive lineman is in contract negotiations. The team has offered the following salary structure:

Time	Salary
0	$6,500,000
1	$5,100,000
2	$5,600,000
3	$6,100,000
4	$7,500,000
5	$8,200,000
6	$9,000,000

Visit us at www.mhhe.com/rwj

All salaries are to be paid in lump sums. The player has asked you as his agent to renegotiate the terms. He wants a $10 million signing bonus payable today and a contract value increase of $2,000,000. He also wants an equal salary paid every three months, with the first paycheck three months from now. If the interest rate is 5.5 percent compounded daily, what is the amount of his quarterly check? Assume 365 days in a year.

60. **Discount Interest Loans [LO4]** This question illustrates what is known as *discount interest*. Imagine you are discussing a loan with a somewhat unscrupulous lender. You want to borrow $25,000 for one year. The interest rate is 13 percent. You and the lender agree that the interest on the loan will be .13 × $25,000 = $3,250. So the lender deducts this interest amount from the loan up front and gives you $21,750. In this case, we say that the discount is $3,250. What's wrong here?

61. **Calculating Annuity Values [LO1]** You are serving on a jury. A plaintiff is suing the city for injuries sustained after a freak street sweeper accident. In the trial, doctors testified that it will be five years before the plaintiff is able to return to work. The jury has already decided in favor of the plaintiff. You are the foreperson of the jury and propose that the jury give the plaintiff an award to cover the following: (a) The present value of two years' back pay. The plaintiff's annual salary for the last two years would have been $41,000 and $44,000, respectively. (b) The present value of five years' future salary. You assume the salary will be $48,000 per year. (c) $100,000 for pain and suffering. (d) $20,000 for court costs. Assume that the salary payments are equal amounts paid at the end of each month. If the interest rate you choose is an 8 percent EAR, what is the size of the settlement? If you were the plaintiff, would you like to see a higher or lower interest rate?

62. **Calculating EAR with Points [LO4]** You are looking at a one-year loan of $10,000. The interest rate is quoted as 9 percent plus three points. A *point* on a loan is simply 1 percent (one percentage point) of the loan amount. Quotes similar to this one are common with home mortgages. The interest rate quotation in this example requires the borrower to pay three points to the lender up front and repay the loan later with 9 percent interest. What rate would you actually be paying here?

63. **Calculating EAR with Points [LO4]** The interest rate on a one-year loan is quoted as 12 percent plus two points (see the previous problem). What is the EAR? Is your answer affected by the loan amount?

64. **EAR versus APR [LO4]** Two banks in the area offer 30-year, $220,000 mortgages at 5.5 percent and charge a $3,500 loan application fee. However, the application fee charged by Insecurity Bank and Trust is refundable if the loan application is denied, whereas that charged by I.M. Greedy and Sons Mortgage Bank is not. The current disclosure law requires that any fees that will be refunded if the applicant is rejected be included in calculating the APR, but this is not required with nonrefundable fees (presumably because refundable fees are part of the loan rather than a fee). What are the EARs on these two loans? What are the APRs?

65. **Calculating EAR with Add-On Interest [LO4]** This problem illustrates a deceptive way of quoting interest rates called *add-on interest*. Imagine that you see an advertisement for Crazy Judy's Stereo City that reads something like this: "$1,000 Instant Credit! 17% Simple Interest! Three Years to Pay! Low, Low Monthly Payments!" You're not exactly sure what all this means and somebody has spilled ink over the APR on the loan contract, so you ask the manager for clarification.

Visit us at www.mhhe.com/rwj

Judy explains that if you borrow $1,000 for three years at 17 percent interest, in three years you will owe:

$$\$1,000 \times 1.17^3 = \$1,000 \times 1.60161 = \$1,601.61$$

Now, Judy recognizes that coming up with $1,601.61 all at once might be a strain, so she lets you make "low, low monthly payments" of $1,601.61/36 = $44.49 per month, even though this is extra bookkeeping work for her.

Is this a 17 percent loan? Why or why not? What is the APR on this loan? What is the EAR? Why do you think this is called add-on interest?

66. **Calculating Annuity Payments [LO1]** This is a classic retirement problem. A time line will help in solving it. Your friend is celebrating her 35th birthday today and wants to start saving for her anticipated retirement at age 65. She wants to be able to withdraw $125,000 from her savings account on each birthday for 20 years following her retirement; the first withdrawal will be on her 66th birthday. Your friend intends to invest her money in the local credit union, which offers 7 percent interest per year. She wants to make equal annual payments on each birthday into the account established at the credit union for her retirement fund.

   a. If she starts making these deposits on her 36th birthday and continues to make deposits until she is 65 (the last deposit will be on her 65th birthday), what amount must she deposit annually to be able to make the desired withdrawals at retirement?

   b. Suppose your friend has just inherited a large sum of money. Rather than making equal annual payments, she has decided to make one lump sum payment on her 35th birthday to cover her retirement needs. What amount does she have to deposit?

   c. Suppose your friend's employer will contribute $3,500 to the account every year as part of the company's profit-sharing plan. In addition, your friend expects a $175,000 distribution from a family trust fund on her 55th birthday, which she will also put into the retirement account. What amount must she deposit annually now to be able to make the desired withdrawals at retirement?

67. **Calculating the Number of Periods [LO2]** Your Christmas ski vacation was great, but it unfortunately ran a bit over budget. All is not lost: You just received an offer in the mail to transfer your $12,000 balance from your current credit card, which charges an annual rate of 19.8 percent, to a new credit card charging a rate of 10.4 percent. How much faster could you pay the loan off by making your planned monthly payments of $225 with the new card? What if there was a 2 percent fee charged on any balances transferred?

68. **Future Value and Multiple Cash Flows [LO1]** An insurance company is offering a new policy to its customers. Typically, the policy is bought by a parent or grandparent for a child at the child's birth. The details of the policy are as follows: The purchaser (say, the parent) makes the following six payments to the insurance company:

First birthday:	$750
Second birthday:	$750
Third birthday:	$850
Fourth birthday:	$850
Fifth birthday:	$950
Sixth birthday:	$950

Visit us at www.mhhe.com/rwj

After the child's sixth birthday, no more payments are made. When the child reaches age 65, he or she receives $250,000. If the relevant interest rate is 10 percent for the first six years and 7 percent for all subsequent years, is the policy worth buying?

69. **Calculating a Balloon Payment [LO2]** You have just arranged for a $1,800,000 mortgage to finance the purchase of a large tract of land. The mortgage has a 7.8 percent APR, and it calls for monthly payments over the next 30 years. However, the loan has an eight-year balloon payment, meaning that the loan must be paid off then. How big will the balloon payment be?

70. **Calculating Interest Rates [LO4]** A financial planning service offers a college savings program. The plan calls for you to make six annual payments of $13,000 each, with the first payment occurring today, your child's 12th birthday. Beginning on your child's 18th birthday, the plan will provide $30,000 per year for four years. What return is this investment offering?

71. **Break-Even Investment Returns [LO4]** Your financial planner offers you two different investment plans. Plan X is a $25,000 annual perpetuity. Plan Y is a 15-year, $35,000 annual annuity. Both plans will make their first payment one year from today. At what discount rate would you be indifferent between these two plans?

72. **Perpetual Cash Flows [LO1]** What is the value of an investment that pays $25,000 every *other* year forever, if the first payment occurs one year from today and the discount rate is 9 percent compounded daily? What is the value today if the first payment occurs four years from today?

73. **Ordinary Annuities and Annuities Due [LO1]** As discussed in the text, an annuity due is identical to an ordinary annuity except that the periodic payments occur at the beginning of each period and not at the end of the period. Show that the relationship between the value of an ordinary annuity and the value of an otherwise equivalent annuity due is:

Annuity due value = Ordinary annuity value $\times$ (1 + r)

Show this for both present and future values.

74. **Calculating Growing Annuities [LO1]** You have 40 years left until retirement and want to retire with $5 million. Your salary is paid annually, and you will receive $50,000 at the end of the current year. Your salary will increase at 3 percent per year, and you can earn a 10 percent return on the money you invest. If you save a constant percentage of your salary, what percentage of your salary must you save each year?

75. **Calculating EAR [LO4]** A check-cashing store is in the business of making personal loans to walk-up customers. The store makes only one-week loans at 8 percent interest per week.

   a. What APR must the store report to its customers? What EAR are customers actually paying?

   b. Now suppose the store makes one-week loans at 8 percent discount interest per week (see Problem 60). What's the APR now? The EAR?

   c. The check-cashing store also makes one-month add-on interest loans at 8 percent discount interest per week. Thus if you borrow $100 for one month (four weeks), the interest will be ($100 $\times$ 1.08^4) − 100 = $36.05. Because this is discount interest, your net loan proceeds today will be $63.95. You must then repay the store $100 at the end of the month. To help you out, though, the store lets you pay off this $100 in installments of $25 per week. What is the APR of this loan? What is the EAR?

76. **Present Value of a Growing Perpetuity [LO1]** What is the equation for the present value of a growing perpetuity with a payment of *C* one period from today if the payments grow by *C* each period?

77. **Rule of 72 [LO4]** Earlier, we discussed the Rule of 72, a useful approximation for many interest rates and periods for the time it takes a lump sum to double in value. For a 10 percent interest rate, show that the "Rule of 73" is slightly better. For what rate is the Rule of 72 exact? (*Hint:* Use the Solver function in Excel.)

78. **Rule of 69.3 [LO4]** A corollary to the Rule of 72 is the Rule of 69.3. The Rule of 69.3 is exactly correct except for rounding when interest rates are compounded continuously. Prove the Rule of 69.3 for continuously compounded interest.

MINICASE

The MBA Decision

Ben Bates graduated from college six years ago with a finance undergraduate degree. Although he is satisfied with his current job, his goal is to become an investment banker. He feels that an MBA degree would allow him to achieve this goal. After examining schools, he has narrowed his choice to either Wilton University or Mount Perry College. Although internships are encouraged by both schools, to get class credit for the internship, no salary can be paid. Other than internships, neither school will allow its students to work while enrolled in its MBA program.

Ben currently works at the money management firm of Dewey and Louis. His annual salary at the firm is $53,000 per year, and his salary is expected to increase at 3 percent per year until retirement. He is currently 28 years old and expects to work for 38 more years. His current job includes a fully paid health insurance plan, and his current average tax rate is 26 percent. Ben has a savings account with enough money to cover the entire cost of his MBA program.

The Ritter College of Business at Wilton University is one of the top MBA programs in the country. The MBA degree requires two years of full-time enrollment at the university. The annual tuition is $58,000, payable at the beginning of each school year. Books and other supplies are estimated to cost $2,000 per year. Ben expects that after graduation from Wilton, he will receive a job offer for about $87,000 per year, with a $10,000 signing bonus. The salary at this job will increase at 4 percent per year. Because of the higher salary, his average income tax rate will increase to 31 percent.

The Bradley School of Business at Mount Perry College began its MBA program 16 years ago. The Bradley School is smaller and less well known than the Ritter College. Bradley offers an accelerated one-year program, with a tuition cost of $75,000 to be paid upon matriculation. Books and other supplies for the program are expected to cost $4,200. Ben thinks that he will receive an offer of $78,000 per year upon graduation, with an $8,000 signing bonus. The salary at this job will increase at 3.5 percent per year. His average tax rate at this level of income will be 29 percent.

Both schools offer a health insurance plan that will cost $3,000 per year, payable at the beginning of the year. Ben has also found that both schools offer graduate housing. His room and board expenses will decrease by $4,000 per year at either school he attends. The appropriate discount rate is 6.5 percent.

QUESTIONS

1. How does Ben's age affect his decision to get an MBA?

2. What other, perhaps nonquantifiable, factors affect Ben's decision to get an MBA?

3. Assuming all salaries are paid at the end of each year, what is the best option for Ben from a strictly financial standpoint?

4. Ben believes that the appropriate analysis is to calculate the future value of each option. How would you evaluate this statement?

5. What initial salary would Ben need to receive to make him indifferent between attending Wilton University and staying in his current position?

6. Suppose, instead of being able to pay cash for his MBA, Ben must borrow the money. The current borrowing rate is 5.4 percent. How would this affect his decision?

Visit us at www.mhhe.com/rwj

INTEREST RATES AND BOND VALUATION

WHEN STATES, CITIES, OR OTHER local governments need to raise money, they turn to the municipal bond market. With about $2.8 trillion in municipal bonds outstanding, it seems that these borrowers reach out to this market quite often! Normally a relatively quiet financial market, the municipal bond market became much more exciting in 2010 and early 2011 because of potential defaults. According to Standard & Poor's (S&P), 110 municipal bonds entered into default during 2010, representing $2.65 billion worth of bonds. What concerned investors even more was the potential for large defaults in the future. States such as California and Illinois were experiencing large deficits, and much bigger municipal bond defaults seemed possible. Congressional leaders further exacerbated the belief that municipal bond defaults could explode when they proposed changing legislation to allow municipalities to declare bankruptcy.

Of course, no municipal bond default to date has exceeded the infamous "Whoops" bonds. Issued by the Washington Public Power Supply System (WPPSS) to fund the construction of five nuclear power plants, WPPSS defaulted on $2.25 billion worth of bonds in 1983, the largest municipal bond default in U.S. history. In the end, investors received only 10 to 40 percent of their original investment.

LEARNING OBJECTIVES

After studying this chapter, you should understand:

LO1 Important bond features and types of bonds.

LO2 Bond values and yields and why they fluctuate.

LO3 Bond ratings and what they mean.

LO4 The impact of inflation on interest rates.

LO5 The term structure of interest rates and the determinants of bond yields.

Our goal in this chapter is to introduce you to bonds. We begin by showing how the techniques we developed in Chapters 5 and 6 can be applied to bond valuation. From there, we go on to discuss bond features and how bonds are bought and sold. One important thing we learn is that bond values depend, in large part, on interest rates. We therefore close the chapter with an examination of interest rates and their behavior.

Bonds and Bond Valuation

When a corporation or government wishes to borrow money from the public on a long-term basis, it usually does so by issuing or selling debt securities that are generically called *bonds*. In this section, we describe the various features of corporate bonds and some of the terminology associated with bonds. We then discuss the cash flows associated with a bond and how bonds can be valued using our discounted cash flow procedure.

BOND FEATURES AND PRICES

As we mentioned in our previous chapter, a bond is normally an interest-only loan, meaning that the borrower will pay the interest every period, but none of the principal will be repaid until the end of the loan. For example, suppose the Beck Corporation wants to borrow $1,000 for 30 years. The interest rate on similar debt issued by similar corporations is 12 percent. Beck will thus pay .12 × $1,000 = $120 in interest every year for 30 years. At the end of 30 years, Beck will repay the $1,000. As this example suggests, a bond is a fairly simple financing arrangement. There is, however, a rich jargon associated with bonds, so we will use this example to define some of the more important terms.

In our example, the $120 regular interest payments that Beck promises to make are called the bond's **coupons**. Because the coupon is constant and paid every year, the type of bond we are describing is sometimes called a *level coupon bond*. The amount that will be repaid at the end of the loan is called the bond's **face value**, or **par value**. As in our example, this par value is usually $1,000 for corporate bonds, and a bond that sells for its par value is called a *par value bond*. Government bonds frequently have much larger face, or par, values. Finally, the annual coupon divided by the face value is called the **coupon rate** on the bond; in this case, because $120/1,000 = 12%, the bond has a 12 percent coupon rate.

The number of years until the face value is paid is called the bond's time to **maturity**. A corporate bond will frequently have a maturity of 30 years when it is originally issued, but this varies. Once the bond has been issued, the number of years to maturity declines as time goes by.

BOND VALUES AND YIELDS

As time passes, interest rates change in the marketplace. The cash flows from a bond, however, stay the same. As a result, the value of the bond will fluctuate. When interest rates rise, the present value of the bond's remaining cash flows declines, and the bond is worth less. When interest rates fall, the bond is worth more.

To determine the value of a bond at a particular point in time, we need to know the number of periods remaining until maturity, the face value, the coupon, and the market interest rate for bonds with similar features. This interest rate required in the market on a bond is called the bond's **yield to maturity (YTM)**. This rate is sometimes called the bond's *yield* for short. Given all this information, we can calculate the present value of the cash flows as an estimate of the bond's current market value.

For example, suppose the Xanth (pronounced "zanth") Co. were to issue a bond with 10 years to maturity. The Xanth bond has an annual coupon of $80. Similar bonds have a yield to maturity of 8 percent. Based on our preceding discussion, the Xanth bond will pay $80 per year for the next 10 years in coupon interest. In 10 years, Xanth will pay $1,000 to the owner of the bond. The cash flows from the bond are shown in Figure 7.1. What would this bond sell for?

As illustrated in Figure 7.1, the Xanth bond's cash flows have an annuity component (the coupons) and a lump sum (the face value paid at maturity). We thus estimate the

coupon
The stated interest payment made on a bond.

face value
The principal amount of a bond that is repaid at the end of the term. Also called *par value*.

coupon rate
The annual coupon divided by the face value of a bond.

maturity
The specified date on which the principal amount of a bond is paid.

yield to maturity (YTM)
The rate required in the market on a bond.

FIGURE 7.1 Cash Flows for Xanth Co. Bond

As shown, the Xanth bond has an annual coupon of $80 and a face, or par, value of $1,000 paid at maturity in 10 years.

market value of the bond by calculating the present value of these two components separately and adding the results together. First, at the going rate of 8 percent, the present value of the $1,000 paid in 10 years is:

Present value = $1,000/1.08^{10}$ = $1,000/2.1589 = $463.19

Second, the bond offers $80 per year for 10 years; the present value of this annuity stream is:

$$\text{Annuity present value} = \$80 \times (1 - 1/1.08^{10})/.08$$
$$= \$80 \times (1 - 1/2.1589)/.08$$
$$= \$80 \times 6.7101$$
$$= \$536.81$$

We can now add the values for the two parts together to get the bond's value:

Total bond value = $463.19 + 536.81 = $1,000

This bond sells for exactly its face value. This is not a coincidence. The going interest rate in the market is 8 percent. Considered as an interest-only loan, what interest rate does this bond have? With an $80 coupon, this bond pays exactly 8 percent interest only when it sells for $1,000.

To illustrate what happens as interest rates change, suppose a year has gone by. The Xanth bond now has nine years to maturity. If the interest rate in the market has risen to 10 percent, what will the bond be worth? To find out, we repeat the present value calculations with 9 years instead of 10, and a 10 percent yield instead of an 8 percent yield. First, the present value of the $1,000 paid in nine years at 10 percent is:

Present value = $1,000/1.10^9$ = $1,000/2.3579 = $424.10

Second, the bond now offers $80 per year for nine years; the present value of this annuity stream at 10 percent is:

$$\text{Annuity present value} = \$80 \times (1 - 1/1.10^9)/.10$$
$$= \$80 \times (1 - 1/2.3579)/.10$$
$$= \$80 \times 5.7590$$
$$= \$460.72$$

We can now add the values for the two parts together to get the bond's value:

Total bond value = $424.10 + 460.72 = $884.82

Therefore, the bond should sell for about $885. In the vernacular, we say that this bond, with its 8 percent coupon, is priced to yield 10 percent at $885.

The Xanth Co. bond now sells for less than its $1,000 face value. Why? The market interest rate is 10 percent. Considered as an interest-only loan of $1,000, this bond pays only 8 percent, its coupon rate. Because this bond pays less than the going rate, investors are willing to lend only something less than the $1,000 promised repayment. Because the bond sells for less than face value, it is said to be a *discount bond.*

The only way to get the interest rate up to 10 percent is to lower the price to less than $1,000 so that the purchaser, in effect, has a built-in gain. For the Xanth bond, the price of $885 is $115 less than the face value, so an investor who purchased and kept the bond would get $80 per year and would have a $115 gain at maturity as well. This gain compensates the lender for the below-market coupon rate.

Another way to see why the bond is discounted by $115 is to note that the $80 coupon is $20 below the coupon on a newly issued par value bond, based on current market conditions. The bond would be worth $1,000 only if it had a coupon of $100 per year. In a sense, an investor who buys and keeps the bond gives up $20 per year for nine years. At 10 percent, this annuity stream is worth:

A good bond site to visit is bonds.yahoo.com, *which has loads of useful information.*

$$\text{Annuity present value} = \$20 \times (1 - 1/1.10^9)/.10$$
$$= \$20 \times 5.7590$$
$$= \$115.18$$

This is just the amount of the discount.

What would the Xanth bond sell for if interest rates had dropped by 2 percent instead of rising by 2 percent? As you might guess, the bond would sell for more than $1,000. Such a bond is said to sell at a *premium* and is called a *premium bond.*

This case is just the opposite of that of a discount bond. The Xanth bond now has a coupon rate of 8 percent when the market rate is only 6 percent. Investors are willing to pay a premium to get this extra coupon amount. In this case, the relevant discount rate is 6 percent, and there are nine years remaining. The present value of the $1,000 face amount is:

Online bond calculators are available at personal.fidelity.com; *interest rate information is available at* money.cnn.com/ markets/bondcenter *and* www.bankrate.com.

$$\text{Present value} = \$1,000/1.06^9 = \$1,000/1.6895 = \$591.89$$

The present value of the coupon stream is:

$$\text{Annuity present value} = \$80 \times (1 - 1/1.06^9)/.06$$
$$= \$80 \times (1 - 1/1.6895)/.06$$
$$= \$80 \times 6.8017$$
$$= \$544.14$$

We can now add the values for the two parts together to get the bond's value:

$$\text{Total bond value} = \$591.89 + 544.14 = \$1,136.03$$

Total bond value is therefore about $136 in excess of par value. Once again, we can verify this amount by noting that the coupon is now $20 too high, based on current market conditions. The present value of $20 per year for nine years at 6 percent is:

$$\text{Annuity present value} = \$20 \times (1 - 1/1.06^9)/.06$$
$$= \$20 \times 6.8017$$
$$= \$136.03$$

This is just as we calculated.

Based on our examples, we can now write the general expression for the value of a bond. If a bond has (1) a face value of F paid at maturity, (2) a coupon of C paid per period, (3) t periods to maturity, and (4) a yield of r per period, its value is:

$$\text{Bond value} = C \times [1 - 1/(1 + r)^t]/r \quad + \qquad F/(1 + r)^t \qquad\qquad \textbf{[7.1]}$$

$$\text{Bond value} = \begin{array}{c}\text{Present value}\\\text{of the coupons}\end{array} \quad + \quad \begin{array}{c}\text{Present value}\\\text{of the face amount}\end{array}$$

EXAMPLE 7.1	**Semiannual Coupons**

In practice, bonds issued in the United States usually make coupon payments twice a year. So, if an ordinary bond has a coupon rate of 14 percent, then the owner will get a total of $140 per year, but this $140 will come in two payments of $70 each. Suppose we are examining such a bond. The yield to maturity is quoted at 16 percent.

Bond yields are quoted like APRs; the quoted rate is equal to the actual rate per period multiplied by the number of periods. In this case, with a 16 percent quoted yield and semiannual payments, the true yield is 8 percent per six months. The bond matures in seven years. What is the bond's price? What is the effective annual yield on this bond?

Based on our discussion, we know the bond will sell at a discount because it has a coupon rate of 7 percent every six months when the market requires 8 percent every six months. So, if our answer exceeds $1,000, we know we have made a mistake.

To get the exact price, we first calculate the present value of the bond's face value of $1,000 paid in seven years. This seven-year period has 14 periods of six months each. At 8 percent per period, the value is:

$$\text{Present value} = \$1,000/1.08^{14} = \$1,000/2.9372 = \$340.46$$

The coupons can be viewed as a 14-period annuity of $70 per period. At an 8 percent discount rate, the present value of such an annuity is:

$$\begin{aligned}\text{Annuity present value} &= \$70 \times (1 - 1/1.08^{14})/.08\\ &= \$70 \times (1 - .3405)/.08\\ &= \$70 \times 8.2442\\ &= \$577.10\end{aligned}$$

The total present value gives us what the bond should sell for:

$$\text{Total present value} = \$340.46 + 577.10 = \$917.56$$

To calculate the effective yield on this bond, note that 8 percent every six months is equivalent to:

$$\text{Effective annual rate} = (1 + .08)^2 - 1 = 16.64\%$$

The effective yield, therefore, is 16.64 percent.

Visit investorguide.com *to learn more about bonds.*

As we have illustrated in this section, bond prices and interest rates always move in opposite directions. When interest rates rise, a bond's value, like any other present value, will decline. Similarly, when interest rates fall, bond values rise. Even if we are considering a bond that is riskless in the sense that the borrower is certain to make all the payments, there is still risk in owning a bond. We discuss this next.

INTEREST RATE RISK

The risk that arises for bond owners from fluctuating interest rates is called *interest rate risk*. How much interest rate risk a bond has depends on how sensitive its price is to interest rate changes. This sensitivity directly depends on two things: the time to maturity and the coupon rate. As we will see momentarily, you should keep the following in mind when looking at a bond:

1. All other things being equal, the longer the time to maturity, the greater the interest rate risk.
2. All other things being equal, the lower the coupon rate, the greater the interest rate risk.

We illustrate the first of these two points in Figure 7.2. As shown, we compute and plot prices under different interest rate scenarios for 10 percent coupon bonds with maturities of 1 year and 30 years. Notice how the slope of the line connecting the prices is much steeper for the 30-year maturity than it is for the 1-year maturity. This steepness tells us that a relatively small change in interest rates will lead to a substantial change in the bond's value. In comparison, the one-year bond's price is relatively insensitive to interest rate changes.

Intuitively, we can see that longer-term bonds have greater interest rate sensitivity because a large portion of a bond's value comes from the $1,000 face amount. The present value of this amount isn't greatly affected by a small change in interest rates if the amount is to be received in one year. Even a small change in the interest rate, however,

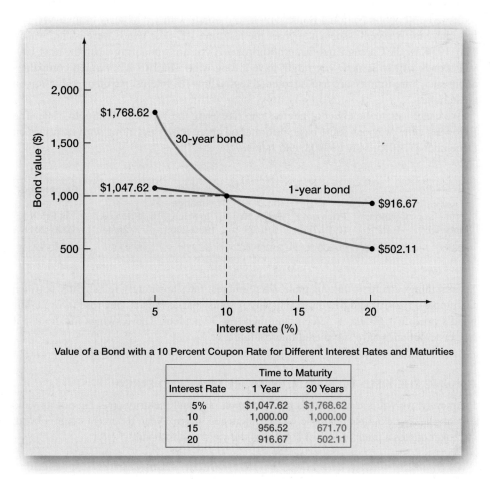

FIGURE 7.2

Interest Rate Risk and Time to Maturity

Value of a Bond with a 10 Percent Coupon Rate for Different Interest Rates and Maturities

	Time to Maturity	
Interest Rate	1 Year	30 Years
5%	$1,047.62	$1,768.62
10	1,000.00	1,000.00
15	956.52	671.70
20	916.67	502.11

once it is compounded for 30 years, can have a significant effect on the present value. As a result, the present value of the face amount will be much more volatile with a longer-term bond.

The other thing to know about interest rate risk is that, like most things in finance and economics, it increases at a decreasing rate. In other words, if we compared a 10-year bond to a 1-year bond, we would see that the 10-year bond has much greater interest rate risk. However, if you were to compare a 20-year bond to a 30-year bond, you would find that the 30-year bond has somewhat greater interest rate risk because it has a longer maturity, but the difference in the risk would be fairly small.

The reason that bonds with lower coupons have greater interest rate risk is essentially the same. As we discussed earlier, the value of a bond depends on the present value of its coupons and the present value of the face amount. If two bonds with different coupon rates have the same maturity, then the value of the one with the lower coupon is proportionately more dependent on the face amount to be received at maturity. As a result, all other things being equal, its value will fluctuate more as interest rates change. Put another way, the bond with the higher coupon has a larger cash flow early in its life, so its value is less sensitive to changes in the discount rate.

Bonds are rarely issued with maturities longer than 30 years. However, low interest rates in recent years have led to the issuance of much longer-term issues. In the 1990s, Walt Disney issued "Sleeping Beauty" bonds with a 100-year maturity. Similarly, Bell-South (now known as AT&T), Coca-Cola, and Dutch banking giant ABN AMRO all issued bonds with 100-year maturities. These companies evidently wanted to lock in the historical low interest rates for a *long* time. The current record holder for corporations looks to be Republic National Bank, which sold bonds with 1,000 years to maturity. Before these fairly recent issues, it appears the last time 100-year bonds were issued was in May 1954, by the Chicago and Eastern Railroad. If you are wondering when the next 100-year bonds will be issued, you might have a long wait. The IRS has warned companies about such long-term issues and threatened to disallow the interest payment deduction on these bonds.

We can illustrate the effect of interest rate risk using the 100-year BellSouth issue. The following table provides some basic information about this issue, along with its prices on December 31, 1995, May 6, 2008, and January 24, 2011:

Maturity	Coupon Rate	Price on 12/31/95	Price on 5/6/08	Percentage Change in Price 1995–2008	Price on 1/24/11	Percentage Change in Price 2008–2011
2095	7.00%	$1,000.00	$1008.40	.8%	$702.95	−30.3%

Several things emerge from this table. First, interest rates apparently fell slightly between December 31, 1995, and May 6, 2008 (why?). After that, however, they rose (why?). The bond's price first gained .8 percent and then lost 30 percent. These swings illustrate that longer-term bonds have significant interest rate risk.

FINDING THE YIELD TO MATURITY: MORE TRIAL AND ERROR

Frequently, we will know a bond's price, coupon rate, and maturity date, but not its yield to maturity. For example, suppose we are interested in a six-year, 8 percent coupon bond. A broker quotes a price of $955.14. What is the yield on this bond?

We've seen that the price of a bond can be written as the sum of its annuity and lump sum components. Knowing that there is an $80 coupon for six years and a $1,000 face value, we can say that the price is:

$$\$955.14 = \$80 \times [1 - 1/(1 + r)^6]/r + 1{,}000/(1 + r)^6$$

where r is the unknown discount rate, or yield to maturity. We have one equation here and one unknown, but we cannot solve it for r explicitly. The only way to find the answer is to use trial and error.

This problem is essentially identical to the one we examined in the last chapter when we tried to find the unknown interest rate on an annuity. However, finding the rate (or yield) on a bond is even more complicated because of the $1,000 face amount.

We can speed up the trial-and-error process by using what we know about bond prices and yields. In this case, the bond has an $80 coupon and is selling at a discount. We thus know that the yield is greater than 8 percent. If we compute the price at 10 percent:

$$\begin{aligned}
\text{Bond value} &= \$80 \times (1 - 1/1.10^6)/.10 + 1{,}000/1.10^6 \\
&= \$80 \times 4.3553 + 1{,}000/1.7716 \\
&= \$912.89
\end{aligned}$$

At 10 percent, the value we calculate is lower than the actual price, so 10 percent is too high. The true yield must be somewhere between 8 and 10 percent. At this point, it's "plug and chug" to find the answer. You would probably want to try 9 percent next. If you did, you would see that this is in fact the bond's yield to maturity.

A bond's yield to maturity should not be confused with its **current yield**, which is simply a bond's annual coupon divided by its price. In the example we just worked, the bond's annual coupon was $80, and its price was $955.14. Given these numbers, we see that the current yield is $80/955.14 = 8.38$ percent, which is less than the yield to maturity of 9 percent. The reason the current yield is too low is that it considers only the coupon portion of your return; it doesn't consider the built-in gain from the price discount. For a premium bond, the reverse is true, meaning that current yield would be higher because it ignores the built-in loss.

Our discussion of bond valuation is summarized in Table 7.1.

Current market rates are available at www.bankrate.com.

current yield
A bond's annual coupon divided by its price.

I.	**Finding the Value of a Bond**
	Bond value $= C \times [1 - 1/(1 + r)^t]/r + F/(1 + r)^t$
	where
	C = Coupon paid each period
	r = Rate per period
	t = Number of periods
	F = Bond's face value
II.	**Finding the Yield on a Bond**
	Given a bond value, coupon, time to maturity, and face value, it is possible to find the implicit discount rate, or yield to maturity, by trial and error only. To do this, try different discount rates until the calculated bond value equals the given value (or let a financial calculator do it for you). Remember that increasing the rate *decreases* the bond value.

TABLE 7.1

Summary of Bond Valuation

EXAMPLE 7.2

Current Events

A bond has a quoted price of $1,080.42. It has a face value of $1,000, a semiannual cou-pon of $30, and a maturity of five years. What is its current yield? What is its yield to ma-turity? Which is bigger? Why?

Notice that this bond makes semiannual payments of $30, so the annual payment is $60. The current yield is thus $60/1,080.42 = 5.55 percent. To calculate the yield to matu-rity, refer back to Example 7.1. In this case, the bond pays $30 every six months and has 10 six-month periods until maturity. So, we need to find r as follows:

$$\$1,080.42 = \$30 \times [1 - 1/(1 + r)^{10}]/r + 1,000/(1 + r)^{10}$$

After some trial and error, we find that r is equal to about 2.1 percent. But, the tricky part is that this 2.1 percent is the yield *per six months*. We have to double it to get the yield to ma-turity, so the yield to maturity is 4.2 percent, which is less than the current yield. The reason is that the current yield ignores the built-in loss of the premium between now and maturity.

EXAMPLE 7.3

Bond Yields

You're looking at two bonds identical in every way except for their coupons and, of course, their prices. Both have 12 years to maturity. The first bond has a 10 percent annual coupon rate and sells for $935.08. The second has a 12 percent annual coupon rate. What do you think it would sell for?

Because the two bonds are similar, they will be priced to yield about the same rate. We first need to calculate the yield on the 10 percent coupon bond. Proceeding as before, we know that the yield must be greater than 10 percent because the bond is selling at a discount. The bond has a fairly long maturity of 12 years. We've seen that long-term bond prices are relatively sensitive to interest rate changes, so the yield is probably close to 10 percent. A little trial and error reveals that the yield is actually 11 percent:

$$\begin{aligned}\text{Bond value} &= \$100 \times (1 - 1/1.11^{12})/.11 + 1,000/1.11^{12} \\ &= \$100 \times 6.4924 + 1,000/3.4985 \\ &= \$649.24 + 285.84 \\ &= \$935.08\end{aligned}$$

With an 11 percent yield, the second bond will sell at a premium because of its $120 coupon. Its value is:

$$\begin{aligned}\text{Bond value} &= \$120 \times (1 - 1/1.11^{12})/.11 + 1,000/1.11^{12} \\ &= \$120 \times 6.4924 + 1,000/3.4985 \\ &= \$779.08 + 285.84 \\ &= \$1,064.92\end{aligned}$$

CALCULATOR HINTS

How to Calculate Bond Prices and Yields Using a Financial Calculator

Many financial calculators have fairly sophisticated built-in bond valuation routines. However, these vary quite a lot in implementation, and not all financial calculators have them. As a result, we will illustrate a simple way to handle bond problems that will work on just about any financial calculator.

To begin, of course, we first remember to clear out the calculator! Next, for Example 7.3, we have two bonds to consider, both with 12 years to maturity. The first one sells for $935.08 and has a 10 percent annual coupon rate. To find its yield, we can do the following:

Enter | 12 | | 100 | −935.08 | 1,000
 | N | I/Y | PMT | PV | FV

Solve for | | 11

Notice that here we have entered both a future value of $1,000, representing the bond's face value, and a payment of 10 percent of $1,000, or $100, per year, representing the bond's annual coupon. Also, notice that we have a negative sign on the bond's price, which we have entered as the present value.

For the second bond, we now know that the relevant yield is 11 percent. It has a 12 percent annual coupon and 12 years to maturity, so what's the price? To answer, we just enter the relevant values and solve for the present value of the bond's cash flows:

Enter | 12 | 11 | 120 | | 1,000
 | N | I/Y | PMT | PV | FV

Solve for | | | | −1,064.92

There is an important detail that comes up here. Suppose we have a bond with a price of $902.29, 10 years to maturity, and a coupon rate of 6 percent. As we mentioned earlier, most bonds actually make semiannual payments. Assuming that this is the case for the bond here, what's the bond's yield? To answer, we need to enter the relevant numbers like this:

Enter | 20 | | 30 | −902.29 | 1,000
 | N | I/Y | PMT | PV | FV

Solve for | | 3.7

Notice that we entered $30 as the payment because the bond actually makes payments of $30 every six months. Similarly, we entered 20 for N because there are actually 20 six-month periods. When we solve for the yield, we get 3.7 percent. The tricky thing to remember is that this is the yield *per six months,* so we have to double it to get the right answer: 2 × 3.7 = 7.4 percent, which would be the bond's reported yield.

SPREADSHEET STRATEGIES

How to Calculate Bond Prices and Yields Using a Spreadsheet

Most spreadsheets have fairly elaborate routines available for calculating bond values and yields; many of these routines involve details we have not discussed. However, setting up a simple spreadsheet to calculate prices or yields is straightforward, as our next two spreadsheets show:

(continued)

	A	B	C	D	E	F	G	H
1								
2		**Using a spreadsheet to calculate bond values**						
3								
4	Suppose we have a bond with 22 years to maturity, a coupon rate of 8 percent, and a yield to							
5	maturity of 9 percent. If the bond makes semiannual payments, what is its price today?							
6								
7	Settlement date:	1/1/00						
8	Maturity date:	1/1/22						
9	Annual coupon rate:	.08						
10	Yield to maturity:	.09						
11	Face value (% of par):	100						
12	Coupons per year:	2						
13	Bond price (% of par):	**90.49**						
14								
15	The formula entered in cell B13 is =PRICE(B7,B8,B9,B10,B11,B12); notice that face value and bond							
16	price are given as a percentage of face value.							

	A	B	C	D	E	F	G	H
1								
2		**Using a spreadsheet to calculate bond yields**						
3								
4	Suppose we have a bond with 22 years to maturity, a coupon rate of 8 percent, and a price of							
5	$960.17. If the bond makes semiannual payments, what is its yield to maturity?							
6								
7	Settlement date:	1/1/00						
8	Maturity date:	1/1/22						
9	Annual coupon rate:	.08						
10	Bond price (% of par):	96.017						
11	Face value (% of par):	100						
12	Coupons per year:	2						
13	Yield to maturity:	**.084**						
14								
15	The formula entered in cell B13 is =YIELD(B7,B8,B9,B10,B11,B12); notice that face value and bond							
16	price are entered as a percentage of face value.							
17								

In our spreadsheets, notice that we had to enter two dates: a settlement date and a maturity date. The settlement date is just the date you actually pay for the bond, and the maturity date is the day the bond actually matures. In most of our problems, we don't explicitly have these dates, so we have to make them up. For example, because our bond has 22 years to maturity, we just picked 1/1/2000 (January 1, 2000) as the settlement date and 1/1/2022 (January 1, 2022) as the maturity date. Any two dates would do as long as they are exactly 22 years apart, but these are particularly easy to work with. Finally, notice that we had to enter the coupon rate and yield to maturity in annual terms and then explicitly provide the number of coupon payments per year.

Concept Questions

7.1a What are the cash flows associated with a bond?

7.1b What is the general expression for the value of a bond?

7.1c Is it true that the only risk associated with owning a bond is that the issuer will not make all the payments? Explain.

More about Bond Features

7.2

In this section, we continue our discussion of corporate debt by describing in some detail the basic terms and features that make up a typical long-term corporate bond. We discuss additional issues associated with long-term debt in subsequent sections.

Securities issued by corporations may be classified roughly as *equity securities* and *debt securities*. At the crudest level, a debt represents something that must be repaid; it is the result of borrowing money. When corporations borrow, they generally promise to make regularly scheduled interest payments and to repay the original amount borrowed (that is, the principal). The person or firm making the loan is called the *creditor* or *lender*. The corporation borrowing the money is called the *debtor* or *borrower*.

From a financial point of view, the main differences between debt and equity are the following:

1. Debt is not an ownership interest in the firm. Creditors generally do not have voting power.
2. The corporation's payment of interest on debt is considered a cost of doing business and is fully tax deductible. Dividends paid to stockholders are *not* tax deductible.
3. Unpaid debt is a liability of the firm. If it is not paid, the creditors can legally claim the assets of the firm. This action can result in liquidation or reorganization, two of the possible consequences of bankruptcy. Thus, one of the costs of issuing debt is the possibility of financial failure. This possibility does not arise when equity is issued.

Information for bond investors can be found at www.investinginbonds.com.

IS IT DEBT OR EQUITY?

Sometimes it is not clear if a particular security is debt or equity. For example, suppose a corporation issues a perpetual bond with interest payable solely from corporate income if and only if earned. Whether this is really a debt is hard to say and is primarily a legal and semantic issue. Courts and taxing authorities would have the final say.

Corporations are adept at creating exotic, hybrid securities that have many features of equity but are treated as debt. Obviously, the distinction between debt and equity is important for tax purposes. So, one reason that corporations try to create a debt security that is really equity is to obtain the tax benefits of debt and the bankruptcy benefits of equity.

As a general rule, equity represents an ownership interest, and it is a residual claim. This means that equity holders are paid after debt holders. As a result of this, the risks and benefits associated with owning debt and equity are different. To give just one example, note that the maximum reward for owning a debt security is ultimately fixed by the amount of the loan, whereas there is no upper limit to the potential reward from owning an equity interest.

LONG-TERM DEBT: THE BASICS

Ultimately, all long-term debt securities are promises made by the issuing firm to pay principal when due and to make timely interest payments on the unpaid balance. Beyond this, a number of features distinguish these securities from one another. We discuss some of these features next.

The maturity of a long-term debt instrument is the length of time the debt remains outstanding with some unpaid balance. Debt securities can be *short-term* (with maturities of one year or less) or *long-term* (with maturities of more than one year).[1] Short-term debt is sometimes referred to as *unfunded debt*.[2]

Debt securities are typically called *notes, debentures,* or *bonds.* Strictly speaking, a bond is a secured debt. However, in common usage, the word *bond* refers to all kinds of secured and unsecured debt. We will therefore continue to use the term generically to refer to long-term debt. Also, usually the only difference between a note and a bond is the original maturity. Issues with an original maturity of 10 years or less are often called notes. Longer-term issues are called bonds.

The two major forms of long-term debt are public issue and privately placed. We concentrate on public-issue bonds. Most of what we say about them holds true for private-issue, long-term debt as well. The main difference between public-issue and privately placed debt is that the latter is directly placed with a lender and not offered to the public. Because this is a private transaction, the specific terms are up to the parties involved.

There are many other dimensions to long-term debt, including such things as security, call features, sinking funds, ratings, and protective covenants. The following table illustrates these features for a bond issued by science and technology giant E. I. du Pont de Nemours (better known as DuPont). If some of these terms are unfamiliar, have no fear. We will discuss them all presently.

Information about individual bonds can be found at www.finra.org/marketdata.

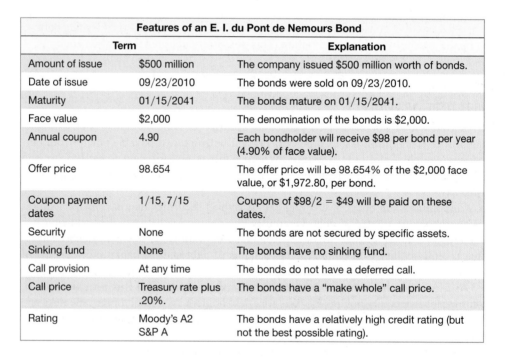

Features of an E. I. du Pont de Nemours Bond		
Term		**Explanation**
Amount of issue	$500 million	The company issued $500 million worth of bonds.
Date of issue	09/23/2010	The bonds were sold on 09/23/2010.
Maturity	01/15/2041	The bonds mature on 01/15/2041.
Face value	$2,000	The denomination of the bonds is $2,000.
Annual coupon	4.90	Each bondholder will receive $98 per bond per year (4.90% of face value).
Offer price	98.654	The offer price will be 98.654% of the $2,000 face value, or $1,972.80, per bond.
Coupon payment dates	1/15, 7/15	Coupons of $98/2 = $49 will be paid on these dates.
Security	None	The bonds are not secured by specific assets.
Sinking fund	None	The bonds have no sinking fund.
Call provision	At any time	The bonds do not have a deferred call.
Call price	Treasury rate plus .20%.	The bonds have a "make whole" call price.
Rating	Moody's A2 S&P A	The bonds have a relatively high credit rating (but not the best possible rating).

Many of these features will be detailed in the bond indenture, so we discuss this first.

---

[1]There is no universally agreed-upon distinction between short-term and long-term debt. In addition, people often refer to *intermediate-term debt,* which has a maturity of more than 1 year and less than 3 to 5, or even 10, years.

[2]The word *funding* is part of the jargon of finance. It generally refers to the long term. Thus, a firm planning to "fund" its debt requirements may be replacing short-term debt with long-term debt.

THE INDENTURE

The **indenture** is the written agreement between the corporation (the borrower) and its creditors. It is sometimes referred to as the *deed of trust.*[3] Usually, a trustee (a bank, perhaps) is appointed by the corporation to represent the bondholders. The trust company must (1) make sure the terms of the indenture are obeyed, (2) manage the sinking fund (described in the following pages), and (3) represent the bondholders in default—that is, if the company defaults on its payments to them.

The bond indenture is a legal document. It can run several hundred pages and generally makes for tedious reading. It is an important document, however, because it generally includes the following provisions:

1. The basic terms of the bonds.
2. The total amount of bonds issued.
3. A description of property used as security.
4. The repayment arrangements.
5. The call provisions.
6. Details of the protective covenants.

We discuss these features next.

Terms of a Bond   Corporate bonds usually have a face value (that is, a denomination) of $1,000, although par values of $2,000 like the DuPont bond have become relatively common. This *principal value* is stated on the bond certificate. So, if a corporation wanted to borrow $1 million, 1,000 bonds would have to be sold. The par value (that is, initial accounting value) of a bond is almost always the same as the face value, and the terms are used interchangeably in practice.

Corporate bonds are usually in **registered form**. For example, the indenture might read as follows:

> **Interest is payable semiannually on July 1 and January 1 of each year to the person in whose name the bond is registered at the close of business on June 15 or December 15, respectively.**

This means that the company has a registrar who will record the ownership of each bond and record any changes in ownership. The company will pay the interest and principal by check mailed directly to the address of the owner of record. A corporate bond may be registered and have attached "coupons." To obtain an interest payment, the owner must separate a coupon from the bond certificate and send it to the company registrar (the paying agent).

Alternatively, the bond could be in **bearer form**. This means that the certificate is the basic evidence of ownership, and the corporation will "pay the bearer." Ownership is not otherwise recorded, and, as with a registered bond with attached coupons, the holder of the bond certificate detaches the coupons and sends them to the company to receive payment.

There are two drawbacks to bearer bonds. First, they are difficult to recover if they are lost or stolen. Second, because the company does not know who owns its bonds, it cannot notify bondholders of important events. Bearer bonds were once the dominant type, but they are now much less common (in the United States) than registered bonds.

indenture
The written agreement between the corporation and the lender detailing the terms of the debt issue.

registered form
The form of bond issue in which the registrar of the company records ownership of each bond; payment is made directly to the owner of record.

bearer form
The form of bond issue in which the bond is issued without record of the owner's name; payment is made to whomever holds the bond.

---

[3]The words *loan agreement* or *loan contract* are usually used for privately placed debt and term loans.

Security　　Debt securities are classified according to the collateral and mortgages used to protect the bondholder.

Collateral is a general term that frequently means securities (for example, bonds and stocks) that are pledged as security for payment of debt. For example, collateral trust bonds often involve a pledge of common stock held by the corporation. However, the term *collateral* is commonly used to refer to any asset pledged on a debt.

Mortgage securities are secured by a mortgage on the real property of the borrower. The property involved is usually real estate—for example, land or buildings. The legal document that describes the mortgage is called a *mortgage trust indenture* or *trust deed*.

Sometimes mortgages are on specific property, such as a railroad car. More often, blanket mortgages are used. A *blanket mortgage* pledges all the real property owned by the company.[4]

Bonds frequently represent unsecured obligations of the company. A **debenture** is an unsecured bond, for which no specific pledge of property is made. The term **note** is generally used for such instruments if the maturity of the unsecured bond is less than 10 or so years when the bond is originally issued. Debenture holders have a claim only on property not otherwise pledged—in other words, the property that remains after mortgages and collateral trusts are taken into account. The DuPont bonds in the table are an example of such an issue.

The terminology that we use here and elsewhere in this chapter is standard in the United States. Outside the United States, these same terms can have different meanings. For example, bonds issued by the British government ("gilts") are called treasury "stock." Also, in the United Kingdom, a debenture is a *secured* obligation.

At the current time, public bonds issued in the United States by industrial and financial companies are typically debentures. However, most utility and railroad bonds are secured by a pledge of assets.

debenture
An unsecured debt, usually with a maturity of 10 years or more.

note
An unsecured debt, usually with a maturity under 10 years.

The Securities Industry and Financial Markets Association (SIFMA) website is www.sifma.org.

Seniority　　In general terms, *seniority* indicates preference in position over other lenders, and debts are sometimes labeled as *senior* or *junior* to indicate seniority. Some debt is *subordinated,* as in, for example, a subordinated debenture.

In the event of default, holders of subordinated debt must give preference to other specified creditors. Usually, this means that the subordinated lenders will be paid off only after the specified creditors have been compensated. However, debt cannot be subordinated to equity.

Repayment　　Bonds can be repaid at maturity, at which time the bondholder will receive the stated, or face, value of the bond; or they may be repaid in part or in entirety before maturity. Early repayment in some form is more typical and is often handled through a sinking fund.

A **sinking fund** is an account managed by the bond trustee for the purpose of repaying the bonds. The company makes annual payments to the trustee, who then uses the funds to retire a portion of the debt. The trustee does this by either buying up some of the bonds in the market or calling in a fraction of the outstanding bonds. This second option is discussed in the next section.

There are many different kinds of sinking fund arrangements, and the details would be spelled out in the indenture. For example:

sinking fund
An account managed by the bond trustee for early bond redemption.

1. Some sinking funds start about 10 years after the initial issuance.
2. Some sinking funds establish equal payments over the life of the bond.

---

[4]Real property includes land and things "affixed thereto." It does not include cash or inventories.

3. Some high-quality bond issues establish payments to the sinking fund that are not sufficient to redeem the entire issue. As a consequence, there is the possibility of a large "balloon payment" at maturity.

The Call Provision   A **call provision** allows the company to repurchase or "call" part or all of the bond issue at stated prices over a specific period. Corporate bonds are usually callable.

Generally, the call price is above the bond's stated value (that is, the par value). The difference between the call price and the stated value is the **call premium**. The amount of the call premium may become smaller over time. One arrangement is to initially set the call premium equal to the annual coupon payment and then make it decline to zero as the call date moves closer to the time of maturity.

Call provisions are often not operative during the first part of a bond's life. This makes the call provision less of a worry for bondholders in the bond's early years. For example, a company might be prohibited from calling its bonds for the first 10 years. This is a **deferred call provision**. During this period of prohibition, the bond is said to be **call protected**.

In recent years, a new type of call provision, a "make-whole" call, has become widespread in the corporate bond market. With such a feature, bondholders receive approximately what the bonds are worth if they are called. Because bondholders don't suffer a loss in the event of a call, they are "made whole."

To determine the make-whole call price, we calculate the present value of the remaining interest and principal payments at a rate specified in the indenture. For example, looking at our DuPont issue, we see that the discount rate is "Treasury rate plus .20%." What this means is that we determine the discount rate by first finding a U.S. Treasury issue with the same maturity. We calculate the yield to maturity on the Treasury issue and then add on .20 percent to get the discount rate we use.

Notice that with a make-whole call provision, the call price is higher when interest rates are lower and vice versa (why?). Also notice that, as is common with a make-whole call, the DuPont issue does not have a deferred call feature. Why might investors not be too concerned about the absence of this feature?

Protective Covenants   A **protective covenant** is that part of the indenture or loan agreement that limits certain actions a company might otherwise wish to take during the term of the loan. Protective covenants can be classified into two types: negative covenants and positive (or affirmative) covenants.

A *negative covenant* is a "thou shalt not" type of covenant. It limits or prohibits actions the company might take. Here are some typical examples:

1. The firm must limit the amount of dividends it pays according to some formula.
2. The firm cannot pledge any assets to other lenders.
3. The firm cannot merge with another firm.
4. The firm cannot sell or lease any major assets without approval by the lender.
5. The firm cannot issue additional long-term debt.

A *positive covenant* is a "thou shalt" type of covenant. It specifies an action the company agrees to take or a condition the company must abide by. Here are some examples:

1. The company must maintain its working capital at or above some specified minimum level.
2. The company must periodically furnish audited financial statements to the lender.
3. The firm must maintain any collateral or security in good condition.

call provision
An agreement giving the corporation the option to repurchase a bond at a specified price prior to maturity.

call premium
The amount by which the call price exceeds the par value of a bond.

deferred call provision
A call provision prohibiting the company from redeeming a bond prior to a certain date.

call-protected bond
A bond that, during a certain period, cannot be redeemed by the issuer.

protective covenant
A part of the indenture limiting certain actions that might be taken during the term of the loan, usually to protect the lender's interest.

Want detailed information about the amount and terms of the debt issued by a particular firm? Check out its latest financial statements by searching SEC filings at www.sec.gov.

This is only a partial list of covenants; a particular indenture may feature many different ones.

Concept Questions

7.2a What are the distinguishing features of debt compared to equity?
7.2b What is the indenture? What are protective covenants? Give some examples.
7.2c What is a sinking fund?

7.3 Bond Ratings

Firms frequently pay to have their debt rated. The two leading bond-rating firms are Moody's and Standard & Poor's (S&P). The debt ratings are an assessment of the creditworthiness of the corporate issuer. The definitions of creditworthiness used by Moody's and S&P are based on how likely the firm is to default and the protection creditors have in the event of a default.

It is important to recognize that bond ratings are concerned *only* with the possibility of default. Earlier, we discussed interest rate risk, which we defined as the risk of a change in the value of a bond resulting from a change in interest rates. Bond ratings do not address this issue. As a result, the price of a highly rated bond can still be quite volatile.

Bond ratings are constructed from information supplied by the corporation. The rating classes and some information concerning them are shown in the following table:

		Investment-Quality Bond Ratings				Low-Quality, Speculative, and/or "Junk" Bond Ratings					
		High Grade		Medium Grade		Low Grade		Very Low Grade			
Standard & Poor's		AAA	AA	A	BBB	BB	B	CCC	CC	C	D
Moody's		Aaa	Aa	A	Baa	Ba	B	Caa	Ca	C	

Moody's	S&P	
Aaa	AAA	Debt rated Aaa and AAA has the highest rating. Capacity to pay interest and principal is extremely strong.
Aa	AA	Debt rated Aa and AA has a very strong capacity to pay interest and repay principal. Together with the highest rating, this group comprises the high-grade bond class.
A	A	Debt rated A has a strong capacity to pay interest and repay principal, although it is somewhat more susceptible to the adverse effects of changes in circumstances and economic conditions than debt in high-rated categories.
Baa	BBB	Debt rated Baa and BBB is regarded as having an adequate capacity to pay interest and repay principal. Whereas it normally exhibits adequate protection parameters, adverse economic conditions or changing circumstances are more likely to lead to a weakened capacity to pay interest and repay principal for debt in this category than in higher-rated categories. These bonds are medium-grade obligations.
Ba; B Caa Ca C	BB; B CCC CC C	Debt rated in these categories is regarded, on balance, as predominantly speculative with respect to capacity to pay interest and repay principal in accordance with the terms of the obligation. BB and Ba indicate the lowest degree of speculation, and Ca, CC, and C the highest degree of speculation. Although such debt is likely to have some quality and protective characteristics, these are outweighed by large uncertainties or major risk exposures to adverse conditions. Issues rated C by Moody's are typically in default.
	D	Debt rated D is in default, and payment of interest and/or repayment of principal is in arrears.

NOTE: At times, both Moody's and S&P use adjustments (called notches) to these ratings. S&P uses plus and minus signs: A+ is the strongest A rating and A− the weakest. Moody's uses a 1, 2, or 3 designation, with 1 being the highest.

The highest rating a firm's debt can have is AAA or Aaa, and such debt is judged to be the best quality and to have the lowest degree of risk. For example, the 100-year BellSouth issue we discussed earlier was rated AAA. This rating is not awarded very often: As of 2011, only four nonfinancial U.S. companies had AAA ratings. AA or Aa ratings indicate very good quality debt and are much more common.

A large part of corporate borrowing takes the form of low-grade, or "junk," bonds. If these low-grade corporate bonds are rated at all, they are rated below investment grade by the major rating agencies. Investment-grade bonds are bonds rated at least BBB by S&P or Baa by Moody's.

Rating agencies don't always agree. To illustrate, some bonds are known as "crossover" or "5B" bonds. The reason is that they are rated triple-B (or Baa) by one rating agency and double-B (or Ba) by another, a "split rating." For example, in December 2010, life science research company Bio-Rad Laboratories sold an issue of 10-year notes rated BBB– by S&P and Ba2 by Moody's.

A bond's credit rating can change as the issuer's financial strength improves or deteriorates. For example, in November 2010, S&P and Moody's downgraded Regions Financial Corporation's long-term debt from investment grade to junk bond status. Bonds that drop into junk territory like this are called *fallen angels*. Regions was downgraded because of large losses on commercial real estate loans and the prospects of even more losses in the future.

Credit ratings are important because defaults really do occur, and when they do, investors can lose heavily. For example, in 2000, AmeriServe Food Distribution, Inc., which supplied restaurants such as Burger King with everything from burgers to giveaway toys, defaulted on $200 million in junk bonds. After the default, the bonds traded at just 18 cents on the dollar, leaving investors with a loss of more than $160 million.

Even worse in AmeriServe's case, the bonds had been issued only four months earlier, thereby making AmeriServe an NCAA champion. Although that might be a good thing for a college basketball team such as the University of Kentucky Wildcats, in the bond market it means "No Coupon At All," and it's not a good thing for investors.

Want to know what criteria are commonly used to rate corporate and municipal bonds? Go to www.standardandpoors. com, www.moodys.com, or www.fitchinv.com.

If you're nervous about the level of debt piled up by the U.S. government, don't go to www.publicdebt.treas. gov *or to* www.brillig.com/ debt_clock! *Learn all about government bonds at* www.ny.frb.org.

Concept Questions

7.3a What does a bond rating say about the risk of fluctuations in a bond's value resulting from interest rate changes?

7.3b What is a junk bond?

Some Different Types of Bonds

7.4

Thus far we have considered only "plain vanilla" corporate bonds. In this section, we briefly look at bonds issued by governments and also at bonds with unusual features.

GOVERNMENT BONDS

The biggest borrower in the world—by a wide margin—is everybody's favorite family member, Uncle Sam. In 2011, the total debt of the U.S. government was $14.1 *trillion,* or about $45,000 per citizen (and growing!). When the government wishes to borrow money for more than one year, it sells what are known as Treasury notes and bonds to the public (in fact, it does so every month). Currently, outstanding Treasury notes and bonds have original maturities ranging from 2 to 30 years.

Most U.S. Treasury issues are just ordinary coupon bonds. Some older issues are callable, and a few have some unusual features. There are two important things to keep in mind, however. First, U.S. Treasury issues, unlike essentially all other bonds, have no default risk because (we hope) the Treasury can always come up with the money to make the payments. Second, Treasury issues are exempt from state income taxes (though not federal income taxes). In other words, the coupons you receive on a Treasury note or bond are taxed only at the federal level.

State and local governments also borrow money by selling notes and bonds. Such issues are called *municipal* notes and bonds, or just "munis." Unlike Treasury issues, munis have varying degrees of default risk, and, in fact, they are rated much like corporate issues. Also, they are almost always callable. The most intriguing thing about munis is that their coupons are exempt from federal income taxes (though not necessarily state income taxes), which makes them very attractive to high-income, high–tax bracket investors.

Because of the enormous tax break they receive, the yields on municipal bonds are much lower than the yields on taxable bonds. For example, in January 2011, long-term Aa-rated corporate bonds were yielding about 5.23 percent. At the same time, long-term Aa munis were yielding about 4.84 percent. Suppose an investor was in a 30 percent tax bracket. All else being the same, would this investor prefer a Aa corporate bond or a Aa municipal bond?

To answer, we need to compare the *aftertax* yields on the two bonds. Ignoring state and local taxes, the muni pays 4.84 percent on both a pretax and an aftertax basis. The corporate issue pays 5.23 percent before taxes, but it pays only $.0523 \times (1 - .30) = .0366$, or 3.7 percent, once we account for the 30 percent tax bite. Given this, the muni has a better yield.

For information on municipal bonds including prices, check out emma.msrb.org.

Another good bond market site is money.cnn.com.

EXAMPLE 7.4   **Taxable versus Municipal Bonds**

Suppose taxable bonds are currently yielding 8 percent, while at the same time, munis of comparable risk and maturity are yielding 6 percent. Which is more attractive to an investor in a 40 percent bracket? What is the break-even tax rate? How do you interpret this rate?

For an investor in a 40 percent tax bracket, a taxable bond yields $8 \times (1 - .40) = 4.8$ percent after taxes, so the muni is much more attractive. The break-even tax rate is the tax rate at which an investor would be indifferent between a taxable and a nontaxable issue. If we let t^* stand for the break-even tax rate, then we can solve for it as follows:

$$.08 \times (1 - t^*) = .06$$
$$1 - t^* = .06/.08 = .75$$
$$t^* = .25$$

Thus, an investor in a 25 percent tax bracket would make 6 percent after taxes from either bond.

ZERO COUPON BONDS

zero coupon bond
A bond that makes no coupon payments and is thus initially priced at a deep discount.

A bond that pays no coupons at all must be offered at a price that is much lower than its stated value. Such bonds are called **zero coupon bonds**, or just *zeroes*.[5]

Suppose the Eight-Inch Nails (EIN) Company issues a $1,000 face value, five-year zero coupon bond. The initial price is set at $508.35. Even though no interest payments are made on the bond, zero coupon bond calculations use semiannual periods to be consistent with coupon bond calculations. Using semiannual periods, it is straightforward to verify

---

[5]A bond issued with a very low coupon rate (as opposed to a zero coupon rate) is an *original-issue discount (OID) bond*.

Year	Beginning Value	Ending Value	Implicit Interest Expense	Straight-Line Interest Expense
1	$508.35	$ 582.01	$ 73.66	$ 98.33
2	582.01	666.34	84.33	98.33
3	666.34	762.90	96.56	98.33
4	762.90	873.44	110.54	98.33
5	873.44	1,000.00	126.56	98.33
Total			$491.65	$491.65

TABLE 7.2

Interest Expense for EIN's Zeroes

that, at this price, the bond yields about 14 percent to maturity. The total interest paid over the life of the bond is $1,000 − 508.35 = $491.65.

For tax purposes, the issuer of a zero coupon bond deducts interest every year even though no interest is actually paid. Similarly, the owner must pay taxes on interest accrued every year, even though no interest is actually received.

The way in which the yearly interest on a zero coupon bond is calculated is governed by tax law. Before 1982, corporations could calculate the interest deduction on a straight-line basis. For EIN, the annual interest deduction would have been $491.65/5 = $98.33 per year.

Under current tax law, the implicit interest is determined by amortizing the loan. We do this by first calculating the bond's value at the beginning of each year. For example, after one year, the bond will have four years until maturity, so it will be worth $1,000/1.07^8 = $582.01; the value in two years will be $1,000/1.07^6 = $666.34; and so on. The implicit interest each year is simply the change in the bond's value for the year. The values and interest expenses for the EIN bond are listed in Table 7.2.

Notice that under the old rules, zero coupon bonds were more attractive because the deductions for interest expense were larger in the early years (compare the implicit interest expense with the straight-line expense).

Under current tax law, EIN could deduct $73.66 in interest paid the first year and the owner of the bond would pay taxes on $73.66 in taxable income (even though no interest was actually received). This second tax feature makes taxable zero coupon bonds less attractive to individuals. However, they are still a very attractive investment for tax-exempt investors with long-term dollar-denominated liabilities, such as pension funds, because the future dollar value is known with relative certainty.

Some bonds are zero coupon bonds for only part of their lives. For example, General Motors has a debenture outstanding that matures on March 15, 2036. For the first 20 years of its life, no coupon payments will be made; but, after 20 years, it will begin paying coupons semiannually at a rate of 7.75 percent per year.

FLOATING-RATE BONDS

The conventional bonds we have talked about in this chapter have fixed-dollar obligations because the coupon rates are set as fixed percentages of the par values. Similarly, the principal amounts are set equal to the par values. Under these circumstances, the coupon payments and principal are completely fixed.

With *floating-rate bonds (floaters),* the coupon payments are adjustable. The adjustments are tied to an interest rate index such as the Treasury bill interest rate or the 30-year Treasury bond rate. The EE Savings Bonds we mentioned in Chapter 5 are a good example of a floater. For EE bonds purchased after May 1, 1997, the interest rate is adjusted every six months. The rate that the bonds earn for a particular six-month period is determined by taking 90 percent of the average yield on ordinary five-year Treasury notes over the previous six months.

The value of a floating-rate bond depends on exactly how the coupon payment adjustments are defined. In most cases, the coupon adjusts with a lag to some base rate. For example, suppose a coupon rate adjustment is made on June 1. The adjustment might be based on the simple average of Treasury bond yields during the previous three months. In addition, the majority of floaters have the following features:

1. The holder has the right to redeem the note at par on the coupon payment date after some specified amount of time. This is called a *put* provision, and it is discussed in the following section.
2. The coupon rate has a floor and a ceiling, meaning that the coupon is subject to a minimum and a maximum. In this case, the coupon rate is said to be "capped," and the upper and lower rates are sometimes called the *collar*.

A particularly interesting type of floating-rate bond is an *inflation-linked* bond. Such bonds have coupons that are adjusted according to the rate of inflation (the principal amount may be adjusted as well). The U.S. Treasury began issuing such bonds in January of 1997. The issues are sometimes called "TIPS," or Treasury Inflation-Protected Securities. Other countries, including Canada, Israel, and Britain, have issued similar securities.

Official information about U.S. inflation-indexed bonds is at www.publicdebt.treas.gov.

OTHER TYPES OF BONDS

Many bonds have unusual or exotic features. So-called catastrophe, or cat, bonds provide an interesting example. In December 2010, Swiss Re, a reinsurance company, issued $170 million in cat bonds (reinsurance companies sell insurance to insurance companies). These cat bonds covered Australian earthquakes, North Atlantic hurricanes, and Californian earthquakes. In the event of one of these triggering events, Swiss Re would receive cash flows to offset its loss.

The largest·single cat bond issue to date is a series of six bonds sold by Merna Reinsurance in 2007. The six bond issues were to cover various catastrophes the company faced due to its reinsurance of State Farm. The six bonds totaled about $1.2 billion in par value, a large portion of the record $7 billion in cat bonds issued during 2007. By 2010, the issuance of cat bonds had fallen to $5 billion, and it was expected to be $5 to $6 billion in 2011.

At this point, cat bonds probably seem pretty risky. It therefore might be surprising to learn that since cat bonds were first issued in 1997, only one has not been paid in full. Because of Hurricane Katrina, bondholders in that one issue lost $190 million.

Another possible bond feature is a *warrant*. A warrant gives the buyer of a bond the right to purchase shares of stock in the company at a fixed price. Such a right would be very valuable if the stock price climbed substantially (a later chapter discusses this subject in greater depth). Because of the value of this feature, bonds with warrants are often issued at a very low coupon rate.

As these examples illustrate, bond features are really limited only by the imaginations of the parties involved. Unfortunately, there are far too many variations for us to cover in detail here. We therefore close this discussion by mentioning a few of the more common types.

Income bonds are similar to conventional bonds, except that coupon payments depend on company income. Specifically, coupons are paid to bondholders only if the firm's income is sufficient. This would appear to be an attractive feature, but income bonds are not very common.

A *convertible bond* can be swapped for a fixed number of shares of stock anytime before maturity at the holder's option. Convertibles are relatively common, but the number has been decreasing in recent years.

A *put bond* allows the *holder* to force the issuer to buy back the bond at a stated price. For example, International Paper Co. has bonds outstanding that allow the holder to force International Paper to buy the bonds back at 100 percent of face value if certain "risk" events happen. One such event is a change in credit rating from investment grade to lower than investment grade by Moody's or S&P. The put feature is therefore just the reverse of the call provision.

Edward I. Altman on Junk Bonds and Leveraged Loans

One of the most important developments in corporate finance over the last 30 years has been the reemergence of publicly owned and traded low-rated corporate debt. Originally offered to the public in the early 1900s to help finance some of our emerging growth industries, these high-yield, high-risk bonds virtually disappeared after the rash of bond defaults during the Depression. Recently, however, the junk bond market has been catapulted from being an insignificant element in the corporate fixed-income market to being one of the fastest-growing and most controversial types of financing mechanisms. Technically, high-yield bonds are bonds issued by companies whose rating given by one or more of the major rating agencies, i.e., Fitch, Moody's or Standard & Poor's, is below investment grade, e.g., below BBB– by S&P.

The term *junk* emanates from the dominant type of low-rated bond issues outstanding prior to 1977 when the "market" consisted almost exclusively of original-issue investment-grade bonds that fell from their lofty status to a higher-default risk, speculative-grade level. These so called fallen angels amounted to about $8.5 billion in 1977. At the end of 2008, fallen angels comprised about 25 percent of the $1 trillion publicly owned junk bond market. The high-yield bond market in Europe began to grow only recently and reached about €175 billion in 2008.

Beginning in 1977, issuers began to go directly to the public to raise debt capital for growth purposes. Early issuers of junk bonds were energy-related firms, cable TV companies, airlines, and assorted other industrial companies. The emerging growth company rationale coupled with relatively high returns to early investors helped legitimize this sector.

By far the most important and controversial aspect of junk bond financing was its role in the corporate restructuring movement from 1985 to 1989. High-leverage transactions and acquisitions, such as leveraged buyouts (LBOs), which occur when a firm is taken private, and leveraged recapitalizations (debt-for-equity swaps), transformed the face of corporate America, leading to a heated debate as to the economic and social consequences of firms' being transformed with debt–equity ratios of at least 6:1. Similar, but less emotional, comments accompanied a second LBO movement in 2004–2007.

These transactions involved increasingly large companies, and the multibillion dollar takeover became fairly common, finally capped by the huge $25+ billion RJR Nabisco LBO in 1989. LBOs were typically financed with about 60 percent senior bank and insurance company debt, about 25–30 percent subordinated public debt (junk bonds), and 10–15 percent equity. The junk bond segment is sometimes referred to as "mezzanine" financing because it lies between the "balcony" senior debt and the "basement" equity. In the most recent LBO binge, however, more than 30 percent of the financing was equity but the transactions were, on average, much larger than in the late 1980s, with only RJR Nabisco from the earlier vintage still in the "top-10 LBOs."

These restructurings resulted in huge fees to advisors and underwriters and huge premiums to the old shareholders who were bought out, and they continued as long as the market was willing to buy these new debt offerings at what appeared to be a favorable risk–return trade-off. The bottom fell out of the market in the last six months of 1989 due to a number of factors including a marked increase in defaults, government regulation against S&Ls holding junk bonds, and at least one highly publicized bankruptcy of a highly leveraged financial restructuring—Federated Department Stores.

The default rate rose dramatically to 4 percent in 1989 and then skyrocketed in 1990 and 1991 to 10.1 percent and 10.3 percent, respectively, with about $19 billion of defaults in 1991. By the end of 1990, the pendulum of growth in new junk bond issues and returns to investors swung dramatically downward as prices plummeted and the new-issue market all but dried up. The year 1991 was a pivotal year in that, despite record defaults, bond prices and new issues rebounded strongly as the prospects for the future brightened.

In the early 1990s, the financial market was questioning the very survival of the junk bond market. The answer as to its survival was a resounding "yes," as the amount of new issues soared to record annual levels of $40 billion in 1992, almost $80 billion in 1993, and in 1997 reached an impressive $119 billion. Coupled with plummeting default rates (under 2.0 percent each year in the 1993–97 period) and attractive returns in these years, the risk–return characteristics have been extremely favorable.

The junk bond market in the late 1990s was a quieter one compared to that of the 1980s, but, in terms of growth and returns, it was healthier than ever before. While the low default rates in 1992–98 helped to fuel new investment funds and new issues, the market experienced its ups and downs in subsequent years. Indeed, default rates started to rise in 1999 and accelerated in 2000–2002. The latter year saw defaults reach record levels as the economy slipped into a recession and investors suffered from the excesses of lending in the late 1990s.

Since the mid-1990s, a "sister" high-yield debt market has developed in the private leveraged loan market. This low-quality market grew enormously in the United States and Europe in the 2005–2007 period and was at least 30 percent larger than the high-yield bond market in 2008. One of the main reasons for the recent growth and popularity of leveraged loans issued by non-investment grade companies was that the issuing bank could

(continued)

easily sell these loans into structured finance vehicles called collateralized loan obligations (CLOs). Usually these private, leveraged loan debt securities have registered lower default rates than high-yield bonds, but there were indications that this usual pattern was going to change due to its greater expansion and liberal terms in the years prior to 2008.

The market for leveraged financing rebounded quickly in 2003 and continued to prosper until the credit crisis of 2007–2008. With the "flight-to-quality" caused by the sub-prime mortgage market meltdown in the second half of 2007 and 2008, returns to investors in high-yield bonds and leveraged loans fell considerably, new issues dried up, and default rates increased from the unusually low-risk years that coincided with the leveraged excesses. Despite these highly volatile events and problems with liquidity, we are convinced that high-yield bonds, and their private debt companion, leveraged loans, will continue in the future to be a major source of corporate debt financing and a legitimate asset class for investors.

Edward I. Altman is Max L. Heine Professor of Finance and Director of Credit and Debt Markets Research at the NYU Salomon Center at the Stern School of Business. He is widely recognized as one of the world's leading experts on bankruptcy and credit analysis as well as the high-yield and distressed debt markets.

A given bond may have many unusual features. Two of the most recent exotic bonds are CoCo bonds, which have a coupon payment, and NoNo bonds, which are zero coupon bonds. CoCo and NoNo bonds are contingent convertible, putable, callable, subordinated bonds. The contingent convertible clause is similar to the normal conversion feature, except the contingent feature must be met. For example, a contingent feature may require that the company stock trade at 110 percent of the conversion price for 20 out of the most recent 30 days. Valuing a bond of this sort can be quite complex, and the yield to maturity calculation is often meaningless. For example, in 2011, a NoNo issued by the American International Group (AIG) was selling at a price of $1,032.50, with a yield to maturity of negative 1.6 percent. At the same time, a NoNo issued by Merrill Lynch was selling for $1,205, which implied a yield to maturity of negative 107 percent!

SUKUK

Worldwide demand for assets that comply with Shariah, or Islamic law and cultural tradition, has grown dramatically. Assets, including deposits at Islamic financial institutions, totaled about $950 billion in 2010 and were expected to grow to $1.6 trillion by 2012. One of the major differences between Western financial practices and shariah is that Islamic law does not permit charging or paying riba, or interest. Given our current discussion about bonds, this means that anyone following shariah cannot buy or issue conventional bonds.

To accommodate the restriction on interest payments, Islamic bonds, or sukuk, have been created. There are many possible structures to sukuk, such as partial ownership in a debt (Sukuk Murabaha) or an asset (Sukuk Al Ijara). In case of a Sukuk Al Ijara, there is a binding promise to repurchase a certain asset by the issuer at maturity. Before the sukuk matures, rent is paid on the asset. While we have noted that traditional bonds can be relatively illiquid, most sukuk are bought and held to maturity. As a result, secondary markets in sukuk are extremely illiquid.

Concept Questions

7.4a Why might an income bond be attractive to a corporation with volatile cash flows? Can you think of a reason why income bonds are not more popular?

7.4b What do you think would be the effect of a put feature on a bond's coupon? How about a convertibility feature? Why?

Bond Markets

7.5

Bonds are bought and sold in enormous quantities every day. You may be surprised to learn that the trading volume in bonds on a typical day is many, many times larger than the trading volume in stocks (by *trading volume* we simply mean the amount of money that changes hands). Here is a finance trivia question: What is the largest securities market in the world? Most people would guess the New York Stock Exchange. In fact, the largest securities market in the world in terms of trading volume is the U.S. Treasury market.

WORK THE WEB

Bond quotes have become more available with the rise of the Internet. One site where you can find current bond prices is cxa.marketwatch.com/finra/MarketData/Default.aspx. We went to the website and searched for bonds issued by Coca-Cola. Here is a look at part of what we found for one of the bonds:

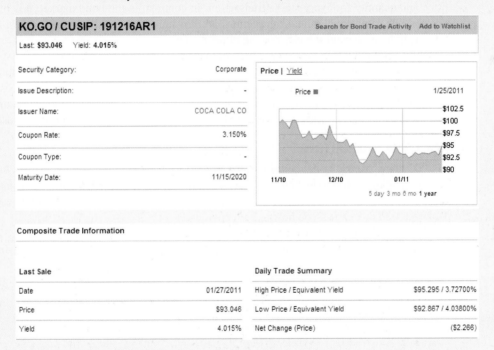

The bond has a coupon rate of 3.15 percent and matures on November 15, 2020. The last sale on this bond was at a price of 93.046 percent of par, which gives a yield to maturity of about 4.015 percent. Not only does the site provide the most recent price and yield information, but it also provides more important information about the bond, such as the credit rating, coupon date, call date, and call price. We'll leave it up to you to have a look at the page and the rest of the information available there.

Questions

1. Go to this website and find the bond shown above. When was this bond issued? What was the size of the bond issue? What were the yield to maturity and price when the bond was issued?
2. If you search for Chevron bonds (CVX), you will find bonds for several companies listed. Why do you think Chevron has bonds issued with different corporate names?

HOW BONDS ARE BOUGHT AND SOLD

As we mentioned all the way back in Chapter 1, most trading in bonds takes place over the counter, or OTC. Recall that this means there is no particular place where buying and selling occur. Instead, dealers around the country (and around the world) stand ready to buy and sell. The various dealers are connected electronically.

One reason the bond markets are so big is that the number of bond issues far exceeds the number of stock issues. There are two reasons for this. First, a corporation would typically have only one common stock issue outstanding (there are exceptions to this that we discuss in our next chapter). However, a single large corporation could easily have a dozen or more note and bond issues outstanding. Beyond this, federal, state, and local borrowing is simply enormous. For example, even a small city would usually have a wide variety of notes and bonds outstanding, representing money borrowed to pay for things like roads, sewers, and schools. When you think about how many small cities there are in the United States, you begin to get the picture!

Because the bond market is almost entirely OTC, it has historically had little or no transparency. A financial market is *transparent* if it is possible to easily observe its prices and trading volume. On the New York Stock Exchange, for example, it is possible to see the price and quantity for every single transaction. In contrast, in the bond market, it is often not possible to observe either. Transactions are privately negotiated between parties, and there is little or no centralized reporting of transactions.

Although the total volume of trading in bonds far exceeds that in stocks, only a small fraction of the total bond issues that exist actually trade on a given day. This fact, combined with the lack of transparency in the bond market, means that getting up-to-date prices on individual bonds can be difficult or impossible, particularly for smaller corporate or municipal issues. Instead, a variety of sources of estimated prices exist and are commonly used.

BOND PRICE REPORTING

To learn more about TRACE, visit www.finra.org.

In 2002, transparency in the corporate bond market began to improve dramatically. Under new regulations, corporate bond dealers are now required to report trade information through what is known as the Trade Report and Compliance Engine (TRACE). Our nearby *Work the Web* box shows you how to get bond quotes.

TRACE bond quotes are available at www.finra.org/marketdata. As shown in Figure 7.3, the Financial Industry Regulatory Authority (FINRA) provides a daily snapshot from

FIGURE 7.3

Sample TRACE Bond Quotations

Most Active Investment Grade Bonds

Issuer Name	Symbol	Coupon	Maturity	Rating Moody's/S&P/Fitch	High	Low	Last	Change	Yield%
DPL CAP TR II	DPL.GE	8.125%	Sep 2031	Baa2 /BBB /BBB	110.000	106.500	110.000	3.504	N/A
CREDIT SUISSE USA INC	CS.JF	6.500%	Jan 2012	Aa1 /A+ /AA-	105.703	105.256	105.592	-0.059	0.621
REGIONS BK ALA MTN FDIC TLGP	RF.GO	3.250%	Dec 2011	Aaa /AAA /AAA	102.660	101.454	101.454	-0.746	1.531
BARCLAYS BK PLC	BCS.IDX	2.500%	Jan 2013	Aa3 /AA- /AA-	102.330	101.449	101.651	0.651	1.648
SARA LEE CORP	SLE.HJ	4.100%	Sep 2020	Baa1 /BBB /BBB	99.764	97.387	97.938	-0.313	4.364
GOLDMAN SACHS GROUP INC	GS.KW	6.600%	Jan 2012	A1 /A /A+	105.807	105.100	105.690	0.106	0.618
TECK RESOURCES LTD	TCK.GL	10.750%	May 2019	Baa2 /BBB /BBB-	130.625	129.500	130.625	1.125	N/A
MERRILL LYNCH CO INC MTN BE	BAC.HRM	5.450%	Feb 2013	A2 /A /A+	107.100	104.960	105.811	-0.400	2.470
BANK OF AMERICA FDIC GTD TLGP	BAC.HGP	3.125%	Jun 2012	Aaa /AAA /AAA	103.610	102.764	103.595	-0.024	0.493
AMERICAN INTL GROUP INC	AIG.PMD	6.400%	Dec 2020	Baa1 /A- /BBB	106.476	105.564	106.155	0.035	5.579

TRACE by reporting the most active issues. The information shown is largely self-explanatory. Notice that the price of the Regions Bank bond dropped about .75 percentage points on this day. What do you think happened to the yield to maturity for this bond? Figure 7.3 focuses on the most active bonds with investment grade ratings, but the most active high-yield and convertible bonds are also available on the website.

If you go to the website and click on a particular bond, you will get a lot of information about the bond, including the credit rating, the call schedule, original issue information, and trade information.

As we mentioned before, the U.S. Treasury market is the largest securities market in the world. As with bond markets in general, it is an OTC market, so there is limited transparency. However, unlike the situation with bond markets in general, trading in Treasury issues, particularly recently issued ones, is very heavy. Each day, representative prices for outstanding Treasury issues are reported.

Figure 7.4 shows a portion of the daily Treasury note and bond listings from the website wsj.com. The entry that begins "2024 Nov 15" is highlighted. This information tells us that the bond will mature in November of 2024. The next column is the coupon rate, which is 7.500 percent for this bond. Treasury bonds all make semiannual payments and have a face value of $1,000, so this bond will pay $37.50 per six months until it matures.

The next two pieces of information are the **bid** and **asked prices**. In general, in any OTC or dealer market, the bid price represents what a dealer is willing to pay for a security, and the asked price (or just "ask" price) is what a dealer is willing to take for it. The difference between the two prices is called the **bid–ask spread** (or just "spread"), and it represents the dealer's profit.

For historical reasons, Treasury prices are quoted in 32nds. Thus, the bid price on the 7.5 percent November 2024 bond, 137:29, actually translates into 137 29/32, or 137.90625 percent of face value. With a $1,000 face value, this price represents $1,379.0625. Because prices are quoted in 32nds, the smallest possible price change is 1/32. This change is called the "tick" size.

The next number quoted is the change in the asked price from the previous day, measured in ticks (in 32nds), so this issue's asked price fell by 49/32 of 1 percent, or 1.53125 percent, of face value from the previous day. Finally, the last number reported is the yield to maturity, based on the asked price. Notice that this is a premium bond because it sells for more than its face value. Not surprisingly, its yield to maturity (3.9133 percent) is less than its coupon rate (7.5 percent).

The very last ordinary bond listed, the 2040 Nov 15, is often called the "bellwether" bond. This bond's yield is the one that is usually reported in the evening news. So, for example, when you hear that long-term interest rates rose, what is really being said is that the yield on this bond went up (and its price went down).

If you examine the yields on the various issues in Figure 7.4, you will clearly see that they vary by maturity. Why this occurs and what it might mean is one of the things we discuss in our next section.

A NOTE ABOUT BOND PRICE QUOTES

If you buy a bond between coupon payment dates, the price you pay is usually more than the price you are quoted. The reason is that standard convention in the bond market is to quote prices net of "accrued interest," meaning that accrued interest is deducted to arrive at the quoted price. This quoted price is called the **clean price**. The price you actually pay, however, includes the accrued interest. This price is the **dirty price**, also known as the "full" or "invoice" price.

An example is the easiest way to understand these issues. Suppose you buy a bond with a 12 percent annual coupon, payable semiannually. You actually pay $1,080 for this bond, so $1,080 is the dirty, or invoice, price. Further, on the day you buy it, the next coupon is due in four months, so you are between coupon dates. Notice that the next coupon will be $60.

The Federal Reserve Bank of St. Louis maintains dozens of online files containing macroeconomic data as well as rates on U.S. Treasury issues. Go to www.stls.frb.org/fred/files.

bid price
The price a dealer is willing to pay for a security.

asked price
The price a dealer is willing to take for a security.

bid–ask spread
The difference between the bid price and the asked price.

Current and historical Treasury yield information is available at www.publicdebt.treas.gov.

clean price
The price of a bond net of accrued interest; this is the price that is typically quoted.

dirty price
The price of a bond including accrued interest, also known as the *full* or *invoice* price. This is the price the buyer actually pays.

FIGURE 7.4

Sample *Wall Street Journal* U.S. Treasury Note and Bond Prices

Source: wsj.com. Reprinted by permission of *The Wall Street Journal,* via Copyright Clearance Center. © 2008 Dow Jones and Company, Inc., January 27, 2011. All Rights Reserved Worldwide.

Treasury Notes and Bonds					
Maturity	**Coupon**	**Bid**	**Asked**	**Chg**	**Asked Yield**
2015 May 15	4.125	110:06	110:07	−6	1.6537
2016 Feb 15	4.500	111:29	111:30	−10	2.0033
2016 May 15	5.125	115:02	115:04	−12	2.0935
2016 Nov 30	2.750	102:00	102:02	−14	2.3709
2017 Feb 28	3.000	103:00	103:01	−15	2.4606
2017 May 15	8.750	136:24	136:27	−20	2.4090
2017 Jul 31	2.375	98:17	98:18	−16	2.6192
2017 Aug 15	4.750	113:02	113:03	−19	2.5658
2018 Aug 15	4.000	107:25	107:27	−22	2.8407
2018 Nov 15	3.750	105:26	105:27	−21	2.9055
2018 Nov 15	9.000	143:09	143:12	−28	2.7741
2019 Feb 15	2.750	98:05	98:06	−22	3.0050
2019 May 15	3.125	100:15	100:15	−22	3.0591
2019 Aug 15	3.625	103:25	103:26	−24	3.1126
2019 Aug 15	8.125	138:12	138:15	−30	2.9927
2019 Nov 15	3.375	101:14	101:15	−24	3.1809
2020 Feb 15	3.625	103:01	103:01	−26	3.2348
2020 May 15	3.500	101:17	101:18	−26	3.3030
2020 Aug 15	2.625	93:28	93:29	−26	3.3766
2020 Aug 15	8.750	145:01	145:04	−33	3.2239
2020 Nov 15	2.625	93:13	93:13	−26	3.4224
2021 Feb 15	7.875	138:12	138:14	−33	3.3411
2021 Nov 15	8.000	140:02	140:04	−37	3.5039
2022 Aug 15	7.250	133:28	133:30	−38	3.6272
2022 Nov 15	7.625	137:20	137:23	−40	3.6603
2023 Feb 15	7.125	132:22	132:24	−41	3.7266
2023 Aug 15	6.250	124:01	124:03	−41	3.8160
2024 Nov 15	7.500	137:29	137:31	−49	3.9133
2025 Feb 15	7.625	139:17	139:18	−50	3.9330
2026 Aug 15	6.750	130:07	130:09	−55	4.0975
2026 Nov 15	6.500	127:10	127:11	−54	4.1263
2027 Nov 15	6.125	122:29	123:00	−55	4.2030
2028 Aug 15	5.500	115:04	115:06	−54	4.2621
2028 Nov 15	5.250	111:28	111:31	−54	4.2829
2029 Feb 15	5.250	111:29	111:31	−54	4.2904
2029 Aug 15	6.125	123:13	123:15	−58	4.2790
2030 May 15	6.250	125:08	125:11	−62	4.3029
2031 Feb 15	5.375	113:17	113:19	−58	4.3517
2036 Feb 15	4.500	99:24	99:26	−62	4.5135
2037 May 15	5.000	107:13	107:15	−68	4.5126
2038 Feb 15	4.375	97:05	97:07	−64	4.5547
2039 Feb 15	3.500	82:23	82:24	−56	4.6009
2040 Feb 15	4.625	100:22	100:24	−66	4.5789
2040 Aug 15	3.875	88:10	88:12	−61	4.5981
2040 Nov 15	4.250	94:13	94:14	−64	4.5952

The accrued interest on a bond is calculated by taking the fraction of the coupon period that has passed, in this case two months out of six, and multiplying this fraction by the next coupon, $60. So, the accrued interest in this example is $2/6 \times \$60 = \$20$. The bond's quoted price (that is, its clean price) would be $\$1,080 - \$20 = \$1,060.$[6]

Concept Questions

7.5a Why do we say bond markets may have little or no transparency?
7.5b In general, what are bid and ask prices?
7.5c What is the difference between a bond's clean price and dirty price?

Inflation and Interest Rates   7.6

So far, we haven't considered the role of inflation in our various discussions of interest rates, yields, and returns. Because this is an important consideration, we consider the impact of inflation next.

REAL VERSUS NOMINAL RATES

In examining interest rates, or any other financial market rates such as discount rates, bond yields, rates of return, and required returns, it is often necessary to distinguish between **real rates** and **nominal rates**. Nominal rates are called "nominal" because they have not been adjusted for inflation. Real rates are rates that have been adjusted for inflation.

real rates
Interest rates or rates of return that have been adjusted for inflation.

nominal rates
Interest rates or rates of return that have not been adjusted for inflation.

To see the effect of inflation, suppose prices are currently rising by 5 percent per year. In other words, the rate of inflation is 5 percent. An investment is available that will be worth $115.50 in one year. It costs $100 today. Notice that with a present value of $100 and a future value in one year of $115.50, this investment has a 15.5 percent rate of return. In calculating this 15.5 percent return, we did not consider the effect of inflation, however, so this is the nominal return.

What is the impact of inflation here? To answer, suppose pizzas cost $5 apiece at the beginning of the year. With $100, we can buy 20 pizzas. Because the inflation rate is 5 percent, pizzas will cost 5 percent more, or $5.25, at the end of the year. If we take the investment, how many pizzas can we buy at the end of the year? Measured in pizzas, what is the rate of return on this investment?

Our $115.50 from the investment will buy us $115.50/5.25 = 22 pizzas. This is up from 20 pizzas, so our pizza rate of return is 10 percent. What this illustrates is that even though the nominal return on our investment is 15.5 percent, our buying power goes up by only 10 percent because of inflation. Put another way, we are really only 10 percent richer. In this case, we say that the real return is 10 percent.

Alternatively, we can say that with 5 percent inflation, each of the $115.50 nominal dollars we get is worth 5 percent less in real terms, so the real dollar value of our investment in a year is:

$$\$115.50/1.05 = \$110$$

What we have done is to *deflate* the $115.50 by 5 percent. Because we give up $100 in current buying power to get the equivalent of $110, our real return is again 10 percent. Because

---

[6]The way accrued interest is calculated actually depends on the type of bond being quoted—for example, Treasury or corporate. The difference has to do with exactly how the fractional coupon period is calculated. In our example here, we implicitly treated the months as having exactly the same length (30 days each, 360 days in a year), which is consistent with the way corporate bonds are quoted. In contrast, for Treasury bonds, actual day counts are used.

we have removed the effect of future inflation here, this $110 is said to be measured in current dollars.

The difference between nominal and real rates is important and bears repeating:

> **The nominal rate on an investment is the percentage change in the number of dollars you have.**
>
> **The real rate on an investment is the percentage change in how much you can buy with your dollars—in other words, the percentage change in your buying power.**

Fisher effect
The relationship between nominal returns, real returns, and inflation.

THE FISHER EFFECT

Our discussion of real and nominal returns illustrates a relationship often called the **Fisher effect** (after the great economist Irving Fisher). Because investors are ultimately concerned with what they can buy with their money, they require compensation for inflation. Let R stand for the nominal rate and r stand for the real rate. The Fisher effect tells us that the relationship between nominal rates, real rates, and inflation can be written as:

$$1 + R = (1 + r) \times (1 + h) \qquad\qquad [7.2]$$

where h is the inflation rate.

In the preceding example, the nominal rate was 15.50 percent and the inflation rate was 5 percent. What was the real rate? We can determine it by plugging in these numbers:

$$1 + .1550 = (1 + r) \times (1 + .05)$$
$$1 + r = 1.1550/1.05 = 1.10$$
$$r = 10\%$$

This real rate is the same as we found before. If we take another look at the Fisher effect, we can rearrange things a little as follows:

$$1 + R = (1 + r) \times (1 + h)$$
$$R = r + h + r \times h \qquad\qquad [7.3]$$

What this tells us is that the nominal rate has three components. First, there is the real rate on the investment, r. Next, there is the compensation for the decrease in the value of the money originally invested because of inflation, h. The third component represents compensation for the fact that the dollars earned on the investment are also worth less because of inflation.

This third component is usually small, so it is often dropped. The nominal rate is then approximately equal to the real rate plus the inflation rate:

$$R \approx r + h \qquad\qquad [7.4]$$

EXAMPLE 7.5	The Fisher Effect

If investors require a 10 percent real rate of return, and the inflation rate is 8 percent, what must be the approximate nominal rate? The exact nominal rate?

The nominal rate is approximately equal to the sum of the real rate and the inflation rate: 10% + 8% = 18%. From the Fisher effect, we have:

$$1 + R = (1 + r) \times (1 + h)$$
$$= 1.10 \times 1.08$$
$$= 1.1880$$

Therefore, the nominal rate will actually be closer to 19 percent.

It is important to note that financial rates, such as interest rates, discount rates, and rates of return, are almost always quoted in nominal terms. To remind you of this, we will henceforth use the symbol R instead of r in most of our discussions about such rates.

INFLATION AND PRESENT VALUES

One question that often comes up is the effect of inflation on present value calculations. The basic principle is simple: Either discount nominal cash flows at a nominal rate or discount real cash flows at a real rate. As long as you are consistent, you will get the same answer.

To illustrate, suppose you want to withdraw money each year for the next three years, and you want each withdrawal to have $25,000 worth of purchasing power as measured in current dollars. If the inflation rate is 4 percent per year, then the withdrawals will simply have to increase by 4 percent each year to compensate. The withdrawals each year will thus be:

$$C_1 = \$25,000(1.04) = \$26,000$$
$$C_2 = \$25,000(1.04)^2 = \$27,040$$
$$C_3 = \$25,000(1.04)^3 = \$28,121.60$$

What is the present value of these cash flows if the appropriate nominal discount rate is 10 percent? This is a standard calculation, and the answer is:

$$PV = \$26,000/1.10 + \$27,040/1.10^2 + \$28,121.60/1.10^3 = \$67,111.65$$

Notice that we discounted the nominal cash flows at a nominal rate.

To calculate the present value using real cash flows, we need the real discount rate. Using the Fisher equation, the real discount rate is:

$$1 + R = (1 + r)(1 + h)$$
$$1 + .10 = (1 + r)(1 + .04)$$
$$r = .0577$$

By design, the real cash flows are an annuity of $25,000 per year. So, the present value in real terms is:

$$PV = \$25,000[1 - (1/1.0577^3)]/.0577 = \$67,111.65$$

Thus, we get exactly the same answer (after allowing for a small rounding error in the real rate). Of course, you could also use the growing annuity equation we discussed in the previous chapter. The withdrawals are increasing at 4 percent per year; so using the growing annuity formula, the present value is:

$$PV = \$26,000\left[\frac{1 - \left(\dfrac{1 + .04}{1 + .10}\right)^3}{.10 - .04}\right] = \$26,000(2.58122) = \$67,111.65$$

This is exactly the same present value we calculated before.

Concept Questions

7.6a What is the difference between a nominal and a real return? Which is more important to a typical investor?

7.6b What is the Fisher effect?

⚡ 7.7 Determinants of Bond Yields

We are now in a position to discuss the determinants of a bond's yield. As we will see, the yield on any particular bond reflects a variety of factors, some common to all bonds and some specific to the issue under consideration.

THE TERM STRUCTURE OF INTEREST RATES

At any point in time, short-term and long-term interest rates will generally be different. Sometimes short-term rates are higher, sometimes lower. Figure 7.5 gives us a long-range perspective on this by showing over two centuries of short- and long-term interest rates. As shown, through time, the difference between short- and long-term rates has ranged from essentially zero to up to several percentage points, both positive and negative.

term structure of interest rates

The relationship between nominal interest rates on default-free, pure discount securities and time to maturity; that is, the pure time value of money.

The relationship between short- and long-term interest rates is known as the **term structure of interest rates**. To be a little more precise, the term structure of interest rates tells us what *nominal* interest rates are on *default-free, pure discount* bonds of all maturities. These rates are, in essence, "pure" interest rates because they involve no risk of default and a single, lump sum future payment. In other words, the term structure tells us the pure time value of money for different lengths of time.

When long-term rates are higher than short-term rates, we say that the term structure is upward sloping; when short-term rates are higher, we say it is downward sloping. The term structure can also be "humped." When this occurs, it is usually because rates increase at first, but then begin to decline as we look at longer- and longer-term rates. The most common shape of the term structure, particularly in modern times, is upward sloping; but the degree of steepness has varied quite a bit.

FIGURE 7.5   U.S. Interest Rates: 1800–2010

SOURCE: Jeremy J. Siegel, *Stocks for the Long Run,* 4th edition, © McGraw-Hill, 2008, updated by the authors.

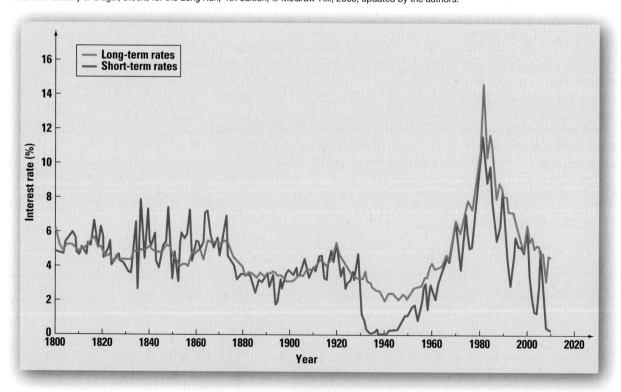

What determines the shape of the term structure? There are three basic components. The first two are the ones we discussed in our previous section: the real rate of interest and the rate of inflation. The real rate of interest is the compensation investors demand for forgoing the use of their money. You can think of it as the pure time value of money after adjusting for the effects of inflation.

The real rate of interest is the basic component underlying every interest rate, regardless of the time to maturity. When the real rate is high, all interest rates will tend to be higher, and vice versa. Thus, the real rate doesn't really determine the shape of the term structure; instead, it mostly influences the overall level of interest rates.

In contrast, the prospect of future inflation strongly influences the shape of the term structure. Investors thinking about lending money for various lengths of time recognize that future inflation erodes the value of the dollars that will be returned. As a result, investors demand compensation for this loss in the form of higher nominal rates. This extra compensation is called the **inflation premium**.

If investors believe the rate of inflation will be higher in the future, then long-term nominal interest rates will tend to be higher than short-term rates. Thus, an upward-sloping term structure may reflect anticipated increases in inflation. Similarly, a downward-sloping term structure probably reflects the belief that inflation will be falling in the future.

The third, and last, component of the term structure has to do with interest rate risk. As we discussed earlier in the chapter, longer-term bonds have much greater risk of loss resulting from changes in interest rates than do shorter-term bonds. Investors recognize this risk, and they demand extra compensation in the form of higher rates for bearing it. This extra compensation is called the **interest rate risk premium**. The longer is the term to maturity, the greater is the interest rate risk, so the interest rate risk premium increases with maturity. However, as we discussed earlier, interest rate risk increases at a decreasing rate, so the interest rate risk premium does as well.[7]

Putting the pieces together, we see that the term structure reflects the combined effect of the real rate of interest, the inflation premium, and the interest rate risk premium. Figure 7.6 shows how these can interact to produce an upward-sloping term structure (in the top part of Figure 7.6) or a downward-sloping term structure (in the bottom part).

In the top part of Figure 7.6, notice how the rate of inflation is expected to rise gradually. At the same time, the interest rate risk premium increases at a decreasing rate, so the combined effect is to produce a pronounced upward-sloping term structure. In the bottom part of Figure 7.6, the rate of inflation is expected to fall in the future, and the expected decline is enough to offset the interest rate risk premium and produce a downward-sloping term structure. Notice that if the rate of inflation was expected to decline by only a small amount, we could still get an upward-sloping term structure because of the interest rate risk premium.

We assumed in drawing Figure 7.6 that the real rate would remain the same. Actually, expected future real rates could be larger or smaller than the current real rate. Also, for simplicity, we used straight lines to show expected future inflation rates as rising or declining, but they do not necessarily have to look like this. They could, for example, rise and then fall, leading to a humped yield curve.

BOND YIELDS AND THE YIELD CURVE: PUTTING IT ALL TOGETHER

Going back to Figure 7.4, recall that we saw that the yields on Treasury notes and bonds of different maturities are not the same. Each day, in addition to the Treasury prices and yields

inflation premium
The portion of a nominal interest rate that represents compensation for expected future inflation.

interest rate risk premium
The compensation investors demand for bearing interest rate risk.

---

[7]In days of old, the interest rate risk premium was called a "liquidity" premium. Today, the term *liquidity premium* has an altogether different meaning, which we explore in our next section. Also, the interest rate risk premium is sometimes called a *maturity risk premium*. Our terminology is consistent with the modern view of the term structure.

FIGURE 7.6

The Term Structure of
Interest Rates

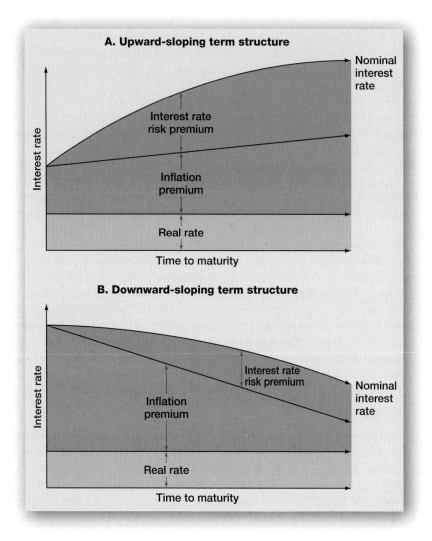

A. Upward-sloping term structure

Nominal interest rate

Interest rate risk premium

Inflation premium

Real rate

Interest rate

Time to maturity

B. Downward-sloping term structure

Interest rate risk premium

Nominal interest rate

Inflation premium

Real rate

Interest rate

Time to maturity

Treasury yield curve
A plot of the yields on
Treasury notes and bonds
relative to maturity.

*Online yield curve
information is available
at* www.bloomberg.com/
markets.

default risk premium
The portion of a nominal
interest rate or bond
yield that represents
compensation for the
possibility of default.

shown in Figure 7.4, *The Wall Street Journal* provides a plot of Treasury yields relative to maturity. This plot is called the **Treasury yield curve** (or just the yield curve). Figure 7.7 shows the yield curve as of January 2011.

As you probably now suspect, the shape of the yield curve reflects the term structure of interest rates. In fact, the Treasury yield curve and the term structure of interest rates are almost the same thing. The only difference is that the term structure is based on pure discount bonds, whereas the yield curve is based on coupon bond yields. As a result, Treasury yields depend on the three components that underlie the term structure—the real rate, expected future inflation, and the interest rate risk premium.

Treasury notes and bonds have three important features that we need to remind you of: They are default-free, they are taxable, and they are highly liquid. This is not true of bonds in general, so we need to examine what additional factors come into play when we look at bonds issued by corporations or municipalities.

The first thing to consider is credit risk—that is, the possibility of default. Investors recognize that issuers other than the Treasury may or may not make all the promised payments on a bond, so they demand a higher yield as compensation for this risk. This extra compensation is called the **default risk premium**. Earlier in the chapter, we saw how bonds were

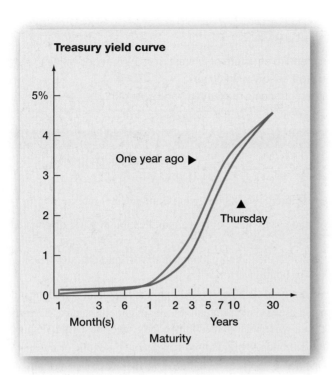

FIGURE 7.7

The Treasury Yield Curve:
January 2011

SOURCE: Reprinted by
permission of *The Wall
Street Journal,* via Copyright
Clearance Center © 2011 by
Dow Jones & Company, Inc.,
2011. All Rights Reserved
Worldwide.

rated based on their credit risk. What you will find if you start looking at bonds of different ratings is that lower-rated bonds have higher yields.

An important thing to recognize about a bond's yield is that it is calculated assuming that all the promised payments will be made. As a result, it is really a promised yield, and it may or may not be what you will earn. In particular, if the issuer defaults, your actual yield will be lower—probably much lower. This fact is particularly important when it comes to junk bonds. Thanks to a clever bit of marketing, such bonds are now commonly called high-yield bonds, which has a much nicer ring to it; but now you recognize that these are really high *promised* yield bonds.

Next, recall that we discussed earlier how municipal bonds are free from most taxes and, as a result, have much lower yields than taxable bonds. Investors demand the extra yield on a taxable bond as compensation for the unfavorable tax treatment. This extra compensation is the **taxability premium**.

Finally, bonds have varying degrees of liquidity. As we discussed earlier, there are an enormous number of bond issues, most of which do not trade regularly. As a result, if you wanted to sell quickly, you would probably not get as good a price as you could otherwise. Investors prefer liquid assets to illiquid ones, so they demand a **liquidity premium** on top of all the other premiums we have discussed. As a result, all else being the same, less liquid bonds will have higher yields than more liquid bonds.

CONCLUSION

If we combine all of the things we have discussed regarding bond yields, we find that bond yields represent the combined effect of no fewer than six things. The first is the real rate of interest. On top of the real rate are five premiums representing compensation for (1) expected future inflation, (2) interest rate risk, (3) default risk, (4) taxability, and (5) lack of liquidity. As a result, determining the appropriate yield on a bond requires careful analysis of each of these effects.

To see how the yield curve has changed over time, check out the "living yield curve" at www.smartmoney.com.

taxability premium
The portion of a nominal interest rate or bond yield that represents compensation for unfavorable tax status.

liquidity premium
The portion of a nominal interest rate or bond yield that represents compensation for lack of liquidity.

Concept Questions

7.7a What is the term structure of interest rates? What determines its shape?

7.7b What is the Treasury yield curve?

7.7c What six components make up a bond's yield?

7.8 Summary and Conclusions

This chapter has explored bonds, bond yields, and interest rates:

1. Determining bond prices and yields is an application of basic discounted cash flow principles.

2. Bond values move in the direction opposite that of interest rates, leading to potential gains or losses for bond investors.

3. Bonds have a variety of features spelled out in a document called the indenture.

4. Bonds are rated based on their default risk. Some bonds, such as Treasury bonds, have no risk of default, whereas so-called junk bonds have substantial default risk.

5. A wide variety of bonds exist, many of which contain exotic or unusual features.

6. Almost all bond trading is OTC, with little or no market transparency in many cases. As a result, bond price and volume information can be difficult to find for some types of bonds.

7. Bond yields and interest rates reflect the effect of six different things: the real interest rate and five premiums that investors demand as compensation for inflation, interest rate risk, default risk, taxability, and lack of liquidity.

In closing, we note that bonds are a vital source of financing to governments and corporations of all types. Bond prices and yields are a rich subject, and our one chapter, necessarily, touches on only the most important concepts and ideas. There is a great deal more we could say, but, instead, we will move on to stocks in our next chapter.

CONNECT TO FINANCE

 |FINANCE

If you are using *Connect*™ *Finance* in your course, get online to take a Practice Test, check out study tools, and find out where you need additional practice.

▼ Chapter 7 Interest Rates and Bond Valuation

Bonds and Bond Valuation

7.1 Bonds and Bond Valuation	eBook	Study	Practice
7.2 More about Bond Features	eBook	Study	Practice
7.3 Bond Ratings	eBook	Study	Practice
7.4 Some Different Types of Bonds	eBook	Study	Practice
7.5 Bond Markets	eBook	Study	Practice
7.6 Inflation and Interest Rates	eBook	Study	Practice
7.7 Determinants of Bond Yields	eBook	Study	Practice

Can you answer the following questions?

Section 7.1   An 8 percent, semiannual coupon bond has a face value of $1,000 and a current market value of $1,030. What is the current yield? (LO 7-2)

Section 7.2   An indenture agreement includes. (LO 7-1)

Section 7.3   The 10-year bonds issued by KP Enterprises were rated as BBB and Baa last year. This year, the bonds are rated as CC and Ca. What term best applies to these bonds today? (LO 7-3)

Section 7.4   What type of bonds is most apt to have a "collar"? (LO 7-1)

Section 7.5   A $100,000 face value Treasury bond is quoted at 101:13. What is the current price of this bond? (LO 7-2)

Section 7.6   Kate wants to earn a 4 percent real rate of return. To do this, what nominal rate must she earn if the inflation rate is 3.6 percent? (LO 7-4)

Section 7.7   The term structure of interest rates is based on what type of bonds? (LO 7-5)

Log on to find out!

CHAPTER REVIEW AND SELF-TEST PROBLEMS

7.1   **Bond Values**   A Microgates Industries bond has a 10 percent coupon rate and a $1,000 face value. Interest is paid semiannually, and the bond has 20 years to maturity. If investors require a 12 percent yield, what is the bond's value? What is the effective annual yield on the bond?

7.2   **Bond Yields**   A Macrohard Corp. bond carries an 8 percent coupon, paid semiannually. The par value is $1,000, and the bond matures in six years. If the bond currently sells for $911.37, what is its yield to maturity? What is the effective annual yield?

ANSWERS TO CHAPTER REVIEW AND SELF-TEST PROBLEMS

7.1   Because the bond has a 10 percent coupon yield and investors require a 12 percent return, we know that the bond must sell at a discount. Notice that, because the bond pays interest semiannually, the coupons amount to $100/2 = $50 every six months. The required yield is 12%/2 = 6% every six months. Finally, the bond matures in 20 years, so there are a total of 40 six-month periods.

The bond's value is thus equal to the present value of $50 every six months for the next 40 six-month periods plus the present value of the $1,000 face amount:

$$\text{Bond value} = \$50 \times [(1 - 1/1.06^{40})/.06] + 1,000/1.06^{40}$$
$$= \$50 \times 15.04630 + 1,000/10.2857$$
$$= \$849.54$$

Notice that we discounted the $1,000 back 40 periods at 6 percent per period, rather than 20 years at 12 percent. The reason is that the effective annual yield on the bond is $1.06^2 - 1 = 12.36\%$, not 12 percent. We thus could have used 12.36 percent per year for 20 years when we calculated the present value of the $1,000 face amount, and the answer would have been the same.

7.2   The present value of the bond's cash flows is its current price, $911.37. The coupon is $40 every six months for 12 periods. The face value is $1,000. So the bond's yield is the unknown discount rate in the following:

$$\$911.37 = \$40 \times [1 - 1/(1 + r)^{12}]/r + 1,000/(1 + r)^{12}$$

The bond sells at a discount. Because the coupon rate is 8 percent, the yield must be something in excess of that.

If we were to solve this by trial and error, we might try 12 percent (or 6 percent per six months):

$$\text{Bond value} = \$40 \times (1 - 1/1.06^{12})/.06 + 1,000/1.06^{12}$$
$$= \$832.32$$

This is less than the actual value, so our discount rate is too high. We now know that the yield is somewhere between 8 and 12 percent. With further trial and error (or a little machine assistance), the yield works out to be 10 percent, or 5 percent every six months.

By convention, the bond's yield to maturity would be quoted as $2 \times 5\% = 10\%$. The effective yield is thus $1.05^2 - 1 = 10.25\%$.

CONCEPTS REVIEW AND CRITICAL THINKING QUESTIONS

1. **Treasury Bonds [LO1]** Is it true that a U.S. Treasury security is risk-free?

2. **Interest Rate Risk [LO2]** Which has greater interest rate risk, a 30-year Treasury bond or a 30-year BB corporate bond?

3. **Treasury Pricing [LO1]** With regard to bid and ask prices on a Treasury bond, is it possible for the bid price to be higher? Why or why not?

4. **Yield to Maturity [LO2]** Treasury bid and ask quotes are sometimes given in terms of yields, so there would be a bid yield and an ask yield. Which do you think would be larger? Explain.

5. **Call Provisions [LO1]** A company is contemplating a long-term bond issue. It is debating whether to include a call provision. What are the benefits to the company from including a call provision? What are the costs? How do these answers change for a put provision?

6. **Coupon Rate [LO1]** How does a bond issuer decide on the appropriate coupon rate to set on its bonds? Explain the difference between the coupon rate and the required return on a bond.

7. **Real and Nominal Returns [LO4]** Are there any circumstances under which an investor might be more concerned about the nominal return on an investment than the real return?

8. **Bond Ratings [LO3]** Companies pay rating agencies such as Moody's and S&P to rate their bonds, and the costs can be substantial. However, companies are not required to have their bonds rated; doing so is strictly voluntary. Why do you think they do it?

9. **Bond Ratings [LO3]** Often, junk bonds are not rated. Why?

10. **Term Structure [LO5]** What is the difference between the term structure of interest rates and the yield curve?

11. **Crossover Bonds [LO3]** Looking back at the crossover bonds we discussed in the chapter, why do you think split ratings such as these occur?

12. **Municipal Bonds [LO1]** Why is it that municipal bonds are not taxed at the federal level, but are taxable across state lines? Why are U.S. Treasury bonds not taxable at the state level? (You may need to dust off the history books for this one.)

13. **Bond Market [LO1]** What are the implications for bond investors of the lack of transparency in the bond market?

14. **Rating Agencies [LO3]** A controversy erupted regarding bond-rating agencies when some agencies began to provide unsolicited bond ratings. Why do you think this is controversial?

15. **Bonds as Equity [LO1]** The 100-year bonds we discussed in the chapter have something in common with junk bonds. Critics charge that, in both cases, the issuers are really selling equity in disguise. What are the issues here? Why would a company want to sell "equity in disguise"?

QUESTIONS AND PROBLEMS

BASIC
(Questions 1–14)

1. **Interpreting Bond Yields [LO1]** Is the yield to maturity on a bond the same thing as the required return? Is YTM the same thing as the coupon rate? Suppose today a 10 percent coupon bond sells at par. Two years from now, the required return on the same bond is 8 percent. What is the coupon rate on the bond then? The YTM?

2. **Interpreting Bond Yields [LO2]** Suppose you buy a 7 percent coupon, 20-year bond today when it's first issued. If interest rates suddenly rise to 15 percent, what happens to the value of your bond? Why?

3. **Valuing Bonds [LO2]** Even though most corporate bonds in the United States make coupon payments semiannually, bonds issued elsewhere often have annual coupon payments. Suppose a German company issues a bond with a par value of €1,000, 25 years to maturity, and a coupon rate of 6.4 percent paid annually. If the yield to maturity is 7.5 percent, what is the current price of the bond?

4. **Bond Yields [LO2]** A Japanese company has a bond outstanding that sells for 87 percent of its ¥100,000 par value. The bond has a coupon rate of 4.3 percent paid annually and matures in 18 years. What is the yield to maturity of this bond?

5. **Coupon Rates [LO2]** Page Enterprises has bonds on the market making annual payments, with nine years to maturity, and selling for $948. At this price, the bonds yield 5.9 percent. What must the coupon rate be on the bonds?

6. **Bond Prices [LO2]** Ninja Co. issued 14-year bonds a year ago at a coupon rate of 6.9 percent. The bonds make semiannual payments. If the YTM on these bonds is 5.2 percent, what is the current bond price?

7. **Bond Yields [LO2]** Stone Sour Corp. issued 20-year bonds two years ago at a coupon rate of 7.1 percent. The bonds make semiannual payments. If these bonds currently sell for 105 percent of par value, what is the YTM?

8. **Coupon Rates [LO2]** Ponzi Corporation has bonds on the market with 14.5 years to maturity, a YTM of 6.1 percent, and a current price of $1,038. The bonds make semiannual payments. What must the coupon rate be on these bonds?

9. **Calculating Real Rates of Return [LO4]** If Treasury bills are currently paying 6 percent and the inflation rate is 2.6 percent, what is the approximate real rate of interest? The exact real rate?

10. **Inflation and Nominal Returns [LO4]** Suppose the real rate is 2.5 percent and the inflation rate is 4.1 percent. What rate would you expect to see on a Treasury bill?

11. **Nominal and Real Returns [LO4]** An investment offers a 13 percent total return over the coming year. Fred Bernanke thinks the total real return on this investment will be only 7 percent. What does Fred believe the inflation rate will be over the next year?

12. **Nominal versus Real Returns [LO4]** Say you own an asset that had a total return last year of 10.7 percent. If the inflation rate last year was 3.7 percent, what was your real return?

Visit us at www.mhhe.com/rwj

13. **Using Treasury Quotes [LO2]** Locate the Treasury issue in Figure 7.4 maturing in August 2029. Is this a note or a bond? What is its coupon rate? What is its bid price? What was the *previous* day's asked price?

14. **Using Treasury Quotes [LO2]** Locate the Treasury bond in Figure 7.4 maturing in August 2029. Is this a premium or a discount bond? What is its current yield? What is its yield to maturity? What is the bid–ask spread?

INTERMEDIATE
(Questions 15–28)

15. **Bond Price Movements [LO2]** Bond X is a premium bond making semiannual payments. The bond pays a 9 percent coupon, has a YTM of 7 percent, and has 13 years to maturity. Bond Y is a discount bond making semiannual payments. This bond pays a 7 percent coupon, has a YTM of 9 percent, and also has 13 years to maturity. What is the price of each bond today? If interest rates remain unchanged, what do you expect the price of these bonds to be one year from now? In three years? In eight years? In 12 years? In 13 years? What's going on here? Illustrate your answers by graphing bond prices versus time to maturity.

16. **Interest Rate Risk [LO2]** Both Bond Sam and Bond Dave have 7 percent coupons, make semiannual payments, and are priced at par value. Bond Sam has 3 years to maturity, whereas Bond Dave has 20 years to maturity. If interest rates suddenly rise by 2 percent, what is the percentage change in the price of Bond Sam? Of Bond Dave? If rates were to suddenly fall by 2 percent instead, what would the percentage change in the price of Bond Sam be then? Of Bond Dave? Illustrate your answers by graphing bond prices versus YTM. What does this problem tell you about the interest rate risk of longer-term bonds?

17. **Interest Rate Risk [LO2]** Bond J is a 3 percent coupon bond. Bond K is a 9 percent coupon bond. Both bonds have 15 years to maturity, make semiannual payments, and have a YTM of 6 percent. If interest rates suddenly rise by 2 percent, what is the percentage price change of these bonds? What if rates suddenly fall by 2 percent instead? What does this problem tell you about the interest rate risk of lower-coupon bonds?

18. **Bond Yields [LO2]** Martin Software has 9.2 percent coupon bonds on the market with 18 years to maturity. The bonds make semiannual payments and currently sell for 106.8 percent of par. What is the current yield on the bonds? The YTM? The effective annual yield?

19. **Bond Yields [LO2]** Coccia Co. wants to issue new 20-year bonds for some much-needed expansion projects. The company currently has 8 percent coupon bonds on the market that sell for $1,075, make semiannual payments, and mature in 20 years. What coupon rate should the company set on its new bonds if it wants them to sell at par?

20. **Accrued Interest [LO2]** You purchase a bond with an invoice price of $1,027. The bond has a coupon rate of 6.8 percent, and there are four months to the next semi-annual coupon date. What is the clean price of the bond?

21. **Accrued Interest [LO2]** You purchase a bond with a coupon rate of 7.3 percent and a clean price of $945. If the next semiannual coupon payment is due in two months, what is the invoice price?

22. **Finding the Bond Maturity [LO2]** Backwater Corp. has 8 percent coupon bonds making annual payments with a YTM of 7.2 percent. The current yield on these bonds is 7.55 percent. How many years do these bonds have left until they mature?

23. **Using Bond Quotes [LO2]** Suppose the following bond quotes for IOU Corporation appear in the financial page of today's newspaper. Assume the bond has a face value of $1,000 and the current date is April 19, 2012. What is the yield to maturity of the bond? What is the current yield?

Company (Ticker)	Coupon	Maturity	Last Price	Last Yield	EST Vol (000s)
IOU (IOU)	6.2	Apr 19, 2028	108.96	??	1,827

24. **Bond Prices versus Yields [LO2]**
    a. What is the relationship between the price of a bond and its YTM?
    b. Explain why some bonds sell at a premium over par value while other bonds sell at a discount. What do you know about the relationship between the coupon rate and the YTM for premium bonds? What about for discount bonds? For bonds selling at par value?
    c. What is the relationship between the current yield and YTM for premium bonds? For discount bonds? For bonds selling at par value?

25. **Interest on Zeroes [LO2]** Pangaea Corporation needs to raise funds to finance a plant expansion, and it has decided to issue 25-year zero coupon bonds to raise the money. The required return on the bonds will be 7 percent.
    a. What will these bonds sell for at issuance?
    b. Using the IRS amortization rule, what interest deduction can the company take on these bonds in the first year? In the last year?
    c. Repeat part (b) using the straight-line method for the interest deduction.
    d. Based on your answers in (b) and (c), which interest deduction method would Pangaea Corporation prefer? Why?

26. **Zero Coupon Bonds [LO2]** Suppose your company needs to raise $45 million and you want to issue 30-year bonds for this purpose. Assume the required return on your bond issue will be 6 percent, and you're evaluating two issue alternatives: a 6 percent semiannual coupon bond and a zero coupon bond. Your company's tax rate is 35 percent.
    a. How many of the coupon bonds would you need to issue to raise the $45 million? How many of the zeroes would you need to issue?
    b. In 30 years, what will your company's repayment be if you issue the coupon bonds? What if you issue the zeroes?
    c. Based on your answers in (a) and (b), why would you ever want to issue the zeroes? To answer, calculate the firm's aftertax cash outflows for the first year under the two different scenarios. Assume the IRS amortization rules apply for the zero coupon bonds.

27. **Finding the Maturity [LO2]** You've just found a 10 percent coupon bond on the market that sells for par value. What is the maturity on this bond?

28. **Real Cash Flows [LO4]** You want to have $2 million in real dollars in an account when you retire in 40 years. The nominal return on your investment is 10 percent and the inflation rate is 3.8 percent. What real amount must you deposit each year to achieve your goal?

29. **Components of Bond Returns [LO2]** Bond P is a premium bond with a 10 percent coupon. Bond D is a 4 percent coupon bond currently selling at a discount. Both bonds make annual payments, have a YTM of 7 percent, and have eight years to maturity. What is the current yield for bond P? For bond D? If interest rates remain unchanged, what is the expected capital gains yield over the next year for bond P? For bond D? Explain your answers and the interrelationships among the various types of yields.

CHALLENGE
(Questions 29–35)

Visit us at www.mhhe.com/rwj

30. Holding Period Yield [LO2] The YTM on a bond is the interest rate you earn on your investment if interest rates don't change. If you actually sell the bond before it matures, your realized return is known as the *holding period yield* (HPY).

   a. Suppose that today you buy an 8 percent annual coupon bond for $1,060. The bond has 19 years to maturity. What rate of return do you expect to earn on your investment?

   b. Two years from now, the YTM on your bond has declined by 1 percent, and you decide to sell. What price will your bond sell for? What is the HPY on your investment? Compare this yield to the YTM when you first bought the bond. Why are they different?

31. Valuing Bonds [LO2] Las Paletas Corporation has two different bonds currently outstanding. Bond M has a face value of $20,000 and matures in 20 years. The bond makes no payments for the first six years, then pays $1,100 every six months over the subsequent eight years, and finally pays $1,400 every six months over the last six years. Bond N also has a face value of $20,000 and a maturity of 20 years; it makes no coupon payments over the life of the bond. If the required return on both these bonds is 6 percent compounded semiannually, what is the current price of bond M? Of bond N?

32. Valuing the Call Feature [LO2] Consider the prices in the following three Treasury issues as of May 15, 2011:

6.500	May 17n	106:10	106:12	−13	5.28
8.250	May 17	103:14	103:16	−3	5.24
12.000	May 17	134:25	134:31	−15	5.32

The bond in the middle is callable in February 2012. What is the implied value of the call feature? (*Hint:* Is there a way to combine the two noncallable issues to create an issue that has the same coupon as the callable bond?)

33. Treasury Bonds [LO2] The following Treasury bond quote appeared in *The Wall Street Journal* on May 11, 2004:

9.125	May 09	100:03	100:04	. . .	−2.15

Why would anyone buy this Treasury bond with a negative yield to maturity? How is this possible?

34. Real Cash Flows [LO4] When Marilyn Monroe died, ex-husband Joe DiMaggio vowed to place fresh flowers on her grave every Sunday as long as he lived. The week after she died in 1962, a bunch of fresh flowers that the former baseball player thought appropriate for the star cost about $7. Based on actuarial tables, "Joltin' Joe" could expect to live for 30 years after the actress died. Assume that the EAR is 9.3 percent. Also, assume that the price of the flowers will increase at 3.7 percent per year, when expressed as an EAR. Assuming that each year has exactly 52 weeks, what is the present value of this commitment? Joe began purchasing flowers the week after Marilyn died.

35. Real Cash Flows [LO4] You are planning to save for retirement over the next 30 years. To save for retirement, you will invest $1,000 a month in a stock account in real dollars and $525 a month in a bond account in real dollars. The effective annual return of the stock account is expected to be 11 percent, and the bond account will earn 7 percent. When you retire, you will combine your money into an account with a 9 percent effective return. The inflation rate over this period is expected to be 4 percent. How much can you withdraw each month from your account in real terms assuming a 25-year withdrawal period? What is the nominal dollar amount of your last withdrawal?

Financing S&S Air's Expansion Plans with a Bond Issue

Mark Sexton and Todd Story, the owners of S&S Air, have decided to expand their operations. They instructed their newly hired financial analyst, Chris Guthrie, to enlist an underwriter to help sell $35 million in new 10-year bonds to finance construction. Chris has entered into discussions with Renata Harper, an underwriter from the firm of Raines and Warren, about which bond features S&S Air should consider and what coupon rate the issue will likely have.

Although Chris is aware of the bond features, he is uncertain about the costs and benefits of some features, so he isn't sure how each feature would affect the coupon rate of the bond issue. You are Renata's assistant, and she has asked you to prepare a memo to Chris describing the effect of each of the following bond features on the coupon rate of the bond. She would also like you to list any advantages or disadvantages of each feature:

QUESTIONS

1. The security of the bond—that is, whether the bond has collateral.

2. The seniority of the bond.

3. The presence of a sinking fund.

4. A call provision with specified call dates and call prices.

5. A deferred call accompanying the call provision.

6. A make-whole call provision.

7. Any positive covenants. Also, discuss several possible positive covenants S&S Air might consider.

8. Any negative covenants. Also, discuss several possible negative covenants S&S Air might consider.

9. A conversion feature (note that S&S Air is not a publicly traded company).

10. A floating-rate coupon.

STOCK VALUATION

WHEN THE STOCK MARKET CLOSED on January 24, 2011, the common stock of McGraw-Hill, publisher of fine quality college textbooks, was going for $38.53 per share. On that same day, stock in First-Energy, an electric utility, closed at $39.43, while stock in Gilead Sciences, a biopharmaceutical company, closed at $38.31. Because the stock prices of these three companies were so similar, you might expect that they would be offering similar dividends to their stockholders, but you would be wrong. In fact, FirstEnergy's annual dividend was $2.20 per share, McGraw-Hill's was $1.00 per share, and Gilead Sciences was paying no dividend at all!

As we will see in this chapter, the dividends currently being paid are one of the primary factors we look at when attempting to value common stocks. However, it is obvious from looking at Gilead Sciences that current dividends are not the end of the story. This chapter explores dividends, stock values, and the connection between the two.

LEARNING OBJECTIVES

After studying this chapter, you should understand:

LO1 How stock prices depend on future dividends and dividend growth.

LO2 How to value stocks using multiples.

LO3 The different ways corporate directors are elected to office.

LO4 How the stock markets work.

In our previous chapter, we introduced you to bonds and bond valuation. In this chapter, we turn to the other major source of financing for corporations: common and preferred stock. We first describe the cash flows associated with a share of stock and then go on to develop a famous result, the dividend growth model. From there, we move on to examine various important features of common and preferred stock, focusing on shareholder rights. We close the chapter with a discussion of how shares of stock are traded and how stock prices and other important information are reported in the financial press.

Common Stock Valuation

A share of common stock is more difficult to value in practice than a bond for at least three reasons. First, with common stock, not even the promised cash flows are known in advance. Second, the life of the investment is essentially forever because common stock has no maturity. Third, there is no way to easily observe the rate of return that the market requires. Nonetheless, as we will see, there are cases in which we can come up with the present value of the future cash flows for a share of stock and thus determine its value.

CASH FLOWS

Imagine that you are considering buying a share of stock today. You plan to sell the stock in one year. You somehow know that the stock will be worth $70 at that time. You predict that the stock will also pay a $10 per share dividend at the end of the year. If you require a 25 percent return on your investment, what is the most you would pay for the stock? In other words, what is the present value of the $10 dividend along with the $70 ending value at 25 percent?

If you buy the stock today and sell it at the end of the year, you will have a total of $80 in cash. At 25 percent:

Present value = ($10 + 70)/1.25 = $64

Therefore, $64 is the value you would assign to the stock today.

More generally, let P_0 be the current price of the stock, and assign P_1 to be the price in one period. If D_1 is the cash dividend paid at the end of the period, then:

$$P_0 = (D_1 + P_1)/(1 + R) \qquad \text{[8.1]}$$

where R is the required return in the market on this investment.

Notice that we really haven't said much so far. If we wanted to determine the value of a share of stock today (P_0), we would first have to come up with the value in one year (P_1). This is even harder to do, so we've only made the problem more complicated.

What is the price in one period, P_1? We don't know in general. Instead, suppose we somehow knew the price in two periods, P_2. Given a predicted dividend in two periods, D_2, the stock price in one period would be:

$$P_1 = (D_2 + P_2)/(1 + R)$$

If we were to substitute this expression for P_1 into our expression for P_0, we would have:

$$P_0 = \frac{D_1 + P_1}{1 + R} = \frac{D_1 + \dfrac{D_2 + P_2}{1 + R}}{1 + R}$$

$$= \frac{D_1}{(1 + R)^1} + \frac{D_2}{(1 + R)^2} + \frac{P_2}{(1 + R)^2}$$

Now we need to get a price in two periods. We don't know this either, so we can procrastinate again and write:

$$P_2 = (D_3 + P_3)/(1 + R)$$

If we substitute this back in for P_2, we have:

$$P_0 = \frac{D_1}{(1 + R)^1} + \frac{D_2}{(1 + R)^2} + \frac{P_2}{(1 + R)^2}$$

$$= \frac{D_1}{(1 + R)^1} + \frac{D_2}{(1 + R)^2} + \frac{\dfrac{D_3 + P_3}{1 + R}}{(1 + R)^2}$$

$$= \frac{D_1}{(1 + R)^1} + \frac{D_2}{(1 + R)^2} + \frac{D_3}{(1 + R)^3} + \frac{P_3}{(1 + R)^3}$$

You should start to notice that we can push the problem of coming up with the stock price off into the future forever. Note that no matter what the stock price is, the present value is essentially zero if we push the sale of the stock far enough away.[1] What we are eventually left with is the result that the current price of the stock can be written as the present value of the dividends beginning in one period and extending out forever:

$$P_0 = \frac{D_1}{(1 + R)^1} + \frac{D_2}{(1 + R)^2} + \frac{D_3}{(1 + R)^3} + \frac{D_4}{(1 + R)^4} + \frac{D_5}{(1 + R)^5} + \cdots$$

We have illustrated here that the price of the stock today is equal to the present value of all of the future dividends. How many future dividends are there? In principle, there can be an infinite number. This means that we still can't compute a value for the stock because we would have to forecast an infinite number of dividends and then discount them all. In the next section, we consider some special cases in which we can get around this problem.

| **EXAMPLE 8.1** | **Growth Stocks** |

You might be wondering about shares of stock in companies such as Yahoo! that currently pay no dividends. Small, growing companies frequently plow back everything and thus pay no dividends. Are such shares worth nothing? It depends. When we say that the value of the stock is equal to the present value of the future dividends, we don't rule out the possibility that some number of those dividends are zero. They just can't *all* be zero.

Imagine a company that has a provision in its corporate charter that prohibits the paying of dividends now or ever. The corporation never borrows any money, never pays out any money to stockholders in any form whatsoever, and never sells any assets. Such a corporation couldn't really exist because the IRS wouldn't like it, and the stockholders could always vote to amend the charter if they wanted to. If it did exist, however, what would the stock be worth?

The stock is worth absolutely nothing. Such a company is a financial "black hole." Money goes in, but nothing valuable ever comes out. Because nobody would ever get any return on this investment, the investment has no value. This example is a little absurd, but it illustrates that when we speak of companies that don't pay dividends, what we really mean is that they are not *currently* paying dividends.

---

[1]The only assumption we make about the stock price is that it is a finite number no matter how far away we push it. It can be extremely large, just not infinitely so. Because no one has ever observed an infinite stock price, this assumption is plausible.

SOME SPECIAL CASES

In a few useful special circumstances, we can come up with a value for the stock. What we have to do is make some simplifying assumptions about the pattern of future dividends. The three cases we consider are the following: (1) The dividend has a zero growth rate, (2) the dividend grows at a constant rate, and (3) the dividend grows at a constant rate after some length of time. We consider each of these separately.

Zero Growth   The case of zero growth is one we've already seen. A share of common stock in a company with a constant dividend is much like a share of preferred stock. From Chapter 6 (Example 6.7), we know that the dividend on a share of preferred stock has zero growth and thus is constant through time. For a zero-growth share of common stock, this implies that:

$$D_1 = D_2 = D_3 = D = \text{constant}$$

So, the value of the stock is:

$$P_0 = \frac{D}{(1 + R)^1} + \frac{D}{(1 + R)^2} + \frac{D}{(1 + R)^3} + \frac{D}{(1 + R)^4} + \frac{D}{(1 + R)^5} + \cdots$$

Because the dividend is always the same, the stock can be viewed as an ordinary perpetuity with a cash flow equal to D every period. The per-share value is thus given by:

$$P_0 = D/R \qquad\qquad\qquad\qquad \textbf{[8.2]}$$

where R is the required return.

For example, suppose the Paradise Prototyping Company has a policy of paying a $10 per share dividend every year. If this policy is to be continued indefinitely, what is the value of a share of stock if the required return is 20 percent? The stock in this case amounts to an ordinary perpetuity, so the stock is worth $10/.20 = $50 per share.

Constant Growth   Suppose we know that the dividend for some company always grows at a steady rate. Call this growth rate g. If we let D_0 be the dividend just paid, then the next dividend, D_1, is:

$$D_1 = D_0 \times (1 + g)$$

The dividend in two periods is:

$$\begin{aligned} D_2 &= D_1 \times (1 + g) \\ &= [D_0 \times (1 + g)] \times (1 + g) \\ &= D_0 \times (1 + g)^2 \end{aligned}$$

We could repeat this process to come up with the dividend at any point in the future. In general, from our discussion of compound growth in Chapter 6, we know that the dividend t periods into the future, D_t, is given by:

$$D_t = D_0 \times (1 + g)^t$$

As we have previously seen, an asset with cash flows that grow at a constant rate forever is called a *growing perpetuity*.

The assumption of steady dividend growth might strike you as peculiar. Why would the dividend grow at a constant rate? The reason is that, for many companies, steady growth in dividends is an explicit goal. For example, in 2010, Procter & Gamble, the Cincinnati-based maker of personal care and household products, increased its dividend by 9.5 percent to $1.93 per share; this increase was notable because it was the 54th in a row. The subject of dividend growth falls under the general heading of dividend policy, so we will defer further discussion of it to a later chapter.

EXAMPLE 8.2   **Dividend Growth**

The Hedless Corporation has just paid a dividend of $3 per share. The dividend of this company grows at a steady rate of 8 percent per year. Based on this information, what will the dividend be in five years?

Here we have a $3 current amount that grows at 8 percent per year for five years. The future amount is thus:

$3 \times 1.08^5 = \$3 \times 1.4693 = \$4.41$

The dividend will therefore increase by $1.41 over the coming five years.

If the dividend grows at a steady rate, then we have replaced the problem of forecasting an infinite number of future dividends with the problem of coming up with a single growth rate, a considerable simplification. In this case, if we take D_0 to be the dividend just paid and g to be the constant growth rate, the value of a share of stock can be written as:

$$P_0 = \frac{D_1}{(1 + R)^1} + \frac{D_2}{(1 + R)^2} + \frac{D_3}{(1 + R)^3} + \cdots$$
$$= \frac{D_0(1 + g)^1}{(1 + R)^1} + \frac{D_0(1 + g)^2}{(1 + R)^2} + \frac{D_0(1 + g)^3}{(1 + R)^3} + \cdots$$

As long as the growth rate, g, is less than the discount rate, r, the present value of this series of cash flows can be written simply as:

$$P_0 = \frac{D_0 \times (1 + g)}{R - g} = \frac{D_1}{R - g} \qquad [8.3]$$

dividend growth model
A model that determines the current price of a stock as its dividend next period divided by the discount rate less the dividend growth rate.

This elegant result goes by a lot of different names. We will call it the **dividend growth model**. By any name, it is easy to use. To illustrate, suppose D_0 is $2.30, R is 13 percent, and g is 5 percent. The price per share in this case is:

$$P_0 = D_0 \times (1 + g)/(R - g)$$
$$= \$2.30 \times 1.05/(.13 - .05)$$
$$= \$2.415/.08$$
$$= \$30.19$$

We can actually use the dividend growth model to get the stock price at any point in time, not just today. In general, the price of the stock as of time t is:

$$P_t = \frac{D_t \times (1 + g)}{R - g} = \frac{D_{t+1}}{R - g} \qquad [8.4]$$

In our example, suppose we are interested in the price of the stock in five years, P_5. We first need the dividend at Time 5, D_5. Because the dividend just paid is $2.30 and the growth rate is 5 percent per year, D_5 is:

$$D_5 = \$2.30 \times 1.05^5 = \$2.30 \times 1.2763 = \$2.935$$

From the dividend growth model, we get the price of the stock in five years:

$$P_5 = \frac{D_5 \times (1 + g)}{R - g} = \frac{\$2.935 \times 1.05}{.13 - .05} = \frac{\$3.0822}{.08} = \$38.53$$

Gordon Growth Company

EXAMPLE 8.3

The next dividend for the Gordon Growth Company will be $4 per share. Investors require a 16 percent return on companies such as Gordon. Gordon's dividend increases by 6 percent every year. Based on the dividend growth model, what is the value of Gordon's stock today? What is the value in four years?

The only tricky thing here is that the next dividend, D_1, is given as $4, so we won't multiply this by $(1 + g)$. With this in mind, the price per share is given by:

$$P_0 = D_1/(R - g)$$
$$= \$4/(.16 - .06)$$
$$= \$4/.10$$
$$= \$40$$

Because we already have the dividend in one year, we know that the dividend in four years is equal to $D_1 \times (1 + g)^3 = \$4 \times 1.06^3 = \$4.764$. The price in four years is therefore:

$$P_4 = D_4 \times (1 + g)/(R - g)$$
$$= \$4.764 \times 1.06/(.16 - .06)$$
$$= \$5.05/.10$$
$$= \$50.50$$

Notice in this example that P_4 is equal to $P_0 \times (1 + g)^4$.

$$P_4 = \$50.50 = \$40 \times 1.06^4 = P_0 \times (1 + g)^4$$

To see why this is so, notice first that:

$$P_4 = D_5/(R - g)$$

However, D_5 is just equal to $D_1 \times (1 + g)^4$, so we can write P_4 as:

$$P_4 = D_1 \times (1 + g)^4/(R - g)$$
$$= [D_1/(R - g)] \times (1 + g)^4$$
$$= P_0 \times (1 + g)^4$$

This last example illustrates that the dividend growth model makes the implicit assumption that the stock price will grow at the same constant rate as the dividend. This really isn't too surprising. What it tells us is that if the cash flows on an investment grow at a constant rate through time, so does the value of that investment.

You might wonder what would happen with the dividend growth model if the growth rate, g, were greater than the discount rate, R. It looks like we would get a negative stock price because $R - g$ would be less than zero. This is not what would happen.

Instead, if the constant growth rate exceeds the discount rate, then the stock price is infinitely large. Why? If the growth rate is bigger than the discount rate, the present value of the dividends keeps getting bigger. Essentially the same is true if the growth rate and the discount rate are equal. In both cases, the simplification that allows us to replace the infinite stream of dividends with the dividend growth model is "illegal," so the answers we get from the dividend growth model are nonsense unless the growth rate is less than the discount rate.

Finally, the expression we came up with for the constant growth case will work for any growing perpetuity, not just dividends on common stock. As we saw in Chapter 6, if C_1 is the next cash flow on a growing perpetuity, then the present value of the cash flows is given by:

Present value $= C_1/(R - g) = C_0(1 + g)/(R - g)$

Notice that this expression looks like the result for an ordinary perpetuity except that we have $R - g$ on the bottom instead of just R.

Nonconstant Growth   The next case we consider is nonconstant growth. The main reason to consider this case is to allow for "supernormal" growth rates over some finite length of time. As we discussed earlier, the growth rate cannot exceed the required return indefinitely, but it certainly could do so for some number of years. To avoid the problem of having to forecast and discount an infinite number of dividends, we will require that the dividends start growing at a constant rate sometime in the future.

For a simple example of nonconstant growth, consider the case of a company that is currently not paying dividends. You predict that, in five years, the company will pay a dividend for the first time. The dividend will be $.50 per share. You expect that this dividend will then grow at a rate of 10 percent per year indefinitely. The required return on companies such as this one is 20 percent. What is the price of the stock today?

To see what the stock is worth today, we first find out what it will be worth once dividends are paid. We can then calculate the present value of that future price to get today's price. The first dividend will be paid in five years, and the dividend will grow steadily from then on. Using the dividend growth model, we can say that the price in four years will be:

$$
\begin{aligned}
P_4 &= D_4 \times (1 + g)/(R - g) \\
&= D_5/(R - g) \\
&= \$.50/(.20 - .10) \\
&= \$5
\end{aligned}
$$

If the stock will be worth $5 in four years, then we can get the current value by discounting this price back four years at 20 percent:

$$
P_0 = \$5/1.20^4 = \$5/2.0736 = \$2.41
$$

The stock is therefore worth $2.41 today.

The problem of nonconstant growth is only slightly more complicated if the dividends are not zero for the first several years. For example, suppose you have come up with the following dividend forecasts for the next three years:

Year	Expected Dividend
1	$1.00
2	$2.00
3	$2.50

After the third year, the dividend will grow at a constant rate of 5 percent per year. The required return is 10 percent. What is the value of the stock today?

In dealing with nonconstant growth, a time line can be helpful. Figure 8.1 illustrates one for this problem. The important thing to notice is when constant growth starts. As we've shown, for this problem, constant growth starts at Time 3. This means we can use our constant growth model to determine the stock price at Time 3, P_3. By far the most common mistake in this situation is to incorrectly identify the start of the constant growth phase and, as a result, calculate the future stock price at the wrong time.

As always, the value of the stock is the present value of all the future dividends. To calculate this present value, we first have to compute the present value of the stock price three years down the road, just as we did before. We then have to add in the present

FIGURE 8.1

Nonconstant Growth

value of the dividends that will be paid between now and then. So, the price in three years is:

$$P_3 = D_3 \times (1 + g)/(R - g)$$
$$= \$2.50 \times 1.05/(.10 - .05)$$
$$= \$52.50$$

We can now calculate the total value of the stock as the present value of the first three dividends plus the present value of the price at Time 3, P_3:

$$P_0 = \frac{D_1}{(1 + R)^1} + \frac{D_2}{(1 + R)^2} + \frac{D_3}{(1 + R)^3} + \frac{P_3}{(1 + R)^3}$$
$$= \frac{\$1}{1.10} + \frac{2}{1.10^2} + \frac{2.50}{1.10^3} + \frac{52.50}{1.10^3}$$
$$= \$.91 + 1.65 + 1.88 + 39.44$$
$$= \$43.88$$

The value of the stock today is thus $43.88.

Supernormal Growth   EXAMPLE 8.4

Chain Reaction, Inc., has been growing at a phenomenal rate of 30 percent per year because of its rapid expansion and explosive sales. You believe this growth rate will last for three more years and will then drop to 10 percent per year. If the growth rate then remains at 10 percent indefinitely, what is the total value of the stock? Total dividends just paid were $5 million, and the required return is 20 percent.

Chain Reaction's situation is an example of supernormal growth. It is unlikely that a 30 percent growth rate can be sustained for any extended time. To value the equity in this company, we first need to calculate the total dividends over the supernormal growth period:

Year	Total Dividends (in millions)
1	$5.00 × 1.3 = $ 6.500
2	6.50 × 1.3 = 8.450
3	8.45 × 1.3 = 10.985

The price at Time 3 can be calculated as:

$$P_3 = D_3 \times (1 + g)/(R - g)$$

where g is the long-run growth rate. So, we have:

$$P_3 = \$10.985 \times 1.10/(.20 - .10) = \$120.835$$

(continued)

To determine the value today, we need the present value of this amount plus the present value of the total dividends:

$$P_0 = \frac{D_1}{(1+R)^1} + \frac{D_2}{(1+R)^2} + \frac{D_3}{(1+R)^3} + \frac{P_3}{(1+R)^3}$$

$$= \frac{\$6.50}{1.20} + \frac{8.45}{1.20^2} + \frac{10.985}{1.20^3} + \frac{120.835}{1.20^3}$$

$$= \$5.42 + 5.87 + 6.36 + 69.93$$

$$= \$87.58$$

The total value of the stock today is thus $87.58 million. If there were, for example, 20 million shares, then the stock would be worth $87.58/20 = $4.38 per share.

Two-Stage Growth   The last case we consider is a special case of nonconstant growth: two-stage growth. Here, the idea is that the dividend will grow at a rate of g_1 for t years and then grow at a rate of g_2 thereafter forever. In this case, the value of the stock can be written as:

$$P_0 = \frac{D_1}{R - g_1} \times \left[1 - \left(\frac{1 + g_1}{1 + R} \right)^t \right] + \frac{P_t}{(1 + R)^t} \qquad \text{[8.5]}$$

Notice that the first term in our expression is the present value of a growing annuity, which we discussed in Chapter 6. In this first stage, g_1 can be greater than R. The second part is the present value of the stock price once the second stage begins at time t.

We can calculate P_t as follows:

$$P_t = \frac{D_{t+1}}{R - g_2} = \frac{D_0 \times (1 + g_1)^t \times (1 + g_2)}{R - g_2} \qquad \text{[8.6]}$$

In this calculation, we need the dividend at time $t + 1$, D_{t+1}, to get the stock price at time t, P_t. Notice that to get it, we grew the current dividend, D_0, at rate g_1 for t periods and then grew it one period at rate g_2. Also, in this second stage, g_2 must be less than R.

EXAMPLE 8.5 | **Two-Stage Growth**

The Highfield Company's dividend is expected to grow at 20 percent for the next five years. After that, the growth is expected to be 4 percent forever. If the required return is 10 percent, what's the value of the stock? The dividend just paid was $2.

There is a fair amount of computation here, but it is mostly just "plug and chug" with a calculator. We can start by calculating the stock price five years from now, P_5:

$$P_5 = \frac{D_6}{R - g_2} = \frac{D_0 \times (1 + g_1)^5 \times (1 + g_2)}{R - g_2}$$

$$= \frac{\$2 \times (1 + .20)^5 \times (1 + .04)}{.10 - .04} = \frac{\$5.18}{.06}$$

$$= \$86.26$$

We then plug this result into our two-stage growth formula to get the price today:

$$P_0 = \frac{D_1}{R - g_1} \times \left[1 - \left(\frac{1 + g_1}{1 + R} \right)^t \right] + \frac{P_t}{(1 + R)^t}$$

$$= \frac{\$2 \times (1 + .20)}{.10 - .20} \times \left[1 - \left(\frac{1 + .20}{1 + .10} \right)^5 \right] + \frac{\$86.26}{(1 + .10)^5}$$

$$= \$66.64$$

CH8 Timeline!!!

Notice that we were given $D_0 = \$2$ here, so we had to grow it by 20 percent for one period to get D_1. Notice also that g_1 is bigger than R in this problem, but that fact does not cause a problem.

COMPONENTS OF THE REQUIRED RETURN

Thus far, we have taken the required return, or discount rate, R, as given. We will have quite a bit to say about this subject in Chapters 12 and 13. For now, we want to examine the implications of the dividend growth model for this required return. Earlier, we calculated P_0 as:

$$P_0 = D_1/(R - g)$$

If we rearrange this to solve for R, we get:

$$R - g = D_1/P_0$$
$$R = D_1/P_0 + g \qquad \qquad \text{[8.7]}$$

This tells us that the total return, R, has two components. The first of these, D_1/P_0, is called the **dividend yield**. Because this is calculated as the expected cash dividend divided by the current price, it is conceptually similar to the current yield on a bond.

The second part of the total return is the growth rate, g. We know that the dividend growth rate is also the rate at which the stock price grows (see Example 8.3). Thus, this growth rate can be interpreted as the **capital gains yield**—that is, the rate at which the value of the investment grows.[2]

To illustrate the components of the required return, suppose we observe a stock selling for \$20 per share. The next dividend will be \$1 per share. You think that the dividend will grow by 10 percent per year more or less indefinitely. What return does this stock offer if this is correct?

The dividend growth model calculates total return as:

$$R = \text{Dividend yield} + \text{Capital gains yield}$$
$$R = \qquad D_1/P_0 \qquad + \qquad g$$

In this case, total return works out to be:

$$R = \$1/20 + 10\%$$
$$= 5\% + 10\%$$
$$= 15\%$$

dividend yield
A stock's expected cash dividend divided by its current price.

capital gains yield
The dividend growth rate, or the rate at which the value of an investment grows.

This stock, therefore, has an expected return of 15 percent.

We can verify this answer by calculating the price in one year, P_1, using 15 percent as the required return. Based on the dividend growth model, this price is:

$$P_1 = D_1 \times (1 + g)/(R - g)$$
$$= \$1 \times 1.10/(.15 - .10)$$
$$= \$1.10/.05$$
$$= \$22$$

---

[2]Here and elsewhere, we use the term *capital gains* a little loosely. For the record, a capital gain (or loss) is, strictly speaking, something defined by the IRS. For our purposes, it would be more accurate (but less common) to use the term *price appreciation* instead of *capital gain.*

Notice that this $22 is $20 × 1.1, so the stock price has grown by 10 percent as it should. If you pay $20 for the stock today, you will get a $1 dividend at the end of the year, and you will have a $22 − 20 = $2 gain. Your dividend yield is thus $1/20 = 5%. Your capital gains yield is $2/20 = 10%, so your total return would be 5% + 10% = 15%.

To get a feel for actual numbers in this context, consider that, according to the 2010 *Value Line Investment Survey,* Procter & Gamble's dividends were expected to grow by 6 percent over the next 5 or so years, compared to a historical growth rate of 12 percent over the preceding 5 years and 11 percent over the preceding 10 years. In 2010, the projected dividend for the coming year was given as $1.95. The stock price at that time was about $67 per share. What is the return investors require on P&G? Here, the dividend yield is 2.9 percent and the capital gains yield is 6 percent, giving a total required return of 8.9 percent on P&G stock.

STOCK VALUATION USING MULTIPLES

An obvious problem with our dividend-based approach to stock valuation is that many companies don't pay dividends. What do we do in such cases? A common approach is to make use of the PE ratio, which we defined in Chapter 3 as the ratio of a stock's price per share to its earnings per share (EPS) over the previous year. The idea here is to have some sort of benchmark or reference PE ratio, which we then multiply by earnings to come up with a price:

$$\text{Price at time } t = P_t = \text{Benchmark PE ratio} \times \text{EPS}_t \qquad [8.8]$$

The benchmark PE ratio could come from one of several possible sources. It could be based on similar companies (perhaps an industry average or median), or it could be based on a company's own historical values. For example, suppose we are trying to value Inactivision, Inc., a video game developer known for its hit *Slack Ops* series. Inactivision does not pay dividends, but after studying the industry, you feel that a PE ratio of 20 is appropriate for a company like this one. Total earnings over the four most recent quarters combined are $2 per share, so you think the stock should sell for 20 × $2 = $40. You might view it as an attractive purchase if it is going for less than $40, but not attractive if it sells for more than $40.

Security analysts spend a lot of time forecasting future earnings, particularly for the coming year. A PE ratio that is based on estimated future earnings is called a *forward* PE ratio. For example, suppose you felt that Inactivision's earnings for the coming year were going to be $2.50, reflecting the growing popularity of the company's *World of Slackcraft* massively multiplayer online role-playing game (MMORPG). In this case, if the current stock price is $40, the forward PE ratio is $40/$2.50 = 16.

Finally, notice that your benchmark PE of 20 applies to earnings over the previous year. If earnings over the coming year turn out to be $2.50, then the stock price one year from today should be 20 × $2.50 = $50. Forecast prices such as this one are often called *target* prices.

Often we will be interested in valuing newer companies that both don't pay dividends and are not yet profitable, meaning that earnings are negative. What do we do then? One answer is to use the price–sales ratio, which we also introduced in Chapter 3. As the name suggests, this ratio is the price per share on the stock divided by sales per share. You use this ratio just like you use the PE ratio, except you use sales per share instead of earnings per share. As with PE ratios, price–sales ratios vary depending on company age and industry. Typical values are in the .8–2.0 range, but they can be much higher for younger, faster-growing companies.

For future reference, our discussion of stock valuation techniques is summarized in Table 8.1.

TABLE 8.1

Summary of Stock Valuation

I.   The General Case

In general, the price today of a share of stock, P_0, is the present value of all of its future dividends, $D_1, D_2, D_3, \ldots$:

$$P_0 = \frac{D_1}{(1 + R)^1} + \frac{D_2}{(1 + R)^2} + \frac{D_3}{(1 + R)^3} + \cdots$$

where R is the required return.

II.   Constant Growth Case

If the dividend grows at a steady rate, g, then the price can be written as:

$$P_0 = \frac{D_1}{R - g}$$

This result is called the *dividend growth model*.

III.   Nonconstant Growth

If the dividend grows steadily after t periods, then the price can be written as:

$$P_0 = \frac{D_1}{(1 + R)^1} + \frac{D_2}{(1 + R)^2} + \cdots + \frac{D_t}{(1 + R)^t} + \frac{P_t}{(1 + R)^t}$$

where

$$P_t = \frac{D_t \times (1 + g)}{(R - g)}$$

IV.   Two-Stage Growth

If the dividend grows at rate g_1 for t periods and then grows at rate g_2 thereafter, then the price can be written as:

$$P_0 = \frac{D_1}{R - g_1} \times \left[1 - \left(\frac{1 + g_1}{1 + R} \right)^t \right] + \frac{P_t}{(1 + R)^t}$$

where

$$P_t = \frac{D_{t+1}}{R - g_2} = \frac{D_0 \times (1 + g_1)^t \times (1 + g_2)}{R - g_2}$$

V.   Valuation Using Multiples

For stocks that don't pay dividends (or have erratic dividend growth rates), we can value them using the PE ratio and/or the price–sales ratio:

P_t = Benchmark PE ratio $\times$ EPS_t

P_t = Benchmark price–sales ratio $\times$ Sales per share$_t$

VI.   The Required Return

The required return, R, can be written as the sum of two things:

$$R = D_1/P_0 + g$$

where D_1/P_0 is the *dividend yield* and g is the *capital gains yield* (which is the same thing as the growth rate in dividends for the steady growth case).

Concept Questions

8.1a What are the relevant cash flows for valuing a share of common stock?

8.1b Does the value of a share of stock depend on how long you expect to keep it?

8.1c What is the value of a share of stock when the dividend grows at a constant rate?

8.2 Some Features of Common and Preferred Stocks

In discussing common stock features, we focus on shareholder rights and dividend payments. For preferred stock, we explain what *preferred* means, and we also debate whether preferred stock is really debt or equity.

COMMON STOCK FEATURES

common stock
Equity without priority for dividends or in bankruptcy.

The term **common stock** means different things to different people, but it is usually applied to stock that has no special preference either in receiving dividends or in bankruptcy.

Shareholder Rights   The conceptual structure of the corporation assumes that shareholders elect directors who, in turn, hire managers to carry out their directives. Shareholders, therefore, control the corporation through the right to elect the directors. Generally, only shareholders have this right.

Directors are elected each year at an annual meeting. Although there are exceptions (discussed next), the general idea is "one share, one vote" (*not* one share*holder,* one vote). Corporate democracy is thus very different from our political democracy. With corporate democracy, the "golden rule" prevails absolutely.[3]

Directors are elected at an annual shareholders' meeting by a vote of the holders of a majority of shares who are present and entitled to vote. However, the exact mechanism for electing directors differs across companies. The most important difference is whether shares must be voted cumulatively or voted straight.

To illustrate the two different voting procedures, imagine that a corporation has two shareholders: Smith with 20 shares and Jones with 80 shares. Both want to be a director. Jones does not want Smith, however. We assume there are a total of four directors to be elected.

cumulative voting
A procedure in which a shareholder may cast all votes for one member of the board of directors.

The effect of **cumulative voting** is to permit minority participation.[4] If cumulative voting is permitted, the total number of votes that each shareholder may cast is determined first. This is usually calculated as the number of shares (owned or controlled) multiplied by the number of directors to be elected.

With cumulative voting, the directors are elected all at once. In our example, this means that the top four vote getters will be the new directors. A shareholder can distribute votes however he or she wishes.

Will Smith get a seat on the board? If we ignore the possibility of a five-way tie, then the answer is yes. Smith will cast $20 \times 4 = 80$ votes, and Jones will cast $80 \times 4 = 320$ votes. If Smith gives all his votes to himself, he is assured of a directorship. The reason is that Jones can't divide 320 votes among four candidates in such a way as to give all of them more than 80 votes, so Smith will finish fourth at worst.

In general, if there are N directors up for election, then $1/(N + 1)$ percent of the stock plus one share will guarantee you a seat. In our current example, this is $1/(4 + 1) = 20\%$. So the more seats that are up for election at one time, the easier (and cheaper) it is to win one.

straight voting
A procedure in which a shareholder may cast all votes for each member of the board of directors.

With **straight voting**, the directors are elected one at a time. Each time, Smith can cast 20 votes and Jones can cast 80. As a consequence, Jones will elect all of the candidates. The

---

[3]The golden rule: Whosoever has the gold makes the rules.

[4]By *minority participation,* we mean participation by shareholders with relatively small amounts of stock.

only way to guarantee a seat is to own 50 percent plus one share. This also guarantees that you will win every seat, so it's really all or nothing.

Buying the Election   EXAMPLE 8.6

Stock in JRJ Corporation sells for $20 per share and features cumulative voting. There are 10,000 shares outstanding. If three directors are up for election, how much does it cost to ensure yourself a seat on the board?

The question here is how many shares of stock it will take to get a seat. The answer is 2,501, so the cost is 2,501 × $20 = $50,020. Why 2,501? Because there is no way the remaining 7,499 votes can be divided among three people to give all of them more than 2,501 votes. For example, suppose two people receive 2,502 votes and the first two seats. A third person can receive at most 10,000 − 2,502 − 2,502 − 2,501 = 2,495, so the third seat is yours.

Many companies have staggered elections for directors. With staggered elections, only a fraction of the directorships (often one-third) are up for election at a particular time. Thus if only two directors are up for election at any one time, it will take $1/(2 + 1) = 33.33\%$ of the stock plus one share to guarantee a seat. Staggered boards are often called *classified* boards because directors are placed into different classes with terms that expire at different times. In recent years, corporations have come under pressure to declassify their boards, meaning that all directors would stand for election every year, and many have done so.

Overall, staggering has two basic effects:

1. Staggering makes it more difficult for a minority to elect a director because there are fewer directors to be elected at one time.
2. Staggering makes takeover attempts less likely to be successful because it makes it more difficult to vote in a majority of new directors.

We should note that staggering may serve a beneficial purpose. It provides "institutional memory"—that is, continuity on the board of directors. This may be important for corporations with significant long-range plans and projects.

Proxy Voting   A **proxy** is the grant of authority by a shareholder to someone else to vote his or her shares. For convenience, much of the voting in large public corporations is actually done by proxy.

As we have seen, with straight voting, each share of stock has one vote. The owner of 10,000 shares has 10,000 votes. Large companies have hundreds of thousands or even millions of shareholders. Shareholders can come to the annual meeting and vote in person, or they can transfer their right to vote to another party.

Obviously, management always tries to get as many proxies as possible transferred to it. However, if shareholders are not satisfied with management, an "outside" group of shareholders can try to obtain votes via proxy. They can vote by proxy in an attempt to replace management by electing enough directors. The resulting battle is called a *proxy fight*.

Classes of Stock   Some firms have more than one class of common stock. Often the classes are created with unequal voting rights. The Ford Motor Company, for example, has Class B common stock, which is not publicly traded (it is held by Ford family interests and

proxy
A grant of authority by a shareholder allowing another individual to vote his or her shares.

trusts). This class has 40 percent of the voting power, even though it represents less than 10 percent of the total number of shares outstanding.

There are many other cases of corporations with different classes of stock. For example, at one time, General Motors had its "GM Classic" shares (the original) and two additional classes, Class E ("GME") and Class H ("GMH"). These classes were created to help pay for two large acquisitions, Electronic Data Systems and Hughes Aircraft. Another good example is Google, the Web search company, which only recently became publicly owned. Google has two classes of common stock, A and B. The Class A shares are held by the public, and each share has one vote. The Class B shares are held by company insiders, and each Class B share has 10 votes. As a result, Google's founders and managers control the company.

Historically, the New York Stock Exchange did not allow companies to create classes of publicly traded common stock with unequal voting rights. Exceptions (like Ford) appear to have been made. In addition, many non-NYSE companies have dual classes of common stock.

A primary reason for creating dual or multiple classes of stock has to do with control of the firm. If such stock exists, management of a firm can raise equity capital by issuing nonvoting or limited-voting stock while maintaining control.

The subject of unequal voting rights is controversial in the United States, and the idea of one share, one vote has a strong following and a long history. Interestingly, however, shares with unequal voting rights are quite common in the United Kingdom and elsewhere around the world.

Other Rights   The value of a share of common stock in a corporation is directly related to the general rights of shareholders. In addition to the right to vote for directors, shareholders usually have the following rights:

1. The right to share proportionally in dividends paid.
2. The right to share proportionally in assets remaining after liabilities have been paid in a liquidation.
3. The right to vote on stockholder matters of great importance, such as a merger. Voting is usually done at the annual meeting or a special meeting.

In addition, stockholders sometimes have the right to share proportionally in any new stock sold. This is called the *preemptive right*.

Essentially, a preemptive right means that a company that wishes to sell stock must first offer it to the existing stockholders before offering it to the general public. The purpose is to give stockholders the opportunity to protect their proportionate ownership in the corporation.

dividends
Payments by a corporation to shareholders, made in either cash or stock.

Dividends   A distinctive feature of corporations is that they have shares of stock on which they are authorized by law to pay dividends to their shareholders. **Dividends** paid to shareholders represent a return on the capital directly or indirectly contributed to the corporation by the shareholders. The payment of dividends is at the discretion of the board of directors.

Some important characteristics of dividends include the following:

1. Unless a dividend is declared by the board of directors of a corporation, it is not a liability of the corporation. A corporation cannot default on an undeclared dividend. As a consequence, corporations cannot become bankrupt because of nonpayment of dividends. The amount of the dividend and even whether it is paid are decisions based on the business judgment of the board of directors.

2. The payment of dividends by the corporation is not a business expense. Dividends are not deductible for corporate tax purposes. In short, dividends are paid out of the corporation's aftertax profits.

3. Dividends received by individual shareholders are taxable. In 2011, the tax rate was 15 percent, but this favorable rate may change. However, corporations that own stock in other corporations are permitted to exclude 70 percent of the dividend amounts they receive and are taxed on only the remaining 30 percent.[5]

PREFERRED STOCK FEATURES

Preferred stock differs from common stock because it has preference over common stock in the payment of dividends and in the distribution of corporation assets in the event of liquidation. *Preference* means only that the holders of the preferred shares must receive a dividend (in the case of an ongoing firm) before holders of common shares are entitled to anything.

Preferred stock is a form of equity from a legal and tax standpoint. It is important to note, however, that holders of preferred stock sometimes have no voting privileges.

preferred stock
Stock with dividend priority over common stock, normally with a fixed dividend rate, sometimes without voting rights.

Stated Value   Preferred shares have a stated liquidating value, usually $100 per share. The cash dividend is described in terms of dollars per share. For example, General Motors "$5 preferred" easily translates into a dividend yield of 5 percent of stated value.

Cumulative and Noncumulative Dividends   A preferred dividend is *not* like interest on a bond. The board of directors may decide not to pay the dividends on preferred shares, and their decision may have nothing to do with the current net income of the corporation.

Dividends payable on preferred stock are either *cumulative* or *noncumulative;* most are cumulative. If preferred dividends are cumulative and are not paid in a particular year, they will be carried forward as an *arrearage*. Usually, both the accumulated (past) preferred dividends and the current preferred dividends must be paid before the common shareholders can receive anything.

Unpaid preferred dividends are *not* debts of the firm. Directors elected by the common shareholders can defer preferred dividends indefinitely. However, in such cases, common shareholders must also forgo dividends. In addition, holders of preferred shares are often granted voting and other rights if preferred dividends have not been paid for some time. For example, as of summer 1996, USAir had failed to pay dividends on one of its preferred stock issues for six quarters. As a consequence, the holders of the shares were allowed to nominate two people to represent their interests on the airline's board. Because preferred stockholders receive no interest on the accumulated dividends, some have argued that firms have an incentive to delay paying preferred dividends; but, as we have seen, this may mean sharing control with preferred stockholders.

Is Preferred Stock Really Debt?   A good case can be made that preferred stock is really debt in disguise, a kind of equity bond. Preferred shareholders receive a stated dividend only; and if the corporation is liquidated, preferred shareholders get a stated value. Often,

---

[5]For the record, the 70 percent exclusion applies when the recipient owns less than 20 percent of the outstanding stock in a corporation. If a corporation owns more than 20 percent but less than 80 percent, the exclusion is 80 percent. If more than 80 percent is owned, the corporation can file a single "consolidated" return and the exclusion is effectively 100 percent.

preferred stocks carry credit ratings much like those of bonds. Furthermore, preferred stock is sometimes convertible into common stock, and preferred stocks are often callable.

In addition, many issues of preferred stock have obligatory sinking funds. The existence of such a sinking fund effectively creates a final maturity because it means that the entire issue will ultimately be retired. For these reasons, preferred stock seems to be a lot like debt. However, for tax purposes, preferred dividends are treated like common stock dividends.

In the 1990s, firms began to sell securities that looked a lot like preferred stocks but were treated as debt for tax purposes. The new securities were given interesting acronyms like TOPrS (trust-originated preferred securities, or toppers), MIPS (monthly income preferred securities), and QUIPS (quarterly income preferred securities), among others. Because of various specific features, these instruments can be counted as debt for tax purposes, making the interest payments tax deductible. Payments made to investors in these instruments are treated as interest for personal income taxes. Until 2003, interest payments and dividends were taxed at the same marginal tax rate. When the tax rate on dividend payments was reduced, these instruments were not included, so individuals must still pay their higher income tax rate on dividend payments received from these instruments.

Concept Questions

8.2a What is a proxy?

8.2b What rights do stockholders have?

8.2c Why is preferred stock called *preferred*?

---

z 8.3 The Stock Markets

Back in Chapter 1, we briefly mentioned that shares of stock are bought and sold on various stock exchanges, the two most important of which are the New York Stock Exchange and the NASDAQ. From our earlier discussion, recall that the stock market consists of a **primary market** and a **secondary market**. In the primary, or new issue, market, shares of stock are first brought to the market and sold to investors. In the secondary market, existing shares are traded among investors.

In the primary market, companies sell securities to raise money. We will discuss this process in detail in a later chapter. We therefore focus mainly on secondary market activity in this section. We conclude with a discussion of how stock prices are quoted in the financial press.

primary market
The market in which new securities are originally sold to investors.

secondary market
The market in which previously issued securities are traded among investors.

dealer
An agent who buys and sells securities from inventory.

broker
An agent who arranges security transactions among investors.

DEALERS AND BROKERS

Because most securities transactions involve dealers and brokers, it is important to understand exactly what is meant by the terms *dealer* and *broker*. A **dealer** maintains an inventory and stands ready to buy and sell at any time. In contrast, a **broker** brings buyers and sellers together but does not maintain an inventory. Thus, when we speak of used car dealers and real estate brokers, we recognize that the used car dealer maintains an inventory, whereas the real estate broker does not.

In the securities markets, a dealer stands ready to buy securities from investors wishing to sell them and sell securities to investors wishing to buy them. Recall from our previous chapter that the price the dealer is willing to pay is called the *bid price*. The price at which the dealer will sell is called the *ask price* (sometimes called the asked, offered, or offering price). The difference between the bid and ask prices is called the *spread,* and it is the basic source of dealer profits.

Dealers exist in all areas of the economy, not just the stock markets. For example, your local college bookstore is probably both a primary and a secondary market textbook dealer. If you buy a new book, this is a primary market transaction. If you buy a used book, this is a secondary market transaction, and you pay the store's ask price. If you sell the book back, you receive the store's bid price (often half of the ask price). The bookstore's spread is the difference between the two prices.

In contrast, a securities broker arranges transactions between investors, matching investors wishing to buy securities with investors wishing to sell securities. The distinctive characteristic of security brokers is that they do not buy or sell securities for their own accounts. Facilitating trades by others is their business.

ORGANIZATION OF THE NYSE

The New York Stock Exchange, or NYSE, popularly known as the Big Board, celebrated its bicentennial a few years ago. It has occupied its current location on Wall Street since the turn of the twentieth century. Measured in terms of the total value of shares listed, it is the largest stock market in the world.

Members   The NYSE has 1,366 exchange **members**. Prior to 2006, the exchange members were said to own "seats" on the exchange, and collectively the members of the exchange were also the owners. For this and other reasons, seats were valuable and were bought and sold fairly regularly. Seat prices reached a record $4 million in 2005.

In 2006, all of this changed when the NYSE became a publicly owned corporation. Naturally, its stock is listed on the NYSE. Now, instead of purchasing seats, exchange members must purchase trading licenses, the number of which is still limited to 1,366. In 2011, a license would set you back a cool $40,000—per year. Having a license entitles you to buy and sell securities on the floor of the exchange. Different members play different roles in this regard.

On April 4, 2007, the NYSE grew even larger when it merged with Euronext to form NYSE Euronext. Euronext was a stock exchange in Amsterdam, with subsidiaries in Belgium, France, Portugal, and the United Kingdom. With the merger, NYSE Euronext became the world's "first global exchange." Further expansion occurred in 2008 when NYSE Euronext merged with the American Stock Exchange. Then, in February 2011, Deutsche Boerse AG, the stock exchange headquartered in Germany, made an offer of $9.53 billion for NYSE Euronext. This deal is far from complete as this is being written because the merger is under scrutiny by European Union antitrust regulators, as well as a lawsuit from at least one NYSE Euronext shareholder.

The largest number of NYSE members are registered as **commission brokers**. The business of a commission broker is to execute customer orders to buy and sell stocks. A commission broker's primary responsibility to customers is to get the best possible prices for their orders. The exact number varies, but usually about 500 NYSE members are commission brokers. NYSE commission brokers typically are employees of brokerage companies such as Merrill Lynch.

Second in number of NYSE members are **specialists**, so named because each of them acts as an assigned dealer for a small set of securities. With a few exceptions, each security listed for trading on the NYSE is assigned to a single specialist. Specialists are also called *market makers* because they are obligated to maintain a fair, orderly market for the securities assigned to them.

Specialists post bid prices and ask prices for securities assigned to them. Specialists make a market by standing ready to buy at bid prices and sell at asked prices when there is a temporary disparity between the flow of buy orders and that of sell orders for a security. In this capacity, they act as dealers for their own accounts.

How big is the bid–ask spread on your favorite stock? Check out the latest quotes at www.bloomberg.com.

member
As of 2011, a member is the owner of a trading license on the NYSE.

commission brokers
NYSE members who execute customer orders to buy and sell stock transmitted to the exchange floor.

specialist
A NYSE member acting as a dealer in a small number of securities on the exchange floor; often called a *market maker.*

floor brokers
NYSE members who execute orders for commission brokers on a fee basis; sometimes called *$2 brokers*.

SuperDOT system
An electronic NYSE system allowing orders to be transmitted directly to the specialist.

floor traders
NYSE members who trade for their own accounts, trying to anticipate temporary price fluctuations.

order flow
The flow of customer orders to buy and sell securities.

Take a virtual field trip to the New York Stock Exchange at www.nyse.com.

specialist's post
A fixed place on the exchange floor where the specialist operates.

Third in number of exchange members are **floor brokers**. Floor brokers are used by commission brokers who are too busy to handle certain orders themselves. Such commission brokers will delegate some orders to floor brokers for execution. Floor brokers are sometimes called *$2 brokers,* a name earned when the standard fee for their service was only $2.

In recent years, floor brokers have become less important on the exchange floor because of the efficient **SuperDOT system** (the *DOT* stands for Designated Order Turnaround), which allows orders to be transmitted electronically directly to the specialist. SuperDOT trading now accounts for a substantial percentage of all trading on the NYSE, particularly on smaller orders.

Finally, a small number of NYSE members are **floor traders** who independently trade for their own accounts. Floor traders try to anticipate temporary price fluctuations and profit from them by buying low and selling high. In recent decades, the number of floor traders has declined substantially, suggesting that it has become increasingly difficult to profit from short-term trading on the exchange floor.

Operations   Now that we have a basic idea of how the NYSE is organized and who the major players are, we turn to the question of how trading actually takes place. Fundamentally, the business of the NYSE is to attract and process **order flow**. The term *order flow* means the flow of customer orders to buy and sell stocks. The customers of the NYSE are the millions of individual investors and tens of thousands of institutional investors who place their orders to buy and sell shares in NYSE-listed companies. The NYSE has been quite successful in attracting order flow. Currently, it is not unusual for well over a billion shares to change hands in a single day.

Floor Activity   It is quite likely that you have seen footage of the NYSE trading floor on television, or you may have visited the NYSE and viewed exchange floor activity from the visitors' gallery (it's worth the trip). Either way, you would have seen a big room, about the size of a basketball gym. This big room is called, technically, "the Big Room." There are a few other, smaller rooms that you normally don't see, one of which is called "the Garage," because that is what it was before it was taken over for trading.

On the floor of the exchange are a number of stations, each with a roughly figure-eight shape. These stations have multiple counters with numerous terminal screens above and on the sides. People operate behind and in front of the counters in relatively stationary positions.

Other people move around on the exchange floor, frequently returning to the many telephones positioned along the exchange walls. In all, you may be reminded of worker ants moving around an ant colony. It is natural to wonder, "What are all those people doing down there (and why are so many wearing funny-looking coats)?"

As an overview of exchange floor activity, here is a quick look at what goes on. Each of the counters at a figure-eight–shaped station is a **specialist's post**. Specialists normally operate in front of their posts to monitor and manage trading in the stocks assigned to them. Clerical employees working for the specialists operate behind the counter. Moving from the many telephones lining the walls of the exchange out to the exchange floor and back again are swarms of commission brokers, receiving telephoned customer orders, walking out to specialists' posts where the orders can be executed, and returning to confirm order executions and receive new customer orders.

To better understand activity on the NYSE trading floor, imagine yourself as a commission broker. Your phone clerk has just handed you an order to sell 20,000 shares of Walmart for a customer of the brokerage company that employs you. The customer wants to sell the stock at the best possible price as soon as possible. You immediately walk (running violates exchange rules) to the specialist's post where Walmart stock is traded.

As you approach the specialist's post where Walmart is traded, you check the terminal screen for information on the current market price. The screen reveals that the last executed trade was at 60.10 and that the specialist is bidding 60 per share. You could immediately sell to the specialist at 60, but that would be too easy.

Instead, as the customer's representative, you are obligated to get the best possible price. It is your job to "work" the order, and your job depends on providing satisfactory order execution service. So, you look around for another broker who represents a customer who wants to buy Walmart stock. Luckily, you quickly find another broker at the specialist's post with an order to buy 20,000 shares. Noticing that the specialist is asking 60.10 per share, you both agree to execute your orders with each other at a price of 60.05. This price is exactly halfway between the specialist's bid and ask prices, and it saves each of your customers .05 × 20,000 = $1,000 as compared to dealing at the posted prices.

For a very actively traded stock, there may be many buyers and sellers around the specialist's post, and most of the trading will be done directly between brokers. This is called trading in the "crowd." In such cases, the specialist's responsibility is to maintain order and to make sure that all buyers and sellers receive a fair price. In other words, the specialist essentially functions as a referee.

More often, however, there will be no crowd at the specialist's post. Going back to our Walmart example, suppose you are unable to quickly find another broker with an order to buy 20,000 shares. Because you have an order to sell immediately, you may have no choice but to sell to the specialist at the bid price of 60. In this case, the need to execute an order quickly takes priority, and the specialist provides the liquidity necessary to allow immediate order execution.

Finally, note that colored coats are worn by many of the people on the floor of the exchange. The color of the coat indicates the person's job or position. Clerks, runners, visitors, exchange officials, and so on wear particular colors to identify themselves. Also, things can get a little hectic on a busy day, with the result that good clothing doesn't last long; the cheap coats offer some protection.

NASDAQ OPERATIONS

In terms of total dollar volume of trading, the second largest stock market in the United States is NASDAQ (say "Naz-dak"). The somewhat odd name originally was an acronym for the National Association of Securities Dealers Automated Quotations system, but NASDAQ is now a name in its own right.

Introduced in 1971, the NASDAQ market is a computer network of securities dealers and others that disseminates timely security price quotes to computer screens worldwide. NASDAQ dealers act as market makers for securities listed on NASDAQ. As market makers, NASDAQ dealers post bid and ask prices at which they accept sell and buy orders, respectively. With each price quote, they also post the number of stock shares that they obligate themselves to trade at their quoted prices.

Like NYSE specialists, NASDAQ market makers trade on an inventory basis—that is, using their inventory as a buffer to absorb buy and sell order imbalances. Unlike the NYSE specialist system, NASDAQ features multiple market makers for actively traded stocks. Thus, there are two key differences between the NYSE and NASDAQ:

1. NASDAQ is a computer network and has no physical location where trading takes place.
2. NASDAQ has a multiple market maker system rather than a specialist system.

over-the-counter (OTC) market
Securities market in which trading is almost exclusively done through dealers who buy and sell for their own inventories.

Traditionally, a securities market largely characterized by dealers who buy and sell securities for their own inventories is called an **over-the-counter (OTC) market**. Consequently, NASDAQ is often referred to as an OTC market. However, in their efforts to promote a distinct image, NASDAQ officials prefer that the term OTC not be used when referring to the NASDAQ market. Nevertheless, old habits die hard, and many people still refer to NASDAQ as an OTC market.

By 2011, NASDAQ had grown to the point that it was, by some measures, bigger than the NYSE. For example, on January 21, 2011, 1.96 billion shares were traded on NASDAQ versus 1.27 billion on the NYSE. In dollars, NASDAQ trading volume for the day was $62.27 billion compared to $38.39 billion for the NYSE.

NASDAQ
(www.nasdaq.com) *has a great website; check it out!*

NASDAQ is actually made up of three separate markets: the NASDAQ Global Select Market, the NASDAQ Global Market, and the NASDAQ Capital Market. As the market for NASDAQ's larger and more actively traded securities, the Global Select Market lists about 1,600 companies (as of early 2011), including some of the best-known companies in the world, such as Microsoft and Intel. Global Market companies are somewhat smaller in size, and NASDAQ lists about 800 of these. Finally, the smallest companies listed on NASDAQ are in the NASDAQ Capital Market; about 500 are currently listed. Of course, as Capital Market companies become more established, they may move up to the Global Market or Global Select Market.

electronic communications network (ECN)
A website that allows investors to trade directly with each other.

ECNs   In a very important development in the late 1990s, the NASDAQ system was opened to so-called **electronic communications networks (ECNs)**. ECNs are basically websites that allow investors to trade directly with one another. Investor buy and sell orders placed on ECNs are transmitted to NASDAQ and displayed along with market maker bid and ask prices. As a result, the ECNs open up NASDAQ by essentially allowing individual investors, not just market makers, to enter orders. As a result, the ECNs act to increase liquidity and competition.

Of course, the NYSE and NASDAQ are not the only places stocks are traded. See our nearby *Work the Web* box for a discussion of somewhat wilder markets.

STOCK MARKET REPORTING

You can get real-time stock quotes on the Web. See finance.yahoo.com *for details.*

In recent years, the reporting of stock prices and related information has increasingly moved from traditional print media, such as *The Wall Street Journal,* to various websites. Yahoo! Finance (finance.yahoo.com) is a good example. We went there and requested a

---

WORK THE WEB

Where do companies go when they can't (or don't want to) meet the listing requirements of the larger stock exchanges? Two options are the Over-the-Counter Bulletin Board (OTCBB) and the Pink Sheets. These two electronic markets are part of the Wild, Wild West of stock trading. The somewhat odd names have simple explanations. The OTCBB began as an electronic bulletin board that was created to facilitate OTC trading in nonlisted stocks. The name "Pink Sheets" just reflects the fact that, at one time, prices for such stocks were quoted on pink sheets of paper.

The well-known markets such as NASDAQ and the NYSE have relatively strict listing requirements. If a company fails to meet these requirements, it can be delisted. The OTCBB and the Pink Sheets, on the other hand, have no listing requirements. The OTCBB does require that companies file financial statements with the SEC (or other relevant agency), but the Pink Sheets does not.

Stocks traded on these markets often have very low prices and are frequently referred to as *penny stocks, microcaps,* or even *nanocaps*. Relatively few brokers do any research on these companies, so information is often spread through word of mouth or the Internet, not the most reliable of sources. In fact, for many stocks, these markets often look like big electronic rumor mills and gossip factories. To get a feel for what trading looks like, we captured a typical screen from the OTCBB website (www.otcbb.com):

Market Statistics   Data delayed 15-20 minutes

OTCBB ▾   Vol Actives ▾   GO

Name	Symbol	Last Price	Chg	% Chg	Open	High	Low	Volume
Greenshift Corp.	GERS	0.0002 ▲	0.0001	100.00%	0.0002	0.0002	0.0001	824.58 m
China Crescent Enterprises Inc.	CCTR	0.002 ▲	0.0001	5.26%	0.002	0.0024	0.0018	603.27 m
Camelot Entertainment Group Inc.	CMGR	0.0001 –	0.00	0.00%	0.0001	0.0002	0.0001	360.40 m
IDO Security Inc.	IDOI	0.0006 ▽	-0.0001	-14.29%	0.0006	0.0007	0.0005	321.39 m
Electric Car Company Inc.	ELCR	0.0001 –	0.00	0.00%	0.0001	0.0002	0.0001	241.10 m
Numobile Inc.	NUBL	0.0009 –	0.00	0.00%	0.001	0.0011	0.0007	143.17 m
Trey Resources Inc.	TYRIA	0.0001 ▽	-0.0001	-50.00%	0.0001	0.0002	0.0001	93.86 m
EcoSystem Corp. NEW	ESYR	0.0001 –	0.00	0.00%	0.0001	0.0002	0.0001	92.07 m
Sunvalley Solar Inc.	SSOL	0.0259 ▲	0.011	73.83%	0.016	0.028	0.016	86.13 m
MultiCell Technologies Inc.	MCET	0.0115 ▲	0.0037	47.44%	0.0081	0.013	0.0081	66.32 m

First, take a look at the returns. Greenshift Corp. had a return at this point in the day of 100 percent! That's not something you see very often. Of course, the big return was generated by a whopping price increase of $.0001 per share. A stock listed on the OTCBB is often the most actively traded stock on any particular day. For example, by the end of this particular day, Intel was the most active stock on NASDAQ, trading about 82.4 million shares. Nine stocks on the OTCBB traded even more shares. Greenshift Corp. led the way with over 824 million shares traded. But, at an average price of, say, $.00015 per share, the total dollar volume in Greenshift was all of $123,600. In contrast, trades in Intel amounted to about $1.7 billion.

The Pink Sheets (www.pinksheets.com) is operated by a privately owned company. To be listed on the Pink Sheets, a company just has to find a market maker willing to trade in the company's stock. Companies list on the Pink Sheets for various reasons. Small companies that do not wish to meet listing requirements are one type. Foreign companies often list on the Pink Sheets because they do not prepare their financial statements according to GAAP, a requirement for listing on U.S. stock exchanges. There are many companies that were formerly listed on bigger stock markets that were either delisted involuntarily or chose to "go dark" for various reasons, including, as we discussed in Chapter 1, the costs associated with Sarbox compliance.

All in all, the OTCBB and Pink Sheets can be pretty wild places to trade. Low stock prices allow for huge percentage returns on small stock price movements. Be advised, however, that attempts at manipulation and fraud are commonplace. Also, stocks on these markets are often thinly traded, meaning there is little volume. It is not unusual for a stock listed on either market to have no trades on a given day. Even two or three days in a row without a trade in a particular stock is not uncommon.

Questions

1. *After the close of the markets (4 p.m. Eastern time), go to finance.yahoo.com and find the stocks on the major exchanges that were the most active during the day. Now go to www.otcbb.com and find the most active stocks traded on the OTCBB for the same day. How many stocks on the OTCBB were more active than the most active stock on the NYSE? The NASDAQ?*
2. *What were the biggest percentage winners and losers on the OTCBB during the current day? How much did the stock price increase or decrease to account for this change?*

Visit us at www.mhhe.com/rwj

stock quote on wholesale club Costco, which is listed on the NASDAQ. Here is a portion of what we found:

Costco Wholesale Corporation (NasdaqGS: COST)

REAL-TIME **72.07** ↓ 0.55 (0.76%) 1:21PM EST

Last Trade:	**72.05**	Day's Range:	71.86 - 72.61
Trade Time:	1:07PM EST	52wk Range:	53.41 - 73.45
Change:	↓ 0.57 (0.78%)	Volume:	1,360,720
Prev Close:	72.62	Avg Vol (3m):	3,049,930
Open:	72.51	Market Cap:	31.45B
Bid:	72.05 x 800	P/E (ttm):	23.78
Ask:	72.06 x 2800	EPS (ttm):	3.03
1y Target Est:	73.25	Div & Yield:	0.82 (1.10%)

Most of this information is self-explanatory. Two prices are reported, one in real time ($72.07) and one with a 15-minute delay ($72.05). Availability of real-time prices for free is a relatively new development. The reported change is from the previous day's closing price. The opening price is the first trade of the day. We see the bid and ask prices of $72.05 and $72.06, respectively, along with the market "depth," which is the number of shares sought at the bid price and offered at the ask price. The "1y Target Est" is the average estimated stock price one year ahead based on estimates from security analysts who follow the stock.

Moving to the second column, we have the range of prices for this day, followed by the range over the previous 52 weeks. Volume is the number of shares traded today, followed by average daily volume over the last three months. Market cap is number of shares outstanding (from the most recent quarterly financial statements) multiplied by the current price per share. P/E is the PE ratio we discussed in Chapter 3. The earnings per share (EPS) used in the calculation is "ttm," meaning "trailing twelve months." Finally, we have the dividend on the stock, which is actually the most recent quarterly dividend multiplied by 4, and the dividend yield. Notice that the yield is just the reported dividend divided by the stock price: $.82/$72.05 = .011 = 1.1%.

Concept Questions

8.3a What is the difference between a securities broker and a securities dealer?

8.3b Which is bigger, the bid price or the ask price? Why?

8.3c How does NASDAQ differ from the NYSE?

8.4 Summary and Conclusions

This chapter has covered the basics of stocks and stock valuation:

1. The cash flows from owning a share of stock come in the form of future dividends. We saw that in certain special cases it is possible to calculate the present value of all the future dividends and thus come up with a value for the stock.

2. As the owner of shares of common stock in a corporation, you have various rights, including the right to vote to elect corporate directors. Voting in corporate elections can be either cumulative or straight. Most voting is actually done by proxy, and a proxy battle breaks out when competing sides try to gain enough votes to elect their candidates for the board.

3. In addition to common stock, some corporations have issued preferred stock. The name stems from the fact that preferred stockholders must be paid first, before common stockholders can receive anything. Preferred stock has a fixed dividend.

4. The two biggest stock markets in the United States are the NYSE and NASDAQ. We discussed the organization and operation of these two markets, and we saw how stock price information is reported in the financial press.

This chapter completes Part 3 of our book. By now, you should have a good grasp of what we mean by *present value*. You should also be familiar with how to calculate present values, loan payments, and so on. In Part 4, we cover capital budgeting decisions. As you will see, the techniques you learned in Chapters 5–8 form the basis for our approach to evaluating business investment decisions.

CONNECT TO FINANCE

If you are using *Connect™ Finance* in your course, get online to take a Practice Test, check out study tools, and find out where you need additional practice.

▼ Chapter 8 Stock Valuation			
8.1 Common Stock Valuation	eBook	Study	Practice
8.2 Some Features of Common and Preferred Stocks	eBook	Study	Practice NPPT 47–48
8.3 The Stock Markets	eBook	Study	Practice

Can you answer the following questions?

Section 8.1 A stock is selling for $11.90 a share given a market return of 14 percent and a capital gains yield of 5 percent. What was the amount of the last annual dividend that was paid? (LO 8-1)

Section 8.2 An 8 percent preferred stock sells for $54 a share. What is the rate of return? (LO 8-1)

Section 8.3 What kind of market is the NYSE? (LO 8-3)

Log on to find out!

Visit us at www.mhhe.com/rwj

CHAPTER REVIEW AND SELF-TEST PROBLEMS

8.1   Dividend Growth and Stock Valuation The Brigapenski Co. has just paid a cash dividend of $2 per share. Investors require a 16 percent return from investments such as this. If the dividend is expected to grow at a steady 8 percent per year, what is the current value of the stock? What will the stock be worth in five years?

8.2   More Dividend Growth and Stock Valuation In Self-Test Problem 8.1, what would the stock sell for today if the dividend was expected to grow at 20 percent per year for the next three years and then settle down to 8 percent per year indefinitely?

ANSWERS TO CHAPTER REVIEW AND SELF-TEST PROBLEMS

8.1   The last dividend, D_0, was \$2. The dividend is expected to grow steadily at 8 percent. The required return is 16 percent. Based on the dividend growth model, we can say that the current price is:

$$P_0 = D_1/(R - g) = D_0 \times (1 + g)/(R - g)$$
$$= \$2 \times 1.08/(.16 - .08)$$
$$= \$2.16/.08$$
$$= \$27$$

We could calculate the price in five years by calculating the dividend in five years and then using the growth model again. Alternatively, we could recognize that the stock price will increase by 8 percent per year and calculate the future price directly. We'll do both. First, the dividend in five years will be:

$$D_5 = D_0 \times (1 + g)^5$$
$$= \$2 \times 1.08^5$$
$$= \$2.9387$$

The price in five years would therefore be:

$$P_5 = D_5 \times (1 + g)/(R - g)$$
$$= \$2.9387 \times 1.08/.08$$
$$= \$3.1738/.08$$
$$= \$39.67$$

Once we understand the dividend model, however, it's easier to notice that:

$$P_5 = P_0 \times (1 + g)^5$$
$$= \$27 \times 1.08^5$$
$$= \$27 \times 1.4693$$
$$= \$39.67$$

Notice that both approaches yield the same price in five years.

8.2   In this scenario, we have supernormal growth for the next three years. We'll need to calculate the dividends during the rapid growth period and the stock price in three years. The dividends are:

$$D_1 = \$2.00 \times 1.20 = \$2.400$$
$$D_2 = \$2.40 \times 1.20 = \$2.880$$
$$D_3 = \$2.88 \times 1.20 = \$3.456$$

After three years, the growth rate falls to 8 percent indefinitely. The price at that time, P_3, is thus:

$$P_3 = D_3 \times (1 + g)/(R - g)$$
$$= \$3.456 \times 1.08/(.16 - .08)$$
$$= \$3.7325/.08$$
$$= \$46.656$$

Visit us at www.mhhe.com/rwj

To complete the calculation of the stock's present value, we have to determine the present value of the three dividends and the future price:

$$P_0 = \frac{D_1}{(1 + R)^1} + \frac{D_2}{(1 + R)^2} + \frac{D_3}{(1 + R)^3} + \frac{P_3}{(1 + R)^3}$$

$$= \frac{\$2.40}{1.16} + \frac{2.88}{1.16^2} + \frac{3.456}{1.16^3} + \frac{46.656}{1.16^3}$$

$$= \$2.07 + 2.14 + 2.21 + 29.89$$

$$= \$36.31$$

CONCEPTS REVIEW AND CRITICAL THINKING QUESTIONS

1. **Stock Valuation [LO1]** Why does the value of a share of stock depend on dividends?
2. **Stock Valuation [LO1]** A substantial percentage of the companies listed on the NYSE and NASDAQ don't pay dividends, but investors are nonetheless willing to buy shares in them. How is this possible given your answer to the previous question?
3. **Dividend Policy [LO1]** Referring to the previous questions, under what circumstances might a company choose not to pay dividends?
4. **Dividend Growth Model [LO1]** Under what two assumptions can we use the dividend growth model presented in the chapter to determine the value of a share of stock? Comment on the reasonableness of these assumptions.
5. **Common versus Preferred Stock [LO1]** Suppose a company has a preferred stock issue and a common stock issue. Both have just paid a $2 dividend. Which do you think will have a higher price, a share of the preferred or a share of the common?
6. **Dividend Growth Model [LO1]** Based on the dividend growth model, what are the two components of the total return on a share of stock? Which do you think is typically larger?
7. **Growth Rate [LO1]** In the context of the dividend growth model, is it true that the growth rate in dividends and the growth rate in the price of the stock are identical?
8. **Voting Rights [LO3]** When it comes to voting in elections, what are the differences between U.S. political democracy and U.S. corporate democracy?
9. **Corporate Ethics [LO3]** Is it unfair or unethical for corporations to create classes of stock with unequal voting rights?
10. **Voting Rights [LO3]** Some companies, such as Reader's Digest, have created classes of stock with no voting rights at all. Why would investors buy such stock?
11. **Stock Valuation [LO1]** Evaluate the following statement: Managers should not focus on the current stock value because doing so will lead to an overemphasis on short-term profits at the expense of long-term profits.
12. **Two-Stage Dividend Growth Model [LO1]** One of the assumptions of the two-stage growth model is that the dividends drop immediately from the high growth rate to the perpetual growth rate. What do you think about this assumption? What happens if this assumption is violated?
13. **Voting Rights [LO3]** In the chapter, we mentioned that many companies have been under pressure to declassify their boards of directors. Why would investors want a board to be declassified? What are the advantages of a classified board?
14. **Price Ratio Valuation [LO2]** What are the difficulties in using the PE ratio to value stock?

Visit us at www.mhhe.com/rwj

BASIC
(Questions 1–13)

1. **Stock Values [LO1]** The Jackson–Timberlake Wardrobe Co. just paid a dividend of $1.45 per share on its stock. The dividends are expected to grow at a constant rate of 6 percent per year indefinitely. If investors require a return of 11 percent on The Jackson–Timberlake Wardrobe Co. stock, what is the current price? What will the price be in three years? In 15 years?

2. **Stock Values [LO1]** The next dividend payment by Blue Cheese, Inc., will be $1.89 per share. The dividends are anticipated to maintain a growth rate of 5 percent forever. If the stock currently sells for $38 per share, what is the required return?

3. **Stock Values [LO1]** For the company in the previous problem, what is the dividend yield? What is the expected capital gains yield?

4. **Stock Values [LO1]** Staal Corporation will pay a $3.40 per share dividend next year. The company pledges to increase its dividend by 4.5 percent per year indefinitely. If you require a return of 11 percent on your investment, how much will you pay for the company's stock today?

5. **Stock Valuation [LO1]** Keenan Co. is expected to maintain a constant 4.8 percent growth rate in its dividends indefinitely. If the company has a dividend yield of 6.9 percent, what is the required return on the company's stock?

6. **Stock Valuation [LO1]** Suppose you know that a company's stock currently sells for $59 per share and the required return on the stock is 11 percent. You also know that the total return on the stock is evenly divided between a capital gains yield and a dividend yield. If it's the company's policy to always maintain a constant growth rate in its dividends, what is the current dividend per share?

7. **Stock Valuation [LO1]** Apocalyptica Corp. pays a constant $8.50 dividend on its stock. The company will maintain this dividend for the next 11 years and will then cease paying dividends forever. If the required return on this stock is 12 percent, what is the current share price?

8. **Valuing Preferred Stock [LO1]** Lane, Inc., has an issue of preferred stock outstanding that pays a $4.75 dividend every year in perpetuity. If this issue currently sells for $93 per share, what is the required return?

9. **Stock Valuation and Required Return [LO1]** Red, Inc., Yellow Corp., and Blue Company each will pay a dividend of $2.65 next year. The growth rate in dividends for all three companies is 5 percent. The required return for each company's stock is 8 percent, 11 percent, and 14 percent, respectively. What is the stock price for each company? What do you conclude about the relationship between the required return and the stock price?

10. **Voting Rights [LO3]** After successfully completing your corporate finance class, you feel the next challenge ahead is to serve on the board of directors of Schenkel Enterprises. Unfortunately, you will be the only person voting for you. If Schenkel has 400,000 shares outstanding, and the stock currently sells for $48, how much will it cost you to buy a seat if the company uses straight voting?

11. **Voting Rights [LO3]** In the previous problem, assume that Schenkel uses cumulative voting, and there are four seats in the current election. How much will it cost you to buy a seat now?

12. **Stock Valuation and PE [LO2]** The Sleeping Flower Co. has earnings of $1.75 per share. The benchmark PE for the company is 18. What stock price would you consider appropriate? What if the benchmark PE were 21?

Visit us at www.mhhe.com/rwj

13. **Stock Valuation and PS [LO2]** TwitterMe, Inc., is a new company and currently
has negative earnings. The company's sales are $1.2 million and there are 130,000
shares outstanding. If the benchmark price–sales ratio is 5.2, what is your estimate
of an appropriate stock price? What if the price–sales ratio were 4.6?

INTERMEDIATE
(Questions 14–31)

14. **Stock Valuation [LO1]** Great Pumpkin Farms just paid a dividend of $3.20 on its
stock. The growth rate in dividends is expected to be a constant 5 percent per year
indefinitely. Investors require a return of 15 percent for the first three years, a return
of 13 percent for the next three years, and a return of 11 percent thereafter. What is
the current share price?

15. **Nonconstant Growth [LO1]** Metallica Bearings, Inc., is a young start-up
company. No dividends will be paid on the stock over the next nine years because
the firm needs to plow back its earnings to fuel growth. The company will pay
a $12 per share dividend in 10 years and will increase the dividend by 5 percent
per year thereafter. If the required return on this stock is 13.5 percent, what is the
current share price?

16. **Nonconstant Dividends [LO1]** Maloney, Inc., has an odd dividend policy. The
company has just paid a dividend of $3 per share and has announced that it will
increase the dividend by $5 per share for each of the next five years, and then never
pay another dividend. If you require a return of 11 percent on the company's stock,
how much will you pay for a share today?

17. **Nonconstant Dividends [LO1]** Lohn Corporation is expected to pay the
following dividends over the next four years: $12, $8, $7, and $2.50. Afterward,
the company pledges to maintain a constant 5 percent growth rate in dividends
forever. If the required return on the stock is 12 percent, what is the current
share price?

18. **Supernormal Growth [LO1]** Janicex Co. is growing quickly. Dividends are
expected to grow at a rate of 24 percent for the next three years, with the growth
rate falling off to a constant 6 percent thereafter. If the required return is 11 percent,
and the company just paid a dividend of $1.90, what is the current share price?

19. **Supernormal Growth [LO1]** Frey Corp. is experiencing rapid growth. Dividends
are expected to grow at 30 percent per year during the next three years, 20 percent
over the following year, and then 6 percent per year indefinitely. The required return
on this stock is 10 percent, and the stock currently sells for $76 per share. What is
the projected dividend for the coming year?

20. **Negative Growth [LO1]** Antiques R Us is a mature manufacturing firm. The company just paid a dividend of $9.40, but management expects to reduce the payout by
4 percent per year indefinitely. If you require a return of 10 percent on this stock,
what will you pay for a share today?

21. **Finding the Dividend [LO1]** Feeback Corporation stock currently sells for
$64 per share. The market requires a return of 11 percent on the firm's stock. If the
company maintains a constant 4.5 percent growth rate in dividends, what was the
most recent dividend per share paid on the stock?

22. **Valuing Preferred Stock [LO1]** E-Eyes.com Bank just issued some new preferred
stock. The issue will pay an annual dividend of $20 in perpetuity, beginning 20
years from now. If the market requires a return of 5.8 percent on this investment,
how much does a share of preferred stock cost today?

23. **Using Stock Quotes [LO3]** You have found the following stock quote for RJW
Enterprises, Inc., in the financial pages of today's newspaper. What was the closing
price for this stock that appeared in *yesterday's* paper? If the company currently has

Visit us at www.mhhe.com/rwj

25 million shares of stock outstanding, what was net income for the most recent four quarters?

| 52-WEEK | | | YLD | | VOL | | NET |
HI	LO	STOCK (DIV)	%	PE	100s	CLOSE	CHG
72.18	53.17	RJW 1.28	2.1	21	17652	??	−.23

24. **Two-Stage Dividend Growth Model [LO1]** Thirsty Cactus Corp. just paid a dividend of $1.30 per share. The dividends are expected to grow at 23 percent for the next eight years and then level off to a growth rate of 6 percent indefinitely. If the required return is 12 percent, what is the price of the stock today?

25. **Two-Stage Dividend Growth Model [LO1]** Chartreuse County Choppers, Inc., is experiencing rapid growth. The company expects dividends to grow at 18 percent per year for the next 11 years before leveling off at 5 percent into perpetuity. The required return on the company's stock is 12 percent. If the dividend per share just paid was $1.94, what is the stock price?

26. **Stock Valuation and PE [LO2]** Sully Corp. currently has an EPS of $2.35, and the benchmark PE for the company is 21. Earnings are expected to grow at 7 percent per year.
    a. What is your estimate of the current stock price?
    b. What is the target stock price in one year?
    c. Assuming the company pays no dividends, what is the implied return on the company's stock over the next year? What does this tell you about the implicit stock return using PE valuation?

27. **Stock Valuation and PE [LO2]** You have found the following historical information for the Daniela Company:

	Year 1	Year 2	Year 3	Year 4
Stock price	$49.50	$58.12	$67.34	$60.25
EPS	2.40	2.58	2.71	2.85

Earnings are expected to grow at 11 percent for the next year. Using the company's historical average PE as a benchmark, what is the target stock price in one year?

28. **Stock Valuation and PE [LO2]** In the previous problem, we assumed that the stock had a single stock price for the year. However, if you look at stock prices over any year, you will find a high and low stock price for the year. Instead of a single benchmark PE ratio, we now have a high and low PE ratio for each year. We can use these ratios to calculate a high and a low stock price for the next year. Suppose we have the following information on a particular company:

	Year 1	Year 2	Year 3	Year 4
High price	$97.90	$121.50	$130.90	$147.53
Low price	72.73	88.84	69.52	116.05
EPS	7.18	8.93	10.01	11.40

Earnings are projected to grow at 6 percent over the next year. What are your high and low target stock prices over the next year?

Visit us at www.mhhe.com/rwj

29. **Stock Valuation and PE [LO2]** Davis, Inc., currently has an EPS of $2 and an earnings growth rate of 8 percent. If the benchmark PE ratio is 22, what is the target share price five years from now?

30. **PE and Terminal Stock Price [LO2]** In practice, a common way to value a share of stock when a company pays dividends is to value the dividends over the next five years or so, then find the "terminal" stock price using a benchmark PE ratio. Suppose a company just paid a dividend of $1.15. The dividends are expected to grow at 20 percent over the next five years. In five years, the estimated payout ratio is 40 percent and the benchmark PE ratio is 21. What is the target stock price in five years? What is the stock price today assuming a required return of 12 percent on this stock?

31. **Stock Valuation and PE [LO2]** Plush Pilots, Inc., has balance sheet equity of $6.4 million. At the same time, the income statement shows net income of $950,000. The company paid dividends of $485,000 and has 190,000 shares of stock outstanding. If the benchmark PE ratio is 16, what is the target stock price in one year?

32. **Capital Gains versus Income [LO1]** Consider four different stocks, all of which have a required return of 17 percent and a most recent dividend of $4.50 per share. Stocks W, X, and Y are expected to maintain constant growth rates in dividends for the foreseeable future of 10 percent, 0 percent, and −5 percent per year, respectively. Stock Z is a growth stock that will increase its dividend by 20 percent for the next two years and then maintain a constant 12 percent growth rate thereafter. What is the dividend yield for each of these four stocks? What is the expected capital gains yield? Discuss the relationship among the various returns that you find for each of these stocks.

CHALLENGE
(Questions 32–38)

33. **Stock Valuation [LO1]** Most corporations pay quarterly dividends on their common stock rather than annual dividends. Barring any unusual circumstances during the year, the board raises, lowers, or maintains the current dividend once a year and then pays this dividend out in equal quarterly installments to its shareholders.

    a. Suppose a company currently pays an annual dividend of $3.60 on its common stock in a single annual installment, and management plans on raising this dividend by 6 percent per year indefinitely. If the required return on this stock is 12 percent, what is the current share price?

    b. Now suppose the company in (a) actually pays its annual dividend in equal quarterly installments; thus, the company has just paid a dividend of $.90 per share, as it has for the previous three quarters. What is your value for the current share price now? (*Hint:* Find the equivalent annual end-of-year dividend for each year.) Comment on whether you think this model of stock valuation is appropriate.

34. **Nonconstant Growth [LO1]** Storico Co. just paid a dividend of $2.25 per share. The company will increase its dividend by 20 percent next year and will then reduce its dividend growth rate by 5 percentage points per year until it reaches the industry average of 5 percent dividend growth, after which the company will keep a constant growth rate forever. If the required return on Storico stock is 12 percent, what will a share of stock sell for today?

35. **Nonconstant Growth [LO1]** This one's a little harder. Suppose the current share price for the firm in the previous problem is $39.52 and all the dividend information remains the same. What required return must investors be demanding on Storico stock? (*Hint:* Set up the valuation formula with all the relevant cash flows, and use trial and error to find the unknown rate of return.)

36. **Constant Dividend Growth Model [LO1]** Assume a stock has dividends that grow at a constant rate forever. If you value the stock using the constant dividend

Visit us at www.mhhe.com/rwj

growth model, how many years worth of dividends constitute one-half of the stock's current price?

37. **Two-Stage Dividend Growth [LO1]** Regarding the two-stage dividend growth model in the chapter, show that the price of a share of stock today can be written as follows:

$$P_0 = \frac{D_0 \times (1 + g_1)}{R - g_1} \times \left[1 - \left(\frac{1 + g_1}{1 + R} \right)^t \right] + \left(\frac{1 + g_1}{1 + R} \right)^t \times \frac{D_0 \times (1 + g_2)}{R - g_2}$$

Can you provide an intuitive interpretation of this expression?

38. **Two-Stage Dividend Growth [LO1]** The chapter shows that in the two-stage dividend growth model, the growth rate in the first stage, g_1, can be greater than or less than the discount rate, R. Can they be exactly equal? (*Hint:* Yes, but what does the expression for the value of the stock look like?)

MINICASE

Stock Valuation at Ragan, Inc.

Ragan, Inc., was founded nine years ago by brother and sister Carrington and Genevieve Ragan. The company manufactures and installs commercial heating, ventilation, and cooling (HVAC) units. Ragan, Inc., has experienced rapid growth because of a proprietary technology that increases the energy efficiency of its units. The company is equally owned by Carrington and Genevieve. The original partnership agreement between the siblings gave each 50,000 shares of stock. In the event either wished to sell stock, the shares first had to be offered to the other at a discounted price.

Although neither sibling wants to sell, they have decided they should value their holdings in the company. To get

started, they have gathered the information about their main competitors in the table below.

Expert HVAC Corporation's negative earnings per share were the result of an accounting write-off last year. Without the write-off, earnings per share for the company would have been $1.10. The ROE for Expert HVAC is based on net income excluding the write-off.

Last year, Ragan, Inc., had an EPS of $3.75 and paid a dividend to Carrington and Genevieve of $48,000 each. The company also had a return on equity of 17 percent. The siblings believe that 14 percent is an appropriate required return for the company.

Ragan, Inc., Competitors					
	EPS	DPS	Stock Price	ROE	R
Arctic Cooling, Inc.	$1.30	$.15	$25.34	9.00%	10.00%
National Heating & Cooling	1.95	.22	29.85	11.00	13.00
Expert HVAC Corp.	−.37	.12	22.13	10.00	12.00
Industry Average	$ .96	$.16	$25.77	10.00%	11.67%

QUESTIONS

1. Assuming the company continues its current growth rate, what is the value per share of the company's stock?

2. To verify their calculations, Carrington and Genevieve have hired Josh Schlessman as a consultant. Josh was previously an equity analyst and covered the HVAC industry. Josh has examined the company's financial statements, as well as examining its competitors. Although Ragan, Inc., currently has a technological advantage, his research indicates that other companies are investigating methods to improve efficiency. Given this, Josh believes

that the company's technological advantage will last only for the next five years. After that period, the company's growth will likely slow to the industry growth average. Additionally, Josh believes that the required return used by the company is too high. He believes the industry average required return is more appropriate. Under this growth rate assumption, what is your estimate of the stock price?

3. What is the industry average price–earnings ratio? What is the price–earnings ratio for Ragan, Inc.? Is this the relationship you would expect between the two ratios? Why?

Visit us at www.mhhe.com/rwj

4. Carrington and Genevieve are unsure how to interpret the price–earnings ratio. After some head scratching, they've come up with the following expression for the price–earnings ratio:

$$\frac{P_0}{E_1} = \frac{1 - b}{R - (\text{ROE} \times b)}$$

Beginning with the constant dividend growth model, verify this result. What does this expression imply about the relationship between the dividend payout ratio, the required return on the stock, and the company's ROE?

5. Assume the company's growth rate slows to the industry average in five years. What future return on equity does this imply, assuming a constant payout ratio?

6. After discussing the stock value with Josh, Carrington and Genevieve agree that they would like to increase the value of the company stock. Like many small business owners, they want to retain control of the company, but they do not want to sell stock to outside investors. They also feel that the company's debt is at a manageable level and do not want to borrow more money. How can they increase the price of the stock? Are there any conditions under which this strategy would not increase the stock price?

Visit us at www.mhhe.com/rwj

9

NET PRESENT VALUE AND OTHER INVESTMENT CRITERIA

WITH THE SUCCESS OF THE POPULAR iPod, iPhone, and iPad, Apple's sales continued to surge in 2010 and were expected to climb even higher. Of course, with greater sales, greater production capacity is needed. In late 2010, Foxconn, the manufacturer of many Apple products, was in the midst of planning a new $10 billion plant in China that would become the new "iPod city." While $10 billion is a large investment, Foxconn was not alone. About the same time, Taiwan Semiconductor Manufacturing announced a new plant in Taiwan that would cost about $9 billion and employ 8,000 people. And Intel announced plans to invest $8 billion for a new plant in Oregon in addition to upgrades of four existing plants.

Foxconn's new plant is an example of a capital budgeting decision. Decisions such as this one, with a price tag of over $10 billion, are obviously major undertakings, and the risks and rewards must be carefully weighed. In this chapter, we discuss the basic tools used in making such decisions.

In Chapter 1, we saw that increasing the value of the stock in a company is the goal of financial management. Thus, what we need to know is how to tell whether a particular investment will achieve that or not. This chapter considers a variety of techniques that are used in practice for this purpose. More important, it shows how many of these techniques can be misleading, and it explains why the net present value approach is the right one.

LEARNING OBJECTIVES

After studying this chapter, you should understand:

LO1 The reasons why the net present value criterion is the best way to evaluate proposed investments.

LO2 The payback rule and some of its shortcomings.

LO3 The discounted payback rule and some of its shortcomings.

LO4 Accounting rates of return and some of the problems with them.

LO5 The internal rate of return criterion and its strengths and weaknesses.

LO6 The modified internal rate of return.

LO7 The profitability index and its relation to net present value.

In Chapter 1, we identified the three key areas of concern to the financial manager. The first of these involved the question: What fixed assets should we buy? We called this the *capital budgeting decision*. In this chapter, we begin to deal with the issues that arise in answering this question.

The process of allocating or budgeting capital is usually more involved than just deciding whether to buy a particular fixed asset. We frequently face broader issues like whether we should launch a new product or enter a new market. Decisions such as these determine the nature of a firm's operations and products for years to come, primarily because fixed asset investments are generally long-lived and not easily reversed once they are made.

The most fundamental decision a business must make concerns its product line. What services will we offer or what will we sell? In what markets will we compete? What new products will we introduce? The answer to any of these questions will require that the firm commit its scarce and valuable capital to certain types of assets. As a result, all of these strategic issues fall under the general heading of capital budgeting. The process of capital budgeting could thus be given a more descriptive (not to mention impressive) name: *strategic asset allocation.*

For the reasons we have discussed, the capital budgeting question is probably the most important issue in corporate finance. How a firm chooses to finance its operations (the capital structure question) and how a firm manages its short-term operating activities (the working capital question) are certainly issues of concern, but the fixed assets define the business of the firm. Airlines, for example, are airlines because they operate airplanes, regardless of how they finance them.

Any firm possesses a huge number of possible investments. Each possible investment is an option available to the firm. Some options are valuable and some are not. The essence of successful financial management, of course, is learning to identify which are which. With this in mind, our goal in this chapter is to introduce you to the techniques used to analyze potential business ventures to decide which are worth undertaking.

We present and compare a number of different procedures used in practice. Our primary goal is to acquaint you with the advantages and disadvantages of the various approaches. As we will see, the most important concept in this area is the idea of net present value. We consider this next.

Net Present Value

In Chapter 1, we argued that the goal of financial management is to create value for the stockholders. The financial manager must thus examine a potential investment in light of its likely effect on the price of the firm's shares. In this section, we describe a widely used procedure for doing this: the net present value approach.

THE BASIC IDEA

An investment is worth undertaking if it creates value for its owners. In the most general sense, we create value by identifying an investment worth more in the marketplace than it costs us to acquire. How can something be worth more than it costs? It's a case of the whole being worth more than the cost of the parts.

For example, suppose you buy a run-down house for $25,000 and spend another $25,000 on painters, plumbers, and so on to get it fixed up. Your total investment is $50,000. When the work is completed, you place the house back on the market and find that it's worth $60,000. The market value ($60,000) exceeds the cost ($50,000) by $10,000. What you have done here is to act as a manager and bring together some fixed assets (a house), some labor (plumbers, carpenters, and others), and some materials (carpeting, paint, and so on). The net result is that you have created $10,000 in value. Put another way, this $10,000 is the *value added* by management.

With our house example, it turned out *after the fact* that $10,000 in value had been created. Things thus worked out nicely. The real challenge, of course, would have been to somehow identify *ahead of time* whether investing the necessary $50,000 was a good idea in the first place. This is what capital budgeting is all about—namely, trying to determine whether a proposed investment or project will be worth more, once it is in place, than it costs.

For reasons that will be obvious in a moment, the difference between an investment's market value and its cost is called the **net present value** of the investment, abbreviated **NPV**. In other words, net present value is a measure of how much value is created or added today by

net present value (NPV)
The difference between an investment's market value and its cost.

267

undertaking an investment. Given our goal of creating value for the stockholders, the capital budgeting process can be viewed as a search for investments with positive net present values.

With our run-down house, you can probably imagine how we would go about making the capital budgeting decision. We would first look at what comparable, fixed-up properties were selling for in the market. We would then get estimates of the cost of buying a particular property and bringing it to market. At this point, we would have an estimated total cost and an estimated market value. If the difference was positive, then this investment would be worth undertaking because it would have a positive estimated net present value. There is risk, of course, because there is no guarantee that our estimates will turn out to be correct.

As our example illustrates, investment decisions are greatly simplified when there is a market for assets similar to the investment we are considering. Capital budgeting becomes much more difficult when we cannot observe the market price for at least roughly comparable investments. The reason is that we then face the problem of estimating the value of an investment using only indirect market information. Unfortunately, this is precisely the situation the financial manager usually encounters. We examine this issue next.

ESTIMATING NET PRESENT VALUE

Imagine we are thinking of starting a business to produce and sell a new product—say, organic fertilizer. We can estimate the start-up costs with reasonable accuracy because we know what we will need to buy to begin production. Would this be a good investment? Based on our discussion, you know that the answer depends on whether the value of the new business exceeds the cost of starting it. In other words, does this investment have a positive NPV?

This problem is much more difficult than our "fixer upper" house example because entire fertilizer companies are not routinely bought and sold in the marketplace, so it is essentially impossible to observe the market value of a similar investment. As a result, we must somehow estimate this value by other means.

Based on our work in Chapters 5 and 6, you may be able to guess how we will go about estimating the value of our fertilizer business. We will first try to estimate the future cash flows we expect the new business to produce. We will then apply our basic discounted cash flow procedure to estimate the present value of those cash flows. Once we have this estimate, we will then estimate NPV as the difference between the present value of the future cash flows and the cost of the investment. As we mentioned in Chapter 5, this procedure is often called **discounted cash flow (DCF) valuation**.

To see how we might go about estimating NPV, suppose we believe the cash revenues from our fertilizer business will be $20,000 per year, assuming everything goes as expected. Cash costs (including taxes) will be $14,000 per year. We will wind down the business in eight years. The plant, property, and equipment will be worth $2,000 as salvage at that time. The project costs $30,000 to launch. We use a 15 percent discount rate on new projects such as this one. Is this a good investment? If there are 1,000 shares of stock outstanding, what will be the effect on the price per share of taking this investment?

From a purely mechanical perspective, we need to calculate the present value of the future cash flows at 15 percent. The net cash inflow will be $20,000 cash income less $14,000 in costs per year for eight years. These cash flows are illustrated in Figure 9.1. As Figure 9.1 suggests, we effectively have an eight-year annuity of $20,000 - 14,000 = $6,000 per year, along with a single lump sum inflow of $2,000 in eight years. Calculating the present value of the future cash flows thus comes down to the same type of problem we considered in Chapter 6. The total present value is:

$$\text{Present value} = \$6,000 \times [1 - (1/1.15^8)]/.15 + (2,000/1.15^8)$$
$$= (\$6,000 \times 4.4873) + (2,000/3.0590)$$
$$= \$26,924 + 654$$
$$= \$27,578$$

discounted cash flow (DCF) valuation
The process of valuing an investment by discounting its future cash flows.

FIGURE 9.1

Project Cash Flows ($000)

Time (years)	0	1	2	3	4	5	6	7	8
Initial cost	−$30								
Inflows		$ 20	$ 20	$ 20	$ 20	$ 20	$ 20	$ 20	$ 20
Outflows		−14	−14	−14	−14	−14	−14	−14	−14
Net inflow		$ 6	$ 6	$ 6	$ 6	$ 6	$ 6	$ 6	$ 6
Salvage									2
Net cash flow	−$30	$ 6	$ 6	$ 6	$ 6	$ 6	$ 6	$ 6	$ 8

When we compare this to the $30,000 estimated cost, we see that the NPV is:

$$\text{NPV} = -\$30,000 + 27,578 = -\$2,422$$

Therefore, this is *not* a good investment. Based on our estimates, taking it would *decrease* the total value of the stock by $2,422. With 1,000 shares outstanding, our best estimate of the impact of taking this project is a loss of value of $2,422/1,000 = $2.42 per share.

Our fertilizer example illustrates how NPV estimates can be used to determine whether an investment is desirable. From our example, notice that if the NPV is negative, the effect on share value will be unfavorable. If the NPV were positive, the effect would be favorable. As a consequence, all we need to know about a particular proposal for the purpose of making an accept–reject decision is whether the NPV is positive or negative.

Given that the goal of financial management is to increase share value, our discussion in this section leads us to the *net present value rule:*

> **An investment should be accepted if the net present value is positive and rejected if it is negative.**

In the unlikely event that the net present value turned out to be exactly zero, we would be indifferent between taking the investment and not taking it.

Two comments about our example are in order. First and foremost, it is not the rather mechanical process of discounting the cash flows that is important. Once we have the cash flows and the appropriate discount rate, the required calculations are fairly straightforward. The task of coming up with the cash flows and the discount rate is much more challenging. We will have much more to say about this in the next several chapters. For the remainder of this chapter, we take it as a given that we have estimates of the cash revenues and costs and, where needed, an appropriate discount rate.

The second thing to keep in mind about our example is that the −$2,422 NPV is an estimate. Like any estimate, it can be high or low. The only way to find out the true NPV would be to place the investment up for sale and see what we could get for it. We generally won't be doing this, so it is important that our estimates be reliable. Once again, we will say more about this later. For the rest of this chapter, we will assume the estimates are accurate.

Using the NPV Rule

EXAMPLE 9.1

Suppose we are asked to decide whether a new consumer product should be launched. Based on projected sales and costs, we expect that the cash flows over the five-year life of the project will be $2,000 in the first two years, $4,000 in the next two, and $5,000 in the last year. It will cost about $10,000 to begin production. We use a 10 percent discount rate to evaluate new products. What should we do here?

(continued)

Given the cash flows and discount rate, we can calculate the total value of the product by discounting the cash flows back to the present:

$$\text{Present value} = (\$2{,}000/1.1) + (2{,}000/1.1^2) + (4{,}000/1.1^3)$$
$$+ (4{,}000/1.1^4) + (5{,}000/1.1^5)$$
$$= \$1{,}818 + 1{,}653 + 3{,}005 + 2{,}732 + 3{,}105$$
$$= \$12{,}313$$

The present value of the expected cash flows is $12,313, but the cost of getting those cash flows is only $10,000, so the NPV is $12,313 − 10,000 = $2,313. This is positive; so, based on the net present value rule, we should take on the project.

As we have seen in this section, estimating NPV is one way of assessing the profitability of a proposed investment. It is certainly not the only way profitability is assessed, and we now turn to some alternatives. As we will see, when compared to NPV, each of the alternative ways of assessing profitability that we will examine is flawed in some key way; so NPV is the preferred approach in principle, if not always in practice.

SPREADSHEET STRATEGIES

Calculating NPVs with a Spreadsheet

Spreadsheets are commonly used to calculate NPVs. Examining the use of spreadsheets in this context also allows us to issue an important warning. Let's rework Example 9.1:

You can get a freeware NPV calculator at www.wheatworks.com.

	A	B	C	D	E	F	G	H
1								
2		Using a spreadsheet to calculate net present values						
3								
4	From Example 9.1, the project's cost is $10,000. The cash flows are $2,000 per year for the first							
5	two years, $4,000 per year for the next two, and $5,000 in the last year. The discount rate is							
6	10 percent; what's the NPV?							
7								
8		Year	Cash Flow					
9		0	-$10,000		Discount rate =		10%	
10		1	2,000					
11		2	2,000		NPV =	$2,102.72	(wrong answer)	
12		3	4,000		NPV =	$2,312.99	(right answer)	
13		4	4,000					
14		5	5,000					
15								
16	The formula entered in cell F11 is =NPV(F9, C9:C14). This gives the wrong answer because the							
17	NPV function actually calculates present values, not net present values.							
18								
19	The formula entered in cell F12 is =NPV(F9, C10:C14) + C9. This gives the right answer because the							
20	NPV function is used to calculate the present value of the cash flows and then the initial cost is							
21	subtracted to calculate the answer. Notice that we added cell C9 because it is already negative.							

In our spreadsheet example, notice that we have provided two answers. By comparing the answers to that found in Example 9.1, we see that the first answer is wrong even though we used the spreadsheet's NPV formula. What happened is that the "NPV" function in our spreadsheet is actually a PV function; unfortunately, one of the original spreadsheet programs many years ago got the definition wrong, and subsequent spreadsheets have copied it! Our second answer shows how to use the formula properly.

The example here illustrates the danger of blindly using calculators or computers without understanding what is going on; we shudder to think of how many capital budgeting decisions in the real world are based on incorrect use of this particular function. We will see another example of something that can go wrong with a spreadsheet later in the chapter.

Concept Questions

9.1a What is the net present value rule?
9.1b If we say an investment has an NPV of $1,000, what exactly do we mean?

The Payback Rule

9.2

It is common in practice to talk of the payback on a proposed investment. Loosely, the *payback* is the length of time it takes to recover our initial investment or "get our bait back." Because this idea is widely understood and used, we will examine it in some detail.

DEFINING THE RULE

We can illustrate how to calculate a payback with an example. Figure 9.2 shows the cash flows from a proposed investment. How many years do we have to wait until the accumulated cash flows from this investment equal or exceed the cost of the investment? As Figure 9.2 indicates, the initial investment is $50,000. After the first year, the firm has recovered $30,000, leaving $20,000. The cash flow in the second year is exactly $20,000, so this investment "pays for itself" in exactly two years. Put another way, the **payback period** is two years. If we require a payback of, say, three years or less, then this investment is acceptable. This illustrates the *payback period rule:*

payback period
The amount of time required for an investment to generate cash flows sufficient to recover its initial cost.

> **Based on the payback rule, an investment is acceptable if its calculated payback period is less than some prespecified number of years.**

In our example, the payback works out to be exactly two years. This won't usually happen, of course. When the numbers don't work out exactly, it is customary to work with fractional years. For example, suppose the initial investment is $60,000, and the cash flows are $20,000 in the first year and $90,000 in the second. The cash flows over the first two years are $110,000, so the project obviously pays back sometime in the second year. After the first year, the project has paid back $20,000, leaving $40,000 to be recovered. To figure out the fractional year, note that this $40,000 is $40,000/$90,000 = 4/9 of the second year's cash flow. Assuming that the $90,000 cash flow is received uniformly throughout the year, the payback would be $1\frac{4}{9}$ years.

Calculating Payback   **EXAMPLE 9.2**

Here are the projected cash flows from a proposed investment:

Year	Cash Flow
1	$100
2	200
3	500

This project costs $500. What is the payback period for this investment?

The initial cost is $500. After the first two years, the cash flows total $300. After the third year, the total cash flow is $800, so the project pays back sometime between the end of Year 2 and the end of Year 3. Because the accumulated cash flows for the first two years are $300, we need to recover $200 in the third year. The third-year cash flow is $500, so we will have to wait $200/$500 = .4 year to do this. The payback period is thus 2.4 years, or about two years and five months.

FIGURE 9.2

Net Project Cash Flows

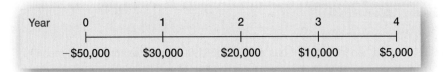

TABLE 9.1

Expected Cash Flows for Projects A through E

Year	A	B	C	D	E
0	−$100	−$200	−$200	−$200	−$ 50
1	30	40	40	100	100
2	40	20	20	100	−50,000,000
3	50	10	10	−200	
4	60		130	200	

Now that we know how to calculate the payback period on an investment, using the payback period rule for making decisions is straightforward. A particular cutoff time is selected—say, two years—and all investment projects that have payback periods of two years or less are accepted, whereas any that pay off in more than two years are rejected.

Table 9.1 illustrates cash flows for five different projects. The figures shown as the Year 0 cash flows are the costs of the investments. We examine these to indicate some peculiarities that can, in principle, arise with payback periods.

The payback for the first project, A, is easily calculated. The sum of the cash flows for the first two years is $70, leaving us with $100 − 70 = $30 to go. Because the cash flow in the third year is $50, the payback occurs sometime in that year. When we compare the $30 we need to the $50 that will be coming in, we get $30/50 = .6; so, payback will occur 60 percent of the way into the year. The payback period is thus 2.6 years.

Project B's payback is also easy to calculate: It *never* pays back because the cash flows never total up to the original investment. Project C has a payback of exactly four years because it supplies the $130 that B is missing in Year 4. Project D is a little strange. Because of the negative cash flow in Year 3, you can easily verify that it has two different payback periods, two years and four years. Which of these is correct? Both of them; the way the payback period is calculated doesn't guarantee a single answer. Finally, Project E is obviously unrealistic, but it does pay back in six months, thereby illustrating the point that a rapid payback does not guarantee a good investment.

ANALYZING THE RULE

When compared to the NPV rule, the payback period rule has some rather severe shortcomings. First, we calculate the payback period by simply adding up the future cash flows. There is no discounting involved, so the time value of money is completely ignored. The payback rule also fails to consider any risk differences. The payback would be calculated the same way for both very risky and very safe projects.

Perhaps the biggest problem with the payback period rule is coming up with the right cutoff period: We don't really have an objective basis for choosing a particular number. Put another way, there is no economic rationale for looking at payback in the first place, so we have no guide for how to pick the cutoff. As a result, we end up using a number that is arbitrarily chosen.

Year	Long	Short
0	−$250	−$250
1	100	100
2	100	200
3	100	0
4	100	0

TABLE 9.2

Investment Projected Cash Flows

Suppose we have somehow decided on an appropriate payback period of two years or less. As we have seen, the payback period rule ignores the time value of money for the first two years. More seriously, cash flows after the second year are ignored entirely. To see this, consider the two investments, Long and Short, in Table 9.2. Both projects cost $250. Based on our discussion, the payback on Long is $2 + (\$50/100) = 2.5$ years, and the payback on Short is $1 + (\$150/200) = 1.75$ years. With a cutoff of two years, Short is acceptable and Long is not.

Is the payback period rule guiding us to the right decisions? Maybe not. Suppose we require a 15 percent return on this type of investment. We can calculate the NPV for these two investments as:

$$\text{NPV(Short)} = -\$250 + (100/1.15) + (200/1.15^2) = -\$11.81$$
$$\text{NPV(Long)} = -\$250 + (100 \times \{[1 - (1/1.15^4)]/.15\}) = \$35.50$$

Now we have a problem. The NPV of the shorter-term investment is actually negative, meaning that taking it diminishes the value of the shareholders' equity. The opposite is true for the longer-term investment—it increases share value.

Our example illustrates two primary shortcomings of the payback period rule. First, by ignoring time value, we may be led to take investments (like Short) that actually are worth less than they cost. Second, by ignoring cash flows beyond the cutoff, we may be led to reject profitable long-term investments (like Long). More generally, using a payback period rule will tend to bias us toward shorter-term investments.

REDEEMING QUALITIES OF THE RULE

Despite its shortcomings, the payback period rule is often used by large and sophisticated companies when they are making relatively minor decisions. There are several reasons for this. The primary reason is that many decisions simply do not warrant detailed analysis because the cost of the analysis would exceed the possible loss from a mistake. As a practical matter, it can be said that an investment that pays back rapidly and has benefits extending beyond the cutoff period probably has a positive NPV.

Small investment decisions are made by the hundreds every day in large organizations. Moreover, they are made at all levels. As a result, it would not be uncommon for a corporation to require, for example, a two-year payback on all investments of less than $10,000. Investments larger than this would be subjected to greater scrutiny. The requirement of a two-year payback is not perfect for reasons we have seen, but it does exercise some control over expenditures and thus limits possible losses.

In addition to its simplicity, the payback rule has two other positive features. First, because it is biased toward short-term projects, it is biased toward liquidity. In other words, a payback rule tends to favor investments that free up cash for other uses quickly. This could be important for a small business; it would be less so for a large corporation. Second, the cash flows that are expected to occur later in a project's life are probably more uncertain. Arguably, a payback period rule adjusts for the extra riskiness of later cash flows, but it does so in a rather draconian fashion—by ignoring them altogether.

We should note here that some of the apparent simplicity of the payback rule is an illusion. The reason is that we still must come up with the cash flows first, and, as we discussed earlier, this is not at all easy to do. Thus, it would probably be more accurate to say that the *concept* of a payback period is both intuitive and easy to understand.

SUMMARY OF THE RULE

To summarize, the payback period is a kind of "break-even" measure. Because time value is ignored, you can think of the payback period as the length of time it takes to break even in an accounting sense, but not in an economic sense. The biggest drawback to the payback period rule is that it doesn't ask the right question. The relevant issue is the impact an investment will have on the value of the stock, not how long it takes to recover the initial investment.

Nevertheless, because it is so simple, companies often use it as a screen for dealing with the myriad minor investment decisions they have to make. There is certainly nothing wrong with this practice. As with any simple rule of thumb, there will be some errors in using it; but it wouldn't have survived all this time if it weren't useful. Now that you understand the rule, you can be on the alert for circumstances under which it might lead to problems. To help you remember, the following table lists the pros and cons of the payback period rule:

Advantages and Disadvantages of the Payback Period Rule	
Advantages	**Disadvantages**
1. Easy to understand.	1. Ignores the time value of money.
2. Adjusts for uncertainty of later cash flows.	2. Requires an arbitrary cutoff point.
	3. Ignores cash flows beyond the cutoff date.
3. Biased toward liquidity.	4. Biased against long-term projects, such as research and development, and new projects.

Concept Questions

9.2a In words, what is the payback period? The payback period rule?

9.2b Why do we say that the payback period is, in a sense, an accounting break-even measure?

⚡ 9.3 The Discounted Payback

discounted payback period
The length of time required for an investment's discounted cash flows to equal its initial cost.

We saw that one shortcoming of the payback period rule was that it ignored time value. A variation of the payback period, the discounted payback period, fixes this particular problem. The **discounted payback period** is the length of time until the sum of the discounted cash flows is equal to the initial investment. The *discounted payback rule* would be:

> **Based on the discounted payback rule, an investment is acceptable if its discounted payback is less than some prespecified number of years.**

To see how we might calculate the discounted payback period, suppose we require a 12.5 percent return on new investments. We have an investment that costs $300 and has

TABLE 9.3

Ordinary and Discounted Payback

Year	Cash Flow		Accumulated Cash Flow	
	Undiscounted	Discounted	Undiscounted	Discounted
1	$100	$89	$100	$ 89
2	100	79	200	168
3	100	70	300	238
4	100	62	400	300
5	100	55	500	355

cash flows of $100 per year for five years. To get the discounted payback, we have to discount each cash flow at 12.5 percent and then start adding them. We do this in Table 9.3. In Table 9.3, we have both the discounted and the undiscounted cash flows. Looking at the accumulated cash flows, we see that the regular payback is exactly three years (look for the highlighted figure in Year 3). The discounted cash flows total $300 only after four years, however, so the discounted payback is four years, as shown.[1]

How do we interpret the discounted payback? Recall that the ordinary payback is the time it takes to break even in an accounting sense. Because it includes the time value of money, the discounted payback is the time it takes to break even in an economic or financial sense. Loosely speaking, in our example, we get our money back, along with the interest we could have earned elsewhere, in four years.

Figure 9.3 illustrates this idea by comparing the *future* value at 12.5 percent of the $300 investment to the *future* value of the $100 annual cash flows at 12.5 percent. Notice that the two lines cross at exactly four years. This tells us that the value of the project's cash flows catches up and then passes the original investment in four years.

Table 9.3 and Figure 9.3 illustrate another interesting feature of the discounted payback period. If a project ever pays back on a discounted basis, then it must have a positive NPV.[2] This is true because, by definition, the NPV is zero when the sum of the discounted cash flows equals the initial investment. For example, the present value of all the cash flows in Table 9.3 is $355. The cost of the project was $300, so the NPV is obviously $55. This $55 is the value of the cash flow that occurs *after* the discounted payback (see the last line in Table 9.3). In general, if we use a discounted payback rule, we won't accidentally take any projects with a negative estimated NPV.

Based on our example, the discounted payback would seem to have much to recommend it. You may be surprised to find out that it is rarely used in practice. Why? Probably because it really isn't any simpler to use than NPV. To calculate a discounted payback, you have to discount cash flows, add them up, and compare them to the cost, just as you do with NPV. So, unlike an ordinary payback, the discounted payback is not especially simple to calculate.

A discounted payback period rule has a couple of other significant drawbacks. The biggest one is that the cutoff still has to be arbitrarily set, and cash flows beyond that point are ignored.[3] As a result, a project with a positive NPV may be found unacceptable because

---

[1]In this case, the discounted payback is an even number of years. This won't ordinarily happen, of course. However, calculating a fractional year for the discounted payback period is more involved than it is for the ordinary payback, and it is not commonly done.

[2]This argument assumes the cash flows, other than the first, are all positive. If they are not, then these statements are not necessarily correct. Also, there may be more than one discounted payback.

[3]If the cutoff were forever, then the discounted payback rule would be the same as the NPV rule. It would also be the same as the profitability index rule considered in a later section.

FIGURE 9.3

Future Value of Project
Cash Flows

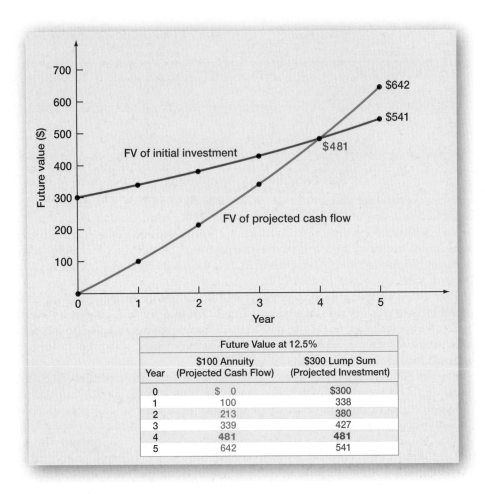

Future Value at 12.5%		
Year	$100 Annuity (Projected Cash Flow)	$300 Lump Sum (Projected Investment)
0	$ 0	$300
1	100	338
2	213	380
3	339	427
4	**481**	**481**
5	642	541

the cutoff is too short. Also, just because one project has a shorter discounted payback than another does not mean it has a larger NPV.

All things considered, the discounted payback is a compromise between a regular pay-back and NPV that lacks the simplicity of the first and the conceptual rigor of the second. Nonetheless, if we need to assess the time it will take to recover the investment required by a project, then the discounted payback is better than the ordinary payback because it considers time value. In other words, the discounted payback recognizes that we could have invested the money elsewhere and earned a return on it. The ordinary payback does not take this into account. The advantages and disadvantages of the discounted payback rule are summarized in the following table:

Advantages and Disadvantages of the Discounted Payback Period Rule	
Advantages	**Disadvantages**
1. Includes time value of money.	1. May reject positive NPV investments.
2. Easy to understand.	2. Requires an arbitrary cutoff point.
3. Does not accept negative estimated NPV investments.	3. Ignores cash flows beyond the cutoff date.
4. Biased toward liquidity.	4. Biased against long-term projects, such as research and development, and new projects.

Calculating Discounted Payback

EXAMPLE 9.3

Consider an investment that costs $400 and pays $100 per year forever. We use a 20 percent discount rate on this type of investment. What is the ordinary payback? What is the discounted payback? What is the NPV?

The NPV and ordinary payback are easy to calculate in this case because the investment is a perpetuity. The present value of the cash flows is $100/.2 = $500, so the NPV is $500 − 400 = $100. The ordinary payback is obviously four years.

To get the discounted payback, we need to find the number of years such that a $100 annuity has a present value of $400 at 20 percent. In other words, the present value annuity factor is $400/100 = 4, and the interest rate is 20 percent per period; so what's the number of periods? If we solve for the number of periods, we find that the answer is a little less than nine years, so this is the discounted payback.

Concept Questions

9.3a In words, what is the discounted payback period? Why do we say it is, in a sense, a financial or economic break-even measure?

9.3b What advantage(s) does the discounted payback have over the ordinary payback?

The Average Accounting Return

9.4 ✗

Another attractive, but flawed, approach to making capital budgeting decisions involves the **average accounting return (AAR)**. There are many different definitions of the AAR. However, in one form or another, the AAR is always defined as:

$$\frac{\text{Some measure of average accounting profit}}{\text{Some measure of average accounting value}}$$

The specific definition we will use is:

$$\frac{\text{Average net income}}{\text{Average book value}}$$

average accounting return (AAR)
An investment's average net income divided by its average book value.

To see how we might calculate this number, suppose we are deciding whether to open a store in a new shopping mall. The required investment in improvements is $500,000. The store would have a five-year life because everything reverts to the mall owners after that time. The required investment would be 100 percent depreciated (straight-line) over five years, so the depreciation would be $500,000/5 = $100,000 per year. The tax rate is 25 percent. Table 9.4 contains the projected revenues and expenses. Net income in each year, based on these figures, is also shown.

To calculate the average book value for this investment, we note that we started out with a book value of $500,000 (the initial cost) and ended up at $0. The average book value during the life of the investment is thus ($500,000 + 0)/2 = $250,000. As long as we use straight-line depreciation, the average investment will always be one-half of the initial investment.[4]

---

[4]We could, of course, calculate the average of the six book values directly. In thousands, we would have ($500 + 400 + 300 + 200 + 100 + 0)/6 = $250.

	Year 1	Year 2	Year 3	Year 4	Year 5
Revenue	$433,333	$450,000	$266,667	$200,000	$133,333
Expenses	200,000	150,000	100,000	100,000	100,000
Earnings before depreciation	$233,333	$300,000	$166,667	$100,000	$ 33,333
Depreciation	100,000	100,000	100,000	100,000	100,000
Earnings before taxes	$133,333	$200,000	$ 66,667	$ 0	−$ 66,667
Taxes (25%)	33,333	50,000	16,667	0	− 16,667
Net income	$100,000	$150,000	$ 50,000	$ 0	−$ 50,000

$$\text{Average net income} = \frac{\$100,000 + 150,000 + 50,000 + 0 - 50,000}{5} = \$50,000$$

$$\text{Average book value} = \frac{\$500,000 + 0}{2} = \$250,000$$

Looking at Table 9.4, we see that net income is $100,000 in the first year, $150,000 in the second year, $50,000 in the third year, $0 in Year 4, and −$50,000 in Year 5. The average net income, then, is:

$$[\$100,000 + 150,000 + 50,000 + 0 + (-50,000)]/5 = \$50,000$$

The average accounting return is:

$$\text{AAR} = \frac{\text{Average net income}}{\text{Average book value}} = \frac{\$50,000}{\$250,000} = 20\%$$

If the firm has a target AAR of less than 20 percent, then this investment is acceptable; otherwise, it is not. The *average accounting return rule* is thus:

> **Based on the average accounting return rule, a project is acceptable if its average accounting return exceeds a target average accounting return.**

As we will now see, the use of this rule has a number of problems.

You should recognize the chief drawback to the AAR immediately. Above all else, the AAR is not a rate of return in any meaningful economic sense. Instead, it is the ratio of two accounting numbers, and it is not comparable to the returns offered, for example, in financial markets.[5]

One of the reasons the AAR is not a true rate of return is that it ignores time value. When we average figures that occur at different times, we are treating the near future and the more distant future in the same way. There was no discounting involved when we computed the average net income, for example.

The second problem with the AAR is similar to the problem we had with the payback period rule concerning the lack of an objective cutoff period. Because a calculated AAR is really not comparable to a market return, the target AAR must somehow be specified. There is no generally agreed-upon way to do this. One way of doing it is to calculate the AAR for the firm as a whole and use this as a benchmark, but there are lots of other ways as well.

---

[5]The AAR is closely related to the return on assets (ROA) discussed in Chapter 3. In practice, the AAR is sometimes computed by first calculating the ROA for each year and then averaging the results. This produces a number that is similar, but not identical, to the one we computed.

The third, and perhaps worst, flaw in the AAR is that it doesn't even look at the right things. Instead of cash flow and market value, it uses net income and book value. These are both poor substitutes. As a result, an AAR doesn't tell us what the effect on share price will be of taking an investment, so it doesn't tell us what we really want to know.

Does the AAR have any redeeming features? About the only one is that it almost always can be computed. The reason is that accounting information will almost always be available, both for the project under consideration and for the firm as a whole. We hasten to add that once the accounting information is available, we can always convert it to cash flows, so even this is not a particularly important fact. The AAR is summarized in the following table:

Advantages and Disadvantages of the Average Accounting Return	
Advantages	**Disadvantages**
1. Easy to calculate. 2. Needed information will usually be available.	1. Not a true rate of return; time value of money is ignored. 2. Uses an arbitrary benchmark cutoff rate. 3. Based on accounting (book) values, not cash flows and market values.

Concept Questions

9.4a What is an average accounting rate of return (AAR)?

9.4b What are the weaknesses of the AAR rule?

The Internal Rate of Return

9.5

We now come to the most important alternative to NPV, the **internal rate of return**, universally known as the **IRR**. As we will see, the IRR is closely related to NPV. With the IRR, we try to find a single rate of return that summarizes the merits of a project. Furthermore, we want this rate to be an "internal" rate in the sense that it depends only on the cash flows of a particular investment, not on rates offered elsewhere.

internal rate of return (IRR)
The discount rate that makes the NPV of an investment zero.

To illustrate the idea behind the IRR, consider a project that costs $100 today and pays $110 in one year. Suppose you were asked, "What is the return on this investment?" What would you say? It seems both natural and obvious to say that the return is 10 percent because, for every dollar we put in, we get $1.10 back. In fact, as we will see in a moment, 10 percent is the internal rate of return, or IRR, on this investment.

Is this project with its 10 percent IRR a good investment? Once again, it would seem apparent that this is a good investment only if our required return is less than 10 percent. This intuition is also correct and illustrates the *IRR rule:*

Based on the IRR rule, an investment is acceptable if the IRR exceeds the required return. It should be rejected otherwise.

Imagine that we want to calculate the NPV for our simple investment. At a discount rate of R, the NPV is:

$$NPV = -\$100 + [110/(1 + R)]$$

Now, suppose we don't know the discount rate. This presents a problem, but we can still ask how high the discount rate would have to be before this project was deemed unacceptable. We know that we are indifferent between taking and not taking this investment when its NPV is just equal to zero. In other words, this investment is *economically* a break-even proposition when the NPV is zero because value is neither created nor destroyed. To find the break-even discount rate, we set NPV equal to zero and solve for R:

$$NPV = 0 = -\$100 + [110/(1 + R)]$$
$$\$100 = \$110/(1 + R)$$
$$1 + R = \$110/100 = 1.1$$
$$R = 10\%$$

This 10 percent is what we already have called the return on this investment. What we have now illustrated is that the internal rate of return on an investment (or just "return" for short) is the discount rate that makes the NPV equal to zero. This is an important observation, so it bears repeating:

> **The IRR on an investment is the required return that results in a zero NPV when it is used as the discount rate.**

The fact that the IRR is simply the discount rate that makes the NPV equal to zero is important because it tells us how to calculate the returns on more complicated investments. As we have seen, finding the IRR turns out to be relatively easy for a single-period investment. However, suppose you were now looking at an investment with the cash flows shown in Figure 9.4. As illustrated, this investment costs $100 and has a cash flow of $60 per year for two years, so it's only slightly more complicated than our single-period example. However, if you were asked for the return on this investment, what would you say? There doesn't seem to be any obvious answer (at least not to us). However, based on what we now know, we can set the NPV equal to zero and solve for the discount rate:

$$NPV = 0 = -\$100 + [60/(1 + IRR)] + [60/(1 + IRR)^2]$$

Unfortunately, the only way to find the IRR in general is by trial and error, either by hand or by calculator. This is precisely the same problem that came up in Chapter 5 when we found the unknown rate for an annuity and in Chapter 7 when we found the yield to maturity on a bond. In fact, we now see that in both of those cases, we were finding an IRR.

In this particular case, the cash flows form a two-period, $60 annuity. To find the unknown rate, we can try some different rates until we get the answer. If we were to start with a 0 percent rate, the NPV would obviously be $120 − 100 = $20. At a 10 percent discount rate, we would have:

$$NPV = -\$100 + (60/1.1) + (60/1.1^2) = \$4.13$$

FIGURE 9.4

Project Cash Flows

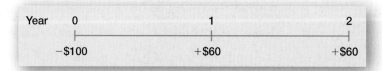

Discount Rate	NPV
0%	$20.00
5	11.56
10	4.13
15	− 2.46
20	− 8.33

TABLE 9.5

NPV at Different Discount Rates

FIGURE 9.5

An NPV Profile

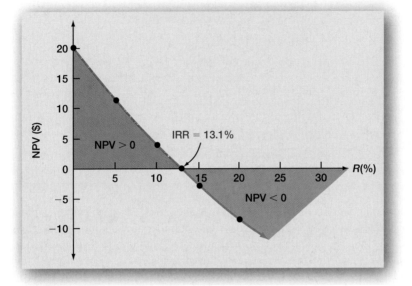

Now, we're getting close. We can summarize these and some other possibilities as shown in Table 9.5. From our calculations, the NPV appears to be zero with a discount rate between 10 percent and 15 percent, so the IRR is somewhere in that range. With a little more effort, we can find that the IRR is about 13.1 percent.[6] So, if our required return were less than 13.1 percent, we would take this investment. If our required return exceeded 13.1 percent, we would reject it.

By now, you have probably noticed that the IRR rule and the NPV rule appear to be quite similar. In fact, the IRR is sometimes simply called the *discounted cash flow,* or *DCF, return.* The easiest way to illustrate the relationship between NPV and IRR is to plot the numbers we calculated for Table 9.5. We put the different NPVs on the vertical axis, or *y*-axis, and the discount rates on the horizontal axis, or *x*-axis. If we had a very large number of points, the resulting picture would be a smooth curve called a **net present value profile.** Figure 9.5 illustrates the NPV profile for this project. Beginning with a 0 percent discount rate, we have $20 plotted directly on the *y*-axis. As the discount rate increases, the NPV declines smoothly. Where will the curve cut through the *x*-axis? This will occur where the NPV is just equal to zero, so it will happen right at the IRR of 13.1 percent.

In our example, the NPV rule and the IRR rule lead to identical accept–reject decisions. We will accept an investment using the IRR rule if the required return is less than 13.1 percent. As Figure 9.5 illustrates, however, the NPV is positive at any discount rate less than 13.1 percent, so we would accept the investment using the NPV rule as well. The two rules give equivalent results in this case.

net present value profile

A graphical representation of the relationship between an investment's NPVs and various discount rates.

---

[6]With a lot more effort (or a personal computer), we can find that the IRR is approximately (to 9 decimal places) 13.066238629 percent—not that anybody would ever want this many decimal places!

EXAMPLE 9.4	**Calculating the IRR**

A project has a total up-front cost of $435.44. The cash flows are $100 in the first year, $200 in the second year, and $300 in the third year. What's the IRR? If we require an 18 percent return, should we take this investment?

We'll describe the NPV profile and find the IRR by calculating some NPVs at different discount rates. You should check our answers for practice. Beginning with 0 percent, we have:

Discount Rate	NPV
0%	$164.56
5	100.36
10	46.15
15	.00
20	− 39.61

The NPV is zero at 15 percent, so 15 percent is the IRR. If we require an 18 percent return, then we should not take the investment. The reason is that the NPV is negative at 18 percent (verify that it is −$24.47). The IRR rule tells us the same thing in this case. We shouldn't take this investment because its 15 percent return is below our required 18 percent return.

At this point, you may be wondering if the IRR and NPV rules always lead to identical decisions. The answer is yes, as long as two very important conditions are met. First, the project's cash flows must be *conventional,* meaning that the first cash flow (the initial investment) is negative and all the rest are positive. Second, the project must be *independent,* meaning that the decision to accept or reject this project does not affect the decision to accept or reject any other. The first of these conditions is typically met, but the second often is not. In any case, when one or both of these conditions are not met, problems can arise. We discuss some of these next.

SPREADSHEET STRATEGIES

Calculating IRRs with a Spreadsheet

Because IRRs are so tedious to calculate by hand, financial calculators and especially spreadsheets are generally used. The procedures used by various financial calculators are too different for us to illustrate here, so we will focus on using a spreadsheet (financial calculators are covered in Appendix D). As the following example illustrates, using a spreadsheet is easy.

	A	B	C	D	E	F	G	H
1								
2		Using a spreadsheet to calculate internal rates of return						
3								
4	Suppose we have a four-year project that costs $500. The cash flows over the four-year life will be							
5	$100, $200, $300, and $400. What is the IRR?							
6								
7		Year	Cash Flow					
8		0	-$500					
9		1	100		IRR =	27.3%		
10		2	200					
11		3	300					
12		4	400					
13								
14								
15	The formula entered in cell F9 is =IRR(C8:C12). Notice that the Year 0 cash flow has a negative							
16	sign representing the initial cost of the project.							
17								

PROBLEMS WITH THE IRR

The problems with the IRR come about when the cash flows are not conventional or when we are trying to compare two or more investments to see which is best. In the first case, surprisingly, the simple question "What's the return?" can become difficult to answer. In the second case, the IRR can be a misleading guide.

Nonconventional Cash Flows   Suppose we have a strip-mining project that requires a $60 investment. Our cash flow in the first year will be $155. In the second year, the mine will be depleted, but we will have to spend $100 to restore the terrain. As Figure 9.6 illustrates, both the first and third cash flows are negative.

To find the IRR on this project, we can calculate the NPV at various rates:

Discount Rate	NPV
0%	−$5.00
10	− 1.74
20	− .28
30	.06
40	− .31

The NPV appears to be behaving in a peculiar fashion here. First, as the discount rate increases from 0 percent to 30 percent, the NPV starts out negative and becomes positive. This seems backward because the NPV is rising as the discount rate rises. It then starts getting smaller and becomes negative again. What's the IRR? To find out, we draw the NPV profile as shown in Figure 9.7.

In Figure 9.7, notice that the NPV is zero when the discount rate is 25 percent, so this is the IRR. Or is it? The NPV is also zero at $33\frac{1}{3}$ percent. Which of these is correct? The answer is both or neither; more precisely, there is no unambiguously correct answer. This is the **multiple rates of return** problem. Many financial computer packages (including a best seller for personal computers) aren't aware of this problem and just report the first IRR that is found. Others report only the smallest positive IRR, even though this answer is no better than any other.

In our current example, the IRR rule breaks down completely. Suppose our required return is 10 percent. Should we take this investment? Both IRRs are greater than 10 percent, so, by the IRR rule, maybe we should. However, as Figure 9.7 shows, the NPV is negative at any discount rate less than 25 percent, so this is not a good investment. When should we take it? Looking at Figure 9.7 one last time, we see that the NPV is positive only if our required return is between 25 percent and $33\frac{1}{3}$ percent.

Nonconventional cash flows can occur in a variety of ways. For example, Northeast Utilities, owner of the Connecticut-located Millstone nuclear power plant, had to shut down the plant's three reactors in November 1995. The reactors were expected to be back online in January 1997. By some estimates, the cost of the shutdown would run about $334 million. In fact, all nuclear plants eventually have to be shut down forever, and the costs associated with decommissioning a plant are enormous, creating large negative cash flows at the end of the project's life.

multiple rates of return
The possibility that more than one discount rate will make the NPV of an investment zero.

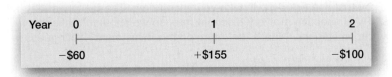

Year	0	1	2
	−$60	+$155	−$100

FIGURE 9.6

Project Cash Flows

FIGURE 9.7

NPV Profile

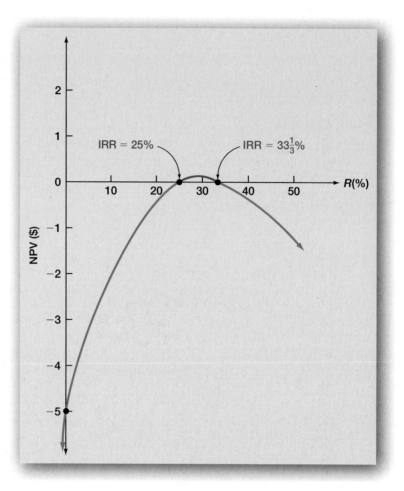

The moral of the story is that when the cash flows aren't conventional, strange things can start to happen to the IRR. This is not anything to get upset about, however, because the NPV rule, as always, works just fine. This illustrates the fact that, oddly enough, the obvious question—What's the rate of return?—may not always have a good answer.

EXAMPLE 9.5   What's the IRR?

You are looking at an investment that requires you to invest $51 today. You'll get $100 in one year, but you must pay out $50 in two years. What is the IRR on this investment?

You're on the alert now for the nonconventional cash flow problem, so you probably wouldn't be surprised to see more than one IRR. However, if you start looking for an IRR by trial and error, it will take you a long time. The reason is that there is no IRR. The NPV is negative at every discount rate, so we shouldn't take this investment under any circumstances. What's the return on this investment? Your guess is as good as ours.

| **"I Think; Therefore, I Know How Many IRRs There Can Be."** | **EXAMPLE 9.6** |

We've seen that it's possible to get more than one IRR. If you wanted to make sure that you had found all of the possible IRRs, how could you do it? The answer comes from the great mathematician, philosopher, and financial analyst Descartes (of "I think; therefore, I am" fame). Descartes' Rule of Sign says that the maximum number of IRRs that there can be is equal to the number of times that the cash flows change sign from positive to negative and/or negative to positive.[7]

In our example with the 25 percent and $33\frac{1}{3}$ percent IRRs, could there be yet another IRR? The cash flows flip from negative to positive, then back to negative, for a total of two sign changes. Therefore, according to Descartes' rule, the maximum number of IRRs is two, and we don't need to look for any more. Note that the actual number of IRRs can be less than the maximum (see Example 9.5).

Mutually Exclusive Investments   Even if there is a single IRR, another problem can arise concerning **mutually exclusive investment decisions**. If two investments, X and Y, are mutually exclusive, then taking one of them means that we cannot take the other. Two projects that are not mutually exclusive are said to be independent. For example, if we own one corner lot, then we can build a gas station or an apartment building, but not both. These are mutually exclusive alternatives.

mutually exclusive investment decisions
A situation in which taking one investment prevents the taking of another.

Thus far, we have asked whether a given investment is worth undertaking. However, a related question comes up often: Given two or more mutually exclusive investments, which one is the best? The answer is simple enough: The best one is the one with the largest NPV. Can we also say that the best one has the highest return? As we show, the answer is no.

To illustrate the problem with the IRR rule and mutually exclusive investments, consider the following cash flows from two mutually exclusive investments:

Year	Investment A	Investment B
0	−$100	−$100
1	50	20
2	40	40
3	40	50
4	30	60

The IRR for A is 24 percent, and the IRR for B is 21 percent. Because these investments are mutually exclusive, we can take only one of them. Simple intuition suggests that investment A is better because of its higher return. Unfortunately, simple intuition is not always correct.

To see why investment A is not necessarily the better of the two investments, we've calculated the NPV of these investments for different required returns:

Discount Rate	NPV(A)	NPV(B)
0%	$60.00	$70.00
5	43.13	47.88
10	29.06	29.79
15	17.18	14.82
20	7.06	2.31
25	− 1.63	− 8.22

[7]To be more precise, the number of IRRs that are bigger than −100 percent is equal to the number of sign changes, or it differs from the number of sign changes by an even number. Thus, for example, if there are five sign changes, there are five IRRs, three IRRs, or one IRR. If there are two sign changes, there are either two IRRs or no IRRs.

FIGURE 9.8

NPV Profiles for Mutually
Exclusive Investments

The IRR for A (24 percent) is larger than the IRR for B (21 percent). However, if you compare the NPVs, you'll see that which investment has the higher NPV depends on our required return. B has greater total cash flow, but it pays back more slowly than A. As a result, it has a higher NPV at lower discount rates.

In our example, the NPV and IRR rankings conflict for some discount rates. If our required return is 10 percent, for instance, then B has the higher NPV and is thus the better of the two even though A has the higher return. If our required return is 15 percent, then there is no ranking conflict: A is better.

The conflict between the IRR and NPV for mutually exclusive investments can be illustrated by plotting the investments' NPV profiles as we have done in Figure 9.8. In Figure 9.8, notice that the NPV profiles cross at about 11 percent. Notice also that at any discount rate less than 11 percent, the NPV for B is higher. In this range, taking B benefits us more than taking A, even though A's IRR is higher. At any rate greater than 11 percent, investment A has the greater NPV.

This example illustrates that when we have mutually exclusive projects, we shouldn't rank them based on their returns. More generally, anytime we are comparing investments to determine which is best, looking at IRRs can be misleading. Instead, we need to look at the relative NPVs to avoid the possibility of choosing incorrectly. Remember, we're ultimately interested in creating value for the shareholders, so the option with the higher NPV is preferred, regardless of the relative returns.

If this seems counterintuitive, think of it this way. Suppose you have two investments. One has a 10 percent return and makes you $100 richer immediately. The other has a 20 percent return and makes you $50 richer immediately. Which one do you like better? We would rather have $100 than $50, regardless of the returns, so we like the first one better.

Calculating the Crossover Rate   EXAMPLE 9.7

In Figure 9.8, the NPV profiles cross at about 11 percent. How can we determine just what this crossover point is? The *crossover rate*, by definition, is the discount rate that makes the NPVs of two projects equal. To illustrate, suppose we have the following two mutually exclusive investments:

Year	Investment A	Investment B
0	−$400	−$500
1	250	320
2	280	340

What's the crossover rate?

To find the crossover, first consider moving out of investment A and into investment B. If you make the move, you'll have to invest an extra $100 (= $500 − 400). For this $100 investment, you'll get an extra $70 (= $320 − 250) in the first year and an extra $60 (= $340 − 280) in the second year. Is this a good move? In other words, is it worth investing the extra $100?

Based on our discussion, the NPV of the switch, NPV(B − A), is:

$$NPV(B − A) = −\$100 + [70/(1 + R)] + [60/(1 + R)^2]$$

We can calculate the return on this investment by setting the NPV equal to zero and solving for the IRR:

$$NPV(B − A) = 0 = −\$100 + [70/(1 + R)] + [60/(1 + R)^2]$$

If you go through this calculation, you will find the IRR is exactly 20 percent. What this tells us is that at a 20 percent discount rate, we are indifferent between the two investments because the NPV of the difference in their cash flows is zero. As a consequence, the two investments have the same value, so this 20 percent is the crossover rate. Check to see that the NPV at 20 percent is $2.78 for both investments.

In general, you can find the crossover rate by taking the difference in the cash flows and calculating the IRR using the difference. It doesn't make any difference which one you subtract from which. To see this, find the IRR for (A − B); you'll see it's the same number. Also, for practice, you might want to find the exact crossover in Figure 9.8. (*Hint:* It's 11.0704 percent.)

Investing or Financing?   Consider the following two independent investments:

Year	Investment A	Investment B
0	−$100	$100
1	130	−130

The company initially pays out cash with investment A and initially receives cash for investment B. While most projects are more like investment A, projects like investment B also occur. For example, consider a corporation conducting a seminar where the participants pay in advance. Because large expenses are frequently incurred at the seminar date, cash inflows precede cash outflows.

For these two projects, suppose the required return for each investment project is 12 percent. According to the IRR decision rule, which, if either, project should we accept? If you calculate the IRRs, you will find that they are 30 percent for both projects.

According to the IRR decision rule, we should accept both projects. However, if we calculate the NPV of B at 12 percent, we get:

$$\$100 − \frac{\$130}{1.12} = −\$16.07$$

FIGURE 9.9   NPV Profile for Investing and Financing Investments

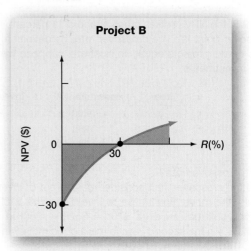

In this case, the NPV and IRR decision rules disagree. To see what's going on, Figure 9.9 shows the NPV profile for each project. As you can see, the NPV profile for B is upward sloping. Thus, the project should be accepted if the required return is *greater* than 30 percent.

When a project has cash flows like investment B's, the IRR is really a rate that you are paying, not receiving. For this reason, we say that the project has *financing type* cash flows, whereas investment A has *investing type* cash flows. You should take a project with financing-type cash flows only if it is an inexpensive source of financing, meaning that its IRR is *lower* than your required return.

REDEEMING QUALITIES OF THE IRR

Despite its flaws, the IRR is very popular in practice—more so than even the NPV. It probably survives because it fills a need that the NPV does not. In analyzing investments, people in general, and financial analysts in particular, seem to prefer talking about rates of return rather than dollar values.

In a similar vein, the IRR also appears to provide a simple way of communicating information about a proposal. One manager might say to another, "Remodeling the clerical wing has a 20 percent return." This may somehow seem simpler than saying, "At a 10 percent discount rate, the net present value is $4,000."

Finally, under certain circumstances, the IRR may have a practical advantage over the NPV. We can't estimate the NPV unless we know the appropriate discount rate, but we can still estimate the IRR. Suppose we didn't know the required return on an investment, but we found, for example, that it had a 40 percent return. We would probably be inclined to take it because it would be unlikely that the required return would be that high. The advantages and disadvantages of the IRR are summarized as follows:

Advantages and Disadvantages of the Internal Rate of Return	
Advantages	**Disadvantages**
1. Closely related to NPV, often leading to identical decisions.	1. May result in multiple answers or not deal with nonconventional cash flows.
2. Easy to understand and communicate.	2. May lead to incorrect decisions in comparisons of mutually exclusive investments.

THE MODIFIED INTERNAL RATE OF RETURN (MIRR)

To address some of the problems that can crop up with the standard IRR, it is often proposed that a modified version be used. As we will see, there are several different ways of calculating a modified IRR, or MIRR, but the basic idea is to modify the cash flows first and then calculate an IRR using the modified cash flows.

To illustrate, let's go back to the cash flows in Figure 9.6: $-\$60$, $+\$155$, and $-\$100$. As we saw, there are two IRRs, 25 percent and $33\frac{1}{3}$ percent. We next illustrate three different MIRRs, all of which have the property that only one answer will result, thereby eliminating the multiple IRR problem.

Method #1: The Discounting Approach   With the discounting approach, the idea is to discount all negative cash flows back to the present at the required return and add them to the initial cost. Then, calculate the IRR. Because only the first modified cash flow is negative, there will be only one IRR. The discount rate used might be the required return, or it might be some other externally supplied rate. We will use the project's required return.

If the required return on the project is 20 percent, then the modified cash flows look like this:

Time 0: $-\$60 + \dfrac{-\$100}{1.20^2} = -\$129.44$

Time 1: $+\$155$

Time 2: $+\$0$

If you calculate the MIRR now, you should get 19.74 percent.

Method #2: The Reinvestment Approach   With the reinvestment approach, we compound *all* cash flows (positive and negative) except the first out to the end of the project's life and then calculate the IRR. In a sense, we are "reinvesting" the cash flows and not taking them out of the project until the very end. The rate we use could be the required return on the project, or it could be a separately specified "reinvestment rate." We will use the project's required return. When we do, here are the modified cash flows:

Time 0: $-\$60$

Time 1: $+0$

Time 2: $-\$100 + (\$155 \times 1.2) = \$86$

The MIRR on this set of cash flows is 19.72 percent, or a little lower than we got using the discounting approach.

Method #3: The Combination Approach   As the name suggests, the combination approach blends our first two methods. Negative cash flows are discounted back to the present, and positive cash flows are compounded to the end of the project. In practice, different discount or compounding rates might be used, but we will again stick with the project's required return.

With the combination approach, the modified cash flows are as follows:

Time 0: $-\$60 + \dfrac{-\$100}{1.20^2} = -\$129.44$

Time 1: $+0$

Time 2: $\$155 \times 1.2 = \$186$

See if you don't agree that the MIRR is 19.87 percent, the highest of the three.

MIRR or IRR: Which Is Better?   MIRRs are controversial. At one extreme are those who claim that MIRRs are superior to IRRs, period. For example, by design, they clearly don't suffer from the multiple rate of return problem.

At the other end, detractors say that MIRR should stand for "meaningless internal rate of return." As our example makes clear, one problem with MIRRs is that there are different ways of calculating them, and there is no clear reason to say one of our three methods is better than any other. The differences are small with our simple cash flows, but they could be much larger for a more complex project. Further, it's not clear how to interpret an MIRR. It may look like a rate of return, but it's a rate of return on a modified set of cash flows, not the project's actual cash flows.

We're not going to take sides. However, notice that calculating an MIRR requires discounting, compounding, or both, which leads to two obvious observations. First, if we have the relevant discount rate, why not calculate the NPV and be done with it? Second, because an MIRR depends on an externally supplied discount (or compounding) rate, the answer you get is not truly an "internal" rate of return, which, by definition, depends on only the project's cash flows.

We *will* take a stand on one issue that frequently comes up in this context. The value of a project does not depend on what the firm does with the cash flows generated by that project. A firm might use a project's cash flows to fund other projects, to pay dividends, or to buy an executive jet. It doesn't matter: How the cash flows are spent in the future does not affect their value today. As a result, there is generally no need to consider reinvestment of interim cash flows.

Concept Questions

9.5a Under what circumstances will the IRR and NPV rules lead to the same accept–reject decisions? When might they conflict?

9.5b Is it generally true that an advantage of the IRR rule over the NPV rule is that we don't need to know the required return to use the IRR rule?

9.6 The Profitability Index

profitability index (PI)
The present value of an investment's future cash flows divided by its initial cost. Also called the benefit–cost ratio.

Another tool used to evaluate projects is called the **profitability index (PI)** or benefit–cost ratio. This index is defined as the present value of the future cash flows divided by the initial investment. So, if a project costs $200 and the present value of its future cash flows is $220, the profitability index value would be $220/200 = 1.1. Notice that the NPV for this investment is $20, so it is a desirable investment.

More generally, if a project has a positive NPV, then the present value of the future cash flows must be bigger than the initial investment. The profitability index would thus be bigger than 1 for a positive NPV investment and less than 1 for a negative NPV investment.

How do we interpret the profitability index? In our example, the PI was 1.1. This tells us that, per dollar invested, $1.10 in value or $.10 in NPV results. The profitability index thus measures "bang for the buck"—that is, the value created per dollar invested. For this reason, it is often proposed as a measure of performance for government or other not-for-profit investments. Also, when capital is scarce, it may make sense to allocate it to projects with the highest PIs. We will return to this issue in a later chapter.

The PI is obviously similar to the NPV. However, consider an investment that costs $5 and has a $10 present value and an investment that costs $100 with a $150 present value.

The first of these investments has an NPV of $5 and a PI of 2. The second has an NPV of $50 and a PI of 1.5. If these are mutually exclusive investments, then the second one is preferred even though it has a lower PI. This ranking problem is similar to the IRR ranking problem we saw in the previous section. In all, there seems to be little reason to rely on the PI instead of the NPV. Our discussion of the PI is summarized as follows:

Advantages and Disadvantages of the Profitability Index	
Advantages	**Disadvantages**
1. Closely related to NPV, generally leading to identical decisions.	1. May lead to incorrect decisions in comparisons of mutually exclusive investments.
2. Easy to understand and communicate.	
3. May be useful when available investment funds are limited.	

Concept Questions

9.6a What does the profitability index measure?

9.6b How would you state the profitability index rule?

The Practice of Capital Budgeting   9.7

Given that NPV seems to be telling us directly what we want to know, you might be wondering why there are so many other procedures and why alternative procedures are commonly used. Recall that we are trying to make an investment decision and that we are frequently operating under considerable uncertainty about the future. We can only *estimate* the NPV of an investment in this case. The resulting estimate can be very "soft," meaning that the true NPV might be quite different.

Because the true NPV is unknown, the astute financial manager seeks clues to help in assessing whether the estimated NPV is reliable. For this reason, firms would typically use multiple criteria for evaluating a proposal. For example, suppose we have an investment with a positive estimated NPV. Based on our experience with other projects, this one appears to have a short payback and a very high AAR. In this case, the different indicators seem to agree that it's "all systems go." Put another way, the payback and the AAR are consistent with the conclusion that the NPV is positive.

On the other hand, suppose we had a positive estimated NPV, a long payback, and a low AAR. This could still be a good investment, but it looks like we need to be much more careful in making the decision because we are getting conflicting signals. If the estimated NPV is based on projections in which we have little confidence, then further analysis is probably in order. We will consider how to evaluate NPV estimates in more detail in the next two chapters.

Large firms often have huge capital budgets. For example, for 2011, ExxonMobil announced that it expected to have about $34 billion in capital outlays during the year, up from $32.2 billion in 2010. About the same time, competitor Chevron announced that it would increase its capital budgeting for 2011 to $26 billion, up from $21.6 billion in 2010. Overall, oil companies projected capital spending of $490 billion worldwide in 2011, an increase of 11 percent over 2010's $442 billion. Other companies with large capital spending budgets included Walmart, which projected capital spending of about $13 to $14 billion

TABLE 9.6　Capital Budgeting Techniques in Practice

A. Historical Comparison of the Primary Use of Various Capital Budgeting Techniques							
	1959	**1964**	**1970**	**1975**	**1977**	**1979**	**1981**
Payback period	34%	24%	12%	15%	9%	10%	5.0%
Average accounting return (AAR)	34	30	26	10	25	14	10.7
Internal rate of return (IRR)	19	38	57	37	54	60	65.3
Net present value (NPV)	—	—	—	26	10	14	16.5
IRR or NPV	19	38	57	63	64	74	81.8

B. Percentage of CFOs Who Always or Almost Always Used a Given Technique in 1999				
Capital Budgeting Technique	**Percentage Always or Almost Always Using**	**Average Score [Scale is 4 (always) to 0 (never)]**		
		Overall	**Large Firms**	**Small Firms**
Internal rate of return	76%	3.09	3.41	2.87
Net present value	75	3.08	3.42	2.83
Payback period	57	2.53	2.25	2.72
Discounted payback period	29	1.56	1.55	1.58
Accounting rate of return	20	1.34	1.25	1.41
Profitability index	12	.83	.75	.88

SOURCES: J.R. Graham and C.R. Harvey, "The Theory and Practice of Corporate Finance: Evidence from the Field," *Journal of Financial Economics,* May–June 2001, pp. 187–244; J.S. Moore and A.K. Reichert, "An Analysis of the Financial Management Techniques Currently Employed by Large U.S. Corporations," *Journal of Business Finance and Accounting,* Winter 1983, pp. 623–45; M.T. Stanley and S.R. Block, "A Survey of Multinational Capital Budgeting," *The Financial Review,* March 1984, pp. 36–51.

for 2011, and semiconductor manufacturer Intel, which projected capital spending of about $5.5 billion for 2011.

According to information released by the Census Bureau in 2010, capital investment for the economy as a whole was $1.375 trillion in 2008, $1.355 trillion in 2007, and $1.31 trillion in 2006. The total for the three years therefore exceeded $3 trillion! Given the sums at stake, it is not too surprising that careful analysis of capital expenditures is something at which successful businesses seek to become adept.

There have been a number of surveys conducted asking firms what types of investment criteria they actually use. Table 9.6 summarizes the results of several of these. Panel A of the table is a historical comparison looking at the primary capital budgeting techniques used by large firms through time. In 1959, only 19 percent of the firms surveyed used either IRR or NPV, and 68 percent used either payback periods or accounting returns. It is clear that by the 1980s, IRR and NPV had become the dominant criteria.

Panel B of Table 9.6 summarizes the results of a 1999 survey of chief financial officers (CFOs) at both large and small firms in the United States. A total of 392 CFOs responded. What is shown is the percentage of CFOs who always or almost always used the various capital budgeting techniques we described in this chapter. Not surprisingly, IRR and NPV were the two most widely used techniques, particularly at larger firms. However, over half of the respondents always, or almost always, used the payback criterion as well. In fact, among smaller firms, payback was used just about as much as NPV and IRR. Less commonly used were discounted payback, accounting rates of return, and the profitability index. For future reference, the various criteria we have discussed are summarized in Table 9.7.

TABLE 9.7

Summary of Investment Criteria

I.   Discounted Cash Flow Criteria

A. *Net present value (NPV):* The NPV of an investment is the difference between its market value and its cost. The NPV rule is to take a project if its NPV is positive. NPV is frequently estimated by calculating the present value of the future cash flows (to estimate market value) and then subtracting the cost. NPV has no serious flaws; it is the preferred decision criterion.

B. *Internal rate of return (IRR):* The IRR is the discount rate that makes the estimated NPV of an investment equal to zero; it is sometimes called the *discounted cash flow (DCF) return*. The IRR rule is to take a project when its IRR exceeds the required return. IRR is closely related to NPV, and it leads to exactly the same decisions as NPV for conventional, independent projects. When project cash flows are not conventional, there may be no IRR or there may be more than one. More seriously, the IRR cannot be used to rank mutually exclusive projects; the project with the highest IRR is not necessarily the preferred investment.

C. *Modified internal rate of return (MIRR):* The MIRR is a modification to the IRR. A project's cash flows are modified by (1) discounting the negative cash flows back to the present; (2) compounding cash flows to the end of the project's life; or (3) combining (1) and (2). An IRR is then computed on the modified cash flows. MIRRs are guaranteed to avoid the multiple rate of return problem, but it is unclear how to interpret them; and they are not truly "internal" because they depend on externally supplied discounting or compounding rates.

D. *Profitability index (PI):* The PI, also called the *benefit–cost ratio,* is the ratio of present value to cost. The PI rule is to take an investment if the index exceeds 1. The PI measures the present value of an investment per dollar invested. It is quite similar to NPV; but, like IRR, it cannot be used to rank mutually exclusive projects. However, it is sometimes used to rank projects when a firm has more positive NPV investments than it can currently finance.

II.   Payback Criteria

A. *Payback period:* The payback period is the length of time until the sum of an investment's cash flows equals its cost. The payback period rule is to take a project if its payback is less than some cutoff. The payback period is a flawed criterion, primarily because it ignores risk, the time value of money, and cash flows beyond the cutoff point.

B. *Discounted payback period:* The discounted payback period is the length of time until the sum of an investment's discounted cash flows equals its cost. The discounted payback period rule is to take an investment if the discounted payback is less than some cutoff. The discounted payback rule is flawed, primarily because it ignores cash flows after the cutoff.

III.   Accounting Criterion

A. *Average accounting return (AAR):* The AAR is a measure of accounting profit relative to book value. It is *not* related to the IRR, but it is similar to the accounting return on assets (ROA) measure in Chapter 3. The AAR rule is to take an investment if its AAR exceeds a benchmark AAR. The AAR is seriously flawed for a variety of reasons, and it has little to recommend it.

Concept Questions

9.7a What are the most commonly used capital budgeting procedures?

9.7b If NPV is conceptually the best procedure for capital budgeting, why do you think multiple measures are used in practice?

Visit us at www.mhhe.com/rwj

9.8 Summary and Conclusions

This chapter has covered the different criteria used to evaluate proposed investments. The seven criteria, in the order we discussed them, are these:

1. Net present value (NPV).
2. Payback period.
3. Discounted payback period.
4. Average accounting return (AAR).
5. Internal rate of return (IRR).
6. Modified internal rate of return (MIRR).
7. Profitability index (PI).

We illustrated how to calculate each of these and discussed the interpretation of the results. We also described the advantages and disadvantages of each of them. Ultimately a good capital budgeting criterion must tell us two things. First, is a particular project a good investment? Second, if we have more than one good project, but we can take only one of them, which one should we take? The main point of this chapter is that only the NPV criterion can always provide the correct answer to both questions.

For this reason, NPV is one of the two or three most important concepts in finance, and we will refer to it many times in the chapters ahead. When we do, keep two things in mind: (1) NPV is always just the difference between the market value of an asset or project and its cost and (2) the financial manager acts in the shareholders' best interests by identifying and taking positive NPV projects.

Finally, we noted that NPVs can't normally be observed in the market; instead, they must be estimated. Because there is always the possibility of a poor estimate, financial managers use multiple criteria for examining projects. The other criteria provide additional information about whether a project truly has a positive NPV.

CONNECT TO FINANCE

If you are using Connect™ Finance in your course, get online to take a Practice Test, check out study tools, and find out where you need additional practice.

▼ Chapter 9 Net Present Value and Other Investment Criteria			Section 9.1
9.1 Net Present Value	eBook	Study	Practice
9.2 The Payback Rule	eBook	Study	Practice
9.3 The Discounted Payback	eBook	Study	Practice
9.4 The Average Accounting Return	eBook	Study	Practice
9.5 The Internal Rate of Return	eBook	Study	Practice
9.6 The Profitability Index	eBook	Study	Practice
9.7 The Practice of Capital Budgeting	eBook	Study	Practice

Can you answer the following questions?

Section 9.1   The net present value rule states that you should accept a project if its net present value_____. (LO 9-1)

Section 9.2   A drawback of the payback method of project analysis is_____. (LO 9-2)

Section 9.3   The discounted payback period for a project will be _____ the payback period for the project given a positive, nonzero discount rate. (LO 9-3)

Section 9.4   What is an advantage of the average accounting return method of project analysis? (LO 9-4)

Section 9.5   A project has an internal rate of return of 10.6 percent. Which one of the following statements must be true based on this information? (LO 9-5)

Section 9.6   What is a benefit–cost ratio? (LO 9-6)

Section 9.7   What method of analysis tends to be least utilized by CFOs, according to the survey conducted in 1999 as presented in your textbook? (LO 9-7)

Log on to find out!

CHAPTER REVIEW AND SELF-TEST PROBLEMS

9.1   **Investment Criteria** This problem will give you some practice calculating NPVs and paybacks. A proposed overseas expansion has the following cash flows:

Year	Cash Flow
0	−$200
1	50
2	60
3	70
4	200

Calculate the payback, the discounted payback, and the NPV at a required return of 10 percent.

9.2   **Mutually Exclusive Investments** Consider the following two mutually exclusive investments. Calculate the IRR for each and the crossover rate. Under what circumstances will the IRR and NPV criteria rank the two projects differently?

Year	Investment A	Investment B
0	−$75	−$75
1	20	60
2	40	50
3	70	15

9.3   **Average Accounting Return** You are looking at a three-year project with a projected net income of $2,000 in Year 1, $4,000 in Year 2, and $6,000 in Year 3. The cost is $12,000, which will be depreciated straight-line to zero over the three-year life of the project. What is the average accounting return (AAR)?

ANSWERS TO CHAPTER REVIEW AND SELF-TEST PROBLEMS

9.1   In the following table, we have listed the cash flow, cumulative cash flow, discounted cash flow (at 10 percent), and cumulative discounted cash flow for the proposed project.

Visit us at www.mhhe.com/rwj

	Cash Flow		Accumulated Cash Flow	
Year	Undiscounted	Discounted	Undiscounted	Discounted
1	$ 50	$ 45.45	$ 50	$ 45.45
2	60	49.59	110	95.04
3	70	52.59	180	147.63
4	200	136.60	380	284.23

Recall that the initial investment was $200. When we compare this to accumulated undiscounted cash flows, we see that payback occurs between Years 3 and 4. The cash flows for the first three years are $180 total, so, going into the fourth year, we are short by $20. The total cash flow in Year 4 is $200, so the payback is 3 + ($20/200) = 3.10 years.

Looking at the accumulated discounted cash flows, we see that the discounted payback occurs between Years 3 and 4. The sum of the discounted cash flows is $284.23, so the NPV is $84.23. Notice that this is the present value of the cash flows that occur after the discounted payback.

9.2   To calculate the IRR, we might try some guesses, as in the following table:

Discount Rate	NPV(A)	NPV(B)
0%	$55.00	$50.00
10	28.83	32.14
20	9.95	18.40
30	− 4.09	7.57
40	−14.80	− 1.17

Several things are immediately apparent from our guesses. First, the IRR on A must be between 20 percent and 30 percent (why?). With some more effort, we find that it's 26.79 percent. For B, the IRR must be a little less than 40 percent (again, why?); it works out to be 38.54 percent. Also, notice that at rates between 0 percent and 10 percent, the NPVs are very close, indicating that the crossover is in that vicinity.

To find the crossover exactly, we can compute the IRR on the difference in the cash flows. If we take the cash flows from A minus the cash flows from B, the resulting cash flows are:

Year	A − B
0	$ 0
1	− 40
2	− 10
3	55

These cash flows look a little odd; but the sign changes only once, so we can find an IRR. With some trial and error, you'll see that the NPV is zero at a discount rate of 5.42 percent, so this is the crossover rate.

The IRR for B is higher. However, as we've seen, A has the larger NPV for any discount rate less than 5.42 percent, so the NPV and IRR rankings will conflict in that range. Remember, if there's a conflict, we will go with the higher NPV. Our decision rule is thus simple: Take A if the required return is less than 5.42 percent, take B if the required return is between 5.42 percent and 38.54 percent (the IRR on B), and take neither if the required return is more than 38.54 percent.

9.3 Here we need to calculate the ratio of average net income to average book value to get the AAR. Average net income is:

Average net income = ($2,000 + 4,000 + 6,000)/3 = $4,000

Average book value is:

Average book value = $12,000/2 = $6,000

So the average accounting return is:

AAR = $4,000/6,000 = 66.67%

This is an impressive return. Remember, however, that it isn't really a rate of return like an interest rate or an IRR, so the size doesn't tell us a lot. In particular, our money is probably not going to grow at a rate of 66.67 percent per year, sorry to say.

CONCEPTS REVIEW AND CRITICAL THINKING QUESTIONS

1. **Payback Period and Net Present Value [LO1, 2]** If a project with conventional cash flows has a payback period less than the project's life, can you definitively state the algebraic sign of the NPV? Why or why not? If you know that the discounted payback period is less than the project's life, what can you say about the NPV? Explain.

2. **Net Present Value [LO1]** Suppose a project has conventional cash flows and a positive NPV. What do you know about its payback? Its discounted payback? Its profitability index? Its IRR? Explain.

3. **Payback Period [LO2]** Concerning payback:
   a. Describe how the payback period is calculated, and describe the information this measure provides about a sequence of cash flows. What is the payback criterion decision rule?
   b. What are the problems associated with using the payback period to evaluate cash flows?
   c. What are the advantages of using the payback period to evaluate cash flows? Are there any circumstances under which using payback might be appropriate? Explain.

4. **Discounted Payback [LO3]** Concerning discounted payback:
   a. Describe how the discounted payback period is calculated, and describe the information this measure provides about a sequence of cash flows. What is the discounted payback criterion decision rule?
   b. What are the problems associated with using the discounted payback period to evaluate cash flows?
   c. What conceptual advantage does the discounted payback method have over the regular payback method? Can the discounted payback ever be longer than the regular payback? Explain.

5. **Average Accounting Return [LO4]** Concerning AAR:
   a. Describe how the average accounting return is usually calculated, and describe the information this measure provides about a sequence of cash flows. What is the AAR criterion decision rule?
   b. What are the problems associated with using the AAR to evaluate a project's cash flows? What underlying feature of AAR is most troubling to you from a financial perspective? Does the AAR have any redeeming qualities?

Visit us at www.mhhe.com/rwj

6. **Net Present Value [LO1]** Concerning NPV:

   a. Describe how NPV is calculated, and describe the information this measure provides about a sequence of cash flows. What is the NPV criterion decision rule?

   b. Why is NPV considered a superior method of evaluating the cash flows from a project? Suppose the NPV for a project's cash flows is computed to be $2,500. What does this number represent with respect to the firm's shareholders?

7. **Internal Rate of Return [LO5]** Concerning IRR:

   a. Describe how the IRR is calculated, and describe the information this measure provides about a sequence of cash flows. What is the IRR criterion decision rule?

   b. What is the relationship between IRR and NPV? Are there any situations in which you might prefer one method over the other? Explain.

   c. Despite its shortcomings in some situations, why do most financial managers use IRR along with NPV when evaluating projects? Can you think of a situation in which IRR might be a more appropriate measure to use than NPV? Explain.

8. **Profitability Index [LO7]** Concerning the profitability index:

   a. Describe how the profitability index is calculated, and describe the information this measure provides about a sequence of cash flows. What is the profitability index decision rule?

   b. What is the relationship between the profitability index and NPV? Are there any situations in which you might prefer one method over the other? Explain.

9. **Payback and Internal Rate of Return [LO2, 5]** A project has perpetual cash flows of C per period, a cost of I, and a required return of R. What is the relationship between the project's payback and its IRR? What implications does your answer have for long-lived projects with relatively constant cash flows?

10. **International Investment Projects [LO1]** In October 2010, automobile manufacturer BMW announced plans to invest $750 million to increase production at its South Carolina plant by 50 percent. BMW apparently felt that it would be better able to compete and create value with U.S-based facilities. Other companies such as Fuji Film and Swiss chemical company Lonza have reached similar conclusions and taken similar actions. What are some of the reasons that foreign manufacturers of products as diverse as automobiles, film, and chemicals might arrive at this same conclusion?

11. **Capital Budgeting Problems [LO1]** What difficulties might come up in actual applications of the various criteria we discussed in this chapter? Which one would be the easiest to implement in actual applications? The most difficult?

12. **Capital Budgeting in Not-for-Profit Entities [LO1]** Are the capital budgeting criteria we discussed applicable to not-for-profit corporations? How should such entities make capital budgeting decisions? What about the U.S. government? Should it evaluate spending proposals using these techniques?

13. **Modified Internal Rate of Return [LO6]** One of the less flattering interpretations of the acronym MIRR is "meaningless internal rate of return." Why do you think this term is applied to MIRR?

14. **Net Present Value [LO1]** It is sometimes stated that "the net present value approach assumes reinvestment of the intermediate cash flows at the required return." Is this claim correct? To answer, suppose you calculate the NPV of a project in the usual way. Next, suppose you do the following:

   a. Calculate the future value (as of the end of the project) of all the cash flows other than the initial outlay assuming they are reinvested at the required return, producing a single future value figure for the project.

   b. Calculate the NPV of the project using the single future value calculated in the previous step and the initial outlay. It is easy to verify that you will get the same NPV as in your original calculation only if you use the required return as the reinvestment rate in the previous step.

15. **Internal Rate of Return [LO5]** It is sometimes stated that "the internal rate of return approach assumes reinvestment of the intermediate cash flows at the internal rate of return." Is this claim correct? To answer, suppose you calculate the IRR of a project in the usual way. Next, suppose you do the following:

   a. Calculate the future value (as of the end of the project) of all the cash flows other than the initial outlay assuming they are reinvested at the IRR, producing a single future value figure for the project.

   b. Calculate the IRR of the project using the single future value calculated in the previous step and the initial outlay. It is easy to verify that you will get the same IRR as in your original calculation only if you use the IRR as the reinvestment rate in the previous step.

QUESTIONS AND PROBLEMS

1. **Calculating Payback [LO2]** What is the payback period for the following set of cash flows?

BASIC
(Questions 1–19)

Year	Cash Flow
0	−$5,500
1	1,300
2	1,500
3	1,900
4	1,400

2. **Calculating Payback [LO2]** An investment project provides cash inflows of $585 per year for eight years. What is the project payback period if the initial cost is $1,700? What if the initial cost is $3,300? What if it is $4,900?

3. **Calculating Payback [LO2]** Buy Coastal, Inc., imposes a payback cutoff of three years for its international investment projects. If the company has the following two projects available, should it accept either of them?

Year	Cash Flow (A)	Cash Flow (B)
0	−$60,000	−$ 70,000
1	23,000	15,000
2	28,000	18,000
3	21,000	26,000
4	8,000	230,000

4. **Calculating Discounted Payback [LO3]** An investment project has annual cash inflows of $3,200, $4,100, $5,300, and $4,500, and a discount rate of 14 percent. What is the discounted payback period for these cash flows if the initial cost is $5,900? What if the initial cost is $8,000? What if it is $11,000?

5. **Calculating Discounted Payback [LO3]** An investment project costs $10,000 and has annual cash flows of $2,900 for six years. What is the discounted payback period if the discount rate is zero percent? What if the discount rate is 5 percent? If it is 19 percent?

Visit us at www.mhhe.com/rwj

6. Calculating AAR [LO4] You're trying to determine whether to expand your business by building a new manufacturing plant. The plant has an installation cost of $12 million, which will be depreciated straight-line to zero over its four-year life. If the plant has projected net income of $1,854,300, $1,907,600, $1,876,000, and $1,329,500 over these four years, what is the project's average accounting return (AAR)?

7. Calculating IRR [LO5] A firm evaluates all of its projects by applying the IRR rule. If the required return is 14 percent, should the firm accept the following project?

Year	Cash Flow
0	−$28,000
1	12,000
2	15,000
3	11,000

8. Calculating NPV [LO1] For the cash flows in the previous problem, suppose the firm uses the NPV decision rule. At a required return of 11 percent, should the firm accept this project? What if the required return is 25 percent?

9. Calculating NPV and IRR [LO1, 5] A project that provides annual cash flows of $17,300 for nine years costs $79,000 today. Is this a good project if the required return is 8 percent? What if it's 20 percent? At what discount rate would you be indifferent between accepting the project and rejecting it?

10. Calculating IRR [LO5] What is the IRR of the following set of cash flows?

Year	Cash Flow
0	−$16,400
1	7,100
2	8,400
3	6,900

11. Calculating NPV [LO1] For the cash flows in the previous problem, what is the NPV at a discount rate of zero percent? What if the discount rate is 10 percent? If it is 20 percent? If it is 30 percent?

12. NPV versus IRR [LO1, 5] Garage, Inc., has identified the following two mutually exclusive projects:

Year	Cash Flow (A)	Cash Flow (B)
0	−$29,000	−$29,000
1	14,400	4,300
2	12,300	9,800
3	9,200	15,200
4	5,100	16,800

a. What is the IRR for each of these projects? Using the IRR decision rule, which project should the company accept? Is this decision necessarily correct?

b. If the required return is 11 percent, what is the NPV for each of these projects? Which project will the company choose if it applies the NPV decision rule?

c. Over what range of discount rates would the company choose project A? Project B? At what discount rate would the company be indifferent between these two projects? Explain.

13. **NPV versus IRR [LO1, 5]** Consider the following two mutually exclusive projects:

Year	Cash Flow (X)	Cash Flow (Y)
0	−$20,000	−$20,000
1	8,850	10,100
2	9,100	7,800
3	8,800	8,700

Sketch the NPV profiles for X and Y over a range of discount rates from zero to 25 percent. What is the crossover rate for these two projects?

14. **Problems with IRR [LO5]** Light Sweet Petroleum, Inc., is trying to evaluate a generation project with the following cash flows:

Year	Cash Flow
0	−$39,000,000
1	63,000,000
2	−12,000,000

a. If the company requires a 12 percent return on its investments, should it accept this project? Why?

b. Compute the IRR for this project. How many IRRs are there? Using the IRR decision rule, should the company accept the project? What's going on here?

15. **Calculating Profitability Index [LO7]** What is the profitability index for the following set of cash flows if the relevant discount rate is 10 percent? What if the discount rate is 15 percent? If it is 22 percent?

Year	Cash Flow
0	−$18,000
1	10,300
2	9,200
3	5,700

16. **Problems with Profitability Index [LO1, 7]** The Angry Bird Corporation is trying to choose between the following two mutually exclusive design projects:

Year	Cash Flow (I)	Cash Flow (II)
0	−$64,000	−$18,000
1	31,000	9,700
2	31,000	9,700
3	31,000	9,700

a. If the required return is 10 percent and the company applies the profitability index decision rule, which project should the firm accept?

b. If the company applies the NPV decision rule, which project should it take?

c. Explain why your answers in (a) and (b) are different.

17. **Comparing Investment Criteria [LO1, 2, 3, 5, 7]** Consider the following two mutually exclusive projects:

Year	Cash Flow (A)	Cash Flow (B)
0	−$350,000	−$50,000
1	45,000	24,000
2	65,000	22,000
3	65,000	19,500
4	440,000	14,600

Visit us at www.mhhe.com/rwj

Whichever project you choose, if any, you require a 15 percent return on your investment.

a. If you apply the payback criterion, which investment will you choose? Why?

b. If you apply the discounted payback criterion, which investment will you choose? Why?

c. If you apply the NPV criterion, which investment will you choose? Why?

d. If you apply the IRR criterion, which investment will you choose? Why?

e. If you apply the profitability index criterion, which investment will you choose? Why?

f. Based on your answers in (a) through (e), which project will you finally choose? Why?

18. **NPV and Discount Rates [LO1]** An investment has an installed cost of $527,800. The cash flows over the four-year life of the investment are projected to be $221,850, $238,450, $205,110, and $153,820. If the discount rate is zero, what is the NPV? If the discount rate is infinite, what is the NPV? At what discount rate is the NPV just equal to zero? Sketch the NPV profile for this investment based on these three points.

19. **MIRR [LO6]** Slow Ride Corp. is evaluating a project with the following cash flows:

Year	Cash Flow
0	−$29,000
1	11,200
2	13,900
3	15,800
4	12,900
5	−9,400

The company uses a 10 percent interest rate on all of its projects. Calculate the MIRR of the project using all three methods.

INTERMEDIATE
(Questions 20–22)

20. **MIRR [LO6]** Suppose the company in the previous problem uses an 11 percent discount rate and an 8 percent reinvestment rate on all of its projects. Calculate the MIRR of the project using all three methods using these interest rates.

21. **NPV and the Profitability Index [LO1, 7]** If we define the NPV index as the ratio of NPV to cost, what is the relationship between this index and the profitability index?

22. **Cash Flow Intuition [LO1, 2]** A project has an initial cost of I, has a required return of R, and pays C annually for N years.

a. Find C in terms of I and N such that the project has a payback period just equal to its life.

b. Find C in terms of I, N, and R such that this is a profitable project according to the NPV decision rule.

c. Find C in terms of I, N, and R such that the project has a benefit–cost ratio of 2.

CHALLENGE
(Questions 23–28)

23. **Payback and NPV [LO1, 2]** An investment under consideration has a payback of seven years and a cost of $875,000. If the required return is 11 percent, what is the worst-case NPV? The best-case NPV? Explain. Assume the cash flows are conventional.

24. **Multiple IRRs [LO5]** This problem is useful for testing the ability of financial calculators and spreadsheets. Consider the following cash flows. How many different IRRs are there? (*Hint:* Search between 20 percent and 70 percent.) When should we take this project?

Visit us at www.mhhe.com/rwj

Year	Cash Flow
0	−$ 3,024
1	17,172
2	−36,420
3	34,200
4	−12,000

25. **NPV Valuation [LO1]** The Yurdone Corporation wants to set up a private cemetery business. According to the CFO, Barry M. Deep, business is "looking up." As a result, the cemetery project will provide a net cash inflow of $97,000 for the firm during the first year, and the cash flows are projected to grow at a rate of 4 percent per year forever. The project requires an initial investment of $1,500,000.

    a. If Yurdone requires an 11 percent return on such undertakings, should the cemetery business be started?

    b. The company is somewhat unsure about the assumption of a 4 percent growth rate in its cash flows. At what constant growth rate would the company just break even if it still required an 11 percent return on investment?

26. **Problems with IRR [LO5]** A project has the following cash flows:

Year	Cash Flow
0	$42,000
1	−21,000
2	−32,000

    What is the IRR for this project? If the required return is 12 percent, should the firm accept the project? What is the NPV of this project? What is the NPV of the project if the required return is 0 percent? 24 percent? What is going on here? Sketch the NPV profile to help you with your answer.

27. **Problems with IRR [LO5]** McKeekin Corp. has a project with the following cash flows:

Year	Cash Flow
0	$ 25,000
1	−11,000
2	7,000

    What is the IRR of the project? What is happening here?

28. **NPV and IRR [LO1, 5]** Anderson International Limited is evaluating a project in Erewhon. The project will create the following cash flows:

Year	Cash Flow
0	−$1,250,000
1	425,000
2	490,000
3	385,000
4	340,000

    All cash flows will occur in Erewhon and are expressed in dollars. In an attempt to improve its economy, the Erewhonian government has declared that all cash flows created by a foreign company are "blocked" and must be reinvested with the government for one year. The reinvestment rate for these funds is 4 percent. If Anderson uses an 11 percent required return on this project, what are the NPV and IRR of the project? Is the IRR you calculated the MIRR of the project? Why or why not?

Visit us at www.mhhe.com/rwj

MINICASE

Bullock Gold Mining

Seth Bullock, the owner of Bullock Gold Mining, is evaluating a new gold mine in South Dakota. Dan Dority, the company's geologist, has just finished his analysis of the mine site. He has estimated that the mine would be productive for eight years, after which the gold would be completely mined. Dan has taken an estimate of the gold deposits to Alma Garrett, the company's financial officer. Alma has been asked by Seth to perform an analysis of the new mine and present her recommendation on whether the company should open the new mine.

Alma has used the estimates provided by Dan to determine the revenues that could be expected from the mine. She has also projected the expense of opening the mine and the annual operating expenses. If the company opens the mine, it will cost $450 million today, and it will have a cash outflow of $95 million nine years from today in costs associated with closing the mine and reclaiming the area surrounding it. The expected cash flows each year from the mine are shown in the table. Bullock Mining has a 12 percent required return on all of its gold mines.

Year	Cash Flow
0	−$450,000,000
1	63,000,000
2	85,000,000
3	120,000,000
4	145,000,000
5	175,000,000
6	120,000,000
7	95,000,000
8	75,000,000
9	−70,000,000

QUESTIONS

1. Construct a spreadsheet to calculate the payback period, internal rate of return, modified internal rate of return, and net present value of the proposed mine.

2. Based on your analysis, should the company open the mine?

3. Bonus question: Most spreadsheets do not have a built-in formula to calculate the payback period. Write a VBA script that calculates the payback period for a project.

MAKING CAPITAL INVESTMENT DECISIONS

IS THERE GREEN IN GREEN? General Electric (GE) thinks so. Through its "Ecomagination" program, the company planned to double research and development spending on green products. In fact, GE invested over $5 billion in its Ecomagination program and announced that it would invest another $10 billion from 2011 to 2015. With products such as a hybrid railroad locomotive (described as a 200-ton, 6,000-horsepower "Prius on rails"), GE's green initiative seems to be paying off. Revenue from the company's green products was $19 billion in 2009, with a target of $20 billion in 2010. Further, revenues from Ecomagination products were growing at twice the rate of the rest of the company's revenues. The company's internal commitment to reduced energy consumption through green "Treasure Hunts" saved it more than $100 million, and, by 2010, the company had reduced water consumption by 30 percent relative to its 2006 baseline, another considerable cost savings.

As you no doubt recognize from your study of the previous chapter, GE's decision to develop and market green technology represents a capital budgeting decision. In this chapter, we further investigate such decisions, how they are made, and how to look at them objectively.

This chapter follows up on our previous one by delving more deeply into capital budgeting. We have two main tasks. First, recall that in the last chapter, we saw that cash flow estimates are the critical input in a net present value analysis, but we didn't say much about where these cash flows come from; so we will now examine this question in some detail. Our second goal is to learn how to critically examine NPV estimates, and, in particular, how to evaluate the sensitivity of NPV estimates to assumptions made about the uncertain future.

LEARNING OBJECTIVES

After studying this chapter, you should understand:

LO1 How to determine the relevant cash flows for a proposed project.

LO2 How to determine if a project is acceptable.

LO3 How to set a bid price for a project.

LO4 How to evaluate the equivalent annual cost of a project.

So far, we've covered various parts of the capital budgeting decision. Our task in this chapter is to start bringing these pieces together. In particular, we will show you how to "spread the numbers" for a proposed investment or project and, based on those numbers, make an initial assessment about whether the project should be undertaken.

In the discussion that follows, we focus on the process of setting up a discounted cash flow analysis. From the last chapter, we know that the projected future cash flows are the key element in such an evaluation. Accordingly, we emphasize working with financial and accounting information to come up with these figures.

In evaluating a proposed investment, we pay special attention to deciding what information is relevant to the decision at hand and what information is not. As we will see, it is easy to overlook important pieces of the capital budgeting puzzle.

We will wait until the next chapter to describe in detail how to go about evaluating the results of our discounted cash flow analysis. Also, where needed, we will assume that we know the relevant required return, or discount rate. We continue to defer in-depth discussion of this subject to Part 5.

10.1 Project Cash Flows: A First Look

The effect of taking a project is to change the firm's overall cash flows today and in the future. To evaluate a proposed investment, we must consider these changes in the firm's cash flows and then decide whether they add value to the firm. The first (and most important) step, therefore, is to decide which cash flows are relevant.

RELEVANT CASH FLOWS

incremental cash flows
The difference between a firm's future cash flows with a project and those without the project.

What is a relevant cash flow for a project? The general principle is simple enough: A relevant cash flow for a project is a change in the firm's overall future cash flow that comes about as a direct consequence of the decision to take that project. Because the relevant cash flows are defined in terms of changes in, or increments to, the firm's existing cash flow, they are called the **incremental cash flows** associated with the project.

The concept of incremental cash flow is central to our analysis, so we will state a general definition and refer back to it as needed:

> **The incremental cash flows for project evaluation consist of *any and all* changes in the firm's future cash flows that are a direct consequence of taking the project.**

This definition of incremental cash flows has an obvious and important corollary: Any cash flow that exists regardless of *whether or not* a project is undertaken is *not* relevant.

THE STAND-ALONE PRINCIPLE

In practice, it would be cumbersome to actually calculate the future total cash flows to the firm with and without a project, especially for a large firm. Fortunately, it is not really necessary to do so. Once we identify the effect of undertaking the proposed project on the firm's cash flows, we need focus only on the project's resulting incremental cash flows. This is called the **stand-alone principle**.

stand-alone principle
The assumption that evaluation of a project may be based on the project's incremental cash flows.

What the stand-alone principle says is that once we have determined the incremental cash flows from undertaking a project, we can view that project as a kind of "minifirm" with its own future revenues and costs, its own assets, and, of course, its own cash flows. We will then be primarily interested in comparing the cash flows from this minifirm to the cost of acquiring it. An important consequence of this approach is that we will be evaluating the proposed project purely on its own merits, in isolation from any other activities or projects.

Concept Questions

10.1a What are the relevant incremental cash flows for project evaluation?
10.1b What is the stand-alone principle?

Incremental Cash Flows

10.2

We are concerned here with only cash flows that are incremental and that result from a project. Looking back at our general definition, we might think it would be easy enough to decide whether a cash flow is incremental. Even so, in a few situations it is easy to make mistakes. In this section, we describe some common pitfalls and how to avoid them.

SUNK COSTS

A **sunk cost**, by definition, is a cost we have already paid or have already incurred the liability to pay. Such a cost cannot be changed by the decision today to accept or reject a project. Put another way, the firm will have to pay this cost no matter what. Based on our general definition of incremental cash flow, such a cost is clearly not relevant to the decision at hand. So, we will always be careful to exclude sunk costs from our analysis.

That a sunk cost is not relevant seems obvious given our discussion. Nonetheless, it's easy to fall prey to the fallacy that a sunk cost should be associated with a project. For example, suppose General Milk Company hires a financial consultant to help evaluate whether a line of chocolate milk should be launched. When the consultant turns in the report, General Milk objects to the analysis because the consultant did not include the hefty consulting fee as a cost of the chocolate milk project.

Who is correct? By now, we know that the consulting fee is a sunk cost: It must be paid whether or not the chocolate milk line is actually launched (this is an attractive feature of the consulting business).

sunk cost
A cost that has already been incurred and cannot be removed and therefore should not be considered in an investment decision.

OPPORTUNITY COSTS

When we think of costs, we normally think of out-of-pocket costs—namely those that require us to actually spend some amount of cash. An **opportunity cost** is slightly different; it requires us to give up a benefit. A common situation arises in which a firm already owns some of the assets a proposed project will be using. For example, we might be thinking of converting an old rustic cotton mill we bought years ago for $100,000 into upmarket condominiums.

If we undertake this project, there will be no direct cash outflow associated with buying the old mill because we already own it. For purposes of evaluating the condo project, should we then treat the mill as "free"? The answer is no. The mill is a valuable resource used by the project. If we didn't use it here, we could do something else with it. Like what? The obvious answer is that, at a minimum, we could sell it. Using the mill for the condo complex thus has an opportunity cost: We give up the valuable opportunity to do something else with the mill.[1]

There is another issue here. Once we agree that the use of the mill has an opportunity cost, how much should we charge the condo project for this use? Given that we paid $100,000, it might seem that we should charge this amount to the condo project. Is this correct? The answer is no, and the reason is based on our discussion concerning sunk costs.

The fact that we paid $100,000 some years ago is irrelevant. That cost is sunk. At a minimum, the opportunity cost that we charge the project is what the mill would sell for today (net of any selling costs) because this is the amount we give up by using the mill instead of selling it.[2]

opportunity cost
The most valuable alternative that is given up if a particular investment is undertaken.

---

[1]Economists sometimes use the acronym TANSTAAFL, which is short for "There ain't no such thing as a free lunch," to describe the fact that only very rarely is something truly free.

[2]If the asset in question is unique, then the opportunity cost might be higher because there might be other valuable projects we could undertake that would use it. However, if the asset in question is of a type that is routinely bought and sold (a used car, perhaps), then the opportunity cost is always the going price in the market because that is the cost of buying another similar asset.

SIDE EFFECTS

Remember that the incremental cash flows for a project include all the resulting changes in the *firm's* future cash flows. It would not be unusual for a project to have side, or spillover, effects, both good and bad. For example, in 2010, the time between the theatrical release of a feature film and the release of the DVD had shrunk to 17 weeks compared to 29 weeks in 1998. Also in 2010, Walt Disney announced that it expected to shorten the time to 13 weeks. This shortened release time was blamed for at least part of the decline in movie theater box office receipts. Of course, retailers cheered the move because it was credited with increasing DVD sales. A negative impact on the cash flows of an existing product from the introduction of a new product is called **erosion**.[3] In this case, the cash flows from the new line should be adjusted downward to reflect lost profits on other lines.

In accounting for erosion, it is important to recognize that any sales lost as a result of launching a new product might be lost anyway because of future competition. Erosion is relevant only when the sales would not otherwise be lost.

Side effects show up in a lot of different ways. For example, one of Walt Disney Company's concerns when it built Euro Disney was that the new park would drain visitors from the Florida park, a popular vacation destination for Europeans.

There are beneficial spillover effects, of course. For example, you might think that Hewlett-Packard would have been concerned when the price of a printer that sold for $500 to $600 in 1994 declined to below $100 by 2011, but such was not the case. HP realized that the big money is in the consumables that printer owners buy to keep their printers going, such as ink-jet cartridges, laser toner cartridges, and special paper. The profit margins for these products are substantial.

erosion
The cash flows of a new project that come at the expense of a firm's existing projects.

NET WORKING CAPITAL

Normally a project will require that the firm invest in net working capital in addition to long-term assets. For example, a project will generally need some amount of cash on hand to pay any expenses that arise. In addition, a project will need an initial investment in inventories and accounts receivable (to cover credit sales). Some of the financing for this will be in the form of amounts owed to suppliers (accounts payable), but the firm will have to supply the balance. This balance represents the investment in net working capital.

It's easy to overlook an important feature of net working capital in capital budgeting. As a project winds down, inventories are sold, receivables are collected, bills are paid, and cash balances can be drawn down. These activities free up the net working capital originally invested. So the firm's investment in project net working capital closely resembles a loan. The firm supplies working capital at the beginning and recovers it toward the end.

FINANCING COSTS

In analyzing a proposed investment, we will *not* include interest paid or any other financing costs such as dividends or principal repaid because we are interested in the cash flow generated by the assets of the project. As we mentioned in Chapter 2, interest paid, for example, is a component of cash flow to creditors, not cash flow from assets.

More generally, our goal in project evaluation is to compare the cash flow from a project to the cost of acquiring that project in order to estimate NPV. The particular mixture of debt and equity a firm actually chooses to use in financing a project is a managerial variable and primarily determines how project cash flow is divided between owners and creditors. This is not to say that financing arrangements are unimportant. They are just something to be analyzed separately. We will cover this in later chapters.

---

[3]More colorfully, erosion is sometimes called *piracy* or *cannibalism*.

OTHER ISSUES

There are some other things to watch out for. First, we are interested only in measuring cash flow. Moreover, we are interested in measuring it when it actually occurs, not when it accrues in an accounting sense. Second, we are always interested in *aftertax* cash flow because taxes are definitely a cash outflow. In fact, whenever we write *incremental cash flows,* we mean aftertax incremental cash flows. Remember, however, that aftertax cash flow and accounting profit, or net income, are entirely different things.

Concept Questions

10.2a What is a sunk cost? An opportunity cost?

10.2b Explain what erosion is and why it is relevant.

10.2c Explain why interest paid is not a relevant cash flow for project evaluation.

Pro Forma Financial Statements and Project Cash Flows

10.3

The first thing we need when we begin evaluating a proposed investment is a set of pro forma, or projected, financial statements. Given these, we can develop the projected cash flows from the project. Once we have the cash flows, we can estimate the value of the project using the techniques we described in the previous chapter.

GETTING STARTED: PRO FORMA FINANCIAL STATEMENTS

Pro forma financial statements are a convenient and easily understood means of summarizing much of the relevant information for a project. To prepare these statements, we will need estimates of quantities such as unit sales, the selling price per unit, the variable cost per unit, and total fixed costs. We will also need to know the total investment required, including any investment in net working capital.

pro forma financial statements
Financial statements projecting future years' operations.

To illustrate, suppose we think we can sell 50,000 cans of shark attractant per year at a price of $4 per can. It costs us about $2.50 per can to make the attractant, and a new product such as this one typically has only a three-year life (perhaps because the customer base dwindles rapidly). We require a 20 percent return on new products.

Fixed costs for the project, including such things as rent on the production facility, will run $12,000 per year.[4] Further, we will need to invest a total of $90,000 in manufacturing equipment. For simplicity, we will assume that this $90,000 will be 100 percent depreciated over the three-year life of the project.[5] Furthermore, the cost of removing the equipment will roughly equal its actual value in three years, so it will be essentially worthless on a market value basis as well. Finally, the project will require an initial $20,000 investment in net working capital, and the tax rate is 34 percent.

In Table 10.1, we organize these initial projections by first preparing the pro forma income statement. Once again, notice that we have *not* deducted any interest expense. This will always be so. As we described earlier, interest paid is a financing expense, not a component of operating cash flow.

---

[4]By *fixed cost,* we literally mean a cash outflow that will occur regardless of the level of sales. This should not be confused with some sort of accounting period charge.

[5]We will also assume that a full year's depreciation can be taken in the first year.

Sales (50,000 units at $4/unit)	$200,000
Variable costs ($2.50/unit)	125,000
	$ 75,000
Fixed costs	12,000
Depreciation ($90,000/3)	30,000
EBIT	$ 33,000
Taxes (34%)	11,220
Net income	$ 21,780

	Year			
	0	1	2	3
Net working capital	$ 20,000	$20,000	$20,000	$20,000
Net fixed assets	90,000	60,000	30,000	0
Total investment	$110,000	$80,000	$50,000	$20,000

We can also prepare a series of abbreviated balance sheets that show the capital requirements for the project as we've done in Table 10.2. Here we have net working capital of $20,000 in each year. Fixed assets are $90,000 at the start of the project's life (Year 0), and they decline by the $30,000 in depreciation each year, ending up at zero. Notice that the total investment given here for future years is the total book, or accounting, value, not market value.

At this point, we need to start converting this accounting information into cash flows. We consider how to do this next.

PROJECT CASH FLOWS

To develop the cash flows from a project, we need to recall (from Chapter 2) that cash flow from assets has three components: operating cash flow, capital spending, and changes in net working capital. To evaluate a project, or minifirm, we need to estimate each of these.

Once we have estimates of the components of cash flow, we will calculate cash flow for our minifirm just as we did in Chapter 2 for an entire firm:

Project cash flow = Project operating cash flow

− Project change in net working capital

− Project capital spending

We consider these components next.

Project Operating Cash Flow   To determine the operating cash flow associated with a project, we first need to recall the definition of operating cash flow:

Operating cash flow = Earnings before interest and taxes

+ Depreciation

− Taxes

To illustrate the calculation of operating cash flow, we will use the projected information from the shark attractant project. For ease of reference, Table 10.3 repeats the income statement in more abbreviated form.

Sales	$200,000
Variable costs	125,000
Fixed costs	12,000
Depreciation	30,000
EBIT	$ 33,000
Taxes (34%)	11,220
Net income	$ 21,780

TABLE 10.3

Projected Income Statement, Abbreviated, Shark Attractant Project

EBIT	$ 33,000
Depreciation	+ 30,000
Taxes	− 11,220
Operating cash flow	$51,780

TABLE 10.4

Projected Operating Cash Flow, Shark Attractant Project

	Year			
	0	1	2	3
Operating cash flow		$51,780	$51,780	$51,780
Changes in NWC	−$ 20,000			+ 20,000
Capital spending	− 90,000			
Total project cash flow	−$110,000	$51,780	$51,780	$71,780

TABLE 10.5

Projected Total Cash Flows, Shark Attractant Project

Given the income statement in Table 10.3, calculating the operating cash flow is straightforward. As we see in Table 10.4, projected operating cash flow for the shark attractant project is $51,780.

Project Net Working Capital and Capital Spending   We next need to take care of the fixed asset and net working capital requirements. Based on our balance sheets, we know that the firm must spend $90,000 up front for fixed assets and invest an additional $20,000 in net working capital. The immediate outflow is thus $110,000. At the end of the project's life, the fixed assets will be worthless, but the firm will recover the $20,000 that was tied up in working capital.[6] This will lead to a $20,000 *inflow* in the last year.

On a purely mechanical level, notice that whenever we have an investment in net working capital, that same investment has to be recovered; in other words, the same number needs to appear at some time in the future with the opposite sign.

PROJECTED TOTAL CASH FLOW AND VALUE

Given the information we've accumulated, we can finish the preliminary cash flow analysis as illustrated in Table 10.5.

Now that we have cash flow projections, we are ready to apply the various criteria we discussed in the last chapter. First, the NPV at the 20 percent required return is:

$$\text{NPV} = -\$110,000 + 51,780/1.2 + 51,780/1.2^2 + 71,780/1.2^3$$
$$= \$10,648$$

---

[6]In reality, the firm would probably recover something less than 100 percent of this amount because of bad debts, inventory loss, and so on. If we wanted to, we could just assume that, for example, only 90 percent was recovered and proceed from there.

Based on these projections, the project creates over $10,000 in value and should be accepted. Also, the return on this investment obviously exceeds 20 percent (because the NPV is positive at 20 percent). After some trial and error, we find that the IRR works out to be about 25.8 percent.

In addition, if required, we could calculate the payback and the average accounting return, or AAR. Inspection of the cash flows shows that the payback on this project is just a little over two years (verify that it's about 2.1 years).[7]

From the last chapter, we know that the AAR is average net income divided by average book value. The net income each year is $21,780. The average (in thousands) of the four book values (from Table 10.2) for total investment is ($110 + 80 + 50 + 20)/4 = $65. So the AAR is $21,780/65,000 = 33.51 percent.[8] We've already seen that the return on this investment (the IRR) is about 26 percent. The fact that the AAR is larger illustrates again why the AAR cannot be meaningfully interpreted as the return on a project.

Concept Questions

10.3a What is the definition of project operating cash flow? How does this differ from net income?

10.3b For the shark attractant project, why did we add back the firm's net working capital investment in the final year?

☒ 10.4 More about Project Cash Flow

In this section, we take a closer look at some aspects of project cash flow. In particular, we discuss project net working capital in more detail. We then examine current tax laws regarding depreciation. Finally, we work through a more involved example of the capital investment decision.

A CLOSER LOOK AT NET WORKING CAPITAL

In calculating operating cash flow, we did not explicitly consider the fact that some of our sales might be on credit. Also, we may not have actually paid some of the costs shown. In either case, the cash flow in question would not yet have occurred. We show here that these possibilities are not a problem as long as we don't forget to include changes in net working capital in our analysis. This discussion thus emphasizes the importance and the effect of doing so.

Suppose that during a particular year of a project we have the following simplified income statement:

Sales	$500
Costs	310
Net income	$190

---

[7]We're guilty of a minor inconsistency here. When we calculated the NPV and the IRR, we assumed that all the cash flows occurred at end of year. When we calculated the payback, we assumed that the cash flows occurred uniformly throughout the year.

[8]Notice that the average total book value is not the initial total of $110,000 divided by 2. The reason is that the $20,000 in working capital doesn't "depreciate."

Depreciation and taxes are zero. No fixed assets are purchased during the year. Also, to illustrate a point, we assume that the only components of net working capital are accounts receivable and payable. The beginning and ending amounts for these accounts are as follows:

	Beginning of Year	End of Year	Change
Accounts receivable	$880	$910	+$30
Accounts payable	550	605	+ 55
Net working capital	$330	$305	−$25

Based on this information, what is total cash flow for the year? We can first just mechanically apply what we have been discussing to come up with the answer. Operating cash flow in this particular case is the same as EBIT because there are no taxes or depreciation; thus, it equals $190. Also, notice that net working capital actually *declined* by $25. This just means that $25 was freed up during the year. There was no capital spending, so the total cash flow for the year is:

$$\text{Total cash flow} = \text{Operating cash flow} - \text{Change in NWC} - \text{Capital spending}$$
$$= \$190 - (-25) - 0$$
$$= \$215$$

Now, we know that this $215 total cash flow has to be "dollars in" less "dollars out" for the year. We could therefore ask a different question: What were cash revenues for the year? Also, what were cash costs?

To determine cash revenues, we need to look more closely at net working capital. During the year, we had sales of $500. However, accounts receivable rose by $30 over the same time period. What does this mean? The $30 increase tells us that sales exceeded collections by $30. In other words, we haven't yet received the cash from $30 of the $500 in sales. As a result, our cash inflow is $500 − 30 = $470. In general, cash income is sales minus the increase in accounts receivable.

Cash outflows can be similarly determined. We show costs of $310 on the income statement, but accounts payable increased by $55 during the year. This means that we have not yet paid $55 of the $310, so cash costs for the period are just $310 − 55 = $255. In other words, in this case, cash costs equal costs less the increase in accounts payable.[9]

Putting this information together, we calculate that cash inflows less cash outflows are $470 − 255 = $215, just as we had before. Notice that:

$$\text{Cash flow} = \text{Cash inflow} - \text{Cash outflow}$$
$$= (\$500 - 30) - (310 - 55)$$
$$= (\$500 - 310) - (30 - 55)$$
$$= \text{Operating cash flow} - \text{Change in NWC}$$
$$= \$190 - (-25)$$
$$= \$215$$

More generally, this example illustrates that including net working capital changes in our calculations has the effect of adjusting for the discrepancy between accounting sales and costs and actual cash receipts and payments.

---

[9]If there were other accounts, we might have to make some further adjustments. For example, a net increase in inventory would be a cash outflow.

Samuel Weaver on Capital Budgeting at The Hershey Company

The capital program at The Hershey Company and most Fortune 500 or Fortune 1,000 companies involves a three-phase approach: planning or budgeting, evaluation, and postcompletion reviews.

The first phase involves identification of likely projects at strategic planning time. These are selected to support the strategic objectives of the corporation. This identification is generally broad in scope with minimal financial evaluation attached. Projects are classified as new product, cost savings, capacity expansion, etc. As the planning process focuses more closely on the short-term plans (or budgets), major capital expenditures are discussed more rigorously. Project costs are more closely honed, and specific projects may be reconsidered.

Each project is then individually reviewed and authorized. Planning, developing, and refining cash flows underlie capital analysis at Hershey. Once the cash flows have been determined, the application of capital evaluation techniques such as those using net present value, internal rate of return, and payback period is routine. Presentation of the results is enhanced using sensitivity analysis, which plays a major role for management in assessing the critical assumptions and resulting impact.

The final phase relates to postcompletion reviews in which the original forecasts of the project's performance are compared to actual results and/or revised expectations.

Capital expenditure analysis is only as good as the assumptions that underlie the project. The old cliché of GIGO (garbage in, garbage out) applies in this case. Incremental cash flows primarily result from incremental sales or margin improvements (cost savings). For the most part, a range of incremental cash flows can be identified from marketing research or engineering studies. However, for a number of projects, correctly discerning the implications and the relevant cash flows is analytically challenging. For example, when a new product is introduced and is expected to generate millions of dollars' worth of sales, the appropriate analysis focuses on the incremental sales after accounting for cannibalization of existing products.

One of the problems that we face at Hershey deals with the application of net present value, NPV, versus internal rate of return, IRR. NPV offers us the correct investment indication when dealing with mutually exclusive alternatives. However, decision makers at all levels sometimes find it difficult to comprehend the result. Specifically, an NPV of, say, $535,000 needs to be interpreted. It is not enough to know that the NPV is positive or even that it is more positive than an alternative. Decision makers seek to determine a level of "comfort" regarding how profitable the investment is by relating it to other standards.

Although the IRR may provide a misleading indication of which project to select, the result is provided in a way that can be interpreted by all parties. The resulting IRR can be mentally compared to expected inflation, current borrowing rates, the cost of capital, an equity portfolio's return, and so on. An IRR of, say, 18 percent is readily interpretable by management. Perhaps this ease of understanding is why surveys indicate that many Fortune 500 or Fortune 1,000 companies use the IRR method (in conjunction with NPV) as a primary evaluation technique.

In addition to the NPV versus IRR problem, there are a limited number of projects for which traditional capital expenditure analysis is difficult to apply because the cash flows can't be determined. When new computer equipment is purchased, an office building is renovated, or a parking lot is repaved, it is essentially impossible to identify the cash flows, so the use of traditional evaluation techniques is limited. These types of "capital expenditure" decisions are made using other techniques that hinge on management's judgment.

Samuel Weaver, Ph.D., is the former director, financial planning and analysis, for Hershey. He is a certified management accountant and certified financial manager. His position combined the theoretical with the pragmatic and involved the analysis of many different facets of finance in addition to capital expenditure analysis.

EXAMPLE 10.1	Cash Collections and Costs

For the year just completed, the Combat Wombat Telestat Co. (CWT) reports sales of $998 and costs of $734. You have collected the following beginning and ending balance sheet information:

	Beginning	**Ending**
Accounts receivable	$100	$110
Inventory	100	80
Accounts payable	100	70
Net working capital	$100	$120

Based on these figures, what are cash inflows? Cash outflows? What happened to each account? What is net cash flow?

Sales were $998, but receivables rose by $10. So cash collections were $10 less than sales, or $988. Costs were $734, but inventories fell by $20. This means that we didn't replace $20 worth of inventory, so costs are actually overstated by this amount. Also, payables fell by $30. This means that, on a net basis, we actually paid our suppliers $30 more than we received from them, resulting in a $30 understatement of costs. Adjusting for these events, we calculate that cash costs are $734 − 20 + 30 = $744. Net cash flow is $988 − 744 = $244.

Finally, notice that net working capital increased by $20 overall. We can check our answer by noting that the original accounting sales less costs (= $998 − 734) are $264. In addition, CWT spent $20 on net working capital, so the net result is a cash flow of $264 − 20 = $244, as we calculated.

DEPRECIATION

As we note elsewhere, accounting depreciation is a noncash deduction. As a result, depreciation has cash flow consequences only because it influences the tax bill. The way that depreciation is computed for tax purposes is thus the relevant method for capital investment decisions. Not surprisingly, the procedures are governed by tax law. We now discuss some specifics of the depreciation system enacted by the tax reform act of 1986. this system is a modification of the **accelerated cost recovery system (ACRS)** instituted in 1981.

accelerated cost recovery system (ACRS)
A depreciation method under U.S. tax law allowing for the accelerated write-off of property under various classifications.

Modified ACRS Depreciation (MACRS)   Calculating depreciation is normally mechanical. Although there are a number of *ifs, ands,* and *buts* involved, the basic idea under MACRS is that every asset is assigned to a particular class. An asset's class establishes its life for tax purposes. Once an asset's tax life is determined, the depreciation for each year is computed by multiplying the cost of the asset by a fixed percentage.[10] The expected salvage value (what we think the asset will be worth when we dispose of it) and the expected economic life (how long we expect the asset to be in service) are not explicitly considered in the calculation of depreciation.

Some typical depreciation classes are given in Table 10.6, and associated percentages (as specified by the IRS) are shown in Table 10.7.[11]

A nonresidential real property, such as an office building, is depreciated over 31.5 years using straight-line depreciation. A residential real property, such as an apartment building, is depreciated straight-line over 27.5 years. Remember that land cannot be depreciated.[12]

---

[10]Under certain circumstances, the cost of the asset may be adjusted before computing depreciation. The result is called the *depreciable basis,* and depreciation is calculated using this number instead of the actual cost.

[11]For the curious, these depreciation percentages are derived from a double-declining balance scheme with a switch to straight-line when the latter becomes advantageous. Further, there is a half-year convention, meaning that all assets are assumed to be placed in service midway through the tax year. This convention is maintained unless more than 40 percent of an asset's cost is incurred in the final quarter. In this case, a midquarter convention is used. The odd-looking rounding is courtesy of the IRS.

[12]There are, however, depletion allowances for firms in extraction-type lines of business (such as mining). These are somewhat similar to depreciation allowances.

TABLE 10.6

Modified ACRS Property Classes

Class	Examples
Three-year	Equipment used in research
Five-year	Autos, computers
Seven-year	Most industrial equipment

TABLE 10.7

Modified ACRS Depreciation Allowances

	Property Class		
Year	Three-Year	Five-Year	Seven-Year
1	33.33%	20.00%	14.29%
2	44.45	32.00	24.49
3	14.81	19.20	17.49
4	7.41	11.52	12.49
5		11.52	8.93
6		5.76	8.92
7			8.93
8			4.46

To illustrate how depreciation is calculated, we consider an automobile costing $12,000. Autos are normally classified as five-year property. Looking at Table 10.7, we see that the relevant figure for the first year of a five-year asset is 20 percent.[13] The depreciation in the first year is thus $12,000 × .20 = $2,400. The relevant percentage in the second year is 32 percent, so the depreciation in the second year is $12,000 × .32 = $3,840, and so on. We can summarize these calculations as follows:

Year	MACRS Percentage	Depreciation		
1	20.00%	.2000 × $12,000 =	$	2,400.00
2	32.00	.3200 × 12,000 =		3,840.00
3	19.20	.1920 × 12,000 =		2,304.00
4	11.52	.1152 × 12,000 =		1,382.40
5	11.52	.1152 × 12,000 =		1,382.40
6	5.76	.0576 × 12,000 =		691.20
	100.00%		$12,000.00	

Notice that the MACRS percentages sum up to 100 percent. As a result, we write off 100 percent of the cost of the asset, or $12,000 in this case.

Book Value versus Market Value   In calculating depreciation under current tax law, the economic life and future market value of the asset are not an issue. As a result, the book value of an asset can differ substantially from its actual market value. For example, with our $12,000 car, book value after the first year is $12,000 less the first year's depreciation of $2,400, or $9,600. The remaining book values are summarized in Table 10.8. After six years, the book value of the car is zero.

Suppose we wanted to sell the car after five years. Based on historical averages, it would be worth, say, 25 percent of the purchase price, or .25 × $12,000 = $3,000. If we actually

---

[13]It may appear odd that five-year property is depreciated over six years. The tax accounting reason is that it is assumed we have the asset for only six months in the first year and, consequently, six months in the last year. As a result, there are five 12-month periods, but we have some depreciation in each of six different tax years.

Year	Beginning Book Value	Depreciation	Ending Book Value
1	$12,000.00	$2,400.00	$9,600.00
2	9,600.00	3,840.00	5,760.00
3	5,760.00	2,304.00	3,456.00
4	3,456.00	1,382.40	2,073.60
5	2,073.60	1,382.40	691.20
6	691.20	691.20	.00

TABLE 10.8

MACRS Book Values

sold it for this, then we would have to pay taxes at the ordinary income tax rate on the difference between the sale price of $3,000 and the book value of $691.20. For a corporation in the 34 percent bracket, the tax liability would be .34 × $2,308.80 = $784.99.[14]

The reason taxes must be paid in this case is that the difference between market value and book value is "excess" depreciation, and it must be "recaptured" when the asset is sold. What this means is that, as it turns out, we overdepreciated the asset by $3,000 − 691.20 = $2,308.80. Because we deducted $2,308.80 too much in depreciation, we paid $784.99 too little in taxes, and we simply have to make up the difference.

Notice that this is *not* a tax on a capital gain. As a general (albeit rough) rule, a capital gain occurs only if the market price exceeds the original cost. However, what is and what is not a capital gain is ultimately up to taxing authorities, and the specific rules can be complex. We will ignore capital gains taxes for the most part.

Finally, if the book value exceeds the market value, then the difference is treated as a loss for tax purposes. For example, if we sell the car after two years for $4,000, then the book value exceeds the market value by $1,760. In this case, a tax saving of .34 × $1,760 = $598.40 occurs.

MACRS Depreciation

EXAMPLE 10.2

The Staple Supply Co. has just purchased a new computerized information system with an installed cost of $160,000. The computer is treated as five-year property. What are the yearly depreciation allowances? Based on historical experience, we think that the system will be worth only $10,000 when Staple gets rid of it in four years. What are the tax consequences of the sale? What is the total aftertax cash flow from the sale?

The yearly depreciation allowances are calculated by just multiplying $160,000 by the five-year percentages found in Table 10.7:

Year	MACRS Percentage	Depreciation	Ending Book Value
1	20.00%	.2000 × $160,000 = $ 32,000	$128,000
2	32.00	.3200 × 160,000 = 51,200	76,800
3	19.20	.1920 × 160,000 = 30,720	46,080
4	11.52	.1152 × 160,000 = 18,432	27,648
5	11.52	.1152 × 160,000 = 18,432	9,216
6	5.76	.0576 × 160,000 = 9,216	0
	100.00%	$160,000	

(continued)

[14]The rules are different and more complicated with real property. Essentially, in this case, only the difference between the actual book value and the book value that would have existed if straight-line depreciation had been used is recaptured. Anything above the straight-line book value is considered a capital gain.

Notice that we have also computed the book value of the system as of the end of each year. The book value at the end of Year 4 is $27,648. If Staple sells the system for $10,000 at that time, it will have a loss of $17,648 (the difference) for tax purposes. This loss, of course, is like depreciation because it isn't a cash expense.

What really happens? Two things. First, Staple gets $10,000 from the buyer. Second, it saves .34 × $17,648 = $6,000 in taxes. So, the total aftertax cash flow from the sale is a $16,000 cash inflow.

AN EXAMPLE: THE MAJESTIC MULCH AND COMPOST COMPANY (MMCC)

At this point, we want to go through a somewhat more involved capital budgeting analysis. Keep in mind as you read that the basic approach here is exactly the same as that in the shark attractant example used earlier. We have just added some real-world detail (and a lot more numbers).

MMCC is investigating the feasibility of a new line of power mulching tools aimed at the growing number of home composters. Based on exploratory conversations with buyers for large garden shops, MMCC projects unit sales as follows:

Year	Unit Sales
1	3,000
2	5,000
3	6,000
4	6,500
5	6,000
6	5,000
7	4,000
8	3,000

The new power mulcher will sell for $120 per unit to start. When the competition catches up after three years, however, MMCC anticipates that the price will drop to $110.

The power mulcher project will require $20,000 in net working capital at the start. Subsequently, total net working capital at the end of each year will be about 15 percent of sales for that year. The variable cost per unit is $60, and total fixed costs are $25,000 per year.

It will cost about $800,000 to buy the equipment necessary to begin production. This investment is primarily in industrial equipment, which qualifies as seven-year MACRS property. The equipment will actually be worth about 20 percent of its cost in eight years, or .20 × $800,000 = $160,000. The relevant tax rate is 34 percent, and the required return is 15 percent. Based on this information, should MMCC proceed?

Operating Cash Flows   There is a lot of information here that we need to organize. The first thing we can do is calculate projected sales. Sales in the first year are projected at 3,000 units at $120 apiece, or $360,000 total. The remaining figures are shown in Table 10.9.

Next, we compute the depreciation on the $800,000 investment in Table 10.10. With this information, we can prepare the pro forma income statements, as shown in Table 10.11. From here, computing the operating cash flows is straightforward. The results are illustrated in the first part of Table 10.13.

Change in NWC   Now that we have the operating cash flows, we need to determine the changes in NWC. By assumption, net working capital requirements change as sales change. In each year, MMCC will generally either add to or recover some of its project net working

Year	Unit Price	Unit Sales	Revenues
1	$120	3,000	$360,000
2	120	5,000	600,000
3	120	6,000	720,000
4	110	6,500	715,000
5	110	6,000	660,000
6	110	5,000	550,000
7	110	4,000	440,000
8	110	3,000	330,000

TABLE 10.9

Projected Revenues, Power Mulcher Project

Year	MACRS Percentage	Depreciation	Ending Book Value
1	14.29%	.1429 × $800,000 = $114,320	$685,680
2	24.49	.2449 × 800,000 = 195,920	489,760
3	17.49	.1749 × 800,000 = 139,920	349,840
4	12.49	.1249 × 800,000 = 99,920	249,920
5	8.93	.0893 × 800,000 = 71,440	178,480
6	8.92	.0892 × 800,000 = 71,360	107,120
7	8.93	.0893 × 800,000 = 71,440	35,680
8	4.46	.0446 × 800,000 = 35,680	0
	100.00%	$800,000	

TABLE 10.10

Annual Depreciation, Power Mulcher Project

TABLE 10.11   Projected Income Statements, Power Mulcher Project

	Year							
	1	2	3	4	5	6	7	8
Unit price	$ 120	$ 120	$ 120	$ 110	$ 110	$ 110	$ 110	$ 110
Unit sales	3,000	5,000	6,000	6,500	6,000	5,000	4,000	3,000
Revenues	$360,000	$600,000	$720,000	$715,000	$660,000	$550,000	$440,000	$330,000
Variable costs	180,000	300,000	360,000	390,000	360,000	300,000	240,000	180,000
Fixed costs	25,000	25,000	25,000	25,000	25,000	25,000	25,000	25,000
Depreciation	114,320	195,920	139,920	99,920	71,440	71,360	71,440	35,680
EBIT	$ 40,680	$ 79,080	$195,080	$200,080	$203,560	$153,640	$103,560	$ 89,320
Taxes (34%)	13,831	26,887	66,327	68,027	69,210	52,238	35,210	30,369
Net income	$ 26,849	$ 52,193	$128,753	$132,053	$134,350	$101,402	$ 68,350	$ 58,951

capital. Recalling that NWC starts out at $20,000 and then rises to 15 percent of sales, we can calculate the amount of NWC for each year as shown in Table 10.12.

As illustrated, during the first year, net working capital grows from $20,000 to .15 × $360,000 = $54,000. The increase in net working capital for the year is thus $54,000 − 20,000 = $34,000. The remaining figures are calculated in the same way.

TABLE 10.12

Changes in Net Working Capital, Power Mulcher Project

Year	Revenues	Net Working Capital	Cash Flow
0		$ 20,000	−$20,000
1	$360,000	54,000	− 34,000
2	600,000	90,000	− 36,000
3	720,000	108,000	− 18,000
4	715,000	107,250	750
5	660,000	99,000	8,250
6	550,000	82,500	16,500
7	440,000	66,000	16,500
8	330,000	49,500	16,500

TABLE 10.13   Projected Cash Flows, Power Mulcher Project

	Year							
	0	**1**	**2**	**3**	**4**	**5**	**6**	**7**	**8**
I. Operating Cash Flow								
EBIT		$ 40,680	$ 79,080	$195,080	$200,080	$203,560	$153,640	$103,560	$89,320
Depreciation		114,320	195,920	139,920	99,920	71,440	71,360	71,440	35,680
Taxes		− 13,831	− 26,887	− 66,327	− 68,027	− 69,210	− 52,238	− 35,210	− 30,369
Operating cash flow		$141,169	$248,113	$268,673	$231,973	$205,790	$172,762	$139,790	$94,631
II. Net Working Capital								
Initial NWC	−$ 20,000								
Change in NWC		−$34,000	−$ 36,000	−$18,000	$ 750	$ 8,250	$ 16,500	$ 16,500	$ 16,500
NWC recovery									49,500
Total change in NWC	−$ 20,000	−$34,000	−$ 36,000	−$18,000	$ 750	$ 8,250	$ 16,500	$ 16,500	$ 66,000
III. Capital Spending								
Initial outlay	−$800,000								
Aftertax salvage									$105,600
Capital spending	−$800,000								$105,600

Remember that an increase in net working capital is a cash outflow, so we use a negative sign in this table to indicate an additional investment that the firm makes in net working capital. A positive sign represents net working capital returning to the firm. Thus, for example, $16,500 in NWC flows back to the firm in Year 6. Over the project's life, net working capital builds to a peak of $108,000 and declines from there as sales begin to drop off.

We show the result for changes in net working capital in the second part of Table 10.13. Notice that at the end of the project's life, there is $49,500 in net working capital still to be recovered. Therefore, in the last year, the project returns $16,500 of NWC during the year and then returns the remaining $49,500 at the end of the year for a total of $66,000.

TABLE 10.14   Projected Total Cash Flows, Power Mulcher Project

	Year								
	0	**1**	**2**	**3**	**4**	**5**	**6**	**7**	**8**
Operating cash flow		$141,169	$248,113	$268,673	$231,973	$205,790	$172,762	$139,790	$ 94,631
Change in NWC	−$ 20,000 −	34,000 −	36,000 −	18,000	750	8,250	16,500	16,500	66,000
Capital spending	− 800,000								105,600
Total project cash flow	−$820,000	$107,169	$212,113	$250,673	$232,723	$214,040	$189,262	$156,290	$266,231
Cumulative cash flow	−$820,000	−$712,831	−$500,718	−$250,045	−$ 17,322	$196,718	$385,980	$542,270	$808,501
Discounted cash flow @ 15%	− 820,000	93,190	160,388	164,822	133,060	106,416	81,823	58,755	87,031

Net present value (15%) = $65,485
Internal rate of return = 17.24%
Payback   = 4.08 years

Capital Spending   Finally, we have to account for the long-term capital invested in the project. In this case, MMCC invests $800,000 at Year 0. By assumption, this equipment will be worth $160,000 at the end of the project. It will have a book value of zero at that time. As we discussed earlier, this $160,000 excess of market value over book value is taxable, so the aftertax proceeds will be $160,000 × (1 − .34) = $105,600. These figures are shown in the third part of Table 10.13.

Total Cash Flow and Value   We now have all the cash flow pieces, and we put them together in Table 10.14. In addition to the total project cash flows, we have calculated the cumulative cash flows and the discounted cash flows. At this point, it's essentially plug-and-chug to calculate the net present value, internal rate of return, and payback.

If we sum the discounted flows and the initial investment, the net present value (at 15 percent) works out to be $65,485. This is positive, so, based on these preliminary projections, the power mulcher project is acceptable. The internal, or DCF, rate of return is greater than 15 percent because the NPV is positive. It works out to be 17.24 percent, again indicating that the project is acceptable.

Looking at the cumulative cash flows, we can see that the project has almost paid back after four years because the table shows that the cumulative cash flow is almost zero at that time. As indicated, the fractional year works out to be $17,322/214,040 = .08, so the payback is 4.08 years. We can't say whether or not this is good because we don't have a benchmark for MMCC. This is the usual problem with payback periods.

Conclusion   This completes our preliminary DCF analysis. Where do we go from here? If we have a great deal of confidence in our projections, there is no further analysis to be done. MMCC should begin production and marketing immediately. It is unlikely that this will be the case. It is important to remember that the result of our analysis is an estimate of NPV, and we will usually have less than complete confidence in our projections. This means we have more work to do. In particular, we will almost surely want to spend some time evaluating the quality of our estimates. We will take up this subject in the next chapter. For now, we look at some alternative definitions of operating cash flow, and we illustrate some different cases that arise in capital budgeting.

10.4a Why is it important to consider changes in net working capital in developing cash flows? What is the effect of doing so?

10.4b How is depreciation calculated for fixed assets under current tax law? What effects do expected salvage value and estimated economic life have on the calculated depreciation deduction?

10.5 Alternative Definitions of Operating Cash Flow

The analysis we went through in the previous section is quite general and can be adapted to just about any capital investment problem. In the next section, we illustrate some particularly useful variations. Before we do so, we need to discuss the fact that there are different definitions of project operating cash flow that are commonly used, both in practice and in finance texts.

As we will see, the different approaches to operating cash flow that exist all measure the same thing. If they are used correctly, they all produce the same answer, and one is not necessarily any better or more useful than another. Unfortunately, the fact that alternative definitions are used does sometimes lead to confusion. For this reason, we examine several of these variations next to see how they are related.

In the discussion that follows, keep in mind that when we speak of cash flow, we literally mean dollars in less dollars out. This is all we are concerned with. Different definitions of operating cash flow simply amount to different ways of manipulating basic information about sales, costs, depreciation, and taxes to get at cash flow.

For a particular project and year under consideration, suppose we have the following estimates:

Sales = $1,500
Costs = $700
Depreciation = $600

With these estimates, notice that EBIT is:

$$\text{EBIT} = \text{Sales} - \text{Costs} - \text{Depreciation}$$
$$= \$1,500 - 700 - 600$$
$$= \$200$$

Once again, we assume that no interest is paid, so the tax bill is:

$$\text{Taxes} = \text{EBIT} \times T$$
$$= \$200 \times .34 = \$68$$

where T, the corporate tax rate, is 34 percent.

When we put all of this together, we see that project operating cash flow, OCF, is:

$$\text{OCF} = \text{EBIT} + \text{Depreciation} - \text{Taxes}$$
$$= \$200 + 600 - 68 = \$732$$

There are some other ways to determine OCF that could be (and are) used. We consider these next.

THE BOTTOM-UP APPROACH

Because we are ignoring any financing expenses, such as interest, in our calculations of project OCF, we can write project net income as:

$$\begin{aligned} \text{Project net income} &= \text{EBIT} - \text{Taxes} \\ &= \$200 - 68 \\ &= \$132 \end{aligned}$$

If we simply add the depreciation to both sides, we arrive at a slightly different and very common expression for OCF:

$$\begin{aligned} \text{OCF} &= \text{Net income} + \text{Depreciation} && \text{[10.1]} \\ &= \$132 + 600 \\ &= \$732 \end{aligned}$$

This is the *bottom-up* approach. Here, we start with the accountant's bottom line (net income) and add back any noncash deductions such as depreciation. It is crucial to remember that this definition of operating cash flow as net income plus depreciation is correct only if there is no interest expense subtracted in the calculation of net income.

For the shark attractant project, net income was $21,780 and depreciation was $30,000, so the bottom-up calculation is:

$$\text{OCF} = \$21,780 + 30,000 = \$51,780$$

This is exactly the same OCF we had previously.

THE TOP-DOWN APPROACH

Perhaps the most obvious way to calculate OCF is:

$$\begin{aligned} \text{OCF} &= \text{Sales} - \text{Costs} - \text{Taxes} && \text{[10.2]} \\ &= \$1,500 - 700 - 68 = \$732 \end{aligned}$$

This is the *top-down* approach, the second variation on the basic OCF definition. Here, we start at the top of the income statement with sales and work our way down to net cash flow by subtracting costs, taxes, and other expenses. Along the way, we simply leave out any strictly noncash items such as depreciation.

For the shark attractant project, the operating cash flow can be readily calculated using the top-down approach. With sales of $200,000, total costs (fixed plus variable) of $137,000, and a tax bill of $11,220, the OCF is:

$$\text{OCF} = \$200,000 - 137,000 - 11,220 = \$51,780$$

This is just as we had before.

THE TAX SHIELD APPROACH

The third variation on our basic definition of OCF is the *tax shield* approach. This approach will be useful for some problems we consider in the next section. The tax shield definition of OCF is:

$$\text{OCF} = (\text{Sales} - \text{Costs}) \times (1 - T) + \text{Depreciation} \times T \qquad \text{[10.3]}$$

where T is again the corporate tax rate. Assuming that $T = 34\%$, the OCF works out to be:

$$\begin{aligned} \text{OCF} &= (\$1,500 - 700) \times .66 + 600 \times .34 \\ &= \$528 + 204 \\ &= \$732 \end{aligned}$$

This is just as we had before.

This approach views OCF as having two components. The first part is what the project's cash flow would be if there were no depreciation expense. In this case, this would-have-been cash flow is $528.

depreciation tax shield
The tax saving that results from the depreciation deduction, calculated as depreciation multiplied by the corporate tax rate.

The second part of OCF in this approach is the depreciation deduction multiplied by the tax rate. This is called the **depreciation tax shield**. We know that depreciation is a noncash expense. The only cash flow effect of deducting depreciation is to reduce our taxes, a benefit to us. At the current 34 percent corporate tax rate, every dollar in depreciation expense saves us 34 cents in taxes. So, in our example, the $600 depreciation deduction saves us $600 × .34 = $204 in taxes.

For the shark attractant project we considered earlier in the chapter, the depreciation tax shield would be $30,000 × .34 = $10,200. The aftertax value for sales less costs would be ($200,000 − 137,000) × (1 − .34) = $41,580. Adding these together yields the value of OCF:

$$OCF = \$41,580 + 10,200 = \$51,780$$

This calculation verifies that the tax shield approach is completely equivalent to the approach we used before.

CONCLUSION

Now that we've seen that all of these approaches are the same, you're probably wondering why everybody doesn't just agree on one of them. One reason, as we will see in the next section, is that different approaches are useful in different circumstances. The best one to use is whichever happens to be the most convenient for the problem at hand.

Concept Questions

10.5a What are the top-down and bottom-up definitions of operating cash flow?
10.5b What is meant by the term *depreciation tax shield*?

10.6 Some Special Cases of Discounted Cash Flow Analysis

To finish our chapter, we look at three common cases involving discounted cash flow analysis. The first case involves investments that are primarily aimed at improving efficiency and thereby cutting costs. The second case we consider comes up when a firm is involved in submitting competitive bids. The third and final case arises in choosing between equipment options with different economic lives.

We could consider many other special cases, but these three are particularly important because problems similar to these are so common. Also, they illustrate some diverse applications of cash flow analysis and DCF valuation.

EVALUATING COST-CUTTING PROPOSALS

One decision we frequently face is whether to upgrade existing facilities to make them more cost-effective. The issue is whether the cost savings are large enough to justify the necessary capital expenditure.

For example, suppose we are considering automating some part of an existing production process. The necessary equipment costs $80,000 to buy and install. The automation will save $22,000 per year (before taxes) by reducing labor and material costs. For simplicity, assume that the equipment has a five-year life and is depreciated to zero on a straight-line basis over that period. It will actually be worth $20,000 in five years. Should we automate? The tax rate is 34 percent, and the discount rate is 10 percent.

As always, the first step in making such a decision is to identify the relevant incremental cash flows. First, determining the relevant capital spending is easy enough. The initial cost is $80,000. The aftertax salvage value is $20,000 × (1 − .34) = $13,200 because the book value will be zero in five years. Second, there are no working capital consequences here, so we don't need to worry about changes in net working capital.

Operating cash flows are the third component to consider. Buying the new equipment affects our operating cash flows in two ways. First, we save $22,000 before taxes every year. In other words, the firm's operating income increases by $22,000, so this is the relevant incremental project operating income.

Second (and it's easy to overlook this), we have an additional depreciation deduction. In this case, the depreciation is $80,000/5 = $16,000 per year.

Because the project has an operating income of $22,000 (the annual pretax cost saving) and a depreciation deduction of $16,000, taking the project will increase the firm's EBIT by $22,000 − 16,000 = $6,000, so this is the project's EBIT.

Finally, because EBIT is rising for the firm, taxes will increase. This increase in taxes will be $6,000 × .34 = $2,040. With this information, we can compute operating cash flow in the usual way:

EBIT	$ 6,000
+ Depreciation	16,000
− Taxes	2,040
Operating cash flow	$19,960

So, our aftertax operating cash flow is $19,960.

It might be somewhat more enlightening to calculate operating cash flow using a different approach. What is actually going on here is very simple. First, the cost savings increase our pretax income by $22,000. We have to pay taxes on this amount, so our tax bill increases by .34 × $22,000 = $7,480. In other words, the $22,000 pretax saving amounts to $22,000 × (1 − .34) = $14,520 after taxes.

Second, the extra $16,000 in depreciation isn't really a cash outflow, but it does reduce our taxes by $16,000 × .34 = $5,440. The sum of these two components is $14,520 + 5,440 = $19,960, just as we had before. Notice that the $5,440 is the depreciation tax shield we discussed earlier, and we have effectively used the tax shield approach here.

We can now finish our analysis. Based on our discussion, here are the relevant cash flows:

		Year				
	0	**1**	**2**	**3**	**4**	**5**
Operating cash flow		$19,960	$19,960	$19,960	$19,960	$19,960
Capital spending	−$80,000					13,200
Total cash flow	−$80,000	$19,960	$19,960	$19,960	$19,960	$33,160

At 10 percent, it's straightforward to verify that the NPV here is $3,860, so we should go ahead and automate.

EXAMPLE 10.3   To Buy or Not to Buy

We are considering the purchase of a $200,000 computer-based inventory management system. It will be depreciated straight-line to zero over its four-year life. It will be worth $30,000 at the end of that time. The system will save us $60,000 before taxes in inventory-related costs. The relevant tax rate is 39 percent. Because the new setup is more efficient than our existing one, we will be able to carry less total inventory and thus free up $45,000 in net working capital. What is the NPV at 16 percent? What is the DCF return (the IRR) on this investment?

We can first calculate the operating cash flow. The aftertax cost savings are $60,000 × (1 − .39) = $36,600. The depreciation is $200,000/4 = $50,000 per year, so the depreciation tax shield is $50,000 × .39 = $19,500. Operating cash flow is thus $36,600 + 19,500 = $56,100 per year.

The capital spending involves $200,000 up front to buy the system. The aftertax salvage is $30,000 × (1 − .39) = $18,300. Finally, and this is the somewhat tricky part, the initial investment in net working capital is a $45,000 *inflow* because the system frees up working capital. Furthermore, we will have to put this back in at the end of the project's life. What this really means is simple: While the system is in operation, we have $45,000 to use elsewhere.

To finish our analysis, we can compute the total cash flows:

	Year				
	0	1	2	3	4
Operating cash flow		$56,100	$56,100	$56,100	$56,100
Change in NWC	$ 45,000				− 45,000
Capital spending	− 200,000				18,300
Total cash flow	−$155,000	$56,100	$56,100	$56,100	$29,400

At 16 percent, the NPV is −$12,768, so the investment is not attractive. After some trial and error, we find that the NPV is zero when the discount rate is 11.48 percent, so the IRR on this investment is about 11.5 percent.

SETTING THE BID PRICE

Early on, we used discounted cash flow analysis to evaluate a proposed new product. A somewhat different (and common) scenario arises when we must submit a competitive bid to win a job. Under such circumstances, the winner is whoever submits the lowest bid.

There is an old joke concerning this process: The low bidder is whoever makes the biggest mistake. This is called the winner's curse. In other words, if you win, there is a good chance you underbid. In this section, we look at how to go about setting the bid price to avoid the winner's curse. The procedure we describe is useful anytime we have to set a price on a product or service.

As with any other capital budgeting project, we must be careful to account for all relevant cash flows. For example, industry analysts estimated that the materials in Microsoft's Xbox 360 cost $470 before assembly. Other items such as the power supply, cables, and controllers increased the materials cost by another $55. At a retail price of $399, Microsoft obviously loses a significant amount on each Xbox 360 it sells. Why would a manufacturer sell at a price well below breakeven? A Microsoft spokesperson stated that the company believed that sales of its game software would make the Xbox 360 a profitable project.

To illustrate how to go about setting a bid price, imagine we are in the business of buying stripped-down truck platforms and then modifying them to customer specifications for resale. A local distributor has requested bids for 5 specially modified trucks each year for the next four years, for a total of 20 trucks in all.

We need to decide what price per truck to bid. The goal of our analysis is to determine the lowest price we can profitably charge. This maximizes our chances of being awarded the contract while guarding against the winner's curse.

Suppose we can buy the truck platforms for $10,000 each. The facilities we need can be leased for $24,000 per year. The labor and material cost to do the modification works out to be about $4,000 per truck. Total cost per year will thus be $24,000 + 5 × (10,000 + 4,000) = $94,000.

We will need to invest $60,000 in new equipment. This equipment will be depreciated straight-line to a zero salvage value over the four years. It will be worth about $5,000 at the end of that time. We will also need to invest $40,000 in raw materials inventory and other working capital items. The relevant tax rate is 39 percent. What price per truck should we bid if we require a 20 percent return on our investment?

We start by looking at the capital spending and net working capital investment. We have to spend $60,000 today for new equipment. The aftertax salvage value is $5,000 × (1 − .39) = $3,050. Furthermore, we have to invest $40,000 today in working capital. We will get this back in four years.

We can't determine the operating cash flow just yet because we don't know the sales price. Thus, if we draw a time line, here is what we have so far:

	Year				
	0	**1**	**2**	**3**	**4**
Operating cash flow		+OCF	+OCF	+OCF	+OCF
Change in NWC	−$40,000				$40,000
Capital spending	− 60,000				−3,050
Total cash flow	−$100,000	+OCF	+OCF	+OCF	+OCF + $43,050

With this in mind, note that the key observation is the following: The lowest possible price we can profitably charge will result in a zero NPV at 20 percent. At that price, we earn exactly 20 percent on our investment.

Given this observation, we first need to determine what the operating cash flow must be for the NPV to equal zero. To do this, we calculate the present value of the $43,050 non-operating cash flow from the last year and subtract it from the $100,000 initial investment:

$100,000 − 43,050/1.20^4 = $100,000 − 20,761 = $79,239

Once we have done this, our time line is as follows:

	Year				
	0	**1**	**2**	**3**	**4**
Total cash flow	−$79,239	+OCF	+OCF	+OCF	+OCF

As the time line suggests, the operating cash flow is now an unknown ordinary annuity amount. The four-year annuity factor for 20 percent is 2.58873, so we have:

NPV = 0 = −$79,239 + OCF × 2.58873

This implies that:

OCF = $79,239/2.58873 = $30,609

So the operating cash flow needs to be $30,609 each year.

We're not quite finished. The final problem is to find out what sales price results in an operating cash flow of $30,609. The easiest way to do this is to recall that operating cash flow can be written as net income plus depreciation (the bottom-up definition). The depreciation here is $60,000/4 = $15,000. Given this, we can determine what net income must be:

$$\text{Operating cash flow} = \text{Net income} + \text{Depreciation}$$
$$\$30,609 = \text{Net income} + \$15,000$$
$$\text{Net income} = \$15,609$$

From here, we work our way backward up the income statement. If net income is $15,609, then our income statement is as follows:

Sales	?
Costs	$94,000
Depreciation	15,000
Taxes (39%)	?
Net income	$15,609

We can solve for sales by noting that:

$$\text{Net income} = (\text{Sales} - \text{Costs} - \text{Depreciation}) \times (1 - T)$$
$$\$15,609 = (\text{Sales} - \$94,000 - \$15,000) \times (1 - .39)$$
$$\text{Sales} = \$15,609/.61 + 94,000 + 15,000$$
$$= \$134,589$$

Sales per year must be $134,589. Because the contract calls for five trucks per year, the sales price has to be $134,589/5 = $26,918. If we round this up a bit, it looks as though we need to bid about $27,000 per truck. At this price, were we to get the contract, our return would be just over 20 percent.

EVALUATING EQUIPMENT OPTIONS WITH DIFFERENT LIVES

The final problem we consider involves choosing among different possible systems, equipment setups, or procedures. Our goal is to choose the most cost-effective. The approach we consider here is necessary only when two special circumstances exist. First, the possibilities under evaluation have different economic lives. Second, and just as important, we will need whatever we buy more or less indefinitely. As a result, when it wears out, we will buy another one.

We can illustrate this problem with a simple example. Imagine we are in the business of manufacturing stamped metal subassemblies. Whenever a stamping mechanism wears out, we have to replace it with a new one to stay in business. We are considering which of two stamping mechanisms to buy.

Machine A costs $100 to buy and $10 per year to operate. It wears out and must be replaced every two years. Machine B costs $140 to buy and $8 per year to operate. It lasts for three years and must then be replaced. Ignoring taxes, which one should we choose if we use a 10 percent discount rate?

In comparing the two machines, we notice that the first is cheaper to buy, but it costs more to operate and it wears out more quickly. How can we evaluate these trade-offs? We can start by computing the present value of the costs for each:

Machine A: $\text{PV} = -\$100 + -10/1.1 + -10/1.1^2 = -\$117.36$
Machine B: $\text{PV} = -\$140 + -8/1.1 + -8/1.1^2 + -8/1.1^3 = -\$159.89$

Notice that *all* the numbers here are costs, so they all have negative signs. If we stopped here, it might appear that A is more attractive because the PV of the costs is less. However, all we have really discovered so far is that A effectively provides two years' worth of stamping service for $117.36, whereas B effectively provides three years' worth for $159.89. These costs are not directly comparable because of the difference in service periods.

We need to somehow work out a cost per year for these two alternatives. To do this, we ask: What amount, paid each year over the life of the machine, has the same PV of costs? This amount is called the **equivalent annual cost (EAC)**.

Calculating the EAC involves finding an unknown payment amount. For example, for machine A, we need to find a two-year ordinary annuity with a PV of −$117.36 at 10 percent. Going back to Chapter 6, we know that the two-year annuity factor is:

$$\text{Annuity factor} = (1 - 1/1.10^2)/.10 = 1.7355$$

For machine A, then, we have:

$$
\begin{aligned}
\text{PV of costs} &= -\$117.36 = \text{EAC} \times 1.7355 \\
\text{EAC} &= -\$117.36/1.7355 \\
&= -\$67.62
\end{aligned}
$$

For machine B, the life is three years, so we first need the three-year annuity factor:

$$\text{Annuity factor} = (1 - 1/1.10^3)/.10 = 2.4869$$

We calculate the EAC for B just as we did for A:

$$
\begin{aligned}
\text{PV of costs} &= -\$159.89 = \text{EAC} \times 2.4869 \\
\text{EAC} &= -\$159.89/2.4869 \\
&= -\$64.29
\end{aligned}
$$

Based on this analysis, we should purchase B because it effectively costs $64.29 per year versus $67.62 for A. In other words, all things considered, B is cheaper. In this case, the longer life and lower operating cost are more than enough to offset the higher initial purchase price.

> **equivalent annual cost (EAC)**
> The present value of a project's costs calculated on an annual basis.

Equivalent Annual Costs   **EXAMPLE 10.4**

This extended example illustrates what happens to the EAC when we consider taxes. You are evaluating two different pollution control options. A filtration system will cost $1.1 million to install and $60,000 annually, before taxes, to operate. It will have to be completely replaced every five years. A precipitation system will cost $1.9 million to install but only $10,000 per year to operate. The precipitation equipment has an effective operating life of eight years. Straight-line depreciation is used throughout, and neither system has any salvage value. Which option should we select if we use a 12 percent discount rate? The tax rate is 34 percent.

We need to consider the EACs for the two systems because they have different service lives and will be replaced as they wear out. The relevant information can be summarized as follows:

	Filtration System	Precipitation System
Aftertax operating cost	−$ 39,600	−$ 6,600
Depreciation tax shield	74,800	80,750
Operating cash flow	$ 35,200	$ 74,150
Economic life	5 years	8 years
Annuity factor (12%)	3.6048	4.9676
Present value of operating cash flow	$ 126,888	$ 368,350
Capital spending	− 1,100,000	− 1,900,000
Total PV of costs	−$ 973,112	−$1,531,650

(continued)

Notice that the operating cash flow is actually positive in both cases because of the large depreciation tax shields. This can occur whenever the operating cost is small relative to the purchase price.

To decide which system to purchase, we compute the EACs for both using the appropriate annuity factors:

Filtration system: $-\$973,112 = \text{EAC} \times 3.6048$

$$\text{EAC} = -\$269,951$$

Precipitation system: $-\$1,531,650 = \text{EAC} \times 4.9676$

$$\text{EAC} = -\$308,328$$

The filtration system is the cheaper of the two, so we select it. In this case, the longer life and smaller operating cost of the precipitation system are not sufficient to offset its higher initial cost.

Concept Questions

10.6a In setting a bid price, we used a zero NPV as our benchmark. Explain why this is appropriate.

10.6b Under what circumstances do we have to worry about unequal economic lives? How do you interpret the EAC?

10.7 Summary and Conclusions

This chapter has described how to put together a discounted cash flow analysis. In it, we covered:

1. The identification of relevant project cash flows: We discussed project cash flows and described how to handle some issues that often come up, including sunk costs, opportunity costs, financing costs, net working capital, and erosion.

2. Preparing and using pro forma, or projected, financial statements: We showed how information from such financial statements is useful in coming up with projected cash flows, and we also looked at some alternative definitions of operating cash flow.

3. The role of net working capital and depreciation in determining project cash flows: We saw that including the change in net working capital was important in cash flow analysis because it adjusted for the discrepancy between accounting revenues and costs and cash revenues and costs. We also went over the calculation of depreciation expense under current tax law.

4. Some special cases encountered in using discounted cash flow analysis: Here we looked at three special issues: evaluating cost-cutting investments, how to go about setting a bid price, and the unequal lives problem.

The discounted cash flow analysis we've covered here is a standard tool in the business world. It is a very powerful tool, so care should be taken in its use. The most important thing is to identify the cash flows in a way that makes economic sense. This chapter gives you a good start in learning to do this.

CONNECT TO FINANCE

McGraw Hill **connect**™ |FINANCE   If you are using *Connect*™ *Finance* in your course, get online to take a Practice Test, check out study tools, and find out where you need additional practice.

▼ Chapter 10 Making Capital Investment Decisions			
10.1 Project Cash Flows: A First Look	eBook	Study	Practice
10.2 Incremental Cash Flows	eBook	Study	Practice
10.3 Pro Forma Financial Statements and Project Cash Flows	eBook	Study	Practice
10.4 More about Project Cash Flow	eBook	Study	Practice
10.5 Alternative Definitions of Operating Cash Flow	eBook	Study	Practice
10.6 Some Special Cases of Discounted Cash Flow Analysis	eBook	Study	Practice

Section Quiz

Can you answer the following questions?

Section 10.1 The analysis of a project based on the project's relevant cash flows is referred to as the _____. (LO 10-1)

Section 10.2 What should NOT be included as an incremental cash flow for a proposed project? (LO 10-1)

Section 10.3 A project has projected sales of $62,000, costs of $48,000, depreciation expense of $6,200, and a tax rate of 34 percent. What is the operating cash flow for this project? (LO 10-1)

Section 10.4 An asset costs $24,000 and is classified as three-year MACRS property. What is the depreciation expense in Year 2? (LO 10-1)

Section 10.5 A firm has sales for the year of $92,000, costs of $46,000, and taxes of $21,000. What is the operating cash flow for the year? (LO 10-1)

Section 10.6 What rate of return will a firm earn if it accepts a project with a sales price per unit set equal to the bid price? (LO 10-3)

Log on to find out!

CHAPTER REVIEW AND SELF-TEST PROBLEMS

10.1 Capital Budgeting for Project X Based on the following information for Project X, should we undertake the venture? To answer, first prepare a pro forma income statement for each year. Next calculate operating cash flow. Finish the problem by determining total cash flow and then calculating NPV assuming a 28 percent required return. Use a 34 percent tax rate throughout. For help, look back at our shark attractant and power mulcher examples.

Project X involves a new type of graphite composite in-line skate wheel. We think we can sell 6,000 units per year at a price of $1,000 each. Variable costs will run about $400 per unit, and the product should have a four-year life.

Fixed costs for the project will run $450,000 per year. Further, we will need to invest a total of $1,250,000 in manufacturing equipment. This equipment is seven-year MACRS property for tax purposes. In four years, the equipment will be worth about

Visit us at www.mhhe.com/rwj

half of what we paid for it. We will have to invest $1,150,000 in net working capital at the start. After that, net working capital requirements will be 25 percent of sales.

10.2 Calculating Operating Cash Flow Mont Blanc Livestock Pens, Inc., has projected a sales volume of $1,650 for the second year of a proposed expansion project. Costs normally run 60 percent of sales, or about $990 in this case. The depreciation expense will be $100, and the tax rate is 35 percent. What is the operating cash flow? Calculate your answer using all of the approaches (including the top-down, bottom-up, and tax shield approaches) described in the chapter.

10.3 Spending Money to Save Money? For help on this one, refer back to the computerized inventory management system in Example 10.3. Here, we're contemplating a new automatic surveillance system to replace our current contract security system. It will cost $450,000 to get the new system. The cost will be depreciated straight-line to zero over the system's four-year expected life. The system is expected to be worth $250,000 at the end of four years after removal costs.

We think the new system will save us $125,000, before taxes, per year in contract security costs. The tax rate is 34 percent. What are the NPV and IRR for buying the new system? The required return is 17 percent.

ANSWERS TO CHAPTER REVIEW AND SELF-TEST PROBLEMS

10.1 To develop the pro forma income statements, we need to calculate the depreciation for each of the four years. The relevant MACRS percentages, depreciation allowances, and book values for the first four years are shown here:

Year	MACRS Percentage	Depreciation	Ending Book Value
1	14.29%	.1429 × $1,250,000 = $178,625	$1,071,375
2	24.49	.2449 × 1,250,000 = 306,125	765,250
3	17.49	.1749 × 1,250,000 = 218,625	546,625
4	12.49	.1249 × 1,250,000 = 156,125	390,500

The projected income statements, therefore, are as follows:

	Year			
	1	2	3	4
Sales	$6,000,000	$6,000,000	$6,000,000	$6,000,000
Variable costs	2,400,000	2,400,000	2,400,000	2,400,000
Fixed costs	450,000	450,000	450,000	450,000
Depreciation	178,625	306,125	218,625	156,125
EBIT	$2,971,375	$2,843,875	$2,931,375	$2,993,875
Taxes (34%)	1,010,268	966,918	996,668	1,017,918
Net income	$1,961,108	$1,876,958	$1,934,708	$1,975,958

Based on this information, here are the operating cash flows:

	Year			
	1	2	3	4
EBIT	$2,971,375	$2,843,875	$2,931,375	$2,993,875
Depreciation	178,625	306,125	218,625	156,125
Taxes	1,010,268	966,918	996,668	1,017,918
Operating cash flow	$2,139,732	$2,183,082	$2,153,332	$2,132,082

We now have to worry about the nonoperating cash flows. Net working capital starts out at $1,150,000 and then rises to 25 percent of sales, or $1,500,000. This is a $350,000 change in net working capital.

Finally, we have to invest $1,250,000 to get started. In four years, the book value of this investment will be $390,500, compared to an estimated market value of $625,000 (half of the cost). The aftertax salvage is thus $625,000 − .34 × ($625,000 − 390,500) = $545,270.

When we combine all this information, the projected cash flows for project X are as follows:

	Year				
	0	1	2	3	4
Operating cash flow		$2,139,732	$2,183,082	$2,153,332	$2,132,082
Change in NWC	−$1,150,000	− 350,000			1,500,000
Capital spending	− 1,250,000				545,270
Total cash flow	−$2,400,000	$1,789,732	$2,183,082	$2,153,332	$4,177,352

With these cash flows, the NPV at 28 percent is:

$$NPV = -\$2,400,000 + 1,789,732/1.28 + 2,183,082/1.28^2$$
$$+ 2,153,332/1.28^3 + 4,177,352/1.28^4$$
$$= \$2,913,649$$

So, this project appears quite profitable.

10.2 First, we can calculate the project's EBIT, its tax bill, and its net income:

$$EBIT = Sales - Costs - Depreciation$$
$$= \$1,650 - 990 - 100 = \$560$$
$$Taxes = \$560 \times .35 = \$196$$
$$Net\ income = \$560 - 196 = \$364$$

With these numbers, operating cash flow is:

$$OCF = EBIT + Depreciation - Taxes$$
$$= \$560 + 100 - 196$$
$$= \$464$$

Using the other OCF definitions, we have:

$$Bottom\text{-}up\ OCF = Net\ income + Depreciation$$
$$= \$364 + 100$$
$$= \$464$$

$$Top\text{-}down\ OCF = Sales - Costs - Taxes$$
$$= \$1,650 - 990 - 196$$
$$= \$464$$

$$Tax\ shield\ OCF = (Sales - Costs) \times (1 - .35) + Depreciation \times .35$$
$$= (\$1,650 - 990) \times .65 + 100 \times .35$$
$$= \$464$$

As expected, all of these definitions produce exactly the same answer.

Visit us at www.mhhe.com/rwj

10.3 The $125,000 pretax saving amounts to $(1 - .34) \times \$125,000 = \$82,500$ after taxes. The annual depreciation of $\$450,000/4 = \$112,500$ generates a tax shield of $.34 \times \$112,500 = \$38,250$ each year. Putting these together, we calculate that the operating cash flow is $\$82,500 + 38,250 = \$120,750$. Because the book value is zero in four years, the aftertax salvage value is $(1 - .34) \times \$250,000 = \$165,000$. There are no working capital consequences, so here are the cash flows:

	Year				
	0	1	2	3	4
Operating cash flow		$120,750	$120,750	$120,750	$120,750
Capital spending	−$450,000				165,000
Total cash flow	−$450,000	$120,750	$120,750	$120,750	$285,750

You can verify that the NPV at 17 percent is −$30,702, and the return on the new surveillance system is only about 13.96 percent. The project does not appear to be profitable.

CONCEPTS REVIEW AND CRITICAL THINKING QUESTIONS

1. **Opportunity Cost [LO1]** In the context of capital budgeting, what is an opportunity cost?

2. **Depreciation [LO1]** Given the choice, would a firm prefer to use MACRS depreciation or straight-line depreciation? Why?

3. **Net Working Capital [LO1]** In our capital budgeting examples, we assumed that a firm would recover all of the working capital it invested in a project. Is this a reasonable assumption? When might it not be valid?

4. **Stand-Alone Principle [LO1]** Suppose a financial manager is quoted as saying, "Our firm uses the stand-alone principle. Because we treat projects like minifirms in our evaluation process, we include financing costs because they are relevant at the firm level." Critically evaluate this statement.

5. **Equivalent Annual Cost [LO4]** When is EAC analysis appropriate for comparing two or more projects? Why is this method used? Are there any implicit assumptions required by this method that you find troubling? Explain.

6. **Cash Flow and Depreciation [LO1]** "When evaluating projects, we're concerned with only the relevant incremental aftertax cash flows. Therefore, because depreciation is a noncash expense, we should ignore its effects when evaluating projects." Critically evaluate this statement.

7. **Capital Budgeting Considerations [LO1]** A major college textbook publisher has an existing finance textbook. The publisher is debating whether to produce an "essentialized" version, meaning a shorter (and lower-priced) book. What are some of the considerations that should come into play?

To answer the next three questions, refer to the following example. In 2003, Porsche unveiled its new sports utility vehicle (SUV), the Cayenne. With a price tag of over $40,000, the Cayenne went from zero to 62 mph in 9.7 seconds. Porsche's decision to enter the SUV market was a response to the runaway success of other high-priced SUVs such as the Mercedes-Benz M-class. Vehicles in this class had generated years of high profits. The Cayenne certainly spiced up the market, and Porsche subsequently introduced the Cayenne Turbo, which goes from zero to 60 mph in 4.4 seconds and has a top speed of 172 mph. The price tag for the Cayenne Turbo in 2011? About $105,000!

Some analysts questioned Porsche's entry into the luxury SUV market. The analysts were concerned not only that Porsche was a late entry into the market, but also that the introduction of the Cayenne would damage Porsche's reputation as a maker of high-performance automobiles.

8. **Erosion [LO1]** In evaluating the Cayenne, would you consider the possible damage to Porsche's reputation erosion?

9. **Capital Budgeting [LO1]** Porsche was one of the last manufacturers to enter the sports utility vehicle market. Why would one company decide to proceed with a product when other companies, at least initially, decide not to enter the market?

10. **Capital Budgeting [LO1]** In evaluating the Cayenne, what do you think Porsche needs to assume regarding the substantial profit margins that exist in this market? Is it likely they will be maintained as the market becomes more competitive, or will Porsche be able to maintain the profit margin because of its image and the performance of the Cayenne?

QUESTIONS AND PROBLEMS

1. **Relevant Cash Flows [LO1]** Parker & Stone, Inc., is looking at setting up a new manufacturing plant in South Park to produce garden tools. The company bought some land six years ago for $5 million in anticipation of using it as a warehouse and distribution site, but the company has since decided to rent these facilities from a competitor instead. If the land were sold today, the company would net $5.3 million. The company wants to build its new manufacturing plant on this land; the plant will cost $12.5 million to build, and the site requires $770,000 worth of grading before it is suitable for construction. What is the proper cash flow amount to use as the initial investment in fixed assets when evaluating this project? Why?

2. **Relevant Cash Flows [LO1]** Winnebagel Corp. currently sells 30,000 motor homes per year at $68,000 each and 12,000 luxury motor coaches per year at $105,000 each. The company wants to introduce a new portable camper to fill out its product line; it hopes to sell 25,000 of these campers per year at $14,000 each. An independent consultant has determined that if Winnebagel introduces the new campers, it should boost the sales of its existing motor homes by 2,400 units per year and reduce the sales of its motor coaches by 1,100 units per year. What is the amount to use as the annual sales figure when evaluating this project? Why?

3. **Calculating Projected Net Income [LO1]** A proposed new investment has projected sales of $750,000. Variable costs are 55 percent of sales, and fixed costs are $164,000; depreciation is $65,000. Prepare a pro forma income statement assuming a tax rate of 35 percent. What is the projected net income?

4. **Calculating OCF [LO1]** Consider the following income statement:

Sales	$682,900
Costs	437,800
Depreciation	110,400
EBIT	?
Taxes (34%)	?
Net income	?

Fill in the missing numbers and then calculate the OCF. What is the depreciation tax shield?

BASIC
(Questions 1–18)

5. **OCF from Several Approaches [LO1]** A proposed new project has projected sales of $125,000, costs of $59,000, and depreciation of $12,800. The tax rate is 35 percent. Calculate operating cash flow using the four different approaches described in the chapter and verify that the answer is the same in each case.

6. **Calculating Depreciation [LO1]** A piece of newly purchased industrial equipment costs $975,000 and is classified as seven-year property under MACRS. Calculate the annual depreciation allowances and end-of-the-year book values for this equipment.

7. **Calculating Salvage Value [LO1]** Consider an asset that costs $640,000 and is depreciated straight-line to zero over its eight-year tax life. The asset is to be used in a five-year project; at the end of the project, the asset can be sold for $175,000. If the relevant tax rate is 35 percent, what is the aftertax cash flow from the sale of this asset?

8. **Calculating Salvage Value [LO1]** An asset used in a four-year project falls in the five-year MACRS class for tax purposes. The asset has an acquisition cost of $6,100,000 and will be sold for $1,300,000 at the end of the project. If the tax rate is 35 percent, what is the aftertax salvage value of the asset?

9. **Calculating Project OCF [LO1]** Keiper, Inc., is considering a new three-year expansion project that requires an initial fixed asset investment of $2.7 million. The fixed asset will be depreciated straight-line to zero over its three-year tax life, after which time it will be worthless. The project is estimated to generate $2,080,000 in annual sales, with costs of $775,000. If the tax rate is 35 percent, what is the OCF for this project?

10. **Calculating Project NPV [LO1]** In the previous problem, suppose the required return on the project is 12 percent. What is the project's NPV?

11. **Calculating Project Cash Flow from Assets [LO1]** In the previous problem, suppose the project requires an initial investment in net working capital of $300,000, and the fixed asset will have a market value of $210,000 at the end of the project. What is the project's Year 0 net cash flow? Year 1? Year 2? Year 3? What is the new NPV?

12. **NPV and Modified ACRS [LO1]** In the previous problem, suppose the fixed asset actually falls into the three-year MACRS class. All the other facts are the same. What is the project's Year 1 net cash flow now? Year 2? Year 3? What is the new NPV?

13. **Project Evaluation [LO1]** Dog Up! Franks is looking at a new sausage system with an installed cost of $480,000. This cost will be depreciated straight-line to zero over the project's five-year life, at the end of which the sausage system can be scrapped for $70,000. The sausage system will save the firm $160,000 per year in pretax operating costs, and the system requires an initial investment in net working capital of $29,000. If the tax rate is 34 percent and the discount rate is 10 percent, what is the NPV of this project?

14. **Project Evaluation [LO1]** Your firm is contemplating the purchase of a new $580,000 computer-based order entry system. The system will be depreciated straight-line to zero over its five-year life. It will be worth $60,000 at the end of that time. You will save $210,000 before taxes per year in order processing costs, and you will be able to reduce working capital by $75,000 (this is a one-time reduction). If the tax rate is 35 percent, what is the IRR for this project?

15. **Project Evaluation [LO1]** In the previous problem, suppose your required return on the project is 15 percent and your pretax cost savings are $200,000 per year. Will you accept the project? What if the pretax cost savings are $150,000 per year? At what level of pretax cost savings would you be indifferent between accepting the project and not accepting it?

16. **Calculating EAC [LO4]** A five-year project has an initial fixed asset investment of $310,000, an initial NWC investment of $30,000, and an annual OCF of –$29,000. The fixed asset is fully depreciated over the life of the project and has no salvage value. If the required return is 11 percent, what is this project's equivalent annual cost, or EAC?

17. **Calculating EAC [LO4]** You are evaluating two different silicon wafer milling machines. The Techron I costs $240,000, has a three-year life, and has pretax operating costs of $63,000 per year. The Techron II costs $420,000, has a five-year life, and has pretax operating costs of $36,000 per year. For both milling machines, use straight-line depreciation to zero over the project's life and assume a salvage value of $40,000. If your tax rate is 35 percent and your discount rate is 10 percent, compute the EAC for both machines. Which do you prefer? Why?

18. **Calculating a Bid Price [LO3]** Dahlia Enterprises needs someone to supply it with 120,000 cartons of machine screws per year to support its manufacturing needs over the next five years, and you've decided to bid on the contract. It will cost you $870,000 to install the equipment necessary to start production; you'll depreciate this cost straight-line to zero over the project's life. You estimate that, in five years, this equipment can be salvaged for $70,000. Your fixed production costs will be $325,000 per year, and your variable production costs should be $10.30 per carton. You also need an initial investment in net working capital of $75,000. If your tax rate is 35 percent and you require a 12 percent return on your investment, what bid price should you submit?

19. **Cost-Cutting Proposals [LO2]** Purple Haze Machine Shop is considering a four-year project to improve its production efficiency. Buying a new machine press for $470,000 is estimated to result in $190,000 in annual pretax cost savings. The press falls in the MACRS five-year class, and it will have a salvage value at the end of the project of $80,000. The press also requires an initial investment in spare parts inventory of $20,000, along with an additional $2,500 in inventory for each succeeding year of the project. If the shop's tax rate is 35 percent and its discount rate is 9 percent, should the company buy and install the machine press?

INTERMEDIATE
(Questions 19–30)

20. **Comparing Mutually Exclusive Projects [LO1]** Lang Industrial Systems Company (LISC) is trying to decide between two different conveyor belt systems. System A costs $240,000, has a four-year life, and requires $75,000 in pretax annual operating costs. System B costs $340,000, has a six-year life, and requires $69,000 in pretax annual operating costs. Both systems are to be depreciated straight-line to zero over their lives and will have zero salvage value. Whichever project is chosen, it will *not* be replaced when it wears out. If the tax rate is 34 percent and the discount rate is 8 percent, which project should the firm choose? ℓ MTB 26, 273.33

21. **Comparing Mutually Exclusive Projects [LO4]** Suppose in the previous problem that LISC always needs a conveyor belt system; when one wears out, it must be replaced. Which project should the firm choose now?

22. **Calculating a Bid Price [LO3]** Consider a project to supply 100 million postage stamps per year to the U.S. Postal Service for the next five years. You have an idle parcel of land available that cost $1,900,000 five years ago; if the land were sold today, it would net you $2,100,000 aftertax. The land can be sold for $2,300,000 after taxes in five years. You will need to install $5.4 million in new manufacturing plant and equipment to actually produce the stamps; this plant and equipment will be depreciated straight-line to zero over the project's five-year life. The equipment can be sold for $500,000 at the end of the project. You will also need $600,000 in initial net working capital for the project, and an additional investment of $50,000 in every

Visit us at www.mhhe.com/rwj

year thereafter. Your production costs are .5 cents per stamp, and you have fixed costs of $1,050,000 per year. If your tax rate is 34 percent and your required return on this project is 12 percent, what bid price should you submit on the contract?

23. **Interpreting a Bid Price [LO3]** In the previous problem, suppose you were going to use a three-year MACRS depreciation schedule for your manufacturing equipment, and you could keep working capital investments down to only $25,000 per year. How would this new information affect your calculated bid price?

24. **Comparing Mutually Exclusive Projects [LO4]** Vandalay Industries is considering the purchase of a new machine for the production of latex. Machine A costs $3,100,000 and will last for six years. Variable costs are 35 percent of sales, and fixed costs are $240,000 per year. Machine B costs $5,300,000 and will last for nine years. Variable costs for this machine are 30 percent of sales and fixed costs are $175,000 per year. The sales for each machine will be $11 million per year. The required return is 10 percent, and the tax rate is 35 percent. Both machines will be depreciated on a straight-line basis. If the company plans to replace the machine when it wears out on a perpetual basis, which machine should you choose?

25. **Equivalent Annual Cost [LO4]** Compact fluorescent lamps (CFLs) have become more popular in recent years, but do they make financial sense? Suppose a typical 60-watt incandescent lightbulb costs $.45 and lasts for 1,000 hours. A 15-watt CFL, which provides the same light, costs $3.40 and lasts for 12,000 hours. A kilowatt-hour of electricity costs $.121, which is about the national average. A kilowatt-hour is 1,000 watts for 1 hour. If you require a 10 percent return and use a light fixture 500 hours per year, what is the equivalent annual cost of each lightbulb?

26. **Break-Even Cost [LO2]** The previous problem suggests that using CFLs instead of incandescent bulbs is a no-brainer. However, electricity costs actually vary quite a bit depending on location and user type (you can get information on your rates from your local power company). An industrial user in West Virginia might pay $.04 per kilowatt-hour whereas a residential user in Hawaii might pay $.25. What's the break-even cost per kilowatt-hour in Problem 25?

27. **Break-Even Replacement [LO2]** The previous two problems suggest that using CFLs is a good idea from a purely financial perspective unless you live in an area where power is relatively inexpensive, but there is another wrinkle. Suppose you have a residence with a lot of incandescent bulbs that are used on average 500 hours a year. The average bulb will be about halfway through its life, so it will have 500 hours remaining (and you can't tell which bulbs are older or newer). At what cost per kilowatt-hour does it make sense to replace your incandescent bulbs today?

28. **Issues in Capital Budgeting [LO1]** The debate regarding CFLs versus incandescent bulbs (see Problems 25–27) has even more wrinkles. In no particular order:

   1. Incandescent bulbs generate a lot more heat than CFLs.

   2. CFL prices will probably decline relative to incandescent bulbs.

   3. CFLs unavoidably contain small amounts of mercury, a significant environmental hazard, and special precautions must be taken in disposing of burned-out units (and also in cleaning up a broken lamp). Currently, there is no agreed-upon way to recycle a CFL. Incandescent bulbs pose no disposal/breakage hazards.

   4. Depending on a light's location (or the number of lights), there can be a non-trivial cost to change bulbs (i.e., labor cost in a business).

   5. Coal-fired power generation accounts for a substantial portion of the mercury emissions in the U.S., though the emissions will drop sharply in the relatively near future.

Visit us at www.mhhe.com/rwj

6. Power generation accounts for a substantial portion of CO_2 emissions in the U.S.

7. CFLs are more energy and material intensive to manufacture. On-site mercury contamination and worker safety are issues.

8. If you install a CFL in a permanent lighting fixture in a building, you will probably move long before the CFL burns out.

9. Another lighting technology based on light-emitting diodes (LEDs) exists and is improving. LEDs are currently much more expensive than CFLs, but costs are coming down. LEDs last much longer than CFLs and use even less power. Plus, LEDs don't contain mercury.

Qualitatively, how do these issues affect your position in the CFL versus incandescent lightbulb debate? Some countries have banned incandescent bulbs. Does your analysis suggest such a move is wise? Are there other regulations short of an outright ban that make sense to you?

29. **Replacement Decisions [LO2]** Your small remodeling business has two work vehicles. One is a small passenger car used for job-site visits and for other general business purposes. The other is a heavy truck used to haul equipment. The car gets 25 miles per gallon (mpg). The truck gets 10 mpg. You want to improve gas mileage to save money, and you have enough money to upgrade one vehicle. The upgrade cost will be the same for both vehicles. An upgraded car will get 40 mpg; an upgraded truck will get 12.5 mpg. The cost of gasoline is $3.70 per gallon. Assuming an upgrade is a good idea in the first place, which one should you upgrade? Both vehicles are driven 12,000 miles per year.

30. **Replacement Decisions [LO2]** In the previous problem, suppose you drive the truck *x* miles per year. How many miles would you have to drive the car before upgrading the car would be the better choice? *Hint:* Look at the relative gas savings.

31. **Calculating Project NPV [LO1]** You have been hired as a consultant for Pristine Urban-Tech Zither, Inc. (PUTZ), manufacturers of fine zithers. The market for zithers is growing quickly. The company bought some land three years ago for $1.4 million in anticipation of using it as a toxic waste dump site but has recently hired another company to handle all toxic materials. Based on a recent appraisal, the company believes it could sell the land for $1.5 million on an aftertax basis. In four years, the land could be sold for $1.6 million after taxes. The company also hired a marketing firm to analyze the zither market, at a cost of $125,000. An excerpt of the marketing report is as follows:

> The zither industry will have a rapid expansion in the next four years. With the brand name recognition that PUTZ brings to bear, we feel that the company will be able to sell 3,800, 4,700, 5,300, and 4,200 units each year for the next four years, respectively. Again, capitalizing on the name recognition of PUTZ, we feel that a premium price of $650 can be charged for each zither. Because zithers appear to be a fad, we feel at the end of the four-year period, sales should be discontinued.

PUTZ believes that fixed costs for the project will be $425,000 per year, and variable costs are 15 percent of sales. The equipment necessary for production will cost $3.5 million and will be depreciated according to a three-year MACRS schedule. At the end of the project, the equipment can be scrapped for $400,000. Net working capital of $125,000 will be required immediately. PUTZ has a 38 percent tax rate, and the required return on the project is 13 percent. What is the NPV of the project?

CHALLENGE
(Questions 31–36)

Visit us at www.mhhe.com/rwj

Ⴘ 32. Project Evaluation [LO1] Aguilera Acoustics, Inc. (AAI), projects unit sales for a
new seven-octave voice emulation implant as follows:

Year	Unit Sales
1	81,000
2	94,000
3	108,000
4	103,000
5	84,000

Production of the implants will require $1,600,000 in net working capital to start
and additional net working capital investments each year equal to 15 percent of
the projected sales increase for the following year. Total fixed costs are $1,500,000
per year, variable production costs are $265 per unit, and the units are priced at
$380 each. The equipment needed to begin production has an installed cost of
$21,000,000. Because the implants are intended for professional singers, this equip-
ment is considered industrial machinery and thus qualifies as seven-year MACRS
property. In five years, this equipment can be sold for about 20 percent of its acquisition cost. AAI is in the 35 percent marginal tax bracket and has a required return
on all its projects of 18 percent. Based on these preliminary project estimates, what
is the NPV of the project? What is the IRR?

33. Calculating Required Savings [LO2] A proposed cost-saving device has an
installed cost of $730,000. The device will be used in a five-year project but is
classified as three-year MACRS property for tax purposes. The required initial
net working capital investment is $55,000, the marginal tax rate is 35 percent, and
the project discount rate is 9 percent. The device has an estimated Year 5 salvage
value of $80,000. What level of pretax cost savings do we require for this project
to be profitable?

34. Financial Break-Even Analysis [LO2] To solve the bid price problem presented in the text, we set the project NPV equal to zero and found the required
price using the definition of OCF. Thus the bid price represents a financial break-
even level for the project. This type of analysis can be extended to many other
types of problems.

   a. In Problem 18, assume that the price per carton is $17 and find the project NPV.
   What does your answer tell you about your bid price? What do you know about the
   number of cartons you can sell and still break even? How about your level of costs?

   b. Solve Problem 18 again with the price still at $17, but find the quantity of
   cartons per year that you can supply and still break even. *Hint:* It's less than
   120,000.

   c. Repeat (b) with a price of $17 and a quantity of 120,000 cartons per year, and
   find the highest level of fixed costs you could afford and still break even. *Hint:*
   It's more than $325,000.

35. Calculating a Bid Price [LO3] Your company has been approached to bid on a
contract to sell 4,200 voice recognition (VR) computer keyboards per year for four
years. Due to technological improvements, beyond that time they will be outdated
and no sales will be possible. The equipment necessary for the production will
cost $3.8 million and will be depreciated on a straight-line basis to a zero salvage
value. Production will require an investment in net working capital of $95,000 to
be returned at the end of the project, and the equipment can be sold for $275,000

Visit us at www.mhhe.com/rwj

at the end of production. Fixed costs are $640,000 per year, and variable costs are $155 per unit. In addition to the contract, you feel your company can sell 9,500, 10,400, 12,500, and 9,800 additional units to companies in other countries over the next four years, respectively, at a price of $310. This price is fixed. The tax rate is 40 percent, and the required return is 10 percent. Additionally, the president of the company will undertake the project only if it has an NPV of $100,000. What bid price should you set for the contract?

36. **Replacement Decisions [LO2]** Suppose we are thinking about replacing an old computer with a new one. The old one cost us $1,300,000; the new one will cost, $1,560,000. The new machine will be depreciated straight-line to zero over its five-year life. It will probably be worth about $300,000 after five years.

     The old computer is being depreciated at a rate of $260,000 per year. It will be completely written off in three years. If we don't replace it now, we will have to replace it in two years. We can sell it now for $420,000; in two years, it will probably be worth $120,000. The new machine will save us $290,000 per year in operating costs. The tax rate is 38 percent, and the discount rate is 12 percent.

     a. Suppose we recognize that if we don't replace the computer now, we will be replacing it in two years. Should we replace now or should we wait? *Hint:* What we effectively have here is a decision either to "invest" in the old computer (by not selling it) or to invest in the new one. Notice that the two investments have unequal lives.

     b. Suppose we consider only whether we should replace the old computer now without worrying about what's going to happen in two years. What are the relevant cash flows? Should we replace it or not? *Hint:* Consider the net change in the firm's aftertax cash flows if we do the replacement.

MINICASE

Conch Republic Electronics, Part 1

Conch Republic Electronics is a midsized electronics manufacturer located in Key West, Florida. The company president is Shelley Couts, who inherited the company. When it was founded over 70 years ago, the company originally repaired radios and other household appliances. Over the years, the company expanded into manufacturing and is now a reputable manufacturer of various electronic items. Jay McCanless, a recent MBA graduate, has been hired by the company's finance department.

One of the major revenue-producing items manufactured by Conch Republic is a smart phone. Conch Republic currently has one smart phone model on the market, and sales have been excellent. The smart phone is a unique item in that it comes in a variety of tropical colors and is preprogrammed to play Jimmy Buffett music. However, as with any electronic item, technology changes rapidly, and the current smart phone has limited features in comparison with newer models. Conch Republic spent $750,000 to develop a prototype for a new smart phone that has all the features of the

existing smart phone but adds new features such as WiFi tethering. The company has spent a further $200,000 for a marketing study to determine the expected sales figures for the new smart phone.

Conch Republic can manufacture the new smart phones for $185 each in variable costs. Fixed costs for the operation are estimated to run $5.3 million per year. The estimated sales volume is 74,000, 95,000, 125,000, 105,000, and 80,000 per year for the next five years, respectively. The unit price of the new smart phone will be $480. The necessary equipment can be purchased for $38.5 million and will be depreciated on a seven-year MACRS schedule. It is believed the value of the equipment in five years will be $5.4 million.

As previously stated, Conch Republic currently manufactures a smart phone. Production of the existing model is expected to be terminated in two years. If Conch Republic does not introduce the new smart phone, sales will be 80,000 units and 60,000 units for the next two years, respectively. The price of the existing smart phone is $310 per unit, with variable costs of $125 each and fixed costs of $1,800,000 per year. If Conch Republic does introduce the new smart phone, sales of the existing smart phone will fall by 15,000 units per year, and the price of the existing units will have to be lowered to $275 each. Net working capital for the smart phones will be 20 percent of sales and will occur with the timing of the cash flows for the year; for example, there is no initial outlay for NWC, but changes in NWC will first occur in Year 1 with the first year's sales. Conch Republic has a 35 percent corporate tax rate and a 12 percent required return.

Shelley has asked Jay to prepare a report that answers the following questions.

QUESTIONS

1. What is the payback period of the project?
2. What is the profitability index of the project?
3. What is the IRR of the project?
4. What is the NPV of the project?

PROJECT ANALYSIS AND EVALUATION

IN THE SUMMER OF 2010, the movie *Repo Men*, starring Jude Law and Forest Whitaker, opened. The movie's advertising slogan was "Consider them your final choice," and many critics and moviegoers agreed. One critic said, "It's a film to be endured more than experienced." Others were even more harsh, saying, "What we need are some cinematic repo men to rip this movie from the theaters" and "As an example of how not to make a movie, *Repo Men* deserves to be studied by film students."

Looking at the numbers, Universal Pictures spent close to $32 million producing the movie, plus millions more for marketing and distribution. Unfortunately for the company, *Repo Men* did poorly at the box office, pulling in only $13.7 million worldwide. In fact, about 4 of 10 movies lose money at the box office, though DVD sales and online views often help the final tally. Of course, there are movies that do quite well. Also in 2010, the Pixar Animation movie *Toy Story 3* raked in about $415 million worldwide at a production cost of $200 million.

So, obviously, Universal Pictures didn't *plan* to lose $18 or so million on *Repo Men*, but it happened. As this particular box office bomb shows, projects don't always go as companies think they will. This chapter explores how this can happen, and what companies can do to analyze and possibly avoid these situations.

LEARNING OBJECTIVES

After studying this chapter, you should understand:

LO1 How to perform and interpret a sensitivity analysis for a proposed investment.

LO2 How to perform and interpret a scenario analysis for a proposed investment.

LO3 How to determine and interpret cash, accounting, and financial break-even points.

LO4 How the degree of operating leverage can affect the cash flows of a project.

LO5 How capital rationing affects the ability of a company to accept projects.

In our previous chapter, we discussed how to identify and organize the relevant cash flows for capital investment decisions. Our primary interest there was in coming up with a preliminary estimate of the net present value for a proposed project. In this chapter, we focus on assessing the reliability of such an estimate and on some additional considerations in project analysis.

We begin by discussing the need for an evaluation of cash flow and NPV estimates. We go on to develop some useful tools for such an evaluation. We also examine additional complications and concerns that can arise in project evaluation.

11.1 Evaluating NPV Estimates

As we discussed in Chapter 9, an investment has a positive net present value if its market value exceeds its cost. Such an investment is desirable because it creates value for its owner. The primary problem in identifying such opportunities is that most of the time we can't actually observe the relevant market value. Instead, we estimate it. Having done so, it is only natural to wonder whether our estimates are at least close to the true values. We consider this question next.

THE BASIC PROBLEM

Suppose we are working on a preliminary discounted cash flow analysis along the lines we described in the previous chapter. We carefully identify the relevant cash flows, avoiding such things as sunk costs, and we remember to consider working capital requirements. We add back any depreciation; we account for possible erosion; and we pay attention to opportunity costs. Finally, we double-check our calculations; when all is said and done, the bottom line is that the estimated NPV is positive.

Now what? Do we stop here and move on to the next proposal? Probably not. The fact that the estimated NPV is positive is definitely a good sign; but, more than anything, this tells us that we need to take a closer look.

If you think about it, there are two circumstances under which a DCF analysis could lead us to conclude that a project has a positive NPV. The first possibility is that the project really does have a positive NPV. That's the good news. The bad news is the second possibility: A project may appear to have a positive NPV because our estimate is inaccurate.

Notice that we could also err in the opposite way. If we conclude that a project has a negative NPV when the true NPV is positive, we lose a valuable opportunity.

PROJECTED VERSUS ACTUAL CASH FLOWS

There is a somewhat subtle point we need to make here. When we say something like "The projected cash flow in Year 4 is $700," what exactly do we mean? Does this mean that we think the cash flow will actually be $700? Not really. It could happen, of course, but we would be surprised to see it turn out exactly that way. The reason is that the $700 projection is based on only what we know today. Almost anything could happen between now and then to change that cash flow.

Loosely speaking, we really mean that if we took all the possible cash flows that could occur in four years and averaged them, the result would be $700. So, we don't really expect a projected cash flow to be exactly right in any one case. What we do expect is that if we evaluate a large number of projects, our projections will be right on average.

FORECASTING RISK

The key inputs into a DCF analysis are projected future cash flows. If the projections are seriously in error, then we have a classic GIGO (garbage in, garbage out) system. In such a case, no matter how carefully we arrange the numbers and manipulate them, the resulting answer can still be grossly misleading. This is the danger in using a relatively sophisticated technique like DCF. It is sometimes easy to get caught up in number crunching and forget the underlying nuts-and-bolts economic reality.

forecasting risk
The possibility that errors in projected cash flows will lead to incorrect decisions. Also known as *estimation risk*.

The possibility that we will make a bad decision because of errors in the projected cash flows is called **forecasting risk** (or *estimation risk*). Because of forecasting risk, there is the danger that we will think a project has a positive NPV when it really does not. How is this possible? It happens if we are overly optimistic about the future, and, as a result, our projected cash flows don't realistically reflect the possible future cash flows.

Forecasting risk can take many forms. For example, Microsoft spent several billion dollars developing and bringing the Xbox game console to market. Technologically more sophisticated, the Xbox was the best way to play against competitors over the Internet. Unfortunately, Microsoft sold only 9 million Xboxes in the first 14 months of sales, at the low end of Microsoft's expected range. The Xbox was arguably the best available game console at the time, so why didn't it sell better? The reason given by analysts was that there were far fewer games made for the Xbox. For example, the Playstation enjoyed a 2-to-1 edge in the number of games made for it.

So far, we have not explicitly considered what to do about the possibility of errors in our forecasts; so one of our goals in this chapter is to develop some tools that are useful in identifying areas where potential errors exist and where they might be especially damaging. In one form or another, we will be trying to assess the economic "reasonableness" of our estimates. We will also be wondering how much damage will be done by errors in those estimates.

SOURCES OF VALUE

The first line of defense against forecasting risk is simply to ask, "What is it about this investment that leads to a positive NPV?" We should be able to point to something specific as the source of value. For example, if the proposal under consideration involves a new product, then we might ask questions such as the following: Are we certain that our new product is significantly better than that of the competition? Can we truly manufacture at lower cost, or distribute more effectively, or identify undeveloped market niches, or gain control of a market?

These are just a few of the potential sources of value. There are many others. For example, in 2004, Google announced a new, free e-mail service: Gmail. Why? Free e-mail service is widely available from big hitters like Microsoft and Yahoo! and, obviously, it's free! The answer is that Google's mail service is integrated with its acclaimed search engine, thereby giving it an edge. Also, offering e-mail lets Google expand its lucrative keyword-based advertising delivery. So, Google's source of value is leveraging its proprietary Web search and ad delivery technologies.

A key factor to keep in mind is the degree of competition in the market. A basic principle of economics is that positive NPV investments will be rare in a highly competitive environment. Therefore, proposals that appear to show significant value in the face of stiff competition are particularly troublesome, and the likely reaction of the competition to any innovations must be closely examined.

To give an example, in 2008, demand for flat screen LCD televisions was high, prices were high, and profit margins were fat for retailers. But, also in 2008, manufacturers of the screens, such as Samsung and Sony, were projected to pour several billion dollars into new production facilities. Thus, anyone thinking of entering this highly profitable market would do well to reflect on what the supply (and profit margin) situation will look like in just a few years. And, in fact, the high prices did not last. By 2011, television sets that had been selling for well over $1,000 only two years before were selling for around $400–$500.

It is also necessary to think about *potential* competition. For example, suppose home improvement retailer Lowe's identifies an area that is underserved and is thinking about opening a store. If the store is successful, what will happen? The answer is that Home Depot (or another competitor) will likely also build a store, thereby driving down volume and profits. So, we always need to keep in mind that success attracts imitators and competitors.

The point to remember is that positive NPV investments are probably not all that common, and the number of positive NPV projects is almost certainly limited for any given firm. If we can't articulate some sound economic basis for thinking ahead of time that we have found something special, then the conclusion that our project has a positive NPV should be viewed with some suspicion.

> **Concept Questions**
>
> **11.1a** What is forecasting risk? Why is it a concern for the financial manager?
> **11.1b** What are some potential sources of value in a new project?

11.2 Scenario and Other What-If Analyses

Our basic approach to evaluating cash flow and NPV estimates involves asking what-if questions. Accordingly, we discuss some organized ways of going about a what-if analysis. Our goal in performing such an analysis is to assess the degree of forecasting risk and to identify the most critical components of the success or failure of an investment.

GETTING STARTED

We are investigating a new project. Naturally, the first thing we do is estimate NPV based on our projected cash flows. We will call this initial set of projections the *base case*. Now, however, we recognize the possibility of error in these cash flow projections. After completing the base case, we thus wish to investigate the impact of different assumptions about the future on our estimates.

One way to organize this investigation is to put upper and lower bounds on the various components of the project. For example, suppose we forecast sales at 100 units per year. We know this estimate may be high or low, but we are relatively certain it is not off by more than 10 units in either direction. We thus pick a lower bound of 90 and an upper bound of 110. We go on to assign such bounds to any other cash flow components we are unsure about.

When we pick these upper and lower bounds, we are not ruling out the possibility that the actual values could be outside this range. What we are saying, again loosely speaking, is that it is unlikely that the true average (as opposed to our estimated average) of the possible values is outside this range.

An example is useful to illustrate the idea here. The project under consideration costs $200,000, has a five-year life, and has no salvage value. Depreciation is straight-line to zero. The required return is 12 percent, and the tax rate is 34 percent. In addition, we have compiled the following information:

	Base Case	Lower Bound	Upper Bound
Unit sales	6,000	5,500	6,500
Price per unit	$80	$75	$85
Variable costs per unit	$60	$58	$62
Fixed costs per year	$50,000	$45,000	$55,000

With this information, we can calculate the base-case NPV by first calculating net income:

Sales	$480,000
Variable costs	360,000
Fixed costs	50,000
Depreciation	40,000
EBIT	$ 30,000
Taxes (34%)	10,200
Net income	$ 19,800

Operating cash flow is thus $30,000 + 40,000 − 10,200 = $59,800 per year. At 12 percent, the five-year annuity factor is 3.6048, so the base-case NPV is:

$$\text{Base-case NPV} = -\$200,000 + 59,800 \times 3.6048$$
$$= \$15,567$$

Thus, the project looks good so far.

SCENARIO ANALYSIS

The basic form of what-if analysis is called **scenario analysis**. What we do is investigate the changes in our NPV estimates that result from asking questions like: What if unit sales realistically should be projected at 5,500 units instead of 6,000?

Once we start looking at alternative scenarios, we might find that most of the plausible ones result in positive NPVs. In this case, we have some confidence in proceeding with the project. If a substantial percentage of the scenarios look bad, the degree of forecasting risk is high and further investigation is in order.

We can consider a number of possible scenarios. A good place to start is with the worst-case scenario. This will tell us the minimum NPV of the project. If this turns out to be positive, we will be in good shape. While we are at it, we will go ahead and determine the other extreme, the best case. This puts an upper bound on our NPV.

To get the worst case, we assign the least favorable value to each item. This means *low* values for items like units sold and price per unit and *high* values for costs. We do the reverse for the best case. For our project, these values would be the following:

scenario analysis
The determination of what happens to NPV estimates when we ask what-if questions.

	Worst Case	Best Case
Unit sales	5,500	6,500
Price per unit	$75	$85
Variable costs per unit	$62	$58
Fixed costs per year	$55,000	$45,000

With this information, we can calculate the net income and cash flows under each scenario (check these for yourself):

Scenario	Net Income	Cash Flow	Net Present Value	IRR
Base case	$19,800	$59,800	$ 15,567	15.1%
Worst case*	− 15,510	24,490	− 111,719	−14.4
Best case	59,730	99,730	159,504	40.9

*We assume a tax credit is created in our worst-case scenario.

What we learn is that under the worst scenario, the cash flow is still positive at $24,490. That's good news. The bad news is that the return is −14.4 percent in this case, and the NPV is −$111,719. Because the project costs $200,000, we stand to lose a little more than half of the original investment under the worst possible scenario. The best case offers an attractive 41 percent return.

The terms *best case* and *worst case* are commonly used, and we will stick with them; but they are somewhat misleading. The absolutely best thing that could happen would be something absurdly unlikely, such as launching a new diet soda and subsequently learning that our (patented) formulation also just happens to cure the common cold. Similarly, the true worst case would involve some incredibly remote possibility of total disaster. We're not claiming that these things don't happen; once in a while they do. Some products, such as personal computers, succeed beyond the wildest expectations; and some turn out to be absolute catastrophes. For example, in April 2010, BP's Gulf of Mexico oil rig *Deepwater Horizon* caught fire and sank following an explosion, leading to a massive oil spill. The leak was finally stopped in July after releasing over 200 million gallons of crude oil into the Gulf. BP's costs associated with the disaster are expected to exceed $40 billion, perhaps by a wide margin. Nonetheless, our point is that in assessing the reasonableness of an NPV estimate, we need to stick to cases that are reasonably likely to occur.

Instead of *best* and *worst,* then, it is probably more accurate to use the words *optimistic* and *pessimistic*. In broad terms, if we were thinking about a reasonable range for, say, unit sales, then what we call the best case would correspond to something near the upper end of that range. The worst case would simply correspond to the lower end.

Not all companies complete (or at least publish) all three estimates. For example, Almaden Minerals, Ltd., made a press release with information concerning its Elk Gold Project in British Columbia. Here is a table of the possible outcomes given by the company:

Project Summary	Base Case	$1,200 Case	Unit
Assumed gold price	1,000	1,200	$US/tr.oz
Tonnes per day treated	500	1,000	tpd
Life	7	9	years
Total tonnes treated	1.1	2.6	MT
Grade	4.14	3.89	g/t
Waste:Ore ratio	16.4	30.1	
Plant recovery	92	92	%
Ounces Au produced	139,198	297,239	tr.oz
Initial capital expense	9.91	17.50	$CADM
Working and preproduction capital	2.27	9.60	$CADM
Waste mining	2.42	1.90	$CAD/tonne waste
Ore mining	8.38	5.87	$CAD/tonne ore
Processing	20.68	14.74	$CAD/tonne ore
Administration and overheads	2.07	1.27	$CAD/tonne ore
Total operating cost	70.30	78.91	$CAD/tonne ore
Pre-tax NPV @ 8%	28.7	67.9	$CADM
Pre-tax IRR	51%	39%	
Max exposure	13.66	33.53	$CADM
Payback, years from start production	1.85	3.30	years
Ratio, gross earnings:max exposure	5.02	6.00	
Ratio, NPV:max exposure	2.10	2.03	

As you can see, the NPV is projected at C$28.7 million in the base case and C$67.9 million in the best case. Unfortunately, Almaden did not release a worst-case analysis, but we hope the company also examined this possibility

As we have mentioned, there are an unlimited number of different scenarios that we could examine. At a minimum, we might want to investigate two intermediate cases by going halfway between the base amounts and the extreme amounts. This would give us five scenarios in all, including the base case.

Beyond this point, it is hard to know when to stop. As we generate more and more possibilities, we run the risk of experiencing "paralysis of analysis." The difficulty is that no matter how many scenarios we run, all we can learn are possibilities—some good and some bad. Beyond that, we don't get any guidance as to what to do. Scenario analysis is thus useful in telling us what can happen and in helping us gauge the potential for disaster, but it does not tell us whether to take a project.

Unfortunately, in practice, even the worst-case scenarios may not be low enough. Two recent examples show what we mean. The Eurotunnel, or Chunnel, may be one of the new wonders of the world. The tunnel under the English Channel connects England to France and covers 24 miles. It took 8,000 workers eight years to remove 9.8 million cubic yards of rock. When the tunnel was finally built, it cost $17.9 billion, or slightly more than twice the original estimate of $8.8 billion. And things got worse. Forecasts called for 16.8 million passengers in the first year, but only 4 million actually used it. Revenue estimates for 2003 were $2.88 billion, but actual revenue was only about one-third of that. The major problems faced by the Eurotunnel were increased competition from ferry services, which dropped their prices, and the rise of low-cost airlines. In 2006, things got so bad that the company operating the Eurotunnel was forced into negotiations with creditors to chop its $11.1 billion debt in half to avoid bankruptcy. The debt reduction appeared to help. In 2007, the Eurotunnel reported its first profit of €1 million ($1.6 million). Of course, this profit paled in comparison to the €204 million in losses accumulated since the Chunnel first opened in 1994.

Another example is the human transporter, or Segway. Trumpeted by inventor Dean Kamen as the replacement for automobiles in cities, the Segway came to market with great expectations. At the end of September 2003, the company recalled all of the transporters due to a mandatory software upgrade. Worse, the company had projected sales of 50,000 to 100,000 units in the first five months of production; but, three years later, only about 23,500 had been sold.

SENSITIVITY ANALYSIS

Sensitivity analysis is a variation on scenario analysis that is useful in pinpointing the areas where forecasting risk is especially severe. The basic idea with a sensitivity analysis is to freeze all of the variables except one and then see how sensitive our estimate of NPV is to changes in that one variable. If our NPV estimate turns out to be very sensitive to relatively small changes in the projected value of some component of project cash flow, then the forecasting risk associated with that variable is high.

sensitivity analysis
Investigation of what happens to NPV when only one variable is changed.

To illustrate how sensitivity analysis works, we go back to our base case for every item except unit sales. We can then calculate cash flow and NPV using the largest and smallest unit sales figures.

Scenario	Unit Sales	Cash Flow	Net Present Value	IRR
Base case	6,000	$59,800	$15,567	15.1%
Worst case	5,500	53,200	−8,226	10.3
Best case	6,500	66,400	39,357	19.7

For comparison, we now freeze everything except fixed costs and repeat the analysis:

Scenario	Fixed Costs	Cash Flow	Net Present Value	IRR
Base case	$50,000	$59,800	$15,567	15.1%
Worst case	55,000	56,500	3,670	12.7
Best case	45,000	63,100	27,461	17.4

What we see here is that given our ranges, the estimated NPV of this project is more sensitive to changes in projected unit sales than it is to changes in projected fixed costs. In fact, under the worst case for fixed costs, the NPV is still positive.

FIGURE 11.1

Sensitivity Analysis for
Unit Sales

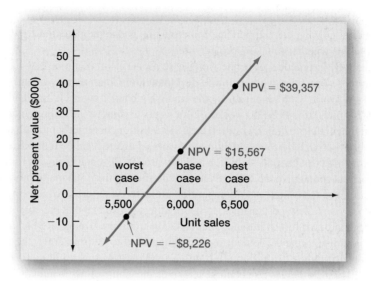

FIGURE 11.1

Sensitivity Analysis for
Unit Sales

The results of our sensitivity analysis for unit sales can be illustrated graphically as in Figure 11.1. Here we place NPV on the vertical axis and unit sales on the horizontal axis. When we plot the combinations of unit sales versus NPV, we see that all possible combinations fall on a straight line. The steeper the resulting line is, the greater the sensitivity of the estimated NPV to changes in the projected value of the variable being investigated.

Sensitivity analysis can produce results that vary dramatically depending on the assumptions. For example, in early 2011, Bard Ventures announced its projections for a molybdenum mine in British Columbia. At a cost of capital of 10 percent and an average molybdenum price of $19 per ton, the NPV of the new mine would be $112 million with an IRR of 12.4 percent. At a high price of $30 per ton, the NPV would be $1.152 billion, and the IRR would be 32.0 percent.

As we have illustrated, sensitivity analysis is useful in pinpointing which variables deserve the most attention. If we find that our estimated NPV is especially sensitive to changes in a variable that is difficult to forecast (such as unit sales), then the degree of forecasting risk is high. We might decide that further market research would be a good idea in this case.

Because sensitivity analysis is a form of scenario analysis, it suffers from the same drawbacks. Sensitivity analysis is useful for pointing out where forecasting errors will do the most damage, but it does not tell us what to do about possible errors.

SIMULATION ANALYSIS

Scenario analysis and sensitivity analysis are widely used. With scenario analysis, we let all the different variables change, but we let them take on only a few values. With sensitivity analysis, we let only one variable change, but we let it take on many values. If we combine the two approaches, the result is a crude form of **simulation analysis**.

simulation analysis
A combination of scenario
and sensitivity analysis.

If we want to let all the items vary at the same time, we have to consider a very large number of scenarios, and computer assistance is almost certainly needed. In the simplest case, we start with unit sales and assume that any value in our 5,500 to 6,500 range is equally likely. We start by randomly picking one value (or by instructing a computer to do so). We then randomly pick a price, a variable cost, and so on.

Once we have values for all the relevant components, we calculate an NPV. We repeat this sequence as much as we desire, probably several thousand times. The result is many NPV estimates that we summarize by calculating the average value and some measure of how spread out the different possibilities are. For example, it would be of some interest to know what percentage of the possible scenarios result in negative estimated NPVs.

Because simulation analysis (or simulation) is an extended form of scenario analysis, it has the same problems. Once we have the results, no simple decision rule tells us what to do. Also, we have described a relatively simple form of simulation. To really do it right, we would have to consider the interrelationships between the different cash flow components. Furthermore, we assumed that the possible values were equally likely to occur. It is probably more realistic to assume that values near the base case are more likely than extreme values, but coming up with the probabilities is difficult, to say the least.

For these reasons, the use of simulation is somewhat limited in practice. However, recent advances in computer software and hardware (and user sophistication) lead us to believe it may become more common in the future, particularly for large-scale projects.

Concept Questions

11.2a What are scenario, sensitivity, and simulation analysis?

11.2b What are the drawbacks to the various types of what-if analysis?

Break-Even Analysis   11.3

It will frequently turn out that the crucial variable for a project is sales volume. If we are thinking of creating a new product or entering a new market, for example, the hardest thing to forecast accurately is how much we can sell. For this reason, sales volume is usually analyzed more closely than other variables.

Break-even analysis is a popular and commonly used tool for analyzing the relationship between sales volume and profitability. There are a variety of different break-even measures, and we have already seen several types. For example, we discussed (in Chapter 9) how the payback period can be interpreted as the length of time until a project breaks even, ignoring time value.

All break-even measures have a similar goal. Loosely speaking, we will always be asking, "How bad do sales have to get before we actually begin to lose money?" Implicitly, we will also be asking, "Is it likely that things will get that bad?" To get started on this subject, we first discuss fixed and variable costs.

FIXED AND VARIABLE COSTS

In discussing break-even, the difference between fixed and variable costs becomes very important. As a result, we need to be a little more explicit about the difference than we have been so far.

Variable Costs   By definition, **variable costs** change as the quantity of output changes, and they are zero when production is zero. For example, direct labor costs and raw material costs are usually considered variable. This makes sense because if we shut down operations tomorrow, there will be no future costs for labor or raw materials.

variable costs
Costs that change when the quantity of output changes.

We will assume that variable costs are a constant amount per unit of output. This simply means that total variable cost is equal to the cost per unit multiplied by the number of units. In other words, the relationship between total variable cost (VC), cost per unit of output (v), and total quantity of output (Q) can be written simply as:

Total variable cost = Total quantity of output × Cost per unit of output

$$VC = Q \times v$$

FIGURE 11.2

Output Level and Variable Costs

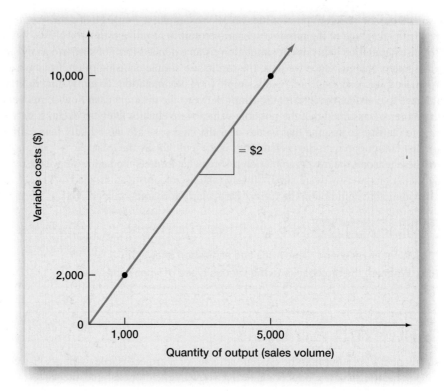

For example, suppose variable costs (v) are \$2 per unit. If total output (Q) is 1,000 units, what will total variable costs (VC) be?

$$VC = Q \times v$$
$$= 1{,}000 \times \$2$$
$$= \$2{,}000$$

Similarly, if Q is 5,000 units, then VC will be $5{,}000 \times \$2 = \$10{,}000$. Figure 11.2 illustrates the relationship between output level and variable costs in this case. In Figure 11.2, notice that increasing output by one unit results in variable costs rising by \$2, so "the rise over the run" (the slope of the line) is given by $\$2/1 = \$2$.

EXAMPLE 11.1   Variable Costs

The Blume Corporation is a manufacturer of pencils. It has received an order for 5,000 pencils, and the company has to decide whether to accept the order. From recent experience, the company knows that each pencil requires 5 cents in raw materials and 50 cents in direct labor costs. These variable costs are expected to continue to apply in the future. What will Blume's total variable costs be if it accepts the order?

In this case, the cost per unit is 50 cents in labor plus 5 cents in material for a total of 55 cents per unit. At 5,000 units of output, we have:

$$VC = Q \times v$$
$$= 5{,}000 \times \$.55$$
$$= \$2{,}750$$

Therefore, total variable costs will be \$2,750.

Fixed Costs   Fixed costs, by definition, do not change during a specified time period. So, unlike variable costs, they do not depend on the amount of goods or services produced during a period (at least within some range of production). For example, the lease payment on a production facility and the company president's salary are fixed costs, at least over some period.

Naturally, fixed costs are not fixed forever. They are fixed only during some particular time, say, a quarter or a year. Beyond that time, leases can be terminated and executives "retired." More to the point, any fixed cost can be modified or eliminated given enough time; so, in the long run, all costs are variable.

Notice that when a cost is fixed, that cost is effectively a sunk cost because we are going to have to pay it no matter what.

fixed costs
Costs that do not change when the quantity of output changes during a particular time period.

Total Costs   Total costs (TC) for a given level of output are the sum of variable costs (VC) and fixed costs (FC):

$$TC = VC + FC$$
$$= v \times Q + FC$$

So, for example, if we have variable costs of $3 per unit and fixed costs of $8,000 per year, our total cost is:

$$TC = \$3 \times Q + \$8,000$$

If we produce 6,000 units, our total production cost will be $3 × 6,000 + $8,000 = $26,000. At other production levels, we have the following:

Quantity Produced	Total Variable Costs	Fixed Costs	Total Costs
0	$ 0	$8,000	$ 8,000
1,000	3,000	8,000	11,000
5,000	15,000	8,000	23,000
10,000	30,000	8,000	38,000

By plotting these points in Figure 11.3, we see that the relationship between quantity produced and total costs is given by a straight line. In Figure 11.3, notice that total costs

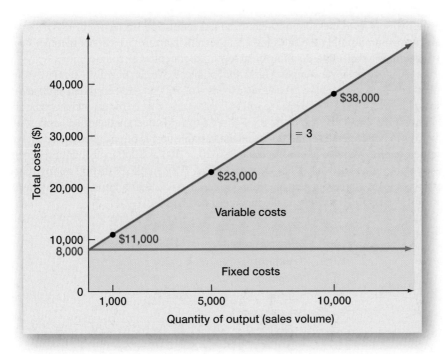

FIGURE 11.3

Output Level and Total Costs

marginal, or incremental, cost
The change in costs that occurs when there is a small change in output.

equal fixed costs when sales are zero. Beyond that point, every one-unit increase in production leads to a $3 increase in total costs, so the slope of the line is 3. In other words, the **marginal**, or **incremental, cost** of producing one more unit is $3.

EXAMPLE 11.2 | Average Cost versus Marginal Cost

Suppose the Blume Corporation has a variable cost per pencil of 55 cents. The lease payment on the production facility runs $5,000 per month. If Blume produces 100,000 pencils per year, what are the total costs of production? What is the average cost per pencil?

The fixed costs are $5,000 per month, or $60,000 per year. The variable cost is $.55 per pencil. So the total cost for the year, assuming that Blume produces 100,000 pencils, is:

$$
\begin{aligned}
\text{Total cost} &= v \times Q + FC \\
&= \$.55 \times 100{,}000 + \$60{,}000 \\
&= \$115{,}000
\end{aligned}
$$

The average cost per pencil is $115,000/100,000 = $1.15.

Now suppose that Blume has received a special, one-shot order for 5,000 pencils. Blume has sufficient capacity to manufacture the 5,000 pencils on top of the 100,000 already produced, so no additional fixed costs will be incurred. Also, there will be no effect on existing orders. If Blume can get 75 cents per pencil for this order, should the order be accepted?

What this boils down to is a simple proposition. It costs 55 cents to make another pencil. Anything Blume can get for this pencil in excess of the 55-cent incremental cost contributes in a positive way toward covering fixed costs. The 75-cent **marginal**, or **incremental, revenue** exceeds the 55-cent marginal cost, so Blume should take the order.

The fixed cost of $60,000 is not relevant to this decision because it is effectively sunk, at least for the current period. In the same way, the fact that the average cost is $1.15 is irrelevant because this average reflects the fixed cost. As long as producing the extra 5,000 pencils truly does not cost anything beyond the 55 cents per pencil, then Blume should accept anything over that 55 cents.

marginal, or incremental, revenue
The change in revenue that occurs when there is a small change in output.

ACCOUNTING BREAK-EVEN

accounting break-even
The sales level that results in zero project net income.

The most widely used measure of break-even is **accounting break-even**. The accounting break-even point is simply the sales level that results in a zero project net income.

To determine a project's accounting break-even, we start off with some common sense. Suppose we retail one-petabyte computer disks for $5 apiece. We can buy disks from a wholesale supplier for $3 apiece. We have accounting expenses of $600 in fixed costs and $300 in depreciation. How many disks do we have to sell to break even—that is, for net income to be zero?

For every disk we sell, we pick up $5 − 3 = $2 toward covering our other expenses (this $2 difference between the selling price and the variable cost is often called the *contribution margin per unit*). We have to cover a total of $600 + 300 = $900 in accounting expenses, so we obviously need to sell $900/2 = 450 disks. We can check this by noting that at a sales level of 450 units, our revenues are $5 × 450 = $2,250 and our variable costs are $3 × 450 = $1,350. Thus, here is the income statement:

Sales	$2,250
Variable costs	1,350
Fixed costs	600
Depreciation	300
EBIT	$ 0
Taxes (34%)	0
Net income	$ 0

FIGURE 11.4

Accounting Break-Even

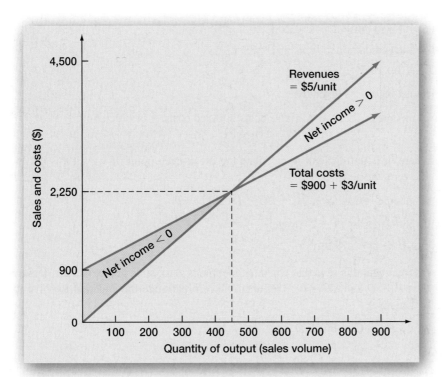

Remember, because we are discussing a proposed new project, we do not consider any interest expense in calculating net income or cash flow from the project. Also, notice that we include depreciation in calculating expenses here, even though depreciation is not a cash outflow. That is why we call it an accounting break-even. Finally, notice that when net income is zero, so are pretax income and, of course, taxes. In accounting terms, our revenues are equal to our costs, so there is no profit to tax.

Figure 11.4 presents another way to see what is happening. This figure looks a lot like Figure 11.3 except that we add a line for revenues. As indicated, total revenues are zero when output is zero. Beyond that, each unit sold brings in another $5, so the slope of the revenue line is 5.

From our preceding discussion, we know that we break even when revenues are equal to total costs. The line for revenues and the line for total costs cross right where output is at 450 units. As illustrated, at any level of output below 450, our accounting profit is negative, and at any level above 450, we have a positive net income.

ACCOUNTING BREAK-EVEN: A CLOSER LOOK

In our numerical example, notice that the break-even level is equal to the sum of fixed costs and depreciation, divided by price per unit less variable costs per unit. This is always true. To see why, we recall all of the following variables:

P = Selling price per unit

v = Variable cost per unit

Q = Total units sold

S = Total sales = $P \times Q$

VC = Total variable costs = $v \times Q$

$$\frac{fc + d}{ppu - vcpu}$$

FC = Fixed costs

D = Depreciation

T = Tax rate

Project net income is given by:

Net income = (Sales − Variable costs − Fixed costs − Depreciation) × (1 − T)

$= (S - \text{VC} - \text{FC} - D) \times (1 - T)$

From here, it is not difficult to calculate the break-even point. If we set this net income equal to zero, we get:

Net income $\overset{\text{SET}}{=} 0 = (S - \text{VC} - \text{FC} - D) \times (1 - T)$

Divide both sides by (1 − T) to get:

$S - \text{VC} - \text{FC} - D = 0$

As we have seen, this says that when net income is zero, so is pretax income. If we recall that $S = P \times Q$ and $\text{VC} = v \times Q$, then we can rearrange the equation to solve for the break-even level:

$$S - \text{VC} = \text{FC} + D$$
$$P \times Q - v \times Q = \text{FC} + D$$
$$(P - v) \times Q = \text{FC} + D$$
$$Q = (\text{FC} + D)/(P - v) \qquad \textbf{[11.1]}$$

This is the same result we described earlier.

USES FOR THE ACCOUNTING BREAK-EVEN

Why would anyone be interested in knowing the accounting break-even point? To illustrate how it can be useful, suppose we are a small specialty ice cream manufacturer with a strictly local distribution. We are thinking about expanding into new markets. Based on the estimated cash flows, we find that the expansion has a positive NPV.

Going back to our discussion of forecasting risk, we know that it is likely that what will make or break our expansion is sales volume. The reason is that, in this case at least, we probably have a fairly good idea of what we can charge for the ice cream. Further, we know relevant production and distribution costs reasonably well because we are already in the business. What we do not know with any real precision is how much ice cream we can sell.

Given the costs and selling price, however, we can immediately calculate the break-even point. Once we have done so, we might find that we need to get 30 percent of the market just to break even. If we think that this is unlikely to occur, because, for example, we have only 10 percent of our current market, then we know our forecast is questionable and there is a real possibility that the true NPV is negative. On the other hand, we might find that we already have firm commitments from buyers for about the break-even amount, so we are almost certain we can sell more. In this case, the forecasting risk is much lower, and we have greater confidence in our estimates.

There are several other reasons why knowing the accounting break-even can be useful. First, as we will discuss in more detail later, accounting break-even and payback period are similar measures. Like payback period, accounting break-even is relatively easy to calculate and explain.

Second, managers are often concerned with the contribution a project will make to the firm's total accounting earnings. A project that does not break even in an accounting sense actually reduces total earnings.

Third, a project that just breaks even on an accounting basis loses money in a financial or opportunity cost sense. This is true because we could have earned more by investing elsewhere. Such a project does not lose money in an out-of-pocket sense. As described in the following pages, we get back exactly what we put in. For noneconomic reasons, opportunity losses may be easier to live with than out-of-pocket losses.

Concept Questions

11.3a How are fixed costs similar to sunk costs?

11.3b What is net income at the accounting break-even point? What about taxes?

11.3c Why might a financial manager be interested in the accounting break-even point?

Operating Cash Flow, Sales Volume, and Break-Even

11.4

Accounting break-even is one tool that is useful for project analysis. Ultimately, however, we are more interested in cash flow than accounting income. So, for example, if sales volume is the critical variable, then we need to know more about the relationship between sales volume and cash flow than just the accounting break-even.

Our goal in this section is to illustrate the relationship between operating cash flow and sales volume. We also discuss some other break-even measures. To simplify matters somewhat, we will ignore the effect of taxes. We start off by looking at the relationship between accounting break-even and cash flow.

ACCOUNTING BREAK-EVEN AND CASH FLOW

Now that we know how to find the accounting break-even, it is natural to wonder what happens with cash flow. To illustrate, suppose the Wettway Sailboat Corporation is considering whether to launch its new Margo-class sailboat. The selling price will be $40,000 per boat. The variable costs will be about half that, or $20,000 per boat, and fixed costs will be $500,000 per year.

The Base Case   The total investment needed to undertake the project is $3,500,000. This amount will be depreciated straight-line to zero over the five-year life of the equipment. The salvage value is zero, and there are no working capital consequences. Wettway has a 20 percent required return on new projects.

Based on market surveys and historical experience, Wettway projects total sales for the five years at 425 boats, or about 85 boats per year. Ignoring taxes, should this project be launched?

To begin, ignoring taxes, the operating cash flow at 85 boats per year is:

$$
\begin{aligned}
\text{Operating cash flow} &= \text{EBIT} + \text{Depreciation} - \text{Taxes} \\
&= (S - \text{VC} - \text{FC} - D) + D - 0 \\
&= 85 \times (\$40,000 - 20,000) - 500,000 \\
&= \$1,200,000 \text{ per year}
\end{aligned}
$$

At 20 percent, the five-year annuity factor is 2.9906, so the NPV is:

$$\text{NPV} = -\$3,500,000 + 1,200,000 \times 2.9906$$
$$= -\$3,500,000 + 3,588,720$$
$$= \$88,720$$

In the absence of additional information, the project should be launched.

Calculating the Break-Even Level   To begin looking a little closer at this project, you might ask a series of questions. For example, how many new boats does Wettway need to sell for the project to break even on an accounting basis? If Wettway does break even, what will be the annual cash flow from the project? What will be the return on the investment in this case?

Before fixed costs and depreciation are considered, Wettway generates $40,000 - 20,000 = \$20,000$ per boat (this is revenue less variable cost). Depreciation is $\$3,500,000/5 = \$700,000$ per year. Fixed costs and depreciation together total $1.2 million, so Wettway needs to sell $(\text{FC} + D)/(P - v) = \$1.2 \text{ million}/20,000 = 60$ boats per year to break even on an accounting basis. This is 25 boats less than projected sales; so, assuming that Wettway is confident its projection is accurate to within, say, 15 boats, it appears unlikely that the new investment will fail to at least break even on an accounting basis.

To calculate Wettway's cash flow in this case, we note that if 60 boats are sold, net income will be exactly zero. Recalling from the previous chapter that operating cash flow for a project can be written as net income plus depreciation (the bottom-up definition), we can see that the operating cash flow is equal to the depreciation, or $700,000 in this case. The internal rate of return is exactly zero (why?).

Payback and Break-Even   As our example illustrates, whenever a project breaks even on an accounting basis, the cash flow for that period will equal the depreciation. This result makes perfect accounting sense. For example, suppose we invest $100,000 in a five-year project. The depreciation is straight-line to a zero salvage, or $20,000 per year. If the project exactly breaks even every period, then the cash flow will be $20,000 per period.

The sum of the cash flows for the life of this project is $5 \times \$20,000 = \$100,000$, the original investment. What this shows is that a project's payback period is exactly equal to its life if the project breaks even every period. Similarly, a project that does better than break even has a payback that is shorter than the life of the project and has a positive rate of return.

The bad news is that a project that just breaks even on an accounting basis has a negative NPV and a zero return. For our sailboat project, the fact that Wettway will almost surely break even on an accounting basis is partially comforting because it means that the firm's "downside" risk (its potential loss) is limited, but we still don't know if the project is truly profitable. More work is needed.

SALES VOLUME AND OPERATING CASH FLOW

At this point, we can generalize our example and introduce some other break-even measures. From our discussion in the previous section, we know that, ignoring taxes, a project's operating cash flow, OCF, can be written simply as EBIT plus depreciation:

$$\text{OCF} = [(P - v) \times Q - \text{FC} - D] + D$$
$$= (P - v) \times Q - \text{FC}$$

[11.2]

For the Wettway sailboat project, the general relationship (in thousands of dollars) between operating cash flow and sales volume is thus:

$$\text{OCF} = (P - v) \times Q - \text{FC}$$
$$= (\$40 - 20) \times Q - 500$$
$$= -\$500 + 20 \times Q$$

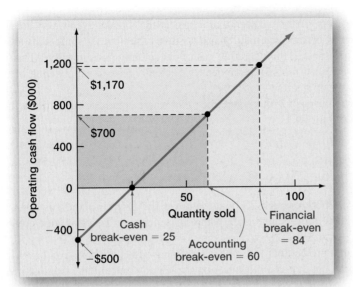

FIGURE 11.5

Operating Cash Flow and
Sales Volume

What this tells us is that the relationship between operating cash flow and sales volume is given by a straight line with a slope of $20 and a y-intercept of $-\$500$. If we calculate some different values, we get:

Quantity Sold	Operating Cash Flow
0	$-\$\ 500$
15	$-\ \ 200$
30	100
50	500
75	1,000

These points are plotted in Figure 11.5, where we have indicated three different break-even points. We discuss these next.

CASH FLOW, ACCOUNTING, AND FINANCIAL BREAK-EVEN POINTS

We know from the preceding discussion that the relationship between operating cash flow and sales volume (ignoring taxes) is:

$$OCF = (P - v) \times Q - FC$$

If we rearrange this and solve for Q, we get:

$$Q = (FC + OCF)/(P - v) \qquad \text{[11.3]}$$

This tells us what sales volume (Q) is necessary to achieve any given OCF, so this result is more general than the accounting break-even. We use it to find the various break-even points in Figure 11.5.

Accounting Break-Even Revisited   Looking at Figure 11.5, suppose operating cash flow is equal to depreciation (D). Recall that this situation corresponds to our break-even point on an accounting basis. To find the sales volume, we substitute the $700 depreciation amount for OCF in our general expression:

$$Q = (FC + OCF)/(P - v)$$
$$= (\$500 + 700)/20$$
$$= 60$$

This is the same quantity we had before.

cash break-even
The sales level that results in a zero operating cash flow.

Cash Break-Even   We have seen that a project that breaks even on an accounting basis has a net income of zero, but it still has a positive cash flow. At some sales level below the accounting break-even, the operating cash flow actually goes negative. This is a particularly unpleasant occurrence. If it happens, we actually have to supply additional cash to the project just to keep it afloat.

To calculate the **cash break-even** (the point where operating cash flow is equal to zero), we put in a zero for OCF:

$$Q = (FC + 0)/(P - v)$$
$$= \$500/20$$
$$= 25$$

Wettway must therefore sell 25 boats to cover the $500 in fixed costs. As we show in Figure 11.5, this point occurs right where the operating cash flow line crosses the horizontal axis.

Notice that a project that just breaks even on a cash flow basis can cover its own fixed operating costs, but that is all. It never pays back anything, so the original investment is a complete loss (the IRR is -100 percent).

financial break-even
The sales level that results in a zero NPV.

Financial Break-Even   The last case we consider is that of **financial break-even**, the sales level that results in a zero NPV. To the financial manager, this is the most interesting case. What we do is first determine what operating cash flow has to be for the NPV to be zero. We then use this amount to determine the sales volume.

To illustrate, recall that Wettway requires a 20 percent return on its $3,500 (in thousands) investment. How many sailboats does Wettway have to sell to break even once we account for the 20 percent per year opportunity cost?

The sailboat project has a five-year life. The project has a zero NPV when the present value of the operating cash flows equals the $3,500 investment. Because the cash flow is the same each year, we can solve for the unknown amount by viewing it as an ordinary annuity. The five-year annuity factor at 20 percent is 2.9906, and the OCF can be determined as follows:

$$\$3,500 = OCF \times 2.9906$$
$$OCF = \$3,500/2.9906$$
$$= \$1,170$$

Wettway thus needs an operating cash flow of $1,170 each year to break even. We can now plug this OCF into the equation for sales volume:

$$Q = (\$500 + 1,170)/20$$
$$= 83.5$$

So, Wettway needs to sell about 84 boats per year. This is not good news.

As indicated in Figure 11.5, the financial break-even is substantially higher than the accounting break-even. This will often be the case. Moreover, what we have discovered is that the sailboat project has a substantial degree of forecasting risk. We project sales of 85 boats per year, but it takes 84 just to earn the required return.

Conclusion   Overall, it seems unlikely that the Wettway sailboat project would fail to break even on an accounting basis. However, there appears to be a very good chance that the true NPV is negative. This illustrates the danger in looking at just the accounting break-even.

What should Wettway do? Is the new project all wet? The decision at this point is essentially a managerial issue—a judgment call. The crucial questions are these:

1. How much confidence do we have in our projections?

TABLE 11.1

Summary of Break-Even Measures

I. The General Break-Even Expression

Ignoring taxes, the relation between operating cash flow (OCF) and quantity of output or sales volume (Q) is:

$$Q = \frac{FC + OCF}{P - v}$$

where

    FC = Total fixed costs
    P = Price per unit
    v = Variable cost per unit

As shown next, this relation can be used to determine the accounting, cash, and financial break-even points.

II. The Accounting Break-Even Point

Accounting break-even occurs when net income is zero. Operating cash flow is equal to depreciation when net income is zero, so the accounting break-even point is:

$$Q = \frac{FC + D}{P - v}$$

A project that always just breaks even on an accounting basis has a payback exactly equal to its life, a negative NPV, and an IRR of zero.

III. The Cash Break-Even Point

Cash break-even occurs when operating cash flow is zero. The cash break-even point is thus:

$$Q = \frac{FC}{P - v}$$

A project that always just breaks even on a cash basis never pays back, has an NPV that is negative and equal to the initial outlay, and has an IRR of −100 percent.

IV. The Financial Break-Even Point

Financial break-even occurs when the NPV of the project is zero. The financial break-even point is thus:

$$Q = \frac{FC + OCF^*}{P - v}$$

where OCF* is the level of OCF that results in a zero NPV. A project that breaks even on a financial basis has a discounted payback equal to its life, a zero NPV, and an IRR just equal to the required return.

2. How important is the project to the future of the company?
3. How badly will the company be hurt if sales turn out to be low? What options are available to the company in this case?

We will consider questions such as these in a later section. For future reference, our discussion of the different break-even measures is summarized in Table 11.1.

Concept Questions

11.4a If a project breaks even on an accounting basis, what is its operating cash flow?

11.4b If a project breaks even on a cash basis, what is its operating cash flow?

11.4c If a project breaks even on a financial basis, what do you know about its *discounted* payback?

⚡ 11.5 Operating Leverage

We have discussed how to calculate and interpret various measures of break-even for a proposed project. What we have not explicitly discussed is what determines these points and how they might be changed. We now turn to this subject.

THE BASIC IDEA

operating leverage
The degree to which a firm or project relies on fixed costs.

Operating leverage is the degree to which a project or firm is committed to fixed production costs. A firm with low operating leverage will have low fixed costs compared to a firm with high operating leverage. Generally speaking, projects with a relatively heavy investment in plant and equipment will have a relatively high degree of operating leverage. Such projects are said to be *capital intensive*.

Anytime we are thinking about a new venture, there will normally be alternative ways of producing and delivering the product. For example, Wettway Corporation can purchase the necessary equipment and build all of the components for its sailboats in-house. Alternatively, some of the work could be farmed out to other firms. The first option involves a greater investment in plant and equipment, greater fixed costs and depreciation, and, as a result, a higher degree of operating leverage.

IMPLICATIONS OF OPERATING LEVERAGE

Regardless of how it is measured, operating leverage has important implications for project evaluation. Fixed costs act like a lever in the sense that a small percentage change in operating revenue can be magnified into a large percentage change in operating cash flow and NPV. This explains why we call it operating "leverage."

The higher the degree of operating leverage, the greater is the potential danger from forecasting risk. The reason is that relatively small errors in forecasting sales volume can get magnified, or "levered up," into large errors in cash flow projections.

From a managerial perspective, one way of coping with highly uncertain projects is to keep the degree of operating leverage as low as possible. This will generally have the effect of keeping the break-even point (however measured) at its minimum level. We will illustrate this point in a bit, but first we need to discuss how to measure operating leverage.

MEASURING OPERATING LEVERAGE

degree of operating leverage (DOL)
The percentage change in operating cash flow relative to the percentage change in quantity sold.

One way of measuring operating leverage is to ask: If quantity sold rises by 5 percent, what will be the percentage change in operating cash flow? In other words, the **degree of operating** leverage (DOL) is defined such that:

Percentage change in OCF = DOL × Percentage change in Q

Based on the relationship between OCF and Q, DOL can be written as:[1]

$$\text{DOL} = 1 + \text{FC/OCF} \qquad \text{[11.4]}$$

---

[1]To see this, note that if Q goes up by one unit, OCF will go up by $(P - v)$. In this case, the percentage change in Q is $1/Q$, and the percentage change in OCF is $(P - v)/\text{OCF}$. Given this, we have:

Percentage change in OCF = DOL × Percentage change in Q

$(P - v)/\text{OCF} = \text{DOL} \times 1/Q$

$\text{DOL} = (P - v) \times Q/\text{OCF}$

Also, based on our definitions of OCF:

$\text{OCF} + \text{FC} = (P - v) \times Q$

Thus, DOL can be written as:

$\text{DOL} = (\text{OCF} + \text{FC})/\text{OCF}$

$= 1 + \text{FC/OCF}$

The ratio FC/OCF simply measures fixed costs as a percentage of total operating cash flow. Notice that zero fixed costs would result in a DOL of 1, implying that percentage changes in quantity sold would show up one for one in operating cash flow. In other words, no magnification, or leverage, effect would exist.

To illustrate this measure of operating leverage, we go back to the Wettway sailboat project. Fixed costs were $500 and $(P - v)$ was $20, so OCF was:

$$OCF = -\$500 + 20 \times Q$$

Suppose Q is currently 50 boats. At this level of output, OCF is $-\$500 + 1,000 = \$500$.

If Q rises by 1 unit to 51, then the percentage change in Q is $(51 - 50)/50 = .02$, or 2%. OCF rises to $520, a change of $P - v = \$20$. The percentage change in OCF is $(\$520 - 500)/500 = .04$, or 4%. So a 2 percent increase in the number of boats sold leads to a 4 percent increase in operating cash flow. The degree of operating leverage must be exactly 2.00. We can check this by noting that:

$$
\begin{aligned}
DOL &= 1 + FC/OCF \\
&= 1 + \$500/500 \\
&= 2
\end{aligned}
$$

This verifies our previous calculations.

Our formulation of DOL depends on the current output level, Q. However, it can handle changes from the current level of any size, not just one unit. For example, suppose Q rises from 50 to 75, a 50 percent increase. With DOL equal to 2, operating cash flow should increase by 100 percent, or exactly double. Does it? The answer is yes, because, at a Q of 75, OCF is:

$$OCF = -\$500 + 20 \times 75 = \$1,000$$

Notice that operating leverage declines as output (Q) rises. For example, at an output level of 75, we have:

$$
\begin{aligned}
DOL &= 1 + \$500/1,000 \\
&= 1.50
\end{aligned}
$$

The reason DOL declines is that fixed costs, considered as a percentage of operating cash flow, get smaller and smaller, so the leverage effect diminishes.

Operating Leverage

EXAMPLE 11.3

The Sasha Corp. currently sells gourmet dog food for $1.20 per can. The variable cost is 80 cents per can, and the packaging and marketing operations have fixed costs of $360,000 per year. Depreciation is $60,000 per year. What is the accounting break-even? Ignoring taxes, what will be the increase in operating cash flow if the quantity sold rises to 10 percent above the break-even point?

The accounting break-even is $420,000/.40 = 1,050,000 cans. As we know, the operating cash flow is equal to the $60,000 depreciation at this level of production, so the degree of operating leverage is:

$$
\begin{aligned}
DOL &= 1 + FC/OCF \\
&= 1 + \$360,000/60,000 \\
&= 7
\end{aligned}
$$

Given this, a 10 percent increase in the number of cans of dog food sold will increase operating cash flow by a substantial 70 percent.

To check this answer, we note that if sales rise by 10 percent, then the quantity sold will rise to $1,050,000 \times 1.1 = 1,155,000$. Ignoring taxes, the operating cash flow will be $1,155,000 \times \$.40 - 360,000 = \$102,000$. Compared to the $60,000 cash flow we had, this is exactly 70 percent more: $\$102,000/60,000 = 1.70$.

OPERATING LEVERAGE AND BREAK-EVEN

We illustrate why operating leverage is an important consideration by examining the Wettway sailboat project under an alternative scenario. At a Q of 85 boats, the degree of operating leverage for the sailboat project under the original scenario is:

$$DOL = 1 + FC/OCF$$
$$= 1 + \$500/1,200$$
$$= 1.42$$

Also, recall that the NPV at a sales level of 85 boats was $88,720, and the accounting break-even was 60 boats.

An option available to Wettway is to subcontract production of the boat hull assemblies. If the company does this, the necessary investment falls to $3,200,000 and the fixed operating costs fall to $180,000. However, variable costs will rise to $25,000 per boat because subcontracting is more expensive than producing in-house. Ignoring taxes, evaluate this option.

For practice, see if you don't agree with the following:

NPV at 20% (85 units) = $74,720

Accounting break-even = 55 boats

Degree of operating leverage = 1.16

What has happened? This option results in a slightly lower estimated net present value, and the accounting break-even point falls to 55 boats from 60 boats.

Given that this alternative has the lower NPV, is there any reason to consider it further? Maybe there is. The degree of operating leverage is substantially lower in the second case. If Wettway is worried about the possibility of an overly optimistic projection, then it might prefer to subcontract.

There is another reason why Wettway might consider the second arrangement. If sales turned out to be better than expected, the company would always have the option of starting to produce in-house at a later date. As a practical matter, it is much easier to increase operating leverage (by purchasing equipment) than to decrease it (by selling off equipment). As we discuss in a later chapter, one of the drawbacks to discounted cash flow analysis is that it is difficult to explicitly include options of this sort in the analysis, even though they may be quite important.

Concept Questions

11.5a What is operating leverage?

11.5b How is operating leverage measured?

11.5c What are the implications of operating leverage for the financial manager?

11.6 Capital Rationing

capital rationing
The situation that exists if a firm has positive NPV projects but cannot find the necessary financing.

Capital rationing is said to exist when we have profitable (positive NPV) investments available but we can't get the funds needed to undertake them. For example, as division managers for a large corporation, we might identify $5 million in excellent projects, but find that, for whatever reason, we can spend only $2 million. Now what? Unfortunately, for reasons we will discuss, there may be no truly satisfactory answer.

SOFT RATIONING

The situation we have just described is called **soft rationing**. This occurs when, for example, different units in a business are allocated some fixed amount of money each year for capital spending. Such an allocation is primarily a means of controlling and keeping track of overall spending. The important thing to note about soft rationing is that the corporation as a whole isn't short of capital; more can be raised on ordinary terms if management so desires.

soft rationing
The situation that occurs when units in a business are allocated a certain amount of financing for capital budgeting.

If we face soft rationing, the first thing to do is to try to get a larger allocation. Failing that, one common suggestion is to generate as large a net present value as possible within the existing budget. This amounts to choosing projects with the largest benefit–cost ratio (profitability index).

Strictly speaking, this is the correct thing to do only if the soft rationing is a one-time event—that is, it won't exist next year. If the soft rationing is a chronic problem, then something is amiss. The reason goes all the way back to Chapter 1. Ongoing soft rationing means we are constantly bypassing positive NPV investments. This contradicts the goal of our firm. If we are not trying to maximize value, then the question of which projects to take becomes ambiguous because we no longer have an objective goal in the first place.

HARD RATIONING

With **hard rationing**, a business cannot raise capital for a project under any circumstances. For large, healthy corporations, this situation probably does not occur very often. This is fortunate because, with hard rationing, our DCF analysis breaks down, and the best course of action is ambiguous.

hard rationing
The situation that occurs when a business cannot raise financing for a project under any circumstances.

The reason DCF analysis breaks down has to do with the required return. Suppose we say our required return is 20 percent. Implicitly, we are saying we will take a project with a return that exceeds this. However, if we face hard rationing, then we are not going to take a new project no matter what the return on that project is, so the whole concept of a required return is ambiguous. About the only interpretation we can give this situation is that the required return is so large that no project has a positive NPV in the first place.

Hard rationing can occur when a company experiences financial distress, meaning that bankruptcy is a possibility. Also, a firm may not be able to raise capital without violating a pre-existing contractual agreement. We discuss these situations in greater detail in a later chapter.

Concept Questions

11.6a What is capital rationing? What types are there?

11.6b What problems does capital rationing create for discounted cash flow analysis?

Visit us at www.mhhe.com/rwj

Summary and Conclusions   11.7

In this chapter, we looked at some ways of evaluating the results of a discounted cash flow analysis; we also touched on some of the problems that can come up in practice:

1. Net present value estimates depend on projected future cash flows. If there are errors in those projections, then our estimated NPVs can be misleading. We called this possibility *forecasting risk*.

2. Scenario and sensitivity analysis are useful tools for identifying which variables are critical to the success of a project and where forecasting problems can do the most damage.

3. Break-even analysis in its various forms is a particularly common type of scenario analysis that is useful for identifying critical levels of sales.

4. Operating leverage is a key determinant of break-even levels. It reflects the degree to which a project or a firm is committed to fixed costs. The degree of operating leverage tells us the sensitivity of operating cash flow to changes in sales volume.

5. Projects usually have future managerial options associated with them. These options may be important, but standard discounted cash flow analysis tends to ignore them.

6. Capital rationing occurs when apparently profitable projects cannot be funded. Standard discounted cash flow analysis is troublesome in this case because NPV is not necessarily the appropriate criterion.

The most important thing to carry away from reading this chapter is that estimated NPVs or returns should not be taken at face value. They depend critically on projected cash flows. If there is room for significant disagreement about those projected cash flows, the results from the analysis have to be taken with a grain of salt.

Despite the problems we have discussed, discounted cash flow analysis is still *the* way of attacking problems because it forces us to ask the right questions. What we have learned in this chapter is that knowing the questions to ask does not guarantee we will get all the answers.

Visit us at www.mhhe.com/rwj

CONNECT TO FINANCE

 |FINANCE

If you are using *Connect™ Finance* in your course, get online to take a Practice Test, check out study tools, and find out where you need additional practice.

Can you answer the following questions?

Section 11.1 The potential for believing that a project has a positive net present value when it does not is referred to as _____. (LO 11-2)

Section 11.2 Marcos Entertainment expects to sell 84,000 theater tickets at $12 each during the coming year. What is the worst-case sales revenue if all estimates are accurate to within a ± 3 percent range? (LO 11-2)

Section 11.3 Delta Tool has projected sales of 8,500 units at a sales price per unit of $9,400. Fixed costs are estimated at $5.2 million, and estimated variable costs per unit are $8,300. What is the amount of the total costs if the firm temporarily stops production? (LO 11-3)

Section 11.4 What is true for a project if that project is operating at its financial break-even point? (LO 11-3)

Section 11.5 A capital-intensive project is one that has a _____. (LO 11-4)

Section 11.6 Pavloki, Inc., has three proposed projects with positive net present values. These projects and their net present values are: Project A−NPV $46,300; Project B−NPV $31,900; Project C−NPV $6,400. If the firm is faced with hard rationing, which of the projects will it accept? (LO 11-5)

Log on to find out!

CHAPTER REVIEW AND SELF-TEST PROBLEMS

Use the following base-case information to work the self-test problems:

A project under consideration costs $750,000, has a five-year life, and has no salvage value. Depreciation is straight-line to zero. The required return is 17 percent, and the tax rate is 34 percent. Sales are projected at 500 units per year. Price per unit is $2,500, variable cost per unit is $1,500, and fixed costs are $200,000 per year.

11.1 Scenario Analysis Suppose you think that the unit sales, price, variable cost, and fixed cost projections given here are accurate to within 5 percent. What are the upper and lower bounds for these projections? What is the base-case NPV? What are the best- and worst-case scenario NPVs?

11.2 Break-Even Analysis Given the base-case projections in the previous problem, what are the cash, accounting, and financial break-even sales levels for this project? Ignore taxes in answering.

ANSWERS TO CHAPTER REVIEW AND SELF-TEST PROBLEMS

11.1 We can summarize the relevant information as follows:

	Base Case	Lower Bound	Upper Bound
Unit sales	500	475	525
Price per unit	$ 2,500	$ 2,375	$ 2,625
Variable cost per unit	$ 1,500	$ 1,425	$ 1,575
Fixed cost per year	$200,000	$190,000	$210,000

Depreciation is $150,000 per year; knowing this, we can calculate the cash flows under each scenario. Remember that we assign high costs and low prices and volume for the worst case and just the opposite for the best case:

Scenario	Unit Sales	Unit Price	Unit Variable Cost	Fixed Costs	Cash Flow
Base case	500	$2,500	$1,500	$200,000	$249,000
Best case	525	2,625	1,425	190,000	341,400
Worst case	475	2,375	1,575	210,000	163,200

Visit us at www.mhhe.com/rwj

At 17 percent, the five-year annuity factor is 3.19935, so the NPVs are:

$$\text{Base-case NPV} = -\$750,000 + 3.19935 \times \$249,000$$
$$= \$46,638$$

$$\text{Best-case NPV} = -\$750,000 + 3.19935 \times \$341,400$$
$$= \$342,258$$

$$\text{Worst-case NPV} = -\$750,000 + 3.19935 \times \$163,200$$
$$= -\$227,866$$

11.2 In this case, we have $200,000 in cash fixed costs to cover. Each unit contributes $2,500 − 1,500 = $1,000 toward covering fixed costs. The cash break-even is thus $200,000/$1,000 = 200 units. We have another $150,000 in depreciation, so the accounting break-even is ($200,000 + 150,000)/$1,000 = 350 units.

To get the financial break-even, we need to find the OCF such that the project has a zero NPV. As we have seen, the five-year annuity factor is 3.19935 and the project costs $750,000, so the OCF must be such that:

$$\$750,000 = \text{OCF} \times 3.19935$$

So, for the project to break even on a financial basis, the project's cash flow must be $750,000/3.19935, or $234,423 per year. If we add this to the $200,000 in cash fixed costs, we get a total of $434,423 that we have to cover. At $1,000 per unit, we need to sell $434,423/$1,000 = 435 units.

CONCEPTS REVIEW AND CRITICAL THINKING QUESTIONS

1. **Forecasting Risk [LO1]** What is forecasting risk? In general, would the degree of forecasting risk be greater for a new product or a cost-cutting proposal? Why?

2. **Sensitivity Analysis and Scenario Analysis [LO1, 2]** What is the essential difference between sensitivity analysis and scenario analysis?

3. **Marginal Cash Flows [LO3]** A co-worker claims that looking at all this marginal this and incremental that is just a bunch of nonsense, saying, "Listen, if our average revenue doesn't exceed our average cost, then we will have a negative cash flow, and we will go broke!" How do you respond?

4. **Operating Leverage [LO4]** At one time at least, many Japanese companies had a "no-layoff" policy (for that matter, so did IBM). What are the implications of such a policy for the degree of operating leverage a company faces?

5. **Operating Leverage [LO4]** Airlines offer an example of an industry in which the degree of operating leverage is fairly high. Why?

6. **Break-Even [LO3]** As a shareholder of a firm that is contemplating a new project, would you be more concerned with the accounting break-even point, the cash break-even point, or the financial break-even point? Why?

7. **Break-Even [LO3]** Assume a firm is considering a new project that requires an initial investment and has equal sales and costs over its life. Will the project reach the accounting, cash, or financial break-even point first? Which will it reach next? Last? Will this ordering always apply?

8. **Capital Rationing [LO5]** How do soft rationing and hard rationing differ? What are the implications if a firm is experiencing soft rationing? Hard rationing?

9. **Capital Rationing [LO5]** Going all the way back to Chapter 1, recall that we saw that partnerships and proprietorships can face difficulties when it comes to raising capital. In the context of this chapter, the implication is that small businesses will generally face what problem?

10. **Scenario Analysis [LO2]** You are at your desk at work when a co-worker excitedly comes to your desk and shows you the scenario analysis that he has just completed for a potential new project. All three scenarios show a positive NPV. He states, "We have to take this project!" What is your initial reaction regarding this new project. Do you believe the results of the scenario analysis?

QUESTIONS AND PROBLEMS

1. **Calculating Costs and Break-Even [LO3]** Night Shades, Inc. (NSI), manufactures biotech sunglasses. The variable materials cost is $10.48 per unit, and the variable labor cost is $6.89 per unit.

   BASIC
   (Questions 1–15)

   a. What is the variable cost per unit?

   b. Suppose NSI incurs fixed costs of $870,000 during a year in which total production is 280,000 units. What are the total costs for the year?

   c. If the selling price is $49.99 per unit, does NSI break even on a cash basis? If depreciation is $490,000 per year, what is the accounting break-even point?

2. **Computing Average Cost [LO3]** K-Too Everwear Corporation can manufacture mountain climbing shoes for $31.85 per pair in variable raw material costs and $22.80 per pair in variable labor expense. The shoes sell for $145 per pair. Last year, production was 120,000 pairs. Fixed costs were $1,750,000. What were total production costs? What is the marginal cost per pair? What is the average cost? If the company is considering a one-time order for an extra 5,000 pairs, what is the minimum acceptable total revenue from the order? Explain.

3. **Scenario Analysis [LO2]** Olin Transmissions, Inc., has the following estimates for its new gear assembly project: price = $1,400 per unit; variable costs = $220 per unit; fixed costs = $3.9 million; quantity = 85,000 units. Suppose the company believes all of its estimates are accurate only to within ±15 percent. What values should the company use for the four variables given here when it performs its best-case scenario analysis? What about the worst-case scenario?

4. **Sensitivity Analysis [LO1]** For the company in the previous problem, suppose management is most concerned about the impact of its price estimate on the project's profitability. How could you address this concern? Describe how you would calculate your answer. What values would you use for the other forecast variables?

5. **Sensitivity Analysis and Break-Even [LO1, 3]** We are evaluating a project that costs $924,000, has an eight-year life, and has no salvage value. Assume that depreciation is straight-line to zero over the life of the project. Sales are projected at 75,000 units per year. Price per unit is $46, variable cost per unit is $31, and fixed costs are $825,000 per year. The tax rate is 35 percent, and we require a 15 percent return on this project.

   a. Calculate the accounting break-even point. What is the degree of operating leverage at the accounting break-even point?

   b. Calculate the base-case cash flow and NPV. What is the sensitivity of NPV to changes in the sales figure? Explain what your answer tells you about a 500-unit decrease in projected sales.

   c. What is the sensitivity of OCF to changes in the variable cost figure? Explain what your answer tells you about a $1 decrease in estimated variable costs.

6. **Scenario Analysis [LO2]** In the previous problem, suppose the projections given for price, quantity, variable costs, and fixed costs are all accurate to within ±10 percent. Calculate the best-case and worst-case NPV figures.

7. **Calculating Break-Even [LO3]** In each of the following cases, calculate the accounting break-even and the cash break-even points. Ignore any tax effects in calculating the cash break-even.

Unit Price	Unit Variable Cost	Fixed Costs	Depreciation
$3,020	$2,275	$9,000,000	$3,100,000
46	41	73,000	150,000
11	4	1,700	930

8. **Calculating Break-Even [LO3]** In each of the following cases, find the unknown variable:

Accounting Break-Even	Unit Price	Unit Variable Cost	Fixed Costs	Depreciation
112,800	$39	$30	$ 820,000	?
165,000	?	27	3,200,000	$1,150,000
4,385	92	?	160,000	105,000

9. **Calculating Break-Even [LO3]** A project has the following estimated data: price = $62 per unit; variable costs = $41 per unit; fixed costs = $15,500; required return = 12 percent; initial investment = $24,000; life = four years. Ignoring the effect of taxes, what is the accounting break-even quantity? The cash break-even quantity? The financial break-even quantity? What is the degree of operating leverage at the financial break-even level of output?

10. **Using Break-Even Analysis [LO3]** Consider a project with the following data: accounting break-even quantity = 13,400 units; cash break-even quantity = 10,600 units; life = five years; fixed costs = $150,000; variable costs = $24 per unit; required return = 12 percent. Ignoring the effect of taxes, find the financial break-even quantity.

11. **Calculating Operating Leverage [LO4]** At an output level of 73,000 units, you calculate that the degree of operating leverage is 2.90. If output rises to 78,000 units, what will the percentage change in operating cash flow be? Will the new level of operating leverage be higher or lower? Explain.

12. **Leverage [LO4]** In the previous problem, suppose fixed costs are $150,000. What is the operating cash flow at 67,000 units? The degree of operating leverage?

13. **Operating Cash Flow and Leverage [LO4]** A proposed project has fixed costs of $84,000 per year. The operating cash flow at 7,500 units is $93,200. Ignoring the effect of taxes, what is the degree of operating leverage? If units sold rise from 7,500 to 8,000, what will be the increase in operating cash flow? What is the new degree of operating leverage?

14. **Cash Flow and Leverage [LO4]** At an output level of 15,000 units, you have calculated that the degree of operating leverage is 2.61. The operating cash flow is $57,000 in this case. Ignoring the effect of taxes, what are fixed costs? What will the operating cash flow be if output rises to 16,000 units? If output falls to 14,000 units?

15. **Leverage [LO4]** In the previous problem, what will be the new degree of operating leverage in each case?

16. **Break-Even Intuition [LO3]** Consider a project with a required return of $R\%$ that costs $\$I$ and will last for N years. The project uses straight-line depreciation to zero over the N-year life; there is no salvage value or net working capital requirements.

    a. At the accounting break-even level of output, what is the IRR of this project? The payback period? The NPV?

    b. At the cash break-even level of output, what is the IRR of this project? The payback period? The NPV?

    c. At the financial break-even level of output, what is the IRR of this project? The payback period? The NPV?

INTERMEDIATE
(Questions 16–24)

17. **Sensitivity Analysis [LO1]** Consider a four-year project with the following information: initial fixed asset investment = $\$420,000$; straight-line depreciation to zero over the four-year life; zero salvage value; price = $\$25$; variable costs = $\$16$; fixed costs = $\$180,000$; quantity sold = 75,000 units; tax rate = 34 percent. How sensitive is OCF to changes in quantity sold?

18. **Operating Leverage [LO4]** In the previous problem, what is the degree of operating leverage at the given level of output? What is the degree of operating leverage at the accounting break-even level of output?

19. **Project Analysis [LO1, 2, 3, 4]** You are considering a new product launch. The project will cost $\$1,400,000$, have a four-year life, and have no salvage value; depreciation is straight-line to zero. Sales are projected at 180 units per year; price per unit will be $\$16,000$, variable cost per unit will be $\$9,800$, and fixed costs will be $\$430,000$ per year. The required return on the project is 12 percent, and the relevant tax rate is 35 percent.

    a. Based on your experience, you think the unit sales, variable cost, and fixed cost projections given here are probably accurate to within ±10 percent. What are the upper and lower bounds for these projections? What is the base-case NPV? What are the best-case and worst-case scenarios?

    b. Evaluate the sensitivity of your base-case NPV to changes in fixed costs.

    c. What is the cash break-even level of output for this project (ignoring taxes)?

    d. What is the accounting break-even level of output for this project? What is the degree of operating leverage at the accounting break-even point? How do you interpret this number?

20. **Project Analysis [LO1, 2]** McGilla Golf has decided to sell a new line of golf clubs. The clubs will sell for $\$825$ per set and have a variable cost of $\$395$ per set. The company has spent $\$150,000$ for a marketing study that determined the company will sell 55,000 sets per year for seven years. The marketing study also determined that the company will lose sales of 10,000 sets of its high-priced clubs. The high-priced clubs sell at $\$1,100$ and have variable costs of $\$650$. The company will also increase sales of its cheap clubs by 12,000 sets. The cheap clubs sell for $\$410$ and have variable costs of $\$185$ per set. The fixed costs each year will be $\$9,200,000$. The company has also spent $\$1,000,000$ on research and development for the new clubs. The plant and equipment required will cost $\$29,400,000$ and will be depreciated on a straight-line basis. The new clubs will also require an increase in net working capital of $\$1,400,000$ that will be returned at the end of the project. The tax rate is 40 percent, and the cost of capital is 10 percent. Calculate the payback period, the NPV, and the IRR.

21. **Scenario Analysis [LO2]** In the previous problem, you feel that the values are accurate to within only ±10 percent. What are the best-case and worst-case NPVs? (*Hint:* The price and variable costs for the two existing sets of clubs are known with certainty; only the sales gained or lost are uncertain.)

22. **Sensitivity Analysis [LO1]** McGilla Golf would like to know the sensitivity of NPV to changes in the price of the new clubs and the quantity of new clubs sold. What is the sensitivity of the NPV to each of these variables?

23. **Break-Even Analysis [LO3]** Hybrid cars are touted as a "green" alternative; however, the financial aspects of hybrid ownership are not as clear. Consider the 2010 Lexus RX 450h, which had a list price of $5,565 (including tax consequences) more than the comparable Lexus RX 350. Additionally, the annual ownership costs (other than fuel) for the hybrid were expected to be $300 more than the traditional sedan. The EPA mileage estimate was 29 mpg for the hybrid and 21 mpg for the traditional sedan.

    a. Assume that gasoline costs $3.25 per gallon and you plan to keep either car for six years. How many miles per year would you need to drive to make the decision to buy the hybrid worthwhile, ignoring the time value of money?

    b. If you drive 15,000 miles per year and keep either car for six years, what price per gallon would make the decision to buy the hybrid worthwhile, ignoring the time value of money?

    c. Rework parts (a) and (b) assuming the appropriate interest rate is 10 percent and all cash flows occur at the end of the year.

    d. What assumption did the analysis in the previous parts make about the resale value of each car?

24. **Break-Even Analysis [LO3]** In an effort to capture the large jet market, Airbus invested $13 billion developing its A380, which is capable of carrying 800 passengers. The plane has a list price of $280 million. In discussing the plane, Airbus stated that the company would break even when 249 A380s were sold.

    a. Assuming the break-even sales figure given is the cash flow break-even, what is the cash flow per plane?

    b. Airbus promised its shareholders a 20 percent rate of return on the investment. If sales of the plane continue in perpetuity, how many planes must the company sell per year to deliver on this promise?

    c. Suppose instead that the sales of the A380 last for only 10 years. How many planes must Airbus sell per year to deliver the same rate of return?

CHALLENGE
(Questions 25–30)

25. **Break-Even and Taxes [LO3]** This problem concerns the effect of taxes on the various break-even measures.

    a. Show that, when we consider taxes, the general relationship between operating cash flow, OCF, and sales volume, Q, can be written as:

$$Q = \frac{FC + \dfrac{OCF - T \times D}{1 - T}}{P - v}$$

    b. Use the expression in part (a) to find the cash, accounting, and financial break-even points for the Wettway sailboat example in the chapter. Assume a 38 percent tax rate.

    c. In part (b), the accounting break-even should be the same as before. Why? Verify this algebraically.

26. **Operating Leverage and Taxes [LO4]** Show that if we consider the effect of taxes, the degree of operating leverage can be written as:

$$DOL = 1 + [FC \times (1 - T) - T \times D]/OCF$$

Notice that this reduces to our previous result if $T = 0$. Can you interpret this in words?

Visit us at www.mhhe.com/rwj

27. **Scenario Analysis [LO2]** Consider a project to supply Detroit with 25,000 tons of machine screws annually for automobile production. You will need an initial $3,600,000 investment in threading equipment to get the project started; the project will last for five years. The accounting department estimates that annual fixed costs will be $850,000 and that variable costs should be $185 per ton; accounting will depreciate the initial fixed asset investment straight-line to zero over the five-year project life. It also estimates a salvage value of $500,000 after dismantling costs. The marketing department estimates that the automakers will let the contract at a selling price of $280 per ton. The engineering department estimates you will need an initial net working capital investment of $360,000. You require a 13 percent return and face a marginal tax rate of 38 percent on this project.

    a. What is the estimated OCF for this project? The NPV? Should you pursue this project?

    b. Suppose you believe that the accounting department's initial cost and salvage value projections are accurate only to within ±15 percent; the marketing department's price estimate is accurate only to within ±10 percent; and the engineering department's net working capital estimate is accurate only to within ±5 percent. What is your worst-case scenario for this project? Your best-case scenario? Do you still want to pursue the project?

28. **Sensitivity Analysis [LO1]** In Problem 27, suppose you're confident about your own projections, but you're a little unsure about Detroit's actual machine screw requirement. What is the sensitivity of the project OCF to changes in the quantity supplied? What about the sensitivity of NPV to changes in quantity supplied? Given the sensitivity number you calculated, is there some minimum level of output below which you wouldn't want to operate? Why?

29. **Break-Even Analysis [LO3]** Use the results of Problem 25 to find the accounting, cash, and financial break-even quantities for the company in Problem 27.

30. **Operating Leverage [LO4]** Use the results of Problem 26 to find the degree of operating leverage for the company in Problem 27 at the base-case output level of 25,000 units. How does this number compare to the sensitivity figure you found in Problem 28? Verify that either approach will give you the same OCF figure at any new quantity level.

MINICASE

Conch Republic Electronics, Part 2

Shelley Couts, the owner of Conch Republic Electronics, had received the capital budgeting analysis from Jay McCanless for the new smart phone the company is considering. Shelley was pleased with the results, but she still had concerns about the new smart phone. Conch Republic had used a small market research firm for the past 20 years, but recently the founder of that firm retired. Because of this, she was not convinced the sales projections presented by the market research firm were entirely accurate. Additionally, because of rapid changes in technology, she was concerned that a competitor could enter the market. This would likely force Conch Republic to lower the sales price of its new smart phone. For these reasons, she

has asked Jay to analyze how changes in the price of the new smart phone and changes in the quantity sold will affect the NPV of the project.

Shelley has asked Jay to prepare a memo answering the following questions.

QUESTIONS

1. How sensitive is the NPV to changes in the price of the new smart phone?

2. How sensitive is the NPV to changes in the quantity sold of the new smart phone?

12

SOME LESSONS FROM CAPITAL MARKET HISTORY

WITH THE S&P 500 UP about 15 percent and the NASDAQ index up about 17 percent in 2010, stock market performance overall was above average for the year. However, investors in telecom company IDT Corporation had to be talking about the 429 percent gain in that stock, and investors in Internet security company VirnetX Holdings had to feel pretty secure following that company's 405 percent gain. Of course, not all stocks increased in value during the year. Stock in First Bancorp fell 80 percent during the year, and stock in Allied Irish Banks dropped 75 percent. These examples show that there were tremendous potential profits to be made during 2010, but there was also the risk of losing money—lots of it. So what should you, as a stock market investor, expect when you invest your own money? In this chapter, we study more than eight decades of market history to find out.

LEARNING OBJECTIVES

After studying this chapter, you should understand:

LO1 How to calculate the return on an investment.

LO2 The historical returns on various important types of investments.

LO3 The historical risks on various important types of investments.

LO4 The implications of market efficiency.

Thus far, we haven't had much to say about what determines the required return on an investment. In one sense, the answer is simple: The required return depends on the risk of the investment. The greater the risk, the greater is the required return.

Having said this, we are left with a somewhat more difficult problem. How can we measure the amount of risk present in an investment? Put another way, what does it mean to say that one investment is riskier than another? Obviously, we need to define what we mean by *risk* if we are going to answer these questions. This is our task in the next two chapters.

From the last several chapters, we know that one of the responsibilities of the financial manager is to assess the value of proposed real asset investments. In doing this, it is important that we first look at what financial investments have to offer. At a minimum, the return we require from a proposed nonfinancial investment must be greater than what we can get by buying financial assets of similar risk.

Our goal in this chapter is to provide a perspective on what capital market history can tell us about risk and return. The most important thing to get out of this chapter is a feel for the numbers. What is a high return? What is a low one? More generally, what returns should we expect from financial assets, and what are the risks of such investments? This perspective is essential for understanding how to analyze and value risky investment projects.

We start our discussion of risk and return by describing the historical experience of investors in U.S. financial markets. In 1931, for example, the stock market lost 43 percent of its value. Just two years later, the stock market gained 54 percent. In more recent memory, the market lost about 25 percent of its value on October 19, 1987, alone. What lessons, if any, can financial managers learn from such shifts in the stock market? We will explore almost a century of market history to find out.

Not everyone agrees on the value of studying history. On the one hand, there is philosopher George Santayana's famous comment: "Those who do not remember the past are condemned to repeat it." On the other hand, there is industrialist Henry Ford's equally famous comment: "History is more or less bunk." Nonetheless, perhaps everyone would agree with Mark Twain's observation: "October. This is one of the peculiarly dangerous months to speculate in stocks in. The others are July, January, September, April, November, May, March, June, December, August, and February."

Two central lessons emerge from our study of market history. First, there is a reward for bearing risk. Second, the greater the potential reward is, the greater is the risk. To illustrate these facts about market returns, we devote much of this chapter to reporting the statistics and numbers that make up the modern capital market history of the United States. In the next chapter, these facts provide the foundation for our study of how financial markets put a price on risk.

The number of websites devoted to financial markets and instruments is astounding—and increasing daily. Be sure to check out the RWJ Web page for links to finance-related sites! (www.mhhe.com/rwj)

Returns

We wish to discuss historical returns on different types of financial assets. The first thing we need to do, then, is to briefly discuss how to calculate the return from investing.

DOLLAR RETURNS

If you buy an asset of any sort, your gain (or loss) from that investment is called the *return on your investment*. This return will usually have two components. First, you may receive some cash directly while you own the investment. This is called the *income component* of your return. Second, the value of the asset you purchase will often change. In this case, you have a capital gain or capital loss on your investment.[1]

To illustrate, suppose the Video Concept Company has several thousand shares of stock outstanding. You purchased some of these shares of stock in the company at the beginning of the year. It is now year-end, and you want to determine how well you have done on your investment.

How did the market do today? Find out at finance.yahoo.com.

First, over the year, a company may pay cash dividends to its shareholders. As a stockholder in Video Concept Company, you are a part owner of the company. If the company is profitable, it may choose to distribute some of its profits to shareholders (we discuss the details of dividend policy in a later chapter). So, as the owner of some stock, you will receive some cash. This cash is the income component from owning the stock.

In addition to the dividend, the other part of your return is the capital gain or capital loss on the stock. This part arises from changes in the value of your investment. For example, consider the cash flows illustrated in Figure 12.1. At the beginning of the year, the stock was selling for $37 per share. If you had bought 100 shares, you would have had a total outlay of $3,700. Suppose that, over the year, the stock paid a dividend of $1.85 per share. By the end of the year, then, you would have received income of:

$$\text{Dividend} = \$1.85 \times 100 = \$185$$

Also, the value of the stock has risen to $40.33 per share by the end of the year. Your 100 shares are now worth $4,033, so you have a capital gain of:

$$\text{Capital gain} = (\$40.33 - 37) \times 100 = \$333$$

---

[1]As we mentioned in an earlier chapter, strictly speaking, what is and what is not a capital gain (or loss) is determined by the IRS. We thus use the terms loosely.

FIGURE 12.1

Dollar Returns

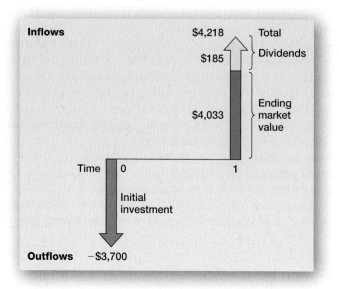

On the other hand, if the price had dropped to, say, $34.78, you would have a capital loss of:

Capital loss = ($34.78 − 37) × 100 = −$222

Notice that a capital loss is the same thing as a negative capital gain.

The total dollar return on your investment is the sum of the dividend and the capital gain:

Total dollar return = Dividend income + Capital gain (or loss)   **[12.1]**

In our first example, the total dollar return is thus given by:

Total dollar return = $185 + 333 = $518

Notice that if you sold the stock at the end of the year, the total amount of cash you would have would equal your initial investment plus the total return. In the preceding example, then:

Total cash if stock is sold = Initial investment + Total return   **[12.2]**

= $3,700 + 518

= $4,218

As a check, notice that this is the same as the proceeds from the sale of the stock plus the dividends:

Proceeds from stock sale + Dividends = $40.33 × 100 + 185

= $4,033 + 185

= $4,218

Suppose you hold on to your Video Concept stock and don't sell it at the end of the year. Should you still consider the capital gain as part of your return? Isn't this only a "paper" gain and not really a cash flow if you don't sell the stock?

The answer to the first question is a strong yes, and the answer to the second is an equally strong no. The capital gain is every bit as much a part of your return as the dividend, and you should certainly count it as part of your return. That you actually decided to keep the stock and not sell (you don't "realize" the gain) is irrelevant because you could have converted it to cash if you had wanted to. Whether you choose to do so or not is up to you.

After all, if you insisted on converting your gain to cash, you could always sell the stock at year-end and immediately reinvest by buying the stock back. There is no net difference between doing this and just not selling (assuming, of course, that there are no tax consequences from selling the stock). Again, the point is that whether you actually cash out and buy sodas (or whatever) or reinvest by not selling doesn't affect the return you earn.

PERCENTAGE RETURNS

It is usually more convenient to summarize information about returns in percentage terms, rather than dollar terms, because that way your return doesn't depend on how much you actually invest. The question we want to answer is this: How much do we get for each dollar we invest?

To answer this question, let P_t be the price of the stock at the beginning of the year and let D_{t+1} be the dividend paid on the stock during the year. Consider the cash flows in Figure 12.2. These are the same as those in Figure 12.1, except that we have now expressed everything on a per-share basis.

Go to www.smartmoney. com/marketmap *for a cool Java applet that shows today's returns by market sector.*

In our example, the price at the beginning of the year was $37 per share and the dividend paid during the year on each share was $1.85. As we discussed in Chapter 8, expressing the dividend as a percentage of the beginning stock price results in the dividend yield:

$$\text{Dividend yield} = D_{t+1}/P_t$$
$$= \$1.85/37 = .05 = 5\%$$

This says that for each dollar we invest, we get five cents in dividends.

The second component of our percentage return is the capital gains yield. Recall (from Chapter 8) that this is calculated as the change in the price during the year (the capital gain) divided by the beginning price:

$$\text{Capital gains yield} = (P_{t+1} - P_t)/P_t$$
$$= (\$40.33 - 37)/37$$
$$= \$3.33/37$$
$$= 9\%$$

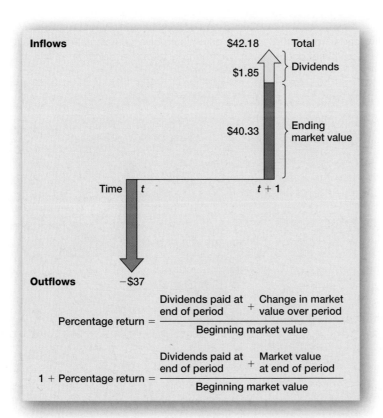

FIGURE 12.2

Percentage Returns

So, per dollar invested, we get nine cents in capital gains.

Putting it together, per dollar invested, we get 5 cents in dividends and 9 cents in capital gains; so we get a total of 14 cents. Our percentage return is 14 cents on the dollar, or 14 percent.

To check this, notice that we invested $3,700 and ended up with $4,218. By what percentage did our $3,700 increase? As we saw, we picked up $4,218 − 3,700 = $518. This is a $518/3,700 = 14% increase.

EXAMPLE 12.1	Calculating Returns

Suppose you bought some stock at the beginning of the year for $25 per share. At the end of the year, the price is $35 per share. During the year, you got a $2 dividend per share. This is the situation illustrated in Figure 12.3. What is the dividend yield? The capital gains yield? The percentage return? If your total investment was $1,000, how much do you have at the end of the year?

Your $2 dividend per share works out to a dividend yield of:

$$\text{Dividend yield} = D_{t+1}/P_t$$
$$= \$2/25 = .08 = 8\%$$

The per-share capital gain is $10, so the capital gains yield is:

$$\text{Capital gains yield} = (P_{t+1} - P_t)/P_t$$
$$= (\$35 - 25)/25$$
$$= \$10/25$$
$$= 40\%$$

The total percentage return is thus 48 percent.

If you had invested $1,000, you would have $1,480 at the end of the year, representing a 48 percent increase. To check this, note that your $1,000 would have bought you $1,000/25 = 40 shares. Your 40 shares would then have paid you a total of 40 × $2 = $80 in cash dividends. Your $10 per share gain would give you a total capital gain of $10 × 40 = $400. Add these together, and you get the $480 increase.

FIGURE 12.3

Cash Flow—An
Investment Example

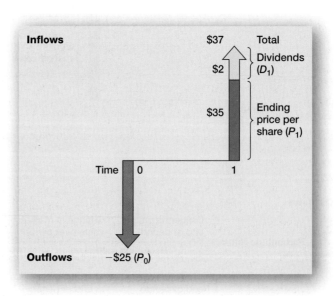

To give another example, stock in Oracle, the well-known enterprise software company, began 2010 at $24.53 per share. Oracle paid dividends of $.20 during 2010, and the stock price at the end of the year was $31.30. What was the return on Oracle for the year? For practice, see if you agree that the answer is 28.41 percent. Of course, negative returns occur as well. For example, again in 2010, petroleum giant BP's stock price at the beginning of the year was $57.97 per share, and dividends of $1.68 were paid. The stock ended the year at $44.17 per share. Verify that the loss was 20.91 percent for the year.

Concept Questions

12.1a What are the two parts of total return?

12.1b Why are unrealized capital gains or losses included in the calculation of returns?

12.1c What is the difference between a dollar return and a percentage return? Why are percentage returns more convenient?

The Historical Record   12.2

Roger Ibbotson and Rex Sinquefield conducted a famous set of studies dealing with rates of return in U.S. financial markets.[2] They presented year-to-year historical rates of return on five important types of financial investments. The returns can be interpreted as what you would have earned if you had held portfolios of the following:

1. *Large-company stocks:* This common stock portfolio is based on the Standard & Poor's (S&P) 500 index, which contains 500 of the largest companies (in terms of total market value of outstanding stock) in the United States.
2. *Small-company stocks:* This is a portfolio composed of the stock corresponding to the smallest 20 percent of the companies listed on the New York Stock Exchange, again as measured by market value of outstanding stock.
3. *Long-term corporate bonds:* This is based on high-quality bonds with 20 years to maturity.
4. *Long-term U.S. government bonds:* This is based on U.S. government bonds with 20 years to maturity.
5. *U.S. Treasury bills:* This is based on Treasury bills (T-bills for short) with a one-month maturity.

For more about market history, visit www.globalfinancialdata.com.

These returns are not adjusted for inflation or taxes; thus, they are nominal, pretax returns.

In addition to the year-to-year returns on these financial instruments, the year-to-year percentage change in the consumer price index (CPI) is also computed. This is a commonly used measure of inflation, so we can calculate real returns using this as the inflation rate.

A FIRST LOOK

Before looking closely at the different portfolio returns, we take a look at the big picture. Figure 12.4 shows what happened to $1 invested in these different portfolios at the end of 1925. The growth in value for each of the different portfolios over the 85-year period ending in 2010 is given separately (the long-term corporate bonds are omitted). Notice that to get everything on a single graph, some modification in scaling is used. As is commonly

---

[2]R.G. Ibbotson and R.A. Sinquefield, *Stocks, Bonds, Bills, and Inflation* [SBBI] (Charlottesville, VA: Financial Analysis Research Foundation, 1982).

FIGURE 12.4   A $1 Investment in Different Types of Portfolios: 1925–2010 (Year-End 1925 = $1)

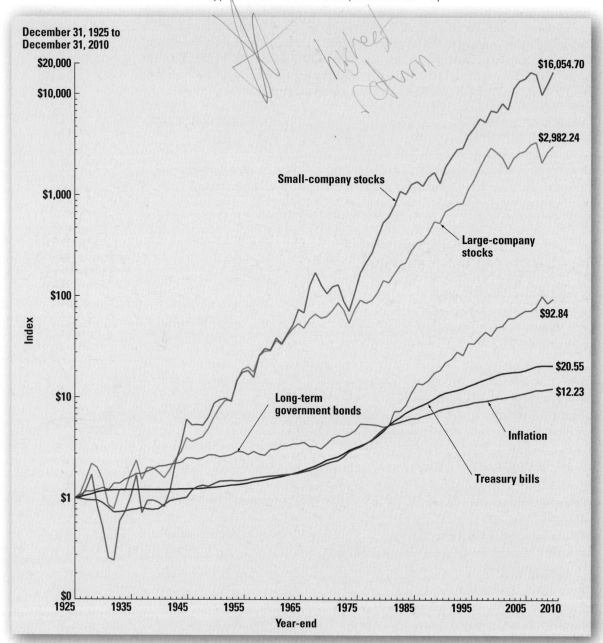

Redrawn from *Stocks, Bonds, Bills, and Inflation: 2011 Yearbook*™, annually updates work by Roger G. Ibbotson and Rex A. Sinquefield (Chicago: Morningstar). All rights reserved.

Go to
bigcharts.marketwatch.com
*to see both intraday and
long-term charts.*

done with financial series, the vertical axis is scaled so that equal distances measure equal percentage (as opposed to dollar) changes in values.[3]

Looking at Figure 12.4, we see that the "small-cap" (short for small-capitalization) investment did the best overall. Every dollar invested grew to a remarkable $16,054.70 over the 85 years. The large-company common stock portfolio did less well; a dollar invested in it grew to $2,982.24.

[3]In other words, the scale is logarithmic.

At the other end, the T-bill portfolio grew to only $20.55. This is even less impressive when we consider the inflation over the period in question. As illustrated, the increase in the price level was such that $12.23 was needed at the end of the period just to replace the original $1.

Given the historical record, why would anybody buy anything other than small-cap stocks? If you look closely at Figure 12.4, you will probably see the answer. The T-bill portfolio and the long-term government bond portfolios grew more slowly than did the stock portfolios, but they also grew much more steadily. The small stocks ended up on top; but as you can see, they grew quite erratically at times. For example, the small stocks were the worst performers for about the first 10 years and had a smaller return than long-term government bonds for over 15 years.

A CLOSER LOOK

To illustrate the variability of the different investments, Figures 12.5 through 12.8 plot the year-to-year percentage returns in the form of vertical bars drawn from the horizontal axis. The

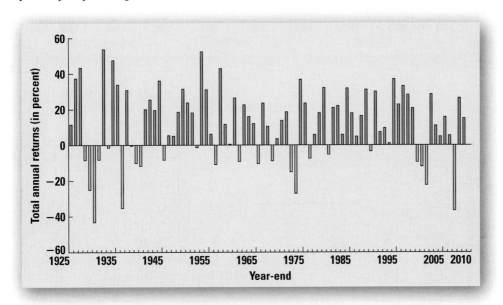

FIGURE 12.5

Year-by-Year Total Returns on Large-Company Common Stocks

Redrawn from *Stocks, Bonds, Bills, and Inflation: 2011 Yearbook™*, annually updates work by Roger G. Ibbotson and Rex A. Sinquefield (Chicago: Morningstar). All rights reserved.

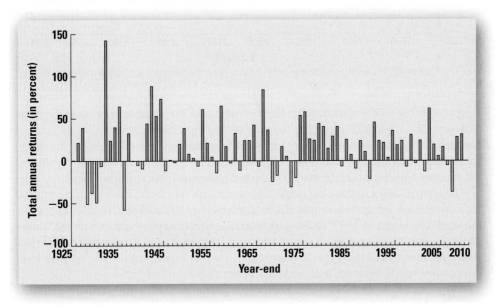

FIGURE 12.6

Year-by-Year Total Returns on Small-Company Stocks

Redrawn from *Stocks, Bonds, Bills, and Inflation: 2011 Yearbook™*, annually updates work by Roger G. Ibbotson and Rex A. Sinquefield (Chicago: Morningstar). All rights reserved.

382   **PART 5**   Risk and Return

FIGURE 12.7

Year-by-Year Total Returns on Bonds and Bills

Redrawn from *Stocks, Bonds, Bills, and Inflation: 2011 Yearbook™*, annually updates work by Roger G. Ibbotson and Rex A. Sinquefield (Chicago: Morningstar). All rights reserved.

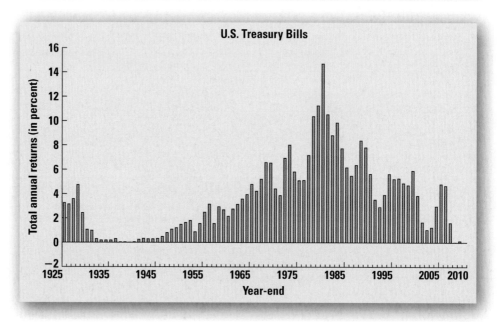

height of the bar tells us the return for the particular year. For example, looking at the long-term government bonds (Figure 12.7), we see that the largest historical return (44.44 percent) occurred in 1982. This was a good year for bonds. In comparing these charts, notice the differences in the vertical axis scales. With these differences in mind, you can see how predictably the Treasury bills (Figure 12.7) behaved compared to the small stocks (Figure 12.6).

The returns shown in these bar graphs are sometimes very large. Looking at the graphs, for example, we see that the largest single-year return is a remarkable 142.87 percent for the small-cap stocks in 1933. In the same year, the large-company stocks returned "only" 52.94 percent. In contrast, the largest Treasury bill return was 15.21 percent in 1981. For future reference, the actual year-to-year returns for the large-company stocks, long-term government bonds, Treasury bills, and the CPI are shown in Table 12.1.

Roger Ibbotson on Capital Market History

The financial markets are the most carefully documented human phenomena in history. Every day, almost 2,000 NYSE stocks are traded, and at least 8,000 more stocks are traded on other U.S. exchanges and electronic crossing networks. Bonds, commodities, futures, and options also provide a wealth of data. These data are available across a wide spectrum of electronic media, including newswires, websites, and market data platforms like Bloomberg. A record actually exists of almost every transaction, providing not only a real-time database but also a historical record extending back, in many cases, more than a century.

The global market adds another dimension to this wealth of data. Over 2,000 stocks trade on Japanese stock markets while the London Exchange reports on over 3,000 domestic and foreign issues a day. Altogether, more than 10 billion shares trade globally on a typical day.

The data generated by these transactions are quantifiable, quickly analyzed and disseminated, and made easily accessible by computer. Because of this, finance has increasingly come to resemble one of the exact sciences. The use of financial market data ranges from the simple, such as using the S&P 500 to compare the performance of a portfolio, to the incredibly complex. For example, only a few decades ago, the bond market was the most staid province on Wall Street. Today, it attracts swarms of traders seeking to exploit arbitrage opportunities—small temporary mispricings—using real-time data and computers to analyze them.

Financial market data are the foundation for the extensive empirical understanding we now have of the financial markets. The following is a list of some of the principal findings of such research:

- Risky securities, such as stocks, have higher average returns than riskless securities such as Treasury bills.
- Stocks of small companies have higher average returns than those of larger companies.
- More liquid stocks have higher valuations, but lower returns than less liquid stocks.
- The cost of capital for a company, project, or division can be estimated using data from the markets.

Because phenomena in the financial markets are so well measured, finance is the most readily quantifiable branch of economics. Researchers are able to do more extensive empirical research than in any other economic field, and the research can be quickly translated into action in the marketplace.

Roger Ibbotson is Professor in the Practice of Management at the Yale School of Management. He is also chairman of Zebra Capital, an equity investment manager. He is the founder of Ibbotson Associates, now a Morningstar, Inc., company and a major supplier of financial data and analysis. An outstanding scholar, he is best known for his original estimates of the historical rates of return realized by investors in different markets.

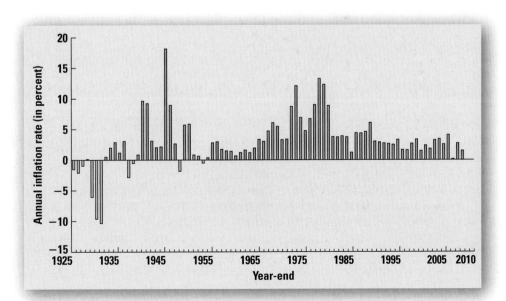

FIGURE 12.8

Year-by-Year Inflation

Redrawn from *Stocks, Bonds, Bills, and Inflation: 2011 Yearbook™*, annually updates work by Roger G. Ibbotson and Rex A. Sinquefield (Chicago: Morningstar). All rights reserved.

TABLE 12.1   Year-to-Year Total Returns: 1926–2010

Year	Large-Company Stocks	Long-Term Government Bonds	U.S. Treasury Bills	Consumer Price Index	Year	Large-Company Stocks	Long-Term Government Bonds	U.S. Treasury Bills	Consumer Price Index
1926	13.75%	5.69%	3.30%	−1.12%	1969	−8.43	−5.63	6.90	6.20
1927	35.70	6.58	3.15	−2.26	1970	3.94	18.92	6.50	5.57
1928	45.08	1.15	4.05	−1.16	1971	14.30	11.24	4.36	3.27
1929	−8.80	4.39	4.47	.58	1972	18.99	2.39	4.23	3.41
1930	−25.13	4.47	2.27	−6.40	1973	−14.69	3.30	7.29	8.71
1931	−43.60	−2.15	1.15	−9.32	1974	−26.47	4.00	7.99	12.34
1932	−8.75	8.51	.88	−10.27	1975	37.23	5.52	5.87	6.94
1933	52.95	1.92	.52	.76	1976	23.93	15.56	5.07	4.86
1934	−2.31	7.59	.27	1.52	1977	−7.16	.38	5.45	6.70
1935	46.79	4.20	.17	2.99	1978	6.57	−1.26	7.64	9.02
1936	32.49	5.13	.17	1.45	1979	18.61	1.26	10.56	13.29
1937	−35.45	1.44	.27	2.86	1980	32.50	−2.48	12.10	12.52
1938	31.63	4.21	.06	−2.78	1981	−4.92	4.04	14.60	8.92
1939	−1.43	3.84	.04	.00	1982	21.55	44.28	10.94	3.83
1940	−10.36	5.70	.04	.71	1983	22.56	1.29	8.99	3.79
1941	−12.02	.47	.14	9.93	1984	6.27	15.29	9.90	3.95
1942	20.75	1.80	.34	9.03	1985	31.73	32.27	7.71	3.80
1943	25.38	2.01	.38	2.96	1986	18.67	22.39	6.09	1.10
1944	19.49	2.27	.38	2.30	1987	5.25	−3.03	5.88	4.43
1945	36.21	5.29	.38	2.25	1988	16.61	6.84	6.94	4.42
1946	−8.42	.54	.38	18.13	1989	31.69	18.54	8.44	4.65
1947	5.05	−1.02	.62	8.84	1990	−3.10	7.74	7.69	6.11
1948	4.99	2.66	1.06	2.99	1991	30.46	19.36	5.43	3.06
1949	17.81	4.58	1.12	−2.07	1992	7.62	7.34	3.48	2.90
1950	30.05	−.98	1.22	5.93	1993	10.08	13.06	3.03	2.75
1951	23.79	−.20	1.56	6.00	1994	1.32	−7.32	4.39	2.67
1952	18.39	2.43	1.75	.75	1995	37.58	25.94	5.61	2.54
1953	−1.07	2.28	1.87	.75	1996	22.96	.13	5.14	3.32
1954	52.23	3.08	.93	−.74	1997	33.36	12.02	5.19	1.70
1955	31.62	−.73	1.80	.37	1998	28.58	14.45	4.86	1.61
1956	6.91	−1.72	2.66	2.99	1999	21.04	−7.51	4.80	2.68
1957	−10.50	6.82	3.28	2.90	2000	−9.10	17.22	5.98	3.39
1958	43.57	−1.72	1.71	1.76	2001	−11.89	5.51	3.33	1.55
1959	12.01	−2.02	3.48	1.73	2002	−22.10	15.15	1.61	2.38
1960	.47	11.21	2.81	1.36	2003	28.89	2.01	.94	1.88
1961	26.84	2.20	2.40	.67	2004	10.88	8.12	1.14	3.26
1962	−8.75	5.72	2.82	1.33	2005	4.91	6.89	2.79	3.42
1963	22.70	1.79	3.23	1.64	2006	15.79	.28	4.97	2.54
1964	16.43	3.71	3.62	.97	2007	5.49	10.85	4.52	4.08
1965	12.38	.93	4.06	1.92	2008	−37.00	41.78	1.24	.09
1966	−10.06	5.12	4.94	3.46	2009	26.46	−25.61	.15	2.72
1967	23.98	−2.86	4.39	3.04	2010	15.06	7.73	.14	1.50
1968	11.03	2.25	5.49	4.72					

Sources: Authors' calculation based on data obtained from *Global Financial Data* and other sources.

Concept Questions

12.2a With 20/20 hindsight, what do you say was the best investment for the period from 1926 through 1935?

12.2b Why doesn't everyone just buy small stocks as investments?

12.2c What was the smallest return observed over the 80 years for each of these investments? Approximately when did it occur?

12.2d About how many times did large-company stocks return more than 30 percent? How many times did they return less than −20 percent?

12.2e What was the longest "winning streak" (years without a negative return) for large-company stocks? For long-term government bonds?

12.2f How often did the T-bill portfolio have a negative return?

Average Returns: The First Lesson

12.3

As you've probably begun to notice, the history of capital market returns is too complicated to be of much use in its undigested form. We need to begin summarizing all these numbers. Accordingly, we discuss how to go about condensing the detailed data. We start out by calculating average returns.

CALCULATING AVERAGE RETURNS

The obvious way to calculate the average returns on the different investments in Table 12.1 is simply to add up the yearly returns and divide by 85. The result is the historical average of the individual values.

For example, if you add up the returns for the large-company stocks in Figure 12.5 for the 85 years, you will get about 10.12. The average annual return is thus 10.12/85 = 11.9%. You interpret this 11.9 percent just like any other average. If you were to pick a year at random from the 85-year history and you had to guess what the return in that year was, the best guess would be 11.9 percent.

AVERAGE RETURNS: THE HISTORICAL RECORD

Table 12.2 shows the average returns for the investments we have discussed. As shown, in a typical year, the small-company stocks increased in value by 16.7 percent. Notice also how much larger the stock returns are than the bond returns.

These averages are, of course, nominal because we haven't worried about inflation. Notice that the average inflation rate was 3.1 percent per year over this 85-year span. The nominal return on U.S. Treasury bills was 3.7 percent per year. The average real return on Treasury bills was thus approximately .6 percent per year; so the real return on T-bills has been quite low historically.

At the other extreme, small stocks had an average real return of about 16.7% − 3.1% = 13.6%, which is relatively large. If you remember the Rule of 72 (Chapter 5), then you know that a quick back-of-the-envelope calculation tells us that 13.6 percent real growth doubles your buying power about every five years. Notice also that the real value of the large-company stock portfolio increased by about 9 percent in a typical year.

TABLE 12.2

Average Annual Returns:
1926–2010

SOURCE: © *Stocks, Bonds,
Bills, and Inflation: 2011
Yearbook™*, annually updates
work by Roger G. Ibbotson
and Rex A. Sinquefield
(Chicago: Morningstar). All
rights reserved.

Investment	Average Return
Large-company stocks	11.9%
Small-company stocks	16.7
Long-term corporate bonds	6.2
Long-term government bonds	5.9
U.S. Treasury bills	3.7
Inflation	3.1

TABLE 12.3

Average Annual Returns
and Risk Premiums:
1926–2010

SOURCE: © *Stocks, Bonds,
Bills, and Inflation: 2011
Yearbook™*, annually updates
work by Roger G. Ibbotson
and Rex A. Sinquefield
(Chicago: Morningstar). All
rights reserved.

Investment	Average Return	Risk Premium
Large-company stocks	11.9%	8.2%
Small-company stocks	16.7	13.0
Long-term corporate bonds	6.2	2.5
Long-term government bonds	5.9	2.2
U.S. Treasury bills	3.7	.0

risk premium

The excess return required
from an investment in
a risky asset over that
required from a risk-free
investment.

RISK PREMIUMS

Now that we have computed some average returns, it seems logical to see how they compare with each other. One such comparison involves government-issued securities. These are free of much of the variability we see in, for example, the stock market.

The government borrows money by issuing bonds in different forms. The ones we will focus on are the Treasury bills. These have the shortest time to maturity of the different government bonds. Because the government can always raise taxes to pay its bills, the debt represented by T-bills is virtually free of any default risk over its short life. Thus, we will call the rate of return on such debt the *risk-free return,* and we will use it as a kind of benchmark.

A particularly interesting comparison involves the virtually risk-free return on T-bills and the very risky return on common stocks. The difference between these two returns can be interpreted as a measure of the *excess return* on the average risky asset (assuming that the stock of a large U.S. corporation has about average risk compared to all risky assets).

We call this the "excess" return because it is the additional return we earn by moving from a relatively risk-free investment to a risky one. Because it can be interpreted as a reward for bearing risk, we will call it a **risk premium**.

Using Table 12.2, we can calculate the risk premiums for the different investments; these are shown in Table 12.3. We report only the nominal risk premiums because there is only a slight difference between the historical nominal and real risk premiums.

The risk premium on T-bills is shown as zero in the table because we have assumed that they are riskless.

THE FIRST LESSON

Looking at Table 12.3, we see that the average risk premium earned by a typical large-company stock is 11.9% − 3.7% = 8.2%. This is a significant reward. The fact that it exists historically is an important observation, and it is the basis for our first lesson: Risky assets, on average, earn a risk premium. Put another way, there is a reward for bearing risk.

Why is this so? Why, for example, is the risk premium for small stocks so much larger than the risk premium for large stocks? More generally, what determines the relative sizes of the risk premiums for the different assets? The answers to these questions are at the heart of modern finance, and the next chapter is devoted to them. For now, we can find part of the answer by looking at the historical variability of the returns on these different investments. So, to get started, we now turn our attention to measuring variability in returns.

Concept Questions

12.3a What do we mean by *excess return* and *risk premium*?
12.3b What was the real (as opposed to nominal) risk premium on the common stock portfolio?
12.3c What was the nominal risk premium on corporate bonds? The real risk premium?
12.3d What is the first lesson from capital market history?

The Variability of Returns: The Second Lesson   12.4 𝕩

We have already seen that the year-to-year returns on common stocks tend to be more volatile than the returns on, say, long-term government bonds. We now discuss measuring this variability of stock returns so we can begin examining the subject of risk.

FREQUENCY DISTRIBUTIONS AND VARIABILITY

To get started, we can draw a *frequency distribution* for the common stock returns like the one in Figure 12.9. What we have done here is to count up the number of times the annual return on the common stock portfolio falls within each 10 percent range. For example, in Figure 12.9, the height of 14 in the range of 10 to 20 percent means that 14 of the 85 annual returns were in that range.

FIGURE 12.9   Frequency Distribution of Returns on Large-Company Stocks: 1926–2010

Source: © *Stocks, Bonds, Bills, and Inflation: 2011 Yearbook™*, annually updates work by Roger G. Ibbotson and Rex A. Sinquefield (Chicago: Morningstar). All rights reserved.

What we need to do now is to actually measure the spread in returns. We know, for example, that the return on small stocks in a typical year was 16.7 percent. We now want to know how much the actual return deviates from this average in a typical year. In other words, we need a measure of how volatile the return is. The **variance** and its square root, the **standard deviation**, are the most commonly used measures of volatility. We describe how to calculate them next.

variance
The average squared difference between the actual return and the average return.

standard deviation
The positive square root of the variance.

Just concept

For an easy-to-read review of basic stats, check out www.robertniles.com.

THE HISTORICAL VARIANCE AND STANDARD DEVIATION

The variance essentially measures the average squared difference between the actual returns and the average return. The bigger this number is, the more the actual returns tend to differ from the average return. Also, the larger the variance or standard deviation is, the more spread out the returns will be.

The way we will calculate the variance and standard deviation will depend on the specific situation. In this chapter, we are looking at historical returns; so the procedure we describe here is the correct one for calculating the *historical* variance and standard deviation. If we were examining projected future returns, then the procedure would be different. We describe this procedure in the next chapter.

To illustrate how we calculate the historical variance, suppose a particular investment had returns of 10 percent, 12 percent, 3 percent, and −9 percent over the last four years. The average return is $(.10 + .12 + .03 − .09)/4 = 4\%$. Notice that the return is never actually equal to 4 percent. Instead, the first return deviates from the average by $.10 − .04 = .06$, the second return deviates from the average by $.12 − .04 = .08$, and so on. To compute the variance, we square each of these deviations, add them up, and divide the result by the number of returns less 1, or 3 in this case. Most of this information is summarized in the following table:

	(1) Actual Return	(2) Average Return	(3) Deviation (1) − (2)	(4) Squared Deviation
	.10	.04	.06	.0036
	.12	.04	.08	.0064
	.03	.04	−.01	.0001
	−.09	.04	−.13	.0169
Totals	.16		.00	.0270

In the first column, we write the four actual returns. In the third column, we calculate the difference between the actual returns and the average by subtracting out 4 percent. Finally, in the fourth column, we square the numbers in the third column to get the squared deviations from the average.

The variance can now be calculated by dividing .0270, the sum of the squared deviations, by the number of returns less 1. Let Var(R), or σ^2 (read this as "sigma squared"), stand for the variance of the return:

$$\text{Var}(R) = \sigma^2 = .027/(4 − 1) = .009$$

The standard deviation is the square root of the variance. So, if SD(R), or σ, stands for the standard deviation of return:

$$\text{SD}(R) = \sigma = \sqrt{.009} = .09487$$

The square root of the variance is used because the variance is measured in "squared" percentages and thus is hard to interpret. The standard deviation is an ordinary percentage, so the answer here could be written as 9.487 percent.

In the preceding table, notice that the sum of the deviations is equal to zero. This will always be the case, and it provides a good way to check your work. In general, if we have T historical returns, where T is some number, we can write the historical variance as:

$$\text{Var}(R) = \frac{1}{T-1}[(R_1 - \bar{R})^2 + \cdots + (R_T - \bar{R})^2] \qquad \text{[12.3]}$$

This formula tells us to do what we just did: Take each of the T individual returns $(R_1, R_2, \ldots)$ and subtract the average return, $\bar{R}$; square the results, and add them all up; and finally, divide this total by the number of returns less 1, $(T - 1)$. The standard deviation is always the square root of $\text{Var}(R)$. Standard deviations are a widely used measure of volatility. Our nearby *Work the Web* box gives a real-world example.

Calculating the Variance and Standard Deviation   EXAMPLE 12.2

Suppose the Supertech Company and the Hyperdrive Company have experienced the following returns in the last four years:

Year	Supertech Return	Hyperdrive Return
2008	−.20	.05
2009	.50	.09
2010	.30	−.12
2011	.10	.20

What are the average returns? The variances? The standard deviations? Which investment was more volatile?

To calculate the average returns, we add up the returns and divide by 4. The results are:

Supertech average return = $\bar{R}$ = .70/4 = .175
Hyperdrive average return = $\bar{R}$ = .22/4 = .055

To calculate the variance for Supertech, we can summarize the relevant calculations as follows:

Year	(1) Actual Return	(2) Average Return	(3) Deviation (1) − (2)	(4) Squared Deviation
2008	−.20	.175	−.375	.140625
2009	.50	.175	.325	.105625
2010	.30	.175	.125	.015625
2011	.10	.175	−.075	.005625
Totals	.70		.000	.267500

Because there are four years of returns, we calculate the variance by dividing .2675 by $(4 - 1) = 3$:

	Supertech	Hyperdrive
Variance (σ^2)	.2675/3 = .0892	.0529/3 = .0176
Standard deviation (σ)	$\sqrt{.0892}$ = .2987	$\sqrt{.0176}$ = .1327

For practice, verify that you get the same answer as we do for Hyperdrive. Notice that the standard deviation for Supertech, 29.87 percent, is a little more than twice Hyperdrive's 13.27 percent; Supertech is thus the more volatile investment.

THE HISTORICAL RECORD

Figure 12.10 summarizes much of our discussion of capital market history so far. It displays average returns, standard deviations, and frequency distributions of annual returns on a common scale. In Figure 12.10, for example, notice that the standard deviation for the small-stock portfolio (32.6 percent per year) is more than 10 times larger than the T-bill portfolio's standard deviation (3.1 percent per year). We will return to these figures momentarily.

WORK THE WEB

Standard deviations are widely reported for mutual funds. For example, the Fidelity Magellan Fund was one of the better-known mutual funds in the United States at the time this was written. How volatile is it? To find out, we went to www.morningstar.com, entered the ticker symbol FMAGX, and clicked the "Risk Measures" link. Here is what we found:

MPT Statistics FMAGX

3-Year	5-Year	10-Year	15-Year

3-Year Trailing	Index	R-Squared	Beta	Alpha	Currency
vs. Best-Fit Index					
FMAGX	Russell Mid Cap Growth TR USD	97.38	1.04	-8.04	USD
vs. Standard Index					
FMAGX	S&P 500 TR	91.52	1.21	-2.64	USD
Category: LG	S&P 500 TR	95.30	1.01	0.37	USD

12/31/2010

Volatility Measures FMAGX

3-Year	5-Year	10-Year	15-Year

3-Year Trailing	Standard Deviation	Mean	Sharpe Ratio	Bear Market Percentile Rank
FMAGX	28.12	-0.28	-0.14	90.00
S&P 500 TR	22.16	-0.04	-0.05	--
Category: LG	22.85	-0.01	-0.03	--

The standard deviation for the Fidelity Magellan Fund is 28.12 percent. When you consider that the average stock has a standard deviation of about 50 percent, this seems like a low number. The reason for the low standard deviation has to do with the power of diversification, a topic we discuss in the next chapter. The mean is the average return, so over the last three years, investors in the Magellan Fund lost .28 percent per year. Also, under the Volatility Measures section, you will see the Sharpe ratio. The Sharpe ratio is calculated as the risk premium of the asset divided by the standard deviation. As such, it is a measure of return relative to the level of risk taken (as measured by standard deviation). The "beta" for the Fidelity Magellan Fund is 1.21. We will have more to say about this number—lots more—in the next chapter.

Questions

1. Go to the Morningstar website at www.morningstar.com. What does the Sharpe ratio measure? What does the Bear Market Percentile Rank measure?
2. Get a quote for the Fidelity Magellan Fund at Morningstar. What are the five sectors that have the highest percentage investment for this fund? What are the five stocks with the highest percentage investment?

FIGURE 12.10   Historical Returns, Standard Deviations, and Frequency Distributions: 1926–2010

Series	Average Return	Standard Deviation	Frequency Distribution
Large-company stocks	11.9%	20.4%	
Small-company stocks	16.7	32.6	*
Long-term corporate bonds	6.2	8.3	
Long-term government bonds	5.9	9.5	
Intermediate-term government bonds	5.5	5.7	
U.S. Treasury bills	3.7	3.1	
Inflation	3.1	4.2	

*The 1933 small-company stocks total return was 142.9 percent.

Source: Modified from *Stocks, Bonds, Bills, and Inflation: 2011 Yearbook™*, annually updates work by Roger G. Ibbotson and Rex A. Sinquefield (Chicago: Morningstar). All rights reserved.

NORMAL DISTRIBUTION

For many different random events in nature, a particular frequency distribution, the **normal distribution** (or *bell curve*), is useful for describing the probability of ending up in a given range. For example, the idea behind "grading on a curve" comes from the fact that exam score distributions often resemble a bell curve.

Figure 12.11 illustrates a normal distribution and its distinctive bell shape. As you can see, this distribution has a much cleaner appearance than the actual return distributions illustrated in Figure 12.10. Even so, like the normal distribution, the actual distributions do appear to be at least roughly mound-shaped and symmetric. When this is true, the normal distribution is often a very good approximation.

normal distribution
A symmetric, bell-shaped frequency distribution that is completely defined by its mean and standard deviation.

FIGURE 12.11

The Normal Distribution

NOTE: Illustrated returns are based on the historical return and standard deviation for a portfolio of large-firm common stocks.

Also, keep in mind that the distributions in Figure 12.10 are based on only 85 yearly observations, whereas Figure 12.11 is, in principle, based on an infinite number. So, if we had been able to observe returns for, say, 1,000 years, we might have filled in a lot of the irregularities and ended up with a much smoother picture in Figure 12.10. For our purposes, it is enough to observe that the returns are at least roughly normally distributed.

The usefulness of the normal distribution stems from the fact that it is completely described by the average and the standard deviation. If you have these two numbers, then there is nothing else to know. For example, with a normal distribution, the probability that we will end up within one standard deviation of the average is about 2/3. The probability that we will end up within two standard deviations is about 95 percent. Finally, the probability of being more than three standard deviations away from the average is less than 1 percent. These ranges and the probabilities are illustrated in Figure 12.11.

To see why this is useful, recall from Figure 12.10 that the standard deviation of returns on the large-company stocks is 20.4 percent. The average return is 11.9 percent. So, assuming that the frequency distribution is at least approximately normal, the probability that the return in a given year is in the range of −8.5 to 32.3 percent (11.9 percent plus or minus one standard deviation, 20.4 percent) is about 2/3. This range is illustrated in Figure 12.11. In other words, there is about one chance in three that the return will be *outside* this range. This literally tells you that, if you buy stocks in large companies, you should expect to be outside this range in one year out of every three. This reinforces our earlier observations about stock market volatility. However, there is only a 5 percent chance (approximately) that we would end up outside the range of −28.9 to 52.7 percent (11.9% plus or minus 2 × 20.4%). These points are also illustrated in Figure 12.11.

THE SECOND LESSON

Our observations concerning the year-to-year variability in returns are the basis for our second lesson from capital market history. On average, bearing risk is handsomely rewarded; but in a given year, there is a significant chance of a dramatic change in value. Thus our second lesson is this: The greater the potential reward, the greater is the risk.

2008: THE BEAR GROWLED AND INVESTORS HOWLED

To reinforce our point concerning stock market volatility, consider that just a few short years ago, 2008 entered the record books as one of the worst years for stock market investors in

FIGURE 12.12

S&P 500 Monthly
Returns: 2008

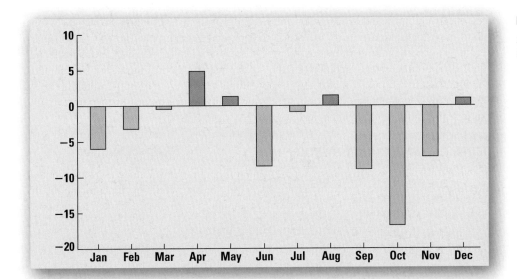

U.S. history. How bad was it? As shown in several exhibits in the chapter (e.g., Table 12.1), the widely followed S&P 500 index plunged 37 percent. Of the 500 stocks in the index, 485 were down for the year.

Over the period 1926–2010, only the year 1931 had a lower return than 2008 (−44 percent versus −37 percent). Making matters worse, the downdraft continued with a further decline of 8.43 percent in January 2009. In all, from November 2007 (when the decline began) through March 2009 (when it ended), the S&P 500 lost 50 percent of its value.

Figure 12.12 shows the month-by-month performance of the S&P 500 during 2008. As indicated, returns were negative in 8 of the 12 months. Most of the damage occurred in the fall, with investors losing almost 17 percent in October alone. Small stocks fared no better. They also fell 37 percent for the year (with a 21 percent drop in October), their worst performance since losing 58 percent in 1937.

As Figure 12.12 suggests, stock prices were highly volatile during the year. Oddly, the S&P had 126 up days and 126 down days (remember the markets are closed weekends and holidays). Of course, the down days were much worse on average. To see how extraordinary volatility was in 2008, consider that there were 18 days during which the value of the S&P changed by more than five percent. There were only 17 such moves between 1956 and 2007!

The drop in stock prices was a global phenomenon, and many of the world's major markets were off by much more than the S&P. China, India, and Russia, for example, all experienced declines of more than 50 percent. Tiny Iceland saw share prices drop by more than 90 percent for the year. Trading on the Icelandic exchange was temporarily suspended on October 9. In what has to be a modern record for a single day, stocks fell by 76 percent when trading resumed on October 14.

Were there any bright spots in 2008 for U.S. investors? The answer is yes because, as stocks tanked, bonds soared, particularly U.S. Treasury bonds. In fact, long-term Treasuries gained 40 percent, while shorter-term Treasury bonds were up 13 percent. Long-term corporate bonds did less well, but still managed to finish in positive territory, up 9 percent. These returns were especially impressive considering that the rate of inflation, as measured by the CPI, was essentially zero.

Of course, stock prices can be volatile in both directions. From March 2009 through February 2011, a period of about 700 days, the S&P 500 doubled in value. This climb was the fastest doubling since 1936 when the S&P did it in just 500 days. So, what lessons should investors take away from this very recent, and very turbulent, bit of capital market history? First, and most obviously, stocks have significant risk! But there is a second, equally important lesson. Depending on the mix, a diversified portfolio of stocks and bonds might have suffered in 2008, but the losses would have been much smaller than those experienced by an all-stock portfolio. In other words, diversification matters, a point we will examine in detail in our next chapter.

USING CAPITAL MARKET HISTORY

Based on the discussion in this section, you should begin to have an idea of the risks and rewards from investing. For example, in early 2011, Treasury bills were paying about .13 percent. Suppose we had an investment that we thought had about the same risk as a portfolio of large-firm common stocks. At a minimum, what return would this investment have to offer for us to be interested?

From Table 12.3, we see that the risk premium on large-company stocks has been 8.2 percent historically, so a reasonable estimate of our required return would be this premium plus the T-bill rate, .13% + 8.2% = 8.3%. This may strike you as being high; but if we were thinking of starting a new business, then the risks of doing so might resemble those of investing in small-company stocks. In this case, the historical risk premium is 13 percent, so we might require as much as 13.1 percent from such an investment at a minimum.

We will discuss the relationship between risk and required return in more detail in the next chapter. For now, you should notice that a projected internal rate of return, or IRR, on a risky investment in the 10 to 20 percent range isn't particularly outstanding. It depends on how much risk there is. This, too, is an important lesson from capital market history.

EXAMPLE 12.3	Investing in Growth Stocks

The term *growth stock* is frequently used as a euphemism for small-company stock. Are such investments suitable for "widows and orphans"? Before answering, you should consider the historical volatility. For example, from the historical record, what is the approximate probability that you will actually lose more than 16 percent of your money in a single year if you buy a portfolio of stocks of such companies?

Looking back at Figure 12.10, we see that the average return on small-company stocks is 16.7 percent and the standard deviation is 32.6 percent. Assuming the returns are approximately normal, there is about a 1/3 probability that you will experience a return outside the range of −15.9 to 49.3 percent (16.7% ± 32.6%).

Because the normal distribution is symmetric, the odds of being above or below this range are equal. There is thus a 1/6 chance (half of 1/3) that you will lose more than −15.9 percent. So you should expect this to happen once in every six years, on average. Such investments can thus be *very* volatile, and they are not well suited for those who cannot afford the risk.

MORE ON THE STOCK MARKET RISK PREMIUM

As we have discussed, the historical stock market risk premium has been substantial. In fact, based on standard economic models, it has been argued that the historical risk premium is *too* big and is thus an overestimate of what is likely to happen in the future.

Of course, any time we use the past to predict the future, there is the danger that the past period we observe isn't representative of what the future will hold. For example, in this chapter, we studied the period 1925–2010. Perhaps investors got lucky over this period and earned particularly high returns. Data from earlier years is available, though it is not of the same quality. With that caveat in mind, researchers have traced returns back to 1802, and the risk premiums seen in the pre-1925 era are perhaps a little smaller, but not dramatically so.

Another possibility is that the U.S. stock market experience was unusually good. Investors in at least some other major countries did not do as well because their financial markets were nearly or completely wiped out because of revolution, war, and/or hyperinflation. A recent study addresses this issue by examining data from 1900–2005 for 17 countries.

Figure 12.13 shows the historical average stock market risk premium for all 17 countries over the 106-year period. Looking at the numbers, the U.S. risk premium is the 8th highest at 7.4 percent (which differs from our earlier estimate because of the differing time periods examined). The overall average risk premium is 7.1 percent. These numbers make it clear that U.S. investors did well, but not exceptionally so relative to investors in many other countries.

So, is the U.S. stock market risk premium estimated from 1925–2010 too high? The evidence seems to suggest that the answer is "maybe a little." One thing we haven't stressed so far is that even with 106 years of data, the average risk premium is still not measured with great precision. From a statistical standpoint, the standard error associated with the U.S.

FIGURE 12.13   Stock Market Risk Premiums for 17 Countries: 1900–2005

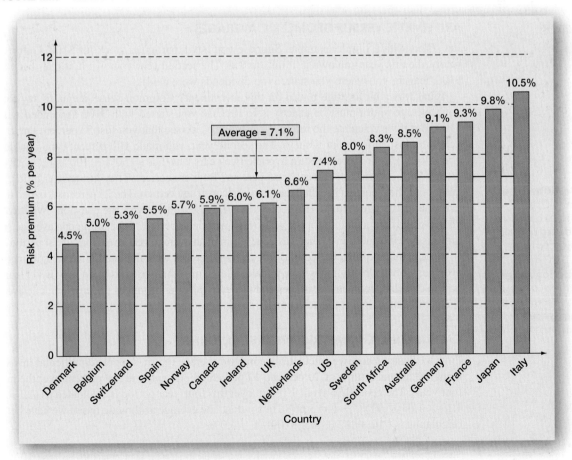

Source: Based on information in Elroy Dimson, Paul Marsh, and Michael Staunton, "The Worldwide Equity Premium: A Smaller Puzzle," in *Handbook of the Equity Risk Premium*, Rajnish Mehra, ed. (Elsevier: 2007).

estimated risk premium of 7.4 percent is about 2 percent.[4] So, even a one standard error range covers 5.4 to 9.4 percent.

Concept Questions

12.4a In words, how do we calculate a variance? A standard deviation?

12.4b With a normal distribution, what is the probability of ending up more than one standard deviation below the average?

12.4c Assuming that long-term corporate bonds have an approximately normal distribution, what is the approximate probability of earning 14.6 percent or more in a given year? With T-bills, roughly what is this probability?

12.4d What is the second lesson from capital market history?

12.5 More about Average Returns

Thus far in this chapter, we have looked closely at simple average returns. But there is another way of computing an average return. The fact that average returns are calculated two different ways leads to some confusion, so our goal in this section is to explain the two approaches and also the circumstances under which each is appropriate.

ARITHMETIC VERSUS GEOMETRIC AVERAGES

Let's start with a simple example. Suppose you buy a particular stock for $100. Unfortunately, the first year you own it, it falls to $50. The second year you own it, it rises back to $100, leaving you where you started (no dividends were paid).

What was your average return on this investment? Common sense seems to say that your average return must be exactly zero because you started with $100 and ended with $100. But if we calculate the returns year-by-year, we see that you lost 50 percent the first year (you lost half of your money). The second year, you made 100 percent (you doubled your money). Your average return over the two years was thus $(-50\% + 100\%)/2 = 25\%$!

So which is correct, 0 percent or 25 percent? Both are correct: They just answer different questions. The 0 percent is called the **geometric average return**. The 25 percent is called the **arithmetic average return**. The geometric average return answers the question "What was your average compound return per year over a particular period?" The arithmetic average return answers the question "What was your return in an average year over a particular period?"

Notice that, in previous sections, the average returns we calculated were all arithmetic averages, so we already know how to calculate them. What we need to do now is (1) learn how to calculate geometric averages and (2) learn the circumstances under which one average is more meaningful than the other.

geometric average return
The average compound return earned per year over a multiyear period.

arithmetic average return
The return earned in an average year over a multiyear period.

CALCULATING GEOMETRIC AVERAGE RETURNS

First, to illustrate how we calculate a geometric average return, suppose a particular investment had annual returns of 10 percent, 12 percent, 3 percent, and -9 percent over the last four years. The geometric average return over this four-year period is calculated as $(1.10 \times 1.12 \times 1.03 \times .91)^{1/4} - 1 = 3.66\%$. In contrast, the average arithmetic return we have been calculating is $(.10 + .12 + .03 - .09)/4 = 4.0\%$.

---

[4]Recall from basic "sadistics" that the standard error of a sample mean is the sample standard deviation divided by the square root of the sample size. In our case, the standard deviation over the 1900–2005 period was 19.6 percent, so the standard error is $.196/\sqrt{106} = .019$.

IN THEIR OWN WORDS ...

Jeremy J. Siegel on Stocks for the Long Run

The most fascinating characteristic about the data on real financial market returns that I collected is the stability of the long-run real equity returns. The compound annual (geometric) real return on U.S. stocks averaged 6.7% per year from 1802 through 2010, and this return had remained remarkably stable over long-term periods. From 1802 through 1871, the real return averaged 7.0%; from 1871, when the Cowles Foundation data became available, through 1925, the real return on stocks averaged 6.6% per year; and since 1925, which the well-known Ibbotson data cover, the real return has averaged 6.4%. Despite the fact that the price level has increased over ten times since the end of the Second World War, real stock returns have still averaged 6.4%.

The long-run stability of real returns on stocks is strongly indicative of *mean reversion of equity return*. Mean reversion means that stock returns can be very volatile in the short run, but show a remarkable stability in the long run. When my research was first published, there was much skepticism of the mean reversion properties of equity market returns, but now this concept is widely accepted for stocks. If mean reversion prevails, portfolios geared for the long term should have a greater share of equities than short-term portfolios. This conclusion has long been the "conventional" wisdom on investing, but it does not follow if stock returns follow a random walk, a concept widely accepted by academics in the 1970s and 1980s.

When my data first appeared, there was also much discussion of "survivorship bias," the fact that the U.S. stock returns are unusually good because the U.S. was the most successful capitalist country. But three British researchers, Elroy Dimson, Paul Marsh, and Michael Staunton, surveyed stock returns in 16 countries since the beginning of the 20th century and wrote up their results in a book entitled *Triumph of the Optimists*. The authors concluded that U.S. stock returns do not give a distorted picture of the superiority of stocks over bonds worldwide.

Jeremy J. Siegel is the Russell E. Palmer Professor of Finance at The Wharton School of the University of Pennsylvania and author of Stocks for the Long Run *and* The Future Investors. *His research covers macroeconomics and monetary policy, financial market returns, and long-term economic trends.*

In general, if we have T years of returns, the geometric average return over these T years is calculated using this formula:

$$\text{Geometric average return} = [(1 + R_1) \times (1 + R_2) \times \ldots \times (1 + R_T)]^{1/T} - 1 \qquad \textbf{[12.4]}$$

This formula tells us that four steps are required:

1. Take each of the T annual returns $R_1, R_2, \ldots, R_T$ and add 1 to each (after converting them to decimals!).
2. Multiply all the numbers from step 1 together.
3. Take the result from step 2 and raise it to the power of $1/T$.
4. Finally, subtract 1 from the result of step 3. The result is the geometric average return.

Calculating the Geometric Average Return — EXAMPLE 12.4

Calculate the geometric average return for S&P 500 large-cap stocks for the first five years in Table 12.1, 1926–1930.

First, convert percentages to decimal returns, add 1, and then calculate their product:

S&P 500 Returns	Product
13.75	1.1375
35.70	×1.3570
45.08	×1.4508
−8.80	×.9120
−25.13	×.7487
	1.5291

Notice that the number 1.5291 is what our investment is worth after five years if we started with a $1 investment. The geometric average return is then calculated as follows:

Geometric average return = $1.5291^{1/5} - 1 = .0887$, or 8.87%

Thus, the geometric average return is about 8.87 percent in this example. Here is a tip: If you are using a financial calculator, you can put $1 in as the present value, $1.5291 as the future value, and 5 as the number of periods. Then, solve for the unknown rate. You should get the same answer we did.

One thing you may have noticed in our examples thus far is that the geometric average returns seem to be smaller. This will always be true (as long as the returns are not all identical, in which case the two "averages" would be the same). To illustrate, Table 12.4 shows the arithmetic averages and standard deviations from Figure 12.10, along with the geometric average returns.

As shown in Table 12.4, the geometric averages are all smaller, but the magnitude of the difference varies quite a bit. The reason is that the difference is greater for more volatile investments. In fact, there is a useful approximation. Assuming all the numbers are expressed in decimals (as opposed to percentages), the geometric average return is approximately equal to the arithmetic average return minus half the variance. For example, looking at the large-company stocks, the arithmetic average is .119 and the standard deviation is .204, implying that the variance is .042. The approximate geometric average is thus .119 − .042/2 = .098, which is quite close to the actual value.

EXAMPLE 12.5   **More Geometric Averages**

Take a look back at Figure 12.4. There, we showed the value of a $1 investment after 85 years. Use the value for the large-company stock investment to check the geometric average in Table 12.4.

In Figure 12.4, the large-company investment grew to $2,982.24 over 85 years. The geometric average return is thus

Geometric average return = $2,982.24^{1/85} - 1 = .0987$, or 9.9%

This 9.9% is the value shown in Table 12.4. For practice, check some of the other numbers in Table 12.4 the same way.

TABLE 12.4

Geometric versus Arithmetic Average Returns: 1926–2010

Series	Average Return		Standard Deviation
	Geometric	**Arithmetic**	
Large-company stocks	9.9%	11.9%	20.4%
Small-company stocks	12.1	16.7	32.6
Long-term corporate bonds	5.9	6.2	8.3
Long-term government bonds	5.5	5.9	9.5
Intermediate-term government bonds	5.4	5.5	5.7
U.S. Treasury bills	3.6	3.7	3.1
Inflation	3.0	3.1	4.2

SOURCE: © *Stocks, Bonds, Bills, and Inflation: 2011 Yearbook™*, annually updates work by Roger G. Ibbotson and Rex A. Sinquefield (Chicago: Morningstar). All rights reserved.

ARITHMETIC AVERAGE RETURN OR GEOMETRIC AVERAGE RETURN?

When we look at historical returns, the difference between the geometric and arithmetic average returns isn't too hard to understand. To put it slightly differently, the geometric average tells you what you actually earned per year on average, compounded annually. The arithmetic average tells you what you earned in a typical year. You should use whichever one answers the question you want answered.

A somewhat trickier question concerns which average return to use when forecasting future wealth levels, and there's a lot of confusion on this point among analysts and financial planners. First, let's get one thing straight: If you *know* the true arithmetic average return, then this is what you should use in your forecast. For example, if you know the arithmetic return is 10 percent, then your best guess of the value of a $1,000 investment in 10 years is the future value of $1,000 at 10 percent for 10 years, or $2,593.74.

The problem we face, however, is that we usually have only *estimates* of the arithmetic and geometric returns, and estimates have errors. In this case, the arithmetic average return is probably too high for longer periods and the geometric average is probably too low for shorter periods. So, you should regard long-run projected wealth levels calculated using arithmetic averages as optimistic. Short-run projected wealth levels calculated using geometric averages are probably pessimistic.

The good news is that there is a simple way of combining the two averages, which we will call *Blume's formula.*[5] Suppose we have calculated geometric and arithmetic return averages from N years of data, and we wish to use these averages to form a T-year average return forecast, $R(T)$, where T is less than N. Here's how we do it:

$$R(T) = \frac{T-1}{N-1} \times \text{Geometric average} + \frac{N-T}{N-1} \times \text{Arithmetic average} \qquad \textbf{[12.5]}$$

For example, suppose that, from 25 years of annual returns data, we calculate an arithmetic average return of 12 percent and a geometric average return of 9 percent. From these averages, we wish to make 1-year, 5-year, and 10-year average return forecasts. These three average return forecasts are calculated as follows:

$$R(1) = \frac{1-1}{24} \times 9\% + \frac{25-1}{24} \times 12\% = 12\%$$

$$R(5) = \frac{5-1}{24} \times 9\% + \frac{25-5}{24} \times 12\% = 11.5\%$$

$$R(10) = \frac{10-1}{24} \times 9\% + \frac{25-10}{24} \times 12\% = 10.875\%$$

Thus, we see that 1-year, 5-year, and 10-year forecasts are 12 percent, 11.5 percent, and 10.875 percent, respectively.

As a practical matter, Blume's formula says that if you are using averages calculated over a long period (such as the 85 years we use) to forecast up to a decade or so into the future, then you should use the arithmetic average. If you are forecasting a few decades into the future (as you might do for retirement planning), then you should just split the difference between the arithmetic and geometric average returns. Finally, if for some reason you are doing very long forecasts covering many decades, use the geometric average.

This concludes our discussion of geometric versus arithmetic averages. One last note: In the future, when we say "average return," we mean arithmetic unless we explicitly say otherwise.

---

[5]This elegant result is due to Marshall Blume ("Unbiased Estimates of Long-Run Expected Rates of Return," *Journal of the American Statistical Association,* September 1974, pp. 634–38).

Concept Questions

12.5a If you wanted to forecast what the stock market is going to do over the next year, should you use an arithmetic or geometric average?

12.5b If you wanted to forecast what the stock market is going to do over the next century, should you use an arithmetic or geometric average?

12.6 Capital Market Efficiency

Capital market history suggests that the market values of stocks and bonds can fluctuate widely from year to year. Why does this occur? At least part of the answer is that prices change because new information arrives, and investors reassess asset values based on that information.

The behavior of market prices has been extensively studied. A question that has received particular attention is whether prices adjust quickly and correctly when new information arrives. A market is said to be "efficient" if this is the case. To be more precise, in an **efficient capital market**, current market prices fully reflect available information. By this we simply mean that, based on available information, there is no reason to believe that the current price is too low or too high.

efficient capital market
A market in which security prices reflect available information.

The concept of market efficiency is a rich one, and much has been written about it. A full discussion of the subject goes beyond the scope of our study of corporate finance. However, because the concept figures so prominently in studies of market history, we briefly describe the key points here.

PRICE BEHAVIOR IN AN EFFICIENT MARKET

To illustrate how prices behave in an efficient market, suppose the F-Stop Camera Corporation (FCC) has, through years of secret research and development, developed a camera with an autofocusing system whose speed will double that of the autofocusing systems now available. FCC's capital budgeting analysis suggests that launching the new camera will be a highly profitable move; in other words, the NPV appears to be positive and substantial. The key assumption thus far is that FCC has not released any information about the new system; so, the fact of its existence is "inside" information only.

Now consider a share of stock in FCC. In an efficient market, its price reflects what is known about FCC's current operations and profitability, and it reflects market opinion about FCC's potential for future growth and profits. The value of the new autofocusing system is not reflected, however, because the market is unaware of the system's existence.

If the market agrees with FCC's assessment of the value of the new project, FCC's stock price will rise when the decision to launch is made public. For example, assume the announcement is made in a press release on Wednesday morning. In an efficient market, the price of shares in FCC will adjust quickly to this new information. Investors should not be able to buy the stock on Wednesday afternoon and make a profit on Thursday. This would imply that it took the stock market a full day to realize the implication of the FCC press release. If the market is efficient, the price of shares of FCC stock on Wednesday afternoon will already reflect the information contained in the Wednesday morning press release.

Figure 12.14 presents three possible stock price adjustments for FCC. In Figure 12.14, Day 0 represents the announcement day. As illustrated, before the announcement, FCC's stock sells for $140 per share. The NPV per share of the new system is, say, $40, so the new price will be $180 once the value of the new project is fully reflected.

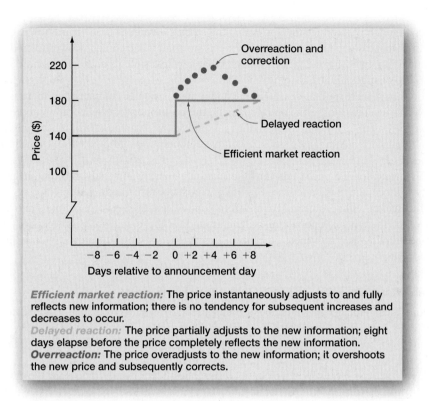

FIGURE 12.14

Reaction of Stock Price to New Information in Efficient and Inefficient Markets

Efficient market reaction: The price instantaneously adjusts to and fully reflects new information; there is no tendency for subsequent increases and decreases to occur.
Delayed reaction: The price partially adjusts to the new information; eight days elapse before the price completely reflects the new information.
Overreaction: The price overadjusts to the new information; it overshoots the new price and subsequently corrects.

The solid line in Figure 12.14 represents the path taken by the stock price in an efficient market. In this case, the price adjusts immediately to the new information and no further changes in the price of the stock take place. The broken line in Figure 12.14 depicts a delayed reaction. Here it takes the market eight days or so to fully absorb the information. Finally, the dotted line illustrates an overreaction and subsequent adjustment to the correct price.

The broken line and the dotted line in Figure 12.14 illustrate paths that the stock price might take in an inefficient market. If, for example, stock prices don't adjust immediately to new information (the broken line), then buying stock immediately following the release of new information and then selling it several days later would be a positive NPV activity because the price is too low for several days after the announcement.

THE EFFICIENT MARKETS HYPOTHESIS

The **efficient markets hypothesis (EMH)** asserts that well-organized capital markets, such as the NYSE, are efficient markets, at least as a practical matter. In other words, an advocate of the EMH might argue that although inefficiencies may exist, they are relatively small and not common.

If a market is efficient, then there is a very important implication for market participants: All investments in that market are *zero* NPV investments. The reason is not complicated. If prices are neither too low nor too high, then the difference between the market value of an investment and its cost is zero; hence, the NPV is zero. As a result, in an efficient market, investors get exactly what they pay for when they buy securities, and firms receive exactly what their stocks and bonds are worth when they sell them.

What makes a market efficient is competition among investors. Many individuals spend their entire lives trying to find mispriced stocks. For any given stock, they study what has

efficient markets hypothesis (EMH)
The hypothesis that actual capital markets, such as the NYSE, are efficient.

Look under the "Contents" link at www.investorhome.com *for more info on the EMH.*

happened in the past to the stock price and the stock's dividends. They learn, to the extent possible, what a company's earnings have been, how much the company owes to creditors, what taxes it pays, what businesses it is in, what new investments are planned, how sensitive it is to changes in the economy, and so on.

Not only is there a great deal to know about any particular company, but there is also a powerful incentive for knowing it—namely, the profit motive. If you know more about some company than other investors in the marketplace, you can profit from that knowledge by investing in the company's stock if you have good news and by selling it if you have bad news.

The logical consequence of all this information gathering and analysis is that mispriced stocks will become fewer and fewer. In other words, because of competition among investors, the market will become increasingly efficient. A kind of equilibrium comes into being with which there is just enough mispricing around for those who are best at identifying it to make a living at it. For most other investors, the activity of information gathering and analysis will not pay.[6]

SOME COMMON MISCONCEPTIONS ABOUT THE EMH

No other idea in finance has attracted as much attention as that of efficient markets, and not all of the attention has been flattering. Rather than rehash the arguments here, we will be content to observe that some markets are more efficient than others. For example, financial markets on the whole are probably much more efficient than real asset markets.

Having said this, however, we can also say that much of the criticism of the EMH is misguided because it is based on a misunderstanding of what the hypothesis says and what it doesn't say. For example, when the notion of market efficiency was first publicized and debated in the popular financial press, it was often characterized by words to the effect that "throwing darts at the financial page will produce a portfolio that can be expected to do as well as any managed by professional security analysts."[7]

Confusion over statements of this sort has often led to a failure to understand the implications of market efficiency. For example, sometimes it is wrongly argued that market efficiency means that it doesn't matter how you invest your money because the efficiency of the market will protect you from making a mistake. However, a random dart thrower might wind up with all of the darts sticking into one or two high-risk stocks that deal in genetic engineering. Would you really want all of your money in two such stocks?

A contest run by *The Wall Street Journal* provides a good example of the controversy surrounding market efficiency. Each month, the *Journal* asked four professional money managers to pick one stock each. At the same time, it threw four darts at the stock page to select a comparison group. In the 147 five-and one-half month contests from July 1990 to September 2002, the pros won 90 times.

The fact that the pros are ahead of the darts by 90 to 57 suggests that markets are not efficient. Or does it? One problem is that the darts naturally tend to select stocks of average risk. The pros, however, are playing to win and naturally select riskier stocks, or so it is argued. If this is true, then, on average, we *expect* the pros to win. Furthermore, the pros'

---

[6]The idea behind the EMH can be illustrated by the following short story: A student was walking down the hall with her finance professor when they both saw a $20 bill on the ground. As the student bent down to pick it up, the professor shook his head slowly and, with a look of disappointment on his face, said patiently to the student, "Don't bother. If it were really there, someone else would have picked it up already." The moral of the story reflects the logic of the efficient markets hypothesis: If you think you have found a pattern in stock prices or a simple device for picking winners, you probably have not.

[7]B. G. Malkiel, *A Random Walk Down Wall Street,* revised and updated ed. (New York: Norton, 2003).

The concept of an efficient market is a special application of the "no free lunch" principle. In an efficient financial market, costless trading policies will not generate "excess" returns. After adjusting for the riskiness of the policy, the trader's return will be no larger than the return of a randomly selected portfolio, at least on average.

This is often thought to imply something about the amount of "information" reflected in asset prices. However, it really doesn't mean that prices reflect all information nor even that they reflect publicly available information. Instead it means that the connection between unreflected information and prices is too subtle and tenuous to be easily or costlessly detected.

Relevant information is difficult and expensive to uncover and evaluate. Thus, if costless trading policies are ineffective, there must exist some traders who make a living by "beating the market." They cover their costs (including the opportunity cost of their time) by trading. The existence of such traders is actually a necessary precondition for markets to become efficient. Without such professional traders, prices would fail to reflect everything that is cheap and easy to evaluate.

Efficient market prices should approximate a random walk, meaning that they will appear to fluctuate more or less randomly. Prices can fluctuate nonrandomly to the extent that their departure from randomness is expensive to discern. Also, observed price series can depart from apparent randomness due to changes in preferences and expectations, but this is really a technicality and does not imply a free lunch relative to current investor sentiments.

Richard Roll is Japan Alumni Professor of International Finance at UCLA. He is a preeminent financial researcher, and he has written extensively in almost every area of modern finance. He is particularly well known for his insightful analyses and great creativity in understanding empirical phenomena.

picks are announced to the public at the start. This publicity may boost the prices of the shares involved somewhat, leading to a partially self-fulfilling prophecy. Unfortunately, the *Journal* discontinued the contest in 2002, so this test of market efficiency is no longer ongoing.

More than anything else, what efficiency implies is that the price a firm will obtain when it sells a share of its stock is a "fair" price in the sense that it reflects the value of that stock given the information available about the firm. Shareholders do not have to worry that they are paying too much for a stock with a low dividend or some other sort of characteristic because the market has already incorporated that characteristic into the price. We sometimes say that the information has been "priced out."

The concept of efficient markets can be explained further by replying to a frequent objection. It is sometimes argued that the market cannot be efficient because stock prices fluctuate from day to day. If the prices are right, the argument goes, then why do they change so much and so often? From our discussion of the market, we can see that these price movements are in no way inconsistent with efficiency. Investors are bombarded with information every day. The fact that prices fluctuate is, at least in part, a reflection of that information flow. In fact, the absence of price movements in a world that changes as rapidly as ours would suggest inefficiency.

THE FORMS OF MARKET EFFICIENCY

It is common to distinguish between three forms of market efficiency. Depending on the degree of efficiency, we say that markets are either *weak form efficient, semistrong form efficient,* or *strong form efficient.* The difference between these forms relates to what information is reflected in prices.

We start with the extreme case. If the market is strong form efficient, then *all* information of *every* kind is reflected in stock prices. In such a market, there is no such thing as inside information. Therefore, in our FCC example, we apparently were assuming that the market was not strong form efficient.

Casual observation, particularly in recent years, suggests that inside information does exist, and it can be valuable to possess. Whether it is lawful or ethical to use that information is another issue. In any event, we conclude that private information about a particular stock may exist that is not currently reflected in the price of the stock. For example, prior knowledge of a takeover attempt could be very valuable.

The second form of efficiency, semistrong form efficiency, is the most controversial. If a market is semistrong form efficient, then all *public* information is reflected in the stock price. The reason this form is controversial is that it implies that a security analyst who tries to identify mispriced stocks using, for example, financial statement information, is wasting time because that information is already reflected in the current price.

The third form of efficiency, weak form efficiency, suggests that, at a minimum, the current price of a stock reflects the stock's own past prices. In other words, studying past prices in an attempt to identify mispriced securities is futile if the market is weak form efficient. Although this form of efficiency might seem rather mild, it implies that searching for patterns in historical prices that will be useful in identifying mispriced stocks will not work (this practice is quite common).

What does capital market history say about market efficiency? Here again, there is great controversy. At the risk of going out on a limb, we can say that the evidence seems to tell us three things. First, prices appear to respond rapidly to new information, and the response is at least not grossly different from what we would expect in an efficient market. Second, the future of market prices, particularly in the short run, is difficult to predict based on publicly available information. Third, if mispriced stocks exist, then there is no obvious means of identifying them. Put another way, simpleminded schemes based on public information will probably not be successful.

Concept Questions

12.6a What is an efficient market?

12.6b What are the forms of market efficiency?

12.7 Summary and Conclusions

This chapter has explored the subject of capital market history. Such history is useful because it tells us what to expect in the way of returns from risky assets. We summed up our study of market history with two key lessons:

1. Risky assets, on average, earn a risk premium. There is a reward for bearing risk.

2. The greater the potential reward from a risky investment, the greater is the risk.

These lessons have significant implications for the financial manager. We will consider these implications in the chapters ahead.

We also discussed the concept of market efficiency. In an efficient market, prices adjust quickly and correctly to new information. Consequently, asset prices in efficient markets are rarely too high or too low. How efficient capital markets (such as the NYSE) are is a matter of debate; but, at a minimum, they are probably much more efficient than most real asset markets.

CONNECT TO FINANCE

 If you are using *Connect™ Finance* in your course, get online to take a Practice Test, check out study tools, and find out where you need additional practice.

▼ Chapter 12 Some Lessons from Capital Market History			
12.1 Returns	eBook	Study	Practice
12.2 The Historical Record	eBook	Study	Practice
12.3 Average Returns: The First Lesson	eBook	Study	Practice
12.4 The Variability of Returns: The Second Lesson	eBook	Study	Practice
12.5 More about Average Returns	eBook	Study	Practice
12.6 Capital Market Efficiency	eBook	Study	Practice

Practice Problems

Can you answer the following questions?

Section 12.1 Chase Bank pays an annual dividend of $1.05 per share on its common stock. One year ago, this stock sold for $48 per share. Today, the stock is priced to sell at $31 per share. What is the capital gains yield? (LO 12-1)

Section 12.2 Which of the following categories of investments had a positive rate of return every year during the period 1926–2010? (LO 12-2)

Section 12.3 The risk premium is computed as the excess return that a security earns over and above the rate for what? (LO 12-2)

Section 12.4 How are risk and reward related? (LO 12-4)

Section 12.5 A stock produced annual rates of return of 11 percent, –17 percent, 2 percent, and 14 percent over the past 4 years, respectively. What is the geometric average return for this period? (LO 12-3)

Section 12.6 Corporate insiders could not benefit financially from the inside information they possess in what type of market? (LO 12-4)

Log on to find out!

CHAPTER REVIEW AND SELF-TEST PROBLEMS

12.1 Recent Return History Use Table 12.1 to calculate the average return over the years 1996 through 2000 for large-company stocks, long-term government bonds, and Treasury bills.

12.2 More Recent Return History Calculate the standard deviation for each security type using information from Problem 12.1. Which of the investments was the most volatile over this period?

Visit us at www.mhhe.com/rwj

ANSWERS TO CHAPTER REVIEW AND SELF-TEST PROBLEMS

12.1 We calculate the averages as follows:

	Actual Returns		
Year	**Large-Company Stocks**	**Long-Term Government Bonds**	**Treasury Bills**
1996	.2296	.0013	.0514
1997	.3336	.1202	.0519
1998	.2858	.1445	.0486
1999	.2104	−.0751	.0480
2000	−.0910	.1722	.0598
Average	.19368	.0726	.0519

12.2 We first need to calculate the deviations from the average returns. Using the averages from Problem 12.1, we get the following values:

	Deviations from Average Returns		
Year	**Large-Company Stocks**	**Long-Term Government Bonds**	**Treasury Bills**
1996	.0357	−.0713	−.0005
1997	.1397	.0476	.0000
1998	.0919	.0719	−.0033
1999	.0165	−.1477	−.0039
2000	−.2847	.0996	.0079
Total	.0000	.0000	.0000

We square these deviations and calculate the variances and standard deviations:

	Squared Deviations from Average Returns		
Year	**Large-Company Stocks**	**Long-Term Government Bonds**	**Treasury Bills**
1996	.0012773	.0050865	.0000003
1997	.0195273	.0022639	.0000000
1998	.0084530	.0051667	.0000112
1999	.0002736	.0218212	.0000155
2000	.0810427	.0099162	.0000618
Variance	.0276691	.0110636	.0000222
Std dev	.1663402	.1051838	.0047104

To calculate the variances, we added up the squared deviations and divided by 4, the number of returns less 1. Notice that the stocks had much more volatility than the bonds with a much larger average return. For large-company stocks, this was a particularly good period: The average return was 19.39 percent.

Visit us at www.mhhe.com/rwj

CONCEPTS REVIEW AND CRITICAL THINKING QUESTIONS

1. **Investment Selection [LO4]** Given that IDT Corporation was up by about 429 percent for 2010, why didn't all investors hold this stock?

2. **Investment Selection [LO4]** Given that First Bancorp was down by 80 percent for 2010, why did some investors hold the stock? Why didn't they sell out before the price declined so sharply?

3. **Risk and Return [LO2, 3]** We have seen that over long periods, stock investments have tended to substantially outperform bond investments. However, it is common to observe investors with long horizons holding entirely bonds. Are such investors irrational?

    no, they may have different liquidity needs.

4. **Market Efficiency Implications [LO4]** Explain why a characteristic of an efficient market is that investments in that market have zero NPVs.

5. **Efficient Markets Hypothesis [LO4]** A stock market analyst is able to identify mispriced stocks by comparing the average price for the last 10 days to the average price for the last 60 days. If this is true, what do you know about the market?

    it's (less than) weak form efficient

6. **Semistrong Efficiency [LO4]** If a market is semistrong form efficient, is it also weak form efficient? Explain.

7. **Efficient Markets Hypothesis [LO4]** What are the implications of the efficient markets hypothesis for investors who buy and sell stocks in an attempt to "beat the market"?

8. **Stocks versus Gambling [LO4]** Critically evaluate the following statement: Playing the stock market is like gambling. Such speculative investing has no social value other than the pleasure people get from this form of gambling.

9. **Efficient Markets Hypothesis [LO4]** Several celebrated investors and stock pickers frequently mentioned in the financial press have recorded huge returns on their investments over the past two decades. Is the success of these particular investors an invalidation of the EMH? Explain.

10. **Efficient Markets Hypothesis [LO4]** For each of the following scenarios, discuss whether profit opportunities exist from trading in the stock of the firm under the conditions that (1) the market is not weak form efficient, (2) the market is weak form but not semistrong form efficient, (3) the market is semistrong form but not strong form efficient, and (4) the market is strong form efficient.

    a. The stock price has risen steadily each day for the past 30 days.

    b. The financial statements for a company were released three days ago, and you believe you've uncovered some anomalies in the company's inventory and cost control reporting techniques that are causing the firm's true liquidity strength to be understated.

    c. You observe that the senior managers of a company have been buying a lot of the company's stock on the open market over the past week.

QUESTIONS AND PROBLEMS

1. **Calculating Returns [LO1]** Suppose a stock had an initial price of $72 per share, paid a dividend of $1.20 per share during the year, and had an ending share price of $79. Compute the percentage total return.

2. **Calculating Yields [LO1]** In Problem 1, what was the dividend yield? The capital gains yield?

BASIC
(Questions 1–12)

Visit us at www.mhhe.com/rwj

Visit us at www.mhhe.com/rwj

3. **Return Calculations [LO1]** Rework Problems 1 and 2 assuming the ending share price is $61.

4. **Calculating Returns [LO1]** Suppose you bought a 6 percent coupon bond one year ago for $920. The bond sells for $940 today.

    a. Assuming a $1,000 face value, what was your total dollar return on this investment over the past year?

    b. What was your total nominal rate of return on this investment over the past year?

    c. If the inflation rate last year was 3 percent, what was your total real rate of return on this investment?

5. **Nominal versus Real Returns [LO2]** What was the average annual return on large-company stock from 1926 through 2010:

    a. In nominal terms?

    b. In real terms?

6. **Bond Returns [LO2]** What is the historical real return on long-term government bonds? On long-term corporate bonds?

7. **Calculating Returns and Variability [LO1]** Using the following returns, calculate the arithmetic average returns, the variances, and the standard deviations for X and Y.

	Returns	
Year	X	Y
1	17%	23%
2	22	34
3	8	11
4	−15	−32
5	10	21

8. **Risk Premiums [LO2, 3]** Refer to Table 12.1 in the text and look at the period from 1970 through 1975.

    a. Calculate the arithmetic average returns for large-company stocks and T-bills over this period.

    b. Calculate the standard deviation of the returns for large-company stocks and T-bills over this period.

    c. Calculate the observed risk premium in each year for the large-company stocks versus the T-bills. What was the average risk premium over this period? What was the standard deviation of the risk premium over this period?

    d. Is it possible for the risk premium to be negative before an investment is undertaken? Can the risk premium be negative after the fact? Explain.

9. **Calculating Returns and Variability [LO1]** You've observed the following returns on Crash-n-Burn Computer's stock over the past five years: 14 percent, −9 percent, 16 percent, 21 percent, and 3 percent.

    a. What was the arithmetic average return on Crash-n-Burn's stock over this five-year period?

    b. What was the variance of Crash-n-Burn's returns over this period? The standard deviation?

10. **Calculating Real Returns and Risk Premiums [LO1]** For Problem 9, suppose the average inflation rate over this period was 3.5 percent and the average T-bill rate over the period was 4.2 percent.

    a. What was the average real return on Crash-n-Burn's stock?

    b. What was the average nominal risk premium on Crash-n-Burn's stock?

11. **Calculating Real Rates [LO1]** Given the information in Problem 10, what was the average real risk-free rate over this time period? What was the average real risk premium?

12. **Effects of Inflation [LO2]** Look at Table 12.1 and Figure 12.7 in the text. When were T-bill rates at their highest over the period from 1926 through 2010? Why do you think they were so high during this period? What relationship underlies your answer?

13. **Calculating Investment Returns [LO1]** You bought one of Great White Shark Repellant Co.'s 8 percent coupon bonds one year ago for $1,030. These bonds make annual payments and mature 14 years from now. Suppose you decide to sell your bonds today, when the required return on the bonds is 7 percent. If the inflation rate was 4.2 percent over the past year, what was your total real return on investment?

INTERMEDIATE
(Questions 13–22)

14. **Calculating Returns and Variability [LO1]** You find a certain stock that had returns of 9 percent, −16 percent, 21 percent, and 17 percent for four of the last five years. If the average return of the stock over this period was 11.3 percent, what was the stock's return for the missing year? What is the standard deviation of the stock's return?

15. **Arithmetic and Geometric Returns [LO1]** A stock has had returns of 14 percent, 18 percent, 26 percent, −19 percent, 34 percent, and −9 percent over the last six years. What are the arithmetic and geometric returns for the stock?

16. **Arithmetic and Geometric Returns [LO1]** A stock has had the following year-end prices and dividends:

Year	Price	Dividend
1	$43.15	–
2	48.13	$.45
3	57.05	.49
4	45.13	.55
5	52.05	.62
6	61.13	.68

What are the arithmetic and geometric returns for the stock?

17. **Using Return Distributions [LO3]** Suppose the returns on long-term corporate bonds are normally distributed. Based on the historical record, what is the approximate probability that your return on these bonds will be less than −2.1 percent in a given year? What range of returns would you expect to see 95 percent of the time? What range would you expect to see 99 percent of the time?

18. **Using Return Distributions [LO3]** Assuming that the returns from holding small-company stocks are normally distributed, what is the approximate probability that your money will double in value in a single year? What about triple in value?

19. **Distributions [LO3]** In Problem 18, what is the probability that the return is less than −100 percent (think)? What are the implications for the distribution of returns?

20. **Blume's Formula [LO1]** Over a 40-year period an asset had an arithmetic return of 11.7 percent and a geometric return of 9.6 percent. Using Blume's formula, what is your best estimate of the future annual returns over 5 years? 10 years? 20 years?

21. **Blume's Formula [LO1, 2]** Assume that the historical return on large-company stocks is a predictor of the future returns. What return would you estimate for large-company stocks over the next year? The next 5 years? 20 years? 30 years?

22. **Calculating Returns [LO2, 3]** Refer to Table 12.1 in the text and look at the period from 1973 through 1980:

    a. Calculate the average return for Treasury bills and the average annual inflation rate (consumer price index) for this period.

Visit us at www.mhhe.com/rwj

b. Calculate the standard deviation of Treasury bill returns and inflation over this period.

c. Calculate the real return for each year. What is the average real return for Treasury bills?

d. Many people consider Treasury bills risk-free. What do these calculations tell you about the potential risks of Treasury bills?

CHALLENGE
(Questions 23–24)

23. Using Probability Distributions [LO3] Suppose the returns on large-company stocks are normally distributed. Based on the historical record, use the NORMDIST function in Excel® to determine the probability that in any given year you will lose money by investing in common stock.

24. Using Probability Distributions [LO3] Suppose the returns on long-term corporate bonds and T-bills are normally distributed. Based on the historical record, use the NORMDIST function in Excel to answer the following questions:

a. What is the probability that in any given year, the return on long-term corporate bonds will be greater than 10 percent? Less than 0 percent?

b. What is the probability that in any given year, the return on T-bills will be greater than 10 percent? Less than 0 percent?

c. In 1979, the return on long-term corporate bonds was −4.18 percent. How likely is it that such a low return will recur at some point in the future? T-bills had a return of 10.56 percent in this same year. How likely is it that such a high return on T-bills will recur at some point in the future?

MINICASE

A Job at S&S Air

You recently graduated from college, and your job search led you to S&S Air. Because you felt the company's business was taking off, you accepted a job offer. The first day on the job, while you are finishing your employment paperwork, Chris Guthrie, who works in Finance, stops by to inform you about the company's 401(k) plan.

A 401(k) plan is a retirement plan offered by many companies. Such plans are tax-deferred savings vehicles, meaning that any deposits you make into the plan are deducted from your current pretax income, so no current taxes are paid on the money. For example, assume your salary will be $50,000 per year. If you contribute $3,000 to the 401(k) plan, you will pay taxes on only $47,000 in income. There are also no taxes paid on any capital gains or income while you are invested in the plan, but you do pay taxes when you withdraw money at retirement. As is fairly common, the company also has a 5 percent match. This means that the company will match your contribution up to 5 percent of your salary, but you must contribute to get the match.

The 401(k) plan has several options for investments, most of which are mutual funds. A mutual fund is a portfolio of assets. When you purchase shares in a mutual fund, you are actually purchasing partial ownership of the fund's assets. The return of the fund is the weighted average of the return of the assets owned by the fund, minus any expenses. The largest expense is typically the management fee, paid to the fund

manager. The management fee is compensation for the manager, who makes all of the investment decisions for the fund.

S&S Air uses Bledsoe Financial Services as its 401(k) plan administrator. Here are the investment options offered for employees:

Company Stock One option in the 401(k) plan is stock in S&S Air. The company is currently privately held. However, when you interviewed with the owners, Mark Sexton and Todd Story, they informed you the company stock was expected to go public in the next three to four years. Until then, a company stock price is simply set each year by the board of directors.

Bledsoe S&P 500 Index Fund This mutual fund tracks the S&P 500. Stocks in the fund are weighted exactly the same as the S&P 500. This means the fund return is approximately the return on the S&P 500, minus expenses. Because an index fund purchases assets based on the composition of the index it is following, the fund manager is not required to research stocks and make investment decisions. The result is that the fund expenses are usually low. The Bledsoe S&P 500 Index Fund charges expenses of .15 percent of assets per year.

Bledsoe Small-Cap Fund This fund primarily invests in small-capitalization stocks. As such, the returns of the fund are more volatile. The fund can also invest 10 percent of its assets in companies based outside the United States. This fund charges 1.70 percent in expenses.

Bledsoe Large-Company Stock Fund This fund invests primarily in large-capitalization stocks of companies based in the United States. The fund is managed by Evan Bledsoe and has outperformed the market in six of the last eight years. The fund charges 1.50 percent in expenses.

Bledsoe Bond Fund This fund invests in long-term corporate bonds issued by U.S.-domiciled companies. The fund is restricted to investments in bonds with an investment-grade credit rating. This fund charges 1.40 percent in expenses.

Bledsoe Money Market Fund This fund invests in short-term, high credit-quality debt instruments, which include Treasury bills. As such, the return on the money market fund is only slightly higher than the return on Treasury bills. Because of the credit quality and short-term nature of the investments, there is only a very slight risk of negative return. The fund charges .60 percent in expenses.

QUESTIONS

1. What advantages do the mutual funds offer compared to the company stock?

2. Assume that you invest 5 percent of your salary and receive the full 5 percent match from S&S Air. What EAR do you earn from the match? What conclusions do you draw about matching plans?

3. Assume you decide you should invest at least part of your money in large-capitalization stocks of companies based in the United States. What are the advantages and disadvantages of choosing the Bledsoe Large-Company Stock Fund compared to the Bledsoe S&P 500 Index Fund?

4. The returns on the Bledsoe Small-Cap Fund are the most volatile of all the mutual funds offered in the 401(k) plan. Why would you ever want to invest in this fund? When you examine the expenses of the mutual funds, you will notice that this fund also has the highest expenses. Does this affect your decision to invest in this fund?

5. A measure of risk-adjusted performance that is often used is the Sharpe ratio. The Sharpe ratio is calculated as the risk premium of an asset divided by its standard deviation. The standard deviation and return of the funds over the past 10 years are listed in the following table. Calculate the Sharpe ratio for each of these funds. Assume that the expected return and standard deviation of the company stock will be 18 percent and 70 percent, respectively. Calculate the Sharpe ratio for the company stock. How appropriate is the Sharpe ratio for these assets? When would you use the Sharpe ratio?

	10-Year Annual Return	Standard Deviation
Bledsoe S&P 500 Index Fund	11.48%	15.82%
Bledsoe Small-Cap Fund	16.68	19.64
Bledsoe Large-Company Stock Fund	11.85	15.41
Bledsoe Bond Fund	9.67	10.83

6. What portfolio allocation would you choose? Why? Explain your thinking carefully.

RETURN, RISK, AND THE SECURITY MARKET LINE

IN FEBRUARY 2011, Home Depot, Campbell Soup Co., and car rental company Avis Budget Group joined a host of other companies in announcing earnings. Home Depot said its fourth quarter profit increased 72 percent from the previous year. The company's EPS was 36 cents per share, easily beating analysts' estimates of 31 cents. For Campbell Soup, the earnings per share were 71 cents, exactly what analysts were predicting. For Avis Budget, analysts had estimated a loss of 7 cents per share, but the company actually lost 36 cents per share. You would expect that these three cases represent good news, no news, and bad news, and usually you would be right. Even so, Home Depot's stock price dropped just over 1 percent, Campbell Soup's stock price dropped by about 3.9 percent, and Avis Budget's stock price increased just under 1 percent.

The stock price reactions do not seem to match what the news for these companies led you to expect. So when is good news really good news? The answer is fundamental to understanding risk and return, and—the good news is—this chapter explores it in some detail.

After studying this chapter, you should understand:

LO1 How to calculate expected returns.

LO2 The impact of diversification.

LO3 The systematic risk principle.

LO4 The security market line and the risk-return trade-off.

In our last chapter, we learned some important lessons from capital market history. Most important, we learned that there is a reward, on average, for bearing risk. We called this reward a *risk premium*. The second lesson is that this risk premium is larger for riskier investments. This chapter explores the economic and managerial implications of this basic idea.

Thus far, we have concentrated mainly on the return behavior of a few large portfolios. We need to expand our consideration to include individual assets. Specifically, we have two tasks to accomplish. First, we have to define risk and discuss how to measure it. We then must quantify the relationship between an asset's risk and its required return.

When we examine the risks associated with individual assets, we find there are two types of risk: systematic and unsystematic. This distinction is crucial because, as we will see, systematic risk affects almost all assets in the economy, at least to some degree, whereas unsystematic risk affects at most a small number of assets. We then develop the principle of diversification, which shows that highly diversified portfolios will tend to have almost no unsystematic risk.

The principle of diversification has an important implication: To a diversified investor, only systematic risk matters. It follows that in deciding whether to buy a particular individual asset, a diversified investor will only be concerned with that asset's systematic risk. This is a key observation, and it allows us to say a great deal about the risks and returns on individual assets. In particular, it is the basis for a famous relationship between risk and return called the *security market line*, or SML. To develop the SML, we introduce the equally famous "beta" coefficient, one of the centerpieces of modern finance. Beta and the SML are key concepts because they supply us with at least part of the answer to the question of how to determine the required return on an investment.

Expected Returns and Variances

In our previous chapter, we discussed how to calculate average returns and variances using historical data. We now begin to discuss how to analyze returns and variances when the information we have concerns future possible returns and their probabilities.

EXPECTED RETURN

We start with a straightforward case. Consider a single period of time—say a year. We have two stocks, L and U, which have the following characteristics: Stock L is expected to have a return of 25 percent in the coming year. Stock U is expected to have a return of 20 percent for the same period.

In a situation like this, if all investors agreed on the expected returns, why would anyone want to hold Stock U? After all, why invest in one stock when the expectation is that another will do better? Clearly, the answer must depend on the risk of the two investments. The return on Stock L, although it is *expected* to be 25 percent, could actually turn out to be higher or lower.

For example, suppose the economy booms. In this case, we think Stock L will have a 70 percent return. If the economy enters a recession, we think the return will be −20 percent. In this case, we say that there are two *states of the economy*, which means that these are the only two possible situations. This setup is oversimplified, of course, but it allows us to illustrate some key ideas without a lot of computation.

Suppose we think a boom and a recession are equally likely to happen, for a 50–50 chance of each. Table 13.1 illustrates the basic information we have described and some additional information about Stock U. Notice that Stock U earns 30 percent if there is a recession and 10 percent if there is a boom.

Obviously, if you buy one of these stocks, say Stock U, what you earn in any particular year depends on what the economy does during that year. However, suppose the probabilities stay the same through time. If you hold Stock U for a number of years, you'll earn 30 percent about half the time and 10 percent the other half. In this case, we say that your **expected return** on Stock U, $E(R_U)$, is 20 percent:

$$E(R_U) = .50 \times 30\% + .50 \times 10\% = 20\%$$

In other words, you should expect to earn 20 percent from this stock, on average.

For Stock L, the probabilities are the same, but the possible returns are different. Here, we lose 20 percent half the time, and we gain 70 percent the other half. The expected return on L, $E(R_L)$, is thus 25 percent:

$$E(R_L) = .50 \times -20\% + .50 \times 70\% = 25\%$$

13.1 ✗

expected return
The return on a risky asset expected in the future.

TABLE 13.1

States of the Economy and Stock Returns

State of Economy	Probability of State of Economy	Rate of Return If State Occurs	
		Stock L	Stock U
Recession	.50	−20%	30%
Boom	.50	70	10
	1.00		

TABLE 13.2

Calculation of Expected Return

(1) State of Economy	(2) Probability of State of Economy	Stock L		Stock U	
		(3) Rate of Return If State Occurs	(4) Product (2) × (3)	(5) Rate of Return If State Occurs	(6) Product (2) × (5)
Recession	.50	−.20	−.10	.30	.15
Boom	.50	.70	.35	.10	.05
	1.00		$E(R_L) = .25 = 25\%$		$E(R_U) = .20 = 20\%$

Table 13.2 illustrates these calculations.

In our previous chapter, we defined the risk premium as the difference between the return on a risky investment and that on a risk-free investment, and we calculated the historical risk premiums on some different investments. Using our projected returns, we can calculate the *projected,* or *expected, risk premium* as the difference between the expected return on a risky investment and the certain return on a risk-free investment.

For example, suppose risk-free investments are currently offering 8 percent. We will say that the risk-free rate, which we label as R_f, is 8 percent. Given this, what is the projected risk premium on Stock U? On Stock L? Because the expected return on Stock U, $E(R_U)$, is 20 percent, the projected risk premium is:

$$\text{Risk premium} = \text{Expected return} - \text{Risk-free rate} \qquad [13.1]$$
$$= E(R_U) - R_f$$
$$= 20\% - 8\%$$
$$= 12\%$$

Similarly, the risk premium on Stock L is $25\% - 8\% = 17\%$.

In general, the expected return on a security or other asset is simply equal to the sum of the possible returns multiplied by their probabilities. So, if we had 100 possible returns, we would multiply each one by its probability and add up the results. The result would be the expected return. The risk premium would then be the difference between this expected return and the risk-free rate.

EXAMPLE 13.1	**Unequal Probabilities**

Look again at Tables 13.1 and 13.2. Suppose you think a boom will occur only 20 percent of the time instead of 50 percent. What are the expected returns on Stocks U and L in this case? If the risk-free rate is 10 percent, what are the risk premiums?

The first thing to notice is that a recession must occur 80 percent of the time (1 − .20 = .80) because there are only two possibilities. With this in mind, we see that Stock U has a 30 percent return in 80 percent of the years and a 10 percent return in 20 percent of the years. To calculate the expected return, we again just multiply the possibilities by the probabilities and add up the results:

$$E(R_U) = .80 \times 30\% + .20 \times 10\% = 26\%$$

Table 13.3 summarizes the calculations for both stocks. Notice that the expected return on L is −2 percent.

The risk premium for Stock U is 26% − 10% = 16% in this case. The risk premium for Stock L is negative: −2% − 10% = −12%. This is a little odd; but, for reasons we discuss later, it is not impossible.

(1) State of Economy	(2) Probability of State of Economy	Stock L		Stock U	
		(3) Rate of Return If State Occurs	(4) Product (2) × (3)	(5) Rate of Return If State Occurs	(6) Product (2) × (5)
Recession	.80	−.20	−.16	.30	.24
Boom	.20	.70	.14	.10	.02
			$E(R_L) = -.02 = -2\%$		$E(R_U) = .26 = 26\%$

TABLE 13.3

Calculation of Expected Return

CALCULATING THE VARIANCE

To calculate the variances of the returns on our two stocks, we first determine the squared deviations from the expected return. We then multiply each possible squared deviation by its probability. We add these up, and the result is the variance. The standard deviation, as always, is the square root of the variance.

To illustrate, let us return to the Stock U we originally discussed, which has an expected return of $E(R_U) = 20\%$. In a given year, it will actually return either 30 percent or 10 percent. The possible deviations are thus $30\% - 20\% = 10\%$ and $10\% - 20\% = -10\%$. In this case, the variance is:

$$\text{Variance} = \sigma^2 = .50 \times (10\%)^2 + .50 \times (-10\%)^2 = .01$$

The standard deviation is the square root of this:

$$\text{Standard deviation} = \sigma = \sqrt{.01} = .10 = 10\%$$

Table 13.4 summarizes these calculations for both stocks. Notice that Stock L has a much larger variance.

When we put the expected return and variability information for our two stocks together, we have the following:

	Stock L	Stock U
Expected return, E(R)	25%	20%
Variance, σ^2	.2025	.0100
Standard deviation, σ	45%	10%

Stock L has a higher expected return, but U has less risk. You could get a 70 percent return on your investment in L, but you could also lose 20 percent. Notice that an investment in U will always pay at least 10 percent.

Which of these two stocks should you buy? We can't really say; it depends on your personal preferences. We can be reasonably sure that some investors would prefer L to U and some would prefer U to L.

You've probably noticed that the way we have calculated expected returns and variances here is somewhat different from the way we did it in the last chapter. The reason is that, in Chapter 12, we were examining actual historical returns, so we estimated the average return and the variance based on some actual events. Here, we have projected *future* returns and their associated probabilities, so this is the information with which we must work.

TABLE 13.4

Calculation of Variance

(1) State of Economy	(2) Probability of State of Economy	(3) Return Deviation from Expected Return	(4) Squared Return Deviation from Expected Return	(5) Product (2) × (4)
Stock L				
Recession	.50	$-.20 - .25 = -.45$	$-.45^2 = .2025$	.10125
Boom	.50	$.70 - .25 = .45$	$.45^2 = .2025$	.10125
				$\sigma_L^2 = .20250$
Stock U				
Recession	.50	$.30 - .20 = .10$	$.10^2 = .01$	.005
Boom	.50	$.10 - .20 = -.10$	$-.10^2 = .01$	.005
				$\sigma_U^2 = .010$

EXAMPLE 13.2   **More Unequal Probabilities**

Going back to Example 13.1, what are the variances on the two stocks once we have unequal probabilities? The standard deviations?

We can summarize the needed calculations as follows:

(1) State of Economy	(2) Probability of State of Economy	(3) Return Deviation from Expected Return	(4) Squared Return Deviation from Expected Return	(5) Product (2) × (4)
Stock L				
Recession	.80	$-.20 - (-.02) = -.18$	.0324	.02592
Boom	.20	$.70 - (-.02) = .72$	.5184	.10368
				$\sigma_L^2 = .12960$
Stock U				
Recession	.80	$.30 - .26 = .04$	.0016	.00128
Boom	.20	$.10 - .26 = -.16$	.0256	.00512
				$\sigma_U^2 = .00640$

Based on these calculations, the standard deviation for L is $\sigma_L = \sqrt{.1296} = .36 = 36\%$. The standard deviation for U is much smaller: $\sigma_U = \sqrt{.0064} = .08$ or 8%.

Concept Questions

13.1a How do we calculate the expected return on a security?

13.1b In words, how do we calculate the variance of the expected return?

---

portfolio

A group of assets such as stocks and bonds held by an investor.

13.2 Portfolios

Thus far in this chapter, we have concentrated on individual assets considered separately. However, most investors actually hold a **portfolio** of assets. All we mean by this is that investors tend to own more than just a single stock, bond, or other asset. Given that this is so, portfolio return and portfolio risk are of obvious relevance. Accordingly, we now discuss portfolio expected returns and variances.

(1) State of Economy	(2) Probability of State of Economy	(3) Portfolio Return If State Occurs	(4) Product (2) × (3)
Recession	.50	.50 × − 20% + .50 × 30% = 5%	.025
Boom	.50	.50 × 70% + .50 × 10% = 40%	.200
			$E(R_p)$ = .225 = 22.5%

TABLE 13.5

Expected Return on an Equally Weighted Portfolio of Stock L and Stock U

PORTFOLIO WEIGHTS

There are many equivalent ways of describing a portfolio. The most convenient approach is to list the percentage of the total portfolio's value that is invested in each portfolio asset. We call these percentages the **portfolio weights**.

For example, if we have $50 in one asset and $150 in another, our total portfolio is worth $200. The percentage of our portfolio in the first asset is $50/$200 = .25. The percentage of our portfolio in the second asset is $150/$200, or .75. Our portfolio weights are thus .25 and .75. Notice that the weights have to add up to 1.00 because all of our money is invested somewhere.[1]

portfolio weight
The percentage of a portfolio's total value that is invested in a particular asset.

PORTFOLIO EXPECTED RETURNS

Let's go back to Stocks L and U. You put half your money in each. The portfolio weights are obviously .50 and .50. What is the pattern of returns on this portfolio? The expected return?

To answer these questions, suppose the economy actually enters a recession. In this case, half your money (the half in L) loses 20 percent. The other half (the half in U) gains 30 percent. Your portfolio return, R_p, in a recession is thus:

$$R_p = .50 \times -20\% + .50 \times 30\% = 5\%$$

Table 13.5 summarizes the remaining calculations. Notice that when a boom occurs, your portfolio will return 40 percent:

$$R_p = .50 \times 70\% + .50 \times 10\% = 40\%$$

As indicated in Table 13.5, the expected return on your portfolio, $E(R_p)$, is 22.5 percent.

We can save ourselves some work by calculating the expected return more directly. Given these portfolio weights, we could have reasoned that we expect half of our money to earn 25 percent (the half in L) and half of our money to earn 20 percent (the half in U). Our portfolio expected return is thus:

$$E(R_p) = .50 \times E(R_L) + .50 \times E(R_U)$$
$$= .50 \times 25\% + .50 \times 20\%$$
$$= 22.5\%$$

Want more information about investing? Visit www.thestreet.com.

This is the same portfolio expected return we calculated previously.

This method of calculating the expected return on a portfolio works no matter how many assets there are in the portfolio. Suppose we had n assets in our portfolio, where n is any number. If we let x_i stand for the percentage of our money in Asset i, then the expected return would be:

$$E(R_p) = x_1 \times E(R_1) + x_2 \times E(R_2) + \cdots + x_n \times E(R_n) \qquad \textbf{[13.2]}$$

---

[1]Some of it could be in cash, of course, but we would then just consider the cash to be one of the portfolio assets.

This says that the expected return on a portfolio is a straightforward combination of the expected returns on the assets in that portfolio. This seems somewhat obvious; but, as we will examine next, the obvious approach is not always the right one.

EXAMPLE 13.3   **Portfolio Expected Return**

Suppose we have the following projections for three stocks:

State of Economy	Probability of State of Economy	Returns If State Occurs		
		Stock A	Stock B	Stock C
Boom	.40	10%	15%	20%
Bust	.60	8	4	0

We want to calculate portfolio expected returns in two cases. First, what would be the expected return on a portfolio with equal amounts invested in each of the three stocks? Second, what would be the expected return if half of the portfolio were in A, with the remainder equally divided between B and C?

Based on what we've learned from our earlier discussions, we can determine that the expected returns on the individual stocks are (check these for practice):

$E(R_A) = 8.8\%$
$E(R_B) = 8.4\%$
$E(R_C) = 8.0\%$

If a portfolio has equal investments in each asset, the portfolio weights are all the same. Such a portfolio is said to be *equally weighted*. Because there are three stocks in this case, the weights are all equal to ⅓. The portfolio expected return is thus:

$E(R_P) = (1/3) \times 8.8\% + (1/3) \times 8.4\% + (1/3) \times 8\% = 8.4\%$

In the second case, verify that the portfolio expected return is 8.5 percent.

PORTFOLIO VARIANCE

From our earlier discussion, the expected return on a portfolio that contains equal investments in Stocks U and L is 22.5 percent. What is the standard deviation of return on this portfolio? Simple intuition might suggest that because half of the money has a standard deviation of 45 percent and the other half has a standard deviation of 10 percent, the portfolio's standard deviation might be calculated as:

$\sigma_P = .50 \times 45\% + .50 \times 10\% = 27.5\%$

Unfortunately, this approach is completely incorrect!

Let's see what the standard deviation really is. Table 13.6 summarizes the relevant calculations. As we see, the portfolio's variance is about .031, and its standard deviation is less than we thought—it's only 17.5 percent. What is illustrated here is that the variance on a portfolio is not generally a simple combination of the variances of the assets in the portfolio.

We can illustrate this point a little more dramatically by considering a slightly different set of portfolio weights. Suppose we put 2/11 (about 18 percent) in L and the other 9/11 (about 82 percent) in U. If a recession occurs, this portfolio will have a return of:

$R_P = (2/11) \times -20\% + (9/11) \times 30\% = 20.91\%$

(1) State of Economy	(2) Probability of State of Economy	(3) Portfolio Return If State Occurs	(4) Squared Deviation from Expected Return	(5) Product (2) × (4)
Recession	.50	5%	$(.05 - .225)^2 = .030625$	.0153125
Boom	.50	40	$(.40 - .225)^2 = .030625$	.0153125
			$\sigma_P^2 = .030625$	
			$\sigma_P = \sqrt{.030625} = 17.5\%$	

TABLE 13.6

Variance on an Equally Weighted Portfolio of Stock L and Stock U

If a boom occurs, this portfolio will have a return of:

$$R_P = (2/11) \times 70\% + (9/11) \times 10\% = 20.91\%$$

Notice that the return is the same no matter what happens. No further calculations are needed: This portfolio has a zero variance. Apparently, combining assets into portfolios can substantially alter the risks faced by the investor. This is a crucial observation, and we will begin to explore its implications in the next section.

Portfolio Variance and Standard Deviation   **EXAMPLE 13.4**

In Example 13.3, what are the standard deviations on the two portfolios? To answer, we first have to calculate the portfolio returns in the two states. We will work with the second portfolio, which has 50 percent in Stock A and 25 percent in each of Stocks B and C. The relevant calculations can be summarized as follows:

State of Economy	Probability of State of Economy	Rate of Return If State Occurs			
		Stock A	Stock B	Stock C	Portfolio
Boom	.40	10%	15%	20%	13.75%
Bust	.60	8	4	0	5.00

The portfolio return when the economy booms is calculated as:

$$E(R_P) = .50 \times 10\% + .25 \times 15\% + .25 \times 20\% = 13.75\%$$

The return when the economy goes bust is calculated the same way. The expected return on the portfolio is 8.5 percent. The variance is thus:

$$\sigma_P^2 = .40 \times (.1375 - .085)^2 + .60 \times (.05 - .085)^2$$
$$= .0018375$$

The standard deviation is thus about 4.3 percent. For our equally weighted portfolio, check to see that the standard deviation is about 5.4 percent.

Concept Questions

13.2a What is a portfolio weight?

13.2b How do we calculate the expected return on a portfolio?

13.2c Is there a simple relationship between the standard deviation on a portfolio and the standard deviations of the assets in the portfolio?

13.3 Announcements, Surprises, and Expected Returns

Now that we know how to construct portfolios and evaluate their returns, we begin to describe more carefully the risks and returns associated with individual securities. Thus far, we have measured volatility by looking at the difference between the actual return on an asset or portfolio, R, and the expected return, $E(R)$. We now look at why those deviations exist.

EXPECTED AND UNEXPECTED RETURNS

To begin, for concreteness, we consider the return on the stock of a company called Flyers. What will determine this stock's return in, say, the coming year?

The return on any stock traded in a financial market is composed of two parts. First, the normal, or expected, return from the stock is the part of the return that shareholders in the market predict or expect. This return depends on the information shareholders have that bears on the stock, and it is based on the market's understanding today of the important factors that will influence the stock in the coming year.

The second part of the return on the stock is the uncertain, or risky, part. This is the portion that comes from unexpected information revealed within the year. A list of all possible sources of such information would be endless, but here are a few examples:

News about Flyers research

Government figures released on gross domestic product (GDP)

The results from the latest arms control talks

The news that Flyers sales figures are higher than expected

A sudden, unexpected drop in interest rates

Based on this discussion, one way to express the return on Flyers stock in the coming year would be:

$$\text{Total return} = \text{Expected return} + \text{Unexpected return}$$
$$R = E(R) + U$$

[13.3]

where R stands for the actual total return in the year, $E(R)$ stands for the expected part of the return, and U stands for the unexpected part of the return. What this says is that the actual return, R, differs from the expected return, $E(R)$, because of surprises that occur during the year. In any given year, the unexpected return will be positive or negative; but, through time, the average value of U will be zero. This simply means that on average, the actual return equals the expected return.

ANNOUNCEMENTS AND NEWS

We need to be careful when we talk about the effect of news items on the return. For example, suppose Flyers's business is such that the company prospers when GDP grows at a relatively high rate and suffers when GDP is relatively stagnant. In this case, in deciding what return to expect this year from owning stock in Flyers, shareholders either implicitly or explicitly must think about what GDP is likely to be for the year.

When the government actually announces GDP figures for the year, what will happen to the value of Flyers's stock? Obviously, the answer depends on what figure is released. More to the point, however, the impact depends on how much of that figure is *new* information.

At the beginning of the year, market participants will have some idea or forecast of what the yearly GDP will be. To the extent that shareholders have predicted GDP, that prediction will already be factored into the expected part of the return on the stock, E(R). On the other hand, if the announced GDP is a surprise, the effect will be part of U, the unanticipated portion of the return. As an example, suppose shareholders in the market had forecast that the GDP increase this year would be .5 percent. If the actual announcement this year is exactly .5 percent, the same as the forecast, then the shareholders don't really learn anything, and the announcement isn't news. There will be no impact on the stock price as a result. This is like receiving confirmation of something you suspected all along; it doesn't reveal anything new.

A common way of saying that an announcement isn't news is to say that the market has already "discounted" the announcement. The use of the word *discount* here is different from the use of the term in computing present values, but the spirit is the same. When we discount a dollar in the future, we say it is worth less to us because of the time value of money. When we discount an announcement or a news item, we say that it has less of an impact on the price because the market already knew much of it.

Going back to Flyers, suppose the government announces that the actual GDP increase during the year has been 1.5 percent. Now shareholders have learned something—namely, that the increase is one percentage point higher than they had forecast. This difference between the actual result and the forecast, one percentage point in this example, is sometimes called the *innovation* or the *surprise*.

This distinction explains why what seems to be good news can actually be bad news (and vice versa). Going back to the companies we discussed in our chapter opener, even though Campbell Soup's earnings were exactly what was expected, the company was facing increased pressures for the rest of the year, and it expected to need heavy price promotions to keep its current customers. Additionally, sales of the company's more profitable condensed soups had fallen because competitors had aggressively lowered the price of ready-to-serve products.

A key idea to keep in mind about news and price changes is that news about the future is what matters. For Avis Budget, while the earnings were much lower than the market expected, the net income for that quarter was lowered dramatically due to one-time acquisition costs and early debt retirement. The company also announced that rental volume increased by 7 percent and revenue from ancillary items grew by 10 percent, both positive indications for the future. For Home Depot, the earnings announcement came on a day when the market turned sour in general. Keep this in mind as you read our next section.

To summarize, an announcement can be broken into two parts: the anticipated, or expected, part and the surprise, or innovation:

Announcement = Expected part + Surprise   **[13.4]**

The expected part of any announcement is the part of the information that the market uses to form the expectation, E(R), of the return on the stock. The surprise is the news that influences the unanticipated return on the stock, U.

Our discussion of market efficiency in the previous chapter bears on this discussion. We are assuming that relevant information known today is already reflected in the expected return. This is identical to saying that the current price reflects relevant publicly available information. We are thus implicitly assuming that markets are at least reasonably efficient in the semistrong form.

Henceforth, when we speak of news, we will mean the surprise part of an announcement and not the portion that the market has expected and therefore already discounted.

Concept Questions

13.3a What are the two basic parts of a return?

13.3b Under what conditions will a company's announcement have no effect on common stock prices?

13.4 Risk: Systematic and Unsystematic

The unanticipated part of the return, that portion resulting from surprises, is the true risk of any investment. After all, if we always receive exactly what we expect, then the investment is perfectly predictable and, by definition, risk-free. In other words, the risk of owning an asset comes from surprises—unanticipated events.

There are important differences, though, among various sources of risk. Look back at our previous list of news stories. Some of these stories are directed specifically at Flyers, and some are more general. Which of the news items are of specific importance to Flyers?

Announcements about interest rates or GDP are clearly important for nearly all companies, whereas news about Flyers's president, its research, or its sales is of specific interest to Flyers. We will distinguish between these two types of events because, as we will see, they have different implications.

SYSTEMATIC AND UNSYSTEMATIC RISK

systematic risk
A risk that influences a large number of assets. Also, market risk.

unsystematic risk
A risk that affects at most a small number of assets. Also, unique or asset-specific risk.

The first type of surprise—the one that affects many assets—we will label **systematic risk**. A systematic risk is one that influences a large number of assets, each to a greater or lesser extent. Because systematic risks have marketwide effects, they are sometimes called *market risks*.

The second type of surprise we will call **unsystematic risk**. An unsystematic risk is one that affects a single asset or a small group of assets. Because these risks are unique to individual companies or assets, they are sometimes called *unique* or *asset-specific risks*. We will use these terms interchangeably.

As we have seen, uncertainties about general economic conditions (such as GDP, interest rates, or inflation) are examples of systematic risks. These conditions affect nearly all companies to some degree. An unanticipated increase, or surprise, in inflation, for example, affects wages and the costs of the supplies that companies buy; it affects the value of the assets that companies own; and it affects the prices at which companies sell their products. Forces such as these, to which all companies are susceptible, are the essence of systematic risk.

In contrast, the announcement of an oil strike by a company will primarily affect that company and, perhaps, a few others (such as primary competitors and suppliers). It is unlikely to have much of an effect on the world oil market, however, or on the affairs of companies not in the oil business, so this is an unsystematic event.

SYSTEMATIC AND UNSYSTEMATIC COMPONENTS OF RETURN

The distinction between a systematic risk and an unsystematic risk is never really as exact as we make it out to be. Even the most narrow and peculiar bit of news about a company ripples through the economy. This is true because every enterprise, no matter how tiny, is a part of the economy. It's like the tale of a kingdom that was lost because one horse lost a shoe. This is mostly hairsplitting, however. Some risks are clearly much more general than others. We'll see some evidence on this point in just a moment.

The distinction between the types of risk allows us to break down the surprise portion, U, of the return on the Flyers stock into two parts. Earlier, we had the actual return broken down into its expected and surprise components:

$$R = E(R) + U$$

We now recognize that the total surprise component for Flyers, U, has a systematic and an unsystematic component, so:

$$R = E(R) + \text{Systematic portion} + \text{Unsystematic portion} \qquad \textbf{[13.5]}$$

Because it is traditional, we will use the Greek letter epsilon, ϵ, to stand for the unsystematic portion. Because systematic risks are often called market risks, we will use the letter m to stand for the systematic part of the surprise. With these symbols, we can rewrite the formula for the total return:

$$R = E(R) + U$$
$$= E(R) + m + \epsilon$$

The important thing about the way we have broken down the total surprise, U, is that the unsystematic portion, ϵ, is more or less unique to Flyers. For this reason, it is unrelated to the unsystematic portion of return on most other assets. To see why this is important, we need to return to the subject of portfolio risk.

Concept Questions

13.4a What are the two basic types of risk?
13.4b What is the distinction between the two types of risk?

Diversification and Portfolio Risk

13.5

We've seen earlier that portfolio risks can, in principle, be quite different from the risks of the assets that make up the portfolio. We now look more closely at the riskiness of an individual asset versus the risk of a portfolio of many different assets. We will once again examine some market history to get an idea of what happens with actual investments in U.S. capital markets.

For more about risk and diversification, visit www.investopedia. com/university.

THE EFFECT OF DIVERSIFICATION: ANOTHER LESSON FROM MARKET HISTORY

In our previous chapter, we saw that the standard deviation of the annual return on a portfolio of 500 large common stocks has historically been about 20 percent per year. Does this mean that the standard deviation of the annual return on a typical stock in that group of 500 is about 20 percent? As you might suspect by now, the answer is no. This is an extremely important observation.

To illustrate the relationship between portfolio size and portfolio risk, Table 13.7 illustrates typical average annual standard deviations for equally weighted portfolios that contain different numbers of randomly selected NYSE securities.

In Column 2 of Table 13.7, we see that the standard deviation for a "portfolio" of one security is about 49 percent. What this means is that if you randomly selected a single NYSE

TABLE 13.7

Standard Deviations of
Annual Portfolio Returns

(1) Number of Stocks in Portfolio	(2) Average Standard Deviation of Annual Portfolio Returns	(3) Ratio of Portfolio Standard Deviation to Standard Deviation of a Single Stock
1	49.24%	1.00
2	37.36	.76
4	29.69	.60
6	26.64	.54
8	24.98	.51
10	23.93	.49
20	21.68	.44
30	20.87	.42
40	20.46	.42
50	20.20	.41
100	19.69	.40
200	19.42	.39
300	19.34	.39
400	19.29	.39
500	19.27	.39
1,000	19.21	.39

These figures are from Table 1 in M. Statman, "How Many Stocks Make a Diversified Portfolio?" *Journal of Financial and Quantitative Analysis* 22 (September 1987), pp. 353–64. They were derived from E.J. Elton and M.J. Gruber, "Risk Reduction and Portfolio Size: An Analytic Solution," *Journal of Business* 50 (October 1977), pp. 415–37.

stock and put all your money into it, your standard deviation of return would typically be a substantial 49 percent per year. If you were to randomly select two stocks and invest half your money in each, your standard deviation would be about 37 percent on average, and so on.

The important thing to notice in Table 13.7 is that the standard deviation declines as the number of securities is increased. By the time we have 100 randomly chosen stocks, the portfolio's standard deviation has declined by about 60 percent, from 49 percent to about 20 percent. With 500 securities, the standard deviation is 19.27 percent, similar to the 20 percent we saw in our previous chapter for the large common stock portfolio. The small difference exists because the portfolio securities and time periods examined are not identical.

THE PRINCIPLE OF DIVERSIFICATION

Figure 13.1 illustrates the point we've been discussing. What we have plotted is the standard deviation of return versus the number of stocks in the portfolio. Notice in Figure 13.1 that the benefit in terms of risk reduction from adding securities drops off as we add more and more. By the time we have 10 securities, most of the effect is already realized; and by the time we get to 30 or so, there is little remaining benefit.

Figure 13.1 illustrates two key points. First, some of the riskiness associated with individual assets can be eliminated by forming portfolios. The process of spreading an investment across assets (and thereby forming a portfolio) is called *diversification*. The **principle of diversification** tells us that spreading an investment across many assets will eliminate some of the risk. The blue shaded area in Figure 13.1, labeled "diversifiable risk," is the part that can be eliminated by diversification.

principle of diversification

Spreading an investment across a number of assets will eliminate some, but not all, of the risk.

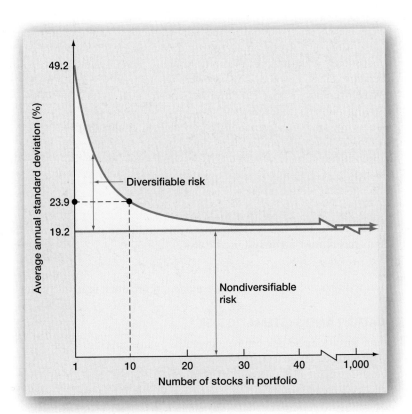

FIGURE 13.1

Portfolio Diversification

The second point is equally important. There is a minimum level of risk that cannot be eliminated simply by diversifying. This minimum level is labeled "nondiversifiable risk" in Figure 13.1. Taken together, these two points are another important lesson from capital market history: Diversification reduces risk, but only up to a point. Put another way, some risk is diversifiable and some is not.

To give a recent example of the impact of diversification, the Dow Jones Industrial Average (DJIA), which is a widely followed stock market index of 30 large, well-known U.S. stocks, was up about 22.7 percent in 2010. As we saw in our previous chapter, this gain represents a good year for a portfolio of large-cap stocks. The biggest individual winners for the year were Caterpillar (up a whopping 65 percent), DuPont (up 48 percent), and McDonald's (up 23 percent). But not all 30 stocks were up: The losers included Hewlett-Packard (down 18 percent), Bank of America (down 11 percent), and Alcoa (down 4 percent). Again, the lesson is clear: Diversification reduces exposure to extreme outcomes, both good and bad.

DIVERSIFICATION AND UNSYSTEMATIC RISK

From our discussion of portfolio risk, we know that some of the risk associated with individual assets can be diversified away and some cannot. We are left with an obvious question: Why is this so? It turns out that the answer hinges on the distinction we made earlier between systematic and unsystematic risk.

By definition, an unsystematic risk is one that is particular to a single asset or, at most, a small group. For example, if the asset under consideration is stock in a single company, the discovery of positive NPV projects such as successful new products and innovative cost savings will tend to increase the value of the stock. Unanticipated lawsuits, industrial accidents, strikes, and similar events will tend to decrease future cash flows and thereby reduce share values.

Here is the important observation: If we held only a single stock, the value of our investment would fluctuate because of company-specific events. If we hold a large portfolio, on the other hand, some of the stocks in the portfolio will go up in value because of positive company-specific events and some will go down in value because of negative events. The net effect on the overall value of the portfolio will be relatively small, however, because these effects will tend to cancel each other out.

Now we see why some of the variability associated with individual assets is eliminated by diversification. When we combine assets into portfolios, the unique, or unsystematic, events—both positive and negative—tend to "wash out" once we have more than just a few assets.

This is an important point that bears repeating:

> **Unsystematic risk is essentially eliminated by diversification, so a portfolio with many assets has almost no unsystematic risk.**

In fact, the terms *diversifiable risk* and *unsystematic risk* are often used interchangeably.

DIVERSIFICATION AND SYSTEMATIC RISK

We've seen that unsystematic risk can be eliminated by diversifying. What about systematic risk? Can it also be eliminated by diversification? The answer is no because, by definition, a systematic risk affects almost all assets to some degree. As a result, no matter how many assets we put into a portfolio, the systematic risk doesn't go away. Thus, for obvious reasons, the terms *systematic risk* and *nondiversifiable risk* are used interchangeably.

Because we have introduced so many different terms, it is useful to summarize our discussion before moving on. What we have seen is that the total risk of an investment, as measured by the standard deviation of its return, can be written as:

$$\text{Total risk} = \text{Systematic risk} + \text{Unsystematic risk} \qquad [13.6]$$

Systematic risk is also called *nondiversifiable risk* or *market risk.* Unsystematic risk is also called *diversifiable risk, unique risk,* or *asset-specific risk.* For a well-diversified portfolio, the unsystematic risk is negligible. For such a portfolio, essentially all of the risk is systematic.

Concept Questions

13.5a What happens to the standard deviation of return for a portfolio if we increase the number of securities in the portfolio?

13.5b What is the principle of diversification?

13.5c Why is some risk diversifiable? Why is some risk not diversifiable?

13.5d Why can't systematic risk be diversified away?

13.6 Systematic Risk and Beta

The question that we now begin to address is this: What determines the size of the risk premium on a risky asset? Put another way, why do some assets have a larger risk premium than other assets? The answer to these questions, as we discuss next, is also based on the distinction between systematic and unsystematic risk.

THE SYSTEMATIC RISK PRINCIPLE

Thus far, we've seen that the total risk associated with an asset can be decomposed into two components: systematic and unsystematic risk. We have also seen that unsystematic risk can be essentially eliminated by diversification. The systematic risk present in an asset, on the other hand, cannot be eliminated by diversification.

Based on our study of capital market history, we know that there is a reward, on average, for bearing risk. However, we now need to be more precise about what we mean by risk. The **systematic risk principle** states that the reward for bearing risk depends only on the systematic risk of an investment. The underlying rationale for this principle is straightforward: Because unsystematic risk can be eliminated at virtually no cost (by diversifying), there is no reward for bearing it. Put another way, the market does not reward risks that are borne unnecessarily.

The systematic risk principle has a remarkable and very important implication:

> **The expected return on an asset depends only on that asset's systematic risk.**

There is an obvious corollary to this principle: No matter how much total risk an asset has, only the systematic portion is relevant in determining the expected return (and the risk premium) on that asset.

MEASURING SYSTEMATIC RISK

Because systematic risk is the crucial determinant of an asset's expected return, we need some way of measuring the level of systematic risk for different investments. The specific measure we will use is called the **beta coefficient**, for which we will use the Greek symbol β. A beta coefficient, or beta for short, tells us how much systematic risk a particular asset has relative to an average asset. By definition, an average asset has a beta of 1.0 relative to itself. An asset with a beta of .50, therefore, has half as much systematic risk as an average asset; an asset with a beta of 2.0 has twice as much.

Table 13.8 contains the estimated beta coefficients for the stocks of some well-known companies. The range of betas in Table 13.8 is typical for stocks of large U.S. corporations. Betas outside this range occur, but they are less common.

The important thing to remember is that the expected return, and thus the risk premium, of an asset depends only on its systematic risk. Because assets with larger betas have greater systematic risks, they will have greater expected returns. Thus, from Table 13.8, an investor who buys stock in Coca-Cola, with a beta of .58, should expect to earn less, on average, than an investor who buys stock in eBay, with a beta of about 1.52.

systematic risk principle
The expected return on a risky asset depends only on that asset's systematic risk.

For more about beta, see www.investools.com *and* moneycentral.msn.com.

beta coefficient
The amount of systematic risk present in a particular risky asset relative to that in an average risky asset.

	Beta Coefficient (β_i)
Kroger Co.	.29
Coca-Cola	.58
3M	.82
Microsoft	1.00
Google	1.08
eBay	1.52
Abercrombie & Fitch	1.68
Bon-Ton Stores, Inc.	2.74

TABLE 13.8

Beta Coefficients for Selected Companies

SOURCE: Yahoo! Finance 2011 (*finance.yahoo.com*).

One cautionary note is in order: Not all betas are created equal. Different providers use somewhat different methods for estimating betas, and significant differences sometimes occur. As a result, it is a good idea to look at several sources. See our nearby *Work the Web* box for more about beta.

WORK THE WEB

You can find beta estimates at many sites on the Web. One of the best is finance.yahoo.com. Here is a snapshot of the "Key Statistics" screen for cosmetics company Revlon (REV):

Stock Price History	
Beta:	2.12
52-Week Change[3]:	-6.50%
S&P500 52-Week Change[3]:	20.18%
52-Week High (May 3, 2010)[3]:	18.79
52-Week Low (Dec 21, 2010)[3]:	9.22
50-Day Moving Average[3]:	10.32
200-Day Moving Average[3]:	11.13

Management Effectiveness	
Return on Assets (ttm):	15.19%
Return on Equity (ttm):	N/A

Balance Sheet	
Total Cash (mrq):	40.50M
Total Cash Per Share (mrq):	0.78
Total Debt (mrq):	1.22B
Total Debt/Equity (mrq):	N/A
Current Ratio (mrq):	1.27
Book Value Per Share (mrq):	-19.11

The reported beta for Revlon is 2.12, which means that Revlon has about twice the systematic risk of a typical stock. You would expect that the company is very risky, and looking at the other numbers, we agree. Revlon's ROA is 15.19 percent, a relatively good number, but the ROE is not reported. Why? If you look at the book value per share, it is negative. In this case, the larger the loss, the larger the ROE! That's not good. Given this, Revlon appears to be a good candidate for a high beta.

Questions

1. As we mentioned, the book value per share of stock for Revlon is negative. What is the current book value per share reported on this website?
2. What growth rate are analysts projecting for Revlon? How does this growth rate compare to the industry?

	EXAMPLE 13.5
Total Risk versus Beta	

Consider the following information about two securities. Which has greater total risk? Which has greater systematic risk? Greater unsystematic risk? Which asset will have a higher risk premium?

	Standard Deviation	Beta
Security A	40%	.50
Security B	20	1.50

From our discussion in this section, Security A has greater total risk, but it has substantially less systematic risk. Because total risk is the sum of systematic and unsystematic risk, Security A must have greater unsystematic risk. Finally, from the systematic risk principle, Security B will have a higher risk premium and a greater expected return, despite the fact that it has less total risk.

PORTFOLIO BETAS

Earlier, we saw that the riskiness of a portfolio has no simple relationship to the risks of the assets in the portfolio. A portfolio beta, however, can be calculated, just like a portfolio expected return. For example, looking again at Table 13.8, suppose you put half of your money in Google and half in Coca-Cola. What would the beta of this combination be? Because Google has a beta of 1.08 and Coca-Cola has a beta of .58, the portfolio's beta, β_p, would be:

$$\beta_p = .50 \times \beta_{Google} + .50 \times \beta_{Coca\text{-}Cola}$$
$$= .50 \times 1.08 + .50 \times .58$$
$$= .83$$

In general, if we had many assets in a portfolio, we would multiply each asset's beta by its portfolio weight and then add the results to get the portfolio's beta.

	EXAMPLE 13.6
Portfolio Betas	

Suppose we had the following investments:

Security	Amount Invested	Expected Return	Beta
Stock A	$1,000	8%	.80
Stock B	2,000	12	.95
Stock C	3,000	15	1.10
Stock D	4,000	18	1.40

What is the expected return on this portfolio? What is the beta of this portfolio? Does this portfolio have more or less systematic risk than an average asset?

(continued)

To answer, we first have to calculate the portfolio weights. Notice that the total amount invested is $10,000. Of this, $1,000/10,000 = 10% is invested in Stock A. Similarly, 20 percent is invested in Stock B, 30 percent is invested in Stock C, and 40 percent is invested in Stock D. The expected return, $E(R_P)$, is thus:

$$E(R_P) = .10 \times E(R_A) + .20 \times E(R_B) + .30 \times E(R_C) + .40 \times E(R_D)$$
$$= .10 \times 8\% + .20 \times 12\% + .30 \times 15\% + .40 \times 18\%$$
$$= 14.9\%$$

Similarly, the portfolio beta, β_P, is:

$$\beta_P = .10 \times \beta_A + .20 \times \beta_B + .30 \times \beta_C + .40 \times \beta_D$$
$$= .10 \times .80 + .20 \times .95 + .30 \times 1.10 + .40 \times 1.40$$
$$= 1.16$$

This portfolio thus has an expected return of 14.9 percent and a beta of 1.16. Because the beta is larger than 1, this portfolio has greater systematic risk than an average asset.

Concept Questions

13.6a What is the systematic risk principle?

13.6b What does a beta coefficient measure?

13.6c True or false: The expected return on a risky asset depends on that asset's total risk. Explain.

13.6d How do you calculate a portfolio beta?

Betas are easy to find on the Web. Try finance.yahoo.com and money.cnn.com.

13.7 The Security Market Line

We're now in a position to see how risk is rewarded in the marketplace. To begin, suppose that Asset A has an expected return of $E(R_A) = 20\%$ and a beta of $\beta_A = 1.6$. Furthermore, suppose that the risk-free rate is $R_f = 8\%$. Notice that a risk-free asset, by definition, has no systematic risk (or unsystematic risk), so a risk-free asset has a beta of zero.

BETA AND THE RISK PREMIUM

Consider a portfolio made up of Asset A and a risk-free asset. We can calculate some different possible portfolio expected returns and betas by varying the percentages invested in these two assets. For example, if 25 percent of the portfolio is invested in Asset A, then the expected return is:

$$E(R_P) = .25 \times E(R_A) + (1 - .25) \times R_f$$
$$= .25 \times 20\% + .75 \times 8\%$$
$$= 11\%$$

Similarly, the beta on the portfolio, β_P, would be:

$$\beta_P = .25 \times \beta_A + (1 - .25) \times 0$$
$$= .25 \times 1.6$$
$$= .40$$

Notice that because the weights have to add up to 1, the percentage invested in the risk-free asset is equal to 1 minus the percentage invested in Asset A.

One thing that you might wonder about is whether it is possible for the percentage invested in Asset A to exceed 100 percent. The answer is yes. This can happen if the investor borrows at the risk-free rate. For example, suppose an investor has $100 and borrows an additional $50 at 8 percent, the risk-free rate. The total investment in Asset A would be $150, or 150 percent of the investor's wealth. The expected return in this case would be:

$$
\begin{aligned}
E(R_P) &= 1.50 \times E(R_A) + (1 - 1.50) \times R_f \\
&= 1.50 \times 20\% - .50 \times 8\% \\
&= 26\%
\end{aligned}
$$

The beta on the portfolio would be:

$$
\begin{aligned}
\beta_P &= 1.50 \times \beta_A + (1 - 1.50) \times 0 \\
&= 1.50 \times 1.6 \\
&= 2.4
\end{aligned}
$$

We can calculate some other possibilities, as follows:

Percentage of Portfolio in Asset A	Portfolio Expected Return	Portfolio Beta
0%	8%	.0
25	11	.4
50	14	.8
75	17	1.2
100	20	1.6
125	23	2.0
150	26	2.4

In Figure 13.2A, these portfolio expected returns are plotted against the portfolio betas. Notice that all the combinations fall on a straight line.

The Reward-to-Risk Ratio   What is the slope of the straight line in Figure 13.2A? As always, the slope of a straight line is equal to "the rise over the run." In this case, as we move out of the risk-free asset into Asset A, the beta increases from zero to 1.6 (a "run"

FIGURE 13.2A

Portfolio Expected Returns and Betas for Asset A

of 1.6). At the same time, the expected return goes from 8 percent to 20 percent, a "rise" of 12 percent. The slope of the line is thus $12\%/1.6 = 7.5\%$.

Notice that the slope of our line is just the risk premium on Asset A, $E(R_A) - R_f$, divided by Asset A's beta, β_A:

$$\text{Slope} = \frac{E(R_A) - R_f}{\beta_A}$$

$$= \frac{20\% - 8\%}{1.6} = 7.5\%$$

What this tells us is that Asset A offers a *reward-to-risk* ratio of 7.5 percent.[2] In other words, Asset A has a risk premium of 7.50 percent per "unit" of systematic risk.

The Basic Argument   Now suppose we consider a second asset, Asset B. This asset has a beta of 1.2 and an expected return of 16 percent. Which investment is better, Asset A or Asset B? You might think that, once again, we really cannot say—some investors might prefer A; some investors might prefer B. Actually, however, we can say: A is better because, as we will demonstrate, B offers inadequate compensation for its level of systematic risk, at least, relative to A.

To begin, we calculate different combinations of expected returns and betas for portfolios of Asset B and a risk-free asset, just as we did for Asset A. For example, if we put 25 percent in Asset B and the remaining 75 percent in the risk-free asset, the portfolio's expected return will be:

$$E(R_P) = .25 \times E(R_B) + (1 - .25) \times R_f$$

$$= .25 \times 16\% + .75 \times 8\%$$

$$= 10\%$$

Similarly, the beta on the portfolio, β_P, would be:

$$\beta_P = .25 \times \beta_B + (1 - .25) \times 0$$

$$= .25 \times 1.2$$

$$= .30$$

Some other possibilities are as follows:

Percentage of Portfolio in Asset B	Portfolio Expected Return	Portfolio Beta
0%	8%	.0
25	10	.3
50	12	.6
75	14	.9
100	16	1.2
125	18	1.5
150	20	1.8

When we plot these combinations of portfolio expected returns and portfolio betas in Figure 13.2B, we get a straight line just as we did for Asset A.

---

[2]This ratio is sometimes called the *Treynor index,* after one of its originators.

FIGURE 13.2B

Portfolio Expected Returns and Betas for Asset B

FIGURE 13.2C

Portfolio Expected Returns and Betas for Both Assets

The key thing to notice is that when we compare the results for Assets A and B, as in Figure 13.2C, the line describing the combinations of expected returns and betas for Asset A is higher than the one for Asset B. This tells us that for any given level of systematic risk (as measured by β), some combination of Asset A and the risk-free asset always offers a larger return. This is why we were able to state that Asset A is a better investment than Asset B.

Another way of seeing that A offers a superior return for its level of risk is to note that the slope of our line for Asset B is:

$$\text{Slope} = \frac{E(R_B) - R_f}{\beta_B}$$

$$= \frac{16\% - 8\%}{1.2} = 6.67\%$$

Thus, Asset B has a reward-to-risk ratio of 6.67 percent, which is less than the 7.5 percent offered by Asset A.

The Fundamental Result   The situation we have described for Assets A and B could not persist in a well-organized, active market, because investors would be attracted to Asset A and away from Asset B. As a result, Asset A's price would rise and Asset B's price would fall. Because prices and returns move in opposite directions, A's expected return would decline and B's would rise.

This buying and selling would continue until the two assets plotted on exactly the same line, which means they would offer the same reward for bearing risk. In other words, in an active, competitive market, we must have the situation that:

$$\frac{E(R_A) - R_f}{\beta_A} = \frac{E(R_B) - R_f}{\beta_B}$$

This is the fundamental relationship between risk and return.

Our basic argument can be extended to more than just two assets. In fact, no matter how many assets we had, we would always reach the same conclusion:

> **The reward-to-risk ratio must be the same for all the assets in the market.**

This result is really not so surprising. What it says is that, for example, if one asset has twice as much systematic risk as another asset, its risk premium will simply be twice as large.

Because all of the assets in the market must have the same reward-to-risk ratio, they all must plot on the same line. This argument is illustrated in Figure 13.3. As shown, Assets A and B plot directly on the line and thus have the same reward-to-risk ratio. If an asset plotted above the line, such as C in Figure 13.3, its price would rise and its expected return would fall until it plotted exactly on the line. Similarly, if an asset plotted below the line, such as D in Figure 13.3, its expected return would rise until it too plotted directly on the line.

The arguments we have presented apply to active, competitive, well-functioning markets. The financial markets, such as the NYSE, best meet these criteria. Other markets, such

FIGURE 13.3

Expected Returns and Systematic Risk

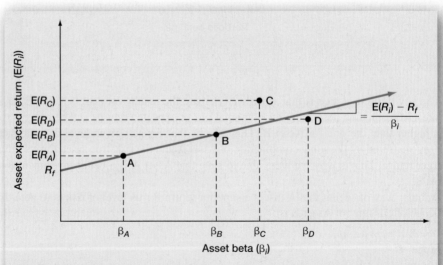

The fundamental relationship between beta and expected return is that all assets must have the same reward-to-risk ratio, $[E(R_i) - R_f]/\beta_i$. This means that they would all plot on the same straight line. Assets A and B are examples of this behavior. Asset C's expected return is too high; asset D's is too low.

as real asset markets, may or may not. For this reason, these concepts are most useful in examining financial markets. We will thus focus on such markets here. However, as we discuss in a later section, the information about risk and return gleaned from financial markets is crucial in evaluating the investments that a corporation makes in real assets.

Buy Low, Sell High

EXAMPLE 13.7

An asset is said to be *overvalued* if its price is too high given its expected return and risk. Suppose you observe the following situation:

Security	Beta	Expected Return
SWMS Co.	1.3	14%
Insec Co.	.8	10

The risk-free rate is currently 6 percent. Is one of the two securities overvalued relative to the other?

To answer, we compute the reward-to-risk ratio for both. For SWMS, this ratio is $(14\% - 6\%)/1.3 = 6.15\%$. For Insec, this ratio is 5 percent. What we conclude is that Insec offers an insufficient expected return for its level of risk, at least relative to SWMS. Because its expected return is too low, its price is too high. In other words, Insec is overvalued relative to SWMS, and we would expect to see its price fall relative to SWMS's. Notice that we could also say SWMS is undervalued relative to Insec.

THE SECURITY MARKET LINE

The line that results when we plot expected returns and beta coefficients is obviously of some importance, so it's time we gave it a name. This line, which we use to describe the relationship between systematic risk and expected return in financial markets, is usually called the **security market line (SML)**. After NPV, the SML is arguably the most important concept in modern finance.

security market line (SML)
A positively sloped straight line displaying the relationship between expected return and beta.

Market Portfolios It will be very useful to know the equation of the SML. There are many different ways we could write it, but one way is particularly common. Suppose we consider a portfolio made up of all of the assets in the market. Such a portfolio is called a market portfolio, and we will express the expected return on this market portfolio as $E(R_M)$.

Because all the assets in the market must plot on the SML, so must a market portfolio made up of those assets. To determine where it plots on the SML, we need to know the beta of the market portfolio, β_M. Because this portfolio is representative of all of the assets in the market, it must have average systematic risk. In other words, it has a beta of 1. We could therefore express the slope of the SML as:

$$\text{SML slope} = \frac{E(R_M) - R_f}{\beta_M} = \frac{E(R_M) - R_f}{1} = E(R_M) - R_f$$

The term $E(R_M) - R_f$ is often called the **market risk premium** because it is the risk premium on a market portfolio.

market risk premium
The slope of the SML—the difference between the expected return on a market portfolio and the risk-free rate.

The Capital Asset Pricing Model To finish up, if we let $E(R_i)$ and β_i stand for the expected return and beta, respectively, on any asset in the market, then we know that asset must plot on the SML. As a result, we know that its reward-to-risk ratio is the same as the overall market's:

$$\frac{E(R_i) - R_f}{\beta_i} = E(R_M) - R_f$$

If we rearrange this, then we can write the equation for the SML as:

$$E(R_i) = R_f + [E(R_M) - R_f] \times \beta_i \qquad [13.7]$$

This result is the famous **capital asset pricing model (CAPM)**.

capital asset pricing model (CAPM)
The equation of the SML showing the relationship between expected return and beta.

The CAPM shows that the expected return for a particular asset depends on three things:

1. *The pure time value of money:* As measured by the risk-free rate, R_f, this is the reward for merely waiting for your money, without taking any risk.
2. *The reward for bearing systematic risk:* As measured by the market risk premium, $E(R_M) - R_f$, this component is the reward the market offers for bearing an average amount of systematic risk in addition to waiting.
3. *The amount of systematic risk:* As measured by β_i, this is the amount of systematic risk present in a particular asset or portfolio, relative to that in an average asset.

By the way, the CAPM works for portfolios of assets just as it does for individual assets. In an earlier section, we saw how to calculate a portfolio's β. To find the expected return on a portfolio, we simply use this β in the CAPM equation.

Figure 13.4 summarizes our discussion of the SML and the CAPM. As before, we plot expected return against beta. Now we recognize that, based on the CAPM, the slope of the SML is equal to the market risk premium, $E(R_M) - R_f$.

This concludes our presentation of concepts related to the risk–return trade-off. For future reference, Table 13.9 summarizes the various concepts in the order in which we discussed them.

FIGURE 13.4

The Security Market Line (SML)

The slope of the security market line is equal to the market risk premium—that is, the reward for bearing an average amount of systematic risk. The equation describing the SML can be written:

$$E(R_i) = R_f + [E(R_M) - R_f] \times \beta_i$$

which is the capital asset pricing model (CAPM).

| Risk and Return | EXAMPLE 13.8 |

Suppose the risk-free rate is 4 percent, the market risk premium is 8.6 percent, and a particular stock has a beta of 1.3. Based on the CAPM, what is the expected return on this stock? What would the expected return be if the beta were to double?

With a beta of 1.3, the risk premium for the stock is 1.3 × 8.6%, or 11.18 percent. The risk-free rate is 4 percent, so the expected return is 15.18 percent. If the beta were to double to 2.6, the risk premium would double to 22.36 percent, so the expected return would be 26.36 percent.

TABLE 13.9

Summary of Risk and Return

I.	**Total Risk**
	The *total risk* of an investment is measured by the variance or, more commonly, the standard deviation of its return.
II.	**Total Return**
	The *total return* on an investment has two components: the expected return and the unexpected return. The unexpected return comes about because of unanticipated events. The risk from investing stems from the possibility of an unanticipated event.
III.	**Systematic and Unsystematic Risks**
	Systematic risks (also called *market risks*) are unanticipated events that affect almost all assets to some degree because the effects are economywide. *Unsystematic risks* are unanticipated events that affect single assets or small groups of assets. Unsystematic risks are also called *unique* or *asset-specific risks*.
IV.	**The Effect of Diversification**
	Some, but not all, of the risk associated with a risky investment can be eliminated by diversification. The reason is that unsystematic risks, which are unique to individual assets, tend to wash out in a large portfolio, but systematic risks, which affect all of the assets in a portfolio to some extent, do not.
V.	**The Systematic Risk Principle and Beta**
	Because unsystematic risk can be freely eliminated by diversification, the *systematic risk principle* states that the reward for bearing risk depends only on the level of systematic risk. The level of systematic risk in a particular asset, relative to the average, is given by the beta of that asset.
VI.	**The Reward-to-Risk Ratio and the Security Market Line**
	The *reward-to-risk ratio* for Asset i is the ratio of its risk premium, $E(R_i) - R_f$, to its beta, β_i: $$\frac{E(R_i) - R_f}{\beta_i}$$ In a well-functioning market, this ratio is the same for every asset. As a result, when asset expected returns are plotted against asset betas, all assets plot on the same straight line, called the *security market line* (SML).
VII.	**The Capital Asset Pricing Model**
	From the SML, the expected return on Asset i can be written: $$E(R_i) = R_f + [E(R_M) - R_f] \times \beta_i$$ This is the *capital asset pricing model* (CAPM). The expected return on a risky asset thus has three components. The first is the pure time value of money (R_f), the second is the market risk premium $[E(R_M) - R_f]$, and the third is the beta for that asset (β_i).

Concept Questions

13.7a What is the fundamental relationship between risk and return in well-functioning markets?

13.7b What is the security market line? Why must all assets plot directly on it in a well-functioning market?

13.7c What is the capital asset pricing model (CAPM)? What does it tell us about the required return on a risky investment?

13.8 The SML and the Cost of Capital: A Preview

Our goal in studying risk and return is twofold. First, risk is an extremely important consideration in almost all business decisions, so we want to discuss just what risk is and how it is rewarded in the market. Our second purpose is to learn what determines the appropriate discount rate for future cash flows. We briefly discuss this second subject now; we will discuss it in more detail in a subsequent chapter.

THE BASIC IDEA

The security market line tells us the reward for bearing risk in financial markets. At an absolute minimum, any new investment our firm undertakes must offer an expected return that is no worse than what the financial markets offer for the same risk. The reason for this is simply that our shareholders can always invest for themselves in the financial markets.

The only way we benefit our shareholders is by finding investments with expected returns that are superior to what the financial markets offer for the same risk. Such an investment will have a positive NPV. So, if we ask, "What is the appropriate discount rate?" the answer is that we should use the expected return offered in financial markets on investments with the same systematic risk.

In other words, to determine whether an investment has a positive NPV, we essentially compare the expected return on that new investment to what the financial market offers on an investment with the same beta. This is why the SML is so important: It tells us the "going rate" for bearing risk in the economy.

THE COST OF CAPITAL

cost of capital
The minimum required return on a new investment.

The appropriate discount rate on a new project is the minimum expected rate of return an investment must offer to be attractive. This minimum required return is often called the **cost of capital** associated with the investment. It is called this because the required return is what the firm must earn on its capital investment in a project just to break even. It can thus be interpreted as the opportunity cost associated with the firm's capital investment.

Notice that when we say an investment is attractive if its expected return exceeds what is offered in financial markets for investments of the same risk, we are effectively using the internal rate of return (IRR) criterion that we developed and discussed in Chapter 9. The only difference is that now we have a much better idea of what determines the required return on an investment. This understanding will be critical when we discuss cost of capital and capital structure in Part 6 of our book.

Concept Questions

13.8a If an investment has a positive NPV, would it plot above or below the SML? Why?

13.8b What is meant by the term *cost of capital?*

Summary and Conclusions

13.9

This chapter has covered the essentials of risk. Along the way, we have introduced a number of definitions and concepts. The most important of these is the security market line, or SML. The SML is important because it tells us the reward offered in financial markets for bearing risk. Once we know this, we have a benchmark against which we can compare the returns expected from real asset investments to determine if they are desirable.

Because we have covered quite a bit of ground, it's useful to summarize the basic economic logic underlying the SML as follows:

1. Based on capital market history, there is a reward for bearing risk. This reward is the risk premium on an asset.

2. The total risk associated with an asset has two parts: systematic risk and unsystematic risk. Unsystematic risk can be freely eliminated by diversification (this is the principle of diversification), so only systematic risk is rewarded. As a result, the risk premium on an asset is determined by its systematic risk. This is the systematic risk principle.

3. An asset's systematic risk, relative to the average, can be measured by its beta coefficient, β_i. The risk premium on an asset is then given by its beta coefficient multiplied by the market risk premium, $[E(R_M) - R_f] \times \beta_i$.

4. The expected return on an asset, $E(R_i)$, is equal to the risk-free rate, R_f, plus the risk premium:

$$E(R_i) = R_f + [E(R_M) - R_f] \times \beta_i$$

   This is the equation of the SML, and it is often called the capital asset pricing model (CAPM).

This chapter completes our discussion of risk and return. Now that we have a better understanding of what determines a firm's cost of capital for an investment, the next several chapters will examine more closely how firms raise the long-term capital needed for investment.

Visit us at www.mhhe.com/rwj

CONNECT TO FINANCE

If you are using *Connect™ Finance* in your course, get online to take a Practice Test, check out study tools, and find out where you need additional practice.

Can you answer the following questions?

Section 13.1 A stock is expected to earn 15 percent in a boom economy and 7 percent in a normal economy. There is a 35 percent chance the economy will boom and a 65 percent chance the economy will be normal. What is the standard deviation of these returns? (LO 13-1)

Section 13.5 Which type of risk can be eliminated through diversification? (LO 13-2)

Section 13.6 Beta is a measure of what? (LO 13-3)

Section 13.7 The slope of the security market line is equal to what? (LO 13-4)

Section 13.8 Where would a negative net present value project appear on a security market line graph? (LO 13-4)

Log on to find out!

Visit us at www.mhhe.com/rwj

CHAPTER REVIEW AND SELF-TEST PROBLEMS

13.1 Expected Return and Standard Deviation This problem will give you some practice calculating measures of prospective portfolio performance. There are two assets and three states of the economy:

State of Economy	Probability of State of Economy	Rate of Return If State Occurs	
		Stock A	Stock B
Recession	.20	−.15	.20
Normal	.50	.20	.30
Boom	.30	.60	.40

What are the expected returns and standard deviations for these two stocks?

13.2 Portfolio Risk and Return Using the information in the previous problem, suppose you have $20,000 total. If you put $15,000 in Stock A and the remainder in Stock B, what will be the expected return and standard deviation of your portfolio?

13.3 Risk and Return Suppose you observe the following situation:

Security	Beta	Expected Return
Cooley, Inc.	1.8	22.00%
Moyer Co.	1.6	20.44

If the risk-free rate is 7 percent, are these securities correctly priced? What would the risk-free rate have to be if they are correctly priced?

13.4 CAPM Suppose the risk-free rate is 8 percent. The expected return on the market is 16 percent. If a particular stock has a beta of .7, what is its expected return based on the CAPM? If another stock has an expected return of 24 percent, what must its beta be?

ANSWERS TO CHAPTER REVIEW AND SELF-TEST PROBLEMS

13.1 The expected returns are just the possible returns multiplied by the associated probabilities:

$$E(R_A) = (.20 \times -.15) + (.50 \times .20) + (.30 \times .60) = 25\%$$
$$E(R_B) = (.20 \times .20) + (.50 \times .30) + (.30 \times .40) = 31\%$$

The variances are given by the sums of the squared deviations from the expected returns multiplied by their probabilities:

$$
\begin{aligned}
\sigma_A^2 &= .20 \times (-.15 - .25)^2 + .50 \times (.20 - .25)^2 + .30 \times (.60 - .25)^2 \\
&= (.20 \times -.40^2) + (.50 \times -.05^2) + (.30 \times .35^2) \\
&= (.20 \times .16) + (.50 \times .0025) + (.30 \times .1225) \\
&= .0700 \\
\sigma_B^2 &= .20 \times (.20 - .31)^2 + .50 \times (.30 - .31)^2 + .30 \times (.40 - .31)^2 \\
&= (.20 \times -.11^2) + (.50 \times -.01^2) + (.30 \times .09^2) \\
&= (.20 \times .0121) + (.50 \times .0001) + (.30 \times .0081) \\
&= .0049
\end{aligned}
$$

The standard deviations are thus:

$$\sigma_A = \sqrt{.0700} = 26.46\%$$
$$\sigma_B = \sqrt{.0049} = 7\%$$

13.2 The portfolio weights are $15,000/20,000 = .75$ and $5,000/20,000 = .25$. The expected return is thus:

$$
\begin{aligned}
E(R_P) &= .75 \times E(R_A) + .25 \times E(R_B) \\
&= (.75 \times 25\%) + (.25 \times 31\%) \\
&= 26.5\%
\end{aligned}
$$

Alternatively, we could calculate the portfolio's return in each of the states:

State of Economy	Probability of State of Economy	Portfolio Return If State Occurs
Recession	.20	$(.75 \times -.15) + (.25 \times .20) = -.0625$
Normal	.50	$(.75 \times .20) + (.25 \times .30) = .2250$
Boom	.30	$(.75 \times .60) + (.25 \times .40) = .5500$

The portfolio's expected return is:

$$E(R_P) = (.20 \times -.0625) + (.50 \times .2250) + (.30 \times .5500) = 26.5\%$$

This is the same as we had before.

The portfolio's variance is:

$$\sigma_P^2 = .20 \times (-.0625 - .265)^2 + .50 \times (.225 - .265)^2$$
$$+ .30 \times (.55 - .265)^2$$
$$= .0466$$

So the standard deviation is $\sqrt{.0466} = 21.59\%$.

13.3 If we compute the reward-to-risk ratios, we get $(22\% - 7\%)/1.8 = 8.33\%$ for Cooley versus 8.4% for Moyer. Relative to that of Cooley, Moyer's expected return is too high, so its price is too low.

If they are correctly priced, then they must offer the same reward-to-risk ratio. The risk-free rate would have to be such that:

$$(22\% - R_f)/1.8 = (20.44\% - R_f)/1.6$$

With a little algebra, we find that the risk-free rate must be 8 percent:

$$22\% - R_f = (20.44\% - R_f)(1.8/1.6)$$
$$22\% - 20.44\% \times 1.125 = R_f - R_f \times 1.125$$
$$R_f = 8\%$$

13.4 Because the expected return on the market is 16 percent, the market risk premium is $16\% - 8\% = 8\%$. The first stock has a beta of .7, so its expected return is $8\% + .7 \times 8\% = 13.6\%$.

For the second stock, notice that the risk premium is $24\% - 8\% = 16\%$. Because this is twice as large as the market risk premium, the beta must be exactly equal to 2. We can verify this using the CAPM:

$$E(R_i) = R_f + [E(R_M) - R_f] \times \beta_i$$
$$24\% = 8\% + (16\% - 8\%) \times \beta_i$$
$$\beta_i = 16\%/8\%$$
$$= 2.0$$

Visit us at www.mhhe.com/rwj

CONCEPTS REVIEW AND CRITICAL THINKING QUESTIONS

1. **Diversifiable and Nondiversifiable Risks [LO3]** In broad terms, why is some risk diversifiable? Why are some risks nondiversifiable? Does it follow that an investor can control the level of unsystematic risk in a portfolio, but not the level of systematic risk?

2. **Information and Market Returns [LO3]** Suppose the government announces that, based on a just-completed survey, the growth rate in the economy is likely to be 2 percent in the coming year, as compared to 5 percent for the past year. Will security prices increase, decrease, or stay the same following this announcement? Does it make any difference whether the 2 percent figure was anticipated by the market? Explain.

3. **Systematic versus Unsystematic Risk [LO3]** Classify the following events as mostly systematic or mostly unsystematic. Is the distinction clear in every case?

   a. Short-term interest rates increase unexpectedly.

   b. The interest rate a company pays on its short-term debt borrowing is increased by its bank.

   c. Oil prices unexpectedly decline.

   d. An oil tanker ruptures, creating a large oil spill.

   e. A manufacturer loses a multimillion-dollar product liability suit.

   f. A Supreme Court decision substantially broadens producer liability for injuries suffered by product users.

4. **Systematic versus Unsystematic Risk [LO3]** Indicate whether the following events might cause stocks in general to change price, and whether they might cause Big Widget Corp.'s stock to change price:

   a. The government announces that inflation unexpectedly jumped by 2 percent last month.

   b. Big Widget's quarterly earnings report, just issued, generally fell in line with analysts' expectations.

   c. The government reports that economic growth last year was at 3 percent, which generally agreed with most economists' forecasts.

   d. The directors of Big Widget die in a plane crash.

   e. Congress approves changes to the tax code that will increase the top marginal corporate tax rate. The legislation had been debated for the previous six months.

5. **Expected Portfolio Returns [LO1]** If a portfolio has a positive investment in every asset, can the expected return on the portfolio be greater than that on every asset in the portfolio? Can it be less than that on every asset in the portfolio? If you answer yes to one or both of these questions, give an example to support your answer.

6. **Diversification [LO2]** True or false: The most important characteristic in determining the expected return of a well-diversified portfolio is the variance of the individual assets in the portfolio. Explain.

7. **Portfolio Risk [LO2]** If a portfolio has a positive investment in every asset, can the standard deviation on the portfolio be less than that on every asset in the portfolio? What about the portfolio beta?

8. **Beta and CAPM [LO4]** Is it possible that a risky asset could have a beta of zero? Explain. Based on the CAPM, what is the expected return on such an asset? Is it possible that a risky asset could have a negative beta? What does the CAPM predict about the expected return on such an asset? Can you give an explanation for your answer?

9. **Corporate Downsizing [LO1]** In recent years, it has been common for companies to experience significant stock price changes in reaction to announcements of massive layoffs. Critics charge that such events encourage companies to fire longtime employees and that Wall Street is cheering them on. Do you agree or disagree?

10. **Earnings and Stock Returns [LO1]** As indicated by a number of examples in this chapter, earnings announcements by companies are closely followed by, and frequently result in, share price revisions. Two issues should come to mind. First, earnings announcements concern past periods. If the market values stocks based on expectations of the future, why are numbers summarizing past performance relevant? Second, these announcements concern accounting earnings. Going back to Chapter 2, such earnings may have little to do with cash flow—so, again, why are they relevant?

QUESTIONS AND PROBLEMS

1. **Determining Portfolio Weights [LO1]** What are the portfolio weights for a portfolio that has 145 shares of Stock A that sell for $45 per share and 110 shares of Stock B that sell for $27 per share?

BASIC
(Questions 1–20)

Visit us at www.mhhe.com/rwj

Visit us at www.mhhe.com/rwj

2. **Portfolio Expected Return [LO1]** You own a portfolio that has $2,950 invested in Stock A and $3,700 invested in Stock B. If the expected returns on these stocks are 8 percent and 11 percent, respectively, what is the expected return on the portfolio?

3. **Portfolio Expected Return [LO1]** You own a portfolio that is 35 percent invested in Stock X, 20 percent in Stock Y, and 45 percent in Stock Z. The expected returns on these three stocks are 9 percent, 17 percent, and 13 percent, respectively. What is the expected return on the portfolio?

4. **Portfolio Expected Return [LO1]** You have $10,000 to invest in a stock portfolio. Your choices are Stock X with an expected return of 12 percent and Stock Y with an expected return of 9.5 percent. If your goal is to create a portfolio with an expected return of 11.1 percent, how much money will you invest in Stock X? In Stock Y?

5. **Calculating Expected Return [LO1]** Based on the following information, calculate the expected return:

State of Economy	Probability of State of Economy	Portfolio Return If State Occurs
Recession	.30	−.14
Boom	.70	.22

6. **Calculating Expected Return [LO1]** Based on the following information, calculate the expected return:

State of Economy	Probability of State of Economy	Portfolio Return If State Occurs
Recession	.20	−.18
Normal	.50	.11
Boom	.30	.29

7. **Calculating Returns and Standard Deviations [LO1]** Based on the following information, calculate the expected return and standard deviation for the two stocks:

State of Economy	Probability of State of Economy	Rate of Return If State Occurs	
		Stock A	Stock B
Recession	.20	.05	−.17
Normal	.55	.08	.12
Boom	.25	.13	.29

8. **Calculating Expected Returns [LO1]** A portfolio is invested 15 percent in Stock G, 55 percent in Stock J, and 30 percent in Stock K. The expected returns on these stocks are 8 percent, 14 percent, and 18 percent, respectively. What is the portfolio's expected return? How do you interpret your answer?

9. **Returns and Variances [LO1]** Consider the following information:

State of Economy	Probability of State of Economy	Rate of Return If State Occurs		
		Stock A	Stock B	Stock C
Boom	.65	.07	.15	.33
Bust	.35	.13	.03	−.06

a. What is the expected return on an equally weighted portfolio of these three stocks?

b. What is the variance of a portfolio invested 20 percent each in A and B and 60 percent in C?

10. **Returns and Standard Deviations [LO1]** Consider the following information:

State of Economy	Probability of State of Economy	Rate of Return If State Occurs		
		Stock A	Stock B	Stock C
Boom	.15	.35	.45	.27
Good	.55	.16	.10	.08
Poor	.25	−.01	−.06	−.04
Bust	.05	−.12	−.20	−.09

$$E_A = R_f + \beta\left(E_R - R_f\right)$$

a. Your portfolio is invested 30 percent each in A and C, and 40 percent in B. What is the expected return of the portfolio?

b. What is the variance of this portfolio? The standard deviation?

11. **Calculating Portfolio Betas [LO4]** You own a stock portfolio invested 35 percent in Stock Q, 25 percent in Stock R, 30 percent in Stock S, and 10 percent in Stock T. The betas for these four stocks are .84, 1.17, 1.11, and 1.36, respectively. What is the portfolio beta?

12. **Calculating Portfolio Betas [LO4]** You own a portfolio equally invested in a risk-free asset and two stocks. If one of the stocks has a beta of 1.27 and the total portfolio is equally as risky as the market, what must the beta be for the other stock in your portfolio?

13. **Using CAPM [LO4]** A stock has a beta of 1.05, the expected return on the market is 10 percent, and the risk-free rate is 3.8 percent. What must the expected return on this stock be?

14. **Using CAPM [LO4]** A stock has an expected return of 10.2 percent, the risk-free rate is 4.5 percent, and the market risk premium is 7.5 percent. What must the beta of this stock be?

15. **Using CAPM [LO4]** A stock has an expected return of 12.4 percent, its beta is 1.17, and the risk-free rate is 4.2 percent. What must the expected return on the market be?

16. **Using CAPM [LO4]** A stock has an expected return of 13.3 percent, its beta is 1.45, and the expected return on the market is 10.5 percent. What must the risk-free rate be?

17. **Using CAPM [LO4]** A stock has a beta of 1.25 and an expected return of 14 percent. A risk-free asset currently earns 2.1 percent.

a. What is the expected return on a portfolio that is equally invested in the two assets?

b. If a portfolio of the two assets has a beta of .93, what are the portfolio weights?

c. If a portfolio of the two assets has an expected return of 9 percent, what is its beta?

d. If a portfolio of the two assets has a beta of 2.50, what are the portfolio weights? How do you interpret the weights for the two assets in this case? Explain.

18. **Using the SML [LO4]** Asset W has an expected return of 12.8 percent and a beta of 1.25. If the risk-free rate is 4.1 percent, complete the following table for portfolios of Asset W and a risk-free asset. Illustrate the relationship between portfolio

Visit us at www.mhhe.com/rwj

expected return and portfolio beta by plotting the expected returns against the betas. What is the slope of the line that results?

Percentage of Portfolio in Asset W	Portfolio Expected Return	Portfolio Beta
0%		
25		
50		
75		
100		
125		
150		

19. **Reward-to-Risk Ratios [LO4]** Stock Y has a beta of 1.3 and an expected return of 15.3 percent. Stock Z has a beta of .70 and an expected return of 9.3 percent. If the risk-free rate is 5.5 percent and the market risk premium is 6.8 percent, are these stocks correctly priced?

20. **Reward-to-Risk Ratios [LO4]** In the previous problem, what would the risk-free rate have to be for the two stocks to be correctly priced?

INTERMEDIATE
(Questions 21–24)

21. **Portfolio Returns [LO2]** Using information from the previous chapter on capital market history, determine the return on a portfolio that is equally invested in large-company stocks and long-term government bonds. What is the return on a portfolio that is equally invested in small-company stocks and Treasury bills?

22. **CAPM [LO4]** Using the CAPM, show that the ratio of the risk premiums on two assets is equal to the ratio of their betas.

23. **Portfolio Returns and Deviations [LO2]** Consider the following information about three stocks:

State of Economy	Probability of State of Economy	Rate of Return If State Occurs		
		Stock A	Stock B	Stock C
Boom	.20	.24	.36	.55
Normal	.55	.17	.13	.09
Bust	.25	.00	−.28	−.45

a. If your portfolio is invested 40 percent each in A and B and 20 percent in C, what is the portfolio expected return? The variance? The standard deviation?

b. If the expected T-bill rate is 3.80 percent, what is the expected risk premium on the portfolio?

c. If the expected inflation rate is 3.50 percent, what are the approximate and exact expected real returns on the portfolio? What are the approximate and exact expected real risk premiums on the portfolio?

24. **Analyzing a Portfolio [LO2]** You want to create a portfolio equally as risky as the market, and you have $1,000,000 to invest. Given this information, fill in the rest of the following table:

Asset	Investment	Beta
Stock A	$195,000	.90
Stock B	$340,000	1.15
Stock C		1.29
Risk-free asset		

25. **Analyzing a Portfolio [LO2, 4]** You have $100,000 to invest in a portfolio containing Stock X and Stock Y. Your goal is to create a portfolio that has an expected return of 17 percent. If Stock X has an expected return of 14.8 percent and a beta of 1.35, and Stock Y has an expected return of 11.2 percent and a beta of .90, how much money will you invest in Stock Y? How do you interpret your answer? What is the beta of your portfolio?

CHALLENGE
(Questions 25–28)

26. **Systematic versus Unsystematic Risk [LO3]** Consider the following information about Stocks I and II:

State of Economy	Probability of State of Economy	Rate of Return If State Occurs	
		Stock I	Stock II
Recession	.25	.02	−.25
Normal	.50	.21	.09
Irrational exuberance	.25	.06	.44

The market risk premium is 7 percent, and the risk-free rate is 4 percent. Which stock has the most systematic risk? Which one has the most unsystematic risk? Which stock is "riskier"? Explain.

27. **SML [LO4]** Suppose you observe the following situation:

Security	Beta	Expected Return
Pete Corp.	1.15	.129
Repete Co.	.84	.102

Assume these securities are correctly priced. Based on the CAPM, what is the expected return on the market? What is the risk-free rate?

28. **SML [LO4]** Suppose you observe the following situation:

State of Economy	Probability of State of Economy	Return If State Occurs	
		Stock A	Stock B
Bust	.25	−.08	−.05
Normal	.60	.13	.14
Boom	.15	.48	.29

a. Calculate the expected return on each stock.
b. Assuming the capital asset pricing model holds and Stock A's beta is greater than Stock B's beta by .25, what is the expected market risk premium?

MINICASE

The Beta for Colgate-Palmolive

Joey Moss, a recent finance graduate, has just begun his job with the investment firm of Covili and Wyatt. Paul Covili, one of the firm's founders, has been talking to Joey about the firm's investment portfolio.

As with any investment, Paul is concerned about the risk of the investment as well as the potential return. More specifically, because the company holds a diversified portfolio,

Paul is concerned about the systematic risk of current and potential investments. One such position the company currently holds is stock in Colgate-Palmolive (CL). Colgate-Palmolive is the well-known manufacturer of consumer products under brand names such as Colgate, Palmolive, Softsoap, Irish Spring, Ajax, and others.

Visit us at www.mhhe.com/rwj

Visit us at www.mhhe.com/rwj

Covili and Wyatt currently uses a commercial data vendor for information about its positions. Because of this, Paul is unsure exactly how the numbers provided are calculated. The data provider considers its methods proprietary, and it will not disclose how stock betas and other information are calculated. Paul is uncomfortable with not knowing exactly how these numbers are being computed and also believes that it could be less expensive to calculate the necessary statistics in-house. To explore this question, Paul has asked Joey to do the following assignments.

QUESTIONS

1. Go to finance.yahoo.com and download the ending monthly stock prices for Colgate-Palmolive for the last 60 months. Use the adjusted closing price, which adjusts for dividend payments and stock splits. Next, download the ending value of the S&P 500 index over the same period. For the historical risk-free rate, go to the St. Louis Federal Reserve website (www.stlouisfed.org) and find the three-month Treasury bill secondary market rate. Download this file. What are the monthly returns, average monthly returns, and standard deviations for Colgate-Palmolive stock, the three-month Treasury bill, and the S&P 500 for this period?

2. Beta is often estimated by linear regression. A model commonly used is called the *market model,* which is:

$$R_t - R_{ft} = \alpha_i + \beta_i [R_{Mt} - R_{ft}] + \varepsilon_t$$

   In this regression, R_t is the return on the stock and R_{ft} is the risk-free rate for the same period. R_{Mt} is the return on a stock market index such as the S&P 500 index. α_i is the regression intercept, and β_i is the slope (and the stock's estimated beta). ε_i represents the residuals for the regression. What do you think is the motivation for this particular regression? The intercept, α_i, is often called *Jensen's alpha*. What does it measure? If an asset has a positive Jensen's alpha, where would it plot with respect to the SML? What is the financial interpretation of the residuals in the regression?

3. Use the market model to estimate the beta for Colgate-Palmolive using the last 36 months of returns (the regression procedure in Excel is one easy way to do this). Plot the monthly returns on Colgate-Palmolive against the index and also show the fitted line.

4. When the beta of a stock is calculated using monthly returns, there is a debate over the number of months that should be used in the calculation. Rework the previous questions using the last 60 months of returns. How does this answer compare to what you calculated previously? What are some arguments for and against using shorter versus longer periods? Also, you've used monthly data, which are a common choice. You could have used daily, weekly, quarterly, or even annual data. What do you think are the issues here?

5. Compare your beta for Colgate-Palmolive to the beta you find on finance.yahoo.com. How similar are they? Why might they be different?

COST OF CAPITAL

WITH OVER 95,000 EMPLOYEES ON FIVE CONTINENTS, Germany-based BASF is a major international company. The company operates in a variety of industries, including agriculture, oil and gas, chemicals, and plastics. In an attempt to increase value, BASF launched Vision 2020, a comprehensive plan that included all functions within the company and challenged and encouraged all employees to act in an entrepreneurial manner. The major financial component of the strategy was that the company expected to earn its weighted average cost of capital, or WACC, plus a premium. So, what exactly is the WACC?

The WACC is the minimum return a company needs to earn to satisfy all of its investors, including stockholders, bondholders, and preferred stockholders. In 2010, for example, BASF pegged its cost of capital at 9 percent and earned a company record premium of €3.9 billion above its cost of capital. In 2011, the company pegged its WACC at 11 percent. In this chapter, we learn how to compute a firm's cost of capital and find out what it means to the firm and its investors. We will also learn when to use the firm's cost of capital, and, perhaps more important, when not to use it.

LEARNING OBJECTIVES

After studying this chapter, you should understand:

LO1 How to determine a firm's cost of equity capital.

LO2 How to determine a firm's cost of debt.

LO3 How to determine a firm's overall cost of capital.

LO4 How to correctly include flotation costs in capital budgeting projects.

LO5 Some of the pitfalls associated with a firm's overall cost of capital and what to do about them.

Suppose you have just become the president of a large company, and the first decision you face is whether to go ahead with a plan to renovate the company's warehouse distribution system. The plan will cost the company $50 million, and it is expected to save $12 million per year after taxes over the next six years.

This is a familiar problem in capital budgeting. To address it, you would determine the relevant cash flows, discount them, and, if the net present value is positive, take on the project; if the NPV is negative, you would scrap it. So far, so good; but what should you use as the discount rate?

From our discussion of risk and return, you know that the correct discount rate depends on the riskiness of the project to renovate the warehouse distribution system. In particular, the new project will have a positive NPV only if its return exceeds what the financial markets offer on investments of similar risk. We called this minimum required return the *cost of capital* associated with the project.[1]

Thus, to make the right decision as president, you must examine what the capital markets have to offer and use this information to arrive at an estimate of the project's cost of capital. Our primary purpose in this chapter is to describe how to go about doing this. There are a variety of approaches to this task, and a number of conceptual and practical issues arise.

One of the most important concepts we develop is that of the *weighted average cost of capital* (WACC). This is the cost of capital for the firm as a whole, and it can be interpreted as the required return on the overall firm. In discussing the WACC, we will recognize the fact that a firm will normally raise capital in a variety of forms and that these different forms of capital may have different costs associated with them.

We also recognize in this chapter that taxes are an important consideration in determining the required return on an investment: We are always interested in valuing the aftertax cash flows from a project. We will therefore discuss how to incorporate taxes explicitly into our estimates of the cost of capital.

14.1 The Cost of Capital: Some Preliminaries

In Chapter 13, we developed the security market line, or SML, and used it to explore the relationship between the expected return on a security and its systematic risk. We concentrated on how the risky returns from buying securities looked from the viewpoint of, for example, a shareholder in the firm. This helped us understand more about the alternatives available to an investor in the capital markets.

In this chapter, we turn things around a bit and look more closely at the other side of the problem, which is how these returns and securities look from the viewpoint of the companies that issue them. The important fact to note is that the return an investor in a security receives is the cost of that security to the company that issued it.

REQUIRED RETURN VERSUS COST OF CAPITAL

When we say that the required return on an investment is, say, 10 percent, we usually mean that the investment will have a positive NPV only if its return exceeds 10 percent. Another way of interpreting the required return is to observe that the firm must earn 10 percent on the investment just to compensate its investors for the use of the capital needed to finance the project. This is why we could also say that 10 percent is the cost of capital associated with the investment.

To illustrate the point further, imagine that we are evaluating a risk-free project. In this case, how to determine the required return is obvious: We look at the capital markets and observe the current rate offered by risk-free investments, and we use this rate to discount the project's cash flows. Thus, the cost of capital for a risk-free investment is the risk-free rate.

If a project is risky, then, assuming that all the other information is unchanged, the required return is obviously higher. In other words, the cost of capital for this project, if it is risky, is greater than the risk-free rate, and the appropriate discount rate would exceed the risk-free rate.

We will henceforth use the terms *required return, appropriate discount rate*, and *cost of capital* more or less interchangeably because, as the discussion in this section suggests, they all mean essentially the same thing. The key fact to grasp is that the cost of capital associated with an investment depends on the risk of that investment. This is one of the most important lessons in corporate finance, so it bears repeating:

The cost of capital depends primarily on the use of the funds, not the source.

---

[1]The term *cost of money* is also used.

It is a common error to forget this crucial point and fall into the trap of thinking that the cost of capital for an investment depends primarily on how and where the capital is raised.

FINANCIAL POLICY AND COST OF CAPITAL

We know that the particular mixture of debt and equity a firm chooses to employ—its capital structure—is a managerial variable. In this chapter, we will take the firm's financial policy as given. In particular, we will assume that the firm has a fixed debt–equity ratio that it maintains. This ratio reflects the firm's *target* capital structure. How a firm might choose that ratio is the subject of a later chapter.

From the preceding discussion, we know that a firm's overall cost of capital will reflect the required return on the firm's assets as a whole. Given that a firm uses both debt and equity capital, this overall cost of capital will be a mixture of the returns needed to compensate its creditors and those needed to compensate its stockholders. In other words, a firm's cost of capital will reflect both its cost of debt capital and its cost of equity capital. We discuss these costs separately in the sections that follow.

Concept Questions

14.1a What is the primary determinant of the cost of capital for an investment?

14.1b What is the relationship between the required return on an investment and the cost of capital associated with that investment?

The Cost of Equity

14.2

We begin with the most difficult question on the subject of cost of capital: What is the firm's overall **cost of equity**? The reason this is a difficult question is that there is no way of directly observing the return that the firm's equity investors require on their investment. Instead, we must somehow estimate it. This section discusses two approaches to determining the cost of equity: the dividend growth model approach and the security market line (SML) approach.

cost of equity
The return that equity investors require on their investment in the firm.

THE DIVIDEND GROWTH MODEL APPROACH

The easiest way to estimate the cost of equity capital is to use the dividend growth model we developed in Chapter 8. Recall that, under the assumption that the firm's dividend will grow at a constant rate, g, the price per share of the stock, P_0, can be written as:

$$P_0 = \frac{D_0 \times (1 + g)}{R_E - g} = \frac{D_1}{R_E - g}$$

where D_0 is the dividend just paid and D_1 is the next period's projected dividend. Notice that we have used the symbol R_E (the E stands for equity) for the required return on the stock.

As we discussed in Chapter 8, we can rearrange this to solve for R_E as follows:

$$R_E = D_1/P_0 + g \qquad \text{[14.1]}$$

Because R_E is the return that the shareholders require on the stock, it can be interpreted as the firm's cost of equity capital.

Implementing the Approach   To estimate R_E using the dividend growth model approach, we obviously need three pieces of information: P_0, D_0, and g.[2] Of these, for a publicly traded, dividend-paying company, the first two can be observed directly, so they are easily obtained. Only the third component, the expected growth rate for dividends, must be estimated.

---

[2]Notice that if we have D_0 and g, we can simply calculate D_1 by multiplying D_0 by $(1 + g)$.

To illustrate how we estimate R_E, suppose Greater States Public Service, a large public utility, paid a dividend of $4 per share last year. The stock currently sells for $60 per share. You estimate that the dividend will grow steadily at a rate of 6 percent per year into the indefinite future. What is the cost of equity capital for Greater States?

Using the dividend growth model, we can calculate that the expected dividend for the coming year, D_1, is:

$$D_1 = D_0 \times (1 + g)$$
$$= \$4 \times 1.06$$
$$= \$4.24$$

Given this, the cost of equity, R_E, is:

$$R_E = D_1/P_0 + g$$
$$= \$4.24/60 + .06$$
$$= 13.07\%$$

The cost of equity is thus 13.07 percent.

Estimating g   To use the dividend growth model, we must come up with an estimate for g, the growth rate. There are essentially two ways of doing this: (1) Use historical growth rates or (2) use analysts' forecasts of future growth rates. Analysts' forecasts are available from a variety of sources. Naturally, different sources will have different estimates, so one approach might be to obtain multiple estimates and then average them.

Alternatively, we might observe dividends for the previous, say, five years, calculate the year-to-year growth rates, and average them. For example, suppose we observe the following for some company:

Growth estimates can be found at www.zacks.com.

Year	Dividend
2007	$1.10
2008	1.20
2009	1.35
2010	1.40
2011	1.55

We can calculate the percentage change in the dividend for each year as follows:

Year	Dividend	Dollar Change	Percentage Change
2007	$1.10	—	—
2008	1.20	$.10	9.09%
2009	1.35	.15	12.50
2010	1.40	.05	3.70
2011	1.55	.15	10.71

Notice that we calculated the change in the dividend on a year-to-year basis and then expressed the change as a percentage. Thus, in 2008 for example, the dividend rose from $1.10 to $1.20, an increase of $.10. This represents a $.10/1.10 = 9.09\%$ increase.

If we average the four growth rates, the result is $(9.09 + 12.50 + 3.70 + 10.71)/4 = 9\%$, so we could use this as an estimate for the expected growth rate, g. Notice that this 9 percent growth rate we have calculated is a simple, or arithmetic, average. Going back to Chapter 12, we also could calculate a geometric growth rate. Here, the dividend grows from $1.10 to $1.55 over a four-year period. What's the compound, or geometric growth rate? See if you don't agree that it's 8.95 percent; you can view this as a simple time value of money problem where $1.10 is the present value and $1.55 is the future value.

As usual, the geometric average (8.95 percent) is lower than the arithmetic average (9 percent), but the difference here is not likely to be of any practical significance. In general, if the dividend has grown at a relatively steady rate, as we assume when we use this approach, then it can't make much difference which way we calculate the average dividend growth rate.

Advantages and Disadvantages of the Approach   The primary advantage of the dividend growth model approach is its simplicity. It is both easy to understand and easy to use. There are a number of associated practical problems and disadvantages.

First and foremost, the dividend growth model is obviously applicable only to companies that pay dividends. This means that the approach is useless in many cases. Furthermore, even for companies that pay dividends, the key underlying assumption is that the dividend grows at a constant rate. As our previous example illustrates, this will never be *exactly* the case. More generally, the model is really applicable only to cases in which reasonably steady growth is likely to occur.

A second problem is that the estimated cost of equity is very sensitive to the estimated growth rate. For a given stock price, an upward revision of g by just one percentage point, for example, increases the estimated cost of equity by at least a full percentage point. Because D_1 will probably be revised upward as well, the increase will actually be somewhat larger than that.

Finally, this approach really does not explicitly consider risk. Unlike the SML approach (which we consider next), there is no direct adjustment for the riskiness of the investment. For example, there is no allowance for the degree of certainty or uncertainty surrounding the estimated growth rate for dividends. As a result, it is difficult to say whether or not the estimated return is commensurate with the level of risk.[3]

THE SML APPROACH

In Chapter 13, we discussed the security market line, or SML. Our primary conclusion was that the required or expected return on a risky investment depends on three things:

1. The risk-free rate, R_f.
2. The market risk premium, $E(R_M) - R_f$.
3. The systematic risk of the asset relative to average, which we called its beta coefficient, β.

Using the SML, we can write the expected return on the company's equity, $E(R_E)$, as:

$$E(R_E) = R_f + \beta_E \times [E(R_M) - R_f]$$

where β_E is the estimated beta. To make the SML approach consistent with the dividend growth model, we will drop the *E*s denoting expectations and henceforth write the required return from the SML, R_E, as:

$$R_E = R_f + \beta_E \times (R_M - R_f) \tag{14.2}$$

---

[3]There is an implicit adjustment for risk because the current stock price is used. All other things being equal, the higher the risk, the lower is the stock price. Further, the lower the stock price, the greater is the cost of equity, again assuming all the other information is the same.

Implementing the Approach   To use the SML approach, we need a risk-free rate, R_f, an estimate of the market risk premium, $R_M - R_f$, and an estimate of the relevant beta, β_E. In Chapter 12, we saw that one estimate of the market risk premium (based on large common stocks) is about 7 percent. U.S. Treasury bills are paying about .10 percent as this chapter is being written, so we will use this as our risk-free rate. Beta coefficients for publicly traded companies are widely available.[4]

Betas and T-bill rates can both be found at www.bloomberg.com.

To illustrate, in Chapter 13, we saw that Abercrombie & Fitch had an estimated beta of 1.68 (Table 13.8). We could thus estimate Abercrombie & Fitch's cost of equity as:

$$R_{A\&F} = R_f + \beta_{A\&F} \times (R_M - R_f)$$
$$= .10\% + 1.68 \times 7\%$$
$$= 11.86\%$$

Thus, using the SML approach, we calculate that Abercrombie & Fitch's cost of equity is about 11.86 percent.

Advantages and Disadvantages of the Approach   The SML approach has two primary advantages. First, it explicitly adjusts for risk. Second, it is applicable to companies other than just those with steady dividend growth. Thus, it may be useful in a wider variety of circumstances.

There are drawbacks, of course. The SML approach requires that two things be estimated: the market risk premium and the beta coefficient. To the extent that our estimates are poor, the resulting cost of equity will be inaccurate. For example, our estimate of the market risk premium, 7 percent, is based on about 100 years of returns on particular stock portfolios and markets. Using different time periods or different stocks and markets could result in very different estimates.

Finally, as with the dividend growth model, we essentially rely on the past to predict the future when we use the SML approach. Economic conditions can change quickly; so as always, the past may not be a good guide to the future. In the best of all worlds, both approaches (the dividend growth model and the SML) are applicable and the two result in similar answers. If this happens, we might have some confidence in our estimates. We might also wish to compare the results to those for other similar companies as a reality check.

EXAMPLE 14.1   **The Cost of Equity**

Suppose stock in Alpha Air Freight has a beta of 1.2. The market risk premium is 7 percent, and the risk-free rate is 6 percent. Alpha's last dividend was $2 per share, and the dividend is expected to grow at 8 percent indefinitely. The stock currently sells for $30. What is Alpha's cost of equity capital?

We can start off by using the SML. Doing this, we find that the expected return on the common stock of Alpha Air Freight is:

$$R_E = R_f + \beta_E \times (R_M - R_f)$$
$$= 6\% + 1.2 \times 7\%$$
$$= 14.4\%$$

---

[4]We can also estimate beta coefficients directly by using historical data. For a discussion of how to do this, see Chapters 10, 11, and 13 in S.A. Ross, R.W. Westerfield, and J.J. Jaffe, *Corporate Finance*, 9th ed. (New York: McGraw-Hill, 2010).

This suggests that 14.4 percent is Alpha's cost of equity. We next use the dividend growth model. The projected dividend is $D_0 \times (1 + g) = \$2 \times 1.08 = \$2.16$, so the expected return using this approach is:

$$R_E = D_1/P_0 + g$$
$$= \$2.16/30 + .08$$
$$= 15.2\%$$

Our two estimates are reasonably close, so we might just average them to find that Alpha's cost of equity is approximately 14.8 percent.

Concept Questions

14.2a What do we mean when we say that a corporation's cost of equity capital is 16 percent?

14.2b What are two approaches to estimating the cost of equity capital?

The Costs of Debt and Preferred Stock

14.3

In addition to ordinary equity, firms use debt and, to a lesser extent, preferred stock to finance their investments. As we discuss next, determining the costs of capital associated with these sources of financing is much easier than determining the cost of equity.

THE COST OF DEBT

The **cost of debt** is the return the firm's creditors demand on new borrowing. In principle, we could determine the beta for the firm's debt and then use the SML to estimate the required return on debt just as we estimated the required return on equity. This isn't really necessary, however.

cost of debt
The return that lenders require on the firm's debt.

Unlike a firm's cost of equity, its cost of debt can normally be observed either directly or indirectly: The cost of debt is simply the interest rate the firm must pay on new borrowing, and we can observe interest rates in the financial markets. For example, if the firm already has bonds outstanding, then the yield to maturity on those bonds is the market-required rate on the firm's debt.

Alternatively, if we know that the firm's bonds are rated, say, AA, then we can simply find the interest rate on newly issued AA-rated bonds. Either way, there is no need to estimate a beta for the debt because we can directly observe the rate we want to know.

There is one thing to be careful about, though. The coupon rate on the firm's outstanding debt is irrelevant here. That rate just tells us roughly what the firm's cost of debt was back when the bonds were issued, not what the cost of debt is today.[5] This is why we have to look at the yield on the debt in today's marketplace. For consistency with our other notation, we will use the symbol R_D for the cost of debt.

---

[5]The firm's cost of debt based on its historical borrowing is sometimes called the *embedded debt cost*.

| EXAMPLE 14.2 | **The Cost of Debt** |

Suppose the General Tool Company issued a 30-year, 7 percent bond 8 years ago. The bond is currently selling for 96 percent of its face value, or $960. What is General Tool's cost of debt?

Going back to Chapter 7, we need to calculate the yield to maturity on this bond. Because the bond is selling at a discount, the yield is apparently greater than 7 percent, but not much greater because the discount is fairly small. You can check to see that the yield to maturity is about 7.37 percent, assuming annual coupons. General Tool's cost of debt, R_D, is thus 7.37 percent.

THE COST OF PREFERRED STOCK

Determining the *cost of preferred stock* is quite straightforward. As we discussed in Chapters 6 and 8, preferred stock has a fixed dividend paid every period forever, so a share of preferred stock is essentially a perpetuity. The cost of preferred stock, R_P, is thus:

$$R_P = D/P_0 \tag{14.3}$$

where D is the fixed dividend and P_0 is the current price per share of the preferred stock. Notice that the cost of preferred stock is simply equal to the dividend yield on the preferred stock. Alternatively, because preferred stocks are rated in much the same way as bonds, the cost of preferred stock can be estimated by observing the required returns on other, similarly rated shares of preferred stock.

| EXAMPLE 14.3 | **Alabama Power Co.'s Cost of Preferred Stock** |

On February 23, 2011, Alabama Power Co. had two issues of ordinary preferred stock with a $100 par value that traded on the NYSE. One issue paid $4.72 annually per share and sold for $84 per share. The other paid $4.60 per share annually and sold for $84.50 per share. What is Alabama Power's cost of preferred stock?

Using the first issue, we calculate that the cost of preferred stock is:

$$R_P = D/P_0$$
$$= \$4.72/84$$
$$= 5.6\%$$

Using the second issue, we calculate that the cost is:

$$R_P = D/P_0$$
$$= \$4.60/84.50$$
$$= 5.4\%$$

So, Alabama Power's cost of preferred stock appears to be about 5.5 percent.

Concept Questions

14.3a Why is the coupon rate a bad estimate of a firm's cost of debt?
14.3b How can the cost of debt be calculated?
14.3c How can the cost of preferred stock be calculated?

The Weighted Average Cost of Capital

14.4 ✗

Now that we have the costs associated with the main sources of capital the firm employs, we need to worry about the specific mix. As we mentioned earlier, we will take this mix, which is the firm's capital structure, as given for now. Also, we will focus mostly on debt and ordinary equity in this discussion.

In Chapter 3, we mentioned that financial analysts frequently focus on a firm's total capitalization, which is the sum of its long-term debt and equity. This is particularly true in determining cost of capital; short-term liabilities are often ignored in the process. We will not explicitly distinguish between total value and total capitalization in the following discussion; the general approach is applicable with either.

THE CAPITAL STRUCTURE WEIGHTS

We will use the symbol E (for equity) to stand for the *market* value of the firm's equity. We calculate this by taking the number of shares outstanding and multiplying it by the price per share. Similarly, we will use the symbol D (for debt) to stand for the *market* value of the firm's debt. For long-term debt, we calculate this by multiplying the market price of a single bond by the number of bonds outstanding.

If there are multiple bond issues (as there normally would be), we repeat this calculation of D for each and then add up the results. If there is debt that is not publicly traded (because it is held by a life insurance company, for example), we must observe the yield on similar publicly traded debt and then estimate the market value of the privately held debt using this yield as the discount rate. For short-term debt, the book (accounting) values and market values should be somewhat similar, so we might use the book values as estimates of the market values.

Finally, we will use the symbol V (for value) to stand for the combined market value of the debt and equity:

$$V = E + D \tag{14.4}$$

If we divide both sides by V, we can calculate the percentages of the total capital represented by the debt and equity:

$$100\% = E/V + D/V \tag{14.5}$$

These percentages can be interpreted just like portfolio weights, and they are often called the *capital structure weights*.

For example, if the total market value of a company's stock were calculated as $200 million and the total market value of the company's debt were calculated as $50 million, then the combined value would be $250 million. Of this total, $E/V = $200 million/250 million = 80\%$, so 80 percent of the firm's financing would be equity and the remaining 20 percent would be debt.

We emphasize here that the correct way to proceed is to use the *market* values of the debt and equity. Under certain circumstances, such as when calculating figures for a privately owned company, it may not be possible to get reliable estimates of these quantities. In this case, we might go ahead and use the accounting values for debt and equity. Although this would probably be better than nothing, we would have to take the answer with a grain of salt.

TAXES AND THE WEIGHTED AVERAGE COST OF CAPITAL

There is one final issue we need to discuss. Recall that we are always concerned with after-tax cash flows. If we are determining the discount rate appropriate to those cash flows, then the discount rate also needs to be expressed on an aftertax basis.

As we discussed previously in various places in this book (and as we will discuss later), the interest paid by a corporation is deductible for tax purposes. Payments to stockholders, such as dividends, are not. What this means, effectively, is that the government pays some of the interest. Thus, in determining an aftertax discount rate, we need to distinguish between the pretax and the aftertax cost of debt.

To illustrate, suppose a firm borrows $1 million at 9 percent interest. The corporate tax rate is 34 percent. What is the aftertax interest rate on this loan? The total interest bill will be $90,000 per year. This amount is tax deductible, however, so the $90,000 interest reduces the firm's tax bill by $.34 \times \$90,000 = \$30,600$. The aftertax interest bill is thus $90,000 - 30,600 = \$59,400$. The aftertax interest rate is thus $59,400/1$ million $= 5.94\%$.

Notice that, in general, the aftertax interest rate is simply equal to the pretax rate multiplied by 1 minus the tax rate. If we use the symbol T_C to stand for the corporate tax rate, then the aftertax rate can be written as $R_D \times (1 - T_C)$. For example, using the numbers from the preceding paragraph, we find that the aftertax interest rate is $9\% \times (1 - .34) = 5.94\%$.

To get a feel for actual, industry-level WACCs, visit www.ibbotson.com.

weighted average cost of capital (WACC)
The weighted average of the cost of equity and the aftertax cost of debt.

Bringing together the various topics we have discussed in this chapter, we now have the capital structure weights along with the cost of equity and the aftertax cost of debt. To calculate the firm's overall cost of capital, we multiply the capital structure weights by the associated costs and add them up. The total is the **weighted average cost of capital (WACC)**:

$$\text{WACC} = (E/V) \times R_E + (D/V) \times R_D \times (1 - T_C) \qquad \textbf{[14.6]}$$

This WACC has a straightforward interpretation. It is the overall return the firm must earn on its existing assets to maintain the value of its stock. It is also the required return on any investments by the firm that have essentially the same risks as existing operations. So, if we were evaluating the cash flows from a proposed expansion of our existing operations, this is the discount rate we would use.

If a firm uses preferred stock in its capital structure, then our expression for the WACC needs a simple extension. If we define P/V as the percentage of the firm's financing that comes from preferred stock, then the WACC is simply:

$$\text{WACC} = (E/V) \times R_E + (P/V) \times R_P + (D/V) \times R_D \times (1 - T_C) \qquad \textbf{[14.7]}$$

where R_P is the cost of preferred stock.

EXAMPLE 14.4 | **Calculating the WACC**

The B.B. Lean Co. has 1.4 million shares of stock outstanding. The stock currently sells for $20 per share. The firm's debt is publicly traded and was recently quoted at 93 percent of face value. It has a total face value of $5 million, and it is currently priced to yield 11 percent. The risk-free rate is 8 percent, and the market risk premium is 7 percent. You've estimated that Lean has a beta of .74. If the corporate tax rate is 34 percent, what is the WACC of Lean Co.?

We can first determine the cost of equity and the cost of debt. Using the SML, we find that the cost of equity is $8\% + .74 \times 7\% = 13.18\%$. The total value of the equity is 1.4 million $\times$ $20 = \$28$ million. The pretax cost of debt is the current yield to maturity on the outstanding debt, 11 percent. The debt sells for 93 percent of its face value, so its current market value is .93 × $5 million = $4.65 million. The total market value of the equity and debt together is $28 million + 4.65 million = $32.65 million.

From here, we can calculate the WACC easily enough. The percentage of equity used by Lean to finance its operations is $28 million/$32.65 million = 85.76%. Because the weights have to add up to 1, the percentage of debt is 1 − .8576 = 14.24%. The WACC is thus:

$$WACC = (E/V) \times R_E + (D/V) \times R_D \times (1 - T_C)$$
$$= .8576 \times 13.18\% + .1424 \times 11\% \times (1 - .34)$$
$$= 12.34\%$$

B.B. Lean thus has an overall weighted average cost of capital of 12.34 percent.

CALCULATING THE WACC FOR EASTMAN CHEMICAL

In this section, we illustrate how to calculate the WACC for Eastman Chemical Co., a leading international chemical company and maker of plastics such as those used in soft drink containers. It was created in 1993, when its former parent company, Eastman Kodak, split off the division as a separate company. Our goal is to take you through, on a step-by-step basis, the process of finding and using the information needed using online sources. As you will see, there is a fair amount of detail involved, but the necessary information is, for the most part, readily available.

Eastman's Cost of Equity   Our first stop is the main screen for Eastman available at finance.yahoo.com (ticker: EMN). As of early 2011, here's what it looked like:

Eastman Chemical Company Common (NYSE: EMN)
After Hours: 89.61 0.00 (0.00%) 4:01PM EST

Last Trade:	**89.61**	Day's Range:	87.50 - 91.20
Trade Time:	4:01PM EST	52wk Range:	51.10 - 97.31
Change:	↓0.90 (0.99%)	Volume:	1,464,370
Prev Close:	90.51	Avg Vol (3m):	916,549
Open:	90.50	Market Cap:	6.34B
Bid:	89.17 x 200	P/E (ttm):	15.12
Ask:	90.08 x 100	EPS (ttm):	5.93
1y Target Est:	101.36	Div & Yield:	1.88 (2.00%)

Next, we went to the "Key Statistics" screen. According to this screen, Eastman has 70.70 million shares of stock outstanding. The book value per share is $23.01, but the stock sells for $89.61. Total equity is therefore about $1.627 billion on a book value basis, but it is closer to $6.335 billion on a market value basis.

Balance Sheet	
Total Cash (mrq):	516.00M
Total Cash Per Share (mrq):	7.30
Total Debt (mrq):	1.60B
Total Debt/Equity (mrq):	98.59
Current Ratio (mrq):	1.91
Book Value Per Share (mrq):	23.01

Stock Price History	
Beta:	2.11
52-Week Change[3]:	53.38%
S&P500 52-Week Change[3]:	20.18%
52-Week High (Feb 17, 2011)[3]:	97.31
52-Week Low (Jul 6, 2010)[3]:	51.10
50-Day Moving Average[3]:	91.44
200-Day Moving Average[3]:	78.60
Share Statistics	
Avg Vol (3 month)[3]:	916,549
Avg Vol (10 day)[3]:	1,071,230
Shares Outstanding[5]:	70.70M
Float:	65.68M
% Held by Insiders[6]:	6.68%
% Held by Institutions[6]:	80.10%
Shares Short (as of Jan 31, 2011)[3]:	5.90M
Short Ratio (as of Jan 31, 2011)[3]:	6.00
Short % of Float (as of Jan 31, 2011)[3]:	8.20%
Shares Short (prior month)[3]:	6.16M

To estimate Eastman's cost of equity, we will assume a market risk premium of 7 percent, similar to what we calculated in Chapter 12. Eastman's beta on Yahoo! is 2.11, which is much higher than the beta of the average stock. To check this number, we went to the well-known *Value Line Investment Survey*, which uses an approach that moderates very large and very small betas. Here, the beta is reported as a much more reasonable 1.25, which is the number we will use. According to the Bonds section of finance.yahoo.com, T-bills were paying about .10 percent. Using the CAPM to estimate the cost of equity, we find:

$$R_E = .001 + 1.25(.07) = .0885 \text{ or } 8.85\%$$

Eastman has paid dividends for only a few years, so calculating the growth rate for the dividend discount model is problematic. However, under the Analyst Estimates link at finance.yahoo.com, we found the following:

Growth Est	EMN	Industry	Sector	S&P 500
Current Qtr.	29.90%	37.70%	25.30%	50.10%
Next Qtr.	3.40%	39.10%	27.80%	37.50%
This Year	10.90%	39.60%	19.70%	19.10%
Next Year	9.60%	16.80%	4.20%	14.30%
Past 5 Years (per annum)	1.14%	N/A	N/A	N/A
Next 5 Years (per annum)	12.35%	14.14%	15.64%	10.43%
Price/Earnings (avg. for comparison categories)	12.28	14.23	12.11	9.42
PEG Ratio (avg. for comparison categories)	0.99	3.73	2.13	1.18

Analysts estimate the growth in earnings per share for the company will be 12.35 percent for the next five years. Remembering that the dividend discount model assumes that the growth rate is into perpetuity, this is a high growth rate. In this case, we will go back to the two-stage dividend growth model and assume that the perpetual growth rate is 5.5 percent. We should also note that this estimate is the growth rate in earnings, not dividends; the link between earnings growth and dividends is discussed in a later chapter. The estimated cost of equity using the two-stage dividend discount model is:

$$P_0 = \frac{\$1.88(1 + .1235)}{R_E - .1235} \times \left[1 - \left(\frac{1 + .1235}{(1 + R_E)}\right)^5\right] + \frac{1}{(1 + R_E)^5} \times \left[\frac{\$1.88(1 + .1235)^5(1 + .055)}{R_E - .055}\right]$$

Solving for R_E, we get 8.48 percent.

Notice that our two estimates for the cost of equity are not identical. This is essentially always the case. Remember that each method of estimating the cost of equity relies on different assumptions, so different estimates of the cost of equity should not surprise us. If the estimates are different, there are two simple solutions. First, we could ignore one of the estimates. We would look at each estimate to see if one of them seemed too high or too low to be reasonable. Second, we could average the two estimates. For Eastman, our estimates of 8.48 percent and 8.85 percent are relatively close, so we will average them to get 8.67 percent as the cost of equity.

Eastman's Cost of Debt   Eastman has eight relatively long-term bond issues that account for essentially all of its long-term debt. To calculate the cost of debt, we will have to combine these eight issues. What we will do is compute a weighted average. We went to www.finra.org/marketdata to find quotes on the bonds. We should note here that finding the yield to maturity for all of a company's outstanding bond issues on a single day is unusual. If you remember our previous discussion of bonds, the bond market is not as liquid as the stock market; on many days, individual bond issues may not trade. To find the book value of the bonds, we went to www.sec.gov and found the 10K report dated December 13, 2010, and filed with the SEC on February 23, 2011. The basic information is as follows:

Coupon Rate	Maturity	Book Value (face value, in millions)	Price (% of par)	Yield to Maturity
7.00%	2012	$ 151	106.432	1.317%
3.00	2015	250	98.789	3.273
6.30	2018	178	112.195	4.419
5.50	2019	250	106.150	4.633
4.50	2021	250	99.423	4.573
7.25	2024	243	113.342	5.765
7.625	2024	54	121.000	5.416
7.60	2027	222	116.450	5.984
		$1,598		

To calculate the weighted average cost of debt, we take the percentage of the total debt represented by each issue and multiply by the yield on the issue. We then add to get the overall weighted average debt cost. We use both book values and market values here for comparison. The results of the calculations are as follows:

Coupon Rate	Book Value (face value, in millions)	Percentage of Total	Market Value (in millions)	Percentage of Total	Yield to Maturity	Book Values	Market Values
7.00%	$ 151	.09	$ 160.71	.09	1.32%	.12%	.12%
3.00	250	.16	246.97	.14	3.27	.51	.47
6.30	178	.11	199.71	.12	4.42	.49	.51
5.50	250	.16	265.38	.15	4.63	.72	.71
4.50	250	.16	248.56	.14	4.57	.72	.66
7.25	243	.15	275.42	.16	5.77	.88	.92
7.625	54	.03	65.34	.04	5.42	.18	.21
7.60	222	.14	258.52	.15	5.98	.83	.90
	$1,598	1.00	$1,720.60	1.00		4.46%	4.51%

As these calculations show, Eastman's cost of debt is 4.46 percent on a book value basis and 4.51 percent on a market value basis. Thus, for Eastman, whether market values or book values are used makes no difference. The reason is simply that the market values and book values are similar. This will often be the case and explains why companies frequently use book values for debt in WACC calculations. Also, Eastman has no preferred stock, so we don't need to consider its cost.

Eastman's WACC   We now have the various pieces necessary to calculate Eastman's WACC. First, we need to calculate the capital structure weights. On a book value basis, Eastman's equity and debt are worth $1.627 billion and $1.598 billion, respectively. The total value is $3.225 billion, so the equity and debt weights are $1.627 billion/3.225 billion = .50 and $1.598 billion/3.225 billion = .50, respectively. Assuming a marginal tax rate of 35 percent, Eastman's WACC is:

$$\text{WACC} = .50 \times 8.67\% + .50 \times 4.46\% \times (1 - .35) = 5.81\%$$

Thus, using book value capital structure weights (and more decimal points than shown here), we get about 5.81 percent for Eastman's WACC.

If we use market value weights, however, the WACC will be higher. To see why, notice that on a market value basis, Eastman's equity and debt are worth $6.335 billion and $1.721 billion, respectively. The capital structure weights are therefore $6.335 billion/8.056 billion = .79 and $1.721 billion/8.056 billion = .21, so the equity percentage is much higher. With these weights (and more decimal points than shown here), Eastman's WACC is:

$$\text{WACC} = .79 \times 8.67\% + .21 \times 4.51\% \times (1 - .35) = 7.44\%$$

Thus, using market value weights, we get about 7.44 percent for Eastman's WACC, which is noticeably larger than the 5.81 percent WACC we got using book value weights.

As this example illustrates, using book values can lead to trouble, particularly if equity book values are used. Going back to Chapter 3, recall that we discussed the market-to-book ratio (the ratio of market value per share to book value per share). This ratio is usually substantially bigger than 1. For Eastman, for example, verify that it's about 3.89; so book values significantly overstate the percentage of Eastman's financing that comes from debt. In addition, if we were computing a WACC for a company that did not have publicly traded stock, we would try to come up with a suitable market-to-book ratio by looking at similar, publicly traded companies, and we would then use this ratio to adjust the book value of the company under consideration. As we have seen, failure to do so can lead to significant underestimation of the WACC.

Our nearby *Work the Web* box explains more about the WACC and related topics.

SOLVING THE WAREHOUSE PROBLEM AND SIMILAR CAPITAL BUDGETING PROBLEMS

Now we can use the WACC to solve the warehouse problem we posed at the beginning of the chapter. However, before we rush to discount the cash flows at the WACC to estimate NPV, we need to make sure we are doing the right thing.

Going back to first principles, we need to find an alternative in the financial markets that is comparable to the warehouse renovation. To be comparable, an alternative must be of the same level of risk as the warehouse project. Projects that have the same risk are said to be in the same risk class.

The WACC for a firm reflects the risk and the target capital structure of the firm's existing assets as a whole. As a result, strictly speaking, the firm's WACC is the appropriate discount rate only if the proposed investment is a replica of the firm's existing operating activities.

WORK THE WEB

So how does our estimate of the WACC for Eastman Chemical compare to others? One place to find estimates for WACC is www.valuepro.net. We went there and found the following information for Eastman:

Online Valuation for EMN - 2 / 23 / 2011

Intrinsic Stock Value: 102.82   [Recalculate]   [Value Another Stock]

Excess Return Period (yrs)	10	Depreciation Rate (% of Rev)	5.43
Revenues ($mil)	6345.0	Investment Rate (% of Rev)	6.14
Growth Rate (%)	10.5	Working Capital (% of Rev)	7.55
Net Oper. Profit Margin (%)	8.44	Short-Term Assets ($mil)	1909.0
Tax Rate (%)	37.770	Short-Term Liab. ($mil)	1072
Stock Price ($)	77.3900	Equity Risk Premium (%)	3
Shares Outstanding (mil)	72.2	Company Beta	1.3125
10-Yr Treasury Yield (%)	5	Value Debt Out. ($mil)	1605
Bond Spread Treasury (%)	1.5	Value Pref. Stock Out. ($mil)	0
Preferred Stock Yield (%)	7.5	Company WACC (%)	7.85

As you can see, ValuePro estimates the WACC (cost of capital) for Eastman as 7.85 percent, which is slightly more than our estimate of 7.44 percent. However, different inputs were used in the computations. For example, ValuePro uses an equity risk premium of only 3 percent. Calculating WACC requires the estimation of various inputs, and you must use your best judgment in these estimates.

Questions

1. Go to www.valuepro.net and look up the current WACC for Eastman Chemical on this website. How has the WACC changed? What are the possible reasons for the change?
2. Celgene (CELG) is a biopharmaceutical company. Would you expect the WACC for this company to be higher or lower than the WACC for Eastman Chemical? Why? Go to www.valuepro. net and find the estimated WACC for CELG. Was your assumption correct?

In broader terms, whether or not we can use the firm's WACC to value the warehouse project depends on whether the warehouse project is in the same risk class as the firm. We will assume that this project is an integral part of the overall business of the firm. In such cases, it is natural to think that the cost savings will be as risky as the general cash flows of the firm, and the project will thus be in the same risk class as the overall firm. More generally, projects like the warehouse renovation that are intimately related to the firm's existing operations are often viewed as being in the same risk class as the overall firm.

We can now see what the president should do. Suppose the firm has a target debt–equity ratio of 1/3. From Chapter 3, we know that a debt–equity ratio of $D/E = 1/3$ implies that E/V is .75 and D/V is .25. The cost of debt is 10 percent, and the cost of equity is 20 percent. Assuming a 34 percent tax rate, the WACC will be:

$$\begin{aligned} \text{WACC} &= (E/V) \times R_E + (D/V) \times R_D \times (1 - T_C) \\ &= .75 \times 20\% + .25 \times 10\% \times (1 - .34) \\ &= 16.65\% \end{aligned}$$

Recall that the warehouse project had a cost of $50 million and expected aftertax cash flows (the cost savings) of $12 million per year for six years. The NPV (in millions) is thus:

$$\text{NPV} = -\$50 + \frac{12}{(1 + \text{WACC})^1} + \cdots + \frac{12}{(1 + \text{WACC})^6}$$

Because the cash flows are in the form of an ordinary annuity, we can calculate this NPV using 16.65 percent (the WACC) as the discount rate as follows:

$$\begin{aligned} \text{NPV} &= -\$50 + 12 \times \frac{1 - [1/(1 + .1665)^6]}{.1665} \\ &= -\$50 + 12 \times 3.6222 \\ &= -\$6.53 \end{aligned}$$

Should the firm take on the warehouse renovation? The project has a negative NPV using the firm's WACC. This means that the financial markets offer superior projects in the same risk class (namely, the firm itself). The answer is clear: The project should be rejected. For future reference, our discussion of the WACC is summarized in Table 14.1.

EXAMPLE 14.5   **Using the WACC**

A firm is considering a project that will result in initial aftertax cash savings of $5 million at the end of the first year. These savings will grow at the rate of 5 percent per year. The firm has a debt–equity ratio of .5, a cost of equity of 29.2 percent, and a cost of debt of 10 percent. The cost-saving proposal is closely related to the firm's core business, so it is viewed as having the same risk as the overall firm. Should the firm take on the project?

Assuming a 34 percent tax rate, the firm should take on this project if it costs less than $30 million. To see this, first note that the PV is:

$$\text{PV} = \frac{\$5 \text{ million}}{\text{WACC} - .05}$$

This is an example of a growing perpetuity as discussed in Chapter 6. The WACC is:

$$\begin{aligned} \text{WACC} &= (E/V) \times R_E + (D/V) \times R_D \times (1 - T_C) \\ &= 2/3 \times 29.2\% + 1/3 \times 10\% \times (1 - .34) \\ &= 21.67\% \end{aligned}$$

The PV is thus:

$$\text{PV} = \frac{\$5 \text{ million}}{.2167 - .05} = \$30 \text{ million}$$

The NPV will be positive only if the cost is less than $30 million.

TABLE 14.1

Summary of Capital Cost Calculations

I.   The Cost of Equity, R_E

    A. Dividend growth model approach (from Chapter 8):

$$R_E = D_1/P_0 + g$$

    where D_1 is the expected dividend in one period, g is the dividend growth rate, and P_0 is the current stock price.

    B. SML approach (from Chapter 13):

$$R_E = R_f + \beta_E \times (R_M - R_f)$$

    where R_f is the risk-free rate, R_M is the expected return on the overall market, and β_E is the systematic risk of the equity.

II.   The Cost of Debt, R_D

    A. For a firm with publicly held debt, the cost of debt can be measured as the yield to maturity on the outstanding debt. The coupon rate is irrelevant. Yield to maturity is covered in Chapter 7.

    B. If the firm has no publicly traded debt, then the cost of debt can be measured as the yield to maturity on similarly rated bonds (bond ratings are discussed in Chapter 7).

III.   The Weighted Average Cost of Capital, WACC

    A. The firm's WACC is the overall required return on the firm as a whole. It is the appropriate discount rate to use for cash flows similar in risk to those of the overall firm.

    B. The WACC is calculated as:

$$\text{WACC} = (E/V) \times R_E + (D/V) \times R_D \times (1 - T_C)$$

    where T_C is the corporate tax rate, E is the *market* value of the firm's equity, D is the *market* value of the firm's debt, and $V = E + D$. Note that E/V is the percentage of the firm's financing (in market value terms) that is equity, and D/V is the percentage that is debt.

PERFORMANCE EVALUATION: ANOTHER USE OF THE WACC

Visit www.sternstewart.com *for more about EVA.*

Performance evaluation is another use of the WACC. Probably the best-known approach in this area is the economic value added (EVA) method developed by Stern Stewart & Co. Companies such as AT&T, Coca-Cola, Quaker Oats, and Briggs & Stratton are among the firms that have been using EVA as a means of evaluating corporate performance. Similar approaches include market value added (MVA) and shareholder value added (SVA).

Although the details differ, the basic idea behind EVA and similar strategies is straightforward. Suppose we have $100 million in capital (debt and equity) tied up in our firm, and our overall WACC is 12 percent. If we multiply these together, we get $12 million. Referring back to Chapter 2, if our cash flow from assets is less than this, we are, on an overall basis, destroying value; if cash flow from assets exceeds $12 million, we are creating value.

In practice, evaluation strategies such as these suffer to a certain extent from problems with implementation. For example, it appears that many companies make extensive use of book values for debt and equity in computing cost of capital. Even so, by focusing on value creation, WACC-based evaluation procedures force employees and management to pay attention to the real bottom line: increasing share prices.

A firm's weighted average cost of capital has important applications other than the discount rate in capital project evaluations. For instance, it is a key ingredient to measure a firm's true economic profit, or what I like to call EVA, standing for economic value added. Accounting rules dictate that the interest expense a company incurs on its debt financing be deducted from its reported profit, but those same rules ironically forbid deducting a charge for the shareholders' funds a firm uses. In economic terms, equity capital is in fact a very costly financing source, because shareholders bear the risk of being paid last, after all other stakeholders and investors are paid first. But according to accountants, shareholders' equity is free.

This egregious oversight has dire practical consequences. For one thing, it means that the profit figure accountants certify to be correct is inherently at odds with the net present value decision rule. For instance, it is a simple matter for management to inflate its reported earnings and earnings per share in ways that actually harm the shareholders by investing capital in projects that earn less than the overall cost of capital but more than the aftertax cost of borrowing money, which amounts to a trivial hurdle in most cases, a couple percentage points at most. In effect, EPS requires management to vault a mere three-foot hurdle when to satisfy shareholders managers must jump a ten-foot hurdle that includes the cost of equity. A prime example of the way accounting profit leads smart managers to do dumb things was Enron, where former top executives Ken Lay and Jeff Skilling boldly declared in the firm's 2000 annual report that they were "laser-focused on earnings per share," and so they were. Bonuses were funded out of book profit, and project developers were paid for signing up new deals and not generating a decent return on investment. Consequently, Enron's EPS was on the rise while its true economic profit—its EVA—measured after deducting the full cost of capital, was plummeting in the years leading up to the firm's demise—the result of massive misallocations of capital to ill-advised energy and new economy projects. The point is, EVA measures economic profit, the profit that actually discounts to net present value, and the maximization of which is every company's most important financial goal; yet, for all its popularity, EPS is just an accounting contrivance that is wholly unrelated to the maximization of shareholder wealth or sending the right decision signals to management.

Starting in the early 1990s, firms around the world—ranging from Coca-Cola, to Briggs & Stratton, Herman Miller, and Eli Lilly in America, Siemens in Germany, Tata Consulting and the Godrej Group out of India, Brahma Beer in Brazil, and many, many more—began to turn to EVA as a new and better way to measure performance and set goals, make decisions and determine bonuses, and to communicate with investors and to teach business and finance basics to managers and employees. Properly tailored and implemented, EVA is a natural way to bring the cost of capital to life and to turn everyone in a company into a capital conscientious, owner-entrepreneur.

Bennett Stewart is a cofounder of Stern Stewart & Co. and also the CEO of EVA Dimensions, a firm providing EVA data, valuation modeling, and hedge fund management. Stewart pioneered the practical development of EVA as chronicled in his book, The Quest for Value.

Concept Questions

14.4a How is the WACC calculated?

14.4b Why do we multiply the cost of debt by $(1 - T_C)$ when we compute the WACC?

14.4c Under what conditions is it correct to use the WACC to determine NPV?

14.5 Divisional and Project Costs of Capital

As we have seen, using the WACC as the discount rate for future cash flows is appropriate only when the proposed investment is similar to the firm's existing activities. This is not as restrictive as it sounds. If we are in the pizza business, for example, and we are thinking of opening a new location, then the WACC is the discount rate to use. The same is true of a retailer thinking of a new store, a manufacturer thinking of expanding production, or a consumer products company thinking of expanding its markets.

Nonetheless, despite the usefulness of the WACC as a benchmark, there will clearly be situations in which the cash flows under consideration have risks distinctly different from those of the overall firm. We consider how to cope with this problem next.

THE SML AND THE WACC

When we are evaluating investments with risks that are substantially different from those of the overall firm, use of the WACC will potentially lead to poor decisions. Figure 14.1 illustrates why.

In Figure 14.1, we have plotted an SML corresponding to a risk-free rate of 7 percent and a market risk premium of 8 percent. To keep things simple, we consider an all-equity company with a beta of 1. As we have indicated, the WACC and the cost of equity are exactly equal to 15 percent for this company because there is no debt.

Suppose our firm uses its WACC to evaluate all investments. This means that any investment with a return of greater than 15 percent will be accepted and any investment with a return of less than 15 percent will be rejected. We know from our study of risk and return, however, that a desirable investment is one that plots above the SML. As Figure 14.1 illustrates, using the WACC for all types of projects can result in the firm's incorrectly accepting relatively risky projects and incorrectly rejecting relatively safe ones.

FIGURE 14.1   The Security Market Line (SML) and the Weighted Average Cost of Capital (WACC)

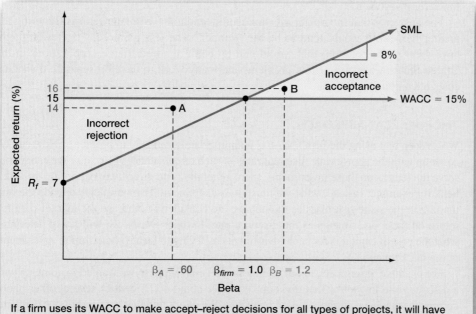

If a firm uses its WACC to make accept–reject decisions for all types of projects, it will have a tendency toward incorrectly accepting risky projects and incorrectly rejecting less risky projects.

For example, consider point A. This project has a beta of $\beta_A = .60$, as compared to the firm's beta of 1.0. It has an expected return of 14 percent. Is this a desirable investment? The answer is yes because its required return is only:

$$
\begin{aligned}
\text{Required return} &= R_f + \beta_A \times (R_M - R_f) \\
&= 7\% + .60 \times 8\% \\
&= 11.8\%
\end{aligned}
$$

However, if we use the WACC as a cutoff, then this project will be rejected because its return is less than 15 percent. This example illustrates that a firm that uses its WACC as a cutoff will tend to reject profitable projects with risks less than those of the overall firm.

At the other extreme, consider point B. This project has a beta of $\beta_B = 1.2$. It offers a 16 percent return, which exceeds the firm's cost of capital. This is not a good investment, however, because, given its level of systematic risk, its return is inadequate. Nonetheless, if we use the WACC to evaluate it, it will appear to be attractive. So the second error that will arise if we use the WACC as a cutoff is that we will tend to make unprofitable investments with risks greater than those of the overall firm. As a consequence, through time, a firm that uses its WACC to evaluate all projects will have a tendency to both accept unprofitable investments and become increasingly risky.

DIVISIONAL COST OF CAPITAL

The same type of problem with the WACC can arise in a corporation with more than one line of business. Imagine, for example, a corporation that has two divisions: a regulated telephone company and an electronics manufacturing operation. The first of these (the phone operation) has relatively low risk; the second has relatively high risk.

In this case, the firm's overall cost of capital is really a mixture of two different costs of capital, one for each division. If the two divisions were competing for resources, and the firm used a single WACC as a cutoff, which division would tend to be awarded greater funds for investment?

The answer is that the riskier division would tend to have greater returns (ignoring the greater risk), so it would tend to be the "winner." The less glamorous operation might have great profit potential that would end up being ignored. Large corporations in the United States are aware of this problem, and many work to develop separate divisional costs of capital.

THE PURE PLAY APPROACH

We've seen that using the firm's WACC inappropriately can lead to problems. How can we come up with the appropriate discount rates in such circumstances? Because we cannot observe the returns on these investments, there generally is no direct way of coming up with a beta, for example. Instead, what we must do is examine other investments outside the firm that are in the same risk class as the one we are considering, and use the market-required return on these investments as the discount rate. In other words, we will try to determine what the cost of capital is for such investments by trying to locate some similar investments in the marketplace.

For example, going back to our telephone division, suppose we wanted to come up with a discount rate to use for that division. What we could do is identify several other phone companies that have publicly traded securities. We might find that a typical phone company has a beta of .80, AA-rated debt, and a capital structure that is about 50 percent debt and 50 percent equity. Using this information, we could develop a WACC for a typical phone company and use this as our discount rate.

Alternatively, if we were thinking of entering a new line of business, we would try to develop the appropriate cost of capital by looking at the market-required returns on companies already in that business. In the language of Wall Street, a company that focuses on a single line of business is called a *pure play*. For example, if you wanted to bet on the price of crude oil by purchasing common stocks, you would try to identify companies that dealt exclusively with this product because they would be the most affected by changes in the price of crude oil. Such companies would be called "pure plays on the price of crude oil."

What we try to do here is to find companies that focus as exclusively as possible on the type of project in which we are interested. Our approach, therefore, is called the **pure play approach** to estimating the required return on an investment. To illustrate, suppose McDonald's decides to enter the personal computer and network server business with a line of machines called McPuters. The risks involved are quite different from those in the fast-food business. As a result, McDonald's would need to look at companies already in the personal computer business to compute a cost of capital for the new division. An obvious pure play candidate would be Dell, which is predominantly in this line of business. HP, on the other hand, would not be as good a choice because its primary focus is elsewhere, and it has many different product lines.

In Chapter 3, we discussed the subject of identifying similar companies for comparison purposes. The same problems we described there come up here. The most obvious one is that we may not be able to find any suitable companies. In this case, how to objectively determine a discount rate becomes a difficult question. Even so, the important thing is to be aware of the issue so that we at least reduce the possibility of the kinds of mistakes that can arise when the WACC is used as a cutoff on all investments.

pure play approach
The use of a WACC that is unique to a particular project, based on companies in similar lines of business.

THE SUBJECTIVE APPROACH

Because of the difficulties that exist in objectively establishing discount rates for individual projects, firms often adopt an approach that involves making subjective adjustments to the overall WACC. To illustrate, suppose a firm has an overall WACC of 14 percent. It places all proposed projects into four categories as follows:

Category	Examples	Adjustment Factor	Discount Rate
High risk	New products	+6%	20%
Moderate risk	Cost savings, expansion of existing lines	+0	14
Low risk	Replacement of existing equipment	−4	10
Mandatory	Pollution control equipment	n/a	n/a

n/a = Not applicable.

The effect of this crude partitioning is to assume that all projects either fall into one of three risk classes or else are mandatory. In the last case, the cost of capital is irrelevant because the project must be taken. With the subjective approach, the firm's WACC may change through time as economic conditions change. As this happens, the discount rates for the different types of projects will also change.

Within each risk class, some projects will presumably have more risk than others, and the danger of making incorrect decisions still exists. Figure 14.2 illustrates this point. Comparing Figures 14.1 and 14.2, we see that similar problems exist; but the magnitude of the potential error is less with the subjective approach. For example, the project labeled A

FIGURE 14.2   The Security Market Line (SML) and the Subjective Approach

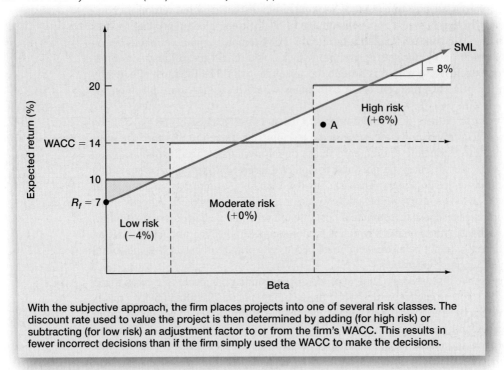

With the subjective approach, the firm places projects into one of several risk classes. The discount rate used to value the project is then determined by adding (for high risk) or subtracting (for low risk) an adjustment factor to or from the firm's WACC. This results in fewer incorrect decisions than if the firm simply used the WACC to make the decisions.

would be accepted if the WACC were used, but it is rejected once it is classified as a high-risk investment. What this illustrates is that some risk adjustment, even if it is subjective, is probably better than no risk adjustment.

It would be better, in principle, to objectively determine the required return for each project separately. However, as a practical matter, it may not be possible to go much beyond subjective adjustments because either the necessary information is unavailable or the cost and effort required are simply not worthwhile.

Concept Questions

14.5a What are the likely consequences if a firm uses its WACC to evaluate all proposed investments?

14.5b What is the pure play approach to determining the appropriate discount rate? When might it be used?

14.6 Flotation Costs and the Weighted Average Cost of Capital

So far, we have not included issue, or flotation, costs in our discussion of the weighted average cost of capital. If a company accepts a new project, it may be required to issue, or float, new bonds and stocks. This means that the firm will incur some costs, which we call *flotation costs*. The nature and magnitude of flotation costs are discussed in some detail in Chapter 15.

Sometimes it is suggested that the firm's WACC should be adjusted upward to reflect flotation costs. This is really not the best approach because, once again, the required return on an investment depends on the risk of the investment, not the source of the funds. This is not to say that flotation costs should be ignored. Because these costs arise as a consequence of the decision to undertake a project, they are relevant cash flows. We therefore briefly discuss how to include them in project analysis.

THE BASIC APPROACH

We start with a simple case. The Spatt Company, an all-equity firm, has a cost of equity of 20 percent. Because this firm is 100 percent equity, its WACC and its cost of equity are the same. Spatt is contemplating a large-scale, $100 million expansion of its existing operations. The expansion would be funded by selling new stock.

Based on conversations with its investment banker, Spatt believes its flotation costs will run 10 percent of the amount issued. This means that Spatt's proceeds from the equity sale will be only 90 percent of the amount sold. When flotation costs are considered, what is the cost of the expansion?

As we discuss in more detail in Chapter 15, Spatt needs to sell enough equity to raise $100 million *after* covering the flotation costs. In other words:

$100 million = $(1 − .10)$ × Amount raised

Amount raised = $100 million$/.90$ = $111.11 million

Spatt's flotation costs are thus $11.11 million, and the true cost of the expansion is $111.11 million once we include flotation costs.

Things are only slightly more complicated if the firm uses both debt and equity. For example, suppose Spatt's target capital structure is 60 percent equity, 40 percent debt. The flotation costs associated with equity are still 10 percent, but the flotation costs for debt are less—say 5 percent.

Earlier, when we had different capital costs for debt and equity, we calculated a weighted average cost of capital using the target capital structure weights. Here we will do much the same thing. We can calculate a weighted average flotation cost, f_A, by multiplying the equity flotation cost, f_E, by the percentage of equity (E/V) and the debt flotation cost, f_D, by the percentage of debt (D/V) and then adding the two together:

$$f_A = (E/V) \times f_E + (D/V) \times f_D \qquad \text{[14.8]}$$
$$= 60\% \times .10 + 40\% \times .05$$
$$= 8\%$$

The weighted average flotation cost is thus 8 percent. What this tells us is that for every dollar in outside financing needed for new projects, the firm must actually raise $1/(1 − .08)$ = $1.087. In our example, the project cost is $100 million when we ignore flotation costs. If we include them, then the true cost is $100 million$/(1 − f_A)$ = $100 million$/.92$ = $108.7 million.

In taking issue costs into account, the firm must be careful not to use the wrong weights. The firm should use the target weights, even if it can finance the entire cost of the project with either debt or equity. The fact that a firm can finance a specific project with debt or equity is not directly relevant. If a firm has a target debt–equity ratio of 1, for example, but chooses to finance a particular project with all debt, it will have to raise additional equity later on to maintain its target debt–equity ratio. To take this into account, the firm should always use the target weights in calculating the flotation cost.

| EXAMPLE 14.6 | **Calculating the Weighted Average Flotation Cost** |

The Weinstein Corporation has a target capital structure that is 80 percent equity, 20 percent debt. The flotation costs for equity issues are 20 percent of the amount raised; the flotation costs for debt issues are 6 percent. If Weinstein needs $65 million for a new manufacturing facility, what is the true cost once flotation costs are considered?

We first calculate the weighted average flotation cost, f_A:

$$f_A = (E/V) \times f_E + (D/V) \times f_D$$
$$= 80\% \times .20 + 20\% \times .06$$
$$= 17.2\%$$

The weighted average flotation cost is thus 17.2 percent. The project cost is $65 million when we ignore flotation costs. If we include them, then the true cost is $65 million/ $(1 - f_A) = \$65$ million/.828 = $78.5 million, again illustrating that flotation costs can be a considerable expense.

FLOTATION COSTS AND NPV

To illustrate how flotation costs can be included in an NPV analysis, suppose the Tripleday Printing Company is currently at its target debt–equity ratio of 100 percent. It is considering building a new $500,000 printing plant in Kansas. This new plant is expected to generate aftertax cash flows of $73,150 per year forever. The tax rate is 34 percent. There are two financing options:

1. A $500,000 new issue of common stock: The issuance costs of the new common stock would be about 10 percent of the amount raised. The required return on the company's new equity is 20 percent.
2. A $500,000 issue of 30-year bonds: The issuance costs of the new debt would be 2 percent of the proceeds. The company can raise new debt at 10 percent.

What is the NPV of the new printing plant?

To begin, because printing is the company's main line of business, we will use the company's weighted average cost of capital to value the new printing plant:

$$\text{WACC} = (E/V) \times R_E + (D/V) \times R_D \times (1 - T_C)$$
$$= .50 \times 20\% + .50 \times 10\% \times (1 - .34)$$
$$= 13.3\%$$

Because the cash flows are $73,150 per year forever, the PV of the cash flows at 13.3 percent per year is:

$$\text{PV} = \frac{\$73,150}{.133} = \$550,000$$

If we ignore flotation costs, the NPV is:

$$\text{NPV} = \$550,000 - 500,000 = \$50,000$$

With no flotation costs, the project generates an NPV that is greater than zero, so it should be accepted.

What about financing arrangements and issue costs? Because new financing must be raised, the flotation costs are relevant. From the information given, we know that the flotation costs are 2 percent for debt and 10 percent for equity. Because Tripleday uses equal amounts of debt and equity, the weighted average flotation cost, f_A, is:

$$f_A = (E/V) \times f_E + (D/V) \times f_D = .50 \times 10\% + .50 \times 2\%$$
$$= 6\%$$

At Hershey, we reevaluate our cost of capital annually or as market conditions warrant. The calculation of the cost of capital essentially involves three different issues, each with a few alternatives:

- *Capital weights*
  Book value or market value weights
  Current or target capital structure

- *Cost of debt*
  Historical (coupon) interest rates
  Market-based interest rates

- *Cost of equity*
  Dividend growth model
  Capital asset pricing model, or CAPM

At Hershey, we calculate our cost of capital officially based on the projected "target" capital structure at the end of our three-year intermediate planning horizon. This allows management to see the immediate impact of strategic decisions related to the planned composition of Hershey's capital pool. The cost of debt is calculated as the anticipated weighted average aftertax cost of debt in that final plan year based on the coupon rates attached to that debt. The cost of equity is computed via the dividend growth model.

We conducted a survey of the 10 food processing companies that we consider our industry group competitors. The results of this survey indicated that the cost of capital for most of these companies was in the 7 to 10 percent range. Furthermore, without exception, all 10 of these companies employed the CAPM when calculating their cost of equity. Our experience has been that the dividend growth model works better for Hershey. We do pay dividends, and we do experience steady, stable growth in our dividends. This growth is also projected within our strategic plan. Consequently, the dividend growth model is technically applicable and appealing to management because it reflects their best estimate of the future long-term growth rate.

In addition to the calculation already described, the other possible combinations and permutations are calculated as barometers. Unofficially, the cost of capital is calculated using market weights, current marginal interest rates, and the CAPM cost of equity. For the most part, and due to rounding the cost of capital to the nearest whole percentage point, these alternative calculations yield approximately the same results.

From the cost of capital, individual project hurdle rates are developed using a subjectively determined risk premium based on the characteristics of the project. Projects are grouped into separate project categories, such as cost savings, capacity expansion, product line extension, and new products. For example, in general, a new product is more risky than a cost savings project. Consequently, each project category's hurdle rate reflects the level of risk and commensurate required return as perceived by senior management. As a result, capital project hurdle rates range from a slight premium over the cost of capital to the highest hurdle rate of approximately double the cost of capital.

Samuel Weaver, Ph.D., was formerly director, financial planning and analysis, for Hershey. He is a certified management accountant and certified financial manager. His position combined the theoretical with the pragmatic and involved the analysis of many different facets of finance in addition to capital expenditure analysis.

Remember, the fact that Tripleday can finance the project with all debt or all equity is irrelevant. Because Tripleday needs $500,000 to fund the new plant, the true cost, once we include flotation costs, is $500,000/(1 − f_A) = $500,000/.94 = $531,915. Because the PV of the cash flows is $550,000, the plant has an NPV of $550,000 − 531,915 = $18,085, so it is still a good investment. However, its value is less than we initially might have thought.

INTERNAL EQUITY AND FLOTATION COSTS

Our discussion of flotation costs to this point implicitly assumes that firms always have to raise the capital needed for new investments. In reality, most firms rarely sell equity at all. Instead, their internally generated cash flow is sufficient to cover the equity portion of their capital spending. Only the debt portion must be raised externally.

The use of internal equity doesn't change our approach. However, we now assign a value of zero to the flotation cost of equity because there is no such cost. In our Tripleday example, the weighted average flotation cost would therefore be:

$$f_A = (E/V) \times f_E + (D/V) \times f_D$$
$$= .50 \times 0\% + .50 \times 2\%$$
$$= 1\%$$

Notice that whether equity is generated internally or externally makes a big difference because external equity has a relatively high flotation cost.

Concept Questions

14.6a What are flotation costs?
14.6b How are flotation costs included in an NPV analysis?

14.7 Summary and Conclusions

This chapter has discussed cost of capital. The most important concept is the weighted average cost of capital, or WACC, which we interpreted as the required rate of return on the overall firm. It is also the discount rate appropriate for cash flows that are similar in risk to those of the overall firm. We described how the WACC can be calculated, and we illustrated how it can be used in certain types of analyses.

We also pointed out situations in which it is inappropriate to use the WACC as the discount rate. To handle such cases, we described some alternative approaches to developing discount rates, such as the pure play approach. We also discussed how the flotation costs associated with raising new capital can be included in an NPV analysis.

CONNECT TO FINANCE

 |FINANCE

If you are using *Connect™ Finance* in your course, get online to take a Practice Test, check out study tools, and find out where you need additional practice.

Can you answer the following questions?

Section 14.2 A firm has paid dividends of $1.02, $1.10, $1.25, and $1.35 over the past 4 years, respectively. What is the average dividend growth rate? (LO 14-1)

Section 14.3 A semiannual, 7 percent bond matures in 14 years and has a face value of $1,000. The market quote on this bond is 101.4. What is the aftertax cost of debt if the tax rate is 35 percent? (LO 14-2)

Section 14.4 Why is the tax rate applied to the cost of debt but not to the cost of equity or preferred stock when computing a firm's weighted average cost of capital? (LO 14-3)

Section 14.5 What approach to a project's costs of capital entails the use of another firm's cost of capital rather than the use of your own firm's cost of capital? (LO 14-5)

Section 14.6 What is the flotation cost of equity for a firm that generates sufficient internal cash flows to cover the equity portion of any capital expenditure? (LO 14-4)

Log on to find out!

CHAPTER REVIEW AND SELF-TEST PROBLEMS

14.1 **Calculating the Cost of Equity** Suppose stock in Watta Corporation has a beta of .80. The market risk premium is 6 percent, and the risk-free rate is 6 percent. Watta's last dividend was $1.20 per share, and the dividend is expected to grow at 8 percent indefinitely. The stock currently sells for $45 per share. What is Watta's cost of equity capital?

14.2 **Calculating the WACC** In addition to the information given in the previous problem, suppose Watta has a target debt–equity ratio of 50 percent. Its cost of debt is 9 percent before taxes. If the tax rate is 35 percent, what is the WACC?

14.3 **Flotation Costs** Suppose in the previous problem Watta is seeking $30 million for a new project. The necessary funds will have to be raised externally. Watta's flotation costs for selling debt and equity are 2 percent and 16 percent, respectively. If flotation costs are considered, what is the true cost of the new project?

ANSWERS TO CHAPTER REVIEW AND SELF-TEST PROBLEMS

14.1 We start off with the SML approach. Based on the information given, the expected return on Watta's common stock is:

$$R_E = R_f + \beta_E \times (R_M - R_f)$$
$$= 6\% + .80 \times 6\%$$
$$= 10.80\%$$

We now use the dividend growth model. The projected dividend is $D_0 \times (1 + g) = \$1.20 \times 1.08 = \$1.296$, so the expected return using this approach is:

$$R_E = D_1/P_0 + g$$
$$= \$1.296/45 + .08$$
$$= 10.88\%$$

Because these two estimates, 10.80 percent and 10.88 percent, are fairly close, we will average them. Watta's cost of equity is approximately 10.84 percent.

14.2 Because the target debt–equity ratio is .50, Watta uses $.50 in debt for every $1 in equity. In other words, Watta's target capital structure is 1/3 debt and 2/3 equity. The WACC is thus:

$$\text{WACC} = (E/V) \times R_E + (D/V) \times R_D \times (1 - T_C)$$
$$= 2/3 \times 10.84\% + 1/3 \times 9\% \times (1 - .35)$$
$$= 9.177\%$$

Visit us at www.mhhe.com/rwj

14.3 Because Watta uses both debt and equity to finance its operations, we first need the weighted average flotation cost. As in the previous problem, the percentage of equity financing is 2/3, so the weighted average cost is:

$$f_A = (E/V) \times f_E + (D/V) \times f_D$$
$$= 2/3 \times 16\% + 1/3 \times 2\%$$
$$= 11.33\%$$

If Watta needs $30 million after flotation costs, then the true cost of the project is $30 million$/(1 - f_A)$ = $30 million/.8867 = $33.83 million.

CONCEPTS REVIEW AND CRITICAL THINKING QUESTIONS

1. **WACC [LO3]** On the most basic level, if a firm's WACC is 12 percent, what does this mean?

2. **Book Values versus Market Values [LO3]** In calculating the WACC, if you had to use book values for either debt or equity, which would you choose? Why?

3. **Project Risk [LO5]** If you can borrow all the money you need for a project at 6 percent, doesn't it follow that 6 percent is your cost of capital for the project?

4. **WACC and Taxes [LO3]** Why do we use an aftertax figure for cost of debt but not for cost of equity?

5. **DCF Cost of Equity Estimation [LO1]** What are the advantages of using the DCF model for determining the cost of equity capital? What are the disadvantages? What specific piece of information do you need to find the cost of equity using this model? What are some of the ways in which you could get this estimate?

6. **SML Cost of Equity Estimation [LO1]** What are the advantages of using the SML approach to finding the cost of equity capital? What are the disadvantages? What specific pieces of information are needed to use this method? Are all of these variables observable, or do they need to be estimated? What are some of the ways in which you could get these estimates?

7. **Cost of Debt Estimation [LO2]** How do you determine the appropriate cost of debt for a company? Does it make a difference if the company's debt is privately placed as opposed to being publicly traded? How would you estimate the cost of debt for a firm whose only debt issues are privately held by institutional investors?

8. **Cost of Capital [LO5]** Suppose Tom O'Bedlam, president of Bedlam Products, Inc., has hired you to determine the firm's cost of debt and cost of equity capital.

    a. The stock currently sells for $50 per share, and the dividend per share will probably be about $5. Tom argues, "It will cost us $5 per share to use the stockholders' money this year, so the cost of equity is equal to 10 percent (= $5/50)." What's wrong with this conclusion?

    b. Based on the most recent financial statements, Bedlam Products' total liabilities are $8 million. Total interest expense for the coming year will be about $1 million. Tom therefore reasons, "We owe $8 million, and we will pay $1 million interest. Therefore, our cost of debt is obviously $1 million/8 million = 12.5%." What's wrong with this conclusion?

    c. Based on his own analysis, Tom is recommending that the company increase its use of equity financing because "debt costs 12.5 percent, but equity costs only 10 percent; thus equity is cheaper." Ignoring all the other issues, what do you think about the conclusion that the cost of equity is less than the cost of debt?

9. **Company Risk versus Project Risk [LO5]** Both Dow Chemical Company, a large natural gas user, and Superior Oil, a major natural gas producer, are thinking of investing in natural gas wells near Houston. Both companies are all equity financed. Dow and Superior are looking at identical projects. They've analyzed their respective investments, which would involve a negative cash flow now and positive expected cash flows in the future. These cash flows would be the same for both firms. No debt would be used to finance the projects. Both companies estimate that their projects would have a net present value of $1 million at an 18 percent discount rate and a −$1.1 million NPV at a 22 percent discount rate. Dow has a beta of 1.25, whereas Superior has a beta of .75. The expected risk premium on the market is 8 percent, and risk-free bonds are yielding 12 percent. Should either company proceed? Should both? Explain.

10. **Divisional Cost of Capital [LO5]** Under what circumstances would it be appropriate for a firm to use different costs of capital for its different operating divisions? If the overall firm WACC were used as the hurdle rate for all divisions, would the riskier divisions or the more conservative divisions tend to get most of the investment projects? Why? If you were to try to estimate the appropriate cost of capital for different divisions, what problems might you encounter? What are two techniques you could use to develop a rough estimate for each division's cost of capital?

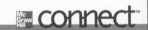

QUESTIONS AND PROBLEMS

1. **Calculating Cost of Equity [LO1]** The Muse Co. just issued a dividend of $2.75 per share on its common stock. The company is expected to maintain a constant 5.8 percent growth rate in its dividends indefinitely. If the stock sells for $59 a share, what is the company's cost of equity?

    BASIC
    (Questions 1–19)

2. **Calculating Cost of Equity [LO1]** The Zombie Corporation's common stock has a beta of 1.2. If the risk-free rate is 4.8 percent and the expected return on the market is 11 percent, what is the company's cost of equity capital?

3. **Calculating Cost of Equity [LO1]** Stock in Dragula Industries has a beta of 1.1. The market risk premium is 7 percent, and T-bills are currently yielding 4.5 percent. The company's most recent dividend was $1.70 per share, and dividends are expected to grow at a 6 percent annual rate indefinitely. If the stock sells for $39 per share, what is your best estimate of the company's cost of equity?

4. **Estimating the DCF Growth Rate [LO1]** Suppose In a Found, Ltd., just issued a dividend of $1.69 per share on its common stock. The company paid dividends of $1.35, $1.43, $1.50, and $1.61 per share in the last four years. If the stock currently sells for $50, what is your best estimate of the company's cost of equity capital using the arithmetic average growth rate in dividends? What if you use the geometric average growth rate?

5. **Calculating Cost of Preferred Stock [LO1]** Holdup Bank has an issue of preferred stock with a $4.25 stated dividend that just sold for $92 per share. What is the bank's cost of preferred stock?

6. **Calculating Cost of Debt [LO2]** Mudvayne, Inc., is trying to determine its cost of debt. The firm has a debt issue outstanding with 18 years to maturity that is quoted at 107 percent of face value. The issue makes semiannual payments and has an embedded cost of 6 percent annually. What is the company's pretax cost of debt? If the tax rate is 35 percent, what is the aftertax cost of debt?

Visit us at www.mhhe.com/rwj

7. **Calculating Cost of Debt [LO2]** Jiminy's Cricket Farm issued a 30-year, 8 percent semiannual bond 3 years ago. The bond currently sells for 93 percent of its face value. The company's tax rate is 35 percent.

   a. What is the pretax cost of debt?

   b. What is the aftertax cost of debt?

   c. Which is more relevant, the pretax or the aftertax cost of debt? Why?

8. **Calculating Cost of Debt [LO2]** For the firm in Problem 7, suppose the book value of the debt issue is $60 million. In addition, the company has a second debt issue on the market, a zero coupon bond with 10 years left to maturity; the book value of this issue is $35 million, and the bonds sell for 57 percent of par. What is the company's total book value of debt? The total market value? What is your best estimate of the aftertax cost of debt now?

9. **Calculating WACC [LO3]** Mullineaux Corporation has a target capital structure of 60 percent common stock, 5 percent preferred stock, and 35 percent debt. Its cost of equity is 12 percent, the cost of preferred stock is 5 percent, and the pretax cost of debt is 7 percent. The relevant tax rate is 35 percent.

   a. What is Mullineaux's WACC?

   b. The company president has approached you about Mullineaux's capital structure. He wants to know why the company doesn't use more preferred stock financing because it costs less than debt. What would you tell the president?

10. **Taxes and WACC [LO3]** Sixx AM Manufacturing has a target debt–equity ratio of .45. Its cost of equity is 13 percent, and its cost of debt is 6 percent. If the tax rate is 35 percent, what is the company's WACC?

11. **Finding the Target Capital Structure [LO3]** Fama's Llamas has a weighted average cost of capital of 9.6 percent. The company's cost of equity is 12 percent, and its pretax cost of debt is 7.9 percent. The tax rate is 35 percent. What is the company's target debt–equity ratio?

12. **Book Value versus Market Value [LO3]** Erna Corp. has 8 million shares of common stock outstanding. The current share price is $73, and the book value per share is $7. Erna Corp. also has two bond issues outstanding. The first bond issue has a face value of $85 million, has a 7 percent coupon, and sells for 97 percent of par. The second issue has a face value of $50 million, has an 8 percent coupon, and sells for 108 percent of par. The first issue matures in 21 years, the second in 6 years.

   a. What are Erna's capital structure weights on a book value basis?

   b. What are Erna's capital structure weights on a market value basis?

   c. Which are more relevant, the book or market value weights? Why?

13. **Calculating the WACC [LO3]** In Problem 12, suppose the most recent dividend was $4.10 and the dividend growth rate is 6 percent. Assume that the overall cost of debt is the weighted average of that implied by the two outstanding debt issues. Both bonds make semiannual payments. The tax rate is 35 percent. What is the company's WACC?

14. **WACC [LO3]** Paget, Inc., has a target debt–equity ratio of 1.25. Its WACC is 9.2 percent, and the tax rate is 35 percent.

   a. If the company's cost of equity is 14 percent, what is its pretax cost of debt?

   b. If instead you know that the aftertax cost of debt is 6.8 percent, what is the cost of equity?

15. **Finding the WACC [LO3]** Given the following information for Lightning Power Co., find the WACC. Assume the company's tax rate is 35 percent.

Debt:	8,000 6.5 percent coupon bonds outstanding, $1,000 par value, 25 years to maturity, selling for 106 percent of par; the bonds make semiannual payments.
Common stock:	310,000 shares outstanding, selling for $57 per share; the beta is 1.05.
Preferred stock:	15,000 shares of 4 percent preferred stock outstanding, currently selling for $72 per share.
Market:	7 percent market risk premium and 4.5 percent risk-free rate.

16. **Finding the WACC [LO3]** Titan Mining Corporation has 8.5 million shares of common stock outstanding, 250,000 shares of 5 percent preferred stock outstanding, and 135,000 7.5 percent semiannual bonds outstanding, par value $1,000 each. The common stock currently sells for $34 per share and has a beta of 1.25, the preferred stock currently sells for $91 per share, and the bonds have 15 years to maturity and sell for 114 percent of par. The market risk premium is 7.5 percent, T-bills are yielding 4 percent, and Titan Mining's tax rate is 35 percent.

   a. What is the firm's market value capital structure?

   b. If Titan Mining is evaluating a new investment project that has the same risk as the firm's typical project, what rate should the firm use to discount the project's cash flows?

17. **SML and WACC [LO1]** An all-equity firm is considering the following projects:

Project	Beta	IRR
W	.60	8.8%
X	.85	9.5
Y	1.15	11.9
Z	1.45	15.0

   The T-bill rate is 4 percent, and the expected return on the market is 11 percent.

   a. Which projects have a higher expected return than the firm's 11 percent cost of capital?

   b. Which projects should be accepted?

   c. Which projects would be incorrectly accepted or rejected if the firm's overall cost of capital were used as a hurdle rate?

18. **Calculating Flotation Costs [LO4]** Suppose your company needs $15 million to build a new assembly line. Your target debt–equity ratio is .60. The flotation cost for new equity is 8 percent, but the flotation cost for debt is only 5 percent. Your boss has decided to fund the project by borrowing money because the flotation costs are lower and the needed funds are relatively small.

   a. What do you think about the rationale behind borrowing the entire amount?

   b. What is your company's weighted average flotation cost, assuming all equity is raised externally?

   c. What is the true cost of building the new assembly line after taking flotation costs into account? Does it matter in this case that the entire amount is being raised from debt?

19. **Calculating Flotation Costs [LO4]** Caughlin Company needs to raise $55 million to start a new project and will raise the money by selling new bonds. The company will generate no internal equity for the foreseeable future. The company has a

target capital structure of 70 percent common stock, 5 percent preferred stock, and 25 percent debt. Flotation costs for issuing new common stock are 9 percent, for new preferred stock, 6 percent, and for new debt, 3 percent. What is the true initial cost figure the company should use when evaluating its project?

INTERMEDIATE
(Questions 20–23)

20. WACC and NPV [LO3, 5] Scanlin, Inc., is considering a project that will result in initial aftertax cash savings of $1.8 million at the end of the first year, and these savings will grow at a rate of 2 percent per year indefinitely. The firm has a target debt–equity ratio of .80, a cost of equity of 12 percent, and an aftertax cost of debt of 4.8 percent. The cost-saving proposal is somewhat riskier than the usual project the firm undertakes; management uses the subjective approach and applies an adjustment factor of +2 percent to the cost of capital for such risky projects. Under what circumstances should the company take on the project?

21. Flotation Costs [LO4] Lorre, Inc., recently issued new securities to finance a new TV show. The project cost $14 million, and the company paid $725,000 in flotation costs. In addition, the equity issued had a flotation cost of 7 percent of the amount raised, whereas the debt issued had a flotation cost of 3 percent of the amount raised. If the company issued new securities in the same proportion as its target capital structure, what is the company's target debt–equity ratio?

22. Calculating the Cost of Debt [LO2] Ying Import has several bond issues outstanding, each making semiannual interest payments. The bonds are listed in the following table. If the corporate tax rate is 34 percent, what is the aftertax cost of Ying's debt?

Bond	Coupon Rate	Price Quote	Maturity	Face Value
1	6.00%	105.86	5 years	$40,000,000
2	7.50	114.52	8 years	35,000,000
3	7.20	113.07	$15\frac{1}{2}$ years	55,000,000
4	6.80	102.31	25 years	50,000,000

23. Calculating the Cost of Equity [LO1] Berta Industries stock has a beta of 1.25. The company just paid a dividend of $.40, and the dividends are expected to grow at 5 percent. The expected return on the market is 12 percent, and Treasury bills are yielding 5.5 percent. The most recent stock price for Berta is $72.

a. Calculate the cost of equity using the DCF method.

b. Calculate the cost of equity using the SML method.

c. Why do you think your estimates in (a) and (b) are so different?

CHALLENGE
(Questions 24–26)

24. Flotation Costs and NPV [LO3, 4] Photochronograph Corporation (PC) manufactures time series photographic equipment. It is currently at its target debt–equity ratio of .80. It's considering building a new $50 million manufacturing facility. This new plant is expected to generate aftertax cash flows of $6.2 million in perpetuity. The company raises all equity from outside financing. There are three financing options:

1. *A new issue of common stock:* The flotation costs of the new common stock would be 8 percent of the amount raised. The required return on the company's new equity is 14 percent.

2. *A new issue of 20-year bonds:* The flotation costs of the new bonds would be 4 percent of the proceeds. If the company issues these new bonds at an annual coupon rate of 8 percent, they will sell at par.

3. *Increased use of accounts payable financing:* Because this financing is part of the company's ongoing daily business, it has no flotation costs, and the company

Visit us at www.mhhe.com/rwj

assigns it a cost that is the same as the overall firm WACC. Management has a target ratio of accounts payable to long-term debt of .15. (Assume there is no difference between the pretax and aftertax accounts payable cost.)

What is the NPV of the new plant? Assume that PC has a 35 percent tax rate.

25. **Flotation Costs [LO4]** Trower Corp. has a debt–equity ratio of .90. The company is considering a new plant that will cost $110 million to build. When the company issues new equity, it incurs a flotation cost of 8 percent. The flotation cost on new debt is 3.5 percent. What is the initial cost of the plant if the company raises all equity externally? What if it typically uses 60 percent retained earnings? What if all equity investment is financed through retained earnings?

26. **Project Evaluation [LO3, 4]** This is a comprehensive project evaluation problem bringing together much of what you have learned in this and previous chapters. Suppose you have been hired as a financial consultant to Defense Electronics, Inc. (DEI), a large, publicly traded firm that is the market share leader in radar detection systems (RDSs). The company is looking at setting up a manufacturing plant overseas to produce a new line of RDSs. This will be a five-year project. The company bought some land three years ago for $4.5 million in anticipation of using it as a toxic dump site for waste chemicals, but it built a piping system to safely discard the chemicals instead. The land was appraised last week for $5.3 million. In five years, the aftertax value of the land will be $5.7 million, but the company expects to keep the land for a future project. The company wants to build its new manufacturing plant on this land; the plant and equipment will cost $32 million to build. The following market data on DEI's securities are current:

Debt:	230,000 7.2 percent coupon bonds outstanding, 25 years to maturity, selling for 108 percent of par; the bonds have a $1,000 par value each and make semiannual payments.
Common stock:	8,800,000 shares outstanding, selling for $71 per share; the beta is 1.1.
Preferred stock:	450,000 shares of 5 percent preferred stock outstanding, selling for $81 per share.
Market:	7 percent expected market risk premium; 5 percent risk-free rate.

DEI uses G.M. Wharton as its lead underwriter. Wharton charges DEI spreads of 8 percent on new common stock issues, 6 percent on new preferred stock issues, and 4 percent on new debt issues. Wharton has included all direct and indirect issuance costs (along with its profit) in setting these spreads. Wharton has recommended to DEI that it raise the funds needed to build the plant by issuing new shares of common stock. DEI's tax rate is 35 percent. The project requires $1,300,000 in initial net working capital investment to get operational. Assume Wharton raises all equity for new projects externally.

a. Calculate the project's initial Time 0 cash flow, taking into account all side effects.

b. The new RDS project is somewhat riskier than a typical project for DEI, primarily because the plant is being located overseas. Management has told you to use an adjustment factor of +2 percent to account for this increased riskiness. Calculate the appropriate discount rate to use when evaluating DEI's project.

c. The manufacturing plant has an eight-year tax life, and DEI uses straight-line depreciation. At the end of the project (that is, the end of Year 5), the plant and equipment can be scrapped for $4.5 million. What is the aftertax salvage value of this plant and equipment?

Visit us at www.mhhe.com/rwj

Visit us at www.mhhe.com/rwj

d. The company will incur $6,800,000 in annual fixed costs. The plan is to manufacture 17,000 RDSs per year and sell them at $10,800 per machine; the variable production costs are $9,400 per RDS. What is the annual operating cash flow (OCF) from this project?

e. DEI's comptroller is primarily interested in the impact of DEI's investments on the bottom line of reported accounting statements. What will you tell her is the accounting break-even quantity of RDSs sold for this project?

f. Finally, DEI's president wants you to throw all your calculations, assumptions, and everything else into the report for the chief financial officer; all he wants to know is what the RDS project's internal rate of return (IRR) and net present value (NPV) are. What will you report?

MINICASE

Cost of Capital for Hubbard Computer, Inc.

You have recently been hired by Hubbard Computer, Inc. (HCI), in its relatively new treasury management department. HCI was founded eight years ago by Bob Hubbard and currently operates 74 stores in the Southeast. The company is privately owned by Bob and his family, and it had sales of $97 million last year.

HCI primarily sells to customers who shop in the stores. Customers come to the store and talk with a sales representative. The sales representative assists the customer in determining the type of computer and peripherals that are necessary for the individual customer's computing needs. After the order is taken, the customer pays for the order immediately, and the computer is made to fill the order. Delivery of the computer averages 15 days, and it is guaranteed in 30 days.

HCI's growth to date has come from its profits. When the company had sufficient capital, it would open a new store. Other than scouting locations, relatively little formal analysis has been used in its capital budgeting process. Bob has just read about capital budgeting techniques and has come to you for help. For starters, the company has never attempted to determine its cost of capital, and Bob would like you to perform the analysis. Because the company is privately owned, it is difficult to determine the cost of equity for the company. Bob wants you to use the pure play approach to estimate the cost of capital for HCI, and he has chosen Dell as a representative company. The following questions will lead you through the steps to calculate this estimate.

QUESTIONS

1. Most publicly traded corporations are required to submit quarterly (10Q) and annual reports (10K) to the SEC detailing the financial operations of the company over the past quarter or year, respectively. These corporate filings are available on the SEC website at www.sec.gov. Go to the SEC website, follow the "Search for Company Filings" link, and search for SEC filings made by Dell. Find the most recent 10Q or 10K, and download the form. Look on the balance sheet to find the book value of debt and the book value of equity. If you look further down the report, you should find a section titled "Long-term Debt and Interest Rate Risk Management" that will provide a breakdown of Dell's long-term debt.

2. To estimate the cost of equity for Dell, go to finance. yahoo.com and enter the ticker symbol DELL. Follow the links to answer the following questions: What is the most recent stock price listed for Dell? What is the market value of equity, or market capitalization? How many shares of stock does Dell have outstanding? What is the most recent annual dividend? Can you use the dividend discount model in this case? What is the beta for Dell? Now go back to finance.yahoo.com and follow the "Bonds" link. What is the yield on three-month Treasury bills? Using the historical market risk premium, what is the cost of equity for Dell using CAPM?

3. You now need to calculate the cost of debt for Dell. Go to www.finra.org/marketdata, enter Dell as the company, and find the yield to maturity for each of Dell's bonds. What is the weighted average cost of debt for Dell using the book value weights and using the market value weights? Does it make a difference in this case if you use book value weights or market value weights?

4. You now have all the necessary information to calculate the weighted average cost of capital for Dell. Calculate this using book value weights and market value weights, assuming Dell has a 35 percent marginal tax rate. Which number is more relevant?

5. You used Dell as a pure play company to estimate the cost of capital for HCI. Are there any potential problems with this approach in this situation?

RAISING CAPITAL

IN AN EAGERLY AWAITED INITIAL PUBLIC OFFERING (IPO), "Government Motors" went public as General Motors on November 18, 2010. Assisted by Morgan Stanley, J.P. Morgan, BofA Merrill Lynch, and Citi, General Motors sold over 500 million shares of stock to the public at a price of $33. Despite the company's recent financial turmoil and subsequent government bailout, the stock price jumped to $34.19 at the end of the day, a 3.6 percent increase. In all, the General Motors offer raised a total of $23.1 billion, the largest IPO in history. Previously the largest IPO had been the Agricultural Bank of China in July 2010, which raised $22.1 billion. In this chapter, we will examine the process by which companies such as General Motors sell stock to the public, the costs of doing so, and the role of investment banks in the process.

LEARNING OBJECTIVES

After studying this chapter, you should understand:

LO1 The venture capital market and its role in the financing of new, high-risk ventures.

LO2 How securities are sold to the public and the role of investment banks in the process.

LO3 Initial public offerings and some of the costs of going public.

LO4 How rights are issued to existing shareholders and how to value those rights.

All firms must, at varying times, obtain capital. To do so, a firm must either borrow the money (debt financing), sell a portion of the firm (equity financing), or both. How a firm raises capital depends a great deal on the size of the firm, its life-cycle stage, and its growth prospects.

In this chapter, we examine some of the ways in which firms actually raise capital. We begin by looking at companies in the early stages of their lives and the importance of venture capital for such firms. We then look at the process of going public and the role of investment banks. Along the way, we discuss many of the issues associated with selling securities to the public and their implications for all types of firms. We close the chapter with a discussion of sources of debt capital.[1]

---

[1]We are indebted to Jay R. Ritter of the University of Florida for helpful comments and suggestions for this chapter.

15.1 The Financing Life Cycle of a Firm: Early-Stage Financing and Venture Capital

One day, you and a friend have a great idea for a new computer software product that helps users communicate using the next-generation meganet. Filled with entrepreneurial zeal, you christen the product Megacomm and set about bringing it to market.

Working nights and weekends, you are able to create a prototype of your product. It doesn't actually work, but at least you can show it around to illustrate your idea. To actually develop the product, you need to hire programmers, buy computers, rent office space, and so on. Unfortunately, because you are both college students, your combined assets are not sufficient to fund a pizza party, much less a start-up company. You need what is often referred to as OPM—other people's money.

Your first thought might be to approach a bank for a loan. You would probably discover, however, that banks are generally not interested in making loans to start-up companies with no assets (other than an idea) run by fledgling entrepreneurs with no track record. Instead your search for capital would likely lead you to the **venture capital (VC)** market.

venture capital (VC)
Financing for new, often high-risk ventures.

VENTURE CAPITAL

The term *venture capital* does not have a precise meaning, but it generally refers to financing for new, often high-risk ventures. For example, before it went public, Google was VC financed. Individual venture capitalists invest their own money; so-called "angels" are usually individual VC investors, but they tend to specialize in smaller deals. Venture capital firms specialize in pooling funds from various sources and investing them. The underlying sources of funds for such firms include individuals, pension funds, insurance companies, large corporations, and even university endowment funds. The broad term *private equity* is often used to label the rapidly growing area of equity financing for nonpublic companies.[2]

Venture capitalists and venture capital firms recognize that many or even most new ventures will not fly, but the occasional one will. The potential profits are enormous in such cases. To limit their risk, venture capitalists generally provide financing in stages. At each stage, enough money is invested to reach the next milestone or planning stage. For example, the *first-stage financing* might be enough to get a prototype built and a manufacturing plan completed. Based on the results, the *second-stage financing* might be a major investment needed to actually begin manufacturing, marketing, and distribution. There might be many such stages, each of which represents a key step in the process of growing the company.

Venture capital firms often specialize in different stages. Some specialize in very early "seed money," or ground floor, financing. In contrast, financing in the later stages might come from venture capitalists specializing in so-called mezzanine-level financing, where *mezzanine level* refers to the level just above the ground floor.

The fact that financing is available in stages and is contingent on specified goals being met is a powerful motivating force for the firm's founders. Often, the founders receive

For a list of well-known VC firms, see www.vfinance.com.

---

[2]So-called vulture capitalists specialize in high-risk investments in established, but financially distressed, firms. Vulgar capitalists invest in firms that have bad taste (OK, we made up this last bit).

relatively little in the way of salary and have substantial portions of their personal assets tied up in the business. At each stage of financing, the value of the founders' stake grows and the probability of success rises.

In addition to providing financing, venture capitalists often actively participate in running the firm, providing the benefit of experience with previous start-ups as well as general business expertise. This is especially true when the firm's founders have little or no hands-on experience in running a company.

SOME VENTURE CAPITAL REALITIES

Although there is a large venture capital market, the truth is that access to venture capital is really very limited. Venture capital companies receive huge numbers of unsolicited proposals, the vast majority of which end up in the circular file unread. Venture capitalists rely heavily on informal networks of lawyers, accountants, bankers, and other venture capitalists to help identify potential investments. As a result, personal contacts are important in gaining access to the venture capital market; it is very much an "introduction" market.

Another simple fact about venture capital is that it is incredibly expensive. In a typical deal, the venture capitalist will demand (and get) 40 percent or more of the equity in the company. Venture capitalists frequently hold voting preferred stock, giving them various priorities in the event that the company is sold or liquidated. The venture capitalist will typically demand (and get) several seats on the company's board of directors and may even appoint one or more members of senior management.

CHOOSING A VENTURE CAPITALIST

The Internet is a tremendous source of venture capital information, both for suppliers and demanders of capital. For example, the site at www.dealflow.com prompts you to search the firm's database as either an entrepreneur (capital seeker) or a venture capitalist (capital supplier).

Some start-up companies, particularly those headed by experienced, previously successful entrepreneurs, will be in such demand that they will have the luxury of looking beyond the money in choosing a venture capitalist. There are some key considerations in such a case, some of which can be summarized as follows:

1. *Financial strength is important:* The venture capitalist needs to have the resources and financial reserves for additional financing stages should they become necessary. This doesn't mean that bigger is necessarily better, however, because of our next consideration.

2. *Style is important:* Some venture capitalists will wish to be very much involved in day-to-day operations and decision making, whereas others will be content with monthly reports. Which are better depends on the firm and also on the venture capitalists' business skills. In addition, a large venture capital firm may be less flexible and more bureaucratic than a smaller "boutique" firm.

3. *References are important:* Has the venture capitalist been successful with similar firms? Of equal importance, how has the venture capitalist dealt with situations that didn't work out?

4. *Contacts are important:* A venture capitalist may be able to help the business in ways other than helping with financing and management by providing introductions to potentially important customers, suppliers, and other industry contacts. Venture capitalist firms frequently specialize in a few particular industries, and such specialization could prove quite valuable.

5. *Exit strategy is important:* Venture capitalists are generally not long-term investors. How and under what circumstances the venture capitalist will "cash out" of the business should be carefully evaluated.

CONCLUSION

If a start-up succeeds, the big payoff frequently comes when the company is sold to another company or goes public. Either way, investment bankers are often involved in the process. We discuss the process of selling securities to the public in the next several sections, paying particular attention to the process of going public.

Concept Questions

15.1a What is venture capital?

15.1b Why is venture capital often provided in stages?

15.2 Selling Securities to the Public: The Basic Procedure

Many rules and regulations surround the process of selling securities. The Securities Act of 1933 is the origin of federal regulations for all new interstate securities issues. The Securities Exchange Act of 1934 is the basis for regulating securities already outstanding. The Securities and Exchange Commission, or SEC, administers both acts.

A series of steps is involved in issuing securities to the public. In general terms, the basic procedure is as follows:

registration statement
A statement filed with the SEC that discloses all material information concerning the corporation making a public offering.

1. Management's first step in issuing any securities to the public is to obtain approval from the board of directors. In some cases, the number of authorized shares of common stock must be increased. This requires a vote of the shareholders.

2. The firm must prepare a **registration statement** and file it with the SEC. The registration statement is required for all public, interstate issues of securities, with two exceptions:

    a. Loans that mature within nine months.

    b. Issues that involve less than $5 million.

Regulation A
An SEC regulation that exempts public issues of less than $5 million from most registration requirements.

The second exception is known as the *small-issues exemption*. In such a case, simplified procedures are used. Under the basic small-issues exemption, issues of less than $5 million are governed by **Regulation A**, for which only a brief offering statement is needed. Normally, however, a registration statement contains many pages (50 or more) of financial information, including a financial history, details of the existing business, proposed financing, and plans for the future.

prospectus
A legal document describing details of the issuing corporation and the proposed offering to potential investors.

3. The SEC examines the registration statement during a waiting period. During this time, the firm may distribute copies of a preliminary **prospectus**. The prospectus contains much of the information in the registration statement, and it is given to potential investors by the firm. The preliminary prospectus is sometimes called a **red herring**, in part because bold red letters are printed on the cover.

red herring
A preliminary prospectus distributed to prospective investors in a new issue of securities.

A registration statement becomes effective on the 20th day after its filing unless the SEC sends a *letter of comment* suggesting changes. In that case, after the changes are made, the 20-day waiting period starts again. It is important to note that the SEC does not consider the economic merits of the proposed sale; it merely makes sure that various rules and regulations are followed. Also, the SEC generally does not check the accuracy or truthfulness of information in the prospectus.

The registration statement does not initially contain the price of the new issue. Usually, a price amendment is filed at or near the end of the waiting period, and the registration becomes effective.

4. The company cannot sell these securities during the waiting period. However, oral offers can be made.

5. On the effective date of the registration statement, a price is determined and a full-fledged selling effort gets under way. A final prospectus must accompany the delivery of securities or confirmation of sale, whichever comes first.

Tombstone advertisements (or, simply, *tombstones*) are used by underwriters during and after the waiting period. An example is reproduced in Figure 15.1. The tombstone contains the name of the issuer (the World Wrestling Federation, now known as World Wrestling Entertainment). It provides some information about the issue, and it lists the investment banks (the underwriters) involved with selling the issue. The role of the investment banks in selling securities is discussed more fully in the following pages.

The investment banks on the tombstone are divided into groups called *brackets* based on their participation in the issue, and the names of the banks are listed alphabetically within each bracket. The brackets are often viewed as a kind of pecking order. In general, the higher the bracket, the greater is the underwriter's prestige. In recent years, the use of printed tombstones has declined, in part as a cost-saving measure.

tombstone
An advertisement announcing a public offering.

Concept Questions

15.2a What are the basic procedures in selling a new issue?

15.2b What is a registration statement?

Find out what firms are going public this week at www.marketwatch.com.

Alternative Issue Methods

15.3

When a company decides to issue a new security, it can sell it as a public issue or a private issue. In the case of a public issue, the firm is required to register the issue with the SEC. However, if the issue is to be sold to fewer than 35 investors, the sale can be carried out privately. In this case, a registration statement is not required.[3]

For equity sales, there are two kinds of public issues: a **general cash offer** and a **rights offer** (or *rights offering*). With a cash offer, securities are offered to the general public. With a rights offer, securities are initially offered only to existing owners. Rights offers are fairly common in other countries, but they are relatively rare in the United States, particularly in recent years. We therefore focus primarily on cash offers in this chapter.

The first public equity issue that is made by a company is referred to as an **initial public offering**, *IPO*, or an *unseasoned new issue*. This issue occurs when a company decides to go public. Obviously, all initial public offerings are cash offers. If the firm's existing shareholders wanted to buy the shares, the firm wouldn't have to sell them publicly in the first place.

general cash offer
An issue of securities offered for sale to the general public on a cash basis.

rights offer
A public issue of securities in which securities are first offered to existing shareholders. Also called a *rights offering*.

initial public offering
A company's first equity issue made available to the public. Also called an *unseasoned new issue* or an *IPO*.

---

[3]A variety of different arrangements can be made for private equity issues. Selling unregistered securities avoids the costs of complying with the Securities Exchange Act of 1934. Regulation significantly restricts the resale of unregistered equity securities. For example, the purchaser may be required to hold the securities for at least one year (or more). Many of the restrictions were significantly eased in 1990 for very large institutional investors, however. The private placement of bonds is discussed in a later section.

FIGURE 15.1

An Example of a
Tombstone
Advertisement

This announcement is neither an offer to sell nor a solicitation of an offer to buy any of these securities.
The offering is made only by the Prospectus.

New Issue

11,500,000 Shares

World Wrestling Federation Entertainment, Inc.

Class A Common Stock

Price $17.00 Per Share

Copies of the Prospectus may be obtained in any State in which this announcement
is circulated from only such of the Underwriters, including the undersigned,
as may lawfully offer these securities in such State.

U.S. Offering

9,200,000 Shares

This portion of the underwriting is being offered in the United States and Canada.

Bear, Stearns & Co. Inc.

Credit Suisse First Boston

Merrill Lynch & Co.

Wit Capital Corporation

Allen & Company Incorporated	Banc of America Securities LLC	Deutsche Banc Alex. Brown
Donaldson, Lufkin & Jenrette	A.G. Edwards & Sons, Inc.	Hambrecht & Quist ING Barings
Prudential Securities	SG Cowen Wasserstein Perella Securities, Inc.	Advest, Inc.
Axiom Capital Management, Inc.	Blackford Securities Corp.	J.C. Bradford & Co.
Joseph Charles & Assoc., Inc.	Chatsworth Securities LLC	Gabelli & Company, Inc.
Gaines, Berland Inc. Jefferies & Company, Inc.	Josephthal & Co. Inc.	Neuberger Berman, LLC
Raymond James & Associates, Inc.		Sanders Morris Mundy
Tucker Anthony Cleary Gull		Wachovia Securities, Inc.

International Offering

2,300,000 Shares

This portion of the underwriting is being offered outside of the United States and Canada.

Bear, Stearns International Limited

Credit Suisse First Boston

Merrill Lynch International

Method	Type	Definition
Public Traditional negotiated cash offer	Firm commitment cash offer	The company negotiates an agreement with an investment banker to underwrite and distribute the new shares. A specified number of shares are bought by underwriters and sold at a higher price.
	Best efforts cash offer	The company has investment bankers sell as many of the new shares as possible at the agreed-upon price. There is no guarantee concerning how much cash will be raised.
	Dutch auction cash offer	The company has investment bankers auction shares to determine the highest offer price obtainable for a given number of shares to be sold.
Privileged subscription	Direct rights offer	The company offers the new stock directly to its existing shareholders.
	Standby rights offer	Like the direct rights offer, this contains a privileged subscription arrangement with existing shareholders. The net proceeds are guaranteed by the underwriters.
Nontraditional cash offer	Shelf cash offer	Qualifying companies can authorize all shares they expect to sell over a two-year period and sell them when needed.
	Competitive firm cash offer	The company can elect to award the underwriting contract through a public auction instead of negotiation.
Private	Direct placement	Securities are sold directly to the purchaser, who, at least until recently, generally could not resell securities for at least two years.

TABLE 15.1

The Methods of Issuing New Securities

IPO information is widely available. Try IPO Central at www.hoovers.com.

A **seasoned equity offering (SEO)** is a new issue for a company with securities that have been previously issued.[4] A seasoned equity offering of common stock can be made by using a cash offer or a rights offer.

These methods of issuing new securities are shown in Table 15.1. They are discussed in Sections 15.4 through 15.8.

seasoned equity offering (SEO)
A new equity issue of securities by a company that has previously issued securities to the public.

Concept Questions

15.3a What is the difference between a rights offer and a cash offer?

15.3b Why is an initial public offering necessarily a cash offer?

Underwriters

If the public issue of securities is a cash offer, **underwriters** are usually involved. Underwriting is an important line of business for large investment firms such as Morgan Stanley. Underwriters perform services such as the following for corporate issuers:

1. Formulating the method used to issue the securities.
2. Pricing the new securities.
3. Selling the new securities.

15.4

underwriters
Investment firms that act as intermediaries between a company selling securities and the investing public.

---

[4]The terms *follow-on offering* and *secondary offering* are also commonly used.

syndicate
A group of underwriters formed to share the risk and to help sell an issue.

Typically, the underwriter buys the securities for less than the offering price and accepts the risk of not being able to sell them. Because underwriting involves risk, underwriters usually combine to form an underwriting group called a **syndicate** to share the risk and to help sell the issue.

In a syndicate, one or more managers arrange, or comanage, the offering. The lead manager typically has the responsibility of dealing with the issuer and pricing the securities. The other underwriters in the syndicate serve primarily to distribute the issue and produce research reports later on. In recent years, it has become fairly common for a syndicate to consist of only a small number of comanagers.

gross spread
Compensation to the underwriter, determined by the difference between the underwriter's buying price and offering price.

The difference between the underwriter's buying price and the offering price is called the **gross spread**, or underwriting discount. It is the basic compensation received by the underwriter. Sometimes, on smaller deals, the underwriter will get noncash compensation in the form of warrants and stock in addition to the spread.[5]

CHOOSING AN UNDERWRITER

A firm can offer its securities to the highest bidding underwriter on a *competitive offer* basis, or it can negotiate directly with an underwriter. Except for a few large firms, companies usually do new issues of debt and equity on a *negotiated offer* basis. The exception is public utility holding companies, which are essentially required to use competitive underwriting.

There is evidence that competitive underwriting is cheaper to use than negotiated underwriting. The underlying reasons for the dominance of negotiated underwriting in the United States are the subject of ongoing debate.

TYPES OF UNDERWRITING

Three basic types of underwriting are involved in a cash offer: firm commitment, best efforts, and Dutch auction.

firm commitment underwriting
The type of underwriting in which the underwriter buys the entire issue, assuming full financial responsibility for any unsold shares.

Firm Commitment Underwriting   In **firm commitment underwriting**, the issuer sells the entire issue to the underwriters, who then attempt to resell it. This is the most prevalent type of underwriting in the United States. This is really just a purchase–resale arrangement, and the underwriter's fee is the spread. For a new issue of seasoned equity, the underwriters can look at the market price to determine what the issue should sell for, and more than 95 percent of all such new issues are firm commitments.

If the underwriter cannot sell all of the issue at the agreed-upon offering price, it may have to lower the price on the unsold shares. Nonetheless, with firm commitment underwriting, the issuer receives the agreed-upon amount, and all the risk associated with selling the issue is transferred to the underwriter.

Because the offering price usually isn't set until the underwriters have investigated how receptive the market is to the issue, this risk is usually minimal. Also, because the offering price usually is not set until just before selling commences, the issuer doesn't know precisely what its net proceeds will be until that time.

Learn more about investment banks at Merrill Lynch (www.ml.com).

To determine the offering price, the underwriter will meet with potential buyers, typically large institutional buyers such as mutual funds. Often, the underwriter and company management will do presentations in multiple cities, pitching the stock in what is known as a *road show*. Potential buyers provide information on the price they would be willing to pay and the number of shares they would purchase at a particular price. This process

---

[5]Warrants are options to buy newly issued stock at a fixed price for some fixed period.

of soliciting information about buyers and the prices and quantities they would demand is known as *bookbuilding*. As we will see, despite the bookbuilding process, underwriters frequently get the price wrong, or so it seems.

Best Efforts Underwriting   In **best efforts underwriting**, the underwriter is legally bound to use "best efforts" to sell the securities at the agreed-upon offering price. Beyond this, the underwriter does not guarantee any particular amount of money to the issuer. This form of underwriting has become uncommon in recent years.

best efforts underwriting
The type of underwriting in which the underwriter sells as much of the issue as possible, but can return any unsold shares to the issuer without financial responsibility.

Dutch Auction Underwriting   With **Dutch auction underwriting**, the underwriter does not set a fixed price for the shares to be sold. Instead, the underwriter conducts an auction in which investors bid for shares. The offer price is determined based on the submitted bids. A Dutch auction is also known by the more descriptive name *uniform price auction*. This approach to selling securities to the public is relatively new in the IPO market and has not been widely used there, but it is very common in the bond markets. For example, it is the sole procedure used by the U.S. Treasury to sell enormous quantities of notes, bonds, and bills to the public.

Dutch auction underwriting
The type of underwriting in which the offer price is set based on competitive bidding by investors. Also known as a *uniform price auction*.

The best way to understand a Dutch or uniform price auction is to consider a simple example. Suppose the Rial Company wants to sell 400 shares to the public. The company receives five bids as follows:

Bidder	Quantity	Price
A	100 shares	$16
B	100 shares	14
C	200 shares	12
D	100 shares	12
E	200 shares	10

Thus, bidder A is willing to buy 100 shares at $16 each, bidder B is willing to buy 100 shares at $14, and so on. The Rial Company examines the bids to determine the highest price that will result in all 400 shares being sold. So, for example, at $14, A and B would buy only 200 shares, so that price is too high. Working our way down, all 400 shares won't be sold until we hit a price of $12, so $12 will be the offer price in the IPO. Bidders A through D will receive shares; bidder E will not.

Learn all about Dutch auction IPOs at www.wrhambrecht.com.

There are two additional important points to observe in our example. First, all the winning bidders will pay $12—even bidders A and B, who actually bid a higher price. The fact that all successful bidders pay the same price is the reason for the name "uniform price auction." The idea in such an auction is to encourage bidders to bid aggressively by providing some protection against bidding a price that is too high.

Second, notice that at the $12 offer price, there are actually bids for 500 shares, which exceeds the 400 shares Rial wants to sell. Thus, there has to be some sort of allocation. How this is done varies a bit; but in the IPO market, the approach has been to simply compute the ratio of shares offered to shares bid at the offer price or better, which, in our example, is $400/500 = .8$, and allocate bidders that percentage of their bids. In other words, bidders A through D would each receive 80 percent of the shares they bid at a price of $12 per share.

THE AFTERMARKET

The period after a new issue is initially sold to the public is referred to as the *aftermarket*. During this time, the members of the underwriting syndicate generally do not sell securities for less than the offering price.

The principal underwriter is permitted to buy shares if the market price falls below the offering price. The purpose of this would be to support the market and stabilize the price against temporary downward pressure. If the issue remains unsold after a time (for example, 30 days), members can leave the group and sell their shares at whatever price the market will allow.[6]

THE GREEN SHOE PROVISION

Green Shoe provision
A contract provision giving the underwriter the option to purchase additional shares from the issuer at the offering price. Also called the *overallotment option*.

Many underwriting contracts contain a **Green Shoe provision** (sometimes called the *overallotment option*), which gives the members of the underwriting group the option to purchase additional shares from the issuer at the offering price.[7] Essentially all IPOs and SEOs include this provision, but ordinary debt offerings generally do not. The stated reason for the Green Shoe option is to cover excess demand and oversubscriptions. Green Shoe options usually last for 30 days and involve 15 percent of the newly issued shares.

In practice, usually underwriters initially go ahead and sell 115 percent of the shares offered. If the demand for the issue is strong after the offering, the underwriters exercise the Green Shoe option to get the extra 15 percent from the company. If demand for the issue is weak, the underwriters buy the needed shares in the open market, thereby helping to support the price of the issue in the aftermarket.

LOCKUP AGREEMENTS

lockup agreement
The part of the underwriting contract that specifies how long insiders must wait after an IPO before they can sell stock.

Although they are not required by law, almost all underwriting contracts contain so-called **lockup agreements.** Such agreements specify how long insiders must wait after an IPO before they can sell some or all of their stock. Lockup periods have become fairly standardized in recent years at 180 days. Thus, following an IPO, insiders can't cash out until six months have gone by, which ensures that they maintain a significant economic interest in the company going public.

Lockup periods are also important because it is not unusual for the number of locked-up shares to exceed the number of shares held by the public, sometimes by a substantial multiple. On the day the lockup period expires, there is the possibility that a large number of shares will hit the market on the same day and thereby depress values. The evidence suggests that, on average, venture capital–backed companies are particularly likely to experience a loss in value on the lockup expiration day.

THE QUIET PERIOD

Once a firm begins to seriously contemplate an IPO, the SEC requires that a firm and its managing underwriters observe a "quiet period." This means that all communications with the public must be limited to ordinary announcements and other purely factual matters. The quiet period ends 40 calendar days after an IPO. The SEC's logic is that all relevant information should be contained in the prospectus. An important result of this requirement is that the underwriter's analysts are prohibited from making recommendations to investors. As soon as the quiet period ends, however, the managing underwriters typically publish research reports, usually accompanied by a favorable "buy" recommendation.

In 2004, two firms experienced notable quiet period–related problems. Just before Google's IPO, an interview with Google cofounders Sergey Brin and Larry Page appeared in *Playboy*. The interview almost caused a postponement of the IPO, but Google was able to amend its prospectus in time. In May 2004, Salesforce.com's IPO was delayed because an interview with CEO Marc Benioff appeared in *The New York Times*. Salesforce.com finally went public two months later.

---

[6]Occasionally, the price of a security falls dramatically when the underwriter ceases to stabilize the price. In such cases, Wall Street humorists (the ones who didn't buy any of the stock) have referred to the period following the aftermarket as the *aftermath*.

[7]The term *Green Shoe provision* sounds quite exotic, but the origin is relatively mundane. The term comes from the name of the Green Shoe Manufacturing Company, which, in 1963, was the first issuer that granted such an option.

Concept Questions

15.4a What do underwriters do?

15.4b What is the Green Shoe provision?

IPOs and Underpricing

15.5

Determining the correct offering price is the most difficult thing an underwriter must do for an initial public offering. The issuing firm faces a potential cost if the offering price is set too high or too low. If the issue is priced too high, it may be unsuccessful and have to be withdrawn. If the issue is priced below the true market value, the issuer's existing shareholders will experience an opportunity loss when the issuer sells shares for less than they are worth.

Underpricing is fairly common. It obviously helps new shareholders earn a higher return on the shares they buy. However, the existing shareholders of the issuing firm are not helped by underpricing. To them, it is an indirect cost of issuing new securities. For example, consider the General Motors IPO we discussed at the beginning of the chapter. The stock opened at $33 and rose to a first-day high of $35.99, before closing at $34.19. Based on these numbers, General Motors was underpriced by about $1.19 per share, which means the company missed out on an additional $568 million or so "left on the table." In 1999, eToys' 8.2-million-share IPO was underpriced by $57 per share, or almost a half a billion dollars in all. eToys could have used the money: It was bankrupt within two years.

IPO UNDERPRICING: THE 1999–2000 EXPERIENCE

Table 15.2, along with Figures 15.2 and 15.3, shows that 1999 and 2000 were extraordinary years in the IPO market. Almost 900 companies went public, and the average first-day return across the two years was about 64 percent. During this time, 194 IPOs doubled, or more than doubled, in value on the first day. In contrast, only 39 did so in the preceding 24 years combined. One company, VA Linux, shot up 698 percent!

The dollar amount raised in 2000, $65 billion, was a record, followed closely by 1999 at just under $65 billion. The underpricing was so severe in 1999 that companies left another $36 billion "on the table," which was substantially more than 1990–1998 combined; and in 2000, the amount was at least $27 billion. In other words, over the two-year period, companies missed out on $63 billion because of underpricing.

October 19, 1999, was one of the more memorable days during this time. The World Wrestling Federation (WWF) (now known as World Wrestling Entertainment, or WWE) and Martha Stewart Omnimedia both went public. When the closing bell rang, it was a clear smack-down as Martha Stewart gained 98 percent on the first day compared to 48 percent for the WWF. If you're interested in finding out how IPOs have done recently, check out our nearby *Work the Web* box.

EVIDENCE ON UNDERPRICING

Figure 15.2 provides a more general illustration of the underpricing phenomenon. What is shown is the month-by-month history of underpricing for SEC-registered IPOs.[8] The

---

[8]The discussion in this section draws on R.G. Ibbotson, J.L. Sindelar, and J.R. Ritter, "The Market's Problems with the Pricing of Initial Public Offerings," *Journal of Applied Corporate Finance* 7 (Spring 1994).

TABLE 15.2

Number of Offerings,
Average First-Day Return,
and Gross Proceeds of
Initial Public Offerings:
1960–2010

Year	Number of Offerings*	Average First-Day Return, %†	Gross Proceeds, $ Millions‡
1960	269	17.8	553
1961	435	34.1	1,243
1962	298	−1.6	431
1963	83	3.9	246
1964	97	5.3	380
1965	146	12.7	409
1966	85	7.1	275
1967	100	37.7	641
1968	368	55.9	1,205
1969	780	12.5	2,605
1970	358	−.70	780
1971	391	21.20	1,655
1972	562	7.50	2,724
1973	105	−17.80	330
1974	9	−7.00	51
1975	12	−0.20	261
1976	26	1.90	214
1977	15	3.60	128
1978	19	12.60	207
1979	39	8.50	313
1980	75	13.90	934
1981	197	6.20	2,367
1982	82	10.60	1,064
1983	524	8.90	11,332
1984	222	2.50	2,841
1985	214	6.20	5,125
1986	481	6.00	15,793
1987	344	5.60	13,300
1988	130	5.40	4,141
1989	122	7.80	5,406
1990	115	10.50	4,325
1991	295	11.70	16,602
1992	416	10.20	22,678
1993	527	12.70	31,599
1994	412	9.80	17,560
1995	461	21.10	30,230
1996	688	17.20	42,425
1997	487	14.00	32,441
1998	318	20.20	34,614
1999	486	69.70	64,927
2000	382	56.20	65,088
2001	79	14.20	34,241
2002	70	8.60	22,136
2003	67	12.30	10,068
2004	184	12.20	32,269
2005	168	10.10	28,593
2006	162	11.90	30,648

TABLE 15.2

(continued)

Year	Number of Offerings*	Average First-Day Return, %†	Gross Proceeds, $ Millions‡
2007	162	13.80	35,762
2008	21	6.40	22,762
2009	43	10.60	13,307
2010	100	8.80	31,291
1960–1969	2,661	21.20	7,988
1970–1979	1,536	7.10	6,663
1980–1989	2,391	6.80	62,303
1990–1999	4,205	21.00	297,441
2000–2010	1,438	23.40	326,165
1960–2010	**12,231**	**16.80**	**692,572**

*The number of offerings excludes IPOs with an offer price of less than $5.00, ADRs, best efforts, units, and Regulation A offers (small issues, raising less than $1.5 million during the 1980s), real estate investment trusts (REITs), partnerships, and closed-end funds. Banks and S&Ls and non-CRSP-listed IPOs are included.

†First-day returns are computed as the percentage return from the offering price to the first closing market price.

‡Gross proceeds data are from Securities Data Co., and they exclude overallotment options but include the international tranche, if any. No adjustments for inflation have been made.

Source: Professor Jay R. Ritter, University of Florida.

period covered is 1960 through 2010. Figure 15.3 presents the number of offerings in each month for the same period.

Figure 15.2 shows that underpricing can be quite dramatic, exceeding 100 percent in some months. In such months, the average IPO more than doubled in value, sometimes in a matter of hours. Also, the degree of underpricing varies through time, and periods of severe underpricing ("hot issue" markets) are followed by periods of little underpricing ("cold issue" markets). For example, in the 1960s, the average IPO was underpriced by 21.2 percent. In the 1970s, the average underpricing was much smaller (7.1 percent), and the amount of underpricing was actually very small or even negative for much of that time. Underpricing in the 1980s ran about 6.8 percent. For 1990–1999, IPOs were underpriced by 21 percent on average, and they were underpriced by 23.4 percent in 2000–2010.

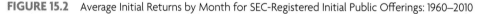

FIGURE 15.2   Average Initial Returns by Month for SEC-Registered Initial Public Offerings: 1960–2010

Source: R.G. Ibbotson, J.L. Sindelar, and J.R. Ritter, "The Market's Problems with the Pricing of Initial Public Offerings," *Journal of Applied Corporate Finance* 7 (Spring 1994), as updated by the authors.

FIGURE 15.3   Number of Offerings by Month for SEC-Registered Initial Public Offerings: 1960–2010

SOURCE: R.G. Ibbotson, J.L. Sindelar, and J.R. Ritter, "The Market's Problems with the Pricing of Initial Public Offerings," *Journal of Applied Corporate Finance* 7 (Spring 1994), as updated by the authors.

From Figure 15.3, it is apparent that the number of IPOs is also highly variable through time. Further, there are pronounced cycles in both the degree of underpricing and the number of IPOs. Comparing Figures 15.2 and 15.3, we see that increases in the number of new offerings tend to follow periods of significant underpricing by roughly six months. This

WORK THE WEB

So how much money have companies left on the table recently? We went to www.hoovers.com to see. Here is what we found for the fourth quarter of 2010:

Money Left On The Table

Company	Lead Underwriter	Offer Price	Pricing Valuation (mil.)	First Trade Price	First Trade Valuation (mil.)	Money on the Table (mil.)
General Motors Company	Morgan Stanley & Co. Incorporated	$33.00	16730	$35.00	$52,500	$956.00
Youku.com Inc.	Goldman Sachs (Asia) L.L.C.	$12.80	427.95	$27.00	$415	$225.10
The Fresh Market, Inc.	Merrill Lynch, Pierce, Fenner & Smith Incorporat	$22.00	448.12	$34.00	$1,632	$158.20
E-Commerce China Dangdang Inc.	Credit Suisse Securities (USA) LLC	$16.00	416.5	$24.50	$417	$144.50
ChinaCache International Holdings Ltd.	Merrill Lynch, Pierce, Fenner & Smith Incorporat	$13.90	181.8	$30.00	$11,191	$97.60

As you can see, General Motors led the list, leaving $956 million on the table. Notice this amount is different from what we reported in the text. The reason is that this website calculates the money left on the table from the first trade price, while we calculate it based on the price at end of the first day of trading.

Questions
1. *Go to www.hoovers.com and find the companies that are currently on the list for leaving money on the table. What company left the most money on the table as a percentage of the value of the company at the offer price?*
2. *Go to www.hoovers.com and find out which companies are expected to begin trading following an IPO. Which companies have filed for an IPO but have yet to start trading?*

The United States is not the only country in which initial public offerings (IPOs) of common stock are underpriced. The phenomenon exists in every country with a stock market, although the extent of underpricing varies from country to country.

In general, countries with developed capital markets have more moderate underpricing than in emerging markets. During the Internet bubble of 1999–2000, however, underpricing in the developed capital markets increased dramatically. In the United States, for example, the average first-day return during 1999–2000 was 65 percent. Since the bursting of the Internet bubble in mid-2000, the level of underpricing in the United States, Germany, and other developed capital markets has returned to more traditional levels.

The underpricing of Chinese IPOs used to be extreme, but in recent years it has moderated. In the 1990s Chinese government regulations required that the offer price could not be more than 15 times earnings, even when comparable stocks had a price–earnings ratio of 45. In 2010, the average first-day return was 40 percent, and there were more IPOs in China, raising more money, than in any other country.

The following table gives a summary of the average first-day returns on IPOs in a number of countries around the world, with the figures collected from a number of studies by various authors.

Country	Sample Size	Time Period	Avg. Initial Return, %	Country	Sample Size	Time Period	Avg. Initial Return, %
Argentina	20	1991–1994	4.40	Jordan	53	1999–2008	149.00
Australia	1,103	1976–2006	19.80	Korea	1,521	1980–2009	63.50
Austria	96	1971–2006	6.50	Malaysia	350	1980–2006	69.60
Belgium	114	1984–2006	13.50	Mexico	88	1987–1994	15.90
Brazil	264	1979–2010	34.40	Netherlands	181	1982–2006	10.20
Bulgaria	9	2004–2007	36.50	New Zealand	214	1979–2006	20.30
Canada	635	1971–2006	7.10	Nigeria	114	1989–2006	12.70
Chile	65	1982–2006	8.40	Norway	153	1984–2006	9.60
China	2,102	1990–2010	137.40	Philippines	123	1987–2006	21.20
Cyprus	51	1999–2002	23.70	Poland	224	1991–2006	22.90
Denmark	145	1984–2006	8.10	Portugal	28	1992–2006	11.60
Egypt	53	1990–2000	8.40	Russia	40	1999–2006	4.20
Finland	162	1971–2006	17.20	Singapore	519	1973–2008	27.40
France	686	1983–2009	10.60	South Africa	285	1980–2007	18.00
Germany	704	1978–2009	25.20	Spain	128	1986–2006	10.90
Greece	373	1976–2009	50.80	Sri Lanka	105	1987–2008	33.50
Hong Kong	1,259	1980–2010	15.40	Sweden	406	1980–2006	27.30
India	2,811	1990–2007	92.70	Switzerland	159	1983–2008	28.00
Indonesia	361	1990–2010	26.30	Taiwan	1,312	1980–2006	37.20
Iran	279	1991–2004	22.40	Thailand	459	1987–2007	36.60
Ireland	31	1999–2006	23.70	Turkey	315	1990–2008	10.60
Israel	348	1990–2006	13.80	United Kingdom	4,205	1959–2009	16.30
Italy	273	1985–2009	16.40	United States	12,165	1960–2010	16.80
Japan	3,078	1970–2009	40.50				

Jay R. Ritter is Cordell Professor of Finance at the University of Florida. An outstanding scholar, he is well known for his insightful analyses of new issues and going public.

probably occurs because companies decide to go public when they perceive that the market is highly receptive to new issues.

Table 15.2 contains a year-by-year summary of underpricing for the years 1960–2010. As indicated, a grand total of 12,231 companies were included in this analysis. The degree of underpricing averaged 16.8 percent overall for the 51 years examined. Securities were overpriced on average in only 5 of the 51 years. At the other extreme, in 1999, the 486 issues were underpriced, on average, by a remarkable 69.7 percent.

TABLE 15.3   Average First-Day Returns, Categorized by Sales, for IPOs: 1980–2010*

Annual Sales of Issuing Firms	1980–1989		1990–1998		1999–2000		2001–2010	
	Number of Firms	First-Day Average Return	Number of Firms	First-Day Average Return	Number of Firms	First-Day Average Return	Number of Firms	First-Day Average Return
0 ≤ sales ≤ $10m	424	10.40%	744	17.40%	334	68.80%	149	5.50%
$10m ≤ sales ≤ $20m	255	8.50	392	18.40	138	80.70	43	7.90
$20m ≤ sales ≤ $50m	495	7.70	792	18.70	154	75.70	143	13.50
$50m ≤ sales ≤ $100m	353	6.60	585	12.90	87	60.40	161	16.30
$100m ≤ sales ≤ $200m	238	4.80	451	11.90	58	39.10	144	14.40
$200m ≤ sales	288	3.40	641	8.60	87	22.60	376	10.60
All	2,053	7.20	3,605	14.80	858	64.40	1,016	11.60

*Sales, measured in millions, are for the last 12 months prior to going public. All sales have been converted into dollars of 2003 purchasing power, using the Consumer Price Index. There are 7,532 IPOs, after excluding IPOs with an offer price of less than $5.00 per share, units, REITs, ADRs, closed-end funds, banks and S&Ls, firms not listed on CRSP, and 20 firms with missing sales. Sales are from Thomson Financial's SDC, Dealogic, EDGAR, and the Graeme Howard-Todd Huxster collection of pre-EDGAR prospectuses. The average first-day return is 18.0%.
SOURCE: Professor Jay R. Ritter, University of Florida.

WHY DOES UNDERPRICING EXIST?

Based on the evidence we've examined, an obvious question is why underpricing continues to exist. As we discuss, there are various explanations; but to date, there is a lack of complete agreement among researchers as to which is correct.

We present some pieces of the underpricing puzzle by stressing two important caveats to our preceding discussion. First, the average figures we have examined tend to obscure the fact that much of the apparent underpricing is attributable to the smaller, more highly speculative issues. This point is illustrated in Table 15.3, which shows the extent of underpricing for IPOs over the period from 1980 through 2010. Here, the firms are grouped based on their total sales in the 12 months prior to the IPO.

As illustrated in Table 15.3, the underpricing tends to be higher for firms with few to no sales in the previous year. These firms tend to be young firms, and such young firms can be very risky investments. Arguably, they must be significantly underpriced, on average, just to attract investors, and this is one explanation for the underpricing phenomenon.

The second caveat is that relatively few IPO buyers will actually get the initial high average returns observed in IPOs, and many will actually lose money. Although it is true that, on average, IPOs have positive initial returns, a significant fraction of them have price drops. Furthermore, when the price is too low, the issue is often "oversubscribed." This means investors will not be able to buy all of the shares they want, and the underwriters will allocate the shares among investors.

The average investor will find it difficult to get shares in a "successful" offering (one in which the price increases) because there will not be enough shares to go around. On the other hand, an investor blindly submitting orders for IPOs tends to get more shares in issues that go down in price.

To illustrate, consider this tale of two investors. Smith knows very accurately what the Bonanza Corporation is worth when its shares are offered. She is confident that the shares are underpriced. Jones knows only that prices usually rise one month after an IPO. Armed with this information, Jones decides to buy 1,000 shares of every IPO. Does he actually earn an abnormally high return on the initial offering?

The answer is no, and at least one reason is Smith. Knowing about the Bonanza Corporation, Smith invests all her money in its IPO. When the issue is oversubscribed, the underwriters have to somehow allocate the shares between Smith and Jones. The net result is that when an issue is underpriced, Jones doesn't get to buy as much of it as he wanted.

Smith also knows that the Blue Sky Corporation IPO is overpriced. In this case, she avoids its IPO altogether, and Jones ends up with a full 1,000 shares. To summarize this tale, Jones gets fewer shares when more knowledgeable investors swarm to buy an underpriced issue and gets all he wants when the smart money avoids the issue.

This is an example of a "winner's curse," and it is thought to be another reason why IPOs have such a large average return. When the average investor "wins" and gets the entire allocation, it may be because those who knew better avoided the issue. The only way underwriters can counteract the winner's curse and attract the average investor is to underprice new issues (on average) so that the average investor still makes a profit.

Another reason for underpricing is that the underpricing is a kind of insurance for the investment banks. Conceivably, an investment bank could be sued successfully by angry customers if it consistently overpriced securities. Underpricing guarantees that, at least on average, customers will come out ahead.

A final reason for underpricing is that before the offer price is established, investment banks talk to big institutional investors to gauge the level of interest in the stock and to gather opinions about a suitable price. Underpricing is a way that the bank can reward these investors for truthfully revealing what they think the stock is worth and the number of shares they would like to buy.

Concept Questions

15.5a Why is underpricing a cost to the issuing firm?

15.5b Suppose a stockbroker calls you up out of the blue and offers to sell you "all the shares you want" of a new issue. Do you think the issue will be more or less underpriced than average?

New Equity Sales and the Value of the Firm

15.6

We now turn to a consideration of seasoned offerings, which, as we discussed earlier, are offerings by firms that already have outstanding securities. It seems reasonable to believe that new long-term financing is arranged by firms after positive net present value projects are put together. As a consequence, when the announcement of external financing is made, the firm's market value should go up. Interestingly, this is not what happens. Stock prices tend to decline following the announcement of a new equity issue, although they tend to not change much following a debt announcement. A number of researchers have studied this issue. Plausible reasons for this strange result include the following:

1. *Managerial information:* If management has superior information about the market value of the firm, it may know when the firm is overvalued. If it does, it will attempt to issue new shares of stock when the market value exceeds the correct value. This will benefit existing shareholders. However, the potential new shareholders are not stupid, and they will anticipate this superior information and discount it in lower market prices at the new-issue date.

2. *Debt usage:* A company's issuing new equity may reveal that the company has too much debt or too little liquidity. One version of this argument says that the equity issue is a bad signal to the market. After all, if the new projects are favorable ones, why should the firm let new shareholders in on them? It could just issue debt and let the existing shareholders have all the gain.

3. *Issue costs:* As we discuss next, there are substantial costs associated with selling securities.

The drop in value of the existing stock following the announcement of a new issue is an example of an indirect cost of selling securities. This drop might typically be on the order of 3 percent for an industrial corporation (and somewhat smaller for a public utility); so, for a large company, it can represent a substantial amount of money. We label this drop the *abnormal return* in our discussion of the costs of new issues that follows.

To give a couple of recent examples, in February 2011, natural gas and crude oil company EOG Recources announced a secondary offering. Its stock fell about 3.9 percent on the day. Also in February 2011, Optimer Pharmaceuticals announced a privately placed secondary offering at a price that was 11 percent less than its then market price. In response, the stock dropped about 9 percent on the day.

Concept Questions

15.6a What are some possible reasons why the price of stock drops on the announcement of a new equity issue?

15.6b Explain why we might expect a firm with a positive NPV investment to finance it with debt instead of equity.

15.7 The Costs of Issuing Securities

Issuing securities to the public isn't free, and the costs of different methods are important determinants of which is used. These costs associated with *floating* a new issue are generically called *flotation costs*. In this section, we take a closer look at the flotation costs associated with equity sales to the public.

THE COSTS OF SELLING STOCK TO THE PUBLIC

The costs of selling stock are classified in the following list and fall into six categories: (1) the gross spread, (2) other direct expenses, (3) indirect expenses, (4) abnormal returns (discussed previously), (5) underpricing, and (6) the Green Shoe option.

THE COSTS OF ISSUING SECURITIES

1. *Gross spread*	The gross spread consists of direct fees paid by the issuer to the underwriting syndicate—the difference between the price the issuer receives and the offer price.
2. *Other direct expenses*	These are direct costs, incurred by the issuer, that are not part of the compensation to underwriters. These costs include filing fees, legal fees, and taxes—all reported on the prospectus.
3. *Indirect expenses*	These costs are not reported on the prospectus and include the costs of management time spent working on the new issue.
4. *Abnormal returns*	In a seasoned issue of stock, the price of the existing stock drops on average by 3 percent on the announcement of the issue. This drop is called the *abnormal return*.
5. *Underpricing*	For initial public offerings, losses arise from selling the stock below the true value.
6. *Green Shoe option*	The Green Shoe option gives the underwriters the right to buy additional shares at the offer price to cover overallotments.

Table 15.4 reports direct costs as a percentage of the gross amount raised for IPOs, SEOs, straight (ordinary) bonds, and convertible bonds sold by U.S. companies over the

TABLE 15.4 Direct Costs as a Percentage of Gross Proceeds for Equity (IPOs and SEOs) and Straight and Convertible Bonds Offered by Domestic Operating Companies: 1990–2008

Proceeds ($ millions)	IPOs				SEOs			
	Number of Issues	Gross Spread	Other Direct Expense	Total Direct Cost	Number of Issues	Gross Spread	Other Direct Expense	Total Direct Cost
2.00–9.99	1,007	9.40%	15.82%	25.22%	515	8.11%	26.99%	35.11%
10.00–19.99	810	7.39	7.30	14.69	726	6.11	7.76	13.86
20.00–39.99	1,422	6.96	7.06	14.03	1,393	5.44	4.10	9.54
40.00–59.99	880	6.89	2.87	9.77	1,129	5.03	8.93	13.96
60.00–79.99	522	6.79	2.16	8.94	841	4.88	1.98	6.85
80.00–99.99	327	6.71	1.84	8.55	536	4.67	2.05	6.72
100.00–199.99	702	6.39	1.57	7.96	1,372	4.34	.89	5.23
200.00–499.99	440	5.81	1.03	6.84	811	3.72	1.22	4.94
500.00 and up	155	5.01	.49	5.50	264	3.10	.27	3.37
Total/Avg	**6,265**	**7.19**	**3.18**	**10.37**	**7,587**	**5.02**	**2.68**	**7.69**

Proceeds ($ millions)	Straight Bonds				Convertible Bonds			
	Number of Issues	Gross Spread	Other Direct Expense	Total Direct Cost	Number of Issues	Gross Spread	Other Direct Expense	Total Direct Cost
2.00–9.99	3,962	1.64	2.40	4.03	14	6.39	3.43	9.82
10.00–19.99	3,400	1.50	1.71	3.20	23	5.52	3.09	8.61
20.00–39.99	2,690	1.25	.92	2.17	30	4.63	1.67	6.30
40.00–59.99	3,345	.81	.79	1.59	35	3.49	1.04	4.54
60.00–79.99	891	1.65	.80	2.44	60	2.79	.62	3.41
80.00–99.99	465	1.41	.57	1.98	16	2.30	.62	2.92
100.00–199.99	4,949	1.61	.52	2.14	82	2.66	.42	3.08
200.00–499.99	3,305	1.38	.33	1.71	46	2.65	.33	2.99
500.00 and up	1,261	.61	.15	.76	7	2.16	.13	2.29
Total/Avg	**24,268**	**1.38**	**.61**	**2.00**	**313**	**3.07**	**.85**	**3.92**

SOURCE: I. Lee, S. Lochhead, J. Ritter, and Q. Zhao, "The Costs of Raising Capital," *Journal of Financial Research* 19 (Spring 1996), updated by the authors.

TABLE 15.5

Direct and Indirect Costs, in Percentages, of Equity IPOs: 1990–2008

Source: I. Lee, S. Lochhead, J. Ritter, and Q. Zhao, "The Costs of Raising Capital," *Journal of Financial Research* 19 (Spring 1996), updated by the authors.

Proceeds ($ millions)	Number of Issues	Gross Spread	Other Direct Expense	Total Direct Cost	Underpricing
2.00–9.99	1,007	9.40%	15.82%	25.22%	20.42%
10.00–19.99	810	7.39	7.30	14.69	10.33
20.00–39.99	1,422	6.96	7.06	14.03	17.03
40.00–59.99	880	6.89	2.87	9.77	28.26
60.00–79.99	522	6.79	2.16	8.94	28.36
80.00–99.99	327	6.71	1.84	8.55	32.92
100.00–199.99	702	6.39	1.57	7.96	21.55
200.00–499.99	440	5.81	1.03	6.84	6.19
500.00 and up	155	5.01	.49	5.50	6.64
Total/Avg	**6,265**	**7.19**	**3.18**	**10.37**	**19.34**

19-year period from 1990 through 2008. These are direct costs only. Not included are indirect expenses, the cost of the Green Shoe provision, underpricing (for IPOs), and abnormal returns (for SEOs).

As Table 15.4 shows, the direct costs alone can be very large, particularly for smaller issues (less than $10 million). On a smaller IPO, for example, the total direct costs amount to 25.22 percent of the amount raised. This means that if a company sells $10 million in stock, it will net only about $7.5 million; the other $2.5 million goes to cover the underwriter spread and other direct expenses. Typical underwriter spreads on an IPO range from about 5 percent up to 10 percent or so, but for well over half of the IPOs in Table 15.4, the spread is exactly 7 percent; so this is, by far, the most common spread.

Overall, four clear patterns emerge from Table 15.4. First, with the possible exception of straight debt offerings (about which we will have more to say later), there are substantial economies of scale. The underwriter spreads are smaller on larger issues, and the other direct costs fall sharply as a percentage of the amount raised—a reflection of the mostly fixed nature of such costs. Second, the costs associated with selling debt are substantially less than the costs of selling equity. Third, IPOs have higher expenses than SEOs, but the difference is not as great as might originally be guessed. Finally, straight bonds are cheaper to float than convertible bonds.

As we have discussed, the underpricing of IPOs is an additional cost to the issuer. To give a better idea of the total cost of going public, Table 15.5 combines the information in Table 15.4 for IPOs with data on the underpricing experienced by these firms. Overall, across all size groups, the total direct costs amount to about 10 percent of the amount raised, and the underpricing amounts to about 19 percent.

Finally, with regard to debt offerings, there is a general pattern in issue costs that is somewhat obscured in Table 15.4. Recall from Chapter 7 that bonds carry different credit ratings. Higher-rated bonds are said to be investment grade, whereas lower-rated bonds are noninvestment grade. Table 15.6 contains a breakdown of direct costs for bond issues after the investment and noninvestment grades have been separated.

Table 15.6 clarifies three things regarding debt issues. First, there are substantial economies of scale here as well. Second, investment-grade issues have much lower direct costs, particularly for straight bonds. Finally, there are fewer noninvestment-grade issues in the smaller size categories, reflecting the fact that such issues are more commonly handled as private placements, which we discuss in a later section.

TABLE 15.6 Average Gross Spreads and Total Direct Costs for Domestic Debt Issues: 1990–2008

Convertible Bonds

Proceeds ($ millions)	Investment Grade				Junk or Not Rated			
	Number of Issues	Gross Spread	Other Direct Expense	Total Direct Cost	Number of Issues	Gross Spread	Other Direct Expense	Total Direct Cost
2.00–9.99	–	–	–	–	14	6.39%	3.43%	9.82%
10.00–19.99	1	14.12%	1.87%	15.98%	23	5.52	3.09	8.61
20.00–39.99	–	–	–	–	30	4.63	1.67	6.30
40.00–59.99	3	1.92	.51	2.43	35	3.49	1.04	4.54
60.00–79.99	6	1.65	.44	2.09	60	2.79	.62	3.41
80.00–99.99	4	.89	.27	1.16	16	2.30	.62	2.92
100.00–199.99	27	2.22	.33	2.55	82	2.66	.42	3.08
200.00–499.99	27	2.03	.19	2.22	46	2.65	.33	2.99
500.00 and up	11	1.94	.13	2.06	7	2.16	.13	2.29
Total/Avg	**79**	**2.15**	**.29**	**2.44**	**299**	**3.31**	**.98**	**4.29**

Straight Bonds

Proceeds ($ millions)	Investment Grade				Junk or Not Rated			
	Number of Issues	Gross Spread	Other Direct Expense	Total Direct Cost	Number of Issues	Gross Spread	Other Direct Expense	Total Direct Cost
2.00–9.99	2,709	.62%	1.28%	1.90%	1,253	2.77%	2.50%	5.27%
10.00–19.99	2,564	.59	1.17	1.76	836	3.15	1.97	5.12
20.00–39.99	2,400	.63	.74	1.37	290	3.07	1.13	4.20
40.00–59.99	3,146	.40	.52	.92	199	2.93	1.20	4.14
60.00–79.99	792	.58	.38	.96	99	3.12	1.16	4.28
80.00–99.99	385	.66	.29	.96	80	2.73	.93	3.66
100.00–199.99	4,427	.54	.25	.79	522	2.73	.68	3.41
200.00–499.99	3,031	.52	.25	.76	274	2.59	.39	2.98
500.00 and up	1,207	.31	.08	.39	54	2.38	.25	2.63
Total/Avg	**20,661**	**.52**	**.35**	**.87**	**3,607**	**2.76**	**.81**	**3.57**

Source: I. Lee, S. Lochhead, J. Ritter, and Q. Zhao, "The Costs of Raising Capital," *Journal of Financial Research* 19 (Spring 1996), updated by the authors.

THE COSTS OF GOING PUBLIC: A CASE STUDY

On March 17, 2011, Cornerstone OnDemand, the Santa Monica–based software company, went public via an IPO. Cornerstone issued 7.5 million shares of stock at a price of $13 each. The lead underwriters on the IPO were Goldman, Sachs & Co. and Barclays Capital, assisted by a syndicate made up of four other investment banks.

Even though the IPO raised a gross sum of $97.5 million, Cornerstone got to keep only $90,538,500 after expenses. The biggest expense was the 7.14 percent underwriter spread, which is ordinary for an offering of this size. Cornerstone sold each of the 7.5 million shares to the underwriters for $12.0718, and the underwriters in turn sold the shares to the public for $13.00 each.

But wait—there's more. Cornerstone spent $15,421 in SEC registration fees, $13,783 in other filing fees, and $150,000 to be listed on the NASDAQ Global Market. The company also spent $2.76 million in legal fees, $1,012,700 on accounting to obtain the necessary audits, $9,350 for a transfer agent to physically transfer the shares and maintain a list of shareholders, $130,000 for printing and engraving expenses, $5,000 in certain legal compliance fees and expenses, and finally, $3,746 in miscellaneous expenses.

As Cornerstone's outlays show, an IPO can be a costly undertaking! In the end, Cornerstone's expenses totaled $11,061,500, of which $6,961,500 went to the underwriters and $4,100,000 went to other parties. All told, the total cost to Cornerstone was 12.2 percent of the issue proceeds.

Concept Questions

15.7a What are the different costs associated with security offerings?

15.7b What lessons do we learn from studying issue costs?

15.8 Rights

When new shares of common stock are sold to the general public, the proportional ownership of existing shareholders is likely to be reduced. However, if a preemptive right is contained in the firm's articles of incorporation, the firm must first offer any new issue of common stock to existing shareholders. If the articles of incorporation do not include a preemptive right, the firm has a choice of offering the issue of common stock directly to existing shareholders or to the public.

An issue of common stock offered to existing stockholders is called a *rights offering* (or *offer*, for short) or a *privileged subscription*. In a rights offering, each shareholder is issued rights to buy a specified number of new shares from the firm at a specified price within a specified time, after which the rights are said to *expire*. The terms of the rights offering are evidenced by certificates known as *share warrants* or *rights*. Such rights are often traded on securities exchanges or over the counter.

Rights offerings have some interesting advantages relative to cash offers. For example, they appear to be cheaper for the issuing firm than cash offers. In fact, a firm can do a rights offering without using an underwriter; whereas, as a practical matter, an underwriter is almost a necessity in a cash offer. Despite this, rights offerings are fairly rare in the United States; however, in many other countries, they are more common than cash offers. Why this is true is a bit of a mystery and the source of much debate; but to our knowledge, no definitive answer exists.

THE MECHANICS OF A RIGHTS OFFERING

To illustrate the various considerations a financial manager faces in a rights offering, we will examine the situation faced by the National Power Company, whose abbreviated initial financial statements are given in Table 15.7.

TABLE 15.7

National Power Company
Financial Statements
Before Rights Offering

NATIONAL POWER COMPANY Balance Sheet			
Assets		**Shareholders' Equity**	
Assets	$15,000,000	Common stock	$ 5,000,000
		Retained earnings	10,000,000
Total	$15,000,000	Total	$15,000,000
Income Statement			
Earnings before taxes		$ 3,030,303	
Taxes (34%)		1,030,303	
Net income		$ 2,000,000	
Shares outstanding		1,000,000	
Earnings per share		$ 2	
Market price per share		$ 20	
Total market value		$20,000,000	

As indicated in Table 15.7, National Power earns $2 million after taxes and has 1 million shares outstanding. Earnings per share are thus $2, and the stock sells for $20, or 10 times earnings (that is, the price–earnings ratio is 10). To fund a planned expansion, the company intends to raise $5 million worth of new equity funds through a rights offering.

To execute a rights offering, the financial management of National Power will have to answer the following questions:

1. What should the price per share be for the new stock?
2. How many shares will have to be sold?
3. How many shares will each shareholder be allowed to buy?

Also, management will probably want to ask this:

4. What is likely to be the effect of the rights offering on the per-share value of the existing stock?

It turns out that the answers to these questions are highly interrelated. We will get to them in just a moment.

The early stages of a rights offering are the same as those for a general cash offer. The difference between a rights offering and a general cash offer lies in how the shares are sold. In a rights offer, National Power's existing shareholders are informed that they own one right for each share of stock they own. National Power will then specify how many rights a shareholder needs to buy one additional share at a specified price.

To take advantage of the rights offering, shareholders have to exercise the rights by filling out a subscription form and sending it, along with payment, to the firm's subscription agent (the subscription agent is usually a bank). Shareholders of National Power will actually have several choices: (1) Exercise their rights and subscribe for some or all of the entitled shares, (2) order some or all of the rights sold, or (3) do nothing and let the rights expire. As we will discuss, this third course of action is inadvisable.

NUMBER OF RIGHTS NEEDED TO PURCHASE A SHARE

National Power wants to raise $5 million in new equity. Suppose the subscription price is set at $10 per share. How National Power arrives at that price we will discuss later; but notice that the subscription price is substantially less than the current $20 per share market price.

At $10 per share, National Power will have to issue 500,000 new shares. This can be determined by dividing the total amount of funds to be raised by the subscription price:

$$\text{Number of new shares} = \frac{\text{Funds to be raised}}{\text{Subscription price}} \qquad \text{[15.1]}$$

$$= \frac{\$5,000,000}{10} = 500,000 \text{ shares}$$

Because stockholders always get one right for each share of stock they own, 1 million rights will be issued by National Power. To determine how many rights will be needed to buy one new share of stock, we can divide the number of existing outstanding shares of stock by the number of new shares:

$$\frac{\text{Number of rights needed}}{\text{to buy a share of stock}} = \frac{\text{Old shares}}{\text{New shares}} \qquad \text{[15.2]}$$

$$= \frac{1,000,000}{500,000} = 2 \text{ rights}$$

Thus, a shareholder will need to give up two rights plus $10 to receive a share of new stock. If all the stockholders do this, National Power will raise the required $5 million.

It should be clear that the subscription price, the number of new shares, and the number of rights needed to buy a new share of stock are interrelated. For example, National Power can lower the subscription price. If it does, more new shares will have to be issued to raise $5 million in new equity. Several alternatives are worked out here:

Subscription Price	Number of New Shares	Number of Rights Needed to Buy a Share of Stock
$20	250,000	4
10	500,000	2
5	1,000,000	1

THE VALUE OF A RIGHT

Rights clearly have value. In the case of National Power, the right to buy a share of stock worth $20 for $10 is definitely worth something. In fact, if you think about it, a right is essentially a call option, and our discussion of such options in later chapters (in the alternate edition of the text) applies here. The most important difference between a right and an ordinary call option is that rights are issued by the firm, so they more closely resemble warrants. In general, the valuation of options, rights, and warrants can be fairly complex, so we defer discussion of this subject to a later chapter. However, we can discuss the value of a right just prior to expiration to illustrate some important points.

Suppose a shareholder of National Power owns two shares of stock just before the rights offering is about to expire. This situation is depicted in Table 15.8. Initially, the price of National Power is $20 per share, so the shareholder's total holding is worth $2 \times \$20 = \$40$. The National Power rights offer gives shareholders with two rights the opportunity to purchase one additional share for $10. The additional share does not carry a right.

The stockholder who has two shares will receive two rights. The holding of the shareholder who exercises these rights and buys the new share will increase to three shares. The total investment will be $\$40 + 10 = \$50$ (the $40 initial value plus the $10 paid to the company).

Initial Position	
Number of shares	2
Share price	$20
Value of holding	$40
Terms of Offer	
Subscription price	$10
Number of rights issued	2
Number of rights for a new share	2
After Offer	
Number of shares	3
Value of holding	$50
Share price	$16.67
Value of one right: Old price − New price	$20 − 16.67 = $3.33

TABLE 15.8

The Value of Rights: The Individual Shareholder

Initial Position	
Number of shares	1 million
Share price	$20
Value of firm	$20 million
Terms of Offer	
Subscription price	$10
Number of rights issued	1 million
Number of rights for a new share	2
After Offer	
Number of shares	1.5 million
Share price	$16.67
Value of firm	$25 million
Value of one right	$20 − 16.67 = $3.33

TABLE 15.9

National Power Company Rights Offering

The stockholder now holds three shares, all of which are identical because the new share does not have a right and the rights attached to the old shares have been exercised. Because the total cost of buying these three shares is $40 + 10 = $50, the price per share must end up at $50/3 = $16.67 (rounded to two decimal places).

Table 15.9 summarizes what happens to National Power's stock price. If all shareholders exercise their rights, the number of shares will increase to 1 million + .5 million = 1.5 million. The value of the firm will increase to $20 million + 5 million = $25 million. The value of each share will thus drop to $25 million/1.5 million = $16.67 after the rights offering.

The difference between the old share price of $20 and the new share price of $16.67 reflects the fact that the old shares carried rights to subscribe to the new issue. The difference must be equal to the value of one right—that is, $20 − 16.67 = $3.33.

An investor holding no shares of outstanding National Power stock who wants to subscribe to the new issue can do so by buying some rights. Suppose an outside investor buys two rights. This will cost $3.33 × 2 = $6.67 (to account for previous rounding). If the investor exercises the rights at a subscription price of $10, the total cost will be $10 + 6.67 = $16.67. In return for this expenditure, the investor will receive a share of the new stock, which, as we have seen, is worth $16.67.

EXAMPLE 15.1   **Exercising Your Rights: Part 1**

In the National Power example, suppose the subscription price is set at $8. How many shares will have to be sold? How many rights will you need to buy a new share? What is the value of a right? What will the price per share be after the rights offer?

To raise $5 million, $5 million/8 = 625,000 shares will need to be sold. There are 1 million shares outstanding, so it will take 1 million/625,000 = 8/5 = 1.6 rights to buy a new share of stock (you can buy five new shares for every eight you own). After the rights offer, there will be 1.625 million shares, worth $25 million altogether, so the per-share value will be $25/1.625 = $15.38. The value of a right in this case is the $20 original price less the $15.38 ending price, or $4.62.

EX RIGHTS

ex-rights date
The beginning of the period when stock is sold without a recently declared right, normally two trading days before the holder-of-record date.

holder-of-record date
The date on which existing shareholders on company records are designated as the recipients of stock rights. Also, the date of record.

National Power's rights have a substantial value. In addition, the rights offering will have a large impact on the market price of National Power's stock. That price will drop by $3.33 on the **ex-rights date**.

The standard procedure for issuing rights involves the firm's setting a **holder-of-record date**. Following stock exchange rules, the stock typically goes ex rights two trading days before the holder-of-record date. If the stock is sold before the ex-rights date—"rights on," "with rights," or "cum rights"—the new owner will receive the rights. After the ex-rights date, an investor who purchases the shares will not receive the rights. This is depicted for National Power in Figure 15.4.

As illustrated, on September 30, National Power announces the terms of the rights offering, stating that the rights will be mailed on, say, November 1 to stockholders of record as of October 15. Because October 13 is the ex-rights date, only shareholders who own the stock on or before October 12 will receive the rights.

EXAMPLE 15.2   **Exercising Your Rights: Part II**

The Lagrange Point Co. has proposed a rights offering. The stock currently sells for $40 per share. Under the terms of the offer, stockholders will be allowed to buy one new share for every five that they own at a price of $25 per share. What is the value of a right? What is the ex-rights price?

You can buy five rights-on shares for 5 × $40 = $200 and then exercise the rights for another $25. Your total investment is $225, and you end up with six ex-rights shares. The ex-rights price per share is $225/6 = $37.50. The rights are thus worth $40 − 37.50 = $2.50 apiece.

EXAMPLE 15.3   **Right On**

In Example 15.2, suppose the rights sell for only $2 instead of the $2.50 we calculated. What can you do?

You can get rich quickly because you have found a money machine. Here's the recipe: Buy five rights for $10. Exercise them and pay $25 to get a new share. Your total investment to get one ex-rights share is 5 × $2 + 25 = $35. Sell the share for $37.50 and pocket the $2.50 difference. Repeat as desired.

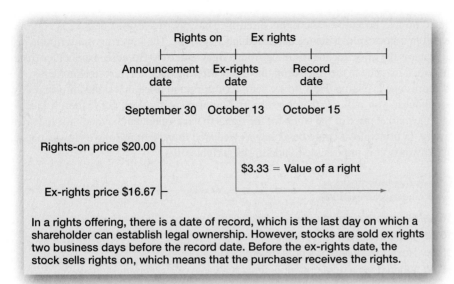

FIGURE 15.4
Ex-Rights Stock Prices

THE UNDERWRITING ARRANGEMENTS

Rights offerings are typically arranged using **standby underwriting**. In standby underwriting, the issuer makes a rights offering, and the underwriter makes a firm commitment to "take up" (that is, purchase) the unsubscribed portion of the issue. The underwriter usually gets a **standby fee** and additional amounts based on the securities taken up.

Standby underwriting protects the firm against undersubscription, which can occur if investors throw away rights or if bad news causes the market price of the stock to fall below the subscription price.

In practice, only a small percentage (fewer than 10 percent) of shareholders fail to exercise valuable rights. This failure can probably be attributed to ignorance or vacations. Furthermore, shareholders are usually given an **oversubscription privilege**, which enables them to purchase unsubscribed shares at the subscription price. The oversubscription privilege makes it unlikely that the corporate issuer would have to turn to its underwriter for help.

standby underwriting
The type of underwriting in which the underwriter agrees to purchase the unsubscribed portion of the issue.

standby fee
An amount paid to an underwriter participating in a standby underwriting agreement.

oversubscription privilege
A privilege that allows shareholders to purchase unsubscribed shares in a rights offering at the subscription price.

EFFECTS ON SHAREHOLDERS

Shareholders can exercise their rights or sell them. In either case, the stockholder will neither win nor lose because of the rights offering. The hypothetical holder of two shares of National Power has a portfolio worth $40. If the shareholder exercises the rights, she or he ends up with three shares worth a total of $50. In other words, with an expenditure of $10, the investor's holding increases in value by $10, which means the shareholder is neither better nor worse off.

On the other hand, if the shareholder sells the two rights for $3.33 each, he or she would obtain $3.33 × 2 = $6.67 and end up with two shares worth $16.67 and the cash from selling the right:

$$
\begin{aligned}
\text{Shares held} &= 2 \times \$16.67 = \$33.33 \\
\text{Rights sold} &= 2 \times \$3.33 \;=\; \underline{6.67} \\
\text{Total} &= \phantom{2 \times \$3.33 = {}}\underline{\$40.00}
\end{aligned}
$$

The new $33.33 market value plus $6.67 in cash is exactly the same as the original holding of $40. Thus, stockholders cannot lose or gain by exercising or selling rights.

It is obvious that after the rights offering, the new market price of the firm's stock will be lower than the price before the rights offering. As we have seen, however, stockholders have suffered no loss because of the rights offering. Thus, the stock price decline is very much like that in a stock split, a device described in Chapter 17. The lower the subscription price, the greater is the price decline resulting from a rights offering. Because shareholders receive rights equal in value to the price drop, the rights offering does *not* hurt stockholders.

There is one last issue. How do we set the subscription price in a rights offering? If you think about it, you will see that the subscription price really does not matter. It has to be below the market price of the stock for the rights to have value; but beyond this, the price is arbitrary. In principle, it could be as low as we cared to make it as long as it was not zero. In other words, it is impossible to underprice a rights offer.

Concept Questions

15.8a How does a rights offering work?

15.8b What questions must financial managers answer in a rights offering?

15.8c How is the value of a right determined?

15.8d When does a rights offering affect the value of a company's shares?

15.8e Does a rights offering cause share prices to decrease? How are existing shareholders affected by a rights offering?

15.9 Dilution

dilution
Loss in existing shareholders' value in terms of ownership, market value, book value, or EPS.

A subject that comes up quite a bit in discussions involving the selling of securities is **dilution**. Dilution refers to a loss in existing shareholders' value. There are several kinds:

1. Dilution of percentage ownership.
2. Dilution of market value.
3. Dilution of book value and earnings per share.

The differences between these three types can be a little confusing, and there are some common misconceptions about dilution, so we discuss it in this section.

DILUTION OF PROPORTIONATE OWNERSHIP

The first type of dilution can arise whenever a firm sells shares to the general public. For example, Joe Smith owns 5,000 shares of Merit Shoe Company. Merit Shoe currently has 50,000 shares of stock outstanding; each share gets one vote. Joe thus controls 10 percent (= 5,000/50,000) of the votes and gets 10 percent of the dividends.

If Merit Shoe issues 50,000 new shares of common stock to the public via a general cash offer, Joe's ownership in Merit Shoe may be diluted. If Joe does not participate in the new issue, his ownership will drop to 5 percent (= 5,000/100,000). Notice that the value of Joe's shares is unaffected; he just owns a smaller percentage of the firm.

Because a rights offering would ensure Joe Smith an opportunity to maintain his proportionate 10 percent share, dilution of the ownership of existing shareholders can be avoided by using a rights offering.

DILUTION OF VALUE: BOOK VERSUS MARKET VALUES

We now examine dilution of value by looking at some accounting numbers. We do this to illustrate a fallacy concerning dilution; we do not mean to suggest that accounting value dilution is more important than market value dilution. As we illustrate, quite the reverse is true.

	Initial	After Taking on New Project	
		With Dilution	**With No Dilution**
Number of shares	1,000,000	1,400,000	1,400,000
Book value	$10,000,000	$12,000,000	$12,000,000
Book value per share (B)	$10	$8.57	$8.57
Market value	$5,000,000	$6,000,000	$8,000,000
Market price (P)	$5	$4.29	$5.71
Net income	$1,000,000	$1,200,000	$1,600,000
Return on equity (ROE)	.10	.10	.13
Earnings per share (EPS)	$1	$.86	$1.14
EPS/P	.20	.20	.20
P/EPS	5	5	5
P/B	.5	.5	.67
Project cost $2,000,000		NPV = −$1,000,000	NPV = $1,000,000

TABLE 15.10

New Issues and Dilution: The Case of Upper States Manufacturing

Suppose Upper States Manufacturing (USM) wants to build a new electricity-generating plant to meet future anticipated demands. As shown in Table 15.10, USM currently has 1 million shares outstanding and no debt. Each share is selling for $5, and the company has a $5 million market value. USM's book value is $10 million total, or $10 per share.

USM has experienced a variety of difficulties in the past, including cost overruns, regulatory delays in building a nuclear-powered electricity-generating plant, and below-normal profits. These difficulties are reflected in the fact that USM's market-to-book ratio is $5/10 = .50 (successful firms rarely have market prices below book values).

Net income for USM is currently $1 million. With 1 million shares, earnings per share are $1, and the return on equity is $1/10 = 10\%$.[9] USM thus sells for five times earnings (the price–earnings ratio is 5). USM has 200 shareholders, each of whom holds 5,000 shares. The new plant will cost $2 million, so USM will have to issue 400,000 new shares ($5 × 400,000 = $2 million). There will thus be 1.4 million shares outstanding after the issue.

The ROE on the new plant is expected to be the same as for the company as a whole. In other words, net income is expected to go up by .10 × $2 million = $200,000. Total net income will thus be $1.2 million. The following will result if the plant is built:

1. With 1.4 million shares outstanding, EPS will be $1.2/1.4 = $.857, down from $1.

2. The proportionate ownership of each old shareholder will drop to 5,000/1.4 million = .36 percent from .50 percent.

3. If the stock continues to sell for five times earnings, then the value will drop to 5 × $.857 = $4.29, representing a loss of $.71 per share.

4. The total book value will be the old $10 million plus the new $2 million, for a total of $12 million. Book value per share will fall to $12 million/1.4 million = $8.57.

If we take this example at face value, then dilution of proportionate ownership, accounting dilution, and market value dilution all occur. USM's stockholders appear to suffer significant losses.

A Misconception   Our example appears to show that selling stock when the market-to-book ratio is less than 1 is detrimental to stockholders. Some managers claim that the resulting dilution occurs because EPS will go down whenever shares are issued when the market value is less than the book value.

---

[9]Return on equity, or ROE, is equal to earnings per share divided by book value per share, or, equivalently, net income divided by common equity. We discuss this and other financial ratios in some detail in Chapter 3.

When the market-to-book ratio is less than 1, increasing the number of shares does cause EPS to go down. Such a decline in EPS is accounting dilution, and accounting dilution will always occur under these circumstances.

Is it also true that market value dilution will necessarily occur? The answer is no. There is nothing incorrect about our example, but why the market price has decreased is not obvious. We discuss this next.

The Correct Arguments   In this example, the market price falls from $5 per share to $4.29. This is true dilution, but why does it occur? The answer has to do with the new project. USM is going to spend $2 million on the new plant. However, as shown in Table 15.10, the total market value of the company is going to rise from $5 million to $6 million, an increase of only $1 million. This simply means that the NPV of the new project is −$1 million. With 1.4 million shares, the loss per share is $1/1.4 = $.71, as we calculated before.

So, true dilution takes place for the shareholders of USM because the NPV of the project is negative, not because the market-to-book ratio is less than 1. This negative NPV causes the market price to drop, and the accounting dilution has nothing to do with it.

Suppose the new project has a positive NPV of $1 million. The total market value rises by $2 million + 1 million = $3 million. As shown in Table 15.10 (third column), the price per share rises to $5.71. Notice that accounting dilution still takes place because the book value per share still falls, but there is no economic consequence of that fact. The market value of the stock rises.

The $.71 increase in share value comes about because of the $1 million NPV, which amounts to an increase in value of about $.71 per share. Also, as shown, if the ratio of price to EPS remains at 5, then EPS must rise to $5.71/5 = $1.14. Total earnings (net income) rises to $1.14 per share × 1.4 million shares = $1.6 million. Finally, ROE will rise to $1.6 million/12 million = 13.33%.

Concept Questions
15.9a What are the different kinds of dilution?
15.9b Is dilution important?

15.10 Issuing Long-Term Debt

The general procedures followed in a public issue of bonds are the same as those for stocks. The issue must be registered with the SEC, there must be a prospectus, and so on. The registration statement for a public issue of bonds, however, is different from the one for common stock. For bonds, the registration statement must indicate an indenture.

Another important difference is that more than 50 percent of all debt is issued privately. There are two basic forms of direct private long-term financing: term loans and private placement.

term loans
Direct business loans of typically one to five years.

Term loans are direct business loans. These loans have maturities of between one year and five years. Most term loans are repayable during the life of the loan. The lenders include commercial banks, insurance companies, and other lenders that specialize in corporate finance. **Private placements** are similar to term loans except that the maturity is longer.

private placements
Loans (usually long-term) provided directly by a limited number of investors.

The important differences between direct private long-term financing and public issues of debt are these:

1. A direct long-term loan avoids the cost of Securities and Exchange Commission registration.

2. Direct placement is likely to have more restrictive covenants.

3. It is easier to renegotiate a term loan or a private placement in the event of a default. It is harder to renegotiate a public issue because hundreds of holders are usually involved.

4. Life insurance companies and pension funds dominate the private placement segment of the bond market. Commercial banks are significant participants in the term loan market.

5. The costs of distributing bonds are lower in the private market.

The interest rates on term loans and private placements are usually higher than those on an equivalent public issue. This difference reflects the trade-off between a higher interest rate and more flexible arrangements in the event of financial distress, as well as the lower costs associated with private placements.

An additional, and very important, consideration is that the flotation costs associated with selling debt are much less than the comparable costs associated with selling equity.

Concept Questions

15.10a What is the difference between private and public bond issues?

15.10b A private placement is likely to have a higher interest rate than a public issue. Why?

Shelf Registration

15.11

To simplify the procedures for issuing securities, in March 1982, the SEC adopted Rule 415 on a temporary basis, and it was made permanent in November 1983. Rule 415 allows shelf registration. Both debt and equity securities can be shelf registered.

Shelf registration permits a corporation to register an offering that it reasonably expects to sell within the next two years and then sell the issue whenever it wants during that two-year period. For example, in February 2011, home builder Beazer Homes announced a shelf registration of $750 million in various securities. This shelf registration was a replacement for the company's 2009 shelf registration. Not all companies can use Rule 415. The primary qualifications are these:

1. The company must be rated investment grade.

2. The firm cannot have defaulted on its debt in the past three years.

3. The aggregate market value of the firm's outstanding stock must be more than $150 million.

4. The firm must not have violated the Securities Act of 1934 in the past three years.

Shelf registration allows firms to use a *dribble* method of new equity issuance. In dribbling, a company registers the issue and hires an underwriter as its selling agent. The company sells shares in "dribs and drabs" from time to time directly via a stock exchange (for example, the NYSE). Companies that have used dribble programs include Wells Fargo & Co., Pacific Gas and Electric, and The Southern Company.

The rule has been controversial. Arguments have been constructed against shelf registration:

1. The costs of new issues might go up because underwriters might not be able to provide as much current information to potential investors as they would otherwise, so investors would pay less. The expense of selling the issue piece by piece might therefore be higher than that of selling it all at once.

shelf registration
Registration permitted by SEC Rule 415, which allows a company to register all issues it expects to sell within two years at one time, with subsequent sales at any time within those two years.

2. Some investment bankers have argued that shelf registration will cause a "market overhang" that will depress market prices. In other words, the possibility that the company may increase the supply of stock at any time will have a negative impact on the current stock price.

Concept Questions

15.11a What is shelf registration?

15.11b What are the arguments against shelf registration?

15.12 Summary and Conclusions

This chapter has looked at how corporate securities are issued. The following are the main points:

1. The costs of issuing securities can be quite large. They are much lower (as a percentage) for larger issues.

2. The direct and indirect costs of going public can be substantial. However, once a firm is public, it can raise additional capital with much greater ease.

3. Rights offerings are cheaper than general cash offers. Even so, most new equity issues in the United States are underwritten general cash offers.

CONNECT TO FINANCE

If you are using *Connect™ Finance* in your course, get online to take a Practice Test, check out study tools, and find out where you need additional practice.

▼ Chapter 15 Raising Capital

15.1 The Financing Life Cycle of a Firm: Early-Stage Financing and Venture Capital	eBook	Study	Practice
15.2 Selling Securities to the Public: The Basic Procedure	eBook	Study	Practice
15.3 Alternative Issue Methods	eBook	Study	Practice
15.4 Underwriters	eBook	Study	Practice
15.5 IPOs and Underpricing	eBook	Study	Practice
15.6 New Equity Sales and the Value of the Firm	eBook	Study	Practice
15.7 The Costs of Issuing Securities	eBook	Study	Practice
15.8 Rights	eBook	Study	Practice
15.9 Dilution	eBook	Study	Practice
15.10 Issuing Long-Term Debt	eBook	Study	Practice
15.11 Shelf Registration	eBook	Study	Practice

NPPT 35–36

Visit us at www.mhhe.com/rwj

Can you answer the following questions?

Section 15.1 What stage of venture capital funding is most apt to provide the funding needed to actually commence the manufacturing operations of a firm? (LO 15-1)

Section 15.2 Smythe Enterprises is issuing securities under Regulation A. Given this, you know that the securities are valued at _____ or less, or are debt securities that mature in less than _____. (LO 15-2)

Section 15.4 The gross spread is defined as the difference between the _____ and the _____. (LO 15-2)

Section 15.7 What is referred to as the abnormal return? (LO 15-3)

Log on to find out!

CHAPTER REVIEW AND SELF-TEST PROBLEMS

15.1 Flotation Costs The L5 Corporation is considering an equity issue to finance a new space station. A total of $15 million in new equity is needed. If the direct costs are estimated at 7 percent of the amount raised, how large does the issue need to be? What is the dollar amount of the flotation cost?

15.2 Rights Offerings The Hadron Corporation currently has 3 million shares outstanding. The stock sells for $40 per share. To raise $20 million for a new particle accelerator, the firm is considering a rights offering at $25 per share. What is the value of a right in this case? The ex-rights price?

ANSWERS TO CHAPTER REVIEW AND SELF-TEST PROBLEMS

15.1 The firm needs to net $15 million after paying the 7 percent flotation costs. So the amount raised is given by:

Amount raised × (1 − .07) = $15 million

Amount raised = $15 million/.93 = $16.129 million

The total flotation cost is thus $1.129 million.

15.2 To raise $20 million at $25 per share, $20 million/25 = 800,000 shares will have to be sold. Before the offering, the firm is worth 3 million × $40 = $120 million. The issue will raise $20 million, and there will be 3.8 million shares outstanding. The value of an ex-rights share will therefore be $140 million/3.8 million = $36.84. The value of a right is thus $40 − 36.84 = $3.16.

CONCEPTS REVIEW AND CRITICAL THINKING QUESTIONS

1. **Debt versus Equity Offering Size [LO2]** In the aggregate, debt offerings are much more common than equity offerings and typically much larger as well. Why?

2. **Debt versus Equity Flotation Costs [LO2]** Why are the costs of selling equity so much larger than the costs of selling debt?

3. **Bond Ratings and Flotation Costs [LO2]** Why do noninvestment-grade bonds have much higher direct costs than investment-grade issues?

4. **Underpricing in Debt Offerings [LO2]** Why is underpricing not a great concern with bond offerings?

   Use the following information to answer the next three questions. Zipcar, the car sharing company, went public in April 2011. Assisted by the investment bank Goldman, Sachs & Co., Zipcar sold 9.68 million shares at $18 each, thereby raising a total

Visit us at www.mhhe.com/rwj

of $174.28 million. By the end of the first day of trading, the stock had zipped to $28 per share, down from a high of $31.50. Based on the end-of-day numbers, Zipcar shares were apparently underpriced by about $10 each, meaning that the company missed out on an additional $96.8 million.

5. **IPO Pricing [LO3]** The Zipcar IPO was underpriced by about 56 percent. Should Zipcar be upset at Goldman over the underpricing?

6. **IPO Pricing [LO3]** In the previous question, how would it affect your thinking to know that the company was incorporated about 10 years earlier, had only $186 million in revenues in 2010, and had never earned a profit? Additionally, the viability of the company's business model was still unproven.

7. **IPO Pricing [LO3]** In the previous two questions, how would it affect your thinking to know that in addition to the 9.68 million shares offered in the IPO, Zipcar had an additional 30 million shares outstanding? Of those 30 million shares, 14.1 million shares were owned by four venture capital firms, and 15.5 million shares were owned by the 12 directors and executive officers.

8. **Cash Offer versus Rights Offer [LO4]** Ren-Stimpy International is planning to raise fresh equity capital by selling a large new issue of common stock. Ren-Stimpy is currently a publicly traded corporation, and it is trying to choose between an underwritten cash offer and a rights offering (not underwritten) to current shareholders. Ren-Stimpy management is interested in minimizing the selling costs and has asked you for advice on the choice of issue methods. What is your recommendation and why?

9. **IPO Underpricing [LO3]** In 1980, a certain assistant professor of finance bought 12 initial public offerings of common stock. He held each of these for approximately one month and then sold. The investment rule he followed was to submit a purchase order for every firm commitment initial public offering of oil and gas exploration companies. There were 22 of these offerings, and he submitted a purchase order for approximately $1,000 in stock for each of the companies. With 10 of these, no shares were allocated to this assistant professor. With 5 of the 12 offerings that were purchased, fewer than the requested number of shares were allocated.

    The year 1980 was very good for oil and gas exploration company owners: On average, for the 22 companies that went public, the stocks were selling for 80 percent above the offering price a month after the initial offering date. The assistant professor looked at his performance record and found that the $8,400 invested in the 12 companies had grown to $10,000, representing a return of only about 20 percent (commissions were negligible). Did he have bad luck, or should he have expected to do worse than the average initial public offering investor? Explain.

10. **IPO Pricing [LO3]** The following material represents the cover page and summary of the prospectus for the initial public offering of the Pest Investigation Control Corporation (PICC), which is going public tomorrow with a firm commitment initial public offering managed by the investment banking firm of Erlanger and Ritter. Answer the following questions:

    a. Assume you know nothing about PICC other than the information contained in the prospectus. Based on your knowledge of finance, what is your prediction for the price of PICC tomorrow? Provide a short explanation of why you think this will occur.

    b. Assume you have several thousand dollars to invest. When you get home from class tonight, you find that your stockbroker, whom you have not talked to for weeks, has called. She has left a message that PICC is going public tomorrow and that she can get you several hundred shares at the offering price if you call her back first thing in the morning. Discuss the merits of this opportunity.

PROSPECTUS   PICC

200,000 SHARES
PEST INVESTIGATION CONTROL CORPORATION

Of the shares being offered hereby, all 200,000 are being sold by the Pest Investigation Control Corporation, Inc. ("the Company"). Before the offering there has been no public market for the shares of PICC, and no guarantee can be given that any such market will develop.

These securities have not been approved or disapproved by the SEC nor has the commission passed upon the accuracy or adequacy of this prospectus. Any representation to the contrary is a criminal offense.

	Price to Public	Underwriting Discount	Proceeds to Company*
Per share	$11.00	$1.10	$9.90
Total	$2,200,000	$220,000	$1,980,000

*Before deducting expenses estimated at $27,000 and payable by the Company.

This is an initial public offering. The common shares are being offered, subject to prior sale, when, as, and if delivered to and accepted by the Underwriters and subject to approval of certain legal matters by their Counsel and by Counsel for the Company. The Underwriters reserve the right to withdraw, cancel, or modify such offer and to reject offers in whole or in part.

Erlanger and Ritter, Investment Bankers
July 12, 2012

Prospectus Summary

The Company	The Pest Investigation Control Corporation (PICC) breeds and markets toads and tree frogs as ecologically safe insect-control mechanisms.
The Offering	200,000 shares of common stock, no par value.
Listing	The Company will seek listing on NASDAQ and will trade over the counter.
Shares Outstanding	As of June 30, 2012, 400,000 shares of common stock were outstanding. After the offering, 600,000 shares of common stock will be outstanding.
Use of Proceeds	To finance expansion of inventory and receivables and general working capital, and to pay for country club memberships for certain finance professors.

Selected Financial Information
(amounts in thousands except per-share data)

	Fiscal Year Ended June 30				As of June 30, 2012	
	2010	2011	2012		Actual	As Adjusted for This Offering
Revenues	$60.00	$120.00	$240.00	Working capital	$ 8	$1,961
Net earnings	3.80	15.90	36.10	Total assets	511	2,464
Earnings per share	.01	.04	.09	Stockholders' equity	423	2,376

QUESTIONS AND PROBLEMS

1. **Rights Offerings [LO4]** Bowman, Inc., is proposing a rights offering. Presently there are 400,000 shares outstanding at $73 each. There will be 50,000 new shares offered at $65 each.

   BASIC
   (Questions 1–8)

   a. What is the new market value of the company?

   b. How many rights are associated with one of the new shares?

   c. What is the ex-rights price?

   d. What is the value of a right?

   e. Why might a company have a rights offering rather than a general cash offer?

2. **Rights Offerings [LO4]** The Clifford Corporation has announced a rights offer to raise $30 million for a new journal, the *Journal of Financial Excess*. This journal will review potential articles after the author pays a nonrefundable reviewing fee of

Visit us at www.mhhe.com/rwj

Visit us at www.mhhe.com/rwj

$5,000 per page. The stock currently sells for $48 per share, and there are 3.9 million shares outstanding.

   a. What is the maximum possible subscription price? What is the minimum?

   b. If the subscription price is set at $43 per share, how many shares must be sold? How many rights will it take to buy one share?

   c. What is the ex-rights price? What is the value of a right?

   d. Show how a shareholder with 1,000 shares before the offering and no desire (or money) to buy additional shares is not harmed by the rights offer.

3. **Rights [LO4]** Red Shoe Co. has concluded that additional equity financing will be needed to expand operations and that the needed funds will be best obtained through a rights offering. It has correctly determined that as a result of the rights offering, the share price will fall from $65 to $63.20 ($65 is the rights-on price; $63.20 is the ex-rights price, also known as the *when-issued* price). The company is seeking $17 million in additional funds with a per-share subscription price equal to $35. How many shares are there currently, before the offering? (Assume that the increment to the market value of the equity equals the gross proceeds from the offering.)

4. **IPO Underpricing [LO3]** The Woods Co. and the Mickelson Co. have both announced IPOs at $40 per share. One of these is undervalued by $9, and the other is overvalued by $4, but you have no way of knowing which is which. You plan to buy 1,000 shares of each issue. If an issue is underpriced, it will be rationed, and only half your order will be filled. If you *could* get 1,000 shares in Woods and 1,000 shares in Mickelson, what would your profit be? What profit do you actually expect? What principle have you illustrated?

5. **Calculating Flotation Costs [LO3]** The Huang Corporation needs to raise $85 million to finance its expansion into new markets. The company will sell new shares of equity via a general cash offering to raise the needed funds. If the offer price is $16 per share and the company's underwriters charge a spread of 8 percent, how many shares need to be sold?

6. **Calculating Flotation Costs [LO3]** In the previous problem, if the SEC filing fee and associated administrative expenses of the offering are $900,000, how many shares need to be sold?

7. **Calculating Flotation Costs [LO3]** The Raven Co. has just gone public. Under a firm commitment agreement, Raven received $17.67 for each of the 15 million shares sold. The initial offering price was $19 per share, and the stock rose to $23.18 per share in the first few minutes of trading. Raven paid $900,000 in direct legal and other costs and $320,000 in indirect costs. What was the flotation cost as a percentage of funds raised?

8. **Price Dilution [LO3]** Canterbury, Inc., has 175,000 shares of stock outstanding. Each share is worth $68, so the company's market value of equity is $11,900,000. Suppose the firm issues 30,000 new shares at the following prices: $68, $65, and $60. What will the effect be of each of these alternative offering prices on the existing price per share?

INTERMEDIATE
(Questions 9–15)

9. **Dilution [LO3]** Teardrop, Inc., wishes to expand its facilities. The company currently has 5 million shares outstanding and no debt. The stock sells for $31 per share, but the book value per share is $7. Net income is currently $3.2 million. The new facility will cost $45 million, and it will increase net income by $900,000.

   a. Assuming a constant price–earnings ratio, what will the effect be of issuing new equity to finance the investment? To answer, calculate the new book value per share, the new total earnings, the new EPS, the new stock price, and the new market-to-book ratio. What is going on here?

b. What would the new net income for the company have to be for the stock price to remain unchanged?

10. **Dilution [LO3]** The Metallica Heavy Metal Mining (MHMM) Corporation wants to diversify its operations. Some recent financial information for the company is shown here:

Stock price	$ 76
Number of shares	40,000
Total assets	$7,500,000
Total liabilities	$3,100,000
Net income	$ 850,000

MHMM is considering an investment that has the same PE ratio as the firm. The cost of the investment is $800,000, and it will be financed with a new equity issue. The return on the investment will equal MHMM's current ROE. What will happen to the book value per share, the market value per share, and the EPS? What is the NPV of this investment? Does dilution take place?

11. **Dilution [LO3]** In the previous problem, what would the ROE on the investment have to be if we wanted the price after the offering to be $76 per share? (Assume the PE ratio remains constant.) What is the NPV of this investment? Does any dilution take place?

12. **Rights [LO4]** Keira Mfg. is considering a rights offer. The company has determined that the ex-rights price would be $83. The current price is $89 per share, and there are 24 million shares outstanding. The rights offer would raise a total of $50 million. What is the subscription price?

13. **Value of a Right [LO4]** Show that the value of a right just prior to expiration can be written as:

$$\text{Value of a right} = P_{RO} - P_X = (P_{RO} - P_S)/(N + 1)$$

where P_{RO}, P_S, and P_X stand for the rights-on price, the subscription price, and the ex-rights price, respectively, and N is the number of rights needed to buy one new share at the subscription price.

14. **Selling Rights [LO4]** Roth Corp. wants to raise $4.5 million via a rights offering. The company currently has 580,000 shares of common stock outstanding that sell for $45 per share. Its underwriter has set a subscription price of $20 per share and will charge the company a spread of 6 percent. If you currently own 5,000 shares of stock in the company and decide not to participate in the rights offering, how much money can you get by selling your rights?

15. **Valuing a Right [LO4]** Knight Inventory Systems, Inc., has announced a rights offer. The company has announced that it will take four rights to buy a new share in the offering at a subscription price of $35. At the close of business the day before the ex-rights day, the company's stock sells for $60 per share. The next morning, you notice that the stock sells for $53 per share and the rights sell for $3 each. Are the stock and the rights correctly priced on the ex-rights day? Describe a transaction in which you could use these prices to create an immediate profit.

Visit us at www.mhhe.com/rwj

S&S Air Goes Public

Mark Sexton and Todd Story have been discussing the future of S&S Air. The company has been experiencing fast growth, and the two see only clear skies in the company's future. However, the fast growth can no longer be funded by internal sources, so Mark and Todd have decided the time is right to take the company public. To this end, they have entered into discussions with the investment bank of Crowe & Mallard. The company has a working relationship with Renata Harper, the underwriter who assisted with the company's previous bond offering. Crowe & Mallard have assisted numerous small companies in the IPO process, so Mark and Todd feel confident with this choice.

Renata begins by telling Mark and Todd about the process. Although Crowe & Mallard charged an underwriter fee of 4 percent on the bond offering, the underwriter fee is 7 percent on all initial stock offerings of the size of S&S Air's offering. Renata tells Mark and Todd that the company can expect to pay about $1,800,000 in legal fees and expenses, $12,000 in SEC registration fees, and $15,000 in other filing fees. Additionally, to be listed on the NASDAQ, the company must pay $100,000. There are also transfer agent fees of $6,500 and engraving expenses of $520,000. The company should also expect to pay $110,000 for other expenses associated with the IPO.

Finally, Renata tells Mark and Todd that to file with the SEC, the company must provide three years' audited financial statements. She is unsure about the costs of the audit. Mark tells Renata that the company provides audited financial statements as part of the bond covenant, and the company pays $300,000 per year for the outside auditor.

QUESTIONS

1. At the end of the discussion, Mark asks Renata about the Dutch auction IPO process. What are the differences in the expenses to S&S Air if it uses a Dutch auction IPO versus a traditional IPO? Should the company go public through a Dutch auction or use a traditional underwritten offering?

2. During the discussion of the potential IPO and S&S Air's future, Mark states that he feels the company should raise $75 million. However, Renata points out that if the company needs more cash in the near future, a secondary offering close to the IPO would be problematic. Instead she suggests that the company should raise $90 million in the IPO. How can we calculate the optimal size of the IPO? What are the advantages and disadvantages of increasing the size of the IPO to $90 million?

3. After deliberation, Mark and Todd have decided that the company should use a firm commitment offering with Crowe & Mallard as the lead underwriter. The IPO will be for $75 million. Ignoring underpricing, how much will the IPO cost the company as a percentage of the funds received?

4. Many employees of S&S Air have shares of stock in the company because of an existing employee stock purchase plan. To sell the stock, the employees can tender their shares to be sold in the IPO at the offering price, or the employees can retain their stock and sell it in the secondary market after S&S Air goes public. Todd asks you to advise the employees about which option is best. What would you suggest to the employees?

Visit us at www.mhhe.com/rwj

FINANCIAL LEVERAGE AND CAPITAL STRUCTURE POLICY

ON FEBRUARY 16, 2011, famed bookseller Borders Group began a new chapter in its corporate life—Chapter 11 bankruptcy. The company had been faced with intense competition from rivals Amazon.com and Barnes & Noble. As a part of the bankruptcy process, the company planned to shut down about 200 of its 462 stores and change its focus to e-books and nonbook products. The company's biggest unsecured creditors were publishing companies. In fact, the six largest publishers were owed a combined $182 million and expected to get back only 25 cents on the dollar. Of course, Borders was not alone. The Honolulu Symphony Orchestra sounded a sour note, filing for Chapter 11 bankruptcy to reorganize its finances in 2009. It was later forced to switch to a Chapter 7 liquidation in February 2011. The assets to be auctioned included two grand pianos, a harpsichord, and 11 cowbells. Even pizza was not immune to bankruptcy. Round Table Pizza, which promised to serve "The Last Honest Pizza," and famed Chicago pizzeria Giordano's, home of "world famous" deep-dish pizza, both filed for bankruptcy within a week of each other in February 2011.

A firm's choice of how much debt it should have relative to equity is known as a capital structure decision. Such a choice has many implications for a firm and is far from being a settled issue in either theory or practice. In this chapter, we discuss the basic ideas underlying capital structures and how firms choose them.

A firm's capital structure is really just a reflection of its borrowing policy. Should we borrow a lot of money, or just a little? At first glance, it probably seems that debt is something to be avoided. After all, the more debt a firm has, the greater is the risk of bankruptcy. What we learn is that debt is really a double-edged sword, and, properly used, debt can be enormously beneficial to a firm.

A good understanding of the effects of debt financing is important simply because the role of debt is so misunderstood, and many firms (and individuals) are far too conservative in their use of debt. Having said this, we can also say that firms sometimes err in the opposite direction, becoming much too heavily indebted, with bankruptcy as the unfortunate consequence. Striking the right balance is what the capital structure issue is all about.

LEARNING OBJECTIVES

After studying this chapter, you should understand:

LO1 The effect of financial leverage.

LO2 The impact of taxes and bankruptcy on capital structure choice.

LO3 The essentials of the bankruptcy process.

Thus far, we have taken the firm's capital structure as given. Debt–equity ratios don't just drop on firms from the sky, of course, so now it's time to wonder where they come from. Going back to Chapter 1, recall that we refer to decisions about a firm's debt–equity ratio as *capital structure decisions.*[1]

For the most part, a firm can choose any capital structure it wants. If management so desired, a firm could issue some bonds and use the proceeds to buy back some stock, thereby increasing the debt–equity ratio. Alternatively, it could issue stock and use the money to pay off some debt, thereby reducing the debt–equity ratio. Activities such as these, which alter the firm's existing capital structure, are called capital *restructurings.* In general, such restructurings take place whenever the firm substitutes one capital structure for another while leaving the firm's assets unchanged.

Because the assets of a firm are not directly affected by a capital restructuring, we can examine the firm's capital structure decision separately from its other activities. This means that a firm can consider capital restructuring decisions in isolation from its investment decisions. In this chapter, then, we will ignore investment decisions and focus on the long-term financing, or capital structure, question.

What we will see in this chapter is that capital structure decisions can have important implications for the value of the firm and its cost of capital. We will also find that important elements of the capital structure decision are easy to identify, but precise measures of these elements are generally not obtainable. As a result, we are only able to give an incomplete answer to the question of what the best capital structure might be for a particular firm at a particular time.

16.1 The Capital Structure Question

How should a firm go about choosing its debt–equity ratio? Here, as always, we assume that the guiding principle is to choose the course of action that maximizes the value of a share of stock. As we discuss next, however, when it comes to capital structure decisions, this is essentially the same thing as maximizing the value of the whole firm, and, for convenience, we will tend to frame our discussion in terms of firm value.

FIRM VALUE AND STOCK VALUE: AN EXAMPLE

The following example illustrates that the capital structure that maximizes the value of the firm is the one financial managers should choose for the shareholders, so there is no conflict in our goals. To begin, suppose the market value of the J.J. Sprint Company is $1,000. The company currently has no debt, and J.J. Sprint's 100 shares sell for $10 each. Further suppose that J.J. Sprint restructures itself by borrowing $500 and then paying out the proceeds to shareholders as an extra dividend of $500/100 = $5 per share.

This restructuring will change the capital structure of the firm with no direct effect on the firm's assets. The immediate effect will be to increase debt and decrease equity. However, what will be the final impact of the restructuring? Table 16.1 illustrates three possible outcomes in addition to the original no-debt case. Notice that in Scenario II, the value of the firm is unchanged at $1,000. In Scenario I, firm value rises to $1,250; it falls by $250, to $750, in Scenario III. We haven't yet said what might lead to these changes. For now, we just take them as possible outcomes to illustrate a point.

Because our goal is to benefit the shareholders, we next examine, in Table 16.2, the net payoffs to the shareholders in these scenarios. We see that, if the value of the firm stays the same, shareholders will experience a capital loss exactly offsetting the extra dividend. This

---

[1] It is conventional to refer to decisions regarding debt and equity as *capital structure decisions.* However, the term *financial structure decisions* would be more accurate, and we use the terms interchangeably.

	No Debt	Debt plus Dividend		
		I	II	III
Debt	$ 0	$ 500	$ 500	$500
Equity	1,000	750	500	250
Firm value	$1,000	$1,250	$1,000	$750

TABLE 16.1

Possible Firm Values: No Debt versus Debt plus Dividend

	Debt plus Dividend		
	I	II	III
Equity value reduction	−$250	−$500	−$750
Dividends	500	500	500
Net effect	+$250	$ 0	−$250

TABLE 16.2

Possible Payoffs to Shareholders: Debt plus Dividend

is Scenario II. In Scenario I, the value of the firm increases to $1,250 and the shareholders come out ahead by $250. In other words, the restructuring has an NPV of $250 in this scenario. The NPV in Scenario III is −$250.

The key observation to make here is that the change in the value of the firm is the same as the net effect on the stockholders. Financial managers can therefore try to find the capital structure that maximizes the value of the firm. Put another way, the NPV rule applies to capital structure decisions, and the change in the value of the overall firm is the NPV of a restructuring. Thus, J.J. Sprint should borrow $500 if it expects Scenario I. The crucial question in determining a firm's capital structure is, of course, which scenario is likely to occur.

CAPITAL STRUCTURE AND THE COST OF CAPITAL

In Chapter 14, we discussed the concept of the firm's weighted average cost of capital, or WACC. You may recall that the WACC tells us that the firm's overall cost of capital is a weighted average of the costs of the various components of the firm's capital structure. When we described the WACC, we took the firm's capital structure as given. Thus, one important issue that we will want to explore in this chapter is what happens to the cost of capital when we vary the amount of debt financing, or the debt–equity ratio.

A primary reason for studying the WACC is that the value of the firm is maximized when the WACC is minimized. To see this, recall that the WACC is the appropriate discount rate for the firm's overall cash flows. Because values and discount rates move in opposite directions, minimizing the WACC will maximize the value of the firm's cash flows.

Thus, we will want to choose the firm's capital structure so that the WACC is minimized. For this reason, we will say that one capital structure is better than another if it results in a lower weighted average cost of capital. Further, we say that a particular debt–equity ratio represents the *optimal capital structure* if it results in the lowest possible WACC. This optimal capital structure is sometimes called the firm's *target* capital structure as well.

Concept Questions

16.1a Why should financial managers choose the capital structure that maximizes the value of the firm?

16.1b What is the relationship between the WACC and the value of the firm?

16.1c What is an optimal capital structure?

℥ 16.2 The Effect of Financial Leverage

The previous section described why the capital structure that produces the highest firm value (or the lowest cost of capital) is the one most beneficial to stockholders. In this section, we examine the impact of financial leverage on the payoffs to stockholders. As you may recall, *financial leverage* refers to the extent to which a firm relies on debt. The more debt financing a firm uses in its capital structure, the more financial leverage it employs.

As we describe, financial leverage can dramatically alter the payoffs to shareholders in the firm. Remarkably, however, financial leverage may not affect the overall cost of capital. If this is true, then a firm's capital structure is irrelevant because changes in capital structure won't affect the value of the firm. We will return to this issue a little later.

THE BASICS OF FINANCIAL LEVERAGE

We start by illustrating how financial leverage works. For now, we ignore the impact of taxes. Also, for ease of presentation, we describe the impact of leverage in terms of its effects on earnings per share, EPS, and return on equity, ROE. These are, of course, accounting numbers and, as such, are not our primary concern. Using cash flows instead of these accounting numbers would lead to precisely the same conclusions, but a little more work would be needed. We discuss the impact on market values in a subsequent section.

Financial Leverage, EPS, and ROE: An Example   The Trans Am Corporation currently has no debt in its capital structure. The CFO, Ms. Morris, is considering a restructuring that would involve issuing debt and using the proceeds to buy back some of the outstanding equity. Table 16.3 presents both the current and proposed capital structures. As shown, the firm's assets have a market value of $8 million, and there are 400,000 shares outstanding. Because Trans Am is an all-equity firm, the price per share is $20.

The proposed debt issue would raise $4 million; the interest rate would be 10 percent. Because the stock sells for $20 per share, the $4 million in new debt would be used to purchase $4 million/20 = 200,000 shares, leaving 200,000. After the restructuring, Trans Am would have a capital structure that was 50 percent debt, so the debt–equity ratio would be 1. Notice that, for now, we assume that the stock price will remain at $20.

To investigate the impact of the proposed restructuring, Ms. Morris has prepared Table 16.4, which compares the firm's current capital structure to the proposed capital structure under three scenarios. The scenarios reflect different assumptions about the firm's EBIT. Under the expected scenario, the EBIT is $1 million. In the recession scenario, EBIT falls to $500,000. In the expansion scenario, it rises to $1.5 million.

To illustrate some of the calculations behind the figures in Table 16.4, consider the expansion case. EBIT is $1.5 million. With no debt (the current capital structure) and no taxes, net income is also $1.5 million. In this case, there are 400,000 shares worth $8 million total. EPS

TABLE 16.3

Current and Proposed Capital Structures for the Trans Am Corporation

	Current	Proposed
Assets	$8,000,000	$8,000,000
Debt	$ 0	$4,000,000
Equity	$8,000,000	$4,000,000
Debt–equity ratio	0	1
Share price	$ 20	$ 20
Shares outstanding	400,000	200,000
Interest rate	10%	10%

Current Capital Structure: No Debt			
	Recession	**Expected**	**Expansion**
EBIT	$500,000	$1,000,000	$1,500,000
Interest	0	0	0
Net income	$500,000	$1,000,000	$1,500,000
ROE	6.25%	12.50%	18.75%
EPS	$ 1.25	$ 2.50	$ 3.75
Proposed Capital Structure: Debt = $4 million			
EBIT	$500,000	$1,000,000	$1,500,000
Interest	400,000	400,000	400,000
Net income	$100,000	$ 600,000	$1,100,000
ROE	2.50%	15.00%	27.50%
EPS	$ .50	$ 3.00	$ 5.50

TABLE 16.4

Capital Structure Scenarios for the Trans Am Corporation

is therefore $1.5 million/400,000 = $3.75. Also, because accounting return on equity, ROE, is net income divided by total equity, ROE is $1.5 million/8 million = 18.75%.[2]

With $4 million in debt (the proposed capital structure), things are somewhat different. Because the interest rate is 10 percent, the interest bill is $400,000. With EBIT of $1.5 million, interest of $400,000, and no taxes, net income is $1.1 million. Now there are only 200,000 shares worth $4 million total. EPS is therefore $1.1 million/200,000 = $5.50, versus the $3.75 that we calculated in the previous scenario. Furthermore, ROE is $1.1 million/4 million = 27.5%. This is well above the 18.75 percent we calculated for the current capital structure.

EPS versus EBIT   The impact of leverage is evident when the effect of the restructuring on EPS and ROE is examined. In particular, the variability in both EPS and ROE is much larger under the proposed capital structure. This illustrates how financial leverage acts to magnify gains and losses to shareholders.

In Figure 16.1, we take a closer look at the effect of the proposed restructuring. This figure plots earnings per share, EPS, against earnings before interest and taxes, EBIT, for the current and proposed capital structures. The first line, labeled "No debt," represents the case of no leverage. This line begins at the origin, indicating that EPS would be zero if EBIT were zero. From there, every $400,000 increase in EBIT increases EPS by $1 (because there are 400,000 shares outstanding).

The second line represents the proposed capital structure. Here, EPS is negative if EBIT is zero. This follows because $400,000 of interest must be paid regardless of the firm's profits. Because there are 200,000 shares in this case, the EPS is −$2 as shown. Similarly, if EBIT were $400,000, EPS would be exactly zero.

The important thing to notice in Figure 16.1 is that the slope of the line in this second case is steeper. In fact, for every $400,000 increase in EBIT, EPS rises by $2, so the line is twice as steep. This tells us that EPS is twice as sensitive to changes in EBIT because of the financial leverage employed.

Another observation to make in Figure 16.1 is that the lines intersect. At that point, EPS is exactly the same for both capital structures. To find this point, note that EPS is equal to EBIT/400,000 in the no-debt case. In the with-debt case, EPS is (EBIT − $400,000)/200,000. If we set these equal to each other, EBIT is:

$$EBIT/400{,}000 = (EBIT - \$400{,}000)/200{,}000$$
$$EBIT = 2 \times (EBIT - \$400{,}000)$$
$$= \$800{,}000$$

[2]ROE is discussed in some detail in Chapter 3.

FIGURE 16.1

Financial Leverage: EPS
and EBIT for the Trans
Am Corporation

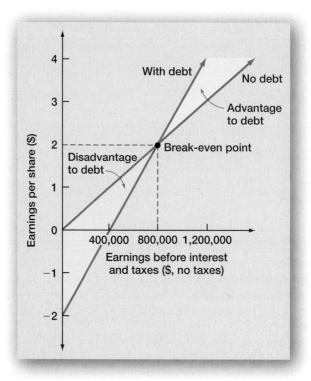

When EBIT is $800,000, EPS is $2 under either capital structure. This is labeled as the break-even point in Figure 16.1; we could also call it the indifference point. If EBIT is above this level, leverage is beneficial; if it is below this point, it is not.

There is another, more intuitive, way of seeing why the break-even point is $800,000. Notice that, if the firm has no debt and its EBIT is $800,000, its net income is also $800,000. In this case, the ROE is 10 percent. This is precisely the same as the interest rate on the debt, so the firm earns a return that is just sufficient to pay the interest.

EXAMPLE 16.1   Break-Even EBIT

The MPD Corporation has decided in favor of a capital restructuring. Currently, MPD uses no debt financing. Following the restructuring, however, debt will be $1 million. The interest rate on the debt will be 9 percent. MPD currently has 200,000 shares outstanding, and the price per share is $20. If the restructuring is expected to increase EPS, what is the minimum level for EBIT that MPD's management must be expecting? Ignore taxes in answering.

To answer, we calculate the break-even EBIT. At any EBIT above this, the increased financial leverage will increase EPS, so this will tell us the minimum level for EBIT. Under the old capital structure, EPS is simply EBIT/200,000. Under the new capital structure, the interest expense will be $1 million × .09 = $90,000. Furthermore, with the $1 million proceeds, MPD will repurchase $1 million/20 = 50,000 shares of stock, leaving 150,000 outstanding. EPS will thus be (EBIT − $90,000)/150,000.

Now that we know how to calculate EPS under both scenarios, we set them equal to each other and solve for the break-even EBIT:

$$\text{EBIT}/200{,}000 = (\text{EBIT} - \$90{,}000)/150{,}000$$
$$\text{EBIT} = 4/3 \times (\text{EBIT} - \$90{,}000)$$
$$= \$360{,}000$$

Verify that, in either case, EPS is $1.80 when EBIT is $360,000. Management at MPD is apparently of the opinion that EPS will exceed $1.80.

CORPORATE BORROWING AND HOMEMADE LEVERAGE

Based on Tables 16.3 and 16.4 and Figure 16.1, Ms. Morris draws the following conclusions:

1. The effect of financial leverage depends on the company's EBIT. When EBIT is relatively high, leverage is beneficial.
2. Under the expected scenario, leverage increases the returns to shareholders, as measured by both ROE and EPS.
3. Shareholders are exposed to more risk under the proposed capital structure because the EPS and ROE are much more sensitive to changes in EBIT in this case.
4. Because of the impact that financial leverage has on both the expected return to stockholders and the riskiness of the stock, capital structure is an important consideration.

The first three of these conclusions are clearly correct. Does the last conclusion necessarily follow? Surprisingly, the answer is no. As we discuss next, the reason is that shareholders can adjust the amount of financial leverage by borrowing and lending on their own. This use of personal borrowing to alter the degree of financial leverage is called **homemade leverage**.

We will now illustrate that it actually makes no difference whether or not Trans Am adopts the proposed capital structure, because any stockholder who prefers the proposed capital structure can simply create it using homemade leverage. To begin, the first part of Table 16.5 shows what will happen to an investor who buys $2,000 worth of Trans Am stock if the proposed capital structure is adopted. This investor purchases 100 shares of stock. From Table 16.4, we know that EPS will be $.50, $3, or $5.50, so the total earnings for 100 shares will be either $50, $300, or $550 under the proposed capital structure.

Now, suppose that Trans Am does not adopt the proposed capital structure. In this case, EPS will be $1.25, $2.50, or $3.75. The second part of Table 16.5 demonstrates how a stockholder who prefers the payoffs under the proposed structure can create them using personal borrowing. To do this, the stockholder borrows $2,000 at 10 percent on her or his own. Our investor uses this amount, along with the original $2,000, to buy 200 shares of stock. As shown, the net payoffs are exactly the same as those for the proposed capital structure.

How did we know to borrow $2,000 to create the right payoffs? We are trying to replicate Trans Am's proposed capital structure at the personal level. The proposed capital structure results in a debt–equity ratio of 1. To replicate this structure at the personal level, the stockholder must borrow enough to create this same debt–equity ratio. Because the stockholder has $2,000 in equity invested, the borrowing of another $2,000 will create a personal debt–equity ratio of 1.

homemade leverage
The use of personal borrowing to change the overall amount of financial leverage to which the individual is exposed.

Proposed Capital Structure			
	Recession	**Expected**	**Expansion**
EPS	$ .50	$ 3.00	$ 5.50
Earnings for 100 shares	50.00	300.00	550.00
Net cost = 100 shares × $20 = $2,000			
Original Capital Structure and Homemade Leverage			
EPS	$ 1.25	$ 2.50	$ 3.75
Earnings for 200 shares	250.00	500.00	750.00
Less: Interest on $2,000 at 10%	200.00	200.00	200.00
Net earnings	$ 50.00	$300.00	$550.00
Net cost = 200 shares × $20 − Amount borrowed = $4,000 − 2,000 − $2,000			

TABLE 16.5

Proposed Capital Structure versus Original Capital Structure with Homemade Leverage

This example demonstrates that investors can always increase financial leverage themselves to create a different pattern of payoffs. It thus makes no difference whether Trans Am chooses the proposed capital structure.

EXAMPLE 16.2 | **Unlevering the Stock**

In our Trans Am example, suppose management adopts the proposed capital structure. Further suppose that an investor who owned 100 shares preferred the original capital structure. Show how this investor could "unlever" the stock to re-create the original payoffs.

To create leverage, investors borrow on their own. To undo leverage, investors must lend money. In the case of Trans Am, the corporation borrowed an amount equal to half its value. The investor can unlever the stock by simply lending money in the same proportion. In this case, the investor sells 50 shares for $1,000 total and then lends the $1,000 at 10 percent. The payoffs are calculated in the following table:

	Recession	Expected	Expansion
EPS (proposed structure)	$ .50	$ 3.00	$ 5.50
Earnings for 50 shares	25.00	150.00	275.00
Plus: Interest on $1,000	100.00	100.00	100.00
Total payoff	$125.00	$250.00	$375.00

These are precisely the payoffs the investor would have experienced under the original capital structure.

Concept Questions

16.2a What is the impact of financial leverage on stockholders?

16.2b What is homemade leverage?

16.2c Why is Trans Am's capital structure irrelevant?

⚡ 16.3 Capital Structure and the Cost of Equity Capital

We have seen that there is nothing special about corporate borrowing because investors can borrow or lend on their own. As a result, whichever capital structure Trans Am chooses, the stock price will be the same. Trans Am's capital structure is thus irrelevant, at least in the simple world we have examined.

Our Trans Am example is based on a famous argument advanced by two Nobel laureates, Franco Modigliani and Merton Miller, whom we will henceforth call M&M. What we illustrated for the Trans Am Corporation is a special case of **M&M Proposition I**. M&M Proposition I states that it is completely irrelevant how a firm chooses to arrange its finances.

M&M Proposition I
The proposition that the value of the firm is independent of the firm's capital structure.

M&M PROPOSITION I: THE PIE MODEL

One way to illustrate M&M Proposition I is to imagine two firms that are identical on the left side of the balance sheet. Their assets and operations are exactly the same. The right sides are different because the two firms finance their operations differently. In this case, we can view the capital structure question in terms of a "pie" model. Why we choose this

FIGURE 16.2

Two Pie Models of Capital Structure

name is apparent from Figure 16.2. Figure 16.2 gives two possible ways of cutting up the pie between the equity slice, E, and the debt slice, D: 40%–60% and 60%–40%. However, the size of the pie in Figure 16.2 is the same for both firms because the value of the assets is the same. This is precisely what M&M Proposition I states: The size of the pie doesn't depend on how it is sliced.

THE COST OF EQUITY AND FINANCIAL LEVERAGE: M&M PROPOSITION II

Although changing the capital structure of the firm does not change the firm's *total* value, it does cause important changes in the firm's debt and equity. We now examine what happens to a firm financed with debt and equity when the debt–equity ratio is changed. To simplify our analysis, we will continue to ignore taxes.

Based on our discussion in Chapter 14, if we ignore taxes, the weighted average cost of capital, WACC, is:

$$\text{WACC} = (E/V) \times R_E + (D/V) \times R_D$$

where $V = E + D$. We also saw that one way of interpreting the WACC is as the required return on the firm's overall assets. To remind us of this, we will use the symbol R_A to stand for the WACC and write:

$$R_A = (E/V) \times R_E + (D/V) \times R_D$$

If we rearrange this to solve for the cost of equity capital, we see that:

$$R_E = R_A + (R_A - R_D) \times (D/E) \qquad \text{[16.1]}$$

This is the famous **M&M Proposition II**, which tells us that the cost of equity depends on three things: the required rate of return on the firm's assets, R_A; the firm's cost of debt, R_D; and the firm's debt–equity ratio, D/E.

Figure 16.3 summarizes our discussion thus far by plotting the cost of equity capital, R_E, against the debt–equity ratio. As shown, M&M Proposition II indicates that the cost of equity, R_E, is given by a straight line with a slope of $(R_A - R_D)$. The y-intercept corresponds to a firm with a debt–equity ratio of zero, so $R_A = R_E$ in that case. Figure 16.3 shows that as the firm raises its debt–equity ratio, the increase in leverage raises the risk of the equity and therefore the required return or cost of equity (R_E).

Notice in Figure 16.3 that the WACC doesn't depend on the debt–equity ratio; it's the same no matter what the debt–equity ratio is. This is another way of stating M&M Proposition I: The firm's overall cost of capital is unaffected by its capital structure. As illustrated, the fact that the cost of debt is lower than the cost of equity is exactly offset by the increase in the cost of equity from borrowing. In other words, the change in the capital structure weights (E/V and D/V) is exactly offset by the change in the cost of equity (R_E), so the WACC stays the same.

M&M Proposition II
The proposition that a firm's cost of equity capital is a positive linear function of the firm's capital structure.

FIGURE 16.3

The Cost of Equity
and the WACC: M&M
Propositions I and II with
No Taxes

$R_E = R_A + (R_A - R_D) \times (D/E)$ by M&M Proposition II

$R_A = \text{WACC} = \left(\dfrac{E}{V}\right) \times R_E + \left(\dfrac{D}{V}\right) \times R_D$

where $V = D + E$

EXAMPLE 16.3   **The Cost of Equity Capital**

The Ricardo Corporation has a weighted average cost of capital (ignoring taxes) of 12 percent. It can borrow at 8 percent. Assuming that Ricardo has a target capital structure of 80 percent equity and 20 percent debt, what is its cost of equity? What is the cost of equity if the target capital structure is 50 percent equity? Calculate the WACC using your answers to verify that it is the same.

According to M&M Proposition II, the cost of equity, R_E, is:

$$R_E = R_A + (R_A - R_D) \times (D/E)$$

In the first case, the debt–equity ratio is $.2/.8 = .25$, so the cost of the equity is:

$$R_E = 12\% + (12\% - 8\%) \times .25$$
$$= 13\%$$

In the second case, verify that the debt–equity ratio is 1.0, so the cost of equity is 16 percent.

We can now calculate the WACC assuming that the percentage of equity financing is 80 percent, the cost of equity is 13 percent, and the tax rate is zero:

$$\text{WACC} = (E/V) \times R_E + (D/V) \times R_D$$
$$= .80 \times 13\% + .20 \times 8\%$$
$$= 12\%$$

In the second case, the percentage of equity financing is 50 percent and the cost of equity is 16 percent. The WACC is:

$$\text{WACC} = (E/V) \times R_E + (D/V) \times R_D$$
$$= .50 \times 16\% + .50 \times 8\%$$
$$= 12\%$$

As we have calculated, the WACC is 12 percent in both cases.

IN THEIR OWN WORDS ...

Merton H. Miller on Capital Structure: M&M 30 Years Later

How difficult it is to summarize briefly the contribution of these papers was brought home to me very clearly after Franco Modigliani was awarded the Nobel Prize in Economics, in part—but, of course, only in part—for his work in finance. The television camera crews from our local stations in Chicago immediately descended upon me. "We understand," they said, "that you worked with Modigliani some years back in developing these M&M theorems, and we wonder if you could explain them briefly to our television viewers." "How briefly?" I asked. "Oh, take 10 seconds," was the reply.

Ten seconds to explain the work of a lifetime! Ten seconds to describe two carefully reasoned articles, each running to more than 30 printed pages and each with 60 or so long footnotes! When they saw the look of dismay on my face, they said, "You don't have to go into details. Just give us the main points in simple, common sense terms."

The main point of the cost-of-capital article was, in principle at least, simple enough to make. It said that in an economist's ideal world, the total market value of all the securities issued by a firm would be governed by the earning power and risk of its underlying real assets and would be independent of how the mix of securities issued to finance it was divided between debt instruments and equity capital. Some corporate treasurers might well think that they could enhance total value by increasing the proportion of debt instruments because yields on debt instruments, given their lower risk, are, by and large, substantially below those on equity capital. But, under the ideal conditions assumed, the added risk to the shareholders from issuing more debt will raise required yields on the equity by just enough to offset the seeming gain from use of low-cost debt.

Such a summary would not only have been too long, but it relied on shorthand terms and concepts that are rich in connotations to economists, but hardly so to the general public. I thought, instead, of an analogy that we ourselves had invoked in the original paper. "Think of the firm," I said, "as a gigantic tub of whole milk. The farmer can sell the whole milk as is. Or he can separate out the cream and sell it at a considerably higher price than the whole milk would bring. (Selling cream is the analog of a firm selling low-yield and hence high-priced debt securities.) But, of course, what the farmer would have left would be skim milk, with low butterfat content, and that would sell for much less than whole milk. Skim milk corresponds to the levered equity. The M&M proposition says that if there were no costs of separation (and, of course, no government dairy support programs), the cream plus the skim milk would bring the same price as the whole milk."

The television people conferred among themselves for a while. They informed me that it was still too long, too complicated, and too academic. "Have you anything simpler?" they asked. I thought of another way in which the M&M proposition is presented that stresses the role of securities as devices for "partitioning" a firm's payoffs among the group of its capital suppliers. "Think of the firm," I said, "as a gigantic pizza, divided into quarters. If, now, you cut each quarter in half into eighths, the M&M proposition says that you will have more pieces, but not more pizza."

Once again whispered conversation. This time, they shut the lights off. They folded up their equipment. They thanked me for my cooperation. They said they would get back to me. But I knew that I had somehow lost my chance to start a new career as a packager of economic wisdom for TV viewers in convenient 10-second sound bites. Some have the talent for it; and some just don't.

The late Merton H. Miller was famous for his pathbreaking work with Franco Modigliani on corporate capital structure, cost of capital, and dividend policy. He received the Nobel Prize in Economics for his contributions shortly after this essay was prepared.

BUSINESS AND FINANCIAL RISK

M&M Proposition II shows that the firm's cost of equity can be broken down into two components. The first component, R_A, is the required return on the firm's assets overall, and it depends on the nature of the firm's operating activities. The risk inherent in a firm's operations is called the **business risk** of the firm's equity. Referring back to Chapter 13, note that this business risk depends on the systematic risk of the firm's assets. The greater a firm's business risk, the greater R_A will be, and, all other things being the same, the greater will be the firm's cost of equity.

business risk
The equity risk that comes from the nature of the firm's operating activities.

The second component in the cost of equity, $(R_A - R_D) \times (D/E)$, is determined by the firm's financial structure. For an all-equity firm, this component is zero. As the firm begins to rely on debt financing, the required return on equity rises. This occurs because the debt financing increases the risks borne by the stockholders. This extra risk that arises from the use of debt financing is called the **financial risk** of the firm's equity.

The total systematic risk of the firm's equity thus has two parts: business risk and financial risk. The first part (the business risk) depends on the firm's assets and operations and is not affected by capital structure. Given the firm's business risk (and its cost of debt), the second part (the financial risk) is completely determined by financial policy. As we have illustrated, the firm's cost of equity rises when the firm increases its use of financial leverage because the financial risk of the equity increases while the business risk remains the same.

financial risk
The equity risk that comes from the financial policy (the capital structure) of the firm.

Concept Questions

16.3a What does M&M Proposition I state?

16.3b What are the three determinants of a firm's cost of equity?

16.3c The total systematic risk of a firm's equity has two parts. What are they?

16.4 M&M Propositions I and II with Corporate Taxes

Debt has two distinguishing features that we have not taken into proper account. First, as we have mentioned in a number of places, interest paid on debt is tax deductible. This is good for the firm, and it may be an added benefit of debt financing. Second, failure to meet debt obligations can result in bankruptcy. This is not good for the firm, and it may be an added cost of debt financing. Because we haven't explicitly considered either of these two features of debt, we realize that we may get a different answer about capital structure once we do. Accordingly, we consider taxes in this section and bankruptcy in the next one.

We can start by considering what happens to M&M Propositions I and II when we consider the effect of corporate taxes. To do this, we will examine two firms: Firm U (unlevered) and Firm L (levered). These two firms are identical on the left side of the balance sheet, so their assets and operations are the same.

We assume that EBIT is expected to be $1,000 every year forever for both firms. The difference between the firms is that Firm L has issued $1,000 worth of perpetual bonds on which it pays 8 percent interest each year. The interest bill is thus $.08 \times \$1,000 = \$80$ every year forever. Also, we assume that the corporate tax rate is 30 percent.

For our two firms, U and L, we can now calculate the following:

	Firm U	Firm L
EBIT	$1,000	$1,000
Interest	0	80
Taxable income	$1,000	$ 920
Taxes (30%)	300	276
Net income	$ 700	$ 644

THE INTEREST TAX SHIELD

To simplify things, we will assume that depreciation is zero. We will also assume that capital spending is zero and that there are no changes in NWC. In this case, cash flow from assets is simply equal to EBIT − Taxes. For Firms U and L, we thus have:

Cash Flow from Assets	Firm U	Firm L
EBIT	$1,000	$1,000
− Taxes	300	276
Total	$ 700	$ 724

We immediately see that capital structure is now having some effect because the cash flows from U and L are not the same even though the two firms have identical assets.

To see what's going on, we can compute the cash flow to stockholders and bondholders:

Cash Flow	Firm U	Firm L
To stockholders	$700	$644
To bondholders	0	80
Total	$700	$724

What we are seeing is that the total cash flow to L is $24 more. This occurs because L's tax bill (which is a cash outflow) is $24 less. The fact that interest is deductible for tax purposes has generated a tax saving equal to the interest payment ($80) multiplied by the corporate tax rate (30 percent): $80 × .30 = $24. We call this tax saving the **interest tax shield**.

interest tax shield
The tax saving attained by a firm from interest expense.

TAXES AND M&M PROPOSITION I

Because the debt is perpetual, the same $24 shield will be generated every year forever. The aftertax cash flow to L will thus be the same $700 that U earns plus the $24 tax shield. Because L's cash flow is always $24 greater, Firm L is worth more than Firm U, the difference being the value of this $24 perpetuity.

Because the tax shield is generated by paying interest, it has the same risk as the debt, and 8 percent (the cost of debt) is therefore the appropriate discount rate. The value of the tax shield is thus:

$$PV = \frac{\$24}{.08} = \frac{.30 \times \$1,000 \times .08}{.08} = .30 \times \$1,000 = \$300$$

As our example illustrates, the present value of the interest tax shield can be written as:

$$\text{Present value of the interest tax shield} = (T_C \times D \times R_D)/R_D$$
$$= T_C \times D \qquad \qquad \text{[16.2]}$$

We have now come up with another famous result, M&M Proposition I with corporate taxes. We have seen that the value of Firm L, V_L, exceeds the value of Firm U, V_U, by the present value of the interest tax shield, $T_C \times D$. M&M Proposition I with taxes therefore states that:

$$V_L = V_U + T_C \times D \qquad \qquad \text{[16.3]}$$

The effect of borrowing in this case is illustrated in Figure 16.4. We have plotted the value of the levered firm, V_L, against the amount of debt, D. M&M Proposition I with corporate taxes implies that the relationship is given by a straight line with a slope of T_C and a y-intercept of V_U.

In Figure 16.4, we have also drawn a horizontal line representing V_U. As indicated, the distance between the two lines is $T_C \times D$, the present value of the tax shield.

FIGURE 16.4

M&M Proposition I
with Taxes

The value of the firm increases as total debt increases because of the interest tax shield.
This is the basis of M&M Proposition I with taxes.

**unlevered cost of
capital**

The cost of capital for a firm
that has no debt.

Suppose that the cost of capital for Firm U is 10 percent. We will call this the **unlevered
cost of capital**, and we will use the symbol R_U to represent it. We can think of R_U as the
cost of capital a firm would have if it had no debt. Firm U's cash flow is $700 every year
forever, and, because U has no debt, the appropriate discount rate is $R_U = 10\%$. The value
of the unlevered firm, V_U, is simply:

$$V_U = \frac{\text{EBIT} \times (1 - T_C)}{R_U}$$
$$= \frac{\$700}{.10}$$
$$= \$7,000$$

The value of the levered firm, V_L, is:

$$V_L = V_U + T_C \times D$$
$$= \$7,000 + .30 \times 1,000$$
$$= \$7,300$$

As Figure 16.4 indicates, the value of the firm goes up by $.30 for every $1 in debt. In
other words, the NPV *per dollar* of debt is $.30. It is difficult to imagine why any corpora-
tion would not borrow to the absolute maximum under these circumstances.

The result of our analysis in this section is the realization that, once we include taxes,
capital structure definitely matters. However, we immediately reach the illogical conclusion that the optimal capital structure is 100 percent debt.

TAXES, THE WACC, AND PROPOSITION II

We can also conclude that the best capital structure is 100 percent debt by examining the
weighted average cost of capital. From Chapter 14, we know that once we consider the

effect of taxes, the WACC is:

$$\text{WACC} = (E/V) \times R_E + (D/V) \times R_D \times (1 - T_C)$$

To calculate this WACC, we need to know the cost of equity. M&M Proposition II with corporate taxes states that the cost of equity is:

$$R_E = R_U + (R_U - R_D) \times (D/E) \times (1 - T_C) \qquad \text{[16.4]}$$

To illustrate, recall that we saw a moment ago that Firm L is worth $7,300 total. Because the debt is worth $1,000, the equity must be worth $7,300 - 1,000 = $6,300. For Firm L, the cost of equity is thus:

$$R_E = .10 + (.10 - .08) \times (\$1,000/6,300) \times (1 - .30)$$
$$= 10.22\%$$

The weighted average cost of capital is:

$$\text{WACC} = (\$6,300/7,300) \times 10.22\% + (1,000/7,300) \times 8\% \times (1 - .30)$$
$$= 9.6\%$$

Without debt, the WACC is over 10 percent; with debt, it is 9.6 percent. Therefore, the firm is better off with debt.

CONCLUSION

Figure 16.5 summarizes our discussion concerning the relationship between the cost of equity, the aftertax cost of debt, and the weighted average cost of capital. For reference, we have included R_U, the unlevered cost of capital. In Figure 16.5, we have the debt–equity

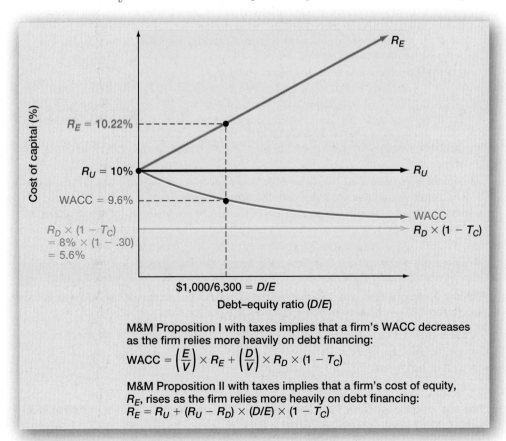

FIGURE 16.5

The Cost of Equity and the WACC: M&M Proposition II with Taxes

M&M Proposition I with taxes implies that a firm's WACC decreases as the firm relies more heavily on debt financing:

$$\text{WACC} = \left(\frac{E}{V}\right) \times R_E + \left(\frac{D}{V}\right) \times R_D \times (1 - T_C)$$

M&M Proposition II with taxes implies that a firm's cost of equity, R_E, rises as the firm relies more heavily on debt financing:

$$R_E = R_U + (R_U - R_D) \times (D/E) \times (1 - T_C)$$

TABLE 16.6

Modigliani and Miller
Summary

I.   The No-Tax Case

  A. Proposition I: The value of the firm levered (V_L) is equal to the value of the firm unlevered (V_U):

$$V_L = V_U$$

   Implications of Proposition I:

   1. A firm's capital structure is irrelevant.

   2. A firm's weighted average cost of capital (WACC) is the same no matter what mixture of debt and equity is used to finance the firm.

  B. Proposition II: The cost of equity, R_E, is:

$$R_E = R_A + (R_A - R_D) \times (D/E)$$

   where R_A is the WACC, R_D is the cost of debt, and D/E is the debt–equity ratio.

   Implications of Proposition II:

   1. The cost of equity rises as the firm increases its use of debt financing.

   2. The risk of the equity depends on two things: the riskiness of the firm's operations *(business risk)* and the degree of financial leverage *(financial risk)*. Business risk determines R_A; financial risk is determined by D/E.

II.   The Tax Case

  A. Proposition I with taxes: The value of the firm levered (V_L) is equal to the value of the firm unlevered (V_U) plus the present value of the interest tax shield:

$$V_L = V_U + T_C \times D$$

   where T_C is the corporate tax rate and D is the amount of debt.

   Implications of Proposition I:

   1. Debt financing is highly advantageous, and, in the extreme, a firm's optimal capital structure is 100 percent debt.

   2. A firm's weighted average cost of capital (WACC) decreases as the firm relies more heavily on debt financing.

  B. Proposition II with taxes: The cost of equity, R_E, is:

$$R_E = R_U + (R_U - R_D) \times (D/E) \times (1 - T_C)$$

   where R_U is the *unlevered cost of capital*—that is, the cost of capital for the firm if it has no debt. Unlike the case with Proposition I, the general implications of Proposition II are the same whether there are taxes or not.

---

ratio on the horizontal axis. Notice how the WACC declines as the debt–equity ratio grows. This illustrates again that the more debt the firm uses, the lower is its WACC. Table 16.6 summarizes the key results of our analysis of the M&M propositions for future reference.

EXAMPLE 16.4   **The Cost of Equity and the Value of the Firm**

This is a comprehensive example that illustrates most of the points we have discussed thus far. You are given the following information for the Format Co.:

$$\text{EBIT} = \$151.52$$
$$T_C = .34$$
$$D = \$500$$
$$R_U = .20$$

The cost of debt capital is 10 percent. What is the value of Format's equity? What is the cost of equity capital for Format? What is the WACC?

This one's easier than it looks. Remember that all the cash flows are perpetuities. The value of the firm if it has no debt, V_U, is:

$$V_U = \frac{\text{EBIT} - \text{Taxes}}{R_U} = \frac{\text{EBIT} \times (1 - T_C)}{R_U}$$

$$= \frac{\$100}{.20}$$

$$= \$500$$

From M&M Proposition I with taxes, we know that the value of the firm with debt is:

$$V_L = V_U + T_C \times D$$

$$= \$500 + .34 \times 500$$

$$= \$670$$

Because the firm is worth $670 total and the debt is worth $500, the equity is worth $170:

$$E = V_L - D$$

$$= \$670 - 500$$

$$= \$170$$

Based on M&M Proposition II with taxes, the cost of equity is:

$$R_E = R_U + (R_U - R_D) \times (D/E) \times (1 - T_C)$$

$$= .20 + (.20 - .10) \times (\$500/170) \times (1 - .34)$$

$$= 39.4\%$$

Finally, the WACC is:

$$\text{WACC} = (\$170/670) \times 39.4\% + (500/670) \times 10\% \times (1 - .34)$$

$$= 14.92\%$$

Notice that this is substantially lower than the cost of capital for the firm with no debt ($R_U = 20\%$), so debt financing is highly advantageous.

Concept Questions

16.4a What is the relationship between the value of an unlevered firm and the value of a levered firm once we consider the effect of corporate taxes?

16.4b If we consider only the effect of taxes, what is the optimal capital structure?

Bankruptcy Costs   16.5

One limiting factor affecting the amount of debt a firm might use comes in the form of *bankruptcy costs*. As the debt–equity ratio rises, so too does the probability that the firm will be unable to pay its bondholders what was promised to them. When this happens, ownership of the firm's assets is ultimately transferred from the stockholders to the bondholders.

In principle, a firm becomes bankrupt when the value of its assets equals the value of its debt. When this occurs, the value of equity is zero, and the stockholders turn over control of the firm to the bondholders. When this takes place, the bondholders hold assets whose value is exactly equal to what is owed on the debt. In a perfect world, there are no costs associated with this transfer of ownership, and the bondholders don't lose anything.

This idealized view of bankruptcy is not, of course, what happens in the real world. Ironically, it is expensive to go bankrupt. As we discuss, the costs associated with bankruptcy may eventually offset the tax-related gains from leverage.

DIRECT BANKRUPTCY COSTS

When the value of a firm's assets equals the value of its debt, then the firm is economically bankrupt in the sense that the equity has no value. However, the formal turning over of the assets to the bondholders is a *legal* process, not an economic one. There are legal and administrative costs to bankruptcy, and it has been remarked that bankruptcies are to lawyers what blood is to sharks.

For example, in September 2008, famed investment bank Lehman Brothers filed for bankruptcy in the largest U.S. bankruptcy to date. As of early 2011, the bankruptcy was still not completed. The direct bankruptcy costs were eye-watering: Lehman was expected to spend almost $2 billion (that's "billion" with a "b") on lawyers, accountants, consultants, and examiners for its U.S. and European operations. The individual costs submitted by one law firm were equally amazing: The firm requested $200,000 for business meals, $439,000 for computerized and other research, $115,000 for local transportation, and $287,000 for copying charges at 10 cents per page. The other costs of bankruptcy may have been even larger. Some experts estimated that because Lehman rushed into bankruptcy it lost out on $75 billion that it could have earned if the sale of many of its assets had been better planned.

Because of the expenses associated with bankruptcy, bondholders won't get all that they are owed. Some fraction of the firm's assets will "disappear" in the legal process of going bankrupt. These are the legal and administrative expenses associated with the bankruptcy proceeding. We call these costs **direct bankruptcy costs**.

These direct bankruptcy costs are a disincentive to debt financing. If a firm goes bankrupt, then, suddenly, a piece of the firm disappears. This amounts to a bankruptcy "tax." So a firm faces a trade-off: Borrowing saves a firm money on its corporate taxes, but the more a firm borrows, the more likely it is that the firm will become bankrupt and have to pay the bankruptcy tax.

INDIRECT BANKRUPTCY COSTS

Because it is expensive to go bankrupt, a firm will spend resources to avoid doing so. When a firm is having significant problems in meeting its debt obligations, we say that it is experiencing financial distress. Some financially distressed firms ultimately file for bankruptcy, but most do not because they are able to recover or otherwise survive.

The costs of avoiding a bankruptcy filing incurred by a financially distressed firm are called **indirect bankruptcy costs**. We use the term **financial distress costs** to refer generically to the direct and indirect costs associated with going bankrupt or avoiding a bankruptcy filing.

The problems that come up in financial distress are particularly severe, and the financial distress costs are thus larger, when the stockholders and the bondholders are different groups. Until the firm is legally bankrupt, the stockholders control it. They, of course, will take actions in their own economic interests. Because the stockholders can be wiped out in a legal bankruptcy, they have a very strong incentive to avoid a bankruptcy filing.

The bondholders, on the other hand, are primarily concerned with protecting the value of the firm's assets and will try to take control away from stockholders. They have a strong incentive to seek bankruptcy to protect their interests and keep stockholders from further dissipating the assets of the firm. The net effect of all this fighting is that a long, drawn-out, and potentially quite expensive legal battle gets started.

direct bankruptcy costs
The costs that are directly associated with bankruptcy, such as legal and administrative expenses.

indirect bankruptcy costs
The costs of avoiding a bankruptcy filing incurred by a financially distressed firm.

financial distress costs
The direct and indirect costs associated with going bankrupt or experiencing financial distress.

Meanwhile, as the wheels of justice turn in their ponderous way, the assets of the firm lose value because management is busy trying to avoid bankruptcy instead of running the business. Normal operations are disrupted, and sales are lost. Valuable employees leave, potentially fruitful programs are dropped to preserve cash, and otherwise profitable investments are not taken.

For example, in 2008, both General Motors and Chrysler were experiencing significant financial difficulty, and many people felt that one or both companies would eventually file for bankruptcy (both later did). As a result of the bad news surrounding them, there was a loss of confidence in the companies' automobiles. A study showed that 75 percent of Americans would not purchase an automobile from a bankrupt company because the company might not honor the warranty, and it might be difficult to obtain replacement parts. This concern resulted in lost potential sales for both companies, which only added to their financial distress.

These are all indirect bankruptcy costs, or costs of financial distress. Whether or not the firm ultimately goes bankrupt, the net effect is a loss of value because the firm chose to use debt in its capital structure. It is this possibility of loss that limits the amount of debt that a firm will choose to use.

Concept Questions

16.5a What are direct bankruptcy costs?

16.5b What are indirect bankruptcy costs?

Optimal Capital Structure

16.6

Our previous two sections have established the basis for determining an optimal capital structure. A firm will borrow because the interest tax shield is valuable. At relatively low debt levels, the probability of bankruptcy and financial distress is low, and the benefit from debt outweighs the cost. At very high debt levels, the possibility of financial distress is a chronic, ongoing problem for the firm, so the benefit from debt financing may be more than offset by the financial distress costs. Based on our discussion, it would appear that an optimal capital structure exists somewhere in between these extremes.

THE STATIC THEORY OF CAPITAL STRUCTURE

The theory of capital structure that we have outlined is called the **static theory of capital structure**. It says that firms borrow up to the point where the tax benefit from an extra dollar in debt is exactly equal to the cost that comes from the increased probability of financial distress. We call this the static theory because it assumes that the firm is fixed in terms of its assets and operations and it considers only possible changes in the debt–equity ratio.

The static theory is illustrated in Figure 16.6, which plots the value of the firm, V_L, against the amount of debt, D. In Figure 16.6, we have drawn lines corresponding to three different stories. The first represents M&M Proposition I with no taxes. This is the horizontal line extending from V_U, and it indicates that the value of the firm is unaffected by its capital structure. The second case, M&M Proposition I with corporate taxes, is represented by the upward-sloping straight line. These two cases are exactly the same as the ones we previously illustrated in Figure 16.4.

The third case in Figure 16.6 illustrates our current discussion: The value of the firm rises to a maximum and then declines beyond that point. This is the picture that we get

static theory of capital structure
The theory that a firm borrows up to the point where the tax benefit from an extra dollar in debt is exactly equal to the cost that comes from the increased probability of financial distress.

FIGURE 16.6   The Static Theory of Capital Structure: The Optimal Capital Structure and the Value of the Firm

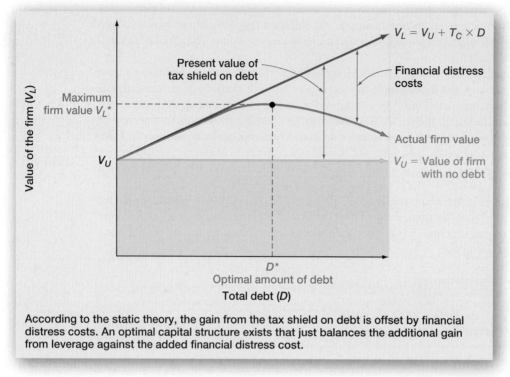

Value of the firm (V_L)

$V_L = V_U + T_C \times D$

Present value of tax shield on debt

Financial distress costs

Maximum firm value V_L^*

Actual firm value

V_U

V_U = Value of firm with no debt

D^*
Optimal amount of debt

Total debt (D)

According to the static theory, the gain from the tax shield on debt is offset by financial distress costs. An optimal capital structure exists that just balances the additional gain from leverage against the added financial distress cost.

from our static theory. The maximum value of the firm, V_L^*, is reached at D^*, so this point represents the optimal amount of borrowing. Put another way, the firm's optimal capital structure is composed of D^*/V_L^* in debt and $(1 - D^*/V_L^*)$ in equity.

The final thing to notice in Figure 16.6 is that the difference between the value of the firm in our static theory and the M&M value of the firm with taxes is the loss in value from the possibility of financial distress. Also, the difference between the static theory value of the firm and the M&M value with no taxes is the gain from leverage, net of distress costs.

OPTIMAL CAPITAL STRUCTURE AND THE COST OF CAPITAL

As we discussed earlier, the capital structure that maximizes the value of the firm is also the one that minimizes the cost of capital. Figure 16.7 illustrates the static theory of capital structure in terms of the weighted average cost of capital and the costs of debt and equity. Notice in Figure 16.7 that we have plotted the various capital costs against the debt–equity ratio, D/E.

Figure 16.7 is much the same as Figure 16.5 except that we have added a new line for the WACC. This line, which corresponds to the static theory, declines at first. This occurs because the aftertax cost of debt is cheaper than equity, so, at least initially, the overall cost of capital declines.

At some point, the cost of debt begins to rise, and the fact that debt is cheaper than equity is more than offset by the financial distress costs. From this point, further increases in debt actually increase the WACC. As illustrated, the minimum WACC* occurs at the point D^*/E^*, just as we described before.

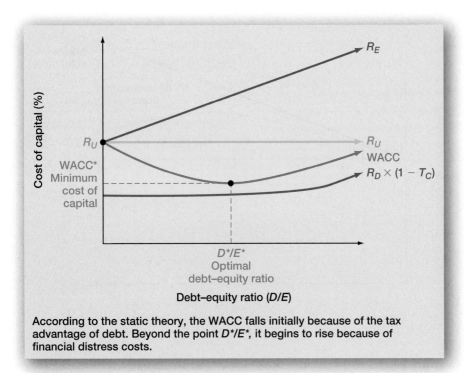

FIGURE 16.7

The Static Theory of
Capital Structure: The
Optimal Capital Structure
and the Cost of Capital

According to the static theory, the WACC falls initially because of the tax advantage of debt. Beyond the point D^*/E^*, it begins to rise because of financial distress costs.

OPTIMAL CAPITAL STRUCTURE: A RECAP

With the help of Figure 16.8, we can recap (no pun intended) our discussion of capital structure and cost of capital. As we have noted, there are essentially three cases. We will use the simplest of the three cases as a starting point and then build up to the static theory of capital structure. Along the way, we will pay particular attention to the connection between capital structure, firm value, and cost of capital.

Figure 16.8 presents the original Modigliani and Miller no-tax, no-bankruptcy argument as Case I. This is the most basic case. In the top part of the figure, we have plotted the value of the firm, V_L, against total debt, D. When there are no taxes, bankruptcy costs, or other real-world imperfections, we know that the total value of the firm is not affected by its debt policy, so V_L is simply constant. The bottom part of Figure 16.8 tells the same story in terms of the cost of capital. Here, the weighted average cost of capital, WACC, is plotted against the debt–equity ratio, D/E. As with total firm value, the overall cost of capital is not affected by debt policy in this basic case, so the WACC is constant.

Next, we consider what happens to the original M&M argument once taxes are introduced. As Case II illustrates, we now see that the firm's value critically depends on its debt policy. The more the firm borrows, the more it is worth. From our earlier discussion, we know this happens because interest payments are tax deductible, and the gain in firm value is just equal to the present value of the interest tax shield.

In the bottom part of Figure 16.8, notice how the WACC declines as the firm uses more and more debt financing. As the firm increases its financial leverage, the cost of equity does increase; but this increase is more than offset by the tax break associated with debt financing. As a result, the firm's overall cost of capital declines.

To finish our story, we include the impact of bankruptcy or financial distress costs to get Case III. As shown in the top part of Figure 16.8, the value of the firm will not be as large as we previously indicated. The reason is that the firm's value is reduced by the present

FIGURE 16.8

The Capital Structure Question

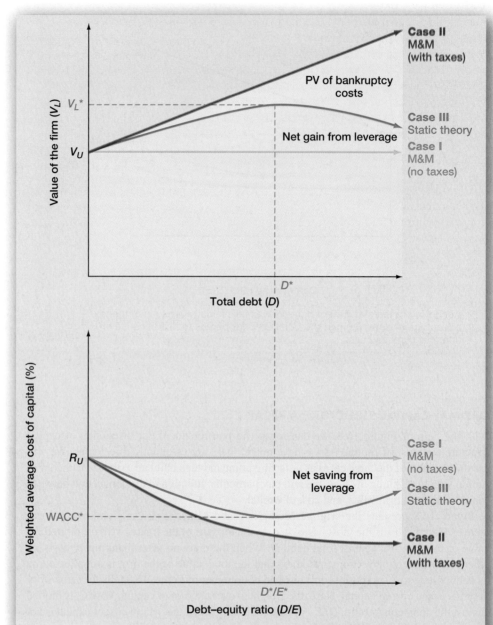

Case I
With no taxes or bankruptcy costs, the value of the firm and its weighted average cost of capital are not affected by capital structures.

Case II
With corporate taxes and no bankruptcy costs, the value of the firm increases and the weighted average cost of capital decreases as the amount of debt goes up.

Case III
With corporate taxes and bankruptcy costs, the value of the firm, V_L, reaches a maximum at D^*, the point representing the optimal amount of borrowing. At the same time, the weighted average cost of capital, WACC, is minimized at D^*/E^*.

value of the potential future bankruptcy costs. These costs grow as the firm borrows more and more, and they eventually overwhelm the tax advantage of debt financing. The optimal capital structure occurs at D^*, the point at which the tax saving from an additional dollar in debt financing is exactly balanced by the increased bankruptcy costs associated with the additional borrowing. This is the essence of the static theory of capital structure.

The bottom part of Figure 16.8 presents the optimal capital structure in terms of the cost of capital. Corresponding to D^*, the optimal debt level, is the optimal debt–equity ratio, D^*/E^*. At this level of debt financing, the lowest possible weighted average cost of capital, $WACC^*$, occurs.

CAPITAL STRUCTURE: SOME MANAGERIAL RECOMMENDATIONS

The static model that we have described is not capable of identifying a precise optimal capital structure, but it does point out two of the more relevant factors: taxes and financial distress. We can draw some limited conclusions concerning these.

Taxes   First of all, the tax benefit from leverage is obviously important only to firms that are in a tax-paying position. Firms with substantial accumulated losses will get little value from the interest tax shield. Furthermore, firms that have substantial tax shields from other sources, such as depreciation, will get less benefit from leverage.

Also, not all firms have the same tax rate. The higher the tax rate, the greater the incentive to borrow.

Financial Distress   Firms with a greater risk of experiencing financial distress will borrow less than firms with a lower risk of financial distress. For example, all other things being equal, the greater the volatility in EBIT, the less a firm should borrow.

In addition, financial distress is more costly for some firms than others. The costs of financial distress depend primarily on the firm's assets. In particular, financial distress costs will be determined by how easily ownership of those assets can be transferred.

For example, a firm with mostly tangible assets that can be sold without great loss in value will have an incentive to borrow more. For firms that rely heavily on intangibles, such as employee talent or growth opportunities, debt will be less attractive because these assets effectively cannot be sold.

Concept Questions

16.6a Can you describe the trade-off that defines the static theory of capital structure?

16.6b What are the important factors in making capital structure decisions?

The Pie Again   16.7

Although it is comforting to know that the firm might have an optimal capital structure when we take account of such real-world matters as taxes and financial distress costs, it is disquieting to see the elegant original M&M intuition (that is, the no-tax version) fall apart in the face of these matters.

Critics of the M&M theory often say that it fails to hold as soon as we add in real-world issues and that the M&M theory is really just that: a theory that doesn't have much to say about the real world that we live in. In fact, they would argue that it is the M&M theory that is irrelevant, not capital structure. As we discuss next, however, taking that view blinds critics to the real value of the M&M theory.

THE EXTENDED PIE MODEL

To illustrate the value of the original M&M intuition, we briefly consider an expanded version of the pie model that we introduced earlier. In the extended pie model, taxes just represent another claim on the cash flows of the firm. Because taxes are reduced as leverage is increased, the value of the government's claim (G) on the firm's cash flows decreases with leverage.

Bankruptcy costs are also a claim on the cash flows. They come into play as the firm comes close to bankruptcy and has to alter its behavior to attempt to stave off the event itself, and they become large when bankruptcy actually takes place. Thus, the value of this claim (B) on the cash flows rises with the debt–equity ratio.

The extended pie theory simply holds that all of these claims can be paid from only one source: the cash flows (CF) of the firm. Algebraically, we must have:

$$\text{CF} = \text{Payments to stockholders} + \text{Payments to creditors}$$
$$+ \text{Payments to the government}$$
$$+ \text{Payments to bankruptcy courts and lawyers}$$
$$+ \text{Payments to any and all other claimants to the cash flows of the firm}$$

The extended pie model is illustrated in Figure 16.9. Notice that we have added a few slices for the additional groups. Notice also the change in the relative sizes of the slices as the firm's use of debt financing is increased.

With the list we have developed, we have not even begun to exhaust the potential claims to the firm's cash flows. To give an unusual example, we might say that everyone reading this book has an economic claim on the cash flows of General Motors. After all, if you are injured in an accident, you might sue GM, and, win or lose, GM will expend some of its cash flow in dealing with the matter. For GM, or any other company, there should thus be a slice of the pie representing potential lawsuits. This is the essence of the M&M intuition

FIGURE 16.9

The Extended Pie Model

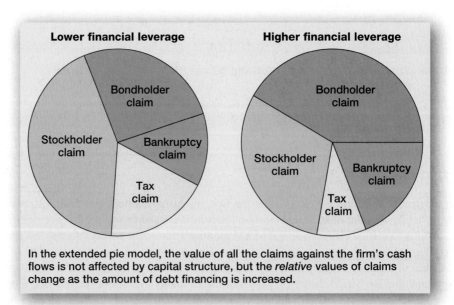

In the extended pie model, the value of all the claims against the firm's cash flows is not affected by capital structure, but the *relative* values of claims change as the amount of debt financing is increased.

and theory: The value of the firm depends on the total cash flow of the firm. The firm's capital structure just cuts that cash flow up into slices without altering the total. What we recognize now is that the stockholders and the bondholders may not be the only ones who can claim a slice.

MARKETED CLAIMS VERSUS NONMARKETED CLAIMS

With our extended pie model, there is an important distinction between claims such as those of stockholders and bondholders, on the one hand, and those of the government and potential litigants in lawsuits on the other. The first set of claims are *marketed claims,* and the second set are *nonmarketed claims.* A key difference is that the marketed claims can be bought and sold in financial markets and the nonmarketed claims cannot.

When we speak of the value of the firm, we are generally referring to just the value of the marketed claims, V_M, and not the value of the nonmarketed claims, V_N. If we write V_T for the total value of *all* the claims against a corporation's cash flows, then:

$$V_T = E + D + G + B + \cdots$$
$$\quad = V_M + V_N$$

The essence of our extended pie model is that this total value, V_T, of all the claims to the firm's cash flows is unaltered by capital structure. However, the value of the marketed claims, V_M, may be affected by changes in the capital structure.

Based on the pie theory, any increase in V_M must imply an identical decrease in V_N. The optimal capital structure is thus the one that maximizes the value of the marketed claims or, equivalently, minimizes the value of nonmarketed claims such as taxes and bankruptcy costs.

Concept Questions

16.7a What are some of the claims to a firm's cash flows?
16.7b What is the difference between a marketed claim and a nonmarketed claim?
16.7c What does the extended pie model say about the value of all the claims to a firm's cash flows?

The Pecking-Order Theory   16.8

The static theory we have developed in this chapter has dominated thinking about capital structure for a long time, but it has some shortcomings. Perhaps the most obvious is that many large, financially sophisticated, and highly profitable firms use little debt. This is the opposite of what we would expect. Under the static theory, these are the firms that should use the *most* debt because there is little risk of bankruptcy and the value of the tax shield is substantial. Why do they use so little debt? The pecking-order theory, which we consider next, may be part of the answer.

INTERNAL FINANCING AND THE PECKING ORDER

The pecking-order theory is an alternative to the static theory. A key element in the pecking-order theory is that firms prefer to use internal financing whenever possible.

A simple reason is that selling securities to raise cash can be expensive, so it makes sense to avoid doing so if possible. If a firm is very profitable, it might never need external financing; so it would end up with little or no debt. For example, in early 2011, Google's balance sheet showed assets of $57.9 billion, of which almost $35 billion was classified as either cash or marketable securities. In fact, Google held so much of its assets in the form of securities that, at one point, it was in danger of being regulated as a mutual fund!

There is a more subtle reason that companies may prefer internal financing. Suppose you are the manager of a firm, and you need to raise external capital to fund a new venture. As an insider, you are privy to a lot of information that isn't known to the public. Based on your knowledge, the firm's future prospects are considerably brighter than outside investors realize. As a result, you think your stock is currently undervalued. Should you issue debt or equity to finance the new venture?

If you think about it, you definitely don't want to issue equity in this case. The reason is that your stock is undervalued, and you don't want to sell it too cheaply. So, you issue debt instead.

Would you ever want to issue equity? Suppose you thought your firm's stock was overvalued. It makes sense to raise money at inflated prices, but a problem crops up. If you try to sell equity, investors will realize that the shares are probably overvalued, and your stock price will take a hit. In other words, if you try to raise money by selling equity, you run the risk of signaling to investors that the price is too high. In fact, in the real world, companies rarely sell new equity, and the market reacts negatively to such sales when they occur.

So, we have a pecking order. Companies will use internal financing first. Then, they will issue debt if necessary. Equity will be sold pretty much as a last resort.

IMPLICATIONS OF THE PECKING ORDER

The pecking-order theory has several significant implications, a couple of which are at odds with our static trade-off theory:

1. *No target capital structure:* Under the pecking-order theory, there is no target or optimal debt–equity ratio. Instead, a firm's capital structure is determined by its need for external financing, which dictates the amount of debt the firm will have.

2. *Profitable firms use less debt:* Because profitable firms have greater internal cash flow, they will need less external financing and will therefore have less debt. As we mentioned earlier, this is a pattern that we seem to observe, at least for some companies.

3. *Companies will want financial slack:* To avoid selling new equity, companies will want to stockpile internally generated cash. Such a cash reserve is known as *financial slack.* It gives management the ability to finance projects as they appear and to move quickly if necessary.

Which theory, static trade-off or pecking order, is correct? Financial researchers have not reached a definitive conclusion on this issue, but we can make a few observations. The trade-off theory speaks more to long-run financial goals or strategies. The issues of tax shields and financial distress costs are plainly important in that context. The pecking-order theory is more concerned with the shorter-run, tactical issue of raising external funds to finance investments. So both theories are useful ways of understanding corporate use of debt. For example, it is probably the case that firms have long-run, target capital structures, but it is also probably true that they will deviate from those long-run targets as needed to avoid issuing new equity.

Concept Questions

16.8a Under the pecking-order theory, what is the order in which firms will obtain financing?

16.8b Why might firms prefer not to issue new equity?

16.8c What are some differences in implications of the static and pecking-order theories?

Observed Capital Structures

16.9

No two firms have identical capital structures. Nonetheless, we see some regular elements when we start looking at actual capital structures. We discuss a few of these next.

The most striking thing we observe about capital structures, particularly in the United States, is that most corporations seem to have relatively low debt–equity ratios. In fact, most corporations use much less debt financing than equity financing. To illustrate, Table 16.7 presents median debt ratios and debt–equity ratios for various U.S. industries classified by SIC code (we discussed such codes in Chapter 3).

In Table 16.7, what is most striking is the wide variation across industries, ranging from essentially no debt for drug and computer companies to relatively heavy debt usage in the airline and cable television industries. Notice that these last two industries are the only ones for which more debt is used than equity, and most of the other industries rely far more heavily on equity than debt. This is true even though many of the companies in these industries pay substantial taxes. Table 16.7 makes it clear that corporations have not, in general, issued debt up to the point that tax shelters have been completely used up, and we conclude that there must be limits to the amount of debt corporations can use. Take a look at our nearby *Work the Web* box for more about actual capital structures.

TABLE 16.7

Capital Structures for U.S. Industries

SOURCE: *Ibbotson Cost of Capital* 2010 Yearbook (Chicago: Morningstar, 2010).

Industry	Ratio of Debt to Total Capital*	Ratio of Debt to Equity	Number of Companies	SIC Code	Representative Companies
Electric utilities	48.54%	94.31%	33	491	American Electric Power, Southern Co.
Computer equipment	9.09	10.02	48	357	Apple, Cisco
Paper	27.75	38.40	24	26	Avery Dennison, Weyerhaeuser
Petroleum refining	32.27	47.65	18	29	Chevron, Sunoco
Airlines	63.92	177.19	10	4512	Delta, Southwest
Pay television	63.56	193.88	5	484	Dish Network, TiVo
Motor vehicles	17.77	21.60	25	371	Ford, Winnebago
Fabric apparel	15.86	18.84	14	23	Guess, Jones Apparel
Department stores	27.40	37.73	8	531	J.C. Penney, Macy's
Eating places	23.40	30.54	42	5812	McDonald's, Papa John's
Drugs	7.80	8.46	194	283	Merck, Pfizer
Steel works	19.96	24.95	9	331	Nucor, U.S. Steel

*Debt is the book value of preferred stock and long-term debt, including amounts due in one year. Equity is the market value of outstanding shares. Total capital is the sum of debt and equity. Median values are shown.

WORK THE WEB

When it comes to capital structure, all companies (and industries) are not created equal. To illustrate, we looked up some capital structure information on United Airlines (UAL) and Johnson & Johnson (JNJ) using the Ratio area of www.reuters.com. United's capital structure looks like this (note that leverage ratios are expressed as percentages on this site):

FINANCIAL STRENGTH

	Company	Industry	Sector	S&P 500
Quick Ratio (MRQ)	0.92	0.78	1.15	0.63
Current Ratio (MRQ)	0.95	0.86	1.45	0.95
LT Debt to Equity (MRQ)	722.06	142.91	49.24	104.85
Total Debt to Equity (MRQ)	876.26	183.58	69.04	150.86
Interest Coverage (TTM)	-0.20	0.04	0.05	16.38

For every dollar of equity, United has long-term debt of $7.2206 and total debt of $8.7626. Compare this result to Johnson & Johnson:

FINANCIAL STRENGTH

	Company	Industry	Sector	S&P 500
Quick Ratio (MRQ)	1.82	1.96	1.83	0.63
Current Ratio (MRQ)	2.05	2.55	2.27	0.95
LT Debt to Equity (MRQ)	16.18	18.29	17.19	104.85
Total Debt to Equity (MRQ)	29.65	22.37	22.30	150.86
Interest Coverage (TTM)	44.64	9.67	2.64	16.38

For every dollar of equity, Johnson & Johnson has only $.1618 of long-term debt and total debt of $.2965. When we examine the industry and sector averages, the differences are again apparent. Although the choice of capital structure is a management decision, it is clearly influenced by industry characteristics.

Questions

1. *The ratios shown for these companies were based on March 2011 figures. Go to www.reuters. com and find the current long-term debt-to-equity and total debt-to-equity ratios for both United Airlines and Johnson & Johnson. How have these ratios changed over this time?*
2. *Go to www.reuters.com and find the long-term debt-to-equity and total debt-to-equity ratios for Bank of America (BAC), Dell (DELL), and Chevron (CVX). Why do you think these three companies use such differing amounts of debt?*

Because different industries have different operating characteristics in terms of, for example, EBIT volatility and asset types, there does appear to be some connection between these characteristics and capital structure. Our story involving tax savings, financial distress costs, and potential pecking orders undoubtedly supplies part of the reason; but, to date, there is no fully satisfactory theory that explains these regularities in capital structures.

Concept Questions

16.9a Do U.S. corporations rely heavily on debt financing?

16.9b What regularities do we observe in capital structures?

A Quick Look at the Bankruptcy Process

16.10

As we have discussed, one consequence of using debt is the possibility of financial distress, which can be defined in several ways:

1. *Business failure:* This term is usually used to refer to a situation in which a business has terminated with a loss to creditors; but even an all-equity firm can fail.

2. *Legal bankruptcy:* Firms or creditors bring petitions to a federal court for bankruptcy. **Bankruptcy** is a legal proceeding for liquidating or reorganizing a business.

3. *Technical insolvency:* Technical insolvency occurs when a firm is unable to meet its financial obligations.

4. *Accounting insolvency:* Firms with negative net worth are insolvent on the books. This happens when the total book liabilities exceed the book value of the total assets.

bankruptcy
A legal proceeding for liquidating or reorganizing a business.

We now very briefly discuss some of the terms and more relevant issues associated with bankruptcy and financial distress.

LIQUIDATION AND REORGANIZATION

Firms that cannot or choose not to make contractually required payments to creditors have two basic options: liquidation or reorganization. **Liquidation** means termination of the firm as a going concern, and it involves selling off the assets of the firm. The proceeds, net of selling costs, are distributed to creditors in order of established priority. **Reorganization** is the option of keeping the firm a going concern; it often involves issuing new securities to replace old securities. Liquidation or reorganization is the result of a bankruptcy proceeding. Which occurs depends on whether the firm is worth more "dead or alive."

liquidation
Termination of the firm as a going concern.

reorganization
Financial restructuring of a failing firm to attempt to continue operations as a going concern.

Bankruptcy Liquidation   Chapter 7 of the Federal Bankruptcy Reform Act of 1978 deals with "straight" liquidation. The following sequence of events is typical:

1. A petition is filed in a federal court. Corporations may file a voluntary petition, or involuntary petitions may be filed against the corporation by several of its creditors.

2. A trustee-in-bankruptcy is elected by the creditors to take over the assets of the debtor corporation. The trustee will attempt to liquidate the assets.

3. When the assets are liquidated, after payment of the bankruptcy administration costs, the proceeds are distributed among the creditors.

4. If any proceeds remain, after expenses and payments to creditors, they are distributed to the shareholders.

The SEC has a good overview of the bankruptcy process in its "Online Publications" section at www.sec.gov.

The distribution of the proceeds of the liquidation occurs according to the following priority list:

1. Administrative expenses associated with the bankruptcy.

2. Other expenses arising after the filing of an involuntary bankruptcy petition but before the appointment of a trustee.

3. Wages, salaries, and commissions.

4. Contributions to employee benefit plans.

5. Consumer claims.

6. Government tax claims.

7. Payment to unsecured creditors.

8. Payment to preferred stockholders.

9. Payment to common stockholders.

absolute priority rule (APR)
The rule establishing priority of claims in liquidation.

This priority list for liquidation is a reflection of the **absolute priority rule (APR)**. The higher a claim is on this list, the more likely it is to be paid. In many of these categories, there are various limitations and qualifications that we omit for the sake of brevity.

Two qualifications to this list are in order. The first concerns secured creditors. Such creditors are entitled to the proceeds from the sale of the security and are outside this ordering. However, if the secured property is liquidated and provides cash insufficient to cover the amount owed, the secured creditors join with unsecured creditors in dividing the remaining liquidated value. In contrast, if the secured property is liquidated for proceeds greater than the secured claim, the net proceeds are used to pay unsecured creditors and others. The second qualification to the APR is that, in reality, what happens, and who gets what, in the event of bankruptcy are subject to much negotiation; as a result, the APR is frequently not followed.

Get the latest on bankruptcy at www.bankruptcydata.com.

Bankruptcy Reorganization   Corporate reorganization takes place under Chapter 11 of the Federal Bankruptcy Reform Act of 1978. The general objective of a proceeding under Chapter 11 is to plan to restructure the corporation with some provision for repayment of creditors. A typical sequence of events follows:

1. A voluntary petition can be filed by the corporation, or an involuntary petition can be filed by creditors.

2. A federal judge either approves or denies the petition. If the petition is approved, a time for filing proofs of claims is set.

3. In most cases, the corporation (the "debtor in possession") continues to run the business.

4. The corporation (and, in certain cases, the creditors) submits a reorganization plan.

5. Creditors and shareholders are divided into classes. A class of creditors accepts the plan if a majority of the class agrees to the plan.

6. After its acceptance by creditors, the plan is confirmed by the court.

7. Payments in cash, property, and securities are made to creditors and shareholders. The plan may provide for the issuance of new securities.

8. For some fixed length of time, the firm operates according to the provisions of the reorganization plan.

The corporation may wish to allow the old stockholders to retain some participation in the firm. Needless to say, this may involve some protest by the holders of unsecured debt.

So-called prepackaged bankruptcies are a relatively common phenomenon. What happens is that the corporation secures the necessary approval of a bankruptcy plan from a majority of its creditors first, and then it files for bankruptcy. As a result, the company enters bankruptcy and reemerges almost immediately.

For example, on November 1, 2009, one of the largest Chapter 11 prepackaged bankruptcies to date began when business lender CIT Group filed. Under the terms of the agreement, stockholders were wiped out entirely and bondholders' claims were reduced by $10.5 billion. At the same time, the maturity on the company's debt was extended by three years. An additional debt reduction occurred when $2.3 billion in "bailout" funds received by the company under the U.S. government's Troubled Assets Relief Program (TARP) were wiped out. Thanks to the prepack, the company moved quickly through the bankruptcy process, emerging from bankruptcy proceedings on December 10, 2009.

In another recent prepack, on November 3, 2010, venerable moviemaker MGM Studios, the company behind such memorable characters as Rocky Balboa and James Bond, filed a prepack bankruptcy. Under the terms of the deal, lenders Credit Suisse and JPMorgan agreed to exchange $4 billion in outstanding debt for the majority of the company's equity when it emerged from bankruptcy. During the bankruptcy process, the company raised another $500 million to fund movies when it came out of bankruptcy. Like Rocky rising from the canvas, the company emerged from bankruptcy on December 10, 2010.

In some cases, the bankruptcy procedure is needed to invoke the "cram-down" power of the bankruptcy court. Under certain circumstances, a class of creditors can be forced to accept a bankruptcy plan even if they vote not to approve it—hence the remarkably apt description "cram down."

In 2005, Congress passed the most significant overhaul of U.S. bankruptcy laws in the last 25 years, the Bankruptcy Abuse Prevention and Consumer Protection Act of 2005 (BAPCPA). Most of the changes were aimed at individual debtors, but corporations were also affected. Before BAPCPA, a bankrupt company had the exclusive right to submit reorganization plans to the bankruptcy court. It has been argued that this exclusivity is one reason some companies have remained in bankruptcy for so long. Under the new law, after 18 months, creditors can submit their own plan for the court's consideration. This change is likely to speed up bankruptcies and also lead to more prepacks.

One controversial change made by BAPCPA has to do with so-called key employee retention plans or KERPs. Strange as it may sound, bankrupt companies routinely give bonus payments to executives, even though the executives may be the same ones who led the company into bankruptcy in the first place. Such bonuses are intended to keep valuable employees from moving to more successful firms, but critics have argued they are often abused. The new law permits KERPs only if the employee in question actually has a job offer from another company.

Recently, Section 363 of the bankruptcy code has been in the news. In a traditional Chapter 11 filing, the bankruptcy plan is described to creditors and shareholders in a prospectus-like disclosure. The plan must then be approved by a vote involving the interested parties. A Section 363 bankruptcy is more like an auction. An initial bidder, known as a *stalking horse,* bids on all or part of the bankrupt company's assets. Other bidders are then invited into the process to determine the highest bid for the company's assets. The main advantage of a Section 363 bankruptcy is speed. Since a traditional bankruptcy requires the approval of interested parties, it is not uncommon for the process to take several years, while a Section 363 bankruptcy is generally much quicker. For example, in the middle of 2009, both General Motors and Chrysler sped through the bankruptcy process in less than 45 days with the help of Section 363 sales.

FINANCIAL MANAGEMENT AND THE BANKRUPTCY PROCESS

It may seem a little odd, but the right to go bankrupt is very valuable. There are several reasons why this is true. First, from an operational standpoint, when a firm files for bankruptcy, there is an immediate "stay" on creditors, usually meaning that payments to creditors will cease, and creditors will have to await the outcome of the bankruptcy process to find out if and how much they will be paid. This stay gives the firm time to evaluate its options, and it prevents what is usually termed a "race to the courthouse steps" by creditors and others.

Beyond this, some bankruptcy filings are actually strategic actions intended to improve a firm's competitive position, and firms have filed for bankruptcy even though they were not insolvent at the time. Probably the most famous example is Continental Airlines. In 1983, following deregulation of the airline industry, Continental found itself competing with newly established airlines that had much lower labor costs. Continental filed for reorganization under Chapter 11 even though it was not insolvent.

Continental argued that, based on pro forma data, it would become insolvent in the future, and a reorganization was therefore necessary. By filing for bankruptcy, Continental was able to terminate its existing labor agreements, lay off large numbers of workers, and slash wages for the remaining employees. In other words, at least in the eyes of critics, Continental essentially used the bankruptcy process as a vehicle for reducing labor costs. Congress subsequently modified bankruptcy laws to make it more difficult, though not impossible, for companies to abrogate a labor contract through the bankruptcy process. For example, Delta Air Lines filed for bankruptcy in 2005, in part to renegotiate the contracts with its union employees.

Other famous examples of strategic bankruptcies exist. For example, Manville (then known as Johns-Manville) and Dow Corning filed for bankruptcies because of expected future losses resulting from litigation associated with asbestos and silicone breast implants, respectively. Similarly, in the then-largest-ever bankruptcy, Texaco filed in 1987 after Pennzoil was awarded a $10.3 billion judgment against the company. Texaco later settled for $3.5 billion and emerged from bankruptcy. As of early 2011, the largest bankruptcies in the United States in terms of assets were the 2008 bankruptcy of Lehman Brothers (with $691 billion in assets) and the collapse of Washington Mutual (with $328 billion in assets), also in 2008. However, the 2003 bankruptcy filing of Italian dairy company Parmalat may have topped them both in terms of relative importance. This company, by itself, represented 1.5 percent of the Italian gross national product!

AGREEMENTS TO AVOID BANKRUPTCY

When a firm defaults on an obligation, it can avoid a bankruptcy filing. Because the legal process of bankruptcy can be lengthy and expensive, it is often in everyone's best interest to devise a "workout" that avoids a bankruptcy filing. Much of the time, creditors can work with the management of a company that has defaulted on a loan contract. Voluntary arrangements to restructure or "reschedule" the company's debt can be and often are made. This may involve *extension,* which postpones the date of payment, or *composition,* which involves a reduced payment.

Concept Questions

16.10a What is the APR?
16.10b What is the difference between liquidation and reorganization?

Summary and Conclusions   16.11

The ideal mixture of debt and equity for a firm—its optimal capital structure—is the one that maximizes the value of the firm and minimizes the overall cost of capital. If we ignore taxes, financial distress costs, and any other imperfections, we find that there is no ideal mixture. Under these circumstances, the firm's capital structure is simply irrelevant.

If we consider the effect of corporate taxes, we find that capital structure matters a great deal. This conclusion is based on the fact that interest is tax deductible and thus generates a valuable tax shield. Unfortunately, we also find that the optimal capital structure is 100 percent debt, which is not something we observe in healthy firms.

We next introduced costs associated with bankruptcy, or, more generally, financial distress. These costs reduce the attractiveness of debt financing. We concluded that an optimal capital structure exists when the net tax saving from an additional dollar in interest just equals the increase in expected financial distress costs. This is the essence of the static theory of capital structure.

We also considered the pecking-order theory of capital structure as an alternative to the static trade-off theory. This theory suggests that firms will use internal financing as much as possible, followed by debt financing if needed. Equity will not be issued if possible. As a result, a firm's capital structure just reflects its historical needs for external financing, so there is no optimal capital structure.

When we examine actual capital structures, we find two regularities. First, firms in the United States typically do not use great amounts of debt, but they pay substantial taxes. This suggests that there is a limit to the use of debt financing to generate tax shields. Second, firms in similar industries tend to have similar capital structures, suggesting that the nature of their assets and operations is an important determinant of capital structure.

CONNECT TO FINANCE

 |FINANCE

If you are using *Connect*™ *Finance* in your course, get online to take a Practice Test, check out study tools, and find out where you need additional practice.

▼ Chapter 16 Financial Leverage and Capital Structure Policy				Section 16.1 Quiz
16.1 The Capital Structure Question	eBook	Study	Practice	
16.2 The Effect of Financial Leverage	eBook	Study	Practice	
16.3 Capital Structure and the Cost of Equity Capital	eBook	Study	Practice	
16.4 M&M Propositions I and II with Corporate Taxes	eBook	Study	Practice	
16.5 Bankruptcy Costs	eBook	Study	Practice	
16.6 Optimal Capital Structure	eBook	Study	Practice	
16.7 The Pie Again	eBook	Study	Practice	
16.8 The Pecking-Order Theory	eBook	Study	Practice	
16.9 Observed Capital Structures	eBook	Study	Practice	
16.10 A Quick Look at the Bankruptcy Process	eBook	Study	Practice	

Visit us at www.mhhe.com/rwj

Visit us at www.mhhe.com/rwj

Can you answer the following questions?

Section 16.1　Maximizing what will maximize shareholder value? (LO 16-1)

Section 16.3　What is most closely related to a firm's use of debt in its capital structure? (LO 16-1)

Section 16.5　Give an example of a direct cost of bankruptcy. (LO 16-3)

Section 16.7　What claims increase when the debt–equity ratio is increased? (LO 16-1)

Log on to find out!

CHAPTER REVIEW AND SELF-TEST PROBLEMS

16.1 **EBIT and EPS**　Suppose the BDJ Corporation has decided in favor of a capital restructuring that involves increasing its existing $80 million in debt to $125 million. The interest rate on the debt is 9 percent and is not expected to change. The firm currently has 10 million shares outstanding, and the price per share is $45. If the restructuring is expected to increase the ROE, what is the minimum level for EBIT that BDJ's management must be expecting? Ignore taxes in your answer.

16.2 **M&M Proposition II (no taxes)**　The Habitat Corporation has a WACC of 16 percent. Its cost of debt is 13 percent. If Habitat's debt–equity ratio is 2, what is its cost of equity capital? Ignore taxes in your answer.

16.3 **M&M Proposition I (with corporate taxes)**　Gypco expects an EBIT of $10,000 every year forever. Gypco can borrow at 7 percent. Suppose Gypco currently has no debt, and its cost of equity is 17 percent. If the corporate tax rate is 35 percent, what is the value of the firm? What will the value be if Gypco borrows $15,000 and uses the proceeds to repurchase stock?

ANSWERS TO CHAPTER REVIEW AND SELF-TEST PROBLEMS

16.1　To answer, we can calculate the break-even EBIT. At any EBIT above this, the increased financial leverage will increase EPS. Under the old capital structure, the interest bill is $80 million $\times$ .09 = $7,200,000. There are 10 million shares of stock; so, ignoring taxes, EPS is (EBIT − $7.2 million)/10 million.

　　Under the new capital structure, the interest expense will be $125 million $\times$ .09 = $11.25 million. Furthermore, the debt rises by $45 million. This amount is sufficient to repurchase $45 million/$45 = 1 million shares of stock, leaving 9 million outstanding. EPS is thus (EBIT − $11.25 million)/9 million.

　　Now that we know how to calculate EPS under both scenarios, we set the two calculations equal to each other and solve for the break-even EBIT:

$$(\text{EBIT} - \$7.2 \text{ million})/10 \text{ million} = (\text{EBIT} - \$11.25 \text{ million})/9 \text{ million}$$
$$\text{EBIT} - \$7.2 \text{ million} = 1.11 \times (\text{EBIT} - \$11.25 \text{ million})$$
$$\text{EBIT} = \$47,700,000$$

Verify that, in either case, EPS is $4.05 when EBIT is $47.7 million.

16.2　According to M&M Proposition II (no taxes), the cost of equity is:

$$R_E = R_A + (R_A - R_D) \times (D/E)$$
$$= 16\% + (16\% - 13\%) \times 2$$
$$= 22\%$$

16.3　With no debt, Gypco's WACC is 17 percent. This is also the unlevered cost of capital. The aftertax cash flow is $10,000 $\times$ (1 − .35) = $6,500, so the value is just
$V_U = \$6,500/.17 = \$38,235.$

After the debt issue, Gypco will be worth the original $38,235 plus the present value of the tax shield. According to M&M Proposition I with taxes, the present value of the tax shield is $T_C \times D$, or $.35 \times \$15,000 = \$5,250$; so the firm is worth $\$38,235 + 5,250 = \$43,485$.

CONCEPTS REVIEW AND CRITICAL THINKING QUESTIONS

1. **Business Risk versus Financial Risk [LO1]** Explain what is meant by *business risk* and *financial risk*. Suppose Firm A has greater business risk than Firm B. Is it true that Firm A also has a higher cost of equity capital? Explain.

2. **M&M Propositions [LO1]** How would you answer in the following debate?

   Q: Isn't it true that the riskiness of a firm's equity will rise if the firm increases its use of debt financing?

   A: Yes, that's the essence of M&M Proposition II.

   Q: And isn't it true that, as a firm increases its use of borrowing, the likelihood of default increases, thereby increasing the risk of the firm's debt?

   A: Yes.

   Q: In other words, increased borrowing increases the risk of the equity *and* the debt?

   A: That's right.

   Q: Well, given that the firm uses only debt and equity financing, and given that the risks of both are increased by increased borrowing, does it not follow that increasing debt increases the overall risk of the firm and therefore decreases the value of the firm?

   A: ??

3. **Optimal Capital Structure [LO1]** Is there an easily identifiable debt–equity ratio that will maximize the value of a firm? Why or why not?

4. **Observed Capital Structures [LO1]** Refer to the observed capital structures given in Table 16.7 of the text. What do you notice about the types of industries with respect to their average debt–equity ratios? Are certain types of industries more likely to be highly leveraged than others? What are some possible reasons for this observed segmentation? Do the operating results and tax history of the firms play a role? How about their future earnings prospects? Explain.

5. **Financial Leverage [LO1]** Why is the use of debt financing referred to as financial "leverage"?

6. **Homemade Leverage [LO1]** What is homemade leverage?

7. **Bankruptcy and Corporate Ethics [LO3]** As mentioned in the text, some firms have filed for bankruptcy because of actual or likely litigation-related losses. Is this a proper use of the bankruptcy process?

8. **Bankruptcy and Corporate Ethics [LO3]** Firms sometimes use the threat of a bankruptcy filing to force creditors to renegotiate terms. Critics argue that in such cases, the firm is using bankruptcy laws "as a sword rather than a shield." Is this an ethical tactic?

9. **Bankruptcy and Corporate Ethics [LO3]** As mentioned in the text, Continental Airlines filed for bankruptcy, at least in part, as a means of reducing labor costs. Whether this move was ethical, or proper, was hotly debated. Give both sides of the argument.

10. **Capital Structure Goal [LO1]** What is the basic goal of financial management with regard to capital structure?

BASIC
(Questions 1–15)

Visit us at www.mhhe.com/rwj

1. **EBIT and Leverage [LO1]** Pendergast, Inc., has no debt outstanding and a total market value of $180,000. Earnings before interest and taxes, EBIT, are projected to be $23,000 if economic conditions are normal. If there is strong expansion in the economy, then EBIT will be 20 percent higher. If there is a recession, then EBIT will be 30 percent lower. Pendergast is considering a $75,000 debt issue with a 7 percent interest rate. The proceeds will be used to repurchase shares of stock. There are currently 6,000 shares outstanding. Ignore taxes for this problem.

    a. Calculate earnings per share (EPS) under each of the three economic scenarios before any debt is issued. Also calculate the percentage changes in EPS when the economy expands or enters a recession.

    b. Repeat part (a) assuming that the company goes through with recapitalization. What do you observe?

2. **EBIT, Taxes, and Leverage [LO2]** Repeat parts (a) and (b) in Problem 1 assuming the company has a tax rate of 35 percent.

3. **ROE and Leverage [LO1, 2]** Suppose the company in Problem 1 has a market-to-book ratio of 1.0.

    a. Calculate return on equity (ROE) under each of the three economic scenarios before any debt is issued. Also calculate the percentage changes in ROE for economic expansion and recession, assuming no taxes.

    b. Repeat part (a) assuming the firm goes through with the proposed recapitalization.

    c. Repeat parts (a) and (b) of this problem assuming the firm has a tax rate of 35 percent.

4. **Break-Even EBIT [LO1]** Rise Against Corporation is comparing two different capital structures: an all-equity plan (Plan I) and a levered plan (Plan II). Under Plan I, the company would have 210,000 shares of stock outstanding. Under Plan II, there would be 150,000 shares of stock outstanding and $2.28 million in debt outstanding. The interest rate on the debt is 8 percent, and there are no taxes.

    a. If EBIT is $500,000, which plan will result in the higher EPS?

    b. If EBIT is $750,000, which plan will result in the higher EPS?

    c. What is the break-even EBIT?

5. **M&M and Stock Value [LO1]** In Problem 4, use M&M Proposition I to find the price per share of equity under each of the two proposed plans. What is the value of the firm?

6. **Break-Even EBIT and Leverage [LO1, 2]** Destin Corp. is comparing two different capital structures. Plan I would result in 10,000 shares of stock and $90,000 in debt. Plan II would result in 7,600 shares of stock and $198,000 in debt. The interest rate on the debt is 10 percent.

    a. Ignoring taxes, compare both of these plans to an all-equity plan assuming that EBIT will be $48,000. The all-equity plan would result in 12,000 shares of stock outstanding. Which of the three plans has the highest EPS? The lowest?

    b. In part (a), what are the break-even levels of EBIT for each plan as compared to that for an all-equity plan? Is one higher than the other? Why?

    c. Ignoring taxes, when will EPS be identical for Plans I and II?

    d. Repeat parts (a), (b), and (c) assuming that the corporate tax rate is 40 percent. Are the break-even levels of EBIT different from before? Why or why not?

7. **Leverage and Stock Value [LO1]** Ignoring taxes in Problem 6, what is the price per share of equity under Plan I? Plan II? What principle is illustrated by your answers?

8. **Homemade Leverage [LO1]** Mudpack, Inc., a prominent consumer products firm, is debating whether to convert its all-equity capital structure to one that is 30 percent debt. Currently, there are 7,000 shares outstanding, and the price per share is $55. EBIT is expected to remain at $27,000 per year forever. The interest rate on new debt is 8 percent, and there are no taxes.

   a. Allison, a shareholder of the firm, owns 100 shares of stock. What is her cash flow under the current capital structure, assuming the firm has a dividend payout rate of 100 percent?

   b. What will Allison's cash flow be under the proposed capital structure of the firm? Assume she keeps all 100 of her shares.

   c. Suppose the company does convert, but Allison prefers the current all-equity capital structure. Show how she could unlever her shares of stock to re-create the original capital structure.

   d. Using your answer to part (c), explain why the company's choice of capital structure is irrelevant.

9. **Homemade Leverage and WACC [LO1]** ABC Co. and XYZ Co. are identical firms in all respects except for their capital structure. ABC is all equity financed with $650,000 in stock. XYZ uses both stock and perpetual debt; its stock is worth $325,000 and the interest rate on its debt is 8 percent. Both firms expect EBIT to be $68,000. Ignore taxes.

   a. Rico owns $48,750 worth of XYZ's stock. What rate of return is he expecting?

   b. Show how Rico could generate exactly the same cash flows and rate of return by investing in ABC and using homemade leverage.

   c. What is the cost of equity for ABC? What is it for XYZ?

   d. What is the WACC for ABC? For XYZ? What principle have you illustrated?

10. **M&M [LO1]** STP Corp. uses no debt. The weighted average cost of capital is 8 percent. If the current market value of the equity is $18 million and there are no taxes, what is EBIT?

11. **M&M and Taxes [LO2]** In the previous question, suppose the corporate tax rate is 35 percent. What is EBIT in this case? What is the WACC? Explain.

12. **Calculating WACC [LO1]** Skillet Industries has a debt–equity ratio of 1.5. Its WACC is 9 percent, and its cost of debt is 5.5 percent. The corporate tax rate is 35 percent.

   a. What is the company's cost of equity capital?

   b. What is the company's unlevered cost of equity capital?

   c. What would the cost of equity be if the debt–equity ratio were 2? What if it were 1.0? What if it were zero?

13. **Calculating WACC [LO1]** Chandeliers Corp. has no debt but can borrow at 6.1 percent. The firm's WACC is currently 9.5 percent, and the tax rate is 35 percent.

   a. What is the company's cost of equity?

   b. If the firm converts to 25 percent debt, what will its cost of equity be?

   c If the firm converts to 50 percent debt, what will its cost of equity be?

   d What is the company's WACC in part (b)? In part (c)?

14. **M&M and Taxes [LO2]** O'Connell & Co. expects its EBIT to be $74,000 every year forever. The firm can borrow at 7 percent. O'Connell currently has no debt, and its cost of equity is 12 percent. If the tax rate is 35 percent, what is the value

of the firm? What will the value be if the company borrows $125,000 and uses the proceeds to repurchase shares?

15. **M&M and Taxes [LO2]** In Problem 14, what is the cost of equity after recapitalization? What is the WACC? What are the implications for the firm's capital structure decision?

INTERMEDIATE
(Questions 16–18)

16. **M&M [LO2]** Tool Manufacturing has an expected EBIT of $73,000 in perpetuity and a tax rate of 35 percent. The firm has $145,000 in outstanding debt at an interest rate of 7.25 percent, and its unlevered cost of capital is 11 percent. What is the value of the firm according to M&M Proposition I with taxes? Should the company change its debt–equity ratio if the goal is to maximize the value of the firm? Explain.

17. **Firm Value [LO2]** Cavo Corporation expects an EBIT of $19,750 every year forever. The company currently has no debt, and its cost of equity is 15 percent.

    a. What is the current value of the company?

    b. Suppose the company can borrow at 10 percent. If the corporate tax rate is 35 percent, what will the value of the firm be if the company takes on debt equal to 50 percent of its unlevered value? What if it takes on debt equal to 100 percent of its unlevered value?

    c. What will the value of the firm be if the company takes on debt equal to 50 percent of its levered value? What if the company takes on debt equal to 100 percent of its levered value?

18. **Homemade Leverage [LO1]** The Veblen Company and the Knight Company are identical in every respect except that Veblen is not levered. Financial information for the two firms appears in the following table. All earnings streams are perpetuities, and neither firm pays taxes. Both firms distribute all earnings available to common stockholders immediately.

	Veblen	Knight
Projected operating income	$ 500,000	$ 500,000
Year-end interest on debt	—	$ 78,000
Market value of stock	$3,100,000	$2,050,000
Market value of debt	—	$1,300,000

    a. An investor who can borrow at 6 percent per year wishes to purchase 5 percent of Knight's equity. Can he increase his dollar return by purchasing 5 percent of Veblen's equity if he borrows so that the initial net costs of the strategies are the same?

    b. Given the two investment strategies in (a), which will investors choose? When will this process cease?

CHALLENGE
(Questions 19–22)

19. **Weighted Average Cost of Capital [LO1]** In a world of corporate taxes only, show that the WACC can be written as $WACC = R_U \times [1 - T_C(D/V)]$.

20. **Cost of Equity and Leverage [LO1]** Assuming a world of corporate taxes only, show that the cost of equity, R_E, is as given in the chapter by M&M Proposition II with corporate taxes.

21. **Business and Financial Risk [LO1]** Assume a firm's debt is risk-free, so that the cost of debt equals the risk-free rate, R_f. Define β_A as the firm's *asset* beta—that is, the systematic risk of the firm's assets. Define β_E to be the beta of the firm's equity. Use the capital asset pricing model (CAPM) along with M&M Proposition II to show that $\beta_E = \beta_A \times (1 + D/E)$, where D/E is the debt–equity ratio. Assume the tax rate is zero.

22. **Stockholder Risk [LO1]** Suppose a firm's business operations are such that they mirror movements in the economy as a whole very closely; that is, the firm's asset beta is 1.0. Use the result of Problem 21 to find the equity beta for this firm for debt–equity ratios of 0, 1, 5, and 20. What does this tell you about the relationship between capital structure and shareholder risk? How is the shareholders' required return on equity affected? Explain.

MINICASE

Stephenson Real Estate Recapitalization

Stephenson Real Estate Company was founded 25 years ago by the current CEO, Robert Stephenson. The company purchases real estate, including land and buildings, and rents the property to tenants. The company has shown a profit every year for the past 18 years, and the shareholders are satisfied with the company's management. Prior to founding Stephenson Real Estate, Robert was the founder and CEO of a failed alpaca farming operation. The resulting bankruptcy made him extremely averse to debt financing. As a result, the company is entirely equity financed, with 12 million shares of common stock outstanding. The stock currently trades at $31.40 per share.

Stephenson is evaluating a plan to purchase a huge tract of land in the southeastern United States for $80 million. The land will subsequently be leased to tenant farmers. This purchase is expected to increase Stephenson's annual pretax earnings by $16 million in perpetuity. Jennifer Weyand, the company's new CFO, has been put in charge of the project. Jennifer has determined that the company's current cost of capital is 10.2 percent. She feels that the company would be more valuable if it included debt in its capital structure, so she is evaluating whether the company should issue debt to entirely finance the project. Based on some conversations with investment banks, she thinks that the company can issue bonds at par value with a 6 percent coupon rate. From her analysis, she also believes that a capital structure in the range of 70 percent equity/30 percent debt would be optimal. If the company goes beyond 30 percent debt, its bonds would carry a lower rating and a much higher coupon because the possibility of financial distress and the associated costs would rise sharply. Stephenson has a 40 percent corporate tax rate (state and federal).

QUESTIONS

1. If Stephenson wishes to maximize its total market value, would you recommend that it issue debt or equity to finance the land purchase? Explain.

2. Construct Stephenson's market value balance sheet before it announces the purchase.

3. Suppose Stephenson decides to issue equity to finance the purchase.
   a. What is the net present value of the project?
   b. Construct Stephenson's market value balance sheet after it announces that the firm will finance the purchase using equity. What would be the new price per share of the firm's stock? How many shares will Stephenson need to issue to finance the purchase?
   c. Construct Stephenson's market value balance sheet after the equity issue but before the purchase has been made. How many shares of common stock does Stephenson have outstanding? What is the price per share of the firm's stock?
   d. Construct Stephenson's market value balance sheet after the purchase has been made.

4. Suppose Stephenson decides to issue debt to finance the purchase.
   a. What will the market value of the Stephenson company be if the purchase is financed with debt?
   b. Construct Stephenson's market value balance sheet after both the debt issue and the land purchase. What is the price per share of the firm's stock?

5. Which method of financing maximizes the per-share stock price of Stephenson's equity?

DIVIDENDS AND PAYOUT POLICY

ON FEBRUARY 16, 2011, cable TV and Internet provider Comcast announced a broad plan to reward stock-holders for the recent success of the firm's business. Under the plan, Comcast would (1) boost its annual dividend by 18 percent from 38 cents per share to 45 cents per share and (2) increase its planned repurchase of Comcast's common stock from $1.2 billion the previous year to $2.1 billion. Investors cheered, bidding up the stock price by about 4 percent on the day of the announcement. Why were investors so pleased? To find out, this chapter explores these actions and their implications for shareholders.

LEARNING OBJECTIVES

After studying this chapter, you should understand:

LO1 Dividend types and how dividends are paid.

LO2 The issues surrounding dividend policy decisions.

LO3 The difference between cash and stock dividends.

LO4 Why share repurchases are an alternative to dividends.

Dividend policy is an important subject in corporate finance, and dividends are a major cash outlay for many corporations. For example, S&P 500 companies paid about $206 billion in dividends in 2010, an increase from the $196 billion paid in 2009, but far below 2008's record dividend payments of $248 billion. AT&T and ExxonMobil were the biggest payers. How much? AT&T paid out about $9.9 billion in dividends during 2010 and ExxonMobil paid out about $8.3 billion. In contrast, about 23 percent of the companies in the S&P 500 paid no dividend at all.

At first glance, it may seem obvious that a firm would always want to give as much as possible back to its shareholders by paying dividends. It might seem equally obvious, how-ever, that a firm could always invest the money for its shareholders instead of paying it out. The heart of the dividend policy question is just this: Should the firm pay out money to its shareholders, or should the firm take that money and invest it for its shareholders?

In this chapter, we will cover a variety of topics related to dividends and corporate payout policies. We first discuss the various types of cash dividends and how they are paid. We ask whether dividend policy matters, and we consider arguments in favor of both high and low dividend payouts. Next, we examine stock repurchases, which have be-come an important alternative to cash dividends. We then bring together several decades of research on dividends and corporate payouts to describe the key trade-offs involved in establishing a payout policy. We conclude the chapter by discussing stock splits and stock dividends.

Cash Dividends and Dividend Payment

The term **dividend** usually refers to cash paid out of earnings. If a payment is made from sources other than current or accumulated retained earnings, the term **distribution**, rather than *dividend*, is used. However, it is acceptable to refer to a distribution from earnings as a dividend and a distribution from capital as a liquidating dividend. More generally, any direct payment by the corporation to the shareholders may be considered a dividend or a part of dividend policy.

Dividends come in several different forms. The basic types of cash dividends are these:

1. Regular cash dividends.
2. Extra dividends.
3. Special dividends.
4. Liquidating dividends.

Later in the chapter, we discuss dividends paid in stock instead of cash. We also consider another alternative to cash dividends: stock repurchase.

dividend
A payment made out of a firm's earnings to its owners, in the form of either cash or stock.

distribution
A payment made by a firm to its owners from sources other than current or accumulated retained earnings.

CASH DIVIDENDS

The most common type of dividend is a cash dividend. Commonly, public companies pay **regular cash dividends** four times a year. As the name suggests, these are cash payments made directly to shareholders, and they are made in the regular course of business. In other words, management sees nothing unusual about the dividend and no reason why it won't be continued.

Sometimes firms will pay a regular cash dividend and an *extra cash dividend*. By calling part of the payment "extra," management is indicating that the "extra" part may or may not be repeated in the future. A *special dividend* is similar, but the name usually indicates that this dividend is viewed as a truly unusual or one-time event and won't be repeated. For example, in December 2004, Microsoft paid a special dividend of $3 per share. The total payout of $32 billion was the largest one-time corporate dividend in history. Founder Bill Gates received about $3 *billion*, which he pledged to donate to charity. To give you another idea of the size of the special dividend, consider that in December, when the dividend was sent to investors, personal income in the United States rose 3.7 percent. Without the dividend, personal income rose only .3 percent, so the dividend payment accounted for about 3 percent of all personal income in the United States for the month! Finally, the payment of a *liquidating dividend* usually means that some or all of the business has been liquidated—that is, sold off.

However it is labeled, a cash dividend payment reduces corporate cash and retained earnings, except in the case of a liquidating dividend (which may reduce paid-in capital).

regular cash dividend
A cash payment made by a firm to its owners in the normal course of business, usually paid four times a year.

For a list of companies that are paying dividends today, go to www.earnings.com.

STANDARD METHOD OF CASH DIVIDEND PAYMENT

The decision to pay a dividend rests in the hands of the board of directors of the corporation. When a dividend has been declared, it becomes a debt of the firm and cannot be rescinded easily. Sometime after it has been declared, a dividend is distributed to all shareholders as of some specific date.

Commonly, the amount of the cash dividend is expressed in terms of dollars per share (*dividends per share*). As we have seen in other chapters, it is also expressed as a percentage

FIGURE 17.1

Example of Procedure for Dividend Payment

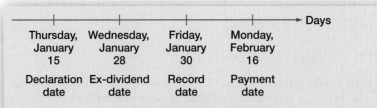

1. *Declaration date*: The board of directors declares a payment of dividends.
2. *Ex-dividend date*: A share of stock goes ex-dividend on the date the seller is entitled to keep the dividend; under NYSE rules, shares are traded ex-dividend on and after the second business day before the record date.
3. *Record date*: The declared dividends are distributable to people who are shareholders of record as of this specific date.
4. *Payment date*: The dividend checks are mailed to shareholders of record.

of the market price (the *dividend yield*) or as a percentage of net income or earnings per share (the *dividend payout*).

DIVIDEND PAYMENT: A CHRONOLOGY

The mechanics of a cash dividend payment can be illustrated by the example in Figure 17.1 and the following description:

declaration date

The date on which the board of directors passes a resolution to pay a dividend.

1. **Declaration date:** On January 15, the board of directors passes a resolution to pay a dividend of $1 per share on February 16 to all holders of record as of January 30.

ex-dividend date

The date two business days before the date of record, establishing those individuals entitled to a dividend.

2. **Ex-dividend date:** To make sure that dividend checks go to the right people, brokerage firms and stock exchanges establish an ex-dividend date. This date is two business days before the date of record (discussed next). If you buy the stock before this date, you are entitled to the dividend. If you buy on this date or after, the previous owner will get the dividend.

   In Figure 17.1, Wednesday, January 28, is the ex-dividend date. Before this date, the stock is said to trade "with dividend" or "cum dividend." Afterward, the stock trades "ex dividend."

   The ex-dividend date convention removes any ambiguity about who is entitled to the dividend. Because the dividend is valuable, the stock price will be affected when the stock goes "ex." We examine this effect in a moment.

date of record

The date by which a holder must be on record to be designated to receive a dividend.

3. **Date of record:** Based on its records, the corporation prepares a list on January 30 of all individuals believed to be stockholders. These are the *holders of record*, and January 30 is the date of record (or record date). The word *believed* is important here. If you buy the stock just before this date, the corporation's records may not reflect that fact because of mailing or other delays. Without some modification, some of the dividend checks will get mailed to the wrong people. This is the reason for the ex-dividend day convention.

date of payment

The date on which the dividend checks are mailed.

4. **Date of payment:** The dividend checks are mailed on February 16.

MORE ABOUT THE EX-DIVIDEND DATE

The ex-dividend date is important and is a common source of confusion. We examine what happens to the stock when it goes ex, meaning that the ex-dividend date arrives. To

FIGURE 17.2

Price Behavior around the
Ex-Dividend Date for a $1
Cash Dividend

Ex date

−t ••• −2 −1 0 +1 +2 ••• t

Price = $10

$1 is the ex-dividend price drop

→ **Price = $9**

The stock price will fall by the amount of the dividend on the ex date
(Time 0). If the dividend is $1 per share, the price will be $10 − 1 = $9
on the ex date:

> Before ex date (Time −1), dividend = $0   Price = $10
> On ex date (Time 0), dividend = $1   Price = $9

illustrate, suppose we have a stock that sells for $10 per share. The board of directors declares a dividend of $1 per share, and the record date is set to be Tuesday, June 12. Based on our previous discussion, we know that the ex date will be two business (not calendar) days earlier, on Friday, June 8.

If you buy the stock on Thursday, June 7, just as the market closes, you'll get the $1 dividend because the stock is trading cum dividend. If you wait and buy it just as the market opens on Friday, you won't get the $1 dividend. What happens to the value of the stock overnight?

If you think about it, you will see that the stock is worth about $1 less on Friday morning, so its price will drop by this amount between close of business on Thursday and the Friday opening. In general, we expect that the value of a share of stock will go down by about the dividend amount when the stock goes ex dividend. The key word here is *about*. Because dividends are taxed, the actual price drop might be closer to some measure of the aftertax value of the dividend. Determining this value is complicated because of the different tax rates and tax rules that apply for different buyers.

The series of events described here is illustrated in Figure 17.2.

| **"Ex" Marks the Day** | **EXAMPLE 17.1** |

The board of directors of Divided Airlines has declared a dividend of $2.50 per share payable on Tuesday, May 30, to shareholders of record as of Tuesday, May 9. Cal Icon buys 100 shares of Divided on Tuesday, May 2, for $150 per share. What is the ex date? Describe the events that will occur with regard to the cash dividend and the stock price.

The ex date is two business days before the date of record, Tuesday, May 9; so the stock will go ex on Friday, May 5. Cal buys the stock on Tuesday, May 2, so Cal purchases the stock cum dividend. In other words, Cal will get $2.50 × 100 = $250 in dividends. The check will be mailed on Tuesday, May 30. Just before the stock does go ex on Friday, its value will drop overnight by about $2.50 per share.

As an example of the price drop on the ex-dividend date, we examine the large dividend paid by investment advisory company Diamond Hill Investment Group in December 2010. The dividend was $13 per share at a time when the stock price was around $85, so the dividend was about 15 percent of the total stock price.

The stock went ex-dividend on November 29, 2010. The stock price chart here shows the change in Diamond Hill stock four days prior to the ex-dividend date and on the ex-dividend date:

The stock closed at $84.86 on November 26 (a Friday) and closed at $72.19 on November 29—a drop of $12.67. With a 15 percent tax rate on dividends, we would have expected a drop of $11.05, so the actual price dropped slightly more than we would have expected (we discuss dividends and taxes in more detail in a subsequent section).

Concept Questions

17.1a What are the different types of cash dividends?

17.1b What are the mechanics of the cash dividend payment?

17.1c How should the price of a stock change when it goes ex dividend?

17.2 Does Dividend Policy Matter?

To decide whether or not dividend policy matters, we first have to define what we mean by dividend *policy*. All other things being the same, of course dividends matter. Dividends are paid in cash, and cash is something that everybody likes. The question we will be discussing here is whether the firm should pay out cash now or invest the cash and pay it out later. Dividend policy, therefore, is the time pattern of dividend payout. In particular, should the firm pay out a large percentage of its earnings now or a small (or even zero) percentage? This is the dividend policy question.

AN ILLUSTRATION OF THE IRRELEVANCE OF DIVIDEND POLICY

A powerful argument can be made that dividend policy does not matter. We illustrate this by considering the simple case of Wharton Corporation. Wharton is an all-equity firm that has existed for 10 years. The current financial managers plan to dissolve the firm in two years. The total cash flows the firm will generate, including the proceeds from liquidation, will be $10,000 in each of the next two years.

Current Policy: Dividends Set Equal to Cash Flow   At the present time, dividends at each date are set equal to the cash flow of $10,000. There are 100 shares outstanding, so the dividend per share is $100. In Chapter 6, we showed that the value of the stock is equal to the present value of the future dividends. Assuming a 10 percent required return, the value of a share of stock today, P_0, is:

$$P_0 = \frac{D_1}{(1+R)^1} + \frac{D_2}{(1+R)^2}$$
$$= \frac{\$100}{1.10} + \frac{100}{1.10^2} = \$173.55$$

The firm as a whole is thus worth $100 \times \$173.55 = \$17,355$.

Several members of the board of Wharton have expressed dissatisfaction with the current dividend policy and have asked you to analyze an alternative policy.

Alternative Policy: Initial Dividend Greater Than Cash Flow   Another possible policy is for the firm to pay a dividend of $110 per share on the first date (Date 1), which is, of course, a total dividend of $11,000. Because the cash flow is only $10,000, an extra $1,000 must somehow be raised. One way to do this is to issue $1,000 worth of bonds or stock at Date 1. Assume that stock is issued. The new stockholders will desire enough cash flow at Date 2 so that they earn the required 10 percent return on their Date 1 investment.[1]

What is the value of the firm with this new dividend policy? The new stockholders invest $1,000. They require a 10 percent return, so they will demand $1,000 \times 1.10 = \$1,100$ of the Date 2 cash flow, leaving only $8,900 to the old stockholders. The dividends to the old stockholders will be as follows:

	Date 1	Date 2
Aggregate dividends to old stockholders	$11,000	$8,900
Dividends per share	110	89

The present value of the dividends per share is therefore:

$$P_0 = \frac{\$110}{1.10} + \frac{89}{1.10^2} = \$173.55$$

This is the same value we had before.

The value of the stock is not affected by this switch in dividend policy even though we have to sell some new stock just to finance the new dividend. In fact, no matter what pattern of dividend payout the firm chooses, the value of the stock will always be the same in this example. In other words, for the Wharton Corporation, dividend policy makes no difference. The reason is simple: Any increase in a dividend at some point in time is exactly offset by a decrease somewhere else; so the net effect, once we account for time value, is zero.

HOMEMADE DIVIDENDS

There is an alternative and perhaps more intuitively appealing explanation of why dividend policy doesn't matter in our example. Suppose individual investor X prefers dividends per share of $100 at both Dates 1 and 2. Would she be disappointed if informed that the firm's management was adopting the alternative dividend policy (dividends of $110 and $89 on the two dates, respectively)? Not necessarily: She could easily reinvest the $10 of unneeded

---

[1] The same results would occur after an issue of bonds, though the arguments would be less easily presented.

funds received on Date 1 by buying more Wharton stock. At 10 percent, this investment would grow to $11 by Date 2. Thus, X would receive her desired net cash flow of $110 − 10 = $100 at Date 1 and $89 + 11 = $100 at Date 2.

Conversely, imagine that investor Z, preferring $110 of cash flow at Date 1 and $89 of cash flow at Date 2, finds that management will pay dividends of $100 at both Dates 1 and 2. This investor can simply sell $10 worth of stock to boost his total cash at Date 1 to $110. Because this investment returns 10 percent, investor Z gives up $11 at Date 2 ($10 × 1.1), leaving him with $100 − 11 = $89.

Our two investors are able to transform the corporation's dividend policy into a different policy by buying or selling on their own. The result is that investors are able to create a **homemade dividend policy**. This means that dissatisfied stockholders can alter the firm's dividend policy to suit themselves. As a result, there is no particular advantage to any one dividend policy the firm might choose.

Many corporations actually assist their stockholders in creating homemade dividend policies by offering *automatic dividend reinvestment plans* (ADRs or DRIPs). McDonald's, Walmart, Sears, and Procter & Gamble, plus over 1,000 more companies, have set up such plans, so they are relatively common. As the name suggests, with such a plan, stockholders have the option of automatically reinvesting some or all of their cash dividend in shares of stock. In some cases, they actually receive a discount on the stock, which makes such a plan very attractive.

homemade dividend policy

The tailored dividend policy created by individual investors who undo corporate dividend policy by reinvesting dividends or selling shares of stock.

For more information on DRIPS, check out the Motley Fool at www.fool.com.

A TEST

Our discussion to this point can be summarized by considering the following true–false test questions:

1. True or false: Dividends are irrelevant.
2. True or false: Dividend policy is irrelevant.

The first statement is surely false, and the reason follows from common sense. Clearly, investors prefer higher dividends to lower dividends at any single date if the dividend level is held constant at every other date. To be more precise regarding the first question, if the dividend per share at a given date is raised while the dividend per share at every other date is held constant, the stock price will rise. The reason is that the present value of the future dividends must go up if this occurs. This action can be accomplished by management decisions that improve productivity, increase tax savings, strengthen product marketing, or otherwise improve cash flow.

The second statement is true, at least in the simple case we have been examining. Dividend policy by itself cannot raise the dividend at one date while keeping it the same at all other dates. Rather, dividend policy merely establishes the trade-off between dividends at one date and dividends at another date. Once we allow for time value, the present value of the dividend stream is unchanged. Thus, in this simple world, dividend policy does not matter because managers choosing either to raise or to lower the current dividend do not affect the current value of their firm. However, we have ignored several real-world factors that might lead us to change our minds; we pursue some of these in subsequent sections.

Concept Questions

17.2a How can an investor create a homemade dividend?

17.2b Are dividends irrelevant?

Real-World Factors Favoring a Low Dividend Payout

The example we used to illustrate the irrelevance of dividend policy ignored taxes and flotation costs. In this section, we will see that these factors might lead us to prefer a low dividend payout.

TAXES

U.S. tax laws are complex, and they affect dividend policy in a number of ways. The key tax feature has to do with the taxation of dividend income and capital gains. For individual shareholders, *effective* tax rates on dividend income are higher than the tax rates on capital gains. Historically, dividends received have been taxed as ordinary income. Capital gains have been taxed at somewhat lower rates, and the tax on a capital gain is deferred until the stock is sold. This second aspect of capital gains taxation makes the effective tax rate much lower because the present value of the tax is less.[2]

Recent tax law changes have led to a renewed interest in the effect of taxes on corporate dividend policies. As we previously noted, historically dividends have been taxed as ordinary income (at ordinary income tax rates). In 2003, under President G.W. Bush, this changed dramatically. Tax rates on dividends and capital gains were lowered from a maximum in the 35–39 percent range to 15 percent, giving corporations a much larger tax incentive to pay dividends. The dividend tax cut has been a contentious issue; however, it has been extended until 2013. Its status after that is uncertain as this is written.

FLOTATION COSTS

In our example illustrating that dividend policy doesn't matter, we saw that the firm could sell some new stock if necessary to pay a dividend. As we mentioned in Chapter 15, selling new stock can be very expensive. If we include flotation costs in our argument, then we will find that the value of the stock decreases if we sell new stock.

More generally, imagine two firms identical in every way except that one pays out a greater percentage of its cash flow in the form of dividends. Because the other firm plows back more, its equity grows faster. If these two firms are to remain identical, then the one with the higher payout will have to periodically sell some stock to catch up. Because this is expensive, a firm might be inclined to have a low payout.

DIVIDEND RESTRICTIONS

In some cases, a corporation may face restrictions on its ability to pay dividends. For example, as we discussed in Chapter 7, a common feature of a bond indenture is a covenant prohibiting dividend payments above some level. Also, a corporation may be prohibited by state law from paying dividends if the dividend amount exceeds the firm's retained earnings.

---

[2] In fact, capital gains taxes can sometimes be avoided altogether. Although we do not recommend this particular tax avoidance strategy, the capital gains tax may be avoided by dying. Your heirs are not considered to have a capital gain, so the tax liability dies when you do. In this instance, you *can* take it with you.

Concept Questions

17.3a What are the tax benefits of low dividends?

17.3b Why do flotation costs favor a low payout?

17.4 Real-World Factors Favoring a High Dividend Payout

In this section, we consider reasons why a firm might pay its shareholders higher dividends even if it means the firm must issue more shares of stock to finance the dividend payments.

In a classic textbook, Benjamin Graham, David Dodd, and Sidney Cottle have argued that firms should generally have high dividend payouts because:

1. "The discounted value of near dividends is higher than the present worth of distant dividends."

2. Between "two companies with the same general earning power and same general position in an industry, the one paying the larger dividend will almost always sell at a higher price."[3]

Two additional factors favoring a high dividend payout have also been mentioned frequently by proponents of this view: the desire for current income and the resolution of uncertainty.

DESIRE FOR CURRENT INCOME

It has been argued that many individuals desire current income. The classic example is the group of retired people and others living on a fixed income (the proverbial widows and orphans). It is argued that this group is willing to pay a premium to get a higher dividend yield. If this is true, then it lends support to the second claim made by Graham, Dodd, and Cottle.

It is easy to see, however, that this argument is not relevant in our simple case. An individual preferring high current cash flow but holding low-dividend securities can easily sell off shares to provide the necessary funds. Similarly, an individual desiring a low current cash flow but holding high-dividend securities can just reinvest the dividend. This is just our homemade dividend argument again. Thus, in a world of no transaction costs, a policy of high current dividends would be of no value to the stockholder.

The current income argument may have relevance in the real world. Here the sale of low-dividend stocks would involve brokerage fees and other transaction costs. These direct cash expenses could be avoided by an investment in high-dividend securities. In addition, the expenditure of the stockholder's own time in selling securities and the natural (though not necessarily rational) fear of consuming out of principal might further lead many investors to buy high-dividend securities.

Even so, to put this argument in perspective, remember that financial intermediaries such as mutual funds can (and do) perform these "repackaging" transactions for individuals at very low cost. Such intermediaries could buy low-dividend stocks and, through a controlled policy of realizing gains, they could pay their investors at a higher rate.

---

[3] B. Graham, D. Dodd, and S. Cottle, *Security Analysis* (New York: McGraw-Hill, 1962).

TAX AND OTHER BENEFITS FROM HIGH DIVIDENDS

Earlier, we saw that dividends were taxed unfavorably for individual investors (at least until very recently). This fact is a powerful argument for a low payout. However, there are a number of other investors who do not receive unfavorable tax treatment from holding high–dividend yield, rather than low–dividend yield, securities.

Corporate Investors   A significant tax break on dividends occurs when a corporation owns stock in another corporation. A corporate stockholder receiving either common or preferred dividends is granted a 70 percent (or more) dividend exclusion. Because the 70 percent exclusion does not apply to capital gains, this group is taxed unfavorably on capital gains.

As a result of the dividend exclusion, high-dividend, low–capital gains stocks may be more appropriate for corporations to hold. As we discuss elsewhere, this is why corporations hold a substantial percentage of the outstanding preferred stock in the economy. This tax advantage of dividends also leads some corporations to hold high-yielding stocks instead of long-term bonds because there is no similar tax exclusion of interest payments to corporate bondholders.

Tax-Exempt Investors   We have pointed out both the tax advantages and the tax disadvantages of a low dividend payout. Of course, this discussion is irrelevant to those in zero tax brackets. This group includes some of the largest investors in the economy, such as pension funds, endowment funds, and trust funds.

CONCLUSION

Overall, individual investors (for whatever reason) may have a desire for current income and may thus be willing to pay the dividend tax. In addition, some very large investors such as corporations and tax-free institutions may have a very strong preference for high dividend payouts.

> **Concept Questions**
>
> **17.4a** Why might some individual investors favor a high dividend payout?
> **17.4b** Why might some nonindividual investors prefer a high dividend payout?

A Resolution of Real-World Factors?   17.5

In the previous sections, we presented some factors that favor a low-dividend policy and others that favor a high-dividend policy. In this section, we discuss two important concepts related to dividends and dividend policy: the information content of dividends and the clientele effect. The first topic illustrates both the importance of dividends in general and the importance of distinguishing between dividends and dividend policy. The second topic suggests that, despite the many real-world considerations we have discussed, the dividend payout ratio may not be as important as we originally imagined.

INFORMATION CONTENT OF DIVIDENDS

To begin, we quickly review some of our earlier discussion. Previously, we examined three different positions on dividends:

1. Based on the homemade dividend argument, dividend policy is irrelevant.

2. Because of tax effects for individual investors and new issue costs, a low-dividend policy is best.
3. Because of the desire for current income and related factors, a high-dividend policy is best.

If you wanted to decide which of these positions is the right one, an obvious way to get started would be to look at what happens to stock prices when companies announce dividend changes. You would find with some consistency that stock prices rise when the current dividend is unexpectedly increased, and they generally fall when the dividend is unexpectedly decreased. What does this imply about any of the three positions just stated?

At first glance, the behavior we describe seems consistent with the third position and inconsistent with the other two. In fact, many writers have argued this. If stock prices rise in response to dividend increases and fall in response to dividend decreases, then isn't the market saying that it approves of higher dividends?

Other authors have pointed out that this observation doesn't really tell us much about dividend policy. Everyone agrees that dividends are important, all other things being equal. Companies cut dividends only with great reluctance. Thus, a dividend cut is often a signal that the firm is in trouble.

More to the point, a dividend cut is usually not a voluntary, planned change in dividend policy. Instead, it usually signals that management does not think that the current dividend policy can be maintained. As a result, expectations of future dividends should generally be revised downward. The present value of expected future dividends falls, and so does the stock price.

In this case, the stock price declines following a dividend cut because future dividends are generally expected to be lower, not because the firm has changed the percentage of its earnings it will pay out in the form of dividends.

For example, on February 22, 2011, bookseller Barnes & Noble announced that it was suspending its $1 per share annual dividend in order to invest in digital products. The stock price was already down about 25 percent from its high over the previous 52 weeks, but shareholders were in for another big shock. On a typical day, about 650,000 shares of the company stock traded hands. Following the announcement, over 2.4 million shares were traded. At one point during the day, the stock was down over 16 percent before settling at a decline of 14.3 percent.

Of course, the phenomenon of a stock price decrease in the face of a dividend cut is not restricted to the United States. In February 2010, German pharmaceutical company Merck KGaA (not to be confused with the U.S. pharmaceutical company Merck, Inc.) announced that it would cut its dividend by a third. In response, the stock dropped by 6.48 euros, or about 10 percent.

In a similar vein, an unexpected increase in the dividend signals good news. Management will raise the dividend only when future earnings, cash flow, and general prospects are expected to rise to such an extent that the dividend will not have to be cut later. A dividend increase is management's signal to the market that the firm is expected to do well. The stock price reacts favorably because expectations of future dividends are revised upward, not because the firm has increased its payout.

In both of these cases, the stock price reacts to the dividend change. The reaction can be attributed to changes in the expected amount of future dividends, not necessarily a change in dividend payout policy. This reaction is called the **information content effect** of the dividend. The fact that dividend changes convey information about the firm to the market makes it difficult to interpret the effect of the dividend policy of the firm.

information content effect
The market's reaction to a change in corporate dividend payout.

THE CLIENTELE EFFECT

In our earlier discussion, we saw that some groups (wealthy individuals, for example) have an incentive to pursue low-payout (or zero-payout) stocks. Other groups (corporations, for example) have an incentive to pursue high-payout stocks. Companies with high payouts will thus attract one group, and low-payout companies will attract another.

These different groups are called *clienteles*, and what we have described is a **clientele effect**. The clientele effect argument states that different groups of investors desire different levels of dividends. When a firm chooses a particular dividend policy, the only effect is to attract a particular clientele. If a firm changes its dividend policy, then it just attracts a different clientele.

What we are left with is a simple supply and demand argument. Suppose 40 percent of all investors prefer high dividends, but only 20 percent of the firms pay high dividends. Here the high-dividend firms will be in short supply; thus, their stock prices will rise. Consequently, low-dividend firms will find it advantageous to switch policies until 40 percent of all firms have high payouts. At this point, the *dividend market* is in equilibrium. Further changes in dividend policy are pointless because all of the clienteles are satisfied. The dividend policy for any individual firm is now irrelevant.

To see if you understand the clientele effect, consider the following statement: In spite of the theoretical argument that dividend policy is irrelevant or that firms should not pay dividends, many investors like high dividends; because of this fact, a firm can boost its share price by having a higher dividend payout ratio. True or false?

The answer is false if clienteles exist. As long as enough high-dividend firms satisfy the dividend-loving investors, a firm won't be able to boost its share price by paying high dividends. An unsatisfied clientele must exist for this to happen, and there is no evidence that this is the case.

> **clientele effect**
> The observable fact that stocks attract particular groups based on dividend yield and the resulting tax effects.

Concept Questions

17.5a How does the market react to unexpected dividend changes? What does this tell us about dividends? About dividend policy?

17.5b What is a dividend clientele? All things considered, would you expect a risky firm with significant but highly uncertain growth prospects to have a low or high dividend payout?

Stock Repurchases: An Alternative to Cash Dividends

17.6

Thus far in our chapter, we have considered cash dividends. However, cash dividends are not the only way corporations distribute cash. Instead, a company can **repurchase** its own stock. Repurchases (or *buybacks*) have become an increasingly popular tool, and the amount spent on repurchases has become huge. For example, during January 2011 alone, about $75 billion in share repurchases were announced, compared to $357 billion in share repurchases in all of 2010. This was in sharp contrast to the $138 billion of repurchases announced in 2009. The record amount of stock buybacks in a year was the $538 billion announced in 2007.

Another way to see how important repurchases have become is to compare them to cash dividends. Consider Figure 17.3, which shows the average ratios of dividends to earnings, repurchases to earnings, and total payout (both dividends and repurchases) to earnings for

> **stock repurchase**
> The purchase, by a corporation, of its own shares of stock; also known as a *buyback*.

FIGURE 17.3

Ratios of Various Payouts
to Earnings

<small>SOURCE: Figure 3 of Brandon
Julio and David Ikenberry,
"Reappearing Dividends,"
*Journal of Applied Corporate
Finance* 16, Fall 2004.</small>

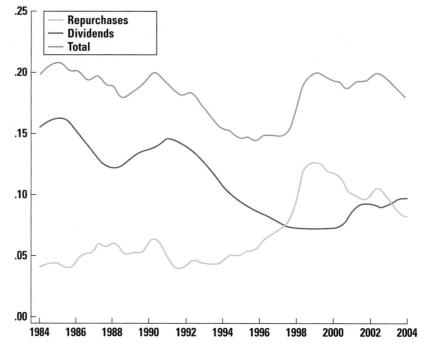

The graph shows the average ratios of repurchases, dividends, and total payout (both repurchases and dividends) to earnings for U.S. industrial companies over the years 1984 to 2004. The graph indicates growth in repurchases over much of the sample period.

U.S. industrial firms over the years from 1984 to 2004. As can be seen, the ratio of repurchases to earnings was far less than the ratio of dividends to earnings in the early years. However, the ratio of repurchases to earnings exceeded the ratio of dividends to earnings by 1998. This trend reversed after 1999, with the ratio of repurchases to earnings falling slightly below the ratio of dividends to earnings by 2004.

Share repurchases are typically accomplished in one of three ways. First, companies may simply purchase their own stock, just as anyone would buy shares of a particular stock. In these *open market purchases*, the firm does not reveal itself as the buyer. Thus, the seller does not know whether the shares were sold back to the firm or to just another investor.

Second, the firm could institute a *tender offer*. Here, the firm announces to all of its stockholders that it is willing to buy a fixed number of shares at a specific price. For example, suppose Arts and Crafts (A&C), Inc., has 1 million shares of stock outstanding, with a stock price of $50 per share. The firm makes a tender offer to buy back 300,000 shares at $60 per share. A&C chooses a price above $50 to induce shareholders to sell, that is, tender, their shares. In fact, if the tender price is set high enough, shareholders may very well want to sell more than the 300,000 shares. In the extreme case where all outstanding shares are tendered, A&C will buy back 3 out of every 10 shares that a shareholder has.

Finally, firms may repurchase shares from specific individual stockholders. This procedure has been called a *targeted repurchase*. For example, suppose the International Biotechnology Corporation purchased approximately 10 percent of the outstanding stock of the Prime Robotics Company (P-R Co.) in April at around $38 per share. At that time, International Biotechnology announced to the Securities and Exchange Commission that it might eventually try to take control of P-R Co. In May, P-R Co. repurchased the International Biotechnology holdings at $48 per share, well above the market price at that time. This offer was not extended to other shareholders.

CASH DIVIDENDS VERSUS REPURCHASE

Imagine an all-equity company with excess cash of $300,000. The firm pays no dividends, and its net income for the year just ended is $49,000. The market value balance sheet at the end of the year is represented here:

Market Value Balance Sheet (before paying out excess cash)			
Excess cash	$ 300,000	Debt	$ 0
Other assets	700,000	Equity	1,000,000
Total	$1,000,000	Total	$1,000,000

There are 100,000 shares outstanding. The total market value of the equity is $1 million, so the stock sells for $10 per share. Earnings per share (EPS) are $49,000/100,000 = $.49, and the price–earnings ratio (PE) is $10/.49 = 20.4.

One option the company is considering is a $300,000/100,000 = $3 per share extra cash dividend. Alternatively, the company is thinking of using the money to repurchase $300,000/10 = 30,000 shares of stock.

If commissions, taxes, and other imperfections are ignored in our example, the stockholders shouldn't care which option is chosen. Does this seem surprising? It shouldn't, really. What is happening here is that the firm is paying out $300,000 in cash. The new balance sheet is represented here:

Market Value Balance Sheet (after paying out excess cash)			
Excess cash	$ 0	Debt	$ 0
Other assets	700,000	Equity	700,000
Total	$700,000	Total	$700,000

If the cash is paid out as a dividend, there are still 100,000 shares outstanding, so each is worth $7.

The fact that the per-share value fell from $10 to $7 is not a cause for concern. Consider a stockholder who owns 100 shares. At $10 per share before the dividend, the total value is $1,000.

After the $3 dividend, this same stockholder has 100 shares worth $7 each, for a total of $700, plus 100 × $3 = $300 in cash, for a combined total of $1,000. This just illustrates what we saw early on: A cash dividend doesn't affect a stockholder's wealth if there are no imperfections. In this case, the stock price simply fell by $3 when the stock went ex dividend.

Also, because total earnings and the number of shares outstanding haven't changed, EPS is still 49 cents. The price–earnings ratio, however, falls to $7/.49 = 14.3. Why we are looking at accounting earnings and PE ratios will be apparent in just a moment.

Alternatively, if the company repurchases 30,000 shares, there are 70,000 left outstanding. The balance sheet looks the same:

Market Value Balance Sheet (after share repurchase)			
Excess cash	$ 0	Debt	$ 0
Other assets	700,000	Equity	700,000
Total	$700,000	Total	$700,000

The company is worth $700,000 again, so each remaining share is worth $700,000/70,000 = $10. Our stockholder with 100 shares is obviously unaffected. For example, if she was so inclined, she could sell 30 shares and end up with $300 in cash and $700 in stock, just as she has if the firm pays the cash dividend. This is another example of a homemade dividend.

In this second case, EPS goes up because total earnings remain the same while the number of shares goes down. The new EPS is $49,000/70,000 = $.70. However, the important thing to notice is that the PE ratio is $10/.70 = 14.3, just as it was following the dividend.

This example illustrates the important point that, if there are no imperfections, a cash dividend and a share repurchase are essentially the same thing. This is just another illustration of dividend policy irrelevance when there are no taxes or other imperfections.

REAL-WORLD CONSIDERATIONS IN A REPURCHASE

The example we have just described shows that a repurchase and a cash dividend are the same thing in a world without taxes and transaction costs. In the real world, there are some accounting differences between a share repurchase and a cash dividend, but the most important difference is in the tax treatment.

Under current tax law, a repurchase has a significant tax advantage over a cash dividend. A dividend is taxed, and a shareholder has no choice about whether or not to receive the dividend. In a repurchase, a shareholder pays taxes only if (1) the shareholder actually chooses to sell and (2) the shareholder has a capital gain on the sale.

For example, suppose a dividend of $1 per share is taxed at ordinary rates. Investors in the 28 percent tax bracket who own 100 shares of the security pay $100 × .28 = $28 in taxes. Selling shareholders would pay far lower taxes if $100 worth of stock were repurchased. This is because taxes are paid only on the profit from a sale. Thus, the gain on a sale would be only $40 if shares sold at $100 were originally purchased at $60. The capital gains tax would be .28 × $40 = $11.20. Note that the recent reductions in dividend and capital gains tax rates do not change the fact that a repurchase has a potentially large tax edge.

To give a few examples of recent repurchase activity, in early 2011, Pfizer announced plans to repurchase $5 billion of its stock, and Intel announced plans for a $10 billion repurchase. Other repurchases announced about the same time, while not quite as large, represented a larger portion of the company's stock. For example, Medco Health Solutions announced it would repurchase about 12 percent of its shares; Unum Group announced it would repurchase about 13 percent of its shares; and GameStop Corporation announced a repurchase of about 17 percent of its shares.

IBM is well known for its aggressive repurchasing policies. In October 2010, it announced a $10 billion share buyback. Since CEO Samuel Palmisano took over in 2003, the company had spent over $68 billion on buybacks through the middle of 2010. In fact, from the beginning of 2003 through 2010, the number of shares in the company fell from 1.72 billion to 1.24 billion. Only ExxonMobil and Microsoft had spent more on buybacks, with Microsoft repurchasing about $103 billion of its own stock from 2000 to 2010.

One thing to note is that not all announced stock repurchase plans are completed. Based on research covering the 2004–2007 period, about 57 percent of all plans were completed.[4]

---

[4]See A.A. Bonaimé, "Mandatory Disclosure and Firm Behavior: Evidence from Share Repurchases," University of Kentucky working paper (2011).

SHARE REPURCHASE AND EPS

You may read in the popular financial press that a share repurchase is beneficial because it causes earnings per share to increase. As we have seen, this will happen. The reason is simply that a share repurchase reduces the number of outstanding shares, but it has no effect on total earnings. As a result, EPS rises.

However, the financial press may place undue emphasis on EPS figures in a repurchase agreement. In our preceding example, we saw that the value of the stock wasn't affected by the EPS change. In fact, the PE ratio was exactly the same when we compared a cash dividend to a repurchase.

Concept Questions

17.6a Why might a stock repurchase make more sense than an extra cash dividend?

17.6b What is the effect of a stock repurchase on a firm's EPS? Its PE?

What We Know and Do Not Know about Dividend and Payout Policies

17.7

DIVIDENDS AND DIVIDEND PAYERS

As we have discussed, there are numerous good reasons favoring a dividend policy of low (or no) payout. Nonetheless, in the United States, aggregate dividends paid are quite large. For example, in 1978, U.S. industrial firms listed on the major exchanges paid $31.3 billion in total dividends. By 2000, that number had risen to $101.6 billion (unadjusted for inflation), an increase of over 200 percent (after adjusting for inflation, the increase is smaller, 22.7 percent, but still substantial).

While we know dividends are large in the aggregate, we also know that the number of companies that pay dividends has declined. Over the same 1978–2000 period, the number of industrial companies paying dividends declined from over 2,000 to just under 1,000, and the percentage of these firms paying dividends declined 65 percent, to just 19 percent.[5]

The fact that aggregate dividends grew while the number of payers fell so sharply seems a bit paradoxical, but the explanation is straightforward: Dividend payments are heavily concentrated in a relatively small set of large firms. In 2000, for example, about 80 percent of aggregate dividends were paid by just 100 firms. The top 25 payers, which include such well-known giants as ExxonMobil and General Electric, collectively paid about 55 percent of all dividends. Thus, the reason that dividends grew while dividend payers shrank is that the decline in dividend payers is almost entirely due to smaller firms, which tend to pay smaller dividends in the first place.

---

[5]These figures and those in the following paragraph are from H. DeAngelo, L. DeAngelo, and D.J. Skinner, "Are Dividends Disappearing? Dividend Concentration and the Consolidation of Earnings," *Journal of Financial Economics* 72 (2004).

FIGURE 17.4

Proportion of Dividend Payers among All U.S. Industrial Firms, 1984–2004

Source: Brandon Julio and David Ikenberry, "Reappearing Dividends," *Journal of Applied Corporate Finance* 16, Fall 2004.

One important reason that the percentage of dividend-paying firms has declined is that the population of firms has changed. There has been a huge increase in the number of newly listed firms over the last 25 or so years. Newly listed firms tend to be younger and less profitable. Such firms need their internally generated cash to fund growth and typically do not pay dividends.

Another factor at work is that firms appear to be more likely to begin making payouts using share repurchases, which are flexible, rather than committing to making cash distributions. Such a policy seems quite sensible given our previous discussions. However, after controlling for the changing mix of firms and the increase in share repurchasing activity, there still appears to be a decreased propensity to pay dividends among certain types of older, better established firms, though further research is needed on this question.

The fact that the number of dividend-paying firms has declined so sharply is an interesting phenomenon. Making matters even more interesting is evidence showing that the trend may have begun to reverse itself. Take a look at Figure 17.4, which shows the percentage of industrial firms paying dividends over the period 1984–2004. As shown, there is a pronounced downward trend, but that trend appears to bottom out in 2000 and then sharply reverse in 2002. So what's going on?

Part of the apparent rebound in Figure 17.4 is probably an illusion. The number of firms listed on the major stock markets dropped sharply, from over 5,000 to under 4,000, during the period 2000–2005. About 2,000 firms delisted over this period, 98 percent of which were not dividend payers. Thus, the percentage of firms paying dividends rose because nonpayers dropped out in large numbers.[6]

However, once we control for the drop-out problem, there is still an increase in the number of dividend payers, but it happens in 2003. As shown in Figure 17.5, the uptick is concentrated in the months following May 2003. What is so special about this month? The answer is that in May 2003, top personal tax rates on dividends were slashed from about 38 to 15 percent. Thus, consistent with our earlier tax arguments, a reduction in personal tax rates led to increases in dividends.

---

[6] These numbers and this explanation are from R. Chetty and E. Saez, "The Effects of the 2003 Dividend Tax Cut on Corporate Behavior: Interpreting the Evidence," *American Economic Review* Papers and Proceedings 96 (2006).

FIGURE 17.5   Regular Dividend Initiations, 2001–2006

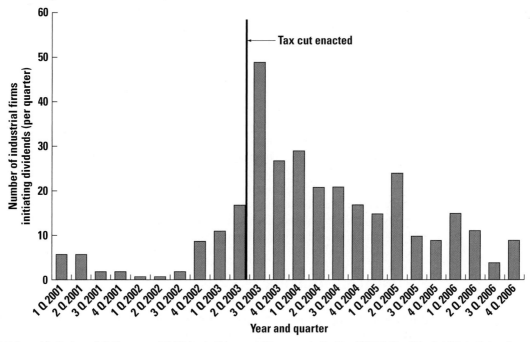

Source: A.P. Brav, J.R. Graham, C.R. Harvey, and R. Michaely, "Managerial Response to the May 2003 Dividend Tax Cut," Duke University working paper (2007).

However, it is important not to read too much into Figure 17.5. It seems clear that the reduction in tax rates did have an effect, but, on balance, what we see is a few hundred firms initiating dividends. There are still thousands of firms that did not initiate dividends, even though the tax rate reduction was very large. Thus, the evidence suggests that tax rates matter, but they are not a primary determinant of dividend policy. This interpretation is consistent with the results of a 2005 survey of financial executives, more than two-thirds of whom said that the tax rate cut probably or definitely would not affect their dividend policies.[7]

A second force that may be at work over time is the maturing of many of the (surviving) newly listed firms we mentioned earlier. As these firms have become better established, their profitability has increased (and, potentially, their investment opportunities have decreased), and they have begun to pay dividends.

A third factor that may be contributing to the increase in the number of dividend payers is a little more subtle. The technology-heavy NASDAQ index plummeted in the spring of 2000 (due to the "dot-com" crash), and it became clear that many newly listed companies were likely to fail. Shortly thereafter, major accounting scandals at companies such as Enron and WorldCom left investors unsure of the trustworthiness of reported earnings. In such an environment, companies may have chosen to initiate dividends in an attempt to signal to investors that they had the cash to make dividend payments now and in the future.

The apparent reversal in the decline of dividend payers is a recent phenomenon, so its significance remains to be seen. It may prove to be just a transient event in the middle of a long decline. We will have to wait and see.

---

[7] See A.P. Brav, J.R. Graham, C.R. Harvey, and R. Michaely, "Managerial Response to the May 2003 Dividend Tax Cut," Duke University working paper (2007).

CORPORATIONS SMOOTH DIVIDENDS

As we previously observed, dividend cuts are frequently viewed as very bad news by market participants. As a result, companies only cut dividends when there is no other acceptable alternative. For the same reason, companies are also reluctant to increase dividends unless they are sure the new dividend level can be sustained.

In practice, what we observe is that dividend-paying companies tend to raise dividends only after earnings have risen, and they don't increase or cut dividends in response to temporary earnings fluctuations. In other words, (1) dividend growth lags earnings growth and (2) dividend growth will tend to be much smoother than earnings growth.

To see how important dividend stability and steady growth are to financial managers, consider that, in 2010, 1,729 companies in the United States increased their dividend payments, while only 145 companies decreased dividend payments. Two companies with long histories of dividend increases are Procter & Gamble and Colgate-Palmolive. At the end of 2010, Procter & Gamble had increased its dividend for 55 consecutive years, and Colgate-Palmolive had increased its dividend for 47 consecutive years. Overall, 42 companies in the S&P 500 had increased dividends for at least 25 consecutive years.

PUTTING IT ALL TOGETHER

Much of what we have discussed in this chapter (and much of what we know about dividends from decades of research) can be pulled together and summarized in the following five observations[8]:

1. Aggregate dividend and stock repurchases are massive, and they have increased steadily in nominal and real terms over the years.
2. Dividends are heavily concentrated among a relatively small number of large, mature firms.
3. Managers are very reluctant to cut dividends, normally doing so only due to firm-specific problems.
4. Managers smooth dividends, raising them slowly and incrementally as earnings grow.
5. Stock prices react to unanticipated changes in dividends.

The challenge now is to fit these five pieces into a reasonably coherent picture. With regard to payouts in general, meaning the combination of stock repurchases and cash dividends, a simple life cycle theory fits points 1 and 2. The key ideas are straightforward. First, relatively young and less profitable firms generally should not make cash distributions. They need the cash to fund investments (and flotation costs discourage the raising of outside cash).

However, as a firm matures, it begins to generate free cash flow (which, you will recall, is internally generated cash flow beyond that needed to fund profitable investment activities). Significant free cash flow can lead to agency problems if it is not distributed. Managers may become tempted to pursue empire building or otherwise spend the excess cash in ways not in the shareholders' best interests. Thus, firms come under pressure to make distributions rather than horde cash. And, consistent with what we observe, we expect large firms with a history of profitability to make large distributions.

Thus, the life cycle theory says that firms trade off the agency costs of excess cash retention against the potential future costs of external equity financing. A firm should begin

---

[8] This list is distilled in part from a longer list in H. DeAngelo and L. DeAngelo, "Payout Policy Pedagogy: What Matters and Why," *European Financial Management* 13 (2007).

making distributions when it generates sufficient internal cash flow to fund its investment needs now and into the foreseeable future.

The more complex issue concerns the type of distribution, cash dividends versus repurchase. The tax argument in favor of repurchases is a clear and strong one. Further, repurchases are a much more flexible option (and managers greatly value financial flexibility), so the question is: Why would firms ever choose a cash dividend?

If we are to answer this question, we have to ask a different question. What can a cash dividend accomplish that a share repurchase cannot? One answer is that when a firm makes a commitment to pay a cash dividend now and into the future, it sends a two-part signal to the markets. As we have already discussed, one signal is that the firm anticipates being profitable, with the ability to make the payments on an ongoing basis. Note that a firm cannot benefit by trying to fool the market in this regard because the firm would ultimately be punished when it couldn't make the dividend payment (or couldn't make it without relying on external financing). Thus, a cash dividend may let a firm distinguish itself from less profitable rivals.

A second, and more subtle, signal takes us back to the agency problem of free cash flow. By committing to pay cash dividends now and in the future, the firm signals that it won't be hoarding cash (or at least not as much cash), thereby reducing agency costs and enhancing shareholder wealth.

This two-part signaling story is consistent with points 3–5 above, but an obvious objection remains. Why don't firms just commit to a policy of setting aside whatever money would be used to pay dividends and use it instead to buy back shares? After all, either way, a firm is committing to pay out cash to shareholders.

A fixed repurchase strategy suffers from two drawbacks. The first is verifiability. A firm could announce an open market repurchase and then simply not do it. By suitably fudging its books, it would be some time before the deception was discovered. Thus, it would be necessary for shareholders to develop a monitoring mechanism, meaning some sort of way for stockholders to know for sure that the repurchase was in fact done. Such a mechanism wouldn't be difficult to build (it could be a simple trustee relationship such as we observe in the bond markets), but it currently does not exist. Of course, a tender offer repurchase needs little or no verification, but such offers have expenses associated with them. The beauty of a cash dividend is that it needs no monitoring. A firm is forced to cut and mail checks four times a year, year in and year out.

A second objection to a fixed repurchase strategy is more controversial. Suppose managers, as insiders, are better able than stockholders to judge whether their stock price is too high or too low. (Note that this idea does not conflict with semistrong market efficiency if inside information is the reason.) In this case, a fixed repurchase commitment forces management to buy back stock even in circumstances when the stock is overvalued. In other words, it forces management into making negative NPV investments.

More research on the cash dividend versus share repurchase question is needed, but the historical trend seems to be favoring continued growth in repurchases relative to dividends.

Total corporate payouts seem to be relatively stable over time at roughly 20 percent of aggregate earnings (see Figure 17.3), but repurchases are becoming a larger portion of that total. The split reached about 50–50 in the latter part of the 1990s, but it looks like aggregate repurchases have recently passed aggregate dividends.

One aspect of aggregate cash dividends that has not received much attention is that there may be a strong legacy effect. Before 1982, the regulatory status of stock repurchases was somewhat murky, creating a significant disincentive. In 1982, the SEC, after years of debate, created a clear set of guidelines for firms to follow, thereby making repurchases much more attractive.

The legacy effect arises because many of the giant firms that pay such a large portion of aggregate dividends were paying dividends before (and perhaps long before) 1982. To the extent that these firms are unwilling to cut their dividends, aggregate cash dividends will be large, but only because of a "lock-in" effect for older firms. If locked-in, legacy payers account for much of the aggregate dividend, what we should observe is (1) a sharply reduced tendency for maturing firms to initiate dividends and (2) a growth in repurchases relative to cash dividends over time. We actually do see evidence of both of these trends; however, legacy effects alone can't account for all cash dividend payers.

The Pros and Cons of Paying Dividends	
Pros	**Cons**
1. Cash dividends can underscore good results and provide support to the stock price.	1. Dividends are taxed to recipients.
2. Dividends may attract institutional investors who prefer some return in the form of dividends. A mix of institutional and individual investors may allow a firm to raise capital at lower cost because of the ability of the firm to reach a wider market.	2. Dividends can reduce internal sources of financing. Dividends may force the firm to forgo positive NPV projects or to rely on costly external equity financing.
3. Stock price usually increases with the announcement of a new or increased dividend.	3. Once established, dividend cuts are hard to make without adversely affecting a firm's stock price.
4. Dividends absorb excess cash flow and may reduce agency costs that arise from conflicts between management and shareholders.	

SOME SURVEY EVIDENCE ON DIVIDENDS

A recent study surveyed a large number of financial executives regarding dividend policy. One of the questions asked was, "Do these statements describe factors that affect your company's dividend decisions?" Table 17.1 shows some of the results.

As shown in Table 17.1, financial managers are very disinclined to cut dividends. Moreover, they are very conscious of their previous dividends and desire to maintain a relatively steady dividend. In contrast, the cost of external capital and the desire to attract "prudent man" investors (those with fiduciary duties) are less important.

TABLE 17.1

Survey Responses on Dividend Decisions*

Source: Adapted from Table 4 of A. Brav, J.R. Graham, C.R. Harvey, and R. Michaely, "Payout Policy in the 21st Century," *Journal of Financial Economics*, 2005.

Policy Statements	Percent Who Agree or Strongly Agree
1. We try to avoid reducing dividends per share.	93.8%
2. We try to maintain a smooth dividend from year to year.	89.6
3. We consider the level of dividends per share that we have paid in recent quarters.	88.2
4. We are reluctant to make dividend changes that might have to be reversed in the future.	77.9
5. We consider the change or growth in dividends per share.	66.7
6. We consider the cost of raising external capital to be smaller than the cost of cutting dividends.	42.8
7. We pay dividends to attract investors subject to "prudent man" investment restrictions.	41.7

*Survey respondents were asked the question, "Do these statements describe factors that affect your company's dividend decisions?"

IN THEIR OWN WORDS ...

Fischer Black on Why Firms Pay Dividends

I think investors simply like dividends. They believe that dividends enhance stock value (given the firm's prospects), and they feel uncomfortable spending out of their capital.

We see evidence for this everywhere: Investment advisers and institutions treat a high-yield stock as both attractive and safe, financial analysts value a stock by predicting and discounting its dividends, financial economists study the relation between stock prices and actual dividends, and investors complain about dividend cuts.

What if investors were neutral toward dividends? Investment advisers would tell clients to spend indifferently from income and capital and, if taxable, to avoid income; financial analysts would ignore dividends in valuing stocks; financial economists would treat stock price and the discounted value of dividends as equal, even when stocks are mispriced; and a firm would apologize to its taxable investors when forced by an accumulated earnings tax to pay dividends. This is not what we observe.

Furthermore, changing dividends seems a poor way to tell the financial markets about a firm's prospects. Public statements can better detail the firm's prospects and have more impact on both the speaker's and the firm's reputations.

I predict that under current tax rules, dividends will gradually disappear.

The late Fischer Black was a partner at Goldman, Sachs & Co., an investment banking firm. Before that, he was a professor of finance at MIT. He is one of the fathers of option pricing theory, and he is widely regarded as one of the preeminent financial scholars. He is well known for his creative ideas, many of which were dismissed at first only to become part of accepted lore when others finally came to understand them. He is sadly missed by his colleagues.

TABLE 17.2

Survey Responses on Dividend Decisions*

SOURCE: Adapted from Table 5 of A. Brav, J.R. Graham, C.R. Harvey, and R. Michaely, "Payout Policy in the 21st Century," *Journal of Financial Economics,* 2005.

Policy Statements	Percent Who Think This Is Important or Very Important
1. Maintaining consistency with our historic dividend policy.	84.1%
2. Stability of future earnings.	71.9
3. A sustainable change in earnings.	67.1
4. Attracting institutional investors to purchase our stock.	52.5
5. The availability of good investment opportunities for our firm to pursue.	47.6
6. Attracting retail investors to purchase our stock.	44.5
7. Personal taxes our stockholders pay when receiving dividends.	21.1
8. Flotation costs to issuing new equity.	9.3

*Survey respondents were asked the question, "How important are the following factors to your company's dividend decision?"

Table 17.2 is drawn from the same survey, but here the responses are to the question, "How important are the following factors to your company's dividend decision?" Not surprisingly given the responses in Table 17.1 and our earlier discussion, the highest priority is maintaining a consistent dividend policy. The next several items are also consistent with our previous analysis. Financial managers are very concerned about earnings stability and future earnings levels in making dividend decisions, and they consider the availability of good investment opportunities. Survey respondents also believed that attracting both institutional and individual (retail) investors was relatively important.

In contrast to our discussion of taxes and flotation costs in the earlier part of this chapter, the financial managers in this survey did not think that personal taxes paid on dividends by shareholders were very important. And even fewer thought that equity flotation costs were relevant.

17.8 Stock Dividends and Stock Splits

stock dividend

A payment made by a firm to its owners in the form of stock, diluting the value of each share outstanding.

Another type of dividend is paid out in shares of stock. This type of dividend is called a **stock dividend**. A stock dividend is not a true dividend because it is not paid in cash. The effect of a stock dividend is to increase the number of shares that each owner holds. Because there are more shares outstanding, each is simply worth less.

A stock dividend is commonly expressed as a percentage; for example, a 20 percent stock dividend means that a shareholder receives one new share for every five currently owned (a 20 percent increase). Because every shareholder receives 20 percent more stock, the total number of shares outstanding rises by 20 percent. As we will see in a moment, the result is that each share of stock is worth about 20 percent less.

stock split

An increase in a firm's shares outstanding without any change in owners' equity.

A **stock split** is essentially the same thing as a stock dividend, except that a split is expressed as a ratio instead of a percentage. When a split is declared, each share is split up to create additional shares. For example, in a three-for-one stock split, each old share is split into three new shares.

SOME DETAILS ABOUT STOCK SPLITS AND STOCK DIVIDENDS

Stock splits and stock dividends have essentially the same impacts on the corporation and the shareholder: They increase the number of shares outstanding and reduce the value per share. The accounting treatment is not the same, however, and it depends on two things: (1) whether the distribution is a stock split or a stock dividend and (2) the size of the stock dividend if it is called a dividend.

By convention, stock dividends of less than 20 to 25 percent are called *small stock dividends*. The accounting procedure for such a dividend is discussed next. A stock dividend greater than this value of 20 to 25 percent is called a *large stock dividend*. Large stock dividends are not uncommon. For example, in October 2010, water heater manufacturer A.O. Smith announced a three-for-two stock split in the form of a 50 percent stock dividend. The same month, automotive supplier Magna International announced a 2-for-1 stock split in the form of a 100 percent stock dividend. Except for some relatively minor accounting differences, a stock dividend has the same effect as a stock split.

Information on upcoming stock splits is available on the splits calendar at www.investmenthouse.com and finance.yahoo.com.

Example of a Small Stock Dividend   The Peterson Co., a consulting firm specializing in difficult accounting problems, has 10,000 shares of stock outstanding, each selling at $66. The total market value of the equity is $66 × 10,000 = $660,000. With a 10 percent stock dividend, each stockholder receives one additional share for each 10 owned, and the total number of shares outstanding after the dividend is 11,000.

Before the stock dividend, the equity portion of Peterson's balance sheet might look like this:

Common stock ($1 par, 10,000 shares outstanding)	$ 10,000
Capital in excess of par value	200,000
Retained earnings	290,000
Total owners' equity	$500,000

A seemingly arbitrary accounting procedure is used to adjust the balance sheet after a small stock dividend. Because 1,000 new shares are issued, the common stock account is increased by $1,000 (1,000 shares at $1 par value each), for a total of $11,000. The market price of $66 is $65 greater than the par value, so the "excess" of $65 $\times$ 1,000 shares = $65,000 is added to the capital surplus account (capital in excess of par value), producing a total of $265,000.

Total owners' equity is unaffected by the stock dividend because no cash has come in or out, so retained earnings are reduced by the entire $66,000, leaving $224,000. The net effect of these machinations is that Peterson's equity accounts now look like this:

Common stock ($1 par, 11,000 shares outstanding)	$ 11,000
Capital in excess of par value	265,000
Retained earnings	224,000
Total owners' equity	$500,000

Example of a Stock Split   A stock split is conceptually similar to a stock dividend, but it is commonly expressed as a ratio. For example, in a three-for-two split, each shareholder receives one additional share of stock for each two held originally, so a three-for-two split amounts to a 50 percent stock dividend. Again, no cash is paid out, and the percentage of the entire firm that each shareholder owns is unaffected.

The accounting treatment of a stock split is a little different from (and simpler than) that of a stock dividend. Suppose Peterson decides to declare a two-for-one stock split. The number of shares outstanding will double to 20,000, and the par value will be halved to $.50 per share. The owners' equity after the split is represented as follows:

Common stock ($.50 par, 20,000 shares outstanding)	$ 10,000
Capital in excess of par value	200,000
Retained earnings	290,000
Total owners' equity	$500,000

For a list of recent stock splits, try www.stocksplits.net.

Note that, for all three of the categories, the figures on the right are completely unaffected by the split. The only changes are in the par value per share and the number of shares outstanding. Because the number of shares has doubled, the par value of each is cut in half.

Example of a Large Stock Dividend   In our example, if a 100 percent stock dividend were declared, 10,000 new shares would be distributed, so 20,000 shares would be outstanding. At a $1 par value per share, the common stock account would rise by $10,000, for a total of $20,000. The retained earnings account would be reduced by $10,000, leaving $280,000. The result would be the following:

Common stock ($1 par, 20,000 shares outstanding)	$ 20,000
Capital in excess of par value	200,000
Retained earnings	280,000
Total owners' equity	$500,000

VALUE OF STOCK SPLITS AND STOCK DIVIDENDS

The laws of logic tell us that stock splits and stock dividends can (1) leave the value of the firm unaffected, (2) increase its value, or (3) decrease its value. Unfortunately, the issues are complex enough that we cannot easily determine which of the three relationships holds.

The Benchmark Case   A strong case can be made that stock dividends and splits do not change either the wealth of any shareholder or the wealth of the firm as a whole. In our preceding example, the equity had a total market value of $660,000. With the small stock dividend, the number of shares increased to 11,000, so it seems that each would be worth $660,000/11,000 = $60.

For example, a shareholder who had 100 shares worth $66 each before the dividend would have 110 shares worth $60 each afterward. The total value of the stock is $6,600 either way; so the stock dividend doesn't really have any economic effect.

After the stock split, there are 20,000 shares outstanding, so each should be worth $660,000/20,000 = $33. In other words, the number of shares doubles and the price halves. From these calculations, it appears that stock dividends and splits are just paper transactions.

Although these results are relatively obvious, reasons are often given to suggest that there may be some benefits to these actions. The typical financial manager is aware of many real-world complexities; for that reason, the stock split or stock dividend decision is not treated lightly in practice.

Popular Trading Range   Proponents of stock dividends and stock splits frequently argue that a security has a proper **trading range**. When the security is priced above this level, many investors do not have the funds to buy the common trading unit of 100 shares, called a *round lot*. Although securities can be purchased in *odd-lot* form (fewer than 100 shares), the commissions are greater. Thus, firms will split the stock to keep the price in this trading range.

For example, Microsoft has split nine times since the company went public in 1986. The stock has split three-for-two on two occasions and two-for-one a total of seven times. So for every share of Microsoft you owned in 1986 when the company first went public, you would own 288 shares as of the most recent stock split. Similarly, since Walmart went public in 1970, it has split its stock two-for-one 11 times, and Dell has split three-for-two once and two-for-one six times since going public in 1988.

Although this argument is a popular one, its validity is questionable for a number of reasons. Mutual funds, pension funds, and other institutions have steadily increased their trading activity since World War II and now handle a sizable percentage of total trading volume (on the order of 80 percent of NYSE trading volume, for example). Because these institutions buy and sell in huge amounts, the individual share price is of little concern.

Furthermore, we sometimes observe share prices that are quite large that do not appear to cause problems. To take a well-known case, Berkshire Hathaway, a widely respected company headed by legendary investor Warren Buffett, sold for as much as $151,650 per share in December 2007. Of course, in March 2011, you could have picked up a share for the bargain price of about $130,000.

Finally, there is evidence that stock splits may actually decrease the liquidity of the company's shares. Following a two-for-one split, the number of shares traded should more than double if liquidity is increased by the split. This doesn't appear to happen, and the reverse is sometimes observed.

REVERSE SPLITS

A less frequently encountered financial maneuver is the **reverse split**. For example, in January 2011, solar power company Evergreen Solar underwent a 1-for-6 reverse stock split, and, in February 2011, PremierWest Bancorp underwent a 1-for-10 reverse split. In a 1-for-10 reverse split, each investor exchanges 10 old shares for one new share. The par value is increased by a factor of 10 in the process. In what will probably be one of the biggest reverse splits ever (in terms of market cap), banking giant Citigroup announced in March 2011 that it would do a 1-for-10 reverse, thereby reducing the number of shares outstanding from 29 billion to 2.9 billion. As with stock splits and stock dividends, a case can be made that a reverse split has no real effect.

trading range
The price range between the highest and lowest prices at which a stock is traded.

reverse split
A stock split in which a firm's number of shares outstanding is reduced.

Given real-world imperfections, three related reasons are cited for reverse splits. First, transaction costs to shareholders may be less after the reverse split. Second, the liquidity and marketability of a company's stock might be improved when its price is raised to the popular trading range. Third, stocks selling at prices below a certain level are not considered respectable, meaning that investors underestimate these firms' earnings, cash flow, growth, and stability. Some financial analysts argue that a reverse split can achieve instant respectability. As was the case with stock splits, none of these reasons is particularly compelling, especially not the third one.

There are two other reasons for reverse splits. First, stock exchanges have minimum price per share requirements. A reverse split may bring the stock price up to such a minimum. For example, NASDAQ delists companies whose stock price drops below $1 per share for 30 days. Following the collapse of the Internet boom in 2001–2002, a large number of Internet-related companies found themselves in danger of being delisted and used reverse splits to boost their stock prices. Second, companies sometimes perform reverse splits and, at the same time, buy out any stockholders who end up with less than a certain number of shares.

For example, in January 2011, Phoenix Footwear Group, Inc., completed a reverse/forward split. In this case, the company first did a 1-for-200 reverse stock split and then repurchased all shares held by stockholders with less than one share of stock, thereby eliminating smaller shareholders (and thus reducing the total number of shareholders). The purpose of the reverse split was to allow the company to "go dark." The reverse split and share repurchase left the company with fewer than 300 shareholders, so it would no longer be required to file periodic reports with the SEC. What made the proposal especially imaginative was that immediately after the reverse split, the company did a 200-for-1 ordinary split to restore the stock to its original cost!

Concept Questions

17.8a What is the effect of a stock split on stockholder wealth?

17.8b How does the accounting treatment of a stock split differ from that used with a small stock dividend?

Visit us at www.mhhe.com/rwj

Summary and Conclusions   17.9

In this chapter, we first discussed the types of dividends and how they are paid. We then defined dividend policy and examined whether or not dividend policy matters. Next, we illustrated how a firm might establish a dividend policy and described an important alternative to cash dividends, a share repurchase.

In covering these subjects, we saw these points:

1. Dividend policy is irrelevant when there are no taxes or other imperfections because shareholders can effectively undo the firm's dividend strategy. Shareholders who receive dividends greater than desired can reinvest the excess. Conversely, shareholders who receive dividends smaller than desired can sell off extra shares of stock.

2. Individual shareholder income taxes and new issue flotation costs are real-world considerations that favor a low dividend payout. With taxes and new issue costs, the firm should pay out dividends only after all positive NPV projects have been fully financed.

3. There are groups in the economy that may favor a high payout. These include many large institutions such as pension plans. Recognizing that some groups prefer a high payout and some prefer a low payout, the clientele effect argument supports the idea that dividend policy responds to the needs of stockholders. For example, if 40 percent of the stockholders prefer low dividends and 60 percent of the stockholders prefer high dividends, approximately 40 percent of companies will have a low dividend payout, and 60 percent will have a high payout. This sharply reduces the impact of any individual firm's dividend policy on its market price.

4. A stock repurchase acts much like a cash dividend, but has a significant tax advantage. Stock repurchases are therefore a very useful part of overall dividend policy.

5. We discussed recent research and thinking on dividend policy. We saw that dividends are heavily concentrated in a relatively small number of larger, older firms and that the use of share repurchases continues to grow. We described a simple life cycle theory of distributions in which firms trade off the agency costs of excess cash retention against the future costs of external equity financing. The implication is that younger firms with significant growth opportunities will not distribute cash, but older, profitable firms with significant free cash flow will do so.

To close our discussion of dividends, we emphasize one last time the difference between dividends and dividend policy. Dividends are important because the value of a share of stock is ultimately determined by the dividends that will be paid. What is less clear is whether the time pattern of dividends (more now versus more later) matters. This is the dividend policy question, and it is not easy to give a definitive answer to it.

Visit us at www.mhhe.com/rwj

CONNECT TO FINANCE

If you are using *Connect™ Finance* in your course, get online to take a Practice Test, check out study tools, and find out where you need additional practice.

▼ Chapter 17 Dividends and Payout Policy			Section 17.1
17.1 Cash Dividends and Dividend Payment	eBook	Study	Practice
17.2 Does Dividend Policy Matter?	eBook	Study	Practice
17.3 Real-World Factors Favoring a Low Dividend Payout	eBook	Study	Practice
17.4 Real-World Factors Favoring a High Dividend Payout	eBook	Study	Practice
17.5 A Resolution of Real-World Factors?	eBook	Study	Practice
17.6 Stock Repurchases: An Alternative to Cash Dividends	eBook	Study	Practice
17.7 What We Know and Do Not Know about Dividend and Payout Policies	eBook	Study	Practice
17.8 Stock Dividends and Stock Splits	eBook	Study	Practice

Can you answer the following questions?

Section 17.1 Dividends are paid to the parties listed as shareholders on what dates? (LO 17-1)

Section 17.3 What factors favor a high dividend payout? (LO 17-2)

Section 17.4 Which parties are most apt to prefer a low dividend payout? (LO 17-2)

Section 17.8 Tomas currently owns 300 shares of Doo Little Corp. How many shares will he own if the firm does a four-for-five reverse stock split? (LO 17-3)

Log on to find out!

CONCEPTS REVIEW AND CRITICAL THINKING QUESTIONS

1. **Dividend Policy Irrelevance [LO2]** How is it possible that dividends are so important, but at the same time, dividend policy is irrelevant?

2. **Stock Repurchases [LO4]** What is the impact of a stock repurchase on a company's debt ratio? Does this suggest another use for excess cash?

3. **Dividend Chronology [LO1]** On Tuesday, December 8, Hometown Power Co.'s board of directors declares a dividend of 75 cents per share payable on Wednesday, January 17, to shareholders of record as of Wednesday, January 3. When is the ex-dividend date? If a shareholder buys stock before that date, who gets the dividends on those shares, the buyer or the seller?

4. **Alternative Dividends [LO1]** Some corporations, like one British company that offers its large shareholders free crematorium use, pay dividends in kind (that is, offer their services to shareholders at below-market cost). Should mutual funds invest in stocks that pay these dividends in kind? (The fundholders do not receive these services.)

5. **Dividends and Stock Price [LO1]** If increases in dividends tend to be followed by (immediate) increases in share prices, how can it be said that dividend policy is irrelevant?

6. **Dividends and Stock Price [LO1]** Last month, Central Virginia Power Company, which had been having trouble with cost overruns on a nuclear power plant that it had been building, announced that it was "temporarily suspending payments due to the cash flow crunch associated with its investment program." The company's stock price dropped from $28.50 to $25 when this announcement was made. How would you interpret this change in the stock price (that is, what would you say caused it)?

7. **Dividend Reinvestment Plans [LO1]** The DRK Corporation has recently developed a dividend reinvestment plan, or DRIP. The plan allows investors to reinvest cash dividends automatically in DRK in exchange for new shares of stock. Over time, investors in DRK will be able to build their holdings by reinvesting dividends to purchase additional shares of the company.

   Over 1,000 companies offer dividend reinvestment plans. Most companies with DRIPs charge no brokerage or service fees. In fact, the shares of DRK will be purchased at a 10 percent discount from the market price.

   A consultant for DRK estimates that about 75 percent of DRK's shareholders will take part in this plan. This is somewhat higher than the average.

   Evaluate DRK's dividend reinvestment plan. Will it increase shareholder wealth? Discuss the advantages and disadvantages involved here.

8. **Dividend Policy [LO1]** For initial public offerings of common stock, 2010 was a relatively slow year, with about $30.7 billion raised by the process. Relatively few of the 94 firms involved paid cash dividends. Why do you think that most chose not to pay cash dividends?

Visit us at www.mhhe.com/rwj

Visit us at www.mhhe.com/rwj

Use the following information to answer the next two questions:

Historically, the U.S. tax code treated dividend payments made to shareholders as ordinary income. Thus, dividends were taxed at the investor's marginal tax rate, which was as high as 38.6 percent in 2002. Capital gains were taxed at a capital gains tax rate, which was the same for most investors and fluctuated through the years. In 2002, the capital gains tax rate stood at 20 percent. In an effort to stimulate the economy, President George W. Bush presided over a tax plan overhaul that included changes in dividend and capital gains tax rates. The new tax plan, which was implemented in 2003, called for a 15 percent tax rate on both dividends and capital gains for investors in higher tax brackets. For lower–tax bracket investors, the tax rate on dividends and capital gains was set at 5 percent through 2007, dropping to zero in 2008.

9. **Ex-Dividend Stock Prices [LO1]** How do you think this tax law change affects ex-dividend stock prices?

10. **Stock Repurchases [LO4]** How do you think this tax law change affected the relative attractiveness of stock repurchases compared to dividend payments?

QUESTIONS AND PROBLEMS

BASIC
(Questions 1–9)

1. **Dividends and Taxes [LO2]** Dark Day, Inc., has declared a $5.10 per share dividend. Suppose capital gains are not taxed, but dividends are taxed at 15 percent. New IRS regulations require that taxes be withheld at the time the dividend is paid. Dark Day sells for $93.85 per share, and the stock is about to go ex dividend. What do you think the ex-dividend price will be?

2. **Stock Dividends [LO3]** The owners' equity accounts for Alexander International are shown here:

Common stock ($.50 par value)	$ 20,000
Capital surplus	285,000
Retained earnings	638,120
Total owners' equity	$933,120

a. If Alexander stock currently sells for $30 per share and a 10 percent stock dividend is declared, how many new shares will be distributed? Show how the equity accounts would change.

b. If Alexander declared a 25 percent stock dividend, how would the accounts change?

3. **Stock Splits [LO3]** For the company in Problem 2, show how the equity accounts will change if:

a. Alexander declares a four-for-one stock split. How many shares are outstanding now? What is the new par value per share?

b. Alexander declares a one-for-five reverse stock split. How many shares are outstanding now? What is the new par value per share?

4. **Stock Splits and Stock Dividends [LO3]** Red Rocks Corporation (RRC) currently has 425,000 shares of stock outstanding that sell for $80 per share. Assuming no market imperfections or tax effects exist, what will the share price be after:

a. RRC has a five-for-three stock split?

b. RRC has a 15 percent stock dividend?

c. RRC has a 42.5 percent stock dividend?

d. RRC has a four-for-seven reverse stock split?

Determine the new number of shares outstanding in parts (a) through (d).

5. **Regular Dividends [LO1]** The balance sheet for Chevelle Corp. is shown here in   **X**
    market value terms. There are 9,000 shares of stock outstanding.

Market Value Balance Sheet			
Cash	$ 43,700	Equity	$353,700
Fixed assets	310,000		
Total	$353,700	Total	$353,700

The company has declared a dividend of $1.40 per share. The stock goes ex divi-
dend tomorrow. Ignoring any tax effects, what is the stock selling for today? What
will it sell for tomorrow? What will the balance sheet look like after the dividends
are paid?

6. **Share Repurchase [LO4]** In the previous problem, suppose Chevelle has an-
    nounced it is going to repurchase $12,600 worth of stock. What effect will this
    transaction have on the equity of the firm? How many shares will be outstanding?
    What will the price per share be after the repurchase? Ignoring tax effects, show
    how the share repurchase is effectively the same as a cash dividend.

7. **Stock Dividends [LO3]** The market value balance sheet for Sci-Fi Crimes Manu-
    facturing is shown here. Sci-Fi Crimes has declared a 25 percent stock dividend.
    The stock goes ex dividend tomorrow (the chronology for a stock dividend is simi-
    lar to that for a cash dividend). There are 14,000 shares of stock outstanding. What
    will the ex-dividend price be?

Market Value Balance Sheet			
Cash	$ 86,000	Debt	$145,000
Fixed assets	630,000	Equity	571,000
Total	$716,000	Total	$716,000

8. **Stock Dividends [LO3]** The company with the common equity accounts shown
    here has declared a 15 percent stock dividend when the market value of its stock is
    $43 per share. What effects on the equity accounts will the distribution of the stock
    dividend have?

Common stock ($1 par value)	$ 385,000
Capital surplus	846,000
Retained earnings	3,720,800
Total owners' equity	$4,951,800

9. **Stock Splits [LO3]** In the previous problem, suppose the company instead decides
    on a four-for-one stock split. The firm's 75-cent per share cash dividend on the new
    (postsplit) shares represents an increase of 10 percent over last year's dividend on
    the presplit stock. What effect does this have on the equity accounts? What was last
    year's dividend per share?

10. **Homemade Dividends [LO2]** You own 1,000 shares of stock in Avondale
    Corporation. You will receive a $1.85 per share dividend in one year. In two years,
    Avondale will pay a liquidating dividend of $58 per share. The required return
    on Avondale stock is 15 percent. What is the current share price of your stock
    (ignoring taxes)? If you would rather have equal dividends in each of the next two

INTERMEDIATE
(Questions 10–12)

Visit us at www.mhhe.com/rwj

Visit us at www.mhhe.com/rwj

years, show how you can accomplish this by creating homemade dividends. *Hint:* Dividends will be in the form of an annuity.

11.   Homemade Dividends [LO2] In the previous problem, suppose you want only $750 total in dividends the first year. What will your homemade dividend be in two years?

✗ 12.   Stock Repurchase [LO4] Rudolph Corporation is evaluating an extra dividend versus a share repurchase. In either case, $11,000 would be spent. Current earnings are $1.40 per share, and the stock currently sells for $58 per share. There are 2,000 shares outstanding. Ignore taxes and other imperfections in answering the first two questions.

    a. Evaluate the two alternatives in terms of the effect on the price per share of the stock and shareholder wealth.

    b. What will be the effect on Rudolph's EPS and PE ratio under the two different scenarios?

    c. In the real world, which of these actions would you recommend? Why?

CHALLENGE   **13.   Expected Return, Dividends, and Taxes [LO2]** The Gecko Company and the
(Questions 13–16)   Gordon Company are two firms whose business risk is the same but that have different dividend policies. Gecko pays no dividend, whereas Gordon has an expected dividend yield of 4 percent. Suppose the capital gains tax rate is zero, whereas the income tax rate is 35 percent. Gecko has an expected earnings growth rate of 15 percent annually, and its stock price is expected to grow at this same rate. If the aftertax expected returns on the two stocks are equal (because they are in the same risk class), what is the pretax required return on Gordon's stock?

14.   Dividends and Taxes [LO2] As discussed in the text, in the absence of market imperfections and tax effects, we would expect the share price to decline by the amount of the dividend payment when the stock goes ex dividend. Once we consider the role of taxes, however, this is not necessarily true. One model has been proposed that incorporates tax effects into determining the ex-dividend price:[9]

$$(P_0 - P_X)/D = (1 - T_P)/(1 - T_G)$$

where P_0 is the price just before the stock goes ex, P_X is the ex-dividend share price, D is the amount of the dividend per share, T_P is the relevant marginal personal tax rate on dividends, and T_G is the effective marginal tax rate on capital gains.

    a. If $T_P = T_G = 0$, how much will the share price fall when the stock goes ex?

    b. If $T_P = 15$ percent and $T_G = 0$, how much will the share price fall?

    c. If $T_P = 15$ percent and $T_G = 30$ percent, how much will the share price fall?

    d. Suppose the only owners of stock are corporations. Recall that corporations get at least a 70 percent exemption from taxation on the dividend income they receive, but they do not get such an exemption on capital gains. If the corporation's income and capital gains tax rates are both 35 percent, what does this model predict the ex-dividend share price will be?

    e. What does this problem tell you about real-world tax considerations and the dividend policy of the firm?

15.   Dividends versus Reinvestment [LO2] National Business Machine Co. (NBM) has $3 million of extra cash after taxes have been paid. NBM has two choices to make use of this cash. One alternative is to invest the cash in financial assets. The

---

[9]N. Elton and M. Gruber, "Marginal Stockholder Tax Rates and the Clientele Effect," *Review of Economics and Statistics* 52 (February 1970).

resulting investment income will be paid out as a special dividend at the end of three years. In this case, the firm can invest in Treasury bills yielding 3 percent or a 5 percent preferred stock. IRS regulations allow the company to exclude from taxable income 70 percent of the dividends received from investing in another company's stock. Another alternative is to pay out the cash now as dividends. This would allow the shareholders to invest on their own in Treasury bills with the same yield, or in preferred stock. The corporate tax rate is 35 percent. Assume the investor has a 31 percent personal income tax rate, which is applied to interest income and preferred stock dividends. The personal dividend tax rate is 15 percent on common stock dividends. Should the cash be paid today or in three years? Which of the two options generates the highest aftertax income for the shareholders?

16. **Dividends versus Reinvestment [LO2]** After completing its capital spending for the year, Carlson Manufacturing has $1,000 extra cash. Carlson's managers must choose between investing the cash in Treasury bonds that yield 6 percent or paying the cash out to investors who would invest in the bonds themselves.

   a. If the corporate tax rate is 35 percent, what personal tax rate would make the investors equally willing to receive the dividend or to let Carlson invest the money?

   b. Is the answer to (a) reasonable? Why or why not?

   c. Suppose the only investment choice is a preferred stock that yields 9 percent. The corporate dividend exclusion of 70 percent applies. What personal tax rate will make the stockholders indifferent to the outcome of Carlson's dividend decision?

   d. Is this a compelling argument for a low dividend payout ratio? Why or why not?

MINICASE

Electronic Timing, Inc.

Electronic Timing, Inc. (ETI), is a small company founded 15 years ago by electronics engineers Tom Miller and Jessica Kerr. ETI manufactures integrated circuits to capitalize on the complex mixed-signal design technology and has recently entered the market for frequency timing generators, or silicon timing devices, which provide the timing signals or "clocks" necessary to synchronize electronic systems. Its clock products originally were used in PC video graphics applications, but the market subsequently expanded to include motherboards, PC peripheral devices, and other digital consumer electronics, such as digital television boxes and game consoles. ETI also designs and markets custom application-specific integrated circuits (ASICs) for industrial customers. The ASIC's design combines analog and digital, or mixed-signal, technology. In addition to Tom and Jessica, Nolan Pittman, who provided capital for the company, is the third primary owner. Each owns 25 percent of the 1 million shares outstanding. The company has several other individuals, including current employees, who own the remaining shares.

Recently, the company designed a new computer motherboard. The company's design is both more efficient and less expensive to manufacture, and the ETI design is expected to become standard in many personal computers. After

investigating the possibility of manufacturing the new motherboard, ETI determined that the costs involved in building a new plant would be prohibitive. The owners also decided that they were unwilling to bring in another large outside owner. Instead, ETI sold the design to an outside firm. The sale of the motherboard design was completed for an aftertax payment of $30 million.

QUESTIONS

1. Tom believes the company should use the extra cash to pay a special one-time dividend. How will this proposal affect the stock price? How will it affect the value of the company?

2. Jessica believes the company should use the extra cash to pay off debt and upgrade and expand its existing manufacturing capability. How would Jessica's proposals affect the company?

3. Nolan favors a share repurchase. He argues that a repurchase will increase the company's P/E ratio, return on assets, and return on equity. Are his arguments correct? How will a share repurchase affect the value of the company?

Visit us at www.mhhe.com/rwj

4. Another option discussed by Tom, Jessica, and Nolan would be to begin a regular dividend payment to shareholders. How would you evaluate this proposal?

5. One way to value a share of stock is the dividend growth, or growing perpetuity, model. Consider the following: The dividend payout ratio is 1 minus b, where b is the "retention" or "plowback" ratio. So, the dividend next year will be the earnings next year, E_1, times 1 minus the retention ratio. The most commonly used equation to calculate the sustainable growth rate is the return on equity times the retention ratio. Substituting these relationships into the dividend growth model, we get the following equation to calculate the price of a share of stock today:

$$P_0 = \frac{E_1(1-b)}{R_s - \text{ROE} \times b}$$

What are the implications of this result in terms of whether the company should pay a dividend or upgrade and expand its manufacturing capability? Explain.

6. Does the question of whether the company should pay a dividend depend on whether the company is organized as a corporation or an LLC?

SHORT-TERM FINANCE AND PLANNING

WITH GASOLINE HITTING $4 PER GALLON in early 2011, sales of hybrid automobiles really began to pick up. For example, in February 2011, the Toyota Prius sat on dealer lots for 36 days, on average, before selling. By March 2011, this period had fallen to 18 days. If you were looking for something a little more upscale, the Lexus CT 200h sat on dealer lots for only four days. And the plug-in hybrid Chevrolet Volt lasted 10 days on dealer lots on average. As this chapter explores, the length of time goods are carried in inventory until they are sold is an important element of short-term financial management, and industries such as the automobile industry pay close attention to it.

LEARNING OBJECTIVES

After studying this chapter, you should understand:

LO1 The operating and cash cycles and why they are important.

LO2 The different types of short-term financial policy.

LO3 The essentials of short-term financial planning.

LO4 The sources and uses of cash on the balance sheet.

To this point, we have described many of the decisions of long-term finance, such as those of capital budgeting, dividend policy, and financial structure. In this chapter, we begin to discuss short-term finance. Short-term finance is primarily concerned with the analysis of decisions that affect current assets and current liabilities.

Frequently, the term *net working capital* is associated with short-term financial decision making. As we describe in Chapter 2 and elsewhere, net working capital is the difference between current assets and current liabilities. Often, short-term financial management is called *working capital management*. These terms mean the same thing.

There is no universally accepted definition of *short-term finance*. The most important difference between short-term and long-term finance is in the timing of cash flows. Short-term financial decisions typically involve cash inflows and outflows that occur within a year or less. For example, short-term financial decisions are involved when a firm orders raw materials, pays in cash, and anticipates selling finished goods in one year for cash. In contrast, long-term financial decisions are involved when a firm purchases a special machine that will reduce operating costs over, say, the next five years.

What types of questions fall under the general heading of short-term finance? To name just a very few:

1. What is a reasonable level of cash to keep on hand (in a bank) to pay bills?
2. How much should the firm borrow in the short term?
3. How much credit should be extended to customers?

This chapter introduces the basic elements of short-term financial decisions. First, we discuss the short-term operating activities of the firm. We then identify some alternative short-term financial policies. Finally, we outline the basic elements in a short-term financial plan and describe short-term financing instruments.

18.1 Tracing Cash and Net Working Capital

Interested in a career in short-term finance? Visit the Treasury Management Association website at www. treasury-management.com.

In this section, we examine the components of cash and net working capital as they change from one year to the next. We have already discussed various aspects of this subject in Chapters 2, 3, and 4. We briefly review some of that discussion as it relates to short-term financing decisions. Our goal is to describe the short-term operating activities of the firm and their impact on cash and working capital.

To begin, recall that *current assets* are cash and other assets that are expected to convert to cash within the year. Current assets are presented on the balance sheet in order of their accounting liquidity—the ease with which they can be converted to cash and the time it takes to convert them. Four of the most important items found in the current asset section of a balance sheet are cash and cash equivalents, marketable securities, accounts receivable, and inventories.

Analogous to their investment in current assets, firms use several kinds of short-term debt, called *current liabilities.* Current liabilities are obligations that are expected to require cash payment within one year (or within the operating period if it is longer than one year). Three major items found as current liabilities are accounts payable, expenses payable (including accrued wages and taxes), and notes payable.

Because we want to focus on changes in cash, we start off by defining *cash* in terms of the other elements of the balance sheet. This lets us isolate the cash account and explore the impact on cash from the firm's operating and financing decisions. The basic balance sheet identity can be written as:

$$\text{Net working capital} + \text{Fixed assets} = \text{Long-term debt} + \text{Equity} \qquad \text{[18.1]}$$

Net working capital is cash plus other current assets, less current liabilities—that is:

$$\text{Net working capital} = (\text{Cash} + \text{Other current assets}) - \text{Current liabilities} \qquad \text{[18.2]}$$

If we substitute this for net working capital in the basic balance sheet identity and rearrange things a bit, we see that cash is:

$$\text{Cash} = \text{Long-term debt} + \text{Equity} + \text{Current liabilities} - \text{Current assets other than cash} - \text{Fixed assets} \qquad \text{[18.3]}$$

This tells us in general terms that some activities naturally increase cash and some activities decrease it. We can list these various activities, along with an example of each, as follows:

ACTIVITIES THAT INCREASE CASH
Increasing long-term debt (borrowing over the long term)
Increasing equity (selling some stock)
Increasing current liabilities (getting a 90-day loan)
Decreasing current assets other than cash (selling some inventory for cash)
Decreasing fixed assets (selling some property)

ACTIVITIES THAT DECREASE CASH
Decreasing long-term debt (paying off a long-term debt)
Decreasing equity (repurchasing some stock)

Decreasing current liabilities (paying off a 90-day loan)

Increasing current assets other than cash (buying some inventory for cash)

Increasing fixed assets (buying some property)

Notice that our two lists are exact opposites. For example, floating a long-term bond issue increases cash (at least until the money is spent). Paying off a long-term bond issue decreases cash.

As we discussed in Chapter 3, those activities that increase cash are called *sources of cash.* Those activities that decrease cash are called *uses of cash.* Looking back at our list, we see that sources of cash always involve increasing a liability (or equity) account or decreasing an asset account. This makes sense because increasing a liability means that we have raised money by borrowing it or by selling an ownership interest in the firm. A decrease in an asset means that we have sold or otherwise liquidated an asset. In either case, there is a cash inflow.

Uses of cash are just the reverse. A use of cash involves decreasing a liability by paying it off, perhaps, or increasing assets by purchasing something. Both of these activities require that the firm spend some cash.

Sources and Uses

EXAMPLE 18.1

Here is a quick check of your understanding of sources and uses: If accounts payable go up by $100, does this indicate a source or a use? What if accounts receivable go up by $100?

Accounts payable are what we owe our suppliers. This is a short-term debt. If it rises by $100, we have effectively borrowed the money, which is a *source* of cash. Receivables are what our customers owe to us, so an increase of $100 in accounts receivable means that we have lent the money; this is a *use* of cash.

Concept Questions

18.1a What is the difference between net working capital and cash?

18.1b Will net working capital always increase when cash increases?

18.1c List five potential sources of cash.

18.1d List five potential uses of cash.

The Operating Cycle and the Cash Cycle   18.2

The primary concern in short-term finance is the firm's short-run operating and financing activities. For a typical manufacturing firm, these short-run activities might consist of the following sequence of events and decisions:

Event	Decision
1. Buying raw materials	1. How much inventory to order
2. Paying cash	2. Whether to borrow or draw down cash balances
3. Manufacturing the product	3. What choice of production technology to use
4. Selling the product	4. Whether credit should be extended to a particular customer
5. Collecting cash	5. How to collect

These activities create patterns of cash inflows and cash outflows. These cash flows are both unsynchronized and uncertain. They are unsynchronized because, for example, the payment of cash for raw materials does not happen at the same time as the receipt of cash from selling the product. They are uncertain because future sales and costs cannot be precisely predicted.

DEFINING THE OPERATING AND CASH CYCLES

We can start with a simple case. One day, call it Day 0, we purchase $1,000 worth of inventory on credit. We pay the bill 30 days later; and after 30 more days, someone buys the $1,000 in inventory for $1,400. Our buyer does not actually pay for another 45 days. We can summarize these events chronologically as follows:

Day	Activity	Cash Effect
0	Acquire inventory	None
30	Pay for inventory	−$1,000
60	Sell inventory on credit	None
105	Collect on sale	+$1,400

look at problem

operating cycle
The period between the acquisition of inventory and the collection of cash from receivables.

inventory period
The time it takes to acquire and sell inventory.

accounts receivable period
The time between sale of inventory and collection of the receivable.

The Operating Cycle   There are several things to notice in our example. First, the entire cycle, from the time we acquire some inventory to the time we collect the cash, takes 105 days. This is called the **operating cycle**.

As we illustrate, the operating cycle is the length of time it takes to acquire inventory, sell it, and collect for it. This cycle has two distinct components. The first part is the time it takes to acquire and sell the inventory. This period, a 60-day span in our example, is called the **inventory period**. The second part is the time it takes to collect on the sale, 45 days in our example. This is called the **accounts receivable period**.

Based on our definitions, the operating cycle is obviously just the sum of the inventory and accounts receivable periods:

$$\text{Operating cycle} = \text{Inventory period} + \text{Accounts receivable period} \qquad \textbf{[18.4]}$$
$$105 \text{ days} = 60 \text{ days} + 45 \text{ days}$$

What the operating cycle describes is how a product moves through the current asset accounts. The product begins life as inventory, it is converted to a receivable when it is sold, and it is finally converted to cash when we collect from the sale. Notice that, at each step, the asset is moving closer to cash.

accounts payable period
The time between receipt of inventory and payment for it.

cash cycle
The time between cash disbursement and cash collection.

The Cash Cycle   The second thing to notice is that the cash flows and other events that occur are not synchronized. For example, we don't actually pay for the inventory until 30 days after we acquire it. The intervening 30-day period is called the **accounts payable period**. Next, we spend cash on Day 30, but we don't collect until Day 105. Somehow, we have to arrange to finance the $1,000 for $105 - 30 = 75$ days. This period is called the **cash cycle**.

The cash cycle, therefore, is the number of days that pass before we collect the cash from a sale, measured from when we actually pay for the inventory. Notice that, based on our definitions, the cash cycle is the difference between the operating cycle and the accounts payable period:

$$\text{Cash cycle} = \text{Operating cycle} - \text{Accounts payable period} \qquad \textbf{[18.5]}$$
$$75 \text{ days} = 105 \text{ days} - 30 \text{ days}$$

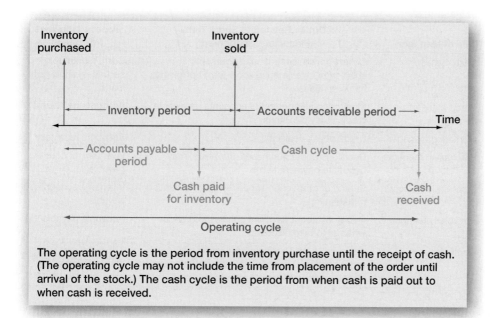

FIGURE 18.1

Cash Flow Time Line and the Short-Term Operating Activities of a Typical Manufacturing Firm

Figure 18.1 depicts the short-term operating activities and cash flows for a typical manufacturing firm by way of a cash flow time line. As shown, the **cash flow time line** presents the operating cycle and the cash cycle in graphical form. In Figure 18.1, the need for short-term financial management is suggested by the gap between the cash inflows and the cash outflows. This is related to the lengths of the operating cycle and the accounts payable period.

The gap between short-term inflows and outflows can be filled either by borrowing or by holding a liquidity reserve in the form of cash or marketable securities. Alternatively, the gap can be shortened by changing the inventory, receivable, and payable periods. These are all managerial options that we discuss in the following sections and in subsequent chapters.

Internet-based bookseller and retailer Amazon.com provides an interesting example of the importance of managing the cash cycle. By early 2011, the market value of Amazon.com was higher than (in fact more than 150 times as much as) that of Barnes & Noble, king of the brick-and-mortar bookstores, even though Amazon's sales were only 5.9 times greater.

How could Amazon.com be worth so much more? There are multiple reasons, but short-term management is one factor. During 2010, Amazon turned over its inventory about 10 times per year, 3 times faster than Barnes & Noble; so its inventory period was dramatically shorter. Even more striking, Amazon charges a customer's credit card when it ships a book, and it usually gets paid by the credit card firm within a day. This means Amazon has a *negative* cash cycle! In fact, during 2010, Amazon's cash cycle was a negative 69 days. Every sale therefore generates a cash inflow that can be put to work immediately.

Amazon is not the only company with a negative cash cycle. Consider aircraft manufacturer Boeing Company. During 2010, Boeing had an inventory period of 145 days and a receivables period of 36 days, so its operating cycle was a lengthy 182 days (the extra day is due to rounding errors). Boeing's cash cycle must be fairly long, right? Wrong. Boeing had a payables period of 235 days, so its cash cycle was a negative 53 days!

THE OPERATING CYCLE AND THE FIRM'S ORGANIZATIONAL CHART

Before we examine the operating and cash cycles in greater detail, it is useful for us to take a look at the people involved in managing a firm's current assets and liabilities. As Table 18.1

cash flow time line
A graphical representation of the operating cycle and the cash cycle.

Learn more about outsourcing accounts management at www.businessdebts.com and www.opiglobal.com.

TABLE 18.1

Managers Who Deal with Short-Term Financial Problems

Title of Manager	Duties Related to Short-Term Financial Management	Assets/Liabilities Influenced
Cash manager	Collection, concentration, disbursement; short-term investments; short-term borrowing; banking relations	Cash, marketable securities, short-term loans
Credit manager	Monitoring and control of accounts receivable; credit policy decisions	Accounts receivable
Marketing manager	Credit policy decisions	Accounts receivable
Purchasing manager	Decisions about purchases, suppliers; may negotiate payment terms	Inventory, accounts payable
Production manager	Setting of production schedules and materials requirements	Inventory, accounts payable
Payables manager	Decisions about payment policies and about whether to take discounts	Accounts payable
Controller	Accounting information about cash flows; reconciliation of accounts payable; application of payments to accounts receivable	Accounts receivable, accounts payable

illustrates, short-term financial management in a large corporation involves a number of different financial and nonfinancial managers. Examining Table 18.1, we see that selling on credit involves at least three different entities: the credit manager, the marketing manager, and the controller. Of these three, only two are responsible to the vice president of finance (the marketing function is usually associated with the vice president of marketing). Thus, there is the potential for conflict, particularly if different managers concentrate on only part of the picture. For example, if marketing is trying to land a new account, it may seek more liberal credit terms as an inducement. However, this may increase the firm's investment in receivables or its exposure to bad-debt risk, and conflict can result.

CALCULATING THE OPERATING AND CASH CYCLES

In our example, the lengths of time that made up the different periods were obvious. If all we have is financial statement information, we will have to do a little more work. We illustrate these calculations next.

To begin, we need to determine various things such as how long it takes, on average, to sell inventory and how long it takes, on average, to collect. We start by gathering some balance sheet information such as the following (in thousands):

Item	Beginning	Ending	Average
Inventory	$2,000	$3,000	$2,500
Accounts receivable	1,600	2,000	1,800
Accounts payable	750	1,000	875

Also, from the most recent income statement, we might have the following figures (in thousands):

Net sales	$11,500
Cost of goods sold	8,200

We now need to calculate some financial ratios. We discussed these in some detail in Chapter 3; here, we just define them and use them as needed.

The Operating Cycle   First of all, we need the inventory period. We spent $8.2 million on inventory (our cost of goods sold). Our average inventory was $2.5 million. We thus turned our inventory over $8.2/2.5$ times during the year:[1]

$$\text{Inventory turnover} = \frac{\text{Cost of goods sold}}{\text{Average inventory}}$$

$$= \frac{\$8.2 \text{ million}}{2.5 \text{ million}} = 3.28 \text{ times}$$

Loosely speaking, this tells us that we bought and sold off our inventory 3.28 times during the year. This means that, on average, we held our inventory for:

$$\text{Inventory period} = \frac{365 \text{ days}}{\text{Inventory turnover}}$$

$$= \frac{365}{3.28} = 111 \text{ days}$$

So, the inventory period is about 111 days. On average, in other words, inventory sat for about 111 days before it was sold.[2]

Similarly, receivables averaged $1.8 million, and sales were $11.5 million. Assuming that all sales were credit sales, the receivables turnover is:[3]

$$\text{Receivables turnover} = \frac{\text{Credit sales}}{\text{Average accounts receivable}}$$

$$= \frac{\$11.5 \text{ million}}{1.8 \text{ million}} = 6.4 \text{ times}$$

If we turn over our receivables 6.4 times, then the receivables period is:

$$\text{Receivables period} = \frac{365 \text{ days}}{\text{Receivables turnover}}$$

$$= \frac{365}{6.4} = 57 \text{ days}$$

The receivables period is also called the *days' sales in receivables* or the *average collection period*. Whatever it is called, it tells us that our customers took an average of 57 days to pay.

The operating cycle is the sum of the inventory and receivables periods:

$$\text{Operating cycle} = \text{Inventory period} + \text{Accounts receivable period}$$

$$= 111 \text{ days} + 57 \text{ days} = 168 \text{ days}$$

This tells us that, on average, 168 days elapse between the time we acquire inventory and, having sold it, collect for the sale.

---

[1]Notice that in calculating inventory turnover here, we use the *average* inventory instead of using the ending inventory as we did in Chapter 3. Both approaches are used in the real world. To gain some practice using average figures, we will stick with this approach in calculating various ratios throughout this chapter.

[2]This measure is conceptually identical to the days' sales in inventory figure we discussed in Chapter 3.

[3]If fewer than 100 percent of our sales were credit sales, then we would just need a little more information—namely, credit sales for the year. See Chapter 3 for more discussion of this measure.

The Cash Cycle   We now need the payables period. From the information given earlier, we know that average payables were $875,000 and cost of goods sold was $8.2 million. Our payables turnover is:

$$\text{Payables turnover} = \frac{\text{Cost of goods sold}}{\text{Average payables}}$$

$$= \frac{\$8.2 \text{ million}}{\$.875 \text{ million}} = 9.4 \text{ times}$$

The payables period is:

$$\text{Payables period} = \frac{365 \text{ days}}{\text{Payables turnover}}$$

$$= \frac{365}{9.4} = 39 \text{ days}$$

Thus, we took an average of 39 days to pay our bills.

Finally, the cash cycle is the difference between the operating cycle and the payables period:

$$\text{Cash cycle} = \text{Operating cycle} - \text{Accounts payable period}$$

$$= 168 \text{ days} - 39 \text{ days} = 129 \text{ days}$$

So, on average, there is a 129-day delay between the time we pay for merchandise and the time we collect on the sale.

| EXAMPLE 18.2 | **The Operating and Cash Cycles** |

You have collected the following information for the Slowpay Company:

Item	Beginning	Ending
Inventory	$5,000	$7,000
Accounts receivable	1,600	2,400
Accounts payable	2,700	4,800

Credit sales for the year just ended were $50,000, and cost of goods sold was $30,000. How long does it take Slowpay to collect on its receivables? How long does merchandise stay around before it is sold? How long does Slowpay take to pay its bills? We can first calculate the three turnover ratios:

$$\text{Inventory turnover} = \$30,000/6,000 = 5 \text{ times}$$
$$\text{Receivables turnover} = \$50,000/2,000 = 25 \text{ times}$$
$$\text{Payables turnover} = \$30,000/3,750 = 8 \text{ times}$$

We use these to get the various periods:

$$\text{Inventory period} = 365/5 \ = 73 \text{ days}$$
$$\text{Receivables period} = 365/25 = 14.6 \text{ days}$$
$$\text{Payables period} = 365/8 \ = 45.6 \text{ days}$$

All told, Slowpay collects on a sale in 14.6 days, inventory sits around for 73 days, and bills get paid after about 46 days. The operating cycle here is the sum of the inventory and receivables periods: 73 + 14.6 = 87.6 days. The cash cycle is the difference between the operating cycle and the payables period: 87.6 − 45.6 = 42 days.

INTERPRETING THE CASH CYCLE

Our examples show that the cash cycle depends on the inventory, receivables, and payables periods. The cash cycle increases as the inventory and receivables periods get longer. It decreases if the company can defer payment of payables and thereby lengthen the payables period.

Unlike Amazon.com, most firms have a positive cash cycle, and they thus require financing for inventories and receivables. The longer the cash cycle, the more financing is required. Also, changes in the firm's cash cycle are often monitored as an early-warning measure. A lengthening cycle can indicate that the firm is having trouble moving inventory or collecting on its receivables. Such problems can be masked, at least partially, by an increased payables cycle; so both cycles should be monitored.

The link between the firm's cash cycle and its profitability can be easily seen by recalling that one of the basic determinants of profitability and growth for a firm is its total asset turnover, which is defined as Sales/Total assets. In Chapter 3, we saw that the higher this ratio is, the greater is the firm's accounting return on assets, ROA, and return on equity, ROE. Thus, all other things being the same, the shorter the cash cycle is, the lower is the firm's investment in inventories and receivables. As a result, the firm's total assets are lower, and total turnover is higher.

Concept Questions

18.2a Describe the operating cycle and the cash cycle. What are the differences?

18.2b What does it mean to say that a firm has an inventory turnover ratio of 4?

18.2c Explain the connection between a firm's accounting-based profitability and its cash cycle.

Some Aspects of Short-Term Financial Policy

18.3

The short-term financial policy that a firm adopts will be reflected in at least two ways:

1. *The size of the firm's investment in current assets:* This is usually measured relative to the firm's level of total operating revenues. A *flexible,* or accommodative, short-term financial policy would maintain a relatively high ratio of current assets to sales. A *restrictive* short-term financial policy would entail a low ratio of current assets to sales.[4]

2. *The financing of current assets:* This is measured as the proportion of short-term debt (that is, current liabilities) and long-term debt used to finance current assets. A restrictive short-term financial policy means a high proportion of short-term debt relative to long-term financing, and a flexible policy means less short-term debt and more long-term debt.

If we take these two areas together, we see that a firm with a flexible policy would have a relatively large investment in current assets, and it would finance this investment with relatively less short-term debt. The net effect of a flexible policy is thus a relatively high level of net working capital. Put another way, with a flexible policy, the firm maintains a higher overall level of liquidity.

---

[4]Some people use the term *conservative* in place of *flexible* and the term *aggressive* in place of *restrictive.*

THE SIZE OF THE FIRM'S INVESTMENT IN CURRENT ASSETS

Short-term financial policies that are flexible with regard to current assets include such actions as:

1. Keeping large balances of cash and marketable securities.
2. Making large investments in inventory.
3. Granting liberal credit terms, which results in a high level of accounts receivable.

Restrictive short-term financial policies would be just the opposite:

1. Keeping low cash balances and making little investment in marketable securities.
2. Making small investments in inventory.
3. Allowing few or no credit sales, thereby minimizing accounts receivable.

Determining the optimal level of investment in short-term assets requires identification of the different costs of alternative short-term financing policies. The objective is to trade off the cost of a restrictive policy against the cost of a flexible one to arrive at the best compromise.

Current asset holdings are highest with a flexible short-term financial policy and lowest with a restrictive policy. So, flexible short-term financial policies are costly in that they require a greater investment in cash and marketable securities, inventory, and accounts receivable. However, we expect that future cash inflows will be higher with a flexible policy. For example, sales are stimulated by the use of a credit policy that provides liberal financing to customers. A large amount of finished inventory on hand ("on the shelf") enables quick delivery service to customers and may increase sales. Similarly, a large inventory of raw materials may result in fewer production stoppages because of inventory shortages.

A more restrictive short-term financial policy probably reduces future sales to levels below those that would be achieved under flexible policies. It is also possible that higher prices can be charged to customers under flexible working capital policies. Customers may be willing to pay higher prices for the quick delivery service and more liberal credit terms implicit in flexible policies.

Managing current assets can be thought of as involving a trade-off between costs that rise and that fall with the level of investment. Costs that rise with increases in the level of investment in current assets are called **carrying costs**. The larger the investment a firm makes in its current assets, the higher its carrying costs will be. Costs that fall with increases in the level of investment in current assets are called **shortage costs**.

In a general sense, carrying costs are the opportunity costs associated with current assets. The rate of return on current assets is very low when compared to that on other assets. For example, the rate of return on U.S. Treasury bills averages about 3 to 4 percent. This is very low compared to the rate of return firms would like to achieve overall. (U.S. Treasury bills are an important component of cash and marketable securities.)

Shortage costs are incurred when the investment in current assets is low. If a firm runs out of cash, it will be forced to sell marketable securities. Of course, if a firm runs out of cash and cannot readily sell marketable securities, it may have to borrow or default on an obligation. This situation is called a *cash-out*. A firm may lose customers if it runs out of inventory (a *stockout*) or if it cannot extend credit to customers.

More generally, there are two kinds of shortage costs:

1. *Trading, or order, costs:* Order costs are the costs of placing an order for more cash (brokerage costs, for example) or more inventory (production setup costs, for example).

carrying costs
Costs that rise with increases in the level of investment in current assets.

shortage costs
Costs that fall with increases in the level of investment in current assets.

2. *Costs related to lack of safety reserves:* These are costs of lost sales, lost customer goodwill, and disruption of production schedules.

The top part of Figure 18.2 illustrates the basic trade-off between carrying costs and shortage costs. On the vertical axis, we have costs measured in dollars; on the horizontal axis, we have the amount of current assets. Carrying costs start out at zero when current assets are zero and then climb steadily as current assets grow. Shortage costs start out very high and then decline as we add current assets. The total cost of holding current assets is the sum of the two. Notice how the combined costs reach a minimum at CA*. This is the optimal level of current assets.

Optimal current asset holdings are highest under a flexible policy. This policy is one in which the carrying costs are perceived to be low relative to shortage costs. This is Case A in Figure 18.2. In comparison, under restrictive current asset policies, carrying costs are perceived to be high relative to shortage costs, resulting in lower current asset holdings. This is Case B in Figure 18.2.

ALTERNATIVE FINANCING POLICIES FOR CURRENT ASSETS

In previous sections, we looked at the basic determinants of the level of investment in current assets, and we thus focused on the asset side of the balance sheet. Now we turn to the financing side of the question. Here we are concerned with the relative amounts of short-term and long-term debt, assuming that the investment in current assets is constant.

An Ideal Case   We start off with the simplest possible case: an "ideal" economy. In such an economy, short-term assets can always be financed with short-term debt, and long-term assets can be financed with long-term debt and equity. In this economy, net working capital is always zero.

Consider a simplified case for a grain elevator operator. Grain elevator operators buy crops after harvest, store them, and sell them during the year. They have high inventories of grain after the harvest and end up with low inventories just before the next harvest.

Bank loans with maturities of less than one year are used to finance the purchase of grain and the storage costs. These loans are paid off from the proceeds of the sale of grain.

The situation is shown in Figure 18.3. Long-term assets are assumed to grow over time, whereas current assets increase at the end of the harvest and then decline during the year. Short-term assets end up at zero just before the next harvest. Current (short-term) assets are financed by short-term debt, and long-term assets are financed with long-term debt and equity. Net working capital—current assets minus current liabilities—is always zero. Figure 18.3 displays a "sawtooth" pattern that we will see again when we get to our discussion of cash management in the next chapter. For now, we need to discuss some alternative policies for financing current assets under less idealized conditions.

Different Policies for Financing Current Assets   In the real world, it is not likely that current assets will ever drop to zero. For example, a long-term rising level of sales will result in some permanent investment in current assets. Moreover, the firm's investments in long-term assets may show a great deal of variation.

A growing firm can be thought of as having a total asset requirement consisting of the current assets and long-term assets needed to run the business efficiently. The total asset requirement may exhibit change over time for many reasons, including (1) a general growth trend, (2) seasonal variation around the trend, and (3) unpredictable day-to-day

FIGURE 18.2

Carrying Costs and
Shortage Costs

Short-term financial policy: the optimal investment in current assets

CA* represents the optimal amount of current assets.
Holding this amount minimizes total costs.

Carrying costs increase with the level of investment in current assets. They
include the costs of maintaining economic value and opportunity costs.
Shortage costs decrease with increases in the level of investment in current
assets. They include trading costs and the costs related to being short of the
current asset (for example, being short of cash). The firm's policy can be
characterized as flexible or restrictive.

A. Flexible policy

A flexible policy is most appropriate when carrying costs are low relative to
shortage costs.

B. Restrictive policy

A restrictive policy is most appropriate when carrying costs are high relative
to shortage costs.

FIGURE 18.3

Financing Policy for an
Ideal Economy

In an ideal world, net working capital is always zero because
short-term assets are financed by short-term debt.

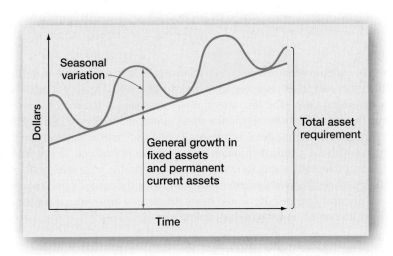

FIGURE 18.4

The Total Asset
Requirement over Time

and month-to-month fluctuations. This fluctuation is depicted in Figure 18.4. (We have not tried to show the unpredictable day-to-day and month-to-month variations in the total asset requirement.)

The peaks and valleys in Figure 18.4 represent the firm's total asset needs through time. For example, for a lawn and garden supply firm, the peaks might represent inventory buildups prior to the spring selling season. The valleys would come about because of lower off-season inventories. Such a firm might consider two strategies to meet its cyclical needs. First, the firm could keep a relatively large pool of marketable securities. As the need for inventory and other current assets began to rise, the firm would sell off marketable securities and use the cash to purchase whatever was needed. Once the inventory was sold and inventory holdings began to decline, the firm would reinvest in marketable securities. This approach is the flexible policy illustrated in Figure 18.5 as Policy F. Notice that the firm essentially uses a pool of marketable securities as a buffer against changing current asset needs.

FIGURE 18.5   Alternative Asset Financing Policies

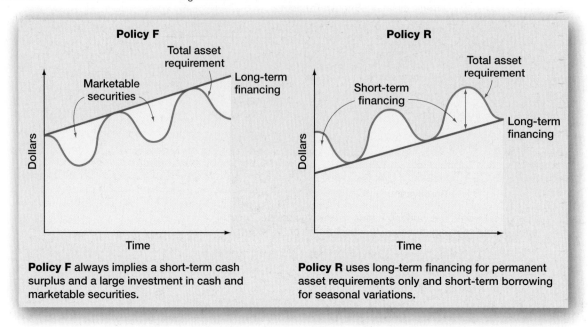

Policy F always implies a short-term cash surplus and a large investment in cash and marketable securities.

Policy R uses long-term financing for permanent asset requirements only and short-term borrowing for seasonal variations.

At the other extreme, the firm could keep relatively little in marketable securities. As the need for inventory and other assets began to rise, the firm would simply borrow the needed cash on a short-term basis. The firm would repay the loans as the need for assets cycled back down. This approach is the restrictive policy illustrated in Figure 18.5 as Policy R.

In comparing the two strategies illustrated in Figure 18.5, notice that the chief difference is the way in which the seasonal variation in asset needs is financed. In the flexible case, the firm finances internally, using its own cash and marketable securities. In the restrictive case, the firm finances the variation externally, borrowing the needed funds on a short-term basis. As we discussed previously, all else being the same, a firm with a flexible policy will have a greater investment in net working capital.

WHICH FINANCING POLICY IS BEST?

What is the most appropriate amount of short-term borrowing? There is no definitive answer. Several considerations must be included in a proper analysis:

1. *Cash reserves:* The flexible financing policy implies surplus cash and little short-term borrowing. This policy reduces the probability that a firm will experience financial distress. Firms may not have to worry as much about meeting recurring, short-run obligations. However, investments in cash and marketable securities are zero net present value investments at best.

2. *Maturity hedging:* Most firms attempt to match the maturities of assets and liabilities. They finance inventories with short-term bank loans and fixed assets with long-term financing. Firms tend to avoid financing long-lived assets with short-term borrowing. This type of maturity mismatching would necessitate frequent refinancing and is inherently risky because short-term interest rates are more volatile than longer-term rates.

3. *Relative interest rates:* Short-term interest rates are usually lower than long-term rates. This implies that it is, on the average, more costly to rely on long-term borrowing as compared to short-term borrowing.

FIGURE 18.6

A Compromise Financing Policy

With a compromise policy, the firm keeps a reserve of liquidity that it uses to initially finance seasonal variations in current asset needs. Short-term borrowing is used when the reserve is exhausted.

The two policies, F and R, we depict in Figure 18.5 are, of course, extreme cases. With F, the firm never does any short-term borrowing; with R, the firm never has a cash reserve (an investment in marketable securities). Figure 18.6 illustrates these two policies along with a compromise, Policy C.

With this compromise approach, the firm borrows in the short term to cover peak financing needs, but it maintains a cash reserve in the form of marketable securities during slow periods. As current assets build up, the firm draws down this reserve before doing any short-term borrowing. This allows for some run-up in current assets before the firm has to resort to short-term borrowing.

CURRENT ASSETS AND LIABILITIES IN PRACTICE

Short-term assets represent a significant portion of a typical firm's overall assets. For U.S. manufacturing, mining, and trade corporations, current assets were about 50 percent of total assets in the 1960s. Today, this figure is closer to 40 percent. Most of the decline is due to more efficient cash and inventory management. Over this same period, current liabilities rose from about 20 percent of total liabilities and equity to almost 30 percent. The result is that liquidity (as measured by the ratio of net working capital to total assets) has declined, signaling a move to more restrictive short-term policies.

Concept Questions

18.3a What keeps the real world from being an ideal one in which net working capital could always be zero?

18.3b What considerations determine the optimal size of the firm's investment in current assets?

18.3c What considerations determine the optimal compromise between flexible and restrictive net working capital policies?

⚡ 18.4 | The Cash Budget

cash budget
A forecast of cash receipts and disbursements for the next planning period.

The **cash budget** is a primary tool in short-run financial planning. It allows the financial manager to identify short-term financial needs and opportunities. An important function of the cash budget is to help the manager explore the need for short-term borrowing. The idea of the cash budget is simple: It records estimates of cash receipts (cash in) and disbursements (cash out). The result is an estimate of the cash surplus or deficit.

SALES AND CASH COLLECTIONS

We start with an example involving the Fun Toys Corporation. We will prepare a quarterly cash budget. We could just as well use a monthly, weekly, or even daily basis. We choose quarters for convenience and also because a quarter is a common short-term business planning period. (Note that, throughout this example, all figures are in millions of dollars.)

All of Fun Toys' cash inflows come from the sale of toys. Cash budgeting for Fun Toys must therefore start with a sales forecast for the coming year, by quarter:

	Q1	**Q2**	**Q3**	**Q4**
Sales (in millions)	$200	$300	$250	$400

Note that these are predicted sales, so there is forecasting risk here, and actual sales could be more or less. Fun Toys started the year with accounts receivable equal to $120.

Fun Toys has a 45-day receivables, or average collection, period. This means that half of the sales in a given quarter will be collected the following quarter. This happens because sales made during the first 45 days of a quarter will be collected in that quarter, whereas sales made in the second 45 days will be collected in the next quarter. Note that we are assuming that each quarter has 90 days, so the 45-day collection period is the same as a half-quarter collection period.

Based on the sales forecasts, we now need to estimate Fun Toys' projected cash collections. First, any receivables that we have at the beginning of a quarter will be collected within 45 days, so all of them will be collected sometime during the quarter. Second, as we discussed, any sales made in the first half of the quarter will be collected, so total cash collections are:

$$\text{Cash collections} = \text{Beginning accounts receivable} + 1/2 \times \text{Sales} \qquad [18.6]$$

For example, in the first quarter, cash collections would be the beginning receivables of $120 plus half of sales, $1/2 \times \$200 = \$100$, for a total of $220.

Because beginning receivables are all collected along with half of sales, ending receivables for a particular quarter will be the other half of sales. First-quarter sales are projected at $200, so ending receivables will be $100. This will be the beginning receivables in the second quarter. Cash collections in the second quarter will thus be $100 plus half of the projected $300 in sales, or $250 total.

Continuing this process, we can summarize Fun Toys' projected cash collections as shown in Table 18.2.

See the Finance Tools section of www.toolkit.com for several useful templates, including a cash flow budget.

TABLE 18.2

Cash Collection for Fun Toys (in Millions)

	Q1	**Q2**	**Q3**	**Q4**
Beginning receivables	$120	→ $100	→ $150	→ $125
Sales	200	300	250	400
Cash collections	− 220	− 250	− 275	− 325
Ending receivables	100	150	125	200

Collections = Beginning receivables + 1/2 × Sales
Ending receivables = Beginning receivables + Sales − Collections
= 1/2 × Sales

In Table 18.2, collections are shown as the only source of cash. Of course, this need not be the case. Other sources of cash could include asset sales, investment income, and receipts from planned long-term financing.

CASH OUTFLOWS

Next, we consider the cash disbursements, or payments. These come in four basic categories:

1. *Payments of accounts payable:* These are payments for goods or services rendered by suppliers, such as raw materials. Generally, these payments will be made sometime after purchases.
2. *Wages, taxes, and other expenses:* This category includes all other regular costs of doing business that require actual expenditures. Depreciation, for example, is often thought of as a regular cost of business; but it requires no cash outflow and is not included.
3. *Capital expenditures:* These are payments of cash for long-lived assets.
4. *Long-term financing expenses:* This category includes, for example, interest payments on long-term debt outstanding and dividend payments to shareholders.

Fun Toys' purchases from suppliers (in dollars) in a quarter are equal to 60 percent of the next quarter's predicted sales. Fun Toys' payments to suppliers are equal to the previous quarter's purchases, so the accounts payable period is 90 days. For example, in the quarter just ended, Fun Toys ordered .60 × $200 = $120 in supplies. This will actually be paid in the first quarter (Q1) of the coming year.

Wages, taxes, and other expenses are routinely 20 percent of sales; interest and dividends are currently $20 per quarter. In addition, Fun Toys plans a major plant expansion (a capital expenditure) costing $100 in the second quarter. If we put all this information together, the cash outflows are as shown in Table 18.3.

THE CASH BALANCE

The predicted *net cash inflow* is the difference between cash collections and cash disbursements. The net cash inflow for Fun Toys is shown in Table 18.4. What we see immediately is that there is a cash surplus in the first and third quarters and a cash deficit in the second and fourth.

	Q1	Q2	Q3	Q4
Payment of accounts (60% of sales)	$120	$180	$150	$240
Wages, taxes, other expenses	40	60	50	80
Capital expenditures	0	100	0	0
Long-term financing expenses (interest and dividends)	20	20	20	20
Total cash disbursements	$180	$360	$220	$340

TABLE 18.3

Cash Disbursements for Fun Toys (in Millions)

	Q1	Q2	Q3	Q4
Total cash collections	$220	$250	$275	$325
Total cash disbursements	180	360	220	340
Net cash inflow	$ 40	−$110	$ 55	−$ 15

TABLE 18.4

Net Cash Inflow for Fun Toys (in Millions)

TABLE 18.5

Cash Balance for Fun Toys (in Millions)

	Q1	Q2	Q3	Q4
Beginning cash balance	$20	$ 60	−$50	$ 5
Net cash inflow	40	− 110	55	− 15
Ending cash balance	$60	−$ 50	$ 5	−$10
Minimum cash balance	− 10	− 10	− 10	− 10
Cumulative surplus (deficit)	$50	−$ 60	−$ 5	−$20

We will assume that Fun Toys starts the year with a $20 cash balance. Furthermore, Fun Toys maintains a $10 minimum cash balance to guard against unforeseen contingencies and forecasting errors. So, the company starts the first quarter with $20 in cash. This amount rises by $40 during the quarter, and the ending balance is $60. Of this, $10 is reserved as a minimum, so we subtract it out and find that the first-quarter surplus is $60 − 10 = $50.

Fun Toys starts the second quarter with $60 in cash (the ending balance from the previous quarter). There is a net cash inflow of −$110, so the ending balance is $60 − 110 = −$50. We need another $10 as a buffer, so the total deficit is −$60. These calculations and those for the last two quarters are summarized in Table 18.5.

At the end of the second quarter, Fun Toys has a cash shortfall of $60. This occurs because of the seasonal pattern of sales (higher toward the end of the second quarter), the delay in collections, and the planned capital expenditure.

The cash situation at Fun Toys is projected to improve to a $5 deficit in the third quarter; but, by year's end, Fun Toys still has a $20 deficit. Without some sort of financing, this deficit will carry over into the next year. We explore this subject in the next section.

For now, we can make the following general comments about Fun Toys' cash needs:

1. Fun Toys' large outflow in the second quarter is not necessarily a sign of trouble. It results from delayed collections on sales and a planned capital expenditure (presumably a worthwhile one).

2. The figures in our example are based on a forecast. Sales could be much worse (or better) than the forecast figures.

Concept Questions

18.4a How would you do a sensitivity analysis (discussed in Chapter 11) for Fun Toys' net cash balance?

18.4b What could you learn from such an analysis?

18.5 Short-Term Borrowing

Fun Toys has a short-term financing problem. It cannot meet the forecast cash outflows in the second quarter using internal sources. How it will finance that shortfall depends on its financial policy. With a very flexible policy, Fun Toys might seek up to $60 million in long-term debt financing.

In addition, note that much of the cash deficit comes from the large capital expenditure. Arguably, this is a candidate for long-term financing. Nonetheless, because we have discussed long-term financing elsewhere, we will concentrate here on two short-term borrowing options: (1) unsecured borrowing and (2) secured borrowing.

UNSECURED LOANS

The most common way to finance a temporary cash deficit is to arrange a short-term unsecured bank loan. Firms that use short-term bank loans often arrange for a line of credit. A **line of credit** is an agreement under which a firm is authorized to borrow up to a specified amount. To ensure that the line is used for short-term purposes, the lender will sometimes require the borrower to pay the line down to zero and keep it there for some period during the year, typically 60 days (called a *cleanup period*).

Short-term lines of credit are classified as either *committed* or *noncommitted.* The latter type is an informal arrangement that allows firms to borrow up to a previously specified limit without going through the normal paperwork (much as they would with a credit card). A *revolving credit arrangement* (or just *revolver*) is similar to a line of credit, but it is usually open for two or more years, whereas a line of credit would usually be evaluated on an annual basis.

Committed lines of credit are more formal legal arrangements that usually involve a commitment fee paid by the firm to the bank (usually the fee is on the order of .25 percent of the total committed funds per year). The interest rate on the line of credit is usually set equal to the bank's prime lending rate plus an additional percentage, and the rate will usually float. A firm that pays a commitment fee for a committed line of credit is essentially buying insurance to guarantee that the bank can't back out of the agreement (absent some material change in the borrower's status).

line of credit
A formal (committed) or informal (noncommitted) prearranged, short-term bank loan.

Compensating Balances   As a part of a credit line or other lending arrangement, banks will sometimes require that the firm keep some amount of money on deposit. This is called a compensating balance. A **compensating balance** is some of the firm's money kept by the bank in low-interest or non-interest-bearing accounts. By leaving these funds with the bank and receiving little or no interest, the firm further increases the effective interest rate earned by the bank on the line of credit, thereby "compensating" the bank. A compensating balance might be on the order of 2 to 5 percent of the amount borrowed.

compensating balance
Money kept by the firm with a bank in low-interest or non-interest-bearing accounts as part of a loan agreement.

Firms also use compensating balances to pay for noncredit bank services such as cash management services. A traditionally contentious issue is whether the firm should pay for bank credit and noncredit services with fees or with compensating balances. Most major firms have now negotiated for banks to use the corporation's collected funds for compensation and use fees to cover any shortfall. Arrangements such as this one and some similar approaches discussed in the next chapter make the subject of minimum balances less of an issue than it once was.

Cost of a Compensating Balance   A compensating balance requirement has an obvious opportunity cost because the money often must be deposited in an account with a zero or low interest rate. For example, suppose that we have a $100,000 line of credit with a 10 percent compensating balance requirement. This means that 10 percent of the amount actually used must be left on deposit in a non-interest-bearing account.

The quoted interest rate on the credit line is 16 percent. Suppose we need $54,000 to purchase some inventory. How much do we have to borrow? What interest rate are we effectively paying?

If we need $54,000, we have to borrow enough so that $54,000 is left over after we take out the 10 percent compensating balance:

$54,000 = (1 - .10) \times$ Amount borrowed

$60,000 = \$54,000/.90 =$ Amount borrowed

The interest on the $60,000 for one year at 16 percent is $60,000 × .16 = $9,600. We're actually getting only $54,000 to use, so the effective interest rate is:

$$\begin{aligned}
\text{Effective interest rate} &= \text{Interest paid/Amount available} \\
&= \$9{,}600/54{,}000 \\
&= 17.78\%
\end{aligned}$$

Notice that what effectively happens here is that we pay 16 cents in interest on every 90 cents we borrow because we don't get to use the 10 cents tied up in the compensating balance. The interest rate is thus .16/.90 = 17.78%, as we calculated.

Several points bear mentioning. First, compensating balances are usually computed as a monthly *average* of the daily balances. This means that the effective interest rate may be lower than our example illustrates. Second, it has become common for compensating balances to be based on the *unused* amount of the credit line. The requirement of such a balance amounts to an implicit commitment fee. Third, and most important, the details of any short-term business lending arrangements are highly negotiable. Banks will generally work with firms to design a package of fees and interest.

Letters of Credit   A *letter of credit* is a common arrangement in international finance. With a letter of credit, the bank issuing the letter promises to make a loan if certain conditions are met. Typically, the letter guarantees payment on a shipment of goods provided that the goods arrive as promised. A letter of credit can be revocable (subject to cancellation) or irrevocable (not subject to cancellation if the specified conditions are met).

SECURED LOANS

Banks and other finance companies often require security for a short-term loan just as they do for a long-term loan. Security for short-term loans usually consists of accounts receivable, inventories, or both.

accounts receivable financing
A secured short-term loan that involves either the assignment or the factoring of receivables.

Accounts Receivable Financing   Accounts receivable financing involves either *assigning* receivables or *factoring* receivables. Under assignment, the lender has the receivables as security, but the borrower is still responsible if a receivable can't be collected. With *conventional factoring,* the receivable is discounted and sold to the lender (the factor). Once it is sold, collection is the factor's problem, and the factor assumes the full risk of default on bad accounts. With *maturity factoring,* the factor forwards the money on an agreed-upon future date.

Factors play a particularly important role in the retail industry. Retailers in the clothing business, for example, must buy large amounts of new clothes at the beginning of the season. Because this is typically a long time before they have sold anything, they wait to pay their suppliers, sometimes 30 to 60 days. If an apparel maker can't wait that long, it turns to factors, who buy the receivables and take over collection. Historically, the garment industry accounted for about 80 percent of all factoring in the United States.

Accounts receivable can now be factored on an open marketplace at www.receivablesxchange.com.

One of the newest types of factoring is called *credit card receivable funding* or *business cash advances*. The way business cash advances work is that a company goes to a factor and receives cash up front. From that point on, a portion of each credit card sale (perhaps 6 to 8 percent) is routed directly to the factor by the credit card processor until the loan is paid off. This arrangement may be attractive to small businesses in particular, but it can be expensive. The typical premium on the advance is about 35 percent—meaning that with a $100,000 loan, $135,000 must be repaid within a relatively short period.

Purchase order financing (or just PO financing) is a popular form of factoring used by small and midsize companies. In a typical scenario, a small business receives a firm order from a customer, but it doesn't have sufficient funds to pay the supplier who manufactures the product. With PO financing, the factor pays the supplier. When the sale is completed and the seller is paid, the factor is repaid. A typical interest rate on purchase order factoring is 3.5 percent for the first 30 days, then 1.25 percent every 10 days after, an annual interest rate above 50 percent.

| Cost of Factoring | EXAMPLE 18.3 |

For the year just ended, LuLu's Pies had an average of $50,000 in accounts receivable. Credit sales were $500,000. LuLu's factors its receivables by discounting them 3 percent—in other words, by selling them for 97 cents on the dollar. What is the effective interest rate on this source of short-term financing?

To determine the interest rate, we first have to know the accounts receivable, or average collection, period. During the year, LuLu's turned over its receivables $500,000/50,000 = 10 times. The average collection period is therefore 365/10 = 36.5 days.

The interest paid here is a form of discount interest (discussed in Chapter 6). In this case, LuLu's is paying 3 cents in interest on every 97 cents of financing. The interest rate per 36.5 days is thus .03/.97 = 3.09%. The APR is 10 × 3.09% = 30.9%, but the effective annual rate is:

$$EAR = 1.0309^{10} - 1 = 35.6\%$$

Factoring is a relatively expensive source of money in this case.

We should note that, if the factor takes on the risk of default by a buyer, then the factor is providing insurance as well as immediate cash. More generally, the factor essentially takes over the firm's credit operations. This can result in a significant saving. The interest rate we calculated is therefore overstated, particularly if default is a significant possibility.

Inventory Loans   **Inventory loans**, short-term loans to purchase inventory, come in three basic forms: blanket inventory liens, trust receipts, and field warehouse financing:

inventory loan
A secured short-term loan to purchase inventory.

1. *Blanket inventory lien:* A blanket lien gives the lender a lien against all the borrower's inventories (the blanket "covers" everything).
2. *Trust receipt:* A trust receipt is a device by which the borrower holds specific inventory in "trust" for the lender. Automobile dealer financing, for example, is done by use of trust receipts. This type of secured financing is also called *floor planning*, in reference to inventory on the showroom floor. However, it is somewhat cumbersome to use trust receipts for, say, wheat grain.
3. *Field warehouse financing:* In field warehouse financing, a public warehouse company (an independent company that specializes in inventory management) acts as a control agent to supervise the inventory for the lender.

OTHER SOURCES

A variety of other sources of short-term funds are employed by corporations. Two of the most important are *commercial paper* and *trade credit.*

Commercial paper consists of short-term notes issued by large, highly rated firms. Typically, these notes are of short maturity, ranging up to 270 days (beyond that limit, the firm must file a registration statement with the SEC). Because the firm issues these directly and because it usually backs the issue with a special bank line of credit, the interest rate the firm obtains is often significantly below the rate a bank would charge for a direct loan.

Another option available to a firm is to increase the accounts payable period; in other words, the firm may take longer to pay its bills. This amounts to borrowing from suppliers in the form of trade credit. This is an extremely important form of financing for smaller businesses in particular. As we discuss in Chapter 20, a firm using trade credit may end up paying a much higher price for what it purchases, so this can be a very expensive source of financing.

Concept Questions

18.5a What are the two basic forms of short-term financing?
18.5b Describe two types of secured loans.

18.6 A Short-Term Financial Plan

To illustrate a completed short-term financial plan, we will assume that Fun Toys arranges to borrow any needed funds on a short-term basis. The interest rate is a 20 percent APR, and it is calculated on a quarterly basis. From Chapter 6, we know that the rate is 20%/4 = 5% per quarter. We will assume that Fun Toys starts the year with no short-term debt.

From Table 18.5, we know that Fun Toys has a second-quarter deficit of $60 million. The firm will have to borrow this amount. Net cash inflow in the following quarter is $55 million. The firm will now have to pay $60 million × .05 = $3 million in interest out of that, leaving $52 million to reduce the borrowing.

Fun Toys still owes $60 million − 52 million = $8 million at the end of the third quarter. Interest in the last quarter will thus be $8 million × .05 = $.4 million. In addition, net inflows in the last quarter are −$15 million; so the company will have to borrow a total of $15.4 million, bringing total borrowing up to $15.4 million + 8 million = $23.4 million. Table 18.6 extends Table 18.5 to include these calculations.

Notice that the ending short-term debt is just equal to the cumulative deficit for the entire year, $20 million, plus the interest paid during the year, $3 million + .4 million = $3.4 million, for a total of $23.4 million.

Our plan is very simple. For example, we ignored the fact that the interest paid on the short-term debt is tax deductible. We also ignored the fact that the cash surplus in the first quarter would earn some interest (which would be taxable). We could add on a number of refinements. Even so, our plan highlights the fact that in about 90 days, Fun Toys will need to borrow $60 million or so on a short-term basis. It's time to start lining up the source of the funds.

Our plan also illustrates that financing the firm's short-term needs will cost about $3.4 million in interest (before taxes) for the year. This is a starting point for Fun Toys to begin evaluating alternatives to reduce this expense. For example, can the $100 million planned expenditure be postponed or spread out? At 5 percent per quarter, short-term credit is expensive.

Also, if Fun Toys' sales are expected to keep growing, then the deficit of $20 million plus will probably also keep growing, and the need for additional financing will be permanent. Fun Toys may wish to think about raising money on a long-term basis to cover this need.

TABLE 18.6

Short-Term Financial Plan for Fun Toys (in Millions)

	Q1	Q2	Q3	Q4
Beginning cash balance	$20	$ 60	$10	$10.0
Net cash inflow	40	− 110	55	− 15.0
New short-term borrowing	—	60	—	15.4
Interest on short-term borrowing	—	—	− 3	− .4
Short-term borrowing repaid	—	—	− 52	—
Ending cash balance	$60	$ 10	$10	$10.0
Minimum cash balance	− 10	− 10	− 10	− 10.0
Cumulative surplus (deficit)	$50	$ 0	$ 0	$ .0
Beginning short-term borrowing	0	0	60	8.0
Change in short-term debt	0	60	− 52	15.4
Ending short-term debt	$ 0	$ 60	$ 8	$23.4

Visit us at www.mhhe.com/rwj

Concept Questions

18.6a In Table 18.6, does Fun Toys have a projected deficit or surplus?

18.6b In Table 18.6, what would happen to Fun Toys' deficit or surplus if the minimum cash balance was reduced to $5?

Summary and Conclusions   18.7

1. This chapter has introduced the management of short-term finance. Short-term finance involves short-lived assets and liabilities. We traced and examined the short-term sources and uses of cash as they appear on the firm's financial statements. We saw how current assets and current liabilities arise in the short-term operating activities and the cash cycle of the firm.

2. Managing short-term cash flows involves the minimizing of costs. The two major costs are carrying costs, the return forgone by keeping too much invested in short-term assets such as cash, and shortage costs, the cost of running out of short-term assets. The objective of managing short-term finance and doing short-term financial planning is to find the optimal trade-off between these two costs.

3. In an ideal economy, the firm could perfectly predict its short-term uses and sources of cash, and net working capital could be kept at zero. In the real world we live in, cash and net working capital provide a buffer that lets the firm meet its ongoing obligations. The financial manager seeks the optimal level of each of the current assets.

4. The financial manager can use the cash budget to identify short-term financial needs. The cash budget tells the manager what borrowing is required or what lending will be possible in the short run. The firm has available to it a number of possible ways of acquiring funds to meet short-term shortfalls, including unsecured and secured loans.

CONNECT TO FINANCE

If you are using *Connect™ Finance* in your course, get online to take a Practice Test, check out study tools, and find out where you need additional practice.

▼ Chapter 18 Short-Term Finance and Planning		Section 18.2	
18.1 Tracing Cash and Net Working Capital	eBook	Study	Practice
18.2 The Operating Cycle and the Cash Cycle	eBook	Study	Practice
18.3 Some Aspects of Short-Term Financial Policy	eBook	Study	Practice
18.4 The Cash Budget	eBook	Study	Practice
18.5 Short-Term Borrowing	eBook	Study	Practice
18.6 A Short-Term Financial Plan	eBook	Study	Practice

Can you answer the following questions?

Section 18.1 Give an example of an action that will increase cash. (LO 18-4)

Section 18.2 A firm has an operating cycle of 64 days and a cash cycle of 21 days. How long will the firm's accounts payable period be if the firm decides to increase its accounts payable period by three days? (LO 18-1)

Section 18.4 Galaxy Sales has a beginning cash balance of $25. During the quarter, the firm had a net cash inflow of $20. What is the cumulative surplus at the end of the quarter if the minimum cash balance is $10? (LO 18-3)

Section 18.5 What type of lending relies on a control agent to supervise inventory on behalf of a lender? (LO 18-3)

Log on to find out!

CHAPTER REVIEW AND SELF-TEST PROBLEMS

18.1 The Operating and Cash Cycles Consider the following financial statement information for the Route 66 Company:

Item	Beginning	Ending
Inventory	$1,273	$1,401
Accounts receivable	3,782	3,368
Accounts payable	1,795	2,025
Net sales	$14,750	
Cost of goods sold	11,375	

Calculate the operating and cash cycles.

18.2 Cash Balance for Greenwell Corporation The Greenwell Corporation has a 60-day average collection period and wishes to maintain a $160 million minimum cash balance. Based on this and the information given in the following cash budget, complete the cash budget. What conclusions do you draw?

GREENWELL CORPORATION Cash Budget (in millions)				
	Q1	**Q2**	**Q3**	**Q4**
Beginning receivables	$240			
Sales	150	$165	$180	$135
Cash collections				
Ending receivables				
Total cash collections				
Total cash disbursements	170	160	185	190
Net cash inflow				
Beginning cash balance	$ 45			
Net cash inflow				
Ending cash balance				
Minimum cash balance				
Cumulative surplus (deficit)				

Visit us at www.mhhe.com/rwj

ANSWERS TO CHAPTER REVIEW AND SELF-TEST PROBLEMS

18.1 We first need the turnover ratios. Note that we use the average values for all balance sheet items and that we base the inventory and payables turnover measures on cost of goods sold:

$$\text{Inventory turnover} = \$11,375/[(1,273 + 1,401)/2] = 8.51 \text{ times}$$
$$\text{Receivables turnover} = \$14,750/[(3,782 + 3,368)/2] = 4.13 \text{ times}$$
$$\text{Payables turnover} = \$11,375/[(1,795 + 2,025)/2] = 5.96 \text{ times}$$

We can now calculate the various periods:

$$\text{Inventory period} = 365 \text{ days}/8.51 \text{ times} = 42.89 \text{ days}$$
$$\text{Receivables period} = 365 \text{ days}/4.13 \text{ times} = 88.38 \text{ days}$$
$$\text{Payables period} = 365 \text{ days}/5.96 \text{ times} = 61.24 \text{ days}$$

So the time it takes to acquire inventory and sell it is about 43 days. Collection takes another 88 days, and the operating cycle is thus 43 + 88 = 131 days. The cash cycle is thus 131 days less the payables period: 131 − 61 = 70 days.

18.2 Because Greenwell has a 60-day collection period, only sales made in the first 30 days of the quarter will be collected in the same quarter. Total cash collections in the first quarter will thus equal 30/90 = ⅓ of sales plus beginning receivables, or ⅓ × $150 + 240 = $290. Ending receivables for the first quarter (and the second-quarter beginning receivables) are the other ⅔ of sales, or ⅔ × $150 = $100. The remaining calculations are straightforward, and the completed budget follows:

GREENWELL CORPORATION Cash Budget (in millions)				
	Q1	**Q2**	**Q3**	**Q4**
Beginning receivables	$240	$100	$110	$120
Sales	150	165	180	135
Cash collections	290	155	170	165
Ending receivables	$100	$110	$120	$ 90
Total cash collections	$290	$155	$170	$165
Total cash disbursements	170	160	185	190
Net cash inflow	$120	−$ 5	−$ 15	−$ 25
Beginning cash balance	$ 45	$165	$160	$145
Net cash inflow	120	− 5	− 15	− 25
Ending cash balance	$165	$160	$145	$120
Minimum cash balance	− 160	− 160	− 160	− 160
Cumulative surplus (deficit)	$ 5	$ 0	−$ 15	−$ 40

The primary conclusion from this schedule is that, beginning in the third quarter, Greenwell's cash surplus becomes a cash deficit. By the end of the year, Greenwell will need to arrange for $40 million in cash beyond what will be available.

CONCEPTS REVIEW AND CRITICAL THINKING QUESTIONS

1. **Operating Cycle [LO1]** What are some of the characteristics of a firm with a long operating cycle?

2. **Cash Cycle [LO1]** What are some of the characteristics of a firm with a long cash cycle?

Visit us at www.mhhe.com/rwj

3. **Sources and Uses [LO4]** For the year just ended, you have gathered the following information about the Holly Corporation:

   a. A $200 dividend was paid.

   b. Accounts payable increased by $500.

   c. Fixed asset purchases were $900.

   d. Inventories increased by $625.

   e. Long-term debt decreased by $1,200.

   Label each as a source or use of cash and describe its effect on the firm's cash balance.

4. **Cost of Current Assets [LO2]** Loftis Manufacturing, Inc., has recently installed a just-in-time (JIT) inventory system. Describe the effect this is likely to have on the company's carrying costs, shortage costs, and operating cycle.

5. **Operating and Cash Cycles [LO1]** Is it possible for a firm's cash cycle to be longer than its operating cycle? Explain why or why not.

   Use the following information to answer Questions 6–10: Last month, BlueSky Airline announced that it would stretch out its bill payments to 45 days from 30 days. The reason given was that the company wanted to "control costs and optimize cash flow." The increased payables period will be in effect for all of the company's 4,000 suppliers.

6. **Operating and Cash Cycles [LO1]** What impact did this change in payables policy have on BlueSky's operating cycle? Its cash cycle?

7. **Operating and Cash Cycles [LO1]** What impact did the announcement have on BlueSky's suppliers?

8. **Corporate Ethics [LO1]** Is it ethical for large firms to unilaterally lengthen their payables periods, particularly when dealing with smaller suppliers?

9. **Payables Period [LO1]** Why don't all firms simply increase their payables periods to shorten their cash cycles?

10. **Payables Period [LO1]** BlueSky lengthened its payables period to "control costs and optimize cash flow." Exactly what is the cash benefit to BlueSky from this change?

QUESTIONS AND PROBLEMS

BASIC
(Questions 1–12)

1. **Changes in the Cash Account [LO4]** Indicate the impact of the following corporate actions on cash, using the letter *I* for an increase, *D* for a decrease, or *N* when no change occurs:

   a. A dividend is paid with funds received from a sale of debt.

   b. Real estate is purchased and paid for with short-term debt.

   c. Inventory is bought on credit.

   d. A short-term bank loan is repaid.

   e. Next year's taxes are prepaid.

   f. Preferred stock is redeemed.

   g. Sales are made on credit.

   h. Interest on long-term debt is paid.

   i. Payments for previous sales are collected.

j. The accounts payable balance is reduced.

k. A dividend is paid.

l. Production supplies are purchased and paid for with a short-term note.

m. Utility bills are paid.

n. Cash is paid for raw materials purchased for inventory.

o. Marketable securities are sold.

2. **Cash Equation [LO3]** Saunders Corp. has a book net worth of $13,205. Long-term debt is $8,200. Net working capital, other than cash, is $4,205. Fixed assets are $17,380. How much cash does the company have? If current liabilities are $1,630, what are current assets?

3. **Changes in the Operating Cycle [LO1]** Indicate the effect that the following will have on the operating cycle. Use the letter *I* to indicate an increase, the letter *D* for a decrease, and the letter *N* for no change:

a. Average receivables goes up.

b. Credit repayment times for customers are increased.

c. Inventory turnover goes from 3 times to 6 times.

d. Payables turnover goes from 6 times to 11 times.

e. Receivables turnover goes from 7 times to 9 times.

f. Payments to suppliers are accelerated.

4. **Changes in Cycles [LO1]** Indicate the impact of the following on the cash and operating cycles, respectively. Use the letter *I* to indicate an increase, the letter *D* for a decrease, and the letter *N* for no change:

a. The terms of cash discounts offered to customers are made less favorable.

b. The cash discounts offered by suppliers are decreased; thus, payments are made earlier.

c. An increased number of customers begin to pay in cash instead of with credit.

d. Fewer raw materials than usual are purchased.

e. A greater percentage of raw material purchases are paid for with credit.

f. More finished goods are produced for inventory instead of for order.

5. **Calculating Cash Collections [LO3]** The Morning Jolt Coffee Company has projected the following quarterly sales amounts for the coming year:

	Q1	Q2	Q3	Q4
Sales	$720	$750	$830	$910

a. Accounts receivable at the beginning of the year are $310. Morning Jolt has a 45-day collection period. Calculate cash collections in each of the four quarters by completing the following:

	Q1	Q2	Q3	Q4
Beginning receivables				
Sales				
Cash collections				
Ending receivables				

b. Rework (a) assuming a collection period of 60 days.

c. Rework (a) assuming a collection period of 30 days.

Visit us at www.mhhe.com/rwj

Visit us at www.mhhe.com/rwj

6. Calculating Cycles [LO1] Consider the following financial statement information for the Schwertzec Corporation:

Item	Beginning	Ending
Inventory	$10,583	$12,412
Accounts receivable	5,130	5,340
Accounts payable	7,205	7,630
Credit sales	$97,381	
Cost of goods sold	69,382	

Calculate the operating and cash cycles. How do you interpret your answer?

7. Factoring Receivables [LO3] Your firm has an average collection period of 29 days. Current practice is to factor all receivables immediately at a 1.25 percent discount. What is the effective cost of borrowing in this case? Assume that default is extremely unlikely.

8. Calculating Payments [LO3] Iron Man Products has projected the following sales for the coming year:

	Q1	Q2	Q3	Q4
Sales	$790	$870	$830	$930

Sales in the year following this one are projected to be 15 percent greater in each quarter.

a. Calculate payments to suppliers assuming that Iron Man places orders during each quarter equal to 30 percent of projected sales for the next quarter. Assume that Iron Man pays immediately. What is the payables period in this case?

	Q1	Q2	Q3	Q4
Payment of accounts	$	$	$	$

b. Rework (a) assuming a 90-day payables period.

c. Rework (a) assuming a 60-day payables period.

9. Calculating Payments [LO3] The Torrey Pine Corporation's purchases from suppliers in a quarter are equal to 75 percent of the next quarter's forecast sales. The payables period is 60 days. Wages, taxes, and other expenses are 20 percent of sales, and interest and dividends are $90 per quarter. No capital expenditures are planned. Projected quarterly sales are shown here:

	Q1	Q2	Q3	Q4
Sales	$1,930	$2,275	$1,810	$1,520

Sales for the first quarter of the following year are projected at $2,150. Calculate the company's cash outlays by completing the following:

	Q1	Q2	Q3	Q4
Payment of accounts				
Wages, taxes, other expenses				
Long-term financing expenses (interest and dividends)				
Total				

10. **Calculating Cash Collections [LO3]** The following is the sales budget for Kulp, Inc., for the first quarter of 2012:

	January	February	March
Sales budget	$195,000	$215,000	$238,000

Credit sales are collected as follows:

65 percent in the month of the sale

20 percent in the month after the sale

15 percent in the second month after the sale

The accounts receivable balance at the end of the previous quarter was $86,000 ($59,000 of which was uncollected December sales).

a. Compute the sales for November.

b. Compute the sales for December.

c. Compute the cash collections from sales for each month from January through March.

11. **Calculating the Cash Budget [LO3]** Here are some important figures from the budget of Nashville Nougats, Inc., for the second quarter of 2012:

	April	May	June
Credit sales	$312,000	$291,200	$350,400
Credit purchases	118,240	141,040	166,800
Cash disbursements			
Wages, taxes, and expenses	43,040	10,800	62,640
Interest	10,480	10,480	10,480
Equipment purchases	74,000	135,000	0

The company predicts that 5 percent of its credit sales will never be collected, 35 percent of its sales will be collected in the month of the sale, and the remaining 60 percent will be collected in the following month. Credit purchases will be paid in the month following the purchase.

In March 2012, credit sales were $196,000 and credit purchases were $134,400. Using this information, complete the following cash budget:

	April	May	June
Beginning cash balance	$112,000		
Cash receipts			
Cash collections from credit sales			
Total cash available			
Cash disbursements			
Purchases			
Wages, taxes, and expenses			
Interest			
Equipment purchases			
Total cash disbursements			
Ending cash balance			

Visit us at www.mhhe.com/rwj

12. **Sources and Uses [LO4]** Below are the most recent balance sheets for Country Kettles, Inc. Excluding accumulated depreciation, determine whether each item is a source or a use of cash and the amount:

COUNTRY KETTLES, INC. Balance Sheet December 31, 2011		
	2010	**2011**
Assets		
Cash	$ 30,400	$ 29,520
Accounts receivable	69,904	73,344
Inventories	60,800	63,736
Property, plant, and equipment	147,000	157,180
Less: Accumulated depreciation	45,730	52,280
Total assets	$262,374	$271,500
Liabilities and Equity		
Accounts payable	$ 44,994	$ 47,118
Accrued expenses	6,280	5,632
Long-term debt	25,600	28,000
Common stock	16,000	20,000
Accumulated retained earnings	$169,500	$170,750
Total liabilities and equity	$262,374	$271,500

INTERMEDIATE
(Questions 13–16)

13. **Costs of Borrowing [LO3]** You've worked out a line of credit arrangement that allows you to borrow up to $50 million at any time. The interest rate is .53 percent per month. In addition, 5 percent of the amount that you borrow must be deposited in a non-interest-bearing account. Assume that your bank uses compound interest on its line of credit loans.

 a. What is the effective annual interest rate on this lending arrangement?

 b. Suppose you need $15 million today and you repay it in six months. How much interest will you pay?

14. **Costs of Borrowing [LO3]** A bank offers your firm a revolving credit arrangement for up to $70 million at an interest rate of 1.9 percent per quarter. The bank also requires you to maintain a compensating balance of 4 percent against the *unused* portion of the credit line, to be deposited in a non-interest-bearing account. Assume you have a short-term investment account at the bank that pays 1.05 percent per quarter, and assume that the bank uses compound interest on its revolving credit loans.

 a. What is your effective annual interest rate (an opportunity cost) on the revolving credit arrangement if your firm does not use it during the year?

 b. What is your effective annual interest rate on the lending arrangement if you borrow $45 million immediately and repay it in one year?

 c. What is your effective annual interest rate if you borrow $70 million immediately and repay it in one year?

15. **Calculating the Cash Budget [LO3]** Wildcat, Inc., has estimated sales (in millions) for the next four quarters as follows:

	Q1	Q2	Q3	Q4
Sales	$160	$175	$190	$215

Visit us at www.mhhe.com/rwj

Sales for the first quarter of the year after this one are projected at $170 million. Accounts receivable at the beginning of the year were $68 million. Wildcat has a 45-day collection period.

Wildcat's purchases from suppliers in a quarter are equal to 45 percent of the next quarter's forecast sales, and suppliers are normally paid in 36 days. Wages, taxes, and other expenses run about 25 percent of sales. Interest and dividends are $12 million per quarter.

Wildcat plans a major capital outlay in the second quarter of $75 million. Finally, the company started the year with a $49 million cash balance and wishes to maintain a $30 million minimum balance.

a. Complete a cash budget for Wildcat by filling in the following:

WILDCAT, INC. Cash Budget (in millions)	Q1	Q2	Q3	Q4
Target cash balance	$30			
Net cash inflow				
Ending cash balance				
Minimum cash balance	30			
Cumulative surplus (deficit)				

b. Assume that Wildcat can borrow any needed funds on a short-term basis at a rate of 3 percent per quarter and can invest any excess funds in short-term marketable securities at a rate of 2 percent per quarter. Prepare a short-term financial plan by filling in the following schedule. What is the net cash cost (total interest paid minus total investment income earned) for the year?

WILDCAT, INC. Short-Term Financial Plan (in millions)	Q1	Q2	Q3	Q4
Target cash balance	$30			
Net cash inflow				
New short-term investments				
Income from short-term investments				
Short-term investments sold				
New short-term borrowing				
Interest on short-term borrowing				
Short-term borrowing repaid				
Ending cash balance				
Minimum cash balance				
Cumulative surplus (deficit)	30			
Beginning short-term investments				
Ending short-term investments				
Beginning short-term debt				
Ending short-term debt				

16. Cash Management Policy [LO3] Rework Problem 15 assuming:

   a. Wildcat maintains a minimum cash balance of $40 million.

   b. Wildcat maintains a minimum cash balance of $20 million.

Based on your answers in (a) and (b), do you think the firm can boost its profit by changing its cash management policy? Are there other factors that must be considered as well? Explain.

CHALLENGE
(Questions 17–18)

17. **Costs of Borrowing [LO3]** In exchange for a $400 million fixed commitment line of credit, your firm has agreed to do the following:

1. Pay 2.1 percent per quarter on any funds actually borrowed.
2. Maintain a 4 percent compensating balance on any funds actually borrowed.
3. Pay an up-front commitment fee of .150 percent of the amount of the line.

Based on this information, answer the following:

a. Ignoring the commitment fee, what is the effective annual interest rate on this line of credit?

b. Suppose your firm immediately uses $130 million of the line and pays it off in one year. What is the effective annual interest rate on this $130 million loan?

18. **Costs of Borrowing [LO3]** Come and Go Bank offers your firm a *discount* interest loan at 9 percent for up to $25 million and, in addition, requires you to maintain a 5 percent compensating balance against the amount borrowed. What is the effective annual interest rate on this lending arrangement?

MINICASE

Piepkorn Manufacturing Working Capital Management

You have recently been hired by Piepkorn Manufacturing to work in the newly established treasury department. Piepkorn Manufacturing is a small company that produces cardboard boxes in a variety of sizes for different purchasers. Gary Piepkorn, the owner of the company, works primarily in the sales and production areas of the company. Currently, the company puts all receivables in one shoe box and all payables in another. Because of the disorganized system, the finance area needs work, and that's what you've been brought in to do.

The company currently has a cash balance of $240,000, and it plans to purchase new box-folding machinery in the fourth quarter at a cost of $445,000. The machinery will be purchased with cash because of a discount offered. The company's policy is to maintain a minimum cash balance of $125,000. All sales and purchases are made on credit.

Gary Piepkorn has projected the following gross sales for each of the next four quarters:

	Q1	Q2	Q3	Q4
Gross sales	$1,240,000	$1,310,000	$1,370,000	$1,450,000

Also, gross sales for the first quarter of next year are projected at $1,290,000. Piepkorn currently has an accounts receivable period of 53 days and an accounts receivable balance of $630,000. Twenty percent of the accounts receivable balance is from a company that has just entered bankruptcy, and it is likely this portion of the accounts receivable will never be collected.

Piepkorn typically orders 50 percent of next quarter's projected gross sales in the current quarter, and suppliers are typically paid in 42 days. Wages, taxes, and other costs run about 30 percent of gross sales. The company has a quarterly interest payment of $130,000 on its long-term debt.

The company uses a local bank for its short-term financial needs. It pays 1.5 percent per quarter in all short-term borrowing and maintains a money market account that pays 1 percent per quarter on all short-term deposits.

Gary has asked you to prepare a cash budget and short-term financial plan for the company under the current policies. He has also asked you to prepare additional plans based on changes in several inputs.

QUESTIONS

1. Use the numbers given to complete the cash budget and short-term financial plan.

2. Rework the cash budget and short-term financial plan assuming Piepkorn changes to a minimum balance of $100,000.

3. You have looked at the credit policy offered by your competitors and have determined that the industry standard credit policy is 1/10, net 40.* The discount will begin to be offered on the first day of the first quarter. You want to examine how this credit policy would affect the cash budget and short-term financial plan. If this credit policy is implemented, you believe that 40 percent of all sales

*If you are not familiar with credit policy quotations, see Chapter 20.

will take advantage of it, and the accounts receivable period will decline to 36 days. Rework the cash budget and short-term financial plan under the new credit policy and a minimum cash balance of $100,000. What interest rate are you effectively offering customers?

4. You have talked to the company's suppliers about the credit terms Piepkorn receives. Currently, the company receives terms of net 45. The suppliers have stated that they would offer new credit terms of 1.5/15, net 40. The discount would begin to be offered on the first day of the first quarter. What interest rate are the suppliers offering the company? Rework the cash budget and short-term financial plan assuming you take the credit terms on all orders and the minimum cash balance is $100,000. Also assume that Piepkorn offers the credit terms in the previous question.

PIEPKORN MANUFACTURING Cash Budget				
	Q1	**Q2**	**Q3**	**Q4**
Target cash balance				
Net cash inflow				
Ending cash balance				
Minimum cash balance				
Cumulative surplus (deficit)				

PIEPKORN MANUFACTURING Short-Term Financial Plan				
	Q1	**Q2**	**Q3**	**Q4**
Target cash balance				
Net cash inflow				
New short-term investments				
Income from short-term investments				
Short-term investments sold				
New short-term borrowing				
Interest on short-term borrowing				
Short-term borrowing repaid				
Ending cash balance				
Minimum cash balance				
Cumulative surplus (deficit)				
Beginning short-term investments				
Ending short-term investments				
Beginning short-term debt				
Ending short-term debt				

Visit us at www.mhhe.com/rwj

19

CASH AND LIQUIDITY MANAGEMENT

IN 2011, NONFINANCIAL S&P 500 companies held cash equivalent to about 8 percent of their market caps, on average. Tech giants Cisco and Microsoft, for example, held about $40.2 billion and $41.3 billion in cash, respectively. In Cisco's case, the cash amounted to well over 40 percent of the company's total market cap. Other companies also had huge amounts of cash, with investment bank Goldman Sachs leading the way. Goldman's cash hoard of almost $100 billion was much bigger than the company's total market cap. In other words, Goldman's cash per share exceeded its stock price!

LEARNING OBJECTIVES

After studying this chapter, you should understand:

LO1 The importance of float and how it affects the cash balances.

LO2 How firms manage their cash and some of the collection, concentration, and disbursement techniques used.

LO3 The advantages and disadvantages to holding cash and some of the ways to invest idle cash.

This chapter is about how firms manage cash. The basic objective in cash management is to keep the investment in cash as low as possible while still keeping the firm operating efficiently and effectively. This goal usually reduces to the dictum "Collect early and pay late." Accordingly, we discuss ways of accelerating collections and managing disbursements.

In addition, firms must invest temporarily idle cash in short-term marketable securities. As we discuss in various places, these securities can be bought and sold in the financial markets. As a group, they have very little default risk, and most are highly marketable. There are different types of these so-called money market securities, and we discuss a few of the most important ones.

Reasons for Holding Cash

19.1

John Maynard Keynes, in his classic work *The General Theory of Employment, Interest, and Money*, identified three motives for liquidity: the speculative motive, the precautionary motive, and the transaction motive. We discuss these next.

THE SPECULATIVE AND PRECAUTIONARY MOTIVES

The **speculative motive** is the need to hold cash in order to be able to take advantage of, for example, bargain purchases that might arise, attractive interest rates, and (in the case of international firms) favorable exchange rate fluctuations.

For most firms, reserve borrowing ability and marketable securities can be used to satisfy speculative motives. Thus, there might be a speculative motive for maintaining liquidity, but not necessarily for holding cash per se. Think of it this way: If you have a credit card with a very large credit limit, then you can probably take advantage of any unusual bargains that come along without carrying any cash.

This is also true, to a lesser extent, for precautionary motives. The **precautionary motive** is the need for a safety supply to act as a financial reserve. Once again, there probably is a precautionary motive for maintaining liquidity. However, given that the value of money market instruments is relatively certain and that instruments such as T-bills are extremely liquid, there is no real need to hold substantial amounts of cash for precautionary purposes.

> **speculative motive**
> The need to hold cash to take advantage of additional investment opportunities, such as bargain purchases.

> **precautionary motive**
> The need to hold cash as a safety margin to act as a financial reserve.

THE TRANSACTION MOTIVE

Cash is needed to satisfy the **transaction motive**, the need to have cash on hand to pay bills. Transaction-related needs come from the normal disbursement and collection activities of the firm. The disbursement of cash includes the payment of wages and salaries, trade debts, taxes, and dividends.

Cash is collected from product sales, the selling of assets, and new financing. The cash inflows (collections) and outflows (disbursements) are not perfectly synchronized, and some level of cash holdings is necessary to serve as a buffer.

As electronic funds transfers and other high-speed, "paperless" payment mechanisms continue to develop, even the transaction demand for cash may all but disappear. Even if it does, however, there will still be a demand for liquidity and a need to manage it efficiently.

> **transaction motive**
> The need to hold cash to satisfy normal disbursement and collection activities associated with a firm's ongoing operations.

COMPENSATING BALANCES

Compensating balances are another reason to hold cash. As we discussed in the previous chapter, cash balances are kept at commercial banks to compensate for banking services the firm receives. A minimum compensating balance requirement may impose a lower limit on the level of cash a firm holds.

COSTS OF HOLDING CASH

When a firm holds cash in excess of some necessary minimum, it incurs an opportunity cost. The opportunity cost of excess cash (held in currency or bank deposits) is the interest income that could be earned in the next best use, such as investment in marketable securities.

Given the opportunity cost of holding cash, why would a firm hold cash in excess of its compensating balance requirements? The answer is that a cash balance must be maintained to provide the liquidity necessary for transaction needs—paying bills. If the firm maintains too small a cash balance, it may run out of cash. If this happens, the firm may have to raise cash on a short-term basis. This could involve, for example, selling marketable securities or borrowing.

Activities such as selling marketable securities and borrowing involve various costs. As we've discussed, holding cash has an opportunity cost. To determine the appropriate cash balance, the firm must weigh the benefits of holding cash against these costs. We discuss this subject in more detail in the sections that follow.

CASH MANAGEMENT VERSUS LIQUIDITY MANAGEMENT

Before we move on, we should note that it is important to distinguish between true cash management and a more general subject, liquidity management. The distinction is a source of confusion because the word *cash* is used in practice in two different ways. First of all, it has its literal meaning: actual cash on hand. However, financial managers frequently use the word to describe a firm's holdings of cash along with its marketable securities, and marketable securities are sometimes called *cash equivalents* or *near-cash*. In our discussion of Cisco's and Microsoft's cash positions at the beginning of the chapter, for example, what was actually being described was their total cash and cash equivalents.

The distinction between liquidity management and cash management is straightforward. Liquidity management concerns the optimal quantity of liquid assets a firm should have on hand, and it is one particular aspect of the current asset management policies we discussed in our previous chapter. Cash management is much more closely related to optimizing mechanisms for collecting and disbursing cash, and it is this subject that we primarily focus on in this chapter.

Concept Questions

19.1a What is the transaction motive, and how does it lead firms to hold cash?

19.1b What is the cost to the firm of holding excess cash?

19.2 Understanding Float

As you no doubt know, the amount of money you have according to your checkbook can be very different from the amount of money that your bank thinks you have. The reason is that some of the checks you have written haven't yet been presented to the bank for payment. The same thing is true for a business. The cash balance that a firm shows on its books is called the firm's *book*, or *ledger, balance*. The balance shown in its bank account as available to spend is called its *available*, or *collected, balance*. The difference between the available balance and the ledger balance, called the **float**, represents the net effect of checks in the process of *clearing* (moving through the banking system).

float
The difference between book cash and bank cash, representing the net effect of checks in the process of clearing.

DISBURSEMENT FLOAT

Checks written by a firm generate *disbursement float*, causing a decrease in the firm's book balance but no change in its available balance. For example, suppose General Mechanics, Inc. (GMI), currently has $100,000 on deposit with its bank. On June 8, it buys some raw materials and pays with a check for $100,000. The company's book balance is immediately reduced by $100,000 as a result.

GMI's bank, however, will not find out about this check until it is presented to GMI's bank for payment on, say, June 14. Until the check is presented, the firm's available balance is greater than its book balance by $100,000. In other words, before June 8, GMI has a zero float:

Float = Firm's available balance − Firm's book balance
= $100,000 − 100,000
= $0

GMI's position from June 8 to June 14 is:

Disbursement float = Firm's available balance − Firm's book balance
= $100,000 − 0
= $100,000

While the check is clearing, GMI has a balance with the bank of $100,000. It can obtain the benefit of this cash during this period. For example, the available balance could be temporarily invested in marketable securities and thus earn some interest. We will return to this subject a little later.

COLLECTION FLOAT AND NET FLOAT

Checks received by the firm create *collection float*. Collection float increases book balances but does not immediately change available balances. For example, suppose GMI receives a check from a customer for $100,000 on October 8. Assume, as before, that the company has $100,000 deposited at its bank and a zero float. It deposits the check and increases its book balance by $100,000 to $200,000. However, the additional cash is not available to GMI until its bank has presented the check to the customer's bank and received $100,000. This will occur on, say, October 14. In the meantime, the cash position at GMI will reflect a collection float of $100,000. We can summarize these events. Before October 8, GMI's position is:

Float = Firm's available balance − Firm's book balance
= $100,000 − 100,000
= $0

GMI's position from October 8 to October 14 is:

Collection float = Firm's available balance − Firm's book balance
= $100,000 − 200,000
= −$100,000

In general, a firm's payment (disbursement) activities generate disbursement float, and its collection activities generate collection float. The net effect—that is, the sum of the total collection and disbursement floats—is the net float. The net float at a point in time is simply the overall difference between the firm's available balance and its book balance. If the net float is positive, then the firm's disbursement float exceeds its collection float, and its available balance exceeds its book balance. If the available balance is less than the book balance, then the firm has a net collection float.

A firm should be concerned with its net float and available balance more than with its book balance. If a financial manager knows that a check written by the company will not clear for several days, that manager will be able to keep a lower cash balance at the bank than might be possible otherwise. This can generate a great deal of money.

For example, take the case of ExxonMobil. The average daily sales of ExxonMobil are about $1 billion. If ExxonMobil's collections could be sped up by a single day, then Exxon-Mobil could free up $1 billion for investing. At a relatively modest .01 percent daily rate, the interest earned would be on the order of $100,000 *per day*.

EXAMPLE 19.1   Staying Afloat

Suppose you have $5,000 on deposit. One day, you write a check for $1,000 to pay for books, and you deposit $2,000. What are your disbursement, collection, and net floats?

After you write the $1,000 check, you show a balance of $4,000 on your books, but the bank shows $5,000 while the check is clearing. The difference is a disbursement float of $1,000.

After you deposit the $2,000 check, you show a balance of $6,000. Your available balance doesn't rise until the check clears. This results in a collection float of −$2,000. Your net float is the sum of the collection and disbursement floats, or −$1,000.

Overall, you show $6,000 on your books. The bank shows a $7,000 balance, but only $5,000 is available because your deposit has not been cleared. The discrepancy between your available balance and your book balance is the net float (−$1,000), and it is bad for you. If you write another check for $5,500, there may not be sufficient available funds to cover it, and it might bounce. This is why financial managers have to be more concerned with available balances than book balances.

For a real-world example of float management services, visit www.carreker.fiserv.com.

FLOAT MANAGEMENT

Float management involves controlling the collection and disbursement of cash. The objective in cash collection is to speed up collections and reduce the lag between the time customers pay their bills and the time the cash becomes available. The objective in cash disbursement is to control payments and minimize the firm's costs associated with making payments.

Total collection or disbursement times can be broken down into three parts: mailing time, processing delay, and availability delay:

1. *Mailing time* is the part of the collection and disbursement process during which checks are trapped in the postal system.
2. *Processing delay* is the time it takes the receiver of a check to process the payment and deposit it in a bank for collection.
3. *Availability delay* refers to the time required to clear a check through the banking system.

Speeding up collections involves reducing one or more of these components. Slowing up disbursements involves increasing one of them. We will describe some procedures for managing collection and disbursement times later. First, we need to discuss how float is measured.

Measuring Float   The size of the float depends on both the dollars and the time delay involved. For example, suppose you mail a check for $500 to another state each month. It takes five days in the mail for the check to reach its destination (the mailing time) and one day for the recipient to get over to the bank (the processing delay). The recipient's bank holds out-of-state checks for three days (availability delay). The total delay is $5 + 1 + 3 = 9$ days.

In this case, what is your average daily disbursement float? There are two equivalent ways of calculating the answer. First, you have a $500 float for nine days, so we say that the total float is $9 \times \$500 = \$4,500$. Assuming 30 days in the month, the average daily float is $\$4,500/30 = \$150$.

Alternatively, your disbursement float is $500 for 9 days out of the month and zero the other 21 days (again assuming 30 days in a month). Your average daily float is thus:

$$\text{Average daily float} = (9 \times \$500 + 21 \times 0)/30$$
$$= 9/30 \times \$500 + 21/30 \times 0$$
$$= \$4,500/30$$
$$= \$150$$

This means that, on an average day, your book balance is $150 less than your available balance, representing a $150 average disbursement float.

Things are only a little more complicated when there are multiple disbursements or receipts. To illustrate, suppose Concepts, Inc., receives two items each month as follows:

Amount	Processing and availability delay	Total float
Item 1: $5,000,000	× 9	= $45,000,000
Item 2: $3,000,000	× 5	= $15,000,000
Total $8,000,000		$60,000,000

The average daily float is equal to:

$$\text{Average daily float} = \frac{\text{Total float}}{\text{Total days}} \qquad \textbf{[19.1]}$$

$$= \frac{\$60 \text{ million}}{30} = \$2 \text{ million}$$

So, on an average day, there is $2 million that is uncollected and not available.

Another way to see this is to calculate the average daily receipts and multiply by the weighted average delay. Average daily receipts are:

$$\text{Average daily receipts} = \frac{\text{Total receipts}}{\text{Total days}} = \frac{\$8 \text{ million}}{30} = \$266,666.67$$

Of the $8 million total receipts, $5 million, or ⅝ of the total, is delayed for nine days. The other ⅜ is delayed for five days. The weighted average delay is thus:

$$\text{Weighted average delay} = (5/8) \times 9 \text{ days} + (3/8) \times 5 \text{ days}$$
$$= 5.625 + 1.875 = 7.50 \text{ days}$$

The average daily float is thus:

$$\text{Average daily float} = \text{Average daily receipts} \times \text{Weighted average delay} \qquad \textbf{[19.2]}$$
$$= \$266,666.67 \times 7.50 \text{ days} = \$2 \text{ million}$$

Some Details   In measuring float, there is an important difference to note between collection and disbursement float. We defined *float* as the difference between the firm's available cash balance and its book balance. With a disbursement, the firm's book balance goes down when the check is *mailed*, so the mailing time is an important component in disbursement float. However, with a collection, the firm's book balance isn't increased until the check is *received*, so mailing time is not a component of collection float.

This doesn't mean that mailing time is not important. The point is that when collection *float* is calculated, mailing time should not be considered. As we will discuss, when total collection *time* is considered, the mailing time is a crucial component.

Also, when we talk about availability delay, how long it actually takes a check to clear isn't really crucial. What matters is how long we must wait before the bank grants availability—that is, use of the funds. Banks actually use availability schedules to determine how long a check is held based on time of deposit and other factors. Beyond this, availability delay can be a matter of negotiation between the bank and a customer. In a similar vein, for outgoing checks, what matters is the date our account is debited, not when the recipient is granted availability.

Cost of the Float   The basic cost of collection float to the firm is simply the opportunity cost of not being able to use the cash. At a minimum, the firm could earn interest on the cash if it were available for investing.

FIGURE 19.1

Buildup of the Float

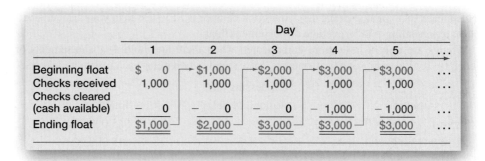

FIGURE 19.2

Effect of Eliminating the Float

	Day			
	t	*t* + 1	*t* + 2	...
Beginning float	$3,000	$ 0	$ 0	...
Checks received	1,000	1,000	1,000	...
Checks cleared (cash available)	− 4,000	− 1,000	− 1,000	...
Ending float	$ 0	$ 0	$ 0	...

Suppose the Lambo Corporation has average daily receipts of $1,000 and a weighted average delay of three days. The average daily float is thus 3 × $1,000 = $3,000. This means that, on a typical day, there is $3,000 that is not earning interest. Suppose Lambo could eliminate the float entirely. What would be the benefit? If it costs $2,000 to eliminate the float, what is the NPV of doing so?

Figure 19.1 illustrates the situation for Lambo. Suppose Lambo starts with a zero float. On a given day, Day 1, Lambo receives and deposits a check for $1,000. The cash will become available three days later on Day 4. At the end of the day on Day 1, the book balance is $1,000 more than the available balance, so the float is $1,000. On Day 2, the firm receives and deposits another check. It will collect three days later on Day 5. At the end of Day 2, there are two uncollected checks, and the books show a $2,000 balance. The bank, however, still shows a zero available balance; so the float is $2,000. The same sequence occurs on Day 3, and the float rises to a total of $3,000.

On Day 4, Lambo again receives and deposits a check for $1,000. However, it also collects $1,000 from the Day 1 check. The change in book balance and the change in available balance are identical, +$1,000; so the float stays at $3,000. The same thing happens every day after Day 4; the float therefore stays at $3,000 forever.[1]

Figure 19.2 illustrates what happens if the float is eliminated entirely on some day *t* in the future. After the float is eliminated, daily receipts are still $1,000. The firm collects the same day because the float is eliminated, so daily collections are also still $1,000. As Figure 19.2 illustrates, the only change occurs the first day. On that day, as usual, Lambo collects $1,000 from the sale made three days before. Because the float is gone, it also collects on the sales made two days before, one day before, and that same day, for an additional $3,000. Total collections on Day *t* are thus $4,000 instead of $1,000.

What we see is that Lambo generates an extra $3,000 on Day *t* by eliminating the float. On every subsequent day, Lambo receives $1,000 in cash just as it did before the float was eliminated. Thus, the only change in the firm's cash flows from eliminating the float is this

---

[1]This permanent float is sometimes called the *steady-state float*.

extra $3,000 that comes in immediately. No other cash flows are affected, so Lambo is $3,000 richer.

In other words, the PV of eliminating the float is simply equal to the total float. Lambo could pay this amount out as a dividend, invest it in interest-bearing assets, or do anything else with it. If it costs $2,000 to eliminate the float, then the NPV is $3,000 − 2,000 = $1,000; so Lambo should do it.

Reducing the Float: Part I   EXAMPLE 19.2

Instead of eliminating the float, suppose Lambo can reduce it to one day. What is the maximum Lambo should be willing to pay for this?

If Lambo can reduce the float from three days to one day, then the amount of the float will fall from $3,000 to $1,000. From our discussion immediately preceding, we see right away that the PV of doing this is just equal to the $2,000 float reduction. Lambo should thus be willing to pay up to $2,000.

Reducing the Float: Part II   EXAMPLE 19.3

Look back at Example 19.2. A large bank is willing to provide the float reduction service for $175 per year, payable at the end of each year. The relevant discount rate is 8 percent. Should Lambo hire the bank? What is the NPV of the investment? How do you interpret this discount rate? What is the most per year that Lambo should be willing to pay?

The PV to Lambo is still $2,000. The $175 would have to be paid out every year forever to maintain the float reduction; so the cost is perpetual, and its PV is $175/.08 = $2,187.50. The NPV is $2,000 − 2,187.50 = −$187.50; therefore, the service is not a good deal.

Ignoring the possibility of bounced checks, the discount rate here corresponds most closely to the cost of short-term borrowing. The reason is that Lambo could borrow $1,000 from the bank every time a check was deposited and pay it back three days later. The cost would be the interest that Lambo would have to pay.

The most Lambo would be willing to pay is whatever charge results in an NPV of zero. This zero NPV occurs when the $2,000 benefit exactly equals the PV of the costs—that is, when $2,000 = C/.08, where C is the annual cost. Solving for C, we find that C = .08 × $2,000 = $160 per year.

Ethical and Legal Questions   The cash manager must work with collected bank cash balances and not the firm's book balance (which reflects checks that have been deposited but not collected). If this is not done, a cash manager could be drawing on uncollected cash as a source of funds for short-term investing. Most banks charge a penalty rate for the use of uncollected funds. However, banks may not have good enough accounting and control procedures to be fully aware of the use of uncollected funds. This raises some ethical and legal questions for the firm.

For example, in May 1985, Robert Fomon, chairman of E.F. Hutton (a large investment bank), pleaded guilty to 2,000 charges of mail and wire fraud in connection with a scheme the firm had operated from 1980 to 1982. E.F. Hutton employees had written checks totaling hundreds of millions of dollars against uncollected cash. The proceeds had then been invested in short-term money market assets. This type of systematic overdrafting of accounts (or check *kiting*, as it is sometimes called) is neither legal nor ethical and is apparently not a widespread practice among corporations. Also, the particular inefficiencies in the banking system that Hutton was exploiting have been largely eliminated.

For its part, E.F. Hutton paid a $2 million fine, reimbursed the government (the U.S. Department of Justice) $750,000, and reserved an additional $8 million for restitution to defrauded banks. We should note that the key issue in the case against Hutton was not its float management per se, but, rather, its practice of writing checks for no economic reason other than to exploit float.

Despite stiff penalties for check kiting, the practice apparently continues. For example, in January 2011, an Oregon car dealer was indicted on charges for check kiting. During a particular nine-day period, over 500 checks totaling more than $19 million were allegedly floated.

ELECTRONIC DATA INTERCHANGE AND CHECK 21: THE END OF FLOAT?

Electronic data interchange (EDI) is a general term that refers to the growing practice of direct, electronic information exchange between all types of businesses. One important use of EDI, often called *financial EDI* or *FEDI*, is to electronically transfer financial information and funds between parties, thereby eliminating paper invoices, paper checks, mailing, and handling. For example, it is now possible to arrange to have your checking account directly debited each month to pay many types of bills, and corporations now routinely directly deposit paychecks into employee accounts. More generally, EDI allows a seller to send a bill electronically to a buyer, thereby avoiding the mail. The buyer can then authorize payment, which also occurs electronically. Its bank then transfers the funds to the seller's account at a different bank. The net effect is that the length of time required to initiate and complete a business transaction is shortened considerably, and much of what we normally think of as float is sharply reduced or eliminated. As the use of FEDI increases (which it will), float management will evolve to focus much more on issues surrounding computerized information exchange and funds transfers.

One of the drawbacks of EDI (and FEDI) is that it is expensive and complex to set up. However, with the growth of the Internet, a new form of EDI has emerged: Internet e-commerce. For example, networking giant Cisco Systems books millions in orders each day on its website from resellers around the world. Firms are also linking to critical suppliers and customers via "extranets," which are business networks that extend a company's internal network. Because of security concerns and lack of standardization, don't look for e-commerce and extranets to eliminate the need for EDI anytime soon. In fact, these are complementary systems that will most likely be used in tandem as the future unfolds.

On October 29, 2004, the Check Clearing Act for the 21st Century, also known as Check 21, took effect. Before Check 21, a bank receiving a check was required to send the physical check to the customer's bank before payment could be made. Now a bank can transmit an electronic image of the check to the customer's bank and receive payment immediately. Previously, an out-of-state check might take three days to clear. But with Check 21, the clearing time is typically one day; and often a check can clear the same day it is written. Thus, Check 21 promises to significantly reduce float.

Concept Questions

19.2a Which would a firm be most interested in reducing, collection or disbursement float? Why?

19.2b How is daily average float calculated?

19.2c What is the benefit from reducing or eliminating float?

Cash Collection and Concentration   19.3

From our previous discussion, we know that collection delays work against the firm. All other things being the same, then, a firm will adopt procedures to speed up collections and thereby decrease collection times. In addition, even after cash is collected, firms need procedures to funnel, or concentrate, that cash where it can be best used. We discuss some common collection and concentration procedures next.

COMPONENTS OF COLLECTION TIME

Based on our previous discussion, we can depict the basic parts of the cash collection process as follows. The total time in this process is made up of mailing time, check-processing delay, and the bank's availability delay.

The amount of time that cash spends in each part of the cash collection process depends on where the firm's customers and banks are located and how efficient the firm is in collecting cash.

CASH COLLECTION

How a firm collects from its customers depends in large part on the nature of the business. The simplest case would be a business such as a restaurant chain. Most of its customers will pay with cash, check, or credit card at the point of sale (this is called *over-the-counter collection*), so there is no problem with mailing delay. Normally, the funds will be deposited in a local bank, and the firm will have some means (discussed later) of gaining access to the funds.

When some or all of the payments a company receives are checks that arrive through the mail, all three components of collection time become relevant. The firm may choose to have all the checks mailed to one location; more commonly, the firm might have a number of different mail collection points to reduce mailing times. Also, the firm may run its collection operation itself or might hire an outside firm that specializes in cash collection. We discuss these issues in more detail in the following pages.

Other approaches to cash collection exist. One that is becoming more common is the preauthorized payment arrangement. With this arrangement, the payment amounts and payment dates are fixed in advance. When the agreed-upon date arrives, the amount is automatically transferred from the customer's bank account to the firm's bank account, which sharply reduces or even eliminates collection delays. The same approach is used by firms that have online terminals, meaning that when a sale is rung up, the money is immediately transferred to the firm's accounts.

LOCKBOXES

When a firm receives its payments by mail, it must decide where the checks will be mailed and how the checks will be picked up and deposited. Careful selection of the number and locations of collection points can greatly reduce collection times. Many firms use special post office boxes called **lockboxes** to intercept payments and speed cash collection.

lockboxes
Special post office boxes set up to intercept and speed up accounts receivable payments.

FIGURE 19.3

Overview of Lockbox
Processing

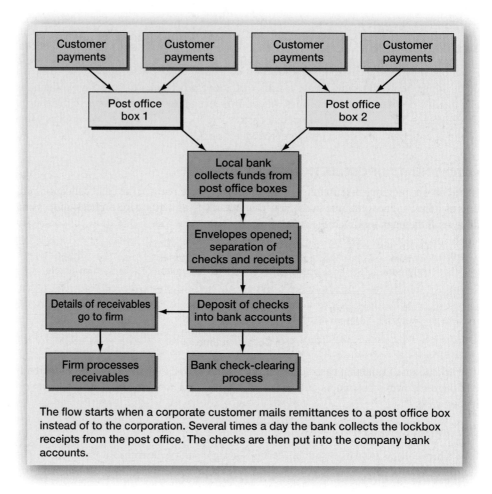

The flow starts when a corporate customer mails remittances to a post office box instead of to the corporation. Several times a day the bank collects the lockbox receipts from the post office. The checks are then put into the company bank accounts.

Figure 19.3 illustrates a lockbox system. The collection process is started by customers mailing their checks to a post office box instead of sending them to the firm. The lockbox is maintained by a local bank. A large corporation may actually maintain more than 20 lockboxes around the country.

In the typical lockbox system, the local bank collects the lockbox checks several times a day. The bank deposits the checks directly into the firm's account. Details of the operation are recorded (in some computer-usable form) and sent to the firm.

A lockbox system reduces mailing time because checks are received at a nearby post office instead of at corporate headquarters. Lockboxes also reduce the processing time because the corporation doesn't have to open the envelopes and deposit checks for collection. In all, a bank lockbox system should enable a firm to get its receipts processed, deposited, and cleared faster than if it were to receive checks at its headquarters and deliver them itself to the bank for deposit and clearing.

Some firms have turned to what are called "electronic lockboxes" as an alternative to traditional lockboxes. In one version of an electronic lockbox, customers use the telephone or the Internet to access their account—say, their credit card account at a bank—review their bill, and authorize payment without paper ever having changed hands on either end of the transaction. Clearly, an electronic lockbox system is far superior to traditional bill payment methods, at least from the biller's perspective. Look for systems like this to continue to grow in popularity.

CASH CONCENTRATION

As we discussed earlier, a firm will typically have a number of cash collection points; as a result, cash collections may end up in many different banks and bank accounts. From here, the firm needs procedures to move the cash into its main accounts. This is called **cash concentration**. By routinely pooling its cash, the firm greatly simplifies its cash management by reducing the number of accounts that must be tracked. Also, by having a larger pool of funds available, a firm may be able to negotiate or otherwise obtain a better rate on any short-term investments.

In setting up a concentration system, firms will typically use one or more *concentration banks*. A concentration bank pools the funds obtained from local banks contained within some geographic region. Concentration systems are often used in conjunction with lockbox systems. Figure 19.4 illustrates how an integrated cash collection and cash concentration system might look. As Figure 19.4 illustrates, a key part of the cash collection and concentration process is the transfer of funds to the concentration bank. There are several options available for accomplishing this transfer. The cheapest is a *depository transfer check (DTC)*, which is a preprinted check that usually needs no signature and is valid only for transferring funds between specific accounts within the *same* firm. The money becomes available one to two days later. *Automated clearinghouse (ACH)* transfers are basically electronic versions of paper checks. These may be more expensive, depending

cash concentration
The practice of and procedures for moving cash from multiple banks into the firm's main accounts.

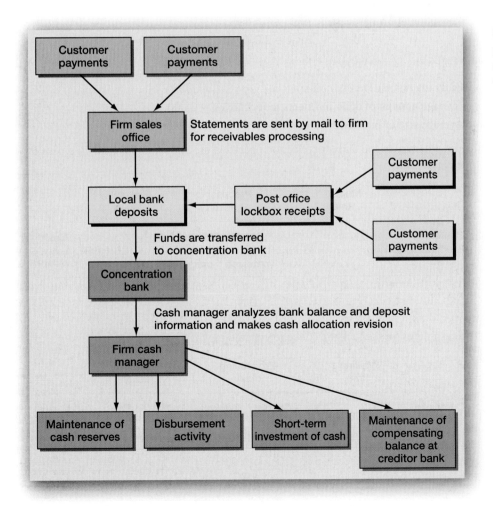

FIGURE 19.4

Lockboxes and Concentration Banks in a Cash Management System

Global Treasury News has current info about cash management, especially for international issues. (www.gtnews.com)

on the circumstances, but the funds are available the next day. The most expensive means of transfer are *wire transfers*, which provide same-day availability. Which approach a firm will choose depends on the number and size of payments. For example, a typical ACH transfer might be $200, whereas a typical wire transfer would be several million dollars. Firms with a large number of collection points and relatively small payments will choose the cheaper route, whereas firms that receive smaller numbers of relatively large payments may choose more expensive procedures.

ACCELERATING COLLECTIONS: AN EXAMPLE

The decision of whether or not to use a bank cash management service incorporating lock-boxes and concentration banks depends on where a firm's customers are located and the speed of the U.S. postal system. Suppose Atlantic Corporation, located in Philadelphia, is considering a lockbox system. Its collection delay is currently eight days.

Atlantic does business in the southwestern part of the country (New Mexico, Arizona, and California). The proposed lockbox system would be located in Los Angeles and operated by Pacific Bank. Pacific Bank has analyzed Atlantic's cash-gathering system and has concluded that it can decrease collection time by two days. Specifically, the bank has come up with the following information on the proposed lockbox system:

Reduction in mailing time	= 1.0 day
Reduction in clearing time	= .5 day
Reduction in firm processing time	= .5 day
Total	= 2.0 days

The following is also known:

Daily interest on Treasury bills	= .025%
Average number of daily payments to lockboxes	= 2,000
Average size of payment	= $600

The cash flows for the current collection operation are shown in the following cash flow time chart:

The cash flows for the lockbox collection operation will be as follows:

Pacific Bank has agreed to operate this lockbox system for a fee of 25 cents per check processed. Should Atlantic give the go-ahead?

We first need to determine the benefit of the system. The average daily collections from the southwestern region are $1.2 million (= 2,000 × $600). The collection time will be decreased by two days, so the lockbox system will increase the collected bank balance by $1.2 million × 2 = $2.4 million. In other words, the lockbox system releases $2.4 million to the firm by reducing processing, mailing, and clearing time by two days. From our earlier discussion, we know that this $2.4 million is the PV of the proposal.

To calculate the NPV, we need to determine the PV of the costs. There are several different ways to proceed. First, at 2,000 checks per day and $.25 per check, the daily cost is $500. This cost will be incurred every day forever. At an interest rate of .025 percent per day, the PV is therefore $500/.00025 = $2 million. The NPV is thus $2.4 million − 2 million = $400,000, and the system appears to be desirable.

Alternatively, Atlantic could invest the $2.4 million at .025 percent per day. The interest earned would be $2.4 million × .00025 = $600 per day. The cost of the system is $500 per day; so, running it obviously generates a profit in the amount of $100 per day. The PV of $100 per day forever is $100/.00025 = $400,000, just as we had before.

Finally, and most simply, each check is for $600 and is available two days sooner if the system is used. The interest on $600 for two days is 2 × $600 × .00025 = $.30. The cost is 25 cents per check, so Atlantic makes a nickel (= $.30 × .25) on every check. With 2,000 checks per day, the profit is $.05 × 2,000 checks = $100 per day, as we calculated.

Accelerating Collections   **EXAMPLE 19.4**

In our example concerning Atlantic Corporation's proposed lockbox system, suppose Pacific Bank wants a $20,000 fixed fee (paid annually) in addition to the 25 cents per check. Is the system still a good idea?

To answer, we need to calculate the PV of the fixed fee. The daily interest rate is .025 percent. The annual rate is therefore $1.00025^{365} − 1 = 9.553\%$. The PV of the fixed fee (which is paid each year forever) is $20,000/.09553 = $209,358. Because the NPV without the fee is $400,000, the NPV with the fee is $400,000 − 209,358 = $190,642. It's still a good idea.

Concept Questions

19.3a What is a lockbox? What purpose does it serve?

19.3b What is a concentration bank? What purpose does it serve?

Managing Cash Disbursements   **19.4**

From the firm's point of view, disbursement float is desirable, so the goal in managing disbursement float is to slow down disbursements. To do this, the firm may develop strategies to *increase* mail float, processing float, and availability float on the checks it writes. Beyond this, firms have developed procedures for minimizing cash held for payment purposes. We discuss the most common of these in this section.

INCREASING DISBURSEMENT FLOAT

As we have seen, slowing down payments comes from the time involved in mail delivery, check processing, and collection of funds. Disbursement float can be increased by writing

For a free cash budgeting spreadsheet, go to www.toolkit.cch.com/tools/tools.asp.

a check on a geographically distant bank. For example, a New York supplier might be paid with checks drawn on a Los Angeles bank. This will increase the time required for the checks to clear through the banking system. Mailing checks from remote post offices is another way firms slow down disbursement.

Tactics for maximizing disbursement float are debatable on both ethical and economic grounds. First, as we discuss in some detail in the next chapter, payment terms frequently offer a substantial discount for early payment. The discount is usually much larger than any possible savings from "playing the float game." In such cases, increasing mailing time will be of no benefit if the recipient dates payments based on the date received (as is common) as opposed to the postmark date.

Beyond this, suppliers are not likely to be fooled by attempts to slow down disbursements. The negative consequences of poor relations with suppliers can be costly. In broader terms, intentionally delaying payments by taking advantage of mailing times or unsophisticated suppliers may amount to avoiding paying bills when they are due—an unethical business procedure.

CONTROLLING DISBURSEMENTS

We have seen that maximizing disbursement float is probably poor business practice. However, a firm will still wish to tie up as little cash as possible in disbursements. Firms have therefore developed systems for efficiently managing the disbursement process. The general idea in such systems is to have no more than the minimum amount necessary to pay bills on deposit in the bank. We discuss some approaches to accomplishing this goal next.

zero-balance account
A disbursement account in which the firm maintains a zero balance, transferring funds in from a master account only as needed to cover checks presented for payment.

Zero-Balance Accounts   With a **zero-balance account** system, the firm, in cooperation with its bank, maintains a master account and a set of subaccounts. When a check written on one of the subaccounts must be paid, the necessary funds are transferred in from the master account. Figure 19.5 illustrates how such a system might work. In this case, the firm maintains two disbursement accounts, one for suppliers and one for payroll. As shown, if the firm does not use zero-balance accounts, then each of these accounts must have a safety stock of cash to meet unanticipated demands. If the firm does use zero-balance accounts, then it can keep one safety stock in a master account and transfer the funds to the two subsidiary accounts as needed. The key is that the total amount of cash held as a buffer is smaller under the zero-balance arrangement, which frees up cash to be used elsewhere.

FIGURE 19.5   Zero-Balance Accounts

No zero-balance accounts

Payroll account   Supplier account

Safety stocks

Two zero-balance accounts

Master account

Safety stock

Cash transfers   Cash transfers

Payroll account   Supplier account

With no zero-balance accounts, separate safety stocks must be maintained, which ties up cash unnecessarily. With zero-balance accounts, the firm keeps a single safety stock of cash in a master account. Funds are transferred into disbursement accounts as needed.

Controlled Disbursement Accounts   With a **controlled disbursement account** system, almost all payments that must be made in a given day are known in the morning. The bank informs the firm of the total, and the firm transfers (usually by wire) the amount needed.

> **controlled disbursement account**
> A disbursement account to which the firm transfers an amount that is sufficient to cover demands for payment.

Concept Questions

19.4a Is maximizing disbursement float a sound business practice?

19.4b What is a zero-balance account? What is the advantage of such an account?

Investing Idle Cash   19.5

If a firm has a temporary cash surplus, it can invest in short-term securities. As we have mentioned at various times, the market for short-term financial assets is called the *money market*. The maturity of short-term financial assets that trade in the money market is one year or less.

Most large firms manage their own short-term financial assets, carrying out transactions through banks and dealers. Some large firms and many small firms use money market mutual funds. These are funds that invest in short-term financial assets for a management fee. The management fee is compensation for the professional expertise and diversification provided by the fund manager.

Among the many money market mutual funds, some specialize in corporate customers. In addition, banks offer arrangements in which the bank takes all excess available funds at the close of each business day and invests them for the firm.

TEMPORARY CASH SURPLUSES

Firms have temporary cash surpluses for various reasons. Two of the most important are the financing of seasonal or cyclical activities of the firm and the financing of planned or possible expenditures.

Seasonal or Cyclical Activities   Some firms have a predictable cash flow pattern. They have surplus cash flows during part of the year and deficit cash flows the rest of the year. For example, Toys "Я" Us, a retail toy firm, has a seasonal cash flow pattern influenced by the holiday season.

A firm such as Toys "Я" Us may buy marketable securities when surplus cash flows occur and sell marketable securities when deficits occur. Of course, bank loans are another short-term financing device. The use of bank loans and marketable securities to meet temporary financing needs is illustrated in Figure 19.6. In this case, the firm is following a compromise working capital policy in the sense we discussed in the previous chapter.

Planned or Possible Expenditures   Firms frequently accumulate temporary investments in marketable securities to provide the cash for a plant construction program, dividend payment, or other large expenditure. Thus, firms may issue bonds and stocks before the cash is needed, investing the proceeds in short-term marketable securities and then selling the securities to finance the expenditures. Also, firms may face the possibility of having to make a large cash outlay. An obvious example would involve the possibility of losing a large lawsuit. Firms may build up cash surpluses against such a contingency.

FIGURE 19.6

Seasonal Cash Demands

Time 1: A surplus cash flow exists. Seasonal demand for assets is low. The surplus cash flow is invested in short-term marketable securities.

Time 2: A deficit cash flow exists. Seasonal demand for assets is high. The financial deficit is financed by selling marketable securities and by bank borrowing.

CHARACTERISTICS OF SHORT-TERM SECURITIES

Given that a firm has some temporarily idle cash, a variety of short-term securities are available for investing. The most important characteristics of these short-term marketable securities are their maturity, default risk, marketability, and taxability.

Maturity   From Chapter 7, we know that for a given change in the level of interest rates, the prices of longer-maturity securities will change more than those of shorter-maturity securities. As a consequence, firms that invest in long-term securities are accepting greater risk than firms that invest in securities with short-term maturities.

We called this type of risk *interest rate risk*. Firms often limit their investments in marketable securities to those maturing in less than 90 days to avoid the risk of losses in value from changing interest rates. Of course, the expected return on securities with short-term maturities is usually less than the expected return on securities with longer maturities.

Default Risk   *Default risk* refers to the probability that interest and principal will not be paid in the promised amounts on the due dates (or will not be paid at all). In Chapter 7, we observed that various financial reporting agencies, such as Moody's Investors Service and Standard and Poor's, compile and publish ratings of various corporate and other publicly held securities. These ratings are connected to default risk. Of course, some securities have negligible default risk, such as U.S. Treasury bills. Given the purposes of investing idle corporate cash, firms typically avoid investing in marketable securities with significant default risk.

Marketability   *Marketability* refers to how easy it is to convert an asset to cash; so marketability and liquidity mean much the same thing. Some money market instruments are much more marketable than others. At the top of the list are U.S. Treasury bills, which can be bought and sold very cheaply and very quickly.

Taxes   Interest earned on money market securities that are not some kind of government obligation (either federal or state) is taxable at the local, state, and federal levels. U.S. Treasury obligations such as T-bills are exempt from state taxation, but other government-backed debt is not. Municipal securities are exempt from federal taxes, but they may be taxed at the state level.

SOME DIFFERENT TYPES OF MONEY MARKET SECURITIES

Money market securities are generally highly marketable and short-term. They usually have low risk of default. They are issued by the U.S. government (for example, U.S. Treasury bills), domestic and foreign banks (for example, certificates of deposit), and business corporations (for example, commercial paper). There are many types in all, and we illustrate only a few of the most common here.

U.S. Treasury bills are obligations of the U.S. government that mature in 30, 90, or 180 days. Bills are sold by auction every week.

Short-term tax-exempts are short-term securities issued by states, municipalities, local housing agencies, and urban renewal agencies. Because these are all considered municipal securities, they are exempt from federal taxes. RANs, BANs, and TANs, for example, are revenue, bond, and tax anticipation notes, respectively. In other words, they represent short-term borrowing by municipalities in anticipation of cash receipts.

Short-term tax-exempts have more default risk than U.S. Treasury issues and are less marketable. Because the interest is exempt from federal income tax, the pretax yield on tax-exempts is lower than that on comparable securities such as Treasury bills. Also, corporations face restrictions on holding tax-exempts as investments.

Commercial paper consists of short-term securities issued by finance companies, banks, and corporations. Typically, commercial paper is unsecured. Maturities range from a few weeks to 270 days.

Check out short-term rates online at www.bloomberg.com.

There is no especially active secondary market in commercial paper. As a consequence, the marketability can be low; however, firms that issue commercial paper will often repurchase it directly before maturity. The default risk of commercial paper depends on the financial strength of the issuer. Moody's and S&P publish quality ratings for commercial paper. These ratings are similar to the bond ratings we discussed in Chapter 7.

Certificates of deposit (CDs) are short-term loans to commercial banks. The most common are jumbo CDs—those in excess of $100,000. There are active markets in CDs of 3-month, 6-month, 9-month, and 12-month maturities.

Repurchase agreements (repos) are sales of government securities (for example, U.S. Treasury bills) by a bank or securities dealer with an agreement to repurchase. Typically, an investor buys some Treasury securities from a bond dealer and simultaneously agrees to sell them back at a later date at a specified higher price. Repurchase agreements usually involve a very short term—overnight to a few days.

Because 70 to 80 percent of the dividends received by one corporation from another are exempt from taxation, the relatively high dividend yields on preferred stock provide a strong incentive for investment. The only problem is that the dividend is fixed with ordinary preferred stock, so the price can fluctuate more than is desirable in a short-term investment. However, money market preferred stock is a fairly recent innovation featuring a floating dividend. The dividend is reset fairly often (usually every 49 days); so this type of preferred has much less price volatility than ordinary preferred, and it has become a popular short-term investment.

Concept Questions

19.5a What are some reasons why firms find themselves with idle cash?

19.5b What are some types of money market securities?

19.5c Why are money market preferred stocks an attractive short-term investment?

19.6 Summary and Conclusions

In this chapter, we have examined cash and liquidity management. We saw the following:

1. A firm holds cash to conduct transactions and to compensate banks for the various services they render.

2. The difference between a firm's available balance and its book balance is the firm's net float. The float reflects the fact that some checks have not cleared and are thus uncollected. The financial manager must always work with collected cash balances and not with the company's book balance. To do otherwise is to use the bank's cash without the bank's knowing it, which raises ethical and legal questions.

3. The firm can make use of a variety of procedures to manage the collection and disbursement of cash in such a way as to speed up the collection of cash and slow down the payments. Some methods to speed up the collection are the use of lockboxes, concentration banking, and wire transfers.

4. Because of seasonal and cyclical activities, to help finance planned expenditures, or as a contingency reserve, firms temporarily hold a cash surplus. The money market offers a variety of possible vehicles for "parking" this idle cash.

Visit us at www.mhhe.com/rwj

CONNECT TO FINANCE

Mc Graw Hill connect™ |FINANCE

If you are using Connect™ Finance in your course, get online to take a Practice Test, check out study tools, and find out where you need additional practice.

▼ Chapter 19 Cash and Liquidity Management			
19.1 Reasons for Holding Cash	eBook	Study	Practice
19.2 Understanding Float	eBook	Study	Practice
19.3 Cash Collection and Concentration	eBook	Study	Practice
19.4 Managing Cash Disbursements	eBook	Study	Practice
19.5 Investing Idle Cash	eBook	Study	Practice

Section Quiz

Can you answer the following questions?

Section 19.1 Cash management is defined as _____. (LO 19-3)

Section 19.2 A firm probably has the most control over what components of collection float? (LO 19-1)

Section 19.3 What is the primary purpose of a lockbox? (LO 19-2)

Log on to find out!

CHAPTER REVIEW AND SELF-TEST PROBLEM

19.1 Float Measurement On a typical day, a firm writes checks totaling $3,000. These checks clear in seven days. Simultaneously, the firm receives $1,700. The cash is available in two days on average. Calculate the disbursement, collection, and net floats. How do you interpret the answer?

ANSWER TO CHAPTER REVIEW AND SELF-TEST PROBLEM

19.1 The disbursement float is 7 days × $3,000 = $21,000. The collection float is 2 days × (−$1,700) = −$3,400. The net float is $21,000 + (−3,400) = $17,600. In other words, at any given time, the firm typically has uncashed checks outstanding of $21,000. At the same time, it has uncollected receipts of $3,400. Thus the firm's book balance is typically $17,600 less than its available balance, for a positive $17,600 net float.

CONCEPTS REVIEW AND CRITICAL THINKING QUESTIONS

1. **Cash Management [LO3]** Is it possible for a firm to have too much cash? Why would shareholders care if a firm accumulates large amounts of cash?

2. **Cash Management [LO3]** What options are available to a firm if it believes it has too much cash? How about too little?

3. **Agency Issues [LO3]** Are stockholders and creditors likely to agree on how much cash a firm should keep on hand?

4. **Motivations for Holding Cash [LO3]** In the chapter opening, we discussed the enormous cash positions of several companies. Why would firms such as these hold such large quantities of cash?

5. **Cash Management versus Liquidity Management [LO3]** What is the difference between cash management and liquidity management?

6. **Short-Term Investments [LO3]** Why is a preferred stock with a dividend tied to short-term interest rates an attractive short-term investment for corporations with excess cash?

7. **Collection and Disbursement Floats [LO1]** Which would a firm prefer: a net collection float or a net disbursement float? Why?

8. **Float [LO1]** Suppose a firm has a book balance of $2 million. At the automatic teller machine (ATM), the cash manager finds out that the bank balance is $2.5 million. What is the situation here? If this is an ongoing situation, what ethical dilemma arises?

9. **Short-Term Investments [LO3]** For each of the short-term marketable securities given here, provide an example of the potential disadvantages the investment has for meeting a corporation's cash management goals:
   a. U.S. Treasury bills.
   b. Ordinary preferred stock.
   c. Negotiable certificates of deposit (NCDs).
   d. Commercial paper.
   e. Revenue anticipation notes.
   f. Repurchase agreements.

10. **Agency Issues [LO3]** It is sometimes argued that excess cash held by a firm can aggravate agency problems (discussed in Chapter 1) and, more generally, reduce incentives for shareholder wealth maximization. How would you frame the issue here?

11. **Use of Excess Cash [LO3]** One option a firm usually has with any excess cash is to pay its suppliers more quickly. What are the advantages and disadvantages of this use of excess cash?

12. **Use of Excess Cash [LO3]** Another option usually available is to reduce the firm's outstanding debt. What are the advantages and disadvantages of this use of excess cash?

13. **Float [LO1]** An unfortunately common practice goes like this (warning: don't try this at home): Suppose you are out of money in your checking account; however, your local grocery store will, as a convenience to you as a customer, cash a check for you. So, you cash a check for $200. Of course, this check will bounce unless you do something. To prevent this, you go to the grocery the next day and cash another check for $200. You take this $200 and deposit it. You repeat this process every day, and, in doing so, you make sure that no checks bounce. Eventually, manna from heaven arrives (perhaps in the form of money from home), and you are able to cover your outstanding checks.

    To make it interesting, suppose you are absolutely certain that no checks will bounce along the way. Assuming this is true, and ignoring any question of legality (what we have described is probably illegal check kiting), is there anything unethical about this? If you say yes, then why? In particular, who is harmed?

QUESTIONS AND PROBLEMS

Visit us at www.mhhe.com/rwj

BASIC
(Questions 1–10)

1. **Calculating Float [LO1]** In a typical month, the Hampton Corporation receives 80 checks totaling $139,000. These are delayed four days on average. What is the average daily float? Assume 30 days in a month.

2. **Calculating Net Float [LO1]** Each business day, on average, a company writes checks totaling $12,000 to pay its suppliers. The usual clearing time for the checks is four days. Meanwhile, the company is receiving payments from its customers each day, in the form of checks, totaling $23,000. The cash from the payments is available to the firm after two days.

    a. Calculate the company's disbursement float, collection float, and net float.

    b. How would your answer to part (a) change if the collected funds were available in one day instead of two?

3. **Costs of Float [LO1]** Purple Feet Wine, Inc., receives an average of $17,000 in checks per day. The delay in clearing is typically three days. The current interest rate is .017 percent per day.

    a. What is the company's float?

    b. What is the most Purple Feet should be willing to pay today to eliminate its float entirely?

    c. What is the highest daily fee the company should be willing to pay to eliminate its float entirely?

4. **Float and Weighted Average Delay [LO1]** Your neighbor goes to the post office once a month and picks up two checks, one for $14,000 and one for $5,000. The larger check takes four days to clear after it is deposited; the smaller one takes three days. Assume 30 days in a month.

a. What is the total float for the month?

b. What is the average daily float?

c. What are the average daily receipts and weighted average delay?

5. **NPV and Collection Time [LO2]** Your firm has an average receipt size of $125. A bank has approached you concerning a lockbox service that will decrease your total collection time by two days. You typically receive 6,400 checks per day. The daily interest rate is .016 percent. If the bank charges a fee of $175 per day, should the lockbox project be accepted? What would the net annual savings be if the service were adopted?

6. **Using Weighted Average Delay [LO1]** A mail-order firm processes 5,300 checks per month. Of these, 60 percent are for $43 and 40 percent are for $75. The $43 checks are delayed two days on average; the $75 checks are delayed three days on average. Assume 30 days in a month.

a. What is the average daily collection float? How do you interpret your answer?

b. What is the weighted average delay? Use the result to calculate the average daily float.

c. How much should the firm be willing to pay to eliminate the float?

d. If the interest rate is 7 percent per year, calculate the daily cost of the float.

e. How much should the firm be willing to pay to reduce the weighted average float to 1.5 days?

7. **Value of Lockboxes [LO2]** Paper Submarine Manufacturing is investigating a lockbox system to reduce its collection time. It has determined the following:

Average number of payments per day	385
Average value of payment	$975
Variable lockbox fee (per transaction)	$.35
Daily interest rate on money market securities	.068%

The total collection time will be reduced by three days if the lockbox system is adopted.

a. What is the PV of adopting the system?

b. What is the NPV of adopting the system?

c. What is the net cash flow per day from adopting? Per check?

8. **Lockboxes and Collections [LO2]** It takes Cookie Cutter Modular Homes, Inc., about six days to receive and deposit checks from customers. Cookie Cutter's management is considering a lockbox system to reduce the firm's collection times. It is expected that the lockbox system will reduce receipt and deposit times to three days total. Average daily collections are $130,000, and the required rate of return is 5 percent per year. Assume 365 days per year.

a. What is the reduction in outstanding cash balances as a result of implementing the lockbox system?

b. What is the dollar return that could be earned on these savings?

c. What is the maximum monthly charge Cookie Cutter should pay for this lockbox system if the payment is due at the end of the month? What if the payment is due at the beginning of the month?

9. **Value of Delay [LO2]** No More Pencils, Inc., disburses checks every two weeks that average $86,000 and take seven days to clear. How much interest can the company earn annually if it delays transfer of funds from an interest-bearing

account that pays .011 percent per day for these seven days? Ignore the effects of compounding interest.

10. **NPV and Reducing Float [LO2]** No More Books Corporation has an agreement with Floyd Bank whereby the bank handles $5 million in collections per day and requires a $350,000 compensating balance. No More Books is contemplating canceling the agreement and dividing its eastern region so that two other banks will handle its business. Banks A and B will each handle $2.5 million of collections per day, and each requires a compensating balance of $200,000. No More Books' financial management expects that collections will be accelerated by one day if the eastern region is divided. Should the company proceed with the new system? What will be the annual net savings? Assume that the T-bill rate is 2.5 percent annually.

INTERMEDIATE
(Questions 11–12)

11. **Lockboxes and Collection Time [LO2]** Bird's Eye Treehouses, Inc., a Kentucky company, has determined that a majority of its customers are located in the Pennsylvania area. It therefore is considering using a lockbox system offered by a bank located in Pittsburgh. The bank has estimated that use of the system will reduce collection time by 1.5 days. Based on the following information, should the lockbox system be adopted?

Average number of payments per day	800
Average value of payment	$750
Variable lockbox fee (per transaction)	$.15
Annual interest rate on money market securities	5.5%

How would your answer change if there were a fixed charge of $5,000 per year in addition to the variable charge? Assume 365 days per year.

12. **Calculating Transactions Required [LO2]** Cow Chips, Inc., a large fertilizer distributor based in California, is planning to use a lockbox system to speed up collections from its customers located on the East Coast. A Philadelphia-area bank will provide this service for an annual fee of $10,000 plus 10 cents per transaction. The estimated reduction in collection and processing time is one day. If the average customer payment in this region is $5,700, how many customers each day, on average, are needed to make the system profitable for Cow Chips? Treasury bills are currently yielding 5 percent per year, and there are 365 days per year.

MINICASE

Cash Management at Webb Corporation

Webb Corporation was founded 20 years ago by its president, Bryan Webb. The company originally began as a mail-order company, but has grown rapidly in recent years, in large part due to its website. Because of the wide geographical dispersion of the company's customers, it currently employs a lockbox system with collection centers in San Francisco, St. Louis, Atlanta, and Boston.

Holly Lennon, the company's treasurer, has been examining the current cash collection policies. On average, each lockbox center handles $175,000 in payments each day. The company's current policy is to invest these payments in short-term marketable securities daily at the collection center banks. Every two weeks, the investment accounts are swept; the proceeds are wire-transferred to Webb's headquarters in Dallas to meet the company's payroll. The investment accounts each earn .012 percent per day, and the wire transfers cost .20 percent of the amount transferred.

Holly has been approached by Third National Bank, located just outside Dallas, about the possibility of setting up a concentration banking system for Webb Corp. Third National will accept each of the lockbox center's daily payments via automated clearinghouse (ACH) transfers in lieu of wire

Visit us at www.mhhe.com/rwj

transfers. The ACH-transferred funds will not be available for use for one day. Once cleared, the funds will be deposited in a short-term account, which will yield .012 percent per day. Each ACH transfer will cost $150. Bryan has asked Holly to determine which cash management system will be the best for the company. As her assistant, Holly has asked you to answer the following questions.

QUESTIONS

1. What is Webb Corporation's total net cash flow available from the current lockbox system to meet payroll?

2. Under the terms outlined by Third National Bank, should the company proceed with the concentration banking system?

3. What cost of ACH transfers would make the company indifferent between the two systems?

Determining the Target Cash Balance

19A

Based on our general discussion of current assets in the previous chapter, the **target cash balance** involves a trade-off between the opportunity costs of holding too much cash (the carrying costs) and the costs of holding too little (the shortage costs, also called **adjustment costs**). The nature of these costs depends on the firm's working capital policy.

If the firm has a flexible working capital policy, it will probably maintain a marketable securities portfolio. In this case, the adjustment, or shortage, costs will be the trading costs associated with buying and selling securities. If the firm has a restrictive working capital policy, it will probably borrow in the short term to meet cash shortages. The costs in this case will be the interest and other expenses associated with arranging a loan.

In our discussion that follows, we will assume the firm has a flexible policy. Its cash management, then, consists of moving money in and out of marketable securities. This is a traditional approach to the subject, and it is a nice way of illustrating the costs and benefits of holding cash. Keep in mind, however, that the distinction between cash and money market investments is becoming increasingly blurred.

For example, how do we classify a money market fund with check-writing privileges? Such near-cash arrangements are becoming more common. It may be that the prime reason they are not universal is regulation limiting their usage. We will return to this subject of such arrangements at various points in the following discussion.

target cash balance
A firm's desired cash level as determined by the trade-off between carrying costs and shortage costs.

adjustment costs
The costs associated with holding too little cash. Also, *shortage costs*.

THE BASIC IDEA

Figure 19A.1 presents the cash management problem for our flexible firm. If a firm tries to keep its cash holdings too low, it will find itself running out of cash more often than is desirable and thus selling marketable securities (and perhaps later buying marketable securities to replace those sold) more frequently than would be the case if the cash balance were higher. Thus trading costs will be high when the cash balance is small. These costs will fall as the cash balance becomes larger.

In contrast, the opportunity costs of holding cash are low if the firm holds little cash. These costs increase as the cash holdings rise because the firm is giving up more interest that could have been earned.

In Figure 19A.1, the sum of the costs is given by the total cost curve. As shown, the minimum total cost occurs where the two individual cost curves cross at point C^*. At this point, the opportunity costs and the trading costs are equal. This point represents the target cash balance, and it is the point the firm should try to find.

Figure 19A.1 is essentially the same as Figure 18.2 in the previous chapter. As we discuss next, however, we can now say more about the optimal investment in cash and the factors that influence it.

Visit us at www.mhhe.com/rwj

FIGURE 19A.1

Cost of Holding Cash

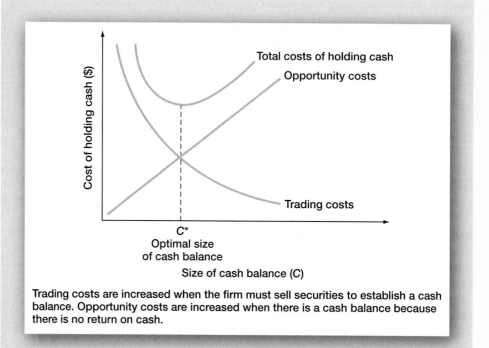

Trading costs are increased when the firm must sell securities to establish a cash balance. Opportunity costs are increased when there is a cash balance because there is no return on cash.

THE BAT MODEL

The Baumol–Allais–Tobin (BAT) model is a classic means of analyzing our cash management problem. We will show how this model can be used to actually establish the target cash balance. It is a straightforward model useful for illustrating the factors in cash management and, more generally, current asset management.

To develop the BAT model, suppose the Golden Socks Corporation starts off at week 0 with a cash balance of $C = \$1.2$ million. Each week, outflows exceed inflows by $600,000. As a result, the cash balance will drop to zero at the end of week 2. The average cash balance will be the beginning balance ($1.2 million) plus the ending balance ($0) divided by 2, or ($1.2 million + 0)/2 = \$600,000, over the two-week period. At the end of week 2, Golden Socks replenishes its cash by depositing another $1.2 million.

As we have described, the simple cash management strategy for Golden Socks boils down to depositing $1.2 million every two weeks. This policy is shown in Figure 19A.2. Notice how the cash balance declines by $600,000 per week. Because the company brings the account up to $1.2 million, the balance hits zero every two weeks. This results in the sawtooth pattern displayed in Figure 19A.2.

Implicitly, we assume that the net cash outflow is the same every day and is known with certainty. These two assumptions make the model easy to handle. We will indicate in the next section what happens when they do not hold.

If C were set higher, say, at $2.4 million, cash would last four weeks before the firm would have to sell marketable securities; but the firm's average cash balance would increase to $1.2 million (from $600,000). If C were set at $600,000, cash would run out in one week, and the firm would have to replenish cash more frequently; but the average cash balance would fall from $600,000 to $300,000.

Because transaction costs (for example, the brokerage costs of selling marketable securities) must be incurred whenever cash is replenished, establishing large initial balances will lower the trading costs connected with cash management. However, the larger the

Visit us at www.mhhe.com/rwj

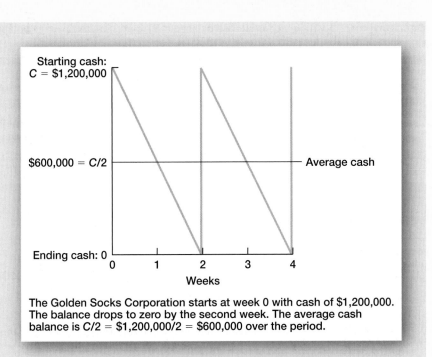

The Golden Socks Corporation starts at week 0 with cash of $1,200,000. The balance drops to zero by the second week. The average cash balance is $C/2 = \$1,200,000/2 = \$600,000$ over the period.

average cash balance, the greater is the opportunity cost (the return that could have been earned on marketable securities).

To determine the optimal strategy, Golden Socks needs to know the following three things:

F = The fixed cost of making a securities trade to replenish cash.
T = The total amount of new cash needed for transaction purposes over the relevant planning period—say, one year.
R = The opportunity cost of holding cash. This is the interest rate on marketable securities.

With this information, Golden Socks can determine the total costs of any particular cash balance policy. It can then determine the optimal cash balance policy.

The Opportunity Costs   To determine the opportunity costs of holding cash, we have to find out how much interest is forgone. Golden Socks has, on average, $C/2$ in cash. This amount could be earning interest at rate R. So the total dollar opportunity costs of cash balances are equal to the average cash balance multiplied by the interest rate:

$$\text{Opportunity costs} = (C/2) \times R \qquad \text{[19A.1]}$$

For example, the opportunity costs of various alternatives are given here, assuming that the interest rate is 10 percent:

Initial Cash Balance	Average Cash Balance	Opportunity Cost (R = .10)
C	$C/2$	$(C/2) \times R$
$4,800,000	$2,400,000	$240,000
2,400,000	1,200,000	120,000
1,200,000	600,000	60,000
600,000	300,000	30,000
300,000	150,000	15,000

Visit us at www.mhhe.com/rwj

In our original case, in which the initial cash balance is $1.2 million, the average balance is $600,000. The interest Golden Socks could have earned on this (at 10 percent) is $60,000, so this is what the firm gives up with this strategy. Notice that the opportunity costs increase as the initial (and average) cash balance rises.

The Trading Costs   To determine the total trading costs for the year, we need to know how many times Golden Socks will have to sell marketable securities during the year. First, the total amount of cash disbursed during the year is $600,000 per week, so $T = \$600,000 \times 52$ weeks $= \$31.2$ million. If the initial cash balance is set at $C = \$1.2$ million, Golden Socks will sell $1.2 million in marketable securities: $T/C = \$31.2$ million$/1.2$ million $= 26$ times per year. It costs F dollars each time, so trading costs are given by:

$$\frac{\$31.2 \text{ million}}{\$1.2 \text{ million}} \times F = 26 \times F$$

In general, the total trading costs will be given by:

$$\text{Trading costs} = (T/C) \times F \qquad \text{[19A.2]}$$

In this example, if F were $1,000 (an unrealistically large amount), the trading costs would be $26,000.

We can calculate the trading costs associated with some different strategies as follows:

Total Amount of Disbursements during Relevant Period	Initial Cash Balance	Trading Costs (F = $1,000)
T	C	$(T/C) \times F$
$31,200,000	$4,800,000	$ 6,500
31,200,000	2,400,000	13,000
31,200,000	1,200,000	26,000
31,200,000	600,000	52,000
31,200,000	300,000	104,000

The Total Cost   Now that we have the opportunity costs and the trading costs, we can calculate the total cost by adding them together:

$$\begin{aligned} \text{Total cost} &= \text{Opportunity costs} + \text{Trading costs} \\ &= (C/2) \times R + (T/C) \times F \end{aligned} \qquad \text{[19A.3]}$$

Using the numbers generated earlier, we have the following:

Cash Balance	Opportunity Costs	+	Trading Costs	=	Total Cost
$4,800,000	$240,000		$ 6,500		$246,500
2,400,000	120,000		13,000		133,000
1,200,000	60,000		26,000		86,000
600,000	30,000		52,000		82,000
300,000	15,000		104,000		119,000

Notice how the total cost starts out at almost $250,000 and declines to about $82,000 before starting to rise again.

The Solution   We can see from the preceding schedule that a $600,000 cash balance results in the lowest total cost of the possibilities presented: $82,000. But what about $700,000 or $500,000 or other possibilities? It appears that the optimal balance is somewhere between

$300,000 and $1.2 million. With this in mind, we could easily proceed by trial and error to find the optimal balance. It is not difficult to find it directly, however, so we do this next.

Take a look back at Figure 19A.1. As the figure is drawn, the optimal size of the cash balance, C^*, occurs right where the two lines cross. At this point, the opportunity costs and the trading costs are exactly equal. So at C^*, we must have that:

Opportunity costs = Trading costs

$$(C^*/2) \times R = (T/C^*) \times F$$

With a little algebra, we can write:

$$C^{*2} = (2T \times F)/R$$

To solve for C^*, we take the square root of both sides to get:

$$C^* = \sqrt{(2T \times F)/R}$$
                                    [19A.4]

This is the optimal initial cash balance.

For Golden Socks, we have $T = \$31.2$ million, $F = \$1,000$, and $R = 10\%$. We can now find the optimal cash balance:

$$C^* = \sqrt{(2 \times \$31,200,000 \times 1,000)/.10}$$
$$= \sqrt{\$624 \text{ billion}}$$
$$= \$789,937$$

We can verify this answer by calculating the various costs at this balance, as well as a little above and a little below:

Cash Balance	Opportunity Costs	+	Trading Costs	=	Total Cost
$850,000	$42,500		$36,706		$79,206
800,000	40,000		39,000		79,000
789,937	39,497		39,497		78,994
750,000	37,500		41,600		79,100
700,000	35,000		44,571		79,571

The total cost at the optimal cash level is $78,994, and it does appear to increase as we move in either direction.

The BAT Model	**EXAMPLE 19A.1**

The Vulcan Corporation has cash outflows of $100 per day, seven days a week. The interest rate is 5 percent, and the fixed cost of replenishing cash balances is $10 per transaction. What is the optimal initial cash balance? What is the total cost?

The total cash needed for the year is 365 days × $100 = $36,500. From the BAT model, we have that the optimal initial balance is:

$$C^* = \sqrt{(2T \times F)/R}$$
$$= \sqrt{(2 \times \$36,500 \times 10)/.05}$$
$$= \sqrt{\$14.6 \text{ million}}$$
$$= \$3,821$$

The average cash balance is $3,821/2 = $1,911, so the opportunity cost is $1,911 × .05 = $96. Because Vulcan needs $100 per day, the $3,821 balance will last $3,821/100 = 38.21 days. The firm needs to resupply the account 365/38.21 = 9.6 times per year, so the trading (order) cost is $96. The total cost is $192.

Visit us at www.mhhe.com/rwj

Conclusion   The BAT model is possibly the simplest and most stripped-down sensible model for determining the optimal cash position. Its chief weakness is that it assumes steady, certain cash outflows. We next discuss a more involved model designed to deal with this limitation.

THE MILLER–ORR MODEL: A MORE GENERAL APPROACH

We now describe a cash management system designed to deal with cash inflows and outflows that fluctuate randomly from day to day. With this model, we again concentrate on the cash balance. But in contrast to the situation with the BAT model, we assume that this balance fluctuates up and down randomly and that the average change is zero.

The Basic Idea   Figure 19A.3 shows how the system works. It operates in terms of an upper limit (U^*) and a lower limit (L) to the amount of cash, as well as a target cash balance (C^*). The firm allows its cash balance to wander around between the lower and upper limits. As long as the cash balance is somewhere between U^* and L, nothing happens.

When the cash balance reaches the upper limit (U^*), as it does at point X, the firm moves $U^* - C^*$ dollars out of the account and into marketable securities. This action moves the cash balance down to C^*. In the same way, if the cash balance falls to the lower limit (L), as it does at point Y, the firm will sell $C^* - L$ worth of securities and deposit the cash in the account. This action takes the cash balance up to C^*.

Using the Model   To get started, management sets the lower limit (L). This limit essentially defines a safety stock; so where it is set depends on how much risk of a cash shortfall the firm is willing to tolerate. Alternatively, the minimum might just equal a required compensating balance.

As with the BAT model, the optimal cash balance depends on trading costs and opportunity costs. Once again, the cost per transaction of buying and selling marketable securities,

Visit us at www.mhhe.com/rwj

FIGURE 19A.3

The Miller–Orr Model

U^* is the upper control limit. L is the lower control limit. The target cash balance is C^*. As long as cash is between L and U^*, no transaction is made.

F, is assumed to be fixed. Also, the opportunity cost of holding cash is R, the interest rate per period on marketable securities.

The only extra piece of information needed is σ^2, the variance of the net cash flow per period. For our purposes, the period can be anything—a day or a week, for example—as long as the interest rate and the variance are based on the same length of time.

Given L, which is set by the firm, Miller and Orr show that the cash balance target, C^*, and the upper limit, U^*, that minimize the total costs of holding cash are:[2]

$$C^* = L + (3/4 \times F \times \sigma^2/R)^{(1/3)} \tag{19A.5}$$

$$U^* = 3 \times C^* - 2 \times L \tag{19A.6}$$

Also, the average cash balance in the Miller–Orr model is:

$$\text{Average cash balance} = (4 \times C^* - L)/3 \tag{19A.7}$$

The derivation of these expressions is relatively complex, so we will not present it here. Fortunately, as we illustrate next, the results are not difficult to use.

For example, suppose $F = \$10$, the interest rate is 1 percent per month, and the standard deviation of the monthly net cash flows is $\$200$. The variance of the monthly net cash flows is:

$$\sigma^2 = \$200^2 = \$40{,}000$$

We assume a minimum cash balance of $L = \$100$. We can calculate the cash balance target, C^*, as follows:

$$
\begin{aligned}
C^* &= L + (3/4 \times F \times \sigma^2/R)^{(1/3)} \\
&= \$100 + (3/4 \times 10 \times 40{,}000/.01)^{(1/3)} \\
&= \$100 + 30{,}000{,}000^{(1/3)} \\
&= \$100 + 311 = \$411
\end{aligned}
$$

The upper limit, U^*, is thus:

$$
\begin{aligned}
U^* &= 3 \times C^* - 2 \times L \\
&= 3 \times \$411 - 2 \times 100 \\
&= \$1{,}033
\end{aligned}
$$

Finally, the average cash balance will be:

$$
\begin{aligned}
\text{Average cash balance} &= (4 \times C^* - L)/3 \\
&= (4 \times \$411 - 100)/3 \\
&= \$515
\end{aligned}
$$

IMPLICATIONS OF THE BAT AND MILLER–ORR MODELS

Our two cash management models differ in complexity, but they have some similar implications. In both cases, all other things being equal, we see that:

1. The greater the interest rate, the lower is the target cash balance.
2. The greater the order cost, the higher is the target balance.

These implications are both fairly obvious. The advantage of the Miller–Orr model is that it improves our understanding of the problem of cash management by considering the effect of uncertainty as measured by the variation in net cash inflows.

---

[2]M.H. Miller and D. Orr, "A Model of the Demand for Money by Firms," *Quarterly Journal of Economics*, August 1966.

Visit us at www.mhhe.com/rwj

The Miller–Orr model shows that the greater the uncertainty is (the higher σ^2 is), the greater is the difference between the target balance and the minimum balance. Similarly, the greater the uncertainty is, the higher is the upper limit and the higher is the average cash balance. These statements all make intuitive sense. For example, the greater the variability is, the greater is the chance that the balance will drop below the minimum. We thus keep a higher balance to guard against this happening.

OTHER FACTORS INFLUENCING THE TARGET CASH BALANCE

Before moving on, we briefly discuss two additional considerations that affect the target cash balance.

First, in our discussion of cash management, we assume cash is invested in marketable securities such as Treasury bills. The firm obtains cash by selling these securities. Another alternative is to borrow cash. Borrowing introduces additional considerations to cash management:

1. Borrowing is likely to be more expensive than selling marketable securities because the interest rate is likely to be higher.
2. The need to borrow will depend on management's desire to hold low cash balances. A firm is more likely to have to borrow to cover an unexpected cash outflow with greater cash flow variability and lower investment in marketable securities.

Second, for large firms, the trading costs of buying and selling securities are small when compared to the opportunity costs of holding cash. For example, suppose a firm has $1 million in cash that won't be needed for 24 hours. Should the firm invest the money or leave it sitting?

Suppose the firm can invest the money at an annualized rate of 7.57 percent per year. The daily rate in this case is about two basis points (.02 percent or .0002).[3] The daily return earned on $1 million is thus .0002 × $1 million = $200. In many cases, the order cost will be much less than this; so a large firm will buy and sell securities very often before it will leave substantial amounts of cash idle.

Concept Questions

19A.1a What is a target cash balance?
19A.1b What is the basic trade-off in the BAT model?
19A.1c Describe how the Miller–Orr model works.

APPENDIX REVIEW AND SELF-TEST PROBLEM

19A.1   The BAT Model Given the following information, calculate the target cash balance using the BAT model:

Annual interest rate	12%
Fixed order cost	$100
Total cash needed	$240,000

What are the opportunity cost of holding cash, the trading cost, and the total cost? What would these be if $15,000 were held instead? If $25,000 were held?

---

[3]A basis point is 1 percent of 1 percent. Also, the annual interest rate is calculated as $(1 + R)^{365} = 1.0757$, implying a daily rate of .02 percent.

ANSWER TO APPENDIX REVIEW AND SELF-TEST PROBLEM

19A.1   From the BAT model, we know that the target cash balance is:

$$C^* = \sqrt{(2T \times F)/R}$$
$$= \sqrt{(2 \times \$240,000 \times 100)/.12}$$
$$= \sqrt{\$400,000,000}$$
$$= \$20,000$$

The average cash balance will be $C^*/2 = \$20,000/2 = \$10,000$. The opportunity cost of holding $10,000 when the going rate is 12 percent is $10,000 × .12 = $1,200. There will be $240,000/20,000 = 12 orders during the year, so the order cost, or trading cost, is also 12 × $100 = $1,200. The total cost is thus $2,400.

   If $15,000 is held, the average balance is $7,500. Verify that the opportunity, trading, and total costs in this case are $900, $1,600, and $2,500, respectively. If $25,000 is held, these numbers are $1,500, $960, and $2,460, respectively.

QUESTIONS AND PROBLEMS

1.   **Changes in Target Cash Balances**   Indicate the likely impact of each of the following on a company's target cash balance. Use the letter *I* to denote an increase and *D* to denote a decrease. Briefly explain your reasoning in each case:

BASIC
(Questions 1–10)

   a. Commissions charged by brokers decrease.

   b. Interest rates paid on money market securities rise.

   c. The compensating balance requirement of a bank is raised.

   d. The firm's credit rating improves.

   e. The cost of borrowing increases.

   f. Direct fees for banking services are established.

2.   **Using the BAT Model**   Given the following information, calculate the target cash balance using the BAT model:

Annual interest rate	4.5%
Fixed order cost	$25
Total cash needed	$10,200

   How do you interpret your answer?

3.   **Opportunity versus Trading Costs**   White Whale Corporation has an average daily cash balance of $1,700. Total cash needed for the year is $64,000. The interest rate is 5 percent, and replenishing the cash costs $8 each time. What are the opportunity cost of holding cash, the trading cost, and the total cost? What do you think of White Whale's strategy?

4.   **Costs and the BAT Model**   Debit and Credit Bookkeepers needs a total of $21,000 in cash during the year for transactions and other purposes. Whenever cash runs low, it sells $1,500 in securities and transfers the cash in. The interest rate is 4 percent per year, and selling securities costs $25 per sale.

   a. What is the opportunity cost under the current policy? The trading cost? With no additional calculations, would you say that Debit and Credit keeps too much or too little cash? Explain.

   b. What is the target cash balance derived using the BAT model?

Visit us at www.mhhe.com/rwj

5. **Determining Optimal Cash Balances** The All Day Company is currently holding $690,000 in cash. It projects that over the next year its cash outflows will exceed cash inflows by $140,000 per month. How much of the current cash holdings should be retained, and how much should be used to increase the company's holdings of marketable securities? Each time these securities are bought or sold through a broker, the company pays a fee of $250. The annual interest rate on money market securities is 3.2 percent. After the initial investment of excess cash, how many times during the next 12 months will securities be sold?

6. **Interpreting Miller–Orr** All Night, Inc., uses a Miller–Orr cash management approach with a lower limit of $43,000, an upper limit of $125,000, and a target balance of $80,000. Explain what each of these points represents; then explain how the system will work.

7. **Using Miller–Orr** Slap Shot Corporation has a fixed cost associated with buying and selling marketable securities of $40. The interest rate is currently .013 percent per day, and the firm has estimated that the standard deviation of its daily net cash flows is $80. Management has set a lower limit of $1,500 on cash holdings. Calculate the target cash balance and upper limit using the Miller–Orr model. Describe how the system will work.

8. **Interpreting Miller– Orr** Based on the Miller–Orr model, describe what will happen to the lower limit, the upper limit, and the spread (the distance between the two) if the variation in net cash flow grows. Give an intuitive explanation for why this happens. What happens if the variance drops to zero?

9. **Using Miller–Orr** The variance of the daily cash flows for the Pele Bicycle Shop is $890,000. The opportunity cost to the firm of holding cash is 4.1 percent per year. What should the target cash level and the upper limit be if the tolerable lower limit has been established as $160,000? The fixed cost of buying and selling securities is $300 per transaction.

10. **Using BAT** Rise Against Corporation has determined that its target cash balance if it uses the BAT model is $5,100. The total cash needed for the year is $31,000, and the order cost is $10. What interest rate must Rise Against be using?

CREDIT AND INVENTORY MANAGEMENT

ON MARCH 11, 2011, a devastating tsunami hit Japan. While business problems in the immediate area were to be expected, they actually extended much further. For example, on March 17, General Motors announced that it would shut down its plant in Shreveport, Louisiana, because of a parts shortage caused by the tsunami. Other carmakers experienced similar problems. Nissan announced that it would shut down four plants in North America for several weeks because of parts shortages, and Honda announced that it would cut shifts at its seven North American plants from eight hours to four hours to conserve parts. In fact, one analyst estimated that the supply of new cars in the United States would likely be affected well into the summer. As these examples show, inventory shortages of things like key parts can cause major problems for businesses, but companies also dislike carrying excessive inventory levels for a variety of reasons. In this chapter, we discuss, among other things, how companies arrive at an optimal inventory level.

LEARNING OBJECTIVES

After studying this chapter, you should understand:

LO1 How firms manage their receivables and the basic components of a firm's credit policies.

LO2 How to analyze the decision by a firm to grant credit.

LO3 The types of inventory and inventory management systems used by firms.

LO4 How to determine the costs of carrying inventory and the optimal inventory level.

20.1 Credit and Receivables

When a firm sells goods and services, it can demand cash on or before the delivery date or it can extend credit to customers and allow some delay in payment. The next few sections provide an idea of what is involved in the firm's decision to grant credit to its customers. Granting credit is making an investment in a customer—an investment tied to the sale of a product or service.

Why do firms grant credit? Not all do, but the practice is extremely common. The obvious reason is that offering credit is a way of stimulating sales. The costs associated with granting credit are not trivial. First, there is the chance that the customer will not pay. Second, the firm has to bear the costs of carrying the receivables. The credit policy decision thus involves a trade-off between the benefits of increased sales and the costs of granting credit.

From an accounting perspective, when credit is granted, an account receivable is created. Such receivables include credit to other firms, called *trade credit*, and credit granted to consumers, called *consumer credit*. About one-sixth of all the assets of U.S. industrial firms are in the form of accounts receivable, so receivables obviously represent a major investment of financial resources by U.S. businesses.

COMPONENTS OF CREDIT POLICY

If a firm decides to grant credit to its customers, then it must establish procedures for extending credit and collecting. In particular, the firm will have to deal with the following components of credit policy:

terms of sale
The conditions under which a firm sells its goods and services for cash or credit.

1. **Terms of sale:** The terms of sale establish how the firm proposes to sell its goods and services. A basic decision is whether the firm will require cash or will extend credit. If the firm does grant credit to a customer, the terms of sale will specify (perhaps implicitly) the credit period, the cash discount and discount period, and the type of credit instrument.

credit analysis
The process of determining the probability that customers will not pay.

2. **Credit analysis:** In granting credit, a firm determines how much effort to expend trying to distinguish between customers who will pay and customers who will not pay. Firms use a number of devices and procedures to determine the probability that customers will not pay; put together, these are called credit analysis.

collection policy
The procedures followed by a firm in collecting accounts receivable.

3. **Collection policy:** After credit has been granted, the firm has the potential problem of collecting the cash, for which it must establish a collection policy.

In the next several sections, we will discuss these components of credit policy that collectively make up the decision to grant credit.

THE CASH FLOWS FROM GRANTING CREDIT

In a previous chapter, we described the accounts receivable period as the time it takes to collect on a sale. There are several events that occur during this period. These events are the cash flows associated with granting credit, and they can be illustrated with a cash flow diagram:

These companies assist businesses with working capital management:
www.treasury.pncbank.com
and www.treasurystrat.
com.

The Cash Flows of Granting Credit

As our time line indicates, the typical sequence of events when a firm grants credit is as follows: (1) The credit sale is made, (2) the customer sends a check to the firm, (3) the firm deposits the check, and (4) the firm's account is credited for the amount of the check.

Based on our discussion in the previous chapter, it is apparent that one of the factors influencing the receivables period is float. Thus, one way to reduce the receivables period is to speed up the check mailing, processing, and clearing. Because we cover this subject elsewhere, we will ignore float in the subsequent discussion and focus on what is likely to be the major determinant of the receivables period: credit policy.

THE INVESTMENT IN RECEIVABLES

The investment in accounts receivable for any firm depends on the amount of credit sales and the average collection period. For example, if a firm's average collection period, ACP, is 30 days, then, at any given time, there will be 30 days' worth of sales outstanding. If credit sales run $1,000 per day, the firm's accounts receivable will then be equal to 30 days $\times$ $1,000 per day = $30,000, on average.

For more on accounts receivable management, visit www.insidearm.com.

As our example illustrates, a firm's receivables generally will be equal to its average daily sales multiplied by its average collection period:

$$\text{Accounts receivable} = \text{Average daily sales} \times \text{ACP} \qquad \textbf{[20.1]}$$

Thus, a firm's investment in accounts receivable depends on factors that influence credit sales and collections.

We have seen the average collection period in various places, including Chapter 3 and Chapter 18. Recall that we use the terms *days' sales in receivables, receivables period*, and *average collection period* interchangeably to refer to the length of time it takes for the firm to collect on a sale.

Concept Questions

20.1a What are the basic components of credit policy?

20.1b What are the basic components of the terms of sale if a firm chooses to sell on credit?

Terms of the Sale   20.2

As we described previously, the terms of a sale are made up of three distinct elements:

1. The period for which credit is granted (the credit period).
2. The cash discount and the discount period.
3. The type of credit instrument.

Within a given industry, the terms of sale are usually fairly standard, but these terms vary quite a bit across industries. In many cases, the terms of sale are remarkably archaic and literally date to previous centuries. Organized systems of trade credit that resemble current practice can be easily traced to the great fairs of medieval Europe, and they almost surely existed long before then.

THE BASIC FORM

The easiest way to understand the terms of sale is to consider an example. Terms such as 2/10, net 60 are common. This means that customers have 60 days from the invoice date (discussed a bit later) to pay the full amount; however, if payment is made within 10 days, a 2 percent cash discount can be taken.

Consider a buyer who places an order for $1,000, and assume that the terms of the sale are 2/10, net 60. The buyer has the option of paying $1,000 × (1 − .02) = $980 in 10 days, or paying the full $1,000 in 60 days. If the terms are stated as just net 30, then the customer has 30 days from the invoice date to pay the entire $1,000, and no discount is offered for early payment.

In general, credit terms are interpreted in the following way:

<take this discount off the invoice price> / <if you pay in this many days>,

<else pay the full invoice amount in this many days>

For more about the credit process for small businesses, see www.newyorkfed. org/education/addpub/ credit.html.

Thus, 5/10, net 45 means take a 5 percent discount from the full price if you pay within 10 days, or else pay the full amount in 45 days.

THE CREDIT PERIOD

credit period
The length of time for which credit is granted.

The **credit period** is the basic length of time for which credit is granted. The credit period varies widely from industry to industry, but it is almost always between 30 and 120 days. If a cash discount is offered, then the credit period has two components: the net credit period and the cash discount period.

The net credit period is the length of time the customer has to pay. The cash discount period is the time during which the discount is available. With 2/10, net 30, for example, the net credit period is 30 days and the cash discount period is 10 days.

invoice
A bill for goods or services provided by the seller to the purchaser.

The Invoice Date   The invoice date is the beginning of the credit period. An **invoice** is a written account of merchandise shipped to the buyer. For individual items, by convention, the invoice date is usually the shipping date or the billing date, *not* the date on which the buyer receives the goods or the bill.

Many other arrangements exist. For example, the terms of sale might be ROG, for *receipt of goods*. In this case, the credit period starts when the customer receives the order. This might be used when the customer is in a remote location.

With EOM dating, all sales made during a particular month are assumed to be made at the end of that month. This is useful when a buyer makes purchases throughout the month, but the seller bills only once a month.

For example, terms of 2/10th, EOM tell the buyer to take a 2 percent discount if payment is made by the 10th of the month; otherwise the full amount is due. Confusingly, the end of the month is sometimes taken to be the 25th day of the month. MOM, for middle of month, is another variation.

Seasonal dating is sometimes used to encourage sales of seasonal products during the off-season. A product sold primarily in the summer (e.g., suntan oil) can be shipped in January with credit terms of 2/10, net 30. However, the invoice might be dated May 1 so that the credit period actually begins at that time. This practice encourages buyers to order early.

Length of the Credit Period   Several factors influence the length of the credit period. Two important ones are the *buyer's* inventory period and operating cycle. All else equal, the shorter these are, the shorter the credit period will be.

As discussed in Chapter 18, the operating cycle has two components: the inventory period and the receivables period. The buyer's inventory period is the time it takes the buyer to acquire inventory (from us), process it, and sell it. The buyer's receivables period is the time it then takes the buyer to collect on the sale. Note that the credit period we offer is effectively the buyer's payables period.

By extending credit, we finance a portion of our buyer's operating cycle and thereby shorten that buyer's cash cycle (see Figure 18.1). If our credit period exceeds the buyer's inventory period, then we are financing not only the buyer's inventory purchases, but part of the buyer's receivables as well.

Furthermore, if our credit period exceeds our buyer's operating cycle, then we are effectively providing financing for aspects of our customer's business beyond the immediate purchase and sale of our merchandise. The reason is that the buyer effectively has a loan from us even after the merchandise is resold, and the buyer can use that credit for other purposes. For this reason, the length of the buyer's operating cycle is often cited as an appropriate upper limit to the credit period.

There are a number of other factors that influence the credit period. Many of these also influence our customer's operating cycles; so, once again, these are related subjects. Among the most important are these:

1. *Perishability and collateral value:* Perishable items have relatively rapid turnover and relatively low collateral value. Credit periods are thus shorter for such goods. For example, a food wholesaler selling fresh fruit and produce might use net seven days. Alternatively, jewelry might be sold for 5/30, net four months.

2. *Consumer demand:* Products that are well established generally have more rapid turnover. Newer or slow-moving products will often have longer credit periods associated with them to entice buyers. Also, as we have seen, sellers may choose to extend much longer credit periods for off-season sales (when customer demand is low).

3. *Cost, profitability, and standardization:* Relatively inexpensive goods tend to have shorter credit periods. The same is true for relatively standardized goods and raw materials. These all tend to have lower markups and higher turnover rates, both of which lead to shorter credit periods. However, there are exceptions. Auto dealers, for example, generally pay for cars as they are received.

4. *Credit risk:* The greater the credit risk of the buyer, the shorter the credit period is likely to be (if credit is granted at all).

5. *Size of the account:* If an account is small, the credit period may be shorter because small accounts cost more to manage, and the customers are less important.

6. *Competition:* When the seller is in a highly competitive market, longer credit periods may be offered as a way of attracting customers.

7. *Customer type:* A single seller might offer different credit terms to different buyers. A food wholesaler, for example, might supply groceries, bakeries, and restaurants. Each group would probably have different credit terms. More generally, sellers often have both wholesale and retail customers, and they frequently quote different terms to the two types.

CASH DISCOUNTS

As we have seen, **cash discounts** are often part of the terms of sale. The practice of granting discounts for cash purchases in the United States dates to the Civil War and is widespread today. One reason discounts are offered is to speed up the collection of receivables. This will have the effect of reducing the amount of credit being offered, and the firm must trade this off against the cost of the discount.

cash discount
A discount given to induce prompt payment. Also, *sales discount*.

Notice that when a cash discount is offered, the credit is essentially free during the discount period. The buyer pays for the credit only after the discount expires. With 2/10, net 30, a rational buyer either pays in 10 days to make the greatest possible use of the free credit or pays in 30 days to get the longest possible use of the money in exchange for giving up the discount. By giving up the discount, the buyer effectively gets $30 - 10 = 20$ days' credit.

Another reason for cash discounts is that they are a way of charging higher prices to customers that have had credit extended to them. In this sense, cash discounts are a convenient way of charging for the credit granted to customers.

Visit the National Association of Credit Management at www.nacm.org.

Cost of the Credit   In our examples, it might seem that the discounts are rather small. With 2/10, net 30, for example, early payment gets the buyer only a 2 percent discount. Does this provide a significant incentive for early payment? The answer is yes because the implicit interest rate is extremely high.

To see why the discount is important, we will calculate the cost to the buyer of not paying early. To do this, we will find the interest rate that the buyer is effectively paying for the trade credit. Suppose the order is for $1,000. The buyer can pay $980 in 10 days or wait another 20 days and pay $1,000. It's obvious that the buyer is effectively borrowing $980 for 20 days and that the buyer pays $20 in interest on the "loan." What's the interest rate?

This interest is ordinary discount interest, which we discussed in Chapter 5. With $20 in interest on $980 borrowed, the rate is $20/980 = 2.0408\%$. This is relatively low, but remember that this is the rate per 20-day period. There are $365/20 = 18.25$ such periods in a year; so, by not taking the discount, the buyer is paying an effective annual rate (EAR) of:

$$EAR = 1.020408^{18.25} - 1 = 44.6\%$$

From the buyer's point of view, this is an expensive source of financing!

Given that the interest rate is so high here, it is unlikely that the seller benefits from early payment. Ignoring the possibility of default by the buyer, the decision of a customer to forgo the discount almost surely works to the seller's advantage.

Trade Discounts   In some circumstances, the discount is not really an incentive for early payment but is instead a *trade discount*, a discount routinely given to some type of buyer. For example, with our 2/10th, EOM terms, the buyer takes a 2 percent discount if the invoice is paid by the 10th, but the bill is considered due on the 10th, and overdue after that. Thus, the credit period and the discount period are effectively the same, and there is no reward for paying before the due date.

The Cash Discount and the ACP   To the extent that a cash discount encourages customers to pay early, it will shorten the receivables period and, all other things being equal, reduce the firm's investment in receivables.

For example, suppose a firm currently has terms of net 30 and an average collection period (ACP) of 30 days. If it offers terms of 2/10, net 30, then perhaps 50 percent of its customers (in terms of volume of purchases) will pay in 10 days. The remaining customers will still take an average of 30 days to pay. What will the new ACP be? If the firm's annual sales are $15 million (before discounts), what will happen to the investment in receivables?

If half of the customers take 10 days to pay and half take 30, then the new average collection period will be:

$$\text{New ACP} = .50 \times 10 \text{ days} + .50 \times 30 \text{ days} = 20 \text{ days}$$

The ACP thus falls from 30 days to 20 days. Average daily sales are $15 million/365 = $41,096 per day. Receivables will thus fall by $41,096 \times 10 = $410,960.

CREDIT INSTRUMENTS

The **credit instrument** is the basic evidence of indebtedness. Most trade credit is offered on *open account*. This means that the only formal instrument of credit is the invoice, which is sent with the shipment of goods and which the customer signs as evidence that the goods have been received. Afterward, the firm and its customers record the exchange on their books of account.

credit instrument
The evidence of indebtedness.

At times, the firm may require that the customer sign a *promissory note*. This is a basic IOU and might be used when the order is large, when there is no cash discount involved, or when the firm anticipates a problem in collections. Promissory notes are not common, but they can eliminate possible controversies later about the existence of debt.

One problem with promissory notes is that they are signed after delivery of the goods. One way to obtain a credit commitment from a customer before the goods are delivered is to arrange a *commercial draft*. Typically, the firm draws up a commercial draft calling for the customer to pay a specific amount by a specified date. The draft is then sent to the customer's bank with the shipping invoices.

If immediate payment is required on the draft, it is called a *sight draft*. If immediate payment is not required, then the draft is a *time draft*. When the draft is presented and the buyer "accepts" it, meaning that the buyer promises to pay it in the future, then it is called a *trade acceptance* and is sent back to the selling firm. The seller can then keep the acceptance or sell it to someone else. If a bank accepts the draft, meaning that the bank is guaranteeing payment, then the draft becomes a *banker's acceptance*. This arrangement is common in international trade, and banker's acceptances are actively traded in the money market.

A firm can also use a conditional sales contract as a credit instrument. With such an arrangement, the firm retains legal ownership of the goods until the customer has completed payment. Conditional sales contracts usually are paid in installments and have an interest cost built into them.

Concept Questions

20.2a What considerations enter the determination of the terms of sale?

20.2b Explain what terms of "3/45, net 90" mean. What is the effective interest rate?

Analyzing Credit Policy   20.3

In this section, we take a closer look at the factors that influence the decision to grant credit. Granting credit makes sense only if the NPV from doing so is positive. We thus need to look at the NPV of the decision to grant credit.

CREDIT POLICY EFFECTS

In evaluating credit policy, there are five basic factors to consider:

1. *Revenue effects:* If the firm grants credit, then there will be a delay in revenue collections as some customers take advantage of the credit offered and pay later. However, the firm may be able to charge a higher price if it grants credit and it may be able to increase the quantity sold. Total revenues may thus increase.

2. *Cost effects:* Although the firm may experience delayed revenues if it grants credit, it will still incur the costs of sales immediately. Whether the firm sells for cash or credit, it will still have to acquire or produce the merchandise (and pay for it).

3. *The cost of debt:* When the firm grants credit, it must arrange to finance the resulting receivables. As a result, the firm's cost of short-term borrowing is a factor in the decision to grant credit.[1]

4. *The probability of nonpayment:* If the firm grants credit, some percentage of the credit buyers will not pay. This can't happen, of course, if the firm sells for cash.

5. *The cash discount:* When the firm offers a cash discount as part of its credit terms, some customers will choose to pay early to take advantage of the discount.

EVALUATING A PROPOSED CREDIT POLICY

To illustrate how credit policy can be analyzed, we will start with a relatively simple case. Locust Software has been in existence for two years, and it is one of several successful firms that develop computer programs. Currently, Locust sells for cash only.

Locust is evaluating a request from some major customers to change its current policy to net one month (30 days). To analyze this proposal, we define the following:

P = Price per unit
v = Variable cost per unit
Q = Current quantity sold per month
Q' = Quantity sold under new policy
R = Monthly required return

For now, we ignore discounts and the possibility of default. Also, we ignore taxes because they don't affect our conclusions.

NPV of Switching Policies   To illustrate the NPV of switching credit policies, suppose we have the following for Locust:

P = $49
v = $20
Q = 100
Q' = 110

If the required return, R, is 2 percent per month, should Locust make the switch?

Currently, Locust has monthly sales of $P \times Q$ = $4,900. Variable costs each month are $v \times Q$ = $2,000, so the monthly cash flow from this activity is:

$$\text{Cash flow with old policy} = (P - v)Q \qquad \text{[20.2]}$$
$$= (\$49 - 20) \times 100$$
$$= \$2,900$$

This is not the total cash flow for Locust, of course, but it is all that we need to look at because fixed costs and other components of cash flow are the same whether or not the switch is made.

---

[1]The cost of short-term debt is not necessarily the required return on receivables, although it is commonly assumed to be. As always, the required return on an investment depends on the risk of the investment, not the source of the financing. The *buyer's* cost of short-term debt is closer in spirit to the correct rate. We will maintain the implicit assumption that the seller and the buyer have the same short-term debt cost. In any case, the time periods in credit decisions are relatively short, so a relatively small error in the discount rate will not have a large effect on our estimated NPV.

If Locust does switch to net 30 days on sales, then the quantity sold will rise to $Q' = 110$. Monthly revenues will increase to $P \times Q'$, and costs will be $v \times Q'$. The monthly cash flow under the new policy will thus be:

$$\text{Cash flow with new policy} = (P - v)\,Q' \qquad\qquad \textbf{[20.3]}$$
$$= (\$49 - 20) \times 110$$
$$= \$3,190$$

Going back to Chapter 10, we know that the relevant incremental cash flow is the difference between the new and old cash flows:

$$\text{Incremental cash inflow} = (P - v)(Q' - Q)$$
$$= (\$49 - 20) \times (110 - 100)$$
$$= \$290$$

This says that the benefit each month of changing policies is equal to the gross profit per unit sold, $P - v = \$29$, multiplied by the increase in sales, $Q' - Q = 10$. The present value of the future incremental cash flows is thus:

$$PV = [(P - v)(Q' - Q)]/R \qquad\qquad \textbf{[20.4]}$$

For Locust, this present value works out to be:

$$PV = (\$29 \times 10)/.02 = \$14,500$$

Notice that we have treated the monthly cash flow as a perpetuity because the same benefit will be realized each month forever.

Now that we know the benefit of switching, what's the cost? There are two components to consider. First, because the quantity sold will rise from Q to Q', Locust will have to produce $Q' - Q$ more units at a cost of $v(Q' - Q) = \$20 \times (110 - 100) = \$200$. Second, the sales that would have been collected this month under the current policy ($P \times Q = \$4,900$) will not be collected. Under the new policy, the sales made this month won't be collected until 30 days later. The cost of the switch is the sum of these two components:

$$\text{Cost of switching} = PQ + v(Q' - Q) \qquad\qquad \textbf{[20.5]}$$

For Locust, this cost would be $\$4,900 + 200 = \$5,100$.

Putting it all together, we see that the NPV of the switch is:

$$\text{NPV of switching} = -[PQ + v(Q' - Q)] + [(P - v)(Q' - Q)]/R \qquad\qquad \textbf{[20.6]}$$

For Locust, the cost of switching is $\$5,100$. As we saw earlier, the benefit is $\$290$ per month, forever. At 2 percent per month, the NPV is:

$$NPV = -\$5,100 + 290/.02$$
$$= -\$5,100 + 14,500$$
$$= \$9,400$$

Therefore, the switch is very profitable.

We'd Rather Fight Than Switch

EXAMPLE 20.1

Suppose a company is considering a switch from all cash to net 30, but the quantity sold is not expected to change. What is the NPV of the switch? Explain.

In this case, $Q' - Q$ is zero, so the NPV is just $-PQ$. What this says is that the effect of the switch is simply to postpone one month's collections forever, with no benefit from doing so.

A Break-Even Application   Based on our discussion thus far, the key variable for Locust is $Q' - Q$, the increase in unit sales. The projected increase of 10 units is only an estimate, so there is some forecasting risk. Under the circumstances, it's natural to wonder what increase in unit sales is necessary to break even.

Earlier, the NPV of the switch was defined as:

$$NPV = -[PQ + v(Q' - Q)] + [(P - v)(Q' - Q)]/R$$

We can calculate the break-even point explicitly by setting the NPV equal to zero and solving for $(Q' - Q)$:

$$NPV = 0 = -[PQ + v(Q' - Q)] + [(P - v)(Q' - Q)]/R$$
$$Q' - Q = PQ/[(P - v)/R - v] \qquad\qquad [20.7]$$

For Locust, the break-even sales increase is thus:

$$Q' - Q = \$4,900/(29/.02 - 20)$$
$$= 3.43 \text{ units}$$

This tells us that the switch is a good idea as long as Locust is confident that it can sell at least 3.43 more units per month.

Concept Questions

20.3a   What are the important effects to consider in a decision to offer credit?
20.3b   Explain how to estimate the NPV of a credit policy switch.

20.4 Optimal Credit Policy

For business reports on credit, visit www.creditworthy.com.

So far, we've discussed how to compute net present values for a switch in credit policy. We have not discussed the optimal amount of credit or the optimal credit policy. In principle, the optimal amount of credit is determined by the point at which the incremental cash flows from increased sales are exactly equal to the incremental costs of carrying the increase in investment in accounts receivable.

THE TOTAL CREDIT COST CURVE

The trade-off between granting credit and not granting credit isn't hard to identify, but it is difficult to quantify precisely. As a result, we can only describe an optimal credit policy.

To begin, the carrying costs associated with granting credit come in three forms:

1. The required return on receivables.
2. The losses from bad debts.
3. The costs of managing credit and credit collections.

We have already discussed the first and second of these. The third cost, the cost of managing credit, consists of the expenses associated with running the credit department. Firms that don't grant credit have no such department and no such expense. These three costs will all increase as credit policy is relaxed.

If a firm has a very restrictive credit policy, then all of the associated costs will be low. In this case, the firm will have a "shortage" of credit, so there will be an opportunity cost.

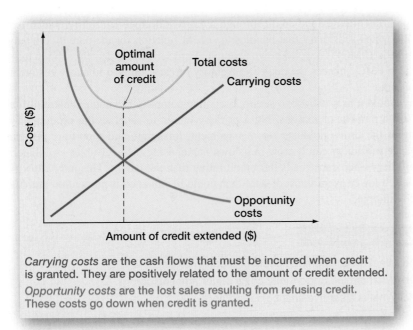

FIGURE 20.1

The Costs of Granting Credit

Carrying costs are the cash flows that must be incurred when credit is granted. They are positively related to the amount of credit extended.

Opportunity costs are the lost sales resulting from refusing credit. These costs go down when credit is granted.

This opportunity cost is the extra potential profit from credit sales that are lost because credit is refused. This forgone benefit comes from two sources: the increase in quantity sold, Q' minus Q, and (potentially) a higher price. The opportunity costs go down as credit policy is relaxed.

The sum of the carrying costs and the opportunity costs of a particular credit policy is called the total **credit cost curve**. We have drawn such a curve in Figure 20.1. As Figure 20.1 illustrates, there is a point where the total credit cost is minimized. This point corresponds to the optimal amount of credit or, equivalently, the optimal investment in receivables.

If the firm extends more credit than this minimum, the additional net cash flow from new customers will not cover the carrying costs of the investment in receivables. If the level of receivables is below this amount, then the firm is forgoing valuable profit opportunities.

In general, the costs and benefits from extending credit will depend on characteristics of particular firms and industries. All other things being equal, for example, it is likely that firms with (1) excess capacity, (2) low variable operating costs, and (3) repeat customers will extend credit more liberally than other firms. See if you can explain why each of these characteristics contributes to a more liberal credit policy.

credit cost curve
A graphical representation of the sum of the carrying costs and the opportunity costs of a credit policy.

ORGANIZING THE CREDIT FUNCTION

Firms that grant credit have the expense of running a credit department. In practice, firms often choose to contract out all or part of the credit function to a factor, an insurance company, or a captive finance company. Chapter 18 discusses factoring, an arrangement in which the firm sells its receivables. Depending on the specific arrangement, the factor may have full responsibility for credit checking, authorization, and collection. Smaller firms may find such an arrangement cheaper than running a credit department.

Firms that manage internal credit operations are self-insured against default. An alternative is to buy credit insurance through an insurance company. The insurance company offers coverage up to a preset dollar limit for accounts. As you would expect, accounts with a higher credit rating merit higher insurance limits. This type of insurance is particularly important for exporters, and government insurance is available for certain types of exports.

captive finance company

A wholly owned subsidiary that handles the credit function for the parent company.

Large firms often extend credit through a **captive finance company**, which is simply a wholly owned subsidiary that handles the credit function for the parent company. Ford Motor Credit (FMC) is a well-known example. Ford sells to car dealers, who in turn sell to customers. FMC finances the dealer's inventory of cars and also finances customers who buy the cars.

Why would a firm choose to set up a separate company to handle the credit function? There are a number of reasons, but a primary one is to separate the production and financing of the firm's products for management, financing, and reporting. For example, the finance subsidiary can borrow in its own name, using its receivables as collateral, and the subsidiary often carries a better credit rating than the parent. This may allow the firm to achieve a lower overall cost of debt than could be obtained if production and financing were commingled.

Concept Questions

20.4a What are the carrying costs of granting credit?

20.4b What are the opportunity costs of not granting credit?

20.4c What is a captive finance subsidiary?

20.5 Credit Analysis

Thus far, we have focused on establishing credit terms. Once a firm decides to grant credit to its customers, it must then establish guidelines for determining who will and who will not be allowed to buy on credit. *Credit analysis* refers to the process of deciding whether or not to extend credit to a particular customer. It usually involves two steps: gathering relevant information and determining creditworthiness.

Credit analysis is important simply because potential losses on receivables can be substantial. Companies report the amount of receivables they expect not to collect on their balance sheets. At the end of 2010, IBM reported that $734 million of accounts receivable were doubtful, and GE reported a staggering $8.1 billion as an allowance for losses.

WHEN SHOULD CREDIT BE GRANTED?

Imagine that a firm is trying to decide whether or not to grant credit to a customer. This decision can get complicated. For example, note that the answer depends on what will happen if credit is refused. Will the customer simply pay cash? Or will the customer not make the purchase at all? To avoid being bogged down by this and other difficulties, we will use some special cases to illustrate the key points.

A One-Time Sale We start by considering the simplest case. A new customer wishes to buy one unit on credit at a price of P per unit. If credit is refused, the customer will not make the purchase.

Furthermore, we assume that, if credit is granted, then, in one month, the customer will either pay up or default. The probability of the second of these events is π. In this case, the probability (π) can be interpreted as the percentage of *new* customers who will not pay. Our business does not have repeat customers, so this is strictly a one-time sale. Finally, the required return on receivables is R per month, and the variable cost is v per unit.

The analysis here is straightforward. If the firm refuses credit, then the incremental cash flow is zero. If it grants credit, then it spends v (the variable cost) this month and expects to collect $(1 - \pi) P$ next month. The NPV of granting credit is:

$$\text{NPV} = -v + (1 - \pi)P/(1 + R) \tag{20.8}$$

For example, for Locust Software, this NPV is:

$$\text{NPV} = -\$20 + (1 - \pi) \times 49/1.02$$

With, say, a 20 percent rate of default, this works out to be:

$$\text{NPV} = -\$20 + .80 \times 49/1.02 = \$18.43$$

Therefore, credit should be granted. Notice that we have divided by $(1 + R)$ here instead of by R because we now assume that this is a one-time transaction.

Our example illustrates an important point. In granting credit to a new customer, a firm risks its variable cost (v). It stands to gain the full price (P). For a new customer, then, credit may be granted even if the default probability is high. For example, the break-even probability in this case can be determined by setting the NPV equal to zero and solving for π:

$$\text{NPV} = 0 = -\$20 + (1 - \pi) \times 49/1.02$$
$$1 - \pi = \$20/49 \times 1.02$$
$$\pi = 58.4\%$$

Locust should extend credit as long as there is a $1 - .584 = 41.6\%$ chance or better of collecting. This explains why firms with higher markups tend to have looser credit terms.

This percentage (58.4%) is the maximum acceptable default probability for a *new* customer. If a returning, cash-paying customer wanted to switch to a credit basis, the analysis would be different, and the maximum acceptable default probability would be much lower.

The important difference is that, if we extend credit to a returning customer, we risk the total sales price (P), because this is what we collect if we don't extend credit. If we extend credit to a new customer, we risk only our variable cost.

Repeat Business   A second, very important factor to keep in mind is the possibility of repeat business. We can illustrate this by extending our one-time sale example. We make one important assumption: A new customer who does not default the first time around will remain a customer forever and never default.

If the firm grants credit, it spends v this month. Next month, it gets nothing if the customer defaults, or it gets P if the customer pays. If the customer pays, then the customer will buy another unit on credit and the firm will spend v again. The net cash inflow for the month is thus $P - v$. In every subsequent month, this same $P - v$ will occur as the customer pays for the previous month's order and places a new one.

It follows from our discussion that, in one month, the firm will receive $0 with probability π. With probability $(1 - \pi)$, however, the firm will have a permanent new customer. The value of a new customer is equal to the present value of $(P - v)$ every month forever:

$$\text{PV} = (P - v)/R$$

The NPV of extending credit is therefore:

$$\text{NPV} = -v + (1 - \pi)(P - v)/R \tag{20.9}$$

For Locust, this is:

$$\text{NPV} = -\$20 + (1 - \pi) \times (49 - 20)/.02$$
$$= -\$20 + (1 - \pi) \times 1,450$$

Even if the probability of default is 90 percent, the NPV is:

$$\text{NPV} = -\$20 + .10 \times 1,450 = \$125$$

Locust should extend credit unless default is a virtual certainty. The reason is that it costs only $20 to find out who is a good customer and who is not. A good customer is worth $1,450, however, so Locust can afford quite a few defaults.

Our repeat business example probably exaggerates the acceptable default probability, but it does illustrate that it will often turn out that the best way to do credit analysis is simply to extend credit to almost anyone. It also points out that the possibility of repeat business is a crucial consideration. In such cases, the important thing is to control the amount of credit initially offered to any one customer so that the possible loss is limited. The amount can be increased with time. Most often, the best predictor of whether or not someone will pay in the future is whether or not they have paid in the past.

CREDIT INFORMATION

Web-surfing students should peruse the Dun & Bradstreet home page. This major supplier of credit information can be found at www.dnb.com.

If a firm wants credit information about customers, there are a number of sources. Information sources commonly used to assess creditworthiness include the following:

1. *Financial statements:* A firm can ask a customer to supply financial statements such as balance sheets and income statements. Minimum standards and rules of thumb based on financial ratios like the ones we discussed in Chapter 3 can then be used as a basis for extending or refusing credit.

2. *Credit reports about the customer's payment history with other firms:* Quite a few organizations sell information about the credit strength and credit history of business firms. The best-known and largest firm of this type is Dun & Bradstreet, which provides subscribers with credit reports on individual firms. Experian is another well-known credit-reporting firm. Ratings and information are available for a huge number of firms, including very small ones. Equifax, Transunion, and Experian are the major suppliers of consumer credit information.

3. *Banks:* Banks will generally provide some assistance to their business customers in acquiring information about the creditworthiness of other firms.

4. *The customer's payment history with the firm:* The most obvious way to obtain information about the likelihood of customers not paying is to examine whether they have settled past obligations (and how quickly).

CREDIT EVALUATION AND SCORING

five Cs of credit
The five basic credit factors to be evaluated: character, capacity, capital, collateral, and conditions.

There are no magical formulas for assessing the probability that a customer will not pay. In very general terms, the classic **five Cs of credit** are the basic factors to be evaluated:

1. *Character:* The customer's willingness to meet credit obligations.
2. *Capacity:* The customer's ability to meet credit obligations out of operating cash flows.
3. *Capital:* The customer's financial reserves.
4. *Collateral:* An asset pledged in the case of default.
5. *Conditions:* General economic conditions in the customer's line of business.

credit scoring
The process of quantifying the probability of default when granting consumer credit.

Credit scoring is the process of calculating a numerical rating for a customer based on information collected; credit is then granted or refused based on the result. For example, a firm might rate a customer on a scale of 1 (very poor) to 10 (very good) on each of the five Cs of credit using all the information available about the customer. A credit score could then be calculated by totaling these ratings. Based on experience, a firm might choose to grant credit only to customers with a score above, say, 30.

Firms such as credit card issuers have developed statistical models for credit scoring. Usually, all of the legally relevant and observable characteristics of a large pool of customers are studied to find their historic relation to defaults. Based on the results, it is possible to determine the variables that best predict whether a customer will pay and then calculate a credit score based on those variables.

Because credit-scoring models and procedures determine who is and who is not creditworthy, it is not surprising that they have been the subject of government regulation. In particular, the kinds of background and demographic information that can be used in the credit decision are limited.

Concept Questions

20.5a What is credit analysis?

20.5b What are the five Cs of credit?

Collection Policy
20.6

Collection policy is the final element in credit policy. Collection policy involves monitoring receivables to spot trouble and obtaining payment on past-due accounts.

MONITORING RECEIVABLES

To keep track of payments by customers, most firms will monitor outstanding accounts. First of all, a firm will normally keep track of its average collection period (ACP) through time. If a firm is in a seasonal business, the ACP will fluctuate during the year; but unexpected increases in the ACP are a cause for concern. Either customers in general are taking longer to pay, or some percentage of accounts receivable are seriously overdue.

The **aging schedule** is a second basic tool for monitoring receivables. To prepare one, the credit department classifies accounts by age.[2] Suppose a firm has $100,000 in receivables. Some of these accounts are only a few days old, but others have been outstanding for quite some time. The following is an example of an aging schedule:

aging schedule
A compilation of accounts receivable by the age of each account.

Aging Schedule		
Age of Account	Amount	Percentage of Total Value of Accounts Receivable
0–10 days	$ 50,000	50%
11–60 days	25,000	25
61–80 days	20,000	20
Over 80 days	5,000	5
	$100,000	100%

If this firm has a credit period of 60 days, then 25 percent of its accounts are late. Whether or not this is serious depends on the nature of the firm's collections and customers. It is often the case that accounts beyond a certain age are almost never collected. Monitoring the age of accounts is very important in such cases.

---

[2]Aging schedules are used elsewhere in business such as inventory tracking.

Firms with seasonal sales will find the percentages on the aging schedule changing during the year. For example, if sales in the current month are very high, then total receivables will also increase sharply. This means that the older accounts, as a percentage of total receivables, become smaller and might appear less important. Some firms have refined the aging schedule so that they have an idea of how it should change with peaks and valleys in their sales.

COLLECTION EFFORT

A firm usually goes through the following sequence of procedures for customers whose payments are overdue:

1. It sends out a delinquency letter informing the customer of the past-due status of the account.
2. It makes a telephone call to the customer.
3. It employs a collection agency.
4. It takes legal action against the customer.

At times, a firm may refuse to grant additional credit to customers until arrearages are cleared up. This may antagonize a normally good customer, which points to a potential conflict between the collections department and the sales department.

In probably the worst case, the customer files for bankruptcy. When this happens, the credit-granting firm is just another unsecured creditor. The firm can simply wait, or it can sell its receivable. For example, when bookseller Borders filed for bankruptcy in 2011, it owed $178.8 million to its vendors and $18.6 million to its landlords. One of the largest vendors was publisher Penguin Putnam, which was owed $41.1 million. Of course, a firm can simply give up on its claim. Another publisher, Wiley, had already written off $9 million in debt for books sold to Borders.

> ### Concept Questions
>
> **20.6a** What tools can a manager use to monitor receivables?
> **20.6b** What is an aging schedule?

20.7 Inventory Management

Like receivables, inventories represent a significant investment for many firms. For a typical manufacturing operation, inventories will often exceed 15 percent of assets. For a retailer, inventories could represent more than 25 percent of assets. From our discussion in Chapter 18, we know that a firm's operating cycle is made up of its inventory period and its receivables period. This is one reason for considering credit and inventory policy in the same chapter. Beyond this, both credit policy and inventory policy are used to drive sales, and the two must be coordinated to ensure that the process of acquiring inventory, selling it, and collecting on the sale proceeds smoothly. For example, changes in credit policy designed to stimulate sales must be accompanied by planning for adequate inventory.

THE FINANCIAL MANAGER AND INVENTORY POLICY

Despite the size of a typical firm's investment in inventories, the financial manager of a firm will not normally have primary control over inventory management. Instead, other functional areas such as purchasing, production, and marketing will usually share decision-making authority regarding inventory. Inventory management has become an increasingly important specialty in its own right, and financial management will often only have input into the decision. For this reason, we will just survey some basics of inventory and inventory policy.

Visit the Society for Inventory Management Benchmarking Analysis at www.simba.org.

INVENTORY TYPES

For a manufacturer, inventory is normally classified into one of three categories. The first category is *raw material*. This is whatever the firm uses as a starting point in its production process. Raw materials might be something as basic as iron ore for a steel manufacturer or something as sophisticated as disk drives for a computer manufacturer.

The second type of inventory is *work-in-progress*, which is just what the name suggests—unfinished product. How big this portion of inventory is depends in large part on the length of the production process. For an airframe manufacturer, for example, work-in-progress can be substantial. The third and final type of inventory is *finished goods*— that is, products ready to ship or sell.

Keep in mind three things concerning inventory types. First, the names for the different types can be a little misleading because one company's raw materials can be another's finished goods. For example, going back to our steel manufacturer, iron ore would be a raw material, and steel would be the final product. An auto body panel stamping operation will have steel as its raw material and auto body panels as its finished goods, and an automobile assembler will have body panels as raw materials and automobiles as finished products.

The second thing to keep in mind is that the various types of inventory can be quite different in terms of their liquidity. Raw materials that are commodity-like or relatively standardized can be easy to convert to cash. Work-in-progress, on the other hand, can be quite illiquid and have little more than scrap value. As always, the liquidity of finished goods depends on the nature of the product.

Finally, a very important distinction between finished goods and other types of inventories is that the demand for an inventory item that becomes a part of another item is usually termed *derived* or *dependent demand* because the firm's need for these inventory types depends on its need for finished items. In contrast, the firm's demand for finished goods is not derived from demand for other inventory items, so it is sometimes said to be *independent*.

INVENTORY COSTS

As we discussed in Chapter 18, two basic types of costs are associated with current assets in general and with inventory in particular. The first of these is *carrying costs*. Here, carrying costs represent all of the direct and opportunity costs of keeping inventory on hand. These include:

1. Storage and tracking costs.
2. Insurance and taxes.
3. Losses due to obsolescence, deterioration, or theft.
4. The opportunity cost of capital on the invested amount.

The sum of these costs can be substantial, ranging roughly from 20 to 40 percent of inventory value per year.

The other type of costs associated with inventory is *shortage costs*. Shortage costs are costs associated with having inadequate inventory on hand. The two components of shortage costs are restocking costs and costs related to safety reserves. Depending on the firm's business, restocking or order costs are either the costs of placing an order with suppliers or the costs of setting up a production run. The costs related to safety reserves are opportunity losses such as lost sales and loss of customer goodwill that result from having inadequate inventory.

A basic trade-off exists in inventory management because carrying costs increase with inventory levels, whereas shortage or restocking costs decline with inventory levels. The basic goal of inventory management is thus to minimize the sum of these two costs. We consider ways to reach this goal in the next section.

Just to give you an idea of how important it is to balance carrying costs with shortage costs, consider the case of Kimberly-Clark, the well-known maker of Kleenex and Huggies. In the fourth quarter of 2010, the company cut production compared to the same period the previous year. Unfortunately, the company underestimated demand and missed out on an estimated $20 million in profit during the quarter.

Concept Questions

20.7a What are the different types of inventory?
20.7b What are three things to remember when examining inventory types?
20.7c What is the basic goal of inventory management?

20.8 Inventory Management Techniques

As we described earlier, the goal of inventory management is usually framed as cost minimization. Three techniques are discussed in this section, ranging from the relatively simple to the very complex.

THE ABC APPROACH

The ABC approach is a simple approach to inventory management in which the basic idea is to divide inventory into three (or more) groups. The underlying rationale is that a small portion of inventory in terms of quantity might represent a large portion in terms of inventory value. For example, this situation would exist for a manufacturer that uses some relatively expensive, high-tech components and some relatively inexpensive basic materials in producing its products.

Figure 20.2 illustrates an ABC comparison of items in terms of the percentage of inventory value represented by each group versus the percentage of items represented. As Figure 20.2 shows, the A Group constitutes only 10 percent of inventory by item count, but it represents over half of the value of inventory. The A Group items are thus monitored closely, and inventory levels are kept relatively low. At the other end, basic inventory items, such as nuts and bolts, also exist; but, because these are crucial and inexpensive, large quantities are ordered and kept on hand. These would be C Group items. The B Group is made up of in-between items.

THE ECONOMIC ORDER QUANTITY MODEL

The economic order quantity (EOQ) model is the best-known approach for explicitly establishing an optimal inventory level. The basic idea is illustrated in Figure 20.3, which plots

FIGURE 20.2

ABC Inventory Analysis

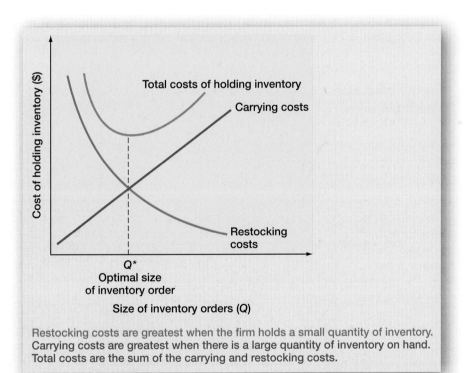

FIGURE 20.3

Costs of Holding
Inventory

the various costs associated with holding inventory (on the vertical axis) against inventory levels (on the horizontal axis). As shown, inventory carrying costs rise and restocking costs decrease as inventory levels increase. From our general discussion in Chapter 18 and our discussion of the total credit cost curve in this chapter, the general shape of the total inventory cost curve is familiar. With the EOQ model, we will attempt to specifically locate the minimum total cost point, Q^*.

In our discussion that follows, an important point to keep in mind is that the actual cost of the inventory itself is not included. The reason is that the *total* amount of inventory the firm needs in a given year is dictated by sales. What we are analyzing here is how much the firm should have on hand at any particular time. More precisely, we are trying to determine what order size the firm should use when it restocks its inventory.

Inventory Depletion   To develop the EOQ, we will assume that the firm's inventory is sold off at a steady rate until it hits zero. At that point, the firm restocks its inventory back to some optimal level. For example, suppose the Eyssell Corporation starts out today with 3,600 units of a particular item in inventory. Annual sales of this item are 46,800 units, which is about 900 per week. If Eyssell sells off 900 units of inventory each week, all the available inventory will be sold after four weeks, and Eyssell will restock by ordering (or manufacturing) another 3,600 and start over. This selling and restocking process produces a sawtooth pattern for inventory holdings; this pattern is illustrated in Figure 20.4. As the figure shows, Eyssell always starts with 3,600 units in inventory and ends up at zero. On average, then, inventory is half of 3,600, or 1,800 units.

The Carrying Costs   As Figure 20.3 illustrates, carrying costs are normally assumed to be directly proportional to inventory levels. Suppose we let Q be the quantity of inventory that Eyssell orders each time (3,600 units); we will call this the *restocking quantity*.

FIGURE 20.4

Inventory Holdings for the Eyssell Corporation

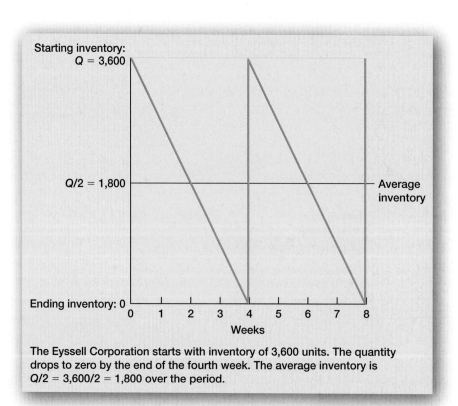

The Eyssell Corporation starts with inventory of 3,600 units. The quantity drops to zero by the end of the fourth week. The average inventory is $Q/2 = 3,600/2 = 1,800$ over the period.

Average inventory would then just be $Q/2$, or 1,800 units. If we let CC be the carrying cost per unit per year, Eyssell's total carrying costs will be:

$$\text{Total carrying costs} = \text{Average inventory} \times \text{Carrying costs per unit}$$
$$= (Q/2) \times \text{CC} \qquad \textbf{[20.10]}$$

In Eyssell's case, if carrying costs were \$.75 per unit per year, total carrying costs would be the average inventory of 1,800 multiplied by \$.75, or \$1,350 per year.

The Restocking Costs   For now, we will focus only on the restocking costs. In essence, we will assume that the firm never actually runs short on inventory, so that costs relating to safety reserves are not important. We will return to this issue later.

Restocking costs are normally assumed to be fixed. In other words, every time we place an order, fixed costs are associated with that order (remember that the cost of the inventory itself is not considered here). Suppose we let T be the firm's total unit sales per year. If the firm orders Q units each time, then it will need to place a total of T/Q orders. For Eyssell, annual sales are 46,800, and the order size is 3,600. Eyssell thus places a total of $46,800/3,600 = 13$ orders per year. If the fixed cost per order is F, the total restocking cost for the year would be:

$$\text{Total restocking cost} = \text{Fixed cost per order} \times \text{Number of orders}$$
$$= F \times (T/Q) \qquad \textbf{[20.11]}$$

For Eyssell, order costs might be \$50 per order, so the total restocking cost for 13 orders would be $\$50 \times 13 = \$650$ per year.

The Total Costs   The total costs associated with holding inventory are the sum of the carrying costs and the restocking costs:

$$\text{Total costs} = \text{Carrying costs} + \text{Restocking costs}$$
$$= (Q/2) \times \text{CC} + F \times (T/Q) \qquad \textbf{[20.12]}$$

Our goal is to find the value of Q, the restocking quantity, that minimizes this cost. To see how we might go about this, we can calculate total costs for some different values of Q. For the Eyssell Corporation, we had carrying costs (CC) of \$.75 per unit per year, fixed costs (F) of \$50 per order, and total unit sales (T) of 46,800 units. With these numbers, here are some possible total costs (check some of these for practice):

Restocking Quantity (Q)	Carrying Costs (Q/2 × CC)	+	Restocking Costs (F × T/Q)	=	Total Costs
500	$ 187.5		$4,680.0		$4,867.5
1,000	375.0		2,340.0		2,715.0
1,500	562.5		1,560.0		2,122.5
2,000	750.0		1,170.0		1,920.0
2,500	937.5		936.0		1,873.5
3,000	1,125.0		780.0		1,905.0
3,500	1,312.5		668.6		1,981.1

Inspecting the numbers, we see that total costs start out at almost \$5,000 and decline to just under \$1,900. The cost-minimizing quantity is about 2,500.

To find the cost-minimizing quantity, we can look back at Figure 20.3. What we notice is that the minimum point occurs right where the two lines cross. At this point, carrying costs and restocking costs are the same. For the particular types of costs we have assumed here, this will always be true; so we can find the minimum point just by setting these costs equal to each other and solving for Q^*:

$$\text{Carrying costs} = \text{Restocking costs}$$
$$(Q^*/2) \times \text{CC} = F \times (T/Q^*) \qquad \text{[20.13]}$$

With a little algebra, we get:

$$Q^{*2} = \frac{2T \times F}{\text{CC}} \qquad \text{[20.14]}$$

To solve for Q^*, we take the square root of both sides to find:

$$Q^* = \sqrt{\frac{2T \times F}{\text{CC}}} \qquad \text{[20.15]}$$

economic order quantity (EOQ)
The restocking quantity that minimizes the total inventory costs.

This reorder quantity, which minimizes the total inventory cost, is called the **economic order quantity (EOQ)**. For the Eyssell Corporation, the EOQ is:

$$
\begin{aligned}
Q^* &= \sqrt{\frac{2T \times F}{\text{CC}}} \\
&= \sqrt{\frac{(2 \times 46{,}800) \times \$50}{.75}} \\
&= \sqrt{6{,}240{,}000} \\
&= 2{,}498 \text{ units}
\end{aligned}
$$

Thus, for Eyssell, the economic order quantity is 2,498 units. At this level, verify that the restocking costs and carrying costs are both $936.75.

EXAMPLE 20.2	**Carrying Costs**

Thiewes Shoes begins each period with 100 pairs of hiking boots in stock. This stock is depleted each period and reordered. If the carrying cost per pair of boots per year is $3, what are the total carrying costs for the hiking boots?

Inventories always start at 100 items and end up at zero, so average inventory is 50 items. At an annual cost of $3 per item, total carrying costs are $150.

EXAMPLE 20.3	**Restocking Costs**

In Example 20.2, suppose Thiewes sells a total of 600 pairs of boots in a year. How many times per year does Thiewes restock? Suppose the restocking cost is $20 per order. What are total restocking costs?

Thiewes orders 100 items each time. Total sales are 600 items per year, so Thiewes restocks six times per year, or about once every two months. The restocking costs would be 6 orders × $20 per order = $120.

EXAMPLE 20.4	**The EOQ**

Based on our previous two examples, what size orders should Thiewes place to minimize costs? How often will Thiewes restock? What are the total carrying and restocking costs? The total costs?

We know that the total number of pairs of boots ordered for the year (T) is 600. The restocking cost (F) is $20 per order, and the carrying cost (CC) is $3. We can calculate the EOQ for Thiewes as follows:

$$
\begin{aligned}
EOQ &= \sqrt{\frac{2T \times F}{CC}} \\
&= \sqrt{\frac{(2 \times 600) \times \$20}{3}} \\
&= \sqrt{8,000} \\
&= 89.44 \text{ units}
\end{aligned}
$$

Because Thiewes sells 600 pairs per year, it will restock $600/89.44 = 6.71$ times. The total restocking costs will be $\$20 \times 6.71 = \$134.16$. Average inventory will be $89.44/2 = 44.72$. The carrying costs will be $\$3 \times 44.72 = \$134.16$, the same as the restocking costs. The total costs are thus $268.33.

EXTENSIONS TO THE EOQ MODEL

Thus far, we have assumed that a company will let its inventory run down to zero and then reorder. In reality, a company will wish to reorder before its inventory goes to zero for two reasons. First, by always having at least some inventory on hand, the firm minimizes the risk of a stockout and the resulting losses of sales and customers. Second, when a firm does reorder, there will be some time lag before the inventory arrives. Thus, to finish our discussion of the EOQ, we consider two extensions: safety stocks and reordering points.

Safety Stocks   A *safety stock* is the minimum level of inventory that a firm keeps on hand. Inventories are reordered whenever the level of inventory falls to the safety stock level. The top of Figure 20.5 illustrates how a safety stock can be incorporated into an EOQ model. Notice that adding a safety stock simply means that the firm does not run its inventory all the way down to zero. Other than this, the situation here is identical to that described in our earlier discussion of the EOQ.

Reorder Points   To allow for delivery time, a firm will place orders before inventories reach a critical level. The *reorder points* are the times at which the firm will actually place its inventory orders. These points are illustrated in the middle of Figure 20.5. As shown, the reorder points simply occur some fixed number of days (or weeks or months) before inventories are projected to reach zero.

One of the reasons that a firm will keep a safety stock is to allow for uncertain delivery times. We can therefore combine our reorder point and safety stock discussions in the bottom part of Figure 20.5. The result is a generalized EOQ model in which the firm orders in advance of anticipated needs and also keeps a safety stock of inventory.

MANAGING DERIVED-DEMAND INVENTORIES

The third type of inventory management technique is used to manage derived-demand inventories. As we described earlier, demand for some inventory types is derived from or dependent on other inventory needs. A good example is given by the auto manufacturing industry, in which the demand for finished products depends on consumer demand, marketing programs, and other factors related to projected unit sales. The demand for inventory items such as tires, batteries, headlights, and other components is then completely determined by the number of autos planned. Materials requirements planning and just-in-time inventory management are two methods for managing demand-dependent inventories.

FIGURE 20.5

Safety Stocks and Reorder Points

A. Safety stocks

With a safety stock, the firm reorders when inventory reaches a minimum level.

B. Reorder points

When there are lags in delivery or production times, the firm reorders when inventory reaches the reorder point.

C. Combined reorder points and safety stocks

By combining safety stocks and reorder points, the firm maintains a buffer against unforeseen events.

Materials Requirements Planning   Production and inventory specialists have developed computer-based systems for ordering and/or scheduling production of demand-dependent types of inventories. These systems fall under the general heading of **materials requirements planning (MRP)**. The basic idea behind MRP is that, once finished goods inventory levels are set, it is possible to determine what levels of work-in-progress inventories must exist to meet the need for finished goods. From there, it is possible to calculate the quantity of raw materials that must be on hand. This ability to schedule backward from finished goods inventories stems from the dependent nature of work-in-progress and raw materials inventories. MRP is particularly important for complicated products for which a variety of components are needed to create the finished product.

Just-in-Time Inventory   **Just-in-time (JIT) inventory** is a modern approach to managing dependent inventories. The goal of JIT is to minimize such inventories, thereby maximizing turnover. The approach began in Japan, and it is a fundamental part of Japanese manufacturing philosophy. As the name suggests, the basic goal of JIT is to have only enough inventory on hand to meet immediate production needs.

The result of the JIT system is that inventories are reordered and restocked frequently. Making such a system work and avoiding shortages requires a high degree of cooperation among suppliers. Japanese manufacturers often have a relatively small, tightly integrated group of suppliers with whom they work closely to achieve the needed coordination. These suppliers are a part of a large manufacturer's (such as Toyota's) industrial group, or *keiretsu*. Each large manufacturer tends to have its own *keiretsu*. It also helps to have suppliers located nearby, a situation that is common in Japan.

The *kanban* is an integral part of a JIT inventory system, and JIT systems are sometimes called *kanban systems*. The literal meaning of *kanban* is "card" or "sign"; but, broadly speaking, a kanban is a signal to a supplier to send more inventory. For example, a kanban can literally be a card attached to a bin of parts. When a worker pulls that bin, the card is detached and routed back to the supplier, who then supplies a replacement bin.

A JIT inventory system is an important part of a larger production planning process. A full discussion of it would necessarily shift our focus away from finance to production and operations management, so we will leave it here.

> **materials requirements planning (MRP)**
> A set of procedures used to determine inventory levels for demand-dependent inventory types such as work-in-progress and raw materials.

> **just-in-time (JIT) inventory**
> A system for managing demand-dependent inventories that minimizes inventory holdings.

Visit us at www.mhhe.com/rwj

Concept Questions

20.8a What does the EOQ model determine for the firm?
20.8b Which cost component of the EOQ model does JIT inventory minimize?

Summary and Conclusions   20.9

This chapter has covered the basics of credit and inventory policy. The major topics we discussed include these:

1. *The components of credit policy:* We discussed the terms of sale, credit analysis, and collection policy. Under the general subject of terms of sale, the credit period, the cash discount and discount period, and the credit instrument were described.

2. *Credit policy analysis:* We developed the cash flows from the decision to grant credit and showed how the credit decision can be analyzed in an NPV setting. The NPV of

granting credit depends on five factors: revenue effects, cost effects, the cost of debt, the probability of nonpayment, and the cash discount.

3. *Optimal credit policy:* The optimal amount of credit the firm should offer depends on the competitive conditions under which the firm operates. These conditions will determine the carrying costs associated with granting credit and the opportunity costs of the lost sales resulting from refusing to offer credit. The optimal credit policy minimizes the sum of these two costs.

4. *Credit analysis:* We looked at the decision to grant credit to a particular customer. We saw that two considerations are very important: the cost relative to the selling price and the possibility of repeat business.

5. *Collection policy:* Collection policy determines the method of monitoring the age of accounts receivable and dealing with past-due accounts. We described how an aging schedule can be prepared and the procedures a firm might use to collect on past-due accounts.

6. *Inventory types:* We described the different inventory types and how they differ in terms of liquidity and demand.

7. *Inventory costs:* The two basic inventory costs are carrying and restocking costs; we discussed how inventory management involves a trade-off between these two costs.

8. *Inventory management techniques:* We described the ABC approach and the EOQ model approach to inventory management. We also briefly touched on materials requirements planning (MRP) and just-in-time (JIT) inventory management.

Visit us at www.mhhe.com/rwj

CONNECT TO FINANCE

 |FINANCE   If you are using *Connect™ Finance* in your course, get online to take a Practice Test, check out study tools, and find out where you need additional practice.

▼ Chapter 20 Credit and Inventory Management			NPPT 40–41
20.1 Credit and Receivables	eBook	Study	Practice
20.2 Terms of the Sale	eBook	Study	Practice
20.3 Analyzing Credit Policy	eBook	Study	Practice
20.4 Optimal Credit Policy	eBook	Study	Practice
20.5 Credit Analysis	eBook	Study	Practice
20.6 Collection Policy	eBook	Study	Practice
20.7 Inventory Management	eBook	Study	Practice
20.8 Inventory Management Techniques	eBook	Study	Practice

Can you answer the following questions?

Section 20.1 What is the difference between the accounts receivable period and the cash collection period? (LO 20-1)

Section 20.2 Marsha can purchase goods for her store on credit terms of 2/10, net 25. What is the effective annual rate that Marsha will pay if she forgoes the discount on a purchase of $8,700? (LO 20-1)

Section 20.7 If Rosie's Formal Attire has too low of an inventory, the firm is most apt to _____. (LO 20-4)

Log on to find out!

CHAPTER REVIEW AND SELF-TEST PROBLEMS

20.1 **Credit Policy** The Cold Fusion Corp. (manufacturer of the Mr. Fusion home power plant) is considering a new credit policy. The current policy is cash only. The new policy would involve extending credit for one period. Based on the following information, determine if a switch is advisable. The interest rate is 2.0 percent per period:

	Current Policy	New Policy
Price per unit	$175	$175
Cost per unit	$130	$130
Sales per period in units	1,000	1,100

20.2 **Credit Where Credit Is Due** You are trying to decide whether or not to extend credit to a particular customer. Your variable cost is $15 per unit; the selling price is $22. This customer wants to buy 1,000 units today and pay in 30 days. You think there is a 15 percent chance of default. The required return is 3 percent per 30 days. Should you extend credit? Assume that this is a one-time sale and that the customer will not buy if credit is not extended.

20.3 **The EOQ** Annondale Manufacturing starts each period with 10,000 "Long John" golf clubs in stock. This stock is depleted each month and reordered. If the carrying cost per golf club is $1, and the fixed order cost is $5, is Annondale following an economically advisable strategy?

ANSWERS TO CHAPTER REVIEW AND SELF-TEST PROBLEMS

20.1 If the switch is made, an extra 100 units per period will be sold at a gross profit of $175 − 130 = $45 each. The total benefit is thus $45 × 100 = $4,500 per period. At 2.0 percent per period forever, the PV is $4,500/.02 = $225,000.

   The cost of the switch is equal to this period's revenue of $175 × 1,000 units = $175,000 plus the cost of producing the extra 100 units: 100 × $130 = $13,000. The total cost is thus $188,000, and the NPV is $225,000 − 188,000 = $37,000. The switch should be made.

20.2 If the customer pays in 30 days, then you will collect $22 × 1,000 = $22,000. There's only an 85 percent chance of collecting this; so you expect to get $22,000 × .85 = $18,700 in 30 days. The present value of this is $18,700/1.03 = $18,155.34. Your cost is $15 × 1,000 = $15,000; so the NPV is $18,155.34 − 15,000 = $3,155.34. Credit should be extended.

20.3 We can answer by first calculating Annondale's carrying and restocking costs. The average inventory is 5,000 clubs, and, because the carrying costs are $1 per club,

Visit us at www.mhhe.com/rwj

total carrying costs are $5,000. Annondale restocks every month at a fixed order cost of $5, so the total restocking costs are $60. What we see is that carrying costs are large relative to reorder costs, so Annondale is carrying too much inventory.

To determine the optimal inventory policy, we can use the EOQ model. Because Annondale orders 10,000 golf clubs 12 times per year, total needs (*T*) are 120,000 golf clubs. The fixed order cost is $5, and the carrying cost per unit (CC) is $1. The EOQ is therefore:

$$
\begin{aligned}
\text{EOQ} &= \sqrt{\frac{2T \times F}{\text{CC}}} \\
&= \sqrt{\frac{(2 \times 120,000) \times \$5}{1}} \\
&= \sqrt{1,200,000} \\
&= 1,095.45 \text{ units}
\end{aligned}
$$

We can check this by noting that the average inventory is about 550 clubs, so the carrying cost is $550. Annondale will have to reorder $120,000/1,095.45 = 109.54 \approx 110$ times. The fixed order cost is $5, so the total restocking cost is also about $550.

CONCEPTS REVIEW AND CRITICAL THINKING QUESTIONS

Visit us at www.mhhe.com/rwj

1. **Credit Instruments [LO1]** Describe each of the following:
   a. Sight draft.
   b. Time draft.
   c. Banker's acceptance.
   d. Promissory note.
   e. Trade acceptance.

2. **Trade Credit Forms [LO1]** In what form is trade credit most commonly offered? What is the credit instrument in this case?

3. **Receivables Costs [LO1]** What costs are associated with carrying receivables? What costs are associated with not granting credit? What do we call the sum of the costs for different levels of receivables?

4. **Five *C*s of Credit [LO1]** What are the five *C*s of credit? Explain why each is important.

5. **Credit Period Length [LO1]** What are some of the factors that determine the length of the credit period? Why is the length of the buyer's operating cycle often considered an upper bound on the length of the credit period?

6. **Credit Period Length [LO1]** In each of the following pairings, indicate which firm would probably have a longer credit period and explain your reasoning.
   a. Firm A sells a miracle cure for baldness; Firm B sells toupees.
   b. Firm A specializes in products for landlords; Firm B specializes in products for renters.
   c. Firm A sells to customers with an inventory turnover of 10 times; Firm B sells to customers with an inventory turnover of 20 times.
   d. Firm A sells fresh fruit; Firm B sells canned fruit.
   e. Firm A sells and installs carpeting; Firm B sells rugs.

7. **Inventory Types [LO3]** What are the different inventory types? How do the types differ? Why are some types said to have dependent demand whereas other types are said to have independent demand?

8. **Just-in-Time Inventory [LO3]** If a company moves to a JIT inventory management system, what will happen to inventory turnover? What will happen to total asset turnover? What will happen to return on equity (ROE)? (*Hint:* Remember the DuPont equation from Chapter 3.)

9. **Inventory Costs [LO3]** If a company's inventory carrying costs are $5 million per year and its fixed order costs are $8 million per year, do you think the firm keeps too much inventory on hand or too little? Why?

10. **Inventory Period [LO3]** At least part of Dell's corporate profits can be traced to its inventory management. Using just-in-time inventory, Dell typically maintains an inventory of three to four days' sales. Competitors such as Hewlett-Packard and IBM have attempted to match Dell's inventory policies, but lag far behind. In an industry where the price of PC components continues to decline, Dell clearly has a competitive advantage. Why would you say that it is to Dell's advantage to have such a short inventory period? If doing this is valuable, why don't all other PC manufacturers switch to Dell's approach?

QUESTIONS AND PROBLEMS

1. **Cash Discounts [LO1]** You place an order for 350 units of inventory at a unit price of $140. The supplier offers terms of 1/10, net 30.

    BASIC
    (Questions 1–12)

    a. How long do you have to pay before the account is overdue? If you take the full period, how much should you remit?

    b. What is the discount being offered? How quickly must you pay to get the discount? If you do take the discount, how much should you remit?

    c. If you don't take the discount, how much interest are you paying implicitly? How many days' credit are you receiving?

2. **Size of Accounts Receivable [LO1]** The Sand Surfer Corporation has annual sales of $38 million. The average collection period is 34 days. What is the average investment in accounts receivable as shown on the balance sheet? Assume 365 days per year.

3. **ACP and Accounts Receivable [LO1]** Kyoto Joe, Inc., sells earnings forecasts for Japanese securities. Its credit terms are 2/10, net 30. Based on experience, 65 percent of all customers will take the discount.

    a. What is the average collection period for Kyoto Joe?

    b. If Kyoto Joe sells 1,300 forecasts every month at a price of $1,750 each, what is its average balance sheet amount in accounts receivable?

4. **Size of Accounts Receivable [LO1]** Skye Flyer, Inc., has weekly credit sales of $17,300, and the average collection period is 36 days. What is the average accounts receivable figure?

5. **Terms of Sale [LO1]** A firm offers terms of 1/10, net 30. What effective annual interest rate does the firm earn when a customer does not take the discount? Without doing any calculations, explain what will happen to this effective rate if:

    a. The discount is changed to 2 percent.

    b. The credit period is increased to 45 days.

    c. The discount period is increased to 15 days.

6. **ACP and Receivables Turnover [LO1]** Rise Above This, Inc., has an average collection period of 33 days. Its average daily investment in receivables is $42,300.

Visit us at www.mhhe.com/rwj

What are annual credit sales? What is the receivables turnover? Assume 365 days per year.

7. **Size of Accounts Receivable [LO1]** Essence of Skunk Fragrances, Ltd., sells 8,200 units of its perfume collection each year at a price per unit of $430. All sales are on credit with terms of 1/10, net 40. The discount is taken by 60 percent of the customers. What is the amount of the company's accounts receivable? In reaction to sales by its main competitor, Sewage Spray, Essence of Skunk is considering a change in its credit policy to terms of 2/10, net 30 to preserve its market share. How will this change in policy affect accounts receivable?

8. **Size of Accounts Receivable [LO1]** The Arizona Bay Corporation sells on credit terms of net 30. Its accounts are, on average, 7 days past due. If annual credit sales are $9.3 million, what is the company's balance sheet amount in accounts receivable?

9. **Evaluating Credit Policy [LO2]** Air Spares is a wholesaler that stocks engine components and test equipment for the commercial aircraft industry. A new customer has placed an order for eight high-bypass turbine engines, which increase fuel economy. The variable cost is $1.9 million per unit, and the credit price is $2.015 million each. Credit is extended for one period, and based on historical experience, payment for about 1 out of every 200 such orders is never collected. The required return is 1.8 percent per period.

    a. Assuming that this is a one-time order, should it be filled? The customer will not buy if credit is not extended.

    b. What is the break-even probability of default in part (a)?

    c. Suppose that customers who don't default become repeat customers and place the same order every period forever. Further assume that repeat customers never default. Should the order be filled? What is the break-even probability of default?

    d. Describe in general terms why credit terms will be more liberal when repeat orders are a possibility.

10. **Credit Policy Evaluation [LO2]** Devour, Inc., is considering a change in its cash-only sales policy. The new terms of sale would be net one month. Based on the following information, determine if Devour should proceed or not. Describe the buildup of receivables in this case. The required return is .95 percent per month.

	Current Policy	New Policy
Price per unit	$720	$720
Cost per unit	$525	$525
Unit sales per month	1,240	1,290

11. **EOQ [LO4]** Redan Manufacturing uses 2,500 switch assemblies per week and then reorders another 2,500. If the relevant carrying cost per switch assembly is $7.50, and the fixed order cost is $1,300, is Redan's inventory policy optimal? Why or why not?

12. **EOQ [LO4]** The Trektronics store begins each week with 300 phasers in stock. This stock is depleted each week and reordered. If the carrying cost per phaser is $38 per year and the fixed order cost is $75, what is the total carrying cost? What is the restocking cost? Should Trektronics increase or decrease its order size? Describe an optimal inventory policy for Trektronics in terms of order size and order frequency.

INTERMEDIATE   13. **EOQ Derivation [LO4]** Prove that when carrying costs and restocking costs are as
(Questions 13–16)   described in the chapter, the EOQ must occur at the point where the carrying costs and restocking costs are equal.

Visit us at www.mhhe.com/rwj

14. **Credit Policy Evaluation [LO2]** The Harrington Corporation is considering a change in its cash-only policy. The new terms would be net one period. Based on the following information, determine if Harrington should proceed or not. The required return is 2.5 percent per period.

	Current Policy	New Policy
Price per unit	$86	$88
Cost per unit	$47	$47
Unit sales per month	3,510	3,620

15. **Credit Policy Evaluation [LO2]** Happy Times currently has an all-cash credit policy. It is considering making a change in the credit policy by going to terms of net 30 days. Based on the following information, what do you recommend? The required return is .95 percent per month.

	Current Policy	New Policy
Price per unit	$150	$154
Cost per unit	$130	$133
Unit sales per month	1,550	1,580

16. **Credit Policy [LO2]** The Silver Spokes Bicycle Shop has decided to offer credit to its customers during the spring selling season. Sales are expected to be 500 bicycles. The average cost to the shop of a bicycle is $390. The owner knows that only 96 percent of the customers will be able to make their payments. To identify the remaining 4 percent, the company is considering subscribing to a credit agency. The initial charge for this service is $750, with an additional charge of $6 per individual report. Should she subscribe to the agency?

17. **Break-Even Quantity [LO2]** In Problem 14, what is the break-even quantity for the new credit policy?

CHALLENGE
(Questions 17–22)

18. **Credit Markup [LO2]** In Problem 14, what is the break-even price per unit that should be charged under the new credit policy? Assume that the sales figure under the new policy is 3,750 units and all other values remain the same.

19. **Credit Markup [LO2]** In Problem 15, what is the break-even price per unit under the new credit policy? Assume all other values remain the same.

20. **Safety Stocks and Order Points [LO1]** Saché, Inc., expects to sell 700 of its designer suits every week. The store is open seven days a week and expects to sell the same number of suits every day. The company has an EOQ of 500 suits and a safety stock of 100 suits. Once an order is placed, it takes three days for Saché to get the suits in. How many orders does the company place per year? Assume that it is Monday morning before the store opens, and a shipment of suits has just arrived. When will Saché place its next order?

21. **Evaluating Credit Policy [LO2]** Solar Engines manufactures solar engines for tractor-trailers. Given the fuel savings available, new orders for 125 units have been made by customers requesting credit. The variable cost is $11,400 per unit, and the credit price is $13,000 each. Credit is extended for one period. The required return is 1.9 percent per period. If Solar Engines extends credit, it expects that 30 percent of the customers will be repeat customers and place the same order every period forever and the remaining customers will be one-time orders. Should credit be extended?

22. **Evaluating Credit Policy [LO2]** In the previous problem, assume that the probability of default is 15 percent. Should the orders be filled now? Assume the number of repeat customers is affected by the defaults. In other words, 30 percent of the customers who do not default are expected to be repeat customers.

Visit us at www.mhhe.com/rwj

MINICASE

Credit Policy at Howlett Industries

Sterling Wyatt, the president of Howlett Industries, has been exploring ways of improving the company's financial performance. Howlett manufactures and sells office equipment to retailers. The company's growth has been relatively slow in recent years, but with an expansion in the economy, it appears that sales may increase more rapidly in the future. Sterling has asked Andrew Preston, the company's treasurer, to examine Howlett's credit policy to see if a change can help increase profitability.

relaxed credit policy and the extension of the credit period to net 45. On the positive side, each of the three policies under consideration would increase sales. The three policies have the drawbacks that default rates would increase, the administrative costs of managing the firm's receivables would increase, and the receivables period would increase. The effect of the credit policy change would impact all four of these variables to different degrees. Andrew has prepared the following table outlining the effect on each of these variables:

	Annual Sales (Millions)	Default Rate (% of Sales)	Administrative Costs (% of Sales)	Receivables Period
Current Policy	$120	1.6%	2.2%	38 days
Option 1	140	2.5	3.2	41 days
Option 2	137	1.8	2.4	51 days
Option 3	150	2.2	3.0	49 days

The company currently has a policy of net 30. As with any credit sales, default rates are always of concern. Because of Howlett's screening and collection process, the default rate on credit is currently only 1.6 percent. Andrew has examined the company's credit policy in relation to other vendors, and he has found three available options.

The first option is to relax the company's decision on when to grant credit. The second option is to increase the credit period to net 45, and the third option is a combination of the

Howlett's variable costs of production are 45 percent of sales, and the relevant interest rate is a 6 percent effective annual rate.

QUESTIONS

1. Which credit policy should the company use?
2. Notice that in option 3, the default rate and administrative costs are above those in option 2. Is this plausible? Why or why not?

20A More about Credit Policy Analysis

This appendix takes a closer look at credit policy analysis by investigating some alternative approaches and by examining the effect of cash discounts and the possibility of nonpayment.

TWO ALTERNATIVE APPROACHES

From our chapter discussion, we know how to analyze the NPV of a proposed credit policy switch. We now discuss two alternative approaches: the one-shot approach and the accounts receivable approach. These are common means of analysis; our goal is to show that these two and our NPV approach are all the same. Afterward, we will use whichever of the three is most convenient.

The One-Shot Approach   Looking back at our example for Locust Software (in Section 20.3), we see that if the switch is not made, Locust will have a net cash flow this month of $(P - v)Q = \$29 \times 100 = \$2,900$. If the switch is made, Locust will invest $vQ' = \$20 \times 110 = \$2,200$ this month and will receive $PQ' = \$49 \times 110 = \$5,390$ next month. Suppose we ignore all other months and cash flows and view this as a one-shot investment.

Is Locust better off with $2,900 in cash this month, or should Locust invest the $2,200 to get $5,390 next month?

The present value of the $5,390 to be received next month is $5,390/1.02 = $5,284.31; the cost is $2,200, so the net benefit is $5,284.31 − 2,200 = $3,084.31. If we compare this to the net cash flow of $2,900 under the current policy, then we see that Locust should switch. The NPV is $3,084.31 − 2,900 = $184.31.

In effect, Locust can repeat this one-shot investment every month and thereby generate an NPV of $184.31 every month (including the current one). The PV of this series of NPVs is:

$$\text{Present value} = \$184.31 + 184.31/.02 = \$9,400$$

This PV is the same as our answer in Section 20.3.

The Accounts Receivable Approach   Our second approach is the one that is most commonly discussed and is very useful. By extending credit, the firm increases its cash flow through increased gross profits. However, the firm must increase its investment in receivables and bear the carrying cost of doing so. The accounts receivable approach focuses on the expense of the incremental investment in receivables as compared to the increased gross profit.

As we have seen, the monthly benefit from extending credit is given by the gross profit per unit $(P − v)$ multiplied by the increase in quantity sold $(Q' − Q)$. For Locust, this benefit is ($49 − 20) × (110 − 100) = $290 per month.

If Locust makes the switch, then receivables will rise from zero (because there are currently no credit sales) to PQ', so Locust must invest in receivables. The necessary investment has two components. The first part is what Locust would have collected under the old policy (PQ). Locust must carry this amount in receivables each month because collections are delayed by 30 days.

The second part is related to the increase in receivables that results from the increase in sales. Because unit sales increase from Q to Q', Locust must produce the latter quantity today even though it won't collect for 30 days. The actual cost to Locust of producing the extra quantity is equal to v per unit, so the investment necessary to provide the extra quantity sold is $v(Q' − Q)$.

In sum, if Locust switches, its investment in receivables will be equal to the $P × Q$ in revenues plus an additional $v(Q' − Q)$ in production costs:

$$\text{Incremental investment in receivables} = PQ + v(Q' − Q)$$

The required return on this investment (the carrying cost of the receivables) is R per month; so, for Locust, the accounts receivable carrying cost is:

$$
\begin{aligned}
\text{Carrying cost} &= [PQ + v(Q' − Q)] × R \\
&= (\$4,900 + 200) × .02 \\
&= \$102 \text{ per month}
\end{aligned}
$$

Because the monthly benefit is $290 and the cost per month is only $102, the net benefit is $290 − 102 = $188 per month. Locust earns this $188 every month, so the PV of the switch is:

$$
\begin{aligned}
\text{Present value} &= \$188/.02 \\
&= \$9,400
\end{aligned}
$$

Again, this is the same figure we previously calculated.

One of the advantages of looking at the accounts receivable approach is that it helps us interpret our earlier NPV calculation. As we have seen, the investment in receivables necessary to make the switch is $PQ + v(Q' − Q)$. If you take a look back at our original NPV calculation, you'll see that this is precisely what we had as the cost to Locust of making the switch. Our earlier NPV calculation thus amounts to a comparison of the incremental investment in receivables to the PV of the increased future cash flows.

Notice one final thing. The increase in accounts receivable is PQ', and this amount corresponds to the amount of receivables shown on the balance sheet. However, the incremental investment in receivables is $PQ + v(Q' - Q)$. It is straightforward to verify that this second quantity is smaller by $(P - v)(Q' - Q)$. This difference is the gross profit on the new sales, which Locust does not actually have to put up in order to switch credit policies.

Put another way, whenever we extend credit to a new customer who would not otherwise buy, all we risk is our cost, not the full sales price. This is the same issue that we discussed in Section 20.5.

EXAMPLE 20A.1   Extra Credit

Looking back at Locust Software, determine the NPV of the switch if the quantity sold is projected to increase by only 5 units instead of 10. What will be the investment in receivables? What is the carrying cost? What is the monthly net benefit from switching?

If the switch is made, Locust gives up $P \times Q = \$4,900$ today. An extra five units have to be produced at a cost of \$20 each, so the cost of switching is $\$4,900 + 5 \times 20 = \$5,000$. The benefit each month of selling the extra five units is $5 \times (\$49 - 20) = \$145$. The NPV of the switch is $-\$5,000 + 145/.02 = \$2,250$, so the switch is still profitable.

The \$5,000 cost of switching can be interpreted as the investment in receivables. At 2 percent per month, the carrying cost is $.02 \times \$5,000 = \$100$. Because the benefit each month is \$145, the net benefit from switching is \$45 per month $(= \$145 - 100)$. Notice that the PV of \$45 per month forever at 2 percent is $\$45/.02 = \$2,250$, as we calculated.

DISCOUNTS AND DEFAULT RISK

We now take a look at cash discounts, default risk, and the relationship between the two. To get started, we define the following:

π = Percentage of credit sales that go uncollected

d = Percentage discount allowed for cash customers

P' = Credit price (the no-discount price)

Notice that the cash price, P, is equal to the credit price, P', multiplied by $(1 - d)$: $P = P'(1 - d)$, or, equivalently, $P' = P/(1 - d)$.

The situation at Locust is now a little more complicated. If a switch is made from the current policy of no credit, then the benefit from the switch will come from both the higher price (P') and, potentially, the increased quantity sold (Q').

Furthermore, in our previous case, it was reasonable to assume that all customers took the credit because it was free. Now, not all customers will take the credit because a discount is offered. In addition, of the customers who do take the credit offered, a certain percentage (π) will not pay.

To simplify the discussion that follows, we will assume that the quantity sold (Q) is not affected by the switch. This assumption isn't crucial, but it does cut down on the work (see Problem 5 at the end of the appendix). We will also assume that all customers take the credit terms. This assumption isn't crucial either. It actually doesn't matter what percentage of the customers take the offered credit.[3]

---

[3]The reason is that all customers are offered the same terms. If the NPV of offering credit is \$100, assuming that all customers switch, then it will be \$50 if only 50 percent of our customers switch. The hidden assumption is that the default rate is a constant percentage of credit sales.

Visit us at www.mhhe.com/rwj

NPV of the Credit Decision   Currently, Locust sells Q units at a price of $P = \$49$. Locust is considering a new policy that involves 30 days' credit and an increase in price to $P' = \$50$ on credit sales. The cash price will remain at $49, so Locust is effectively allowing a discount of $(\$50 - 49)/50 = 2\%$ for cash.

What is the NPV to Locust of extending credit? To answer, note that Locust is already receiving $(P - v)Q$ every month. With the new, higher price, this will rise to $(P' - v)Q$, assuming that everybody pays. However, because π percent of sales will not be collected, Locust will collect on only $(1 - \pi) \times P'Q$; so net receipts will be $[(1 - \pi)P' - v] \times Q$.

The net effect of the switch for Locust is thus the difference between the cash flows under the new policy and those under the old policy:

Net incremental cash flow $= [(1 - \pi)P' - v] \times Q - (P - v) \times Q$

Because $P = P' \times (1 - d)$, this simplifies to:[4]

$$\text{Net incremental cash flow} = P'Q \times (d - \pi) \qquad \textbf{[20A.1]}$$

If Locust makes the switch, the cost in terms of the investment in receivables is just $P \times Q$ because $Q = Q'$. The NPV of the switch is thus:

$$\text{NPV} = -PQ + P'Q \times (d - \pi)/R \qquad \textbf{[20A.2]}$$

For example, suppose that, based on industry experience, the percentage of "deadbeats" (π) is expected to be 1 percent. What is the NPV of changing credit terms for Locust? We can plug in the relevant numbers as follows:

$$\begin{aligned} \text{NPV} &= -PQ + P'Q \times (d - \pi)/R \\ &= -\$49 \times 100 + 50 \times 100 \times (.02 - .01)/.02 \\ &= -\$2,400 \end{aligned}$$

Because the NPV of the change is negative, Locust shouldn't switch.

In our expression for NPV, the key elements are the cash discount percentage (d) and the default rate (π). One thing we see immediately is that, if the percentage of sales that goes uncollected exceeds the discount percentage, then $d - \pi$ is negative. Obviously, the NPV of the switch would then be negative as well. More generally, our result tells us that the decision to grant credit here is a trade-off between getting a higher price, thereby increasing sales revenues, and not collecting on some fraction of those sales.

With this in mind, note that $P'Q \times (d - \pi)$ is the increase in sales less the portion of that increase that won't be collected. This is the incremental cash inflow from the switch in credit policy. If d is 5 percent and π is 2 percent, for example, then, loosely speaking, revenues are increasing by 5 percent because of the higher price, but collections rise by only 3 percent because the default rate is 2 percent. Unless $d > \pi$, we will actually have a decrease in cash inflows from the switch.

A Break-Even Application   Because the discount percentage (d) is controlled by the firm, the key unknown in this case is the default rate (π). What is the break-even default rate for Locust Software?

---

[4]To see this, note that the net incremental cash flow is:

Net incremental cash flow $= [(1 - \pi)P' - v] \times Q - (P - v) \times Q$
$$= [(1 - \pi)P' - P] \times Q$$

Because $P = P' \times (1 - d)$, this can be written as:

Net incremental cash flow $= [(1 - \pi)P' - (1 - d)P'] \times Q$
$$= P'Q \times (d - \pi)$$

Visit us at www.mhhe.com/rwj

We can answer by finding the default rate that makes the NPV equal to zero:

$$\text{NPV} = 0 = -PQ + P'Q \times (d - \pi)/R$$

Rearranging things a bit, we have:

$$PR = P'(d - \pi)$$
$$\pi = d - R \times (1 - d)$$

For Locust, the break-even default rate works out to be:

$$\pi = .02 - .02 \times (.98)$$
$$= .0004$$
$$= .04\%$$

This is quite small because the implicit interest rate Locust will be charging its credit customers (2 percent discount interest per month, or about $.02/.98 = 2.0408\%$) is only slightly greater than the required return of 2 percent per month. As a result, there's not much room for defaults if the switch is going to make sense.

Concept Questions

20A.1a What is the incremental investment that a firm must make in receivables if credit is extended?

20A.1b Describe the trade-off between the default rate and the cash discount.

APPENDIX REVIEW AND SELF-TEST PROBLEMS

20A.1 **Credit Policy** Rework Chapter Review and Self-Test Problem 20.1 using the one-shot and accounts receivable approaches. As before, the required return is 2.0 percent per period, and there will be no defaults. Here is the basic information:

	Current Policy	New Policy
Price per unit	$175	$175
Cost per unit	$130	$130
Sales per period in units	1,000	1,100

20A.2 **Discounts and Default Risk** The De Long Corporation is considering a change in credit policy. The current policy is cash only, and sales per period are 2,000 units at a price of $110. If credit is offered, the new price will be $120 per unit, and the credit will be extended for one period. Unit sales are not expected to change, and all customers are expected to take credit. De Long anticipates that 4 percent of its customers will default. If the required return is 2 percent per period, is the change a good idea? What if only half the customers take the offered credit?

ANSWERS TO APPENDIX REVIEW AND SELF-TEST PROBLEMS

20A.1 As we saw earlier, if the switch is made, an extra 100 units per period will be sold at a gross profit of $175 - 130 = \$45$ each. The total benefit is thus $\$45 \times 100 = \$4,500$ per period. At 2.0 percent per period forever, the PV is $\$4,500/.02 = \$225,000$.

Visit us at www.mhhe.com/rwj

The cost of the switch is equal to this period's revenue of $175 × 1,000 units = $175,000 plus the cost of producing the extra 100 units, 100 × $130 = $13,000. The total cost is thus $188,000, and the NPV is $225,000 − 188,000 = $37,000. The switch should be made.

For the accounts receivable approach, we interpret the $188,000 cost as the investment in receivables. At 2.0 percent per period, the carrying cost is $188,000 × .02 = $3,760 per period. The benefit per period we calculated as $4,500; so the net gain per period is $4,500 − 3,760 = $740. At 2.0 percent per period, the PV of this is $740/.02 = $37,000.

Finally, for the one-shot approach, if credit is not granted, the firm will generate ($175 − 130) × 1,000 = $45,000 this period. If credit is extended, the firm will invest $130 × 1,100 = $143,000 today and receive $175 × 1,100 = $192,500 in one period. The NPV of this second option is $192,500/1.02 − 143,000 = $45,725.49. The firm is $45,725.49 − 45,000 = $725.49 better off today and in each future period because of granting credit. The PV of this stream is $725.49 + 725.49/.02 = $37,000 (allowing for a rounding error).

20A.2   The costs per period are the same whether or not credit is offered; so we can ignore the production costs. The firm currently has sales of, and collects, $110 × 2,000 = $220,000 per period. If credit is offered, sales will rise to $120 × 2,000 = $240,000.

Defaults will be 4 percent of sales, so the cash inflow under the new policy will be .96 × $240,000 = $230,400. This amounts to an extra $10,400 every period. At 2 percent per period, the PV is $10,400/.02 = $520,000. If the switch is made, De Long will give up this month's revenues of $220,000; so the NPV of the switch is $300,000. If only half of the customers take the credit, then the NPV is half as large: $150,000. So, regardless of what percentage of customers take the credit, the NPV is positive. Thus, the change is a good idea.

QUESTIONS AND PROBLEMS

1. **Evaluating Credit Policy [LO2]** Bismark Co. is in the process of considering a change in its terms of sale. The current policy is cash only; the new policy will involve one period's credit. Sales are 25,000 units per period at a price of $450 per unit. If credit is offered, the new price will be $472. Unit sales are not expected to change, and all customers are expected to take the credit. Bismark estimates that 3 percent of credit sales will be uncollectible. If the required return is 2.5 percent per period, is the change a good idea?

    BASIC
    (Questions 1–5)

2. **Credit Policy Evaluation [LO2]** The Johnson Company sells 2,400 pairs of running shoes per month at a cash price of $99 per pair. The firm is considering a new policy that involves 30 days' credit and an increase in price to $100 per pair on credit sales. The cash price will remain at $99, and the new policy is not expected to affect the quantity sold. The discount period will be 20 days. The required return is .75 percent per month.

    a. How would the new credit terms be quoted?

    b. What investment in receivables is required under the new policy?

    c. Explain why the variable cost of manufacturing the shoes is not relevant here.

    d. If the default rate is anticipated to be 8 percent, should the switch be made? What is the break-even credit price? The break-even cash discount?

3. **Credit Analysis [LO2]** Silicon Wafers, Inc. (SWI), is debating whether or not to extend credit to a particular customer. SWI's products, primarily used in the manufacture of semiconductors, currently sell for $975 per unit. The variable cost is $540 per unit. The order under consideration is for 15 units today; payment is promised in 30 days.

    a. If there is a 20 percent chance of default, should SWI fill the order? The required return is 2 percent per month. This is a one-time sale, and the customer will not buy if credit is not extended.

    b. What is the break-even probability in part (a)?

    c. This part is a little harder. In general terms, how do you think your answer to part (a) will be affected if the customer will purchase the merchandise for cash if the credit is refused? The cash price is $910 per unit.

4. **Credit Analysis [LO2]** Consider the following information about two alternative credit strategies:

	Refuse Credit	Grant Credit
Price per unit	$64	$69
Cost per unit	$32	$33
Quantity sold per quarter	5,800	6,400
Probability of payment	1.0	.90

    The higher cost per unit reflects the expense associated with credit orders, and the higher price per unit reflects the existence of a cash discount. The credit period will be 90 days, and the cost of debt is .75 percent per month.

    a. Based on this information, should credit be granted?

    b. In part (a), what does the credit price per unit have to be to break even?

    c. In part (a), suppose we can obtain a credit report for $1.50 per customer. Assuming that each customer buys one unit and that the credit report correctly identifies all customers who will not pay, should credit be extended?

5. **NPV of Credit Policy Switch [LO2]** Suppose a corporation currently sells Q units per month for a cash-only price of P. Under a new credit policy that allows one month's credit, the quantity sold will be Q' and the price per unit will be P'. Defaults will be π percent of credit sales. The variable cost is v per unit and is not expected to change. The percentage of customers who will take the credit is α, and the required return is R per month. What is the NPV of the decision to switch? Interpret the various parts of your answer.

Visit us at www.mhhe.com/rwj

21

INTERNATIONAL CORPORATE FINANCE

IN EARLY 2011, the Japanese yen had reached levels not seen in years, which was not necessarily good news for Japanese auto manufacturers. In the six months ending September 2010, Honda announced that it lost about ¥49 billion ($592 million). Over the same period, Nissan lost about ¥55 billion ($665 million), and Toyota lost about ¥120 billion ($1.45 billion). Nissan's response was the most dramatic among these carmakers. In July 2010, the company said it would move production of its Micra compact to Thailand. Then, in early 2011, the company further announced that it would move production of 100,000 units of its Rogue crossover to the United States in 2012 and move production of its Leaf electric car to the United States in 2013 when its new plant in Tennessee was completed. In this chapter, we explore the important role played by currencies and exchange rates in international finance, along with a number of other key topics.

LEARNING OBJECTIVES

After studying this chapter, you should understand:

LO1 How exchange rates are quoted, what they mean, and the difference between spot and forward exchange rates.

LO2 Purchasing power parity, interest rate parity, unbiased forward rates, uncovered interest rate parity, and the international Fisher effect and their implications for exchange rate changes.

LO3 The different types of exchange rate risk and ways firms manage exchange rate risk.

LO4 The impact of political risk on international business investing.

Corporations with significant foreign operations are often called *international corporations* or *multinationals*. Such corporations must consider many financial factors that do not directly affect purely domestic firms. These include foreign exchange rates, differing interest rates from country to country, complex accounting methods for foreign operations, foreign tax rates, and foreign government intervention.

The basic principles of corporate finance still apply to international corporations; like domestic companies, these firms seek to invest in projects that create more value for the shareholders than they cost and to arrange financing that raises cash at the lowest possible cost. In other words, the net present value principle holds for both foreign and domestic operations, although it is usually more complicated to apply the NPV rule to foreign investments.

One of the most significant complications of international finance is foreign exchange. The foreign exchange markets provide important information and opportunities for an international corporation when it undertakes capital budgeting and financing decisions. As we will discuss, international exchange rates, interest rates, and inflation rates are closely related. We will spend much of this chapter exploring the connection between these financial variables.

We won't have much to say here about the role of cultural and social differences in international business. Neither will we be discussing the implications of differing political and economic systems. These factors are of great importance to international businesses, but it would take another book to do them justice. Consequently, we will focus only on some purely financial considerations in international finance and some key aspects of foreign exchange markets.

21.1 Terminology

See www.adr.com for more.

American Depositary Receipt (ADR)
A security issued in the United States representing shares of a foreign stock and allowing that stock to be traded in the United States.

cross-rate
The implicit exchange rate between two currencies (usually non-U.S.) quoted in some third currency (usually the U.S. dollar).

Eurobonds
International bonds issued in multiple countries but denominated in a single currency (usually the issuer's currency).

Eurocurrency
Money deposited in a financial center outside of the country whose currency is involved.

foreign bonds
International bonds issued in a single country, usually denominated in that country's currency.

gilts
British and Irish government securities.

A common buzzword for the student of business finance is *globalization*. The first step in learning about the globalization of financial markets is to conquer the new vocabulary. As with any specialty, international finance is rich in jargon. Accordingly, we get started on the subject with a highly eclectic vocabulary exercise.

The terms that follow are presented alphabetically, and they are not all of equal importance. We choose these particular ones because they appear frequently in the financial press or because they illustrate the colorful nature of the language of international finance.

1. An **American Depositary Receipt (ADR)** is a security issued in the United States that represents shares of a foreign stock, allowing that stock to be traded in the United States. Foreign companies use ADRs, which are issued in U.S. dollars, to expand the pool of potential U.S. investors. ADRs are available in two forms for a large and growing number of foreign companies: company sponsored, which are listed on an exchange, and unsponsored, which usually are held by the investment bank that makes a market in the ADR. Both forms are available to individual investors, but only company-sponsored issues are quoted daily in newspapers.

2. The **cross-rate** is the implicit exchange rate between two currencies (usually non-U.S.) when both are quoted in some third currency, usually the U.S. dollar.

3. A **Eurobond** is a bond issued in multiple countries, but denominated in a single currency, usually the issuer's home currency. Such bonds have become an important way to raise capital for many international companies and governments. Eurobonds are issued outside the restrictions that apply to domestic offerings and are syndicated and traded mostly from London. Trading takes place anywhere there is a buyer and a seller.

4. **Eurocurrency** is money deposited in a financial center outside of the country whose currency is involved. For instance, Eurodollars—the most widely used Eurocurrency—are U.S. dollars deposited in banks outside the U.S. banking system.

5. **Foreign bonds**, unlike Eurobonds, are issued in a single country and are usually denominated in that country's currency. Often, the country in which these bonds are issued will draw distinctions between them and bonds issued by domestic issuers, including different tax laws, restrictions on the amount issued, and tougher disclosure rules.

   Foreign bonds often are nicknamed for the country where they are issued: Yankee bonds (United States), Samurai bonds (Japan), Rembrandt bonds (the Netherlands), Bulldog bonds (Britain). Partly because of tougher regulations and disclosure requirements, the foreign bond market hasn't grown in past years with the vigor of the Eurobond market.

6. **Gilts**, technically, are British and Irish government securities, although the term also includes issues of local British authorities and some overseas public sector offerings.

7. The **London Interbank Offered Rate (LIBOR)** is the rate that most international banks charge one another for loans of Eurodollars overnight in the London market. LIBOR is a cornerstone in the pricing of money market issues and other short-term debt issues by both government and corporate borrowers. Interest rates are frequently quoted as some spread over LIBOR, and they then float with the LIBOR rate.

London Interbank Offered Rate (LIBOR)
The rate most international banks charge one another for overnight Eurodollar loans.

8. There are two basic kinds of **swaps**: interest rate and currency. An interest rate swap occurs when two parties exchange a floating-rate payment for a fixed-rate payment or vice versa. Currency swaps are agreements to deliver one currency in exchange for another. Often, both types of swaps are used in the same transaction when debt denominated in different currencies is swapped.

swaps
Agreements to exchange two securities or currencies.

Concept Questions

21.1a What are the differences between a Eurobond and a foreign bond?

21.1b What are Eurodollars?

For current LIBOR rates, see www.bloomberg.com.

Foreign Exchange Markets and Exchange Rates

21.2

The **foreign exchange market** (also called the forex or FX market) is undoubtedly the world's largest financial market. It is the market where one country's currency is traded for another's. Most of the trading takes place in a few currencies: the U.S. dollar ($), the British pound sterling (£), the Japanese yen (¥), and the euro (€). Table 21.1 lists some of the more common currencies and their symbols.

foreign exchange market
The market in which one country's currency is traded for another's.

The foreign exchange market is an over-the-counter market, so there is no single location where traders get together. Instead, market participants are located in the major commercial and investment banks around the world. They communicate using computer

Country	Currency	Symbol
Australia	Dollar	A$
Canada	Dollar	Can$
China	Yuan (Renminbi)	元
Denmark	Krone	DKr
EMU (Eurozone)	Euro	€
India	Rupee	Rs
Iran	Rial	Rl
Japan	Yen	¥
Kuwait	Dinar	KD
Mexico	Peso	Ps
Norway	Krone	NKr
Saudi Arabia	Riyal	SR
Singapore	Dollar	S$
South Africa	Rand	R
Sweden	Krona	SKr
Switzerland	Franc	SF
United Kingdom	Pound	£
United States	Dollar	$

TABLE 21.1

International Currency Symbols

WORK THE WEB

You just returned from your dream vacation to Jamaica and feel rich because you have 10,000 Jamaican dollars left over. You now need to convert this to U.S. dollars. How much will you have? You can look up the current exchange rate and do the conversion yourself, or simply work the Web. We went to www.xe.com and used the currency converter on the site to find out. This is what we found:

CURRENCY CONVERTER WIDGET

Looks like you left Jamaica just before you ran out of money.

Questions

1. *Using this currency converter, what is the current US$/Jamaican$ exchange rate?*
2. *The website www.xe.com also lists cross-rates. What is the current ¥/€ cross-rate?*

terminals, telephones, and other telecommunications devices. For example, one communications network for foreign transactions is maintained by the Society for Worldwide Interbank Financial Telecommunication (SWIFT), a Belgian not-for-profit cooperative. Using data transmission lines, a bank in New York can send messages to a bank in London via SWIFT regional processing centers.

The many different types of participants in the foreign exchange market include the following:

1. Importers who pay for goods using foreign currencies.
2. Exporters who receive foreign currency and may want to convert to the domestic currency.
3. Portfolio managers who buy or sell foreign stocks and bonds.
4. Foreign exchange brokers who match buy and sell orders.
5. Traders who "make a market" in foreign currencies.
6. Speculators who try to profit from changes in exchange rates.

Visit SWIFT at www.swift.com.

EXCHANGE RATES

exchange rate
The price of one country's currency expressed in terms of another country's currency.

An **exchange rate** is simply the price of one country's currency expressed in terms of another country's currency. In practice, almost all trading of currencies takes place in terms of the U.S. dollar. For example, both the Swiss franc and the Japanese yen are traded with their prices quoted in U.S. dollars. Exchange rates are constantly changing. Our nearby *Work the Web* box shows you how to get up-to-the-minute rates.

Exchange Rate Quotations   Figure 21.1 reproduces exchange rate quotations as they appeared in *The Wall Street Journal* in 2011. The second column (labeled "in US$") gives the number of dollars it takes to buy one unit of foreign currency. Because this is the price in dollars of a foreign currency, it is called a *direct* or *American quote* (remember

Currencies

U.S.-dollar foreign-exchange rates in late New York trading

FIGURE 21.1

Exchange Rate Quotations

SOURCE: Reprinted by permission of *The Wall Street Journal*, © 2011 Dow Jones & Company, Inc., January 31, 2011. All Rights Reserved Worldwide.

Country/currency	Fri in US$	Fri per US$	US$ vs, YTD chg (%)
Americas			
Argentina peso✻	.2503	3.9952	0.6
Brazil real	.5944	1.6824	1.4
Canada dollar	.9990	1.0010	0.3
1-mos forward	.9984	1.0016	0.3
3-mos forward	.9970	1.0030	0.3
6-mos forward	.9948	1.0052	0.3
Chile peso	.002064	484.50	3.5
Colombia peso	.0005349	1869.51	-2.6
Ecuador US dollar	1	1	unch
Mexico peso✻	.0819	12.2055	-1.1
Peru new sol	.3606	2.773	-1.2
Uruguay peso†	.05060	19.76	-0.6
Venezuela b. fuerte	.232851	4.2946	unch
Asia-Pacific			
Australian dollar	.9930	1.0070	2.9
China yuan	.1519	6.5821	-0.1
Hong Kong dollar	.1284	7.7885	0.2
India rupee	.02178	45.914	2.7
Indonesia rupiah	.0001108	9025	0.2
Japan yen	.012176	82.13	1.1
1-mos forward	.012178	82.12	1.1
3-mos forward	.012185	82.07	1.1
6-mos forward	.012199	81.97	1.2
Malaysia ringgit	.3273	3.0553	-0.9
New Zealand dollar	.7722	1.2950	0.8
Pakistan rupee	.01168	85.616	-0.1
Philippines peso	.0227	44.092	1.0
Singapore dollar	.7783	1.2849	0.1
South Korea won	.0008961	1115.95	-0.5
Taiwan dollar	.03439	29.078	-0.3
Thailand baht	.03218	31.075	3.4

Country/currency	Fri in US$	Fri per US$	US$ vs, YTD chg (%)
Vietnam dong	.00005129	19498	unch
Europe			
Czech Rep. koruna	.05613	17.816	-4.8
Denmark krone	.1826	5.4765	-1.8
Euro area euro	1.3609	.7348	-1.8
Hungary forint	.004983	200.68	-3.6
Norway krone	.1720	5.8140	-0.2
Poland zloty	.3446	2.9019	-2.1
Russia ruble‡	.03354	29.815	-2.5
Sweden krona	.1532	6.5274	-2.9
Switzerland franc	1.0617	.9419	0.8
1-mos forward	1.0619	.9417	0.8
3-mos forward	1.0626	.9411	0.8
6-mos forward	1.0636	.9402	0.9
Turkey lira✻✻	.6194	1.6144	4.7
UK pound	1.5861	.6305	-1.7
1-mos forward	1.5858	.6306	-1.7
3-mos forward	1.5849	.6310	-1.7
6-mos forward	1.5832	.6316	-1.7
Middle East/Africa			
Bahrain dinar	2.6522	.3770	unch
Egypt pound✻	.1707	5.8575	0.9
Israel shekel	.2721	3.6751	4.3
Jordan dinar	1.4119	.7083	unch
Kuwait dinar	3.5742	.2798	-0.6
Lebanon pound	.0006634	1507.39	0.5
Saudi Arabia riyal	.2666	3.7509	unch
South Africa rand	.1390	7.1942	8.6
UAE dirham	.2722	3.6738	unch
SDR††	1.5643	.6393	-1.6

✻Floating rate †Financial §Government rate ‡Russian Central Bank rate ✻✻Rebased as of Jan 1, 2005 ††Special Drawing Rights (SDR); from the International Monetary Fund; based on exchange rates for U.S., British and Japanese currencies.

---

that "Americans are direct"). For example, the Australian dollar is quoted at .9930, which means you can buy one Australian dollar with U.S. $.9930.

The third column shows the *indirect*, or European, exchange rate (even though the currency may not be European). This is the amount of foreign currency per U.S. dollar. The Australian dollar is quoted here at 1.0070, so you can get 1.0070 Australian dollars for one U.S. dollar. Naturally, this second exchange rate is just the reciprocal of the first one (possibly with a little rounding error), 1/.9930 = 1.0070.

Get up-to-the-minute exchange rates at www.xe.com *and* www.exchangerate.com.

Cross-Rates and Triangle Arbitrage   Using the U.S. dollar as the common denominator in quoting exchange rates greatly reduces the number of possible cross-currency quotes. For example, with five major currencies, there would potentially be 10 exchange rates instead of just 4.[1] Also, the fact that the dollar is used throughout decreases inconsistencies in the exchange rate quotations.

---

[1]There are four exchange rates instead of five because one exchange rate would involve the exchange of a currency for itself. More generally, it might seem that there should be 25 exchange rates with five currencies. There are 25 different combinations, but, of these, 5 involve the exchange of a currency for itself. Of the remaining 20, half are redundant because they are just the reciprocals of another exchange rate. Of the remaining 10, 6 can be eliminated by using a common denominator.

EXAMPLE 21.1   **A Yen for Euros**

Suppose you have $1,000. Based on the rates in Figure 21.1, how many Japanese yen can you get? Alternatively, if a Porsche costs €100,000 (recall that € is the symbol for the euro), how many dollars will you need to buy it?

The exchange rate in terms of yen per dollar (third column) is 82.13. Your $1,000 will thus get you:

$1,000 × 82.13 yen per $1 = 82,130 yen

Because the exchange rate in terms of dollars per euro (second column) is 1.3609, you will need:

€100,000 × $1.3609 per € = $136,090

Earlier, we defined the cross-rate as the exchange rate for a non-U.S. currency expressed in terms of another non-U.S. currency. For example, suppose we observe the following for the euro (€) and the Swiss franc (SF):

€ per $1 = 1.00
SF per $1 = 2.00

Suppose the cross-rate is quoted as:

€ per SF = .40

What do you think?

The cross-rate here is inconsistent with the exchange rates. To see this, suppose you have $100. If you convert this to Swiss francs, you will receive:

$100 × SF 2 per $1 = SF 200

If you convert this to euros at the cross-rate, you will have:

SF 200 × €.4 per SF 1 = €80

However, if you just convert your dollars to euros without going through Swiss francs, you will have:

$100 × €1 per $1 = €100

What we see is that the euro has two prices, €1 per $1 and €.80 per $1, with the price we pay depending on how we get the euros.

To make money, we want to buy low and sell high. The important thing to note is that euros are cheaper if you buy them with dollars because you get 1 euro instead of just .8. You should proceed as follows:

1. Buy 100 euros for $100.
2. Use the 100 euros to buy Swiss francs at the cross-rate. Because it takes .4 euros to buy a Swiss franc, you will receive €100/.4 = SF 250.
3. Use the SF 250 to buy dollars. Because the exchange rate is SF 2 per dollar, you receive SF 250/2 = $125, for a round-trip profit of $25.
4. Repeat steps 1 through 3.

This particular activity is called *triangle arbitrage* because the arbitrage involves moving through three different exchange rates:

To prevent such opportunities, it is not difficult to see that because a dollar will buy you either 1 euro or 2 Swiss francs, the cross-rate must be:

$$(€1/\$1)/(SF\ 2/\$1) = €1/SF\ 2$$

That is, the cross-rate must be one euro per two Swiss francs. If it were anything else, there would be a triangle arbitrage opportunity.

Shedding Some Pounds

EXAMPLE 21.2

Suppose the exchange rates for the British pound and Swiss franc are:

    Pounds per $1 = .60
    SF per $1 = 2.00

The cross-rate is three francs per pound. Is this consistent? Explain how to make some money.

The cross-rate should be SF 2.00/£.60 = SF 3.33 per pound. You can buy a pound for SF 3 in one market, and you can sell a pound for SF 3.33 in another. So, we want to first get some francs, then use the francs to buy some pounds, and then sell the pounds. Assuming you have $100, you could:

1. Exchange dollars for francs: $100 × 2 = SF 200.
2. Exchange francs for pounds: SF 200/3 = £66.67.
3. Exchange pounds for dollars: £66.67/.60 = $111.12.

This would result in an $11.12 round-trip profit.

For international news and events, visit www.ft.com.

Types of Transactions   There are two basic types of trades in the foreign exchange market: spot trades and forward trades. A **spot trade** is an agreement to exchange currency "on the spot," which actually means that the transaction will be completed or settled within two business days. The exchange rate on a spot trade is called the **spot exchange rate**. Implicitly, all of the exchange rates and transactions we have discussed so far have referred to the spot market.

A **forward trade** is an agreement to exchange currency at some time in the future. The exchange rate that will be used is agreed upon today and is called the **forward exchange rate**. A forward trade will normally be settled sometime in the next 12 months.

If you look back at Figure 21.1, you will see forward exchange rates quoted for some of the major currencies. For example, the spot exchange rate for the Swiss franc is SF 1 = $1.0617. The 180-day (6-month) forward exchange rate is SF 1 = $1.0636. This means you can buy a Swiss franc today for $1.0617, or you can agree to take delivery of a Swiss franc in 180 days and pay $1.0636 at that time.

Notice that the Swiss franc is more expensive in the forward market ($1.0636 versus $1.0617). Because the Swiss franc is more expensive in the future than it is today, it is said

spot trade
An agreement to trade currencies based on the exchange rate today for settlement within two business days.

spot exchange rate
The exchange rate on a spot trade.

forward trade
An agreement to exchange currency at some time in the future.

forward exchange rate
The agreed-upon exchange rate to be used in a forward trade.

to be selling at a *premium* relative to the dollar. For the same reason, the dollar is said to be selling at a *discount* relative to the Swiss franc.

Why does the forward market exist? One answer is that it allows businesses and individuals to lock in a future exchange rate today, thereby eliminating any risk from unfavorable shifts in the exchange rate.

EXAMPLE 21.3   **Looking Forward**

Suppose you are expecting to receive a million British pounds in six months, and you agree to a forward trade to exchange your pounds for dollars. Based on Figure 21.1, how many dollars will you get in six months? Is the pound selling at a discount or a premium relative to the dollar?

In Figure 21.1, the spot exchange rate and the 180-day forward rate in terms of dollars per pound are $1.5861 = £1 and $1.5832 = £1, respectively. If you expect £1 million in 180 days, you will get £1 million × $1.5832 per pound = $1.5832 million. Because it is less expensive to buy a pound in the forward market than in the spot market ($1.5832 versus $1.5861), the pound is said to be selling at a discount relative to the dollar.

As we mentioned earlier, it is standard practice around the world (with a few exceptions) to quote exchange rates in terms of the U.S. dollar. This means rates are quoted as the amount of currency per U.S. dollar. For the remainder of this chapter, we will stick with this form. Things can get extremely confusing if you forget this. Thus when we say things like "the exchange rate is expected to rise," it is important to remember that we are talking about the exchange rate quoted as units of foreign currency per dollar.

Concept Questions

21.2a What is triangle arbitrage?
21.2b What do we mean by the 90-day forward exchange rate?
21.2c If we say that the exchange rate is SF 1.90, what do we mean?

21.3 Purchasing Power Parity

purchasing power parity (PPP)
The idea that the exchange rate adjusts to keep purchasing power constant among currencies.

Now that we have discussed what exchange rate quotations mean, we can address an obvious question: What determines the level of the spot exchange rate? In addition, because we know that exchange rates change through time, we can ask the related question: What determines the rate of change in exchange rates? At least part of the answer in both cases goes by the name of **purchasing power parity (PPP)**: the idea that the exchange rate adjusts to keep purchasing power constant among currencies. As we discuss next, there are two forms of PPP, *absolute* and *relative*.

ABSOLUTE PURCHASING POWER PARITY

The basic idea behind *absolute purchasing power parity* is that a commodity costs the same regardless of what currency is used to purchase it or where it is selling. This is a straightforward concept. If a beer costs £2 in London, and the exchange rate is £.60 per dollar, then a beer costs £2/.60 = $3.33 in New York. In other words, absolute PPP says that $1 will buy you the same number of, say, cheeseburgers anywhere in the world.

More formally, let S_0 be the spot exchange rate between the British pound and the U.S. dollar today (Time 0), and remember that we are quoting exchange rates as the amount of foreign currency per dollar. Let P_{US} and P_{UK} be the current U.S. and British prices, respectively, on a particular commodity—say, apples. Absolute PPP simply says that:

$$P_{UK} = S_0 \times P_{US}$$

This tells us that the British price for something is equal to the U.S. price for that same thing multiplied by the exchange rate.

The rationale behind PPP is similar to that behind triangle arbitrage. If PPP did not hold, arbitrage would be possible (in principle) if apples were moved from one country to another. For example, suppose apples are selling in New York for $4 per bushel, whereas in London the price is £2.40 per bushel. Absolute PPP implies that:

$$
\begin{aligned}
P_{UK} &= S_0 \times P_{US} \\
£2.40 &= S_0 \times \$4 \\
S_0 &= £2.40/\$4 = £.60
\end{aligned}
$$

That is, the implied spot exchange rate is £.60 per dollar. Equivalently, a pound is worth $1/£.60 = $1.67.

Suppose that, instead, the actual exchange rate is £.50. Starting with $4, a trader could buy a bushel of apples in New York, ship it to London, and sell it there for £2.40. Our trader could then convert the £2.40 into dollars at the prevailing exchange rate, $S_0 = £.50$, yielding a total of £2.40/.50 = $4.80. The round-trip gain would be 80 cents.

Because of this profit potential, forces are set in motion to change the exchange rate and/or the price of apples. In our example, apples would begin moving from New York to London. The reduced supply of apples in New York would raise the price of apples there, and the increased supply in Britain would lower the price of apples in London.

In addition to moving apples around, apple traders would be busily converting pounds back into dollars to buy more apples. This activity would increase the supply of pounds and simultaneously increase the demand for dollars. We would expect the value of a pound to fall. This means that the dollar would be getting more valuable, so it would take more pounds to buy one dollar. Because the exchange rate is quoted as pounds per dollar, we would expect the exchange rate to rise from £.50.

For absolute PPP to hold absolutely, several things must be true:

1. The transactions costs of trading apples—shipping, insurance, spoilage, and so on—must be zero.
2. There must be no barriers to trading apples—no tariffs, taxes, or other political barriers.
3. Finally, an apple in New York must be identical to an apple in London. It won't do for you to send red apples to London if the English eat only green apples.

Given the fact that the transactions costs are not zero and that the other conditions are rarely exactly met, it is not surprising that absolute PPP is really applicable only to traded goods, and then only to very uniform ones.

For this reason, absolute PPP does not imply that a Mercedes costs the same as a Ford or that a nuclear power plant in France costs the same as one in New York. In the case of the cars, they are not identical. In the case of the power plants, even if they were identical, they are expensive and would be very difficult to ship. On the other hand, we would be surprised to see a significant violation of absolute PPP for gold.

Examples of violations of purchasing power parity are not too hard to find. In late 2010, for example, the Blu-ray Diamond Edition of the *Beauty and the Beast* DVD sold for about $36 in New York. At the same time, it sold for KRW27,500 ($25) in Seoul and £16.83 ($25) in London. In some countries, the DVD was more expensive. It sold for HK$325 ($42) in Hong Kong and THB1,334 ($45) in Bangkok. Looking for something a little more upscale? A Dries Van Noten Square tassel club scarf sold for $222 in New York, £165 ($259) in London, and ¥23,100 ($284) in Tokyo.

RELATIVE PURCHASING POWER PARITY

As a practical matter, a relative version of purchasing power parity has evolved. *Relative purchasing power parity* does not tell us what determines the absolute level of the exchange rate. Instead, it tells what determines the *change* in the exchange rate over time.

The Basic Idea   Suppose the British pound–U.S. dollar exchange rate is currently $S_0 =$ £.50. Further suppose that the inflation rate in Britain is predicted to be 10 percent over the coming year, and (for the moment) the inflation rate in the United States is predicted to be zero. What do you think the exchange rate will be in a year?

If you think about it, you see that a dollar currently costs .50 pounds in Britain. With 10 percent inflation, we expect prices in Britain to generally rise by 10 percent. So we expect that the price of a dollar will go up by 10 percent, and the exchange rate should rise to £.50 × 1.1 = £.55.

If the inflation rate in the United States is not zero, then we need to worry about the *relative* inflation rates in the two countries. For example, suppose the U.S. inflation rate is predicted to be 4 percent. Relative to prices in the United States, prices in Britain are rising at a rate of 10% − 4% = 6% per year. So we expect the price of the dollar to rise by 6 percent, and the predicted exchange rate is £.50 × 1.06 = £.53.

The Result   In general, relative PPP says that the change in the exchange rate is determined by the difference in the inflation rates of the two countries. To be more specific, we will use the following notation:

S_0 = Current (Time 0) spot exchange rate (foreign currency per dollar)

$E(S_t)$ = Expected exchange rate in t periods

h_{US} = Inflation rate in the United States

h_{FC} = Foreign country inflation rate

Based on our preceding discussion, relative PPP says that the expected percentage change in the exchange rate over the next year, $[E(S_1) − S_0]/ S_0$, is:

$$[E(S_1) − S_0]/S_0 = h_{FC} − h_{US} \qquad \text{[21.1]}$$

In words, relative PPP simply says that the expected percentage change in the exchange rate is equal to the difference in inflation rates. If we rearrange this slightly, we get:

$$E(S_1) = S_0 × [1 + (h_{FC} − h_{US})] \qquad \text{[21.2]}$$

This result makes a certain amount of sense, but care must be used in quoting the exchange rate.

In our example involving Britain and the United States, relative PPP tells us that the exchange rate will rise by $h_{FC} − h_{US}$ = 10% − 4% = 6% per year. Assuming the difference in inflation rates doesn't change, the expected exchange rate in two years, $E(S_2)$, will therefore be:

$$E(S_2) = E(S_1) \times (1 + .06)$$
$$= .53 \times 1.06$$
$$= .562$$

Notice that we could have written this as:

$$E(S_2) = .53 \times 1.06$$
$$= .50 \times (1.06 \times 1.06)$$
$$= .50 \times 1.06^2$$

In general, relative PPP says that the expected exchange rate at some time in the future, $E(S_t)$, is:

$$E(S_t) = S_0 \times [1 + (h_{FC} - h_{US})]^t \qquad [21.3]$$

As we will see, this is a very useful relationship.

Because we don't really expect absolute PPP to hold for most goods, we will focus on relative PPP in our following discussion. Henceforth, when we refer to PPP without further qualification, we mean relative PPP.

<table>
<tr><td>**It's All Relative**</td><td align="right">**EXAMPLE 21.4**</td></tr>
</table>

Suppose the Japanese exchange rate is currently 105 yen per dollar. The inflation rate in Japan over the next three years will run, say, 2 percent per year, whereas the U.S. inflation rate will be 6 percent. Based on relative PPP, what will the exchange rate be in three years?

Because the U.S. inflation rate is higher, we expect that a dollar will become less valuable. The exchange rate change will be $2\% - 6\% = -4\%$ per year. Over three years, the exchange rate will fall to:

$$E(S_3) = S_0 \times [1 + (h_{FC} - h_{US})]^3$$
$$= 105 \times [1 + (-.04)]^3$$
$$= 92.90$$

Currency Appreciation and Depreciation   We frequently hear things like "the dollar strengthened (or weakened) in financial markets today" or "the dollar is expected to appreciate (or depreciate) relative to the pound." When we say that the dollar strengthens or appreciates, we mean that the value of a dollar rises, so it takes more foreign currency to buy a dollar.

What happens to the exchange rates as currencies fluctuate in value depends on how exchange rates are quoted. Because we are quoting them as units of foreign currency per dollar, the exchange rate moves in the same direction as the value of the dollar: It rises as the dollar strengthens, and it falls as the dollar weakens.

Relative PPP tells us that the exchange rate will rise if the U.S. inflation rate is lower than the foreign country's. This happens because the foreign currency depreciates in value and therefore weakens relative to the dollar.

Concept Questions

21.3a What does absolute PPP say? Why might it not hold for many types of goods?

21.3b According to relative PPP, what determines the change in exchange rates?

21.4 Interest Rate Parity, Unbiased Forward Rates, and the International Fisher Effect

The next issue we need to address is the relationship between spot exchange rates, forward exchange rates, and interest rates. To get started, we need some additional notation:

F_t = Forward exchange rate for settlement at time t

R_{US} = U.S. nominal risk-free interest rate

R_{FC} = Foreign country nominal risk-free interest rate

As before, we will use S_0 to stand for the spot exchange rate. You can take the U.S. nominal risk-free rate, R_{US}, to be the T-bill rate.

COVERED INTEREST ARBITRAGE

Suppose we observe the following information about U.S. and Swiss currency in the market:

S_0 = SF 2.00
F_1 = SF 1.90
R_{US} = 10%
R_S = 5%

where R_S is the nominal risk-free rate in Switzerland. The period is one year, so F_1 is the 360-day forward rate.

Do you see an arbitrage opportunity here? There is one. Suppose you have $1 to invest, and you want a riskless investment. One option you have is to invest the $1 in a riskless U.S. investment such as a 360-day T-bill. If you do this, then, in one period, your $1 will be worth:

$ value in 1 period = \$1 \times (1 + R_{US})$
                    = \$1.10

For exchange rates and even pictures of non-U.S. currencies, see www.travlang.com/money.

Alternatively, you can invest in the Swiss risk-free investment. To do this, you need to convert your $1 to Swiss francs and simultaneously execute a forward trade to convert francs back to dollars in one year. The necessary steps would be as follows:

1. Convert your $1 to $1 \times S_0$ = SF 2.00.
2. At the same time, enter into a forward agreement to convert Swiss francs back to dollars in one year. Because the forward rate is SF 1.90, you will get $1 for every SF 1.90 that you have in one year.
3. Invest your SF 2.00 in Switzerland at R_S. In one year, you will have:

SF value in 1 year = SF 2.00 \times (1 + R_S)
                   = SF 2.00 \times 1.05
                   = SF 2.10

4. Convert your SF 2.10 back to dollars at the agreed-upon rate of SF 1.90 = $1. You end up with:

$ value in 1 year = SF 2.10/1.90
                  = \$1.1053

Notice that the value in one year resulting from this strategy can be written as:

$$\begin{aligned} \text{\$ value in 1 year} &= \$1 \times S_0 \times (1 + R_S)/F_1 \\ &= \$1 \times 2 \times 1.05/1.90 \\ &= \$1.1053 \end{aligned}$$

The return on this investment is apparently 10.53 percent. This is higher than the 10 percent we get from investing in the United States. Because both investments are risk-free, there is an arbitrage opportunity.

To exploit the difference in interest rates, you need to borrow, say, $5 million at the lower U.S. rate and invest it at the higher Swiss rate. What is the round-trip profit from doing this? To find out, we can work through the steps outlined previously:

1. Convert the $5 million at SF 2 = $1 to get SF 10 million.
2. Agree to exchange Swiss francs for dollars in one year at SF 1.90 to the dollar.
3. Invest the SF 10 million for one year at $R_S = 5\%$. You end up with SF 10.5 million.
4. Convert the SF 10.5 million back to dollars to fulfill the forward contract. You receive SF 10.5 million/1.90 = $5,526,316.
5. Repay the loan with interest. You owe $5 million plus 10 percent interest, for a total of $5.5 million. You have $5,526,316, so your round-trip profit is a risk-free $26,316.

The activity that we have illustrated here goes by the name of *covered interest arbitrage*. The term *covered* refers to the fact that we are covered in the event of a change in the exchange rate because we lock in the forward exchange rate today.

INTEREST RATE PARITY

If we assume that significant covered interest arbitrage opportunities do not exist, then there must be some relationship between spot exchange rates, forward exchange rates, and relative interest rates. To see what this relationship is, note that, in general, Strategy 1, from the preceding discussion, investing in a riskless U.S. investment, gives us $1 + R_{US}$ for every dollar we invest. Strategy 2, investing in a foreign risk-free investment, gives us $S_0 \times (1 + R_{FC})/F_1$ for every dollar we invest. Because these have to be equal to prevent arbitrage, it must be the case that:

$$1 + R_{US} = S_0 \times (1 + R_{FC})/F_1$$

Rearranging this a bit gets us the famous **interest rate parity (IRP)** condition:

$$F_1/S_0 = (1 + R_{FC})/(1 + R_{US}) \tag{21.4}$$

There is a very useful approximation for IRP that illustrates very clearly what is going on and is not difficult to remember. If we define the percentage forward premium or discount as $(F_1 - S_0)/S_0$, then IRP says that this percentage premium or discount is *approximately* equal to the difference in interest rates:

$$(F_1 - S_0)/S_0 = R_{FC} - R_{US} \tag{21.5}$$

Very loosely, what IRP says is that any difference in interest rates between two countries for some period is just offset by the change in the relative value of the currencies, thereby eliminating any arbitrage possibilities. Notice that we could also write:

$$F_1 = S_0 \times [1 + (R_{FC} - R_{US})] \tag{21.6}$$

In general, if we have t periods instead of just one, the IRP approximation is written as:

$$F_t = S_0 \times [1 + (R_{FC} - R_{US})]^t \tag{21.7}$$

interest rate parity (IRP)
The condition stating that the interest rate differential between two countries is equal to the percentage difference between the forward exchange rate and the spot exchange rate.

EXAMPLE 21.5 | **Parity Check**

Suppose the exchange rate for Japanese yen, S_0, is currently ¥120 = $1. If the interest rate in the United States is R_{US} = 10% and the interest rate in Japan is R_J = 5%, then what must the forward rate be to prevent covered interest arbitrage?

From IRP, we have:

$$F_1 = S_0 \times [1 + (R_J - R_{US})]$$
$$= ¥120 \times [1 + (.05 - .10)]$$
$$= ¥120 \times .95$$
$$= ¥114$$

Notice that the yen will sell at a premium relative to the dollar (why?).

FORWARD RATES AND FUTURE SPOT RATES

unbiased forward rates (UFR)
The condition stating that the current forward rate is an unbiased predictor of the future spot exchange rate.

In addition to PPP and IRP, we need to discuss one more basic relationship. What is the connection between the forward rate and the expected future spot rate? The **unbiased forward rates (UFR)** condition says that the forward rate, F_1, is equal to the *expected* future spot rate, $E(S_1)$:

$$F_1 = E(S_1)$$

With t periods, UFR would be written as:

$$F_t = E(S_t)$$

Loosely, the UFR condition says that, on average, the forward exchange rate is equal to the future spot exchange rate.

If we ignore risk, then the UFR condition should hold. Suppose the forward rate for the Japanese yen is consistently lower than the future spot rate by, say, 10 yen. This means that anyone who wanted to convert dollars to yen in the future would consistently get more yen by not agreeing to a forward exchange. The forward rate would have to rise to interest anyone in a forward exchange.

Similarly, if the forward rate were consistently higher than the future spot rate, then anyone who wanted to convert yen to dollars would get more dollars per yen by not agreeing to a forward trade. The forward exchange rate would have to fall to attract such traders.

For these reasons, the forward and actual future spot rates should be equal to each other on average. What the future spot rate will actually be is uncertain, of course. The UFR condition may not hold if traders are willing to pay a premium to avoid this uncertainty. If the condition does hold, then the 180-day forward rate that we see today should be an unbiased predictor of what the exchange rate will actually be in 180 days.

How are the international markets doing? Find out at www.marketwatch.com.

PUTTING IT ALL TOGETHER

We have developed three relationships, PPP, IRP, and UFR, that describe the interaction between key financial variables such as interest rates, exchange rates, and inflation rates. We now explore the implications of these relationships as a group.

Uncovered Interest Parity   To start, it is useful to collect our international financial market relationships in one place:

PPP: $E(S_1) = S_0 \times [1 + (h_{FC} - h_{US})]$

IRP: $F_1 = S_0 \times [1 + (R_{FC} - R_{US})]$

UFR: $F_1 = E(S_1)$

We begin by combining UFR and IRP. Because we know that $F_1 = E(S_1)$ from the UFR condition, we can substitute $E(S_1)$ for F_1 in IRP. The result is:

$$\text{UIP: } E(S_1) = S_0 \times [1 + (R_{FC} - R_{US})] \tag{21.8}$$

This important relationship is called **uncovered interest parity** (UIP), and it will play a key role in our international capital budgeting discussion that follows. With t periods, UIP becomes:

$$E(S_t) = S_0 \times [1 + (R_{FC} - R_{US})]^t \tag{21.9}$$

uncovered interest parity (UIP)
The condition stating that the expected percentage change in the exchange rate is equal to the difference in interest rates.

The International Fisher Effect   Next, we compare PPP and UIP. Both of them have $E(S_1)$ on the left-hand side, so their right-hand sides must be equal. We thus have that:

$$S_0 \times [1 + (h_{FC} - h_{US})] = S_0 \times [1 + (R_{FC} - R_{US})]$$
$$h_{FC} - h_{US} = R_{FC} - R_{US}$$

This tells us that the difference in returns between the United States and a foreign country is just equal to the difference in inflation rates. Rearranging this slightly gives us the **international Fisher effect** (IFE):

$$\text{IFE: } R_{US} - h_{US} = R_{FC} - h_{FC} \tag{21.10}$$

international Fisher effect (IFE)
The theory that real interest rates are equal across countries.

The IFE says that *real* rates are equal across countries.[2]

The conclusion that real returns are equal across countries is really basic economics. If real returns were higher in, say, Brazil than in the United States, money would flow out of U.S. financial markets and into Brazilian markets. Asset prices in Brazil would rise and their returns would fall. At the same time, asset prices in the United States would fall and their returns would rise. This process acts to equalize real returns.

Having said all this, we need to note a couple of things. First of all, we really haven't explicitly dealt with risk in our discussion. We might reach a different conclusion about real returns once we do, particularly if people in different countries have different tastes and attitudes toward risk. Second, there are many barriers to the movement of money and capital around the world. Real returns might be different in two different countries for long periods of time if money can't move freely between them.

Despite these problems, we expect that capital markets will become increasingly internationalized. As this occurs, any differences in real rates that do exist will probably diminish. The laws of economics have very little respect for national boundaries.

Concept Questions

21.4a What is covered interest arbitrage?

21.4b What is the international Fisher effect?

---

[2]Notice that our result here is in terms of the approximate real rate, $R - h$ (see Chapter 7), because we used approximations for PPP and IRP. For the exact result, see Problem 18 at the end of the chapter.

21.5 International Capital Budgeting

Kihlstrom Equipment, a U.S.-based international company, is evaluating an overseas investment. Kihlstrom's exports of drill bits have increased to such a degree that it is considering building a distribution center in France. The project will cost €2 million to launch. The cash flows are expected to be €.9 million per year for the next three years.

The current spot exchange rate for euros is €.5. Recall that this is euros per dollar, so a euro is worth $1/.5 = $2. The risk-free rate in the United States is 5 percent, and the risk-free rate in "euroland" is 7 percent. Note that the exchange rate and the two interest rates are observed in financial markets, not estimated.[3] Kihlstrom's required return on dollar investments of this sort is 10 percent.

Should Kihlstrom take this investment? As always, the answer depends on the NPV; but how do we calculate the net present value of this project in U.S. dollars? There are two basic methods:

1. *The home currency approach:* Convert all the euro cash flows into dollars, and then discount at 10 percent to find the NPV in dollars. Notice that for this approach, we have to come up with the future exchange rates to convert the future projected euro cash flows into dollars.

2. *The foreign currency approach:* Determine the required return on euro investments, and then discount the euro cash flows to find the NPV in euros. Then convert this euro NPV to a dollar NPV. This approach requires us to somehow convert the 10 percent dollar required return to the equivalent euro required return.

The difference between these two approaches is primarily a matter of when we convert from euros to dollars. In the first case, we convert before estimating the NPV. In the second case, we convert after estimating NPV.

It might appear that the second approach is superior because we have to come up with only one number, the euro discount rate. Furthermore, because the first approach requires us to forecast future exchange rates, it probably seems that there is greater room for error with this approach. As we illustrate next, however, based on our previous results, the two approaches are really the same.

METHOD 1: THE HOME CURRENCY APPROACH

To convert the project future cash flows into dollars, we will invoke the uncovered interest parity, or UIP, relation to come up with the projected exchange rates. Based on our earlier discussion, the expected exchange rate at time t, $E(S_t)$, is:

$$E(S_t) = S_0 \times [1 + (R_€ - R_{US})]^t$$

where $R_€$ stands for the nominal risk-free rate in euroland. Because $R_€$ is 7 percent, R_{US} is 5 percent, and the current exchange rate (S_0) is €.5:

$$E(S_t) = .5 \times [1 + (.07 - .05)]^t$$
$$= .5 \times 1.02^t$$

---

[3]For example, the interest rates might be the short-term Eurodollar and euro deposit rates offered by large money center banks.

The projected exchange rates for the drill bit project are thus:

Year	Expected Exchange Rate
1	€.5 × 1.02^1 = €.5100
2	€.5 × 1.02^2 = €.5202
3	€.5 × 1.02^3 = €.5306

Using these exchange rates, along with the current exchange rate, we can convert all of the euro cash flows to dollars (note that all of the cash flows in this example are in millions):

Year	(1) Cash Flow in €mil	(2) Expected Exchange Rate	(3) Cash Flow in $mil (1)/(2)
0	−€2.0	€.5000	−$4.00
1	.9	.5100	1.76
2	.9	.5202	1.73
3	.9	.5306	1.70

To finish off, we calculate the NPV in the ordinary way:

$$\text{NPV}_\$ = -\$4 + \$1.76/1.10 + \$1.73/1.10^2 + \$1.70/1.10^3$$
$$= \$.3 \text{ million}$$

So, the project appears to be profitable.

METHOD 2: THE FOREIGN CURRENCY APPROACH

Kihlstrom requires a nominal return of 10 percent on the dollar-denominated cash flows. We need to convert this to a rate suitable for euro-denominated cash flows. Based on the international Fisher effect, we know that the difference in the nominal rates is:

$$R_€ - R_{US} = h_€ - h_{US}$$
$$= 7\% - 5\% = 2\%$$

The appropriate discount rate for estimating the euro cash flows from the drill bit project is approximately equal to 10 percent plus an extra 2 percent to compensate for the greater euro inflation rate.

If we calculate the NPV of the euro cash flows at this rate, we get:

$$\text{NPV}_€ = -€2 + €.9/1.12 + €.9/1.12^2 + €.9/1.12^3$$
$$= €.16 \text{ million}$$

The NPV of this project is €.16 million. Taking this project makes us €.16 million richer today. What is this in dollars? Because the exchange rate today is €.5, the dollar NPV of the project is:

$$\text{NPV}_\$ = \text{NPV}_€/S_0 = €.16/.5 = \$.3 \text{ million}$$

This is the same dollar NPV that we previously calculated.

The important thing to recognize from our example is that the two capital budgeting procedures are actually the same and will always give the same answer.[4] In this second

---

[4]Actually, there will be a slight difference because we are using the approximate relationships. If we calculate the required return as 1.10 × (1 + .02) − 1 = 12.2%, then we get exactly the same NPV. See Problem 18 for more detail.

approach, the fact that we are implicitly forecasting exchange rates is simply hidden. Even so, the foreign currency approach is computationally a little easier.

UNREMITTED CASH FLOWS

The previous example assumed that all aftertax cash flows from the foreign investment could be remitted to (paid out to) the parent firm. Actually, substantial differences can exist between the cash flows generated by a foreign project and the amount that can actually be remitted, or "repatriated," to the parent firm.

A foreign subsidiary can remit funds to a parent in many forms, including the following:

1. Dividends.
2. Management fees for central services.
3. Royalties on the use of trade names and patents.

However cash flows are repatriated, international firms must pay special attention to remittances because there may be current and future controls on remittances. Many governments are sensitive to the charge of being exploited by foreign national firms. In such cases, governments are tempted to limit the ability of international firms to remit cash flows. Funds that cannot currently be remitted are sometimes said to be *blocked*.

Concept Questions

21.5a What financial complications arise in international capital budgeting? Describe two procedures for estimating NPV in the case of an international project.
21.5b What are blocked funds?

21.6 Exchange Rate Risk

exchange rate risk
The risk related to having international operations in a world where relative currency values vary.

Exchange rate risk is the natural consequence of international operations in a world where relative currency values move up and down. Managing exchange rate risk is an important part of international finance. As we discuss next, there are three different types of exchange rate risk, or exposure: short-run exposure, long-run exposure, and translation exposure. Chapter 23 contains a more detailed discussion of the issues raised in this section.

SHORT-RUN EXPOSURE

The day-to-day fluctuations in exchange rates create short-run risks for international firms. Most such firms have contractual agreements to buy and sell goods in the near future at set prices. When different currencies are involved, such transactions have an extra element of risk.

For example, imagine that you are importing imitation pasta from Italy and reselling it in the United States under the Impasta brand name. Your largest customer has ordered 10,000 cases of Impasta. You place the order with your supplier today, but you won't pay until the goods arrive in 60 days. Your selling price is $6 per case. Your cost is 8.4 euros per case, and the exchange rate is currently €1.50; so it takes 1.50 euros to buy $1.

At the current exchange rate, your cost in dollars of filling the order is €8.4/1.5 = $5.60 per case, so your pretax profit on the order is 10,000 × ($6 − 5.60) = $4,000. However, the exchange rate in 60 days will probably be different, so your profit will depend on what the future exchange rate turns out to be.

For example, if the rate goes to €1.6, your cost is €8.4/1.6 = $5.25 per case. Your profit goes to $7,500. If the exchange rate goes to, say, €1.4, then your cost is €8.4/1.4 = $6, and your profit is zero.

The short-run exposure in our example can be reduced or eliminated in several ways. The most obvious way is by entering into a forward exchange agreement to lock in an exchange rate. For example, suppose the 60-day forward rate is €1.58. What will be your profit if you hedge? What profit should you expect if you don't?

If you hedge, you lock in an exchange rate of €1.58. Your cost in dollars will thus be €8.4/1.58 = $5.32 per case, so your profit will be 10,000 × ($6 − 5.32) = $6,800. If you don't hedge, then, assuming that the forward rate is an unbiased predictor (in other words, assuming the UFR condition holds), you should expect that the exchange rate will actually be €1.58 in 60 days. You should expect to make $6,800.

Alternatively, if this strategy is not feasible, you could simply borrow the dollars today, convert them into euros, and invest the euros for 60 days to earn some interest. Based on IRP, this amounts to entering into a forward contract.

LONG-RUN EXPOSURE

In the long run, the value of a foreign operation can fluctuate because of unanticipated changes in relative economic conditions. For example, imagine that we own a labor-intensive assembly operation located in another country to take advantage of lower wages. Through time, unexpected changes in economic conditions can raise the foreign wage levels to the point where the cost advantage is eliminated or even becomes negative.

The impact of changes in exchange rate levels can be substantial. For example, during early 2011, the U.S. dollar continued to weaken against other currencies. This meant domestic manufacturers took home more for each dollar's worth of sales they made, which can lead to big profit swings. For example, during 2010, Coca-Cola estimated that it gained about $151 million due to currency swings. The dramatic effect of exchange rate movements on profitability is also shown by the analysis done by Iluka Resources, Ltd., an Australian mining company, which stated that a one-cent movement in the Australian dollar–U.S. dollar exchange rate would change its net income by $5 million.

Hedging long-run exposure is more difficult than hedging short-term risks. For one thing, organized forward markets don't exist for such long-term needs. Instead, the primary option that firms have is to try to match up foreign currency inflows and outflows. The same thing goes for matching foreign currency–denominated assets and liabilities. For example, a firm that sells in a foreign country might try to concentrate its raw material purchases and labor expense in that country. That way, the dollar values of its revenues and costs will move up and down together. Probably the best examples of this type of hedging are the so-called transplant auto manufacturers such as BMW, Honda, Mercedes, and Toyota, which now build a substantial portion of the cars they sell in the United States, thereby obtaining some degree of immunization against exchange rate movements.

For example, BMW produces 160,000 cars in South Carolina and exports about 100,000 of them. The costs of manufacturing the cars are paid mostly in dollars; when BMW exports the cars to Europe, it receives euros. When the dollar weakens, these vehicles become more profitable for BMW. At the same time, BMW exports about 217,000 cars to the United States each year. The costs of manufacturing these imported cars are mostly in euros, so they become less profitable when the dollar weakens. Taken together, these gains and losses tend to offset each other and provide BMW with a natural hedge.

Of course, this type of hedge can fail when exchange rates move dramatically, as happened with the recent slide of the dollar. For example, BMW was expected to lose about €450 million ($673.5 million) in 2008 because of the euro–dollar exchange rate. In response, the company announced plans to increase its U.S. production to 240,000 vehicles by 2012. And in 2010, BMW announced plans to increase purchases of auto parts from Mexico from its current $615 million per year to $2.4 billion per year beginning in 2012. Similarly, Mercedes-Benz expanded its plant in Alabama, and Volkswagen announced it would begin planning for its first U.S. plant. Of course, if demand for a good is high enough elsewhere, a company can simply avoid a particular currency. For example, Porsche announced it would reduce shipments to the United States, opting to sell its vehicles in other countries where the exchange rate was more favorable.

Similarly, a firm can reduce its long-run exchange rate risk by borrowing in the foreign country. Fluctuations in the value of the foreign subsidiary's assets will then be at least partially offset by changes in the value of the liabilities.

TRANSLATION EXPOSURE

When a U.S. company calculates its accounting net income and EPS for some period, it must "translate" everything into dollars. This can create some problems for the accountants when there are significant foreign operations. In particular, two issues arise:

1. What is the appropriate exchange rate to use for translating each balance sheet account?
2. How should balance sheet accounting gains and losses from foreign currency translation be handled?

To illustrate the accounting problem, suppose we started a small foreign subsidiary in Lilliputia a year ago. The local currency is the gulliver, abbreviated GL. At the beginning of the year, the exchange rate was GL 2 = $1, and the balance sheet in gullivers looked like this:

Assets	GL 1,000	Liabilities	GL 500
		Equity	500

At two gullivers to the dollar, the beginning balance sheet in dollars was as follows:

Assets	$500	Liabilities	$250
		Equity	250

Lilliputia is a quiet place, and nothing at all actually happened during the year. As a result, net income was zero (before consideration of exchange rate changes). However, the exchange rate did change to 4 gullivers = $1 purely because the Lilliputian inflation rate is much higher than the U.S. inflation rate.

Because nothing happened, the accounting ending balance sheet in gullivers is the same as the beginning one. However, if we convert it to dollars at the new exchange rate, we get:

Assets	$250	Liabilities	$125
		Equity	125

Notice that the value of the equity has gone down by $125, even though net income was exactly zero. Despite the fact that absolutely nothing really happened, there is a $125 accounting loss. How to handle this $125 loss has been a controversial accounting question.

One obvious and consistent way to handle this loss is simply to report the loss on the parent's income statement. During periods of volatile exchange rates, this kind of treatment can dramatically impact an international company's reported EPS. This is purely an accounting phenomenon; but, even so, such fluctuations are disliked by some financial managers.

The current approach to handling translation gains and losses is based on rules set out in the Financial Accounting Standards Board (FASB) *Statement of Financial Accounting Standards No. 52* (FASB 52), issued in December 1981. For the most part, FASB 52 requires that all assets and liabilities be translated from the subsidiary's currency into the parent's currency using the exchange rate that currently prevails.

Any translation gains and losses that occur are accumulated in a special account within the shareholders' equity section of the balance sheet. This account might be labeled something like "unrealized foreign exchange gains (losses)." The amounts involved can be substantial, at least from an accounting standpoint. For example, IBM's December 31, 2010, fiscal year-end balance sheet shows an increase in equity in the amount of $643 million for translation adjustments related to assets and liabilities of non-U.S. subsidiaries. These gains and losses are not reported on the income statement. As a result, the impact of translation gains and losses will not be recognized explicitly in net income until the underlying assets and liabilities are sold or otherwise liquidated.

MANAGING EXCHANGE RATE RISK

For a large multinational firm, the management of exchange rate risk is complicated by the fact that there can be many different currencies involved in many different subsidiaries. A change in some exchange rate will likely benefit some subsidiaries and hurt others. The net effect on the overall firm depends on its net exposure.

For example, suppose a firm has two divisions. Division A buys goods in the United States for dollars and sells them in Britain for pounds. Division B buys goods in Britain for pounds and sells them in the United States for dollars. If these two divisions are of roughly equal size in terms of their inflows and outflows, then the overall firm obviously has little exchange rate risk.

In our example, the firm's net position in pounds (the amount coming in less the amount going out) is small, so the exchange rate risk is small. However, if one division, acting on its own, were to start hedging its exchange rate risk, then the overall firm's exchange rate risk would go up. The moral of the story is that multinational firms have to be conscious of their overall positions in a foreign currency. For this reason, management of exchange rate risk is probably best handled on a centralized basis.

Concept Questions
21.6a What are the different types of exchange rate risk?
21.6b How can a firm hedge short-run exchange rate risk? Long-run exchange rate risk?

Political Risk

One final element of risk in international investing is **political risk**. Political risk refers to changes in value that arise as a consequence of political actions. This is not a problem faced exclusively by international firms. For example, changes in U.S. tax laws and regulations may benefit some U.S. firms and hurt others, so political risk exists nationally as well as internationally.

Some countries do have more political risk than others, however. When firms operate in these riskier countries, the extra political risk may lead the firms to require higher returns on overseas investments to compensate for the possibility that funds may be blocked, critical operations interrupted, and contracts abrogated. In the most extreme case, the possibility of outright confiscation may be a concern in countries with relatively unstable political environments.

Political risk also depends on the nature of the business; some businesses are less likely to be confiscated because they are not particularly valuable in the hands of a different owner. An assembly operation supplying subcomponents that only the parent company

21.7

political risk
Risk related to changes in value that arise because of political actions.

A great site for evaluating the political risk of a country is www.cia.gov/cia/publications/factbook.

uses would not be an attractive "takeover" target, for example. Similarly, a manufacturing operation that requires the use of specialized components from the parent is of little value without the parent company's cooperation.

Natural resource developments, such as copper mining or oil drilling, are just the opposite. Once the operation is in place, much of the value is in the commodity. The political risk for such investments is much higher for this reason. Also, the issue of exploitation is more pronounced with such investments, again increasing the political risk.

Political risk can be hedged in several ways, particularly when confiscation or nationalization is a concern. The use of local financing, perhaps from the government of the foreign country in question, reduces the possible loss because the company can refuse to pay the debt in the event of unfavorable political activities. Based on our discussion in this section, structuring the operation in such a way that it requires significant parent company involvement to function is another way to reduce political risk.

Concept Questions

21.7a What is political risk?

21.7b What are some ways of hedging political risk?

21.8 Summary and Conclusions

The international firm has a more complicated life than the purely domestic firm. Management must understand the connection between interest rates, foreign currency exchange rates, and inflation, and it must become aware of many different financial market regulations and tax systems. This chapter is intended to be a concise introduction to some of the financial issues that come up in international investing.

Our coverage has been necessarily brief. The main topics we discussed are the following:

1. *Some basic vocabulary:* We briefly defined some exotic terms such as *LIBOR* and *Eurocurrency*.

2. *The basic mechanics of exchange rate quotations:* We discussed the spot and forward markets and how exchange rates are interpreted.

3. *The fundamental relationships between international financial variables*:

   a. Absolute and relative purchasing power parity, PPP.

   b. Interest rate parity, IRP.

   c. Unbiased forward rates, UFR.

   Absolute purchasing power parity states that $1 should have the same purchasing power in each country. This means that an orange costs the same whether you buy it in New York or in Tokyo.

   Relative purchasing power parity means that the expected percentage change in exchange rates between the currencies of two countries is equal to the difference in their inflation rates.

   Interest rate parity implies that the percentage difference between the forward exchange rate and the spot exchange rate is equal to the interest rate differential. We showed how covered interest arbitrage forces this relationship to hold.

   The unbiased forward rates condition indicates that the current forward rate is a good predictor of the future spot exchange rate.

Visit us at www.mhhe.com/rwj

4. *International capital budgeting:* We showed that the basic foreign exchange relationships imply two other conditions:

a. Uncovered interest parity.

b. The international Fisher effect.

By invoking these two conditions, we learned how to estimate NPVs in foreign currencies and how to convert foreign currencies into dollars to estimate NPV in the usual way.

5. *Exchange rate and political risk:* We described the various types of exchange rate risk and discussed some commonly used approaches to managing the effect of fluctuating exchange rates on the cash flows and value of the international firm. We also discussed political risk and some ways of managing exposure to it.

CONNECT TO FINANCE

If you are using *Connect™ Finance* in your course, get online to take a Practice Test, check out study tools, and find out where you need additional practice.

▼ Chapter 21 International Corporate Finance					Section 21.2
21.1 Terminology			eBook	Study	Practice
21.2 Foreign Exchange Markets and Exchange Rates			eBook	Study	Practice
21.3 Purchasing Power Parity			eBook	Study	Practice
21.4 Interest Rate Parity, Unbiased Forward Rates, and the International Fisher Effect			eBook	Study	Practice
21.5 International Capital Budgeting			eBook	Study	Practice
21.6 Exchange Rate Risk			eBook	Study	Practice
21.7 Political Risk			eBook	Study	Practice

Can you answer the following questions?

Section 21.1 United Travel is exchanging a fixed-rate payment for Foreign Travel's variable-rate payment. This exchange is called a(n)_____. (LO 21-1)

Section 21.3 Roger purchased a cell phone in Canada for Can$189. The exchange rate is $1 = Can$1.08. If absolute purchasing power parity exists, what is the price of this same phone in the United States? (LO 21-2)

Section 21.6 When will a U.S. firm recognize for income statement purposes any accounting gain or loss the firm has from converting a firm's foreign balance sheet into U.S. dollars? (LO 21-3)

Log on to find out!

Visit us at www.mhhe.com/rwj

Visit us at www.mhhe.com/rwj

CHAPTER REVIEW AND SELF-TEST PROBLEMS

21.1 Relative Purchasing Power Parity The inflation rate in the United States is projected at 3 percent per year for the next several years. The New Zealand inflation rate is projected to be 5 percent during that time. The exchange rate is currently NZ\$ 1.66. Based on relative PPP, what is the expected exchange rate in two years?

21.2 Covered Interest Arbitrage The spot and 360-day forward rates on the Swiss franc are SF 2.1 and SF 1.9, respectively. The risk-free interest rate in the United States is 6 percent, and the risk-free rate in Switzerland is 4 percent. Is there an arbitrage opportunity here? How would you exploit it?

ANSWERS TO CHAPTER REVIEW AND SELF-TEST PROBLEMS

21.1 Based on relative PPP, the expected exchange rate in two years, $E(S_2)$, is:

$$E(S_2) = S_0 \times [1 + (h_{NZ} - h_{US})]^2$$

where h_{NZ} is the New Zealand inflation rate. The current exchange rate is NZ\$ 1.66, so the expected exchange rate is:

$$E(S_2) = \text{NZ\$ } 1.66 \times [1 + (.05 - .03)]^2$$
$$= \text{NZ\$ } 1.66 \times 1.02^2$$
$$= \text{NZ\$ } 1.73$$

21.2 Based on interest rate parity, the forward rate should be (approximately):

$$F_1 = S_0 \times [1 + (R_{FC} - R_{US})]$$
$$= 2.1 \times [1 + (.04 - .06)]$$
$$= 2.06$$

Because the forward rate is actually SF 1.9, there is an arbitrage opportunity.

   To exploit the arbitrage opportunity, you first note that dollars are selling for SF 1.9 each in the forward market. Based on IRP, this is too cheap because they should be selling for SF 2.06. So you want to arrange to buy dollars with Swiss francs in the forward market. To do this, you can:

1. *Today:* Borrow, say, \$1 million for 360 days. Convert it to SF 2.1 million in the spot market, and buy a forward contract at SF 1.9 to convert it back to dollars in 360 days. Invest the SF 2.1 million at 4 percent.

2. *In one year:* Your investment has grown to SF 2.1 million × 1.04 = SF 2.184 million. Convert this to dollars at the rate of SF 1.9 = \$1. You will have SF 2.184 million/1.9 = \$1,149,474. Pay off your loan with 6 percent interest at a cost of \$1 million × 1.06 = \$1,060,000 and pocket the difference of \$89,474.

CONCEPTS REVIEW AND CRITICAL THINKING QUESTIONS

1. Spot and Forward Rates [LO1] Suppose the exchange rate for the Swiss franc is quoted as SF 1.50 in the spot market and SF 1.53 in the 90-day forward market.

a. Is the dollar selling at a premium or a discount relative to the franc?

b. Does the financial market expect the franc to strengthen relative to the dollar? Explain.

c. What do you suspect is true about relative economic conditions in the United States and Switzerland?

2. **Purchasing Power Parity [LO2]** Suppose the rate of inflation in Mexico will run about 3 percent higher than the U.S. inflation rate over the next several years. All other things being the same, what will happen to the Mexican peso–U.S. dollar exchange rate? What relationship are you relying on in answering?

3. **Exchange Rates [LO1]** The exchange rate for the Australian dollar is currently A$1.40. This exchange rate is expected to rise by 10 percent over the next year.

   a. Is the Australian dollar expected to get stronger or weaker?

   b. What do you think about the relative inflation rates in the United States and Australia?

   c. What do you think about the relative nominal interest rates in the United States and Australia? Relative real rates?

4. **Yankee Bonds [LO3]** Which of the following most accurately describes a Yankee bond?

   a. A bond issued by General Motors in Japan with the interest payable in U.S. dollars.

   b. A bond issued by General Motors in Japan with the interest payable in yen.

   c. A bond issued by Toyota in the United States with the interest payable in yen.

   d. A bond issued by Toyota in the United States with the interest payable in dollars.

   e. A bond issued by Toyota worldwide with the interest payable in dollars.

5. **Exchange Rates [LO1]** Are exchange rate changes necessarily good or bad for a particular company?

6. **International Risks [LO4]** At one point, Duracell International confirmed that it was planning to open battery-manufacturing plants in China and India. Manufacturing in these countries allows Duracell to avoid import duties of between 30 and 35 percent that have made alkaline batteries prohibitively expensive for some consumers. What additional advantages might Duracell see in this proposal? What are some of the risks to Duracell?

7. **Multinational Corporations [LO3]** Given that many multinationals based in many countries have much greater sales outside their domestic markets than within them, what is the particular relevance of their domestic currency?

8. **Exchange Rate Movements [LO3]** Are the following statements true or false? Explain why.

   a. If the general price index in Great Britain rises faster than that in the United States, we would expect the pound to appreciate relative to the dollar.

   b. Suppose you are a German machine tool exporter, and you invoice all of your sales in foreign currency. Further suppose that the euroland monetary authorities begin to undertake an expansionary monetary policy. If it is certain that the easy money policy will result in higher inflation rates in euroland relative to those in other countries, you should use the forward markets to protect yourself against future losses resulting from the deterioration in the value of the euro.

   c. If you could accurately estimate differences in the relative inflation rates of two countries over a long period while other market participants were unable to do so, you could successfully speculate in spot currency markets.

9. **Exchange Rate Movements [LO3]** Some countries encourage movements in their exchange rate relative to those of some other country as a short-term means of addressing foreign trade imbalances. For each of the following scenarios, evaluate the

impact the announcement would have on an American importer and an American exporter doing business with the foreign country:

a. Officials in the administration of the U.S. government announce that they are comfortable with a rising euro relative to the dollar.

b. British monetary authorities announce that they feel the pound has been driven too low by currency speculators relative to the dollar.

c. The Brazilian government announces that it will print billions of new reais and inject them into the economy in an effort to reduce the country's unemployment rate.

10. **International Capital Market Relationships [LO2]** We discussed five international capital market relationships: relative PPP, IRP, UFR, UIP, and the international Fisher effect. Which of these would you expect to hold most closely?

QUESTIONS AND PROBLEMS

Visit us at www.mhhe.com/rwj

BASIC
(Questions 1–13)

1. **Using Exchange Rates [LO1]** Take a look back at Figure 21.1 to answer the following questions:

   a. If you have $100, how many euros can you get?

   b. How much is one euro worth?

   c. If you have 5 million euros, how many dollars do you have?

   d. Which is worth more, a New Zealand dollar or a Singapore dollar?

   e. Which is worth more, a Mexican peso or a Chilean peso?

   f. How many Mexican pesos can you get for a euro? What do you call this rate?

   g. Per unit, what is the most valuable currency of those listed? The least valuable?

2. **Using the Cross-Rate [LO1]** Use the information in Figure 21.1 to answer the following questions:

   a. Which would you rather have, $100 or £100? Why?

   b. Which would you rather have, 100 Swiss francs (SF) or £100? Why?

   c. What is the cross-rate for Swiss francs in terms of British pounds? For British pounds in terms of Swiss francs?

3. **Forward Exchange Rates [LO1]** Use the information in Figure 21.1 to answer the following questions:

   a. What is the six-month forward rate for the Japanese yen in yen per U.S. dollar? Is the yen selling at a premium or a discount? Explain.

   b. What is the three-month forward rate for Canadian dollars in U.S. dollars per Canadian dollar? Is the dollar selling at a premium or a discount? Explain.

   c. What do you think will happen to the value of the dollar relative to the yen and the Canadian dollar, based on the information in the figure? Explain.

4. **Using Spot and Forward Exchange Rates [LO1]** Suppose the spot exchange rate for the Canadian dollar is Can$1.05 and the six-month forward rate is Can$1.07.

   a. Which is worth more, a U.S. dollar or a Canadian dollar?

   b. Assuming absolute PPP holds, what is the cost in the United States of an Elkhead beer if the price in Canada is Can$2.50? Why might the beer actually sell at a different price in the United States?

   c. Is the U.S. dollar selling at a premium or a discount relative to the Canadian dollar?

    d. Which currency is expected to appreciate in value?

    e. Which country do you think has higher interest rates—the United States or Canada? Explain.

5. **Cross-Rates and Arbitrage [LO1]** Suppose the Japanese yen exchange rate is ¥80 = $1, and the British pound exchange rate is £1 = $1.58.

    a. What is the cross-rate in terms of yen per pound?

    b. Suppose the cross-rate is ¥129 = £1. Is there an arbitrage opportunity here? If there is, explain how to take advantage of the mispricing and the potential arbitrage profit.

6. **Interest Rate Parity [LO2]** Use Figure 21.1 to answer the following questions: Suppose interest rate parity holds, and the current six-month risk-free rate in the United States is 1.4 percent. What must the six-month risk-free rate be in Great Britain? In Japan? In Switzerland?

7. **Interest Rates and Arbitrage [LO2]** The treasurer of a major U.S. firm has $30 million to invest for three months. The interest rate in the United States is .24 percent per month. The interest rate in Great Britain is .29 percent per month. The spot exchange rate is £.631, and the three-month forward rate is £.633. Ignoring transaction costs, in which country would the treasurer want to invest the company's funds? Why?

8. **Inflation and Exchange Rates [LO2]** Suppose the current exchange rate for the Polish zloty is Z 2.86. The expected exchange rate in three years is Z 2.94. What is the difference in the annual inflation rates for the United States and Poland over this period? Assume that the anticipated rate is constant for both countries. What relationship are you relying on in answering?

9. **Exchange Rate Risk [LO3]** Suppose your company imports computer motherboards from Singapore. The exchange rate is given in Figure 21.1. You have just placed an order for 30,000 motherboards at a cost to you of 233.5 Singapore dollars each. You will pay for the shipment when it arrives in 90 days. You can sell the motherboards for $195 each. Calculate your profit if the exchange rate goes up or down by 10 percent over the next 90 days. What is the break-even exchange rate? What percentage rise or fall does this represent in terms of the Singapore dollar versus the U.S. dollar?

10. **Exchange Rates and Arbitrage [LO2]** Suppose the spot and six-month forward rates on the Norwegian krone are Kr 5.78 and Kr 5.86, respectively. The annual risk-free rate in the United States is 3.8 percent, and the annual risk-free rate in Norway is 5.7 percent.

    a. Is there an arbitrage opportunity here? If so, how would you exploit it?

    b. What must the six-month forward rate be to prevent arbitrage?

11. **The International Fisher Effect [LO2]** You observe that the inflation rate in the United States is 2.6 percent per year and that T-bills currently yield 3.4 percent annually. What do you estimate the inflation rate to be in:

    a. Australia, if short-term Australian government securities yield 4 percent per year?

    b. Canada, if short-term Canadian government securities yield 7 percent per year?

    c. Taiwan, if short-term Taiwanese government securities yield 9 percent per year?

12. **Spot versus Forward Rates [LO1]** Suppose the spot and three-month forward rates for the yen are ¥79.12 and ¥78.64, respectively.

    a. Is the yen expected to get stronger or weaker?

    b. What would you estimate is the difference between the annual inflation rates of the United States and Japan?

Visit us at www.mhhe.com/rwj

13. **Expected Spot Rates [LO2]** Suppose the spot exchange rate for the Hungarian forint is HUF 204.32. The inflation rate in the United States will be 1.9 percent per year. It will be 4.5 percent in Hungary. What do you predict the exchange rate will be in one year? In two years? In five years? What relationship are you using?

INTERMEDIATE
(Questions 14–16)

14. **Capital Budgeting [LO2]** Lakonishok Equipment has an investment opportunity in Europe. The project costs €12 million and is expected to produce cash flows of €1.8 million in Year 1, €2.6 million in Year 2, and €3.5 million in Year 3. The current spot exchange rate is $1.36/€; the current risk-free rate in the United States is 2.3 percent, compared to that in Europe of 1.8 percent. The appropriate discount rate for the project is estimated to be 13 percent, the U.S. cost of capital for the company. In addition, the subsidiary can be sold at the end of three years for an estimated €8.9 million. What is the NPV of the project?

15. **Capital Budgeting [LO2]** You are evaluating a proposed expansion of an existing subsidiary located in Switzerland. The cost of the expansion would be SF 21 million. The cash flows from the project would be SF 5.9 million per year for the next five years. The dollar required return is 12 percent per year, and the current exchange rate is SF 1.09. The going rate on Eurodollars is 5 percent per year. It is 4 percent per year on Euroswiss.

    a. What do you project will happen to exchange rates over the next four years?

    b. Based on your answer in (a), convert the projected franc flows into dollar flows and calculate the NPV.

    c. What is the required return on franc flows? Based on your answer, calculate the NPV in francs and then convert to dollars.

16. **Translation Exposure [LO3]** Atreides International has operations in Arrakis. The balance sheet for this division in Arrakeen solaris shows assets of 27,000 solaris, debt in the amount of 11,000 solaris, and equity of 16,000 solaris.

    a. If the current exchange ratio is 1.50 solaris per dollar, what does the balance sheet look like in dollars?

    b. Assume that one year from now the balance sheet in solaris is exactly the same as at the beginning of the year. If the exchange rate is 1.60 solaris per dollar, what does the balance sheet look like in dollars now?

    c. Rework part (b) assuming the exchange rate is 1.41 solaris per dollar.

CHALLENGE
(Questions 17–18)

17. **Translation Exposure [LO3]** In the previous problem, assume the equity increases by 1,250 solaris due to retained earnings. If the exchange rate at the end of the year is 1.54 solaris per dollar, what does the balance sheet look like?

18. **Using the Exact International Fisher Effect [LO2]** From our discussion of the Fisher effect in Chapter 7, we know that the actual relationship between a nominal rate, R, a real rate, r, and an inflation rate, h, can be written as:

    $$1 + r = (1 + R)/(1 + h)$$

    This is the *domestic* Fisher effect.

    a. What is the nonapproximate form of the international Fisher effect?

    b. Based on your answer in (a), what is the exact form for UIP? (*Hint:* Recall the exact form of IRP and use UFR.)

    c. What is the exact form for relative PPP? (*Hint:* Combine your previous two answers.)

    d. Recalculate the NPV for the Kihlstrom drill bit project (discussed in Section 21.5) using the exact forms for UIP and the international Fisher effect. Verify that you get precisely the same answer either way.

Visit us at www.mhhe.com/rwj

MINICASE

S&S Air Goes International

Mark Sexton and Todd Story, the owners of S&S Air, have been in discussions with a light aircraft dealer in Monaco about selling the company's planes in Europe. Jarek Jachowicz, the dealer, wants to add S&S Air to his current retail line. Jarek has told Mark and Todd that he feels the retail sales will be approximately €5 million per month. All sales will be made in euros, and Jarek will retain 5 percent of retail sales as a commission, which will be paid in euros. Because the planes will be customized to order, the first sales will take place in one month. Jarek will pay S&S Air for the order 90 days after it is filled. This payment schedule will continue for the length of the contract between the two companies.

Mark and Todd are confident the company can handle the extra volume with its existing facilities, but they are unsure about the potential financial risks of selling their planes in Europe. In their discussion with Jarek, they found that the current exchange rate is \$1.35/€. At the current exchange rate, the company would spend 80 percent of the sales on production costs. This number does not reflect the sales commission paid to Jarek.

Mark and Todd have decided to ask Chris Guthrie, the company's financial analyst, to prepare an analysis of the proposed international sales. Specifically, they ask Chris to answer the following questions.

QUESTIONS

1. What are the pros and cons of the international sales? What additional risks will the company face?

2. What happens to the company's profits if the dollar strengthens? What if the dollar weakens?

3. Ignoring taxes, what are S&S Air's projected gains or losses from this proposed arrangement at the current exchange rate of \$1.35/€? What happens to profits if the exchange rate changes to \$1.25/€? At what exchange rate will the company break even?

4. How could the company hedge its exchange rate risk? What are the implications for this approach?

5. Taking all factors into account, should the company pursue the international sales further? Why or why not?

Visit us at www.mhhe.com/rwj

MATHEMATICAL TABLES

TABLE A.1   Future value of $1 at the end of t periods $= (1 + r)^t$

Period	Interest Rate								
	1%	**2%**	**3%**	**4%**	**5%**	**6%**	**7%**	**8%**	**9%**
1	1.0100	1.0200	1.0300	1.0400	1.0500	1.0600	1.0700	1.0800	1.0900
2	1.0201	1.0404	1.0609	1.0816	1.1025	1.1236	1.1449	1.1664	1.1881
3	1.0303	1.0612	1.0927	1.1249	1.1576	1.1910	1.2250	1.2597	1.2950
4	1.0406	1.0824	1.1255	1.1699	1.2155	1.2625	1.3108	1.3605	1.4116
5	1.0510	1.1041	1.1593	1.2167	1.2763	1.3382	1.4026	1.4693	1.5386
6	1.0615	1.1262	1.1941	1.2653	1.3401	1.4185	1.5007	1.5869	1.6771
7	1.0721	1.1487	1.2299	1.3159	1.4071	1.5036	1.6058	1.7138	1.8280
8	1.0829	1.1717	1.2668	1.3686	1.4775	1.5938	1.7182	1.8509	1.9926
9	1.0937	1.1951	1.3048	1.4233	1.5513	1.6895	1.8385	1.9990	2.1719
10	1.1046	1.2190	1.3439	1.4802	1.6289	1.7908	1.9672	2.1589	2.3674
11	1.1157	1.2434	1.3842	1.5395	1.7103	1.8983	2.1049	2.3316	2.5804
12	1.1268	1.2682	1.4258	1.6010	1.7959	2.0122	2.2522	2.5182	2.8127
13	1.1381	1.2936	1.4685	1.6651	1.8856	2.1329	2.4098	2.7196	3.0658
14	1.1495	1.3195	1.5126	1.7317	1.9799	2.2609	2.5785	2.9372	3.3417
15	1.1610	1.3459	1.5580	1.8009	2.0789	2.3966	2.7590	3.1722	3.6425
16	1.1726	1.3728	1.6047	1.8730	2.1829	2.5404	2.9522	3.4259	3.9703
17	1.1843	1.4002	1.6528	1.9479	2.2920	2.6928	3.1588	3.7000	4.3276
18	1.1961	1.4282	1.7024	2.0258	2.4066	2.8543	3.3799	3.9960	4.7171
19	1.2081	1.4568	1.7535	2.1068	2.5270	3.0256	3.6165	4.3157	5.1417
20	1.2202	1.4859	1.8061	2.1911	2.6533	3.2071	3.8697	4.6610	5.6044
21	1.2324	1.5157	1.8603	2.2788	2.7860	3.3996	4.1406	5.0338	6.1088
22	1.2447	1.5460	1.9161	2.3699	2.9253	3.6035	4.4304	5.4365	6.6586
23	1.2572	1.5769	1.9736	2.4647	3.0715	3.8197	4.7405	5.8715	7.2579
24	1.2697	1.6084	2.0328	2.5633	3.2251	4.0489	5.0724	6.3412	7.9111
25	1.2824	1.6406	2.0938	2.6658	3.3864	4.2919	5.4274	6.8485	8.6231
30	1.3478	1.8114	2.4273	3.2434	4.3219	5.7435	7.6123	10.063	13.268
40	1.4889	2.2080	3.2620	4.8010	7.0400	10.286	14.974	21.725	31.409
50	1.6446	2.6916	4.3839	7.1067	11.467	18.420	29.457	46.902	74.358
60	1.8167	3.2810	5.8916	10.520	18.679	32.988	57.946	101.26	176.03

continued on next page

10%	12%	14%	15%	16%	18%	20%	24%	28%	32%	36%
1.1000	1.1200	1.1400	1.1500	1.1600	1.1800	1.2000	1.2400	1.2800	1.3200	1.3600
1.2100	1.2544	1.2996	1.3225	1.3456	1.3924	1.4400	1.5376	1.6384	1.7424	1.8496
1.3310	1.4049	1.4815	1.5209	1.5609	1.6430	1.7280	1.9066	2.0972	2.3000	2.5155
1.4641	1.5735	1.6890	1.7490	1.8106	1.9388	2.0736	2.3642	2.6844	3.0360	3.4210
1.6105	1.7623	1.9254	2.0114	2.1003	2.2878	2.4883	2.9316	3.4360	4.0075	4.6526
1.7716	1.9738	2.1950	2.3131	2.4364	2.6996	2.9860	3.6352	4.3980	5.2899	6.3275
1.9487	2.2107	2.5023	2.6600	2.8262	3.1855	3.5832	4.5077	5.6295	6.9826	8.6054
2.1436	2.4760	2.8526	3.0590	3.2784	3.7589	4.2998	5.5895	7.2058	9.2170	11.703
2.3579	2.7731	3.2519	3.5179	3.8030	4.4355	5.1598	6.9310	9.2234	12.166	15.917
2.5937	3.1058	3.7072	4.0456	4.4114	5.2338	6.1917	8.5944	11.806	16.060	21.647
2.8531	3.4785	4.2262	4.6524	5.1173	6.1759	7.4301	10.657	15.112	21.199	29.439
3.1384	3.8960	4.8179	5.3503	5.9360	7.2876	8.9161	13.215	19.343	27.983	40.037
3.4523	4.3635	5.4924	6.1528	6.8858	8.5994	10.699	16.386	24.759	36.937	54.451
3.7975	4.8871	6.2613	7.0757	7.9875	10.147	12.839	20.319	31.691	48.757	74.053
4.1772	5.4736	7.1379	8.1371	9.2655	11.974	15.407	25.196	40.565	64.359	100.71
4.5950	6.1304	8.1372	9.3576	10.748	14.129	18.488	31.243	51.923	84.954	136.97
5.0545	6.8660	9.2765	10.761	12.468	16.672	22.186	38.741	66.461	112.14	186.28
5.5599	7.6900	10.575	12.375	14.463	19.673	26.623	48.039	85.071	148.02	253.34
6.1159	8.6128	12.056	14.232	16.777	23.214	31.948	59.568	108.89	195.39	344.54
6.7275	9.6463	13.743	16.367	19.461	27.393	38.338	73.864	139.38	257.92	468.57
7.4002	10.804	15.668	18.822	22.574	32.324	46.005	91.592	178.41	340.45	637.26
8.1403	12.100	17.861	21.645	26.186	38.142	55.206	113.57	228.36	449.39	866.67
8.9543	13.552	20.362	24.891	30.376	45.008	66.247	140.83	292.30	593.20	1178.7
9.8497	15.179	23.212	28.625	35.236	53.109	79.497	174.63	374.14	783.02	1603.0
10.835	17.000	26.462	32.919	40.874	62.669	95.396	216.54	478.90	1033.6	2180.1
17.449	29.960	50.950	66.212	85.850	143.37	237.38	634.82	1645.5	4142.1	10143.
45.259	93.051	188.88	267.86	378.72	750.38	1469.8	5455.9	19427.	66521.	*
117.39	289.00	700.23	1083.7	1670.7	3927.4	9100.4	46890.	*	*	*
304.48	897.60	2595.9	4384.0	7370.2	20555.	56348.	*	*	*	*

*The factor is greater than 99,999.

TABLE A.2   Present value of $1 to be received after t periods $= 1/(1 + r)^t$

Period	1%	2%	3%	4%	5%	6%	7%	8%	9%
					Interest Rate				
1	.9901	.9804	.9709	.9615	.9524	.9434	.9346	.9259	.9174
2	.9803	.9612	.9426	.9246	.9070	.8900	.8734	.8573	.8417
3	.9706	.9423	.9151	.8890	.8638	.8396	.8163	.7938	.7722
4	.9610	.9238	.8885	.8548	.8227	.7921	.7629	.7350	.7084
5	.9515	.9057	.8626	.8219	.7835	.7473	.7130	.6806	.6499
6	.9420	.8880	.8375	.7903	.7462	.7050	.6663	.6302	.5963
7	.9327	.8706	.8131	.7599	.7107	.6651	.6227	.5835	.5470
8	.9235	.8535	.7894	.7307	.6768	.6274	.5820	.5403	.5019
9	.9143	.8368	.7664	.7026	.6446	.5919	.5439	.5002	.4604
10	.9053	.8203	.7441	.6756	.6139	.5584	.5083	.4632	.4224
11	.8963	.8043	.7224	.6496	.5847	.5268	.4751	.4289	.3875
12	.8874	.7885	.7014	.6246	.5568	.4970	.4440	.3971	.3555
13	.8787	.7730	.6810	.6006	.5303	.4688	.4150	.3677	.3262
14	.8700	.7579	.6611	.5775	.5051	.4423	.3878	.3405	.2992
15	.8613	.7430	.6419	.5553	.4810	.4173	.3624	.3152	.2745
16	.8528	.7284	.6232	.5339	.4581	.3936	.3387	.2919	.2519
17	.8444	.7142	.6050	.5134	.4363	.3714	.3166	.2703	.2311
18	.8360	.7002	.5874	.4936	.4155	.3503	.2959	.2502	.2120
19	.8277	.6864	.5703	.4746	.3957	.3305	.2765	.2317	.1945
20	.8195	.6730	.5537	.4564	.3769	.3118	.2584	.2145	.1784
21	.8114	.6598	.5375	.4388	.3589	.2942	.2415	.1987	.1637
22	.8034	.6468	.5219	.4220	.3418	.2775	.2257	.1839	.1502
23	.7954	.6342	.5067	.4057	.3256	.2618	.2109	.1703	.1378
24	.7876	.6217	.4919	.3901	.3101	.2470	.1971	.1577	.1264
25	.7798	.6095	.4776	.3751	.2953	.2330	.1842	.1460	.1160
30	.7419	.5521	.4120	.3083	.2314	.1741	.1314	.0994	.0754
40	.6717	.4529	.3066	.2083	.1420	.0972	.0668	.0460	.0318
50	.6080	.3715	.2281	.1407	.0872	.0543	.0339	.0213	.0134

continued on next page

10%	12%	14%	15%	16%	18%	20%	24%	28%	32%	36%
.9091	.8929	.8772	.8696	.8621	.8475	.8333	.8065	.7813	.7576	.7353
.8264	.7972	.7695	.7561	.7432	.7182	.6944	.6504	.6104	.5739	.5407
.7513	.7118	.6750	.6575	.6407	.6086	.5787	.5245	.4768	.4348	.3975
.6830	.6355	.5921	.5718	.5523	.5158	.4823	.4230	.3725	.3294	.2923
.6209	.5674	.5194	.4972	.4761	.4371	.4019	.3411	.2910	.2495	.2149
.5645	.5066	.4556	.4323	.4104	.3704	.3349	.2751	.2274	.1890	.1580
.5132	.4523	.3996	.3759	.3538	.3139	.2791	.2218	.1776	.1432	.1162
.4665	.4039	.3506	.3269	.3050	.2660	.2326	.1789	.1388	.1085	.0854
.4241	.3606	.3075	.2843	.2630	.2255	.1938	.1443	.1084	.0822	.0628
.3855	.3220	.2697	.2472	.2267	.1911	.1615	.1164	.0847	.0623	.0462
.3505	.2875	.2366	.2149	.1954	.1619	.1346	.0938	.0662	.0472	.0340
.3186	.2567	.2076	.1869	.1685	.1372	.1122	.0757	.0517	.0357	.0250
.2897	.2292	.1821	.1625	.1452	.1163	.0935	.0610	.0404	.0271	.0184
.2633	.2046	.1597	.1413	.1252	.0985	.0779	.0492	.0316	.0205	.0135
.2394	.1827	.1401	.1229	.1079	.0835	.0649	.0397	.0247	.0155	.0099
.2176	.1631	.1229	.1069	.0930	.0708	.0541	.0320	.0193	.0118	.0073
.1978	.1456	.1078	.0929	.0802	.0600	.0451	.0258	.0150	.0089	.0054
.1799	.1300	.0946	.0808	.0691	.0508	.0376	.0208	.0118	.0068	.0039
.1635	.1161	.0829	.0703	.0596	.0431	.0313	.0168	.0092	.0051	.0029
.1486	.1037	.0728	.0611	.0514	.0365	.0261	.0135	.0072	.0039	.0021
.1351	.0926	.0638	.0531	.0443	.0309	.0217	.0109	.0056	.0029	.0016
.1228	.0826	.0560	.0462	.0382	.0262	.0181	.0088	.0044	.0022	.0012
.1117	.0738	.0491	.0402	.0329	.0222	.0151	.0071	.0034	.0017	.0008
.1015	.0659	.0431	.0349	.0284	.0188	.0126	.0057	.0027	.0013	.0006
.0923	.0588	.0378	.0304	.0245	.0160	.0105	.0046	.0021	.0010	.0005
.0573	.0334	.0196	.0151	.0116	.0070	.0042	.0016	.0006	.0002	.0001
.0221	.0107	.0053	.0037	.0026	.0013	.0007	.0002	.0001	*	*
.0085	.0035	.0014	.0009	.0006	.0003	.0001	*	*	*	*

*The factor is zero to four decimal places.

TABLE A.3   Present value of an annuity of $1 per period for t periods $= [1 - 1/(1 + r)^t]/r$

Number of Periods	Interest Rate								
	1%	2%	3%	4%	5%	6%	7%	8%	9%
1	.9901	.9804	.9709	.9615	.9524	.9434	.9346	.9259	.9174
2	1.9704	1.9416	1.9135	1.8861	1.8594	1.8334	1.8080	1.7833	1.7591
3	2.9410	2.8839	2.8286	2.7751	2.7232	2.6730	2.6243	2.5771	2.5313
4	3.9020	3.8077	3.7171	3.6299	3.5460	3.4651	3.3872	3.3121	3.2397
5	4.8534	4.7135	4.5797	4.4518	4.3295	4.2124	4.1002	3.9927	3.8897
6	5.7955	5.6014	5.4172	5.2421	5.0757	4.9173	4.7665	4.6229	4.4859
7	6.7282	6.4720	6.2303	6.0021	5.7864	5.5824	5.3893	5.2064	5.0330
8	7.6517	7.3255	7.0197	6.7327	6.4632	6.2098	5.9713	5.7466	5.5348
9	8.5660	8.1622	7.7861	7.4353	7.1078	6.8017	6.5152	6.2469	5.9952
10	9.4713	8.9826	8.5302	8.1109	7.7217	7.3601	7.0236	6.7101	6.4177
11	10.3676	9.7868	9.2526	8.7605	8.3064	7.8869	7.4987	7.1390	6.8052
12	11.2551	10.5753	9.9540	9.3851	8.8633	8.3838	7.9427	7.5361	7.1607
13	12.1337	11.3484	10.6350	9.9856	9.3936	8.8527	8.3577	7.9038	7.4869
14	13.0037	12.1062	11.2961	10.5631	9.8986	9.2950	8.7455	8.2442	7.7862
15	13.8651	12.8493	11.9379	11.1184	10.3797	9.7122	9.1079	8.5595	8.0607
16	14.7179	13.5777	12.5611	11.6523	10.8378	10.1059	9.4466	8.8514	8.3126
17	15.5623	14.2919	13.1661	12.1657	11.2741	10.4773	9.7632	9.1216	8.5436
18	16.3983	14.9920	13.7535	12.6593	11.6896	10.8276	10.0591	9.3719	8.7556
19	17.2260	15.6785	14.3238	13.1339	12.0853	11.1581	10.3356	9.6036	8.9501
20	18.0456	16.3514	14.8775	13.5903	12.4622	11.4699	10.5940	9.8181	9.1285
21	18.8570	17.0112	15.4150	14.0292	12.8212	11.7641	10.8355	10.0168	9.2922
22	19.6604	17.6580	15.9369	14.4511	13.1630	12.0416	11.0612	10.2007	9.4424
23	20.4558	18.2922	16.4436	14.8568	13.4886	12.3034	11.2722	10.3741	9.5802
24	21.2434	18.9139	16.9355	15.2470	13.7986	12.5504	11.4693	10.5288	9.7066
25	22.0232	19.5235	17.4131	15.6221	14.0939	12.7834	11.6536	10.6748	9.8226
30	25.8077	22.3965	19.6004	17.2920	15.3725	13.7648	12.4090	11.2578	10.2737
40	32.8347	27.3555	23.1148	19.7928	17.1591	15.0463	13.3317	11.9246	10.7574
50	39.1961	31.4236	25.7298	21.4822	18.2559	15.7619	13.8007	12.2335	10.9617

continued on next page

10%	12%	14%	15%	16%	18%	20%	24%	28%	32%	36%
.9091	.8929	.8772	.8696	.8621	.8475	.8333	.8065	.7813	.7576	.7353
1.7355	1.6901	1.6467	1.6257	1.6052	1.5656	1.5278	1.4568	1.3916	1.3315	1.2760
2.4869	2.4018	2.3216	2.2832	2.2459	2.1743	2.1065	1.9813	1.8684	1.7663	1.6735
3.1699	3.0373	2.9137	2.8550	2.7982	2.6901	2.5887	2.4043	2.2410	2.0957	1.9658
3.7908	3.6048	3.4331	3.3522	3.2743	3.1272	2.9906	2.7454	2.5320	2.3452	2.1807
4.3553	4.1114	3.8887	3.7845	3.6847	3.4976	3.3255	3.0205	2.7594	2.5342	2.3388
4.8684	4.5638	4.2883	4.1604	4.0386	3.8115	3.6046	3.2423	2.9370	2.6775	2.4550
5.3349	4.9676	4.6389	4.4873	4.3436	4.0776	3.8372	3.4212	3.0758	2.7860	2.5404
5.7590	5.3282	4.9464	4.7716	4.6065	4.3030	4.0310	3.5655	3.1842	2.8681	2.6033
6.1446	5.6502	5.2161	5.0188	4.8332	4.4941	4.1925	3.6819	3.2689	2.9304	2.6495
6.4951	5.9377	5.4527	5.2337	5.0286	4.6560	4.3271	3.7757	3.3351	2.9776	2.6834
6.8137	6.1944	5.6603	5.4206	5.1971	4.7932	4.4392	3.8514	3.3868	3.0133	2.7084
7.1034	6.4235	5.8424	5.5831	5.3423	4.9095	4.5327	3.9124	3.4272	3.0404	2.7268
7.3667	6.6282	6.0021	5.7245	5.4675	5.0081	4.6106	3.9616	3.4587	3.0609	2.7403
7.6061	6.8109	6.1422	5.8474	5.5755	5.0916	4.6755	4.0013	3.4834	3.0764	2.7502
7.8237	6.9740	6.2651	5.9542	5.6685	5.1624	4.7296	4.0333	3.5026	3.0882	2.7575
8.0216	7.1196	6.3729	6.0472	5.7487	5.2223	4.7746	4.0591	3.5177	3.0971	2.7629
8.2014	7.2497	6.4674	6.1280	5.8178	5.2732	4.8122	4.0799	3.5294	3.1039	2.7668
8.3649	7.3658	6.5504	6.1982	5.8775	5.3162	4.8435	4.0967	3.5386	3.1090	2.7697
8.5136	7.4694	6.6231	6.2593	5.9288	5.3527	4.8696	4.1103	3.5458	3.1129	2.7718
8.6487	7.5620	6.6870	6.3125	5.9731	5.3837	4.8913	4.1212	3.5514	3.1158	2.7734
8.7715	7.6446	6.7429	6.3587	6.0113	5.4099	4.9094	4.1300	3.5558	3.1180	2.7746
8.8832	7.7184	6.7921	6.3988	6.0442	5.4321	4.9245	4.1371	3.5592	3.1197	2.7754
8.9847	7.7843	6.8351	6.4338	6.0726	5.4509	4.9371	4.1428	3.5619	3.1210	2.7760
9.0770	7.8431	6.8729	6.4641	6.0971	5.4669	4.9476	4.1474	3.5640	3.1220	2.7765
9.4269	8.0552	7.0027	6.5660	6.1772	5.5168	4.9789	4.1601	3.5693	3.1242	2.7775
9.7791	8.2438	7.1050	6.6418	6.2335	5.5482	4.9966	4.1659	3.5712	3.1250	2.7778
9.9148	8.3045	7.1327	6.6605	6.2463	5.5541	4.9995	4.1666	3.5714	3.1250	2.7778

TABLE A.4   Future value of an annuity of $1 per period for t periods $= [(1 + r)^t - 1]/r$

Number of Periods	Interest Rate								
	1%	2%	3%	4%	5%	6%	7%	8%	9%
1	1.0000	1.0000	1.0000	1.0000	1.0000	1.0000	1.0000	1.0000	1.0000
2	2.0100	2.0200	2.0300	2.0400	2.0500	2.0600	2.0700	2.0800	2.0900
3	3.0301	3.0604	3.0909	3.1216	3.1525	3.1836	3.2149	3.2464	3.2781
4	4.0604	4.1216	4.1836	4.2465	4.3101	4.3746	4.4399	4.5061	4.5731
5	5.1010	5.2040	5.3091	5.4163	5.5256	5.6371	5.7507	5.8666	5.9847
6	6.1520	6.3081	6.4684	6.6330	6.8019	6.9753	7.1533	7.3359	7.5233
7	7.2135	7.4343	7.6625	7.8983	8.1420	8.3938	8.6540	8.9228	9.2004
8	8.2857	8.5830	8.8932	9.2142	9.5491	9.8975	10.260	10.637	11.028
9	9.3685	9.7546	10.159	10.583	11.027	11.491	11.978	12.488	13.021
10	10.462	10.950	11.464	12.006	12.578	13.181	13.816	14.487	15.193
11	11.567	12.169	12.808	13.486	14.207	14.972	15.784	16.645	17.560
12	12.683	13.412	14.192	15.026	15.917	16.870	17.888	18.977	20.141
13	13.809	14.680	15.618	16.627	17.713	18.882	20.141	21.495	22.953
14	14.947	15.974	17.086	18.292	19.599	21.015	22.550	24.215	26.019
15	16.097	17.293	18.599	20.024	21.579	23.276	25.129	27.152	29.361
16	17.258	18.639	20.157	21.825	23.657	25.673	27.888	30.324	33.003
17	18.430	20.012	21.762	23.698	25.840	28.213	30.840	33.750	36.974
18	19.615	21.412	23.414	25.645	28.132	30.906	33.999	37.450	41.301
19	20.811	22.841	25.117	27.671	30.539	33.760	37.379	41.446	46.018
20	22.019	24.297	26.870	29.778	33.066	36.786	40.995	45.762	51.160
21	23.239	25.783	28.676	31.969	35.719	39.993	44.865	50.423	56.765
22	24.472	27.299	30.537	34.248	38.505	43.392	49.006	55.457	62.873
23	25.716	28.845	32.453	36.618	41.430	46.996	53.436	60.893	69.532
24	26.973	30.422	34.426	39.083	44.502	50.816	58.177	66.765	76.790
25	28.243	32.030	36.459	41.646	47.727	54.865	63.249	73.106	84.701
30	34.785	40.568	47.575	56.085	66.439	79.058	94.461	113.28	136.31
40	48.886	60.402	75.401	95.026	120.80	154.76	199.64	259.06	337.88
50	64.463	84.579	112.80	152.67	209.35	290.34	406.53	573.77	815.08
60	81.670	114.05	163.05	237.99	353.58	533.13	813.52	1253.2	1944.8

continued on next page

10%	12%	14%	15%	16%	18%	20%	24%	28%	32%	36%
1.0000	1.0000	1.0000	1.0000	1.0000	1.0000	1.0000	1.0000	1.0000	1.0000	1.0000
2.1000	2.1200	2.1400	2.1500	2.1600	2.1800	2.2000	2.2400	2.2800	2.3200	2.3600
3.3100	3.3744	3.4396	3.4725	3.5056	3.5724	3.6400	3.7776	3.9184	4.0624	4.2096
4.6410	4.7793	4.9211	4.9934	5.0665	5.2154	5.3680	5.6842	6.0156	6.3624	6.7251
6.1051	6.3528	6.6101	6.7424	6.8771	7.1542	7.4416	8.0484	8.6999	9.3983	10.146
7.7156	8.1152	8.5355	8.7537	8.9775	9.4420	9.9299	10.980	12.136	13.406	14.799
9.4872	10.089	10.730	11.067	11.414	12.142	12.916	14.615	16.534	18.696	21.126
11.436	12.300	13.233	13.727	14.240	15.327	16.499	19.123	22.163	25.678	29.732
13.579	14.776	16.085	16.786	17.519	19.086	20.799	24.712	29.369	34.895	41.435
15.937	17.549	19.337	20.304	21.321	23.521	25.959	31.643	38.593	47.062	57.352
18.531	20.655	23.045	24.349	25.733	28.755	32.150	40.238	50.398	63.122	78.998
21.384	24.133	27.271	29.002	30.850	34.931	39.581	50.895	65.510	84.320	108.44
24.523	28.029	32.089	34.352	36.786	42.219	48.497	64.110	84.853	112.30	148.47
27.975	32.393	37.581	40.505	43.672	50.818	59.196	80.496	109.61	149.24	202.93
31.772	37.280	43.842	47.580	51.660	60.965	72.035	100.82	141.30	198.00	276.98
35.950	42.753	50.980	55.717	60.925	72.939	87.442	126.01	181.87	262.36	377.69
40.545	48.884	59.118	65.075	71.673	87.068	105.93	157.25	233.79	347.31	514.66
45.599	55.750	68.394	75.836	84.141	103.74	128.12	195.99	300.25	459.45	700.94
51.159	63.440	78.969	88.212	98.603	123.41	154.74	244.03	385.32	607.47	954.28
57.275	72.052	91.025	102.44	115.38	146.63	186.69	303.60	494.21	802.86	1298.8
64.002	81.699	104.77	118.81	134.84	174.02	225.03	377.46	633.59	1060.8	1767.4
71.403	92.503	120.44	137.63	157.41	206.34	271.03	469.06	812.00	1401.2	2404.7
79.543	104.60	138.30	159.28	183.60	244.49	326.24	582.63	1040.4	1850.6	3271.3
88.497	118.16	158.66	184.17	213.98	289.49	392.48	723.46	1332.7	2443.8	4450.0
98.347	133.33	181.87	212.79	249.21	342.60	471.98	898.09	1706.8	3226.8	6053.0
164.49	241.33	356.79	434.75	530.31	790.95	1181.9	2640.9	5873.2	12941.	28172.
442.59	767.09	1342.0	1779.1	2360.8	4163.2	7343.9	22729.	69377.	*	*
1163.9	2400.0	4994.5	7217.7	10436.	21813.	45497.	*	*	*	*
3043.8	7471.6	18535.	29220.	46058.	*	*	*	*	*	*

*The factor is greater than 99,999.

TABLE A.5   Cumulative normal distribution

d	N(d)	d	N(d)	d	N(d)	d	N(d)	d	N(d)	d	N(d)
−3.00	.0013	−1.58	.0571	−.76	.2236	.06	.5239	.86	.8051	1.66	.9515
−2.95	.0016	−1.56	.0594	−.74	.2297	.08	.5319	.88	.8106	1.68	.9535
−2.90	.0019	−1.54	.0618	−.72	.2358	.10	.5398	.90	.8159	1.70	.9554
−2.85	.0022	−1.52	.0643	−.70	.2420	.12	.5478	.92	.8212	1.72	.9573
−2.80	.0026	−1.50	.0668	−.68	.2483	.14	.5557	.94	.8264	1.74	.9591
−2.75	.0030	−1.48	.0694	−.66	.2546	.16	.5636	.96	.8315	1.76	.9608
−2.70	.0035	−1.46	.0721	−.64	.2611	.18	.5714	.98	.8365	1.78	.9625
−2.65	.0040	−1.44	.0749	−.62	.2676	.20	.5793	1.00	.8413	1.80	.9641
−2.60	.0047	−1.42	.0778	−.60	.2743	.22	.5871	1.02	.8461	1.82	.9656
−2.55	.0054	−1.40	.0808	−.58	.2810	.24	.5948	1.04	.8508	1.84	.9671
−2.50	.0062	−1.38	.0838	−.56	.2877	.26	.6026	1.06	.8554	1.86	.9686
−2.45	.0071	−1.36	.0869	−.54	.2946	.28	.6103	1.08	.8599	1.88	.9699
−2.40	.0082	−1.34	.0901	−.52	.3015	.30	.6179	1.10	.8643	1.90	.9713
−2.35	.0094	−1.32	.0934	−.50	.3085	.32	.6255	1.12	.8686	1.92	.9726
−2.30	.0107	−1.30	.0968	−.48	.3156	.34	.6331	1.14	.8729	1.94	.9738
−2.25	.0122	−1.28	.1003	−.46	.3228	.36	.6406	1.16	.8770	1.96	.9750
−2.20	.0139	−1.26	.1038	−.44	.3300	.38	.6480	1.18	.8810	1.98	.9761
−2.15	.0158	−1.24	.1075	−.42	.3372	.40	.6554	1.20	.8849	2.00	.9772
−2.10	.0179	−1.22	.1112	−.40	.3446	.42	.6628	1.22	.8888	2.05	.9798
−2.05	.0202	−1.20	.1151	−.38	.3520	.44	.6700	1.24	.8925	2.10	.9821
−2.00	.0228	−1.18	.1190	−.36	.3594	.46	.6772	1.26	.8962	2.15	.9842
−1.98	.0239	−1.16	.1230	−.34	.3669	.48	.6844	1.28	.8997	2.20	.9861
−1.96	.0250	−1.14	.1271	−.32	.3745	.50	.6915	1.30	.9032	2.25	.9878
−1.94	.0262	−1.12	.1314	−.30	.3821	.52	.6985	1.32	.9066	2.30	.9893
−1.92	.0274	−1.10	.1357	−.28	.3897	.54	.7054	1.34	.9099	2.35	.9906
−1.90	.0287	−1.08	.1401	−.26	.3974	.56	.7123	1.36	.9131	2.40	.9918
−1.88	.0301	−1.06	.1446	−.24	.4052	.58	.7190	1.38	.9162	2.45	.9929
−1.86	.0314	−1.04	.1492	−.22	.4129	.60	.7257	1.40	.9192	2.50	.9938
−1.84	.0329	−1.02	.1539	−.20	.4207	.62	.7324	1.42	.9222	2.55	.9946
−1.82	.0344	−1.00	.1587	−.18	.4286	.64	.7389	1.44	.9251	2.60	.9953
−1.80	.0359	−.98	.1635	−.16	.4364	.66	.7454	1.46	.9279	2.65	.9960
−1.78	.0375	−.96	.1685	−.14	.4443	.68	.7518	1.48	.9306	2.70	.9965
−1.76	.0392	−.94	.1736	−.12	.4522	.70	.7580	1.50	.9332	2.75	.9970
−1.74	.0409	−.92	.1788	−.10	.4602	.72	.7642	1.52	.9357	2.80	.9974
−1.72	.0427	−.90	.1841	−.08	.4681	.74	.7704	1.54	.9382	2.85	.9978
−1.70	.0446	−.88	.1894	−.06	.4761	.76	.7764	1.56	.9406	2.90	.9981
−1.68	.0465	−.86	.1949	−.04	.4840	.78	.7823	1.58	.9429	2.95	.9984
−1.66	.0485	−.84	.2005	−.02	.4920	.80	.7881	1.60	.9452	3.00	.9987
−1.64	.0505	−.82	.2061	.00	.5000	.82	.7939	1.62	.9474	3.05	.9989
−1.62	.0526	−.80	.2119	.02	.5080	.84	.7995	1.64	.9495		
−1.60	.0548	−.78	.2177	.04	.5160						

This table shows the probability [N(d)] of observing a value less than or equal to d. For example, as illustrated, if d is −.24, then N(d) is .4052.

KEY EQUATIONS

CHAPTER 2

1. The balance sheet identity or equation:

Assets = Liabilities
+ Shareholders' equity   [2.1]

2. The income statement equation:

Revenues − Expenses = Income   [2.2]

3. The cash flow identity:

Cash flow from assets =
Cash flow to creditors +   [2.3]
Cash flow to stockholders

where

a. Cash flow from assets = Operating cash flow (OCF) − Net capital spending − Change in net working capital (NWC)

    (1) Operating cash flow = Earnings before interest and taxes (EBIT) + Depreciation − Taxes

    (2) Net capital spending = Ending net fixed assets − Beginning net fixed assets + Depreciation

    (3) Change in net working capital = Ending NWC − Beginning NWC

b. Cash flow to creditors = Interest paid − Net new borrowing

c. Cash flow to stockholders = Dividends paid − Net new equity raised

CHAPTER 3

1. The current ratio:

$$\text{Current ratio} = \frac{\text{Current assets}}{\text{Current liabilities}} \quad [3.1]$$

2. The quick or acid-test ratio:

$$\text{Quick ratio} = \frac{\text{Current assets} - \text{Inventory}}{\text{Current liabilities}} \quad [3.2]$$

3. The cash ratio:

$$\text{Cash ratio} = \frac{\text{Cash}}{\text{Current liabilities}} \quad [3.3]$$

4. The ratio of net working capital to total assets:

Net working capital to total assets
$$= \frac{\text{Net working capital}}{\text{Total assets}} \quad [3.4]$$

5. The interval measure:

Interval measure
$$= \frac{\text{Current assets}}{\text{Average daily operating costs}} \quad [3.5]$$

6. The total debt ratio:

Total debt ratio
$$= \frac{\text{Total assets} - \text{Total equity}}{\text{Total assets}} \quad [3.6]$$

7. The debt–equity ratio:

Debt–equity ratio
$$= \text{Total debt/Total equity} \quad [3.7]$$

8. The equity multiplier:

Equity multiplier
$$= \text{Total assets/Total equity} \quad [3.8]$$

9. The long-term debt ratio:

Long-term debt ratio
$$= \frac{\text{Long-term debt}}{\text{Long-term debt} + \text{Total equity}} \quad [3.9]$$

10. The times interest earned (TIE) ratio:

$$\text{Times interest earned ratio} = \frac{\text{EBIT}}{\text{Interest}} \quad [3.10]$$

11. The cash coverage ratio:

Cash coverage ratio
$$= \frac{\text{EBIT} + \text{Depreciation}}{\text{Interest}} \quad [3.11]$$

12. The inventory turnover ratio:

Inventory turnover
$$= \frac{\text{Cost of goods sold}}{\text{Inventory}} \quad [3.12]$$

13. The average days' sales in inventory:

Days' sales in inventory
$$= \frac{365 \text{ days}}{\text{Inventory turnover}} \quad [3.13]$$

14. The receivables turnover ratio:
Receivables turnover
$$= \frac{\text{Sales}}{\text{Accounts receivable}} \qquad [3.14]$$

15. The days' sales in receivables:
Days' sales in receivables
$$= \frac{365 \text{ days}}{\text{Receivables turnover}} \qquad [3.15]$$

16. The net working capital (NWC) turnover ratio:
$$\text{NWC turnover} = \frac{\text{Sales}}{\text{NWC}} \qquad [3.16]$$

17. The fixed asset turnover ratio:
$$\text{Fixed asset turnover} = \frac{\text{Sales}}{\text{Net fixed assets}} \qquad [3.17]$$

18. The total asset turnover ratio:
$$\text{Total asset turnover} = \frac{\text{Sales}}{\text{Total assets}} \qquad [3.18]$$

19. Profit margin:
$$\text{Profit margin} = \frac{\text{Net income}}{\text{Sales}} \qquad [3.19]$$

20. Return on assets (ROA):
$$\text{Return on assets} = \frac{\text{Net income}}{\text{Total assets}} \qquad [3.20]$$

21. Return on equity (ROE):
$$\text{Return on equity} = \frac{\text{Net income}}{\text{Total equity}} \qquad [3.21]$$

22. The price–earnings (PE) ratio:
$$\text{PE ratio} = \frac{\text{Price per share}}{\text{Earnings per share}} \qquad [3.22]$$

23. The market-to-book ratio:
Market-to-book ratio
$$= \frac{\text{Market value per share}}{\text{Book value per share}} \qquad [3.23]$$

24. Enterprise value:
Enterprise value = Total market value of the stock +
Book value of all liabilities −
Cash   [3.24]

25. The EBITDA ratio:
$$\text{EBITDA ratio} = \frac{\text{Enterprise value}}{\text{EBITDA}} \qquad [3.25]$$

26. The Du Pont identity:
$$\text{ROE} = \underbrace{\frac{\text{Net income}}{\text{Sales}} \times \frac{\text{Sales}}{\text{Assets}}}_{\text{Return on assets}} \times \frac{\text{Assets}}{\text{Equity}} \qquad [3.26]$$

ROE = Profit margin
× Total asset turnover
× Equity multiplier

CHAPTER 4

1. The dividend payout ratio:
Dividend payout ratio
= Cash dividends/Net income   [4.1]

2. The internal growth rate:
$$\text{Internal growth rate} = \frac{\text{ROA} \times b}{1 - \text{ROA} \times b} \qquad [4.2]$$

3. The sustainable growth rate:
$$\text{Sustainable growth rate} = \frac{\text{ROE} \times b}{1 - \text{ROE} \times b} \qquad [4.3]$$

CHAPTER 5

1. The future value of $1 invested for t periods at rate of r per period:
$$\text{Future value} = \$1 \times (1 + r)^t \qquad [5.1]$$

2. The present value of $1 to be received t periods in the future at a discount rate of r:
$$\text{PV} = \$1 \times [1/(1 + r)^t] = \$1/(1 + r)^t \qquad [5.2]$$

3. The relationship between future value and present value (the basic present value equation):
$$\text{PV} \times (1 + r)^t = \text{FV}_t \qquad [5.3]$$
$$\text{PV} = \text{FV}_t/(1 + r)^t = \text{FV}_t \times [1/(1 + r)^t]$$

CHAPTER 6

1. The present value of an annuity of C dollars per period for t periods when the rate of return or interest rate is r:
Annuity present value
$$= C \times \left(\frac{1 - \text{Present value factor}}{r}\right)$$
$$= C \times \left\{\frac{1 - [1/(1 + r)^t]}{r}\right\} \qquad [6.1]$$

2. The future value factor for an annuity:
Annuity FV factor
$$= (\text{Future value factor} - 1)/r \qquad [6.2]$$
$$= [(1 + r)^t - 1]/r$$

3. Annuity due value = Ordinary annuity value
$$\times (1 + r) \qquad [6.3]$$

4. Present value for a perpetuity:
$$\text{PV for a perpetuity} = C/r = C \times (1/r) \qquad [6.4]$$

5. Growing annuity present value
$$= C \left[\frac{1 - \left(\dfrac{1 + g}{1 + r}\right)^t}{r - g}\right] \qquad [6.5]$$

6. Growing perpetuity present value
$$= \frac{C}{r - g} \qquad [6.6]$$

7. Effective annual rate (EAR), where m is the number of times the interest is compounded during the year:
$$\text{EAR} = [1 + (\text{Quoted rate}/m)]^m - 1 \qquad [6.7]$$

8. Effective annual rate (EAR), where q stands for the continuously compounded quoted rate:
$$\text{EAR} = e^q - 1 \qquad [6.8]$$

CHAPTER 7

1. Bond value if bond has (1) a face value of F paid at maturity, (2) a coupon of C paid per period, (3) t periods to maturity, and (4) a yield of r per period:

    Bond value
    $$= C \times [1 - 1/(1 + r)^t]/r + F/(1 + r)^t \qquad \textbf{[7.1]}$$
    Bond value
    $$= \frac{\text{Present value}}{\text{of the coupons}} + \frac{\text{Present value}}{\text{of the face amount}}$$

2. The Fisher effect:
    $$1 + R = (1 + r) \times (1 + h) \qquad \textbf{[7.2]}$$
    $$R = r + h + r \times h \qquad \textbf{[7.3]}$$
    $$R \approx r + h \qquad \textbf{[7.4]}$$

CHAPTER 8

1. The dividend growth model:
    $$P_0 = \frac{D_0 \times (1 + g)}{R - g} = \frac{D_1}{R - g} \qquad \textbf{[8.3]}$$

2. Required return:
    $$R = D_1/P_0 + g \qquad \textbf{[8.7]}$$

CHAPTER 9

1. Net present value (NPV):
    NPV = Present value of future cash flows
         − Investment cost

2. Payback period:
    Payback period = Number of years that pass before the sum of an investment's cash flows equals the cost of the investment

3. Discounted payback period:
    Discounted payback period = Number of years that pass before the sum of an investment's *discounted* cash flows equals the cost of the investment

4. The average accounting return (AAR):
    $$\text{AAR} = \frac{\text{Average net income}}{\text{Average book value}}$$

5. Internal rate of return (IRR):
    IRR = Discount rate of required return such that the net present value of an investment is zero

6. Profitability index:
    $$\text{Profitability index} = \frac{\text{PV of cash flows}}{\text{Cost of investment}}$$

CHAPTER 10

1. Bottom-up approach to operating cash flow (OCF):
    $$\text{OCF} = \text{Net income} + \text{Depreciation} \qquad \textbf{[10.1]}$$

2. Top-down approach to operating cash flow (OCF):
    $$\text{OCF} = \text{Sales} - \text{Costs} - \text{Taxes} \qquad \textbf{[10.2]}$$

3. Tax shield approach to operating cash flow (OCF):
    $$\text{OCF} = (\text{Sales} - \text{Costs}) \times (1 - T)$$
    $$+ \text{Depreciation} \times T \qquad \textbf{[10.3]}$$

CHAPTER 11

1. Accounting break-even level:
    $$Q = (FC + D)/(P - v) \qquad \textbf{[11.1]}$$

2. Relationship between operating cash flow (OCF) and sales volume:
    $$Q = (FC + OCF)/(P - v) \qquad \textbf{[11.3]}$$

3. Cash break-even level:
    $$Q = FC/(P - v)$$

4. Financial break-even level:
    $$Q = (FC + OCF^*)/(P - v)$$

    where

    $$OCF^* = \text{Zero NPV cash flow}$$

5. Degree of operating leverage (DOL):
    $$\text{DOL} = 1 + FC/OCF \qquad \textbf{[11.4]}$$

CHAPTER 12

1. Variance of returns, Var(R) or σ^2:
    $$\text{Var}(R) = \frac{1}{T - 1}[(R_1 - \overline{R})^2 + \cdots$$
    $$+ (R_T - \overline{R})^2] \qquad \textbf{[12.3]}$$

2. Standard deviation of returns, SD(R) or σ:
    $$\text{SD}(R) = \sqrt{\text{Var}(R)}$$

CHAPTER 13

1. Risk premium:
    Risk premium = Expected return
                  − Risk-free rate $\qquad \textbf{[13.1]}$

2. Expected return on a portfolio:
    $$E(R_P) = x_1 \times E(R_1) + x_2 \times E(R_2) + \cdots$$
    $$+ x_n \times E(R_n) \qquad \textbf{[13.2]}$$

3. The reward-to-risk ratio:
    $$\text{Reward-to-risk ratio} = \frac{E(R_i) - R_f}{\beta_i}$$

4. The capital asset pricing model (CAPM):
    $$E(R_i) = R_f + [E(R_M) - R_f] \times \beta_i \qquad \textbf{[13.7]}$$

CHAPTER 14

1. Required return on equity, R_E (dividend growth model):
    $$R_E = D_1/P_0 + g \qquad \textbf{[14.1]}$$

2. Required return on equity, R_E (CAPM):
    $$R_E = R_f + \beta_E \times (R_M - R_f) \qquad \textbf{[14.2]}$$

3. Required return on preferred stock, R_P:
$$R_P = D/P_0 \qquad \textbf{[14.3]}$$

4. The weighted average cost of capital (WACC):
$$\text{WACC} = (E/V) \times R_E + (D/V) \times R_D \\ \times (1 - T_C) \qquad \textbf{[14.6]}$$

5. Weighted average flotation cost, f_A:
$$f_A = \frac{E}{V} \times f_E + \frac{D}{V} \times f_D \qquad \textbf{[14.8]}$$

CHAPTER 15

1. Rights offerings:
   a. Number of new shares:
   $$\text{Number of new shares} \\ = \frac{\text{Funds to be raised}}{\text{Subscription price}} \qquad \textbf{[15.1]}$$

   b. Number of rights needed:
   $$\text{Number of rights needed to buy a share of stock} \\ = \frac{\text{Old shares}}{\text{New shares}} \qquad \textbf{[15.2]}$$

   c. Value of a right:
   $$\text{Value of a right} = \text{Rights-on price} - \text{Ex-rights price}$$

CHAPTER 16

1. Modigliani–Miller propositions (no taxes):
   a. Proposition I:
   $$V_L = V_U$$
   b. Proposition II:
   $$R_E = R_A + (R_A - R_D) \times (D/E) \qquad \textbf{[16.1]}$$

2. Modigliani–Miller propositions (with taxes):
   a. Value of the interest tax shield:
   $$\text{Present value of the interest tax shield} \\ = (T_C \times D \times R_D)/R_D \qquad \textbf{[16.2]} \\ = T_C \times D$$
   b. Proposition I:
   $$V_L = V_U + T_C \times D \qquad \textbf{[16.3]}$$
   c. Proposition II:
   $$R_E = R_U + (R_U - R_D) \times (D/E) \\ \times (1 - T_C) \qquad \textbf{[16.4]}$$

CHAPTER 18

1. The operating cycle:
   $$\text{Operating cycle} = \text{Inventory period} \\ + \text{Accounts receivable period} \qquad \textbf{[18.4]}$$

2. The cash cycle:
   $$\text{Cash cycle} = \text{Operating cycle} \\ - \text{Accounts payable period} \qquad \textbf{[18.5]}$$

CHAPTER 19

1. Float measurement:
   a. Average daily float:
   $$\text{Average daily float} = \frac{\text{Total float}}{\text{Total days}} \qquad \textbf{[19.1]}$$

   b. Average daily float:
   $$\text{Average daily float} \\ = \text{Average daily receipts} \\ \times \text{Weighted average delay} \qquad \textbf{[19.2]}$$

2. The Baumol–Allais–Tobin (BAT) model:
   a. Opportunity costs:
   $$\text{Opportunity costs} = (C/2) \times R \qquad \textbf{[19A.1]}$$
   b. Trading costs:
   $$\text{Trading costs} = (T/C) \times F \qquad \textbf{[19A.2]}$$
   c. Total cost:
   $$\text{Total cost} = \text{Opportunity costs} \\ + \text{Trading costs} \qquad \textbf{[19A.3]}$$
   d. The optimal initial cash balance:
   $$C^* = \sqrt{(2T \times F)/R} \qquad \textbf{[19A.4]}$$

3. The Miller–Orr model:
   a. The optimal cash balance:
   $$C^* = L + (3/4 \times F \times \sigma^2/R)^{1/3} \qquad \textbf{[19A.5]}$$
   b. The upper limit:
   $$U^* = 3 \times C^* - 2 \times L \qquad \textbf{[19A.6]}$$

CHAPTER 20

1. The size of receivables:
   $$\text{Accounts receivable} \\ = \text{Average daily sales} \times \text{ACP} \qquad \textbf{[20.1]}$$

2. NPV of switching credit terms:
   a. Present value of switching:
   $$\text{PV} = [(P - v)(Q' - Q)]/R \qquad \textbf{[20.4]}$$
   b. Cost of switching:
   $$\text{Cost of switching} = PQ + v(Q' - Q) \qquad \textbf{[20.5]}$$
   c. NPV of switching:
   $$\text{NPV of switching} = -[PQ + v(Q' - Q)] \\ + [(P - v) \qquad \textbf{[20.6]} \\ \times (Q' - Q)]/R$$

3. NPV of granting credit:
   a. With no repeat business:
   $$\text{NPV} = -v + (1 - \pi)P/(1 + R) \qquad \textbf{[20.8]}$$
   b. With repeat business:
   $$\text{NPV} = -v + (1 - \pi)(P - v)/R \qquad \textbf{[20.9]}$$

4. The economic order quantity (EOQ) model:

   a. Total carrying costs:

      Total carrying costs

      = Average inventory

        × Carrying costs per unit

      $= (Q/2) \times CC$ **[20.10]**

   b. Total restocking costs:

      Total restocking costs

      = Fixed cost per order

        × Number of orders $= F \times (T/Q)$ **[20.11]**

   c. Total costs:

      Total costs = Carrying costs

          + Restocking costs

      $= (Q/2) \times CC$

         $+ F \times (T/Q)$ **[20.12]**

   d. The optimal order size Q^*:

$$Q^* = \sqrt{\frac{2T \times F}{CC}}$$ **[20.15]**

CHAPTER 21

1. Purchasing power parity (PPP):

$$E(S_t) = S_0 \times [1 + (h_{FC} - h_{US})]^t$$ **[21.3]**

2. Interest rate parity (IRP):

   a. Exact, single period:

$$F_1/S_0 = (1 + R_{FC})/(1 + R_{US})$$ **[21.4]**

   b. Approximate, multiperiod:

$$F_t = S_0 \times [1 + (R_{FC} - R_{US})]^t$$ **[21.7]**

3. Uncovered interest parity (UIP):

$$E(S_t) = S_0 \times [1 + (R_{FC} - R_{US})]^t$$ **[21.9]**

4. International Fisher effect (IFE):

$$R_{US} - h_{US} = R_{FC} - h_{FC}$$ **[21.10]**

ANSWERS TO SELECTED END-OF-CHAPTER PROBLEMS

CHAPTER 2

2. $218,400
7. Average rate = 32.43%
   Marginal rate = 39%
10. −$70
14. a. $66,535
   b. $17,400
   c. $6,200
   d. $635
18. a. Tax_{Growth} = $14,090
22. a. 2010 = $2,325
   2011 = $2,999
   b. $31
   c. Fixed assets sold = $88
   Cash flow from assets = $2,653
   d. Debt retired = $252
   Cash flow to creditors = $168

CHAPTER 3

2. Net income = $1,440,000
   ROA = 9.23%
   ROE = 15.48%
6. EPS = $3.79
   DPS = $1.21
   BVPS = $33.10
   Market-to-book ratio = 2.39 times
   PE ratio = 20.83 times
   P/S ratio = 2.44 times
10. 65.33 days
18. $151.94
22. Firm A: 16.36%
   Firm B: 18.46%
26. a. 1.32 times; 1.24 times
   b. .78 times; .73 times
   c. .51 times; .45 times
   d. .85 times
   e. 9.32 times
   f. 24.09 times
   g. .33 times; .34 times
   h. .49 times; .52 times
   i. 1.49 times; 1.52 times
   j. 5.71 times
   k. 7.96 times

l. 11.93%
m. 10.13%
n. 15.44%

CHAPTER 4

2. −$575
5. $786.90
12. 5.54%
16. 8.70%
19. 1.36 times
21. Sustainable growth rate = 12.09%
   New borrowing = $8,219.78
   Internal growth rate = 4.85%

CHAPTER 5

2. $8,630.69; $15,999.00; $373,155.46;
   $292,942.90
6. 8.87%
10. $154,256,258
14. 10.74%
18. $547,651.21; $192,874.26

CHAPTER 6

2. @ 5%: PV_X = $33,608.71
   PV_Y = $31,605.18
   @ 15%: PV_X = $23,334.07
   PV_Y = $24,470.73
6. $348,058.92
10. $517,241.38
14. First National EAR = 14.03%
   First United EAR = 13.96%
18. $21,354.60
22. APR = 1,733.33%
   EAR = 313,916,515.69%
26. $38,446.08
30. 6.77% semiannual
   3.33% quarterly
   1.10% monthly
38. $2,966,204
42. $401,039.60

46. Profit = $7,931.22
Break-even = 15.67%
50. $47,823.03
54. $1,554.38
58. PV of lease payments = $15,780.17
PV of purchase = $19,219.83
Break-even resale price = $22,136.63
60. EAR = 14.94%
64. Refundable fee:
APR = 5.64%
EAR = 5.79%
Nonrefundable fee:
APR = 5.50%
EAR = 5.64%
70. 8.87%
74. 16.67%

CHAPTER 7

4. 5.45%
8. 6.50%
12. 6.75%
26. a. 45,000 coupon bonds; 265,122 zeroes
b. $46,350,000; $265,122,140
c. Coupon bonds = $1,755,000 outflow
Zero coupon = $959,175 inflow
28. $13,010.95

CHAPTER 8

2. 9.97%
6. $3.08
10. $9,600,048
14. $48.54
18. $63.30
20. $64.46

CHAPTER 9

4. 1.98 years; 2.57 years; 3.55 years
8. @ 11%: NPV = $3,028.55
@ 25%: NPV = −$3,168.00
12. a. IRR_A = 18.56%
IRR_B = 17.42%
b. NPV_A = $4,042.42
NPV_B = $5,008.56
c. Crossover rate = 14.83%
16. a. PI_I = 1.205
PI_I = 1.340
b. NPV_I = $13,092.41
NPV_{II} = $6,122.46
22. a. $C = I/N$
b. $C > I/\text{PVIFA}_{R\%,N}$
c. $C > 2.0 * I/\text{PVIFA}_{R\%,N}$

CHAPTER 10

2. $397,700,000
8. $1,213,928
12. CF_0 = −$3,000,000
CF_1 = $1,163,218.50
CF_2 = $1,268,302.50
CF_3 = $1,494,729.00
NPV = $113,589.51
16. −$116,176.80
22. $.03644

CHAPTER 11

2. Total costs = $8,308,000
Marginal cost = $54.65
Average cost = $69.23
Minimum revenue = $273,250
8. D = 195,200
P = $53.30
VC = $31.57
12. OCF = $60,130
DOL = 3.495
18. DOL = 1.4967
DOL_A = 2.7143
22. $\Delta NPV/\Delta P$ = $160,657.82
$\Delta NPV/\Delta Q$ = $1,256.05
30. DOL = 1.2079
ΔOCF = +4.83%

CHAPTER 12

2. R_D = 1.67%
R_C = 9.72%
6. r_G = 2.72%; r_C = 3.01%
16. R_A = 9.53%
R_G = 8.35%
20. 11.48%; 11.22%; 10.68%

CHAPTER 13

2. 9.67%
6. 10.60%
10. a. 9.96%
b. σ_P^2 = .01848
σ_P = 13.59%
14. .76
18. Slope of SML = .0696
24. C = $336,046.51
R_F = $128,953.49
26. β_I = 1.21
σ_I = 8.62%
β_{II} = .75
σ_{II} = 24.40%

CHAPTER 14

2. 12.24%
4. R_A = 9.36%; R_G = 9.35%
8. Book value = $95,000,000
Market value = $75,750,000
Aftertax cost = 5.13%
12. a. E/V = .2932
D/V = .7068
b. E/V = .8106
D/V = .1894
16. a. D/V = .3305
P/V = .0489
E/V = .6206
b. 9.87%
20. Break-even cost = $20,454,545

CHAPTER 15

2. a. $48; anything greater than $0
b. 697,674; 5.59
c. $47.24; $.76
6. 5,835,598
8. No change;
declines by $.44;
declines by $1.17
14. $36,516.49

CHAPTER 16

2. a. $1.74; $2.49; $2.99
b. $2.02; $3.30; $4.15
6. a. $3.90; $3.71; $4.00
b. $54,000; $54,000
c. $54,000
d. $2.34; $2.23; $2.40
$54,000; $54,000; $54,000
10. $1,440,000
12. a. 17.14%
b. 11.39%
c. 19.05%; 15.22%; 11.39%
16. $482,113.64

CHAPTER 17

2. a. 4,000 new shares
b. 10,000 new shares
4. a. $48.00
b. $69.57
c. $56.14
d. $140.00
e. 708,333; 488,750; 605,625; 242,857
8. Shares outstanding = 442,750
Capital surplus = $3,271,500
10. P_0 = $45.47; D = $27.97

CHAPTER 18

2. Cash = $1,450
Current assets = $7,285
4. a. *I,I*
b. *I,N*
c. *D,D*
d. *D,D*
e. *D,N*
f. *I,I*
6. Operating cycle = 80.11 days
Cash cycle = 41.09 days
8. a. $261.00; $249.00; $279.00; $272.55
b. $237.00; $261.00; $249.00; $279.00
c. $245.00; $257.00; $259.00; $276.85
10. a. $180,000
b. $168,571.43
c. $187,464.29; $204,035.71; $226,950
14. a. 4.27%
b. 7.91%
c. 7.82%
18. 10.47%

CHAPTER 19

2. a. $48,000
−$46,000
$2,000
b. $48,000
−$23,000
$25,000
6. a. $25,016
b. 2.54 days
c. $25,016
d. $4.64
e. $14,787
10. NPV = $4,950,000
Net savings = $123,750

APPENDIX 19A

19A.2 $3,366.50
19A.4 **a.** Opportunity cost = $30
Trading cost = $350
b. $5,123.48
19A.10 2.38%

CHAPTER 20

2. $3,539,726
6. Sales = $467,863.64
Accounts receivable turnover = 11.0606 times
10. NPV = $107,265.79
12. Carrying cost = $5,700
Order cost = $3,900

EOQ = 248.15
Orders = 62.86 per year
16. Net savings = $4,050

APPENDIX 20A

20A.2 **a.** 1/20, net 30
b. $240,000
d. NPV = −$2,477,600
Break-even price = $108.42
Break-even discount = 8.68%
20A.4 **b.** $70.45
c. NPV = $151,131.30

CHAPTER 21

6. Great Britain: 1.57%
Japan: 1.21%
Switzerland: 1.22%
10. **b.** Krone 5.8347
12. **b.** U.S. 2.4% greater

USING THE HP 10B AND TI BA II PLUS FINANCIAL CALCULATORS

This appendix is intended to help you use your Hewlett-Packard HP 10B or Texas Instruments TI BA II Plus financial calculator to solve problems encountered in an introductory finance course. It describes the various calculator settings and provides keystroke solutions for nine selected problems from this book. Please see your owner's manual for more complete instructions. For more examples and problem-solving techniques, please see *Financial Analysis with an Electronic Calculator,* 7th edition, by Mark A. White (New York: McGraw-Hill, 2007).

CALCULATOR SETTINGS

Most calculator errors in introductory finance courses are the result of inappropriate settings. Before beginning a calculation, you should ask yourself the following questions:

1. Did I clear the financial registers?
2. Is the compounding frequency set to once per period?
3. Is the calculator in END mode?
4. Did I enter negative numbers using the +/− key?

Clearing the Registers

All calculators have areas of memory, called registers, where variables and intermediate results are stored. There are two sets of financial registers, the time value of money (TVM) registers and the cash flow (CF) registers. These must be cleared before beginning a new calculation. On the Hewlett-Packard HP 10B, pressing {CLEAR ALL} clears both the TVM and the CF registers.[1] To clear the TVM registers on the TI BA II Plus, press 2nd {CLR TVM}. Press 2nd {CLR Work} from within the cash flow worksheet to clear the CF registers.

Compounding Frequency

Both the HP 10B and the TI BA II Plus are hard-wired to assume monthly compounding, that is, compounding 12 times per period. Because very few problems in introductory finance courses make this assumption, you should change this default setting to once per period. On the HP 10B, press 1 {P/YR}. To verify that the default has been changed, press the key, then press and briefly hold the **INPUT** key.[2] The display should read "1P_Yr".

On the TI BA II Plus, you can specify both payment frequency and compounding frequency, although they should normally be set to the same number. To set both to once per period, press the key sequence 2nd {P/Y} 1 **ENTER**, then press ↓ 1 **ENTER**. Pressing 2nd {QUIT} returns you to standard calculator mode.

END Mode and Annuities Due

In most problems, payment is made at the end of a period, and this is the default setting (end mode) for both the HP 10B and the TI BA II Plus. *Annuities due* assume payments are made at the *beginning* of each period (begin mode). On the HP 10B, pressing {BEG/END} toggles between begin and end mode. Press the key sequence 2nd {BGN} 2nd [SET] 2nd {QUIT} to accomplish the same task on the TI BA II Plus. Both calculators will indicate on the display that your calculator is set for begin mode.

---

[1]The key is colored orange and serves as a Shift key for the functions in curly brackets.

[2]This is the same keystroke used to clear all registers; pretty handy, eh?

Sign Changes

Sign changes are used to identify the direction of cash inflows and outflows. Generally, cash inflows are entered as positive numbers and cash outflows are entered as negative numbers. To enter a negative number on either the HP 10B or the TI BA II Plus, first press the appropriate digit keys and then press the change sign key, +/− . Do *not* use the minus sign key, − , as its effects are quite unpredictable.

SAMPLE PROBLEMS

This section provides keystroke solutions for selected problems from the text illustrating the nine basic financial calculator skills.

1. Future Value or Present Value of a Single Sum

Compute the future value of $2,250 at a 17 percent annual rate for 30 years.

HP 10B		TI BA II PLUS	
-2,250.00 **PV**		-2,250.00 **PV**	
30.00 **N**		30.00 **N**	
17.00 **I/YR**		17.00 **I/Y**	
FV 249,895.46		**CPT** **FV** 249,895.46	

The future value is $249,895.46.

2. Present Value or Future Value of an Ordinary Annuity

Betty's Bank offers you a $20,000, seven-year term loan at 11 percent annual interest. What will your annual loan payment be?

HP 10B		TI BA II PLUS	
-20,000.00 **PV**		-20,000.00 **PV**	
7.00 **N**		7.00 **N**	
11.00 **I/YR**		11.00 **I/Y**	
PMT 4,244.31		**CPT** **PMT** 4,244.31	

Your annual loan payment will be $4,244.31.

3. Finding an Unknown Interest Rate

Assume that the total cost of a college education will be $75,000 when your child enters college in 18 years. You presently have $7,000 to invest. What rate of interest must you earn on your investment to cover the cost of your child's college education?

HP 10B		TI BA II PLUS	
-7,000.00 **PV**		-7,000.00 **PV**	
18.00 **N**		18.00 **N**	
75,000.00 **FV**		75,000.00 **FV**	
I/YR 14.08		**CPT** **I/Y** 14.08	

You must earn an annual interest rate of at least 14.08 percent to cover the expected future cost of your child's education.

4. Finding an Unknown Number of Periods

One of your customers is delinquent on his accounts payable balance. You've mutually agreed to a repayment schedule of $374 per month. You will charge 1.4 percent per month interest on the overdue balance. If the current balance is $12,000, how long will it take for the account to be paid off?

HP 10B		TI BA II PLUS	
-12,000.00 **PV**		-12,000.00 **PV**	
1.40 **I/YR**		1.40 **I/Y**	
374.00 **PMT**		374.00 **PMT**	
N 42.90		**CPT** **N** 42.90	

The loan will be paid off in 42.90 months.

5. Simple Bond Pricing

Mullineaux Co. issued 11-year bonds one year ago at a coupon rate of 8.25 percent. The bonds make semiannual payments. If the YTM on these bonds is 7.10 percent, what is the current bond price?

HP 10B		TI BA II PLUS	
41.25 **PMT**		41.25 **PMT**	
1,000.00 **FV**		1,000.00 **FV**	
20.00 **N**		20.00 **N**	
3.55 **I/YR**		3.55 **I/Y**	
PV -1,081.35		**CPT** **PV** -1,081.35	

Because the bonds make semiannual payments, we must halve the coupon payment (8.25 ÷ 2 = 4.125 ==> $41.25), halve the YTM (7.10 ÷ 2 ==> 3.55), and double the number of periods (10 years remaining × 2 = 20 periods). Then, the current bond price is $1,081.35.

6. Simple Bond Yields to Maturity

Vasicek Co. has 12.5 percent coupon bonds on the market with eight years left to maturity. The bonds make annual payments. If one of these bonds currently sells for $1,145.68, what is its YTM?

HP 10B		TI BA II PLUS	
-1,145.68	**PV**	-1,145.68	**PV**
125.00	**PMT**	125.00	**PMT**
1,000.00	**FV**	1,000.00	**FV**
8.00	**N**	8.00	**N**
I/YR	9.79	**CPT** **I/Y**	9.79

The bond has a yield to maturity of 9.79 percent.

7. Cash Flow Analysis

What are the IRR and NPV of the following set of cash flows? Assume a discount rate of 10 percent.

YEAR	CASH FLOW
0	−$1,300
1	400
2	300
3	1,200

HP 10B		TI BA II PLUS		
-1,300.00	**CFj**	**CF**		
400.00	**CFj**	**2nd** {CLR Work}		
1.00	{Nj}	-1,300.00	**ENTER**	↓
300.00	**CFj**	400.00	**ENTER**	↓
1.00	{Nj}	1.00	**ENTER**	↓
1,200.00	**CFj**	300.00	**ENTER**	↓
1.00	{Nj}	1.00	**ENTER**	↓
{IRR/YR}	17.40	1,200.00	**ENTER**	↓
10.00	**I/YR**	1.00	**ENTER**	↓
{NPV}	213.15	**IRR** **CPT**	17.40	
		NPV		
		10.00	**ENTER**	
		↓ **CPT**	213.15	

The project has an IRR of 17.40 percent and an NPV of $213.15.

8. Loan Amortization

Prepare an amortization schedule for a three-year loan of $24,000. The interest rate is 16 percent per year, and the loan calls for equal annual payments. How much interest is paid in the third year? How much total interest is paid over the life of the loan?

To prepare a complete amortization schedule, you must amortize each payment one at a time:

HP 10B					TI BA II PLUS			
	-24,000.00	**PV**			-24,000.00	**PV**		
	16.00	**I/YR**			16.00	**I/Y**		
	3.00	**N**			3.00	**N**		
	PMT	10,686.19			**CPT** **PMT**	10,686.19		
1.00 **INPUT** {AMORT}	=	3,840.00	<== Interest		**2nd** {AMORT} **2nd** {CLR Work}			
	=	6,846.19	<== Principal					
	=	-17,153.81	<== Balance	1.00 **ENTER** ↓				
2.00 **INPUT** {AMORT}	=	2,744.61	<== Interest	1.00 **ENTER** ↓	-17,153.81	<== Balance		
	=	7,941.58	<== Principal	↓	6,846.19	<== Principal		
	=	-9,212.23	<== Balance	↓	3,840.00	<== Interest		
				↓				

(Continued)

Interest of $1,473.96 is paid in the third year.

Enter both a beginning and an ending period to compute the total amount of interest or principal paid over a particular period of time.

HP 10B			TI BA II PLUS		
-24,000.00 **PV**			-24,000.00 **PV**		
16.00 **I/YR**			16.00 **I/Y**		
3.00 **N**			3.00 **N**		
PMT 10,686.19			**CPT** **PMT** 10,686.19		
1.00 **INPUT**			**2nd** {AMORT} **2nd** {CLR Work}		
3.00 {AMORT} = 8,058.57 <== Interest			1.00 **ENTER** ↓		
= 24,000.00 <== Principal			3.00 **ENTER** ↓ 0.00 <== Balance		
= 0.00 <== Balance			↓ 24,000.00 <== Principal		
			↓ 8,058.57 <== Interest		

Total interest of $8,058.57 is paid over the life of the loan.

9. Interest Rate Conversions

Find the effective annual rate, EAR, corresponding to a 7 percent annual percentage rate, APR, compounded quarterly.

HP 10B	TI BA II PLUS
4.00 {P/YR}	**2nd** {IConv}
7.00 {NOM%}	7.00 **ENTER**
{EFF%} 7.19	↓ ↓
	4.00 **ENTER**
	↑ **CPT** 7.19

The effective annual rate equals 7.19 percent.

NAME INDEX

Page numbers followed by n refer to notes.

I

EQUATION INDEX

A

accounts receivable, 661
accounts receivable period, 596
acid-test ratio, 58
announcement, 421
annuity due, 162
average accounting return, 277–278
average collection period, 62
average daily float, 630

B

balance sheet identity, 22
benchmark PE ratio, 245
bond value, 194
break-even
    accounting, 355–356, 361
    cash, 360, 361
    financial, 360, 361
    general expression, 359, 361

C

capital asset pricing model, 436
capital gains yield, 243
capital intensity ratio, 99
carrying costs, 679
cash, 594
cash collections, 608
cash coverage ratio, 61
cash cycle, 596, 600
cash flow from assets, 32
cash ratio, 59
collection float, 629
common financial ratios, 67
cost of equity, 452
current ratio, 57

D

days' sales in inventory, 61
days' sales in receivables, 62
debt–equity ratio, 60
degree of operating leverage, 362–363
disbursement float, 629
dividend growth rate, 451
dividend payout ratio, 98
dividend yield, 243
dividends per share, 26
DuPont identity, 69

E

earnings per share, 26
economic order quantity, 680
effective annual yield, 166–167
equity multiplier, 60
equivalent annual cost, 329
expected exchange rate, 712–713
expected return, 413

F

fixed asset turnover ratio, 63
float, 629
    average daily, 630
future value, 124
    factor, 124, 134

G

geometric average return, 396–397

H

historical variance, 388–389

I

income statement, 25
interest coverage ratio, 60–61
interest rate parity, 709
internal growth rate, 107
internal rate of return, 279–280
international Fisher effect, 711
interval measure, 59
inventory period, 599
inventory turnover ratio, 61

L

long-term debt ratio, 60

M

market-to-book ratio, 66

N

net incremental cash flow, 693
net present value, 279–280
net working capital, 594
net working capital to total assets, 59
net working capital turnover ratio, 63

O

operating cash flow, 357–358
operating cycle, 596

P

payable period, 600
payables turnover ratio, 62–63
plowback ratio, 98
portfolio beta, 429–430
portfolio return, 417
present value, 130
    annuity, 156
    basic, 134
    factor, 134
    interest factors, 131–132
    perpetuity, 163
price–earnings ratio, 65
    benchmark, 245
price–sales ratio, 65
profit margin, 64

Q

quick ratio, 58

R

receivables period, 599
receivables turnover ratio, 62
restocking cost, 679
retention ratio, 98
return on assets, 64
return on equity, 64, 68
risk premium, 414

S

security market line, 435
shareholders' equity, 24
standard deviation of the return, 388
stock valuation
    constant growth model, 237
    dividend growth model, 238
    nonconstant growth, 240–242
    required return, 243
    zero growth, 237
sustainable growth rate, 107

SUBJECT INDEX

Note: Key terms are in **boldface;** page numbers followed by n refer to notes.